lonely planet

Greece

Northern
Greece
(p235)

Central
Greece
(p187)

Evia & the
Sporades
(p603)

Northeastern
Aegean Islands
(p538)

Ionian
Islands
(p629)

Athens &
Around
(p64)

Peloponnese
(p130)

Saronic
Gulf Islands
(p300)

Cyclades
(p319)

Dodecanese
(p465)

Crete
(p414)

THIS EDITION WRITTEN AND

Kate Armstro   is Deliso,
Victoria   ters

Contents

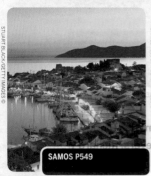

ANCIENT DELOS P397

MYKONOS P335

SAMOS P549

GREEK CUISINE P711

Contents

UNDERSTAND

SURVIVAL GUIDE

SPECIAL FEATURES

Welcome to Greece

Experience endless miles of aquamarine coastline, sun-bleached ancient ruins, strong feta and stronger ouzo. The Greek landscape thrills, and Greek people are passionate about politics, coffee, art and gossiping.

Naturally Inviting

It's easy to understand how so many myths of gods and giants originated in this vast and varied landscape, with wide open skies and a sea speckled with islands, where days melt from one to the next, while you relish the white-sand and palm-fringed beaches. Greece is a magnet for anyone who enjoys the great outdoors. Wander along cobbled, Byzantine footpaths, hike into volcanoes, watch for dolphins and sea turtles and cycle through lush forests. Discover world-class kitesurfing, diving and rock-climbing locations or simply hop on a boat and set sail into the glittering blue beyond.

Culturally Rich

Step into the ring where Olympic athletes competed. Gaze at Meteora's monasteries, perched atop towering rock pinnacles. Contemplate the Oracle's insights from the grandeur of Delphi or take in a starlit drama at an ancient outdoor theatre. In the most unexpected places you'll encounter thought-provoking modern art, the melancholic throb of *rembetika* (blues songs) and collections of ancient marble sculptures dredged up from beneath the Aegean. Greece balances its past, present and future in a way managed by few other countries. The result is a nation with endless cultural pursuits.

Sumptuous Feasting

Greeks pride themselves on their cuisine and will go out of their way to ensure you are well fed. The tang of homemade tzatziki and the aroma of souvlaki grilling are just the beginning. Taste-test your way through regional cheeses – from crumbling feta to honeyed soft cheeses and sharp, hard rounds. Dig into rich layers of *mousakas* and sip crisp wine from grapes ripened under the hot Mediterranean sun. The Italian legacy of pasta is paired with Greek specialties like lobster, while Turkish spices find their way into delicate sweets. Mussels are steamed in ouzo, bread is baked with olives and fish is cooked straight from the sea.

Socially Spirited

Greeks are truly social beings. Their families are extended and they are quick to welcome in newcomers, whether for a coffee, a shot of ouzo, a chorus on the bouzouki or a heated debate. Greeks are passionate, if nothing else, and this passion continues to drive society forward despite the current economic turmoil. Life is lived to the fullest, even at the most difficult of times, and herein lies the secret of how a country, seemingly riddled with challenges, is full of people who remain so in love with life.

Why I Love Greece

By Korina Miller, Author

I first visited Greece as an 18-year-old, sleeping on the decks of slow-moving ferries, living on olives and feta, and constantly salt-crusted from swimming in the deep blue Aegean. But it was a starlit performance at the 3rd-century Theatre of Epidavros that sealed my love of the country. Watching the ancient Greek drama unfold before me as I sat on stone seats worn smooth by thousands of years of use, I felt caught in a moment that seemed to sidestep time. I love Greece because magical moments like that one aren't so hard to find here.

For more about our authors, see page 768

Above: Oia (p385), Santorini

Greece

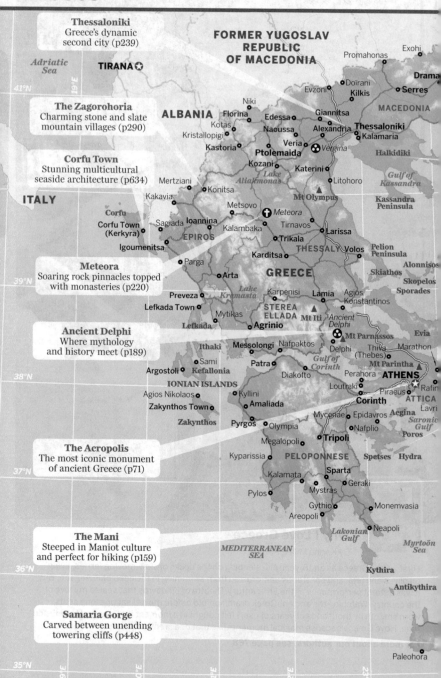

Thessaloniki
Greece's dynamic second city (p239)

The Zagorohoria
Charming stone and slate mountain villages (p290)

Corfu Town
Stunning multicultural seaside architecture (p634)

Meteora
Soaring rock pinnacles topped with monasteries (p220)

Ancient Delphi
Where mythology and history meet (p189)

The Acropolis
The most iconic monument of ancient Greece (p71)

The Mani
Steeped in Maniot culture and perfect for hiking (p159)

Samaria Gorge
Carved between unending towering cliffs (p448)

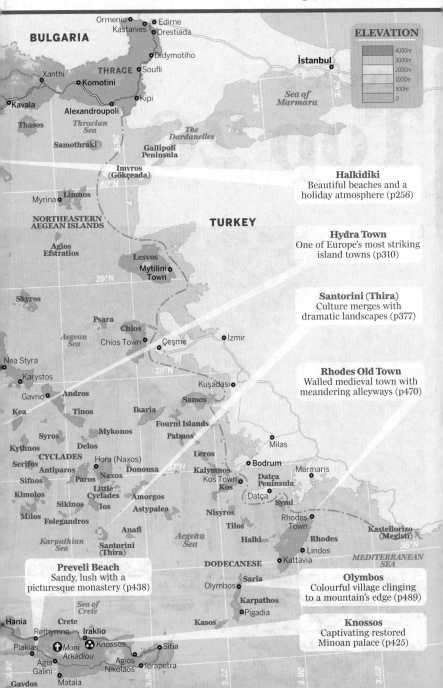

N 0 ——— 100km
0 ——— 50miles

ELEVATION

4000m
3000m
2000m
1000m
500m
0

BULGARIA

Ormenio • Edirne
Kastanies • Orestiada

• Didymotiho

İstanbul

Xanthi **THRACE** Soufli
• Komotini

Kavala
Alexandroupoli • Kipi

Thasos *Thracian Sea*

Samothraki *The Dardanelles*

Gallipoli Peninsula

Sea of Marmara

Imvros (Gökçeada)

Halkidiki
Beautiful beaches and a
holiday atmosphere (p256)

40°N

Myrina • Limnos

**NORTHEASTERN
AEGEAN ISLANDS**

TURKEY

Hydra Town
One of Europe's most striking
island towns (p310)

Agios
Efstratios

39°N Lesvos
Mytilini
Town

Skyros

Santorini (Thira)
Culture merges with
dramatic landscapes (p377)

Psara
Chios
Chios Town • Çeşme • İzmir

*Aegean
Sea*

Rhodes Old Town
Walled medieval town with
meandering alleyways (p470)

Nea Styra

38°N

Karystos

Gavrio • **Andros**
Kuşadası •
Kea **Tinos** **Samos**

Ikaria

Syros **Mykonos** **Fourni Islands**
Kythnos **Delos** **Patmos**
Serifos **CYCLADES** Hora (Naxos)
Antiparos Donousa **Leros** Milas
Sifnos **Paros** Naxos **Kalymnos** • Bodrum
Kimolos **Little** **Kos Town** **Datça** Marmaris
Sikinos **Cyclades** **Amorgos** Kos **Peninsula**
Milos **Ios** • Datça
Folegandros **Astypalea** **Symi**
Anafi **Nisyros**
*Karpathian
Sea* **Tilos** Rhodes
Santorini **Halki** Town **Kastellorizo**
(Thira) *Aegean* **Rhodes** (Megisti)
Sea • Lindos
DODECANESE • Kattavia *MEDITERRANEAN
SEA*
36°N

Preveli Beach
Sandy, lush with a
picturesque monastery (p438)

Saria

Olymbos •

Olymbos
Colourful village clinging
to a mountain's edge (p489)

Hania *Sea of
Crete*
Rethymno **Crete** Iraklio **Kasos**
Plakias *Moni
Arkadiou* *Knossos* • Sitia

Knossos
Captivating restored
Minoan palace (p425)

Agia
Galini Agios
Gavdos Matala Nikolaos • Ierapetra

24°N

Greece's
Top 20

1

Experiencing the Acropolis

1 There's a reason the Acropolis (p71) remains the quintessential landmark of Western civilisation – it is spectacular. Whether experienced during an early morning stroll up its flanks or from a dinnertime terrace with the Parthenon all lit up and glorious, the Acropolis embodies a harmony, power and beauty that speak to all generations. Look beyond the Parthenon and you'll find more intimate spots such as the exquisite, tiny Temple of Athena Nike (p75), while the Acropolis Museum (p78) cleverly showcases the ethereal grace of the Acropolis' surviving treasures. Below left: Parthenon (p75)

Meteora

2 You're not likely to forget the first moment the magnificent Meteora (p220) comes into view – soaring pillars of rock that jut heavenward, and a handful of monasteries at the summit (some dating from the 14th century). The rope ladders that once enabled the monks to reach the top have long been replaced by steps carved into the rock. Today, these spectacular stone towers beckon rock climbers from around the world. Below right: Moni Agias Varvaras Rousanou (p222)

RICARDO DE MATTOS/GETTY IMAGES ©

JAANA ELEFTHERIOU/GETTY IMAGES ©

WILL & DENI MCINTYRE/GETTY IMAGES ©

Ancient Delphi

3 Arrive early to catch the magic of the sun's rays pouring over the Sanctuary of Athena Pronea at Delphi (p189), the centre of the ancient Greek world. Only three columns remain of the magnificent sanctuary, but that's enough to let your imagination soar. Nearby, the Sacred Way meanders past the Temple of Apollo where the Delphic Oracle uttered prophecies that sent armies to battle and made lovers swoon.

Cutting-Edge Capital

4 Life in Athens (p64) is a magnificent mash-up of the ancient and the modern. Beneath the majestic facades of venerable landmarks, the city teems with life and creativity. And Athenians love to get out and enjoy it all. Galleries and clubs hold the exhibitions, performances and installations of the city's booming arts scene. Trendy restaurants and humble tavernas rustle up fine, fine fare. Ubiquitous cafes fill with stylin' locals, and moods run from punk rock to haute couture. Discos and bars abound and swing deep into the night. Above top right: Brettos bar (p112)

Santorini Sunsets

5 There's more to Santorini (Thira; p377) than sunsets, but this remarkable island, shaped by the fire of prehistoric eruptions, has made the celebratory sunset its own. On summer evenings the clifftop towns of Fira and Oia are packed with visitors awed by the vast blood-red canvas of the cliff face as the sun struts its stuff. You can catch the sunset without the crowds from almost anywhere along the cliff edge. And if you miss sundown, you can always face east at first light for some fairly stunning sunrises too... Above right: Oia (p385)

Rhodes' Old Town

6 Getting lost in Rhodes' Old Town (p470) is a must. Away from the crowds, meander down twisting, cobbled alleyways with archways above and squares opening up ahead. In these hidden corners the imagination takes off with flights of medieval fancy. Explore the ancient Knights' Quarter, the old Jewish neighbourhood or the Turkish Quarter. Hear traditional live music in tiny tavernas or dine on fresh seafood at atmospheric outdoor restaurants. Wander along the top of the city walls, with the sea on one side and a bird's-eye view into this living museum.

Easter Festivities

7 The Greek calendar is chock-full of festivals. By far, the biggest event of the Greek Orthodox Church is Easter, when villages and towns come to life with fireworks, street dancing, huge outdoor lamb roasts and plenty of ouzo shots. Begin with the candlelit processions of flower-filled biers marking the start of the celebration on Good Friday; by Saturday night you'll be shouting *Hristos Anesti* (Christ is Risen) and cracking red-dyed eggs. The best spot to join in the festivities is Patmos in the Dodecanese.

Bottom: Easter procession at Mt Athos (p259)

Cuisine

8 You don't have to be a fan of octopus and ouzo to enjoy Greek cuisine. Visit Thessaloniki for Eastern spiciness and Corfu or the Dodecanese for pasta galore. Traditional bakeries will leave your mouth watering with honey-drenched pastries; Leros has one of the best. Village restaurants will satisfy you with home-cooked roasts, fresh fish and salads picked from the back garden, while chefs in Athens or Santorini mix traditional recipes with creative flavours. Try mezedhes, little dishes that let you taste-test your way through the menu.

Island Hopping

9 From the spirited nightlife and celebrity hideaways of Kos and los, to the isolated sandy coasts of far-flung specks such as Anafi, jumping from island to island is a must. Peppered with ancient ruins (try Delos), mystical castles (head to Rhodes), lush scenery and rare wildlife (visit Lesvos), the islands are spread like jewels across the sea. Pinpoint those that take your fancy and join the dots by speeding over the Aegean on catamarans or swaying on old-fashioned ferry boats. You won't regret a saltwater-splashed second of it. Above: Kalymnos (p517)

Samaria Gorge

10 The gaping gorge of Samaria (p448), starting at Omalos and running down through an ancient riverbed to the Libyan Sea, is the most-trod canyon in Crete – and with good reason. The magnificent gorge is home to varied wildlife, soaring birds of prey and a dazzling array of wildflowers in spring. It's a full day's walk (about six hours down), and you'll have to start early, but it certainly builds character. To get more solitude, try lesser-known gorges such as Imbros Gorge, which runs roughly parallel to Samaria.

Colourful Thessaloniki

11 Stylish Thessaloniki (p239) remains northern Greece's liveliest town, thanks to its universities, cultural scene, arts and nightlife. There's little hassle and getting about by foot is easy. Take the city in at dusk from the viewing station up by the Byzantine walls in the old quarter, known as Ano Poli (Upper Town). It's a neighbourhood full of colourful, winding little streets marked by white-plastered houses, lazy cats and Byzantine churches.

Hydra

12 Everyone approaches Hydra (p309) by sea. There is no airport, there are no cars. As you sail in, you find, simply, a stunningly preserved stone village with white-gold houses filling a natural cove and hugging the edges of surrounding mountains. Then you join the ballet of port life. Sailboats, caïques and megayachts fill Hydra's quays and a people-watching potpourri fills the ubiquitous harbourside cafes. Here, a mere hour and a half from Athens, you'll find a great cappuccino, rich naval and architectural history, and the raw seacoast beckoning you for a swim.

Knossos

13 Rub shoulders with the ghosts of the Minoans, a Bronze Age people that attained an astonishingly high level of civilisation and ruled large parts of the Aegean from their capital in Knossos (p425) some 4000 years ago. Until the site's excavation in the early 20th century, an extraordinary wealth of frescoes, sculptures, jewellery, seals and other remnants lay buried under the Cretan soil. Despite a controversial partial reconstruction, Knossos remains one of the most important archaeological sites in the Mediterranean and is Crete's most visited tourist attraction.

Preveli Beach

14 Crete's Preveli Beach (p438) comprises one of Greece's most instantly recognisable stretches of sand. Bisected by a freshwater river and flanked by cliffs concealing sea caves, Preveli is lapped by the Libyan Sea, with clear pools of water along its palm-lined riverbank that are perfect for cool dips. The beach lies under the sacred gaze of a magnificent monastery perched high above. Once the centre of anti-Ottoman resistance and later a shelter for Allied soldiers, this tranquil building offers magnificent views.

The Zagorohoria

15 After passing through a seemingly endless array of tunnels, the Egnatia Odos highway brings you into rugged Epiros, home of the Pindos Mountains and the Zagorohoria (p290) – an immaculately preserved region of traditional villages spread along the ridges of Europe's deepest canyon, the Vikos Gorge. Here, the air is clear, fresh and cool, and the views astounding. You can explore the region by hiking or mountain biking, or simply get cosy by the fire in one of the many rustic B&Bs dotting the region. Below: Vikos Gorge (p293)

Corfu

16 The story of Corfu (p631) is written across the facades of its main town's buildings. This is a place that crams a remarkable mix of architecture into its small compass. Stroll past Byzantine fortresses, neoclassical British buildings of the 19th century, Parisian-style arcades, Orthodox church towers, and the narrow, sun-dappled streets of the Venetian Old Town. Beyond town, Corfu is lush green mountains, rolling countryside and dramatic coastlines. And if the architecture and scenery aren't enough, come for the Italian-influenced food!

Halkidiki & Mt Athos

17 Northern Greece's 'three fingers' are outstretched in the Aegean: the Halkidiki Peninsula (p256) has great beaches, nightlife, camping spots and some serious history. The first finger, Kassandra, buzzes in summer with open-air discos and fleshed-out beaches. The second, Sithonia, is quieter, drawing escapists to its sandy shores. Ouranoupoli on the third finger, Athos, offers family-friendly beaches, while the monasteries of the forested Mt Athos (p259) have preserved their Byzantine rituals for over 1000 years. Above top: Mt Athos

Hiking the Mani

18 Although it can no longer be described as 'remote', the Mani (p159) holds a magic unlike anywhere else in Greece. For centuries, the feuding families here were a law unto themselves, contributing to the unique Maniot culture. The Mani's footpaths and landscape beckon hikers from around the world. With everything from rugged rocky highlands and hidden lush-green oases to small fishing tavernas and severe rock-solid tower houses, this pocket of the Peloponnese is well worth exploring. Above: Vathia (p163)

Olymbos

19 Let your mind drift from the sandy coast to the interior, where secluded mountaintop villages guard unique cultures. Olymbos (p489) looks precarious at best, perched high above the rocky shoreline. After the day-trippers have gone home, the village exudes a certain quietness. Along cobbled alleyways, women bake bread in communal ovens and men whittle on doorsteps. They've dressed the same way for centuries and speak a language nearly lost. In a shrinking world, there aren't many places like this left. Soak up the magic while it still survives.

Ancient Olympia

20 The atmosphere at the site (p176) of the first Olympics is almost magical. Feel the watchful eye of Zeus as you tour the ruins, imagining the thousands of men that gathered to compete with hands full of offerings. The historical significance of this site is both humbling and inspiring. You may even be motivated to run a lap or two.

Need to Know

For more information, see Survival Guide (p725)

Currency
Euro (€)

Language
Greek

Money
ATMS widely available. Credit cards accepted in larger establishments and destinations. Cash necessary in villages and on smaller islands.

Visas
Generally not required for stays of up to 90 days; however travellers from some nations may require a visa; double-check with the Greek embassy.

Mobile Phones
Local SIM cards can be used in European and Australian phones. Most other phones can be set to roaming. US/Canadian phones need to have a dual- or tri-band system.

Time
East European Time (GMT/UTC plus two hours)

When to Go

- Dry climate
- Warm summer, mild winter
- Mild summer, very cold winter

Thessaloniki GO May–Nov

Corfu GO May–Sep

Athens GO May–Sep

Rhodes GO Apr–Sep

Iraklio GO May–Oct

High Season
(May–Aug)

➡ Everything is in full swing and transport is plentiful.

➡ Accommodation sometimes costs twice as much.

➡ Crowds and temperatures soar.

➡ This also applies to Easter.

Shoulder
(Apr & Sep)

➡ Accommodation prices can drop by 20%.

➡ Temperatures are milder.

➡ Internal flights and ferries have reduced schedules.

➡ Few crowds.

Low Season
(Oct–Mar)

➡ Many hotels, sights and restaurants shut, especially on islands.

➡ Accommodation costs up to 50% less than during high season.

➡ Ferry schedules are skeletal.

➡ Temperatures drop; Athens and Crete can see snow.

Useful Websites

EOT (Greek National Tourist Organisation; www.gnto.gr) Concise tourist information.

Greek Travel Pages (www.gtp.gr) Access to ferry schedules and accommodation.

Lonely Planet (www.lonelyplanet.com) Destination information, hotel bookings and traveller forum.

Ministry of Culture (www.culture.gr) For cultural events and sights.

Important Numbers

In Greece, the area code must be dialled, meaning you always dial the full 10-digit telephone number. The international access code is ⌨00.

Country code	⌨30
Ambulance	⌨166
Highway rescue (ELPA)	⌨104
Police	⌨100
Tourist police	⌨171

Exchange Rates

Australia	A$1	€0.70
Canada	C$1	€0.74
Japan	¥100	€0.77
New Zealand	NZ$1	€0.60
UK	£1	€1.16
USA	US$1	€0.77

For current exchange rates see www.xe.com.

Daily Costs
Budget: Less than €60

➡ Dorm beds €10 to €20 and domatia (Greek B&B) from €25.

➡ Markets and street stalls offer good prices.

➡ Your euros will stretch further in shoulder season.

Midrange: €60-100

➡ Double rooms in midrange hotels €35 to €60.

➡ Plenty of local tavernas with hearty midrange fare.

➡ Majority of sights have reasonable entrance fees.

Top End: Over €150

➡ Double rooms in top hotels from €90.

➡ Excellent dining; some accompanied by Michelin stars.

➡ Activities like diving and sailing available.

➡ Nightlife and cocktail bars abound.

Opening Hours

Opening hours vary throughout the year. We've provided high-season opening hours; hours decrease significantly in the shoulder and low seasons, when many places shut completely.

Banks 8.30am-2.30pm Mon-Thu, 8am-2pm Fri

Restaurants 11am-noon & 7pm-1am

Cafes 10am-midnight

Bars 8pm-late

Clubs 10pm-4am

Post Offices 7.30am-2pm Mon-Fri (rural), 7.30am-8pm Mon-Fri, 7.30am-2pm Sat (urban)

Shops 8am-3pm Mon, Wed & Sat, 8am-2.30pm & 5-8pm Tue, Thu & Fri

Arriving in Greece

Eleftherios Venizelos International Airport, Athens (p734)

➡ Express buses operate 24 hours between the airport, city centre and Piraeus.

➡ Half-hourly metro trains run between the city centre and airport from 5.30am to 11.30pm.

➡ Taxis to the city centre cost €30 (one hour).

Makedonia Airport, Thessaloniki (p254)

➡ Bus 78 runs half-hourly from the airport to the city's main bus station, via the train station.

➡ Taxis to the city centre cost €12.

Safety in Greece

➡ Greece is generally a very safe place to visit. Despite the recent high profile coverage in the media, protests and rioting are rare and generally confined to specific areas which are easily avoidable for tourists. The major risks are pickpockets in the large cities and taxi drivers willing to charge you extortionate rates from airports to the city centres.

➡ Other less common dangers include dodgy drinking water on many of the islands, the possibility of spiked drinks in Athens and at international party resorts, and heatstroke on unshaded, sun-drenched beaches. If you board a private boat, always ensure it has adequate life jackets, and be vigilant about your belongings when lounging on busy, popular beaches; leave passports behind in hotel safes. Potentially risky activities aren't limited to diving and mountain climbing; getting behind the wheel of a car in Greece also requires extra caution.

For much more on **getting around**, see p736

First Time Greece

For more information, see Survival Guide (p725)

Checklist

➡ Check the validity of your passport.

➡ Make any necessary bookings for accommodation and travel.

➡ Check airline baggage restrictions, including for regional flights.

➡ Inform credit/debit card company of your travel plans.

➡ Organise travel insurance.

➡ Check if you'll be able to use your mobile (cell) phone.

What to Pack

➡ Waterproof money belt

➡ Credit and debit cards

➡ Driver's licence

➡ Phrasebook

➡ Diving qualifications

➡ Phone charger

➡ Power adapter

➡ Lock/padlock

➡ Lightweight raincoat

➡ Seasickness remedies

➡ Mosquito repellent

➡ Swimwear, snorkel and fins

➡ Clothes pegs and laundry line

➡ Earplugs

Top Tips for Your Trip

➡ If at all possible, visit in the shoulder seasons – late spring or early autumn. The weather is softer and the crowds are slim.

➡ Be sure to visit a few out-of-the-way villages where you can still find full-on, unself-conscious traditional culture. The best way to do this is to rent a car and explore. Stop for lunch, check out the local shops and test out your Greek.

➡ Visit at least one local coffee shop, one seafood taverna next to a port and one traditional live-music venue. This is where you'll experience Greek culture at its most potent.

Sleeping

Reserving your accommodation out of season is important, as in some locations many hotels close for months on end. In high season it's equally essential as hotels can be fully booked well in advance.

➡ **Hotels** Classed from A through E, with A being five-star resort-style hotels and E having shared baths and questionable hot water.

➡ **Domatia** The Greek equivalent of the British B&B, minus the breakfast. Nowadays, many are purpose-built with fully equipped kitchens.

➡ **Campgrounds** Found in the majority of regions and islands and often include hot showers, communal kitchen, restaurants and swimming pools.

What to Wear

Athenians are well-groomed and the younger crowd is trendy, so keep your smart clothes for the city. Nevertheless, in Athens and other metropolises such as Rhodes, Thessaloniki and Iraklio, you'll get away with shorts or jeans and casual tops. Bars or fashionable restaurants require more effort – the scene is stylish rather than dressy. Think tops and trousers rather than T-shirts and cut-offs. In out-of-the-way places you can wear casual clothing; in summer, the heat will make you want to run naked; bring quick-drying tank-tops and cool dresses. Sturdy walking shoes are a must for the cobbled roads.

Money

In cities and large hotels, restaurants and shops, you can usually use debit and credit cards. Visa and MasterCard are widely accepted in Greece. American Express and Diners Club are accepted in larger tourist areas but unheard of elsewhere. In smaller, family-run places, particularly in out-of-the-way locations, cards won't be accepted and you'll need to have cash. Most towns have ATMS but they can often be out-of-order for days at a time. It's therefore wise (and necessary) to carry extra cash in a safe place like a money belt. (Note, card companies often put an automatic block on cards after the first withdrawal abroad as an antifraud mechanism. To avoid this happening, inform your bank of your travel plans.)

For more information, see p730.

Bargaining

Bargaining is acceptable in flea markets and markets, but elsewhere you are expected to pay the stated price.

Tipping

➡ **Restaurants** If a service charge is included, a small tip is appreciated. If there's no service charge, leave 10% to 20%.

➡ **Taxis** Round up the fare by a couple of euros. There's a small fee for handling bags; this is an official charge, not a tip.

➡ **Bellhops** Bellhops in hotels or stewards on ferries expect a small gratuity of €1 to €3.

Language

Tourism is big business in Greece and being good business people, many Greeks have learned the tools of the trade – English. In cities and popular towns, you can get by with less than a smattering of Greek; in smaller villages or out-of-the-way islands and destinations, a few phrases in Greek will go a long way. Wherever you are, Greeks will hugely appreciate your efforts to speak their language.

Etiquette

➡ **Eating & Dining** Meals are commonly laid in the middle of the table and shared. Always accept an offer of a drink as it's a show of goodwill. Don't insist on paying if invited out; it insults your hosts. In restaurants, the pace of service might feel slow; dining is a drawn-out experience in Greece and it's impolite to rush waitstaff.

➡ **Photography** In churches, avoid using a flash or photographing the main altar, which is considered taboo. At archaeological sites, you'll be stopped from using a tripod which marks you as a professional and thereby requires special permissions.

➡ **Places of Worship** If you plan to visit churches, carry a shawl or long sleeves and a long skirt or trousers to cover up in a show of respect.

➡ **Body Language** If you feel you're not getting a straight answer, you might need literacy in Greek body language. 'Yes' is a swing of the head and 'no' is a curt raising of the head or eyebrows, often accompanied by a 'ts' click-of-the-tongue sound.

Eating

Like much of Europe, the Greeks dine late and many restaurants don't open their doors for dinner until after 7pm. You will only need reservations in the most popular restaurants and these can usually be made a day in advance.

➡ **Taverna** Informal and often specialising in seafood, chargrilled meat or traditional home-style baked dishes.

➡ **Estiatorio** More formal restaurant serving similar fare to tavernas or international cuisine.

➡ **Mezedhopoleio** Serves mezedhes (appetisers); an *ouzerie* is similar but serves a round of ouzo with a round of mezedhes.

➡ **Kafeneio** One of Greece's oldest traditions, serving coffee, spirits and little else.

What's New

Ancient Akrotiri

Closed for years, this spectacular site has reopened within a protective enclosure. A once flourishing Minoan settlement, its buildings, ceramics and frescoes have been dug out from under the ash of Santorini's catastrophic volcanic eruption in 1613. The ruins are all the more accessible with new boardwalks crossing over and through the city, from where you can look down and watch archeologists still at work. Take one of the free tours now offered; the history and mystery of this place is truly intriguing. (p388)

Santorini Brewing Company

Unfiltered, unpasturised and preservative-free, Santorini's newest tipple is quickly recognisable for the donkey on its label. Red Donkey is ale, Yellow is lager and Crazy Donkey is Greece's first IPA. Take a tour. Buy the T-shirt. Savour the beer.

Ladadika

Thessaloniki's historic district of Ladadika has brushed off its somewhat twee, gentrified persona and reemerged as a lively nightlife scene with fab eateries, live-music venues and some of the city's top accommodation. (p251)

Funky Gourmet

The name does not lie. With an art deco lounge and dining area filled with contemporary art and designer lighting, this fresh Athens restaurant has more degustation menus than you could shake a smoked ice-cream sandwich at. There is nothing ordinary about this place. (p108)

Old Town of Xanthi

Until recently just a dreamy place of faded grandeur with narrow, winding lanes and pastel, timber-framed houses, Old Xanthi has got a new lease on life. In the evening, the beautiful streets are all the more captivating with lots of atmospheric bars and *mezedopoleia* (cafes serving small plates) spilling out into the little streets. (p276)

The Art Scene

Artists across Greece are using their work as a means of responding to the country's economic crisis. The result is a flourishing art scene. The number of art collectives in Athens has topped 50 with an ever-growing number of temporary exhibits and pop-up galleries appearing in empty shops and restaurants.

Cleaner Beaches

With 393 beaches and nine marinas receiving the much coveted Blue Flag in 2014 for cleanliness, Greece now ranks second in a list of 49 countries worldwide. To choose where to stretch out your towel, visit www.blueflag.org.

The Original Marathon

In 2013 the number of foreigners entering the annual Athens Classic Marathon climbed by 25% as runners clamor to follow the original 42.195km course of the news-bearing foot soldier from ancient Athens. If you're keen to do the same next November, register early at www.athens classicalmarathon.org.

For more recommendations and reviews, see lonelyplanet.com/greece

If You Like...

Art

For the oldest artistic expressions, countless archaeological museums contain ancient sculptures and bronze statues, often dredged up from the Aegean.

Byzantine iconography This art is thriving in galleries around the country where artists create exquisite, gold-hued creations; check out galleries at Ouranoupoli near Mt Athos, on Patmos and in Rhodes' Old Town.

National Museum of Contemporary Art This is an excellent starting point, however, you can witness the capital's flourishing modern art scene at numerous events and galleries. (p89)

Art Space This atmospheric gallery is housed in the wine caverns of one of Santorini's oldest vineyards. Showing some of the country's top current artists, it's one of Greece's largest art galleries. (p388)

National Art Gallery Home to a rich collection spanning Greece's creative history, this gallery (p71) is currently being expanded by over 11,000 square metres and is due to reopen by 2016. While it's closed, visit the gallery's offshoots including the National Sculpture Gallery (p71).

Walking

Stroll along the ancient promenade in Athens, hike a windswept donkey-trail or wander an ancient footpath beneath olive and cypress trees.

Crete's gorges Hikers flock to the spectacular Samaria Gorge (p449); its nearby cousins, the slender Imbros Gorge and lush Agia Irini Gorge are equally breathtaking.

Mt Olympus Follow trails from ancient times up thickly forested slopes towards the cloud-covered peak, once the lair of the Ancient Greek pantheon. (p266)

Pelion Peninsula Follow donkey trails that zigzag over rolling hills to quiet, sandy coves and quaint villages. (p209)

Museums

While it can't be denied that many Greek museums are dusty affairs, there are some modern, well-maintained gems to thoroughly impress you.

Acropolis Museum Treasures unearthed from the neighbouring Acropolis are on display in these state-of-the-art exhibition halls. (p78)

Benaki Museum A private museum filled to the gills with Bronze Age finds from Mycenae and Thessaly, works by El Greco and stunning collections of Greek regional costumes. (p88)

Iraklio Archaeological Museum A collection spanning 5500 years, but most famous for its Minoan collection, including the gob-smacking frescoes from Knossos. (p419)

Regional Cuisine

From rich *mousakas* to grilled souvlaki and honey-laced baklava, Greek cuisine has a homemade authenticity.

Ottoman influence The Turkish influence is felt strongly in the kitchens of Thessaloniki and northern Greece, with *yiaourtlou* kebab (grilled beef on pitta bread with Greek yoghurt) to patisseries piled high with *loukoumi* (Turkish delight).

Italian influence The Italians left behind pastas that the Greeks have added to their own dishes; try *makarounes* (homemade pasta cooked with cheese and onions) and visit Corfu Town where some of the finest homemade pasta is rolled out.

Seafood Harbourside kitchens land everything from mackerel to cuttlefish, squid and sea urchins; have yours grilled, fried, baked or stuffed with cheese and herbs. Fill yourself to the gills at 1500 BC (p384) on Santorini and Nireas on Rhodes (p477).

Live Music

Clubs throughout the country host traditional *rembetika* bands, playing evocative Greek blues. Live music is often accompanied by dining or ouzo.

Thessaloniki From traditional *bouzoukia* to major international acts, plus music in the strangest places, from jazz trios in bookstores to punk bands in anarchist dive bars. (p250)

Cafe Chantant At this atmospheric club in Rhodes' Old Town musicians whip up energetic tunes and locals sway and shoot ouzo from long wooden tables. (p478)

Rockwave Festival Big-name bands and massive crowds gather outside in a park; it's every rocker's dream. (p95)

Shopping

Leather Strappy sandals, handbags, belts, Cretan boots – Greek leather goods are great quality, support the local economy and look good. Shop for and test drive these goods in Hania. (p439)

Market stalls Hats, olives, art, jewellery, clothing and postcards – Greek markets are like giant jumble sales with the food markets in particular being cultural eye-openers and tummy-pleasers. Athens is a market wonderland. (p118)

Silver Ioannina has a long tradition of producing ornate handcrafted silver goods that shine in the Greek sunlight. (p289)

Top Hora (p337), Mykonos
Bottom Blue Caves (p664), Zakynthos

Month by Month

January

Most of the islands are snoozing during the winter months. However, the capital and surrounding mainland is awake and welcomes visitors with festivals that aren't really aimed at tourists. Expect local insight and warmth from hospitality (rather than the sun).

Feast of Agios Vasilios (St Basil)

The first day of January sees a busy church ceremony followed by gifts, singing, dancing and feasting. The *vasilopita* (golden glazed cake for New Year's Eve) is cut; if you're fortunate enough to get the slice containing a coin, you'll supposedly have a lucky year.

Epiphany (Blessing of the Waters)

The day of Christ's baptism by St John is celebrated throughout Greece on 6 January. Seas, lakes and rivers are all blessed, with the largest ceremony held at Piraeus.

Gynaikokratia

The villages of the prefectures of Rodopi, Kilkis and Seres in Northern Greece hold a day of role reversal on 8 January. Women spend the day in *kafeneia* (coffee houses) while the men stay at home to do the housework.

February

While February is an unlikely time to head to Greece, if you like a party and can time your visit with Carnival, it's well worth it.

Carnival Season

Carnival season kicks off three weeks prior to the fasting of Lent, from mid-January to late February or early March. A host of minor events leads up to a wild weekend of costume parades, colourful floats, feasting and traditional dancing. Celebrations see distinct regional variations; the Patra Carnival is the largest, while the most bizarre is on Skyros.

Clean Monday (Shrove Monday)

On the first day of Lent (a day which is referred to as Kathara Deftera), people take to the hills throughout Greece to enjoy picnicking and kite-flying.

March

The islands are still sleepy but the weather is warming up, making March a quiet, relaxed time to visit. Although the national calendar is quiet, there are countless religious festivals that towns and entire islands celebrate with great gusto.

Independence Day

The anniversary of the hoisting of the Greek flag by independence supporters at Moni Agias Lavras is celebrated with parades and dancing on 25 March. This act of revolt marked the start of the War of Independence.

April

In Greece, the biggest day of the year is Easter when the country, particularly the islands, shakes off its winter slumber. The holiday weekend is busy with Greeks hopping on planes and boats and booking out hotels; be sure to reserve well in advance.

 Orthodox Easter

Communities joyously celebrate Jesus' resurrection beginning with candlelit processions on Good Friday. One of the most impressive of these processions climbs Lykavittos Hill in Athens. The Lenten fast ends after 40 days on Easter Sunday with the cracking of red-dyed Easter eggs, fire-crackers, feasting and dancing. The Monastery of St John the Theologian on Patmos is a great place to witness it.

Festival of Agios Georgios (St George)

The feast day of St George, the country's patron saint and the patron saint of shepherds, falls on 23 April or the first Tuesday following Easter. It's celebrated with particular exuberance in Arahova, near Delphi. Expect dancing, feasting and a general party atmosphere.

May

If you're planning to head out on hiking trails, May is a great time to visit. Temperatures are still relatively mild and wildflowers create a huge splash of colour. Local greens, vegies and produce fill Greek kitchens.

May Day

The first of May is marked by a mass exodus from towns for picnics in the country. Wildflowers are gathered and made into wreaths to decorate houses. As a day associated with workers' rights, recent years have also seen mass walkouts and strikes on this day.

June

For festival-goers looking for contemporary acts rather than traditional village parties, June is hopping on the mainland. Top national and international performers fill atmospheric stages with dance, music and drama.

Navy Week

Celebrating their long relationship with the sea, fishing villages and ports throughout the country host historical re-enactments and parties in early June.

Nafplion Festival

Featuring Greek and international performers, this classical music festival in the Peloponnese uses the Palamidi fortress as one of its atmospheric concert venues. Check out www.nafplionfestival.gr for dates and details.

Feast of St John the Baptist

The country is ablaze with bonfires on 24 June as Greeks light up the wreaths they made on May Day.

Rockwave Festival

Rockwave has major international artists (such as Moby, The Killers and Mötley Crüe) and massive crowds. It's held in late June on a huge parkland at the edge of Athens. See www.rockwavefestival.gr for more.

Hellenic Festival

The most prominent Greek summer festival features local and international music, dance and drama staged at the ancient Odeon of Herodes Atticus on the slopes of the Acropolis in Athens and at the world famous Theatre of Epidavros, near Nafplio in the Peloponnese. Events run from June through August. Get details and tickets at www.greekfestival.gr.

July

Temperatures soar and life buzzes on the islands' beaches, while outdoor cinemas and giant beach clubs continue to draw visitors to Athens' nightlife. If you're staying anywhere near the water, fill your belly with seafood that's hauled in daily.

Wine & Culture Festival

Held at Evia's coastal town of Karystos, this festival runs through July and August and includes theatre, traditional dancing, music and visual-art exhibits. It ends with a sampling of every local wine imaginable.

☆ Delphi Cultural Festival

Every July, the European Cultural Centre of Delphi hosts a 10-day cultural festival with fine arts, a sculpture park and drama performances at its own open-air theatre.

August

Respect the heat of August; expect to do just a little bit less, move a little more slowly and relax just a little more fully. If you're planning to travel mid-month, reserve well ahead as Greeks take to the roads and boats in large numbers.

☆ August Moon Festival

Under the brightest moon of the year, historical venues in Athens open with free moonlit performances. Watch theatre, dance and music at venues such as the Acropolis or Roman Agora. The festival is also celebrated at other towns and sites around the country; check locally for details.

🎆 Feast of the Assumption

Assumption Day is celebrated with family reunions on 15 August; the whole population is seemingly on the move on either side of the big day. Thousands also make a pilgrimage to Tinos to its miracle-working icon of Panagia Evangelistria.

November

Autumn sees temperatures drop and the islands quieten down, although city life continues apace. Olive-picking is in full swing in places like Crete and feta production picks up, giving you the opportunity to taste some seriously fresh cheese.

🎆 Thessaloniki International Film Festival

Around 150 films are crammed into 10 days of screenings around the city in mid-November. The focus is on independent filmmakers and the festival is gaining increasing notoriety. For details, check out www.filmfestival.gr.

Plan Your Trip
Itineraries

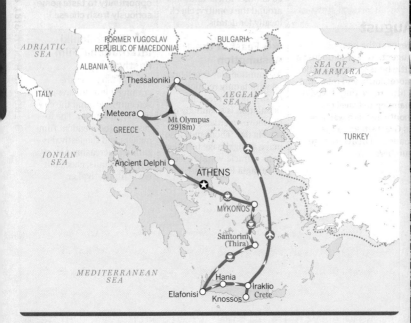

DENNIS K. JOHNSON/GETTY IMAGES ©

The Grand Tour

2 WEEKS

First trip to Greece? This tour takes in some of the country's biggest sights, best beaches and cultural highs. You'll also treat your appetite to the full array of Greek cuisine, from contemporary Athens restaurants to regional island cheese and herbs and northern, Ottoman-inspired dishes. (Not to mention Santorini's wine and beer scene.) If you want a more leisurely pace, choose just one of the islands and spend a bit longer stretched out on a beach.

Begin with a couple of days in **Athens**, home to some of the world's most important ancient sites and museums. Take in the markets, contemporary art scene and brilliant nightlife. From here catch a ferry to chic **Mykonos**, famous for its colourful harbour, bars and beaches. Visit the tiny, sacred island of Delos on a day trip to explore its ancient ruins. Hop on another ferry to spectacular **Santorini**. The dramatic, sheer cliffs of its volcanic caldera offer an amazing perch for watching the sun sink into the sea. There are also excellent local wineries, fascinating ruins and volcanic sand lapped by the Aegean.

Hora (p337), Mykonos

It's not far from here to Crete, where you should rent a car and before you do anything else, head south to **Elafonisi** beach – Crete's most stunning stretch of sand. From there, journey back up along the northern coast to charming **Hania**, with its beautiful harbour and labyrinth of backstreets and then on to the capital **Iraklio** and the nearby magnificent Minoan ruins of **Knossos**.

From Iraklio hop on a flight to cool, cultured **Thessaloniki** in northern Greece. Check out the impressive Roman and Byzantine architecture, sample some Ottoman-inspired cuisine (particularly the pastries!) and enjoy the vivacious arts scene. From here, work off the pastries on the nearby slopes of **Mt Olympus** (2918m), Greece's highest peak and first national park. You'll encounter a huge diversity of plant and bird life along these ancient trails. Next visit the mesmerising monasteries of **Meteora**, perched high on narrow pinnacles of rock and once the home of hermit monks. Your last stop is at unforgettable **ancient Delphi**, former home of the mysterious Delphic oracle and steeped in atmosphere. From Delphi it's a short trip back to Athens.

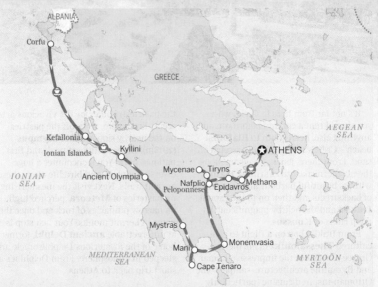

DAVID C TOMLINSON/GETTY IMAGES ©

Ionians & the Peloponnese

3 WEEKS

If you've a hankering for island life along with beautiful medieval towns, ancient historic sights and dramatic scenery, a tour of the Ionian Islands and the neighbouring Peloponnesian peninsula will more than satisfy you. This is doubly true if you're keen to toss some outdoor activities into your trip.

Begin your tour in **Corfu**, where you can easily spend a couple of days wandering through the amazing blend of Italian, French and British architecture in Corfu Old Town, indulging in gourmet cuisine, exploring picturesque coastal villages and lounging on fantastic sandy beaches. If you want to expend a bit more energy, Corfu is also a great place for windsurfing, or try biking in the island's mountainous interior. From Corfu, hop on a ferry to **Kefallonia**. Stay overnight in the picturesque village of Fiskardo, kayak to isolated golden beaches and sample the island's well-reputed local wine.

From Kefallonia, it's a short ferry ride to **Kyllini** on the Peloponnesian peninsula. Visit the sanctuary of **Ancient Olympia**, and stand in the stadium that hosted the first Olympic Games. Stay overnight in the town and take in some of the excellent museums. Head south to the captivating, World Heritage–listed ruins of **Mystras**. This massive ancient fortress town was the last stronghold of the Byzantine Empire.

Continue south to the rugged and remote **Mani**, to encounter villages filled with fascinating architecture and the remnants of the unique Maniot culture. This region is a haven for hikers with the dramatic Taÿgetos Mountains and tiny, isolated coves. It's also home to one of mainland Europe's most southerly points at **Cape Tenaro**, made famous in Homer's *Iliad*. Follow the coast east to spectacular **Monemvasia** and spend at least a day exploring the medieval cobbled alleyways and a night staying in atmospheric lodgings within the walls of its medieval town.

Next head north to graceful **Nafplio** with its mansions, museums and lively port. From here, it's easy to do day trips to the impressive acropolis at **Tiryns** and the citadel of **Mycenae**. East of here is the ancient theatre of **Epidavros**, where it's well worth taking in some star-lit classical performances. Then hop on ferry from nearby **Methana** to end your journey in **Athens**.

OLIVIERO OLIVIERI/GETTY IMAGES ©

Top: Lourdata (p653), Kefallonia
Bottom: Theatre of Epidavros (p146)

2 WEEKS Crete & the Dodecanese

Once considered out-of-the-way, Crete's eastern half has some fantastic sights and excellent towns that are making it an increasingly magnetic region. From here it's a short hop to the neighbouring Dodecanese, with their wealth of diversity and speedy catamaran services that makes island hopping a joy.

Begin in **Iraklio**, taking in the excellent archaeological museum and making a day trip to the impressive Minoan ruins of **Knossos**. En route take in the surrounding **Peza** wine region, which is nestled amid a landscape of shapely hills, sunbaked slopes and lush valleys. From Iraklio head east along the northern coast to the relaxed resort-town of **Agios Nikolaos**, which dishes out charm and hip ambience in equal portions. This makes a great base for exploring the surrounding region. Check out **Golden Beach** (Voulisma Beach) and **Istron Bay** for long stretches of sand, and the massive fortress on **Spinalonga Island**, a fascinating spot that's just a short ferry ride across the Gulf of Mirabello. Visit the surrounding Minoan ruins, such as **Malia**, a palace still filled with mysteries, and rent a bike to explore the tranquil villages of the fertile **Lasithi Plateau**, lying snugly between mountain ranges and home to Zeus' birthplace.

Continue on to **Sitia** from where you can head for the white sand of **Vaï**, Europe's only natural palm-forest beach. You can also head south from here to **Kato Zakros** to hike through the dramatic Valley of the Dead.

From Sitia, get settled on a 10-hour ferry ride to **Rhodes**. Spend a couple of days exploring Rhodes Town's walled medieval Old Town and checking out its burgeoning nightlife. Visit some of the surrounding beaches and stunning Byzantine chapels. Catch one of the daily catamarans to lush **Nisyros** to explore deep within its bubbling caldera and then carry on to **Patmos** to experience its artistic and religious vibe and to visit the cave where St John wrote the Book of Revelations. There are also some laidback beaches here and excellent restaurants. Backtrack to **Kos** to spend a final couple of days on gorgeous, sandy **Kefalos Bay** and to sip coffee and cocktails in Kos Town's lively squares. From Kos Town you can catch onward flights to **Athens**.

TOM PFEIFFER/VOLCANODISCOVERY/GETTY IMAGES ©

ALBERTO COTO/GETTY IMAGES ©

Top: Stefanos volcano crater (p504), Nisyros
Bottom: Vaï beach (p460), Crete

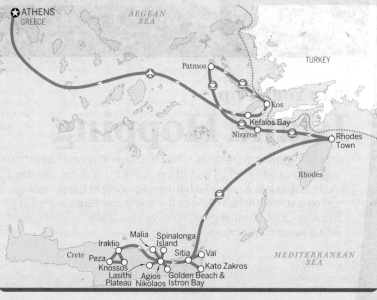

Spinalonga Island (p457), Crete

Plan Your Trip

Island Hopping

In Greece, getting there really is half the adventure and island hopping remains an essential part of the Greek experience. Whether you're sailing into a colourful harbour, listening to the pounding surf on a sun-drenched deck, or flying low over azure waters in a propeller-driven twin-engine plane, you will undoubtedly be filled with a sense of adventure.

Island Highlights

Best for Culture

Delos A stunning archaeological site.

Karpathos Experience Olymbos' Dorian-based culture.

Patmos See the cave where St John wrote the Book of Revelations.

Rhodes Roam around the medieval Old Town.

Crete Explore the Minoan palace of Knossos.

Best for Activities

Mykonos Dive with dolphins.

Crete Hike Europe's longest gorge.

Karpathos Try world-class kitesurfing.

Kefallonia Kayak to a remote cove or beach.

Best During Low-Season

Santorini Watch gorgeous sunsets.

Hydra Escape from Athens.

Crete Medieval cities and mountain villages.

Lesvos Find yourself on this isolated island.

Best for Drinking & Dining

Santorini Taste test at local wineries.

Ios Home to top restaurants.

Ikaria Seafood galore.

Corfu Braised meat, risottos and pasta.

Planning Essentials

While the local laissez-faire attitude is worth emulating while island hopping, a little bit of planning can also take you a long way. Deciding where and when you want to go and getting your head around routes and schedules before you go will take the work out of your holiday.

Travelling in Greece is that much more enjoyable when you have room to be somewhat flexible and to go with the flow. While transport information is always vulnerable to change, it seems nowhere is this truer than in Greece. Everything from windy weather to striking workers mean planes and boats are regularly subject to delays and cancellations at short notice. Ferry and airline timetables change from year to year and season to season, with ferry companies often 'winning' contracts to operate different routes annually. When island hopping, it's important to remember that no timetable is watertight.

When to Go

High Season

Over the Easter week and from June until September, lots of boats and planes connect the islands to one another and to the mainland. During this time, the tourist infrastructure is in full swing. However, transport and hotels can sometimes be booked up months in advance. This is mainly true of the most popular islands and where distances are greater. For example, overnight ferries to and from Athens are best purchased at least a couple weeks in advance if you're wanting anything more than deck class.

Low Season

Out of high season, planning ahead is essential. The number of boats and planes is quite limited and many hoteliers and restaurant owners close shop and head to Athens. In the dead of winter, all but the most popular islands are virtually closed. Before heading off, always check that transport links are up running and book hotels to ensure that they're open. And don't go expecting a dip in the sea, unless you're immune to cold water.

Shoulder Season

April, May, September and October are excellent times to hop through the islands. The weather is spring-like; most accommodation, restaurants and sights are open; and transport – though slightly limited – makes it possible to reach most destinations. Most importantly, you won't be fighting the crowds and everything is relatively cheap.

Travelling by Sea

The Fleet

With a network covering every inhabited island, the Greek ferry system is vast and varied. The slow rust-buckets that used to ply the seas are nearly a thing of the past. You'll still find slow boats, but high-speed ferries are increasingly more common and cover most of the popular routes. Local ferries, excursion boats and tiny, private fishing boats called caïques often connect neighbouring islands and islets. You'll also find water taxis that will take you to isolated beaches and coves. At the other end of the spectrum, hydrofoils and catamarans can cut down travel time drastically. Hydrofoils have seen their heyday but continue to link some of the more remote islands and island groups. Catamarans have taken to the sea in a big way, offering more comfort and coping better with poor weather conditions.

For long-haul ferry travel, it is still possible to board one of the slow boats chugging between the islands and to curl up on deck in your sleeping bag to save a night's accommodation, but Greece's domestic ferry scene has undergone a radical transformation in the past decade and these days you can also travel in serious comfort and at a decent speed. The trade off is, of course, that long-haul sea travel can be quite expensive. A bed for the night in a cabin from Piraeus to Rhodes can be more expensive than a discounted airline ticket.

Ticketing

As ferries are prone to delays and cancellations, for short trips it's often best not to purchase a ticket until it has been confirmed that the ferry is leaving. During high season, or if you need to reserve a car space, you should book in advance. High-speed boats like catamarans tend to sell out long before the slow chuggers. For overnight ferries it's always best to book in advance, particularly if you want a cabin or particular type of accommodation. If a service is cancelled you can usually transfer your ticket to the next available service with that company.

Many ferry companies have online booking services or you can purchase tickets from their local offices and most travel agents in Greece. Agencies selling tickets line the waterfront of most ports, but rarely is there one that sells tickets for every boat, and often an agency is reluctant to give you information about a boat they do not sell tickets for. Most have timetables displayed outside; check these for the next departing boat or ask the *limenarhio* (port police).

ISLAND FINDER

ISLAND	FOOD	FAMILY-FRIENDLY	NIGHTLIFE	BEACHES	CULTURE	ACTIVITIES	EASY ACCESS
Amorgos					✓	✓	
Corfu	✓	✓		✓	✓		✓
Crete		✓		✓	✓	✓	✓
Hydra					✓	✓	✓
Ios	✓		✓	✓			✓
Kefallonia	✓	✓		✓			✓
Kos	✓	✓	✓	✓	✓		✓
Lefkada				✓	✓	✓	✓
Milos				✓	✓	✓	
Mykonos			✓	✓			✓
Naxos	✓	✓	✓	✓	✓	✓	✓
Paros	✓	✓	✓	✓		✓	✓
Rhodes	✓	✓	✓		✓		✓
Samos	✓	✓		✓	✓	✓	✓
Santorini	✓		✓	✓	✓	✓	✓
Sifnos	✓				✓	✓	
Skiathos			✓	✓			✓
Thasos		✓		✓	✓	✓	✓
Zakynthos				✓	✓	✓	✓

Top: Kassiopi (p640), Corfu

Bottom: Corfu Town (p634)

Ferry Routes

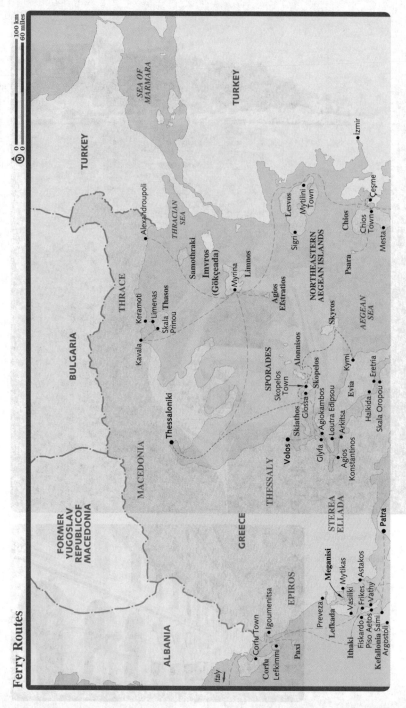

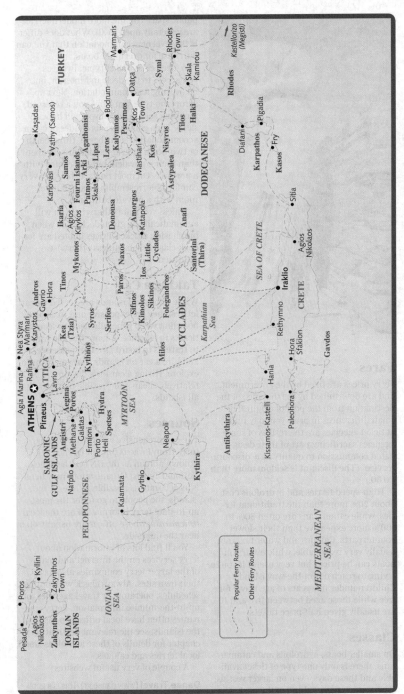

Popular Ferry Routes

Other Ferry Routes

House of Cleopatra, Ancient Delos (p397)

Fares

Ferry prices are fixed by the government, and are determined by the distance of the destination from the port of origin. The small differences in price you may find at ticket agencies are the results of some agencies sacrificing part of their designated commission to qualify as a 'discount service'. (The discount is seldom more than €0.50.)

High-speed ferries and hydrofoils cost about 20% more than the traditional ferries, while catamarans are often 30% to 100% more expensive than their slower counterparts. Caïques and water taxis are usually very reasonable, while excursion boats can be pricey but very useful if you're trying to reach out-of-the-way islands. Children under five years of age travel for free while those aged between five and 10 are usually given half-price tickets.

Classes

On smaller boats, hydrofoils and catamarans, there is only one type of ticket available and these days, even on larger vessels, classes are largely a thing of the past. The public spaces on the more modern ferries are generally open to all. What does differ is the level of accommodation that you can purchase for overnight boats.

A 'deck class' ticket typically gives you access to the deck and interior, but no overnight accommodation. Next up, aeroplane-type seats give you a reserved, reclining seat in which you will hope to sleep. Then come various shades of cabin accommodation: four-berth, three-berth or two-berth interior cabins are cheaper than their equivalent outside cabins with a porthole. On most boats, cabins are very comfortable, resembling a small hotel room with a private bathroom.

Unless you state otherwise, you will automatically be given deck class when purchasing a ticket. Prices quoted are for deck-class tickets, unless otherwise indicated.

Taking a Car

While almost all islands are served by car ferries, they are expensive and to ensure boarding you'll generally need to secure tickets in advance. A more flexible way to travel is to board as a foot passenger and hire a car on islands that you want to explore. Hiring a car for a day or two is relatively cheap and possible on virtually all islands.

Sources

The comprehensive weekly list of departures from Piraeus put out by the EOT (known abroad as the GNTO, the Greek National Tourist Organisation) in Athens is as accurate as possible. While on the islands, the people to go to for the most up-to-date ferry information are the local *limenarhio*, whose offices are usually on or near the quayside.

You'll find lots of information about ferry services on the internet and many of the larger ferry companies also have their own sites. Always check with online schedules, operators or travel agencies for up-to-the-minute information. Ferry companies often have local offices on many of the islands; see the relevant destination chapter for details of these as well as small, local ferries and caïques.

A couple of very useful websites:

Danae Travel (www.danae.gr) This is a good site for booking boat tickets.

GETTING YOUR SEA LEGS

Even those with the sturdiest stomachs can feel seasick when a boat hits rough weather. Here are a few tips to calm your tummy:

➡ Gaze at the horizon, not the sea. Don't read or stare at objects that your mind will assume are stable.

➡ Drink plenty and eat lightly. Many people claim ginger biscuits and ginger tea settle the stomach.

➡ Don't use binoculars.

➡ If possible stay in the fresh air – don't go below deck and avoid hydrofoils where you are trapped indoors.

➡ Try to keep your mind occupied.

➡ If you know you're prone to seasickness, consider investing in acupressure wrist bands before you leave.

Greek Travel Pages (www.gtp.gr) Has a useful search program and links for ferries.

Travelling by Air

The Squadron

A flight can save you hours at sea and offers extraordinary views across the island groups. While the largest and most popular islands tend to have airports, many of the smaller ones don't. Flights between the islands tend to be short and aeroplanes small, often making for a bumpy ride. The vast majority of domestic flights are handled by the country's national carrier, Olympic Air (p734), and its main competitor **Aegean Airlines** (☑ 801 112 0000; www. aegeanair.com). Both offer regular services and competitive rates. In addition to these national airlines, there are a number of smaller outfits running seaplanes or complementing the most popular routes.

Ticketing & Fares

The easiest way to book tickets is online, via the carriers themselves. You can also purchase flight tickets in most travel agencies in Greece. Olympic Air has offices in the towns flights depart from, as well as in other major towns. The prices listed here are for full-fare economy, and include domestic taxes and charges. There are discounts for return tickets when travelling midweek (between Monday and Thursday), and bigger discounts for trips that include a Saturday night away. You'll find full details and information on timetables on the airlines' websites.

Sources

Up-to-date information on timetables is best found online. Airlines often have local offices on the islands.

➡ **Aegean Airlines** (www.aegeanair.com)

➡ **Athens Airways** (www.athensairways.com)

➡ **Greek Travel Pages** (www.gtp.gr)

➡ **Olympic Air** (www.olympicair.com)

➡ **Sky Express** (www.skyexpress.gr)

Plan Your Trip
Cruising

With more than 1400 islands scattered across it, Greece's gorgeous azure water practically begs to be navigated. Not surprisingly, cruising is an increasingly popular way of seeing the country. Not only does cruising remove the stress of sorting out your own interisland transport, accommodation, meals and itinerary, it also gets you out on the sea with the *meltemi* (dry northerly wind) at your back and another island always on the horizon. Depending on the cruise you choose, it can also open doors to cultural tours and experiences otherwise not available, and take you to destinations where you might not have ventured.

Great Cruise Lines for...

Culture
Silversea runs exclusive tours that include language and cooking classes, guest lectures and entertainment from local ports.

Freedom
Azamara offers cruises with top service and few organised activities.

Luxury
Seadream Yacht Club offers ultra-pampering with nearly as many crew as guests.

Mature Travellers
Saga Tours does return cruises from the UK for people aged over 50.

Small & Personalised Trips
Variety Cruises has a maximum of 50 guests and the sea as its swimming pool.

Unconventional Trips
Star Clippers runs cruises on the world's largest fully rigged tall ships.

Choosing a Cruise

Cruises aren't what they used to be and certainly no longer the domain of blue-rinses and slot-machines. Catering to a discerning, ever-growing clientele, cruises are often geared to specific interests and niches. Greater competition also means better facilities, more varied excursions, worthwhile on-board diversions and increased dining options. Whether you're in the 30-something crowd, travelling with kids, after a little luxury or just want a no-frills adventure, if the idea of boarding a cruise ship appeals to you, chances are there's a perfect liner out there waiting.

Ship Size

Forget what you've heard, size does matter – at least when you're choosing a cruise ship. A ship's size says a lot about the experience it's offering; megaships can seem more like floating resorts, with a few thousand people on-board, while tiny liners cater to fewer than 50 passengers.

Large or Megaships
➡ Accommodate 1000-plus people.
➡ Nonstop activities and complete amenities.

CRUISING INDEPENDENTLY

Yachting is an amazing way to sail the seas, offering the freedom to visit remote and uninhabited islands. If you can't afford to buy a yacht, there are several other options. You can hire a bare boat (a yacht without a crew) if two crew members have a sailing certificate. Prices start at €1700 per week; check out **Set Sail Holidays** (www.setsail.co.uk). If you'd rather have someone else do the sailing for you, Trekking Hellas (p741) offers a fully crewed, fully loaded yacht that sleeps 10 from €3800 per day. **Tasemaro** (www.tasemarosailing.eu) takes up to four passengers, allowing you to be as involved as you like in the sailing. Prices start from €840/1280 per single/double per week.

Hellenic Yachting Server (www.yachting.gr) has general information on sailing around the islands and lots of links, including information on chartering yachts.

The sailing season is from April to October, although July to September is most popular. Unfortunately, it also happens to be when the *meltemi* (dry northerly wind) is at its strongest. This isn't an issue in the Ionian Sea, where the main summer wind is the *maïstros*, a light to moderate northwesterly that rises in the afternoon and usually dies away at sunset.

➡ Casinos, restaurants, spas, theatres, children's clubs, discos, bars, cafes and shops.

➡ Often unable to squeeze into some of the smaller islands' harbours and so visit the largest, most popular ports.

➡ Can seem to dwarf an island with its passengers more than doubling the destination's population.

Medium or Midsized Ships

➡ Cater for 400 to 1000 passengers.

➡ Usually more focused on the destination, with more port stops, more excursions and fewer on-board activities.

➡ Spa, pool, restaurants and bars.

➡ More often able to dock in small island harbours.

Small

➡ Itineraries are often more varied as they can stop at small, out-of-the-way ports.

➡ Often concentrate on a particular cruise niche, such as luxury or activity-based adventure.

➡ Don't expect a pool, spa, large cabin or plethora of dining options.

Itineraries

International cruises tend to visit Greece in combination with ports from other countries – usually Italy, Turkey and Croatia, often beginning at one port and ending at another. Greece-based cruises usually focus solely on ports within Greece and offer round trips. These cruises are often much more destination focused, with one or two stops each day. The crew are usually Greek, adding to the feel of authenticity, and cuisine and entertainment is more locally based with a bit of international flavour thrown in. Some Greek-based cruise lines worth checking out include:

➡ **Golden Star** (www.golden-star-cruises.com)

➡ **Louis Cruises** (www.louiscruises.com)

➡ **Variety Cruises** (www.varietycruises.com)

➡ **Windstar Cruises** (www.windstarcruises.com)

Popular Greek Ports of Call

➡ **Piraeus** The nearest port to Athens, allowing cruisers to explore ancient sites and experience contemporary Greece.

➡ **Mykonos** Famous for its nightlife and glamour; it's worth stopping overnight to take this in.

➡ **Delos** Ancient ruins cover this tiny island. Explore it on a half-day stop.

➡ **Corfu** Fantastic architecture and activity-based excursions to stunning beaches.

➡ **Santorini** Visit villages and beaches, hike volcanoes and enjoy sunset cocktail bars.

➡ **Crete** Atmospheric Hania or Iraklio are perfect for excursions to Knossos.

➡ **Katakolon** The nearest port to soaring Mt Olympus.

➡ **Nafplio** The magnificent site of Mycenae.

➡ **Itea** The closest port to the inspiring site of ancient Delphi.

➡ **Rhodes** A bustling medieval walled city can be explored when docked at the Old Town.

➡ **Patmos** An artistic haven and pilgrim site where St John wrote the Book of Revelations.

Excursions

Excursions are often what make cruises worthwhile and are designed to help you make the most of your sometimes brief visits ashore. Ensure that you factor in the cost of any excursions from the get-go. Excursions are generally most valuable when sights are not near the port or if a cultural expert is leading the tour. Where all of the sights are near the harbour, it's often just as worthwhile and more relaxing to go exploring on your own. If you plan to explore alone, it's worth double-checking before you book; some larger cruise boats dock at distant ports and it's difficult to

reach the island's sights or main towns independently.

Excursions are usually booked before you depart or else when you first board the ship. They're offered on a first-come, first-served basis and are generally very popular, so if you're choosing your cruise based on the excursions on offer, it's important to book them as soon as possible. Tours generally range from €35 to €60 for a half-day or €70 to €110 for a full day. Activity-based tours such as mountain biking or kayaking tend to be more, with a half-day around €100.

Budgeting

Cruise prices vary greatly depending on the time of year. Booking during the low season will get you good deals but means you will probably only have the opportunity to visit the largest and busiest ports

WHO'S WHO IN THE WATER

COMPANY	CONTACT	SHIP SIZE	CRUISE LENGTH	DESTINATIONS	BUDGET
Azamara	www.azamaracruises.com	medium	7-10 days	Greece, Turkey, Italy	$
Celebrity Cruises	www.celebrity.com	mega	10-13 days	Greece, Italy, Turkey, France	$
Costa Cruise Lines	www.costacruises.com	large	7-9 days	Greece, Italy, Turkey, Croatia	$
Crystal Cruises	www.crystalcruises.com	large	7-12 days	Greece, Italy, Turkey	$$
Cunard Line	www.cunard.com	large	7-21 days	Greece, Italy, Croatia, Turkey, UK, Spain	$
Golden Star	www.golden-star-cruises.com	medium	3-7 days	Greece, Turkey	$
Holland America Line	www.hollandamerica.com	large	6-12 days	Italy, Greece, Spain	$
Louis Cruises	www.louiscruises.com	medium & large	3-7 days	Greece, Turkey	$
MSC	www.msccruises.com	large	7-10 days	Greece, Turkey, Croatia, Italy	$
Oceania Cruises	www.oceaniacruises.com	medium	10-12 days	Greece, Turkey, Italy, Spain	$$$
Princess Cruises	www.princess.com	medium & large	6-24 days	Greece, Italy	$
Regent Seven Sea Cruises	www.rssc.com	medium	10-20 days	Greece, Italy, Turkey	$$$

as smaller islands virtually close out of season.

Budget cruises can be anywhere from €60 to €144 per day, midrange from €145 to €359 and luxury liners begin at €360 and go up to as much as €560 per day. Prices on cruises include meals, on-board activities, entertainment, port fees and portage but there are sometimes additional fuel charges. You also need to budget for airfare, tips, alcohol, pre- and post-cruise accommodation and excursions. Deals to look out for include two-for-one offers, prices including airfare or hotels and early-bird rates.

Booking

If you are confident manoeuvring your way around websites and know what you want from your cruise, booking online can be a straightforward option. It's certainly worth looking online for virtual tours and reviews, but a knowledgeable travel agent can help you through the plethora of options available and advise you on extra excursion charges and surcharges that you may miss when booking online.

There are often great rates for booking early and this allows you more choice in choosing cabins, excursions, dining options and so forth. While you can get great last-minute deals, you need to be willing and able to be flexible about dates and options. Booking your airfare through the cruise line may also mean you're collected at the airport and taken to the ship and if your flight or luggage is delayed, they'll wait or transport you to the first port.

Choosing a Cabin

Standard cabins are akin to very small hotel rooms, with fully equipped en suites, a double bed and somewhere to unpack. The cheapest option is an 'inside cabin' (ie no window). If you get claustrophobic, you can pay significantly more for an 'outside cabin' where you get either a window or porthole. Prices tend to climb with each floor on the ship but so does the ship's movement. If you suffer from seasickness, choose a lower deck where it's less rocky.

Cabin pricing is for double-occupancy; if you're travelling solo you pay a surcharge and if you're travelling as a group of three or four and willing to share a cabin, you can receive substantial discounts. Bunks are referred to as upper and lower berths, otherwise there is a double bed or twin beds that can be pushed together to make a double. Family rooms are sometimes available by having connecting cabins.

Things to check are how close your cabin is located to the disco and, if you're paying extra for a window, whether or not your view is likely to be blocked by a lifeboat.

Life on Board

Embarking: What to Expect

➡ A check-in time that's two or three hours before sailing.

➡ Your passport to be taken for immigration processing.

➡ The first day's program and a deck map, found in your cabin.

➡ The offer of a tour of the ship.

➡ A safety drill – legally required on all ships.

➡ The opportunity to set up an on-board credit account.

➡ Your dining-room table assignment.

Meals

Set mealtimes and seating assignments are still the norm on most ships and you will be able to choose your preferred dinnertime and table size when you book. Many ships continue to have formal dining evenings with dress codes. Some smaller ships have an all-casual policy while others have alternative dining options for those not interested in attending the formal evenings.

Tipping

Firstly, don't tip the captain or officers; it would be akin to tipping your dentist or airline pilot. On the final day of your cruise, you'll likely find tipping guidelines in your cabin, usually around €8 per person per day. Tipping is not required but makes up a huge part of the service staffs' wage and is expected.

Central Market (p108), Athens

Plan Your Trip
Eat Like a Local

Greeks love to eat out and share impossibly big meals with family and friends. Meals are drawn out, casual and convivial affairs. Some of the best and most authentic food is found at humble no-frills places. Whether you are eating seafood at a rickety table by the sea, trying modern Greek fare under the floodlit Acropolis or boiled goat in a village taverna, dining out in Greece is never just about what you eat, but the whole sensory experience.

When to Go

Food Seasons

Many olive oil producers, wineries, agricultural cooperatives and cheese makers are visitor-friendly year-round.

Food Festivals

Annual festivals celebrate local specialities and harvest seasons.

Fishermen's festivals (August to October) include the sardine festival on Lesvos and Ithaki's *maridha* (whitebait) festival.

In the Peloponnese, Leonidio's Aubergine Festival is held in August.

Aegina's pistachio industry celebrates Fistiki Fest mid-September.

Raki or *tsikoudia* festivals are held in Voukolies and other Cretan villages in November, when olive oil is produced.

Best Markets

Year-round, visit Athens' Central Market, Thessaloniki's Modiano Market and Hania's historic Agora, or find rotating weekly farmers markets.

Food Experiences

Dining on fresh fish and seafood at a rustic seaside taverna is one of Greece's enduring delights.

Take a cue from the locals and go straight to the source, heading to seaside fishing hamlets for fresh fish or mountain villages for local meat. Seek out tavernas that produce their own vegetables, wine and oil, where the fried potatoes are hand-cut, or the fish caught by the owner (or his cousin etc), though these places are becoming rare.

Enjoy traditional fare and the lively atmosphere at the tavernas inside Greece's bustling central markets.

Meals of a Lifetime

➡ **Varoulko** (p108) Stellar seafood by one of Greece's star chefs, with Acropolis views.

➡ **1800** (p387) Innovative seafood in stylish surrounds with stunning cliff-top vistas over Santorini's caldera.

➡ **Portes** (p443) Cretan food with flair and ambience in a narrow alleyway under Hania's Old Town city walls.

➡ **Levantis** (p347) Superb modern Greek cuisine with an Aegean bent in a delightful courtyard garden on Paros.

➡ **Katogi** (p376) Tantalising and inventive mezedhes (appetisers) in lively and delightful garden surrounds on Ios.

➡ **Klimataria** (p641) Stellar example of fresh, simple food from the humble taverna, in Corfu's fishing village of Benitses.

➡ **Thalassaki** (p328) Artful use of local produce and outstanding seafood in a charming seaside setting on Tinos.

➡ **Hotzas** (☑22710 42787; Kondyli 3; mains from €6) Exquisite traditional and fusion dishes in a classic stone taverna in Chios.

➡ **Hatzikelis** (p477) Fish harpooned by free-divers and filleted in front you in a chandelier-lit gem on Rhodes.

➡ **Paparouna** (p248) Inventive contemporary Greek fare in Thessaloniki's lively Ladadika dining precinct.

Cheap Treats

➡ **Souvlaki** Greece's favourite fast food, both the *gyros* and skewered meat versions wrapped in pitta bread, with tomato, onion and lashings of tzatziki.

➡ **Pies** Bakeries make endless variations of *tyropita* (cheese pie) and *spanakopita* (spinach pie) and other pies.

➡ **Street food** Includes *koulouria* (fresh pretzel-style bread) and seasonal snacks such as roasted chestnuts or corn.

Cooking Courses

Well-known Greece-based cooking writers and chefs run cooking workshops on several islands and in Athens, mostly during spring and autumn.

PRICE RANGES

Price indicators in this guide refer to the average cost of a main course:

€ Under €10

€€ €10–20

€€€ Over €20

➡ **Glorious Greek Kitchen Cooking School** (www.dianekochilas.com) Diane Kochilas runs week-long courses on her ancestral island, Ikaria, in July and August, as well as classes and culinary tours in Athens, Crete and the Cyclades.

➡ **Kea Artisanal** (www.keartisanal.com) Aglaia Kremezi and her friends open their kitchens and gardens on the island of Kea for cooking workshops.

➡ **Crete's Culinary Sanctuaries** (www.cookingincrete.com) Nikki Rose combines cooking classes, organic farm tours and cultural excursions around Crete.

Cook it at Home

Leave room in your baggage for local treats (customs and quarantine rules permitting) such as olives and extra virgin olive oil from small, organic producers; aromatic Greek thyme honey; dried oregano, mountain tea or camomile flowers; and dried barley rusks. A jar of fruit preserves, or 'spoon sweets' make an easy dessert poured atop Greek yoghurt or ice cream.

Local Specialities

From cheese and olive oil to the raw ingredients on your plate, you will find many regional variations and specialities on your travels. Crete is a popular foodie destination, with distinct culinary traditions, but the islands and mainland offer their own culinary treats. Be sure to ask about local dishes, cheese and produce.

How to Eat & Drink

Greece's relaxed and hospitable dining culture makes it easy to get into the local spirit.

Dolmadhes (stuffed vine leaves)

Given the long summers and mild winters, alfresco dining is central to the dining experience – with tables set up on pavements, roads, squares and beaches.

Greece doesn't have a big breakfast tradition, unless you count coffee and a cigarette, and maybe a *koulouri* or *tyropita* eaten on the run. You will find Western-style breakfasts in hotels and tourist areas.

When to Eat

Greeks eat late, rarely having dinner before sunset in summer. This coincides with shop closing hours, so restaurants often don't fill until after 10pm. Get in by 9pm to avoid the crowds.

While changes in working hours are affecting traditional meal patterns, lunch is still usually the big meal of the day, starting after 2pm.

Most tavernas open all day, but some upmarket restaurants open for dinner only.

Where to Eat

Steer away from 'tourist' restaurants and go where locals eat. As a general rule, avoid places on the main tourist drags,

Hora, Mykonos (p337)

especially those with touts outside and big signs with photos of food. Be wary of hotel recommendations, as some have deals with particular restaurants.

Tavernas are casual, good-value, often family-run (and child-friendly) places, where the waiter arrives with a paper tablecloth and plonks a basket of bread and cutlery on the table.

Don't judge a place by its decor (or view). Go for places with a smaller selection (where food is more likely to be freshly cooked) rather than those with impossibly extensive menus.

Restaurant Guide

➡ The classic Greek **taverna** has a few specialist variations – the **psarotaverna** (serving fish and seafood), and **hasapotaverna** or **psistaria** (for chargrilled or spit-roasted meat).

➡ A **mayirio** (cookhouse) specialises in traditional one-pot stews and baked dishes (*mayirefta*).

➡ An **estiatorio** serves upmarket international cuisine or Greek classics in a more formal setting.

➡ A **mezedhopoleio** offers lots of mezedhes (appetisers). In a similar vein, the **ouzerie** serves mezedhes (traditionally arriving with each round of ouzo) while regional variations focusing on the local firewater include the **rakadhiko** (serving *raki*) in Crete, and the **tsipouradhiko** (serving *tsipouro*) in the north.

OUZO TIME?

Ouzo – Greece's famous liquor – has come to embody a way of eating and socialising, enjoyed with mezedhes (appetisers) during lazy, extended summer afternoons. Sipped slowly and ritually to cleanse the palate between dishes, ouzo is usually served in small bottles or *karafakia* (carafes) with a bowl of ice cubes to dilute it (turning it a cloudy white).

Ouzo is made from distilled grapes with residuals from fruit, grains and potatoes and flavoured with spices, primarily aniseed, giving it that liquorice flavour. The best ouzo is produced in Lesvos (Mytilini).

ETIQUETTE & TABLE MANNERS

➡ Greek tavernas can be disarmingly and refreshingly laid-back. The dress code is generally casual, but in upmarket places locals dress to impress.

➡ Service can be slow (and patchy) by Western standards, but there's no rushing you out of there, either.

➡ Tables are not generally cleared until you ask for the bill, which in traditional places arrives with complimentary fruit or sweets or a shot of liquor. Receipts may be placed on the table at the start of the meal in case tax inspectors visit.

➡ Greeks drink with meals (the drinking age is 16), but public drunkenness is uncommon and frowned upon.

➡ Book for upmarket restaurants, but reservations are unnecessary in most tavernas.

➡ Service charges are included in the bill, but most people leave a small tip or round up the bill; 10% to 15% is acceptable. If you want to split the bill, it is best you work it out among your group – Greeks are more likely to argue over whose turn it is to pick up the tab.

➡ Greeks are generous and proud hosts. Don't refuse a coffee or drink – it's a gesture of hospitality and goodwill. If you're invited out, the host normally pays. If you are invited to someone's home, it is polite to take a small gift (flowers or sweets) and pace yourself, as you will be expected to eat everything on your plate.

➡ Smoking is banned in enclosed public spaces, including restaurants and cafes, but outdoor spaces are still open slather.

Menu Advice

Menus with prices must be displayed outside restaurants. English menus are fairly standard but off the beaten track you may encounter Greek-only menus. Many places display big trays of the day's *mayirefta* or encourage you to see what's cooking in the kitchen.

Bread and occasionally small dips or nibbles are served on arrival (you're not given a choice, and it's added to the bill).

Don't stick to the three-course paradigm – locals often share a range of starters and mains (or starters can be the whole meal). Dishes may arrive in no particular order.

Frozen ingredients, especially seafood, are usually flagged on the menu (an asterisk or 'kat' on Greek menu).

Fish is usually sold per kilogram rather than per portion, and is generally cooked whole rather than filleted. It is customary to go into the kitchen to select your fish (go for firm flesh and glistening eyes). Check the weight (raw) so there are no surprises on the bill.

Snorkelling, Ionian Islands (p629)

Plan Your Trip
Outdoor Activities

Greece has long been graced with an enormous expanse of blue water and warm winds; a profusion of undersea life; dramatic cliff faces; flourishing forests, groves and meadows; and an endless string of ancient walkways. It's only more recently that visitors have looked up from their sunloungers to notice. Whether you're a novice kitesurfer or avid cyclist, want to hike into deep gorges or ski from lofty heights, opportunities abound.

Best For...

Hiking

Samaria Gorge Trek among towering cliffs and wildflowers.

Andros Follow well-worn footpaths across hills to deep valleys.

Nisyros Hike through lush foliage and deep into the caldera.

Samos Wander through woods and swim under waterfalls.

Skopelos Walk through olive groves and pristine meadows.

Experts

Santorini Offers a pathway of canyons and swim-through sand caverns for divers.

Naxos Hike to the Cave of Zeus.

Paros Shangri-la for kitesurfing.

Peloponnese Cycle mountainous roads.

Novices

Vasiliki Learn how to windsurf.

Ios Dive schools catering to first-timers.

Poros Waterskiing beginners.

Paxi Walks through ancient olive groves.

Kos Cycle on the flat.

Water Activities

Diving & Snorkelling

Snorkelling can be enjoyed just about anywhere along the coast of Greece and equipment is cheaply available. Especially good spots to don your fins are Monastiri on Paros; Paleokastritsa on Corfu; Xirokambos Bay on Leros; and anywhere off the coast of Kastellorizo (Megisti). Many dive schools also use their boats to take groups of snorkellers to prime spots.

Greek law insists that diving be done under the supervision of a diving school in order to protect the many antiquities in the depths of the Mediterranean and Aegean Seas. Until recently dive sites were severely restricted, but many more have been opened up and diving schools have flourished. You'll find schools on the islands of Corfu, Evia, Leros, Milos, Mykonos, Paros, Rhodes, Santorini and Skiathos; in Agios Nikolaos and Rethymno in Crete; in Glyfada near Athens; and in Parga on the mainland.

The **Professional Association of Diving Instructors** (PADI; www.padi.com) has lots of useful information, including a list of all PADI-approved dive centres in Greece.

Windsurfing

Windsurfing is a very popular water sport in Greece. Hrysi Akti on Paros, and Vasiliki on Lefkada vie for the position of the best windsurfing beach. According to some, Vasiliki is one of the best places in the world to learn the sport.

There are numerous other prime locations around the islands and many water adventure outlets rent equipment. Check out Kalafatis Beach on Mykonos; Agios Georgios on Naxos; Mylopotas Beach on Ios; Cape Prasonisi in southern Rhodes; around Tingaki on Kos and Kokkari on Samos.

You'll find sailboards for hire almost everywhere. Hire charges range from €10 to €25, depending on the gear and the location. If you are a novice, most places that rent equipment also give lessons. Sailboards can be imported freely from other EU countries, but importing boards from other destinations, such as Australia and the USA, is subject to regulations.

Kitesurfing & Surfing

With near-constant wind and ideal conditions, Paros' Pounda beach is a magnet for kitesurfing's top talent, attracting both the Professional Kiteboard Riders Association championships and the Kiteboard Pro World Tour. With a shallow side, this is also an great place to learn the art of surfing. Mikri Vigla on Naxos is also an excellent spot, with courses off the gorgeous white-sand beach.

Waterskiing

Given the relatively calm and flat waters of most island locations and the generally warm waters of the Mediterranean, waterskiing can be a very pleasant activity. August can be a tricky month, when the *meltemi* (dry northerly wind) can make conditions difficult in the central Aegean. Poros, near Athens, is a particularly well-organised locale, with an organisation, **Passage** (☑22980 42540; www.passage.gr; Neorion Bay), hosting a popular school and slalom centre.

White-Water Rafting

The popularity of white-water rafting and other river adventure sports has grown rapidly in recent years as more and more urban Greeks, particularly Athenians, head off in search of a wilderness experience.

Trekking Hellas (p741) offers half-a-dozen possibilities, including the Ladonas and Alfios Rivers in the Peloponnese, the Arahthos River in Epiros and the Aheloos River in Thessaly. **Eco Action** (☑210 331 7866; www.ecoaction.gr; Agion Anargyron, Psyrri) offers rafting and kayaking on the Ladonas River, which hosted the kayaking at the 2004 Olympics, as well as on another three rivers throughout Greece.

Land Activities

Hiking

The majority of Greece is mountainous and, in many ways, a hikers' paradise. The most popular routes are well walked and maintained; however, the **EOS** (Greek Alpine Club; ☑210 321 2429; Plateia Kapnikareas 2, Athens) is grossly underfunded and consequently many of the lesser-known paths are overgrown and inadequately marked. You'll find EOS branches in Epiros, Crete (Greek Mountaineering Association) and Evia (Halkida Alpine Club).

The Lousios Gorge and the Mani, both in the Peloponnese, are two of the best places in Greece to explore on foot.

Hiking on the islands is particularly rewarding. On small islands you will encounter a variety of paths, including *kalderimia*, which are cobbled or flagstone paths that have linked settlements since Byzantine times. Other paths include *monopatia* (shepherd's or monk's trails) that link settlements with sheepfolds or link remote settlements via rough unmarked trails. Be aware that shepherd or animal trails can be very steep and difficult to navigate.

If you're going to be venturing off the beaten track, a good map is essential. Unfortunately, most of the tourist maps sold around the islands are completely inadequate. The best hiking maps for the islands are produced by **Anavasi** (www.anavasi.gr) and **Terrain** (www.terrainmaps.gr), both Greece-based companies.

Spring (April to May) is the best time for hiking; the countryside is green and fresh

---

DIVING INTO HISTORY

In the last half decade, Greek diving laws have relaxed to allow divers to visit many more underwater locations. While most divers and dive companies are heralding this as a positive move, historians and archaeologists are increasingly alarmed and calling for a return to the law prior to 2007, which strictly limited diving to a handful of areas. Their reason? The looting of underwater archaeological sites.

Greece's underwater world holds a wealth of historic discoveries. Over the centuries, a great many statues on land were melted down to make weapons and coins. Consequently, many of the largest ancient statues you'll see in Greek museums have been salvaged from the watery depths in the past century. The sea is now the country's largest archaeological site left. Approximately 100 known underwater sites are protected; however, historians claim there are likely to be thousands more yet to be discovered. Greece's ocean bed is a graveyard to countless shipwrecks dating all the way back to Classical times, which are considered both fascinating dive sites and archaeological hotbeds.

Despite a law dating back to 1932 that asserts that all found artefacts belong to the state, divers are said to be surfacing with sculptures, jewellery, warrior helmets and more. Meanwhile, archaeologists claim that the removal of even the most seemingly mundane objects can affect and eventually destroy sites.

The moral for divers? Don't become another masked and finned pirate. Look but don't touch.

from the winter rains, and carpeted with wildflowers. Autumn (September to October) is another good time, but July and August, when the temperatures are constantly up around 40°C, are not much fun at all. Whatever time of year you opt to set out, you will need to come equipped with a good pair of walking boots to handle the rough, rocky terrain, a wide-brimmed hat, a water bottle and a high UV-factor sunscreen.

A number of companies run organised hikes. The biggest is Trekking Hellas (p741), which offers a variety of hikes ranging from a four-hour stroll through the Lousios Valley to a week-long hike around Mt Olympus and Meteora. The company also runs hikes in Crete and the Cyclades.

Cycling

With over 4000km of coastal road on the mainland alone and 80% of mountainous terrain, Greece is gaining popularity as a cycling destination. While it's possible to rent a bike for a day, many people choose cycling as their main form of transport. Bicycles can usually be taken on trains and ferries for free and there are an increasing number of tour companies specialising in cycling holidays.

Cycle Greece (www.cyclegreece.gr) runs road- and mountain-bike tours across most of Greece for various skill levels. **Hooked on Cycling** (www.hookedoncycling.co.uk/Greece/greece.html) offers boat and bike trips through the islands and tours of the

TOP ISLAND HIKES

ISLAND GROUP	DESTINATION	SKILL LEVEL	DESCRIPTION
Crete	Samaria Gorge	easy to medium	One of Europe's most popular hikes with 500m vertical walls, countless wildflowers and endangered wildlife (impassable from mid-Oct–mid-Apr)
Crete	Zakros & Kato Zakros	easy to medium	Passing through the mysterious Valley of the Dead, this trail leads to a remote Minoan palace site
Cyclades	Tragaea, Naxos	easy to medium	A broad central plain of olive groves, unspoiled villages and plenty of trails
Cyclades	Filoti, Naxos	medium to difficult	A strenuous climb to the Cave of Zeus (a natural cavern on the slopes of Mt Zeus)
Dodecanese	Tilos	easy to medium	Countless traditional trails along dramatic clifftops and down to isolated beaches; a bird-lover's paradise
Dodecanese	Nisyros	easy to medium	A lush volcanic island with hikes that lead into the hissing craters of Mt Polyvotis
Evia	Steni	medium to difficult	Day hikes and more serious trekking opportunities up Mt Dirfys, Evia's highest mountain
Ionian Islands	Paxi	easy	Paths along ancient olive groves and snaking dry-stone walls; perfect for escaping the crowds
Ionian Islands	Ithaki	easy to medium	Mythology fans can hike between sites linked to the Trojan War hero Odysseus
Northeastern Aegean Islands	Samos	easy to medium	Explore the quiet interior of this Aegean Island with its mountain villages and the forested northern slopes of Mt Ambelos
Saronic Gulf Islands	Hydra	easy	A vehicle-free island with a well-maintained network of paths to beaches and monasteries
Sporades	Alonnisos	easy	A network of established trails that lead to pristine beaches

Hiking, Samaria Gorge (p448), Crete

GETTING MORE INFO

Diving Greece (www.diving-greece.net) For dive centres, sites, links and articles.

Trekking Hellas (www.trekking.gr) Hiking, white-water rafting.

Snow Report (www.snowreport.gr) For snow conditions.

and August most cyclists break between noon and 4pm to avoid sunstroke and dehydration.

Skiing

Greece provides some of the cheapest skiing in Europe. There are 16 resorts dotted around the mountains of mainland Greece, mainly in the north. The main skiing areas are Mt Parnassos, 195km northwest of Athens, and Mt Vermio, 110km west of Thessaloniki. There are no foreign package holidays to these resorts; they are used mainly by Greeks. They have all the basic facilities and can be a pleasant alternative to the glitzy resorts of northern Europe.

The season depends on snow conditions but runs approximately from January to the end of April. For further information pick up a copy of *Greece: Mountain Refuges & Ski Centres* from an EOT (Greek National Tourist Organisation) office. Information may also be obtained from the **Hellenic Skiing Federation** (210 323 0182; press@ski.org.gr; Karageorgi Servias 7, Syntagma, Athens).

mainland. **Bike Greece** (www.bikegreece.com) specialises in mountain biking, with various week-long tours for beginners and the experienced.

Much of Greece is very remote. Be sure to carry puncture-repair and first-aid kits with you. Motorists are notoriously fast and not always travelling in the expected lane, and extra caution on corners and narrow roads is well warranted. In July

Plan Your Trip
Travel with Children

Greece doesn't cater to kids in the way that some countries do – you won't find endless theme parks and children's menus. Instead, children are simply welcomed and included wherever you go. Greeks will generally make a fuss over your kids, who may find themselves receiving many small gifts and treats. Children are actively encouraged to join in most experiences, and teaching them a few Greek words will make them even more appreciated.

Best Regions for Kids

Athens
With ruins to clamber over, plus museums and child-geared sights to explore, Athens is great for kids. You'll also find big parks and gardens, a variety of cuisines and family-friendly hotels.

Crete
The island's beaches are long and sandy, Knossos ignites kids' imaginations, and you can explore from a single base, sidestepping the need to pack up and move around.

Dodecanese
The magical forts and castles, glorious beaches, laid-back islands, and speedy catamarans linking the Dodecanese daily make it ideal for families. And the Italian influence means an abundance of kid-friendly pasta dishes.

Northern Greece
Offers slightly lower summertime temperatures, Ottoman patisseries and Halkidiki's beaches. Laid-back Ioannina makes a great base and Parga is popular with families. Sithonia is less crowded but also less family friendly than the rest of Halkidiki.

Greece for Kids
Sights & Activities

While even the most modern Greek museums are often quite simply filled to the gills with relics and objects that not all children are going to appreciate, the settings are often intriguing as kids wander through the ancient palace-like buildings. The stories behind the objects can also captivate kids – ancient statues hauled up from the depth of the sea or helmets worn by gladiators. Generally more popular than the museums are the many ancient sights where kids enjoy climbing and exploring.

The beach is one of the best sources of entertainment for children in Greece. In summer, many of the larger, popular beaches have boogie boards, surfboards, snorkelling gear and windsurfing equipment for rent. Many also offer lessons or trips on boats or giant, rubber, air-filled bananas. While some beaches have steep drop-offs or strong currents, there is generally a calmer side to each island or a shallow, protected bay that locals can direct you to.

Most towns will have at least a small playground, while larger cities often have fantastic, modern play parks. In many cases, you can admire children's innate ability to overcome language barriers through play while you enjoy a coffee and pastry at the park's attached cafe. Some of the larger and more popular locations (such as Rhodes, Crete and Athens) also have water parks.

Dining Out

Greek cuisine is all about sharing; ordering lots of mezedhes (small dishes) lets your children try the local cuisine and find their favourites. You'll also find lots of kid-friendly options like pizza and pasta, omelettes, chips, bread, savoury pies and yoghurt.

The fast service in most restaurants is good news when it comes to feeding hungry kids. Tavernas are very family-friendly affairs and the owners will generally be more than willing to cater to your children's tastes. Ingredients like nuts and dairy find their way into lots of dishes so if your children suffer from any severe allergies, it's best to ask someone to write this down for you clearly in plain Greek to show restaurant staff.

Accommodation

Many hotels let small children stay for free and will squeeze an extra bed in the room. In all but the smallest hotels, travel cots can often be found, but it's always best to check this in advance. In larger hotels, cities and resorts, there are often package deals for families and these places are generally set up to cater to kids with childcare options, adjoining rooms, paddling pools, cots and highchairs.

Safety

Greece is a safe and easy place to travel with children. Greek children are given a huge amount of freedom and can often be seen playing in squares and playgrounds late into the night. Nevertheless, it's wise to be extra vigilant with children when travelling, and to ensure they always know where to go and who to approach for help. This is especially true on beaches or playgrounds where it's easy for children to become disoriented. It's also prudent not to have your children use bags, clothing, towels etc with their name or personal information (such as national flag) stitched onto them; this kind of information could be used by potential predators.

Dangers children are far more likely to encounter are heat stroke, water-borne bugs and illness, mosquito bites, and cuts and scrapes from climbing around on ancient ruins and crumbling castles. Most islands have a clinic of some sort, although hours may be irregular so it's handy to carry a first-aid kid with basic medicine and bandages.

Children's Highlights

Keep Busy

➡ **Boat trips** Whether it's zipping over the sea in a catamaran, bobbing up and down in a fishing boat or sailing on a day trip to a secluded bay.

➡ **Kayaking** Paddle alongside dolphins and visit pirate coves off Kefallonia.

➡ **Beach time** Jump waves, build sandcastles and snorkel.

➡ **Cycling** Use pedal-power along the flat, bike-friendly roads of Kos.

Explore

➡ **Acropolis** (p71) The home of the Greek gods is perfect for exploring early in the day.

➡ **Medieval castles** (p467) The island of Rhodes is packed with crumbling castles perched on cliffs above the sea; perfect for climbing and make-believe.

➡ **Knossos** (p425) Young imaginations go into overdrive when let loose in this labyrinth.

➡ **Nisyros' volcano** (p501) See it hiss and hear it bubble.

Eat Up

➡ **Yemista** Vegies (usually tomatoes) stuffed with rice.

➡ **Pastitsio** Buttery macaroni baked with minced lamb.

➡ **Tzatziki** A sauce or dip made from cucumber, yoghurt and garlic.

➡ **Loukoumadhes** Ball-shaped doughnuts served with honey and cinnamon.

➡ **Galaktoboureko** Custard-filled pastry.

➡ **Politiko pagoto** Constantinople-style (slightly chewy) ice-cream made with mastic.

WHAT TO PACK

➡ Travel highchair (either a deflatable booster seat or a cloth one that attaches to the back of a chair; these are light and easy to pack away)

➡ Lightweight pop-up cot for babies (if travelling to remote locations)

➡ Car seats (rental agencies are not always reliable for these, particularly on small islands or with local agencies)

➡ Plastic cups and cutlery for little ones

➡ Medicine, inhalers etc along with prescriptions

➡ Motion sickness medicine and mosquito repellent

➡ Hats, waterproof sunscreen, sunglasses and water bottles

Cool Culture

➡ **Carnival season** Fancy dress, parades and traditional dancing will keep even the oldest kids enthralled.

➡ **Football** Snag tickets for a game to catch some national spirit.

➡ **Hellenic Children's Museum** (p94) An excellent diversion in Athens. Kids can join in Greek cooking and craft classes.

Planning

The shoulder seasons (April/May and September/October) are great times to travel with children because the weather is milder and the crowds thinner. An excellent way to prepare your kids for their holiday and to encourage an active interest in the destination is by introducing them to some books or DVDs ahead of time. Lots of younger children enjoy stories of Greek gods and Greek myths while slightly older kids will enjoy movies like *Mamma Mia* or *Lara Croft: Tomb Raider* for their Greek settings. You can also find children's books about life in Greece that include a few easy phrases that your kids can try out.

If your kids aren't old enough to walk on their own for long, consider a sturdy carrying backpack; pushchairs (strollers) are a struggle in towns and villages with slippery cobblestones and high pavements. Nevertheless, if the pushchair is a sturdy, off-road style, with a bit of an extra push you should be OK.

Travel on ferries, buses and trains is free for children under four. They pay half-fare up to the age of 10 (ferries) or 12 (buses and trains). Full fares apply otherwise. On domestic flights, you'll pay 10% of the adult fare to have a child under two sitting on your knee. Kids aged two to 12 pay half-fare. If you plan to hire a car, it's wise to bring your own car seat or booster seat as many of the smaller local agencies won't have these.

Fresh milk is available in large towns and tourist areas, but harder to find on smaller islands. Supermarkets are the best place to look. Formula is available almost everywhere, as is condensed and heat-treated milk. Disposable nappies are also available everywhere, although it's wise to take extra supplies of all of these things to out-of-the-way islands in case of local shortages.

Matt Barrett has been dispensing his knowledge of Greece across the internet for years. His website **Travel Guide to Greece** (www.greektravel.com) has lots of useful tips for parents, while his daughter Amarandi has put together some tips for kids at **Greece 4 Kids** (www.greece4kids.com).

Regions at a Glance

Athens & Around

Ancient Ruins
Nightlife
Museums

Ancient Ruins

Roaming the hilltop ruins of the Acropolis is a must, while watching traditional Greek drama unfold at the Odeon of Herodes Atticus will send shivers down any theatregoer's spine. Athens and its surrounds are littered with ruins to explore, from the Agora in the city's heart to the Temple of Poseidon on Cape Sounion.

Nightlife

You don't have to be a night owl to appreciate Athens after dark (but it helps). This city refuses to snooze, with thousands dancing to foreign DJs at glamorous beachside clubs, intimate *rembetika* clubs where you can soak up Greek blues and ouzo, and everything in between.

Museums

Athens is a major contributor in the world's museum scene, from the expansive, stunning collection at the Byzantine Museum to the National Archaeological Museum's floors of antiquities, or the ultramodern Acropolis Museum which houses long-lost treasures from the site.

p64

Peloponnese

Ancient Ruins
Architecture
Activities

Ancient Ruins

The Peloponnese is packed with inspiring sites that bring the past to life. Visit the sanctuary of Ancient Olympia – birthplace of the Olympic Games. Explore the citadels of Mycenae and Tiryns, or take in a show at the theatre of Epidavros.

Architecture

From Byzantine cities to Venetian fortresses, this region is peppered with architectural gems. Walk across the causeway to Monemvasia, a magical castle off the coast, or explore traditional tower houses from the 17th century. The offerings are diverse and fascinating.

Activities

Put on your walking shoes. The Mani, the peninsula's rugged and remote southern region, is a popular place to amble, with mountains tumbling down to gorgeous coastal views. Northwest of here, hike through the Lousios Gorge to find charming village monasteries.

p130

Central Greece

Ancient Sites
Activities
Beaches

Ancient Sites

This region is home to two of Greece's most atmospheric architectural sites. The sanctuary of Delphi rests on the slopes of Mt Parnassos with views of olive groves and the sea. Nearby, Meteora's monasteries sit atop towering pinnacles of rock, built by 14th century monks.

Activities

Follow cobblestone trails past villages and in and out of forests on the Pelion Peninsula; raft over rapids or kayak on the Aheloos River; and follow in Hercules' footsteps, exploring the green depths of Iti National Park.

Beaches

Central Greece keeps its beautiful beaches a bit of a secret. Low-key resorts dot the Gulf of Corinth and the Pelion Peninsula where hidden, sandy coves and long stretches of sand await the intrepid.

p187

Northern Greece

Food & Wine
Activities
Beaches

Food & Wine

The mezedhes culture here is stronger than anywhere else in Greece, with a spiciness brought by refugees from the Anatolian Peninsula in Turkey. You'll also encounter mussel pilaf, crayfish, lots of cheese, and wine from Macedonian vineyards. Try Ottoman sweets in Thessaloniki's cafes and patisseries.

Activities

The story of Zeus takes you hiking into the clouds atop Mt Olympus, Greece's highest peak. In Zagorohoria, hike between 46 preserved hamlets steeped in legend in the Pindos Mountains.

Beaches

With sandy beaches, island getaways and towns with strong Italian-village influences, Parga typifies the region's resorts – popular yet relaxed, good for families yet also great for nightlife. And if you just want to escape, head for the remote sandy coves of Halkidiki.

p235

Saronic Gulf Islands

Activities
Architecture
Museums

Activities

Diving is magical in these waters. Dolphin safaris, sunken pirate ships and underwater caves are just the start. When dry land beckons, Poros, Hydra and Spetses have forests to explore and hilltops to climb.

Architecture

Hydra has taken good care of herself. Tiers of traditional buildings sweep down to the pretty harbour, and serene, ancient monasteries dot nearby hilltops. Next door on Spetses, see traditional boat building and impressive, deep-rooted mansions.

Museums

Hydra's museums include a fully restored hilltop mansion, eclectic naval collections and a museum filled with gold-encrusted ecclesiastic paraphernalia. At Spetses, see a traditional seafarer's home and at Baltiza, a museum of sea craft, from caïques to yachts.

p300

Cyclades

Ancient Ruins
Cuisine
Nightlife

Ancient Ruins

As one of the country's most important archeological sites, the sacred relics of Delos are protected and showcased on their own private island. The Minoan city of Akrotiki on Santorini is equally atmospheric.

Cuisine

Smoked eel and ham, Mykonian prosciutto, handmade soft cheeses and local wild mushrooms fill the menus on Mykonos and Paros. Kitchens are filled with creative culinary flair and modern takes on traditional foods, making it hard not to spend your day fantasising about your next meal.

Nightlife

The nightlife on Mykonos is legendary. It's a glamorous scene that's always entertaining. Ios is less swanky but very full-on, with wall-to-wall clubs and nonstop beach parties. Quieter Santorini has cocktail bars over the caldera with unparalleled sunset views.

p319

Crete

Ancient Ruins
Activities
Beaches

Ancient Ruins

The ruins of the Minoan civilisation grace this island, including the spectacular restored palace of Knossos and the labyrinth referred to in Greek mythology. At remote sites, there's a lingering sense of mystery.

Activities

The Samaria is Europe's longest gorge, and one of Crete's most popular draws. The island also boasts other quieter, equally dramatic gorges for hiking and rock climbing, and a mountainous interior with hermit caves and an allegedly haunted woodland to explore.

Beaches

Crete's beaches are palm-fringed stretches of powder-soft sand; some are packed with sun worshippers while others are isolated oases, but all are worth sinking your toes into.

p414

Dodecanese

Architecture
Activities
Cuisine

Architecture

This island group offers a huge amount of architectural eye candy: fairytale castles on the hilltops, frescoed Byzantine churches and Rhodes' walled, medieval Old Town. There are mountain villages tucked away from pirates, ruins of ancient temples and Italian-inspired harbour towns.

Activities

Some of the world's top rock climbing, kite-surfing, beach-combing, diving and walking is packed into the Dodecanese. Follow ancient footpaths to see endangered birdlife, hike into the caldera of a bubbling volcano or hang ten on a surfboard.

Cuisine

Mix Greek cuisine with long-term Italian influences and get scrumptious results; pizzas, pastas, stews and stuffed vegies, local cheeses, honey, wild greens and herbs, seafood and grilled meats are all here. The Dodecanese is also home to organic-farm-based restaurants and top-notch chefs.

p465

Northeastern Aegean Islands

Activities
Cuisine
Beaches

Activities

The clear water that laps these islands is perfect for diving into. You'll also be beckoned to hike to wooded waterfalls, wade through rivers and explore old-growth forests on foot or by bicycle.

Cuisine

Dining daily on fresh seafood is a way of life here. Venus clams, sea urchins, crayfish, grilled cod and lobster are all washed down with plenty of ouzo and Samos' sweet, local wine. Wherever you go, there'll be locally sourced, home-made meals including grills, cheeses, pies and puddings.

Beaches

From the remote, white-pebbled coast on Ikaria to hidden coves on the Fourni Islands, pristine sandy stretches on Chios and seaside resorts on Samos, you're never far from a beach on the aquamarine Aegean.

p538

Evia & the Sporades

Activities
Cuisine
Nightlife

Activities

Soak in thermal waters at local beaches or spas, watch for dolphins as you bob on the waters of a marine park, and hike through olive groves and pretty meadows. The region's also renowned for excellent scuba diving.

Cuisine

Don't miss the local honey, especially the *elatos* (fir) and *pefko* (pine) varieties. You'll also find amazingly fresh fish – select it directly from the nets and dine on the dock. Locally grown vegies and pressed olive oil add up to home cooking like *yiayia* makes it.

Nightlife

Nightlife isn't always about clubbing. Here it's about listening to some of the country's top bouzouki players and watching the sun sink over the horizon from low-key wine bars.

p603

Ionian Islands

Architecture
Activities
Cuisine

Architecture

Corfu Town is a symphony of pastel-hued Venetian mansions, French arcades and British neoclassical architecture, earning it a reputation as one of Greece's loveliest towns. For good measure, there's also a 6th-century fortress. Corfu is dotted with other historic mansions while neighbouring islands have traditional whitewashed villages and ancient windmills.

Activities

Kayak to remote coves, windsail across the blue Aegean, wander among ancient olive groves and hike through the mountains. Continuous stretches of gorgeous coastline and quiet interiors lure the adventurous.

Cuisine

Soft braised meat, plenty of garlic, home-made bread, seafood risottos and hand-rolled pasta allude to an Italian influence in the kitchen. Without a history of Turkish rule, Corfiot cuisine is distinctive and delicious.

p629

On the
Road

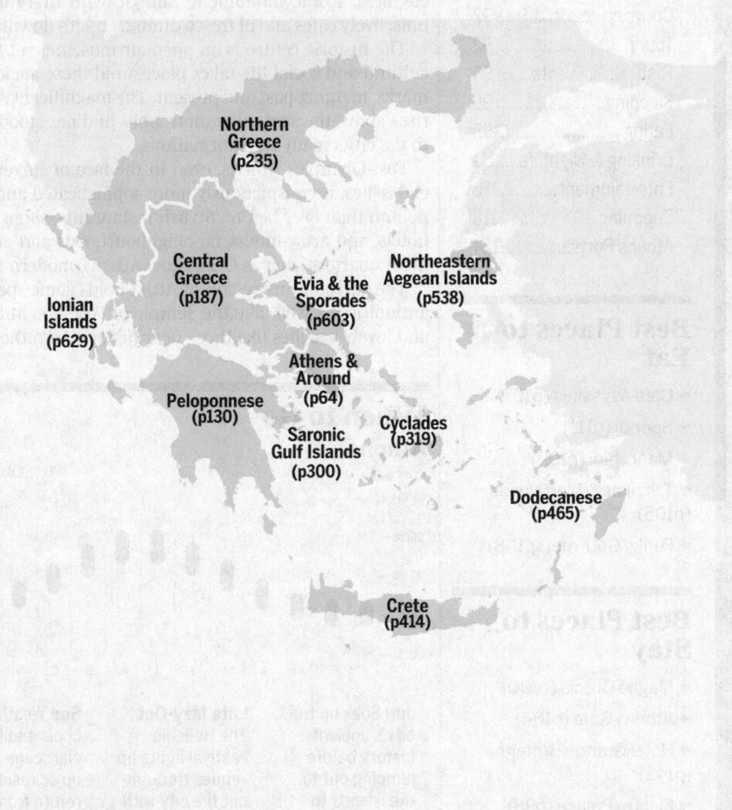

Northern Greece (p235)

Central Greece (p187)

Ionian Islands (p629)

Evia & the Sporades (p603)

Northeastern Aegean Islands (p538)

Athens & Around (p64)

Peloponnese (p130)

Saronic Gulf Islands (p300)

Cyclades (p319)

Dodecanese (p465)

Crete (p414)

Athens & Around

Best Places to Eat

➡ Café Avyssinia (p107)

➡ Spondi (p111)

➡ Mani Mani (p109)

➡ Tzitzikas & Mermingas (p105)

➡ Funky Gourmet (p108)

Best Places to Stay

➡ Magna Grecia (p100)

➡ Athens Gate (p104)

➡ Hotel Grande Bretagne (p143)

➡ Electra Palace (p98)

➡ NEW Hotel (p96)

Why Go?

Ancient and modern, with equal measures of grunge and grace, bustling Athens (Αθήνα) is a heady mix of history and edginess. Iconic monuments mingle with first-rate museums, lively cafes and al fresco dining, and it's downright fun.

The historic centre is an open-air museum, yet the city's cultural and social life takes place amid these ancient landmarks, merging past and present. The magnificent Acropolis rises above the sprawling metropolis and has stood witness to the city's many transformations.

Post-Olympics Athens, even in the face of current financial issues, is conspicuously more sophisticated and cosmopolitan than ever before. Stylish restaurants, shops and hip hotels, and artsy-industrial neighbourhoods and entertainment quarters such as Gazi, show Athens' modern face.

The surrounding region of Attiki holds some spectacular antiquities as well, like the Temple of Poseidon at Sounion, and lovely beaches like those near historic Marathon.

When to Go
Athens

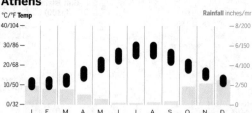

Jun Soak up the city's ancient history before jumping out to the islands to soak up the sun.

Late May-Oct The Hellenic Festival lights up venues throughout the city with drama and music.

Sep Weather cools and the social scene heats up as residents return from the islands.

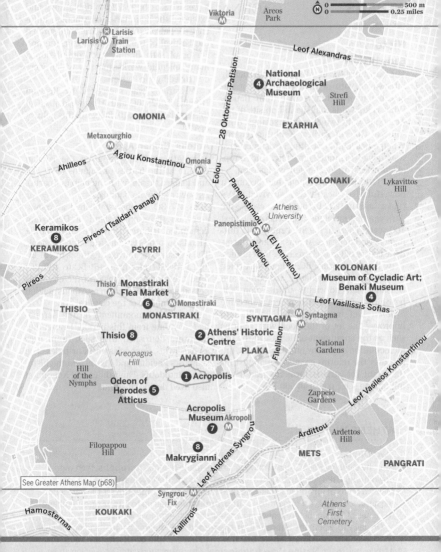

Athens Highlights

1 Climb to the awe-inspiring **Acropolis** (p71)

2 Promenade around Plaka, Monastiraki and Thisio in **Athens' historic centre** (p81)

3 Live it up with Athens' hot **nightlife** (p111): lively bars, jamming discos, chic beach clubs and moonlit cinemas

4 Compare superb antiquities and contemporary art at the **National Archaeological Museum** (p88), the **Museum of Cycladic Art** (p89), the **Benaki Museum** (p88) and Athens' multicultural centres

5 Catch an **Athens Festival** (p95) show at the Odeon of Herodes Atticus

6 Shop till you drop in the **Monastiraki Flea Market** (p118), or any of the boutiques

7 Enjoy the majesty of the Parthenon sculptures at the **Acropolis Museum** (p78)

8 Dine out in **Thisio** (p107), **Keramikos** (p107) or **Makrygianni** (p109) with a view of the floodlit Acropolis

ATHENS

ΑΘHNA

POP 3.8 MILLION

History

Early History

The early history of Athens is inextricably interwoven with mythology, making it impossible to disentangle fact from fiction. What is known is that the hilltop site of the Acropolis, with two abundant springs, drew some of Greece's earliest Neolithic settlers. When a peaceful agricultural existence gave way to war-orientated city states, the Acropolis provided an ideal defensive position.

By 1400 BC the Acropolis had become a powerful Mycenaean city. It survived a Dorian assault in 1200 BC but didn't escape the dark age that enveloped Greece for the next 400 years. Then, in the 8th century BC, during a period of peace, Athens became the artistic centre of Greece, excelling in ceramics.

By the 6th century BC, Athens was ruled by aristocrats and generals. Labourers and peasants had no rights until Solon, the harbinger of Athenian democracy, became *arhon* (chief magistrate) in 594 BC and improved the lot of the poor, with reforms such as the annulment of debts and the implementation of trial by jury. Continuing unrest over the reforms created the pretext for the tyrant Peisistratos, formerly head of the military, to seize power in 560 BC.

Peisistratos built a formidable navy and extended the boundaries of Athenian influence. A patron of the arts, he inaugurated the Festival of the Great Dionysia, the precursor of Attic drama, and commissioned many splendid works, most of which were destroyed by the Persians.

Peisistratos was succeeded by his son Hippias in 528 BC and Athens rid itself of this oppressor in 510 BC with the help of Sparta.

Athens' Golden Age

After Athens finally repulsed the Persian Empire at the battles of Salamis (480 BC) and Plataea (again, with the help of Sparta), its power knew no bounds.

In 477 BC Athens established a confederacy on the sacred island of Delos and demanded tributes from the surrounding islands to protect them from the Persians. The treasury was moved to Athens in 461 BC and Pericles (ruler from 461 BC to 429 BC) used the money to transform the city. This period has become known as Athens' golden age, the pinnacle of the classical era.

Most of the monuments on the Acropolis today date from this period. Drama and literature flourished with such luminaries as Aeschylus, Sophocles and Euripides. The sculptors Pheidias and Myron and the historians Herodotus, Thucydides and Xenophon also lived during this time.

ATHENS IN...

Two Days

Start by climbing Plaka's early morning streets to the glorious **Acropolis**, then wind down through the **Ancient Agora**. Explore **Plaka** and the **Monastiraki Flea Market**, taking a break at an Adrianou cafe. Head to the **Acropolis Museum** for the Parthenon masterpieces. Amble around the **grand promenade**, then up to **Filopappou Hill** and the cafes of **Thisio**, before dinner at a restaurant with Acropolis views.

On day two, watch the **changing of the guard** at Syntagma before heading through the gardens to the **Panathenaic Stadium** and the **Temple of Olympian Zeus**. Take a trolleybus to the **National Archaeological Museum**, then catch an evening show at the historic **Odeon of Herodes Atticus**, or head to **Gazi** for dinner and nightlife.

Four Days

With a couple more days, visit the **Benaki Museum**, the **Museum of Cycladic Art** and the **Byzantine & Christian Museum** before lunch and shopping in **Kolonaki**. Take the *teleferik* (funicular railway) or climb **Lykavittos Hill** for panoramic views. Catch a **movie by moonlight** at one of Athens' outdoor cinemas, or hit the **cocktail bars** around Plateia Karytsi and Plateia Agia Irini, or a **rembetika club** in winter.

On day four explore the dynamic **central market** and the **Keramikos** site. Trip along the coast to Cape Sounion's **Temple of Poseidon** or save your energy for summer nightlife at Glyfada's **beach bars**.

CONTEST FOR ATHENS

As the myth goes, Athena won the honour of being Athens' namesake and patron deity in a battle with Poseidon. After Kekrops, a Phoenician, founded a city on a huge rock near the sea, the gods of Olympus proclaimed that it should be named after the deity who could provide the most valuable legacy for mortals. Athena (goddess of wisdom, among other things) produced an olive tree, symbol of peace and prosperity. Poseidon (god of the sea) struck a rock with his trident and a saltwater spring emerged (some versions of the myth say he made a horse). The gods judged that Athena's gift would better serve the citizens of Athens with nourishment, oil and wood. To this day the goddess dominates Athens' mythology and the city's great monuments are dedicated to her.

Rivalry with Sparta

Sparta did not let Athens revel in its new-found glory. The jockeying for power between them led to the Peloponnesian Wars in 431 BC, which dragged on until 404 BC, when Sparta gained the upper hand. Athens was never to return to its former glory. The 4th century BC did, however, produce three of the West's greatest orators and philosophers: Socrates, Plato and Aristotle.

In 338 BC Athens, along with the other city states of Greece, was conquered by Philip II of Macedon. After Philip's assassination, his son Alexander the Great favoured Athens over other city states. After Alexander's untimely death, Athens passed in quick succession through the hands of his generals.

Roman & Byzantine Rule

The Romans defeated the Macedonians and in 186 BC attacked Athens after it sided against them in a botched rebellion in Asia Minor. They destroyed the city walls and took precious sculptures to Rome. During three centuries of peace under Roman rule known as the 'Pax Romana', Athens continued to be a major seat of learning and the Romans adopted Hellenistic culture. Many wealthy young Romans attended Athens' schools and anybody who was anybody in Rome at the time spoke Greek. The Roman emperors, particularly Hadrian, graced Athens with many grand buildings. Christianity became the official religion of Athens and worship of the 'pagan' Greek gods was outlawed.

After the subdivision of the Roman Empire into east and west, Athens remained an important cultural and intellectual centre until Emperor Justinian closed its schools of philosophy in AD 529. The city declined, and between 1200 and 1450, Athens was continually invaded: by the Franks, Catalans, Florentines and Venetians, all preoccupied with grabbing principalities from the crumbling Byzantine Empire.

Ottoman Rule & Independence

Athens was captured by the Turks in 1456, and nearly 400 years of Ottoman rule followed. The Acropolis became the home of the Turkish governor, the Parthenon was converted into a mosque and the Erechtheion became a harem.

On 25 March 1821 the Greeks launched the War of Independence (declaring independence in 1822). Fierce fighting broke out in the streets of Athens, which changed hands several times. Britain, France and Russia eventually stepped in and destroyed the Turkish-Egyptian fleet in the famous Battle of Navarino in October 1827.

Initially the city of Nafplio was named Greece's capital. After elected president Ioannis Kapodistrias was assassinated in 1831, Britain, France and Russia again intervened, declaring Greece a monarchy. The throne was given to 17-year-old Prince Otto of Bavaria, who transferred his court to Athens. It became the Greek capital in 1834 and was little more than a sleepy town of about 6000, with many residents having fled after the 1827 siege. Bavarian architects created imposing neoclassical buildings, tree-lined boulevards and squares. The best surviving examples are on Leoforos Vasilissis Sofias and Panepistimiou.

Otto was overthrown in 1862 after a period of power struggles, including British and French occupation of Piraeus aimed at quashing the 'Great Idea', Greece's doomed expansionist goal. The imposed sovereign was Danish Prince William, crowned Prince George in 1863.

Greater Athens

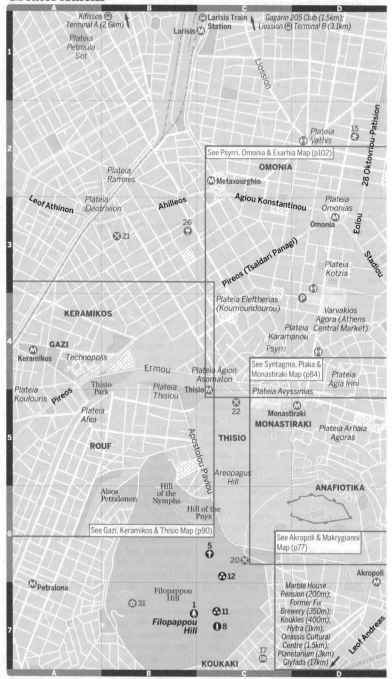

Kifissos (R)
Terminal A (2.6km)

Plateia
Petroula
Sot

Larisis Train Station

Larisis (M)

Gagarin 205 Club (1.5km);
Liossion (R) Terminal B (3.1km)

Liossion

28 Oktovriou-Patision

Plateia
Vathis 15

See Psyrri, Omonia & Exarhia Map (p102)

OMONIA

Plateia
Rammes

(M) Metaxourghio

Agiou Konstantinou

Plateia
Omonias

Leof Athinon

Plateia
Eleotrivion

Ahilleos

Omonia (M)

Omonia

Eolou

26

21

Pireos (Tsaldari Panagi)

Plateia
Kotzia

Stadiou

KERAMIKOS

Plateia Eleftherias
(Koumoundourou)

Varvakios
Agora (Athens
Central Market)

GAZI

Plateia
Karamanou

(M)
Keramikos

Technopolis

Ermou

Plateia Agion
Asomaton

Psyrri

See Syntagma, Plaka &
Monastiraki Map (p84)

Plateia
Agia Irini

Plateia
Koulouris

Pireos

Thisio
Park

Plateia
Thisiou

Thisio (M)

Plateia Avyssinias

Plateia
Afea

22

Monastiraki

MONASTIRAKI

Plateia Arhaia
Agoras

ROUF

Apostolou Pavlou

THISIO

Areopagus
Hill

ANAFIOTIKA

Alsos
Petralonon

Hill
of the
Nymphs

Hill of the
Pnyx

See Gazi, Keramikos & Thisio Map (p90)

See Akropoli & Makrygianni
Map (p77)

5

(M) Petralona

31

Filopappou
Hill

1

Filopappou
Hill

20

12

11

8

Akropoli (M)

Marble House
Pension (200m);
Former Fix
Brewery (350m);
Koukles (400m);
Hytra (1km);
Onassis Cultural
Centre (1.5km);
Planetarium (3km);
Glyfada (17km)

Leof Andreas

17

KOUKAKI

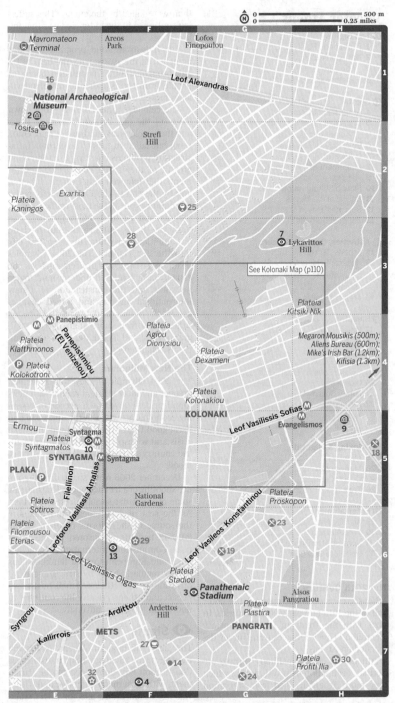

0 — 500 m
0 — 0.25 miles

Mavromateon Terminal

Areos Park

Lofos Finopoulou

Leof Alexandras

16

National Archaeological Museum

2   6

Tositsa

Strefi Hill

Plateia Kaningos

Exarhia

25

28

7 Lykavittos Hill

See Kolonaki Map (p110)

Panepistimio

Panepistimiou (El Venizelou)

Plateia Klafthmonos

Plateia Kolokotroni

Plateia Agiou Dionysiou

Plateia Kitsiki Nik

Plateia Dexameni

Megaron Mousikis (500m);
Aliens Bureau (600m);
Mike's Irish Bar (1.2km);
Kifisia (1.3km)

Plateia Kolonakiou

KOLONAKI

Leof Vasilissis Sofias

Evangelismos

9

18

Ermou

Syntagma

10

Plateia Syntagmatos

SYNTAGMA

Syntagma

PLAKA

Filellinon

Leoforos Vasilissis Amalias

Plateia Sotiros

Plateia Filomousou Eterias

National Gardens

Plateia Proskopon

23

Leof Vasileos Konstantinou

19

Leof Vasilissis Olgas

13

29

Plateia Stadiou

3 Panathenaic Stadium

Plateia Plastira

Alsos Pangratiou

Syngrou

Ardittou

Kallirrois

METS

Ardettos Hill

27

14

PANGRATI

32

4

24

Plateia Profiti Ilia

30

Greater Athens

The 20th Century

Athens grew steadily throughout the latter half of the 19th and early 20th centuries. In 1923, with the Treaty of Lausanne, nearly one million Greek refugees from Turkey descended on Athens.

Athens suffered appallingly during the German occupation of WWII, during which time more Athenians died from starvation than were killed by the enemy. This suffering continued in the bitter civil war that followed.

The industrialisation program that was launched in the 1950s, with the help of US aid, brought another population boom, as people from the islands and mainland villages moved to Athens in search of work.

The colonels' junta (1967–74) tore down many of the old Turkish houses of Plaka and the neoclassical buildings of King Otto's time, but failed to tackle the chronic infrastructure problems resulting from the rapid growth of the 1950s. The elected governments that followed didn't do much better, and by the end of the 1980s the city had a reputation as one of the most traffic-clogged, polluted and dysfunctional in Europe.

In the 1990s authorities embarked on an ambitious program to drag the city into the 21st century. The 2004 Olympics deadline fast-tracked projects such as the expansion of road and underground metro networks and the construction of a new international airport, and forced changes across the public and private sectors. As Athens absorbed more than 600,000 migrants, legal and illegal, the city's social fabric also changed.

The New Millenium

The 2004 Olympics legacy was a cleaner, greener and more efficient capital with newfound pride, buoyed by a decade of booming economic growth. But the optimism and fiscal good times were short-lived: financial crisis and widespread disenchantment with the country's governance darkened Athens' mood.

December 2008 riots, sparked by the police shooting of a teenage boy in Exarhia, saw some of the worst social unrest in decades. As the seat of government, and therefore the source of the reforms required by the 2010–13 bailouts (sponsored by the European Commission, International Monetary Fund and European Central Bank), Athens is now regularly beset by strikes and demonstrations. Nevertheless, small businesses persist and Athens' creative life continues to flourish in the face of adversity.

◉ Sights

The heart of modern Athens is **Plateia Syntagmatos** (Syntagma Sq; translated as Constitution Sq), dominated by the Parliament, with most major sights located within walking distance (see p98 for a DIY walking tour). South of Syntagma, the old Turkish quarter in **Plaka** is virtually all that existed when Athens was declared capital of Greece. Its paved, narrow streets nestle into the northeastern slope of the Acropolis and encompass many of the city's ancient sites. Touristy in the extreme, Plaka is still the most character-filled part of Athens.

Centred on busy **Plateia Monastirakiou** (Monastiraki Sq), the area just west of Syntagma is the city's grungier but nonetheless atmospheric market district. **Psyrri** (psee-ree), just north of Monastiraki, has a bit of a bar-and-restaurant quarter. The **Thisio** neighbourhood's Apostolou Pavlou is a lovely green pedestrian promenade under the Acropolis, with a host of cafes and youth-filled bars. The red neon-lit chimney stacks at the renovated gasworks in **Gazi** illuminate the city's densest nightlife district, packed with bars and restaurants. It is one of the burgeoning gay-friendly neighbourhoods of Athens.

Kolonaki, tucked beneath **Lykavittos Hill** east of Syntagma, is undeniably chic. Its streets are full of classy boutiques and art galleries, as well as dozens of cafes and trendy restaurants. To the east of the Acropolis, **Pangrati** is an unpretentious residential neighbourhood. The quiet neighbourhoods of **Makrygianni** and **Koukaki**, south of the Acropolis, around the Acropolis Museum, are refreshingly untouristy.

The commercial district around **Omonia** was once one of the city's smarter areas, but despite ongoing efforts to clean it up, it is still super-seedy, especially at night – exercise caution. **Exarhia**, the bohemian, graffiti-covered neighbourhood squashed between the Polytechnio and Strefi Hill, is a lively spot popular with students, artists and left-wing intellectuals.

The swank suburbs of **Kifisia** (inland) and **Glyfada** (seaside) have their own shopping, cafe and nightlife scenes.

The Athens basin is surrounded by mountains, bounded to the north by **Mt Parnitha**, the northeast by **Mt Pendeli**, the west by **Mt Egaleo** and the east by **Mt Ymittos**. Downtown Athens is dominated by its much smaller hills.

Athens boasts a large number of fine neoclassical buildings dating from the period after Independence. Foremost are the celebrated neoclassical trilogy on Panepistimiou, halfway between Omonia and Syntagma: the **National Library** (Map p102; ☎210 338 2541; www.nlg.gr; Panepistimiou 32, Syntagma; ⊙9am-8pm Mon-Thu, 9am-2pm Fri & Sat; M Panepistimio) FREE, **Athens University** (Map p102; ⊙closed to public; M Panepistimio), and **Athens Academy**.

At the time of research the **National Art Gallery** (Map p68; ☎210 723 5937; www.nationalgallery.gr; Leoforos Vasileos Konstantinou 50, Kolonaki; M Evangelismos) was closed for two years' renovation. The **National Sculpture Gallery** (Glyptotheque; ☎210 770 9855; Army Park, Katehaki; adult/child €3/free; M Katehaki), 8km southeast, was slated to reopen in late 2013.

Acropolis

Acropolis HISTORIC SITE

(Map p84; ☎210 321 0219; http://odysseus.culture.gr; adult/concession/child €12/6/free; ⊙8am-8pm, reduced in low season; M Akropoli) The Acropolis is the most important ancient site in the Western world. Crowned by the Parthenon, it stands sentinel over Athens, visible from almost everywhere within the city. Its monuments of Pentelic marble gleam white in the midday sun and gradually take on a honey hue as the sun sinks, while at night they stand brilliantly illuminated above the city. A glimpse of this magnificent sight cannot fail to exalt your spirit.

Inspiring as these monuments are, they are but faded remnants of Pericles' city. Pericles spared no expense – only the best materials, architects, sculptors and artists were good enough for a city dedicated to the cult of Athena. The city was a showcase of lavishly coloured colossal buildings and of gargantuan statues, some of bronze, others of marble plated with gold and encrusted with precious stones.

The Acropolis was first inhabited in Neolithic times (4000–3000 BC). The first temples were built during the Mycenaean era in homage to the goddess Athena. People lived on the Acropolis until the late 6th century BC, but in 510 BC the Delphic oracle declared that it should be the province of the gods.

After all the buildings on the Acropolis were reduced to ashes by the Persians on the eve of the Battle of Salamis (480 BC), Pericles set about his ambitious rebuilding program. He transformed the Acropolis into a city of temples, which has come to be regarded as the zenith of classical Greek achievement.

The Acropolis

Cast your imagination back in time, two and a half millennia ago, and envision the majesty of the Acropolis. Its famed and hallowed monument, the Parthenon, dedicated to the goddess Athena, stood proudly over a small city, dwarfing the population with its graceful grandeur. In the Acropolis' heyday in the 5th century BC, pilgrims and priests worshipped at the temples illustrated here (most of which still stand in varying states of restoration). Many were painted brilliant colours and were abundantly adorned with sculptural masterpieces crafted from ivory, gold and semiprecious stones.

As you enter the site today, elevated on the right, perches one of the Acropolis' best-restored buildings: the diminutive **Temple of Athena Nike 1**. Follow the Panathenaic Way through the Propylaia and up the slope toward the Parthenon – icon of the Western world. Its **majestic columns 2** sweep up to some of what were the finest carvings of their time: wraparound **pediments, metopes and a frieze 3**. Stroll around the temple's exterior and take in the spectacular views over Athens and Piraeus below.

As you circle back to the centre of the site, you will encounter those renowned lovely ladies, the **Caryatids 4** of the Erechtheion. On the Erechtheion's northern face, the oft-forgotten **Temple of Poseidon 5** sits alongside ingenious **Themistocles' Wall 6**. Wander to the Erechtheion's western side to find Athena's gift to the city: **the olive tree 7**.

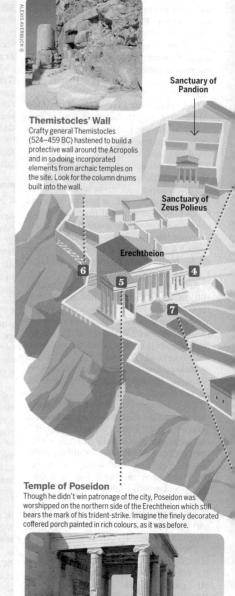

Sanctuary of Pandion

Themistocles' Wall
Crafty general Themistocles (524–459 BC) hastened to build a protective wall around the Acropolis and in so doing incorporated elements from archaic temples on the site. Look for the column drums built into the wall.

Sanctuary of Zeus Polieus

Erechtheion

Temple of Poseidon
Though he didn't win patronage of the city, Poseidon was worshipped on the northern side of the Erechtheion which still bears the mark of his trident-strike. Imagine the finely decorated coffered porch painted in rich colours, as it was before.

TOP TIP

» **The Acropolis** is a must-see for every visitor to Athens. Avoid the crowds by arriving first thing in the morning or late in the day.

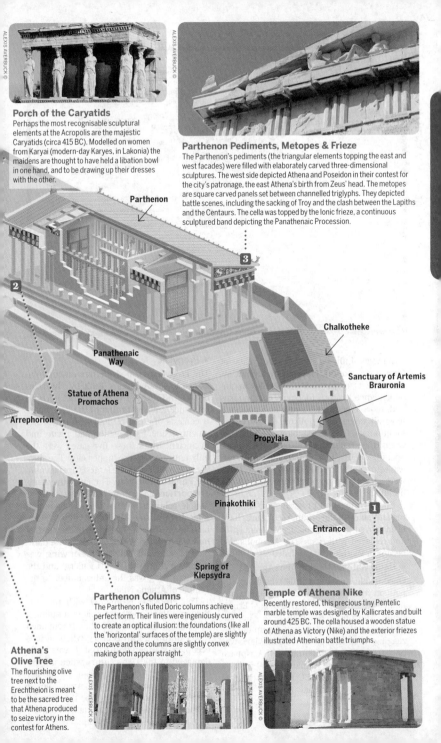

Porch of the Caryatids
Perhaps the most recognisable sculptural elements at the Acropolis are the majestic Caryatids (circa 415 BC). Modelled on women from Karyai (modern-day Karyes, in Lakonia) the maidens are thought to have held a libation bowl in one hand, and to be drawing up their dresses with the other.

Parthenon Pediments, Metopes & Frieze
The Parthenon's pediments (the triangular elements topping the east and west facades) were filled with elaborately carved three-dimensional sculptures. The west side depicted Athena and Poseidon in their contest for the city's patronage, the east Athena's birth from Zeus' head. The metopes are square carved panels set between channelled triglyphs. They depicted battle scenes, including the sacking of Troy and the clash between the Lapiths and the Centaurs. The cella was topped by the Ionic frieze, a continuous sculptured band depicting the Panathenaic Procession.

Parthenon

Chalkotheke

Sanctuary of Artemis Brauronia

Panathenaic Way

Statue of Athena Promachos

Arrephorion

Propylaia

Pinakothiki

Entrance

Spring of Klepsydra

Parthenon Columns
The Parthenon's fluted Doric columns achieve perfect form. Their lines were ingeniously curved to create an optical illusion: the foundations (like all the 'horizontal' surfaces of the temple) are slightly concave and the columns are slightly convex making both appear straight.

Athena's Olive Tree
The flourishing olive tree next to the Erechtheion is meant to be the sacred tree that Athena produced to seize victory in the contest for Athens.

Temple of Athena Nike
Recently restored, this precious tiny Pentelic marble temple was designed by Kallicrates and built around 425 BC. The cella housed a wooden statue of Athena as Victory (Nike) and the exterior friezes illustrated Athenian battle triumphs.

Acropolis

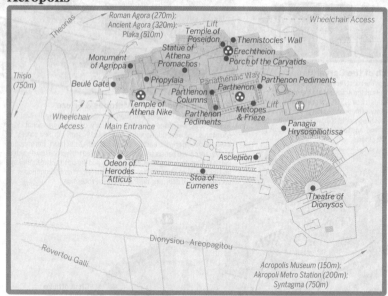

Ravages inflicted during the years of foreign occupation, pilfering by foreign archaeologists, inept renovations following Independence, visitors' footsteps, earthquakes and, more recently, acid rain and pollution have all taken their toll on the surviving monuments. The worst blow was in 1687 when the Venetians attacked the Turks, opening fire on the Acropolis and causing an explosion in the Parthenon, where the Turks were storing gunpowder, damaging all the buildings.

Major restoration programs are continuing and many of the original sculptures have been moved to the Acropolis Museum (p78) and replaced with casts. The Acropolis also became a World Heritage–listed site in 1987.

➡ Beulé Gate & Monument of Agrippa

Once inside the site, a little way along the path on your left you will see the Beulé Gate, named after the French archaeologist Ernest Beulé, who uncovered it in 1852. The 8m-high pedestal on the left, halfway up the zig-zagging ramp leading to the Propylaia, was once topped by the Monument of Agrippa, a bronze statue of the Roman general riding a chariot, erected in 27 BC to commemorate victory in the Panathenaic Games.

➡ Propylaia

The Propylaia formed the monumental entrance to the Acropolis. Built by Mnesicles between 437 BC and 432 BC, its architectural brilliance ranks with that of the Parthenon. It consists of a central hall with two wings on either side. Each section had a gate, and in ancient times these five gates were the only entrances to the 'upper city'. The middle gate (which was the largest) opened onto the **Panathenaic Way**. The imposing **western portico** of the Propylaia consisted of six double columns, Doric on the outside and Ionic on the inside. The fourth column along has been restored. The ceiling of the **central hall** was painted with gold stars on a dark-blue background. The **northern wing** was used as a *pinakothiki* (art gallery) and the southern wing was the antechamber to the Temple of Athena Nike.

The Propylaia is aligned with the Parthenon – the earliest example of a building designed in relation to another. It remained intact until the 13th century, when various occupiers started adding to it. It was badly damaged in the 17th century when a lightning strike set off an explosion in another Turkish gunpowder store. Archaeologist Heinrich Schliemann paid for the removal of one of its appendages – a Frankish tower –

in the 19th century. Reconstruction took place between 1909 and 1917, and again after WWII.

➡ Temple of Athena Nike

The exquisitely proportioned small Temple of Athena Nike stands on a platform perched atop the steep southwest edge of the Acropolis, to the right of the Propylaia. The temple was dismantled piece by piece in 2003 in a controversial move to restore it offsite and is now resplendent after its painstaking reassembly. The Turks also took it apart in 1686 and put a huge cannon on the platform. It was carefully reconstructed between 1836 and 1842, but was taken apart again 60 years later because the platform was crumbling.

Designed by Kallicrates, the temple was built of Pentelic marble between 427 BC and 424 BC. The building is almost square, with four graceful Ionic columns at either end. Only fragments remain of the frieze, which had scenes from mythology, the Battle of Plataea (479 BC) and Athenians fighting Boeotians and Persians. Parts of the frieze are in the Acropolis Museum, as are some relief sculptures, including the beautiful depiction of Athena Nike fastening her sandal. The temple housed a wooden statue of Athena.

➡ Statue of Athena Promachos

Continuing ahead along the Panathenaic Way you will see, to your left, the foundations of pedestals for the statues that once lined the path, including one that held Pheidias' 9m-high statue of Athena Promachos (*promachos* means 'champion'). Symbolising Athenian invincibility against the Persians, the helmeted goddess held a shield in her left hand and a spear in her right. The statue was carted off to Constantinople by Emperor Theodosius in AD 426. By 1204 it had lost its spear, so the hand appeared to be gesturing. This led the inhabitants to believe that the statue had beckoned the Crusaders to the city, so they smashed it to pieces.

➡ Parthenon

The Parthenon is the monument that more than any other epitomises the glory of Ancient Greece. Parthenon means 'virgin's apartment' and it is dedicated to Athena Parthenos, the goddess embodying the power and prestige of the city. The largest Doric temple ever completed in Greece, and the only one built completely of Pentelic marble (apart from the wood in its roof), it took 15 years to complete.

Built on the highest part of the Acropolis, the Parthenon had a dual purpose – to house the great statue of Athena commissioned by Pericles, and to serve as the new treasury. It was built on the site of at least four earlier temples dedicated to Athena. It was designed by Iktinos and Kallicrates to be the pre-eminent monument of the Acropolis and was completed in time for the Great Panathenaic Festival of 438 BC.

The temple consisted of eight fluted Doric **columns** at either end and 17 on each side. To achieve perfect form, its lines were ingeniously curved to create an optical illusion – the foundations are slightly concave and the columns are slightly convex to make both look straight. Supervised by Pheidias, the sculptors Agoracritos and Alcamenes worked on the architectural sculptures of the Parthenon, including the pediments, frieze and metopes, which were brightly coloured and gilded.

The **metopes** on the eastern side depicted the Olympian gods fighting the giants, and on the western side they showed Theseus leading the Athenian youths into battle against the Amazons. The southern metopes illustrated the contest of the Lapiths and Centaurs at a marriage feast, while the northern ones depicted the sacking of Troy.

ℹ ENTERING THE ACROPOLIS

There are several entry points to the Acropolis. From the south, walk along Dionysiou Areopagitou to the stairs just beyond the Odeon of Herodes Atticus to reach the **main entrance**, or go through the **Theatre of Dionysos entrance** near the Akropoli metro station, and wind your way up from there. Anyone carrying a backpack or large bag (including camera bags) must use the main entrance and leave bags at the cloakroom. The main approach from Plaka is along the path that is a continuation of Dioskouron.

People in wheelchairs can access the site via a cage lift rising vertically up the rock face on the northern side. Go to the main entrance for this.

Arrive as early as possible, or go late in the afternoon; it gets incredibly crowded. Also, wear shoes with rubber soles – the paths around the site are uneven and slippery.

> ### ℹ ACROPOLIS PASS & ENTRY HOURS
>
> The Acropolis admission includes entry to Athens' main ancient sites: the Theatre of Dionysos, Ancient Agora, Roman Agora, Hadrian's Library, Keramikos and the Temple of Olympian Zeus. The ticket is valid for four days; otherwise individual site fees apply. With the changes in government budgets, it will pay to double-check hours as they fluctuate from year to year. Check http://odysseus.culture.gr for free-admission holidays.

Much of the **frieze** depicting the Panathenaic Procession (see boxed text, p78) was damaged in the explosion of 1687 or later defaced by the Christians, but the greatest existing part (over 75m long) consists of the controversial Parthenon Marbles, taken by Lord Elgin and now in the British Museum in London. The British government continues to ignore campaigns for their return.

The **ceiling** of the Parthenon, like that of the Propylaia, was painted blue and gilded with stars. At the eastern end was the holy **cella** (inner room of a temple), into which only a few privileged initiates could enter. Here stood the statue for which the temple was built – the **Athena Polias** (Athena of the City), considered one of the wonders of the ancient world. Designed by Pheidias and completed in 432 BC, it was gold-plated over an inner wooden frame and stood almost 12m high on its pedestal. The face, hands and feet were made of ivory, and the eyes were fashioned from jewels. Clad in a long gold dress with the head of Medusa carved in ivory on her breast, the goddess held a statuette of Nike (the goddess of victory) in her right hand, and in her left a spear with a serpent at its base. On top of her helmet was a sphinx with griffins in relief at either side.

In AD 426 the statue was taken to Constantinople, where it disappeared. There is a Roman copy (the Athena Varvakeion) in the National Archaeological Museum.

➡ **Erechtheion**

Although the Parthenon was the most impressive monument of the Acropolis, it was more a showpiece than a sanctuary. That role fell to the Erechtheion, built on the part of the Acropolis held most sacred, where Poseidon struck the ground with his trident, and where Athena produced the olive tree. Named after Erechtheus, a mythical king of Athens, the temple housed the cults of Athena, Poseidon and Erechtheus.

The Erechtheion is immediately recognisable by the six larger-than-life maiden columns, the **Caryatids** (so called because they were modelled on women from Karyai, modern-day Karyes, in Lakonia), that support its southern portico. Those you see are plaster casts. The originals (except for one removed by Lord Elgin, and now in the British Museum) are in the Acropolis Museum.

The Erechtheion was part of Pericles' plan, but the project was postponed after the outbreak of the Peloponnesian Wars. Work did not start until 421 BC, eight years after his death, and was completed around 406 BC.

Architecturally it is the most unusual monument of the Acropolis, a supreme example of Ionic architecture ingeniously built on several levels to counteract the uneven bedrock. The main temple is divided into two cellae – one dedicated to Athena, the other to Poseidon – representing a reconciliation of the two deities after their contest. In Athena's cella stood an olive-wood statue of Athena Polias holding a shield adorned with a gorgon's head. It was this statue on which the sacred peplos was placed at the culmination of the Great Panathenaic Festival.

The northern porch consists of six Ionic columns; on the floor are the fissures supposedly left by the thunderbolt sent by Zeus to kill Erechtheus. To the south of here was the Cecropion – King Cecrops' burial place.

Except for a small temple of Rome and Augustus, which is no longer in existence, the Erechtheion was the last public building erected on the Acropolis in antiquity.

◉ South Slope of the Acropolis & Makrygianni

★ **Theatre of Dionysos** HISTORIC SITE
(Map p84; ☏ 210 322 4625; Dionysiou Areopagitou; adult/child €2/free, free with Acropolis pass; ⊙ 8am-8pm, reduced low season; Ⓜ Akropoli) The tyrant Peisistratos introduced the annual Festival of the Great Dionysia during the 6th century BC, and held it in the world's first theatre on the south slope of the Acropolis. The original theatre on this site was a timber structure, and masses of people attended the contests, where men clad in goatskins

sang and danced, followed by feasting and revelry.

Drama as we know it dates back to these contests. At one of them, Thespis left the ensemble and took centre stage for a solo performance, an act considered to be the first true dramatic performance – hence the term 'thespian'.

During the golden age in the 5th century BC, the annual festival was one of the state's major events. Politicians sponsored dramas by writers such as Aeschylus, Sophocles and Euripides, with some light relief provided by the bawdy comedies of Aristophanes. People came from all over Attica, with their expenses met by the state.

The theatre was reconstructed in stone and marble by Lycurgus between 342 BC and 326 BC, with a seating capacity of 17,000 spread over 64 tiers, of which about 20 survive. Apart from the front row, the seats were built of Piraeus limestone and were occupied by ordinary citizens, although women were confined to the back rows. The front row's 67 Pentelic marble thrones were reserved for festival officials and important

Akropoli & Makrygianni

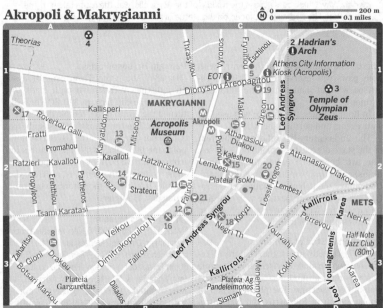

Akropoli & Makrygianni

PANATHENIAC PROCESSION

The biggest event in ancient Athens was the Panathenaic Procession, the climax of the Panathenaia Festival held to venerate the goddess Athena. Colourful scenes of the Procession are depicted in the 160m-long Parthenon frieze in the Acropolis Museum.

There were actually two festivals. The Lesser Panathenaic Festival took place annually on Athena's birthday, but the Great Panathenaic Festival was held on every fourth anniversary of the goddess' birth.

The Great Panathenaic Festival began with dancing, followed by athletic, dramatic and musical contests. On the final day, the Panathenaic Procession began at Keramikos, led by men carrying animals sacrificed to Athena, followed by maidens carrying *rhytons* (horn-shaped drinking vessels) and musicians playing a fanfare for the girls of noble birth who held aloft the sacred *peplos* (a glorious saffron-coloured shawl). The Panathenaic Way, which cuts across the middle of the Acropolis, was the route taken by the procession. The *peplos* was placed on the statue of Athena Polias in the Erechtheion in the festival's grand finale.

priests. The grandest one in the centre, with lions' paws, was reserved for the Priest of Dionysos, who sat shaded from the sun under a canopy.

In Roman times, the theatre was used for state events and performances.

The 2nd-century-BC **reliefs** at the rear of the stage depict the exploits of Dionysos. The two hefty men (who still have their heads) are *selini*, worshippers of the mythical Selinos, the debauched father of the satyrs, whose favourite pastime was charging up mountains with his oversized phallus in lecherous pursuit of nymphs.

Asclepion & Stoa of Eumenes RUIN
(Map p77) Directly above the Theatre of Dionysos, steps lead to the Asclepion, a temple that was built around a sacred spring. The worship of Asclepius, the physician son of Apollo, began in Epidavros and was introduced to Athens in 429 BC at a time when plague was sweeping the city; people sought cures here.

Beneath the Asclepion is the Stoa of Eumenes, a colonnade built by Eumenes II, King of Pergamum (197–159 BC), as a shelter and promenade for theatre audiences.

★Odeon of Herodes Atticus HISTORIC SITE
(Map p84; ☑210 324 1807; www.greekfestival.gr for Athens Festival) The path continues west from the Asclepion to the Odeon of Herodes Atticus, built in AD 161 by wealthy Roman Herodes Atticus in memory of his wife Regilla. It was excavated in 1857–58 and completely restored between 1950 and 1961. Performances of drama, music and dance are held here during the Athens Festival.

Panagia Hrysospiliotissa HISTORIC SITE
(Map p84) Above the Theatre of Dionysos, an indistinct rock-strewn path leads to a grotto in the cliff face. In 320 BC Thrasyllos turned the grotto into a temple dedicated to Dionysos. The tiny Panagia Hrysospiliotissa (Chapel of Our Lady of the Cavern) is now a poignant little place with old pictures and icons on the walls. Above the chapel are two Ionic columns, the remains of Thrasyllos' temple. It is closed to visitors except on its name day, 15 August.

★Acropolis Museum MUSEUM
(Map p77; ☑210 900 0901; www.theacropolis museum.gr; Dionysiou Areopagitou 15, Makrygianni; adult/concession €5/3; ⊙8am-8pm Tue-Sun, to 10pm Fri Apr-Oct, 9am-5pm Mon-Thu, to 10pm Fri, 9am-8pm Sat & Sun Nov-Mar; Ⓜ Akropoli) The long-awaited Acropolis Museum opened with much fanfare in 2009 in the southern foothills of the Acropolis. Ten times larger than the former on-site museum, the imposing modernist building brings together surviving treasures of the Acropolis, including items formerly held in other museums or storage, as well as pieces returned from foreign museums. The **restaurant** has superb views (and is surprisingly good value) and there's a fine museum **shop**.

Designed by US-based architect Bernard Tschumi, with Greek architect Michael Photiadis, the €130-million museum cleverly showcases layers of history, floating above the ruins and with the Acropolis visible above, thus allowing visitors to see the masterpieces in context.

While the collection covers the Archaic and Roman periods, the emphasis is on the

Acropolis of the 5th century BC, considered the apotheosis of Greece's artistic achievement.

★ Filopappou Hill
PARK

(Map p68; M Akropoli) Also called the Hill of the Muses, Filopappou Hill – along with the Hills of the Pnyx and Nymphs – was, according to Plutarch, where Thesues and the Amazons did battle. Inhabited from prehistoric times to the post-Byzantine era, today the pine-clad slopes are a relaxing place for a stroll. They offer excellent views of Attica and the Saronic Gulf, well-signed ruins and some of the very best vantage points for photographing the Acropolis.

The hill is identifiable to the southwest of the Acropolis by the **Monument of Filopappos** (Map p68) crowning its summit. The monument was built between AD 114 and 116 in honour of Julius Antiochus Filopappos, who was a prominent Roman consul and administrator.

The paved path to the top starts near the *periptero* (kiosk) on Dionysiou Areopagitou. After 250m, it passes the excellent **Church of Agios Dimitrios Loumbardiaris** (Map p68), which contains fine frescoes and continues past **Socrates' prison** (Map p68), the **Shrine of the Muses** (Map p68) and on up to the top.

Areopagus Hill
PARK

(Map p84; M Monastiraki) This rocky outcrop below the Acropolis has great views over the Ancient Agora. According to mythology, it was here that Ares was tried by the council of the gods for the murder of Halirrhothios, son of Poseidon. The council accepted his defence of justifiable deicide on the grounds that he was protecting his daughter, Alcippe, from unwanted advances.

ATHENS & AROUND SIGHTS

MUSEUM TOUR: ACROPOLIS MUSEUM

As you enter the grounds of the museum, look through the plexiglass floor to see the **ruins of an ancient Athenian neighbourhood**, which have been cleverly incorporated into the museum design after being uncovered during excavations.

Finds from the slopes of the Acropolis are on display in the **foyer gallery**, which has an ascending glass floor that emulates the climb up to the sacred hill, while allowing glimpses of the ruins below. Exhibits include painted vases and votive offerings from the sanctuaries where gods were worshipped, and more recent objects found in excavations of the settlement, including two clay statues of Nike at the entrance.

Bathed in natural light, the 1st-floor **Archaic Gallery** is a veritable forest of statues, mostly votive offerings to Athena. These include stunning examples of 6th-century *kore* (maiden) – statues of young women in draped clothing and elaborate braids, usually carrying a pomegranate, wreath or bird. Most were recovered from a pit on the Acropolis, where the Athenians buried them after the Battle of Salamis.

The 570 BC youth bearing a calf is one of the rare male statues found. There are also bronze figurines and finds from temples predating the Parthenon, which were destroyed by the Persians, including wonderful pedimental sculptures from earlier temples, such as Heracles slaying the Lernaian Hydra and a lioness devouring a bull.

Five **Caryatids**, the maiden columns that held up the Erechtheion (the sixth is in the British Museum), and a giant floral *akrotirion* (a decorative element placed on the brick at the end of a gable of a classical building) that once crowned the southern ridge of the Parthenon pediment are on this floor.

The museum's crowning glory is the top-floor **Parthenon Gallery**, a glass atrium built in alignment with the temple, and a virtual replica of the cella of the Parthenon, which can be seen from the gallery. It showcases the temple's sculptures, metopes and 160m-long frieze, which for the first time in more than 200 years is shown in sequence as one narrative about the Panathenaic Procession. The Procession starts at the southwest corner of the temple, with two groups splitting off and meeting on the east side for the delivery of the *peplos* to Athena. Interspersed between the golden-hued originals are stark-white plaster replicas of the missing pieces – the controversial Parthenon Marbles hacked off by Lord Elgin in 1801 and later sold to the British Museum (more than half the frieze is in London). The sight makes a compelling case for their reunification.

Don't miss the **movie** describing the history of the Acropolis.

The hill became the place where murder, treason and corruption trials were heard before the Council of the Areopagus. In AD 51 St Paul delivered his famous 'Sermon to an Unknown God' from this hill and gained his first Athenian convert, Dionysos, who became patron saint of the city.

Hill of the Pnyx
PARK

(Map p90; M Thisio) North of Filopappou, this rocky hill was the meeting place of the Democratic Assembly in the 5th century BC, where the great orators Aristides, Demosthenes, Pericles and Themistocles addressed assemblies. This less-visited site offers great views over Athens and a peaceful walk.

Hill of the Nymphs
PARK

(Map p90; M Thisio) Northwest of Hill of the Pnyx, this hill is home to the old Athens observatory, built in 1842.

◉ North of the Acropolis: Monastiraki & Keramikos

★ Ancient Agora
HISTORIC SITE

(Map p84; ☑ 210 321 0185; http://odysseus.culture .gr; Adrianou; adult/child €4/free, free with Acropolis pass; ◷ 11am-3pm Mon, 8am-3pm Tue-Sun; M Monastiraki) The heart of ancient Athens was the Agora, the lively, crowded focal point of administrative, commercial, political and social activity. Socrates expounded his philosophy here, and in AD 49 St Paul came here to win converts to Christianity.

First developed as a public site in the 6th century BC, the Agora was devastated by the Persians in 480 BC, but a new one was built in its place almost immediately. It was flourishing by Pericles' time and continued to do so until AD 267, when it was destroyed by the Herulians, a Gothic tribe from Scandinavia. The Turks built a residential quarter on the site, but this was demolished by archaeologists after Independence and later excavated to classical and, in parts, Neolithic levels.

The site today is a lush, refreshing break from congested city streets, and is dotted with beautiful monuments and a good museum. There most convenient entrance is the northern entrance from Adrianou. See the tour of Ancient Agora on p83.

★ Roman Agora & Tower of the Winds
RUIN

(Map p84; ☑ 210 324 5220; cnr Pelopida & Eolou, Monastiraki; adult/child €2/1, free with Acropolis pass; ◷ 8am-3pm; M Monastiraki) Entrance to the Roman Agora is through the well-preserved Gate of Athena Archegetis, which is flanked by four Doric columns. It was erected sometime during the 1st century AD and financed by Julius Caesar. The well-preserved, extraordinary Tower of the Winds was built in the 1st century BC by a Syrian astronomer named Andronicus.

The octagonal monument of Pentelic marble is an ingenious construction that functioned as a sundial, weather vane, water clock and compass. Each side represents a point of the compass, and has a relief of a figure floating through the air, which depicts the wind associated with that particular point. Beneath each of the reliefs are the faint markings of sundials. The weather vane, which disappeared long ago, was a bronze Triton that revolved on top of the tower. The Turks allowed dervishes to use the tower.

The rest of the ruins are hard to make sense of. To the right of the entrance are the foundations of a 1st-century public latrine. In the southeast area are the foundations of a propylon and a row of shops.

★ Keramikos
HISTORIC SITE

(Map p90; ☑ 210 346 3552; Ermou 148, Keramikos; adult/child incl museum €2/free, free with Acropolis pass; ◷ 8am-5pm Mon-Fri to 3pm Sat & Sun, reduced low season; M Thisio) The city's cemetery from the 12th century BC to Roman times, Keramikos was originally a settlement for potters who were attracted by the clay on the banks of the River Iridanos. Because of frequent flooding, the area was ultimately converted to a cemetery. Rediscovered in 1861 during the construction of Pireos St, Keramikos is now a lush, tranquil site with a fine museum.

Once inside, head for the small knoll ahead to the right, where you'll find a plan of the site. A path leads down to the right from the knoll to the remains of the city wall built by Themistocles in 479 BC, and rebuilt by Konon in 394 BC. The wall is broken by the foundations of two gates; tiny signs mark each one.

The first, the Sacred Gate, spanned the Sacred Way and was the one by which pilgrims from Eleusis entered the city during the annual Eleusian procession. The second, the Dipylon Gate, northeast of the Sacred Gate, was the city's main entrance and where the Panathenaic Procession began. It was also where the city's prostitutes gathered to offer their services to jaded travellers.

From a platform outside the Dipylon Gate, Pericles gave his famous speech extolling the virtues of Athens and honouring those who died in the first year of the Peloponnesian Wars.

Between the Sacred and Dipylon Gates are the foundations of the **Pompeion**, used as a dressing room for participants in the Panathenaic Procession.

Leading off the Sacred Way to the left as you head away from the city is the **Street of Tombs**. This avenue was reserved for the tombs of Athens' most prominent citizens. The surviving stelae (grave slabs) are now in the National Archaeological Museum, and what you see are mostly replicas. The astonishing array of funerary monuments, and their bas reliefs, warrant close examination. Ordinary citizens were buried in the areas bordering the Street of Tombs. One well-preserved stela (up the stone steps on the northern side) shows a little girl with her pet dog. The site's largest stela is that of sisters Demetria and Pamphile.

The small but excellent **Keramikos museum** has remarkable stelae and sculptures from the site, as well as a good collection of vases and terracotta figurines.

★ **Museum of Islamic Art**   MUSEUM
(Map p90; ☑210 325 1311; Agion Asomaton 22 & Dipylou 12, Keramikos; adult/concession €7/5; ☺9am-5pm Thu-Sun; Ⓜ Thisio) This museum showcases one of the world's most significant collections of Islamic art. Housed in two restored neoclassical mansions near Keramikos, it exhibits more than 8000 items covering the 12th to 19th centuries, including weavings, carvings, prayer rugs, tiles and ceramics. On the 3rd floor is a 17th-century reception room with an inlaid marble floor from a Cairo mansion.

You can see part of the Themistoklean wall in the basement.

Hadrian's Library   RUIN
(Map p84; ☑210 324 9350; Areos, Monastiraki; adult/child €2/free, free with Acropolis pass; ☺8am-3pm, reduced hr in low season; Ⓜ Monastiraki) To the north of the Roman Agora is this vast 2nd-century-AD library, the largest structure erected by Hadrian. It included a cloistered courtyard bordered by 100 columns and there was a pool in the centre. As well as books, the building housed music and lecture rooms and a theatre. Last admission is 30 minutes before closing.

Church of Agios Eleftherios BYZANTINE CHURCH
(Little Metropolis; Map p84; Plateia Mitropoleos, Monastiraki; Ⓜ Monastiraki) This 12th-century church is considered one of the city's finest. It is built partly of Pentelic marble and decorated with an external frieze of symbolic beasts in bas relief. Originally dedicated to the Panagia Gorgoepikoos (meaning 'Virgin swift to answer prayers'), it was once the city's cathedral, but now stands in the shadows of the much larger new **cathedral**.

Church of Kapnikarea   BYZANTINE CHURCH
(Map p84; Ermou, Monastiraki; ☺8am-2pm Tue, Thu & Fri; Ⓜ Monastiraki) This small 11th-century structure stands smack in the middle of the Ermou shopping strip. It was saved from the bulldozers and restored by Athens University. Its dome is supported by four large Roman columns.

Turkish Baths   BATHHOUSE
(Map p84; ☑210 324 4340; Kyrristou 8, Monastiraki; admission €2; ☺8am-3pm Wed-Mon; Ⓜ Monastiraki) This beautifully refurbished 17th-century hammam is the only surviving public bathhouse in Athens and one of the few remnants of Ottoman times. A helpful free audio tour takes you back to the bathhouse's glory days.

ANCIENT PROMENADE

The once traffic-choked streets around Athens' historic centre were transformed into a spectacular 3km-long pedestrian promenade for the 2004 Olympics and connect the city's most significant ancient sites. Locals and tourists alike come out in force for an evening *volta* (walk) along the stunning heritage trail – one of Europe's longest pedestrian precincts – under the floodlit Acropolis.

The **grand promenade** starts at Dionysiou Areopagitou, opposite the Temple of Olympian Zeus, and continues along the southern foothills of the Acropolis, all the way to the Ancient Agora, branching off from Thisio to Keramikos and Gazi, and north along Adrianou to Monastiraki and Plaka.

⦿ Southeast of the Acropolis

★ Temple of Olympian Zeus RUIN

(Map p77; ☑210 922 6330; adult/child €2/free, free with Acropolis pass; ☉8am-3pm; Ⓜ Syntagma, Akropoli) You can't miss this striking marvel, smack in the centre of Athens. It is the largest temple in Greece and was begun in the 6th century BC by Peisistratos, but was abandoned for lack of funds. Various other leaders had stabs at completing it, but it was left to Hadrian to complete the work in AD 131. In total, it took more than 700 years to build.

The temple is impressive for the sheer size of its 104 Corinthian columns (17m high with a base diameter of 1.7m), of which 15 remain – the fallen column was blown down in a gale in 1852. Hadrian put a colossal statue of Zeus in the cella and, in typically immodest fashion, placed an equally large one of himself next to it.

★ Hadrian's Arch MONUMENT

(Map p77; cnr Leoforos Vasilissis Olgas & Leoforos Vasilissis Amalias; Ⓜ Syntagma) FREE The Roman emperor Hadrian had a great affection for Athens. Although he did his fair share of spiriting its classical artwork to Rome, he also embellished the city with many monuments influenced by classical architecture. His arch is a lofty monument of Pentelic marble that stands where busy Leoforos Vasilissis Olgas and Leoforos Vasilissis Amalias meet. Hadrian erected it in AD 132, probably to commemorate the consecration of the Temple of Olympian Zeus.

The inscriptions show that it was also intended as a dividing point between the ancient and Roman city. The northwest frieze reads, 'This is Athens, the Ancient city of Theseus', while the southeast frieze states, 'This is the city of Hadrian, and not of Theseus'.

★ Panathenaic Stadium HISTORIC SITE

(Map p68; ☑210 752 2984; www.panathenaicstadium.gr; Leoforos Vasileos Konstantinou, Pangrati; adult/child €3/1.50; ☉8am-7pm, reduced hr in low season; Ⓜ Akropoli) The grand Panathenaic Stadium lies between two pine-covered hills between the neighbourhoods of Mets and Pangrati. It was originally built in the 4th century BC as a venue for the Panathenaic athletic contests. It's said that at Hadrian's inauguration in AD 120, 1000 wild animals were sacrificed in the arena. Later, the seats were rebuilt in Pentelic marble by Herodes Atticus.

After hundreds of years of disuse, the stadium was completely restored in 1895 by wealthy Greek benefactor Georgios Averof to host the first modern Olympic Games the following year. It's a faithful replica of the original Panathenaic Stadium, comprising seats of Pentelic marble for 70,000 spectators, a running track and a central area for field events. It made a stunning backdrop to the archery competition and the marathon finish during the 2004 Olympics. It's occasionally used for concerts and public events, and the annual Athens marathon finishes here.

Roman Baths RUIN

(Map p84; Leoforos Vasilissis Amalias; Ⓜ Syntagma) FREE Excavation work to create a ventilation shaft for the metro uncovered the well-preserved ruins of a large Roman bath complex. The baths, which extend into the National Gardens, were established near the Ilissos river after the Herulian raids in the 3rd century AD; they were destroyed and repaired again in the 5th or 6th century.

⦿ Syntagma & Plaka

★ National Gardens GARDENS

(Map p110; entrances on Leoforos Vasilissis Sofias & Leoforos Vasilissis Amalias, Syntagma; ☉7am-dusk; Ⓜ Syntagma) A delightful, shady refuge during summer, the National Gardens were formerly the royal gardens designed by Queen Amalia. There's a large children's **playground**, a duck pond and a shady **cafe**.

Zappeio Gardens GARDENS

(Map p68; entrances on Leoforos Vasilissis Amalias & Leoforos Vasilissis Olgas, Syntagma; Ⓜ Syntagma) These gardens sit between the National Gardens and the Panathenaic Stadium and are laid out in a network of wide walkways around the grand **Zappeio Palace**. The palace was built in the 1870s and hosts conferences and exhibitions. A pleasant cafe, restaurant and the open-air Aigli cinema (p117) are alongside the palace.

Plateia Syntagmatos SQUARE

(Syntagma Sq; Map p68; Ⓜ Syntagma) Athens' central square (Syntagma, or Constitution Sq) is named for the constitution granted, after uprisings, by King Otto on 3 September 1843. Today, the square serves as a major

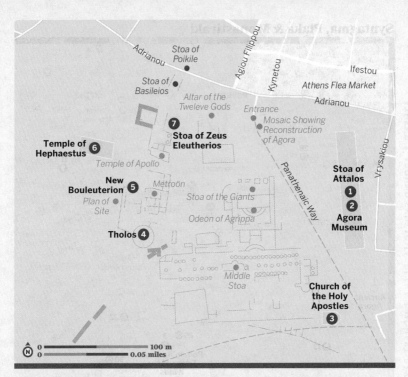

Site Tour
Ancient Agora

LENGTH TWO HOURS
SEE ANCIENT AGORA (P80)

As you enter the Agora, make your way to the magnificent **① Stoa of Attalos**. This two-storied stoa (covered walkway or portico), built by King Attalos II of Pergamum (159–138 BC), served as the first-ever shopping arcade. It has 45 Doric columns on the ground floor and Ionic columns on the upper. Originally, its facade was painted red and blue. People gathered here every four years to watch the Panathenaic Procession.

The excellent **② Agora Museum**, inside the stoa, is a good place to make sense of the site. It holds a model of the Agora and many outstanding finds, and is surrounded by an-cient statues of the gods.

Continue to the southern end of the site to the **③ Church of the Holy Apostles**, built in the early 10th century to commemorate St Paul's teaching in the Agora. Between 1954 and 1957 it was stripped of its 19th-century additions and restored to its original form. It contains fine Byzantine frescoes.

Heading north across the site, you'll pass the circular **④ Tholos** where the heads of government met, and what was the **⑤ New Bouleuterion** (Council House), where the Senate met.

Go to the western edge of the Agora for the striking **⑥ Temple of Hephaestus**, the best-preserved Doric temple in Greece. Dedicated to Hephaestus, god of the forge, the temple was one of the first of Pericles' projects and was built in 449 BC by Iktinos, one of the architects of the Parthenon. It has 34 columns and a frieze on the eastern side depicting nine of the Twelve Labours of Heracles. In AD 1300 it was converted into the Church of Agios Georgios. The last serv-ice was held in 1834 in honour of King Otto's arrival in Athens.

To the northeast of the temple, you'll pass the foundation of the **⑦ Stoa of Zeus Eleu-therios**, one of the places where Socrates expounded his philosophy.

Syntagma, Plaka & Monastiraki

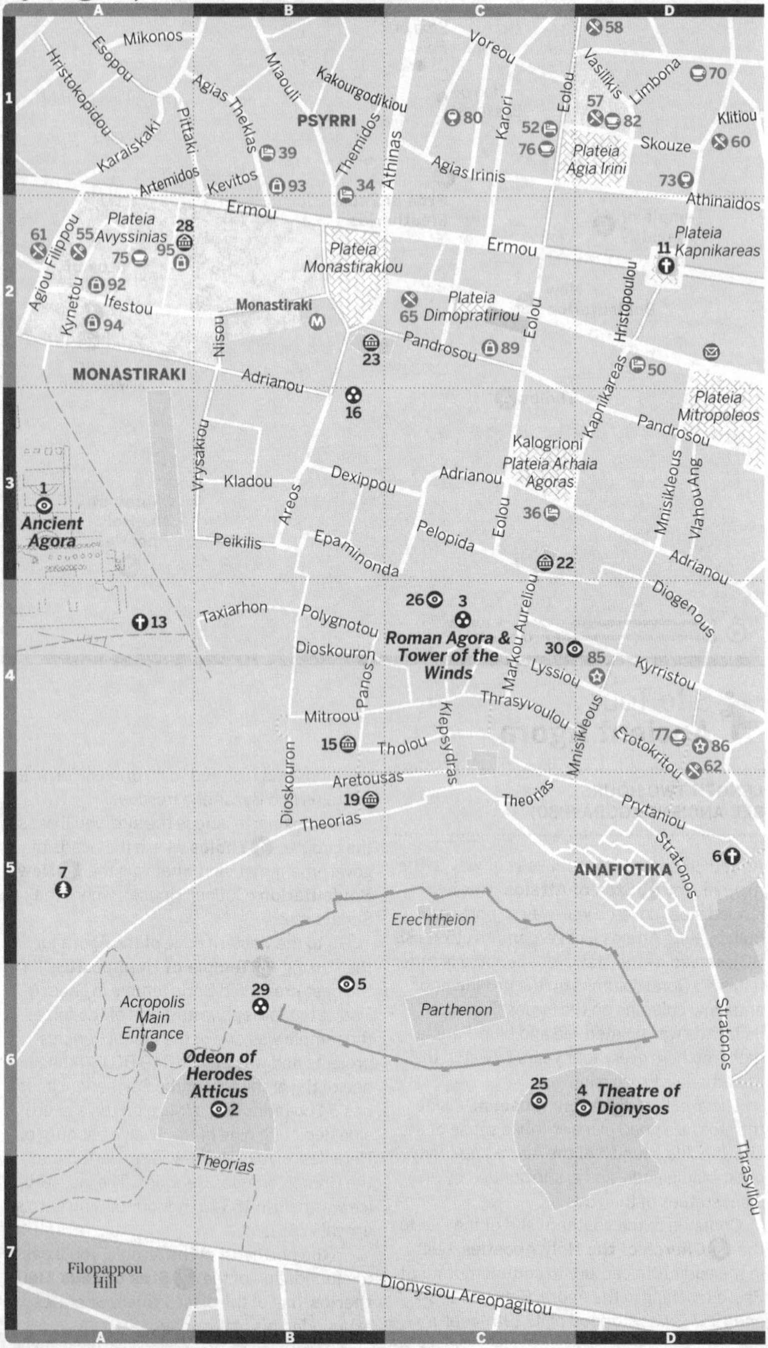

Mikonos
Hristokopidou
Esopou
Karaiskaki
Pittaki
Agias Thekias
Miaouli
Kakourgodikiou
Voreou
Eolou
Karori
Vasilikis
Limbona
70
58

PSYRRI

Themidos
Athinas
Agias Irinis
80
57
52
82
Plateia
Agia Irini
Klitiou
Skouze
60

Artemidos
Kevitos
39
93
34
76
73

Ermou
Ermou
Plateia
Kapnikareas
11

Agiou Filippou
61
55
Plateia
Avyssinias
28
95
75
Plateia
Monastirakiou
Histopoulou

Kynetou
92
Ifestou
94

MONASTIRAKI
Nisou
Monastiraki
M
23
Plateia
Dimopratiriou
65
Pandrosou
89
Kapnikareas
Pandrosou
50
Plateia
Mitropoleos

Adrianou
16

Vrysakiou
Kladou
Dexippou
Adrianou
Plateia Arhaia
Agoras
Kalogrioni
Eolou
36
Mnisikleous
Vlahou-Ang
Adrianou

1
Ancient
Agora
Areos
Peikilis
Epaminonda
Pelopida
22
Diogenous

Taxiarhon
13
Polygnotou
Dioskouron
26 3
Roman Agora &
Tower of the
Winds
30 85
Markou Avreliou
Lyssiou
Kyrristou

Paros
Mitroou
Thrasyvoulou
Mnisikleous
77 86
Erotokritou
62

15
Tholou
Aretousas
19
Theorias
Prytaniou
Stratonos
6

Dioskouron
Theorias
ANAFIOTIKA

7

Erechtheion

Acropolis
Main
Entrance
29
5
Parthenon
Stratonos

Odeon of
Herodes
Atticus
2
25
4 Theatre of
Dionysos

Theorias

Thrasyllou

7
Filopappou
Hill
Dionysiou Areopagitou

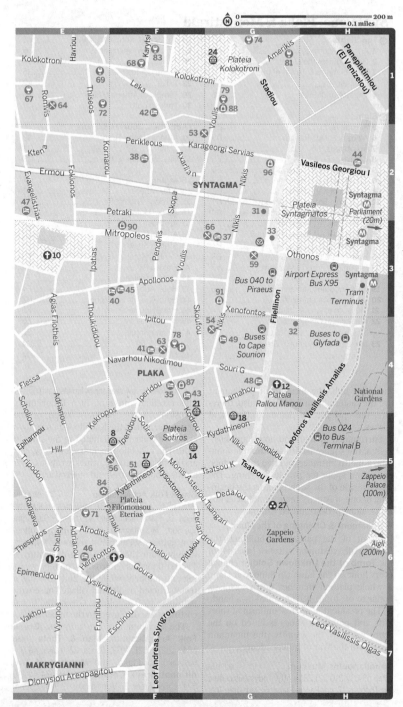

Syntagma, Plaka & Monastiraki

◎ Top Sights

◎ Sights

◎ Activities, Courses & Tours

◎ Sleeping

transport hub, the location of parliament (on the eastern, uphill side) and also, therefore, the epicentre of demonstrations and strikes.

Surrounded by high-end hotels and businesses, the square istelf has a marble fountain, a metro entrance and two cafes, which are prime spots for people watching. The western side of the square marks the beginning of one of Athens' main commercial districts, along pedestrianised Ermou.

➡ Paliament & Changing of the Guard

In front of the parliament building, the traditionally costumed *evzones* (guards) of the **Tomb of the Unknown Soldier** change every hour on the hour. On Sunday at 11am, a whole platoon marches down Vasilissis Sofias to the tomb, accompanied by a band.

The presidential guards' uniform of short kilts and pom-pom shoes is based on the attire worn by the *klephts* (the mountain fighters of the War of Independence).

Kanellopoulos Museum MUSEUM
(Map p84; ☎210 321 2313; http://odysseus.culture
.gr; Theorias 12, cnr Panos, Plaka; ☉9am-4pm Tue-

Sun, reduced hr low season; Ⓜ Monastiraki) **FREE** This excellent museum, in a 19th-century mansion on the northern slope of the Acropolis, houses the Kanellopoulos family's extensive collection, donated to the state in 1976. The collection includes jewellery, clay and stone vases and figurines, weapons, Byzantine icons, bronzes and objets d'art.

Greek Folk Art Museum MUSEUM
(Map p84; ☎210 322 9031; www.melt.gr; Kydathineon 17, Plaka; adult/child €2/free; ☉9am-2pm Tue-Sun; Ⓜ Syntagma) This superb collection gathers secular and religious folk art, mainly from the 18th and 19th centuries. The 1st floor has embroidery, pottery, weaving and puppets, while the 2nd floor has a reconstructed traditional village house with paintings by Theophilos. Greek traditional costumes are displayed on the upper levels.

The museum has two annexes: **Greek Folk Art Museum: Man & Tools** (Map p84; ☎210 321 4972; Panos 22, Plaka; Ⓜ Monastiraki), in Plaka, and **Museum of Traditional Greek Ceramics** (Map p84; ☎210 324 2066; Areos 1, Monastiraki; ☉9am-2.30pm

Wed-Mon; Ⓜ Monastiraki) at the old mosque in Monastiraki.

National Historical Museum MUSEUM
(Map p84; ☑ 210 323 7617; www.nhmuseum.gr; Stadiou 13, Syntagma; adult/child €3/free, Sun free; ☺ 9am-2pm Tue-Sun; Ⓜ Syntagma) Specialising in memorabilia from the War of Independence, this museum houses Byron's helmet and sword, a series of paintings depicting events leading up to the war and a collection of photographs and royal portraits. The museum is housed in the old Parliament building, on the steps of which Prime Minister Theodoros Deligiannis was assassinated in 1905.

Jewish Museum MUSEUM
(Map p84; ☑ 210 322 5582; www.jewishmuseum.gr; Nikis 39, Plaka; adult/child €6/free; ☺ 9am-2.30pm Mon-Fri, 10am-2pm Sun; Ⓜ Syntagma) This museum traces the history of the Jewish community in Greece back to the 3rd century BC through an impressive collection of documents and religious and folk art. It includes a small reconstruction of a synagogue.

Church of Agii Theodori BYZANTINE CHURCH
(Map p102; cnr Dragatsaniou & Agion Theodoron, Syntagma; Ⓜ Panepistimio) This 11th-century church behind Plateia Klafthmonos has a tiled dome and walls decorated with a pretty terracotta frieze of animals and plants.

Agios Nikolaos Rangavas BYZANTINE CHURCH
(Map p84; ☑ 210 322 8193; Prytaniou 1, cnr Epiharmou, Plaka; ☺ 8am-noon & 5-8pm; Ⓜ Akropoli, Monastiraki) This lovely 11th-century church was part of the palace of the Rangavas family, who counted among them Michael I, emperor of Byzantium. The church bell was the first installed in Athens after liberation from the Turks (who banned them), and was the first to ring in 1833 to announce the freedom of Athens.

Church of Sotira Lykodimou BYZANTINE CHURCH
(Map p84; Fillelinon, Plateia Rallou Manou, Plaka; Ⓜ Syntagma) Now the Russian Orthodox Cathedral, this unique 11th-century church is the only octagonal Byzantine church and has an imposing dome.

BYZANTINE ATHENS

Very little Byzantine architecture remains in Athens. The most important Byzantine building is the World Heritage–listed, 11th-century **Moni Dafniou** (☑ 210 581 1558; ☺ 9am-2pm Tue & Fri) **FREE** at Dafni, 10km northwest of Athens. One of the oldest churches in Athens is the 10th-century **Church of the Holy Apostles** (Map p84; Monastiraki) in the Ancient Agora.

The most important city-centre Byzantine churches are listed in the Sights section, and do not have set opening hours.

Other churches worth seeing are the 11th- to 12th-century **Church of Agia Ekaterini**, in Plaka near the choregic **Lysikrates Monument** (Map p84), and the 15th-century Church of Agios Dimitrios Loumbardiaris (p79) on Filopappou Hill. The lovely Byzantine monastery, **Moni Kaisarianis** (Monastery of Kaisariani; ☑ 210 723 6619; Mt Hymettos; adult/child €2/free; ☺ 8.30am-2.45pm Tue-Sun, grounds 8.30am-sunset Tue-Sun), 5km east of the city, is also worth a visit.

◎ Thisio

Herakleidon Museum   MUSEUM
(Map p90; ☑ 210 346 1981; www.herakleidon-art.gr; Herakleidon 16, Thisio; adult/child €6/free; ☺ 1-9pm Fri, 11am-7pm Sat & Sun; Ⓜ Thisio) This superb private museum showcases how art, mathematics and philosophy interrelate. The permanent collection includes one of the world's biggest collections of MC Escher, as well as Victor Vasarely, in a beautifully restored neoclassical mansion. Extensive educational programs include excellent two-hour guided tour-seminars in English, available with advance booking (€25, minimum of 10 participants required).

◎ Exarhia

★ **National Archaeological Museum**   MUSEUM
(Map p68; ☑ 210 821 7717; www.namuseum.gr; 28 Oktovriou-Patision 44, Exarhia; adult/concession €7/3; ☺ 1-8pm Mon, 8am-8pm Tue-Sat, 8am-3pm Sun; Ⓜ Viktoria; ☒ 2, 4, 5, 9 or 11 Polytechnio stop) One of the world's most important museums, the National Archaeological Museum houses the world's finest collection of Greek antiquities. Treasures offering a view of Greek art and history, dating from the Neolithic era to classical periods, include exquisite sculptures, pottery, jewellery, frescoes and artefacts found throughout Greece. The exhibits are displayed largely thematically and are beautifully presented.

The museum also has a superb pottery collection on its upper floor, which traces the development of pottery from the Bronze Age through Attic red-figured pottery (late 5th to early 4th centuries BC). Among the treasures, see six Panathenaic amphorae, presented to the winners of the Panathenaic Games. They contained oil from the sacred olive trees of Athens and victors might have received up to 140 of them.

Allow plenty of time to view the vast and spectacular collections (more than 11,000 items) housed in this enormous (8000-sq-metre) 19th-century neoclassical building. It could take several visits to appreciate the museum's holdings, but it's possible to see the highlights in a half-day (see the tour on p96). The museum also hosts world-class temporary exhibitions.

The museum is a 10-minute walk from Viktoria metro station, or catch trolleybus 2, 4, 5, 9 or 11 from outside St Denis Cathedral on Panepistimiou and get off at the Polytechnio stop.

◎ Kolonaki

★ **Benaki Museum**   MUSEUM
(Map p110; ☑ 210 367 1000; www.benaki.gr; Koumbari 1, cnr Leoforos Vasilissis Sofias, Kolonaki; adult/concession €7/5, free Thu; ☺ 9am-5pm Wed & Fri, to midnight Thu & Sat, to 3pm Sun; Ⓜ Syntagma, Evangelismos) Greece's finest private museum contains the vast collection of Antonis Benakis, accumulated during 35 years of avid collecting in Europe and Asia. The collection includes Bronze Age finds from Mycenae and Thessaly; works by El Greco; ecclesiastical furniture brought from Asia Minor; pottery, copper, silver and woodwork from Egypt, Asia Minor and Mesopotamia; and a stunning collection of Greek regional costumes.

The museum has expanded into several branches to house its vast and diverse collections and is a major player in the city's arts scene. It hosts a full schedule of rotating exhibitions.

The **Benaki Museum Pireos Annexe** (Map p90; ☑ 210 345 3111; www.benaki.gr; Pireos 138, cnr Andronikou, Rouf; admission €4-6; ☻10am-6pm Thu & Sun, to 10pm Fri & Sat, closed Aug; ⓜKeramikos) hosts regular visual arts, cultural and historical exhibitions as well as major international shows. The impressive former industrial building has a cafe and excellent gift shop.

★**Museum of Cycladic Art**   MUSEUM
(Map p110; ☑ 210 722 8321; www.cycladic.gr; Neofytou Douka 4, cnr Leoforos Vasilissis Sofias, Kolonaki; adult/child €7/free, half-price Mon; ☻10am-5pm Mon, Wed, Fri & Sat, 10am-8pm Thu, 11am-5pm Sun; ⓜEvangelismos) This exceptional private museum boasts the largest independent collection of distinctive Cycladic art and holds excellent periodic exhibitions. The 1st-floor Cycladic collection, dating from 3000 BC to 2000 BC, includes the marble figurines that inspired many 20th-century artists, such as Picasso and Modigliani, with their simplicity and purity of form. The rest of the museum features Greek and Cypriot art dating from 2000 BC to the 4th century AD.

The 4th-floor exhibition, Scenes from Daily Life in Antiquity, includes artefacts and films depicting life in Ancient Greece.

★**Byzantine & Christian Museum** MUSEUM
(Map p110; ☑ 210 721 1027; www.byzantinemuseum.gr; Leoforos Vasilissis Sofias 22, Kolonaki; adult/concession/child €4/2/free; ☻9am-6pm Tue-Sun,

reduced hr low season; ⓜEvangelismos) This outstanding museum – on the grounds of former Villa Ilissia, an urban oasis – presents a priceless collection of Christian art from the 3rd to 20th centuries. Thematic snapshots of the Byzantine and post-Byzantine world are exceptionally presented in expansive, well-lit multilevel galleries, and clearly arranged chronologically with English translations. The collection includes icons, frescoes, sculptures, textiles, manuscripts, vestments and mosaics.

The villa grounds include ancient ruins such as the Peisistratos aqueduct, and sit next to **Aristotle's Lyceum**.

National Museum of Contemporary Art   GALLERY
(Map p110; ☑ 210 924 2111; www.emst.gr; cnr Vassileos Georgiou B 17 -19 & Rigillis, Athens Conservatory, Kolonaki; adult/child €3/free; ☻11am-7pm Tue, Wed & Fri-Sun, to 10pm Thu; ⓜSyngrou-Fix) This museum shows top-notch rotating exhibitions of Greek and international contemporary art. Exhibitions include paintings, installations, photography, video and new media, as well as experimental architecture. In early 2014 the museum is slated to open in spectacularly renovated quarters at the former **Fix Brewery** (cnr Kallirois & Frantzi; ⓜSyngrou-Fix) on Leoforos Syngrou.

Lykavittos Hill   LANDMARK
(Map p68; ⓜEvangelismos) Lykavittos means 'Hill of Wolves' and derives from ancient times when the hill was surrounded by countryside and its pine-covered slopes were inhabited by wolves. A path leads to the summit from the top of Loukianou for the finest

---

FREE MUSEUMS

Kanellopoulos Museum (p86) Fine collections from throughout Greek history.

Museum of Greek Popular Instruments (Map p84; ☑ 210 325 4119; www.instruments-museum.gr; Diogenous 1-3, Plaka; ☻10am-2pm Tue & Thu-Sun, noon-6pm Wed; ⓜMonastiraki) **FREE** Displays and recordings of a wide selection of traditional instruments and costumes, including those of the great masters of Greek music. Concerts are held in the courtyard on weeknights in summer. A restored hammam in the gift shop is one of the few surviving private Turkish baths in Athens.

Epigraphical Museum (Map p68; ☑ 210 821 7637; http://odysseus.culture.gr; Tositsa 1, Exarhia; ☻8.30am-3pm Tue-Sun; ⓜViktoria) **FREE** The most significant collection of Greek inscriptions on a veritable library of stone tablets next to the National Archaeological Museum.

Centre of Folk Art & Tradition (Map p84; ☑ 210 324 3987; www.cityofathens.gr; Hatzimihali Angelikis 6, Plaka; ☻9am-1pm & 5-9pm Tue-Fri, 9am-1pm Sat & Sun; ⓜSyntagma) **FREE** Stunning Plaka mansion with interesting periodic exhibitions.

Gazi, Keramikos & Thisio

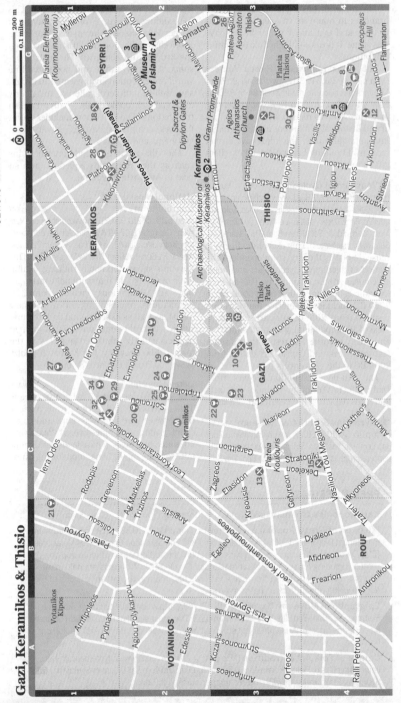

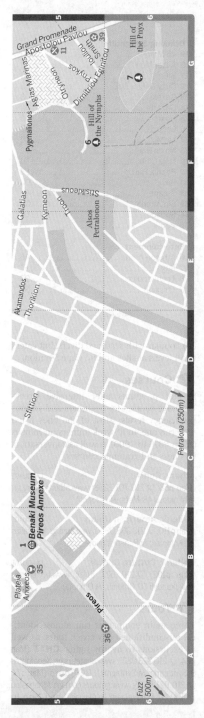

panoramas of the city and the Attic basin – the *nefos* (pollution haze) permitting. Alternatively, take the **funicular railway** (☏ 210 721 0701; return €6; ☉ 9am-3am, half-hourly), or *teleferik*, from the top of Ploutarhou in Kolonaki. Perched on the summit is the little **Chapel of Agios Georgios**, floodlit like a beacon over the city at night.

Open-air **Lykavittos Theatre**, northeast of the summit, hosts concerts in summer.

◉ Mets

Athens' First Cemetery   CEMETERY
(Map p68; Anapafseos, Trivonianou, Mets; ☉ 7.30am-sunset; Ⓜ Syngrou-Fix) This resting place of many famous Greeks and philhellenes is a peaceful spot to explore. Famous names include the archaeologist Heinrich Schliemann (1822–90), whose mausoleum is decorated with scenes from the Trojan War. Most of the tombstones and mausoleums are lavish in the extreme. Works of art include Halepas' *Sleeping Maiden* sculpture on the tomb of a young girl.

◉ The Coast

Glyfada, about 17km southeast of Athens, marks the beginning of a stretch of coastline known as the **Apollo Coast**, which has a string of fine beaches and upmarket resorts running south to Cape Sounion. Much of the summer nightlife takes place here.

Most beaches are privately run and charge admission (€4 to €15 per adult). They're usually open between 8am and dusk May to October (later during heatwaves), and have sunbeds and umbrellas (additional charge in some places), changing rooms, children's playgrounds and cafes.

The flashiest and most exclusive summer playground is **Astir Beach** (☏ 210 890 1621; www.astir-beach.com; adult/child €15/8 Mon-Fri, €25/13 Sat & Sun), with water sports, shops and restaurants. You can even book online.

The following can be reached by tram and then buses from Glyfada or Voula:

Akti Tou Iliou (☏ 210 985 5169; Alimo; adult/child €6/3 Mon-Fri, €8/4 Sat & Sun)

Asteras Beach (☏ 210 894 1620; www.asterascomplex.com; Glyfada; adult/child €6/3 Mon-Fri, €7/3 Sat & Sun)

Yabanaki (☏ 210 897 2414; www.yabanaki.gr; Varkiza; adult/child €7/4.50 Mon-Fri, €8/4.50 Sat & Sun)

Gazi, Keramikos & Thisio

There are free beaches at Palio Faliro (Edem), Kavouri and Glyfada. There is also good (free) swimming at Shinias, Marathon and Vravrona in the north, though these take much longer to get to and are best reached by car.

Swim year-round at **Limni Vouliagmenis** (☑ 210 896 2239; Leoforos Vouliagmenis; adult/child €8/5; ⊙ 7am-8pm; ⬛ A2 [E2 express in summer] to Plateia Glyfada stop [aka Plateia Katraki Vasos], then ⬛ 114), a part-saltwater, part-springwater lake where the temperature usually doesn't fall below 20°C. It is set dramatically against a jutting cliff, just off the coast, and has an old-world atmosphere thanks to the regular clientele of elderly citizens dressed in bathing caps and towelling gowns.

🏃 Activities

Aegean Dive Centre DIVING
(☑ 210 894 5409; www.adc.gr; Zamanou 53, cnr Pandoras, Glyfada; PADI certification from €390, day/night dives €35/100) Organises dives between Vouliagmeni and Cape Sounion.

Planet Blue Dive Centre DIVING
(☑ 229 202 6446; www.planetblue.gr; Velpex Factory, Lavrio; PADI certification from €300, dives €35-

80) Popular with seasoned divers, but caters to all levels at sites around Cape Sounion.

🎓 Courses

Several programs offer intensive Greek-language courses for beginners and various proficiency levels. Most of the ones listed here run one- to 10-week immersion courses (from €370 to €900) as well as conversation, business and grammar courses.

Athens Centre LANGUAGE
(Map p68; ☑ 210 701 2268; www.athenscentre.gr; Arhimidous 48, Mets; Ⓜ Akropoli)

Hellenic American Union LANGUAGE
(Map p110; ☑ 210 368 0900; www.hau.gr; Massalias 22, Kolonaki; Ⓜ Panepistimio)

Hellenic Culture Centre LANGUAGE
(Map p102; ☑ 210 523 8149; www.hcc.edu.gr; Halkokondyli 50, Omonia; Ⓜ Omonia)

🧭 Tours

Three main companies run almost identical air-conditioned city coach tours, as well as excursions to nearby sights: **CHAT** (Map p84; ☑ 210 323 0827; www.chatours.gr; Xenofontos 9, Syntagma; Ⓜ Syntagma), **GO Tours** (Map p77; ☑ 210 921 9555; www.gotours.com.gr; Athanasiou Diakou 20, Makrygianni; Ⓜ Akropoli) and **Hop In**

ARTS EXPLOSION

Recent years have brought a burgeoning of the arts scene in Athens. Even as the city struggles with other aspects of political or social life, Greece's musicians, performing artists and visual artists remain hard at work and a new breed of multi-use gallery has sprung up to host all of the disciplines. Some feel like museums, others more like nightclubs, and for others it just depends on the time of day.

Theocharakis Foundation for the Fine Arts & Music (Map p110; 210 361 1206; www.thf.gr; Leoforos Vasilissis Sofias 9, Kolonaki; adult/child €6/free; 10am-6pm Mon, Wed & Fri-Sun, to 10pm Thu; M Syntagma) This excellent centre has three levels of exhibition space featuring local and international 20th- and 21st-century artists, a theatre, an art shop and a pleasant cafe. Music performances are held between September and May.

Taf (The Art Foundation; Map p84; 210 323 8757; www.theartfoundation.gr; Normanou 5, Monastiraki; 1pm-midnight; M Monastiraki) The central courtyard cafe at Taf, surrounded by crumbling 1870s brick buildings, fills with an eclectic young crowd. The rest functions as an art, music and theatre space where performances and screenings are often free.

Six DOGS (Map p84; 210 321 0510; www.sixdogs.gr; Avramiotou 6, Monastiraki; M Monastiraki) Six degrees of separation, indeed. The rustic rear garden courtyard here is the place for quiet chats with coffee and drinks, while the bar jams the lane to the front at night...theatre and art, too.

Onassis Cultural Centre (213 017 8000, box office 210 900 5800; www.sgt.gr; Leoforos Syngrou 107-109, Neos Kosmos; M Syngrou-Fix) The multimillion-euro visual and performing arts centre hosts big-name productions and installations. It's 1.5km southwest of the Syngrou-Fix metro station.

Bios (Map p90; www.bios.gr; Pireos 84, Gazi; M Thisio) In an industrial Bauhaus building near Gazi, this avant-garde multilevel warren has a bar, live performances, art and new-media exhibitions, a basement club, a tiny arthouse cinema and a roof garden.

Technopolis (Map p90; 210 346 7322; www.technopolis-athens.com; Pireos 100, Gazi; M Keramikos) The superbly converted Athens gasworks complex presents multimedia exhibitions, concerts and special events.

Art Events

Art-Athina (www.art-athina.gr) International contemporary art fair in May.

Athens Biennial (www.athensbiennial.org) Every two years from June to October.

ReMap (http://remapkm.com) Parallel event to the Biennial, exhibiting around town.

Art Galleries

Get a full list of galleries and art spaces at www.athensartmap.net; alternatively, pick up an *Athens Contemporary Art Map* at galleries and cafes around town.

AD Gallery (Map p102; 210 322 8785; www.adgallery.gr; Pallados 3, Psyrri; noon-9pm Tue-Fri, noon-4pm Sat, closed Aug; M Monastiraki)

CAN (Map p110; 210 339 0833; www.can-gallery.com; Anagnostopoulou 42, Kolonaki; 11am-3pm & 5pm-8pm Tue-Fri, 11am-4pm Sat, closed Aug; M Syntagma)

Bernier-Eliades (Map p90; 210 341 3935; www.bernier-eliades.gr; Eptachalkou 11, Thisio; 10.30am-6.30pm Tue-Fri, noon-4pm Sat; M Thisio)

Qbox Gallery (Map p102; 211 119 9991; www.qbox.gr; Armodiou 10, Monastiraki; noon-6pm Tue-Fri, noon-4pm Sat; M Omonia, Monastiraki)

Andreas Melas & Helena Papadopoulos Gallery (Map p102; 210 325 1881; http://melaspapadopoulos.com; Epikourou 26, cnr Korinis, Psyrri; noon-6pm Tue-Fri, noon-4pm Sat; M Omonia, Monastiraki)

Medusa Art Gallery (Map p110; 210 724 4552; www.medusaartgallery.com; Xenokratous 7, Kolonaki; M Evangelismos)

ATHENS FOR CHILDREN

Athens is short on playgrounds but there is plenty to keep kids amused. The shady National Gardens (p82) has a playground, duck pond and mini zoo. There is also a fully enclosed shady playground in the Zappeio Gardens (p82).

The **Hellenic Children's Museum** (Map p84; ☑ 210 331 2995; www.hcm.gr; Kydathineon 14, Plaka; ◷ 10am-2pm Tue-Fri, 10am-3pm Sat & Sun; Ⓜ Syntagma) **FREE** is more of a play centre, with a games room and a number of 'exhibits', such as a mock-up of a metro tunnel, for children to explore. Workshops range from baking to bubble making. Parents must supervise children.

The **Museum of Greek Children's Art** (Map p84; ☑ 210 331 2621; www.childrensart museum.gr; Kodrou 9, Plaka; ◷ 10am-2pm Tue-Sat, 11am-2pm Sun, closed Aug; Ⓜ Syntagma) **FREE** has a room set aside where children can let loose their creative energy, or learn about Ancient Greece.

Attica Zoological Park (☑ 210 663 4724; www.atticapark.gr; Yalou, Spata; adult/child €15/11; ◷ 9am-sunset) has an expanding collection of big cats, birds, reptiles and other animals, including a monkey forest and Cheetahland. The 19-hectare site is near the airport, east of the city.

You can always escape the heat and amuse the kids with a virtual-reality tour of Ancient Greece at the **Hellenic Cosmos** (☑ 212 254 0000; www.hellenic-cosmos.gr; Pireos 254, Tavros; per show adult €5-10, child €3-8, day pass adult/child €15/12; ◷ 9am-4pm Mon-Fri, 10am-3pm Sun, closed 2 weeks mid-Aug; underground rail Kalithea), or explore the universe at the impressive **Planetarium** (☑ 210 946 9600; www.eugenfound.edu.gr; Leoforos Syngrou 387, Palio Faliro; adult €6-8, child €4-5; ◷ 5.30-8.30pm Wed-Fri, 10.30am-8.30pm Sat & Sun, closed mid-Jul–late Aug). At the **War Museum** (Map p110; ☑ 210 725 2975; www.warmuseum .gr; Rizari 2, cnr Leoforos Vasilissis Sofias, Kolonaki; adult/child €3/1.50; ◷ 9.30am-5pm Tue-Sun; Ⓜ Evangelismos), kids can climb into the cockpit of a WWII plane and other aircraft in the courtyard.

Further afield, the enormous **Allou Fun Park & Kidom** (☑ 210 425 6999; www.allou .gr; cnr Leoforos Kifisou & Petrou Rali, Renti; admission free, rides €2-4; ◷ 5-11pm Mon-Fri, 10am-midnight Sat & Sun) is Athens' biggest amusement-park complex. Kidom is aimed at younger children.

Sightseeing (Map p77; ☑ 210 428 5500; www. hopin.com; Syngrou 19, Makrygianni; Ⓜ Akropoli).

Tours include a half-day sightseeing tour of Athens (from €68), usually doing little more than pointing out all the major sights and stopping at the Acropolis. Half-day trips go to Ancient Corinth (€58) and Cape Sounion (€43); day tours to Delphi (€91), the Corinth Canal, Mycenae, Nafplio and Epidavros (similar prices); and cruises to Aegina, Poros and Hydra (including lunch €99). Hotels act as booking agents and often offer discounts.

CitySightseeing Athens BUS TOUR
(Map p84; ☑ 210 922 0604; www.city-sightseeing. com; Plateia Syntagmatos, Syntagma; adult/child €15/6.50; ◷ every 30min 9am-8pm; Ⓜ Syntagma) Open-top double-decker buses cruise around town on a 90-minute circuit starting at Syntagma. You can get on and off at 15 stops on a 24-hour ticket.

Trekking Hellas WALKING TOUR
(Map p68; ☑ 210 331 0323; www.trekking.gr; Saripolou 10, Exarhia; Ⓜ Viktoria) Activities range from Athens walking tours (€39) to trekking in the Peloponnese.

Athens: Adventures GUIDED TOUR
(☑ 210 922 4044; www.athensadventures.gr) With a base at Athens Backpackers, this operator offers a €6 Athens walking tour and daytrips to Nafplio, Delphi and Sounio.

This is My Athens GUIDED TOUR
(www.thisisathens.org) This is a volunteer program that pairs you with a local to show you around for two hours. Must book online 72 hours ahead.

Athens Segway Tours GUIDED TOUR
(Map p77; ☑ 210 322 2500; www.athenssegway tours.com; Eschinou 9, Plaka; 2hr tour €59; Ⓜ Akropoli) Zip through town on a Segway.

Alternative Athens GUIDED TOUR
(📞 6948405242; www.alternative-athens.com) Experience-based tours and workshops to get off the beaten path.

Athens Happy Train MINI-TRAIN TOUR
(Map p84; 📞210 725 5400; www.athenshappy train.com; Plateia Syntagmatos, Syntagma; adult/child €6/4; ⊙every 30min 9am-midnight; Ⓜ Syntagma) Stops include the Acropolis, Monastiraki and the Panathenaic Stadium. Tours take one hour if you don't get off, or you can get on and off over five hours. Trains leave from the top of Ermou every 30 minutes.

☆☆ Festivals & Events

Hellenic Festival PERFORMING ARTS FESTIVAL
(www.greekfestival.gr; ⊙late May-Oct) Greece's premier cultural festival features a top line-up of local and international music, dance and theatre.

Major shows in its **Athens Festival** take place at the superb Odeon of Herodes Atticus (p78), one of the world's prime historic venues, with the floodlit Acropolis as a backdrop. Events are also held in modern venues around town.

Its **Epidavros Festival** presents local and international productions of Ancient Greek drama at the famous ancient Theatre of Epidavros (p146) in the Peloponnese, two hours west of Athens, on Friday and Saturday nights in July and August. Check the festival website for special **KTEL buses** (📞210 513 4588; return €23) to Epidavros.

Book tickets online, by phone, at the **Hellenic Festival Box Office** (Map p102; 📞210 327 2000; Arcade, Panepistimiou 39, Syntagma; ⊙8.30am-4pm Mon-Fri, 9am-2pm Sat; underground rail Panepistimio), or at Public and Papasotiriou stores. Though available at theatre box offices, queues at performances can be very long or may be sold out. Half-price student discounts (with ID) for most performances.

European Jazz Festival MUSIC FESTIVAL
(www.cityofathens.gr; ⊙late May-early Jun) Run by the City of Athens, which also organises other free summer concerts and dance performances across the city, such as the **International Dance Festival**.

Rockwave Festival MUSIC FESTIVAL
(📞210 882 0426; www.rockwavefestival.gr; ⊙Jun-Jul) Annual international rock show held at Terra Vibe, a parkland venue on the outskirts of Athens in Malakassa. Special buses from town, and cheap camping.

August Moon Festival PERFORMING ARTS FESTIVAL
Every August on the night of the full moon, musical performances are held at key historic venues, including the Acropolis, the Roman Agora and other sites around Greece.

Athens International Film Festival FILM FESTIVAL
(📞210 606 1413; www.aiff.gr; ⊙Sep) Features retrospectives, premieres and international art films and documentaries.

🛏 Sleeping

Athens has a full range of options, though service is not always up to expectations. Plaka is most popular with travellers. High-end hotels cluster around Syntagma. Some excellent smaller hotels dot the quiet neighbourhoods of Makrygianni and Koukaki. Around Omonia some hotels have been upgraded, but there is still a general seediness (think drugs and prostitution), especially at night.

Book ahead in July and August. Prices quoted are for high season; get considerable discounts in low season, for longer stays and online. No-smoking rules are often laxly enforced, if at all.

🛏 Syntagma & Plaka

Hotel Adonis HOTEL $
(Map p84; 📞210 324 9737; www.hotel-adonis.gr; 3 Kodrou St, Plaka; s/d/tr incl breakfast €60/70/85; ✳@☎; Ⓜ Syntagma) This comfortable pension on a quiet pedestrian street in Plaka has basic, clean rooms with TVs. Bathrooms are small but have been excellently renovated. Take in great Acropolis views from 4th-floor rooms and the rooftop terrace where breakfast is served. No credit cards.

Acropolis House Pension PENSION $
(Map p84; 📞210 322 2344; www.acropolishouse. gr; Kodrou 6-8, Plaka; d/tr/q incl breakfast from €60/90/116; ✳☎; Ⓜ Syntagma) This atmospheric family-run pension is in a beautifully preserved, 19th-century house, which retains many original features and has lovely painted walls. There are discounts for stays of three days or more. Some rooms have private bathrooms across the hall.

Niki Hotel HOTEL $
(Map p84; 📞210 322 0913; www.nikihotel.gr; Nikis 27, Syntagma; s/d/tr incl breakfast from €56/65/90; ✳@☎; Ⓜ Syntagma) This small hotel bordering Plaka has contemporary design and furnishings. The rooms are well

appointed and there is a two-level suite for families (€140), with balconies offering Acropolis views.

Arethusa Hotel
HOTEL $

(Map p84; ☑ 210 322 9431; www.arethusahotel.gr; Mitropoleos 6, cnr Nikis, Syntagma; s/d incl breakfast €50/70; ☎; Ⓜ Syntagma) Arethusa is a basic, central choice.

Student & Travellers' Inn
HOSTEL $

(Map p84; ☑ 210 324 4808; www.studenttravellersinn.com; Kydathineon 16, Plaka; dm €20-25, s/d/tr €57/73/90, without bathroom €50/65/81; ❄ @ ☎; Ⓜ Syntagma) Its location in the heart of Plaka makes this long-established hostel popular with visitors of all ages. There's a mix of very basic dorms and rooms, some with private bathroom and air-conditioning, though shared bathrooms are run-down and complaints about cleanliness are common. It's got a pleasant, shady courtyard and a helpful travel service.

★ NEW Hotel
BOUTIQUE HOTEL $$

(Map p84; ☑ 210 628 4565; www.yeshotels.gr; Filellinon 16, Plaka; d incl breakfast from €123; ℙ ❄ ☎; Ⓜ Syntagma) Whether you dig the groovy, top-designer Campana Brothers furniture or the pillow menu (tell 'em how you like it!), you'll find some sort of decadent treat here to tickle your fancy. Part of a renowned local design-hotel group, NEW Hotel is the latest entry on the high-end Athens scene.

Central Hotel
BOUTIQUE HOTEL $$

(Map p84; ☑ 210 323 4357; www.centralhotel.gr; Apollonos 21, Plaka; d incl breakfast from €90; ❄ @; Ⓜ Syntagma) This stylish hotel has been tastefully decorated in light, contemporary tones. It has comfortable rooms with all the mod cons and good bathrooms. There is a lovely roof terrace with Acropolis views, a small spa and sun lounges. As its name suggests, Central Hotel is in a great location between Syntagma and Plaka.

Athens Cypria Hotel
HOTEL $$

(Map p84; ☑ 210 323 8034; www.athenscypria.com; Diomias 5, Syntagma; d €89; ❄ @ ☎; Ⓜ Syntagma) Tucked in a side street off Ermou, this small, family-friendly hotel is a little characterless, but it is modern and comfortable, with good facilities and a very handy location. Some rooms have balconies but no great view. There are family rooms (from €170).

🏃 Museum Tour
National Archaeological Museum

LENGTH TWO HOURS
SEE NATIONAL ARCHAEOLOGICAL MUSEUM (P88)

Ahead of you as you enter the museum is the ❶ **Prehistoric collection**, showcasing some of the most important pieces of Mycenaean, Neolithic and Cycladic art, many in solid gold. The fabulous collection of ❷ **Mycenaean antiquities** (gallery 4) is the museum's tour de force. The first cabinet holds the celebrated gold ❸ **Mask of Agamemnon**, unearthed at Mycenae, and bronze daggers with intricate representations of the hunt. The exquisite ❹ **Vaphio gold cups**, with scenes of men taming wild bulls, are regarded as among the finest surviving examples of Mycenaean art.

The ❺ **Cycladic collection** (gallery 6) includes superb figurines of the 3rd and 2nd millennia BC that inspired artists such as Picasso.

The galleries to the left of the entrance house the oldest, most significant pieces of the sculpture collection. The colossal 600 BC Naxian marble ❻ **Sounion Kouros** (room 8) stood before Poseidon's temple in Sounion. Gallery 15 is dominated by the incredible 460 BC bronze ❼ **statue of Zeus or Poseidon**, found in the sea off Evia. It depicts one of the gods (no one really knows which) with his arms outstretched.

The 200 BC ❽ **statue of Athena Varvakeion** (gallery 20) is the most famous copy – much reduced in size – of the colossal statue of Athena Polias by Pheidias that once stood in the Parthenon.

In gallery 21 the striking 2nd-century-BC ❾ **statue of horse and young rider**, recovered from a shipwreck off Cape Artemision in Evia, stands opposite exquisite works such as the ❿ **statue of Aphrodite**.

Upstairs, the spectacular ⓫ **Minoan frescoes** from Santorini (Thira) were uncovered in the prehistoric settlement of Akrotiri, which was buried by a volcanic eruption in the late 16th century BC.

NATIONAL ARCHAEOLOGICAL MUSEUM

First Floor

Cypriot Collection

Pottery Collection

Pottery Collection

Panathenaic Amphorae

Thira Gallery

Lift

Minoan Frescoes 11

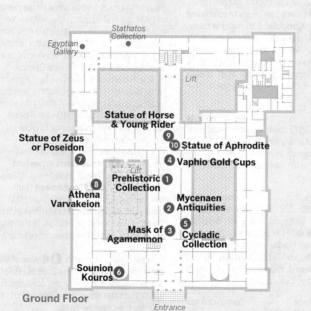

Ground Floor

Stathatos Collection

Egyptian Gallery

Lift

Lift

Statue of Horse & Young Rider

9

10 Statue of Aphrodite

Statue of Zeus or Poseidon

7

4 Vaphio Gold Cups

1 Prehistoric Collection

Lift

8

Athena Varvakeion

2 Mycenaen Antiquities

Mask of 3 Agamemnon

5 Cycladic Collection

Sounion 6 Kouros

Entrance

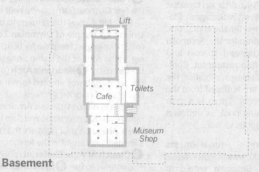

Basement

Lift

Toilets

Cafe

Museum Shop

Adrian Hotel
HOTEL $$

(Map p84; ☑ 210 322 1553; www.douros-hotels. com; Adrianou 74, Plaka; s/d/tr incl breakfast €95/115/135; ❋ @ 🛜; Ⓜ Monastiraki) This tiny hotel right in the heart of Plaka serves breakfast on a lovely shady terrace with Acropolis views. The well-equipped rooms are pleasant if a bit worn. Third-floor rooms are the best, with large balconies overlooking the square.

Hotel Phaedra
HOTEL $$

(Map p84; ☑ 210 323 8461; www.hotelphaedra. com; Herefontos 16, Plaka; d/tr €80/90; ❋ @ 🛜; Ⓜ Akropoli) Many of the rooms at this small, family-run hotel have balconies overlooking a church or the Acropolis. The hotel is tastefully furnished, though rooms vary from small to snug. Some rooms have private bathrooms across the hall (d/tr €60/70). A great rooftop terrace, friendly staff and a good location make this one of the better deals in Plaka.

Hotel Hermes
BOUTIQUE HOTEL $$

(Map p84; ☑ 210 323 5514; www.hermeshotel.gr; Apollonos 19, Plaka; d/q incl breakfast €120/195; ❋ @ 🛜; Ⓜ Syntagma) Hermes is next to the Central Hotel, with similar amenities, but not quite as swish.

Hotel Achilleas
BUSINESS HOTEL $$

(Map p84; ☑ 210 323 3197; www.achilleashotel. gr; Leka 21, Syntagma; s/d/q incl breakfast €105/125/135; ❋ @ 🛜; Ⓜ Syntagma) This conveniently located business-style hotel has a sleek lobby with marble chequerboard floors and well-appointed rooms, some of which open onto garden balconies.

★ Electra Palace
LUXURY HOTEL $$$

(Map p84; ☑ 210 337 0000; www.electrahotels.gr; Navarhou Nikodimou 18, Plaka; d/ste incl breakfast from €185/255; P ❋ @ 🛜 ⊠; Ⓜ Syntagma) Plaka's smartest hotel is one for the romantics. You can have breakfast under the Acropolis on your balcony (higher-end rooms) and dinner in the chic rooftop restaurant. Completely refurbished with classic elegance, the well-appointed rooms are buffered from the sounds of the city streets. There is a gym and an indoor swimming pool, as well as a rooftop pool with Acropolis views.

Hotel Grande Bretagne
LUXURY HOTEL $$$

(Map p84; ☑ 210 333 0000; www.grandebretagne. gr; Vasileos Georgiou 1, Syntagma; r/ste from €295/600; P ❋ @ 🛜; Ⓜ Syntagma) If you aspire to the best, *the* place to stay in Athens

🚶 Walking Tour
Central Athens

START SYNTAGMA
END MONASTIRAKI FLEA MARKET
LENGTH 3.5KM; TWO HOURS

Start in ❶ **Plateia Syntagmatos** (p82). The square has been a favourite place for protests ever since the rally that led to the granting of a constitution on 3 September 1843, declared by King Otto from the balcony of the royal palace (now Parliament). In 1944 the first round of the civil war began here after police opened fire on a communist rally, and in 1954 it was the location of the first demonstration demanding the *enosis* (union) of Cyprus with Greece.

The historic Hotel Grande Bretagne, the most illustrious of Athens' hotels, was built in 1862. The Nazis made it their headquarters during WWII, and in 1944 the hotel was the scene of an attempt to blow up Winston Churchill.

Left of the metro entrance, find a section of the ❷ **Peisistratos aqueduct**, which was unearthed during excavations. In front of the ❸ **Parliament** (p86) the much-photographed *evzones* (the presidential guards) stand sentinel at the Tomb of the Unknown Soldier. The changing of the guard takes place every hour on the hour.

Walk through the lush ❹ **National Gardens** (p82) and exit to the Zappeio Palace, which was used as the Olympic village in 2004. Pass the playground and go left until you see the crossing to the ❺ **Panathenaic Stadium** (p82), where the first Olympic Games were held in 1896.

Walk back along the gardens to the striking ❻ **Temple of Olympian Zeus** (p82), the largest temple ever built. Teetering on the edge of the traffic alongside the temple is ❼ **Hadrian's Arch** (p82), the ornate gateway erected to mark the boundary of Hadrian's Athens.

Cross Leoforos Vasilissis Amalias, head right towards Lysikratous and turn left into Plaka. Ahead on your right are the ruins of a Roman monument in the forecourt of the ❽ **Church of Agia Ekaterini** (p88).

Continue to the ❾ **Lysikrates Monument**. Built in 334 BC to commemorate a win in a choral festival, it's the earliest-

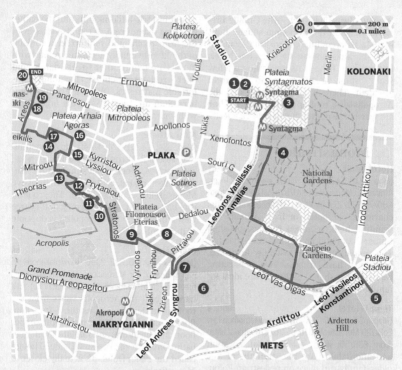

known monument using Corinthian capitals externally. The reliefs depict the battle between Dionysos and the Tyrrhenian pirates, whom the god had transformed into dolphins. It stands in what was once part of the Street of Tripods (Modern Tripodon), where winners of ancient dramatic and choral contests dedicated their tripod trophies to Dionysos. In the 18th century the monument was incorporated into the library of a French Capuchin convent, in which Lord Byron stayed in 1810–11 and wrote *Childe Harold*. The convent was destroyed by fire in 1890.

Facing the monument, turn left and then right into Epimenidou. At the top of the steps, turn right into Stratonos, which skirts the Acropolis. Just ahead you will see the ⑩ **Church of St George of the Rock**, which marks the entry to the ⑪ **Anafiotika quarter**. The picturesque maze of little whitewashed houses is the legacy of stonemasons from the small Cycladic island of Anafi, who were brought in to build the king's palace after Independence. It's a peaceful spot, with brightly painted olive-oil cans brimming with flowers in the tiny gardens in summer.

Continue past the tiny ⑫ **Church of Agios Simeon**. It looks like a dead end but

persevere and you will emerge at the Acropolis road. Turn right and then left into Prytaniou, veering right after 50m into Tholou. The yellow-ochre building at Tholou 5 is the ⑬ **old Athens University**, built by the Venetians. The Turks used it as public offices and it housed Athens University from 1837 to 1841.

Continue down to the ruins of the ⑭ **Roman Agora** (p80). To the right of the Tower of the Winds on Kyrristou is the ⑮ **Turkish Baths** (p81). Meanwhile, the ⑯ **Museum of Greek Popular Instruments** (p89), on Diogenous, has one of Athens' only remaining private hammams in its gift shop. Turning onto Pelopida, you'll see the gate of the Muslim Seminary, built in 1721 and destroyed in a fire in 1911, and the ⑰ **Fethiye Mosque**, on the site of the Agora.

Follow the road around the Agora to the ruins of ⑱ **Hadrian's Library** (p81). Next to them is the ⑲ **Museum of Traditional Greek Ceramics** (p86), housed in the 1759 Mosque of Tzistarakis. After Independence it lost its minaret and was used as a prison.

You're now in Monastiraki, the colourful, chaotic square teeming with street vendors. To the left is ⑳ **Monastiraki Flea Market** (p118).

is – and always has been – the Grande Bretagne, right on the Syntagma square. Built in 1862 to accommodate visiting heads of state, it ranks among the grandest hotels in the world. Though its renovation is a few years distant, it still retains its old-world grandeur. There is a divine **spa**, and the Acropolis-view rooftop **restaurant** and **bar** are worth a visit, even if you aren't a guest.

Monastiraki

Hotel Cecil
HOTEL **$**

(Map p102; ☑210 321 7079; www.cecilhotel.gr; Athinas 39, Monastiraki; s/d/tr/q incl breakfast from €60/75/120/155; ❄@☎; Ⓜ Monastiraki) This charming old hotel on busy Athinas has beautiful high, moulded ceilings, polished timber floors and an original cage-style lift. The simple rooms are tastefully furnished, but don't have fridges. Two connecting rooms with a shared bathroom are ideal for families.

Tempi Hotel
HOTEL **$**

(Map p84; ☑210 321 3175; www.tempihotel.gr; Eolou 29, Monastiraki; d/tr €57/67, s/d without bathroom €38/50; ❄☎; Ⓜ Monastiraki) Location and affordability are the strengths of this older, family-run place on pedestrian Eolou. Front balconies overlook Plateia Agia Irini, the scene of some of Athens' best nightlife, and side views get the Acropolis. Basic rooms have satellite TV, but bathrooms are primitive. Top-floor rooms are small and quite a hike. There is a communal kitchen.

★ Magna Grecia
BOUTIQUE HOTEL **$$**

(Map p84; ☑210 324 0314; www.magnagrecia hotel.com; Mitropoleos 54, Monastiraki; d incl breakfast €90-140, tr from €120; ❄☎; Ⓜ Monastiraki) This intimate boutique hotel, in a re-stored historic building opposite the cathedral, has magnificent Acropolis views from the front rooms and rooftop terrace. Each of the 12 individually decorated rooms with murals are named after Greek islands, and offer excellent amenities, including comfortable mattresses, DVD players and minibars. Staff are friendly and the hotel drips with character.

A for Athens
HOTEL **$$**

(Map p84; ☑210 324 4244; http://aforathens. com; Miaouli 2, Monastiraki; d from €130; ❄☎; Ⓜ Monastiraki) Modern but simple, A for Athens makes a good, central base right above Monastiraki's central square. The rooftop cafe-bar is grand, with sweeping 360-degree views that take in the Acropolis (as do some of the rooms).

Plaka Hotel
HOTEL **$$**

(Map p84; ☑210 322 2096; www.plakahotel.gr; Kapnikareas 7, cnr Mitropoleos, Monastiraki; d incl breakfast from €135; ❄☎; Ⓜ Monastiraki) It's hard to beat the Acropolis views from the rooftop garden, as well as those from top-floor rooms. Tidy rooms have light timber floors and furniture, and satellite TV, though bathrooms are on the small side. Though called the Plaka Hotel, it's actually closer to Monastiraki.

Thisio

Phidias Hotel
HOTEL **$**

(Map p90; ☑210 345 9511; www.phidias.gr; Apostolou Pavlou 39, Thisio; s/d/tr incl breakfast €57/70/80; ❄☎; Ⓜ Thisio) Smack dab midway along Thisio's grand pedestrianised promenade, this hotel and its friendly management offer straight-up, no-frills rooms in a great location.

STUDIOS & APARTMENTS

For longer stays or for families, a furnished studio or apartment may offer the best value.

Near the Acropolis, there are excellent simple apartments in various configurations, with daily cleaning, at **Athens Studios** (Map p77; ☑210 923 5811; www.athensstudios.gr; Veïkou 3a, Makrygianni; apt incl breakfast €80-120; @☎; Ⓜ Akropoli).

In Psyrri, Athens Style (p101) has well-equipped studios on the upper level, with kitchenettes, flat-screen TVs, stylish bathrooms and balconies with Acropolis views.

Book ahead for a superbly renovated, spacious apartment or whole house through **Boutique Athens** (☑6985083556; www.boutiqueathens.com; apt €80-210, min 2-night stay; ❄☎; Ⓜ Thisio), with locations all over town. In Psyrri, its massive roof garden with Acropolis views has sunbeds, a barbecue and a beer fridge.

Psyrri, Omonia & Exarhia

Athens Style HOSTEL $
(Map p84; ☑210 322 5010; www.athenstyle.com; Agias Theklas 10, Psyrri; dm €18-26, s/d €51/75, apt from €84; ❋@; Ⓜ Monastiraki) This bright and arty place has friendly staff, well-equipped studio apartments and hostel beds within walking distance of the metro, major sights and nightlife. Each dorm has lockers; some balconies have Acropolis views. Murals bedeck reception, and the cool basement lounge with its pool table, home cinema and internet corner holds art exhibitions. The small Acropolis-view rooftop bar hosts evening happy hours.

City Circus HOSTEL $
(Map p102; ☑213 023 7244; www.citycircus.gr; Sarri 16, Psyrri; dm incl breakfast €27-30, d €60-90; ❋⏶) Athens' newest hostel promises good things and delivers. Bright, well-designed rooms with modern bathrooms are configured as dorms or private rooms, some with kitchens. The attitude is jaunty and helpful.

Hotel Attalos HOTEL $
(Map p102; ☑210 321 2801; www.attaloshotel.com; Athinas 29, Psyrri; s/d/tr from €56/70/80; ❋@⏶; Ⓜ Monastiraki) Though decor has never been its strong point, this nonetheless comfortable hotel is very central. Its best feature remains the rooftop bar with wonderful views of the Acropolis. Rooms at the back have balconies (add €9) with Acropolis views.

Hotel Exarchion HOTEL $
(Map p102; ☑210 380 0731; www.exarchion.com; Themistokleous 55, Exarhia; d/tr/q incl breakfast from €40/50/64; ❋@; Ⓜ Omonia) Right in the heart of bohemian Exarhia, this straightforward but comfortable 1960s high-rise hotel offers clean, updated, well-equipped rooms, some with balconies. There's a rooftop cafe-bar and plenty of dining and entertainment options at your doorstep.

Fresh Hotel BOUTIQUE HOTEL $$
(Map p102; ☑210 524 8511; www.freshhotel.gr; Sofokleous 26, cnr Klisthenous, Omonia; r/ste incl breakfast from €104/250; ❋⏶❄; Ⓜ Omonia) The first of the hip hotels to open in the gritty Omonia area, this is a cool place so long as you're happy to ignore the working girls in the streets outside. Expect chic design and brightly coloured rooms plus a fantastic

ℹ **AIRPORT HOTELS**

If you need to catch an early flight, there are only two hotels near the airport: the **Sofitel** (☑210 354 4000; www.sofitel.com; Airport; d from €168), at the terminal, and the **Holiday Inn** (☑210 668 9100; www.hiathens.com; Peania, near Airport; d from €90), a 15-minute free shuttle ride away.

Acropolis-view rooftop, with pool, bar and restaurant.

Melia BUSINESS HOTEL $$
(Map p102; ☑210 332 0100; www.melia.com; Halkokondyli 14, cnr 28 Oktovriou-Patision, Omonia; d from €76; ❋⏶❄; Ⓜ Omonia) Professional staff, sleek rooms and a rooftop Acropolis view with bar-pool-spa make Melia a great hideout. It's midway between Omonia and Exarhia.

Ochre & Brown BOUTIQUE HOTEL $$$
(Map p102; ☑210 331 2940; www.oandbhotel.com; Leokoriou 7, Psyrri; d €135-300, ste €225-580; ❋⏶; Ⓜ Thisio) In Psyrri's main trendy hotel, step outside to the city's liveliest shopping district in nearby Monastiraki or retreat into luxurious solitude.

Akropoli, Makrygianni & Koukaki

★**Athens Backpackers** HOSTEL $
(Map p77; ☑210 922 4044; www.backpackers.gr; Makri 12, Makrygianni; dm incl breakfast €24-28, 2-/4-/6-person apt €95/125/155; ❋@⏶; Ⓜ Akropoli) The popular rooftop bar with cheap drinks and Acropolis views is a major drawcard of this modern and friendly Australian-run backpacker favourite, right near the Acropolis metro. There's a barbecue in the courtyard, a well-stocked kitchen and a busy social scene. Spotless dorms with private bathrooms and lockers have bedding, but use of towels cost €2. The same management runs well-priced modern apartments nearby.

Art Gallery Hotel PENSION $
(Map p77; ☑210 923 8376; www.artgalleryhotel.gr; Erehthiou 5, Koukaki; s/d/tr/q from €50/60/70/80; ❋⏶; Ⓜ Syngrou-Fix) Staying in this quaint, family-run place feels like staying in a home. Original furniture from the 1960s decorates the communal areas. Some rooms are a bit

Psyrri, Omonia & Exarhia

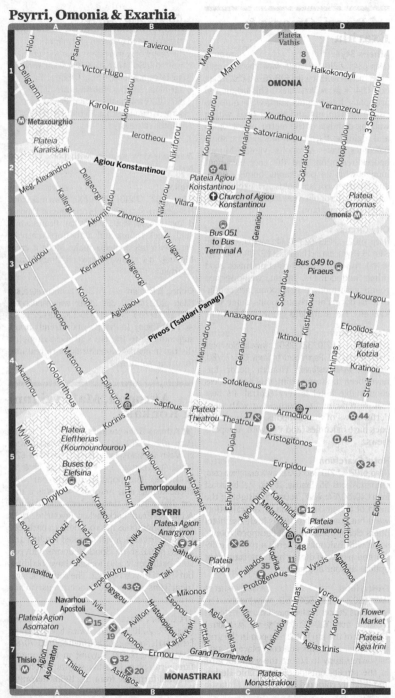

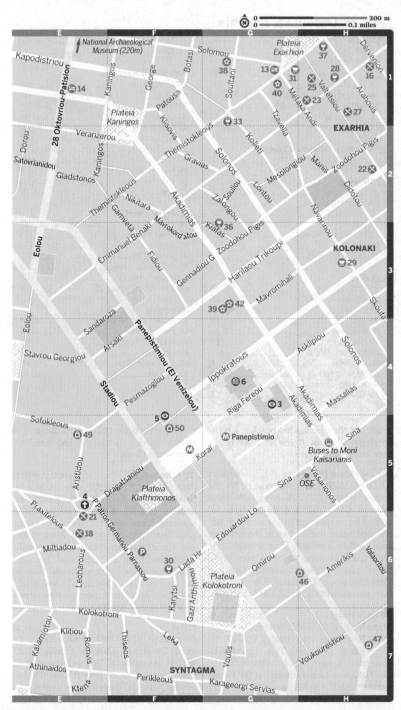

Psyrri, Omonia & Exarhia

small, but the upstairs balcony has a bit of an Acropolis view. A few cheaper rooms have shared bathrooms.

Marble House Pension PENSION $
(☎ 210 923 4058; www.marblehouse.gr; Zini 35a, Koukaki; s/d/tr €35/45/55, d/tr/q with shared bathroom €40/50/60; ✻@🛜; ⓂSyngrou-Fix) Tucked into a quiet cul-de-sac is one of Athens' best-value budget hotels. Rooms have been artfully updated, with wrought-iron beds, and bathrooms are sleek marble. All rooms have a fridge and ceiling fans and some have air-con (€9 extra). It is a fair walk from the tourist drag, but close to the metro.

★**Hera Hotel** BOUTIQUE HOTEL $$
(Map p77; ☎ 210 923 6682; www.herahotel.gr; Falirou 9, Makrygianni; d incl breakfast €130-160, ste €225; ✻@🛜; ⓂAkropoli) This elegant boutique hotel, a short walk from the Acropolis and Plaka, was totally rebuilt but the formal interior design is in keeping with the lovely neoclassical facade. There's lots of brass and

timber, and stylish classic furnishings. The rooftop garden, restaurant and bar have spectacular views.

★**Athens Gate** BUSINESS HOTEL $$
(Map p77; ☎ 210 923 8302; www.athensgate.gr; Leoforos Syngrou Andrea 10, Makrygianni; d incl breakfast €125-165; ✻@🛜; ⓂAkropoli) With stunning views over the Temple of Olympian Zeus from the spacious front rooms, and a central (if busy) location, this totally refurbished hotel is a great find. The chic, stylish rooms are immaculate and have all the mod cons, staff are friendly and breakfast is served on the superb rooftop terrace with 360-degree Athens views.

Hotel Tony HOTEL $$
(Map p68; ☎ 210 923 0561; www.hoteltony.gr; Zaharitsa 26, Koukaki; s/d/tr/apt €65/85/95/130; ✻@🛜; ⓂSyngrou-Fix) The well-maintained, clean rooms here all have fridges, TV and air-con (€9 extra). Tony also has roomy, well-equipped apartments nearby (€130 to €140).

Herodion   HOTEL $$$
(Map p77; ☑210 923 6832; www.herodion.com;
Rovertou Galli 4, Makrygianni; s/d incl breakfast
€155/170; ❋@🛜; ⓂAkropoli) This smart
four-star hotel is geared towards the well-
heeled traveller and businessperson. Rooms
are small but decked out with all the trim-
mings and have super-comfortable beds.
The rooftop spa and lounge have unbeatable
Acropolis and museum views.

Philippos Hotel   HOTEL $$$
(Map p77; ☑210 922 3611; www.philipposhotel.
com; Mitseon 3, Makrygianni; s/d/tr incl breakfast
€110/158/171; ❋@🛜; ⓂAkropoli) A popular
favourite, Philippos offers small and well-
appointed rooms near the Acropolis. The
double on the roof has a private terrace.

🛏 Kolonaki

★**Periscope**   BOUTIQUE HOTEL $$
(Map p110; ☑210 729 7200; www.periscope.gr;
Haritos 22, Kolonaki; d incl breakfast from €87;
❋🛜; ⓂEvangelismos) Right in chic Kolonaki
overlooking Lykavittos, Periscope is a design
hotel with industrial decor. Clever gadgets
are sprinkled throughout, including the
lobby slide show and aerial shots of the city
on the ceilings. Korres organic toiletries and
the trendy **Pbox** restaurant add to the vibe.
The penthouse's private rooftop spa has sen-
sational views.

Camping

The *Camping in Greece* booklet, produced
by EOT (Greek National Tourist Organisa-
tion), and www.travelling.gr list sites in the
Attica region. Most campgrounds near Ath-
ens offer basic facilities and are not general-
ly up to European standards. If you must, try
the closest, **Athens Camping** (☑210 581 4114;
www.campingathens.com.gr; Leoforos Athinon 198,
Haidari; camp sites per adult/tent/car €8.50/5/4;
⊙year-round; 🛜), 7km west of the city centre
on the road to Corinth. Better camping op-
tions are further afield, at Shinias and Cape
Sounion.

🍴 Eating

Athens' vibrant restaurant scene is marked
by a delightful culture of casual, convivial al
fresco dining. Getting together to eat, drink
and talk is the main source of entertain-
ment for Greeks, so you are spoilt for choice.
A new generation of chefs draws inspiration
from Greece's regional cuisine and local
produce; this results in an interesting blend

of culinary sophistication and grandma's
home-style cooking. Trendy nouveau-Greek
restaurants compete alongside traditional
tavernas, *ouzeries* (places that serve ouzo
and light snacks) and quaint old-style
mayiria (cook houses).

It's hard to avoid eating in Plaka if you are
staying there, but the food is generally over-
priced and ho-hum. Gazi and Monastiraki
have many modern tavernas that are con-
venient for lining your belly before a night
out in nearby clubs. Also in Monastiraki, the
end of Mitropoleos is a souvlaki hub, with
musicians adding to the area's bustling at-
mosphere. *Mezedhopoleia* (restaurants spe-
cialising in mezedhes) and more-upmarket
restaurants can be found around Adrianou.
Exarhia's popular eateries cater largely to
locals, while chic Kolonaki has some of the
best fine-dining options. At high-end restau-
rants, reservations are essential.

🍴 Syntagma & Plaka

★**Tzitzikas & Mermingas**   MEZEDHES $
(Map p84; ☑210 324 7607; Mitropoleos 12-14, Syn-
tagma; mezedhes €6-11; ⊙lunch & dinner; ⓂSyn-
tagma) Greek merchandise lines the walls of
this cheery, modern *mezedhopoleio* that sits
smack in the middle of central Athens. It
serves a tasty range of delicious and creative
mezedhes (like the honey-drizzled, bacon-
wrapped cheese one) to a bustling crowd of
locals.

★**Avocado**   VEGETARIAN $
(Map p84; ☑210 323 7878; www.avocadoathens.
com; Nikis 30, Plaka; mains €6.50-9.50; ⊙11am-
10pm Mon-Sat, to 7pm Sun; 🛜✎; ⓂSyntagma)
This new entry on the downtown scene of-
fers a full array of vegan, gluten-free and or-
ganic treats – a rarity in Greece. Next to an
organic market, and with a tiny front patio,
you can enjoy everything from sandwiches
to quinoa with eggplant or mixed veg coco-
nut curry. Fresh juices and mango lassis are
all made on the spot.

Glykis   MEZEDHES $
(Map p84; ☑210 322 3925; Angelou Geronta 2,
Plaka; mezedhes €5.50-6; ⊙10.30am-1.30am;
ⓂAkropoli) In a quiet corner of Plaka, this
low-key *mezedhopoleio* with a shady court-
yard is mostly frequented by students and
locals. It has a tasty selection of mezedhes,
including traditional dishes such as *briam*
(oven-baked vegetable casserole) and cuttle-
fish in wine.

STREET FOOD

From vendors selling *koulouria* (fresh pretzel-style bread) and grilled corn or chestnuts, to the raft of fast-food offerings, there's no shortage of snacks on the run in Athens. You can't go wrong with *tiropites* (cheese pies) at **Ariston** (Map p84; ☑ 210 322 7626; Voulis 10, Syntagma; pies €1.40-2; ⊙ 10am-4pm Mon-Fri; Ⓜ Syntagma), which has been around since 1910. Greece's favourite savoury snack is souvlaki, packing more punch for €2.50 than anything else. We list purveyors in most neighbourhoods. One of the best is tiny **Kostas** (Map p84; ☑ 210 323 2971; Plateia Agia Irini 2, Monastiraki; souvlaki €2; ⊙ 9am-5pm; Ⓜ Monastiraki), with its signature spicy tomato sauce, in the pleasant square opposite Agia Irini church.

Doris   TAVERNA $
(Map p102; ☑ 210 323 2671; Praxitelous 30, Syntagma; mains €4-9; ⊙ 8am-6.30pm Mon-Sat; Ⓜ Panepistimio) This Athens institution started as a *galaktopoleio* (dairy store) in 1947 and became a traditional *mayirio* catering to city workers. Classic marble tables, historical photos and old-style waiters give it a yesteryear ambience. Choose from trays of daily specials. Finish off with renowned *loukoumadhes* (ball-shaped doughnuts served with honey and cinnamon).

Pure Bliss   CAFE $
(Map p84; ☑ 210 325 0360; www.purebliss.gr; Romvis 24a, Syntagma; snacks €3-9; ⊙ 10am-1am Mon-Sat, 5-9pm Sun; 🛜; Ⓜ Syntagma) 🍃 Enjoy the laid-back vibe at one of the few places in Athens where you can get organic fairtrade coffee, exotic teas and soy products. There's a range of healthy salads, sandwiches, smoothies and mostly organic food, wine and cocktails.

Meatropoleos 3   SOUVLAKI $
(Map p84; ☑ 210 324 1805; www.meatropoleos3.com; Mitropoloeos 3; mains €8-9, souvlaki €1.50; ⊙ noon-midnight) Lay into grilled meats before a night on the town.

Paradosiako   TAVERNA $$
(Map p84; ☑ 210 321 4121; Voulis 44a, Plaka; mains €5-12; ⊙ lunch & dinner; 🛜; Ⓜ Syntagma) For great traditional fare, you can't beat this inconspicuous, no-frills taverna on the periphery of Plaka, with a few tables on the footpath. There's a basic menu but it's best to choose from the daily specials, which include fresh seafood such as prawn saganaki.

Palia Taverna Tou Psara   TAVERNA $$
(Map p84; ☑ 210 321 8734; www.psaras-taverna.gr; Erehtheos 16, Plaka; mains €12-24; ⊙ 11am-12.30am Wed-Mon; Ⓜ Akropoli) Away from the main hustle of Plaka, this taverna is a cut above

the rest and fills tables cascading across the street. It is known as the best seafood taverna in Plaka (fish €65 per kilogram).

🍴 Monastiraki

Kalnterimi   TAVERNA $
(Map p102; ☑ 210 331 0049; www.kalnterimi.gr; Plateia Agion Theodoron, cnr Skouleniou, Monastiraki; mains €5-8; ⊙ lunch & dinner; Ⓜ Panepistimio) Find your way behind the Church of Agii Theodori to this hidden open-air taverna offering Greek food at its most authentic. Everything is fresh cooked and delicious: you can't go wrong. Hand-painted tables spill onto the footpath along a pedestrian street and give a feeling of peace in one of the busiest parts of the city.

Mama Roux   INTERNATIONAL $
(Map p84; ☑ 213 004 8382; Eolou 48-50, Monastiraki; mains €5-10; ⊙ 9am-midnight Tue-Sat, to 5pm Mon, noon-5pm Sun; 🛜; Ⓜ Monastiraki) Downtown's hottest cheap-eats restaurant fills up with locals digging into a fresh, delicious mix of food, from real burritos and Cajun specials to whopping American-style burgers. Reserve ahead for this popular hangout, with Santorini's Yellow Donkey beer on tap and Sunday jazz brunches.

Melilotos   GREEK $
(Map p84; ☑ 210 322 2458; www.melilotos.gr; Kalamiotou 19, Monastiraki; mains €6.50-8.50; ⊙ noon-6pm Mon, noon-1am Tue-Sat, 2-10pm Sun) Great, affordable Greek food with a dram of wine makes a fun start to a night out in the area's bar quarter. Specials rotate daily.

Kalipateira   MEZEDHES $
(Map p102; ☑ 210 321 4152; Astingos 8, Monastiraki; dishes €4-10; ⊙ lunch & dinner; Ⓜ Monastiraki) In a neoclassical building overlooking an archaeological dig, young Athenians gather for long sessions over mezedhes and carafes

of ouzo. *Rembetika* (Greek blues) Thursday to Sunday.

Ouzou Melathron
TAVERNA $

(Map p84; ☑ 210 324 0716; Agiou Filipou 10, cnr Astingos, Monastiraki; mezedhes €5-7; ⊗ noon-late; Ⓜ Monastiraki) The famous *ouzerie* chain from Thessaloniki has been a hit since it opened right in the middle of the Monastiraki marketplace. It's a buzzing, unpretentious spot serving tasty mezedhes from a whimsical menu.

Thanasis
SOUVLAKI $

(Map p84; ☑ 210 324 4705; Mitropoleos 69, Monastiraki; gyros €2.50; ⊗ 8.30am-2.30am; Ⓜ Monastiraki) In the heart of Athens' souvlaki hub, at the end of Mitropoleos, Thanasis is known for its kebabs on pitta with grilled tomato and onions.

★ Café Avyssinia
MEZEDHES $$

(Map p84; ☑ 210 321 7047; www.avissinia.gr; Kynetou 7, Monastiraki; mains €10-16; ⊗ 11am-1am Tue-Sat, to 7pm Sun; Ⓜ Monastiraki) Hidden away on colourful Plateia Avyssinias, in the middle of the flea market, this bohemian *mezedhopoleio* gets top marks for atmosphere, food and friendly service. It specialises in regional Greek cuisine, from warm fava to eggplants baked with tomato and cheese, and has a great selection of ouzo, *raki* (Cretan firewater) and *tsipouro* (distilled spirit similar to ouzo but usually stronger).

There is acoustic live Greek music on weekends. Snag fantastic Acropolis views upstairs.

Kuzina
MODERN GREEK $$

(Map p68; ☑ 210 324 0133; www.kuzina.gr; Adrianou 9, Monastiraki; mains €12-25; ⊗ lunch & dinner; Ⓜ Thisio) Light streams through plate-glass windows, warming the crowded tables in winter. Or eat outside on pedestrianised, people-watching Adrianou in summer. Expect inventive Greek fusion, such as Cretan pappardelle or chicken with figs and sesame.

✕ Gazi, Thisio & Keramikos

Kanella
TAVERNA $

(Map p90; ☑ 210 347 6320; Leoforos Konstantinoupoleos 70, Gazi; dishes €7-10; ⊗ 1.30pm-late; Ⓜ Keramikos) Homemade village-style bread, mismatched retro crockery and brown-paper tablecloths set the tone for this trendy, modern taverna serving regional Greek cui-

sine. Friendly staff serve daily specials such as lemon lamb with potatoes, and an excellent zucchini and avocado salad.

To Steki tou Ilia
TAVERNA $

(Map p90; ☑ 210 345 8052; Eptahalkou 5, Thisio; chops per portion/kg €9/30; ⊗ 8pm-late; Ⓜ Thisio) You'll often see people waiting for a table at this *psistaria* (restaurant serving grilled food), famous for its tasty grilled lamb and pork chops. With tables under the trees on the quiet pedestrian strip opposite the church, it's a no-frills place with barrel wine and simple dips, chips and salads.

Jamon
TAPAS $

(Map p90; ☑ 210 346 4120; www.jamon.gr; Elasidon 15, Gazi; tapas €1.75-7; ⊗ 2pm-late; Ⓜ Keramikos) Scrumptious tapas and paella (€10), served with Spanish wines and flare, streetside by a gregarious owner.

Gevomai Kai Magevomai
TAVERNA $

(Map p90; ☑ 210 345 2802; www.gevome-magevome.gr; Nileos 11, Thisio; mains €6-11; ⊗ lunch & dinner; ☎; Ⓜ Thisio) Stroll off the pedestrian way to find this small corner taverna with marble-topped tables. Neighbourhood denizens know it as one of the best places for home-cooked, simple food with the freshest ingredients.

Oina Perdamata
TAVERNA $

(Map p90; ☑ 210 341 1461; Vasiliou tou Megalou 10, Gazi; mains €6-9; ⊗ lunch & dinner; ☎; Ⓜ Keramikos) Unpretentious, fresh daily specials are the hallmark of this simple spot off busy Pireos. Try staples such as fried cod with garlic dip and roast vegetables, or pork stew, rabbit and rooster.

★ Athiri
MODERN GREEK $$

(Map p90; ☑ 210 346 2983; www.athirirestaurant.gr; Plateon 15, Keramikos; mains €16-19; ⊗ 8pm-1am Tue-Sat, 6pm-midnight Sun; Ⓜ Thisio) Athiri's lovely garden courtyard is a verdant surprise in this pocket of Keramikos, The small but innovative menu plays on Greek regional classics. Try Santorini fava and the hearty beef stew with *myzithra* (sheep's-milk cheese) and handmade pasta from Karpathos.

Filistron
MEZEDHES $$

(Map p90; ☑ 210 346 7554; Apostolou Pavlou 23, Thisio; mezedhes €8-14; ⊗ lunch & dinner Tue-Sun; Ⓜ Thisio) It's wise to book a prized table on the rooftop terrace of this excellent *mezedhopoleio*, which enjoys breathtaking Acropolis and Lykavittos views. Specialising in regional cuisine, it has a great range of tasty mezedhes and an extensive Greek wine list.

Dirty Ginger
MODERN GREEK

(Map p90; ☑ 210 342 3809; www.dirtyginger.gr; Triptolemou 46, Gazi; mains €10-15; ☺ dinner May-Oct; Ⓜ Keramikos) A summer favourite, with tables around the giant palm tree in the colourfully lit courtyard, this 'postmodern taverna' is big on meat dishes. It's not the place for a quiet meal as it progressively morphs into a lively bar.

Sardelles
SEAFOOD $$

(Map p90; ☑ 210 347 8050; Persefonis 15, Gazi; fish dishes €10-17; ☺ lunch & dinner; Ⓜ Keramikos) Dig into simply cooked seafood mezedhes at tables outside, opposite the illuminated gasworks. Nice touches include fishmonger paper tablecloths and souvenir pots of basil. Meat eaters can venture next door to its counterpart, Butcher Shop (Map p90; ☑ 210 341 3440; Persefonis 19, Gazi; Ⓜ Keramikos).

★ Funky Gourmet
MODERN MEDITERRANEAN $$$

(Map p68; ☑ 210 524 2727; www.funkygourmet. com; Paramithias 3, cnr Salaminas, Keramikos; set menu from €68; ☺ 8-11.30pm Tue-Sat) Noveau gastronomy meets fresh Mediterranean ingredients at this Michelin-starred restaurant. Elegant lighting, refinement and sheer joy in food make this a worthwhile stop for any foodie. The degustation menus can be paired with wines. Book ahead.

★ Varoulko
SEAFOOD $$$

(Map p90; ☑ 210 522 8400; www.varoulko.gr; Pireos 80, Keramikos; mains €35-60; ☺ from 8.30pm Mon-Sat; Ⓜ Thisio, Keramikos) For a heady Greek dining experience, try the Michelin-starred combination of Acropolis views and delicious seafood. Service can be spotty but the wine list and rooftop terrace are enviable.

✖ Psyrri, Omonia & Exarhia

The streets around the colourful and bustling Varvakios Agora (Central Market; Map p102; Athinas, Omonia; ☺ Mon-Sat; Ⓜ Monastiraki) are a sensory delight. The meat and fish market fills the historic building on the eastern side, and the fruit and vegetable market is across the road. The meat market might sound like a strange place to go for a meal, but its tavernas, such as Papandreou (Map p102; ☑ 213 008 2242; Aristogitonos 1; mains €7-8; ☺ 24hr; Ⓜ Omonia, Monastiraki),

are an Athenian institution. Clients range from hungry market workers to elegant couples emerging from nightclubs in search of a bowl of hangover-busting *patsas* (tripe soup).

★ Diporto Agoras
TAVERNA $

(Map p102; ☑ 210 321 1463; cnr Theatrou & Sokratous; plates €5-6; ☺ 8am-6pm Mon-Sat, closed 1-20 Aug) This quirky old taverna is one of the dining gems of Athens. There's no signage, only two doors leading to a rustic cellar where there's no menu, just a few dishes that haven't changed in years. The house speciality is *revythia* (chickpeas), usually followed by grilled fish and washed down with wine from one of the giant barrels lining the wall. The often-erratic service is part of the appeal.

Kimatothrafstis
CAFE $

(Map p102; ☑ 213 030 8274; Harilaou Trikoupi 49, Exarhia; small/large plate €3/6; ☺ 8am-11pm, closed dinner Sun; Ⓜ Omonia) This great-value, bright and casual modern cafe with communal tables dishes out a range of home-style Greek cooking and alternative fare. Choose from the buffet of the day's offerings. Plates come in two sizes: big and small.

Barbagiannis
TAVERNA $

(Map p102; ☑ 210 330 0185; Emmanuel Benaki 94, Exarhia; mains €5-7; ☺ lunch & dinner Mon-Sat, to 7pm Sun; Ⓜ Omonia) An Exarhia institution, this low-key *mayirio* is popular with students and those wanting good-value home-style Greek food.

Oxo Nou
CRETAN $

(Map p102; ☑ 210 380 1778; Emmanuel Benaki 63-65, cnr Metaxa, Exarhia; mains €8-11; ☺ 3pm-late; Ⓜ Omonia) Super Cretan food has finally found its way to central Athens.

Ivis
MEZEDHES $

(Map p102; ☑ 210 323 2554; Navarhou Apostoli 19, Psyrri; mezedhes €4-10; Ⓜ Thisio) This cosy corner *mezedhopoleio*, with its bright, arty decor, has a small but delicious range of simple, freshly cooked mezedhes. Ask for the daily specials as there's only a rough Greek hand-written menu. A good ouzo selection lights things up.

Rozalia
TAVERNA $

(Map p102; ☑ 210 330 2933; Valtetsiou 58, Exarhia; mains €5-11; Ⓜ Omonia) An Exarhia favourite on a lively pedestrian strip, this family-run taverna serves grills and home-style fare.

Taverna tou Psyrri
TAVERNA $

(Map p102; ☑ 210 321 4923; Eshylou 12, Psyrri; mains €6-8; ☺ closed 2 weeks Aug; Ⓜ Monastiraki) This cheerful taverna just off Plateia Iroön turns out decent, no-frills, traditional food.

★ Yiantes
TAVERNA $$

(Map p102; ☑ 210 330 1369; Valtetsiou 44, Exarhia; mains €9-12; ☺ lunch & dinner; Ⓜ Omonia) This modern eatery with its white linen and fresh-cut flowers set in a lovely garden courtyard is upmarket for Exarhia, but the food is superb and made with largely organic produce. Try interesting greens such as *almirikia*, the perfectly grilled fish, or delicious mussels and calamari with saffron.

✕ Akropoli, Makrygianni & Koukaki

★ Mani Mani
GREEK $$

(Map p77; ☑ 210 921 8180; www.manimani.com.gr; Falirou 10, Makrygianni; mains €10-16, mezedhes €7.50; ☺ 3pm-12.30am Tue-Fri, from 1pm Sat, 1-5.30pm Sun, closed Jul & Aug; Ⓜ Akropoli) Head upstairs to the relaxing, cheerful dining rooms of this delightful modern restaurant, which specialises in regional cuisine from Mani in the Peloponnese. The ravioli with Swiss chard, chervil and cheese, and the tangy Mani sausage with orange are standouts. Almost all dishes can be ordered as half portions (at half-price), allowing you to sample widely.

Trapezaria
MODERN GREEK $$

(Map p77; ☑ 210 921 3500; www.trapezaria.gr; Negri 1, Makrygianni; mains €8-15; ☺ dinner Mon-Sat; Ⓜ Akropoli) In an unassuming spot, this stylish contemporary Greek restaurant packs in locals in search of good, affordable eats, served with style. The wine list is remarkable.

Aglio, Olio & Peperoncino
ITALIAN $$

(Map p77; ☑ 210 921 1801; Porinou 13, Makrygianni; mains €15-25; ☺ noon-midnight Mon-Fri, 8pm-2am Sat, 2-7pm Sun; Ⓜ Akropoli) Hardly the most obvious place for a restaurant, but this hidden gem behind the metro is a great choice for no-frills classic Italian pastas and a cosy, trattoria ambience.

Strofi
GREEK $$

(Map p77; ☑ 210 921 4130; www.strofi.gr; Rovertou Galli 25, Makrygianni; mains €11-15; Ⓜ Akropoli) Book ahead for a Parthenon view from the rooftop of this exquisitely renovated townhouse. Food is simple Greek, but the setting, with elegant white linen and sweet service, elevates the experience to romantic levels.

★ Hytra
MEDITERRANEAN $$$

(☑ 217 707 1118, 210 331 6767; www.hytra.gr; Onassis Cultural Centre, Syngrou 107-109; mains €29-31; ☺ dinner Tue-Sun) Routinely voted one of Athens' top restaurants, Hytra has recently moved into the Onassis Cultural Centre. Book ahead for exquisitely presented Greek food with a modern twist. In summer there's also a branch at the Westin Athens Astir Palace Beach Resort in coastal Vouliagmeni.

Dionysos
MEDITERRANEAN $$$

(Map p68; ☑ 210 923 1939; www.dionysoszonars.gr; Rovertou Galli 43, Makrygianni;; mains €18-28; ☺ restaurant noon-1am, cafe 8am-1am; Ⓜ Akropoli) Location, location, location. Eat here for the fantastic sweep of plate glass looking out onto the unblemished south slope of the Acropolis. Food is pricey but service is attentive... Date night?

✕ Kolonaki & Pangrati

★ Oikeio
MEDITERRANEAN $

(Map p110; ☑ 210 725 9216; Ploutarhou 15, Kolonaki; mains €7-13; ☺ 1pm-2.30am Mon-Sat; Ⓜ Evangelismos) With excellent home-style cooking, this modern taverna lives up to its name (meaning 'homey'). It's decorated like a cosy bistro on the inside, and tables on the footpath allow people-watching without the normal Kolonaki bill. Pastas, salads and international fare are tasty, but try the *mayirefta* (ready-cooked meals) specials such as the excellent stuffed zucchini. Book ahead.

Filippou
TAVERNA $

(Map p110; ☑ 210 721 6390; Xenokratous 19, Kolonaki; mains €8-12; ☺ lunch & dinner, closed Sat night & Sun; Ⓜ Evangelismos) Why mess with what works? Filippou has been dishing out yummy Greek dishes since 1923. A chance for a little soul cooking, with white linen, in the heart of Kolonaki.

Mavro Provato
MEZEDHES $

(Map p68; ☑ 210 722 3466; www.tomauroprovato.gr; Arrianou 31-33, Pangrati; dishes €4-12; ☺ lunch & dinner) Book ahead for this wildly popular modern *mezedhopoleio* in Pangrati.

Kalamaki Kolonaki
SOUVLAKI $

(Map p110; ☑ 210 721 8800; Ploutarhou 32, Kolonaki; mains €7; ☺ 12.30pm-2am; Ⓜ Evangelismos) Order by the *kalamaki* (skewer; €1.70),

Kolonaki

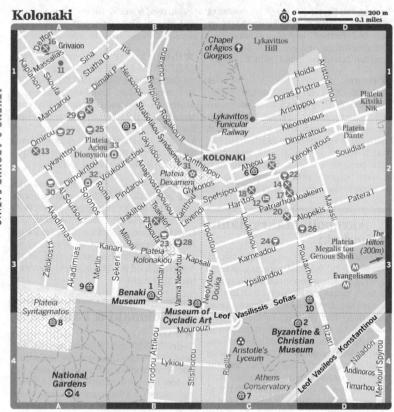

add on some salad and pittas, and you've got great quick eats with all the requisite people-watching at Kolonaki's standout souvlaki joint.

⭐ Yozen
DESSERTS $

(Map p110; ☑ 210 360 3196; Tsakalof 7, Kolonaki; frozen yoghurt from €3; ☺ 11am-late; Ⓜ Syntagma) Kolonaki's newest trend: frozen Greek yoghurt. And it's totally delicious. Flavours range from undoctored pure yoghurt to a rotating menu of fruit, chocolate and other inspirations. Homemade spoon sweets compete with liquid chocolate and the standard range of candy bits as toppings.

Nice N' Easy
CAFE $

(Map p110; ☑ 210 361 7201; www.niceneasy.gr; Omirou 60, Kolonaki; sandwiches €5-10; ☺ lunch & dinner daily, breakfast Sat & Sun; Ⓜ Panepistimio) 🖋 Dig into organic, fresh sandwiches, salads and brunch treats such as huevos rancheros

beneath images of Louis Armstrong and Marilyn Monroe.

Kavatza
TAVERNA $

(Map p110; ☑ 210 724 1862; Spefsipou 10, Kolonaki; mains €4-8; ☺ lunch & dinner; Ⓜ Evangelismos) Straight, value-for-money Greek dishes.

Cucina Povera
MEDITERRANEAN $$

(Map p68; ☑ 210 756 6008; www.cucinapovera.gr; Efforionos 13, Pangrati; mains €9-14; ☺ dinner Tue-Sat, brunch Sun; Ⓜ Evangelismos) Dishes can be occasionally (but not consistently) incandescent, such as the salad with avocado, pear and goat cheese. The dining room embodies relaxed hipness, and the wine list rocks.

Café Boheme
CAFE $$

(Map p110; ☑ 210 360 8018; Omirou 36, Kolonaki; mains €9-15; ☺ lunch & dinner; Ⓜ Panepistimiou) A jazzy, brasserie-feeling spot, it also has a great wine selection.

Kolonaki

Capanna   ITALIAN $$

(Map p110; ☑ 210 724 1777; Ploutarhou 38 & Haritos 42, Kolonaki; mains €10-17; ⊙ 1pm-1am Tue-Sun; Ⓜ Evangelismos) One of Kolonaki's newest restaurants, Capanna hugs a corner, with tables wrapping around the footpath in summer. Cuisine is fresh Italian, from enormous pizzas to gnocchi with Gorgonzola. Hearty eating with attentive service and a goblet of wine.

Alatsi   CRETAN $$

(Map p68; ☑ 210 721 0501; Vrasida 13, Ilissia; mains €12-17; ⊙ 1pm-1am Mon-Sat; Ⓜ Evangelismos) Alatsi represents the new breed of trendy upscale restaurants, serving traditional Cretan cuisine, such as *gamopilafo* (wedding pilaf) with lamb or rare *stamnagathi* (wild greens), to fashionable Athenians.

Il Postino   ITALIAN $$

(Map p110; ☑ 210 364 1414; Grivaion 3, Kolonaki; pasta €8-12; Ⓜ Panepistimio) In the mood for a plate of homemade gnocchi with pesto before a night out clubbing? Sneak into this little side street and sup under old photos of Roma.

★ Spondi   MEDITERRANEAN $$$

(Map p68; ☑ 210 756 4021; www.spondi.gr; Pyrronos 5, Pangrati; mains €35-50; ⊙ 8pm-late) Two Michelin-starred Spondi is consistently voted Athens' best restaurant, and the accolades are totally deserved. It offers Mediterranean haute cuisine, with heavy French influences, in a relaxed, chic setting in a charming old house. Choose from the menu or a range of set dinner and wine *prix fixes*.

The restaurant has a lovely bougainvillea-draped garden. Book ahead, and take a cab – it's hard to reach on public transport.

⚲ Drinking & Nightlife

One Athenian (and Greek) favoured pastime is going for coffee. Athens' ubiquitous, packed cafes have Europe's most expensive coffee (between €3 and €5). You're essentially hiring the chair and can linger for hours. Many daytime cafes and restaurants turn into bars and clubs at night.

⚲ Syntagma, Plaka & Monastiraki

The city's hottest scene masses around Plateia Karytsi north of Syntagma, and Plateia Agia Irini in Monastiraki. A cafe-thick area in Monastiraki is Adrianou, along the Ancient Agora, where people fill shady tables. Multi-use spaces Taf (p93) and Six DOGS (p93) morph from gallery to cafe to overflowing bar.

★ Tailor Made
CAFE, BAR

(Map p84; ☑ 213 004 9645; www.tailormade.gr; Plateia Agia Irini 2, Monastiraki; Ⓜ Monastiraki) This popular new micro-roastery offers its array of coffee blends as well as hand-pressed teas. Find the full gamut from pea-berry coffee to rooibos tea, as well as home-made desserts (€5) and sandwiches (€6). Cheerful Athenians spill from the mod-art-festooned interior to the tables alongside the flower market. At night it turns into a happening cocktail and wine bar.

Faust
BAR

(Map p84; ☑ 210 323 4095; www.faust.gr; Kalami-otou 11 & Athinaidos 12; ⊙ Sep-May; Ⓜ Monastiraki) One of the city's hottest new bars, Faust – just a tiny hole in the wall – also hosts live music, cabarets and art shows.

Barley Cargo
BAR

(Map p84; ☑ 210 323 0445; Kolokotroni 6, Syntagma; Ⓜ Syntagma) This fantastic beer bar offers over 150 different versions of the sweet elixir, many of them from Greek microbreweries. Or sip a Trappist brew at one of the wooden-barrel tables.

Drunk Sinatra
COCKTAIL BAR

(Map p84; ☑ 210 331 3733; Thiseos 16, Syntagma; Ⓜ Syntagma) Athens' newest hipster hang also serves a mean cocktail.

Melina
CAFE

(Map p84; Lyssiou 22, Plaka; Ⓜ Akropoli, Monastiraki) An ode to the great Merkouri, Melina offers charm and intimacy out of the hectic centre.

ⓘ TOP NIGHTLIFE TIPS

➡ Expect bars to begin filling after 11pm and stay open till late.

➡ Right now, Gazi and the areas around Plateia Karytsi (north of Syntagma) and Plateia Agia Irini (Monastiraki) have the most action, while Kolonaki steadfastly attracts the trendier set.

➡ With the current strapped financial climate in Athens, watch your back, wherever you go.

➡ For the best dancing in summer, cab it to the beach clubs – city locations close earlier.

Seven Jokers
BAR

(Map p84; Voulis 7, Syntagma; Ⓜ Syntagma) Lively and central Seven Jokers anchors the party block, also shared by spacious 42 (around the corner) which serves cocktails in wood-panelled splendour.

Baba Au Rum
COCKTAIL BAR

(Map p84; Klitiou 6, Syntagma; Ⓜ Syntagma) Fab cocktail mixologists concoct the tipples of your dreams.

Bartessera
BAR

(Map p84; Kolokotroni 25, Syntagma; Ⓜ Syntagma) This cool bar-cafe with great music hides out at the end of a narrow arcade.

Brettos
BAR

(Map p84; Kydathineon 41, Plaka; Ⓜ Akropoli) You won't find any happening bars in Plaka, but Brettos is a delightful old bar and distillery with a stunning wall of colourful bottles and huge barrels. Sample its home brands of wine, ouzo, brandy and other spirits.

Booze Cooperativa
CAFE, BAR

(Map p84; ☑ 211 400 0863; www.boozecooperativa.com; Kolokotroni 57, Syntagma; ⊙ 10am-late Mon-Fri, from 3pm Sat, from noon Sun; 🛜; Ⓜ Monastiraki) By day, this laid-back arty hangout is full of young Athenians playing chess and backgammon and working on their Macs; later it transforms into a happening bar that rocks till late. The basement hosts art exhibitions and there's a theatre upstairs.

Gin Joint
COCKTAIL BAR

(Map p102; Lada 1, Syntagma; Ⓜ Syntagma) They call it Gin Joint for a reason: sample 60 gins or other fancy beverages, some with historical notes on their origin.

Galaxy Bar
BAR

(Map p84; Stadiou 10, Syntagma; ⊙ Mon-Sat; Ⓜ Syntagma) Not to be confused with the Hilton's sky bar, this sweet little wood-panelled place has a homey saloon feel.

Sixx
CLUB

(Map p84; ☑ 6979470638; Amerikis 6, Syntagma; ⊙ 11pm-7am Thu-Sat; Ⓜ Syntagma) If you just can't call it a night...DJs party till dawn.

Oinoscent
WINE BAR

(Map p84; ☑ 210 322 9374; www.oinoscent.gr; Voulis 45-47, Plaka; Ⓜ Syntagma) Drop in for a vast array of Greek and international wines, or pick up a bottle for the road.

SUMMER CLUBS

In summer much of the city's serious nightlife moves to glamorous, enormous seafront clubs. Many sit on the tram route, which runs to 2.30am on Friday and Saturday. If you book for dinner you don't pay cover; otherwise admission ranges from €10 to €20 and includes one drink. Glam up to get in.

Akrotiri (210 985 9147; www.akrotirilounge.gr; Vasileos Georgiou B5, Agios Kosmas) This massive, top beach club holds 3000 people in bars, a restaurant and lounges over different levels. Jamming party nights bring top resident and visiting DJs. Pool parties rock during the day.

Balux (210 894 1620; www.baluxcafe.com; Leoforos Poseidonos 58, Glyfada) This glamorous club-restaurant-lounge right on the beach must be seen to be believed, with poolside chaises, four-poster beds with flowing nets, and a night-time line-up of top DJs next door at **Akanthus** (210 968 0800; www.akanthus.gr).

Island (210 965 3563; www.islandclubrestaurant.gr; Varkiza, 27th km, Athens–Sounion Rd) Dreamy classic summer club-restaurant on the seaside with superb island decor.

Toy   COCKTAIL BAR
(Map p84; Plateia Karytsi 10, Syntagma; M Syntagma) Thirty-somethings gather at this old favourite for coffee by day and glam cocktails by night.

James Joyce   PUB
(Map p102; 210 323 5055; Astingos 12, Monastiraki; M Monastiraki) The Guinness is free flowing at this Irish pub with decent food (mains €9 to €14), live music and loads of travellers and expats.

🍷 Gazi, Thisio & Keramikos

Get off the metro at Keramikos and you'll be smack in the middle of the thriving Gazi scene. In Thisio, cafes along the pedestrian promenade Apostolou Pavlou have great Acropolis views, and those along pedestrianised Iraklidon pack 'em in at night.

★ Gazarte   BAR
(Map p90; 210 346 0347; www.gazarte.gr; Voutadon 32-34, Gazi; M Keramikos) Upstairs you'll find a cinema-sized screen playing videos, amazing city views taking in the Acropolis, mainstream music and a trendy 30-something crowd. Occasional live music, and has a cinema and restaurant to boot.

Hoxton   BAR
(Map p90; Voutadon 42, Gazi; M Keramikos) Join the hip, artsy crowd here for shoulder-to-shoulder hobnobbing amid original art, iron beams and leather sofas.

Gazaki   BAR
(Map p90; Triptolemou 31, Gazi; M Keramikos) This Gazi trailblazer opened before the neighbourhood had become *the* place to be. Friendly locals crowd the great rooftop bar.

Nixon Bar   BAR
(Map p90; Agisilaou 61b, Keramikos; M Thisio) More chic than most, Nixon Bar serves up food and cocktails and sits next door to swinging **Belafonte**.

MoMix   COCKTAIL BAR
(Map p90; 6974350179; http://momix.gr; Keleou 1-5, Gazi; M Keramikos) Athens' first molecular mixology bar.

A Liar Man   BAR
(Map p90; www.aliarman.gr; Sofroniou 2, Gazi; M Keramikos) A tiny hideout with a more hushed vibe.

Pixi   CLUB
(Map p90; 210 342 3751; http://pixi.gr; Evmolpidon 11, Gazi; M Keramikos) Good DJs and flashing lights for the younger set.

45 Moires   BAR
(Map p90; Iakhou 18, cnr Voutadon, Gazi; M Keramikos) Go deep into hard rock and enjoy terrace views of Gazi's neon-lit chimneys and the Acropolis.

Venue   CLUB
(Map p90; 210 342 2606; www.venue-club.com; Tzaferi 11, cnr Andronikou, Rouf; ⊙ Sep-May; M Keramikos) Arguably the city's biggest dance club with the biggest dance parties by the world's biggest DJs.

Sin Athina
CAFE

(Map p90; ☑ 210 345 5550; www.sinathina.gr; Iraklidon 2, Thisio; Ⓜ Thisio) Location, location, location! This little cafe-bar sits at the junction of the two pedestrianised cafe strips, and has a sweeping view up to the Acropolis.

Peonia Herbs
TEAHOUSE

(Map p90; ☑ 210 341 0260; Amfiktyonos 12, Thisio; ☺ 10am-4pm Mon-Fri, to 3pm Sat; Ⓜ Thisio) There's an instantly calming, smoke-free aura to this herb shop and tearoom.

Loop
BAR

(Map p90; ☑ 210 324 7666; Plateia Agion Asomaton 3; Ⓜ Thisio) Folks gather in a semi-industrial area to rock out to top DJs.

Kolonaki

Kolonaki has two main strips of bars: the top end of Skoufa, and among the crowds squeezing into tiny bars on Haritos.

★ Rock'n'Roll
CLUB

(Map p110; ☑ 210 721 7127; Plateia Kolonakiou, Kolonaki; Ⓜ Evangelismos) A Kolonaki classic, this upscale crowd pleaser lives up to its name. Saturday afternoon dance parties get wild, and each night has different DJed sets. Popular with the trendy Kolonaki crowd, it has a good vibe, but 'face control' can be strict.

Da Capo
CAFE

(Map p110; Tsakalof 1, Kolonaki; Ⓜ Syntagma) Da Capo anchors the cafes on the main square and is *the* place to be seen. It's self-serve if you can find a table.

Mai Tai
BAR

(Map p110; Ploutarhou 18, Kolonaki; Ⓜ Evangelismos) Join Kolonaki's best dressed as they pack into this narrow bar and spill out into the street beyond. It's a place to see and be seen.

Filion
CAFE

(Map p110; Skoufa 34, Kolonaki; Ⓜ Syntagma) Despite its unassuming decor, Filion consistently attracts the intellectual set: artists, writers and film-makers.

Doors
BAR

(Map p110; Karneadou 25-29, Kolonaki; Ⓜ Evangelismos) Drop in for some dinner theatre on weekdays, and drinks every night. Doors is next to La Boom, an '80s disco that moves to Agios Kosmas (near Akrotiri) in summer.

Petite Fleur
CAFE

(Map p110; Omirou 44, Kolonaki; Ⓜ Panepistimio) Petite Fleur serves up large mugs of hot chocolate and speciality cappucinos in a quiet, almost-Parisian ambience.

City
BAR

(Map p110; Haritos 43, Kolonaki; Ⓜ Evangelismos) One of the best bars on hopping Haritos, City makes an excellent *mastiha* cocktail.

Rosebud
BAR

(Map p110; Omirou 60, cnr Skoufa, Kolonaki; Ⓜ Panepistimiou) Kolonaki professionals and chicsters cram this straight-up cocktail bar, which also offers vegetarian snacks.

To Tsai
TEAHOUSE

(Map p110; ☑ 210 338 8941; Alexandrou Soutsou 19, Kolonaki; ☺ 6am-9pm Mon-Sat, daily in winter; Ⓜ Syntagma) Get a Zen vibe as you sip tea at natural wood tables and, on a lively day, a bit of Dixieland jazz will be tinkling in the background. Light meals (€6 to €8) include soup and grilled chicken.

Psyrri, Omonia & Exarhia

Exarhia is a good bet for youthful, lively bars on Plateia Exarhion. The cheap bar precinct on nearby Mesolongiou is popular with students and anarchists. Note, however, that Omonia at night is especially dangerous these days.

Vox
BAR

(Map p102; Themistokleous 80, Exarhia; Ⓜ Omonia) Vox is a good place to start on the square – linger over coffee during the day, or join the crowd of liquoring locals at night.

Alexandrino
COCKTAIL BAR

(Map p102; Emmanuel Benaki 69, Exarhia; Ⓜ Omonia) Imagine a small, French bistro with excellent wines and cocktails.

Blue Fox
BAR

(Map p68; Asklipiou 91, Exarhia; Ⓜ Omonia) You might not expect this in Athens, but Blue Fox is great for '50s-era swing and rockabilly, complete with Vespas and poodle skirts.

Tralala
BAR

(Map p68; Asklipiou 45, Exarhia; Ⓜ Panepistimio) Actors frequent cool Tralala with its original artwork, lively owners and gregarious atmosphere.

Ginger Ale
CAFE, BAR

(Map p102; ☎210 330 1246; Themistokleous 80, Exarhia; Ⓜ Omonia) 🍷 Dip back in time to a '50s veneered coffee shop cum rocking nightspot. Sip espresso by day and catch a rotating line-up of live acts by night.

Tsin Tsin
COCKTAIL BAR

(Map p102; ☎210 384 1460; Kiafas 6, Exarhia; Ⓜ Omonia) Teeny, tiny and out of the way, but the bartender is a true mixologist.

Tranzistor
BAR

(Map p102; ☎210 322 8658; Protogenous 10, Psyrri; Ⓜ Monastiraki) Sidle up to the backlit bar or relax at tables outside.

Circus
CAFE, COCKTAIL BAR

(Map p102; www.circusbar.gr; Navarinou 11, Exarhia; Ⓜ Panepistimiou) Presided over by a Ganesh-style wire elephant, Circus has relaxed coffees by day and cocktails by night.

Mo Better
BAR

(Map p102; Kolleti 32, cnr Themistokleous, Exarhia; Ⓜ Omonia) Tickle your ears with classic rock in a neoclassical building.

Second Skin
BAR

(Map p102; www.secondskinclub.gr; Plateia Agion Anargyron 5, Psyrri; Ⓜ Thisio) Athens' premier Goth-Industrial venue holds torture garden parties and the like.

Floral
CAFE

(Map p102; Themistokleous 80, Exarhia; ☎; Ⓜ Omonia) Floral is sleekly modern with grey-toned images of retro life and, you guessed it, flowers on the walls. Locals come to buy books, chat and people-watch.

🍺 Akropoli & Makrygianni

Duende
BAR

(Map p77; Tzireon 2, Makrygianni; Ⓜ Akropoli) This intimate pub feels almost like a Parisian brasserie and is tucked away on a quiet side street.

Odeon Cafe
CAFE

(Map p68; ☎210 922 3414; Markou Mousourou 19, Mets; Ⓜ Akropoli) This delightful slice of local

---

GAY & LESBIAN ATHENS

For the most part, Athens' gay and lesbian scene is relatively low-key, though the **Athens Pride** (www.athenspride.eu) march, held in June, has been an annual event since 2005. Check out www.athensinfoguide.com, www.gay.gr or a copy of the *Greek Gay Guide* booklet at *periptera* (newspaper kiosks).

For nightlife, Gazi has become Athens' gay and lesbian hub, with a gay triangle emerging near the railway line on Leoforos Konstantinoupoleos and Megalou Alexandrou. Gay and gay-friendly clubs around town are also in Makrygianni, Psyrri, Metaxourghio and Exarhia.

Sodade (Map p90; ☎210 346 8657; www.sodade.gr; Triptolemou 10, Gazi; Ⓜ Keramikos) In Gazi, tiny, sleek Sodade is super-fun for dancing.

S-cape (Map p90; ☎210 341 1003; www.s-cape-club.blogspot.com; Megalou Alexandrou 139, Gazi; Ⓜ Keramikos) Stays packed with the younger crowd.

Noiz Club (Map p90; ☎210 342 4771; www.noizclub.gr; Evmolpidon 41, Gazi; Ⓜ Keramikos)

BIG (Map p90; www.barbig.gr; Falesias 12, Gazi; ⊙Tue-Sun; Ⓜ Keramikos) Hub of Athens' lively bear scene.

Magaze (Map p84; ☎210 324 3740; Eolou 33, Monastiraki; Ⓜ Monastiraki) Gay-friendly Magaze has Acropolis views from footpath tables.

Loukoumi (Map p84; Plateia Avyssinias 3, Monastiraki; Ⓜ Monastiraki) Daytime coffee and a night scene with DJs and live music.

Lamda Club (Map p77; ☎210 942 4202; Lembesi 15, cnr Leoforos Syngrou, Makrygianni; Ⓜ Akropoli) Busy, three-level Lamda Club is not for the faint of heart.

Mirovolos (Map p68; ☎210 522 8806; Giatrakou 12, Metaxourghio; Ⓜ Metaxourghio) Popular lesbian cafe-bar-restaurant.

Koukles (☎694 755 7443; Zan Moreas 32, Koukaki) The drag show here rocks.

The popular gay beach **Limanakia** is below the rocky coves near Varkiza. Take the tram or A2/E2 express bus to Glyfada, then bus 115 or 116 to the Limnakia B stop.

life is a simple corner coffee shop with quietly chatting friends sitting beneath ivy winding over the footpath. Occasional live music.

Tiki Athens
BAR

(Map p77; ☑ 210 923 6908; www.tikiathens.com; Falirou 15, Makrygianni; ☺ 4.30pm-late; Ⓜ Akropoli) Funky '50s decor, lots of varied music, an Asian-inspired menu and an alternative young crowd make this a fun place for a drink.

☆ Entertainment

English-language entertainment information appears daily in the *Kathimerini* supplement in the *International Herald Tribune; Athens News* and *Athens Plus* also have listings. Check out entertainment websites for events and concerts around town. Athens' thriving multi-use spaces host all manner of goings-on.

☆ Greek Music

Athens has some of the best *rembetika* (Greek blues) in intimate, evocative venues. Most close May to September, so in summer try live-music tavernas around Plaka and Psyrri. Performances usually include both *rembetika* and *laïka* (urban popular music), start at around 11.30pm and do not have a cover charge, though drinks can be expensive. There's also live music most weekends at Café Avyssinia (p107).

★ Stoa Athanaton
REMBETIKA

(Map p102; ☑ 210 321 4362; Sofokleous 19, Central Market; ☺ 3-6pm & midnight-6am Mon-Sat, closed Jun-Sep; Ⓜ Monastiraki, Panepistimio, Omonia) This legendary club occupies a hall above the central meat market. Popular for classic *rembetika* and *laïka* from a respected band of musicians, it often starts from midafternoon. Access is by a lift in the arcade.

Perivoli Tou Ouranou
REMBETIKA

(☑ 210 323 5517; Lysikratous 19, Plaka; ☺ 9pm-late Thu-Sun, closed Jul-Sep; Ⓜ Akropoli) A favourite rustic, old-style Plaka music haunt with dinner (mains €18 to €29).

Kavouras
REMBETIKA

(Map p102; ☑ 210 381 0202; Themistokleous 64, Exarhia; ☺ 11pm-late Thu-Sat, closed Jul & Aug; Ⓜ Omonia) Above Exarhia's popular souvlaki joint, this lively club usually plays until dawn for a student crowd.

Palea Plakiotiki Taverna Stamatopoulos
TRADITIONAL MUSIC

(Map p84; ☑ 210 322 8722; www.stamatopoulostavern.gr; Lyssiou 26, Plaka; ☺ 7pm-2am Mon-Sat, 11am-2am Sun; Ⓜ Monastiraki) This Plaka institution with live music nightly fills up late with locals; arrive early for a table.

Mostrou
TRADITIONAL MUSIC

(Map p84; ☑ 210 322 5558; Mnisikleous 22, cnr Lyssiou, Plaka; ☺ 9pm-late Thu-Sun; Ⓜ Monastiraki) Popular full-sized stage and dance floor; in summer, there's more sedate live music on the terrace.

Paliogramofono
TRADITIONAL MUSIC

(Map p102; ☑ 210 323 1409; Navarhou Apostoli 8, Psyrri; Ⓜ Thisio) One of Psyrri's many music tavernas, with decent food.

☆ Rock Music

Athens has a healthy rock-music scene and many European tours stop here. In summer check Rockwave and other festival schedules.

★ Gagarin 205 Club
LIVE MUSIC

(☑ 213 024 8358; www.gagarin205.gr; Liossion 205, Thymarakia; Ⓜ Agios Nikolaos) Friday and Saturday night gigs feature leading rock and underground bands

---

BOUZOUKIA

Greek *bouzoukia* or *skyladika* (literally 'dog houses', a mocking term for second-rate places with crooning singers) is a one-of-a-kind thing. Athens' grandest incarnation is a decadent circus for adults. These glitzy cabaret-style venues host famous headliners, exotic dancers, costumes, aerialists, glitter, the works! Women dancing the sinewy *tsifteteli* (belly dance) are showered with expensive trays of carnations and revellers party till sunrise. Check listings for what's on, or try glam **Athinon Arena** (Map p90; ☑ 210 347 1111; www.athenspantheon.com; Pireos 166, Rouf; ☺ Fri & Sat; Ⓜ Petraluna) if you have a bankroll (buy table tickets in advance, pricey bottles once you're there) and an appetite for adventure.

DON'T MISS

SUMMER CINEMA

One of the delights of hot summer nights in Athens is the enduring tradition of open-air cinema, where you can watch the latest Hollywood or art-house flick under moonlight. Many refurbished original outdoor cinemas are still operating in gardens and on rooftops around Athens, with modern sound systems.

The most historic outdoor cinema is **Aigli** (Map p68; ☑ 210 336 9369; www.aegli zappiou.gr; Zappeio Gardens, Syntagma; Ⓜ Syntagma) in the verdant Zappeio Gardens, where you can watch a movie in style with a glass of wine.

Kolonaki's **Dexameni** (Map p110; ☑ 210 362 3942; Plateia Dexameni, Kolonaki; Ⓜ Evangelismos) is in a peaceful square.

Try to nab a seat with Acropolis views on the rooftop of Plaka's **Cine Paris** (Map p84; ☑ 210 322 0721; www.cineparis.gr; Kydathineon 22, Plaka; Ⓜ Syntagma), or meander around the foothills of the Acropolis to **Thission** (Map p90; ☑ 210 342 0864; http://cine-thisio.gr; Apostolou Pavlou 7, Thisio; Ⓜ Thisio).

AN Club LIVE MUSIC
(Map p102; ☑ 210 330 5056; www.anclub.gr; Solomou 13-15, Exarhia; Ⓜ Omonia) A small spot for lesser-known international and local rock bands.

Mike's Irish Bar LIVE MUSIC
(☑ 210 777 6797; www.mikesirishbar.com; Sinopis 6, Ambelokipi; Ⓜ Ambelokipi) A long-time favourite of the expatriate community, with live music most nights.

Fuzz LIVE MUSIC
(☑ 210 345 0817; www.fuzzclub.gr; Pireos 209, Tavros; Ⓜ Petraluna) Fuzz jams with international acts such as the Wailers and Gypsy punk band Gogol Bordello.

☆ Jazz & World Music

★ **Half Note Jazz Club** JAZZ
(Map p68; ☑ 210 921 3310; www.halfnote.gr; Trivonianou 17, Mets; Ⓜ Akropoli) Athens' stylish, principal and most serious jazz venue hosts an array of international musicians.

Cafe Alavastron LIVE MUSIC
(Map p68; ☑ 210 756 0102; www.cafealavastron.gr; Damareos 78, Pangrati) A mix of modern jazz, ethnic and quality Greek music in a casual, intimate setting.

Theatre & Performing Arts

In summer the main cultural happening is the Hellenic Festival (p95).

★ **Megaron Mousikis** PERFORMING ARTS
(Athens Concert Hall; ☑ 210 728 2333; www. megaron.gr; Kokkali 1, cnr Leoforos Vasilissis Sofias, Ilissia; ⊗ box office 10am-6pm Mon-Fri, to 2pm Sat; Ⓜ Megaro Mousikis) The city's state-of-the-art

concert hall presents a rich winter program of operas and concerts featuring world-class international and Greek performers.

Greek National Opera OPERA
(Ethniki Lyriki Skini; Map p102; ☑ 210 366 2100; www. nationalopera.gr) The season runs from November to June. Performances are usually held at the **Olympia Theatre** (Map p102; ☑ 210 361 2461; Akadimias 59, Exarhia; Ⓜ Panepistimio) or the Odeon of Herodes Atticus (p78) in summer.

National Theatre THEATRE
(Map p102; ☑ 210 528 8100; www.n-t.gr; Agiou Konstantinou 22-24, Omonia; Ⓜ Omonia) Performances of contemporary plays and ancient theatre in one of the city's finest neoclassical buildings, in venues around town and, in summer, in ancient theatres across Greece.

Dora Stratou Dance Theatre TRADITIONAL DANCE
(Map p68; ☑ 210 324 4395; www.grdance.org; Filopappou Hill; adult/child €15/5; ⊙ performances 9.30pm Wed-Fri, 8.15pm Sat & Sun Jun-Sep; Ⓜ Petralona, Akropoli) Every summer this company performs its repertoire of Greek folk dances at its open-air theatre on the western side of Filopappou Hill. It also runs folk-dancing workshops in summer.

Sport

Athens' most popular sports are basketball – see the **Hellenic Basketball Association** (www.basket.gr) – and football. Greece's top football teams are Athens-based Panathinaikos and AEK, and Piraeus-based Olympiakos, all three of which are in the European Champions League. Check club websites, English-language press, www.greeksoccer. com or www.tickethour.gr.

WHAT'S ON IN ATHENS

For comprehensive events listings, with links to online ticket sales points, try the following:

www.breathtakingathens.gr Athens tourism site.

www.elculture.gr Arts and culture listings.

www.tickethour.com Also has sports matches.

www.tickethouse.gr Rockwave and other festivals.

www.ticketservices.gr Range of events.

🛍 Shopping

Central Athens is one big bustling shopping hub, with an eclectic mix of stores and speciality shopping strips. The central shopping street is Ermou, the pedestrian street lined with mainstream fashion stores running from Syntagma to Monastiraki.

Top-brand international designers and jewellers surround Syntagma, from the Attica department store past pedestrian Voukourestiou to the fashion boutiques of Kolonaki. Plaka and Monastiraki are rife with souvenir stores and streetwear. The main streets are Kydathineon and Adrianou. Big department stores dot Stadiou from Syntagma to Omonia. Kifisia and Glyfada also have excellent high-end shopping.

Find a delectable array of food and spices at the colourful **central market** (Varvakios Agora; Map p102; Athinas , btwn Sofokleous & Evripidou; ☉ 7am-3pm Mon-Sat; Ⓜ Monastiraki, Panepistimio, Omonia), and all manner of housewares in the surrounding streets.

★ Monastiraki Flea Market   MARKET
(Map p84; Adrianou, Monastiraki; ☉ daily; Ⓜ Monastiraki) This traditional market has a festive atmosphere. Permanent antique and collectables shops are open all week, while the streets around the station and Adrianou fill with vendors selling jewellery, handicrafts and bric-a-brac.

★ Mastiha Shop   FOOD, BEAUTY
(Map p102; ☎ 210 363 2750; www.mastihashop.com; Panepistimiou 6, Syntagma; ☉ 9am-9pm; Ⓜ Syntagma) Mastic, the medicinal resin from rare mastic trees produced only on the island of Chios, is the key ingredient in everything in this store, from natural skin products to a liqueur that's divine when served chilled.

★ Anavasi   BOOKS
(☎ 210 321 8104; www.anavasi.gr; Voulis 32, Apollonos, Syntagma; ☉ 9.30am-5.30pm Mon & Wed, to 8.30pm Tue, Thu & Fri, 10am-3pm Sat; Ⓜ Syntagma) Great travel bookshop with an extensive range of Greece maps and walking and activity guides.

Mompso   ACCESSORIES
(Map p102; ☎ 210 323 0670; www.mompso.com; Athinas 33, Psyrri; Ⓜ Monastiraki) Find all manner of equestrian supplies and traditional accessories for donkeys (beaded headdresses), shepherds (bronze bells) and country folk (walking sticks).

Xylouris   MUSIC
(Map p102; ☎ 210 322 2711; www.xilouris.gr; Arcade, Panepistimiou 39, Panepistimio; Ⓜ Syntagma) This music treasure trove is run by the family of Cretan legend Nikos Xylouris. They can guide you through the comprehensive range of Greek music, including select and rare recordings. Also has a branch at the Museum of Greek Popular Instruments (p89).

Apivita   BEAUTY
(Map p110; ☎ 210 364 0760; www.apivita.com; Solonos 26, Kolonaki; Ⓜ Syntagma) Apivita's flagship store has the full range of its excellent natural beauty products and an express spa downstairs for pampering on the run.

To Pantopoleion   FOOD & DRINK
(Map p102; ☎ 210 323 4612; Sofokleous 1, Omonia; Ⓜ Panepistimio) Expansive store selling traditional food products from all over Greece, from Santorini capers to boutique olive oils, Cretan rusks, jars of goodies for edible souvenirs and Greek wines and spirits.

Ekavi   GAMES
(Map p84; ☎ 210 323 7740; www.manopoulos.com; Mitropoleos 36, Syntagma; Ⓜ Syntagma) If you're hooked on the local sport, there's a huge selection of backgammon boards, as well as great chess pieces depicting the battles of Troy etc.

Aristokratikon   FOOD
(Map p84; ☎ 210 322 0546; www.aristokratikon.com; Voulis 7, Syntagma; Ⓜ Syntagma) Chocaholics will be thrilled by the dazzling array of handmade chocolates at this tiny store.

Amorgos
HANDICRAFTS

(Map p84; 210 324 3836; www.amorgosart.gr; Kodrou 3, Plaka; MSyntagma) Charming store crammed with Greek folk art, trinkets, ceramics, embroidery and woodcarved furniture made by the owner.

Parthenis
CLOTHING

(Map p110; 210 363 3158; www.orsalia-parthenis. gr; Dimokritou 20, cnr Tsakalof, Kolonaki; MSyntagma) Totally Greek and totally natural, these women's clothes designed by a father-and-daughter team are high-quality, classic silhouettes in natural fibres.

Melissinos Art
SHOES

(Map p84; 210 321 9247; www.melissinos-art.com; Agias Theklas 2, Psyrri; MMonastiraki) Pantelis Melissinos continues the sandal-making tradition of his famous poet/sandal-maker father Stavros, whose customers included the Beatles, Sophia Loren and Jackie Onassis. Pantelis' daughter runs excellent Olgianna Melissinos (Map p84; 210 331 1925; Normanou 7, Monastiraki; MMonastiraki), with a wide range of leather goods. Can be made to order.

John Samuelin
MUSIC

(Map p84; 210 321 2433; www.musicshop.gr; Ifestou 36, Monastiraki; MMonastiraki) This central spot is jam-packed with Greek and other musical instruments.

Eleftheroudakis
BOOKS

Syntagma (Map p102; 210 325 8440; Panepistimiou 15, Syntagma; MSyntagma); Plaka (Map p84; 210 323 1401; Nikis 20, Plaka; MSyntagma) Has a section dedicated to English-language books.

Public
BOOKS, ELECTRONICS

(Map p84; 210 324 6210; Plateia Syntagmatos, Syntagma; ; MSyntagma) This multimedia behemoth includes computers, stationery and English-language books (3rd floor).

Centre of Hellenic Tradition
HANDICRAFTS

(Map p84; 210 321 3023; Pandrosou 36, Monastiraki; MMonastiraki) Traditional ceramics, sculpture and handicrafts from all parts of Greece.

❶ Information

DANGERS & ANNOYANCES

Crime has heightened in Athens with the onset of the financial crisis. Though violent street crime remains relatively rare, travellers should be alert on the streets, especially at night, and beware the traps listed here.

Streets surrounding Omonia have become markedly seedier, with an increase in prostitutes and junkies; avoid the area, especially at night.

Pickpockets

Favourite hunting grounds are the metro, particularly the Piraeus–Kifisia line, and crowded streets around Omonia, Athinas and the Monastiraki Flea Market.

Taxi Scams

➸ Most (but not all) rip-offs involve taxis picked up from ranks at the airport, train stations, bus terminals and particularly the port of Piraeus. At Piraeus, avoid the drivers at the port exit asking if you need a taxi; hail one off the street.

➸ Some drivers don't turn on the meter and demand whatever they think they can get away with; others claim you gave them a smaller bill than you did and short-change you. Only negotiate a set fare if you have some idea of the cost.

➸ Some drivers may try to persuade you that the hotel you want to go to is full, even if you have a booking.

Bar Scams

➸ Scammers target tourists in central Athens, particularly around Syntagma. One scam goes like this: friendly Greek approaches solo male traveller; friendly Greek reveals that he, too, is from out of town or does the 'I have a cousin in Australia' routine and suggests they go to a bar for a drink. Before they know it, women appear, more drinks are ordered and the conman disappears, leaving the traveller to pay an exorbitant bill. Smiles disappear and the atmosphere turns threatening.

➸ Some bars lure intoxicated males with talk of sex and present them with outrageous bills.

➸ Some bars and clubs serve what are locally known as bombes, adulterated drinks diluted with cheap illegal imports or methanol-based spirit substitutes. They leave you feeling decidedly low the next day.

EMERGENCY

Police (100)

Police Station Central (210 770 5711/17; Leoforos Alexandras 173, Ambelokipi; MAmbelokipi); Syntagma (210 725 7000; Mimnermou 6-8; MSyntagma).

Tourist Police (210 920 0724, 24hr 171; Veïkou 43-45, Koukaki; 8am-10pm; MSyngrou-Fix)

Visitor Emergency Assistance (112) Toll-free 24-hour service in English.

INTERNET ACCESS

Most hotels have internet access and wifi. Free wireless hotspots are at Syntagma, Thisio, Gazi and the port of Piraeus. Buy prepaid internet cards for your laptop at OTE (Greece's main telecommunications carrier) shops or Germanos stores.

LEFT LUGGAGE

Most hotels store luggage free for guests, although many simply pile bags in a hallway. Storage facilities are also at the airport and at Omonia, Monastiraki and Piraeus metro stations.

MEDIA

Kathimerini (www.ekathimerini.com) English edition of *Kathimerini*, published daily (except Sunday) with the *International Herald Tribune*, with news, arts, cinema listings and daily ferry schedules.

Athens News (www.athensnews.gr) Friday; entertainment listings.

Athens Plus Weekly English news and entertainment newspaper; published Fridays by *Kathimerini* and online.

MEDICAL SERVICES

Ambulance/First-aid Advice (☑ 166)

Pharmacies (☑ in Greek 1434) Check pharmacy windows for details of the nearest duty pharmacy. There's a 24-hour pharmacy at the airport.

SOS Doctors (☑ 210 821 1888, 1016; ☺ 24hr) Pay service with English-speaking doctors.

MONEY

Major banks have branches around Syntagma, and ATMs blanket the city.

Eurochange Syntagma (☑ 210 331 2462; Karageorgi Servias 2, Syntagma; ☺ 8am-9pm; ⓜ Syntagma); Monastiraki (☑ 210 322 2657; Areos 1, Monastiraki; ⓜ Monastiraki) Exchanges travellers cheques and arranges money transfers.

National Bank of Greece (☑ 210 334 0500; cnr Karageorgi Servias & Stadiou, Syntagma; ⓜ Syntagma) Has a 24-hour automated exchange machine.

POST

Syntagma Post Office (Map p84; Plateia Syntagmatos, Syntagma; ☺ 7.30am-8pm Mon-Fri, 7.30am-2pm Sat; ⓜ Syntagma)

TELEPHONE

Public phones allow international calls. Purchase phonecards at kiosks, and reasonably priced SIM cards at mobile shops.

TOURIST INFORMATION

EOT (Greek National Tourist Organisation; Map p77; ☑ 210 331 0716, 210 331 0347; www.visitgreece.gr; Dionysiou Areopagitou 18-20, Makrygianni; ☺ 8am-8pm Mon-Fri, 10am-4pm Sat & Sun May-Sep, 9am-7pm Mon-Fri Oct-Apr; ⓜ Akropoli) Free Athens map, transport information and *Athens & Attica* booklet. At the time of research, its airport branch was closed.

Athens Airport Information Desk This 24-hour desk has Athens info, booklets and Athens Spotlighted discount card for goods and services at the airport and around town.

Athens City Information Kiosk (www.breath takingathens.com) Airport (☑ 210 353 0390; airport; ☺ 8am-8pm; ⓜ Airport); Acropolis (Map p77; Acropolis; ☺ 9am-9pm Jun-Aug; ⓜ Akropoli) Maps, transport information and all Athens info.

USEFUL WEBSITES

Two Greek-language sites are useful if you have a webpage translator: **Athinorama** (www.athino rama.gr) and **Athens Voice** (www.athensvoice. gr). They both have print editions as well.

Athens Official Visitor Site (www.breathtaking athens.gr) Athens Tourism and Economic Development Agency site with what's-on listings.

Arts and Culture (www.elculture.gr) Bilingual, including theatre, music and cinema listings.

Ministry of Culture (www.culture.gr) Museums, archaeological sites and cultural events.

Short Videos (www.athensliving.net) Clips of Athens life.

❶ Getting There & Away

AIR

Modern Eleftherios Venizelos International Airport (p734), at Spata, 27km east of Athens, has all the modern conveniences, including 24-hour luggage storage in the arrivals hall and a children's playroom and a small archaeological museum above the check-in hall for passing time.

Average domestic one-way fares range from €56 to €140, but vary dramatically depending on season. Olympic Air has flights to all islands with airports, and the more popular are also serviced by Aegean Airlines and Athens Airways.

Aegean Airlines (☑ 801 112 0000, 210 626 1000; www.aegeanair.com)

Athens Airways (☑ 801 801 4000, 210 669 6600; www.athensairways.com)

Olympic Air (☑ 801 801 0101, 210 355 0500; www.olympicair.com)

Sky Express (☑ 281 022 3500; www.sky express.gr) Cretan airline with flights around Greece.

BOAT

Most ferry, hydrofoil and high-speed catamaran services to the islands leave from Athens' massive port at Piraeus.

Some services for Evia and the Cyclades also depart from smaller ports at Rafina and Lavrio.

Purchase tickets at booths on the quay next to each ferry, over the phone or online; also, travel agencies selling tickets surround each port.

BUS

Athens has two main intercity (IC) **KTEL** (☎14505; www.ktel.org) bus stations, 5km and 7km to the north of Omonia. Pick up timetables at the tourist office.

Kifissos Terminal A (☎210 512 4910; Kifisou 100, Peristeri; Ⓜ Agios Antonios) Buses to Thessaloniki, the Peloponnese, Ionian Islands and destinations in western Greece such as Igoumenitsa, Ioannina, Kastoria and Edessa, among other places. Bus 051 goes to central Athens (junction of Zinonos and Menandrou, near Omonia) every 15 minutes from 5am to midnight. Taxis to Syntagma cost about €8.

Liossion Terminal B (☎210 831 7153; Liossion 260, Thymarakia; Ⓜ Agios Nikolaos) Buses to central and northern Greece, such as Trikala (for Meteora), Delphi, Larissa, Thiva and Volos. To get here take bus 024 from outside the main gate of the National Gardens on Amalias and ask to get off at Praktoria KTEL. Get off the bus at Liossion 260, turn right onto Gousiou and you'll see the terminal. There is no public transport here from 11.40pm to 5am; taxis to Syntagma cost about €8.

Mavromateon Terminal (Map p68; ☎210 822 5148, 210 880 8000; cnr Leoforos Alexandras & 28 Oktovriou-Patision, Pedion Areos; Ⓜ Viktoria) Buses for destinations in southern Attica leave from here, about 250m north of the National Archaeological Museum. Buses to Rafina, Lavrio and Marathon leave from the northern section of the Mavromateon terminal (just 150m to the north).

Key Buses from Kifissos Terminal A

DESTINATION	TIME	FARE	FREQUENCY
Alexandroupoli	11hr	€71	1 daily
Corfu*	9½hr	€46	3 daily
Epidavros	2½hr	€14	3 daily
Igoumenitsa	7½hr	€47	4 daily
Ioannina	7hr	€39	7 daily
Ithaki*	7½hr	€52	2 daily
Kalavryta	3hr	€18	2 daily
Kefallonia*	7hr	€55	4 daily
Lefkada	5½hr	€36	4 daily
Monemvasia	6hr	€29	2 daily
Nafplio	2½hr	€13	hourly
Olympia	5½hr	€31	2 daily
Patra	3hr	€22	half-hourly
Thessaloniki	7hr	€42	12 daily
Zakynthos*	6hr	€38	4 daily

*includes ferry ticket

Key Buses from Liossion Terminal B

DESTINATION	TIME	FARE	FREQUENCY
Agios Konstantinos	2½hr	€15	hourly
Delphi	3hr	€17	5 daily
Halkida	1¼hr	€7	half-hourly
Karpenisi	4½hr	€25	3 daily
Paralia Kymis	4½hr	€15	1 daily
Trikala	4½hr	€28	6 daily
Volos	4½hr	€25	11 daily

Key Buses from Mavromateon Terminal

DESTINATION	TIME	FARE	FREQUENCY
Cape Sounion (coastal road)	1½hr	€7.50	half-hourly
Lavrio port	1½hr	€5.20	half-hourly
Marathon	1¼hr	€4.50	half-hourly
Rafina port	1hr	€2.40	half-hourly

CAR & MOTORCYCLE

Attiki Odos (Attiki Rd), Ethniki Odos (National Rd) and various ring roads facilitate getting in and out of Athens.

The airport has all major car-hire companies, and the top end of Leoforos Syngrou, near the Temple of Olympian Zeus, is dotted with firms. Local companies tend to offer better deals than the multinationals. Expect to pay €45 per day, less for three or more days.

Avis (☎210 322 4951; www.avis.gr; Leoforos Vasilissis Amalias 46, Makrygianni; Ⓜ Akropoli)

Budget (☎210 922 4200; www.budget -athens.gr; Leoforos Syngrou 23, Makrygianni; Ⓜ Akropoli)

Europcar (☎210 921 1444; www.europcar -greece.gr; Leoforos Syngrou 25, Makrygianni; Ⓜ Akropoli)

Hertz (☎210 922 0102; www.hertz.gr; Leoforos Syngrou 12, Makrygianni; Ⓜ Akropoli)

Kosmos (☎210 923 4696; www.kosmos-car rental.com; Leoforos Syngrou 9, Makrygianni; Ⓜ Akropoli)

Motorent (☎210 923 4939; www.motorent.gr; Rovertou Galli 1, Makrygianni; Ⓜ Akropoli) From 50cc to 250cc (from €16 per day); must have motorcycle licence and nerves of steel.

TRAIN

Intercity (IC) trains to central and northern Greece depart from the central **Larisis train station**, about 1km northwest of Plateia Omonias.

For the Peloponnese, take the suburban rail to Kiato and change for other OSE services there, or check for available lines at the Larisis station. At time of research, the Patra line was closed for work. OSE buses replace its services.

Note: at the time of research, Greece's train system was in a state of flux due to the financial crisis. International trains are discontinued, and domestic schedules/fares should be confirmed online or at **OSE** (☑ 1110, 210 362 4405, 210 362 4402; www.ose.gr; Sina 6, Syntagma; ☉ 8am-3pm Mon-Sat; Ⓜ Panepistimio). The chart is only a loose guide.

DESTINATION	TIME	FARE	FREQUENCY
Alexandroupoli	12¼hr	€40	1 daily (via Thessaloniki)
Alexandroupoli (IC)	11hr	€65	2 daily (via Thessaloniki)
Corinth (suburban rail)	1hr 20min	€8	13 daily
Kiato (suburban rail)*	1hr 40min	€8	13 daily
Kiato-Patra	2hr	€8.50	5 daily
Kiato-Patra (IC)	1hr 40min	€9	4 daily
Thessaloniki	6hr	€25	1 daily
Thessaloniki (IC)	5hr	€45	6 daily
Volos	6½hr	€16	1 daily (via Larisa)
Volos (IC)	5hr	€30	6 daily (via Larisa)

*from Kiato, change to regular or intercity (IC) services

❶ Getting Around

TO/FROM THE AIRPORT

The metro and suburban rail provide quick connections to central Athens. The bus is cheapest, though it takes longer. The suburban rail also goes to Piraeus.

Bus

Express buses operate 24 hours between the airport and the city centre, Piraeus and KTEL bus terminals. At the airport, buy tickets (€5; not valid for other forms of public transport) at the booth near the stops.

Plateia Syntagmatos Bus X95, one to 1½ hours, every 30 minutes, 24 hours. The Syntagma stop is on Othonos St.

Kifissos Terminal A bus station Bus X93, one hour, every 30 minutes, 24 hours.

Metro line 3 at Ethniki Amyna station Bus X94, 25 minutes, every 10 minutes, 7.30am to 11.30pm.

Piraeus Bus X96, 1½ hours, every 20 minutes, 24 hours. To Plateia Karaïskaki.

Kifisia Bus X92, about 45 minutes, every 45 minutes, 24 hours.

Metro line 2 at Dafni station Bus X97, one hour, every 30 minutes, 24 hours.

Metro

Metro line 3 goes to the airport. Some trains terminate early at Doukissis Plakentias, where you get out and wait till an airport train (displayed on the train and platform screen) comes along. Trains run every 30 minutes, leaving Monastiraki between 5.50am and midnight, and the airport between 5.30am and 11.30pm.

Airport tickets costs €8 per adult or €14 return (return valid 48 hours). The fare for two or more passengers is €7 each, so purchase tickets together (same with suburban rail). Tickets are valid for all forms of public transport for 90 minutes (revalidate your ticket on final mode of transport).

Suburban Rail

Take the suburban rail (one hour, same price as the metro but return ticket is valid for a month) from central Athens (Larisis) station then change trains for the airport at Ano Liosia, or Nerantziotissa (on metro line 1). The metro also connects at Doukissis Plakentias (line 3). Trains to the airport run from 6am to midnight; trains from the airport to Athens run from 5.10am to 11.30pm; trains run every 15 minutes from Nerantziotissa. Suburban rail also goes from the airport to Piraeus (change trains at Nerantziotissa) and Kiato in the Peloponnese (via Corinth).

Taxi

Fixed fares are posted. Expect day/night €35/50 to the city centre, and €47/65 to Piraeus. Both trips should take at least an hour, longer with heavy traffic. Check www.athens airporttaxi.com for more info.

BICYCLE

Even experienced cyclists might find Athens' roads a challenge, with no cycle lanes and often reckless drivers. Day rental costs about €12.

Funky Rides (☑ 211 710 9366; www.funkyride. gr; Dimitrakopoulou 1, Koukaki; Ⓜ Akropoli)

CAR & MOTORCYCLE

Athens' notorious traffic congestion, confusing signage, impatient/erratic drivers and one-way streets make for occasionally nightmarish driving.

Contrary to what you see, parking is actually illegal alongside kerbs marked with yellow lines, on footpaths and in pedestrian malls. Paid parking areas require tickets available from kiosks.

PUBLIC TRANSPORT

Athens has an extensive and inexpensive integrated public transport network of buses, metro, trolleybuses and trams. Get maps at tourist offices or online: **Athens Urban Transport Organisation** (OASA; ☑185; www.oasa.gr; ☉6.30am-11.30pm Mon-Fri, 7.30am-10.30pm Sat & Sun).

Tickets

Tickets good for 90 minutes (€1.40), 24 hours (€4) and seven days (€14) are valid for all forms of public transport except for airport services. Bus/trolleybus-only tickets (€1.20) cannot be used on the metro. Children under six travel free; people under 18 and over 65 pay half-fare. Buy tickets in metro stations or transport kiosks or most *periptera*. Validate the ticket in the machine as you board your transport of choice.

Bus & Trolleybus

Local express buses, regular buses and electric trolleybuses operate every 15 minutes from 5am to midnight. The free OASA map shows most routes.

Piraeus Buses

Piraeus buses operate 24 hours (every 20 minutes from 6am to midnight, and then hourly):

From Syntagma (bus 040) At the corner of Syntagma and Filellinon to Akti Xaveriou

From Omonia (bus 049) At the Omonia end of Athinas to Plateia Themistokleous

Metro

The metro works well and posted maps are self-explanatory (icons and English translations). Trains operate from 5am to midnight (every four minutes during peak periods and every 10 minutes off peak); on Friday and Saturday, lines 2 and 3 run until 2am. Get information at www.isap.gr and www.ametro.gr. All stations have wheelchair access.

Line 1 (Green) The old Kifisia–Piraeus line is known as the Ilektriko and travels slower than the others and above ground. Transfer at Omonia and Attiki for line 2, Monastiraki for line 3 and Nerantziotissa for suburban rail. The hourly all-night bus service (bus 500 Piraeus–Kifisia) follows this route, with bus stops located outside the train stations.

Line 2 (Red) Runs from Agios Antonios in the northwest to Agios Dimitrios in the southeast. Attiki and Omonia connect with line 1, Syntagma connects with line 3.

Line 3 (Blue) Runs northeast from Egaleo to Doukissis Plakentias, with the airport train continuing from there. Transfer for line 1 at Monastiraki and line 2 at Syntagma.

ⓘ TRAVEL PASS

For short-stay visitors, 24-hour/3-day tickets (€4/14) allow unlimited travel on all public transport inside Athens, excluding airport services. Tourist passes (three days/one week €20/50) also include one airport round trip and are only available at the airport or bus stations.

Train

Fast **suburban rail** (☑1110; www.trainose.gr) links Athens with the airport, Piraeus, the outer regions and the northern Peloponnese. It connects to the metro at Larisis, Doukissis Plakentias and Nerantziotissa stations, and goes from the airport to Kiato (€14, 1¾ hours).

Tram

Athens' **tram** (www.tramsa.gr) offers a slow, scenic coastal journey to Faliro and Voula, via Glyfada.

Trams run from Syntagma to Faliro (45 minutes), Syntagma to Voula (one hour) and Faliro to Voula from 5.30am to 1am Sunday to Thursday (every 10 minutes), and from 5.30am to 2.30am on Friday and Saturday (every 40 minutes).

The Syntagma terminus is on Leoforos Vasilissis Amalias, opposite the National Gardens, with ticket vending machines on platforms.

TAXI

Despite the large number of yellow taxis, it can be tricky getting one, especially during rush hour. Thrust your arm out vigorously...and still you may have to shout your destination to the driver to see if he or she is interested. Make sure the meter is on.

If a taxi picks you up while already carrying passengers, the fare is not shared: each person pays the fare on the meter minus any diversions to drop others (note what it's at when you get in). Short trips around central Athens cost around €5. Taxi services include **Athina 1** (☑210 921 2800), **Enotita** (☑18388) and **Parthenon** (Map p84; ☑210 532 3000). Costs:

→ flag fall €1.19

→ ports, train and bus station surcharge €1.07

→ airport surcharge €3.79

→ day rate (tariff 1 on the meter) €0.68 per km

→ night rate (tariff 2 on the meter) €1.19 per km (midnight to 5am)

→ baggage €0.40 per item over 10kg

→ holiday tariff (Easter and Christmas) €1 to €2

→ minimum fare €3.16

→ booking a radio taxi €1.88

ATHENS PORTS

Piraeus   Πειραιάς

POP 163,910

The highlights of Greece's main port and ferry hub, Piraeus, are the otherworldly rows of ferries, ships and hydrofoils filling its seemingly endless quays. Piraeus, 10km southwest of central Athens, is the biggest port in the Mediterranean (with more than 20 million passengers passing through annually), the hub of the Aegean ferry network, the centre of Greece's maritime trade and the base for its large merchant navy. While technically a separate city, these days Piraeus virtually melds into the urban sprawl of Athens.

Central Piraeus is not a place where visitors choose to linger because it's congested with traffic. Beyond its shipping offices, banks and public buildings, you find a jumble of pedestrian precincts, shopping strips and rather grungy areas. The most attractive quarter lies to the east around **Zea Marina** and touristy **Mikrolimano** harbour, which is lined with cafes, restaurants and bars.

Piraeus has been the port of Athens since classical times, when Themistocles transferred his Athenian fleet from the exposed port of Phaleron (modern Faliro) to the security of Piraeus in the 5th century BC. It was eventually overtaken by other ports, and during medieval and Turkish times, it diminished into a tiny fishing village. Its resurgence began in 1834 when Athens became the capital of independent Greece. To kill time, visit the **Piraeus Archaeological Museum** (📞 210 452 1598; Harilaou Trikoupi 31; admission €3; ⊙ 8.30am-3pm Tue-Sun) with its magnificent statue of Apollo, or the **Hellenic Maritime Museum** (📞 210 451 6264; Akti Themistokleous, Plateia Freatidas, Zea Marina; admission €3; ⊙ 8.30am-1pm Tue-Sun).

Piraeus

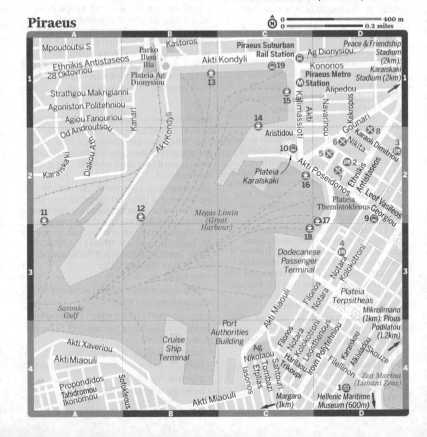

🛏 Sleeping

If you're catching an early ferry you can stay in Piraeus instead of central Athens, but many hotels around Megas Limin (Great Harbour) are shabby and aimed at sailors and clandestine liaisons. Don't sleep out: Piraeus is probably one of the most dangerous places in Greece to do so.

Hotel Triton
HOTEL $

(📞 210 417 3457; www.htriton.gr; Tsamadou 8; d/tr incl breakfast from €57/86; ✳ @ ; Ⓜ Piraeus) This simple, conveniently located hotel with helpful staff is a treat compared to the usual run-down joints in Piraeus. Some rooms overlook the bustling market square. There's one family suite (€132).

Pireaus Dream Hotel
HOTEL $

(📞 210 411 0555; www.piraeusdream.gr; Filonos 79-81; s/d/tr incl breakfast €55/60/90; ✳ @ ; Ⓜ Piraeus) With quiet rooms starting on the 4th floor, this renovated hotel is about 500m from the metro.

Piraeus Theoxenia
LUXURY HOTEL $$

(📞 210 411 2550; www.theoxeniapalace.com; Karaoli Dimitriou 23; d/tr incl breakfast from €110/150; ✳ @ 🛜 ; Ⓜ Piraeus) Pireaus' swanky, central hotel with plump bathrobes and satellite TV; get the best deals online.

🍴 Eating & Drinking

The Great Harbour is backed by lots of gritty cafes and fast-food joints; better food and ambience hide away in the backstreets or further afield around Mikrolimano harbour, Zea Marina and along the waterfront promenade at Freatida.

Mandragoras
DELI $

(📞 210 417 2961; Gounari 14; ⊘ 7.30am-4pm Mon, Wed & Sat, to 8pm Tue, Thu & Fri; Ⓜ Piraeus) This superb delicatessen offers a fine selection of gourmet cheeses, ready-made mezedhes, spices, olive oils and preserved foods.

★ Margaro
SEAFOOD $$

(📞 210 451 4226; Hatzikiriakou 126; mains €6-21; ⊘ noon-midnight Sep-Jul) It's worth a taxi ride to this long-time local favourite known for its fresh crayfish, eaten in a giant pile. See what's fresh and indulge in this off-the-beaten-path, casual gem.

Rakadiko
TAVERNA $$

(📞 210 417 8470; Karaoli Dimitriou 5, Stoa Kouvelou; mains €9-17; ⊘ lunch & dinner Tue-Sat) Dine quietly under grapevines on mezedhes from all over Greece. Live *rembetika* on weekends.

Plous Podilatou
SEAFOOD $$

(📞 210 413 7910; www.plous-podilatou.gr; Akti Koumoundourou 42, Mikrolimano; mains €12-20) This modern restaurant in Mikrolimano has a Mediterranean menu, with an emphasis on well-prepared fresh fish and seafood.

General Market
MARKET $

(Dimosthenous; ⊘ 6am-4pm Mon-Fri) Broad range of food and bric-a-brac.

Piraikon
SUPERMARKET $

(Ippokratous 1; ⊘ 8am-8pm Mon-Fri, to 4pm Sat) Convenient for provisioning for longer trips.

ℹ Information

There are luggage lockers at the metro station (€3 for 24 hours), and free wifi around the port.

ATHENS & AROUND PIRAEUS

Piraeus

MONEY

ATMs and money changers line the Great Harbour.
Emporiki Bank (cnr Antistaseos & Makras Stoas)
National Bank of Greece (cnr Antistaseos & Tsamadou)

Getting There & Away

The metro and suburban rail lines from Athens terminate at the northeastern corner of the Great Harbour on Akti Kalimassioti. Most ferry departure points are a short walk over the footbridge from here. A left turn out of the metro station leads 250m to Plateia Karaïskaki, the terminus for airport buses.

BOAT

Piraeus is the busiest port in Greece, with a bewildering array of departures, including daily service to most island groups. The exceptions are the Ionians, with only boats to Kythira (for the other islands sail from Patra and Igoumenitsa), and the Sporades plus Kea (Tzia) and Andros in the Cyclades (which sail from Rafina and Lavrio). Piraeus ferries also serve the Peloponnese (Methana, Ermioni, Porto Heli, Monemvasia and Gythio).

Always check departure docks with the ticketing agent.

Note that there are two departure points for Crete at Piraeus port: ferries for Iraklio leave from the western end of Akti Kondyli, but ferries for other Cretan ports occasionally dock there as well, or in other places.

Schedules & Tickets All ferry companies have online timetables and booths on the quays. Ferry schedules are reduced in April, May and October, and are radically cut in winter, especially to smaller islands. Find schedules and buy tickets online (www.greekferries.gr, www.openseas.gr, www.ferries.gr or company websites), at travel agents or phone companies directly. In this book, we list ferry schedules in the relevant island/destination chapters.
Piraeus Port Authority (1441; www.olp.gr) also has schedule information.

BUS

The **X96 Piraeus–Athens Airport Express** (€5) leaves from the southwestern corner of Plateia Karaïskaki and also stops on Kalimassioti. **Bus 040** goes from Leoforos Vasileos Geourgiou to Athens.

METRO

The fastest and most convenient link between the Great Harbour and Athens is the metro (€1.40, 30 minutes, every 10 minutes, 5am to midnight), near the ferries at the northern end of Akti Kalimassioti. Take extra care as the section between Piraeus and Monastiraki is notorious for pickpockets.

TRAIN

Piraeus is also connected to the suburban rail, whose terminus is located opposite the metro station. To get to the airport or the Peloponnese, you need to change trains at Nerantziotissa.

Getting Around

The port is massive and a **free shuttle bus** runs regularly along the quay nearest the metro station (see signposted maps).

The city of Piraeus has its own network of buses. The services likely to interest travellers are buses 904 and 905 between Zea Marina and the metro station.

Rafina   Ραφήνα

Rafina, on Attica's east coast, is Athens' main fishing port and the second-most important port for passenger ferries. It is far smaller than Piraeus and less confusing – and fares are about 20% cheaper – but it does take an hour on the bus to get here.

Getting There & Away

BUS

Frequent **KTEL buses** (Rafina 22940 23440, info 210 880 8080/8000; www.ktelattikis.gr) run from Athens to Rafina (€2.40, one hour) between 5.45am and 10.30pm, departing Athens' Mavromateon bus terminal. Buses from Athens Airport (€3, 45 minutes) leave from in front of the arrivals hall, near the Sofitel. Both stop on the Rafina quay.

BOAT

Rafina Port Authority (229 402 8888; www.rafinaport.gr) has information on ferries. See the destination island chapter for ticketing specifics.

Boat Services from Rafina

DESTINATION	TIME	FARE	FREQUENCY
Andros	2½hr	€16	4-8 daily
Evia (Marmari)	1hr	€7	2-4 daily
Ios*	4hr	€55	5 weekly
Mykonos	4½hr	€25	2-3 daily
Mykonos*	2hr 10min	€49	2 daily
Naxos*	3hr	€52	1 daily
Paros	5hr	€29	1 daily
Paros*	3hr	€50	1 daily
Santorini (Thira)*	4¾hr	€69	1 daily
Tinos*	1¾hr	€49-54.50	4-5 daily
Tinos	4hr	€23	4 daily

*high-speed services

Lavrio · Λαύριο

Lavrio, an industrial town on the coast 60km southeast of Athens, is the port for ferries to Kea and Kythnos and high-season catamarans to the western Cyclades. In antiquity, it was an important mining town. The silver mines here funded the great classical-building boom in Athens and helped build the fleet that defeated the Persians. Some of the underground shafts and mining galleries are still visible. Lavrio has also become a windsurfing spot.

The town has a small **Archaeological Museum** (☑ 229 202 2817; Sepieri; admission €2; ☉10am-3pm Tue-Sun) and a **Mineralogical Museum** (☑ 229 302 6270; Iroön Polytehniou; admission €1.20; ☉10am-noon Wed, Sat & Sun).

Lavrio has many fish tavernas and *ouzeries,* as well as a great fish market.

❶ Getting There & Away

BUS

Buses (p126) to Lavrio (€5.20, two hours, every 30 minutes) run from the Mavromateon terminal in Athens. Airport buses (€5, one hour) leave from the front of the arrivals hall near the Sofitel, and you must change buses at Markopoulo. Both stop on the Lavrio quay.

BOAT

Lavrio Port Authority (☑ 229 202 5249) has ferry information.

DESTINATION	TIME	FARE	FREQUENCY
Kea (Tzia)	1¼hr	€10	4 daily
Kythnos	2hr	€10	2 daily
Syros	5hr	€18	2 weekly
Limnos	10½hr	€30	2 weekly

TAXI

Lavrio taxis (☑ 6981040085, 229 202 5871) to the airport (€40, 30 minutes), central Athens (€50, one hour) and Piraeus (€60, 1½ hours).

AROUND ATHENS

Until the 7th century, Attica was home to a number of smaller kingdoms, such as those at Eleusis (Elefsina), Ramnous and Brauron (Vravrona). The remains of these cities continue to be among the region's attractions, although they pale alongside the superb Temple of Poseidon at Cape Sounion.

An agricultural and wine-growing region with several large population centres, Attica has some fine beaches, particularly along the Apollo Coast and at Shinias, near Marathon.

❶ SHORTCUTS

Because of Lavrio's, and especially Rafina's, close proximity to Athens' airport, if you are going to the northern Cyclades it is often fastest to travel straight from the airport to the port, bypassing Athens and Piraeus completely.

Many of these places can be reached (often with some difficulty, as schedules can be infrequent) by regular city buses or KTEL services from the Mavromateon terminal. It's easiest to go with your own wheels.

Cape Sounion

The Ancient Greeks certainly knew how to choose a site for a temple. Nowhere is this more evident than at Cape Sounion, 70km south of Athens. The **Temple of Poseidon** (☑ 229 203 9363; adult/child €4/free; ☉9.30am-8pm) stands on a craggy spur that plunges 65m down to the sea. Built in 444 BC it is constructed of local marble from Agrilesa, and its slender columns, of which 16 remain, are Doric. It is thought that the temple was built by Iktinos, the architect of the Temple of Hephaestus in Athens' Ancient Agora.

Mt Parnitha

The **Mt Parnitha National Park** (www.parnitha-ng.gr), about 25km north of Athens, is the highest mountain range surrounding the city, and serves as the 'lungs' of Athens. Tragically, more than 4200 hectares of century-old fir and pine forest was razed in devastating fires in 2007. The state has since tripled the area designated as national park and launched a reforestation program.

Mt Parnitha comprises a number of smaller peaks, the highest of which is **Karavola** (1413m). The park is crisscrossed by walking trails, is a popular hiking and mountain-biking destination, and has two shelters for hikers. Find the Road Editions hiking map of the area. There are many caves and much wildlife, including red deer.

Marathon & Around

The plain surrounding the unremarkable small town of Marathon, 42km northeast of Athens, is the site of one of the most celebrated

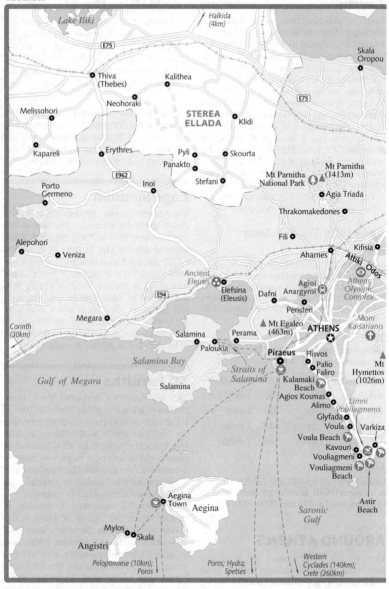

battles in world history. In 490 BC an army of
9000 Greeks and 1000 Plataeans defeated the
25,000-strong Persian army. The Greeks were
indebted to the ingenious tactics of Miltiades,
who altered the conventional battle formation
so that there were fewer soldiers in the centre,
but more in the wings. This lulled the Persians
into thinking the Greeks were going to be a
pushover. They broke through in the centre
but were then ambushed by the soldiers in the
wings. At the end of the day, 6000 Persians
and only 192 Greeks lay dead. After the battle,

thon Tomb (☎229 405 5462; site & museum adult/child €3/free; ◷8.30am-3pm Tue-Sun), 4km before the town. Nearer to town, the site's excellent **museum** (☎22940 55155) displays local discoveries, including Neolithic pottery from the Cave of Pan, finds from the Tomb of the Athenians and well-preserved statues from an Egyptian sanctuary.

The ruins of the ancient port of **Ramnous** (☎22940 63477; adult/child €2/free; ◷8.30am-3pm) lie about 10km northeast of Marathon. The evocative and secluded site stands on a picturesque plateau overlooking the sea. Among the ruins are the remains of the Doric Temple of Nemesis (435 BC) and a fortress. There is no public transport to the site.

The long, sandy, pine-fringed beach at **Shinias** is the best in this part of Attica.

Vravrona

In Vravrona the **Sanctuary of Artemis** (☎22990 27020; adult/child €3/free; ◷8am-2.45pm Tue-Sun), originally a Neolithic settlement, came to be revered by worshippers of Artemis, the goddess of the hunt and protector of women in childbirth and newborns. The current temple ruins date from approximately 420 BC. The museum houses exceptional finds from the sanctuary.

Elefsina

The **Ancient Eleusis** (☎210 554 6019; adult/child €3/free; ◷8.30am-3pm Tue-Sun) ruins lie beside the industrial town of Elefsina, 22km west of Athens. In ancient times it nestled on the slopes of a low hill close to the shore of the Saronic Gulf, built around the Sanctuary of Demeter. The site dates to Mycenaean times, when the cult of Demeter began. By classical times it was celebrated with a huge annual festival. In the 4th century AD, Roman emperor Theodosius closed it.

Peania

Perhaps Peania's biggest claim to fame was as the birthplace of Greek statesman Demosthenes (384–322 BC). Today the area is known primarily for remarkable **Koutouki Cave** (☎210 664 2910; www.culture.gr; adult/child €5/free; ◷9am-3pm Mon-Fri, 9.30am-2.30pm Sat & Sun) and the **Vorres Museum** (☎210 664 2520; www.culture.gr; Parodos Diadohou Konstantinou 4, Peania; adult/child €4.40/free; ◷10am-2pm Sat & Sun).

Pheidippides ran to Athens to announce the victory. After shouting 'Enikesame!' ('We won!') he collapsed and died. This is the origin of today's marathon race.

The 192 men who fell at Marathon were cremated and buried in the collective **Mara-**

Peloponnese

Why Go?

The Peloponnese (pe-lo-*po*-nih-sos; Πελοπόννησος) is the stuff of which legends are made. Numerous myths were born and borne out here – it is where many Greek gods or heroes strutted their stuff (and aired their buffed bodies). Today this region is far from a fable. It boasts historical sites, with classical temples, Mycenaean palaces, Byzantine cities and Frankish and Venetian fortresses.

The region's natural playground truly mesmerises, with lofty, snowcapped mountains, lush gorges, valleys of citrus groves and vineyards, cypress trees and sun-speckled beaches. For centuries Greeks fought hard against invaders of their Peloponnese paradise, but today foreigners are far from repelled.

Filoxenia (hospitality) is as strong here as anywhere in the country and the cuisine is among Greece's best. The locals claim to have the best of everything to give. And that's no myth.

Best Places to Eat

➡ Antica Gelateria di Roma (p143)

➡ Voula's Yesterday & Today (p164)

➡ Zerzova (p149)

➡ Elies (p165)

Best Places to Stay

➡ Elies (p165)

➡ Pirgos Mavromichali Hotel (p161)

➡ Pension Marianna (p142)

➡ Mpelleiko (p148)

When to Go
Nafplio

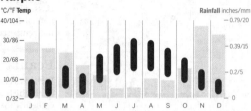

Apr-Jun Wildflower paradise; the perfect time for do-it-yourself explorations.

Sep & Oct Enjoy the beaches and sun when the summer crowds have long gone.

Easter Religious festivities and cuisine in Orthodox Easter week are unforgettable.

History

Since ancient times the Peloponnese has played a major role in Greek history. When the Minoan civilisation declined after 1450 BC, the focus of power in the ancient Aegean world moved from Crete to the hill-fortress palaces of Mycenae and Tiryns in the Peloponnese. As elsewhere in Greece, the 400 years following the Dorian conquests in the 12th century BC are known as the Dark Ages. When the region emerged from darkness in the 7th century BC, Athens' arch rival, Sparta, had surpassed Mycenae as the most powerful city in the Peloponnese. The period of peace and prosperity under Roman rule (146 BC to around AD 250) was shattered by a series of invasions by Goths, Avars and Slavs.

The Byzantines were slow to make inroads into the Peloponnese, only becoming firmly established during the 9th century. In 1204, after the fall of Constantinople to the Crusaders, the Frankish Crusader chiefs William de Champlitte and Geoffrey de Villehardouin divided the region into 12 fiefs, which they parcelled out to various barons of France, Flanders and Burgundy. These fiefs were overseen by de Villehardouin, the self-appointed Prince of the 'Morea', as the region was called in medieval times, perhaps because mulberry trees grow so well in the area (*mouria* means mulberry tree).

The Byzantines gradually won back the Morea and, although the empire as a whole was now in terminal decline, a glorious renaissance took place in the area, centred on Mystras, which became the region's seat of government.

The Morea fell to the Turks in 1460 and hundreds of years of power struggles between the Turks and Venetians followed. The Venetians had long coveted the Morea and succeeded in establishing profitable trading ports at Methoni, Pylos, Koroni and Monemvasia.

The Greek War of Independence supposedly began in the Peloponnese, when Bishop Germanos of Patra raised the flag of revolt near Kalavryta on 25 March 1821. The Egyptian army, under the leadership of Ibrahim Pasha, brutally restored Turkish rule in 1825.

In 1827 the Triple Alliance of Great Britain, France and Russia, moved by Greek suffering and the activities of philhellenes (Byron's death in 1824 was particularly influential), came to the rescue of the Greeks by destroying the Turkish-Egyptian fleet at the Battle of Navarino, ending Turkish domination of the area.

The Peloponnese became part of the independent state of Greece, and Nafplio (in Argolis) became the first national capital. Ioannis Kapodistrias, Greece's first president, was assassinated on the steps of Nafplio's Church of St Spyridon in October 1831, and the new king, Otto, moved the capital to Athens in 1834.

Like the rest of Greece, the Peloponnese suffered badly during WWII. Part of this history is vividly and tragically illustrated in the mountain town of Kalavryta, where nearly all males aged over 15 were massacred.

The civil war (1944–9) brought widespread destruction and, in the 1950s, many villagers migrated to Athens, Australia, Canada, South Africa and the USA.

ⓘ Information

Since the Greek financial crisis, the hours of museums and sites in the Peloponnese are particularly vulnerable to change, particularly extended summer hours; it's best to check beforehand.

ⓘ Getting There & Away

BUS

Note: there is a difference between Corinth Isthmus (the canal) and Corinth (the city). Although it's plonked on a main road on the Peloponnese side of the Corinth Canal, the **Corinth Isthmus (Peloponnese) KTEL bus station** (☑ 27410 75410, Athens 210 512 4919), located near the canal ('isthmus'), is the spot to change for buses south to the rest of the Peloponnese. This includes **Pyrgos**, **Patra**, and **Olympia**. No formal timetables are available; most buses from Athens heading to the Peloponnese stop here.

Exceptions depart from the **KTEL Korinthos bus station** (☑ 27410 75425; www.ktel-korinthias.gr; Dimocratias 4) in Corinth (city), which is the departure point for buses to **Ancient Corinth** (€1.60, 20 minutes, seven daily Monday to Saturday), **Nemea** (€4.50, one hour, seven daily, one Sunday), **Isthmia** (€1.60, 15 minutes, three daily) and Loutraki (for **Corinth Isthmus**; €1.70, 10 minutes, half-hourly). You can also catch all these buses from the corner of Aratou and Ethnikis Andistasis.

TRAIN

At the time of writing the OSE train services in the Peloponnese were off the rails. Only one line (Athens–Patra) was operating, but even this had a replacement bus service between Kiato and Patra. Simply put: KTEL buses are a more convenient option to access the region.

Peloponnese Highlights

1 Soak up the past and present of **Nafplio** (p139) and **Monemvasia** (p155)

2 Marvel at the sanctuary of **Ancient Olympia** (p176), birthplace of the Olympic Games

3 Walk in the remote and rugged **Mani** (p159) and marvel at the Maniot tower houses

4 Hike to the monasteries of **Lousios Gorge** (p148) and discover the delights of charming mountain-top villages **Stemnitsa** (p148), **Dimitsana** (p148), **Karitena** (p150) and **Andritsena** (p178)

5 Meander through the magical **Mystras** (p154), a World Heritage–listed site

6 Explore the historic sites of **Ancient Mycenae** (p137), **Ancient Nemea** (p136) and **Epidavros** (p145)

7 Meander up the dramatic **Vouraïkos Gorge** (p183) on the unique rack-and-pinion train to the historic village of Kalavryta

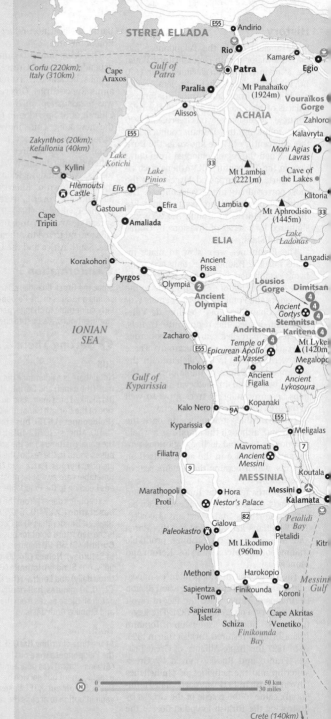

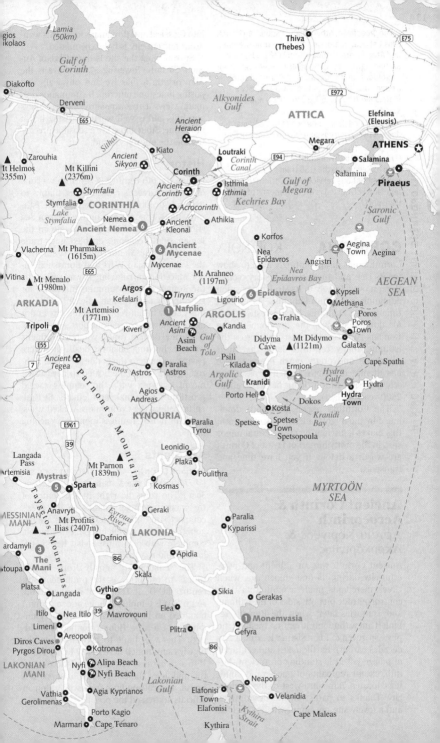

The *proastiako*, Athens handy suburban train, runs between Kiato, Corinth (city) train station and Athens international airport (€12, 1½ hours, around eight daily, timetables change regularly). To get to/from the Corinth (city) train station, a handy bus shuttles between Corinth city's Plateia Kentriki (€1.50, 20 minutes) and the station.

A small local train runs two to three times daily between Pyrgos and Olympia (for Ancient Olympia).

For **Diakofto** (to catch the rack-and-pinion train to Kalavryta) the OSE train's current replacement bus service from Corinth (not regular KTEL buses) is the only means of public transport.

CORINTHIA ΚΟΡΙΝΘΙΑ

Corinthia has disappointingly little to show for its rich and tumultuous history (something it owes largely to its strategic position adjoining the Corinth Isthmus). Throughout time several empires have wrestled here for dominance over the Peloponnese: the Romans constructed a vast wall across the isthmus, many centuries later the Turks overran it and pretty much everyone else has attempted to carve a canal across it (the schedule slipped a little bit behind – about 2600 years, in fact).

The Corinthia region was once dominated by the mighty, ancient city of Corinth; this makes a fascinating visit. Several minor sites in the pretty hinterland west of Corinth are worth a detour if you have time and transport.

Ancient Corinth & Acrocorinth

Αρχαία Κόρινθος & Ακροκόρινθος

Ancient Corinth was an affluent and powerful city during its first golden age, when Greek merchants made a mint from their control of trade on both sides of the isthmus and, centuries later, when the Romans rebuilt it anew (but only after first trashing the place in revenge for resisting its rule a few decades earlier). Earthquakes and centuries of pillage left little standing of Ancient Corinth, except remnants of once-grand buildings, located 7km southwest of the modern city. Thanks to paths, on-site descriptions and a lovely site museum (which is divided into Classical and Roman periods), this wondrous ancient city is not to be missed.

Surrounding the site is the village of Ancient Corinth. Towering 575m above is the Acrocorinth, a massive and physically imposing limestone outcrop. It commands dramatic views across the surrounding valleys and hills and is well worth perusing if you have time. Stout shoes are a sensible precaution on the uneven ground.

History

During the 6th century BC Corinth was one of Ancient Greece's richest cities, thanks to its strategic position on the Corinth Isthmus. Its twin ports, one on the Aegean Sea (Kenchreai, near Kechries) and one on the Ionian side (Lecheon), enabled it to trade throughout the Mediterranean. It survived the Peloponnesian Wars and flourished under Macedonian rule, but it was sacked by the Roman consul Mummius in 146 BC for rebelling against Roman rule. In 44 BC Julius Caesar began rebuilding the city and it again became a prosperous port.

During Roman times, when Corinthians weren't clinching business deals, they were paying homage to the goddess of love, Aphrodite, in a temple dedicated to her (which meant partying with the temple's sacred prostitutes, both male and female). St Paul, perturbed by the Corinthians' wicked ways, spent 18 mostly fruitless months preaching here.

◎ Sights

Ancient Corinth   ARCHAEOLOGICAL SITE
(☏ 27410 31207; site & museum €6; ⊗ 8.30am-3pm) The ruins lie right in the centre of the modern village. Thanks to the area's compact size (although excavations are ongoing), and the excellent signs in English, complete with diagrams, a visit here is enjoyable and rewarding.

The remains are mostly from Roman times. An exception is the prominent 5th-century-BC Doric **Temple of Apollo**. To the south of this temple is a huge **agora** (forum) bounded on its southern side by the foundations of a **stoa** (long colonnaded building). This was built to accommodate the bigwigs summoned here in 337 BC by Philip II to sign oaths of allegiance to Macedon. In the middle of the central row of shops is a **bema**, a marble podium from which Roman officials addressed the people.

At the eastern end of the *agora* are the remains of the **Julian Basilica**. To the north is the **Lower Peirene fountain** – the Upper Peirene fountain is on Acrocorinth. According to mythology, Peirene wept so much when her son Kenchrias was killed by Artemis that the gods, rather than let all the precious water go to waste, turned her into a fountain (actually, it's a spring). The water tanks, or cisterns, are concealed in a fountain house with a six-arched facade.

West of the fountain, steps lead to the **Lecheon road**, once the main thoroughfare to the port of Lecheon. On the east side of the road is the **Peribolos of Apollo**, a courtyard flanked by Ionic columns, some of which have been restored. Nearby is a **public latrine**, where some seats remain.

South of the museum is **Temple E** (also known as Temple of Octavia; Pausanias describes it as being dedicated to Octavia, sister of Augustus). Several columns remain.

The site's **museum** has three main rooms: the first two exhibit fine Greek and Roman statues, mosaics, figurines, reliefs and friezes. The third room, the museum's latest addition, houses the finds of excavations at the nearby Sanctuary of Asklepios, a temple from the 5th century BC. Some interesting pieces include grave markers and votive genitalia from the 4th century BC.

Opposite the site entrance is the **ancient theatre**, constructed in the 5th century BC for up to 15,000 spectators, and altered various times, and the **odeion** (indoor theatre), a Roman construction from the 1st century AD. You view both sites from the road.

Acrocorinth

RUIN

(☉8am-3pm) **FREE** The sheer bulk of limestone known as Acrocorinth was one of the finest natural fortifications in Ancient Greece. It remains an impressive ruin to this day, commanding wonderful views over the surrounding region.

The original fortress was built in ancient times, but it has been modified many times over the years by a string of invaders. The ruins are a medley of imposing Roman, Byzantine, Frankish, Venetian and Turkish ramparts, harbouring remains of Byzantine chapels, Turkish houses and mosques.

On the higher of Acrocorinth's two summits is the **Temple of Aphrodite**, where sacred courtesans (exactly how they differed from the less-holy variety isn't clear) catered to the desires of the insatiable Corinthians. Little remains of the temple, but the views are tremendous.

CORINTH CANAL
ΔΙΩΡΥΓΑ ΤΗΣ ΚΟΡΙΝΘΟΥ

The concept of cutting a canal through the Corinth Isthmus to link the Ionian and Aegean Seas was first proposed by Periander, tyrant of Ancient Corinth at the end of the 7th century BC. The magnitude of the task defeated him, so he opted instead to build a *diolkos* (paved slipway), across which sailors dragged small ships on rollers, a method used until the 13th century.

In the intervening years many leaders, including Alexander the Great and Caligula, toyed with the canal idea, but it was Nero who actually began digging in AD 67. In true megalomaniac fashion, he struck the first blow himself, using a golden pickaxe. He then left it to 6000 Jewish prisoners to do the hard work. The project was soon halted by invasions by the Gauls. It was not until the 19th century (1883–93) that a French engineering company completed the canal.

The Corinth Canal, cut through solid rock, is over 6km long and 23m wide. The vertical sides rise 90m above the water. The canal did much to elevate Piraeus' status as a major Mediterranean port. It's an impressive sight, particularly when a ship is passing through.

If you're feeling adventurous, **Zulu Bungy Jump** (📞932702535; www.zulubungy.com; €60; ☉10am-5pm Wed-Sun Jun-Sep) offers the chance to see the canal walls from a unique angle.

If you have your own transport, head to nearby Isthmia to the **submersible bridge**, one of two bridges crossing the canal (the other is near Loutraki). It gives an excellent perspective of the canal and the nearby banks are great viewing points if you're lucky enough to see a ship pass over the submerged bridge.

Any bus from Athens passes over the bridge and stops at the KTEL Corinth Isthmus, 200m from the canal.

It's a butt-kicking – but doable – 4km up-hill hike to the fortress, as there's no bus. Try to grab a lift or take a village taxi.

Ancient Nemea
Αρχαία Νεμέα

Ancient Nemea (☑ 27460 22739; site, museum & stadium adult/concession €4/2, site & museum adult/concession €3/2; ☺ museum 8am-3pm, museum closed Mon morning), 31km southwest of Corinth, lies on the northeastern edge of modern Nemea. This stunning site is growing in popularity, helped by the fact that a two-day 'Modern Nemea' Games occurs for two days each Olympic year in June. According to mythology it was around this area that Hercules carried out the first of his labours – the slaying of the lion that had been sent by Hera to destroy Nemea. The lion became the constellation Leo (each of the 12 labours is related to a sign of the zodiac).

Like Olympia, Nemea was not a city but a sanctuary and venue for the biennial Nemean Games, held in honour of Zeus. These games were hosted by the nearby city of Kleonai, and they became one of the great Panhellenic festivals. Three original columns of the 4th-century-BC Doric **Temple of Zeus** survive, and have been joined by two more columns reassembled by an American team. Other ruins include a **bathhouse**, probably used by athletes to oil up pre-competition, and a **hostelry**.

The site's **museum** has two models of the ancient site – the first shows what it would have looked like in 573 BC, the second in AD 500 – and explanations in English. The jewel of the collection, quite literally, is the **Gold of Aidonia**, an exquisite assortment of gold rings, seals and beads from the site of Aidonia, near Nemea. Don't miss the video that explains the extraordinarily advanced race-starting mechanism (English subtitles).

The **stadium** (stadium only adult/concession €2/1; ☺ 8am-3pm) is 500m back along the road, and was once connected to the sanctuary by a sacred road. The athletes' starting line is still in place, together with the distance markers. Look out for ancient 'graffiti' in the tunnel used by athletes (note: the tunnel is slightly hidden).

ⓘ Getting There & Away

Nemea is best visited with your own transport. Buses to/from Corinth Isthmus (€4.50, one hour, around four to five daily, fewer on Sunday) will stop outside the site on the way to modern Nemea, a busy agricultural service town about 4km northwest of the site.

ARGOLIS ΑΡΓΟΛΙΔΑ

The Argolis Peninsula, which separates the Saronic and Argolic Gulfs, is a veritable treasure trove for archaeology buffs, history lovers and those after a fascinating frolic. The town of Argos, from which the region takes its name, is thought to be the longest continually inhabited town in Greece. Argolis was the seat of power of the Mycenaean empire that ruled Greece from 1600 to 1100 BC. Its citadels, Mycenae and Tiryns, are two of the region's major attractions, along with the famous Theatre of Epidavros. The de-

---

UNTANGLING THE SPRAWLING VINE ROUTES

The Nemea region, in the rolling hills southwest of Corinth, is one of Greece's premier wine-producing areas, famous for its full-bodied reds, produced from the local *agioritiko* grape. Look out also for wine made from *roditis*, a local variety of white grape.

Nemea has been known for its fine wines since Mycenaean times, when nearby Phlius supplied the wine for the royal court at Mycenae. Half a dozen or so wineries provide tastings for visitors (usually free, some by appointment). They include **Skouras** (☑ 27510 23688; www.skouraswines.com; ☺ 9am-3pm Mon-Fri, 10am-6pm Sat, 11am-3pm Sun), northwest of Argos, **Ktima Palivou** (☑ 27460 24190; www.palivos.gr; Ancient Nemea; ☺ 8.30am-5pm) and **Lafkioti** (☑ 27460 31000; www.lafkiotis.gr; Ancient Kleonai; ☺ 11am-4pm), 3km east of Ancient Nemea.

North of Nemea in pretty hill country, **Gaia Wines** (☑ 27460 31000; www.gaia-wines. gr; Koutsi; ☺ by appointment) produces unfiltered wines, including *appellation d'origine contrôlée* (AOC) varieties.

Nearby is the dramatically located **Domaine Helios** (☑ 21062 16811; www.semeliwines. com; ☺ by appointment), which produces various varieties of reds, whites and a rosé.

lightful old Venetian town of Nafplio makes a perfect base from which to explore.

Argos   Αργος

POP 22,200

The ancient town of Argos stretches back an astonishing 6000 years. Today most vestiges of its past glory lie buried beneath the existing modern town. Overshadowed by its stunning neighbour, Nafplio (12km away), Argos is an extremely pleasant, bustling town; it's worth a detour for the archaeological museum, as well as the ruins and fortress out of town. The market on Tsokri (Wednesday and Saturday) is also fun.

◉ Sights

Archaeological Museum of Argos   MUSEUM
(☑ 27510 68819; Plateia Agiou Petrou; adult/concession €2/1; ◷ 8am-3pm Tue-Sun) The archaeological museum, on the edge of the central square, spans three floors and includes a pretty garden. The collection includes some outstanding and complete Roman mosaics and sculptures, as well as bronze objects from Mycenaean tombs. Highlights include the statuette of a goddess, the mosaic of the four seasons in the courtyard, a suit of bronze armour from the 8th century BC and some fine Neolithic, Mycenaean and Geometric pottery, including some Argive grey and brown vases dating to before 1600 BC.

Roman Ruins   RUIN
(◷ 8am-3pm) FREE Impressive Roman ruins straddle both sides of a road (Tripolis). The star attraction is the **theatre**, which could seat up to 20,000 people (more than at Epidavros). It dates from Classical times but was greatly modified by the Romans. Nearby are the remains of a 1st-century-AD **odeion** (a smaller theatre) and **Roman baths**. Opposite is the **Ancient Agora**. Signage provides clear diagrams and contextualises the setting. To get there from the central square, head south along Danaou for about 500m and then turn right onto Theatrou.

Fortress of Larissa   FORT
FREE The impressive Fortress of Larissa that looms over Argos is a conglomeration of Byzantine, Frankish, Venetian and Turkish architecture, standing on the foundations of the city's principal ancient citadel. A road leads you to the top of the fortress; it's signposted from the centre and northern end of town and winds around the back of

the fortress for 5km. Ongoing excavations are taking place; take care while visiting.

❶ Getting There & Away

Just south of the central square, **KTEL Argolis** (☑ 27510 67324; www.ktel-argolidas.gr; Kapodistriou 8) has bus services to Nafplio (€1.60, 30 minutes, hourly), Mycenae (€1.60, 30 minutes, three daily) and Nemea (€3, one hour, two on Thursdays only).

There are also bus services to Athens between 5.30am and 8.30pm (€12, two hours, hourly) via Corinth Isthmus (€5, 50 minutes), and to Tripoli (€7, one hour, four daily except Sunday).

Ancient Mycenae   Αρχαία Μυκήνες

In the barren foothills of Mt Agios Ilias (750m) and Mt Zara (600m) stand the sombre and mighty ruins of **Ancient Mycenae** (☑ 27510 76585; admission €8; ◷ 8am-6pm Mon-Fri, to 3pm Sat & Sun winter). For 400 years (1600–1200 BC) this vestige of a kingdom was the most powerful in Greece, holding sway over the Argolid (the modern-day prefecture of Argolis) and influencing the other Mycenaean kingdoms.

History

World Heritage–listed Mycenae is synonymous with the names Homer and Schliemann. In the 9th century BC Homer told in his epic poems, the 'Iliad' and the 'Odyssey', of 'well-built Mycenae, rich in gold'. These poems were, until the 19th century, regarded as no more than gripping and beautiful legends. But in the 1870s the amateur archaeologist Heinrich Schliemann (1822–90), despite derision from professional archaeologists, struck gold, first at Troy then at Mycenae. (Although, owing to doubts about the provenance of some of his information and even allegations that he falsified some finds to fit his theories, his reputation has since suffered.)

In Mycenae, myth and history are inextricably linked. According to Homer, the city of Mycenae was founded by Perseus, the son of Danae and Zeus. Perseus' greatest heroic deed was the killing of the hideous snake-haired Medusa, whose looks literally petrified the beholder. Eventually, the dynasty of Perseus was overthrown by Pelops, a son of Tantalus. The Mycenaean Royal House of Atreus was probably descended from Pelops, although myth and history are

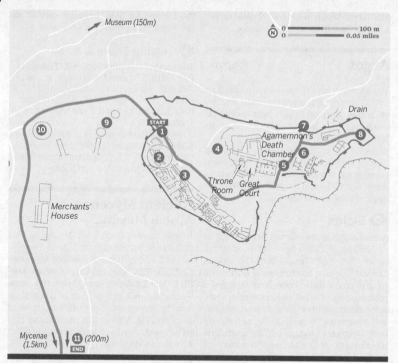

Museum (150m)

100 m
0.05 miles

Drain

START
1

10

9

2

4

7

8

3

6

5

Agamemnon's
Death
Chamber

Throne
Room

Great
Court

Merchants'
Houses

Mycenae
(1.5km)

11
END

(200m)

Site Tour
Citadel of Mycenae

START LION GATE
END MUSEUM
LENGTH 2.5KM; 2 HOURS

Enter through the dramatic ❶ **Lion Gate**, a solid construction of massive stone blocks over which rear two large lionesses. This motif is believed to have been the insignia of the Royal House of Atreus.

Inside the citadel, ❷ **Grave Circle A** is on the right. This was the royal cemetery and had six grave shafts. Five shafts were excavated by Schliemann between 1874 and 1876, uncovering magnificent gold treasures, including a well-preserved gold death mask. Schliemann sent a telegram to the Greek king stating, 'I have gazed upon the face of Agamemnon', but the mask turned out to belong to an unknown king.

South of Grave Circle A are the remains of a group of ❸ **houses**. In one was discovered the famous Warrior Vase, regarded by Schliemann as one of his greatest discoveries because it offered a glimpse of what Mycenae's legendary warriors looked like.

Follow the main path to ❹ **Agamemnon's Palace**, centred on the Great Court. The rooms to the north were private royal apartments where it is thought that Agamemnon was murdered. On the palace's southeastern side is the ❺ **megaron** (reception hall) and, beyond this, the ❻ **artisans' quarters**.

On the northern boundary of the citadel is the ❼ **Postern Gate**, through which, it is said, Orestes escaped after murdering his mother. In the far northeastern corner of the citadel is the ❽ **secret cistern**.

Until the late 15th century BC the Mycenaeans put their royal dead into shaft graves. They then used a new form of burial – the behive-shaped tholos tomb. Return via the ❾ **tholos tombs** of Aegisthus and Clytaemnestra and the nearby ❿ **Grave Circle B**.

Visit the museum, then head back along the road to modern Mycenae to the ⓫ **Treasury of Atreus**, or tomb of Agamemnon. A 40m-long passage leads to this immense beehive-shaped chamber.

AGAMEMNON, KING OF MYCENAE

Agamemnon is one of the principal characters in the 'Iliad' and crops up regularly in Greek legend. The son of Atreus and the king of Mycenae, he later led the Greeks during the Trojan War. Agamemnon and his brother Menelaus married Clytemnestra and Helen respectively, both daughters of the King of Sparta.

According to legend, Paris, the son of the Trojan king, stole Helen away. This was the catalyst for the Trojan War, as Agamemnon called on Greek princes to unite in a war of revenge. Around this time Artemis, the goddess of hunting, also sought revenge from Agamemnon and stalled the departing warships with adverse winds. To make peace with Artemis, Agamemnon was forced to sacrifice his daughter, Iphigenia. Artemis set the seas right again, and the Greek ships sailed for Troy, where a 10-year siege ensued. In the war's final year, Agamemnon had a jealous quarrel with Achilles over the attentions of a captive female, which could have cost the Greeks the war.

Finally, however, Agamemnon returned home victorious with his war spoils, which included the Trojan princess Cassandra. His victory was short-lived; on his return home he was murdered by his wife and her lover, Aegisthus. Years later Agamemnon's daughter, Electra, and her brother, Orestes, avenged their father's death by murdering Aegisthus and Clytemnestra.

so intertwined, and the genealogical line so complex, that no one really knows. Whatever the bloodlines, by Agamemnon's time the Royal House of Atreus was the most powerful of the Achaeans (Homer's name for the Greeks). It eventually came to a sticky end, fulfilling the curse that had been cast because of Pelops' misdeeds.

The historical facts are that Mycenae was first settled by Neolithic people in the 6th millennium BC. Between 2100 and 1900 BC, during the Bronze Age, Greece was invaded by people of Indo-European heritage who had crossed Anatolia via Troy to Greece. The invaders brought an advanced culture to then-primitive Mycenae and other mainland settlements. This new civilisation is now referred to as the Mycenaean, named after its most powerful kingdom. The other kingdoms included Pylos, Tiryns, Corinth and Argos, all in the Peloponnese. Evidence of Mycenaean civilisation has also been found at Thiva (Thebes) and Athens.

The city of Mycenae consisted of a fortified citadel and surrounding settlement. Due to the sheer size of the citadel walls (13m high and 7m thick), formed by stone blocks weighing 6 tonnes in places, the Ancient Greeks believed they must have been built by a Cyclops, one of the giants described in the 'Odyssey'.

Archaeological evidence indicates that the palaces of the Mycenaean kingdoms declined some time around 1200 BC and the palace itself was set ablaze around 1100 BC. Whether the destruction was the work of outsiders or due to internal division between the various Mycenaean kingdoms remains unresolved.

🛈 Getting There & Away

Three daily buses (excluding Sunday) head to Mycenae from Nafplio (€2.60, one hour) and Argos (€1.60, 30 minutes). The buses stop in the village and at the ancient site.

Other bus services, such as Athens–Nafplio, stop at the village of Fihtio on the main road, leaving you 3km from Mycenae village (from where it's another 2km or so to the site of Ancient Mycenae).

Nafplio · Ναύπλιο

POP 14,200

Nafplio, located 12km southeast of Argos on the Argolic Gulf, is one of Greece's prettiest and most romantic towns. It occupies a knockout location – on a small port beneath the towering Palamidi fortress – and is graced with attractive narrow streets, elegant Venetian houses, neoclassical mansions and interesting museums. Both overseas visitors and weekending Athenians flock to this lively, upwardly mobile place. It's full of quayside cafes, posh boutiques and many comfortable hotels and guesthouses (but it does get somewhat overcrowded in high season and holidays).

Nafplio was the first capital of Greece after Independence (between 1833 and 1834) and has been a major port since the Bronze Age. So strategic was its position that it had

Nafplio

200 m
0.1 miles

Argolic Gulf

Bourtzi (100m)

Boats to Bourtzi

Plateia Filellinon

Farmakopoulou

Akti Miaouli

Vyronos

Miniati

Plateia Syntagmatou

Staikopoulou

Spiliadou

30 Noemvriou

Plateia Poliko

Nosokomiou

Zygomala

Efthimiopoulou

Akronafplia

Argolic Gulf

Vasileos Alexandrou

Bouboulinas

Olgas

Ypsilandou

Amalias

Blesi

Sofroni

Vasileos Konstantinou

Platonos

Church of Agios Spyridon

Plateia Agios Spiridonos

Potamianou

Polizoidou

Town Hall

Plapouta

Kapodistriou

Plateia Kapodistria

Sidiras Merarhias

Flessa

Syngrou

Neas Kiou

Dervenakion

Vasileos Konstantinou

25 Martiou

Navarinou

Kilkis

Vas Georgiou

Irakleous

Thisseos

Stadium

Train Station

Tolo (10km); Epidavros(30km)

Karathona Beach (3km)

Arvanitia Beach

1
2
3
4
5
6
7
8
9
10
11
12
13
14
15
16
17
18
19
20
21
22
23
24
25
26
27
28
29

Nafplio

three fortresses – the massive principal fortress of Palamidi, the smaller Akronafplia and the diminutive Bourtzi on an islet west of the old town.

With good bus connections and services, the town is an ideal base from which to explore many nearby ancient sites.

⊙ Sights & Activities

Palamidi Fortress   FORT
(☎27520 28036; admission €4; ⊙8am-7.30pm May–mid-Oct, to 3pm mid-Oct-Apr) This vast and spectacular citadel stands on a 216m-high outcrop of rock with excellent views down onto the sea and surrounding land. It was built by the Venetians between 1711 and 1714, and is regarded as a masterpiece of military architecture. Within its walls stands a series of independent bastions, strategically located across the hill. The most important, and best preserved, is the western **Agios Andreas Bastion**, which stands at the top of the steps from town. It was the home of the garrison commander, and it is named after the tiny church in the interior courtyard. There are wonderful views over the Akronafplia and the old town from the bastion walls.

The **Miltiades Bastion**, to the northeast, is the largest of the bastions. It was used as a prison for condemned criminals from 1840 to 1920. War of Independence hero Theodoros Kolokotronis spent several years here after being condemned for treason.

There are two main approaches to the fortress. You can go via the road (taxis cost about €8 one way) or the energetic can tackle the seemingly endless steps that begin southeast of the bus station. The exact number of steps is an issue of much conjecture. Locals claim that there are 999 steps, which has prompted many travellers to conduct independent counts. Most report a considerably lower figure. Locals respond that the 999 steps are to the Church of Agios Andreas. Whatever the number, climb early and take water.

Akronafplia Fortress   FORT
Rising above the old part of town, the Akronafplia fortress is the oldest of Nafplio's three castles, although there's much less to see here than at the other two forts. The lower sections of the walls date back to the Bronze Age. Until the arrival of the Venetians, the town was restricted to within its walls. The Turks called it İç Kale (meaning 'inner castle'). It was used as a political prison from 1936 to 1956.

There's a lift up to the fortress from Plateia Poliko Nosokomiou at the western edge of town (it accesses the Nafplia Palace hotel complex). The old gateway to the fortress, crowned with a fine Venetian lion emblem, is at the top of Potamianou above Hotel Marianna.

Bourtzi   FORT
(boat €4 return) The island fortress of Bourtzi lies about 600m west of the town's port.

Most of the existing structure was built by the Venetians. Boats to the island leave from the northeastern end of Akti Miaouli.

Peloponnese Folklore Foundation Museum
MUSEUM

(☑ 27520 28379; www.pli.gr; Vasileos Alexandrou 1; admission €2; ⏱ 9.30am-2.30pm Wed-Mon) Nafplio's award-winning museum is a beautifully arranged collection of folk costumes and household items from Nafplio's former times. Established by the philanthropic owner, it's not to be missed. A lovely gift shop is on the ground floor.

War Museum
MUSEUM

(Amalias 22; ⏱ 9am-2pm Tue-Sun) **FREE** Traces Greece's military history from the War of Independence onwards through a collection of photographs, paintings, uniforms and assorted weaponry.

Archaeological Museum
MUSEUM

(☑ 27520 27502; Plateia Syntagmatos; adult/concession €3/2; ⏱ noon-4pm Mon, 9am-4pm Tue-Sun) Overlooking Plateia Syntagmatos, this museum reopened in 2009 following seven years of renovations. It features fine exhibits over two light and airy floors. The oldest exhibits, fire middens, date from 32,000 BC. Another highlight is the only bronze armour from near Mycenae in existence, dating from the 12th to 13th centuries BC.

National Gallery – Alexandros Soutzos Museum
GALLERY

(Sidiras Merarhias 23; adult/concession €3/2, free Mon; ⏱ 10am-3pm Mon, Thu & Sat, 10am-3pm & 5-8pm Wed & Fri, 10am-3pm Sun) This arm of the Athens National Gallery is housed in a stunningly restored neoclassical building. It features works on the 1821 Greek War of Independence, including works by Greek painters Vryzakis and Tsokos, considered the most important artists of the postwar years.

Cruise to Saronic Gulf Islands
BOAT TOUR

(☑ 27250 59430; www.pegasuscruises.gr; one way/return €20/34; ⏱ late Apr-late Sep) Pegasus Cruises offers popular full-day trips to the islands of Hydra and Spetses from Tolo, 10km southeast of Nafplio. You stop off for a couple of hours in each place. You can take a taxi to/from Tolo (€12) or one of the early/late buses to Tolo may get you there and back, depending on the schedule. There are at least two weekly departures (more in July and August); any travel agency sells tickets.

Nafplio Bike
BICYCLE RENTAL

(www.nafplio-bike.gr; Kipou 2; per day €15; ⏱ 9am-9pm Mon-Sat) This is the place to hire city and trekking bikes. Hourly rates also available.

Beaches

Arvanitia Beach is a small pebble beach just 10 minutes' walk south of town, tucked beside the Akronafplia fortress. If you're feeling energetic, you can follow a path east around the coast for about an hour (roughly 3km) to sandy **Karathona Beach**, at the far side of the Palamidi fortress. The walk is extremely pretty, as would be the beach if it weren't for the litter.

Festivals & Events

Nafplio is a good base for visits to Epidavros for performances at the famous theatre during the Epidavros Festival in July and August, part of the larger cultural Hellenic Festival (p95).

Classical Music Festival
MUSIC

(www.nafplionfestival.gr) Nafplio hosts a classical music festival between late May and July, featuring Greek and international performers. The Palamidi fortress is one of the concert venues. Check the website for exact dates.

Sleeping

Hotel Byron
PENSION $

(☑ 27520 22351; www.byronhotel.gr; Platonos 2; d incl breakfast €50-70; ❉) Occupying a fine Venetian building, the Byron is a reliable favourite, with friendly management, neat rooms, iron bedsteads and period furniture. Breakfast costs €5.

Pension Dimitris Bekas
PENSION $

(☑ 27520 24594; Efthimiopoulou 26; s/d/tr €20/30/40) Nafplio's only 'true' budget option – homey rooms around the owners' house with a top-value location on the slopes of the Akronafplia.

Hotel Leto
HOTEL $

(☑ 27520 28093; www.leto-hotel.com; Zygomala 28; s/d/tr €40/55/65) More personality on the outside than the inside (the interiors are c 1980s) but it's in an attractive position in the old part of town.

★ Pension Marianna
HOTEL $$

(☑ 27520 24256; www.pensionmarianna.gr; Potamianou 9; s €50, d €65-75, tr €85, q €100 incl

BOUTIQUE HOTELS

Nafplio's streets burst with boutique hotels. These renovated former mansions vary in style, though most have four to eight (often cramped) rooms with contemporary, period or kitsch furnishings. Prices include cable TV. Note: all have steep internal stairs. We love the following:

Aetoma (☑ 27520 27373; www.nafplionhotel.com; Plateia Agios Spiridonos 2; d €80-120 incl breakfast; ❋ 🛜) Intimate and comfortable, with dark, heavy and stylish furnishings. Generous traditional breakfast.

Adiandi (☑ 27520 22073; www.hotel-adiandi.com; Othonos 31; r incl breakfast €70-110; ❋ 🛜) Rooms in this fun and upmarket place are quirkily decorated with artistic door bedheads and contemporary decor. A funky cafe-cum-breakfast-room is downstairs.

Amymone (☑ 27520 99477; www.amymone.gr; Othonos 39; r incl breakfast €70-105; @ 🛜) The sister hotel of Adiandi, where you have breakfast, this place is an interior designer's delight – funkily colourful and colourfully funky.

breakfast; 🅿 ❋ 🛜) For value and hospitality, it doesn't get better than this. The welcoming owner-hosts, the warm Zotos brothers, epitomise Greek *filoxenia* and serve up conviviality, travel advice and delicious breakfasts (comprising homemade produce where possible). The comfortable, squeaky-clean rooms open onto terraces where you can feast on the killer view from your hilltop position.

Heights come at a small cost – several flights of stairs. Parking is available on the road behind leading up to the fortress. Rates are €5 less per person without breakfast.

Grand Sarai
BOUTIQUE HOTEL **$$**
(☑ 27520 22563; www.grandsarainafplio.com; Fotomara & Potamianou 3; s €60-130, d €70-160) Nafplio's newest kid on the block is a beautifully renovated building that errs on modern interiors. It's sleek without being kitsch and sports blonde-wood floors and tasteful bathrooms. Also has a lift and a small bar. Delightful breakfasts using local produce are served in an intimate setting downstairs.

Hotel Perivoli
BOUTIQUE HOTEL **$$**
(☑ 27520 47905; www.hotelperivoli.com; Pirgiotika; r €120-130; ❋) Around 8.5km from Nafplio (follow signs to Pirgiotika), this boutique resort-style place has a stunning rural view, overlooking olive and citrus groves. The 12 sleek rooms have direct access to a pool and all the mod-cons. It has its own small restaurant; breakfasts serve up local produce. Minimum two-night stays June to September.

Hotel Grande Bretagne
LUXURY HOTEL **$$**
(☑ 27520 96200; www.grandebretagne.com.gr; Plateia Filellinon; s/d/tr incl breakfast from €95/130/145; ❋ 🛜) Nafplion elegance – this is a plush, traditionally styled period hotel, right in the heart of the waterfront-cafe action.

✖ Eating

Although full of reasonable eateries, Nafplio won't blow your culinary mind. Go beyond the tourist eateries along Staïkopoulou and you'll discover some surprises.

Carrefour (cnr Syngrou & Flessa) is the only central supermarket.

Antica Gelateria di Roma
GELATERIA **$**
(☑ 27520 23520; www.anticagelateria.gr; cnr Farmakopoulou & Komninou; snacks from €2) The only 'true' gelato shop in Nafplio, where Italian gelati maestros Marcello, Claudia or Monica Raffo greet you with: '*Bongiorno* – this is an *Italian* gelati shop!' Only natural and local products are used and it's all made on the premises.

In any case, you'll see and smell (and we'll bet, soon taste) the smorgasbord of the best (yes, best) traditional gelati outside Italy. The panini (rolls) are good for a picnic lunch, too.

Mezedopoleio O Noulis
MEZEDHES **$**
(☑ 27520 25541; Moutzouridou 22; mezedhes €4-10; ☺ lunch Mon-Sat Oct-Apr, lunch & dinner May-Sep) A tasty and fresh – if slightly pricy – range of mezedhes. Having said that, the tasting plate of 10 different morsels (€9) is a meal in itself.

Nafplios
TAVERNA **$**
(☑ 27520 97999; cnr Bouboublinas & Syngrou; mains €7-10; ☺ lunch & dinner) This unpretentious, buzzing place overlooks a car park.

Hearty dishes – all traditional – are served up from large pans.

To Omorfo Tavernaki   GREEK $
(☑ 27520 25944; Vasilissis Olgas 1; mains €8-15) Slightly smaller servings of homemade delights in a convivial restaurant adorned with antique oddments. The mezedhes plates are particularly good.

Alaloum   GREEK $$
(☑ 27520 29883; Papanikolaou 10; mains €10-18) Situated in a lovely spot overlooking a leafy square, Alaloum serves up excellent (and very generous portions of) Greek Mediterranean fare.

Fougaro   GREEK $$
(www.fougaro.gr; Asklipiou 98; mains €8-12) Cultural and coffee snobs should sniff out this place, a lovely cafe-restaurant-cum-cultural-space in one. There's a gift shop and a relaxing space set around a courtyard for lunch and dinner gourmet Greek eats. It's 3km from Nafplio in a converted factory, on the road to Epidavros. Look for the chimney ('fougaro').

Arapakos   SEAFOOD $$
(☑ 27520 27675; www.arapakos.gr; Bouboulinas 81; fish per 1kg €35-65) For fish lovers, this is the best spot to hook onto for seafood. Prices are by the kilogram, so be sure to check first.

🍸 Drinking & Nightlife

Wander the old town to cafe- and bar-hop the lively scene. You could start at **O Mavros Gatos** (Sofroni 1; ⊘ 8.30am-late), which has a DJ from 9pm, or hang out with creative stalwarts at **Cafe Rosso** (Komninou 5), where every tabletop is different, and then finish the evening in style at **3Sixty** (Papanikolaou

26), an ultra-smart cafe-bar-restaurant with an excellent wine cellar.

🛍 Shopping

Nafplio shopping is a delight, with boutiques and jewellery workshops and wonderful regional products such as worry beads, honey, wine and handicrafts.

Glykos Pirasmos   FOOD
(Plapouta 10) *The* place for delicious homemade cookies, baklava and *loukoumi* (Turkish delight) sweets.

Karonis   WINE
(☑ 27520 24446; www.karoniswineshop.gr; Amalias 5) Wine enthusiasts can find a fine selection of wines from all over the country, especially Nemean reds and spirits. Wine tastings offered.

Museum of the Komboloi   SOUVENIRS
(☑ 27520 21618; www.komboloi.gr; Staïkopoulou 25; adult/concession €3/free; ⊘ 9.30am-8pm, hrs change seasonally) This shop – with a private museum above – sells *komboloï* (worry beads), evil-eye charms and amulets.

Odyssey   BOOKS
(☑ 27520 23430; Plateia Syntagmatos) Stocks international newspapers, maps and a small selection of novels in English, French and German.

ℹ Information

Hospital (☑ 27520 361100; cnr Asklipiou & Poti)

National Bank of Greece (Plateia Syntagmatos) Has ATMs.

Post Office (cnr Syngrou & Sidiras Merarhias; ⊘ 7.30am-2pm Mon-Fri)

PEREGRINATIONS OF PAUSANIAS

Lonely Planet and its alternatives were beaten to the publishing of guidebooks by nearly 20 centuries. The traveller and geographer Pausanias wrote what is believed to be the first – and most definitive – 'guidebook' for tourists in the 2nd century AD. His work, *Description of Greece* (sometimes known as *Tour* or *Itinerary of Greece*), is a series of 10 volumes in which he describes most of Greece as seen at the time (between AD 143 and 161), covering the regions of Attica, Beotia, Phocis and Ozolian Locris, plus the regions that make up much of the Peloponnese: Corinthia, Lakonia, Messinia, Elia, Achaïa and Arkadia. Classical Greek scholars, historians and archaeologists regard it as an extremely important historical work for its insight into places, people, monuments and sites, as well as associated facts and legends. Pausanias is believed to be from Lydia in Asia Minor and travelled extensively throughout Greece, Macedonia, Italy and parts of Asia and Africa.

Staikos Tours (☑27520 27950; Bouboulinas 50) A helpful and reliable travel agent that is happy to answer general tourist enquiries. Also arranges ferry tickets.

To Kentrikou (Plateia Syntagmatos; ☉7.30am-late) A bar-internet spot where for the price of a drink or two you can happily browse away.

Tourist Police (☑27520 98727/8; Eleftherias 2)

ⓘ Getting There & Away

The **KTEL Argolis bus station** (☑27520 27323; www.ktel-argolidas.gr; Syngrou) has buses to Athens (€13.10, 2½ hours, hourly) via Corinth Isthmus (Peloponnese) KTEL bus station (€6.50, 1½ hours), as well as buses to Argos (€1.60, 30 minutes, half-hourly), Tolo (€1.60, 15 minutes, hourly), Epidavros (€2.60, 45 minutes, four daily, one Sunday), Mycenae (€2.60, one hour, two daily except Sunday), Kranidi (€8, two hours, three daily except weekends) and Galatas (€8.20, two hours, two daily except weekends). Other destinations include Tripoli (€6, 1½ hours, two daily).

ⓘ Getting Around

For taxis call ☑27520 24120 or head to the rank on Syngrou. Car-hire agencies include the following.

Avis (☑27520 24160; Bouboulinas 51)
Bounos Rent a Car (☑27520 24390; www.bounos-carrental.com; Syngrou)
Hermes Car Rental (☑27520 25308; www.hermestravel.gr; Sigrou 18)

Tiryns Τίρυνθα

Situated 4km from Nafplio, just to the east of the Nafplio–Argos road, is the impressive acropolis of **Tiryns** (☑27520 22657; adult/concession €3/2; ☉8am-7pm summer, to 3pm winter), an important and underrated Mycenaean acropolis and the apogee of Mycenaean architectural achievement, especially its massive walls. In parts they are 7m thick and, according to mythology, were built by the Cyclops.

Tiryns shares equal billing on the World Heritage list with Mycenae, although Tiryn's setting is less awe-inspiring. The layout of some of the ruins is easy to make out, and there are few crowds. As yet, the site has no signs or descriptions; it's worth buying a guidebook, such as *Tiryns* (by Dr Alkestis Papademetriou; €8), at the ticket office. While further excavations continue, visitors are limited to exploring the Upper and Lower Citadels. Make sure you ask about the location of the gallery, an impressively shaped

tunnel (you can view it from one end, but can't enter).

Any Nafplio–Argos bus can drop you outside the site.

Epidavros Επίδαυρος

In its day **Epidavros** (☑27530 22009; admission €6; ☉8am-8pm Apr-Oct, to 5pm Nov-Mar), 30km east of Nafplio, was famed and revered as far away as Rome as a place of miraculous healing. Visitors came great distances to this sanctuary of Asclepius (god of medicine) to seek a cure for their ailments. (Epidavros is sometimes referred to on signs as Sanctuary of Asklepios.)

Today visitors are more likely to flock to the site for its amazingly well-preserved theatre, which remains a venue during the Hellenic Festival for Classical Greek theatre (along with more modern plays, opera and music), first performed here up to 2000 years ago. The site occupies a glorious setting amid pine-clad hills. Not surprisingly, Epidavros is a protected World Heritage site.

If visiting Epidavros on your own by car, do not be confused by the sign to P Epidavros (Paleia Epidavros) – this means Ancient Epidavros. To confuse matters more, the so-called 'small theatre' used for some festival performances is located here; the 'large theatre' referred to on festival programs is at the main site, signed as Theatre of Edipavros.

History

Legend has it that Asclepius was the son of Apollo and Coronis. While giving birth to Asclepius, Coronis was struck by a thunderbolt and killed. Apollo took his son to Mt Pelion, where the physician Chiron instructed the boy in the healing arts.

Apollo was worshipped at Epidavros in Mycenaean and Archaic times, but by the 4th century BC he had been superseded by his son. Epidavros became acknowledged as the birthplace of Asclepius. Although the afflicted worshipped Asclepius at sanctuaries throughout Greece, the two most important were at Epidavros and on the island of Kos. The fame of the sanctuary spread, and when a plague raged in Rome, Livy and Ovid came to Epidavros to seek help.

It is believed that licks from snakes were one of the curative practices at the sanctuary. Asclepius is normally shown with a serpent, which – by renewing its skin – symbolises rejuvenation. Other treatments provided at the sanctuary involved diet instruction, herbal medicines and occasionally even surgery. The sanctuary also served as an entertainment venue and every four years, during the Festival of Asclepieia, Epidavros hosted dramas and athletic competitions.

◉ Sights

Theatre of Epidavros   HISTORIC SITE

Today it's the 3rd-century theatre, not the sanctuary, that pulls the crowds to Epidavros. It is one of the best-preserved Classical Greek structures, renowned for its amazing acoustics; a coin dropped in the centre can be heard from the highest seat. Built of limestone, the theatre seats up to 14,000 people. Its entrance is flanked by restored **Corinthian pilasters**. It's used for performances of ancient Greek drama during the annual Hellenic Festival (p95).

Sanctuary   RUIN

The ruins of the sanctuary are less crowded than the theatre. In the south is the huge **katagogeion**, a hostelry for pilgrims and patients. To the west is the large **banquet hall** in which the Romans built an **odeum**. It was here that the Festival of Asclepieia took place. Opposite is the **stadium**, venue for the festival's athletic competitions. This is one of several areas under reconstruction; at the time of writing one side was completed.

To the north are the foundations of the **Temple of Asclepius** and next to them is the **abaton**. The therapies practised here seemed to have depended on the influence of the mind upon the body. It is believed that patients were given a pep talk by a priest on the powers of Asclepius, then put to sleep in the *abaton* to dream of a visitation by the god. The dream would hold the key to the healing process.

East is the **Sanctuary of Egyptian Gods**, which indicates that the cult of Asclepius was an adaptation of the cult of Imhotep, worshipped in Egypt for his healing powers. To the southwest of the Temple of Asclepius are the remains of the **tholos** (built 360–320 BC), the function of which is unknown.

Set among the green foothills of Mt Arahneo, the air redolent with herbs and pine trees, it's easy to see how the sanctuary would have had a beneficial effect upon the ailing.

At the time of writing, some of the buildings, including the *tholos* and *abaton,* were in the process of being partially reconstruct-ed. This entails adding sections of columns and, in some places, re-creating parts of ruins in their entirety.

Museum   MUSEUM

The museum, between the sanctuary and the theatre, houses statues, stone inscriptions recording miraculous cures, surgical instruments, votive offerings and partial reconstructions of the sanctuary's once-elaborate *tholos.* Unfortunately, it's light on in the way of written information but some of the statuary and the chunks of marble do hint at the sanctuary's former status. After the theatre, the *tholos* is considered to have been the site's most impressive building and fragments of beautiful, intricately carved reliefs from its ceiling are also displayed. Most of the statues are copies (the real ones are in the National Archaeological Museum in Athens).

✲✲ Festivals & Events

Epidavros Festival   THEATRE

(✆ 27530 22026; www.greekfestival.gr/en; ◷ 9am-2pm & 5-8pm Mon-Thu, 9.30am-9.30pm Fri & Sat summer) The Epidavros Theatre is the venue for performances staged (with both modern theatre and Ancient Greek dramas) during the annual Epidavros Festival in July and August (exact dates vary), part of the larger cultural Hellenic Festival. Tickets can be bought in Epidavros at the site office or from the Hellenic Festival box office (p95) in Athens. Prices vary according to seating, and student discounts are available. There are special bus services available from Athens (around €23, two hours) and Nafplio (around €8, 45 minutes).

🛏 Sleeping & Eating

There is a choice of restaurants on the main street of Ligourio, several kilometres from Epidavros.

Hotel Avaton   HOTEL $

(✆ 27530 22178; s/d/tr incl breakfast €45/55/65; 🅿 ✳) If you're planning an early morning visit to the site, this small, clean and modern hotel is the best accommodation option. It's just 1km away, at the junction of the roads to Kranidi and the site of Epidavros.

❶ Getting There & Away

There are buses from Nafplio to Epidavros (€3, 45 minutes, four daily except Sundays) and two to three daily buses to Athens from nearby Ligourio (around €13, 2½ hours). **Taxis** (☎ 27530 23322) from Ligourio cost around €6; we don't recommended walking to Epidavros from here, as it's along a main road.

Southwest Argolis

Very few travellers take the time to venture to the southwestern heel of the Argolis peninsula, centred on the agricultural service town of **Kranidi**, 90km southeast of Nafplio. The region is famous for its pomegranates, which appreciate the mild winter temperatures around here. These spectacular ruby-red fruits ripen in November.

The small resorts of **Porto Heli**, 4km south of Kranidi, and **Ermioni**, 4km east of Kranidi, offer convenient connections to the Saronic Gulf islands of Hydra and Spetses.

About 1km west of the village of Didyma, don't miss the **Didyma Caves** (admission free) FREE, two extraordinary sinkholes. The caves collapsed thousands of years ago, leaving large crater-like holes. One hides a sensational surprise – a tiny Byzantine church, constructed under a crevice. The caves are well signposted.

❶ Getting There & Away

BOAT

Hydrofoils change each season; at the time of writing **Hellenic Seaways** (☎ 27540 32408; www.hellenicseaways.gr) was running the show. Normally, regular boats depart from Porto Heli to Piraeus via Spetses and Hydra, and from Ermioni to Piraeus via Hydra. Caïques shuttle between Galatas and Poros (€1, five minutes; €1.50 between midnight and 5am).

BUS

There are **bus services** (☎ 27540 21237) between Kranidi and Nafplio (€9, two hours, three daily except Sunday), and local buses from Kranidi to Ermioni (€1.85, 10 minutes, one to two daily) and Porto Heli (€1.85, 10 minutes, one to two daily).

ARKADIA ΑΡΚΑΔΙΑ

The picturesque rural prefecture of Arkadia occupies much of the central Peloponnese. Its name evokes images of grassy meadows, forested mountains, gurgling streams and shady grottoes. According to mythology, it was a favourite haunt of Pan.

Almost encircled by mountain ranges, Arkadia was remote enough in ancient times to remain largely untouched by the battles and intrigues of the rest of Greece, and was the only region of the Peloponnese not conquered by the Dorians. The region is dotted with crumbling medieval villages, remote monasteries and Frankish castles, and is popular among outdoor-loving visitors. It also has 100km or so of rugged and unspoilt coastline on the Argolic Gulf, running south from the pretty town of Kiveri to Leonidio.

❶ Getting There & Away

KTEL Arcadia in Tripoli is the departure point for buses to Stemnitsa (€5, one hour, one daily Monday to Friday), Dimitsana (€6.50, 1½ hours, one daily) and Andritsena (€8.60, 1½ hours, one daily) via the turn-off to Karitena.

This office also handles buses to Athens (via Corinth Isthmus, €15, hourly). There are also buses to Olympia (€12.40, one daily), Pyrgos (€14, one daily), Nafplio (€6.70, two daily) and Patra (€16.20, one to two daily). The **bus stop** (☎ 27102 42086) on Lagopati handles departures to Sparta and Kalamata.

Central Arkadia

The area to the west of Tripoli is a tangle of medieval villages, precipitous ravines and narrow roads that wind their way through the valleys of the Menalon Mountains. This is the heart of the Arkadia prefecture, and you'll find it's an area with some of the most breathtaking scenery in the Peloponnese. The region is high above sea level and nights

BOAT SERVICES FROM SOUTHWEST ARGOLIS

DESTINATION	PORT	TIME	FARE	FREQUENCY
Hydra	Ermioni	20-40min	€9.50	3-4 daily
Hydra	Porto Heli	1hr	€15	3-4 daily
Poros	Methana	30min	€4.30	1 daily
Spetses*	Porto Heli	15min	€5.50	3-4 daily
Spetses*	Ermioni	20-30min	€7.50	2-3 daily

*high-speed service

can be chilly, even in summer. Snow is common in winter.

Your own transport is highly recommended here, with public transport to the three most important villages – Karitena, Stemnitsa and Dimitsana – doable but inconvenient.

Stemnitsa   Στεμνίτσα

POP 200

Stemnitsa (stem-*nee*-tsah), 16km north of Karitena, is a striking and beautiful village of stone houses and Byzantine churches. There are several monasteries in the area in the Lousios Gorge along the riverbank to/from the site of **Ancient Gortys**.

The town boasts a small **folk art museum** (with irregular opening times) and a silversmiths' school. There are an incredible 40 churches in and around the hills vicinity. Ask around for the keys to the central ones.

🛏 Sleeping & Eating

Sarakiniotis Rooms   PENSION $
(☑ 6974451200; www.sarakiniotis.gr; s/d/tr €45/55/65; ❋) Among the town's few budget options are these basic, slightly dark rooms, though they're not great value.

★ **Mpelleiko**   B&B $$
(☑ 6976607967; www.mpelleiko.gr; s/d/tr incl breakfast €65/75/85; ☎) Superior in design and with a lofty location, this superbly renovated house is perched behind the village and is by far the most original and beautiful of all sleeping options. The ultra-hospitable and knowledgeable English-speaking owner, Nena, has converted her family home (dating from 1650) into a stylish, contemporary guesthouse. You can even sleep in the former 'donkey basement'.

Breakfast includes homemade, organic produce and is served in a beautiful room with an open fireplace. For directions, enquire at the jam shop at the southern end of town signified by a 'B&B' sign.

Xenonas Tsarbou   BOUTIQUE HOTEL $$
(☑ 27950 81406; www.xenonas-tsarbou.gr; d incl breakfast from €70; ℗ ☎) This slick-feeling place is a little incongruous in its converted historic stone building. Slightly cramped but smart rooms with gold and velvet trimmings. The ground floor boasts a cosy bar with fireplace.

I Stemnitsa   TAVERNA $
(☑ 27950 81371; mains €4-14; ⊘ lunch & dinner) It may be the only taverna open year-round in Stemnitsa, but you could do worse. Tables are under giant brollies and good, honest (if slighly repetitive) dishes are on offer. The local butcher owns the establishment, so expect quality, hearty cuts of meat.

❶ Getting There & Away

There is one bus each weekday to/from Tripoli (€4.10, one hour). The bus to Tripoli heads to Dimitsana (€5). A taxi to Dimitsana costs around €10, Podromos (walking starting point) €15, Ancient Gortys €25 and the Monastery of Filosofos €20. Times change seasonally.

Dimitsana   Δημητσάνα

POP 340

Built amphitheatrically on two hills at the beginning of the Lousios Gorge, Dimitsana (dih-mi-*tsah*-nah), 11km north of Stem-

---

GORGE YOURSELF

Hiking

Hiking is a popular activity in these magnificent surroundings. There are some splendid walks along the **Lousios Gorge**; the most accessible departure points are from Stemnitsa or Dimitsana. Walks vary from one hour to long (and hilly) day trips, where you can hike the entire length of the gorge, taking in monasteries including Prodomou and New and Old Philosophou. Other walks extend beyond the gorge to mountain villages. A range of walks is outlined in the excellent publication *Walker's Map of the River Lousios Valley* (€7.50), available at the Open-Air Water Power Museum (p149) in Dimitsana.

Rafting & Kayaking

Based in the village of Dimitsana, **Trekking Hellas of Arcadia** (☑ 6974459753, 27910 25978; www.trekkinghellas.gr) offers various activities, including white-water rafting (€50 to €80) on the Lousios and Alfios Rivers and hiking along the gorge (€20 to €50). Minimum rates apply.

Caution: river activities must not be taken lightly. Fatal accidents can and do occur.

WORTH A TRIP

SUSTAINABLE FOOD SOJOURN

All foodies should head to Zerzova (☑ 6932847358, 27950 31753; Panaghia; mains €6-15; ☺ lunch & dinner Fri-Mon Sep-May) ✆, a tiny eatery located 14km southwest of Dimitsana. Why? It ticks all the right boxes. Sustainable practices? Tick – the husband-and-wife team collect all wild herbs and cultivate their own produce. Home cooking? Tick – even Greek grandmothers are happy to come here. Traditional? Tick again – it's in a lovely old building with a cellar below. In a village with only seven residents, crowds nevertheless flock here for this place's simple charm (for it is simple)...and much more.

nitsa, is a delightful medieval village. This small place played a significant role in the country's struggle for self-determination. Its Greek school, founded in 1764, was an important spawning ground for the ideas leading to the uprisings against the Turks. Its students included Bishop Germanos of Patra and Patriarch Gregory V, who was hanged by the Turks in retaliation for the massacre in Tripoli. The village also had a number of gunpowder factories and a branch of the secret Filiki Eteria (Friendly Society), where Greeks met to discuss the revolution.

◉ Sights

Open-Air Water Power Museum — MUSEUM
(☑ 27950 31630; www.piop.gr; adult €3; ☺ 10am-6pm Wed-Mon Mar-Oct, to 5pm Wed-Mon Nov-Feb) It may sound of marginal interest but this excellent little museum offers an illuminating insight into the region's pre-industrial past. It occupies the old Agios Yiannis mill complex, 1.5km south of town (signposted), where a spring-fed stream once supplied power for a succession of mills spread down the hillside.

⛏ Sleeping & Eating

Amanites — BOUTIQUE HOTEL $$
(☑ 27950 31090; www.amanites.gr; r €80-100, weekends €120; P ☎) This lovely place, a converted historic home, has seven elegant rooms with heavy drapes and tasteful fabrics. Four rooms have front-facing balconies, others a kitchenette. Delightful English-speaking owner. Prices are considerably lower outside high season (winter).

Tsiapa Rooms to Rent — PENSION $$
(☑ 27950 31583; www.xenonastsiapas.gr; d €60; ☎) These simple but so-clean-you-could-eat-off-the-floor rooms also boast fridges and hotplates. The communal living room has a fireplace – perfect for a cold evening.

There is little to distinguish the village tavernas – all serve reasonable fare, such as rooster in red wine and *fasoladha* (bean soup).

ⓘ Getting There & Away

There are one to two buses each weekday from Tripoli to Dimitsana (€5, 1½ hours) and one each weekday from Dimitsana to Tripoli. A taxi to Stemnitsa costs €10, to Monastery of Filosofos €15, and to Ancient Gortys €25.

Kynouria   Κυνουρία

Kynouria is the coastal region of Arkadia. It covers a narrow strip of territory that stretches south from the tiny village of Kiveri, 41km east of Tripoli, to Kosmas, perched high in the Parnonas Mountains. Much of the land is incredibly rugged, with a narrow coastal plain and very little fertile ground.

In ancient times the region was contested by Argos and Sparta – the Argives held sway in the north and the Spartans controlled the south. The easiest access is from Argos.

Leonidio   Λεωνίδιο

POP 3200

Leonidio, 76km south of Argos, has a dramatic setting at the mouth of the Badron Gorge. The village is famous for its Tsakonian aubergines (eggplants) and summer **Aubergine Festival**. Its tiny Plateia 25 Martiou is an archetypal, unspoilt, whitewashed Greek village square. If you are lucky, you might find an elder who still speaks Tsakonika, a highly distinctive dialect dating back to the time of ancient Sparta.

There are some reasonably pleasant beaches to be found at the nearby seaside village of Plaka, 5km from Leonidio. If this tiny fishing port takes your fancy, you can dig in for the night at **Hotel Dionysos** (☑ 6970804050, 27570 23455; s €30-35, d & tr €45-50; ❄). All four tavernas here can be recommended for their seafood and traditional offerings.

WORTH A TRIP

KARITENA   ΚΑΡΙΤΑΙΝΑ

If tiny medieval villages are your thing, then it's worth popping into Karitena (kar-eet-eh-nah), a tiny settlement that sits high above the Megalopoli–Andritsena road. You can climb the stepped path up to the 13th-century Frankish castle, perched atop a massive rock. En route is the delightful Byzantine church, **Agios Nikolaos**. The castle was captured by Greek forces under Kolokotronis early in the War of Independence and became a key stronghold as the war unfolded.

Before the advent of the euro, Karitena was known as the home of the wonderful arched stone bridge over the Alfios River that adorned the 5000 drachma note. The old bridge now sits beneath a large modern concrete bridge.

One daily bus plies the route between Karitena and Tripoli (€6, one hour) via Megalopoli. One bus continues to Andritsena (€2.60) – check the schedule at Café Vrenthi. (Note: some buses arrive/depart from the crossroads below the village, from where it's an arduous walk to the village.)

There are buses up and down the coast to/from Argos (€8, 2¼ hours, two daily) and Tripoli (€9.20, 2½ hours, two weekdays, one on weekends). In summer, buses head between Plaka and Leonidio (€1.60, 10 minutes). The KTEL bus station is at the **Café Bar 2Porto** (☑ 27570 22255; Thioporto).

South of Leonidio

The road south from Leonidio over the Parnonas Mountains to the village of Geraki in Lakonia, 48km away, is one of the most scenic in the Peloponnese. For the first 12km, the road snakes west up the **Badron Gorge**, climbing slowly away from the river until at times the water is no more than a speck of silver far below. The road then leaves the Badron and climbs rapidly towards Kosmas on dramatic hairpin bends that make the Monaco Formula One circuit seem like an airstrip.

Just before the top of the climb, there's a sealed road to the left leading to **Moni Panagias Elonis**, a remarkable little monastery perched precariously on the mountainside. Visitors are welcome, provided they are suitably dressed.

It's another 14km from the monastery to the peaceful, beautiful mountain village of **Kosmas**. There are several sleeping options here, including **Selinounta Studios** (☑ 6979001030; www.selinounta.gr; Central Sq, Kosmas; s/d/tr/q €50/55/60), where you can watch the village world go by from one of five studios (with cooking facilities) housed in a beautiful stone building. Ask at the shop next door (a little English is spoken). Even if you don't stay overnight, it's worth trying the town speciality (goat) at a taverna beneath the huge plane trees in the square.

After Kosmas the road descends – more gently this time – to the village of **Geraki**. A brief pause is warranted to visit the quaint churches and to see the locals at play in the busy square. From here you can head 40km west to Sparta, or continue south through Skala, Molai and Sikia, also in Lakonia, to Monemvasia.

Aside from one weekly bus (€3, Wednesday), there is no public transport between Leonidio and Kosmas.

LAKONIA   ΛΑΚΩΝΙΑ

The region of Lakonia occupies almost identical boundaries to the powerful mountain-skirted kingdom ruled by King Menelaus in Mycenaean times. It is home to legends, including the city of Sparta and the spectacular ruins of Mystras, the Byzantine Empire's last stronghold.

Dominating the landscape are two huge mountain ranges, the Taÿgetos Mountains in the west and the Parnonas Mountains in the east. These taper away to create the central and eastern fingers of the Peloponnese.

English speakers can thank the Lakonians for the word 'laconic'.

Sparta   Σπάρτη

POP 16,200

The gridlike streets of modern Sparta (spartee) are in line with its ancient precursor's image of discipline, although fortunately not deprivation. It is an easy-going, if unremarkable, town that lies at the heart of the Evrotas Valley, surrounded by olive and citrus groves, while the Taÿgetos Mountains, snowcapped until early June, provide a stunning backdrop to the west.

The town was refounded in 1834 on the orders of King Otto, who had just made the decision to move his court from Nafplio to Athens.

Mindful of history, Otto and his court felt that since Athens was to be rebuilt to reflect its former glory, so too should Sparta. There's a pleasant-enough square and a fascinating oil museum, and a few ruins attesting to its ancient pre-eminence. Most visitors head to the nearby site of Mystras, but it's worth spending at least a few hours here.

◎ Sights

Ancient Sparta
RUIN

A wander around ancient Sparta's meagre ruins bears testimony to the accuracy of Thucydides' prophecy in *The Histories*: 'If the city of the Lacedaemonians were destroyed, and only its temples and the foundations of its buildings left, remote posterity would greatly doubt whether their power were ever equal to their renown'.

For despite a grand sense of history, the ruins are not like counterparts around Greece, being thinly spread across a site at the northern end of town. It's worth going here, however, for the impressive views of the snowcapped Taÿgetos Mountains.

To get here, head to the **King Leonidas statue** that stands belligerently at the northern end of Paleologou. West of here, signs point the way to the acropolis.

Within the site, signs point left (west) through olive groves to the 2nd- or 3rd-century-BC **ancient theatre**, the site's most discernible ruin.

The main cobbled path leads north to the **acropolis** (some of which is fenced off), passing the **Byzantine Church of Christ the Saviour** on the way to the hilltop **Sanctuary of Athena Halkioitou**, an ancient temple. Some

Sparta

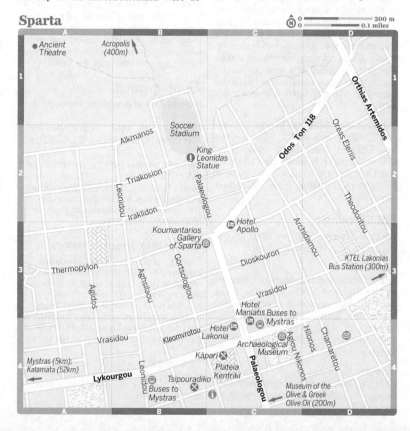

PELOPONNESE SPARTA

of the most important finds in the town's archaeological museum were unearthed here. Alternatively, you can see and approach the theatre from here.

Archaeological Museum MUSEUM
(☑ 27310 28575; cnr Lykourgou & Agiou Nikonos; adult €2; ☺ 8am-3pm Tue-Sun) Sparta's old-style archaeological museum sits in a beautiful park setting with a fountain and an orange grove. Its artefacts are from Sparta's illustrious past, including votive sickles that Spartan boys dedicated to Artemis Orthia, heads and torsos of various deities, a statue thought to be the great King Leonidas, and masks and grave stelae. Mosaics from Hellenistic and Roman Sparta are also on show.

Museum of the Olive & Greek Olive Oil MUSEUM
(☑ 27310 89315; www.piop.gr; Othonos Amalias 129; adult/concession €3/1.50; ☺ 10am-6pm Mar–mid-Oct, 10am-5pm mid-Oct–Feb Wed-Mon) This stunningly designed museum shows and tells you everything you could want to know about olives. The high-quality explanations in English trace the history of the olive from its first appearance in the Mediterranean to the modern day. There are some magnificent antique olive presses, as well as a series of working models that demonstrate changes in pressing technology. The downstairs cafe serves good coffee.

Koumantarios Gallery of Sparta GALLERY
(☑ 27310 81557; Paleologou 123; ☺ 8am-3pm Wed-Mon) `FREE` An annex of the National Art Gallery, the quaint Koumantarios art gallery holds a permanent collection of around 40 paintings on a rotating basis, plus temporary exhibitions.

🛏 Sleeping

The closest campgrounds are 2km from central Sparta, or near Mystras village.

Hotel Lakonia HOTEL $
(☑ 27310 28951; www.lakoniahotel.gr; Palaeologou 89; s/d incl breakfast €40/55; ❄ 🛜) The 32 cutting-edge rooms best suit sleek geeks, and are far from spartan. Two-tone chairs, spot lighting and portal access are a few of the mod cons. Double-glazed windows cut out any street noise.

Hotel Apollo HOTEL $
(☑ 27310 22491; fax 27310 23936; Thermopylon 84; s/d/tr €30/35/40) A reasonable, plain but spruce budget option.

Hotel Maniatis HOTEL $$
(☑ 27310 22665; www.maniatishotel.gr; Paleologou 72-76; s/d incl breakfast €80/100; ❄ 🛜) Light and pleasant rooms have more designer shapes than a NYC contemporary-design exhibition, and the service is efficient. The upmarket Zeys restaurant (mains €7 to €17) is attached.

Eating

Tsipouradiko TAVERNA $
(☑ 27310 83585; Evangelistrias 50; €6-10; ☺ lunch Mon-Sat, dinner daily) This atmospheric spot has been renovated to look like an old-style shop and *tsipouradiko* – traditional barrels, china pieces and old cans line the walls. There's an amazing backyard and all sorts of nooks and crannies. As for the food? Traditional *mayirefta* (ready-cooked meals) and grills. A must.

Kápari MEDITERRANEAN $$
(Caper; ☑ 2731 300520; www.kaparirestaurant.gr; mains €5-15) A refreshing change to Sparta's tired taverna scene, this clean, friendly spot does some great Mediterranean dishes – lovely salads, excellent seafood and grills – with modern presentation (but that does not mean minimalist servings. Far from it.).

ℹ Information

National Bank of Greece (cnr Paleologou & Dioskouron)

Police (☑ 27310 24852; Evangelistrias 83-91)

Post Office (Archidamou 10; ☺ 7.30am-2pm Mon-Fri)

Revanche Internet Cafe (Gortsologou 51; per hr €2; ☺ 9am-late)

Sparta Tourism (☑ 27310 28166; www.sparti. gr; Evangelistrias 83-91; ☺ 8am-3pm Mon-Fri) This small office has helpful staff; shares an office with the local police.

ℹ Getting There & Away

Sparta's well-organised **KTEL Lakonia bus station** (☑ 27310 26441; cnr Lykourgou & Thivronos) has buses to Athens (€19.50, 3¼ hours, nine daily) via Corinth (two hours), and buses to Gythio (€4.30, one hour, six daily), Neapoli (€14.20, three hours, three daily), Tripoli (€5.40, one hour, nine daily), Geraki (€4, 45 minutes, three daily) and Monemvasia (€10, two hours, four daily).

Travelling to Kalamata (€3.20, one hour, one or two daily) involves changing buses at Artemisia (€3.20, 40 minutes) on the Messinian side of the Langada Pass.

Departures to the Mani peninsula include buses to Gerolimenas (€10.30, 2¼ hours, three daily), Areopoli (€6.90, two hours, three daily) and a 9am service to the Diros Caves (€8); the return times change.

Mystras   Μυστράς

The captivating ruins of churches, libraries, strongholds and palaces in the fortress town of Mystras (miss-*trahss*), a World Heritage–listed site, spill from a spur of the Taÿgetos Mountains 7km west of Sparta. It's among the most important historical sites in the Peloponnese. This is where the Byzantine Empire's richly artistic and intellectual culture made its last stand before an invading Ottoman army, almost 1000 years after its foundation.

Note: most facilities for the traveller are in Mystras village, 1km or so below the ancient site of Mystras.

History

The Frankish leader Guillaume de Villehardouin built the fortress in 1249. When the Byzantines won back the Morea from the Franks, Emperor Michael VIII Palaeologos made Mystras its capital and seat of government. Settlers from the surrounding plains began to move here, seeking refuge from the invading Slavs. From this time until Dimitrios surrendered to the Turks in 1460, a despot of Morea (usually a son or brother of the ruling Byzantine emperor) lived and reigned at Mystras.

While the empire plunged into decline elsewhere, Mystras enjoyed a renaissance under the despots. Gemistos Plethon (1355–1452) founded a school of humanistic philosophy here and his enlightened ideas, including the revival of the teachings of Plato and Pythagoras, attracted intellectuals from all corners of Byzantium. After the Turks occupied Mystras, Plethon's pupils

Mystras

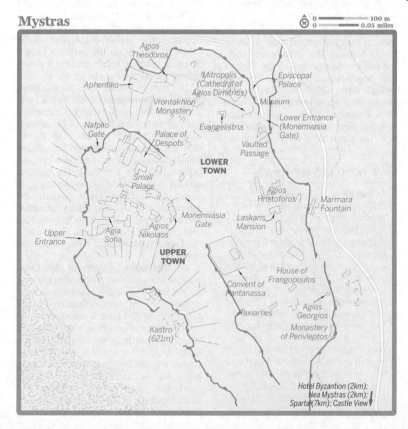

N   0 ————— 100 m
0 ————— 0.05 miles

Agios Theodoros
Mitropolis (Cathedral of Agios Dimitrios)
Episcopal Palace
Aphentiko
Vrontokhion Monastery
Museum
Nafplio Gate
Evangelistria
Lower Entrance (Monemvasia Gate)
Palace of Despots
Vaulted Passage
LOWER TOWN
Small Palace
Agios Hristoforos
Marmara Fountain
Monemvasia Gate
Laskaris Mansion
Upper Entrance
Agia Sofia
Agios Nikolaos
UPPER TOWN
House of Frangopoulos
Convent of Pantanassa
Agios Georgios
Taxiarhes
Monastery of Perivleptos
Kastro (621m)
Hotel Byzantion (2km); Nea Mystras (2km); Sparta (7km); Castle View

moved to Rome and Florence, where they made a significant contribution to the Italian Renaissance. Art and architecture also flourished, as seen in the town's splendid buildings and frescoes.

Mystras declined under Turkish rule, but thrived again after the Venetians captured it in 1687 and developed a flourishing silk industry, with the population swelling to 40,000. The Turks recaptured it in 1715 and from then it was downhill all the way; the Russians burnt it in 1770, the Albanians in 1780 and Ibrahim Pasha torched what was left in 1825. By the time of Independence it was a largely abandoned ruin. Much restoration has taken place since the 1950s (and continues to this day) and in 1989 it was declared a World Heritage site.

⊙ Sights

Mystras   RUIN
(☏ 23315 25363; adult €5; ⊙ 8.30am-5.30pm Mon-Sat, to 3pm Sun, sometimes longer in summer)

➡ **Kastro & Upper Town**

From opposite the upper entrance ticket office, a path (signposted '*kastro*') leads up to the fortress. The fortress was built by the Franks and extended by the Turks. The path descends from the ticket office leading to **Agia Sofia**, which served as the palace church, and where some frescoes survive. Steps descend from here to a T-junction.

A left turn leads to the **Nafplio Gate**. Near the gate, but closed for restoration at

---

ℹ TACKLING MYSTRAS

At least half a day is needed to do justice to the ruins of Mystras. Wear sensible shoes and bring plenty of water. The site is divided into three sections – the *kastro* (the fortress on the summit), the *hora* (upper town) and the *kato hora* (lower town). You can approach the ruins from either direction – top to bottom or vice versa (both options are quite strenuous).

If you have transport and start at the top and walk down, you'll need to return to your car at the end of your visit – or do the top half first, then drive to the bottom and do the lower section (this involves walking uphill; you can use the same ticket to re-enter). If you catch a taxi from Sparta, it's best to head to the top and wander downhill.

---

the time of writing, is the huge **Palace of Despots**, a complex of several buildings constructed at different times.

From the palace, a winding, cobbled path leads down to the **Monemvasia Gate**, the entrance to the lower town.

➡ **Lower Town**

Through the Monemvasia Gate, turn right for the well-preserved, 14th-century **Convent of Pantanassa**. This features a beautifully ornate stone-carved facade and is still maintained by nuns, Mystras' only inhabitants. It's an elaborate, perfectly proportioned building – never overstated. The exquisite, richly coloured, 15th-century frescoes here are among the finest examples of late-Byzantine art. Look out for the tiny stamped silver and gold votive offerings beneath the large icon of the Virgin. You'll find images of eyes, ears, legs, arms, breasts and even houses stamped onto these small tablets, depending on the (usually health-related) problems for which the faithful are hoping for supernatural help. There is a wonderful view of the pancake-flat and densely cultivated plain of Lakonia from the columned terrace on the northern facade. The nuns ask that, before entering, you cover bare legs with the cloths provided.

The path continues down to the **Monastery of Perivleptos**, built into a rock. Inside, the 14th-century frescoes, preserved virtually intact, equal those of Pantanassa. The church has a very high dome and in the centre is the Pantokrator (the Byzantine depiction of Christ as the universal, all-powerful ruler), surrounded by the Apostles, and the Virgin flanked by two angels.

As you continue down towards the Mitropolis, you will pass **Agios Georgios**, one of Mystras' many private chapels. Further down, and above the path on the left, is the **Laskaris Mansion**, a typical Byzantine house.

The **Mitropolis** (Cathedral of Agios Dimitrios) is a complex of buildings enclosed by a high wall. The original church was built in the 1200s, but was greatly altered in the 15th century. The church stands in an attractive courtyard surrounded by stoae and balconies. Its impressive ecclesiastical ornaments and furniture include a marble iconostasis, an intricately carved wooden throne and a marble slab in the floor featuring a two-headed eagle (symbol of Byzantium) located exactly on the site where Emperor Constantine XI was crowned. The church also has some fine frescoes. The adjoining small but modern **museum** houses some quirky pieces, including female hair, buttons and embroidery, and other everyday items of Mystras' inhabitants.

Beyond the Mitropolis is the **Vrontokhion Monastery**. This was once the wealthiest monastery of Mystras, the focus of cultural activities and the burial place of the despots. Of its two churches, **Agios Theodoros** and **Aphentiko**, the latter is the most impressive, with striking frescoes.

Outside the lower entrance to Mystras is a *kantina* (mobile cafe) selling snacks and drinks.

🛏 Sleeping & Eating

In addition to the following options, there are some upmarket guesthouses around the village and a couple of cafes and tavernas.

Hotel Byzantion   HOTEL **$$**
(✉ 27310 83309; www.byzantionhotel.gr; s/d/tr €40/50/65; P ❄ @ ☎) Located in the centre of the modern village of Nea Mystras, this appealing 26-room option is an alternative to sleeping in Sparta. Management is helpful, there's a delightful garden in the rear, and the bright rooms have balconies offering arresting valley or mountain views. It's about 1km from the site.

Castle View   CAMPGROUND **$**
(✉ 27310 83303; www.castleview.gr; camp sites per adult/tent/car €6/4/4, 2-person bungalow €25; ☉ Apr-Oct; ☎ ☎) This campground receives positive reader feedback. It's about 1km before Nea Mystras village and set among olive trees. Buses will stop here if you ask.

ℹ Getting There & Away

To get a bus to Mystras (€1.60, 30 minutes, seven daily) from Sparta, you can do so at the stop next to the OTE building on Lykourgou, or at the stop on Leonidou. Alternatively, a radio taxi from Sparta to Mystras' lower entrance (Xenia Restaurant) costs around €10, slightly more to the upper entrance.

Monemvasia   Μονεμβάσια

Vast, imposing, spectacular Monemvasia (mo-nem-vah-*see*-ah or mo-nem-*vah*-see-ah) is the Greek equivalent to France's Mont Saint-Michel. This perfect fortress is an iceberg-like slab of rock moored off the coast, with sheer cliffs rising hundreds of metres from the sea, and a single, highly defendable causeway.

These days Monemvasia incorporates both the rock, whose medieval village is enclosed within the walls of the rock's *kastro*, plus the modern mainland village of Gefyra just across the causeway. In summer both places brim with visitors (only around 7 people live in the *kastro*). Fortunately the extraordinary visual impact of the medieval village in particular – and the delights of exploring it – override the effects of mass tourism. The staunch communist poet Yiannis Ritsos was born here.

From Gefyra you can see little of the fortress. But cross the causeway and follow the road that curves around the side of the rock and you will come to the official entrance, a narrow tunnel in a massive fortifying wall. The tunnel is L-shaped, so the magical town is concealed until you emerge into its narrow artery (with a maze to explore) on the other side.

History

The rock island of Monemvasia was part of the mainland until it was cut off by an earthquake in AD 375. Its name means 'single entry' (*moni* – single, *emvasia* – entry), as there is only one way into the medieval town.

During the 6th century, barbarian incursions forced inhabitants of the surrounding area to retreat to this natural rock fortress. By the 13th century it had become the principal commercial centre of Byzantine Morea, complementing Mystras, the spiritual centre. It was famous throughout Europe for its highly praised Malvasia-grape wine.

The Franks, Venetians and Turks all invaded in the following centuries. During the War of Independence its Turkish inhabitants were massacred after their surrender, following a three-month siege.

⊙ Sights

Kastro – Medieval Town   HISTORIC AREA
'You can find everything you want in this city – except water', observed an 18th-century Turkish traveller. In fact, the Kastro is almost wholly surrounded by ocean, while precious fresh water was stored in underground cisterns, many of which have been converted into rooms within hotels.

These days, the narrow, cobbled main street is lined with souvenir shops and tavernas, flanked by winding stairways that

WORTH A TRIP

LANGADA PASS   ΟΡΕΙΝΗ ΔΙΑΒΑΣΗ ΛΑΓΚΑΔΑ

If you have time and your own wheels, the 59km Sparta–Kalamata road is one of the most stunning, if time consuming and winding, routes in Greece, crossing the Taÿgetos Mountains by way of the Langada Pass.

The climb begins in the village of **Trypi**, 9km west of Sparta, where the road enters the dramatic **Langada Gorge**. To the north is the site where the ancient Spartans left babies too weak or deformed to become good soldiers to die (see the boxed text, p679).

The road then follows the course of the Langada River before climbing sharply through a series of hairpin bends to emerge in a sheltered valley. This is a good spot to stop for a stroll among the plane trees along the riverbank. The road then climbs steeply once more, to the high point of 1524m, crossing the boundary from Lakonia into Messinia on the way. The descent to Kalamata is equally dramatic.

weave between a complex network of stone houses with walled gardens and courtyards. The main street leads to the central square and the **Cathedral of Christ in Chains**, dating from the 13th century. Opposite is the **Church of Agios Pavlos**, built in 956. Further along the main street is the **Church of Myrtidiotissa**, virtually in ruins, but still with a small altar and a defiantly flickering candle. Overlooking the sea is the whitewashed 16th-century **Church of Panagia Hrysafitissa**.

The path to the **fortress** and the **upper town** is signposted up the steps to the left of the central square. The upper town is now a vast and fascinating jumbled ruin, except for the **Church of Agia Sofia**, which perches on the edge of a sheer cliff.

Monemvasia
Archaeological Museum   MUSEUM
(☑ 27320 61403; adult/concession €2/1; ⏱ 8.30am-3pm Tue-Sun winter, 9am-4pm Tue-Sun summer) This small museum, housed in the village's oldest surviving (former) temple, Agios Andreas (AD 596), displays a detailed map of Monemvasia, useful for orientating yourself. It also houses finds unearthed in the course of excavations and building around the old town. The star turn is the **templon** (chancel screen) from an 11th-century church near the sea gate. Other objects of note include a marble door frame from the Church of Agia Sofia and plenty of fine ceramics.

🛏 Sleeping

There's no truly budget accommodation in the *kastro* itself but considering where you are, some places offer excellent value. Prices are far from rock solid; they alter drastically depending on good ol' supply and demand.

The hotels are nearly identical – boutique in manner, and stylishly furnished in timber and muted materials throughout.

A torch (flashlight) and sensible shoes are a good idea for those staying in the cobbled, dimly lit *kastro*.

If the *kastro* doesn't give you the urge to splurge, there are cheaper hotels and numerous domatia in Gefyra.

Monopati Rooms & Apartments   B&B $$
(☑ 27320 61772; www.byzantine-escapade.com; Monemvasia; apt €70-85, 'little house' €110-140) These two delightful stone options ooze personality, as do the hospitable owners. Stylish decor fills the apartments' quirky spaces, and both include kitchenettes. Rates vary according to the number of people staying. Good deals for long-term stays. Breakfast, which can be served where you like it, when you like it, costs €6.

Hotel Byzantino   HOTEL $$
(☑ 27320 61351; www.hotelbyzantino.com; Monemvasia; r €70-135; ❄) This range of atmospheric rooms offers a great experience of traditional *kastro* – they occupy around five different buildings. This means they come in varying shapes, sizes and prices (from cheaper rooms with no views to smarter digs with sea-facing balconies); most are decked out in antiques. Breakfast costs €6. Pricing can be a bit fluid.

Malvasia Hotel   HOTEL $$
(☑ 27320 61160; http://en.malvasiahotel-traditional.gr; d from €70) The Malavasia features a range of atmospheric rooms of all shapes and sizes spread around the village. Room prices start at around €70 (double) with breakfast in its older style rooms, and from €90 in the renovated buildings. Some are slightly dingy; others are delightful.

The Flower of Monemvasia HOTEL $$

(☑ 27320 61395; www.flower-hotel.gr; Gefyra; s/d/tr incl breakfast €68/80/100; [P][❄][🗘]) Located in mainland Gefyra, opposite Monemvasia's *kastro*, this clean, modern spot is a far cry from the region's more traditional offerings. Nearly all 20 rooms have sea views and some have kitchenettes. Prices are significantly lower outside high season.

New Malvasia HOTEL $$

(☑ 27230 63007/8; www.malvasia-hotel.gr; r incl breakfast €75-110; [❄][🗘]) The so-called 'New Malvasia' (confusingly sometimes called simply the Malvasia) is the newer of the Malvasia-clan hotels and is at the far end of the village. Its 16 small rooms are simple and modern, housed in an historic building. Breakfast is served in its quaint cafe.

Hotel Lazareto HOTEL $$$

(☑ 27320 61991; www.lazareto.gr; Monemvasia; d € 170-280, ste €365; [❄]) Located outside the fortress walls, just over the causeway, and occupying the handsome stone buildings of a former quarantine hospital, Lazareto is the most luxurious choice in the area. The furnishings in the well-equipped rooms are stylishly muted. It's a 15-minute walk to the *kastro* from here. Prices include breakfast.

🍴 Eating

Three tavernas sit cheek to cheek in Monemvasia's old town: **Matoula** (☑ 27320 61660; mains €8-13), **Marianthi** (☑ 27320 61371; mains €8-13) and **To Kanoni** (☑ 27320 61387; mains €7-12). You can't really go wrong with any – choose between them for dish type (all traditional Greek) or ambience. (The village cats like all of them, too.)

Self-caterers will find most things at the Lefkakis supermarket, just past the post office in Gefyra.

ℹ Information

All the practicalities are located in Gefyra. The main street is 23 Iouliou, which runs south around the coast from the causeway, while Spartis runs north up the coast and becomes the road to Molai.

Malvasia Travel (☑ 27320 61752; ⊙ 7.30am-2.30pm & 5.15-6.15pm, to 8pm summer Mon-Sat), just before the causeway in Geyfra, acts as the bus stop and also sells tickets (it may open specially; don't panic if it doesn't stick to its stated opening hours). Several ATMs and the **post office** (⊙ 7.30am-2pm Mon-Fri) are nearby. The **police** (☑ 27320 61210; Spartis 137) are located on Spartis.

ℹ Getting There & Away

Buses leave from outside Malvasia Travel just over the causeway in Gefyra. There are buses to Athens (€30, six hours, at least two daily) via Sparta (€10, 2½ hours), Tripoli (€15.50, 3½ hours) and Corinth Isthmus (€22.90, 4½ hours). If running, ferries stop at Monemvasia between June and September before heading to Crete (via Kythira). Enquire at the travel agency of **Panagiotis Angelakos** (☑ 27320 61219), next to the petrol station, over the causeway.

ℹ Getting Around

The medieval *kastro* of Monemvasia is pedestrian only, but cars and motorcycles can cross the causeway. Parking is available along the narrow road skirting the rock. Alternatively, park in Gefyra to avoid the tight squeeze.

A **shuttle bus** (⊙ 8am-midnight Jun-Sep, Christmas & Easter) ferries visitors between Gefyra and the *kastro*.

Neapoli Νεάπολη

POP 2727

Neapoli (neh-ah-po-lih), close to the southern tip of the eastern prong of the Peloponnese, is the departure point for the Ionian Island of Kythira, clearly visible across the bay. You also pass through Neapoli to see the Cave of Kastania.

From March to December, two daily ferries run between Neapoli and Diakofti on Kythira (per person/car €11/44, 1¼ hours). Tickets are sold at **Vatika Bay Shipping Agency** (☑ 27340 24004; ⊙ 9am-9pm summer, 2hr before boat rest of year), 350m before the small bridge. Leave plenty of time to find the place and buy the ticket.

KTEL (☑ 27340 23222; www.ktel-lakonias.gr) has buses from Neapoli to Athens (€34, three daily) via Sparta (€14.20, three hours) and Molai (€7, 1¼ hours). Molai is the place to change buses for Monemvasia.

Nearby, the small island of **Elafonisi** is renowned for its white beaches and visiting loggerhead turtles. Regular ferries make the 10-minute trip from a small port, Viglafia, around 13km west of Neapoli.

The Cave of Kastania Σπήλαιο Καστανιάς

The extraordinary **Cave of Kastania** (☑ 27343 22226; adult/concession €7/3; ⊙ 10am-4.30pm Sat & Sun summer), located at the end of a spectacularly winding 17km route northeast of Neapoli (allow half an hour), contains one of the best examples of rare stalactites and stalagmites in Europe. The stalactites are estimated to be around three million years old; 1cm of a stalactite takes 100 years to form. You can view around 1,500 sq metres of stalactites as you walk around a raised and lit 300m circuit. Large sections of the cave still remain unexplored. Tours in English depart hourly (last tour 4.30pm). The guide's rote-like spiel won't sate (or create) wannabe scientists; information focuses on the comic resemblance of the formations rather than geological facts. But don't let this detract from the awe-inspiring experience.

Keep in mind that opening hours and tour times can be extremely flexible; check for a notice on the front window of the town hall in Neapoli.

Gythio   Γύθειο
POP 4700

Once the port of ancient Sparta, Gythio (*yee*-thih-o) is the gateway to the Lakonian Mani. This attractive fishing town, with its pastel-coloured, 19th-century buildings, has suffered through the recent economic crisis. It lacks the bustle it once had and businesses are struggling. Nevertheless, it's a charming spot. Six kilometres of sandy beaches extend from the village of Mavrovouni, 2km south of Gythio.

⊙ Sights

Marathonisi Islet   HISTORIC SITE
According to mythology, tranquil pine-shaded Marathonisi is ancient Cranae, where Paris (prince of Troy) and Helen (wife of Menelaus) consummated the affair that sparked the Trojan Wars. A small 18th-century Tzanetakis Grigorakis tower (no longer open to visitors) sits in the centre of the island.

Shadow Theatre Museum   MUSEUM
(☑ 2733 022 064; www.hassanakos.gr; Kalkandi 4; ⊙ 10.30am-2pm Mon, Wed, Thu & Sat, 5.30-8.30pm Tue & Fri) **FREE** This beautiful little studio-cum-museum-cum-shop is run by personable local artist Giorgos Hassanako. The gallery pays homage to traditional shadow puppets with an historical overview of shadow puppetry (unfortunately, in Greek only), plus a range of the artist's own creations, including satirical puppets (Greek politicians!).

🛏 Sleeping

In addition to the following, you can try your luck at the range of studios at Mavrovouni Beach.

Saga Pension   HOTEL $
(☑ 27330 23220; www.sagapension.gr; Kranais; d €50; ❄ 🐾) This is a good-value, saga-free, comfortable place, where some rooms have balconies. The pleasant French owner speaks English. It's 150m from the port,

---

MYTHOLOGY MADE PELOPONNEASY

If you are interested in treading the real landscape of Greek mythology, the Peloponnese is home to many of its fabled places.

It takes some getting used to seeing so many road signs to places of legend, such as Mycenae, Tiryns and Nestor's Palace; homes to Homer's heroes and villains in the 'Iliad', and places of real historical as well as mythological interest.

If you want to find the entrance to the Underworld, try exploring along the Styx River in northeastern Arkadia, known to modern Greeks as the Mavroneri River. Or perhaps you'd prefer to see Aphrodite's birthplace, off a magnificent spot on the remote island of Kythira.

Even the territory itself is named after a mythical figure – Pelops – who, according to legend, became king of Elia after sneakily defeating the previous king Oimanaos in a chariot race (by tampering with his chariot wheels) and to whom subsequent rulers from the area were desperate to prove a blood line.

Gods and demigods sported here, too, including Pan, who sexually harassed nymphs in bucolic Arkadia, and Hercules, who worked as a kind of supernatural pest controller, ridding the country around Argos of the many-headed Hydra and strangling the fearsome Nemean Lion at Nemea. According to the ancient Greek writer Plutarch, even Zeus himself celebrated here, after beating his father Cronos at wrestling, by holding the first ever Olympics at Ancient Olympia.

overlooking Marathonisi Islet. The upmarket Saga Restaurant (mains €9 to €15, fish per 1kg €40 to €60) is below. Breakfast €5.

Matina's PENSION $
(☎ 27330 22518; s/d/tr €25/30/40) A clean and comfortable budget option in a great location, right in the heart of town. Owner Matina speaks no English but is welcoming.

Camping Meltemi CAMPGROUND $
(☎ 27330 23260; www.campingmeltemi.gr; camp sites per tent/adult €5.50/6, bungalows €30-60; ☺ Apr-Oct; ☎ ⚏) Very well organised and the pick of the three campgrounds at Mavrovouni. Three kilometres southwest of Gythio, it's right behind the beach and sites are set among 3000 well-tended olive trees. The bungalows include kitchen, air-con and TV. Buses to Areopoli stop outside.

Xenia Karlaftis Rooms to Rent PENSION $
(☎ 27330 22719; opposite Marathonisi islet; s/d/tr €25/30/40) This long-standing budget option is slightly tired but keeps on keeping on. The communal kitchen area has a fridge and stove for making tea and coffee. Voula, the owner, also keeps neat apartments in nearby Mavrovoumi.

✖ Eating

Seafood is the obvious choice, and the waterfront on Akti Vasileos Pavlou is lined with numerous fish tavernas, especially on Kranais, where tourists walk the gauntlet of waiters touting for custom. But if anywhere has been affected by the crisis, it's here, it seems. You can no longer assume the fish has been supplied that day.

Palai (o) Polis TAVERNA $
(☎ 27330 23322; Irakeous 10; mains €6-8; ☺ lunch & dinner) We like this eatery for its attractive decor – the traditional objects and chandeliers are a stylish take on traditional Greek. Choose from the tasty daily specials on show. Ask the owner to explain the pun in the title.

Poulikakos Restaurant-Grill TAVERNA $
(☎ 27330 22792; mains €6-14, fish per 1kg €40-60; ☺ lunch) You know the deal: Greek favourites for lovers of traditional cuisine. Decor is basic, helpings are gargantuan, quality is good and prices are reasonable.

Taverna O Potis TAVERNA $
(☎ 27330 23245; mains €7-15; ☺ closed Thu winter) This shipshape place, opposite Marathonisi

Islet, has a spotless kitchen and generous helpings.

ℹ Information

Police (☎ 27330 22100; Akti Vasileos Pavlou)
Post Office (cnr Ermou & Arheou Theatrou)

ℹ Getting There & Away

BOAT
LANE Lines (www.lane.gr; per person/car €23/60) has one weekly ferry to Crete via Kythira and Antikythira. Check the ever-changing schedule with Rozakis Travel (p159), on the waterfront.

BUS
The **KTEL Lakonia bus station** (☎ 27330 22228; http://ktel-lakonias.gr; cnr Vasileos Georgios & Evrikleos) is northwest along the waterfront, near Jande Café. Services run north to Athens (€23.80, 4½ hours, six daily) or via Sparta (€4.30, one hour) and Tripoli (€9.70); and south to Areopoli (€2.60, 30 minutes, four daily), Gerolimenas (€6, 1¼ hours, three daily), the Diros Caves (€3.70, one hour, one daily) and Vathia (€6.80, 1½ hours, two weekly).

Helpful staff will explain the best way to see some of the Mani from Gythio (return) in one day. Getting to Kalamata can be fiddly; it involves taking onward connections from either Itilo (€3.80, 45 minutes) or Sparta. There are only two buses daily (5am and 1pm) except Sunday to Itilo (the 1pm bus may require a change at Areopoli). For Monemvasia, change at Sparta.

ℹ Getting Around

Taxis can be found opposite the bus station.
Rozakis Travel (☎ 27330 22207; rosakigy@otenet.gr; Pavlou 5) has cars for hire.

THE MANI H MANH

The Mani, the region covering the central peninsula in the south of the Peloponnese, is a wild, rugged place. Greeks from elsewhere will tell you, so are its people. Such was the formidable reputation of the inhabitants of the remote inner Mani that many would-be occupiers opted in the end to leave them alone.

The people of the Mani regard themselves as direct descendants of the Spartans. After the decline of Sparta, citizens loyal to the principles of Lycurgus (founder of Sparta's constitution) chose to withdraw to the mountains rather than serve under foreign masters. Later, refugees from occupying powers joined these people, who became known as Maniots, from the Greek word 'mania'. For centuries the Maniots were a law unto themselves, renowned for their fierce independence, resentment of attempts to govern them and for their bitter, spectacularly murderous internal feuds. Dotted around the territory, particularly in the inner Mani, you'll find bizarre tower settlements that were built as refuges during clan wars from the 17th century onwards.

Until Independence the Maniots lived in clans led by chieftains. Fertile land was so scarce that it was fiercely fought over. Blood feuds were a way of life.

The Turks failed to subdue the Maniots, who eagerly participated in the War of Independence. But, after 1834, although reluctant to relinquish their independence, they became part of the new kingdom.

It's worth including this region in your itinerary. The steep tumbling skirts of the Taÿgetos Mountains (threaded with wonderful walking trails) and the tiny coves and ports nestling beside them make for some memorably dramatic scenery. As well as the towers, there are magnificent churches and caves.

The Mani is generally divided into the **Messinian Mani** (or outer Mani) and the **Lakonian Mani** (or inner Mani). The Messinian Mani starts southeast of Kalamata and runs south between the coast and the Taÿgetos Mountains, while the Lakonian Mani covers the rest of the peninsula south of Itilo.

Lakonian Mani

Grey rock, mottled with defiant clumps of green scrub, characterises the Scottish-like mountains of inner Mani. Cultivatable land is at a premium here, and supports little more than a few stunted olives and figs. The wild flowers that cloak the valleys in spring exhibit nature's resilience by sprouting from the rocks.

The indented coast's sheer cliffs plunge into the sea, and rocky outcrops shelter pebbled beaches. This wild and barren landscape is broken only by austere and imposing stone towers, many now being restored, which still stand sentinel over the region.

With your own vehicle you can explore the Mani by the loop road that runs down the west coast from the main town, Areopoli, to Gerolimenas, and return via the

---

ⓘ ITILO BUS INTERCHANGE

To travel between Lakonian and Messinian Mani, you must change buses at Itilo. **Itilo** (*eet*-ih-lo), 11km north of Areopoli, was the medieval capital of the Mani and traditionally regarded as the border between outer and inner Mani. There are two buses daily (except Sunday) to Areopoli (€1.60, 20 minutes) and Kalamata (€4, 2¼ hours). Areopoli–Itilo buses go via Nea Itilo and Limeni.

---

east coast (or vice versa). Public transport exists, although it's limited.

Areopoli   Αρεόπολη

POP 800

Areopoli (ah-reh-*o*-po-lih), capital of the Mani, is aptly named after Ares, the god of war. Dominating the main square, Plateia Athanaton, is a statue of Petrobey Mavromihalis, who proclaimed the Maniot insurrection against the Turks. Konstantinos and Georgios Mavromihalis (1765–1848), who assassinated Kapodistrias, belonged to the same family. The town retains many other reminders of its rumbustious past.

◉ Sights & Activities

Churches

There are some fine examples of Maniot architecture to be found in the narrow alleyways surrounding Plateia 17 Martiou.

Church of Taxiarhes   CHURCH

On the southern side of the square is the 18th-century Church of Taxiarhes. Its four-storey bell tower marks it as the most important of Areopoli's many churches. Look out for the extremely well-preserved relief carvings above the main door.

Church of Agios Ioannis   CHURCH

The much older Church of Agios Ioannis, on the southern edge of Areopoli's old town, contains a series of frescoes relating the life of Jesus. It was built by the Mavromihalis family.

Tower Houses

There are numerous examples of tower houses – some in poor condition, while others have been converted into smart accommodation. The **Mavromihalis Tower** (Tzani Tzanaki), south of Plateia 17 Martiou, was once the mightiest tower in town, but now it stands sadly derelict.

Pikoulakis Tower House Museum MUSEUM
(⊙8.30am-2.30pm Tue-Sun) FREE At the southern end of town (ask for directions), the Pikoulakis Tower House Museum is a must-see. Housed in a restored tower, the museum contains exquisite Byzantine pieces from Mani churches, including superb manuscripts and jewellery.

Walking Routes
There is some fabulous walking in the area – look for the signs in the main square. Hikers should be experienced in using compasses and equipment as the routes may not be maintained.

🛏 Sleeping

Hotel Kouris HOTEL $
(⊘27330 51340; hotel_kouris@yahoo.gr; Plateia Athanaton; s/d incl breakfast €35/55) Out of place against the Maniot towers, this concrete block is characterless, but a useful budget fallback.

Londas Pension B&B $$
(⊘27330 51360; www.londas.com; near Church of Taxiarhes; s/d/tr incl breakfast €65/75/103, s/d without bathroom €56/65) This 200-year-old tower is the undisputed king of the castle: stylish whitewashed rooms tastefully decorated in an antique and modern fusion. The small sign is hard to spot near the Church of Taxiarhes. Minimum two-night stay; promotes 'crisis prices'. The owners will help organise walks in the mountains.

Areos Polis BOUTIQUE HOTEL $$
(⊘27330 51028; www.areospolis.gr; s/d/tr incl breakfast from €40/70/80; ❋🛜) This boutique(ish) option is on the main square. Each room is unique and varies from the more modern to those with cast-iron bedsteads and frilly bits.

🍴 Eating & Drinking

Eating options are a bit limited in Areopoli; there are a couple of tavernas in the main square, and on the street leading to the church.

For self-caterers, the small Koilakos supermarket is near Plateia Athanaton.

Barba Petros TAVERNA $
(⊘27330 51205; mains €8-12; ⊙lunch & dinner) This long-standing taverna has been in the family since 1917. The current grandchild/

owner and his daughter run the show. This is the place to pig out in every sense – the owner breeds his own pigs, and other meats are sourced locally. It's a smallish menu but go for the daily recommendations.

Aula BAR
(cocktails €7-8; ⊙9am-late) Yes, we know you're in Greece. But for a refreshing touch of Mexico, head to this funky little bar in the middle of historic Areopoli – it shakes up some of the region's best margaritas (€7).

🛍 Shopping

Invincible Mani BOOKS
(⊘27330 53670; Plateia Athanaton) Has an excellent selection of hiking maps and books on the region.

ℹ Information

The town is split into two parts: the new upper town, around Plateia Athanaton; and the old lower town, around Plateia 17 Martiou. The two squares are linked by a 'main' lane (formerly Kapetan Matapan but no longer officially referred to). There is no tourist office or tourist police.

National Bank of Greece (Petrobey Mavromihali) The only bank in town; has an ATM.

Post Office (Petrobey Mavromihali; ⊙7.30am-2pm Mon-Fri) At the northern edge of town.

ℹ Getting There & Away

The **bus station** (⊘27330 51229; Plateia Athanaton) is situated near the high school at the town's northern end. There are buses to Gythio (€2.60, 30 minutes, four daily), which proceed to Athens (€27). There are bus services to Itilo (€1.60, 20 minutes, two daily Monday to Saturday) via Limeni, to Gerolimenas (€3.40, 45 minutes, three daily), the Diros Caves (€1.60, 15 minutes, 10.15am; returns at 12.45pm), Lagia (€3.70, 40 minutes, one daily) and Vathia (€4.20, one hour, three weekly).

Limeni Λιμένι

The tiny village of Limeni is 3km north of Areopoli on the southern flank of beautiful **Limeni Bay**.

If this little gem draws you in (warning: quite likely in fair weather), consider spending a night at **Pirgos Mavromichali Hotel** (⊘27330 51042; www.pirgosmavromichali.gr; d incl breakfast €120, ste €250; ❋🛜), Limeni's newest addition. The owner has beautifully converted his family's 300-year-old tower house into 13 chic rooms with mod cons.

In a glorious location set out over water, Takis (☑ 27330 51327; fish per 1kg €50-65; ⊘lunch & dinner Apr-Oct) lures in diners; it's the place for quality (if pricey) fish in the area. But the result is good, according to modest Takis, 'because I love what I do'.

Diros Caves   Σπήλαιο Διρού

These extraordinary caves (☑ 27330 52222; adult/child €12/7; ⊘10am-5pm Jun-Sep, to 3pm Oct-May) are 11km south of Areopoli, and signposted near the village of Pyrgos Dirou.

The natural entrance to the caves is on the beach and locals like to believe the legend that they extend as far north as Sparta (speleologists have so far estimated the caves to be around 14km; tourists enter to 1.2km, the first 300m on foot and the remaining section by boat). They were inhabited in Neolithic times, but were abandoned after an earthquake in 4 BC and weren't rediscovered until 1895. Systematic exploration began in 1949. The caves are famous for their stalactites and stalagmites, which have fittingly poetic names such as the Palm Forest, Crystal Lily and the Three Wise Men.

Unfortunately, the half-hour guided tour through the caves is disappointingly brief (and in Greek only, unless you are lucky) – it covers only the lake section and bypasses the most spectacular formations of the dry area.

The nearby Neolithic Museum of Diros (☑ 27330 52233; adult/concession €2/1; ⊘8.30am-3pm Tue-Sun) houses items found in the adjoining Neolithic Alepotrypa Cave. Unfortunately, the cave itself is off limits.

Pyrgos Dirou to Gerolimenas
Πύργος Διρού προς Γερολιμένας

Journeying south down Mani's west coast from Pyrgos Dirou to Gerolimenas, the barren mountain landscape is broken only by deserted settlements with mighty towers. A right turn 9km south of Pyrgos Dirou leads down to the Bay of Mezapos, sheltered to the east by the frying-pan-shaped Tigani peninsula. The ruins on the peninsula are those of the Castle of Maina, built by the Frankish leader Guillaume de Villehardouin in 1248 and subsequently adapted by the Byzantines.

Kita, 13km south of Pyrgos Dirou, bristles with the ruins of war towers and fortified houses. It was the setting for the last great interfamily feud recorded in the Mani,

which erupted in 1870 and required the intervention of the army, complete with artillery, to force a truce.

Gerolimenas   Γερολιμένας
POP 55

Gerolimenas (yeh-ro-lih-*meh*-nahss) is a tranquil fishing village built around a small, sheltered bay at the southwestern tip of the peninsula. It's the perfect place for scenic seclusion.

🛏 Sleeping & Eating

There is a small supermarket on the promenade, and a couple of cafes and tavernas.

Hotel Akrogiali   HOTEL $
(☑ 27330 54204; www.gerolimenas-hotels.com; s €25-30, d €30-40, tr €45-60, 2-4-person apt €50-100; ✳) The Akrogiali has a great setting overlooking the bay on the western edge of town. It offers various sleeping options, from OK doubles in the traditional hotel building to squishier rooms in a newer stone wing, and one- and two-room apartments nearby. Breakfast costs €6.

Kyrimi B&B   B&B $$
(☑ 27330 53078; www.kyrimi.com; r incl breakfast €85; ✳) Not to be confused with Hotel Kirimai (which is next door), this new kid on the block offers a range of smart rooms with wooden and marble trim and a pleasant communal lounge area and outdoor patio.

Hotel Kirimai   LUXURY HOTEL $$$
(☑ 27330 54288; www.kyrimai.gr; d €110-200, ste €260-300; P✳✳) The luxurious Kirimai holds some sway when it comes to status-seeking Athenians. It sits in an idyllic setting at the far southern end of the harbour. The stone-floored, timber-beamed rooms are individually finished with decor-magazine flair. Its restaurant (mains €15 to €25) is open to nonguests.

ⓘ Getting There & Away

There are three buses daily from Gerolimenas to Areopoli (€5, 45 minutes), and on to Athens (€30), Gythio (€10, 1¼ hours) and Sparta (2¼ hours). The bus stop is outside Hotel Akrotenaritis; tickets are bought on board.

Gerolimenas to Porto Kagio
Γερολιμένας προς Πόρτο Κάγιο

South of Gerolimenas, the road continues 4km to the small village of Alika, where it divides. One road leads across the mountains to the east coast, and the other goes south to Vathia and Porto Kagio. The southern road follows the coast, passing pebbly beaches. It then climbs steeply inland to **Vathia**, the most dramatic of the traditional Mani villages, comprising a cluster of closely packed tower houses perched on a rocky spur.

A turn-off to the right 9km south of Alika leads to **Marmari**, with its two sandy beaches, while the main road cuts across the peninsula to the tiny east-coast fishing village of **Porto Kagio**, set on a perfect horseshoe bay. The village's three competing accommodation options are in as remote a place as you'll find anywhere in the Peloponnese.

A 10-minute walk will take you to a peninsula, on which perches the tiny **St Nicholas** church. Hardier walkers should head to one of Europe's southernmost points, **Cape Tenaro** (or Cape Matapan), where the beautiful lighthouse has been recently restored. The cape has been an important location for millennia and was first mentioned by Homer in *The Iliad*. Follow the signs from Porto Kagio; from the car park it's a solid 45-minute walk. You'll pass some Roman ruins – look out for the stunning wave-patterned, circular mosaic.

For a seafood dinner, choose from three waterfront tavernas (open all day in high season). Prices are much the same for all (mains €7 to €17, fish per kilogram €40 to €70).

🛏 Sleeping

Hotel Psamathous HOTEL **$**
(☑ 27330 55221; www.portokayio.com; Porto Kagio; d €50, tr €70-80, incl breakfast ; ❄) This Flintstones-style (modern Maniot) place is owned by the crowd at Porto Taverna. Set back from the waterfront, it has stone-platform beds, mezzanines and a nearly-but-not-quite-there designer touch.

Porto Kale GUESTHOUSE **$**
(☑ 6980755528, 27330 54202; Porto Kagio; d/tr €50/65) A good option in Porto Kagio – simple but with an appealing range of clean and stylish rooms.

Akrotiri Domatia GUESTHOUSE **$$**
(☑ 27330 52013; www.porto-kagio.com; Porto Kagio; d/tr incl breakfast €75/85) Set right on the waterfront – the best rooms are those at the front, which have balconies and overlook the glorious bay (the other rooms are less superior). Owner Nikos also runs boat trips.

East Coast

The east coast is even more rugged and barren than the west. The main town is the formidable-looking **Lagia**, 12km northeast of the Alika turn-off. Perched some 400m above sea level, it was once the chief town of the southeastern Mani. Some of its towers are now derelict (although many are being renovated).

From Lagia, the road winds down with spectacular views of the little fishing harbour of **Agios Kyprianos** – a short diversion from the main road. The next village is **Kokala**, a busy place with two pebbled beaches. The best beach is further north at **Nyfi**, where a turn-off to the right leads to sheltered **Alipa Beach**. Continuing north, a turn-off beyond Flomohori descends to **Kotronas**, while the main road cuts back across the peninsula to Areopoli.

There are a couple of seasonal hotels in Kokala and Kotronas, but nothing worth stopping for.

Public transport is limited – there's one daily bus service between Areopoli and Lagia (around €4, 40 minutes).

Messinian Mani

The Messinian Mani, or outer Mani, lies to the north of its Lakonian counterpart, sandwiched between the Taÿgetos Mountains and the west coast of the Mani peninsula. Kalamata lies at the northern end of the peninsula. The rugged coast is scattered with small coves and beaches, and backed by mountains that remain snowcapped until late May. There are glorious views and hiking opportunities. Useful for walkers is the Anavasi hiking map, *Mani - Kardamyli - Stoupa, Aghios Nikolaos; 1:25,000.*

Stoupa Στούπα

POP 625
The former fishing village of Stoupa, 10km south of Kardamyli, is a resort village teetering on the verge of overdevelopment, and a magnet for (mainly British) package tourists. Although not as picturesque as Kardamyli, it does have two pleasant beaches.

Celebrated author Nikos Kazantzakis lived here for a while and based the protagonist of his novel *Zorba the Greek* on Alexis Zorbas, a coal-mine supervisor in Pastrova, near Stoupa.

🛏 Sleeping & Eating

Stoupa's growing band of pensions and custom-built domatia tend to be block booked by package-tour operators. Travel agencies may be able to help you.

There are supermarkets on the main road behind Stoupa.

Hotel Lefktron HOTEL $$
(📞 27210 77322; www.lefktron-hotel.gr; s/d incl breakfast from €80/87; ◷ Apr-Oct; ❋ 🛜 ☒) Signposted off the southern approach road to Stoupa.

Hotel Stoupa HOTEL $$
(📞 27210 77308; www.hotel-stoupa.gr; s/d incl breakfast €65/75; ❋) It's simple but clean and comfortable and is Stoupa's only hotel open in winter. It's a couple of blocks behind the beach.

★ **Voula's Yesterday & Today** MEDITERRANEAN $$
(📞 27210 77535; www.voula-yesterdayandtoday.gr; mains €7-12.50; ◷ dinner May-Oct) The indomitable Voula, in her words, 'cooks from her heart'. She serves up traditional foods from a bygone era with her personal, more contemporary take. Menu treats include smoked pork dishes (€12.50) and superb homemade pies. She houses exhibits on the Mani and has her own recipe book – the culmination of clients asking for her secrets. Don't miss it.

Taverna Akrogiali TAVERNA $$
(📞 27210 77335; mains €7-14, fish per 1kg €35-60; ◷ breakfast, lunch & dinner; 🛜) This taverna – a popular local meeting spot – has a top location at the southern end of the beach, and an extensive menu that's strong on seafood (platters for €14) and good local dishes. The elderly matriarch still oversees kitchen proceedings.

ℹ Information

Stoupa is 1km west of the main Areopoli– Kalamata road, connected by roads both north and south of town. Both roads lead to the larger of Stoupa's main beaches – a crescent of golden sand. There is no tourist office.

Katerina's Supermarket (📞 27210 77777) Doubles as the post office; it also changes money and sells phonecards.

Thomeas Travel (📞 27210 77689; www.thomeastravel.gr) Changes money and organises car hire, excursions to sites, ferry and air tickets. Also has a good book exchange.

ℹ Getting There & Away

Stoupa is on the main Itilo–Kalamata bus route. One bus (two in summer) heads daily to Itilo (40 minutes) and around four to Kalamata (€4.40, 1½ hours). There are bus stops at the junctions of both the southern and northern approach roads, but the buses don't go into town.

Kardamyli Καρδαμύλη
POP 300

It's easy to see why Kardamyli (kahr-dah-mee-lih) was one of the seven cities offered to Achilles by Agamemnon. This tiny village has one of the prettiest settings in the Peloponnese, nestled between the blue waters of the Messinian Gulf and the Taÿgetos Mountains. The **Vyros Gorge**, which emerges just north of town, runs to the foot of **Mt Profitis Ilias** (2407m), the highest peak of the Taÿgetos. Today the gorge and surrounding areas are very popular with hikers. Visitor numbers can swell in summer. More recently, Kardamyli has been put on the map by the American film industry – it was the setting for the third of the *Before* series featuring Ethan Hawke and Julie Delpy (*Before Midnight*, released in 2013).

🏃 Activities

Hiking has become Kardamyli's biggest drawcard. The hills behind the village are criss-crossed with an extensive network of colour-coded walking trails. Many guesthouses in the village can supply you with route maps (of varying detail and quality). Most of the hikes around here are strenuous, so strong footwear is essential to support your ankles on the often relentlessly rough ground, particularly if you venture into the boulder-strewn gorge itself. You will also need to carry plenty of drinking water.

Many of the walking trails pass through the mountain village of **Exohorio**, which is perched on the edge of the Vyros Gorge at an altitude of 450m. For nonwalkers the village is also accessible by road, and it's a good place to get into a spot of more gentle exploration. The turn-off to Exohorio is 3km south of Kardamyli.

2407 Mountain Activities OUTDOORS
(📞 27210 73752; www.2407m.com) 🏞 For those who don't want to go it alone, the cool Action Jacksons at 2407 Mountain Activities offer a range of fabulous activities, including hiking (from €30 per person; minimum four people), a rock-climbing centre (on a

real 80m-high rock) and mountain-bike trips (€20 to €30) venturing into 'secret' forested and rocky regions in and around the Taÿgetos Mountains. A full-day trip to the Taÿgetos peak costs €100. The owners have cleared old donkey paths and are proud to have a 'traveller, not tourist attitude'. They don't enter villages en masse, for example, and prefer to stick to their secret locations. The office is halfway along the main street.

🛏 Sleeping

There are plenty of domatia signs along the main road. Prices are considerably lower outside high season.

Olympia Koumounakou Rooms PENSION $
(☎27210 73623; s/d €35/45) Olympia loves her budget travellers (as they do her) and offers clean, comfortable rooms and a communal kitchen.

**Volvere Studios
(Stratis Bravakos Rooms)** APARTMENT $
(☎27210 73326; www.yvolvere.gr; d/tr €40/55) Volvere, directly opposite Olympia, is also great value for spotless studio apartments with kitchenettes.

★Elies APARTMENT $$
(☎27210 73140; www.elieshotel.gr; 2-person apt €120, 4-person apt €140-170, 6-person apt €220; ❄ 🛜) Live out your image of quintessential Greece (dreamy sigh): tasteful provincial-style stone maisonettes, with stylish 'haven't-missed-a-beat' interiors, all nestled within an olive grove (which turns into a car park during high season - the only let-down). It's situated 1km north of the village, a pebble's throw from Ritsa Beach. At a discrete distance is Elies taverna.

Kalamitsi Hotel HOTEL $$
(☎27210 73131; www.kalamitsi-hotel.gr; d/ste €110/160) Situated 1km south of town, the Kalamitsi is a lovely, modern, stone-built hotel with serene, well-appointed rooms (family bungalows also available for €220). Within its shady grounds are paths leading to a secluded pebbly beach. Home-cooked dinners and fresh buffet breakfasts are available to guests.

Hotel Vardia HOTEL $$
(☎27210 73777; www.vardia-hotel.gr; studio €80, apt €115-165; �
Mar-Nov; @ 🛜) March into this relaxing and stylish stone hotel (near a former sentry tower and situated high

behind the village beyond the ancient Kardamyli). The 18 well-appointed studio-style rooms have exceptional views of the Messinian Gulf. For those with transport, it's worth tackling the hill. Entrance is at the southern end of town.

🍴 Eating

There's no shortage of eating options in and around Kardamyli. The inland villages of Saidona, Mileu and Exochori also have some excellent tavernas.

There are two supermarkets side by side at the northern edge of the village.

Elies TAVERNA $
(☎27210 73140; mains €6-13; ☉lunch Apr-Oct, dinner 15 Jun-15 Sep) Location, location. Right by Ritsa beach, 1km north of town, and nestled in olive groves, it's got the atmosphere of a provincial Mediterranean private garden with top-quality nosh to boot. In good weather, allow time in your travels to wile away an afternoon.

O Perivoulis TAVERNA $
(☎27210 73713; mains €7-11; ☉dinner Tue-Sun, closed Dec) What it lacks in seaside (it's in the village), it makes up for with a cosy interior, pretty garden and excellent taverna dishes that incorporate local ingredients where possible.

Taverna Dioskouri TAVERNA $
(☎27210 73236; www.dioskuri.gr; mains €7-14; ☉lunch & dinner) A safe option with nothing over the top, except for the friendly owner and the clifftop view – it overlooks the ocean from the hillside just south of town.

ℹ Information

Kardamyli is on the main Areopoli–Kalamata road. The central square, Plateia 25 Martiou 1821, lies at the northern end of the main thoroughfare.

Kardamyli's main pebble-and-stone beach is off the road to Kalamata; turn left beyond the bridge on the northern edge of town. The road up to Old (or Upper) Kardamyli is on the right before the bridge. The **post office** (☉7.30am-2pm Mon-Fri) is on the main strip.

The useful www.kardamili-greece.com website can provide some information.

ℹ Getting There & Around

Kardamyli is on the main bus route from Itilo to Kalamata (around €4, one hour, two to four daily, more in summer). The bus stops at the central square at the northern end of the main thoroughfare, and at the bookshop at the southern end.

Two weekly buses head to Exohorio (€1.60, runs to changing times); most travellers prefer to take a taxi (around €18). The helpful folk in **Cafe Plateia** (⏺27210 73067) at the western end of town can tell you schedules.

MESSINIA ΜΕΣΣΗΝΙΑ

The beaches in the southwestern corner of the Peloponnese in Messinia are extremely pleasant, and while villages such as Koroni have felt the weight of package tourism, the old Venetian towns of Pylos and Methoni still remain delightful hideaways.

Messinia's boundaries were established in 371 BC following the defeat of Sparta by the Thebans at the Battle of Leuctra. The defeat ended almost 350 years of Spartan domination of the Peloponnese – during which time Messinian exiles founded the city of Messinia in Sicily – and meant the Messinians were left free to develop their kingdom in the region stretching west from the Taÿgetos Mountains. Their capital was ancient Messini, about 25km northwest of Kalamata on the slopes of Mt Ithomi.

Kalamata Καλαμάτα

POP 54,100

Kalamata is Messinia's capital and the second-largest city in the Peloponnese. Compared to its more peaceful surrounds, it is a less-inspiring destination for visitors, but museum lovers and shoppers will be satisfied. Built on the site of ancient Pharai, the city takes its modern name from a miracle-working icon of the Virgin Mary known as *kalo mata* (good eye). It was discovered in the stables of the Ottoman aga (governor), who converted to Christianity as a result of the miracles it was believed to have performed. The icon now resides inside the city's oversized cathedral, the Church of Ypapantis.

Below the *kastro* is the small but attractive old town, which was almost totally destroyed by the Turks during the War of Independence and rebuilt by French engineers in the 1830s. On 14 September 1986 Kalamata was devastated by an earthquake; 20 people were killed, hundreds were injured and more than 10,000 homes were destroyed.

⊙ Sights

Kastro FORT
(⊙8am-2pm Mon-Fri, 9am-3pm Sat & Sun) FREE
Looming over the town is the 13th-century *kastro*. Remarkably, it survived the 1986 earthquake. The entry gate is its most impressive feature. There's not much else to see, but there are good views from the battlements.

Archaeological Museum of Messenia MUSEUM
(⏺27210 83485; www.archmusmes.gr; Benaki & Agiou Ioannou; admission €3; ⊙1.30-8pm Mon & 8am-8pm Tue-Sun summer, 8.30am-3pm Tue-Sun winter) This wonderful child-friendly museum, recently reopened after years of renovation, is a must-visit, especially if you are struggling to get your head around Greece's ancient history and treasures. The displays are divided into provincial regions – Kalamata, Pylia, Messini and Trifylia – and you follow a trail that snakes among the exhibits revealing everything from sculptures and mosaics to descriptions and images. It's just north of Plateia 23 Martiou.

Historical & Folklore Museum of Kalamata MUSEUM
(⏺27210 28449; Ioannou 12, cnr Kyriakou; adult/concession €2/1; ⊙9am-1pm Tue-Sat, 10am-1pm Sun) This eggshell-blue building holds an exquisite collection of donated local artefacts – from tools and looms to household items and clothes – that offer a thorough insight into Kalamata's bygone era. It's professionally run and well worth supporting.

Military Museum MUSEUM
(⏺27210 21219; Mitropolitou Meletiou 10; ⊙9am-2pm Tue-Sat, plus 6-8pm Wed, 11am-2pm Sun) FREE This museum's displays span a broad chronological sweep of Greek history from the Turkish occupation (depicted in grisly paintings) to the 21st century. National servicemen take guided tours (English speakers are supposedly available but, unfortunately, all signage is in Greek).

✪ Festivals & Events

Kalamata International Dance Festival MUSIC
(www.kalamatadancefestival.gr) In July each year, this festival draws crowds to its quality performances of traditional music and dance. Venues include the amphitheatre of the *kastro*. See the website for dates and prices.

Kalamata

🛏 Sleeping & Eating

There's a shortage of good sleeping options
in Kalamata. The waterfront east of Faron is
lined with characterless C-class (two-star) hotels. The Marina is the best place for seafood
and tavernas, with varying styles and prices.

Hotel Rex   HOTEL $$
(☑ 27210 94440; www.rexhotel.gr; Aristomenous 26;
d/ste incl breakfast from €100/200; ❋ 🛜) The
Rex stands unchallenged as the best address
(with the slowest lift) in Kalamata. It occu-
pies a fine neoclassical building, and offers
travellers comfortable – if slightly cramped –
modern rooms. The corner room 403 has
good rooftop views.

Hotel Haikos   HOTEL $$
(☑ 27210 88902; www.haikos.gr; Navarino 115;
s/d/tr incl breakfast €50/70/80) One of the
best choices along the beachfront is this
business-like, modern hotel, which has had
a recent makeover. Rooms at the front can
catch the street noise.

I Milopetra   MEDITERRANEAN $
(☑ 27210 98950; mains €5-10; ⊗ 8am-late) A
cosmopolitan, upmarket cafe with an olive
theme, in a handy location near Plateia 23
Martiou in the old town. Serves gourmet
snacks and olive-based products. And (bonus) it's strictly no-smoking inside.

Food Market   MARKET $
(Nedontos) Self-caterers should visit the
large food market across the bridge from
the KTEL Messinia bus station. Kalamata is
noted for its olives, olive oil and figs.

Aragma   GREEK $
(☑ 27210 97949; Salaminos 50, Marina; mains
€6-15) This pleasant spot is all things to all

KALAMATA OLIVES

Kalamata gives its name to the prized Kalamata olive, a plump, purple-black variety that is found in delicatessens around the world and is also grown extensively (although not exclusively) in neighbouring Lakonia. The region's reliable winter rains and hot summers make for perfect olive-growing conditions.

The Kalamata tree is distinguished from the common olive (grown for oil) by the size of its leaves. Like its fruit, the leaves of the Kalamata are twice the size of other varieties and a darker shade of green.

Unlike other varieties, Kalamata olives can't be picked green. They ripen in late November and must be hand-picked to avoid bruising. You can buy and sample these famous olives at the markets in Kalamata.

people – a cafe, ouzerie and *mezedopoleio* (small plates). Serves up good traditional dishes and, according to many, some of the best fresh calamari around.

❶ Information

National Bank of Greece (Aristomenous, Central Sq, cnr Akrita and Navarinou)

Post Office (cnr Olgas & Navarinou; ⊙ 7.30am-2pm Mon-Fri)

The Web (Stathmou 19; per hr €2.20; ⊙ 24hr) Good internet (if you can elbow your way through the the testosterone haze…read, young gamers).

Tourist Police (☑ 27210 44680; Messinis; ⊙ 8am-9pm Mon-Fri)

❶ Getting There & Away

AIR

Airlines that fly to Kalamata change with the wind, it seems. At the time of writing, **Aegean Airlines** (www.aegeanair.com) operated flights between Kalamata and Athens and Thessaloniki from June through September.

BOAT

Between June and September, a weekly ferry service operated by LANE Lines runs from Kalamata to Crete (per person/car €25/56) via Kythira (per person/car €17/46). Contact **SMAN Travel/Maniatis** (☑ 27210 20704; smantrv@otenet.gr; cnr Likourgou & Psaron 148), by the port, for the schedule.

BUS

KTEL Messinia bus station (☑ 27210 28581; www.ktelmessinias.gr; Artemidos) has buses to Athens (€23, 4½ hours, 12 daily) via Corinth Isthmus (€16, 2½ hours). It also has buses to Tripoli (€8.10, 1¼ hours, five daily), Kyparissia (€7, 1¼ hours, four weekdays) and Patra (€23, four hours, two daily) via Pyrgos (€14, two hours).

Heading west, there are buses to Koroni (€5, 1½ hours, six daily), Finikounda (€6, 1¾ hours, one daily), Methoni (€6.10, 1½ hours, five daily) and Pylos (€5, 1¼ hours, five daily).

Heading east across the Langada Pass to Sparta (€5, one to two daily) involves changing buses at Artemisia. Two to four daily buses head to Itilo (€7.40, 2¼ hours) in Messinian Mani via Kardamyli (€4, one hour) and Stoupa (€4.40, 1¼ hours).

Note: weekend services for all routes are greatly reduced or nonexistent.

❶ Getting Around

TO/FROM THE AIRPORT

Kalamata's airport is 10.5km west of the city, near Messini. There is no airport shuttle bus. A taxi costs around €20.

BUS

Local buses leave from the KTEL Messinia bus station. The most useful service is bus 1, which goes south to the seafront and then east along Navarinou as far as the Filoxenia Hotel. Buy tickets (€1.20) from kiosks or the driver.

CAR & MOTORCYCLE

Kalamata is a good place to rent a vehicle, due to hot competition between the agencies at the waterfront end of Faron. Recommended options:

Avis (☑ 27210 20352; Kesari 2)

Verga Rent a Car (☑ 27210 95190; Faron 202)

Ancient Messini
Αρχαία Μεσσήνη

POP 350

The fascinating ruins of Ancient Messini lie scattered across a small valley below the pretty village of Mavromati, 25km northwest of Kalamata. The village takes its name from the fountain in the central square; the water gushes from a hole in the rock that looks like a black eye (*mavro mati* in Greek). More recently 'Mavromati' is referred to infrequently and the name 'Ancient Messini' is used to refer to both the historic site and the village itself.

History

Ancient Messini was founded in 371 BC after the Theban general Epaminondas defeated Sparta at the Battle of Leuctra, freeing the Messinians from almost 350 years of Spartan rule. Built on the site of an earlier stronghold, the new Messinian capital was one of a string of defensive positions designed to keep watch over Sparta. Epaminondas himself helped to plan the fortifications, which were based on a massive wall that stretched 9km around the surrounding ridges and completely enclosed the town.

Apart from its defensive potential, Ancient Messini was also favoured by the gods. According to local myth, Zeus was born here – not Crete – and raised by the nymphs Neda and Ithomi, who bathed him in the same spring that gives the modern village its name.

◎ Sights

Ancient Messini   HISTORIC SITE
(☑ 27240 51201; www.ancientmessene.gr; museum & site €5; ☺ 8am-sunset) The best views of this beautiful site are from the village central square, and it's worth briefly examining the layout before heading down for a closer look at the site itself. Access is by a road near the museum, about 300m northwest of the square.

The **museum** (adult €2; ☺ 8.30am-4pm Tue-Sun, later in summer), situated above the site on the village road, houses a small and interesting collection of finds from Ancient Messini, mainly statues recovered from the *asklepion* (ancient medical complex). They include two statues assumed to be of Machaon and Podaleiros, the sons of Asclepius. They are thought to be the work of the sculptor Damophon, who specialised in oversized statues of gods and heroes and was responsible for many of the statues that once adorned Ancient Messini.

Before heading down to the site, it's worth continuing another 800m along the road past the museum to view the celebrated **Arcadian Gate**. This unusual circular gate guarded the ancient route to Megalopoli – now the modern road north to Meligalas and Zerbisia – which runs through the gate. Running uphill from the gate is the finest surviving section of the mighty defensive wall built by Epaminondas. It remains impressive, studded with small, square forts, and is well worth the gentle uphill walk from the village.

The site itself is still emerging from the valley floor as ongoing, thorough excavations are taking place. At the time of research, these included the impressive **agora** (marketplace) and the stunning **amphitheatre**, part of which was being reconstructed for contemporary use – keep an ear open for forthcoming performances.

Elsewhere, the **asklepion** complex lay at the heart of the ancient city. This extensive complex was centred on a **Doric temple** that once housed a golden statue of Ithomi. The modern awning west of the temple protects the **artemision**, where fragments of an enormous statue of Artemis Orthia were found. The structures to the east of the *asklepion* include the **ekklesiasterion**, which once acted as an assembly hall. Two **amphitheatres** provide an evocative glimpse into the site.

Don't miss heading further downhill from the *asklepion* to the wonderfully imposing **stadium**, which is surrounded by the ruins of an enormous **gymnasium**.

You can buy entry tickets at both the site and the museum.

🛏 Sleeping & Eating

Likourgos Rooms   GUESTHOUSE $
(☑ 27240 51297; roomslykourgos@yahoo.gr; d/tr €45/60) If you are taken by the superb vistas and want to stay, try this spacious and comfortable modern option, where the front rooms afford glimpses of the ruins. The helpful owner, Victoria, speaks some English.

Taverna Ithomi   TAVERNA $
(☑ 27240 51298; www.ithomi.gr; mains €6-12; ☺ lunch & dinner daily Feb-Nov, Sat & Sun only Dec & Jan) Besides a couple of local *kafeneia* (coffee houses), this is the only eatery in town and offers traditional cuisine. Friendly owner Nikos is the local 'man in the know'.

❶ Getting There & Away

There are two buses between Ancient Messini/ Mavromati and Kalamata (€3, one hour, Monday, Wednesday and Friday only), one in the early morning, the other in the afternoon, to a changing schedule. Check at the Taverna Ithomi.

Koroni   Κορώνη
POP 1700

Koroni (ko-*ro*-nih) is a lovely Venetian port town on Messinia Bay, 43km southwest of Kalamata. Medieval mansions and churches line the town's quaint, narrow and winding streets. These lead to a promontory, on which perches an extensive castle and monastery.

◉ Sights & Activities

Castle   CASTLE
Much of the old castle is occupied by the **Timios Prodromos Convent**. If open, you can enter (a strict dress code applies). Note the castle's impressive Gothic entrance. The small promontory beyond the castle is a tranquil place for a stroll, with lovely views over the Messinian Gulf to the Taÿgetos Mountains.

Zaga Beach   BEACH
Koroni's main attraction is Zaga Beach, a long sweep of golden sand just south of the town. It takes about 20 minutes to walk to here – you can cut through the castle or go via the road. Ask locals for directions.

Koroni also sees loggerhead turtles, which lay their eggs near Zaga.

⊨ Sleeping & Eating

Accommodation is a bit limited in Koroni. Most of the rooms are spread around a cluster of domatia by the sea, at the eastern end of the main street. There are more domatia overlooking Zaga Beach, but they are often booked out in summer.

Hotel Diana   HOTEL $
(⏲ tel/fax 27250 22312; www.dianahotel-koroni.gr; s/d €30/40; ✹ ☏) This place is blessed (or otherwise) with Byzantine gold-plated bar stools, icons and the like. Rooms are not quite as glossy – they are simple but adequate. It's off the central square, almost on the seafront. Breakfast costs €5.

Sofotel   HOTEL $
(⏲ 27250 22230; www.koroni-holidays.com; d €60; ✹) Not to everyone's taste are these modern, gold-trimmed and ornament-filled (if spotless) digs. Some rooms have balconies.

Camping Koroni   CAMPGROUND $
(⏲ 27250 22119; www.koronicamping.com; camp sites per adult/tent & car €8/8; ☏ ✹) Located only 200m from Koroni, near the beach and with good facilities.

Zaga Apartments   APARTMENT $$
(⏲ 6973754036, 27250 22722; www.zaga.gr; Zaga Beach; 2-/4-/6-person apt €70/85/125; ⊙ 15 May–end Sep; 🅿 ✹) Personable apartments with

kitchen facilities and balconies and views over Zaga Beach.

Agia Playa   TAVERNA $
(Falanthi; mains €6-13; ⊙ dinner, closed Mon Oct) This pretty place, around 5km from Koroni in Falanthi, is out of a child's storybook: fountains, vines, plane trees, a stream. As for the food? Grills and other bites, but you'll not much care with this setting. Follow the nymphs – we swear they're here somewhere.

ⓘ Information

The main street (formal name Perikli Ralli, but few know it) runs east from the central square, one block back from the sea.

There is no tourist office, but the large town map on the cathedral wall shows the location of both banks and the **post office** (⊙ 7.30am-2pm Mon-Fri), all of which are nearby.

ⓘ Getting There & Away

Buses will drop you in the central square outside the Church of Agios Dimitrios, one block back from the harbour. There are five buses daily to Kalamata (€5, 1½ hours) and one to Athens (€27.20). Tickets can be bought from the barber shop, near the main square.

Methoni   Μεθώνη
POP 1169

Methoni (meh-*tho*-nih), 12km south of Pylos, was another of the seven cities offered to Achilles by Agamemnon. Homer described it as 'rich in vines'. Today it's a pretty seaside town with a popular beach, next to which crouches a sturdy 15th-century Venetian fortress.

◉ Sights

Fortress   FORT
(⊙ 8am-3pm) **FREE** This splendid *kastro*, a great example of military architecture, is vast and romantic. Within the walls are a Turkish bath, a cathedral, a house, a cistern, parapets and underground passages.

The vast fortification is built on a promontory south of the modern town and is surrounded on three sides by the sea and separated from the mainland by a moat. The medieval port town, which was located within the fortress walls, was the Venetians' first, and their longest-held possession, in the Peloponnese. It was also a stopover for pilgrims en route to the Holy Land. During medieval times the twin fortresses of Methoni and Koroni were known as 'the Eyes of the Serene Republic'.

A short causeway leads from the fortress to the diminutive octagonal **Bourtzi fortress** on an adjacent islet.

🛏 Sleeping & Eating

Apartments Melina   APARTMENT $$
(☑ 27230 31505; www.methoni-apartments.gr; studio €60, 2-/3-/4-person apt €70/85/85, 6-person 'villa' €100) A gem – immaculate, spacious apartments right across from the beach, with a perfumed garden of roses, vines and palms, and ultrafriendly English-speaking owners, Kathy and Spiros.

Hotel Achilles   HOTEL $$
(☑ 27230 31819; achilleshotel@hotmail.com; s/d €55/70; ☺ year-round; ❄) The smartest of a range of small family hotels in town, with 13 comfortable modern rooms and a pleasant outdoor terrace. There's a light, airy dining area, too. Breakfast costs €6.

Nonda's   GREEK $
(☑ 27230 31791; mains €2-8.50; ☺ dinner) Nonda's is the undisputed king of the castle among locals for souvlaki. Great grilled meats, too. Forget the ambience – it's a sterile, barn-like place – but the generous, fresh portions (plus the best Greek salads) make it worth a visit. (And - *burp* - for the record, we heartily agree with those in the know).

Taverna Klimataria   TAVERNA $
(☑ 27230 31544; Miaouli; mains €7-10; ☺ lunch & dinner May-Oct) Locals are in agreement: this is the place to head for traditional dishes. It's in an old home, with seating on the front porch or in a courtyard. Typical choices include onion pie and stuffed zucchini flowers. The treat – a gavros starter – is complimentary.

🛈 Information

The road from Pylos forks on the edge of town to create Methoni's two main streets, which then run parallel through town to the fortress. As you come from Pylos, the fork to the right is the main shopping street. It has numerous shops, *kafeneia*, a National Bank of Greece (and ATE Bank ATM) and a nearby supermarket. The left fork leads directly to the fortress car park, passing the **post office** (☺ 7.30am-2pm Mon-Fri) on the way.

There is no tourist office or tourist police; in emergencies contact the regular **police** (☑ 27230 31203).

🛈 Getting There & Away

Buses depart from Methoni from the fork at the Pylos end of town where the two main streets meet. Buses travel to Pylos (€1.60, 15 minutes, three to six daily) and on to Kalamata (€6, 1½ hours). Services also run to Finikounda (€2.60, 15 minutes, one to two daily, none on Sundays). Unbelievably, there is no bus between Methoni and Koroni; you must change at Finikounda – if the timetable works, that is. The bus to Kalamata stops at Harakopio, 4.5km from Koroni. For bus information call ☑ 27230 22230.

Pylos   Πύλος
POP 2760

Pylos (*pee*-loss), on the coast 51km southwest of Kalamata, presides over the southern end of an immense bay. With its huge natural harbour almost enclosed by the Sfaktiria Islet, a delightful tree-shaded central square, two castles and surrounding pine-covered hills, Pylos is one of the most picturesque towns in the Peloponnese.

From the bay on 20 October 1827, the British, French and Russian fleets, under the command of Admiral Codrington, fired at point-blank range on Ibrahim Pasha's combined Turkish, Egyptian and Tunisian fleet, sinking 53 ships and killing 6000 men, with negligible losses on the Allies' side.

The attack was known as the Battle of Navarino (which is the town's former name) and was decisive in the War of Independence, but it was not meant to have been a battle at all. The Allied fleet wanted to achieve no more than to persuade Ibrahim Pasha and his fleet to leave, but things got somewhat out of hand. George IV, on hearing the news, described it as a 'deplorable misunderstanding'.

🎯 Sights & Activities

Neo Kastro   CASTLE
(☑ 27230 22955; adult €3; ☺ 8.30am-3pm Tue-Sun) There are castles on each side of Navarino Bay, but this is the more accessible of them, situated on the hilltop at the southern edge of town, off the road to Methoni. It was built by the Turks in 1573 and later used as a launching pad for the invasion of Crete. It remains in good condition, especially the formidable surrounding walls. Within its walls are a citadel, a mosque converted into a church and a courtyard surrounded by dungeons (used as a prison until the 1900s). At the time of research, there were plans to

move the town's small **archaeological museum** (☑ 27230 22448; €2; ☺ 8am-3pm Tue-Sun) to this site.

René Puaux Exhibition MUSEUM
(☺ 8.30am-3pm Tue-Sun) Recently relocated from the castle to a stunning red mansion, this collection of pictures depicts the Battle of Navarino and was donated by René Puaux (1878–1937), who bequeathed his collection of porcelain, engravings and lithographs on condition that it be exhibited at Pylos, near the battle's location.

Club Boats BOAT TOUR
(☑ 6972263565, 27230 23155; www.pyloscruises. gr; kiosk on the quay; ☺ Jun-Sep) Runs boat tours around the Bay of Navarino and to Sfaktiria Islet (silt-covered wrecks of sunken Turkish ships are discernible in the clear waters). The price depends on the number of passengers, but reckon on about €15 per person (minimum numbers apply).

🛌 Sleeping

Karalís Beach Hotel HOTEL $$
(☑ 27230 23021; www.karalisbeach.gr; Paralia; s/d/tr €75/90/110) Pylos' clear winner in the rather noncompetitive hotel stakes. It's hard not to like this place for the setting alone – under the castle walls, clinging to a cliff over the water. Rooms are small but stylish with beige tones. Those at the front have balconies.

Hotel Miramare HOTEL $$
(☑ 27230 22751; www.miramarepylos.gr; Tsamadou 3; d incl breakfast €60; P ❀) Deceptively large with 35 simple but airy rooms, this marine-themed spot is in a prime location, overlooking the water. It's popular with groups so you may need to book ahead.

🍴 Eating

There are plenty of tavernas with standard favourites, so if you're the kind of person who smells sea air and craves fish, you will be very satisfied. Prices tend to fluctuate greatly depending on the season.

Restaurant Grigoris TAVERNA $
(☑ 27230 22621; mains €5-12) Nestled under plane trees on the corner of the central square (and over the road under a terrace), this charming eatery hits the spot. Round off your appetite with a selection from the chef's stove-top displays, then sit back and watch the world go by. Sigh. Greece at its best.

Koukos TAVERNA $
(☑ 27230 22950; mains €7-10) A plain, unpretentious and good-ol'-fashioned taverna serving hearty portions of grills and oven-baked dishes to a changing menu. It's a short walk up the hill above the port – ask for directions in the plaza.

ⓘ Information

Everything of importance is within walking distance of the central square, Plateia Trion Navarhon (Square of the Three Admirals), down by the seafront.

ATE Bank (Plateia Trion Navarhon) With ATM.

Computerra (Papaflessa Sq; per hr €2.20; ☺ 10am-late) The place for internet and a drink.

National Bank of Greece (Plateia Trion Navarhon) With ATM.

Police Station (☑ 27230 23016) On the central square.

Post Office (Nileos; ☺ 7.30am-2pm Mon-Fri)

ⓘ Getting There & Away

The **KTEL Messinia bus station** (☑ 27230 22230) is on the inland side of the central square. From the bus station, there are services to Kalamata (€5, 1¼ hours, four to seven daily), Kyparissia (€6.10, 1¼ hours, two to four daily) via Nestor's Palace and Hora (€2, 35 minutes), Methoni (€1.60, 20 minutes, three to four daily) and Finikounda (€1.80, 30 minutes, three services daily, none on Sunday). There are two daily buses to Athens (€28, five hours). For Patra there's one connection a day at Kyparissia. Services are reduced, if existent, on weekends. Frustratingly, there's no bus between Pylos and Koroni.

Gialova Γιάλοβα
POP 275

The village of Gialova lies 8km north of Pylos on the northeastern edge of Navarino Bay. It boasts a fine sandy beach and safe swimming in the sheltered waters of the bay. The Gialova Lagoon is a prime birdwatching site in winter.

🛌 Sleeping & Eating

Camping Erodios CAMPGROUND $
(☑ 27230 23269; www.erodioss.gr; camp sites per adult/tent/car €7/5/4, 2-/4-bed cabins €65/75; ☎) Neat as a pin, this campground has a good stretch of beach on Navarino Bay and great facilities. It's northwest of the village on the road leading out to the Gialova Lagoon and Paleokastro.

Hotel-Restaurant Zoe   HOTEL **$$**
(☎27230 22025; www.zoeresort.com; r incl break-
fast from €65, apt from €85; ✳❄) This once-
small family-run place on the seafront
near the pier is morphing into a constantly
expanding resort. We like the older hotel
rooms with the small front balcony, al-
though they're potentially noisy if Zoe's out-
door taverna rocks on. The resort section is
modern, but lacks shade.

Elia   MEDITERRANEAN **$**
(☎27230 23503; www.elia-gialova.gr; mains €6-15;
⊙Feb-Oct) This is a gourmet-Greek–cum-
contemporary-Mediterranean eatery. The
smoked pork and octopus can only be out-
done by the ambience, with its trendy de-
signer lights and flower boxes.

❶ Getting There & Away

There are several buses a day south to Pylos
(€2, 15 minutes) and several north to Kyparissia
via Nestor's Palace and Hora. A taxi between Gia
lova and Pylos costs around €15.

Around Gialova

◉ Sights

Paleokastro   RUIN
The ruins of this ancient castle lie 5km west
of Gialova on rugged **Koryphasion Hill**, a for-
midable natural defensive position overlook-
ing the northern entrance to Navarino Bay.

The road to the castle is signposted on the
northern edge of the village. It crosses the
narrow spit of land that separates Navarino

Bay from the Gialova Lagoon, and finishes
at a car park at the southern end of the hill.
Signs point to a rough track that snakes up
the steep hillside to the castle entrance.

The castle was built by the Franks at the
end of the 13th century and sits on the site
of the acropolis of Ancient Pylos. It was oc-
cupied in 1381 by Spanish mercenaries from
Navarra, after whom the bay is named.

The car park is also the starting point for a
track that skirts around the base of Korypha-
sion Hill to **Voidokilia Beach**. This beauti-
ful, sandy horseshoe bay is presumed to be
Homer's 'sandy Pylos', where Telemachus
was warmly welcomed when he came to ask
wise old King Nestor the whereabouts of his
long-lost father, Odysseus, King of Ithaca.

There's another path up to the castle from
the southern side of the beach that passes
Nestor's Cave. According to mythology,
this is the cave where Hermes hid the cattle
he stole from Apollo. This small cave boasts
a few stalactites.

Voidokilia Beach can also be approached
by road from the village of **Petrohori**, 6km
north of Gialova off the road to Hora.

Nestor's Palace   RUIN
(☎27630 31437) At the time of research, Nes-
tor's Palace was closed due to site upgrades
but due to open at the end of 2014.

Nestor's Palace is so called because it is
believed to have been the court of the mythi-
cal hero Nestor, who took part in the voyage
of the Argonauts and fought in the Trojan
War. It's the best preserved of all Mycenaean
palaces. Originally a two-storey building, the
palace's walls stand 1m high, giving a good

BIRDWATCHING & THE GIALOVA LAGOON

The best, and most accessible, birdwatching site in the Peloponnese is the Gialova
Lagoon. Between September and March the lagoon is home to up to 20,000 assorted
waterbirds, while many others pause here on their spring migration between Africa and
Eastern Europe.

The Hellenic Ornithological Society has recorded here 265 of around 400 species
found in Greece, including 10 species of duck and eight types of heron. Waders descend
in their thousands, along with flamingos and glossy ibises. Birds of prey include the
internationally threatened imperial eagle, plus ospreys, peregrine falcons and harriers.

The lagoon and associated wetlands cover 700 hectares at the northern end of Na-
varino Bay, separated from the bay by a narrow spit of land leading out to Koryphasion
Hill. They are fed by two freshwater streams that flow into the reed beds on the northern
and eastern flanks of the lagoon and empty into Navarino Bay, below Koryphasion Hill.

The wetlands and surrounding coastal habitats were declared a protected area in
1997. The old pump house, former nerve centre of an ill-considered drainage scheme,
has been converted into an information centre and is the starting point for two walking
trails that guide visitors through a range of habitats.

idea of the layout of a Mycenaean palace complex. The main palace, in the middle, was a building of many rooms. The largest room, the **throne room**, was where the king dealt with state business. In the centre was a large, circular hearth surrounded by four ornate columns that supported a 1st-floor balcony. Some of the fine frescoes discovered here are housed in the museum in the nearby village of Hora. Surrounding the throne is the sentry box, pantry, waiting room, a vestibule and, most fascinating, a bathroom with a terracotta tub still in place.

The most important finds were 1200 or so Linear B script tablets, the first discovered on the mainland. Some are in Hora's museum. The site was excavated later than the other Mycenaean sites, between 1952 and 1965. An excellent guidebook by Carl Blegen, who led the excavations, is sold at the site (€5).

Nestor's Palace is 17km north of modern Pylos.

Hora Archaeological Museum MUSEUM
(☑ 27632 31358; adult €3; ⊗ 8.30am-3pm Tue-Sun)
Hora's fascinating musuem, 4km northeast of Nestor's Palace, houses finds from the site and other Mycenaean artefacts from Messinia. The prize pieces are the incomplete frescoes from the throne rooms at Nestor's Palace and the Linear B tablets (the latter are copies).

Buses from Pylos to Kyparissia stop at Hora.

OLYMPIA   ΟΛΥΜΠΙΑ

Most people come to Olympia for one reason: to visit the historically important and impressive site of Ancient Olympia, birthplace of the Olympic Games, in the region's western prefecture. Elia (Ελιά) is otherwise largely an agricultural area.

Ancient Elia took its name from the mythical King Helios. Its capital was the city of Elis, now a forgotten ruin on the road from Gastouni to Lake Pinios. When the Franks arrived, they made Andravida the capital of their principate of Morea. Pyrgos is the dull modern capital.

❶ Getting There & Around

There are regular bus services into the region. From Pyrgos, there are seven buses daily to Athens (€27.70, four hours), 10 daily to Patra (€10, two hours), and two daily to Andritsena (€6.20, two hours) and Kalamata (€13.10, two hours). The schedule is reduced on weekends.

Buses to Olympia depart from Pyrgos (€2.20, 30 minutes).

There's a small train on the branch line from Pyrgos to Olympia (around €2, 40 minutes, two daily).

Tholos to Olympia

Heading north into Elia from Messinia, the mountains to the east give way to populated plains fringed by golden-sand beaches. Elia's coastline comprises long stretches of beaches, interspersed here and there by pebbled shores and rocky outcrops. Unfortunately, behind the beaches, buildings are increasingly impeding potentially pretty views. Among the best southern beaches are **Tholos**, **Kakovatos** and **Kouroutas**. There is seaside accommodation available in each village, but most of it is in uninspiring concrete buildings.

Olympia   Ολυμπία
POP 1000

With countless overpriced souvenir shops and eateries, the modern village of Olympia (o-lim-bee-*ah*) panders unashamedly to the hundreds of thousands of tourists who pour through on their way to Ancient Olympia. Despite this, the town is far from kitsch. Only 500m south of the well-kept leafy streets, over the Kladeos River, is Ancient Olympia. Although the site's surrounds were tragically burnt in the 2007 bushfires, rendering it devoid of trees, Ancient Olympia survived, thanks to the efforts of locals and firefighters; it remains a luxuriantly green, beautiful and historically important site.

◎ Sights

Three museums focus on Ancient Olympia (and Olympics) mania. The Archaeological Museum of Olympia and Museum of the History of the Olympic Games in Antiquity are not to be missed; the Museum of the History of Excavations in Olympia is okay if you have time to kill or interest to satisfy. And this is before you hit the Olympic site itself.

Entrance times to Ancient Olympia and to the museums change annually, seasonally and at whim, it seems; check with your hotel on arrival. You can buy a joint ticket for the Olympic site and the Archaeological Museum. A handy website to the area is www.ancientolympiahotels.gr.

Museum of the History of the Olympic Games in Antiquity
MUSEUM

(⊙ 12.30-7.30pm Mon, 8am-7.30pm Tue-Sun May-Oct, 10am-5pm Mon, 8am-3pm Tue-Fri) **FREE** This museum, opened in 2004 (after the Athens Olympics), is a beautifully presented space depicting the history of all things athletic, as well as of the Nemean, Panathenaic and, of course, Olympic Games. The sculptures, mosaics and other displays all pay tribute to athletes and athleticism. Women, and their involvement (or lack of), are also acknowledged.

Museum of the History of Excavations in Olympia
MUSEUM

(⊙ 1.30-8pm Mon, 8am-8pm Tue-Sun Apr-Oct, 10am-5pm Mon, 8am-3pm Tue-Fri) **FREE** Next to the Museum of the History of the Olympic Games in Antiquity, and housed in a small historic building, this museum will appeal more to archaeology and history buffs. It displays items relating to the site's German excavations in the 19th century.

★ Archaeological Museum of Olympia
MUSEUM

(☑ tel/fax 26240 22742; adult/concession €6/3, incl site visit €9/5; ⊙ 10am-5pm Mon, 8am-8pm Tue-Fri, reduced hours in winter) This superb museum – Ancient Olympia's archaeological site museum – about 200m north of the sanctuary's ticket kiosk, is a great place to start or end your visit to the site of Ancient Olympia.

The museum includes a scale model of the site, and spectacular (if not complete) reassembled pediments and metopes from the Temple of Zeus. The **eastern pediment** depicts the chariot race between Pelops and Oinomaos, the **western pediment** shows the fight between the Centaurs and Lapiths,

PELOPONNESE OLYMPIA

THE OLYMPIC GAMES

The Olympics were undoubtedly the Ancient World's biggest sporting event. During the Games, warring states briefly halted their squabbles and victorious competitors won great fame and considerable fortune. The origins of Olympia date back to Mycenaean times. The Great Goddess, identified as Rea, was worshipped here in the 1st millennium BC. By the Classical era Rea had been superseded by her son Zeus. A small regional festival, which probably included athletic events, began in the 11th century BC.

The first official quadrennial Olympic Games were declared in 776 BC by King Iphitos of Elis. By 676 BC they were open to all Greek males, and they reached the height of their prestige in 576 BC. The Games were held in honour of Zeus, popularly acclaimed as their founder, and took place around the first full moon in August.

The athletic festival lasted five days and included wrestling, chariot and horse racing, the pentathlon (wrestling, discus and javelin throwing, long jump and running) and the pancratium (a vicious form of fisticuffs).

Originally only Greek-born males were allowed to participate, but later Romans were permitted. Slaves and women were not allowed to enter the sanctuary as participants or spectators. Women trying to sneak in were thrown from a nearby rock.

The event served purposes besides athletic competition. Writers, poets and historians read their works to large audiences, and the citizens of various city states got together. Traders clinched business deals and city state leaders talked in an atmosphere of festivity that was conducive to resolving differences through discussion, rather than battle.

The Games continued during the first years of Roman rule. By this time, however, their importance had declined and, thanks to Nero, they had become less sporting. In AD 67 Nero entered the chariot race with 10 horses, ordering that other competitors could have no more than four. Despite this advantage he fell and abandoned the race, yet was still declared the winner by the judges.

The Games were held for the last time in AD 394, before they were banned by Emperor Theodosius I as part of a purge of pagan festivals. In AD 426 Theodosius II decreed that the temples of Olympia be destroyed.

The modern Olympic Games were instituted in 1896 and, other than during WWI and WWII, have been held every four years in different cities around the world ever since, including (to much celebration in Greece) the 2004 Athens Olympics. The Olympic flame is lit at the ancient site and carried by runners to the city where the Games are held.

Ancient Olympia

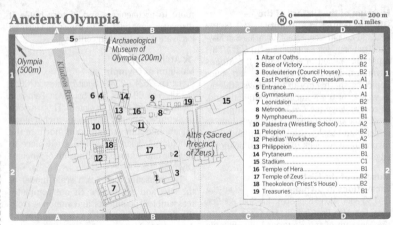

N 0 ———— 200 m
0 ———— 0.1 miles

1 Altar of Oaths	B2
2 Base of Victory	B2
3 Bouleuterion (Council House)	B2
4 East Portico of the Gymnasium	A1
5 Entrance	A1
6 Gymnasium	A1
7 Leonidaion	B2
8 Metroön	B1
9 Nymphaeum	B1
10 Palaestra (Wrestling School)	A2
11 Pelopion	B2
12 Pheidias' Workshop	A2
13 Philippeion	B1
14 Prytaneum	B1
15 Stadium	C1
16 Temple of Hera	B1
17 Temple of Zeus	B2
18 Theokoleon (Priest's House)	B2
19 Treasuries	B1

and the **metopes** depict the Twelve Labours of Hercules.

Don't miss the 4th-century Parian marble statue of **Hermes of Praxiteles**, a masterpiece of classical sculpture from the Temple of Hera. Hermes was charged with taking the infant Dionysos to Mt Nysa.

You'll also find intriguing collections of tiny, but beautifully crafted, votive offerings discovered on the site, and the sculptured **Head of Hera**.

Ancient Olympia   HISTORIC SITE
(☑26240 22517; adult/child €6/3, site & museum €9/5; ⊙8am-8pm Mon-Fri, 8am-3pm Sat & Sun, reduced hours in winter) Held every four years until their abolition by killjoy Emperor Theodosius I in AD 393, the Olympic Games were held here for at least 1000 years. The World Heritage–listed site of Ancient Olympia is still a recognisable complex of temples, priests' dwellings and public buildings. The site contains excellent explanatory boards, with depictions of what the buildings would have looked like, along with a plan and description in English.

Ancient Olympia is signposted from the modern village. The entrance is beyond the bridge over the Kladeos River. Thanks to Theodosius II and various earthquakes, little remains of the magnificent buildings of Ancient Olympia, but enough exists to sustain an absorbing visit in an idyllic, leafy setting; allow a minimum of half a day. A visit to the archaeological museum (p175) beforehand will help with visualising the ancient buildings.

The first ruin encountered is the **gymnasium**, which dates from the 2nd century BC.

South of here is the partly restored **palaestra** (wrestling school), where contestants practised and trained. The next building was the **theokoleon** (priests' house). Behind it is **Pheidias' workshop**, where the gargantuan ivory-and-gold Statue of Zeus, one of the Seven Wonders of the Ancient World, was sculpted. The workshop was identified by archaeologists after the discovery of tools and moulds. Beyond the theokoleon is the **leonidaion**, an elaborate structure that accommodated dignitaries.

The altis, or **Sacred Precinct of Zeus**, lies east of the path. Its most important building was the immense 5th-century Doric **Temple of Zeus**, which enshrined Pheidias' statue, later removed to Constantinople by Theodosius II (where it was destroyed by fire in AD 475). One column has been restored and re-erected, and helps put into perspective its sheer size.

South of the Temple of Zeus is the **bouleuterion** (council house), which contains the **altar of oaths**, where competitors swore to obey the rules decreed by the Olympic Senate.

The **stadium** lies to the east of the *altis* and is entered through an archway. The start and finish lines of the 120m sprint track and the judges' seats still survive. The stadium could seat at least 45,000 spectators. Slaves and women spectators had to be content to watch from the Hill of Cronos.

To the north of the Temple of Zeus was the **pelopion**, a small, wooded hillock with an altar to Pelops. It was surrounded by a wall containing the remains of its Doric portico. Many artefacts now displayed in the museum were found on the hillock.

Further north is the 6th-century Doric **Temple of Hera**, the site's most intact structure. Hera was worshipped along with Rea until the two were superseded by Zeus.

To the east of this temple is the **nymphaeum**, erected by the wealthy Roman banker Herodes Atticus in AD 156–60. Typical of buildings financed by Roman benefactors, it was grandiose, consisting of a semicircular building with Doric columns flanked at each side by a circular temple. The building contained statues of Herodes Atticus and his family. Despite its elaborate appearance, the nymphaeum had a practical purpose; it was a fountain house supplying Olympia with fresh spring water.

Beyond the nymphaeum and up a flight of stone steps, a row of 12 **treasuries** stretched to the stadium, each erected by a city state for use as a storehouse and marking the northern boundaries of the *altis*.

At the bottom of these steps are the scant remains of the 5th-century-BC **metroön**, a temple dedicated to Rea, the mother of the gods. Apparently the ancients worshipped Rea in this temple with orgies.

The foundations of the **philippeion**, west of the Temple of Hera, are the remains of a circular construction with Ionic columns built by Philip of Macedon to commemorate the Battle of Chaironeia (338 BC), where he defeated a combined army of Athenians and Thebans. The building contained statues of Philip and his family.

North of the *philippeion* was the **prytaneum**, the magistrate's residence. Here, winning athletes were entertained and feasted.

Tours

To really make the site come alive – to visualise the buffed and oiled athletes, the visiting all-male crowds, the dignitaries and the pomp and ceremony of the ancient Games – it's well worth considering hiring a guide, especially if there are a few of you. Tours usually include both the site and museum, but any preference will be catered for. Recommended guides include **Niki Vlachou** (6972426085, 26240 23630; www.olympictours.gr; 2½-3hr tour incl museum €120), who speaks English and French, **Agelos Koutras** (26240 22602), and **Marieta Kolotourou** (26250 23596), who speaks English and Spanish.

Sleeping

A self-drive day trip to Olympia from as far as Athens, Nafplio or Kalamata is time-consuming and relatively arduous. We suggest you factor at least one night to stay here. Alternatively, Stemnitsa or Dimitsana make excellent overnight stopovers on the way to Ancient Olympia if you are heading on the east–west route across the region.

Hotel Pelops   HOTEL $
(26240 22543; www.hotelpelops.gr; Varela 2; s/d/tr incl breakfast €40/50/70;   @   ) Opposite the church, this is among the town's best contenders, with comfortable rooms. The delightful Greek-Australian owners, the Spiliopoulos family, provide friendly, knowledgeable service and a decent breakfast. And, hurrah, there's tea and coffee facilities in each room.

Hotel Kronio   HOTEL $
(26240 22188; www.hotelkronio.gr; Tsoureka 1; s/d/tr incl breakfast €39/45/55;   @   ) The helpful, multilingual owner, Panagiotis, is a bonus to this pleasant spot with its excellent-value bright and airy rooms.

Pension Posidon   PENSION $
(26240 22567; www.pensionposidon.gr; Stefanopoulou 9; s €35, d €40-45, tr €50 incl breakfast;   ) A helpful couple run this centrally located, cosy spot where rooms are simple but pleasant and have balconies. Breakfast costs €5.

Camping Diana   CAMPGROUND $
(26240 22314; www.campingdiana.gr; camp sites per adult/tent/car €8/6/5;   ) A well-run place, with delightful elderly, multilingual owners and luxuriant tree canopy; clearly signposted 250m west of the village. Open all year.

Hotel Hermes   PENSION $
(26240 22577; hermes72@otenet.gr; s/d/tr incl breakfast €25/30/35;   ) This friendly, family-run budget option has seven basic, but spotless, rooms with linoleum floors. A taverna is attached. It's after the BP petrol station on the right as you enter town from the south.

Best Western Europa   HOTEL $$
(26240 22650; www.hoteleuropa.gr; Drouva 1; s/d/tr incl breakfast €75/95/110;   @   ) This franchise is popular with groups. Rooms vary in size and quality – the larger rooms with balcony vistas are more luxurious. A bar, swimming pool and a decent pool-side taverna, under the shade of olive trees, help push it over the line.

🍴 Eating

There are no outstanding favourites among Olympia's restaurants; with so many one-off customers passing through, they lack incentive to strive for excellence. You're better off heading to the outer villages such as Floka, 1.5km north.

Self-caterers will find a good supermarket near the Shell petrol station.

Takis Tyropitas BAKERY $
(Praxitelis Kondilis 36; snacks €1.50; ⊙7am-3pm) This nondescript blink-and-you'll-miss-it takeaway joint has been here for 24 years, and with good reason. Owner Takis makes the best *tyropita* (cheese pie) and other homemade treats in the Pelops – some would say, Greece.

Taverna Thea TAVERNA $
(☑26240 23264; mains €6.50-12; ⊙lunch May-Oct, dinner year-round) It's worth the effort to venture the winding route to the small village of Floka, 1.5km north of Olympia, for hearty traditional taverna fare. Enjoy the grills, zucchini balls and views of Floka from the large terrace. That is, if the locals don't beat you to it.

Mithos KEBAB $
(☑6970605395; mains €6-10; ⊙lunch & dinner) A locally recommended place off the tourist drag. The place to get your chops around some quality grills.

The Garden Taverna GREEK $$
(☑26240 22650; Best Western Hotel Europa International; mains €9.50-15; ⊙lunch & dinner May-Sep) Don't be put off by the fact it's in the gardens of a hotel. This outdoor eatery offers excellent grills and more standard tourist fare (moussaka, pasta) in a lovely setting under olive trees and by a pool. In fine weather, it's a lovely way to get your taste of the Mediterranean.

ⓘ Information

Cafe Zeus (Praxitelous Kondyli; ⊙8am-late Mar-Nov) One of several cafes with wi-fi access.
National Bank of Greece (cnr Praxitelous Kondyli & Stefanopoulou)
Post Office (Pierre Coubertin 3)

ⓘ Getting There & Away

BUS

There is no direct service from Olympia to Athens; you must catch these in Pyrgos. Fourteen or so buses (reduced schedule on weekends) go

to Pyrgos (€2.30, 30 minutes) – allow time to connect for services to Athens. From Olympia there are two buses east to Tripoli (€14.30, three hours) and one to Dimitsana (around €7, 2½ hours) on Monday to Friday; on all other days, it goes to Karkalou, about 5km from Dimitsana. Note: for tickets to Tripoli, you must reserve your seat with **KTEL Pyrgos** (☑26210 20600; www.ktelileias.gr) one day prior to travel; hotels will call on your behalf.

CAR

There are three possible routes between Olympia and Athens and/or Nafplio. The first is along the main northern coastal road via Patra, and the second is via the toll road, direction Tripoli, via Megalopoli and Kalo Nero. The final is via the toll road, direction Tripoli. After the Artemisio tunnel follow the sign to the right for Ancient Olympia (Archaia Olympia) and follow the road through the mountains of Arkadia. This route is extremely winding. Note: all routes are quite arduous; ask hotels for time estimates (and add at least an hour for speed differences and photo stops).

TRAIN

Olympia train services head to/from Pyrgos only – there are two to three local departures daily (€1, 30 minutes). From here, it's best to catch a bus.

Andritsena   Ανδρίτσαινα

POP 575

The village of Andritsena, situated 65km southeast of Pyrgos, hovers on a hillside overlooking the valley of the Alfios River. Crumbling stone houses, some with rickety wooden balconies, flank the village's narrow cobbled streets and a stream bubbles its way through the central square, Plateia Agnostopoulou. Keep an eye out for the fountain emerging from the trunk of a huge plane tree. Andritsena makes an appealing base from which to visit the magnificent Temple of Epicurean Apollo at Vasses, a World Heritage–listed site, located 14km from the village.

⊙ Sights

Nikolopoulos Andritsena Library LIBRARY, MUSEUM
(☑26260 22242; ⊙8.30am-2pm Tue-Sat) `FREE`
You don't need to be a reader to appreciate the stunning legacy of Nikolopoulos at this library. In 1838 he donated 4000 rare books to his father's home town to establish a school. It was one of Europe's largest private book collections at the time. There's

a 1502 edition and a 1657 Bible. The nearby village of Stemnitsa donated another 4000 books, now on display, along with manuscripts from Greece's 1821 Independence movement. Don't miss the short explanatory video in English. Located behind Hotel Theoxenia.

Folk Museum
MUSEUM

(⊙11am-2pm & 6-8pm) This much-advertised, but rarely open, Folk Museum contains a quaint collection of local items, from furniture to traditional clothing. For entry, you must ring the telephone displayed on the door.

Temple of Epicurean Apollo at Vasses
HISTORIC SITE

(☑26260 22275; adult €3; ⊙8am-8pm Apr-Oct, to 6pm Nov-Mar) Situated 14km from Andritsena, on a wild, isolated spot overlooking rugged mountains and hills, the World Heritage-listed Vasses, with its Temple of Epicurean Apollo, is one of Greece's most romantic and atmospheric archaeological sites. The road from Andritsena climbs along a mountain ridge, taking you through increasingly dramatic scenery, until you arrive at the temple, which stands at an altitude of 1200m.

The striking and well-preserved temple is robbed of some of its splendour and immediate visual impact by the giant (and semipermanent) steel-girded tent enclosing it, as it undergoes a superslow restoration program, but it's magnificent all the same.

The temple was built in 420 BC by the people of nearby Figalia, who dedicated it to Apollo Epicurus (the Helper) for delivering them from the plague. Designed by Iktinos, the architect of the Parthenon, the temple combines Doric and Ionic columns and a single Corinthian column – the earliest example of this order.

No public buses run to Vasses. You could try to arrange a group to share a taxi.

🛏 Sleeping & Eating

For somewhere to eat, try any of the casual tavernas and grill places spread along the main street.

Epikourios Apollon
HOTEL $$

(☑26260 22840; www.epikoureios-apollon.gr; Plateia Agnostopoulou; s/d/tr incl breakfast €40/60/75; ⊙year-round; 🛜) This guesthouse-cum-hotel has simple but cheerful rooms overlooking the central square or the valley behind.

WINERY STOPOVER

Nemea's wine country is not the only region of the Peloponnese to produce a decent drop. **Mercouri Estate** (☑26210 41601; www.mercouri.gr; tastings €10; ⊙9am-2pm Mon-Sat), 1km north of Korakohori village and about 15km from Pyrgos, is another worthwhile winery. This handsome estate produces a dry white Foloi, and a prize-winning rich red, its flagship Domaine Mercouri. It also runs tours of the grounds (reservations required).

ⓘ Information

Both the ATE Bank (with an ATM) and the post office are found near the central square.

ⓘ Getting There & Away

There are buses to Pyrgos (around €6.20, 1½ hours, two daily except weekends), and to Athens (€24, two hours, two daily) via Karitena, Megalopoli, Tripoli and Corinth Isthmus.

Kyllini
Κυλλήνη

The port of Kyllini (kih-*lee*-nih), 78km southwest of Patra, warrants a mention merely as the jumping-off point for ferries to Kefallonia and Zakynthos. Most people arrive on buses from Patra to board the ferries.

There are boats to Zakynthos (per person/car €6.50/29.90, 1¼ hours, up to four daily in summer) and to Poros (per person/car €11.50/61, 1½ hours, up to four daily in summer) and Argostoli (two hours, one daily summer only) on Kefallonia. See www.ionianferries.gr as schedules change regularly.

From Pyrgos (€6, one hour) there are two daily buses to Kyllini, and three to four buses daily from the KTEL Zakynthos bus station in Patra (€8, 1¼ hours). Some connect with ferries to Zakynthos (bus and ferry €15.90). Note, however, doing the reverse trip that there are no buses from Kyllini to Patra. A **taxi** (☑6973535678) to Patra costs around €60.

ACHAÏA
ΑΧΑΪΑ

Foreign visitors are slowly discovering the delights of Achaïa. The spectacular region hides a string of coastal resorts, some high and skiable mountain country (reached on a fantastic rack-and-pinion railway) and a bustling capital, Patra.

Achaïa owes its name to the Achaeans, an Indo-European branch of migrants who settled on mainland Greece and established what is more commonly known as the Mycenaean civilisation. When the Dorians arrived, the Achaeans were pushed into this northwestern corner of the Peloponnese, displacing the original Ionians.

Legend has it that the Achaeans founded 12 cities, which later developed into the powerful Achaean Federation that survived until Roman times. Principal among these cities were the ports of Patra and Egio (on the coast of the Gulf of Corinth).

Patra (Patras)   Πάτρα

POP 168,000

The largest city in the Peloponnese, and Achaïa's capital, Patra is named after King Patreas, who ruled Achaïa around 1100 BC. Despite an eventful 3000 years of history, Patra is often dismissed by travellers. Many pass straight through, boarding or disembarking from boats that sail between here, Italy and some Ionian Islands.

There's no doubt Patra is feeling the crisis, evidenced by closed shops, lack of tourist office and scrappy port-side streets. Nevertheless, on the city's more attractive pedestrian hub, you'll find a cosmopolitan city with a vibrant cafe and clubbing scene (helped by the presence of Patra's 20,000 university students), some interesting sites and a busy arts-and-culture community.

Patra's cityscape is dominated by a former port (note: the new ferry port is located south of town), bland 1950s concrete tenements and a few surviving 19th-century neoclassical buildings. But the city also has attractive squares and architectural landmarks, such as the Apollon Theatre, the impressive archaeological museum and the Rio–Andirio suspension bridge, an engineering feat that links the city with western continental Greece.

◎ Sights & Activities

Archaeological Museum of Patras   MUSEUM
(☑26104 20645; cnr Amerikis & Patras-Athens National Rd; ◎8.30am-3pm Tue-Sun) FREE This space-age museum, with shiny metallic domes and contemporary buildings, is the country's second-largest museum. Its col-

lections – across three themed halls (private life, public life and cemeteries) – feature objects from prehistoric to Roman times (including extraordinary mosaics, sarcophagi and jewellery) from Patra and surrounds. The museum also includes a particularly significant collection of Mycenaean swords. Note that the museum is located 7km out of town.

Kastro   CASTLE
(◎8.30am-3pm Tue-Sun) FREE The *kastro* stands on the site of the acropolis of ancient Patrai. The Romans were the first to build a fort here around AD 550, but the present structure is of Frankish origin, remodelled many times over the centuries by the Byzantines, Venetians and Turks. It was in use as a defensive position until WWII. Set in an attractive pencil-pine park, it is reached by climbing the 190-plus steps at the southeastern end of Agiou Nikolaou. Great views of Zakynthos and Kefallonia are the reward.

Church of Agios Andreas   CHURCH
(Agiou Andreou) Seating 5500 people, this church is one of the largest in the Balkans. It houses religious icons and paintings, plus St Andreas' skull, along with part of the cross on which he was crucified.

Hammam   BATHHOUSE
(☑2610 274 267; Boukaouri 29; ◎9am-9pm Mon-Sat winter only) This *hammam* (Turkish baths) is a privately run venture, but you can scrub up as the Turks did before you in AD 1500.

✦ Festivals & Events

Patra's citizens party hard during the annual **Patras Carnival** (www.carnivalpatras.gr). This program features a host of minor events leading up to a wild weekend of costume parades, colourful floats and celebrations in late February or early March. The event draws big crowds, so hotel reservations are essential if you want to stay overnight. Dates change annually, so check the website.

🛏 Sleeping

Prices double at Carnival time.

Pension Nikos   HOTEL $
(☑2610 623 757; cnr Patreos 3 & Agiou Andreou 121; s/d/tr €30/40/55, s/d without bathroom €25/35; ❄) This centrally located, '60s-style budget option has flaking shutters on the outside, but inside Nikos runs a tight ship

with clean rooms on several floors and a reasonable roof terrace.

Maison Grecque BOUTIQUE HOTEL **$$**

(☎2610 241 212; www.mghotels.gr; 25 Martiou St 116; s/d/tr incl breakfast €65/85/135) As the name might suggest, this smart, boutique spot has a touch of 'sleek Greek' pretension. Each room is decked out uniquely (with an original ceiling fresco or two thrown in) – think dark hues with metalic touches – and one or two of the rooms are slightly claustrophic. The rest, however, are sophisticated and smart.

It's in a handy location, a five-minute walk from the pedestrianised centre.

Hotel Marie Palace HOTEL **$$**

(☎2610 331 302; www.mariepalace.gr; Gounari 6; s/d incl breakfast €40/60; ❄📶) The helpful, friendly staff here make up for any shortfalls in the simple but clean rooms, which are popular with budget-minded business travellers. Rooms at the front have balconies, but can be noisy at night.

Hotel Byzantino HOTEL **$$**

(☎2610 243 000; www.byzantino-hotel.gr; Riga Fereou 106; s/d/tr incl breakfast €75/85/100; ❄📶) The Byzantino is a change from Patra's concrete monoliths. This graceful and restored neoclassical building features reasonable

Patra

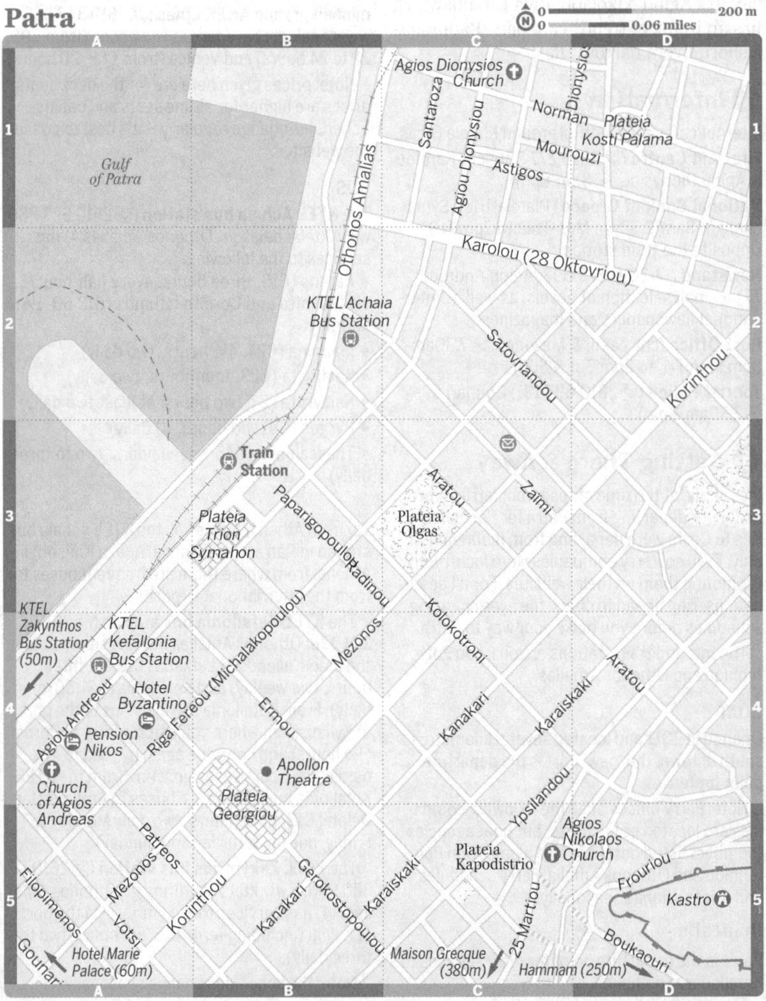

0 200 m
0 0.06 miles
A
B
C
D
1
2
3
4
5
Gulf of Patra
Agios Dionysios Church
Santaroza
Agiou Dionysiou
Dionysiou
Norman
Plateia Kosti Palama
Mourouzi
Astigos
Othonos Amalias
Karolou (28 Oktovriou)
KTEL Achaia Bus Station
Satovriandou
Korinthou
Train Station
Paparigopoulou
Aratou
Zaimi
Plateia Olgas
Plateia Trion Symahon
Radinou
Kolokotroni
Riga Fereou (Michalakopoulou)
Mezonos
KTEL Zakynthos Bus Station (50m)
KTEL Kefallonia Bus Station
Hotel Byzantino
Agiou Andreou
Pension Nikos
Ermou
Kanakari
Karaiskaki
Aratou
Church of Agios Andreas
Apollon Theatre
Plateia Georgiou
Ypsilandou
Agios Nikolaos Church
Plateia Kapodistrio
Patreos
Mezonos
Korinthou
Gerokostopoulou
Karaiskaki
Kanakari
Frouriou
Kastro
Filopimenos
Votsi
25 Martiou
Boukaouri
Gounari
Hotel Marie Palace (60m)
Maison Grecque (380m)
Hammam (250m)

rooms with fancy bedsteads, wooden floors and period furniture.

 ## Eating

To do frappé (Greek-style iced coffee) with the best of 'em, head along Agiou Nikolaou; new trendy cafes also line the newly pedestrianised Riga Fereou (Michalakopoulou). For good eating options head southeast to Trion Navarhon. Cheap student eateries are along Gerokostopoulou.

Drinking & Nightlife

Around sunset Patra transforms into a cosmopolitan, sharp-dressing, buzzy, cafe-lined city. Try Agiou Nikolaou, Riga Fereou, which has an influx of trendy cafe-bars. Radinou is a short, lively, narrow alley.

 ## Information

Internet cafes are plentiful around Plateia Olgas.
First Aid Centre (☑ 2610 277 386; cnr Karolou & Agiou Dionysiou; ⊘ 8am-8pm)
National Bank of Greece (Plateia Trion Symachon; ⊘ 8am-2.30pm Mon-Thu, to 2pm Fri) Opposite the train station.
Newstand (☑ 2610 273 092; Agiou Andreou 77) A small selection of novels, as well as international newspapers and magazines.
Post Office (cnr Zaïmi & Mezonos; ⊘ 7.30am-8pm Mon-Fri, to 2pm Sat & Sun)
Tourist Police (☑ 2610 695 191; Gounari 52; ⊘ 7.30am-9pm)

 ## Getting There & Away

Incredibly, at the time of research, ferries were no longer departing from Patra for Corfu; ferries to Corfu were departing from Igounemitsa only. Even so, ferry companies were incorrectly promoting them on their websites. For all destinations, ring ahead to check the ever-changing schedules before you make your way to Patra.

The bus and train stations are on Iroön Polytehniou and Othonos Amalias.

BOAT

Opened in 2011 and located several kilometres south of town, the 'new' port is the departure point for ferries.

Note: Ferry offices of all the following companies are located at the ports, but boat agencies (numbers listed here) are also along Iroön Polytehniou and Othonos Amalia. Ferry schedules and prices change seasonally.

Domestic

Patra is the departure point for ferry services to Kefallonia and Ithaki.

Strintzis Lines (☑ 2610 240 000; www.strinzisferries.gr) has services to Kefallonia (Sami; two daily, 2¾ hours, per person/car €18.80/64). The same services head to Ithaki (Pisoaetos; two daily, 3½ hours, €19).

International

Patra is Greece's main port for ferry services to Italy – Ancona, Bari, Brindisi and Venice. Some of these ferries may stop at Igoumenitsa and Corfu, but under no circumstances are you permitted a free stopover on Corfu.

Superfast/Blue Star Ferries (☑ 2610 622 500; www.superfast.com; Othonos Amalias 12) runs trips to Ancona (from €78, 21 hours) and Bari (from €75, 15½ hours).

Minoan Lines (☑ 261 042 6000; www.minoan.gr) and **ANEK Lines** (☑ 2610 343 655; www.anek.gr) have ferries to Ancona (from €95, 22 to 24 hours) and Venice (from €65, 20 hours).

Note: prices given here are for the deck seats; prices are higher for airline seats and cabins. Schedules change regularly – it's best to consult the websites.

BUS

The **KTEL Achaia bus station** (☑ 2610 623 886; www.ktelachaias.gr; Othonos Amalias 4) has services to the following:

➡ Athens (€19, three hours, every half-hour) via Diakofto and Corinth Isthmus (€12.60, 1½ hours)

➡ Ioannina (€24, 4½ hours, two daily)

➡ Kalamata (€23, four hours, two daily)

➡ Kalavryta (€7, two hours, at least two daily)

➡ Pyrgos (€9, two hours, 10 daily)

➡ Thessaloniki (€45, seven hours, two to three daily)

To/from Athens, buses link the KTEL Achaia bus station in Patra with Terminal A (aka Kiffisou) in Athens, from where there are frequent buses to/from the international airport.

The **KTEL Kefallonia bus station** (☑ 2610 274 938; Othonos Amalias 58) has services to the Ionian islands of Lefkada (€16.20, three hours, two weekly) and Kefallonia (€21.50, one daily). From Kefallonia travel by bus to the port of Kyllini, from where you catch a ferry to Poros (1½ hours) and continue again by road to Argostoli (one hour). Also departing from the KTEL Kefallonia bus station are buses to Amfissa (for Delphi; €13, three hours, two daily Monday to Friday, one on Saturday and Sunday).

The **KTEL Zakynthos bus station** (☑ 2610 220 993; www.ktel-zakynthos.gr; Othonos Amalias 84) has services to Zakynthos, via the port of Kyllini (including ferry €16, 3½ hours, two to three daily).

Note: the schedules change seasonally.

TRAIN

There are six trains a day to Athens (€17). At the time of research, a replacement bus heads as far as Kiato, from where you take the *proastiako*. Note: on arrival in Athens you can use your *proastiako* ticket for 1½ hours on the metro, but to do this you must validate the ticket or you will be fined.

🛈 Getting Around

Hertz (☑ 2610 220 990; www.hertz.gr; Akti Dimaion 40) Recommended, reliable car-hire outlet.

Zahlorou   Ζαχλωρού

POP 40

The picturesque settlement of Zahlorou, the halfway stop on the Diakofto–Kalavryta train line, straddles both sides of a river and a railway line. Some people take the train to this point and walk back to Diakofto – the walk, much of it on the track itself, takes up to four hours.

From here, you can also hike up to **Moni Megalou Spileou** (Monastery of the Great Cavern; ☑ 26920 23130; ☺ 8am-noon & 1pm-sunset winter, 8am-1pm & 2pm-sunset summer) **FREE**, a monastery (the 3km-long walk takes about an hour). The original monastery was destroyed in 1934 when gunpowder stored during the War of Independence exploded. The new monastery houses illuminated gospels and relics, and the miraculous icon of the Virgin Mary, supposedly discovered in the nearby cavern by St Theodore and St Simeon in AD 362.

Of the two budget sleeping options right on the station platform, **Zachlorou** (☑ 6983125616, 26920 22789; www.zachlorou.gr; r from €40) is the preferred option over the sootier **Hotel Romantzo** (☑ 6986885779, 26920 22758; r from €35), but we're not talking first-class services at either. A better option is **Taverna Oneiro** (☑ 6945776821, 26920 23772; www.villa-oneiro.gr; r incl breakfast from €50; ☺ Oct-May), with nine wood-trimmed ski-lodge-style studios.

All Diakofto–Kalavryta trains stop briefly at Zahlorou. You can drive to Zahlorou on a narrow road leading off the Diakofto–Kalavryta road. The turn-off is 7.5km north of Kalavryta.

DIAKOFTO–KALAVRYTA RAILWAY

One of the unmissable journeys to make in the Peloponnese is aboard the tiny, unique **train** (☑ 6986307176, 26910 43206; one way/return €9.50/19) running along the railway from Diakofto to Kalavryta. It takes travellers on an unforgettable ride through the dramatic **Vouraïkos Gorge**. The train climbs over 700m in 22.5km, using a rack-and-pinion (cog) system for traction on the steep sections, effectively clamping itself to the notched girder you can see running between the rails. Built by an Italian company between 1885 and 1895, the railway was a remarkable feat of engineering for its time, with only a handful of equivalents around the world (most notably in the Swiss Alps). Between 2007 and 2009 the trains were off the tracks as the entire rails and cog sections were replaced, and four new modern trains were constructed to replace the former carriages.

As you head through the gorge, the line switches back and forth under a leafy canopy of plane trees and clings to a narrow ledge overhanging the river, passing through seven curving tunnels along the way.

The journey takes just over an hour, stopping en route at Zahlorou. There are departures daily to a changing schedule. A good website to check its status (run by a passionate trainspotter) is www.odontotos.com.

The original steam engines that first plied the route were replaced in the early 1960s by diesel cars, but the old engines can still be seen outside Diakofto and Kalavryta stations.

Note: Regular KTEL buses do not stop in Diakofto. To get there, catch the only 'working' train line: Corinth–Patra. (Though OSE buses currently run in place of trains for the Diakofto-Kiato section). On leaving Diakofto, you can catch the same replacement bus service west to Patra or, to head east, take the replacement bus service to Kiato, from where you catch the *proastiako* train, either one stop to Corinth or as far as Athens airport.

Kalavryta   Καλάβρυτα

POP 1800

Perched 756m above sea level, Kalavryta (kah-*lah*-vrih-tah) is a delightful resort town with fresh mountain air, gushing springs and a tree-shaded square. The town is especially popular among Athenians, who arrive in numbers on weekends and during the winter ski season. As such, prices can be a bit higher here than in other villages.

Two relatively recent historical events have assured Kalavryta a place in the hearts of all Greeks. First, despite plenty of evidence that fighting had already begun elsewhere, the official version of the War of Independence states that the revolt against the Turks began here on 25 March 1821, when Bishop Germanos of Patra raised the Greek flag at Moni Agias Lavras, 6km from town. Second, on 13 December 1943, in one of the worst atrocities of WWII, the Nazis set fire to the town and massacred nearly all its male inhabitants over the age of 15 (498 people) as punishment for resistance activity. The hands of the old cathedral clock stand eternally at 2.34, the time the massacre began. The event is solemnly and movingly recorded in the old schoolhouse, now a museum dedicated to the memory of those killed both in this event and in the region (about 700 people in total).

The area is said to have a unique blue butterfly species, found only in the area, and the region is also becoming popular for birdwatchers.

☉ Sights

Museum of the Kalavryta Holocaust   MUSEUM

(☑ 26920 23646; www.dmko.gr; 1-5 Syngrou; admission €3; ☉ 9am-4pm Tue-Sun) This extraordinary museum should be a compulsory first stop for all visitors to the town. The country's only Holocaust museum, it is a most powerful tribute to the memory of the estimated 700 people killed by the German army in the region during WWII, especially the 498 people who died in the 13 December 1943 slaughter. It's a dignified, understated, yet extremely evocative account of the struggle between the occupying forces and partisan fighters in the area, and the events running up to the massacre – an atrocity reported to be partly put in motion by the partisans' execution of a group of German prisoners.

Whatever you do, don't pass by the videos on continuous loop dotted throughout the exhibition. These are the accounts of surviving townspeople who escaped death, some after being locked with their mothers in the schoolhouse (now the museum building), apparently to be burned alive. The wall covered with pictures of the dead Kalavryta villagers is an especially striking memorial.

Martyrs' Monument   MONUMENT

A huge white cross on a cypress-covered hillside just east of town marks the site of the 1943 massacre. Beneath this imposing monument is a poignant little shrine to the victims. It's signposted off Konstantinou.

🛏 Sleeping

Lodges are dotted outside the town; the town itself has few hotel options. Peak period here is the ski season (November to April), when reservations are essential. Bookings are also required on weekends throughout the year, when Athenians come to enjoy the cool mountain air. Prices are slashed by as much as 50% at other times. The hotels association website, www.kalavrita-hotels.gr, lists some good options.

The cheapest options are the domatia on the streets behind the train station.

Hotel Kynaitha   HOTEL $$

(☑ 26920 22609; www.kynaitha.gr; Ethnikis Andistasis 11; s/d/tr/ste incl breakfast €65/85/98/145; ❄ 🛜) Modern and comfortable with spacious and attractively furnished rooms boasting gleaming-white bathrooms and posh toiletries.

Finday Boutique Hotel   BOUTIQUE HOTEL $$

(☑ 26920 24552; www.findayhotel.gr; r incl breakfast from €60) This upmarket choice is great for longer stays, with elegant rooms and studios boasting chic trimmings – quilts and cast-iron beds – plus lovely views of town. It's a Greek favourite with honeymooning couples.

Hotel Filoxenia   HOTEL $$

(☑ 26920 22422; www.hotelfiloxenia.gr; Ethnikis Andistasis 10; s/d/tr incl breakfast €70/90/110; ⚑ ❄ 🛜) Kind of like an old-fashioned ski lodge – old, brown and a bit daggy, but comfortable and friendly. Rooms have balconies. Rates are considerably cheaper on weekdays.

Hotel Helmos HOTEL **$$**
(☑26920 29222; www.hotelhelmos.gr; Plateia Eleftherias 1; s/d/tr €80/110/145; 🌐🔌📶) Housed in one of the village's stunning original buildings, this renovated option has slightly cramped rooms, but with creature comforts and contemporary surrounds.

✕ Eating

Most places to eat are on 25 Martiou: head from top to bottom and go where the Greeks go. Even out of ski season Kalavryta is one of *the* weekend places for Athenians, so it has an abundance of trendy bars and cafes.

To Spitikou TAVERNA **$**
(☑26920 24260; mains €6-12; ⊙lunch & dinner) Opposite the bus station and off the beaten track, this cosy place with a ski-lodge feel serves up great-quality traditional taverna meals, many made by the owner's mother.

Gri Gri Café SWEETS **$**
(25 Martiou; snacks €1.50-4; ⊙8am-8pm) Opposite the museum you'll find this good (less fashion-conscious) family-run spot. Recommended for its sweet or savoury homemade snacks, such as cheese pie, baklava and tasty *crèma* (sweet, set custard).

Ellinikon BAKERY **$**
(snacks €1.50-4) This terrific bakery is near the petrol station on the road out of town towards Patra and Klitoria. It has ideal picnic fare: wonderful bread, mini pizzas and dozens of types of sweet pastries.

ℹ Information

The train station is on the northern edge of town, opposite the museum. To the right of the museum is Syngrou/25 Martiou, a pedestrian precinct. To the left of the museum is Konstantinou.

The central square, Plateia Kalavrytou, is two blocks up from the train station.

There is no tourist office.

National Bank of Greece (25 Martiou) Just before Plateia Kalavrytou.

Post Office (⊙7.30am-2pm Mon-Fri) Behind Plateia Kalavrytou.

ℹ Getting There & Around

The rack-and-pinion train to/from Diakofto via Zahlorou runs to a changing timetable.

There are buses to Patra (€8, two hours, three daily on weekdays, two on weekends), Athens (€17, three hours, at least one to two daily) and Klitoria (€3, one to two daily). The **bus station**

(☑26920 22224) is 200m before the entrance to town (from Diakofto approach road), beside the Jetoil petrol station.

Kalavryta's **taxi rank** (☑26920 22127) is in front of the train station.

Most of the attractions are out of town, so it's very handy to have your own transport.

Around Kalavryta

Kalavryta and its surrounding mountains feature several interesting sites. While some are just outside the town, others are further afield but doable in a car. Roads are winding and rather slow going, but afford varied and stunning scenery.

◉ Sights & Activities

Moni Agias Lavras MONASTERY
(☑26920 22363; ⊙10am-1pm & 3-4pm winter, 10am-1pm & 4-5pm summer) The original 10th-century monastery that stood here was burnt down by the Nazis. The new monastery has a small museum where the banner standard (the flag that started Greece's War of Independence) is displayed along with monastic memorabilia. The monastery is around 6km southwest of Kalavryta. A taxi from Kalavryta costs €20 return with half an hour to see the monastery.

Cave of the Lakes CAVE
(☑26920 31588; www.kastriacave.gr; adult/child €9/4.50; ⊙9.30am-4.30pm, longer hours in summer) The remarkable Cave of the Lakes lies 16.5km south of Kalavryta near the village of Kastria. The cave features in Greek mythology and is mentioned in the writings of the ancient traveller Pausanias, but its whereabouts remained unknown in modern times until 1964 when locals investigated, having noticed water pouring from the roof of a smaller cave. They discovered a large bat-filled cavern at the start of a 2km-long cave carved out by a subterranean river.

The cavern is now reached by an artificial entrance, which is the starting point for a 500m boardwalk that snakes up the riverbed. You must go with a guide on the 35-minute tour (in Greek). The lakes are a series of 13 stone basins formed by mineral deposits over the millennia.

Getting to the cave is difficult without your own transport. A taxi from Kalavryta costs around €40 return (the taxi will wait for you). Check opening hours – they change regularly.

Trout Farms & Restaurants
TROUT FARMS

A pleasant afternoon's eating can be had in the tiny village of Planitero, about 20km south of Kalavryta (6km north of the village of Klitoria), where half a dozen trout restaurants and several trout farms – all offering similar fare (trout €8 to €11) – line the banks of the Aroanios River, many under the shade of plane trees.

The turn-off to Planitero is signposted to the left, about 4km short of Klitoria.

Ski Centre
SKIING

(☑26920 24451; www.kalavrita-ski.gr; ☺9am-4pm Dec-Apr) With 12 runs and seven lifts (two chairlifts), the Ski Centre (elevation 1700m to 2340m) is 14km east of Kalavryta on Mt Helmos (2355m). There's no overnight accommodation but it rents skis and snowboard equipment (€20 to €25 for boots and skis or snowboard). In Kalavryta try **Ski Time Center** (☑26920 22030; Agiou Alexiou) for ski hire.

There's no public transport from Kalavryta. A taxi costs €40 return. The season lasts from December to April, snow permitting.

Central Greece

Includes ➡

Best Places to Eat

➡ Taverna Vakhos (p196)

➡ Bebelis (p199)

➡ Taverna Orea Ammoudia (p214)

➡ Georgaras Restaurant (p216)

Best Places to Stay

➡ Lost Unicorn Hotel (p215)

➡ Hotel Ganimede (p199)

➡ Mansion Karagiannopoulou (p216)

➡ Doupiani House (p225)

Why Go?

Ancient Greece's 'centre' of the Earth – Delphi – is these days among Greece's most visited places for the archaeological site, ancient footpaths and vistas of the Corinthian Gulf. Delphi is rivalled in popularity only by Meteora, the breathtaking outcroppings of rocky towers topped by teetering monasteries (and rock climbers).

The central Greece (κεντρική Ελλάδα) region also holds many underrated surprises. Alpine meadows and valleys cover the Evritania mountain range, making it perfect for skiing, white-water rafting and breezy summer hikes. And it doesn't get much better than the beautiful Pelion Peninsula, home to Jason and the Argonauts, and criss-crossed with historic cobblestone paths linking lush mountain hamlets with coves and beaches that rival the best islands (yes! ssshhhhh!).

And speaking of 'good, better, best'? The region's good-natured people serve up hospitality, superb experiences and great cuisine.

There's no better place to navel gaze.

When to Go
Delphi

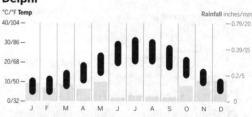

Apr & May Wild herbs and flowers mingle in alpine meadows.

Sep Stable, sunny weather and fewer crowds.

Orthodox Easter Villages that follow traditional customs, with parades and copious food.

DELPHI & STEREA ELLADA

Greek mythology and history seem to mingle in the rugged and scenic landscape of Sterea Ellada (Στερεά Ελλάδα). On the slopes of Mt Parnassos sits Delphi, regarded by the ancient Greeks as the centre of the world. The land stretches east to Attica, where legendary King Oedipus met his fate, and west to Messolongi, where British bard Lord Byron died of fever during the Greek War of Independence. The region acquired its name, meaning Mainland Greece, in 1827, as part of the newly formed Greece.

Thiva (Thebes) Θήβα

Thiva, the birthplace of Hercules and Dionysos, was a powerful city state in 400 BC during Greece's golden age, occupying a strategic position between northern Greece and the Peloponnese. The tragic fate of its

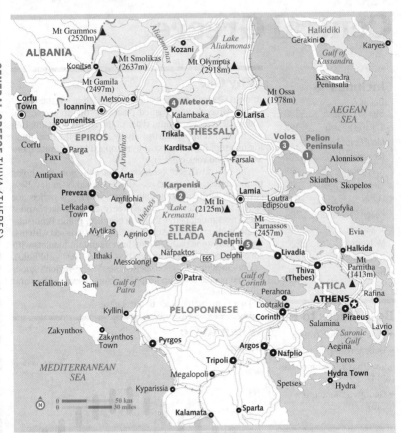

Central Greece Highlights

1 Wander along former donkey paths to the sea on the **Pelion Peninsula** (p209)

2 Feast on fresh trout from mountain streams near **Karpenisi** (p202)

3 Try a *tsipouro* or three with the locals in **Volos** (p207)

4 Climb the monastery-topped rock pinnacles at **Meteora** (p220), following ancient footpaths to hidden caves

5 Meditate over the last light of day at the Sanctuary of Athena Pronea in **Ancient Delphi** (p191)

royal dynasty, centred on the myth of Oedipus, rivalled that of ancient Mycenae.

After the Trojan War in the 12th century BC, Thiva became the dominant city of the Boeotia region. Thiva's glorious run ended in 335 BC, however, when it was sacked by Alexander the Great for siding with the Persians.

Although present-day Thiva has few vestiges of its past glory – except for a wonderful archaeological museum which has been inexplicably closed for the last few years – Greek history diehards might head here for posterity; the centre is a pleasant enough place to wander around for an hour or so.

🛈 Getting There & Away

Buses operate to Athens (€8, 1½ hours, hourly) from Thiva's central **bus station** (☑ 22620 27512; KTEL Thiva), 500m south of Plateia Agios Kalotinis. Trains from **Thiva station** (☑ 22620 27531; www.trainose.gr), 500m north of the museum, depart for Athens (normal/express/intercity €5/9/10.30, 75/70/60 minutes, 10 daily) and Thessaloniki (normal/express/intercity €16.70/25/33, 4/5/5.5 hours, one daily).

Delphi   Δελφοί

POP 1020

If the ancient Greeks hadn't chosen Delphi (from *delphis,* womb) as their navel of the Earth and built the Sanctuary of Apollo here, someone else would have thought of a good reason to make this eagle's-nest town a tourist attraction. Its location on a precipitous cliff edge is spectacular and, despite its overt commercialism and the constant passage of tour buses through the modern village, it still has a special feel. Delphi is 178km northwest of Athens and is the base for exploring one of Greece's major tourist sites.

History

Delphi reached its height between the 6th and 4th centuries BC, when multitudes of pilgrims came to the sanctuary to consult the oracle.

Delphi was protected by the Amphictyonic League, a federation of 12 tribal states (that unified most of southern Greece), which took control of the sanctuary following the First Sacred War (595–586 BC), making Delphi an autonomous state that enjoyed great prosperity from numerous benefactors, including the kings of Lydia and Egypt, and Hadrian.

The influence of the oracle had a major impact on political and intellectual life, determining – directly or otherwise through the prophecies – such decisions as the establishment of colonies and wars.

The sanctuary survived fire (548 BC) and earthquake (373 BC), and in the 3rd century BC it was conquered by the Aetolians, and then by the Romans in 191 BC. Although the Roman Sulla plundered the sanctuary in 86 BC, other emperors, fascinated by its reputation, kept the rituals at Delphi alive well into the 2nd century AD, when the oracle's influence began to dwindle. The sanctuary was finally abolished by the Byzantine emperor Theodosius in the late 4th century AD. By the 7th century a new village, Kastri, had appeared over the ancient site. Much of what is known about Delphi today comes from the notes of 2nd-century AD Athenian geographer Pausanius.

⊙ Sights

Ancient Delphi   RUIN

(☑ 22650 82312; www.culture.gr; site or museum €6, combined adult/student €9/5; ⊙ 7.30am-8pm summer, 8am-3pm winter) Of all the archaeological sites in Greece, Ancient Delphi is the one with the most potent 'spirit of place'. Built on the slopes of Mt Parnassos, overlooking the Gulf of Corinth and extending into a valley of cypress and olive trees, this World Heritage site's allure lies both in its stunning setting and its inspiring ruins. The ancient Greeks regarded Delphi as the centre of the world – according to mythology, Zeus released two eagles at opposite ends of the world and they met here.

Check ahead for opening hours as these are subject to change. In summer, visit the site early to avoid the crowds and the heat. Don't head into the site just before closing time; staff are already rounding visitors up by then and you won't be permitted a thorough visit.

➡ **Sanctuary of Apollo**

The Sanctuary of Apollo, considered the heart of the oracle, is on the left of the main road as you walk towards Arahova. One hundred metres to the right of the museum (follow the pavement), notice the brickwork of the Roman **agora**.

From the main entrance, the steps on your right lead to the Sacred Way, which winds gradually up to the foundations of the Doric Temple of Apollo. Entering the site, you pass several **stone bases**. The first is the pedes-

Sterea Ellada

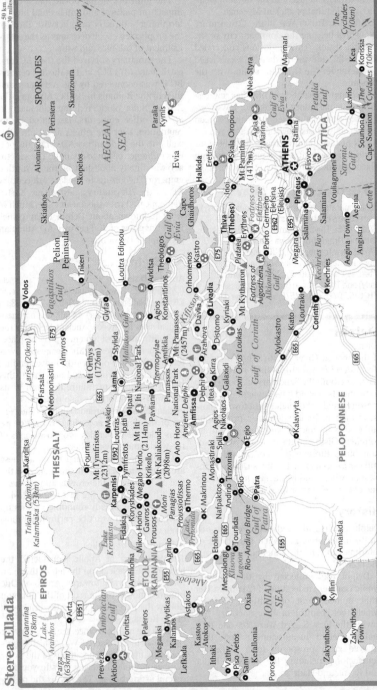

50 km
30 miles

SPORADES

Skyros

Skantzoura

Peristera

Alonnisos

AEGEAN
SEA

Skopelos

Skiathos

Pelion
Peninsula

Trikeri

Loutra Edipsou

Pagasitikos
Gulf

Volos

Glyfa

Arkitsa

Paralia
Kymis

Kymis

Nea Styra

Marmari

Kea
Korissia

The
Cyclades
(10km)

The
Cyclades
(10km)

Evia

Theologos

Agios
Konstantinos

Cape
Ghaidhoros

Gulf of
Evia

Eretria

Halkida

Lavrio

Sounion
Cape Sounion

Petalia
Gulf

ATTICA

Saronic
Gulf

Crete

Aegina

Angistri

Aegina Town

Salamina

Piraeus

ATHENS

Flisvos

Voula

Vouliagmeni

Kechries

Kechries Bay

Megara

Loutraki

Corinth

Kiato

Xylokastro

Gulf of Corinth

E65

PELOPONNESE

Kalavryta

Amaliada

Kyllini

IONIAN
SEA

Zakynthos

Zakynthos
Town

Poros

Sami

Kefallonia

Piso Aetos

Vathy

Ithaki

Atokos

Kastos

Lefkada

Meganisi

Mytikas

Kalamos

Astakos

Oxia

Messolongi
Klisova
Lagoon

Etoliko

Rio-Andirio Bridge

Gulf of
Patra

Rio

Patra

Andirio Trizonia

Nafpaktos

K Makrinou

Thermo

Lake
Trihonida

Moni
Proussiotissas

Panagias

Agrinio

Amfilohia

Vonitsa

Arta

Preveza
Aktion

Parga
(63km)

Ioannina
(18km)

Lake
Arahthos

Ambracian
Gulf

E951

EPIROS

ETOLO-
AKARNANIA

Lake
Kremasta

Acheloos

E65

E55

Fidakia

Koryshades

Mikro Horio

Gavros

Karpenisi

Mt Tymfristos
(2312m)

Fourna

Tymfristos

E952

Loutras

Makri

Ipati

Lamia

E65

Megalo Horio

Mt Iti
Krikello
Mt Kaliakouda
(2098m)

Mt Iti National Park

Pavliani

Ipati

Thermopylae

Amfiklia

Mt Parnassos
(2457m)

Kiriaki

Davlia

Kifissos

Livadia

Orhomenos

Kastro

Inoi

Mt Parnitha
(1413m)

Skala Oropou

Agia
Marina

Rafina

Erithres

Plataea

Fortress of
Eleftherae

Thiva
(Thebes)

E75

Porto Germeno

Fortress of
Agosthena

Mt Kythairon

Alkionides
Gulf

Kirra

Galaxidi

Itea

Agios
Nikolaos

Spilia

Delphi

Ancient Delphi

Amfissa

Ano Hora

Monastiraki

Spilia

Distomo

Arahova

Moni Osios Loukas

Parnassos
National Park

Tourlida

Kisova

E65

Almyros

Farsala

Neomonastiri

Karditsa

THESSALY

Larisa (20km);
E75

Trikala (20km);
Kalambaka (53km)

Mt Orthys
(1726m)

Stylida

Maliakos Gulf

Iti National Park

Mt Tymfristos
(1726m)

Eleftsina
(Eleusis)

E962

E95

Voula

Kea

N

0

0

tal that held the statue of a bull dedicated by the city of Corfu (Kerkyra). Just beyond it, on the right, are the remains of the Votive Offering of Lacedaemon, commemorating a battle victory. The next two semicircular structures on either side of the Sacred Way were erected by the Argives (people of Argos). To their right stood the Kings of Argos Monument.

In ancient times the Sacred Way was lined with treasuries and statues given by grateful city states – Athens, Sikyon, Siphnos, Knidos and Thiva (Thebes) etc – not only as thanks to Apollo, but as a kind of PR machine to show their wealth and might. To the north of the reconstructed Athenian Treasury are the foundations of the **bouleuterion** (council house).

The 4th-century BC **Temple of Apollo** dominated the entire sanctuary with a statue of Apollo and a hearth where an eternal flame burned. On the temple vestibule were inscriptions of Greek philosophers, such as 'Know Thyself' and 'Nothing in Excess', known as the Delphic Commandments.

Above the temple is the well-preserved 4th-century BC **theatre**, which was restored by the Pergamenon kings in the 1st century BC, yielding magnificent views from the top row. Plays were performed here during the Pythian Festival, held, like the Olympic Games, every four years. From the theatre the path continues to the **stadium**, the best preserved in all of Greece. Check out the sprinters' etched-stone starting blocks at the eastern end. On occasion, stadium access is limited because of possible rockslides.

From the Sanctuary of Apollo, the paved path towards Arahova runs parallel to the main road and leads to the **Castalian Spring** on the left, where pilgrims cleansed themselves before consulting the oracle (closed at the time of research due to work to secure falling rocks).

➡ Gymnasium

Across the road, to the south, west of the Sanctuary of Athena Pronea, you will find the remains of the ancient gymnasium. Two running tracks occupied an upper terrace here; on a lower terrace, boxers and wrestlers practised their art and then cooled off in the large, spring-fed circular **pool**, which is still visible among the ruins.

➡ Sanctuary of Athena Pronea

After the gymnasium is the Sanctuary of Athena Pronea, the site of the 4th-century BC **tholos** (rotunda), the most striking of Delphi's monuments. This graceful circular structure comprised 20 columns on a three-stepped podium; three of its columns were re-erected in the 1940s. The white portions of each column are the original marble; the darker portions are new material. To its west, the foundations of the Temple of Athena Pronea are all that remain of a rectangular structure that was heavily damaged by the same rockslides and earthquake that levelled much of the *tholos*.

THE DELPHIC ORACLE

The Delphic oracle was considered one of the most important religious (and political) sanctuaries in Greece. Worshippers flocked here from far and wide to consult the god Apollo on serious decisions. Apollo's instrument of communication was the *pythia*, or priestess, usually an older woman, who sat on a tripod in the Temple of Apollo.

During visitations and consultations, the priestess chewed laurel leaves, and entered a trance after inhaling vapours from a chasm below. Archaeologists believe this could have been ethylene wafting through a crack from a fault line (carried by water running underground). Her vapour-inspired, if somewhat vague, answers were spoken in tongue then 'translated' by the priests of Apollo. In fact, the oracle's reputation for infallibility may have rested with the often ambiguous or cryptic answers. Wars were fought, marriages sealed, leaders chosen and journeys begun on the strength of the oracle's visions. And, after all, the prophecies were the will of a god, so the oracle's reputation remained throughout antiquity.

Legend holds that one priestess suffered for her vagueness. When Alexander the Great visited, hoping to hear a prophecy that he would soon conquer the ancient world, the priestess refused direct comment, instead asking that he return later. Enraged, he dragged her by the hair out of the chamber until she screamed, 'Let go of me; you're unbeatable'. He quickly dropped her, saying, 'I have my answer'.

Delphi Town

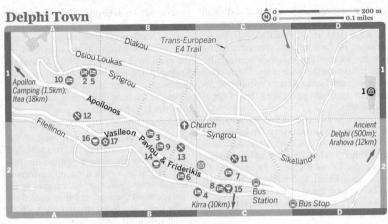

Delphi Town

Delphi Museum　　　　　　　　　MUSEUM
(☏ 22650 82312; www.culture.gr; adult site or
museum €6, combined adult/student €9/5;
⊙ 9am-4pm summer, 8am-2.45pm winter) From
around the 8th century BC, Ancient Delphi
managed to amass a considerable treasure
trove, much of it reflected in its magnificent
museum.

Upon entering the museum, you'll first
notice (in room 5) the *Sphinx of the Naxians*, dating from 560 BC. Also residing here
are well-preserved parts of the frieze from
the Siphnian treasury, which depicts not
only the battle between the gods and the giants, but also the Judgment of Paris (far-left
corner as you enter), who was called upon
to decide which goddess was most beautiful
(he chose Aphrodite). In room 3 are two fine
examples of 6th-century BC *kouroi* (statues
of young men), the 'twins of Argos'.

In the rooms to the left are fragments of
metopes (figures within the frieze) from the
Athenian treasury depicting the Labours of

Hercules, the Exploits of Theseus and the
Battle of the Amazons (room 7). Further on
you can't miss the tall Acanthus Column of
Dancers (room 11), with three women dancing around its top. Next to it is the omphalos,
a sculpted cone that once stood at what was
considered the centre of the world. In the
end room is the celebrated, life-size Bronze
Charioteer, which commemorates a victory
in the Pythian Games of 478 or 474 BC.

🏃 Activities

Two popular **day hikes**, both part of the E4
European long-distance path, start and end
at Delphi. The first connects two ancient sites,
the **Temple of Apollo** and **Korykeon Cave**,
a sacred mountain cave-shrine for Pan. This
wonderful cavern comprises a natural amphitheatre filled with stalactites and stalagmites.
You can walk as far as 80m inside (caution:
it can be slippery). Many hikers hire a taxi
in Arahova as far as Kalyvia (around €25),
hike to the cave (500m) and return to Delphi

along a well-marked path (four hours). Along the way, there are awesome views of Delphi, the Amfissa plain and Galaxidi.

A second hike meanders through the shady olives groves – the largest continuous olive grove in Greece – that stretch from Delphi to ancient Kirra on the Gulf of Corinth, and takes three to four hours. After lunch or a swim, return by bus (around €2) to Delphi. The E4 trailhead is marked 100m east of the Hotel Acropole.

A useful and excellent website is www.delphi.gr. Keen walkers should download the guide *Walking on the Footsteps of History: Trekking the Delphi Pathways* in the 'Hiking' section.

☞ Tours

Excellent English-language tours of Delphi are offered by charismatic **Penny Kolomvotsos** (☑ 6944644427; kpagona@hotmail.com), who also speaks German and brings the site alive; **Christina Stoli** (☑ 6944987411); and **Vicki Tsonis** (☑ 6945494583), who also speaks French.

🛏 Sleeping

Rooms Pitho   PENSION **$**
(☑ 22650 82850; www.pithohotel.gr; Vasileon Pavlou & Friderikis 40a; s/d/tr incl breakfast from €40/55/65; ✳🛜) Pitho's eight modern rooms, excellent service and location – about halfway along the street above a gift shop – and extremely friendly owners make it a top budget choice. Because it's incorporated into a home-style lodging, it's quieter than some hotels.

Hotel Sibylla   HOTEL **$**
(☑ 22650 82335; www.sibylla-hotel.gr; Vasileon Pavlou & Friderikis 9; s €24, d €26-30, tr €35-40; ✳🛜) An excellent budget choice, cosy Sibylla has delightful owners and seven light and spotless rooms, all with fans, and several with views across to the gulf.

Sunview Pension   PENSION **$**
(☑ 22650 82349; dkal@otenet.gr; Apollonos 84; s/d/tr incl breakfast from €30/40/45; P✳🛜) This basic but pleasant pension commands a stunning location in upper Delphi, with brightly painted rooms and friendly family owners who treat it like their own home, which it happens to be.

Arion Hotel   HOTEL **$**
(☑ 22650 82097; www.ariondelphihotel.com; Syngrou 29; s/d/tr/q incl breakfast €35/45/55/65;

✳@🛜) Offers comfort and value in a quiet location at the back of town.

Hotel Hermes   HOTEL **$**
(☑ 22650 82318; www.hermeshotel.com.gr; Vasileon Pavlou & Friderikis 27; s/d incl breakfast €40/50; ✳) The family-run Hermes is in the heart of Delphi. Most of the wood-shuttered rooms have balconies facing the gulf but the marble floors can mean noisy corridors. Views from the breakfast lounge are splendid.

Chrissa Camping   CAMPGROUND **$**
(☑ 22650 82020; www.chrissacamping.gr; camp sites per person/tent/car €6.50/6/3.50) About 6km west of modern Delphi.

Delphi Camping   CAMPGROUND **$**
(☑ 22650 82209; www.delphicamping.com; sites per person/tent/car €6.70/5/3.90; P🛜🏊) About 4.5km from Delphi towards Itea.

Apollon Camping   CAMPGROUND **$**
(☑ 22650 82762; www.apolloncamping.gr; camp sites per person/tent €8.50/4; P@🛜🏊) Only 2km west of modern Delphi.

Hotel Apollonia   HOTEL **$$**
(☑ 22650 82919; www.hotelapollonia.gr; Syngrou 37-39; s/d incl breakfast €75/90; ✳@🛜) The swank Apollonia has an intimate feel to it, tucked away on Delphi's upper Syngrou street. Rooms are quite modern with elegant dark-wood furnishings, carpet, large bathrooms and balcony views over all of Delphi.

Hotel Leto   HOTEL **$$**
(☑ 22650 82302; www.leto-delphi.gr; Apollonos 15; s/d/tr incl breakfast €48/60/78; ✳🛜) If the traditional Greek motif is getting you down, head to these compact but smartly decorated digs where the slick lighting and cream-and-orange trim make it one of the town's most contemporary choices.

Fedriades Hotel   HOTEL **$$**
(☑ 22650 82370; www.fedriades.com; Vasileon Pavlou & Friderikis 46; s/d/tr incl breakfast €46/59/73; ✳🛜) The Fedriades is a reliable bet with small, neat but bright and modern motel-style rooms and extra-friendly staff. Enthusiastic and helpful owner Babis will help with onward routes; breakfast includes some homemade treats. The lobby is a pleasant place to lounge after a site visit.

Hotel Acropole   HOTEL **$$**
(☑ 22650 82675; www.delphi.com.gr; Filellinon 13; s/d/tr incl breakfast €51/55/74; ✳🛜) On the quieter street below the main drag, the

Ancient Delphi

The pretty, hillside-strewn ruins of Delphi were in use for over 1500 years (8th century BC to 4th century AD), but the period from the 6th to the 4th century BC was particularly active. Visitors can still walk in the footsteps of past pilgrims and, with a bit of imagination, re-create the experience of this ancient place.

The sanctuary was adorned with many buildings and dedications to Apollo erected by Greek city states. Worshippers purified themselves in the Castalian Spring (now closed to the public), paid a *pelanos* (tribute) and, if they hadn't brought one with them, purchased a votive offering from **The Roman Market** . Then they wandered up the **Sacred Way** towards the Temple of Apollo.

En route they passed thousands of dedications, including statues, sculptures and small temples (treasuries). Treasuries, including the **Athenian Treasury** , were constructed by victorious city states and filled with the spoils of war. The nearby **omphalos**  (navel stone), a symbol of the centre of the earth, was left by archaeologists where it was found.

Next, visitors would pass the **Rock of the Sibyl** before arriving at the Stoa of the Athenians, behind which is an extraordinary **polygonal wall** .

Finally, they arrived at the **Temple of Apollo** in the centre of the sanctuary, where consultations with the oracle took place and the Pythia's chants were interpreted by the priests of Apollo. The **theatre** 8 behind the temple held drama and music competitions.

TOP TIPS

➡ Visit in the morning or late afternoon to beat the heat and crowds.

➡ Allow time to visit the stadium, which is located further uphill.

➡ Wear comfortable shoes and a hat, and bring drinking water.

➡ Opening hours are subject to change, so check ahead.

➡ Don't miss the Delphi Museum, which helps to contextualise the site.

Athenian Treasury

The impressive Athenian Treasury is one of many important treasury buildings here. Built to commemorate the Athenians' victory against the Persians at the battle of Marathon in 490 BC, it was reconstructed in the early 1900s.

Omphalos

Delphi was considered the *omphalos* (navel) of the world. After releasing two eagles, Zeus threw down a stone to mark the place they met. There was also an omphalos in the adyton (temple chamber) where the Pythia pronounced her oracles.

KATE ARMSTRONG ©

Siphnian Treasury

The Bouleuterion

The Sacred Way

The Sacred Way (so-named in modern times by archaeologists) leads to the Temple of Apollo. It was lined with thousands of monuments, statues and treasuries that commemorated victories (usually in war, sometimes the Games).

KATE ARMSTRONG ©

To Delphi Museum

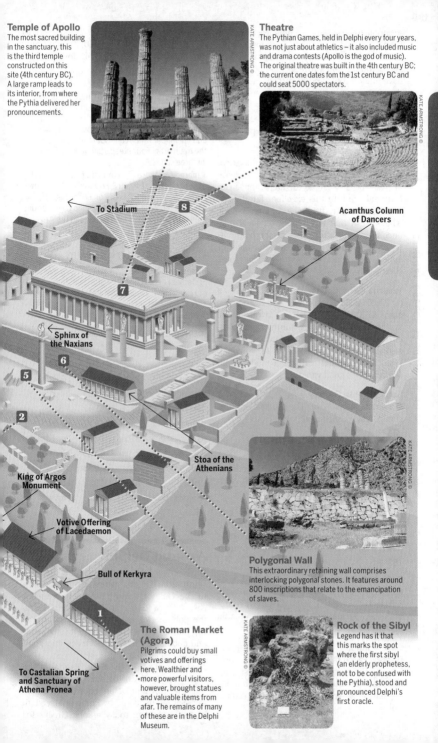

Temple of Apollo
The most sacred building in the sanctuary, this is the third temple constructed on this site (4th century BC). A large ramp leads to its interior, from where the Pythia delivered her pronouncements.

Theatre
The Pythian Games, held in Delphi every four years, was not just about athletics – it also included music and drama contests (Apollo is the god of music). The original theatre was built in the 4th century BC; the current one dates fom the 1st century BC and could seat 5000 spectators.

To Stadium

8

Acanthus Column of Dancers

7

Sphinx of the Naxians

6

5

2

King of Argos Monument

Votive Offering of Lacedaemon

Stoa of the Athenians

Bull of Kerkyra

1

To Castalian Spring and Sanctuary of Athena Pronea

Polygonal Wall
This extraordinary retaining wall comprises interlocking polygonal stones. It features around 800 inscriptions that relate to the emancipation of slaves.

The Roman Market (Agora)
Pilgrims could buy small votives and offerings here. Wealthier and more powerful visitors, however, brought statues and valuable items from afar. The remains of many of these are in the Delphi Museum.

Rock of the Sibyl
Legend has it that this marks the spot where the first sibyl (an elderly prophetess, not to be confused with the Pythia), stood and pronounced Delphi's first oracle.

Acropole has a ski-lodge ambience, though it hasn't changed its 'on piste' wear for a while. The rooms are pleasant and most have wood and wrought-iron fittings. Top-floor rooms have angled roofs and great views across to the gulf.

Eating

Eating in Delphi can be a so-so experience. Try these worthy exceptions.

Taverna Vakhos
TAVERNA $

(22650 83186; www.vakhos.com; Apollonos 31; mains €6-11; 🛜) Take the steps above the National Bank to this excellent family taverna featuring traditional local fare. Ask for what's fresh that day – they get local produce if possible and gather the herbs themselves. If nothing appeals, make a meal of appetisers alone, eg *formaela,* the local cheese (€6).

Taverna Gargadouas
TAVERNA $

(22650 82488; Vasileon Pavlou & Friderikis; mains €7-10) Easily the local favourite for grilled meats. The house summer speciality is *provatina* (slow-roasted lamb). You can also tuck into a combo of pasta, souvlaki, salad and seasonal fruit for a modest €13. Generally, it's good value.

Souvlaki Pita Gyros
KEBAB $

(Apollonos; mains €2-6) The budget option: cheap, fast, fresh, go. Opposite Hotel Leto.

🍷 Drinking & Nightlife

There are plenty of cafe-bars along Vasileon Pavlou & Friderikis, and while the rest of Delphi sleeps, one main-street club provides plenty of DJ dancing into the wee hours.

Cafe Ihor
CAFE

(22650 83095; Vasileon Pavlou & Friderikis 61; ⊙10am-late; 🛜) Funky, contemporary-style place with wi-fi access and great verandah views.

Café Agora
CAFE

(22650 83116; www.agoracafe.gr; Vasileon Pavlou & Friderikis; breakfast & snacks €2-10; 🛜) Along with the wi-fi and great verandah views, this also serves up good pizza and crêpes.

Café Apollon
KAFENEIO

(Vasileon Pavlou & Friderikis; ⊙7am-10pm) Apollon has the cheapest coffee, the worst English and no internet now or ever, but it's a charming, traditional *kafeneio* (coffee house).

Club Katoi
CLUB

(6932526578; admission €5-10) Delphi's only late-night spot to let your hair down.

🛈 Information

Almost everything you'll need in Delphi is on Vasileon Pavlou & Friderikis. Delphi's other through roads are Apollonos, which runs north of and parallel to Vasileon Pavlou & Friderikis, and Filellinon, which runs south and parallel to the main drag. Four steep stairways connect to all three roads.

Incredibly, there is no tourist office. The **post office** (Vasileon Pavlou & Friderikis; ⊙7.30am-2pm) and several ATMs are on Friderikis. The small medical centre is on Apollonos. For serious medical matters, it's best to head to the **Amfissa hospital** (22650 22222).

🛈 Getting There & Away

Buses (22650 82317; Vasileon Pavlou & Friderikis) depart from the at the eastern end of Friderikis. Travellers to Kalambaka/Meteora should find better connections via Lamia and Trikala, rather than Larisa.

DESTINATION	TIME	FARE	FREQUENCY
Amfissa	30min	€2.10	6 daily
Arahova	20min	€1.60	1-5 daily
Athens	3hr	€15.10	1-5 daily
Galaxidi	45min	€3.50	1-4 daily
Itea	30min	€1.90	4-5 daily
Lamia	2hr	€9.10	1 daily
Larisa	3½hr	€20	1 daily
Livadia	55min	€4.20	1-5 daily
Nafpaktos	2½hr	€9.70	3 daily
Patra	4hr	€14	1 daily
Thessaloniki	5hr	€35	1 daily
Thiva	1¼hr	€8	1-5 daily

Around Delphi

Olive groves and clear skies mark the road south from Delphi, which stretches 18km to the Gulf of Corinth where it branches east to Kirra (2km). This was ancient Kirra, the port of Delphi, now a quiet suburb of the market town of Itea, with a long sand-and-pebble beach, very clean sea and good beachside camping.

The town of Amfissa (the capital of the new Municipality of Delphi) sits in the foothills 21km west of Delphi on the road to Lamia. Sacked in 338 BC by Philip of Macedon, it's better known today among Greeks for its marvellous green olives, ancient castle, a beautiful and well-preserved Byzantine church, Agios Sotiras (Church of the Saviour), and the small but beautiful **Archaeological Museum** (✏22650 23344; adult/child €2/1; ⊙8am-2.30pm Tue-Sat) featuring a wonderful collection that puts Delphi and surrounds into context.

Heading west from Delphi towards Amfissa and Itea, the 19th-century convent of **Moni Profiti Ilia** (✏22650 35002; ⊙8am-2pm & 4pm-sunset) rests on a hillside overlooking the Gulf of Corinth. The turn-off is marked with a small cross and '3km' sign.

Parnassos National Park
Εθνικός Δρυμός Παρνασσού

Established in 1938, **Parnassos National Park** (www.routes.gr), to the north of Delphi and Arahova, has three peaks over 2300m: Liakoura (2457m), the highest, Tsarkos (2416m) and Gerondovrachos (2396m). Kouvelos (1882m) is a popular rock-climbing face. Mt Parnassos is part of the elaborate E4 European long-distance path (*orivatiko monopati)* from Gibraltar to Cyprus, also known as the European Ramblers Path, or E4 European Path. See the **European Ramblers Association** (www.era-ewv-ferp.org) website for more information.

Between 800m and 1800m, the slopes of Parnassos support Kefallonian fir, spruce and juniper, interspersed with yellow-flowered shrubs, plum trees and the rare purple-flowered *Daphne jasminea*. Above the tree line are meadows of fescue grass. Spring flowers including crocuses, squills, tulips, orchids and irises sprouting from the limestone rocks. Greece's most common mammals – foxes, hares, squirrels and jackals – may be seen, as well as vultures, passerines and hawks.

🏃 Activities

Hiking
The most popular ascent on Parnassos is to Liakoura. The route begins at the Parnassos refuge (1990m), 20km north of Arahova and 25km south of Amfiklia. For information, you can contact the local mountain guide **Nikos Chatzis** (✏6938008699) or the **Amfissa Greek Mountaineering Club** (✏6974824456; eosamfissas@gmail.com).

Skiing
For more information, see www.snow-report.gr. The **Parnassos Ski Centre**

(✏22340 22694; www.parnassos-ski.gr/en; ⊙Nov-May) handles ski and snowboard operations for the most popular slope on the mountain, **Kelaria** (1950m). At last count, there were 13 lifts covering more than 20 ski runs and alpine trails. The centre is 24km from Arahova and 17km from Amfiklia. It has hip cafes and restaurants, a safety network and medical centre, along with ski and snowboarding schools. For accommodation, it's best to stay in Arahova; most of the lodges on the plateau before the centre are private. Adjacent to Kelaria are the steeper slopes of **Fterolakkas** (six lifts), popular with extreme skiers.

❶ Getting There & Away

There is no public transport between Arahova and the ski centre. A taxi from Delphi costs around €45.

Arahova
Αράχωβα

POP 3240

Arahova (ah-*ra*-ho-vah), only 12km from Delphi, rests on a rocky spur of Mt Parnassos at an altitude of 960m. Although primarily a fashionable winter resort for skiers, the stepped alleyways of the mountain town hide a rugged charm.

Arahova's shops sell embroidery, hand-woven bags and *flokati* (shaggy woollen rugs). The town is also noted for its cheese, honey, *hilopites* (fettuccine-style pasta) and red wine.

THE OEDIPUS CROSSROADS

Travellers can still see the spot 'where three roads meet', as described by the ancient playwright Sophocles. This fateful junction was where proud Oedipus encountered his father, King Laius, thus fulfilling the powerful Delphic oracle's tragic prophecy that he would unknowingly murder his father and marry his mother.

To find the actual Oedipus crossroads (heading west from Livadia towards Delphi), look first for the road sign to Distomo and, 1km on, for a sign to Davlia. Proceed uphill another 1.5km to the car park (P) on the right. Look down and to the right to see visible traces of an ancient crossing, perhaps the narrow meeting of roads and fate.

DISTOMO

Distomo is remembered throughout Greece for the massacre of 10 June 1944, when Nazi troops killed 218 villagers in a door-to-door reprisal for a guerrilla ambush in nearby Steiri. In 1966 the German government erected a dramatic white-marble war memorial, with inscriptions in both Greek and German.

✸ Festivals & Events

Festival of Agios Georgios   STREET CARNIVAL
Held in town around 23 April (if this date falls during Lent, the festival is postponed until the following Easter Tuesday). It's a joyous three-day celebration with virtually the entire village in costume, dancing and singing, a tug-of-war contest and, on the last day, feasting on roasted lamb, all compliments of the town.

🛏 Sleeping

Room prices in Arahova can jump about 50% on winter weekends and holidays, from November to April.

Xenonas Maria   HOTEL $
(✆22670 31803; www.mariarooms.com; d/tr €50/65) Atmospheric, old-style, split-level rooms, and lots of red carpets and fur-covered trims. Behind town hall. Open all year.

Hotel Likoria   HOTEL $$
(✆22670 31180; www.likoria.gr; r/tr incl breakfast from €60/85; P❄@🛜) Off the main road, 250m northwest of Plateia Xenias, the low-key Likoria feels more like a country inn. Rooms are quite traditional, with carpeting, huge soft beds and shuttered doors opening to large balconies. The friendly English-speaking staff are a plus.

Pension Alexandros   PENSION $$
(✆22670 32884; www.alexandrosgr.com; r from €80; ⊘Sep–mid-May; ❄🛜) Upscale mansion, antiques and murals, behind Plateia Lakka.

🍴 Eating

Taverna Agnandio   TAVERNA $
(mains €7-12) This handsome Greek eatery, 30m east of Plateia Lakka, has a let's-dig-in-here-for-the-afternoon ambience and serves a daily selection of oven-ready dishes and grills.

To Yefira Taverna   TAVERNA $
(✆22670 31917; mains €8-13; ⊘lunch & dinner) By the bridge, with a lovely view of the tower, this basic, colourful spot whips up home fare, including good *pites* (pies) and moussakas.

Taverna Karamalis   TAVERNA $
(mains €5-14) The decor is tasteful, with olive-green rush chairs and views. *Hilopites* are good here (though don't expect much beyond a tomato salsa). Good daily specials.

Taverna Panagiota   TAVERNA $$
(✆22670 32735; mains €9-25; ⊘lunch Fri-Sun, dinner Thu-Sun, lunch & dinner daily winter) Unless you drive, it's a mere 263 steps up to this cosy, upmarket taverna behind Agios Georgios church. Tasty traditional Greek oven dishes fill the tables, and in winter there's always a fire going.

ⓘ Information

The **post office** (Plateia Xenias) is near ATMs, and the entire village is a wi-fi hotspot.

ⓘ Getting There & Away

The daily buses that run between Athens and Delphi stop at Arahova's Plateia Xenias (€15.10, 2½ hours).

Moni Osios Loukas
Μόνη Οσίου Λούκα

The World Heritage–listed monastery **Moni Osios Loukas** (Monastery of St Luke; ✆22670 22228; admission €3; ⊘8am-6pm summer, to 5pm winter) is 23km southeast of Arahova, between the villages of Distomo and Kyriaki. Its principal church contains some of Greece's finest Byzantine frescoes. Modest dress is required (no shorts).

The monastery is dedicated to a local hermit who was canonised for his healing and prophetic powers. The monastic complex includes two churches. The interior of the larger, **Agios Loukas**, is a glorious symphony of marble and mosaics with icons by Michael Damaskinos, the 16th-century Cretan painter.

In the main body of the church, the light is partially blocked by the ornate marble window decorations, creating striking contrasts of light and shade. Walk around the corner to find several fine frescoes that brighten up the crypt where St Luke is buried.

Nearby, is the smaller 10th-century Agia Panagia (Church of the Virgin Mary).

To get here from Delphi, you can take the Livadia/Athens bus as far as the Distomo crossing (€2.10, 35 minutes, five daily), then walk or hitch the 2km to Distomo. Alternatively, taxis will get you to the monastery from Distomo (€20 return), Livadia (€30 return) or Delphi (€40 return); for an extra charge, the taxi will wait an hour at the monastery. Coming from Livadia, one daily bus heads to Moni Osios Loukas (€3.50, 30 minutes).

Galaxidi   Γαλαξίδι

POP 2010

The prettiest of the low-key resorts on the Gulf of Corinth, Galaxidi is graced with narrow cobblestone streets, handsome stone mansions and two small harbours, and makes a pleasant base from which to visit Delphi. A forested headland, opposite the waterfront, is fringed by a 1.5km walking path and pebbled coves popular with swimmers. The town is reasonably tranquil except during summer and holiday weekends, when its charm is tested by car loads of Athenians. Galaxidi's most prosperous period was between 1830 and 1910 when it was a major centre for building caïques (small boats).

◉ Sights

Nautical Historical Museum   MUSEUM
(☑ 22650 41795; Plateia Manousakia; adult/child €5/free; ⊙ 10.10am-1.30pm & 5.30-8.30pm Jun-Sep, 10.10am-4.15pm Oct-May) The excellent Nautical Historical Museum documents Greece's maritime history and Galaxidi's unique ship-building lore, and includes several splendid ship figureheads.

Church of Agios Nikolaos   CHURCH
The carved-wood iconostasis in the Church of Agios Nikolaos is one of Greece's finest. Follow the English signs for the museum and church.

Moni Metamorfosis   MONASTERY
The little 13th-century Moni Metamorfosis stands amid olive groves and cypress trees, 4km inland from Galaxidi. From this vantage point there are terrific views down to the Gulf of Corinth. To reach it, go under the flyover and take the road opposite.

🛏 Sleeping

In summer, several of the waterfront cafes have rooms to let, though they're not great value.

Hotel Galaxidi   HOTEL $
(☑ 22650 41850; www.hotelgalaxidi.gr; r incl breakfast €50; 🕏) Seventies-style pine and low beds in an unfussy environment.

★ **Hotel Ganimede**   BOUTIQUE HOTEL $$
(☑ 6937154567, 22650 41328; www.ganimede.gr; Nik Gourgouris 20; s/d/tr incl breakfast €55/75/95; ❄🕏) This courtyard hotel in a 19th-century captain's house offers a range of slightly dated but charming pastel-shaded rooms with wood-panelled ceilings and period furniture. What it's best known for, however, are the gut-busting breakfasts from owner Chrisoula – think homemade jams, cheeses, fresh-squeezed juices and breads from the family bakery.

MiraMare Studios   STUDIO $$
(☑ 6937154567; studio d €75) These lovely bright and airy studios, equipped with small kitchenettes and balconies, are a pebble's throw from the waterfront action.

To Spitaki   PENSION $$
(☑ 6977512238, 22650 41257; www.tospitaki.com; d €70-110, f €120-160, incl breakfast; ℗ ➡ ❄ @) Its name meaning 'little house' in Greek, this converted 1850s stone ouzerie (ouzo bar) is one of four neighbouring properties, each complete with kitchen and pretty flower garden, halfway between the port and the main square.

Arhontiko Art Hotel   BOUTIQUE HOTEL $$
(☑ 22650 42292; www.archontikoarthotel.gr; s €45, d €50-70 incl breakfast; ℗ 🕏) Near the old harbour, this mansion hasn't had a makeover in a while, but quirky themed rooms – think 'sun room' with a round bed, 'moon room' with a mirrored ceiling and a boat-shaped bed anchored in the 'navy room' – are kind of fun.

🍴 Eating

Bebelis   TAVERNA $
(mains €6.50-12; ⊙ Sep-May) Fresh flowers and lace curtains and its location – a couple of blocks from the 'new harbour' – add a touch of taverna class to Galaxidi. Proud owner Bebelis (the owner's nickname) offers a lovely go-slow experience; the menu's photos accurately reflect the tasty specialities.

Albatross
TAVERNA **$**

(☑ 22650 42233; Konstadinou Satha 36; mains €6-8; ☺lunch & dinner) We love this little place near the Church of Agios Nikolaos, run by a long-standing couple. The generous offerings of mezedhes (try the dolmadhes – stuffed vine leaves) along with a few oven-ready dishes are always tasty and cheap.

Skeletovrachos
SEAFOOD **$$**

(mains €10-20, fish per kg €36-50) The owner's son is the chef at this reliable spot (named after a former sea captain). Seafood is the go and the menu is 'naughty' – think 'aphrodisiacs' – from oysters and shrimps, to the likes of 'immoral rice' (you guessed it, a spicy dish). Saucy gimmickry aside, it's good quality.

ⓘ Information

The post office and a bank are on Nikolaou Mama. All the cafes have wi-fi access.

ⓘ Getting There & Away

The **bus stop** (☑ 22650 42087) is on Plateia Manousakia. There are buses to Delphi (€3.50, 45 minutes, four daily), Athens (€18.70, 3½ hours, four daily) and Patra (€10.10, 1¾ hours, two daily). For Delphi and Athens, you must change bus in Itea; ticket prices cover the entire journey.

Nafpaktos   Ναύπακτος
POP 13,300

West of Galaxidi, the coastal highway winds in and out of a number of seaside towns and villages, including picturesque Monastiraki, 12km before the bustling town of Nafpaktos. Nafpaktos spreads out from a handsome circular-walled harbour, dotted with plane trees, trendy cafes and a good **swimming**

BRIDGE TO PATRA

The striking Rio–Andirio suspension bridge connects mainland Andirio and Rio in the Peloponnese, a crossing formerly only made by ferry. Despite the steep toll (€13.20 each way), getting to Patra and beyond couldn't be easier. If you're not in a hurry, a ferry (€6) also departs from under the bridge (follow the signs) every 20 minutes and you get a great view of the bridge's underbelly.

---

beach (Psani). An open market takes place every Saturday.

Nafpaktos was known as Lepanto in medieval times, and it was here on 7 October 1571 that the naval battle of Lepanto took place between the Ottoman Empire and the combined navies of the Vatican, Spain and Venice. The decisive victory over the Turks temporarily ended their naval domination of the Mediterranean.

The Spanish author Cervantes fought in the battle of Lepanto (and lost an arm). A small statue on the waterfront honours him, along with a Greek hero, Giorgos Anemogiannis (1796–1821), who, during the Greek War of Independence, tried to burn the Turkish fleet that was moored in the harbour (he failed and was killed by the Turks).

⊙ Sights

Botsari Museum
MUSEUM

(☺9am-1.30pm) **FREE** Battle aficionados must head to the Venetian-style Tower of Botsaris, currently a museum run by the Botsaris Foundation (the owners). It houses a collection of replicas of paintings and engravings, made by the most famous artists of that era (Vasari, Tintoretto and the like), recording the Battle of Lepanto. Ring the bell during opening hours.

Castle
CASTLE

The town's well-preserved fortress and Venetian *kastro* (castle) are fascinating. The *kastro* is protected by a series of five terraced stone walls built by a succession of conquerors (Doric, Roman, Byzantine, Venetian and Turk). It was closed at time of research for maintenance, but the walk and views alone are well worth checking out

🛏 Sleeping & Eating

Hotel Akti
HOTEL **$$**

(☑ 26340 28464; www.akti.gr; Grimbovo Beach; s/d/tr/ste €55/70/90/160; ✱🐾) The Akti's exterior looks like a pastel colour chart with balconies. Inside this delightful surprise are beautiful rugs and antiques galore and rooms that are high, wide and comfortable. Delightful English-speaking owner, Giorgos.

Evinos
MEDITERRANEAN **$**

(mains €6-9.50; ☺lunch & dinner, closed lunch summer) A twist of gourmet hits Nafpaktos' eateries at this pleasant spot, the name of which translates as 'good wine'. Don't expect any plate smashing here – it's not traditional. There's international bites – pastas

BUS SERVICES FROM NAFPAKTOS

DESTINATION	STATION	TIME	FARE	FREQUENCY
Athens via Rio–Andirio	Nafpaktos	3hr	€21	2 daily
Delphi	Fokida	3hr	€12	3 daily
Galaxidi	Fokida	1½hr	€7.40	3-4 daily
Itea	Fokida	2hr	€9	3 daily
Lamia	Nafpaktos	3½hr	€14.50	1 daily
Messolongi	Nafpaktos	50min	€5	3-4 daily
Patra	Nafpaktos	30min	€3.30	2-8 daily Mon-Sat
Thessaloniki	Nafpaktos	6hr	€44	2 daily

and risotti – plus traditional dishes with a twist, such as haloumi torta. A lovely setting, though not by the sea.

ⓘ Getting There & Away

Nafpaktos has two bus stations. The **KTEL Nafpaktos station** (☑ 26340 27224; cnr Manassi & Botsari) is behind the large Church of Agios Dimitrios. The **KTEL Fokida station** (☑ 26340 27241; cnr Kefalourisou & Asklipiou) is 400m further east.

Messolongi   Μεσολόγγι

POP 14,400

From a distance, Messolongi's flat landscape lacks the siren's irresistible draw. The town skirts the motionless **Klisova Lagoon**, the largest natural wetland in Greece, a favourite winter stopover for thousands of migrating birds and an important breeding ground for the endangered Dalmatian pelican – not to mention a pilgrimage site for birdwatchers and photographers, thanks to the remarkable *pelades* (stilt huts) in the water. The town centre is anything but motionless, with the pedestrian lanes around the central square lined with lively bars and tavernas.

History

During the War of Independence (1821–30), Britain's philhellenic bard Lord Byron arrived in Messolongi with the intention of organising the troops and supporting the Greek war effort. After months of vain attempts, Byron contracted a fever and died on 19 April 1824, his immediate aims unfulfilled.

Byron's death spurred international forces to hasten the end of the War of Independence, making him, to this day, a Greek national hero. Many men bear the name Byron

(Vyronas in Greek) and most Greek towns have a street named after him.

In the spring of 1826, under the helm of Egyptian general Ibrahim, Messolongi was captured by the Turks. Their year-long siege drove 9000 men, women and children to escape on the night of 22 April 1826 through what is now called the Gate of Exodus. Many took refuge on nearby Mt Zygos, only to be caught or killed by an Albanian mercenary force. A smaller group remained behind to detonate explosives as the Turks approached. This tragic exodus was immortalised in Dionysios Solomos' epic poem 'I Eleftheri Poliorkimeni' (The Free Besieged).

◉ Sights

Garden of the Heroes   GARDEN
(☺ 8am-8pm) Just beyond the Gate of Exodus is the Garden of Heroes, translated incorrectly as 'Heroes' Tombs' on the road sign. This memorial garden was established by the first governor of Greece following independence, Ioannis Kapodistrias, who issued the following decree (the Greek text of which is on the marble slab to the right as you enter the garden): '...within these walls of the city of Messolongi lie the bones of those brave men, who fell bravely while defending the city...it is our duty to gather together, with reverence, the holy remains of these men and to lay them to rest in a memorial where our country may, each year, repay its debt of gratitude.'

A **statue of Lord Byron** features prominently in the garden. When Byron died, the Greeks were heartbroken at the loss of a British nobleman who had given his life for their freedom. At the end of a national 21-day mourning period, Byron's embalmed body was returned to England, but his heart was kept by the Greeks and is buried be-

TOURLIDA ΤΟΥΡΛΙΔΑ

From Messolongi, you can drive, walk or cycle across the surreal **Klisova Lagoon** on the 5km-long causeway to visit the sandy hamlet of **Tourlida**, with **Alikes Taverna** (☑ 26310 22189; www.alykes.eu; mains €5-10) worth a stop for excellent grilled eel, and clean and breezy **Domatia Iliovasilema** (☑ 6977928335, 26310 51408; d/tr/q €40/50/60; P ✱) making it easy to stay overnight.

neath the statue. The English authorities at the time refused Byron's burial at Westminster Abbey.

Museum of History & Art MUSEUM
(☑ 26310 22134; Plateia Markou Botsari; ⊙ 9am-1.30pm & 4-6pm) FREE This museum is dedicated to the revolution and features a collection of Byron memorabilia and paintings. The passionate ticket seller has clocked up over 26 years in his chair.

Diexodos Museum–Picture Gallery GALLERY
(☑ 26310 51260; www.diexodos.com.gr; Razikotsika 23; ⊙ 10.30am-1pm Wed-Sun) FREE A labour of love of a local lawyer who restored the 18th-century mansion, the beautiful Deixodos Museum–Picture Gallery houses a private collection of paintings, and hosts temporary exhibitions and cultural events.

🛏 Sleeping & Eating

Any of the *ouzeries* and eateries along and near Razikotsika are reliable bets; *heli* (eel) and *avgotaraho* (grey mullet) are the culinary 'go' here.

Hotel Avra HOTEL $
(☑ 26310 22284; www.hotelavramesolongi.gr; Harilaou Trikoupi; s/d/tr €40/55/75; ✱) The 16-room Avra is tidy and comfortable; rear-facing rooms avoid the din of the adjacent central Plateia Markou Botsari.

Allotino TAVERNA $
(Razikotsika 7; mains €7-13; ⊙ lunch & dinner; 🔊) A good choice along pedestrian-friendly Razikotsika, this handsome eatery serves a selection of traditional dishes – *allotino* means 'something from the past'.

ℹ Information

Messolongi is the capital of the prefecture of Etolo-Akarnania. The central square, Plateia Markou Botsari, is dominated by the gallery and mayoral office on its eastern side. Several of the surrounding cafes have free wi-fi.

ℹ Getting There & Away

The **KTEL Messolongi station** (☑ 26310 22371) is outside the walled town, near the arched Gate of Exodus. There are regular buses to Athens (€24, 3½ hours, 10 daily) via Rio–Andirio, as well as buses to Patra (€6, one hour, eight daily), Nafpaktos (€5, 50 minutes, four daily), Amfissa (€13.20, three hours, one daily) and Mytikas (€9, 1½ hours, one daily).

Karpenisi Καρπενήσι

POP 7350

Karpenisi, the underrated, attractive capital of the mountainous prefecture of Evritania, lies in the well-wooded foothills of Mt Tymfristos (2312m), or Velouchi, between Lamia and Lake Kremasta. Not surprisingly, given its billing as the 'Switzerland of Greece', the town has an alpine-village feel, with chalet-style lodgings, churches and tavernas. Opportunities abound for outdoor activities. For the less action-orientated, driving through the forest to steep villages and monasteries is equally rewarding.

🏃 Activities

Karpenisi Ski Centre SKIING
(☑ 22370 23506; www.snowreport.gr/karpenissi) The Karpenisi ski centre on Mt Tymfristos operates four lifts with five runs (not six lifts and 11 runs as often promoted) from November to March. Karpenisi is also a mecca for hikers, rafters, mountain bikers and rock climbers.

A couple of companies offer extreme sports from white-water rafting, snowboarding and canyoning to rock climbing, river hiking and mountain biking. Unfortunately, however, these are mainly for groups. **Trekking Hellas** (☑ 22370 25940; www.trekking.gr) is your best bet for groups of around four people. Prices vary according to activity, and include equipment and transport.

You can also hike the E4 trail between Karpenisi and Krikello.

🛏 Sleeping

Hotel Galini HOTEL $
(☑ 22370 22914; www.galini-hotel.com; Riga Fereou 3; s/d incl breakfast €25/40) The side-street

Galini is a great budget choice, with simple rooms and friendly owners. From the *plateia*, walk 100m down Tsitsara.

Deluxe Hotel Anesis   HOTEL **$$**
(☑ 22370 80700; www.anesis.gr; Zinopoulou 50; s €50-55, d €55-65, tr €65-75, incl breakfast; ❋ ☎ ☜) The nearest thing to a Swiss chalet without the snow, this slightly twee, warm place is nevertheless handsome, with a welcoming lobby and warm rooms.

✖ Eating & Drinking

Surprisingly, there is a limited range of good-quality eating options in town itself, although if you have your own wheels, it's fun to choose from one of many good tavernas that are dotted between Karpenisi and Megalo Horio/Gavros.

Taverna En Elladi   TAVERNA **$**
(☑ 22370 22235; www.enelladi-tavern.gr; Kotsidou 4; mains €6-12) This earns marks for its handy location, just above the main square. The food is reasonable, too – hearty homemade soups, along with oven-ready dishes such as veal En Elladi (veal with potatoes and cheese, €8).

Taverna Panorama   TAVERNA **$**
(☑ 22370 25976; Riga Fereou 18; mains €6-13) It's all about the food and less about the ambience in this cavernous space with a leafy outdoor terrace. The huge menu features plenty of grilled lamb and pork, plus a hearty goat soup (€7).

Saloon Park   BAR, CAFE
(Karpenisi–Prousos road) A popular, if incongruous, bar-cafe 3km south of town. The unmistakable theme is the American Old West, with a Jack Daniels–meets-ouzo ambience. A stable is attached.

❶ Information

Several banks around the central square have ATMs.

Hospital (☑ 22373 50100; Ethnikis Antistasis 9)
Phoenix Internet Café (Kosma Aitolou; per hr €2; ☉ 11am-late)
Police (☑ 22370 23666; Pavlou Bakogianni 2)
Post Office (cnr Agiou Nikolaou & Athanasiou Karpenisiotou; ☉ 7.30am-2pm)

❶ Getting There & Away

Karpenisi's **KTEL bus station** (☑ 22370 80013/4) is 1.5km southeast of town. Buses run to Athens (€25, five hours, two daily) and Lamia (€7.20, 1½ hours, two daily).

Around Karpenisi

From Karpenisi a scenic mountain road leads south for 34km towards the village of Prousos and the 12th-century **Moni Panagias Proussiotissas** (☑ 22370 80705). Pilgrims flock here on 23 August for the Feast of the Assumption, to drink holy water from the spring and to step into the cavelike *katholikon* (principal church of a monastery), which claims to have a miracle-working icon of the Virgin Mary.

Just 14km south of Karpenisi are the twin villages of **Mikro Horio** (Little Village), with a couple of good tavernas, and **Megalo Horio** (Big Village). This scenic village boasts traditional stone houses and a charming **Folklore Museum** (☉ 10am-2.30pm Fri-Sun Sep-Jul, 10.30am-2.30pm & 6-8pm Aug) **FREE**.

Megalo Horio is also the starting point for the all-day hike to **Mt Kaliakouda** (2098m) and back. If you fancy something more level, you can take a satisfying stroll along the banks of the Karpenisiotis River on a footpath that begins opposite the village bus terminal.

Back on the main road, at the foot of Megalo Horio, the riverside **Gavros** attracts Karpenisi families in search of a good meal in the countryside, or a stroll along the Karpenisiotis River.

With your own transport, you can visit the restored village of **Koryshades**, reached by a marked turn-off about 3km southwest of Karpenisi.

⏩ Sleeping & Eating

Pension Agrambeli   PENSION **$$**
(☑ 22370 41148; www.agrampeli.gr; Gavros; d/tr from €60/70, ste €75-120, incl breakfast; @ ☎ ☎) This uniquely decorated mountain lodging

---

FERRIES TO IONIAN ISLANDS FROM ASTAKOS

The only reason to head to Astakos (Αστακός) is as a convenient stepping stone for access to the Ionian Islands, via the daily ferry to Kefallonia (Sami) in summer (around €10, three hours). A few cafes, domatia and tavernas line the small waterfront, but best-in-show goes to **Poseidon Palace** (mains €6-12), where cook-proprietor Kristos claims, 'Have everything, simple souvlaki, great fish, what you like'.

in Gavros overlooks the river and Mt Talakondia. The seven rooms vary in size and features, some with iron beds and locally made rugs, others with kitchens and fireplaces.

Taverna To Spiti tou Psara
TAVERNA $

(Fisherman's House, Gavros; mains €6.50-9; ☺ lunch & dinner) At this nearby and excellent riverside taverna, a house speciality is fresh *pestrofa* (grilled wild trout; €8.50). The handmade *pites* (€4), baked lamb (€9) and the owner's house-made wine justify the trip from Karpenisi.

❶ Getting There & Away

BUS

Two local buses depart Karpenisi (on Tuesday, Thursday and Saturday) for Megalo Horio, Mikro Horio and Gavros (€1.60, 25 minutes). Two buses head to Prousos (€3.40, 50 minutes); if you take the 5.45am bus, you can catch the 3pm return service. Check at **KTEL** (22370 80013/4) as these are subject to change.

TAXI

From Karpenisi's central *plateia* it's €17 to Gavros, Megalo Horio or Mikro Horio; to Prousos, about €35 (one way). A driver will wait for you for €10 per hour.

Lamia   Λαμία

POP 52,000

Lamia is the capital of the prefecture of Fthiotida, midway between Delphi and Meteora. Lamia rarely figures on travellers' itineraries, but it's a vibrant and lively place year-round. Life here revolves around the town's rambling squares, and it is famous for its *kokoretsi* (lambs' intestines), *kourabiedes* (almond shortcake) and *xynogalo* (sour milk). It's the gateway to the Iti National Park.

◉ Sights

There's a bustling street market on Riga Fereou and its side streets every Saturday morning.

Fortress
FORT

Lamia's *frourio* is worth the hike just for the views. Within it is the **Archaeological Museum** (☑ 22310 29992; admission €2; ☺ 8.30am-3pm Tue-Sun), chock-a-block with amazing finds from Neolithic to Roman times, including some classical, Hellenistic and Roman children's toys.

Gorgopotamos Railway Bridge
BRIDGE

The original Gorgopotamos Railway Bridge, 7km south of Lamia, was blown up by a coalition of British and Greek guerrilla forces on 25 November 1942, in order to delay the German advance, and is considered one of the greatest acts of sabotage of the time. The spectacular attack put the Greek underground on the map, and forced the Germans to divert resources away from the Russian front. The reconstructed bridge spans a deep ravine, with the replacement piers in stark contrast to the originals.

Thermopylae
HISTORIC SITE

About 20km southeast of Lamia is the narrow pass of Thermopylae where, in 480 BC, Leonidas and a band of 300 brave Spartans managed to temporarily halt the invading Persian army of Xerxes. There's little here now, except for a statue of Leonidas. It honours the heroic battle site where the Spartans ultimately perished against overwhelming odds.

Sleeping & Eating

The southern end of Plateia Laou is full of excellent-value *psistarias* (restaurants serving grilled meat) with whole lambs, goats and pigs adorning the windows. *Ouzeries* line a pedestrian street 50 metres west of here.

Hotel Athina
HOTEL $

(☑ 22310 27700; www.hotelsline.gr/athina; Rozaki Angeli 41; s/d/tr incl breakfast €40/55/70; ❷❀❢) The efficient, friendly and family-managed Athina has modern tile-floored rooms, large bathrooms, comfortable beds and, remarkably, its own parking. It's handy to Plateias Laou and Eleftherias.

Fitilis Restaurant
TAVERNA $

(☑ 22310 26761; Plateia Laou 6; mains €6-12) On a lovely square, Fitilis serves classic *mayirefta* (ready-cooked) dishes at value-for-money prices. If you're lucky, there might be slow-cooked goat, which sizzles over an open, antique wood oven.

ℹ Information

Six banks, all with ATMs, encircle Plateia Parkou.
Police Station (☎ 22310 22431; Patroklou)
Post Office (Athanasiou Diakou) Opposite Plateia Parkou.

ℹ Getting There & Away

BUS

All buses depart from the **KTEL bus station** (☎ 22310 51345/6; Taygetou), 2.5km southwest of the centre. A taxi between the centre and the bus station costs €5.

For Iti National Park, head to Ipati (€2.20, 40 minutes, nine daily).

DESTINATION	TIME	FARE	FREQUENCY
Agios Konstantinos	50min	€4.30	hourly
Amfissa	1½hr	€7.10	1-2 daily
Athens	3hr	€20.50	hourly
Delphi*	2hr	€9.20	1-2 daily
Karpenisi	1¾hr	€7.20	2-3 daily
Larisa	1½hr	€12.70	6 daily
Patra	3hr	€18.80	3 daily
Thessaloniki	4hr	€25.80	6 daily
Trikala**	2hr	€11.80	6 daily
Volos	2hr	€12.70	2 daily

* change in Amfissa
** change for Meteora & Kalambaka

TRAIN

Lamia's main train station is 6km west of the town centre at Lianokladi. Train tickets should be purchased in Lamia from the **OSE ticket office** (☎ 22310 44883; Konstadinopoleos, Kon/Poleos), where an OSE shuttle bus links with the Lianokladi train station.

Regular trains from here run to both Athens and Thessaloniki.

Iti National Park
Εθνικός Δρυμός Οίτης

Iti is one of Greece's most beautiful but least developed national parks. It's a verdant region with forests of fir and black pine, meadows and snow-melt pools fringed by marsh orchids, and home to woodpeckers, eagles, deer and boar. According to mythology, Hercules built his own funeral pyre on Mt Iti, before joining his divine peers on Mt Olympus.

Trails are not uniformly well marked, though a good day hike begins clearly at Ipa-
ti and climbs to a refuge (Trapeza at 1850m) near the Pyrgos summit (2152m). Other day hikes reach the villages of Kastania and Kapnohori. For information about hikes on Mt Iti, contact the **Hellenic Federation of Mountaineering** (☎ 21036 45904; www.eooa.gr) in Athens. Also, check out Road Editions Map No 43, *Iti,* or Anavasi Map No 2.3, *Central Greece: Giona, Iti, Vardhousia.*

The bordering village of **Ipati**, 22km west of Lamia and 8km south of the Karpenisi–Lamia road, has the remains of a fortress and is (along with Pavliani to the south) a starting point for hikes on Mt Iti. The hub of the village is the tree-shaded central square, Plateia Ainianon, flanked by traditional *kafeneia* (coffee houses). Just past here, too, is the lovely 15th-century **Agathon Monastery** (☉ sunrise-sunset).

The gorgeous and shady village of **Loutra Ipatis** is home to a summer sulphur spa.

🛏 Sleeping & Eating

Hotel Alexakis　　　　　　　HOTEL **$**
(☎ 22310 59380; www.alexakis.gr; Loutra Ipatis; s/d incl breakfast €35/50; P ✻ @) The immaculate, newly renovated Alexakis boasts contemporary rooms, a lovely terrace and broad views of Mt Iti. The delightful, friendly owners, Julia and Sofia, epitomise *filoxenia* (hospitality).

I Mouries　　　　　　　TAVERNA **$**
(www.lymouries.gr; Loutra Ipatis; mains €6-8; ☉ lunch & dinner; 🐾) A cosy village spot with fabulous *mayirefta* dishes and excellent daily grills (each day, a different meat).

Agios Konstantinos
Αγιος Κωνσταντίνος
POP 3410

The pretty village of Agios Konstantinos, on the main Athens–Thessaloniki route, is one of the three mainland ports (along with Volos and Thessaloniki) that serve the islands of Skiathos, Skopelos and Alonnisos, which make up the northern Sporades.

Two English-speaking travel agencies on the plaza in front of the port sell ferry tickets: **Bilalis Travel** (☎ 22350 31614; www.bta.gr; Karaiskaki 4) and **Alkyon** (☎ 21038 32545).

ℹ Getting There & Away

BOAT

Hellenic Seaways operates the crossings to Skiathos (per person/car €37/75), Skopelos (per person/car €49.50/80) and Alonnisos (per person/car €49.50/80). In summer, a boat departs daily to a changing schedule. Between October and April, a small passenger boat ferries foot passengers only.

BUS

From the **KTEL bus station** (☑ 22350 32223), 200m south of the ferry landing, there are buses to Athens (€16, 2½ hours, hourly) and Lamia (€4.70, one hour, nine daily). For Patra and Thessaloniki, you must change at Lamia.

METEORA & THESSALY

The region of Thessaly (Θεσσαλία) occupies much of east-central Greece between the Pindos Mountains and the Aegean Sea. The fertile and river-fed Thessalian plain supported one of the earliest neolithic settlements on the continent. Today, it boasts two of Greece's most extraordinary natural phenomena: the lofty monastery-capped rock pinnacles of Meteora, and the lush Pelion Peninsula. The mountains and alpine meadows around Elati are destinations for outdoor enthusiasts.

Larisa   Λάρισα

POP 162,600

Occupying the east bank of the ancient Pinios River, Larisa is a major transport, military and service hub for the vast agricultural plain of Thessaly. Despite its workaday feel, it is a vibrant university town, with bustling cafeterias, shops galore and numerous fountains. Larisa has been inhabited for nearly 10,000 years, and remnants of its layered Byzantine and Ottoman pasts are dotted about town.

☉ Sights

You can gaze at the ongoing archaeological excavation of a well-preserved 3rd-century BC ancient **theatre** in the city centre, 100m north of Plateia Sarka. Nearby, the **acropolis** on Agios Ahillios Hill dates from Neolithic times (6000 BC).

Municipal Art Gallery of Larisa   GALLERY
(☑ 24106 16266; Pinakothiki Katsigra, cnr Papandreou & Kliou Patera; admission €3; ☉ 10am-2pm Tue-Sun) Houses a superb private collection of contemporary Greek art that's second only to the National Art Gallery in Athens.

🛏 Sleeping

Hotel Metropol   HOTEL $$
(☑ 24105 37161; www.hotelmetropol.gr; Rousvelt 14; s/d/f incl breakfast €45/60/75; P ❄ @ 🛜) Should you linger in Larisa, you'll find large rooms decorated with the owner's paintings at this dated, but adequate, business-style hotel, between Plateia Kentriki (Central Sq) and Ethnarhou Makariou.

ℹ Information

There are several banks around Plateia Mihail Sapka.
Hospital (☑ 24102 30031; Tsakalof 1)
K-Net (☑ 24105 39355; Rousvelt 24; per hr €2; ☉ 24hr) Internet access.
Municipal Tourism Office (☑ 24106 18189; ereot@otenet.gr; Ipirou 58; ☉ 7.30am-3pm Mon-Fri)
Police Station (☑ 100; Papandreou 14)
Post Office (cnr Papanastasiou & Athanasiou Diakou)

ℹ Getting There & Away

BUS

Buses leave Larisa's **KTEL station** (☑ 24105 67600; cnr Georgiadou & Olympou) for Athens (€28, four hours, eight daily), Thessaloniki (€15, two hours, seven daily), Volos (€5.30, one hour, 10 to 12 daily) and Ioannina (€18.70, four hours, three daily).

From the branch **KTEL Trikalon station** (☑ 24106 10124; Iroön Polytechniou), near the

---

WORTH A TRIP

AROUND LARISA

If you have time, it's a pleasant drive 28km northeast of Larisa to the **Vale of Tembi**, a dramatic gorge cut by the Pinios River between Mt Olympus and Mt Ossa that was sacred to Apollo in ancient times. A small bridge connects the car park with 13th-century **Agia Paraskevi** church and, 2km further on, the ruins of a **medieval fortress**.

The picturesque village of **Ambelakia**, 5km up a winding road from the village of Tembi, was a prosperous textile centre in the 18th century. A few dozen of the original 600 mansions remain, and walking the cobbled streets is a pleasure.

Thessaly

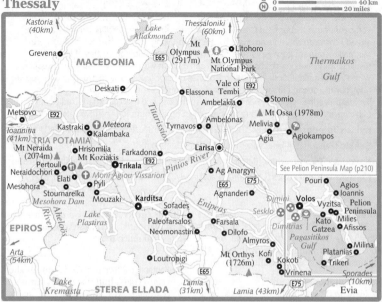

junction with Gazi Anthimou, buses run regularly to/from Trikala (€6.30, one hour, hourly). For Meteora, take the Trikala bus, then change for Kalambaka.

TRAIN

Express and normal trains pass daily through Larisa's **train station** (☑ 24102 36250; cnr 28 Octovriou & Iroön Polytechniou) to/from Thessaloniki (normal €6.70, 1¾ hours, express €15 to €20, 1½ hours) and Athens (normal €23, express €28 to €36, 3½ hours, three daily). You can buy tickets at the **OSE office** (☑ 24105 90239; Papakyriazi 35-37; ☺ 9am-2pm Tue & Thu, 9am-2pm & 5-9pm Wed & Fri).

Volos   Βόλος

POP 85,000

Once called ancient Iolkos, Volos was the mythic home of Jason and his band of Argonauts. These days, Volos is a large and bustling university city on the northern shores of the Pagasitikos Gulf, and its function as the gateway to the Pelion Peninsula or the Sporades draws travellers to the city.

◎ Sights

Archaeological Museum   MUSEUM
(☑ 24210 25285; Athanasaki 1; admission €2; ☺ 8.30am-3pm) This excellent museum is

set in a pretty rose garden and houses area finds from Dimini and Sesklo, along with an impressive collection of painted grave stelae from the nearby Hellenistic site of Dimitrias. Recorded commentaries are available; leave your passport as security.

Tsalapatas Brickworks Museum   MUSEUM
(☑ 24210 29844; old town; admission €3; ☺ 10am-6pm Wed-Mon 1 Mar-15 Oct, to 5pm 16 Oct-28 Feb) From 1926 until 1975, the Tsalapatas Rooftile and Brickworks was part of the cultural fabric of Volos. In 2006 the restored plant opened as the handsome Tsalapatas Brickworks Museum with brick-making machinery, grinding mills and massive kilns on display.

⌂ Sleeping

The nearest campgrounds to Volos – **Camping Hellas** (☑ 24230 22267; www.campinghellas.gr; camp sites per adult/tent €7/4; @ ⬚) and **Sikia Camping** (☑ 24230 22279; www.camping-sikia.gr; camp sites per adult/tent €5.50/3.60; @ ⬚) – are side by side at Kato Gatzea, 17km away, on the west coast of the Pelion Peninsula. Both are well-managed facilities, each with restaurant, minimarket and beach bar. July and August may require bookings.

THE TSIPOURADHIKA

Volos is famous throughout Greece for its *ouzeries* and *tsipouradhika*. If you have not already come across one, an *ouzerie* (strictly speaking, called a *tsipouradhiko*) is a type of small restaurant serving various plates of mezedhes and tiny bottles of *tsipouro*, a distilled spirit, like ouzo but stronger. You can dilute it with water if you prefer it weaker. When you've finished one round of mezedhes or *tsipouro*, you keep ordering until you've had your fill (or can't stand up!). The basic rule: don't expect a drink without a plate. Typical mezedhes include grilled *ohtapodi* (octopus) and fried calamari. Traditional *tsipouradhika* were open during the day only. Some of our old-time favourites in Volos:

Kyklos Tsipouradiko (☎ 24210 20872; Mikrasiaton 85; mezedhes €2-6; ⊙ Mon-Sat)

Sesklo (Papakiriazi 44; mezedhes from €3.50; ⊙ 11am-6pm)

Kavouras Tsipouradiko (Gatziagiri 8; drink & mezedhes plate €3-4; ⊙ 11am-6pm Mon-Sat)

Kerasia Tsipouradiko (Cherry Tree; Papakiriazi 40; mezedhes €3-5; ⊙ 9am-6pm)

Hotel Jason HOTEL $
(☎ 24210 26075; www.jason-hotel.gr; s/d/tr €25/45/60) One of Volos' few real budget hotels, it offers simple rooms with few frills; the upside is its close proximity to the port.

Hotel Philippos HOTEL $
(☎ 24210 37607; www.philippos.gr; Solonos 9; s/d/tr incl breakfast €45/55/65) This respectable spot has professional staff and a large foyer. Rooms are basic, but neat.

Hotel Kipseli HOTEL $$
(☎ 24210 24420; www.hotelkipseli.gr; Agiou Nikolaou 1; s/d/ste incl breakfast from €55/65/75; ❀ ⊛ 🖥) This boutique lodging, with a great boardwalk location near the quay, is smart and modern, with handsome rooms. Its central location can mean noise, however. The rooftop bar has the best night views of the harbour.

Volos Palace Hotel HOTEL $$
(☎ 24210 76501; www.volospalace.gr; Xenothontos; r incl breakfast €98-118, ste €150-170; 🅿 ⊛ 🖥) This rambling upmarket chain hotel is of the heavy-drape-thick-carpet variety with professional receptionists. However, it's showing signs of wear and tear. Front rooms are opposite the modern amphitheatre, which can be a blessing or a curse depending on what show is playing. Good deals can be arranged, however.

✖ Eating

Stafylos GREEK $
(Malounas 6 ; mains €7-10; ⊙ lunch & dinner) Your welcome is a small glass of *tsipouro* and some olives and a tomato dip before you've even ordered. There are lovely dishes from all over Greece, including a delicious apaki pork marinated in spices (typical of Crete), snails and much more.

Plagios MEDITERRANEAN $$
(cnr Kontaratou & Skirou; mains €9-25) An alternative to Volos' traditional *tsipouradhika* (place that serves ouzo and light snacks) scene, this smart place has a low-key snob factor and touts itself as an all-day bar-restaurant. It adds a touch of contemporary gourmet to the Greek cuisine.

🍷 Drinking & Nightlife

For a night of music, drinking and dancing, head to the revitalised old industrial district known as the Palaia (note: single women shouldn't go here alone). Most of Volos seems to booze the evenings away in the city centre, especially around Koumoundourou and Kontaratou.

★ Bar Balthassar BAR
(☎ 6949383200; Oikonomaki 76) Balthassar – named after a former Italian beer-making monk – is a mellow beer-and-sausage hangout that features fine Belgian ales and assorted planetary brews. Located in Volos' cool cafe district.

Thalasses CLUB
(☎ 24210 87577; Pagasson 68; ⊙ May-Sep) In the Palaia district, Thalasses features live bouzouki music, drinks and dancing, but don't bother showing up before midnight.

🛍 Shopping

Ekonomou O Papous FOOD
(☎ 24210 34606; Anthimou Gazi 135) Charming shop with only one item for sale: *louk-*

oumi, a traditional Greek version of Turkish delight.

ℹ Information

Parking in Volos can be tricky. Head straight for a parking lot; the one on the quay (€1.50 per hour) is the most convenient. There are several ATMs on Argonafton, Iasonos and Dimitriados.

Post Office (cnr Dimitriados & Agiou Nikolaou) Near Agios Nikolaos church.

Tourist Police (☎ 24210 39065; 28 Octovriou 179) Locals also refer to the street name for 28 Octovriou as Alexandras.

Volos General Hospital (☎ 24210 94200; Polymeri 134) Located near the Archaeological Museum.

Volos Information Centre & Hotels' Association of Magnesia (☎ 24210 30940; www.voloinfo.gr; cnr Grigoriou Lambraki & Sekeri; ⊙ 8am-4pm Mon-Fri, to 2pm Sat) Just opposite the KTEL bus station, this modern facility offers hotel information, town maps and bus, train and ferry schedules, along with helpful travel tips for the Pelion Peninsula.

Web (Iasonos 137; per hr €2.20; ⊙ 24hr) Internet shop. Many waterfront cafe-bars also have free wi-fi.

ℹ Getting There & Away

BOAT

Volos is a gateway to the northern Sporades isles of Skiathos, Skopelos and Alonnisos. Ferries arrive and depart from the far end of the dock; hydrofoils from the near end. The following are high-season schedules. Note: these change regularly.

DESTINATION	TIME	FARE	FREQUENCY
Alonnisos	5½hr	€27.50	2 daily
Alonnisos*	3hr	€48	1 daily
Skiathos	2hr	€23	1 daily
Skiathos*	1½hr	€37.50	3 daily
Skopelos (Skopelos Town)	4hr	€27.50	1 weekly
Skopelos (Glossa)*	2hr	€40	1 daily
Skopelos (Skopelos Town)*	3hr	€48	4 daily

*high-speed service

BUS

From the **KTEL Volos bus station** (☎ 24210 33254; www.ktelvolou.gr; cnr Zachou & Almyrou), opposite the tourist info centre, buses depart for Athens (€28, 4½ hours, 10 daily),

Larisa (€5.30, one hour, eight daily), Thessaloniki (€19, 2½ hours, eight to nine daily), Trikala (€14, 2½ hours, four daily) and Ioannina (€24, 4½ hours, three daily).

For buses to the Pelion Peninsula, see p210.

TRAIN

The atmospheric Volos **train station** (☎ 24210 24056; Papadiamanti) is 200m northwest of Plateia Riga Fereou. Nine trains run daily to Larisa (€34, one hour), which is the place to catch connections to Athens (normal/express €19/36, seven daily) and Thessaloniki (normal/express €12/22, hourly), although check whether these are still running, as there were mumblings about their cessation at time of research. You can also check schedules and buy tickets at the **OSE outlet** (Dimitriados; ⊙ 8am-4pm Mon-Fri) near the university.

ℹ Getting Around

Cars can be hired from **Hertz** (☎ 24210 22544; stvolos@herz.gr), at the port next to the fish market, and **Avis** (☎ 24210 22880; avisvolos@otenet.gr; Argonafton 41).

Around Volos

Just west of Volos are two major archaeological sites, both dating from early Greek civilisation in Thessaly. The first is **Dimini** (☎ 24210 85960; admission €2; ⊙ 8.30am-2.30pm Tue-Sun), a late Neolithic site (4800–4500 BC) inhabited to the Bronze Age, complete with traces of streets and houses and a wonderful *tholos* (Mycenaean tomb shaped like a beehive). The second is **Sesklo** (☎ 24210 95172; admission €2; ⊙ 8.30am-2.30pm Tue-Sun), with remains of the oldest acropolis in Greece (6000 BC). The architecture at both sites typifies the complex agrarian communities that could sustain much larger populations than those of their Palaeolithic hunter-gatherer ancestors.

Pelion Peninsula
Πήλιον Ορος

The Pelion Peninsula lies to the east and south of Volos. It's formed by a dramatic mountain range, where the highest peak is Pourianos Stavros (1624m). The largely inaccessible eastern flank consists of high cliffs that plunge into the sea. The gentler western flank coils around the Pagasitikos Gulf. The interior is a green wonderland where trees heavy with fruit vie with wild olive groves and forests of horse chestnut, oak, walnut, eucalyptus and beech to reach the light of day. The villages tucked away in this profuse foliage are characterised by whitewashed, half-timbered houses with overhanging balconies, grey slate roofs and old winding footpaths.

Many lodgings in the Pelion are traditional *arhontika* (stone mansions), tastefully converted into pensions and reasonably priced. The peninsula has an enduring tradition of regional cooking, often flavoured with mountain herbs. Local specialities include *fasoladha* (bean soup), *kouneli stifadho, spetsofaï* (stewed pork sausages and peppers) and *tyropsomo* (cheese bread).

For accommodation, you can expect the higher July and August rates quoted here to drop by at least 30% at other times.

History

In mythology the Pelion was inhabited by *kentavri* (centaurs) – half-man, half-horse creatures who took delight in drinking wine,

defflowering virgins and generally ripping up the countryside. Not all were random reprobates, however – Chiron, considered the wisest of the group, was renowned for his skill in medicine.

The Turkish occupation did not extend into the inaccessible central and eastern parts of the Pelion and, as a result, the western coastal towns were abandoned in favour of mountain villages. In these remote settlements, culture and the economy flourished; silk and wool were exported to many places in Europe. The Orthodox Church at the time was instrumental in maintaining Kryfa Skolia (Hidden Schools). Like many remote areas in Greece, the Pelion became a spawning ground for ideas that culminated in the War of Independence.

ⓘ Getting There & Away

Buses to villages throughout the Pelion leave from the Volos bus station.

Pelion Peninsula

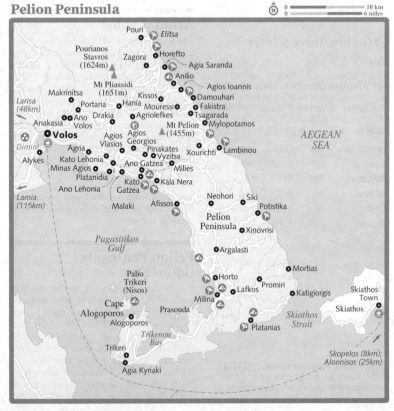

DESTINATION	TIME	FARE	FREQUENCY
Agios Ioannis	2hr	€6.60	1-2 daily
Kala Nera	50min	€1.70	15 daily
Makrinitsa (via Portaria)	45min	€1.60	6-8 daily
Milina (via Argalasti and Horto)	1½hr	€4.60	3-5 daily
Pinakates	1hr	€2.40	2 weekdays
Platanias	2hr	€6.40	2-4 daily
Pouri	1¾hr	€5	2-3 daily
Trikeri	3hr	€7.60	1-2 daily
Tsagarada	1½hr	€5.10	1-3 daily
Vyzitsa (via Milies)	1hr 10min	€2.80	4-6 daily
Zagora (via Hania)	1½hr	€4.30	1-3 daily

Northwest Pelion

VOLOS TO MAKRINITSA

Taking the northeastern route from Volos to Makrinitsa, the road climbs 6km to the village of **Anakasia** (just after Ano Volos), where there's the fascinating **Theophilos Museum** (Anakasia; ☉8am-2.30pm Mon-Fri) **FREE**, a converted mansion featuring works of native artist Theophilos Hatzimichael (1866–1934), who wandered the Pelion region trading his artwork for food. The upstairs wall murals reflect local scenes and personal visions.

Portaria, 2km east of Makrinitsa, is 12km northeast of Volos. True to Pelion form, its *plateia* has a splendid old plane tree, and the little 13th-century **Church of Panagia of Portaria** has fine frescoes.

🛏 Sleeping & Eating

Midrange to upmarket places line Portaria.

Arhontiko Kritsa   HOTEL $
(☑24280 99418; Portaria; s/d €40/50) For its unpretentious, old-fashioned modesty, we like Arhontiko Kritsa (not to be confused with Hotel Kritsa, which is also in the centre), where you have a choice of the creaky, atmospheric old building with three inter-connecting rooms, or newer '80s-style rooms.

Hotel Despotiko   BOUTIQUE HOTEL $$$
(☑24280 99046; www.despotiko.gr; Portaria; r from €100; ☏☀) For an upmarket experience (with varied reviews about service), try

this handsomely converted mansion. Website promotions sometimes available.

Kritsa Hotel Restaurant   GREEK $
(☑24280 99121; www.hotel-kritsa.gr; Portaria; mains €6-14) Head to the Portaria *plateia* to find this welcoming spot, set under plane trees and serving outstanding Pelion favourites such as slow-cooked 'lamb-in-the-jug' (€11) and roasted wild greens with egg (€8).

MAKRINITSA   ΜΑΚΡΙΝΙΤΣΑ

POP 650

Clinging to a mountainside, Makrinitsa is aptly called the Balcony of Pelion. From a distance, the traditional houses give the impression that they're stacked on top of one another. Up close, the whitewashed structures are threaded with steep stairs crowded with geraniums, hydrangeas and roses. Further up, the path leads to more than 50 stone water fountains. It is one of the loveliest of the Pelion villages and, because of its proximity to Volos, also the most visited.

The village is a pedestrian zone; a bus terminus and shaded car park mark the entrance. The central square is anchored by a massive plane tree with a kid-friendly hollow, a marble fountain and the tiny chapel of Agia Panagia.

⊙ Sights

Museum of Folk Art   MUSEUM
(admission €2; ☉10am-4.30pm Tue-Sun) This restored 1844 mansion has well-displayed relics, including an old *tsipouro* still, a Victrola phonograph 'talking machine' and a hidden water fountain built into a stone wall.

🛏 Sleeping & Eating

Several hotels are scattered around the village. Prices listed here can increase by 50% on winter weekends. Stop for the views at the main square, but look beyond it for the best eateries.

Arhontiko Repana   GUESTHOUSE $
(☑24280 99067; www.repana.gr; s/d/tr incl breakfast from €45/55/75; ☏) For hospitality and value, we love this friendly, family-run place. Rooms are homely, comfortable and decked out with wood and red carpets. One has an open fireplace.

Sisilianou Arhontiko   GUESTHOUSE $$
(☑24280 99556; www.arhontiko-sisilianou.gr; d incl breakfast €75-90; ☏) This elegant rebuilt mansion has rooms of varying sizes (the

CENTRAL GREECE PELION PENINSULA

TOP FIVE QUIRKY MUSEUMS OF THE PELION

Part of the Pelion Peninsula's character derives from its rugged geography and virtual isolation, and the region is well known for its unique art, cuisine and architecture. Much of that exceptional spirit is captured in a handful of small private museums, each one a minor revelation of the people and the land. Check out these gems:

➡ **Museum of the Olive** (p216)

➡ **Serpentine Organic Garden** (p215)

➡ **Theophilos Museum** (p211)

➡ **Skolio tou Riga Museum** (Hellinomouseion; ☑ 24260 23708; ⊙ 9am-2pm & 6-8pm)

➡ **Old Radio Museum** (p218)

small are a bit claustrophobic) and is decorated in period furniture with well-appointed bathrooms. Room 7 has mountain views from the bed. If you're lucky, the owner's father, Nico, might take you on a Sunday outing.

Taverna Alpha-Beta TAVERNA $
(mains €7-11; ⊙ Tue-Sun) Taverna A-B, 150m past the square, makes the most of strictly local and seasonal produce and meat in mountain favourites such as rabbit in red-wine sauce, along with well-made appetisers and salads. The view from the verandah merits a glass of the house red by itself.

Taverna Leonidas TAVERNA $
(mains €6-10; ⊙ lunch & dinner daily, closed Mon-Fri in winter) Just past the square, this is a good choice for local fare and views below.

Northeast Pelion

ZAGORA ΖΑΓΟΡΑ
POP 3821

From Hania, the road zigzags down through chestnut trees to a junction leading to Zagora, the largest of the Pelion villages and a major fruit-growing centre – it's the apple capital of Greece. Until blight ruined the silk industry in 1850, the town exported fine silk around the continent. Two War of Independence landmarks – the museum and library – have their roots in Zagora.

For medical emergencies, contact the **Zagora Health Centre** (☑ 24260 22591) and, for internet use, drop by **Ylien Cafe** (Plateia Agios Georgios) on the main square.

🛏 Sleeping & Eating

Arhontiko Dhrakopoulou HOSTEL $
(☑ 24260 23566; fax 24260 23460; r incl breakfast €40) The local women's association manages

this homey lodging, next to Plateia Agios Georgios. A local flower designates each of five simply furnished rooms.

Arhontiko Stamou GUESTHOUSE $$
(☑ 24260 23880; www.stamou-hotel.com; s €55, d €55-70, tr €55-70, incl breakfast; P @ ☎) Arhontiko Stamou, off Plateia Agios Georgios, is a handsome and spacious villa (c. 1863) that shares the courtyard with the mellow Café Anemella (Greek for silkworm). The knowledgeable owner will point you in the right direction.

Taverna Niki TAVERNA $
(Meintani; mains €4-7.50) In Plateia Sotira, flower-draped Taverna Niki is excellent for *mayirefta*, grills and salads (Niki is a chef).

AROUND ZAGORA
The laid-back village of **Pouri**, which spills down a steep mountainside to a small bay, is home to a few tavernas clustered beneath the church. Just 3km down the hill, Pouri boasts two fine swimming beaches, pebbly **Elitsa** and sandy **Analipsi**.

⊙ Sights

Popotech Workshop GALLERY
(☑ 6945447878; www.popotech.blogspot.com) **FREE** A couple of kilometres south of Pouri is Popotech Workshop, where Irish and Dutch transplants Gemma and Gary create unique jewellery, ceramics and found-metal sculpture. You'll spot their quirky sculptures from the road.

🛏 Sleeping & Eating

Panorama Rooms B&B $$
(☑ 6938810309, 24260 23168; r incl breakfast €60; P) If this end-of-the-road nest appeals, consider lingering at the lovely Panorama Rooms, where apple farmers Vasiliki and

Theoharis stock a common kitchen with the family's homemade cheese.

Taverna Plimari
TAVERNA **$**

(Analipsi beach; mains €7-10; ☺ Easter-Oct) Three kilometres down the hill, on sandy Analipsi beach, is the superb Taverna Plimari, where, as the owner says as he views his olive trees and water, 'if someone wants to live their dream in Greece, this is the place'.

ZAGORA TO KISSOS

Picturesque villages adorn the road from Zagora to Tsagarada, one of the most scenically spectacular in the Pelion. The village of **Anilio** ('sunless' in Greek) rests in the shadow of a ridge of chestnut and walnut trees, a rich source for the **Anilion Women's Agricultural Group** (☑ 24260 31329) at the northern end of the village, which makes and sells wonderful jams and pastries.

The flower-draped village of **Kissos** is built on steep terraces surrounding the 18th-century **Church of Agia Marina**, where the frescoes are considered the finest in the Pelion.

In Kissos stop for lunch or dinner at **Taverna 5F** (O Makis; mains €4-8; ☺ lunch & dinner), great for dolmadhes, or at **Taverna Klimataria** (mains €6.50-9.50) for *spetsofai* (€7.50).

HOREFTO
ΧΟΡΕΥΤΟ

Eight kilometres downhill from Zagora, Horefto is a low-key resort with palm trees and a long sandy beach. It's also the mythical home of Chiron, a roving centaur who healed the sick in the days when doctors still made house calls. The main beach is very decent, while isolated **Agia Serandabeach** fills a beautiful cove 2km south, with a simple domatia and taverna nearby.

🛏 Sleeping & Eating

Hotel Cleopatra
HOTEL **$**

(☑ 24260 22606; s/d €35/50; P ❄ 🛜) This vine-adorned hotel has spacious tile-and-wood rooms, balconies and overhead fans, making it good value. It's opposite the beach as you enter Horefto.

Hotel Aeolos
HOTEL **$$**

(☑ 24260 23260; d/apt from €80/100; ❄ @ 🛜 ⛶) An elegant in-town spot.

Marabou Hotel
HOTEL **$$**

(☑ 24260 23710; www.marabouhotel.gr; s/d/ste €45/70/110; P ❄ @) Marabou Hotel is a comfortable hotel that sits on a green hillside 250m from the beach.

Taverna O Petros
TAVERNA **$**

(mains €4-7) This reliable seaside eatery starts you out with a complimentary shot of local *tsipouro* and mezes, and serves up fine fish grills and a variety of meat and veg dishes, including cheesy local favourite *hortopita*.

Taverna Ta Delfinia
GREEK **$**

(mains €4-8) The spot for local *mayirefta*.

AGIOS IOANNIS
ΑΓΙΟΣ ΙΩΑΝΝΗΣ
POP 660

Agios Ioannis is the busiest of the eastern coastal resorts, but there's still plenty of room. Small hotels, tavernas and pizzerias line the waterfront, and two sandy beaches are just a short walk north (Plaka) and south (Papa Nero).

🛏 Sleeping & Eating

Katerina's Apartments
APARTMENT **$**

(☑ 6945762183, 24260 31159; www.pilio-katerina.gr; s/d/f from €35/45/90; ☺ Apr-Oct; ❄ 🛜) A narrow lane south of Papa Nero opens to a cosy courtyard anchored by a lemon and orange tree at this welcoming, family-run gem. Rooms are light, tidy and charming and have small kitchenettes.

Camping Papa Nero
CAMPGROUND **$**

(☑ 24260 31319; www.campingpapanero.com; camp sites per adult/tent/car €6/4/5) Clean and shaded, south of the waterfront.

The Magic Balcony
GUESTHOUSE **$$**

(☑ 6979114086; www.magicbalcony.com; s/d/apt from €50/60/120; ☺ Apr-Oct) This supremely peaceful place is run by hospitable, eco-friendly folks with vast local knowledge. Choose between doubles with arty flourishes and anatomical mattresses, and larger apartments with separate bedrooms and grand living rooms that include fireplace and leather couches.

Hotel Anesis
HOTEL **$$**

(☑ 24260 31123; www.hotelanesis.gr; s/d/tr incl breakfast €60/75/90; ❄ @ 🛜) Along with its appealing location away from the street, this has dated but pleasant pastel-toned rooms, though bathrooms are smallish. Breakfast is served on a vine-shaded terrace overlooking the sea.

Hotel Kentrikon
HOTEL **$$**

(☑ 24260 31232; www.bungalows-kentrikon.gr; s/d/ste from €91/104/234; P ❄ @ 🛜 ⛶) A reasonable choice with a strange mix of luxurious suites and some faded studio-style rooms.

Sofokles Hotel
HOTEL $$

(☑ 24260 31230; www.sofokleshotel.com; r incl breakfast €115; ❄ ☎ ☒) This inviting, recently renovated hotel features smart, well-appointed rooms with wood and marble touches, small balconies and a vine-covered breakfast terrace opposite the beach.

★ Taverna Orea Ammoudia
GREEK $

(mains €4-8; ☺ May-Oct; ☎) Spread out under lush foliage at the southern end of Papa Nero beach, this efficient family taverna does excellent oven-ready mains such as baked cod, chicken and potatoes, lamb grills and unusual salads such as *kritama* (tomatoes with sea herbs). An outdoor bar serves up cool drinks and ice cream in summer.

Taverna Akrogiali
SEAFOOD $

(www.akrogialipelion.gr; mains €8-10; ☺ lunch & dinner May-Oct) A favourite of the Volos locals who love their seafood dishes, including *rizi tou psara* (seafood risotto, or a Greek version of paella; €8). The owner says 'our food is honest' – think Greek produce and realistic prices.

Taverna Poseidonas
SEAFOOD $

(mains €7-10, fish per kg €25-45; ☺ lunch & dinner) The owners are proud of their local reputation for serving only their own catch. In addition to the usual by-the-kilo offerings, you can sample oven-ready standbys.

DAMOUHARI & MOURESSI
ΝΤΑΜΟΥΧΑΡΗ & ΜΟΥΡΕΣΙ

Picturesque **Damouhari** is next to a rambling grove of olive trees bordering a pebble beach and protected cove that once shielded the hamlet from passing pirate ships. According to local lore, the village got its name from the expression *dos mou hari* (give me grace). The little church of **Agios Nikolaos** contains several fine frescoes (Apostolis at the taverna next door keeps the key). Damouhari enjoyed brief fame from the 2008 movie *Mamma Mia!* (with Meryl Streep), which borrowed the secluded port for two weeks of filming. Damouhari is also the starting point for a beautiful 4km walk to **Fakistra Beach**.

Nestled off the main road, 3km north of Tsagarada, is the mellow village of **Mouressi**, known for its cherries, chestnuts and *mouria* (mulberries). There are great views of the Aegean from the lime-tree-shaded *plateia*.

🛏 Sleeping & Eating

Old Silk Store
GUESTHOUSE $

(☑ 6937156780, 24260 49086; www.pelionet.gr; Mouressi; d €55; ☺ mid-Apr–mid-Oct) The rambling Old Silk Store is showing its age these days but it's a 19th-century neoclassical gem with a personable owner, British transplant Jill Sleeman. There's a range of traditional-style rooms in an overgrown garden setting, with an available breakfast of homemade goodies. There's even a resident donkey, Boy George. Breakfast costs €7.50.

Hotel Damouhari
HOTEL $$

(☑ 24260 49840; www.damouchari.gr; Damouhari; r from €85; ℗ ☒) Hotel Damouhari is right on the beach and its range of unique stone rooms, which face a garden, are quaint and creaky and filled with quirky antiques and paraphernalia. The Kleopatra Miramar bar brims with nautical finds and is the spot for a post-beach drink.

Domatia Victoria
PENSION $$

(☑ 24260 49872; Damouhari; d €60; ❄ @) One of two very decent domatia in Damouhari. Good views of the bay.

Taverna O Vangelis
TAVERNA $

(Mouressi; mains €6-9) Hard-working cook, server and chatty host Vangelis has a loyal following for his good grills (pork chops €6) and rich *spetsofaï* (€4.50).

Taverna Karagatsi
TAVERNA $

(Damouhari; mains €4-9) Flower-in-his-ear cook Apostolis serves up fine taverna standards, plus big Greek salads and tasty mezedhes such as *taramasalata* (a thick purée of fish roe, potato, oil and lemon juice), all overlooking the tiny bay below.

Taverna To Tavernaki
TAVERNA $

(Mouressi; mains €5.50-9) Opposite the petrol station and well regarded for *mayirefta*.

TSAGARADA
ΤΣΑΓΚΑΡΑΔΑ
POP 710

Tsagarada (tsag-ah-*rah*-dah, sometimes written as Tsangarada) nestles in oak and plane forests. This rambling and spread-out village comprises the four separate communities of Agio Taxiarhes, Agios Stefanos, Agia Kyriaki and Agia Paraskevi, the largest of the group, just north of the main Volos–Milies–Tsagarada road. The plane tree in Agia Paraskevi's *plateia* is said to be one of the largest and oldest in Greece. There is an ATM next to the post office.

Hotels, domatia and tavernas dot rambling Tsagarada.

◉ Sights

Serpentine Organic Garden GARDEN
(☑ 24260 49060; www.serpentin-garden.com; Taxiadhes; admission by donation) Serpentine Organic Garden is a one-woman labour of love, the inspiration of Doris who, over 30 years, has created a virtual museum of all things green and flowering, including rare trees and roses, along with sustainable vegetable, berry and herb gardens. Doris offers bed-and-board volunteer internships, part of World Wide Opportunities on Organic Farms, and opens to visitors by appointment only.

🛏 Sleeping & Eating

Villa Ton Rodon GUESTHOUSE $
(☑ 24260 49340; www.villatonrodon.gr; Agia Paraskevi; s/d/tr incl breakfast €35/50/60; ℗) This simple, unpretentious but comfortable pine-clad spot is surrounded by the friendly owners' garden. It's 50m down a small path off the main road (signed).

★ Lost Unicorn Hotel HOTEL $$
(☑ 6979795252, 24260 49930; www.lostunicorn.com; Agia Paraskevi; s/d incl breakfast from €70/90; ⊘ Apr-Oct; ℗ ✳ @ 🛜) Lost Unicorn Hotel features Persian carpets, slow-swirling fans and antique-outfitted rooms in an elegant and well-appointed 19th-century mansion set in a beautiful glade. The Greek and English owners, Christos and Clare, keep things informal and make a breakfast worthy of the scenery, complete with singing nightingales. In summer, the magical dining room serves as a restaurant dishing up international cuisine (Christos is a trained chef; mains €10 to €18).

Aleka's House GUESTHOUSE $$
(☑ 24260 49380; www.alekashouse.gr; Tsagarada; d/tr incl breakfast €85/100; ℗ ✳ 🛜) Attractive Aleka's House is in a smart spot and is one of the few accommodation options in the region to open all year. It also has a cafeteria and lovely restaurant with local produce; worth going for the daily specials.

Taverna To Agnanti TAVERNA $
(Agio Taxiarches; mains €7-13) This atmospheric eatery cooks up the likes of pork leg and lamb, risotto with shrimps and spaghetti with octopus. Located to the right of the

CENTRAL GREECE PELION PENINSULA

WALKING IN THE PELION

The Pelion is a hiking mecca, and a centuries-old network of frequently restored *kalderimia* (cobbled mule pathways) connect most mountain and seaside villages around the region. The presence of many of the wonderful walking trails, former donkey routes, is thanks to the 'Friends of the Kalderimi' (www.friendsofthekalderimi.org), which is dedicated to maintaining and restoring these historic cobblestone paths.

In the north, two relatively simple and unguided hikes begin near **Tsagarada**. From the square of Agia Paraskevi, it's two hours down to the small bay at Damouhari. And from the village of **Xourichti**, 4km south of Agia Paraskevi, a good cross-ridge path leads to the village of **Milies**, a hike of nearly three hours. A beautiful forest hike begins above the road at Fakistra Beach and follows the coast to Plaka Beach in about two hours.

In the south, a wonderful downhill trek is from **Promiri** to **Platania**. Here too, **Lafkos** to **Milina** is a classic hike, where you can see both sides of the peninsula. **Argalasti** to **Kalamos** and **Lefokastro** is a popular walk.

The most useful of all resources are the websites www.pilionwalks.com, run by passionate expat walkers, with excellent circuit hikes, and http://walking-pelion.blogspot.com, by an ultra-dedicated Greek local (who is currently mapping the region with a GPS). *A Hiker's Guide to Mount Pelion* by local Nikos Haratsis is available in English (ask around in Volos). A long-standing publication, *Walks in the Pelion* by Lance Chilton, has online updates (www.marengowalks.com/Pilionbk.html). For maps, the detailed 1:25,000 Anavasi Map *Central Pelion* is available in Volos bookshops, as is the excellent Terrain Map No 218, *Central Pelion*. Several accommodation places sell a wonderful map, *Pelion Walks* (€5 to €6), outlining seven different walks around Tsagarada.

small fountain you see as you enter Plateia Taxiarhes.

MYLOPOTAMOS   ΜΥΛΟΠΟΤΑΜΟΣ

Scenic Mylopotamos is divided by a rocky outcrop, with a natural tunnel connecting two small beautiful beaches. It's 7km along the road from Tsagarada's Agia Paraskevi.

🛏 Sleeping & Eating

Diakoumis Rooms   GUESTHOUSE **$$**

(☑ 24260 49203; s/d/tr from €50/70/80, apt €90; P ❋ 🛜) At Diakoumis Rooms, just 1km before the village and beach, genial owners Stathis and Athina have made the most of the dramatic cliff-side lodging. Light and airy stone-floored rooms have clear views of the bay and beyond, as well as four self-catering apartments.

Taverna Angelika   TAVERNA **$**

(mains €6-10) Taverna Angelika is a regular stop for many Pelion residents who appreciate the good food and wine, not to mention the breezy view.

West-Central Pelion

VOLOS TO PINAKATES, VYZITSA & MILIES

From Volos, the west-coast road heads south through the touristy villages of Agria and Ano Lehonia, where a branch road leads inland to Agios Vlasios, Pinakates, Vyzitsa and Milies, while the main road continues to neighbouring Kato Gatzea, Ano Gatzea and Kala Nera. After the tortuous and narrow roads of the eastern Pelion villages, this stretch of road is a blessing.

Two nearby attractions merit a stop. The **Little Train of Pelion** begins its old-fashioned run at Ano Lehonia. One of its quaint station stops is Ano Gatzea, home to the inviting **Museum of the Olive** (☑ 6945854310, 24230 22009; www.mouseioelias.gr; ⊙ 8am-5pm, or when train pulls in) FREE, set in an old stone mansion with detailed displays of picking tools and ladders, presses and storage vessels, plus a small shop.

PINAKATES   ΠΙΝΑΚΑΤΕΣ

POP 100

An old plane tree anchors Plateia Agios Dimitrios, home to the church, two tavernas, a small fountain, ceramic shop and wood-oven bakery. Pristine Pinakates only acquired electricity in 1973 and, from the looks of it, things haven't gotten out of hand.

🛏 Sleeping & Eating

Hotel Ta Xelidonakia   HOTEL **$$**

(Little Swallows; ☑ 24230 86920; www.pinakates.com; d/tr incl breakfast €100/120; P @ 🛜 ❄) This beautifully restored classic mansion balances history and comfort in grand fashion. The verandah is anchored by a 3000L chestnut wine barrel.

Taverna Drosia   TAVERNA **$**

(mains €4-8.50; ⊙ dinner) This eatery is an extension of a family house and serves Pelion favourites such as baked goat and *spetsofaï*, with good local wine always on hand.

O Pileas   TAVERNA **$**

(mains €5.50-8.50) One of two tavernas in town, popular with locals for village fare.

VYZITSA   ΒΥΖΙΤΣΑ

POP 280

Handsome Vyzitsa's cobbled pathways wind between traditional (these days upmarket) slate-roofed mansions. To reach its shady central square and tavernas, walk up the cobbled path beside Thetis Café.

🛏 Sleeping & Eating

Hotel Stoikos   HOTEL **$**

(☑ 24230 86406; www.hotelstoikos.gr; s/d/tr from €40/50/60; P ❋ 🛜) This well-managed place has a traditional look, especially with the beamed ceilings and stained glass of the spacious upper-floor rooms (great views). It's good value in pricey Vyzitsa.

Mansion Karagiannopoulou   GUESTHOUSE **$$**

(☑ 6945479570, 24230 86717; www.karagiannopoulou.com; d €60-80, tr from €70, incl breakfast; 🛜) This beautiful guesthouse ingeniously combines traditional and modern, boasting stunning sitting rooms and bedrooms.

Georgaras Restaurant   GREEK **$**

(www.georgarasvizitsa.gr; mains €7-11; ⊙ lunch & dinner May-Sep, dinner weekends Oct-Apr) *The* pick of Vyzitsa's eateries has a menu featuring salads, stews and soups, along with stuffed pork with orange, and *kouneli stifadho*. It claims its clients say, 'If you visit Vyzitsa and you don't eat there, is as bad as visiting Athens for the first time and not seeing the Acropolis'. It's a big statement, but we like the experience.

🛍 Shopping

Esperides   FOOD

(Vizitsa) The place for edible souvenirs. It comprises a group of 10 women who handmake traditional jams.

MILIES   ΜΗΛΙΕΣ
POP 640

Beautiful Milies (mih-lih-*ess*) has a ubiquitous shady square and a plethora of fountains. The village played a major role in the intellectual and cultural awakening that led to Greek independence. It was the birthplace of Anthimos Gazis (1761–1828), who organised revolutionary forces in Thessaly in 1821 and toured mountain villages of the Pelion inspiring local resistance and leadership.

Milies is also the start/end point for the Little Train. The walk down to the old station is very pretty and well worth doing (note: there are many steps).

◎ Sights & Activities

Agios Taxiarhes   CHURCH
On the central square is Agios Taxiarhes, a church with beautiful 18th-century frescoes. It's extraordinary for the 48 internal ceramic 'jars' that enhance acoustics, and for the unique frescoes, completed by one monk over 33 years.

Milies Museum   MUSEUM
(☑ 24230 86602; ☺ 10am-2.30pm & 6.30-9pm Wed-Sun) **FREE** Milies Museum houses a display of local crafts and costumes.

🛏 Sleeping & Eating

Palios Stathmos   GUESTHOUSE $$
(Old Station; ☑ 24230 86425; www.paliosstathmos .com; s/d incl breakfast from €40/60) Nestled among a grove of plane trees, Palios Stathmos is a comfortable pension that recalls a bygone era, but only from the balconied rooms facing the narrow-gauge railway station.

Taverna Panorama   TAVERNA $
(mains €5-7.50) This cosy grill serves up Pelion favourites such as zucchini pie, pork chops in wine and *spetsofaï*. It's located about 200m north of the central square (and nearly covered in climbing roses).

Anna Na Ena Milo   CAFE $
(snacks €3-6; ☺ 9am-late) A cosy crepe-and-jam cafe; owners Nicoletta and Nicos make everything (the cheesecake is delicious).

Korbas Bakery   BAKERY $
(snacks €1.50-4) Head here for gastronomic highlights – try the scrumptious *tyropsomo* (cheese bread) and *eliopsomo* (olive bread). It's located on the main road.

South Pelion
SOUTH TO TRIKERI

The southern part of the Pelion has a wide-open feel to it, with sparsely forested hills, olive groves and lovely beaches. Before heading inland after Kala Nera, the road skirts the little coastal fishing village of Afissos, winds up through to the attractive farming community of Argalasti, and then forks – the left fork continues inland, the right goes to the coastal resorts of Horto and Milina. From Milina the road branches southeast towards Platanias and southwest to Trikeri.

There is an end-of-the-world feel about this part of the Pelion, especially as the road from Milina to Trikeri becomes more and more desolate. Residents pride themselves on their tradition as seafarers, fighters against the Turks in the War of Independence, and upholders of traditional customs and dress.

THE LITTLE TRAIN

In 1895 a 13km railway line was built between Volos and Ano Lehonia. By 1903 the narrow-gauge line was extended to Milies, making the town a prosperous centre of commerce. **To Trenaki** (☑ 24210 39723; www.trainose.gr; adult/child €18/10; ☺ daily Aug & Sep, Sat & Sun Apr-Jul & Oct), the steam train that used to chug along this route, retired formally in 1971, but was revived in 1997 as a weekend and holiday tourist attraction. The popular four-carriage train leaves Ano Lehonia at 10am and returns around 3pm, leaving you time to stroll around Milies.

A restored Belgian coal-burning locomotive pulled the train when the route first re-opened. But in 2000 a new diesel engine went into service after the train operators grew tired of following the smoke-belching original with a water tanker to put out the frequent grass fires started by airborne sparks. Despite the environmental upgrade, To Trenaki is still called *Moudzouris*, an affectionate term meaning 'the smudger'. Note: check schedules and departure times as these change annually.

HORTO & MILINA   ΧΟΡΤΟ & ΜΗΛΙΝΑ

Milina is the larger of these two coastal villages, and sees many package tourists. Both are on a quiet part of the peninsula with pristine water and a few inviting pebble beaches.

◉ Sights & Activities

Old Radio Museum   MUSEUM

(☑ 6970374922; ⊙ daily 16 May-14 Sep, Sat & Sun 15 Sep-15 May) **FREE** If you're one of those people who think nostalgia isn't what it used to be, turn your dial to this spot, in the village of Lafkos, 5km east of Milina, to check out one collector's pre-digital love affair with the original wireless.

⊨ Sleeping & Eating

Hotel Leda   HOTEL $$

(☑ 24210 27931; www.ledahotel.gr; Horto; r €80; ⊙ Apr-Oct; P ✱ ❋ ⊜ ⊠) Look for the resort-style bungalows at Hotel Leda, complete with beach bar and pool.

Ouzerie Vangelis   OUZERIE

(Milina) One of a cluster of tavernas next to Milina's main jetty, is excellent for seafood mezedhes and *tsipouro*.

ⓘ Information

Milina Holidays (☑ 24230 65020; www. milina-holidays.com) Resourceful George Fleris of Milina Holidays on the waterfront can help with accommodation, as well as arranging bike and boat hire, plus day cruises to nearby Palio Trikeri (adult/child €25/15).

AGIA KYRIAKI   ΑΓΙΑ ΚΥΡΙΑΚΗ

This is the last stop on the Pelion Peninsula, a steep 2km drive off the main road, or a quick 1km walk down a cobblestone path. This fishing village sees few tourists, and the bright, orange-coloured boats are put to good use by a hard-working population of around 200. The Agia Kyriaki Hotel (☑ 24210 91112, 6978771831; www.agiakyriaki. gr; s/d incl breakfast €35/50; ⊙ May-Sep) has a stunning setting, and there are three fish tavernas in a row, facing the opposite shores of Evia. Manolas is known for its lobster spaghetti.

PALIO TRIKERI   ΠΑΛΙΟ ΤΡΙΚΕΡΙ

If you really must go that one step further to get away from it all, then head for this little island with a year-round population of 15, just off the coast; it's often called Nisos (Island) for short. To reach tiny Nisos from the fishing village of Alogoporos, a five-minute boat ride away (€2 per person), telephone Nikos at Taverna Diavlos (☑ 6976851056; mains €5-10; ⊙ Feb-Nov) on Nisos. There are a couple of domatia at the taverna. Wild camping is possible as well, but the main activities on Palio Trikeri are explaining to locals why you're there, and then explaining to yourself why you're leaving.

PLATANIAS   ΠΛΑΤΑΝΙΑΣ

Platanias (plah-tah-nih-*ahs*) was a popular resort until the hydrofoil service stopped in 2001, allowing it to return to its low-key roots. There's a good sand-and-pebble beach, a campground and a few tavernas and domatia.

🏃 Activities

Africana   BOAT TOUR

(☑ 6939848464, 6973496818; www.africana-cruises.gr; adult/child €25/12.50) From roughly early June through to the end of August, an excursion boat, the *Africana*, makes runs (if there are people) between Platanias and the island of Skiathos. The 100-passenger boat departs Platanias at 9.30am and returns at 5.30pm.

⊨ Sleeping

Olive Store Cottage   GUESTHOUSE $$

(☑ 6945575360; www.holidaylettings.co.uk/rent als/pelion/347420; cottage for 2 €100) To prolong the extraordinary end-of-the-earth feeling, head 4km north of Platanias for this beautiful self-catering cottage run by two enthusiastic expats and keen walkers.

Trikala   Τρίκαλα

POP 81,000

The first thing you might notice about Trikala (*tree*-kah-lah) are the bicycles. Half the town, young and old, seems to be pedalling around on their treadlies. Roughly halfway between Karditsa and Kalambaka, Trikala was once ancient Trikki, and home to Asclepius, the god of healing. A statue honouring the mythic doctor stands on a small bridge by the main square. Trikala is an attractive and bustling agricultural centre.

◉ Sights

Fortress of Trikala   FORT

It is worth a wander up to the gardens surrounding the restored Byzantine fort. An adjacent cafe-bar overlooks the town. Walk

400m up Sarafi from the central square and look for the sign pointing right.

Sanctuary of Asclepius   RUIN
Asclepius' sanctuary ruins are located before the turn to the Fortress of Trikala.

Varousi   NEIGHBOURHOOD
More interesting is the old Turkish quarter of Varousi, just east of the fortress. It's a fascinating area of narrow streets and fine old houses with overhanging balconies. At the corner of Anagiron and Virvou, peek at the fine murals within the 16th-century church of **Agioi Anargiri**. Another 200m up the hill from Varousi, you'll find the **Chapel of Profitis Ilias**.

Koursoun Tzami   MOSQUE
(⊙8am-2pm Mon-Fri) The Koursoun Tzami was built in the 16th century by Sinan Pasha, the same architect who built the Blue Mosque in İstanbul. The mosque was restored in the mid-1990s with EU funding. From the bus station head south and follow the river for 300m.

🛏 Sleeping

Hotel Panellinion   HOTEL $$
(🖉24310 73545; www.hotelpanellinion.com; Plateia Riga Fereou; s/d incl breakfast €45/60; ❄ 🕏) Dating from 1914, this restored and spacious neoclassical hotel is filled with traditional memorabilia, including old telephones and beautiful rugs. It's located just opposite the river.

Hotel Achilleon   HOTEL $$
(Asklinniou 2; s/d incl breakfast €50/60; 🕏) Highly professional staff and situated right on the plaza, this large place has a 1970s art-deco touch and comfortable rooms.

✗ Eating

Trikala's cafe life is centred on the northern end of Asklipiou and across the river in the old Manavika district. Ypsilanti is flanked by tavernas and *tsipouradhika*. For quick eats, head to Plateia Kitrilaki, where you'll find good €2 souvlakia (cubes of meat on skewers) plates.

Kebab Karthoutsos   KEBAB $
(🖉24310 38084; Ioulietas Adam 5; mains €3-6) This long-standing place, handy to Plateia Riga Fereou, grills a great pork kebab (served on paper), *horta* (wild greens), feta and local wine, all for around €10 per head.

Taverna Palia Istoria   TAVERNA $
(🖉24319 77627; Ypsilanti 3; mains €7-13.50) If businessmen are anything to go by, this is a popular place for its grills served with cream and mustard sauces...but it can also put a slightly gourmet twist on tradition with the likes of *Salata Cleopatra* (salad with figs, pine nuts and balsamic vinegar; €6).

🍺 Drinking & Nightlife

On weekend nights, the idea in Trikala seems to be to tank up on coffee along Asklipiou until midnight, then cross the bridge to the humming Manavika district for mojitos, mezedhes and music. This three-block maze of narrow passageways and outdoor tables jumps with lamp-lit music bars, small *ouzeries* and all-night cafes.

For authentic Greek *rembetika* (blues), follow the locals to **Aparhes Bar** (🖉24310 75800; Manavika; ⊙Fri & Sat), along the riverbank.

❶ Information

Banks with ATMs ring the squares on either side of the river. Most cafes around Plateia Riga Fereou offer free wi-fi.

Neos Kosmos Internet Cafe (Vyronos 20; per hr €2; ⊙8am-midnight) Has wi-fi and several fast computers.

Police Station (🖉24310 63013; Sidiras Merarhias)

Post Office (Sarafi 13) Next to Plateia Riga Fereou.

❶ Getting There & Away

BUS

Buses depart from Trikala's **KTEL bus station** (🖉24310 73130; Rizargio), 4km south of town. A shuttle (€0.60) runs from the **ticket office** (cnr Othonos & Garivaldi).

DESTINATION	TIME	FARE	FREQUENCY
Athens	4½hr	€28	7 daily
Elati	1hr	€3.40	1-2 daily
Ioannina	2½hr	€15	2 daily
Kalambaka	30min	€2.30	hourly
Lamia	2hr	€12	7 daily
Larisa	1hr	€6.30	hourly
Thessaloniki	3hr	€19	5 daily
Volos	2¼hr	€14	4 daily

TRAIN

From Trikala **train station** (🖉24317 70666) there are trains to Kalambaka (€1.80, 15 minutes, five daily), Larisa (€5.80, one hour, two daily),

Athens (IC €17.80, four hours, two daily) and Thessaloniki (€14.10, three hours, one daily).

Around Trikala

About 18km southwest of Trikala is the village of Pyli, 'gate' in Greek, opening to a spectacular gorge and one of Greece's more inviting wilderness areas.

At the gorge's entrance is the 13th-century **Church of Porta Panagia**, with an impressive pair of mosaic icons and a marble iconostasis. To reach it, cross the footbridge over the river and turn left.

The 16th-century **Moni Agiou Vissarion** stands on a slope of Mt Koziakas, 5km from Pyli. To get here, cross the bridge over the river and follow the sign uphill for 500m.

Meteora   Μετέωρα

The World Heritage–listed Meteora (meh-*teh*-o-rah) is an extraordinary place, and one of the most visited in all of Greece. The massive pinnacles of smooth rock are ancient and yet could be the setting for a futuristic science-fiction tale. The monasteries atop them add to the strange and beautiful landscape.

Meteora, Kastraki & Kalambaka

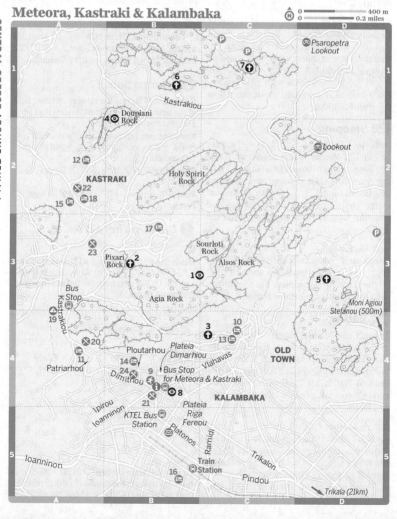

Each monastery is built around a central courtyard surrounded by monks' cells, chapels and a refectory. In the centre of each courtyard is the *katholikon*.

An excellent booklet, *The Footpaths of Meteora* by Andonis Kalogirou (Kritiki Publishers), is available from the no-name souvenir shop at Patriachou Dimitriou 1, Kalambaka. Several maps are available, including Orama Editions' 1:8000 *Meteora*.

History

The name Meteora derives from the Greek adjective *meteoros*, which means 'suspended in the air'; the word 'meteor' is from the same root.

From the 11th century, hermit monks lived in the scattered caverns of Meteora. By the 14th century, the Byzantine power of the Roman Empire was on the wane and Turkish incursions into Greece were on the rise, so monks began to seek safe havens away from the bloodshed. The inaccessibility of the rocks of Meteora made them an ideal retreat.

The earliest monasteries were reached by climbing removable ladders. Later, windlasses were used so monks could be hauled up in nets. A story goes that when curious visitors asked how frequently the ropes were replaced, the monks' stock reply was 'when the Lord lets them break'.

These days, access to the monasteries is by steps that were hewn into the rocks in the 1920s, and by a convenient access road.

◉ Sights

Before setting out to the area's monasteries, decide on a route. If you start early, you can see several, if not all, *mones* (monasteries) in one day.

The main sealed road surrounding the entire Meteora complex of rocks and monasteries is about 15km in length; with your own transport, you can easily visit them all.

Alternatively, take the bus (€1.20, 20 minutes) that departs from Kalambaka and Kastraki at 9am, and returns at 1pm (12.40pm on weekends). That's enough time to explore three monasteries – Moni Megalou Meteorou, Moni Varlaam and Moni Agias Varvaras Rousanou. Perhaps the best route is to take the bus one way to the top and then work your way down and around on foot, finishing at either Moni Agiou Nikolaou on the Kastraki side, or at Moni Agios Triados on the Kalambaka side.

Keen walkers should definitely explore the area on foot on the old and once-secret *monopatia* (monk paths).

Walking and climbing around the rocks can be thirsty work. In summer mobile canteens sell drinks and snacks at some monastery car parks.

Moni Agiou Nikolaou MONASTERY
(Monastery of St Nikolaou Anapafsa; ☑ 24320 22375; ⊙ 9am-3.30pm Sat-Thu Nov-Mar, to 2pm Apr-Oct) Moni Agiou Nikolaou is the nearest *moni* to Kastraki, just 2km from the village square to the steep steps leading to the *moni*. Many people bypass this, but they shouldn't. The monastery was built in the 15th century, and the exceptional frescoes in its *katholikon* were painted by the monk Theophanes Strelizas from Crete. Especially beautiful is the 1527 fresco *The Naming of Animals by Adam in Paradise*.

Meteora, Kastraki & Kalambaka

Moni Megalou Meteorou MONASTERY
(Grand Meteoron; ☑24320 22278; ⊘9am-5pm Wed-Mon Apr-Oct, to 4pm Thu-Mon Nov-Mar) The best known of the monasteries in Meteora, Moni Megalou Meteorou, is an imposing form built on the highest rock in the valley, 613m above sea level. Founded by St Athanasios in the 14th century, it became the richest and most powerful monastery thanks to the Serbian emperor Symeon Uros, who turned all his wealth over to the monastery and became a monk. Its *katholikon* has a magnificent 12-sided central dome. Its striking series of frescoes entitled *Martyrdom of Saints* depicts the graphic persecution of Christians by the Romans.

Moni Varlaam MONASTERY
(☑24320 22277; ⊘9am-4pm Sat-Thu Apr-Oct, Sat-Wed Nov-Mar) About 700m down from Moni Megalou, Moni Varlaam has a small museum, an original rope-basket (until the 1930s the method for hauling up provisions and monks) and fine late-Byzantine frescoes by Frangos Kastellanos. The mural *The Blessed Sisois at the Tomb of Alexander the Great* shows the great conqueror as a humble skeleton. Look just above the door, past the candles.

For a panoramic break, visit the rambling **Psaropetra lookout**, located 300m east of the signposted fork northeast of Moni Varlaam.

Moni Agias Varvaras Rousanou MONASTERY
(⊘9am-6pm Thu-Tue Apr-Oct, to 2pm Nov-Mar) Access to Moni Agias Varvaras Rousanou is via a small wooden bridge. The beautiful coloured-glass-illuminated *katholikon* is the highlight here, with superb frescoes of the *Resurrection* (on your left entering) and *Transfiguration* (on your right). The imposing steep structure of Rousanou is itself a stunning accomplishment, and is today home to an order of around 15 nuns. If you're there near closing, listen for the call to vespers.

Moni Agias Triados MONASTERY
(Holy Trinity Monastery; ☑24320 22220; ⊘9am-5pm Fri-Wed Apr-Oct, 10am-4pm Fri-Tue Nov-Mar) Of all the monasteries in Meteora, Moni Agias Triados has the most remote feel, plus the longest approach. It was featured in the 1981 James Bond film *For Your Eyes Only*. The views here are extraordinary, and the small 17th-century *katholikon* is beautiful, in particular the *Judgement of Pilate* and the *Hospitality of Abraham*. A well-marked 1km *monopati* leads back to Kalambaka.

Moni Agiou Stefanou MONASTERY
(☑24320 22279; ⊘9am-1.30pm & 3.30-5.30pm Tue-Sun Apr-Oct, 9.30am-1pm & 3-5pm Nov-Mar) The newest of the monastery's two *katholikon* of Moni Agiou Stefanou was built in 1798 and is dedicated to St Charalambos. In recent years, Greek hagiographer Vlassios Tsotsonis has been repainting the *katholikon* (depicting the Life of Christ) with beautiful results. Efficient nuns do a thriving trade selling religious souvenirs. The monastery is at the very end of the road, 1.5km beyond Agias Triados.

THE METEORA: GEOLOGY OF A ROCK FOREST

The jutting pinnacles and cliffs of the Meteora were once sediments of an inland sea. About 10 million years ago vertical tectonic movements pushed the entire region out of the sea at a sloping angle. The same tectonic movements caused the flanking mountains to move closer, exerting extreme pressure on the hardened sedimentary deposits. The Meteora developed netlike fissures and cracks. The weathering and erosion that followed formed the towering outcrops of rock that now vault heavenwards. The rocks were conglomerates of many types: limestone, marble, serpentinite and metamorphic, interspersed with layers of sand and shale.

By the dawn of human civilisation, the rocks had weathered and eroded into fantastic shapes; the sandstone and shale washed away, isolating blocks of rock and cliffs. Where erosion was less extreme, caves and overhangs appeared in the rock face.

As early as the 11th century AD, these awesome natural caves had become the solitary abodes of hermit monks. Eventually, 24 monasteries were built on these pinnacles. Today, six are active religious sites, occupied by monks or nuns and visited by the faithful and curious alike.

VISITING THE MONASTERIES

Entry to each monastery is €3 and dress codes apply: no bare shoulders are allowed, men must wear trousers and women must wear skirts below the knee (wrap-around skirts are generally provided at the entrances). Before planning your route, double-check days and opening hours; the monks are an independent lot, and no two monasteries keep exactly the same hours. The following is a list of closures as at the time of research:

Moni Agiou Nikolaou Closed Friday

Moni Megalou Meteorou Closed Tuesday (and Wednesday November to March)

Moni Varlaam Closed Friday (and Thursday November to March)

Moni Agias Varvaras Rousanou Closed Wednesday

Moni Agias Triados Closed Thursday (and Wednesday November to March)

Moni Agiou Stefanou Closed Monday

Activities

Walking

Keen walkers will be in their element exploring several days' worth of *monopatia* that thread through the region. Good maps outline routes.

The geological heart of Meteora is considered the **Adhrakhti**, or obelisk, a striking column visible from anywhere in Kastraki. A 1km path up the gully will deposit you there in about 20 minutes from Kastraki's central square.

Nearby, on the east-facing side of the Pixari rock face, closer to Kastraki, look for the cave-chapel of **Agiou Andonios**. To the left of the chapel, in the hollows and cavities of the rock face, are the **Askitaria** (cave hermitages), complete with hanging ladders and nesting doves. The Askitaria were occupied until the early 20th century by solitary monks, and they remain a testament to the original spirit of Meteora.

Elsewhere, lovely walks head along the path above Alsos House (p224) to the monasteries of **Agia Triada** and **Agios Stefanos**.

Rock Climbing

Meteora has been a mecca for European rock climbers for several years. Climbers of various skill levels can choose routes from more than 100 peaks and towers with names such as the Tower of the Holy Ghost, the Great Saint, the Devil's Tower, the Corner of Madness and the Iron Edge. Best times weather-wise are mid-March to mid-June and mid-August to mid-November.

A typical guided climb averages three hours, and costs start from €40 per person, depending on routes and the degree of difficulty. Most climbs reach heights between 90m and 200m. A beginners' route takes about two hours on **Doupiani Rock**. (All equipment, including harness, shoes and helmet, is included in prices.)

For assisted climbs, contact mountaineering instructor Kostas Liolios (p223) or **Lazaros Botelis** (☑ 6948043655, 24320 79165; meteora.guide@gmail.gr; Kastraki).

Tours

English-language tours of Meteora are offered by knowledgeable **Ekaterini Kaiki** (☑ 6973890701; www.katerinakaiki.com; up to 4 people from €120), who also speaks Italian; **Kostas Liolios** (☑ 6972567582; ksts_liolios@yahoo.com; Kalambaka), also a climbing instructor; and long-time guide **Christos Konis** (☑ 6972825212), who also speaks French and Italian.

Kalambaka   Καλαμπακά

POP 8620

Kalambaka, the gateway to Meteora, is almost entirely modern, having been burned to the ground by the Nazis in WWII. It takes at least a day to see all of the monasteries of Meteora, so you'll need to spend the night either in Kalambaka or the village of Kastraki.

Sights & Activities

First-time visitors to Kalambaka will be amazed at the vertical rocks that guard the northern edge of the town. There is a bustling market every Friday.

Church of the Assumption of the Virgin Mary
CHURCH

(admission €1.50; ⊙8am-1pm & 3-8pm) It's worth finding your way to this 7th-century Byzantine cathedral, a three-aisle basilica with superb frescoes dating to the 14th century. (Note: don't be confused with the church in the centre). At 6.30pm you can hear the vespers.

🛏 Sleeping

Rooms are plentiful in Kalambaka, though it's best to avoid noisy Trikalon.

★ Alsos House
PENSION $

(☑24320 24097; www.alsoshouse.gr; Kanari 5; s/d/tr incl breakfast €35/45/65, f incl breakfast €75-80, apt €80-100; P❉@🛜) The well-managed Alsos House has a communal kitchen, laundry, and wide views of the rocks. It's 500m from the centre and a stone's throw from wonderful *monopati*. Welcoming English-speaking owner Yiannis Karakantas wants the best for his guests; he knows as much about the area as the monks do about their prayers.

Guest House Elena
BOUTIQUE HOTEL $

(☑6976562529, 24320 77789; www.elenaguesthouse.gr; Kanari 3; s/d/tr incl breakfast from €40/50/60, ste €100; P❉@🛜) Period furnishings in lovely rooms with an intimate atmosphere; multilingual owner.

Hotel Meteora
PENSION $

(☑24320 22367; www.hotel-meteora.blogspot.com; Ploutarhou 14; s/d/tr incl breakfast €25/30/45; P❉@🛜) On a quiet cul-de-sac below the rocks, this is a reliable budget option. Reports of great breakfasts with homegrown produce. Guests have use of a swimming pool at a relative's large hotel.

Monastiri Guest House
BOUTIQUE HOTEL $

(☑24320 23952; www.monastiri-guesthouse.gr; Agios Kostantinos Elenis; s/d/tr/ste incl breakfast €45/55/75/100; P❉🛜) Behind the railway station, this converted stone mansion has colourful decorations, long poster-beds and light and airy bathrooms. The handsome wood-and-stone lobby sports a fireplace and bar.

🍴 Eating

For quick eats and *gyros* (rotisserie-cooked meat skewers, usually served with pitta bread), roam the block south of Plateia Riga Fereou.

Taverna To Paramithi
TAVERNA $

(☑24320 24441; Patriarhou Dimitriou 14; mains €5.50-8; ⊙lunch & dinner Mar-Dec) Along with very good grills and fresh pasta served in a convivial environment, owner-cooks Makis and Eleni bring in fresh seafood daily and cook up good classic dishes. Local musicians often end the night here, with guitar or bouzouki in hand (and possibly a glass of the tasty house wine or some homemade *tsipouro*).

Restaurant Meteora
GREEK $

(www.restaurant-meteora.gr; Oikonomou 2; €7.50-10; ⊙lunch) Yes, it's on the main square (read obvious). And ok, it caters to group travel (read touristy). But this charming place, run by a third-generation family and housed in a stunning building displaying bits and pieces from a bygone era, is a lovely spot for local dishes. You file past the pots in the kitchen and choose what you want.

Panorama
GREEK $$

(www.meeoronpanorama.gr; mains €8-12) It's a large place (which is a bit overwhelming if you're eating alone), but true to its name, it offers beautiful vistas. The cuisine is excellent, especially the grills. The lamb in paper is worth trying.

ℹ Information

Banks with ATMs surround the central Plateia Riga Fereou on Trikalon. There is also a currency-exchange window next to the post office.

Health Care Centre (☑24320 22222; Pindou)

Post Office (Trikalon 24)

Visit Meteora (www.visitmeteora.travel; Patriarchou Dimitriou 2; ⊙9am-9pm) Run by a young crowd, this new private tourist office aims to be all things to all tourists. It's a useful first stop to the area – it provides maps, and can arrange guided tours, transport and activities.

Tourist Police (☑24320 78516; cnr Ipirou & Pindou)

ℹ Getting There & Away

BUS

Kalambaka's **KTEL bus station** (☑24320 22432; Ikonomou) is 50m down from the main square and fountain, and is the arrival/departure point for regular Trikala bus connections. Travellers to Delphi should go via Trikala (not

Larisa), taking the 8am bus, and changing to the 9am Amfissa/Delphi bus.

DESTINATION	TIME	FARE	FREQUENCY
Athens	5hr	€29	6 daily except weekends
Ioannina	2½hr	€12.50	2 daily
Lamia (change in Trikala)	2hr	€14.10	7 daily
Thessaloniki	3½hr	€20	5 daily
Trikala	30min	€2.30	hourly
Volos (change in Trikala)	2½hr	€16	4 daily

TRAIN

Trains depart from the Kalambaka **train station** (☑ 24320 22451). For trains to Athens, Thessaloniki and Volos you may need to change at Paleofarsalos.

DESTINATION	TIME	FARE	FREQUENCY
Athens (normal)	5½hr	€18.30	1 daily
Athens (IC)	4½hr	€18.30	1 daily
Thessaloniki	4hr	€15.20	1 daily
Volos	1½hr	€9.40	1 daily

❶ Getting Around

BICYCLE

Bikes (€8) and motorcycles (€18) can be hired for the day from **Hobby Shop** (hobbyshop@hotmail.gr; Patriarhou Dimitriou 28).

BUS

Every two hours buses for Kastraki (€1) leave from beside the Plateia Dimarhiou fountain. Two daily Meteora-bound buses (€1.60) depart from the KTEL station (also picking tourists up at the town hall) between May and September. Ask at the KTEL office for the schedule.

TAXI

From opposite the fountain, taxis go to Kastraki (€3.50) and all the monasteries (for example, Moni Megalou Meteorou for around €10). Some drivers speak English, German or Italian, and you arrange a taxi tour from about €20 per hour.

Kastraki   Καστράκι

POP 1200

Kastraki is less than 2km from Kalambaka, but its location right under the rocks gives it an otherworldly feel. As a base for exploring the Meteora monasteries, or climbing the rocks themselves, Kastraki is a good choice.

🛏 Sleeping

★ Doupiani House   PENSION $

(☑ 24320 75326; www.doupianihouse.com; s/d/tr incl breakfast €40/50/60; P ❄ @ 🛜) The delightful Doupiani House has the lot: spotless, tastefully decorated rooms, with balconies or garden access. Its location – just outside the village – provides a window to Meteora; it boasts one of the region's best panoramic views. There's breakfast on the terrace, birdsong and attentive hosts, Toula and Thanasis.

Hotel Tsikeli   HOTEL $

(☑ 24320 22438; www.tsikelihotel.gr; s €35, d €45-50, incl breakfast; P ❄ 🛜) Simple rooms with wood and marble trim, large balconies and a grassy front garden. Carpeted corridors are a plus to keeping noise levels down.

Rooms Ziogas Vasiliki   PENSION $

(☑ 24320 24037; www.ziogasrooms.com; s/d/tr from €25/35/40; P ❄ 🛜) This friendly budget option is clean and airy, and there are great views from several rooms facing the rocks. Breakfast costs €5.

Vrachos Camping   CAMPGROUND $

(☑ 24320 22293; www.campingmeteora.gr; camp sites per tent/adult €7.50/free; ✦) A well-shaded campground on the Kalambaka–Kastraki road with excellent facilities.

Dellas Boutique Hotel   BOUTIQUE HOTEL $$

(☑ 24320 78260; www.dellasboutiquehotel.com; s €55, d €60-78, tr €85, incl breakfast; ☉ Apr-Sep) While it doesn't boast a wide-angled panoramic view, this handsome place between Kastraki and Kalambaka receives accolades for its elegant, tidy rooms and high service standards. Prices vary according to the views.

Pyrgos Adrachti   BOUTIQUE HOTEL $$

(☑ 24320 22275; www.hotel-adrachti.gr; s €40, d €50-69, tr €80; P ❄ 🛜) Slick and cool sums up this boutique hotel – think designer-style touches throughout the rooms, bar and common areas, and an up-close-and-personal rock experience. Plus there's a tidy garden to relax in post-activities. It's at the northern end of the village, nestled under the rocks; ask for directions.

✗ Eating

Taverna Paradisos
TAVERNA $

(24320 22723; mains €6.50-9) The traditional meals at the roomy Paradisos will have you '*nostimo*-ing!' (exclaiming 'delicious!') all the way through your dishes, thanks to local and high-quality ingredients and owner-chef Koula's magic touch. Excellent fried zucchini.

Taverna Meteora Vavitsas
TAVERNA $

(24230 22285; mains €6-10) Opposite Hotel Kastraki, this popular meat-and-more-meat taverna is set back in a leafy brick terrace.

Cafe Milios
SWEETS $

This cafe is one of the few places where you can buy *soutzouki*, a traditional sweet made by dipping a string over and over into grape juice to create a jelly-like roll. It's worth buying some (by weight) to support the labour alone. Ask for directions.

ℹ Information

Kastraki's only internet place is **All Time Café** (per hr €2; ⊙ 9am-midnight), on the main road opposite Taverna Paradisos.

DAVID C TOMLINSON/GETTY IMAGES ©

Natural Havens

An island escape requires certain ingredients – powder-soft sand between your toes, crystalline water warm enough to dive into headlong, and that sensation of having sidestepped real life. Throw in verdant forests, crumbling castles and vivid sunsets and it becomes slightly surreal. Sun-drenched and plentiful, the Greek islands are heavenly.

Contents
➡ Island Candy
➡ Sand Castles
➡ Natural Attractions

Above: Shipwreck Beach, Navagio Bay (p664), Zakynthos

1. Santorini (p377) 2. Rhodes Town (p470) 3. Hydra (p309)
4. Lesvos (p568)

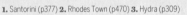

MARTIN CHILD/GETTY IMAGES ©

KAROLOS TRIVIZAS/GETTY IMAGES ©

Island Candy

The Greek Islands have been kissed by Mother Nature. Delve into the islands' interiors for breathtaking forests, unexpected wildlife and volcanic moonscapes. Explore their coastlines for magnificent sea-hewn landscapes and inspiring marine life. These are the backdrops from your dreams.

Santorini (Thira)

Santorini isn't just about sunsets, but it could be. Sipping a cocktail on a balcony that stretches out over the caldera, while the sun sinks and the cliffs dazzle red and orange, is undeniable island bliss.

Rhodes

The beauty of Rhodes has drawn artists and conquerors throughout the ages, resulting in a cultural history as striking as its windswept coastline. An ancient acropolis, countless Byzantine chapels and crumbling fairytale-like castles will fill your days, while evenings offer musicians playing in evocative local bars.

Hydra

A preserved stone village and a bubbling port, all within shooting distance of Athens, makes Hydra one of Greece's most popular islands. Unbelievably, life carries on here as it has for centuries, with simple tavernas, no cars, and a raw coastline daring you to jump into the water.

Lesvos (Mytilini)

Massive Lesvos is varied: rolling olive groves and cool pine forests, arid plains, salt marshes and one of the world's few petrified forests found outside the USA. The hot springs gush some of the warmest water in Europe.

Sand Castles

While it's true that Greece is more than beaches, its shoreline is the icing on this destination. And in very Greek-style, the beaches offer something for everyone. With long, easy-to-reach stretches coveted by sun-worshipers and out-of-the-way pebbled coves full of sealife, you'll find somewhere to stretch out your towel.

Sandy Stretches

Crete is well known for its beaches and it's impossible to choose just one. This island has more than its fair share of the country's top sandy stretches. Tropical Elafonisi with its pink sand, photogenic Preveli with freshwater pools, end-of-the-world Falasarna and palm-forested Vaï will all compete for your attention.

The famed volcanic beaches of **Santorini** have red or black coloured sand. Vlyhada Beach is long and strewn with pumice stones. In a small cove nearby, Red Beach rests dramatically beneath deep vermilion-coloured cliffs.

To the east, the majestic Kefalos Bay of **Kos** is no secret, but anyone who feels the warmth of this 12km stretch of magnificent sand underfoot quickly appreciates that some things really are worth sharing. The bay is divided into several beaches, each with its own character. Some offer parties, others tranquillity.

Corfu is popular for its readily accessible sea-lapped sand. The west coast's Paleokastritsa is a chain of charming coves tucked between tall cliffs with craggy mountaintops and olive trees towering above. Find your own quiet patch and dig in your toes.

1. Kathisma beach (p649), Lefkada
2. Santorini (p377)
3. Naxos (p352)

Secret Stashes of Sand

Despite the popularity of its beaches, Greece has managed to keep a few gorgeous stretches quiet. Visit **Ikaria**, a magical island with soft sand and white-pebble pockets of paradise. It's easy to find isolated stretches and even the well-patronised beaches are far more laid back than your typical island resort.

The west coast of **Lefkada** offers everything to fulfil a beach-lover's dreams. Remote, breathtaking beaches, many with few facilities, where locals sell olives, wine and honey. Who'd guess that you were so close to the bustling mainland?

With lush greenery and Mt Zeus as a backdrop, laid-back **Naxos** offers two indulgences – local liqueur and idyllic white-sand beaches. Stretch out and sip kitron on the endless Agia Anna, or follow the age-old tradition of watching for pirates from isolated Mikri Vigla.

BEST BEACHES FOR...

Swimming Myrtos Beach, Assos; Preveli Beach, Crete

Snorkelling Monastiri, Paros; Paleokastritsa, Corfu; Xirokambos Bay, Leros

Kids Kambos Beach, Patmos; Halkidiki Peninsula, Northern Greece

Solitude Porto Katsiki, Lefkada; Vaï, Crete

Beach Bars Kritika Beach, Kos; Glyfada, Athens

Wildlife The beaches of Lesvos and Skyros

Natural Attractions

You may have planned to spend your entire holiday lazing on the beach, but when you hear talk of Greece's mysterious gorges and rugged peaks, the only way to satisfy your curiosity is to get up and get out there. Hike through the infamous Samaria Gorge; hop on a boat to look for monk seals, sea turtles and dolphins; wander along ancient Byzantine stone paths; or scale Mt Olympus.

1. Myrina (p580), Limnos
The hilltop castle's ruins date from the 13th century.

2. Paxi (p643)
Paxi is one of the Ionians' most idyllic islands.

3. Olymbos (p489), Karpathos
Perched above the island's rocky shoreline, this traditional village guards a unique culture.

4. Bay of Laganas (p664), Zakynthos
The National Marine Park of Zakynthos is home to the endangered loggerhead turtle.

5. Samaria Gorge (p448), Crete
The 16km-long trail is a 'must do' experience for hikers.

Matala's 'hippie' caves (p431), Crete

Northern Greece

Best Places to Eat

➡ Paparouna (p248)

➡ Castello Restaurant (p298)

➡ Kivotos (p258)

➡ Sta Riza (p294)

➡ Sapore Cucine Italiana (p283)

Best Places to Stay

➡ Colors Central Ladadika (p247)

➡ Arhontiko Dilofo (p293)

➡ Salvator Villas & Spa Hotel (p298)

➡ Cavo Olympo Luxury Resort & Spa (p265)

Why Go?

Vast northern Greece (βόρεια Ελλάδα) has the country's wildest terrain, and widest variety of cultures, cuisines and legacies. Its major city, Thessaloniki, is a hip metropolis with arguably the best nightlife in southeast Europe.

The region stretches from the sandy Ionian coast over Epiros' stark mountains, through Macedonia's lakes and vineyards, and across Thrace's mountains and plains all the way to Turkey. It has been for centuries a stomping ground for major civilisations such as the Macedonians, Thracians, Romans, Byzantines, Slavs and Turks. This mixed heritage has graced the region with spectacular churches, monasteries, castles, towers and museums.

For urban action, start with Thessaloniki or Ioannina. Beach-lovers will love the Halkidiki Peninsula's clear waters, the golden 'Epirot Riviera' and beaches east of Mt Olympus. Outdoor activities abound from the Vikos Gorge to the Prespa Lakes, protected Evros Delta and Dadia Forest Reserve. And, something is always happening, whatever the season.

When to Go
Thessaloniki

Jun-Aug Hit the beaches at Halkidiki or around Parga in Epirus.

Sep-Nov Dig Thessaloniki's culture scene, at film fests art exhibits and alternative bars.

Dec-Mar Cultivate a ski-lodge glow in Zagorohoria or celebrate a Mt Athos monastic Christmas.

Northern Greece Highlights

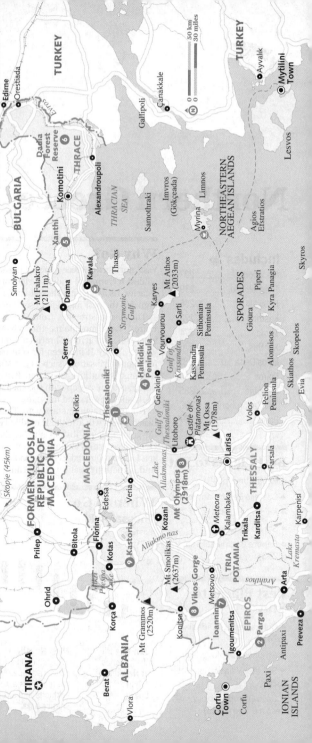

1 Enjoy fine dining, live music, Byzantine churches, ruins and museums in exuberant **Thessaloniki** (p239)

2 Dive clear Ionian waters at Venetian-flavoured **Parga** (p297)

3 Contemplate snow-capped Mt Olympus and the sandy Aegean coast from atop the **Castle of Platamonas** (p266)

4 Chill out on Sithonia's beaches or decamp with Athos' monks on the wildly varied **Halkidiki Peninsula** (p256)

5 Partake in Xanthi's riotous **winter carnival** (p276)

6 See circling vultures and hawks at Thrace's **Dadia Forest Reserve** (p281)

7 Buy handcrafted local silver and explore the castle quarter of **Ioannina** (p285)

8 Hike one of Europe's grandest canyons, the **Vikos Gorge** (p293)

9 Cycle, kayak, or simply sit back and breathe in **Kastoria's** (p272) enigmatic lake

MACEDONIA ΜΑΚΕΔΟΝΙΑ

Although for many foreigners the word Macedonia (in Greek, mah-keh-dho-*nee*-ah) conjures up only ancient conqueror Alexander the Great, Greece's biggest province has major modern attractions to rival the museums and key historical sites Pella and Vergina. Thessaloniki, Greece's sophisticated second city, has fantastic dining and nightlife, while the Halkidiki Peninsulas just east offer fine sandy coves and big beaches, and the 1000-year-old Athonite monastic community.

Macedonia's other big-ticket sights include legendary Mt Olympus, Greece's highest peak at 2918m and a great place for hiking; and just opposite, more beaches stretch down the wooded Pieria coast, punctuated by a clifftop Byzantine castle at Platamonas. Traces of this heritage meet shimmering waters again in Macedonia's far northwest, where grand basilica ruins and frescoed church grottoes meet the Prespa Lakes, and in quiet Kastoria, with its sublime Byzantine shrines set above an elliptical lake of its own.

Macedonia's kaleidoscope of landscapes – from mountains and deep forests to arid plains and wetland marshes – make it ideal for nature buffs, food lovers and outdoors adventurers. Florina has Greece's best red peppers and highlands where brown bears amble, while Veria is famous for its peaches; the nearby vineyards produce excellent wines. Birdwatchers will enjoy scanning for pelicans, cormorants and migrating birds at the lakes and saltwater estuaries (where tasty fish are plentiful too).

History

Although life in Macedonia goes back 700,000 years, it's best known for the powerful Macedonian civilisation that peaked with Alexander the Great (d 323 BC), who conquered as far as India. Deemed barbarians by cultivated Athenians, the Macedonians subjugated Greece under Alexander's father, Philip II, yet adopted Greek mores. Alexander spread the Greek culture and language widely, creating a Hellenistic soc\iety that would be absorbed by the Romans. Later, after their empire split into eastern and western halves in the 4th century AD, the Greek-speaking Byzantine Empire emerged.

Thessaloniki became Byzantium's second city, a vital commercial, cultural and strategic centre on the Balkan trade routes. However, 6th- and 7th-century-AD Slavic migrations brought new populations and challenges. The empire frequently battled with the medieval Bulgarian kingdom from the 9th century to the 11th century. In 1018 Emperor Basil II finally defeated Bulgarian Tsar Samuel, who had ruled much of the southern Balkans from Macedonia's Mikri Prespa Lake.

After Serbian rule in the 14th century, Macedonia and the Balkans were overrun by the Ottoman Turks. The Ottoman system distinguished subjects by religion, not race, causing strife in the late 19th century, when guerrilla movements arose to fight the Turks, pledging to annex Macedonia for Greece, Bulgaria or even an independent 'Macedonia for the Macedonians'; in the very early 20th century, great powers such as Britain favoured the latter.

Ottoman atrocities against Macedonia's Christian populations presaged the First Balkan War of 1912, in which Greece, Bulgaria and Serbia drove the Turks from Macedonia; however, the Bulgarians were unhappy with their share, and declared war on their former allies in 1913 (the Second Balkan War). Bulgaria's quick defeat lost its allotted portions of eastern Macedonia and Thrace, and Greece was the big winner, taking half of geographical Macedonia, with Serbia taking 38%. Bulgaria was left with 13%. Newly created Albania received a sliver around Ohrid and the Prespa lakes.

In 1923, with the massive Greek–Turkish population exchanges, the government resettled many Anatolian Greek refugees in Macedonia, displacing the indigenous (non-Greek) populations. A vigorous program for assimilating non-Greeks was already under way, primarily through education and the church. In WWII Greece was occupied by the Nazis, who deported and killed most of Macedonia's significant Sephardic Jewish population. After, during the Greek Civil War (1944–49), authorities targeted 'communist supporters' – often a label for ethnic minorities – causing the expulsion of thousands of (Slavic) Macedonians, many of them children, as well as Bulgarians and others. Greek Macedonia today is thus different from what it was even 60 years ago.

NORTHERN GREECE MACEDONIA

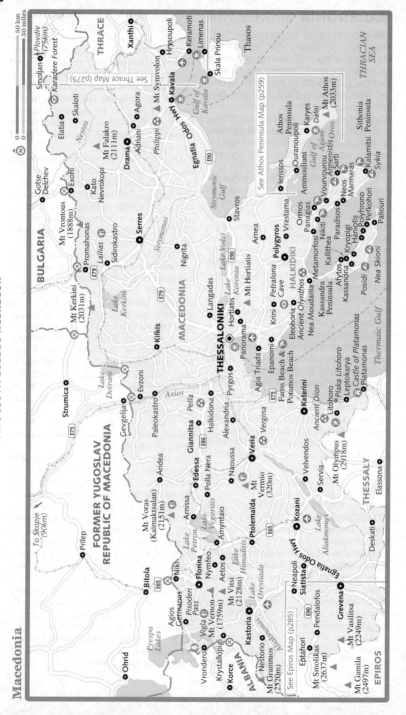

Thessaloniki Θεσσαλονίκη

POP 325,182

Immensely likable Thessaloniki (thess-ah-lo-*nee*-kih) has never been more fun, cultured or affordable than it is right now. Greece's second city has excellent restaurants, museums and sights, plus an increasingly hip and inventive nightlife scene fleshed out by many thousands of Greek and foreign university students. Thessaloniki's a great base, as it provides easy connections by air, land and sea with numerous national and international destinations. And, as a safe and walkable small city, it has none of Athens' problems, either.

Travellers always seem to return to Thessaloniki, and it's indeed outfitted with enduring symbols of a glorious history; these include the White Tower on the cafe-lined waterfront, erstwhile Ottoman structures, and lengthy Byzantine walls culminating at the Ano Poli (Upper Town), an enchanting neighbourhood of colourful old houses, where Byzantine churches peek from winding alleyways. Grand structures include the 5th-century Church of Agios Dimitrios, the enormous Roman Rotunda and Roman Emperor Galerius' 3rd-century palace ruins.

Most recently, during digs for the long-awaited Metro, extensive portions of the 6th-century central street and *tetraphylon* (monumental gate) were discovered, sparking fervent debates over how to reconcile modern development with buried historical riches.

History

Thessaloniki was named for a woman who herself was named to commemorate a military victory, that of her father, Philip II, over a tribe in Thessaly with the help of crack Thessalian horsemen. Thessaloniki married the Macedonian general Kassandros, who named the city after her in 316 BC – ensuring that the royal daughter's name would forever be on the lips of all who would ever experience the city.

In 168 BC the Romans conquered Macedon. Thessaloniki's importance was enhanced by its ideal location on the Thermaic Gulf, east–west Via Egnatia, and the Axios/Vardar River valley leading north. Under Galerius, Thessaloniki became the eastern imperial capital; with the empire's division in 395 AD, it became Byzantium's second city, a flourishing Constantinople in miniature.

However, it was also frequently attacked by Goths, Slavs, Saracens and Crusaders. Still, Thessaloniki remained a cultural centre. It bore the 9th-century monks Cyril and Methodius (creators of Glagolitic, precursor to Cyrillic), who expanded Orthodox Byzantine literary culture among the Slavs, and the great 14th-century theologian St Gregory Palamas.

In 1430, the Ottoman Turks captured Thessaloniki; after 1492, they resettled Sephardic Jews fleeing the Inquisition here, adding to the city's diversity.

With the 1821 Independence War only a partial success, 19th-century Thessaloniki became a lurid hub for intrigue, secret societies and mutually antagonistic rebels and reformers. Along with Greek revolutionaries, these included the pro-Bulgarian Internal Macedonian Revolutionary Organisation (IMRO), and the Young Turks, who wanted Western-style reforms for the empire. Indeed, one Young Turk and Thessaloniki native, Mustafa Kemal (Atatürk) would become modern Turkey's founding father.

Thessaloniki suffered successive tragedies over the following four decades. The August 1917 fire burned most of it, and ethnic diversity shrank with the 1923 population exchanges. During the WWII Nazi occupation, Thessaloniki's Jews were deported to concentration camps and other non-Greeks were expelled following the Greek Civil War. By 1950, Thessaloniki was learning to become a Greek city again.

◉ Sights

Thessaloniki's Byzantine and ancient sites (and its museums) constitute its major attractions. Steadily refurbished Ottoman structures also appeal. Thessaloniki's former Jewish population is attested by some surviving buildings and a small, mostly elderly community. Find *Jewish Sites in Thessaloniki: Brief History and Guide* by Rena Molho and Vilma Hastaoglou-Martinidi (Lycabettus Press) at bookshops and the Jewish Museum.

White Tower   HISTORIC BUILDING

(Lefkos Pyrgos; ☑2310 267 832; www.lpth.gr; ⊙8.30am-3pm Tue-Sun) The history of Thessaloniki's most famous landmark, the pacific White Tower, is actually bathed in blood. In 1826 Ottoman Sultan Mahmud II massacred rebellious janissaries (elite troops of forcibly Islamicised Christian boys) here. After the 1913 Greek reconquest, the 'bloody tower'

Thessaloniki

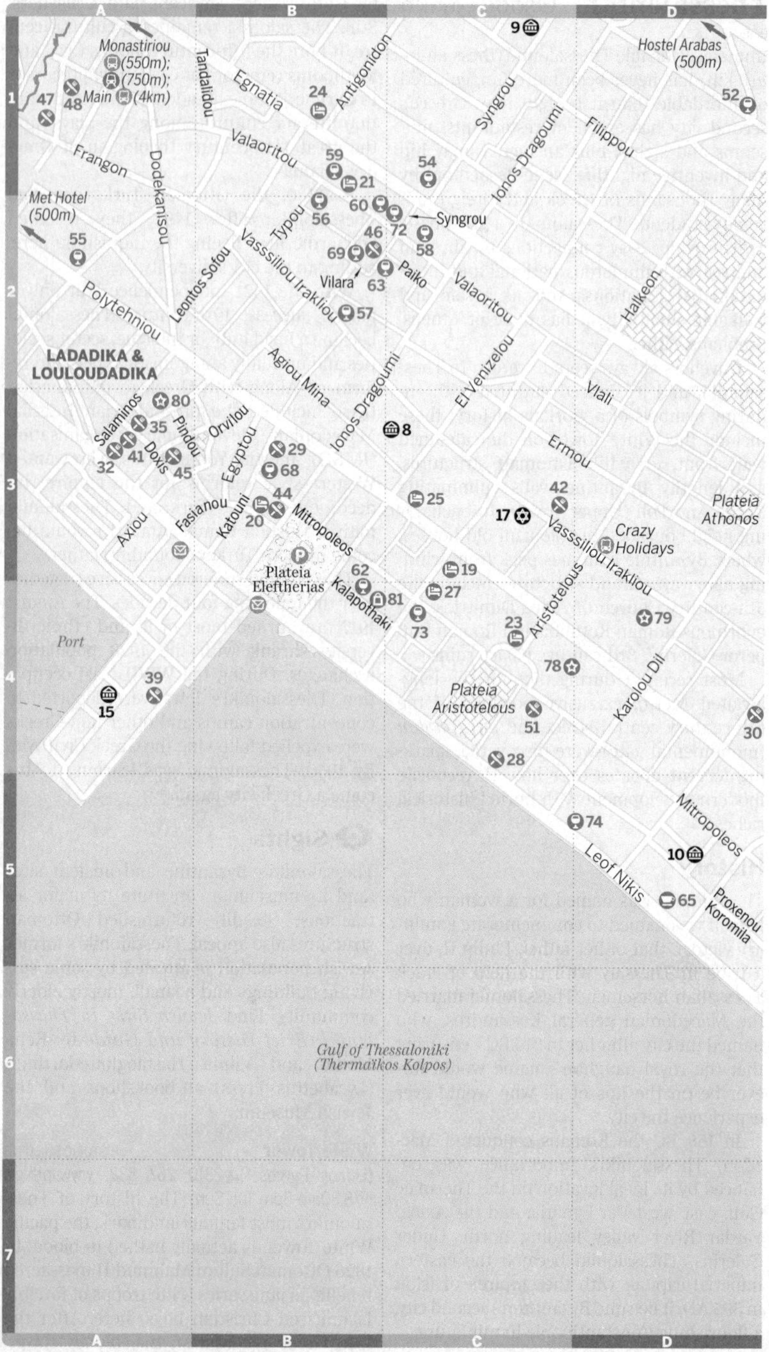

NORTHERN GREECE THESSALONIKI

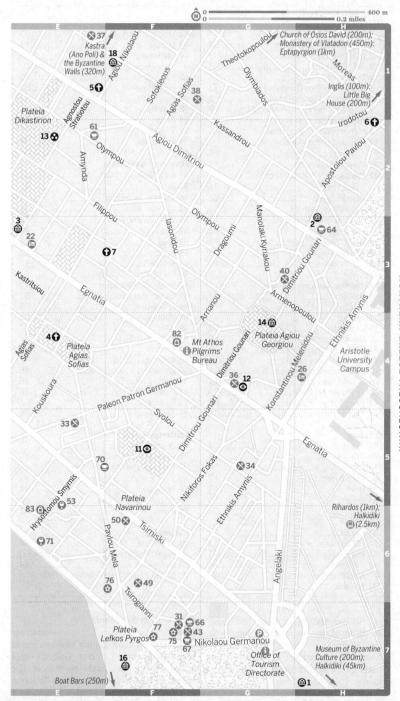

Thessaloniki

was whitewashed to expunge this grisly past. Although the whitewash is long gone, the name stuck.

The tower's interactive museum presents Thessaloniki's history through multimedia displays.

Palace, Arch & Rotunda of Galerius   HISTORIC AREA

FREE Three major Roman monuments of early-4th-century Emperor Galerius spill across Egnatia at Plateia Navarinou. The ruined **Palace of Galerius** (Plateia Navarinou; ◷ 8.30am-3pm Tue-Sun), sprawling east–west across the square, contains floor mosaics, columns and some walls. North of Egnatia at Kamara, the Arch of Galerius (AD 303) celebrates a victory over the Persians, with carved, lunging soldiers.

North of this arch is the Rotunda (Mausoleum; ☎2310 218 720; Plateia Agiou Georgiou; ☺8am-5pm Tue-Sun). Galerius built this hulking brick structure as his future mausoleum, but he died in retirement in today's Serbia. Constantine the Great made it Thessaloniki's first church (Agios Georgios); the Ottomans made it a mosque (note the restored minaret). Some frescoes survive inside.

Roman Agora   RUIN
(Plateia Dikastirion; ☺8am-3pm Tue-Sun) FREE
The Agora lies north of Plateia Aristotelous, on Plateia Dikastirion. In the 3rd century BC, Macedonians made it a commercial centre and the Romans maintained this function. An English-language placard explains the site, which contains clustered shop walls and mosaic floor remnants.

In summer, it hosts the city-sponsored Urban Picnic, which livens up the ruins with free food and live music.

Kastra (Ano Poli) &
the Byzantine Walls   HISTORIC AREA
FREE The Kastra (Castle), also called Ano Poli (Upper Town), contains important Byzantine churches and timber-framed, pastel-painted houses with overhanging upper storeys. Panoramic views of the city and gulf are had from the Byzantine Walls' eastern edge, in the pyrgos (tower). The tower – recently renovated and opened to visitors – is a marvellously atmospheric structure. Ascend it for expansive views.

Emperor Theodosius (AD 379–475) built these walls according to his own great Constantinopolitan wall system. They were rebuilt in the 14th century and in 1821 the Turks removed marble stones from the Jewish cemetery to strengthen them further. You can walk them from opposite the university (Panepistimio Aristotelion) almost all the way uphill.

Only Ano Poli (then, the Turkish Quarter) largely survived the 1917 fire – although it originated there, the wind swept the flames towards the sea. Today, it's a refuge for Thessaloniki's leftists and lazing cats, with a quiet residential charm.

Church of Agios Dimitrios   CHURCH
(☎2310 270 008; Agiou Dimitriou 97; ☺8am-10pm) This enormous 5th-century structure honours Thessaloniki's patron saint. A Roman soldier, Dimitrios was killed around AD 303 at this former Roman bath site, on orders of Emperor Galerius, infamous persecutor of Christians. The martyrdom site is now an eerie underground crypt, open daytime hours and for a Friday-night service. Dimitrios's relics, returned from Italy in 1980, occupy a silver reliquary inside.

The Ottomans made Agios Dimitrios a mosque, plastering over frescoes. After the 1913 Greek reconquest the plaster was removed, revealing Thessaloniki's finest church mosaics. While the 1917 fire was very damaging, five 8th-century mosaics survive, spanning the altar.

Church of Agia Sofia   CHURCH
(Plateia Agias Sofias; ☺7am-1pm & 5-6.30pm) This 8th-century church occupying Plateia Agias Sofias was modelled on its İstanbul namesake. Its dome has a striking mosaic of the Ascension of Christ. Built over a previous 3rd-century church, it's notable for the cross-basilica style associated with middle-Byzantine architecture.

Church of the Panagia Ahiropiitos CHURCH
(☺7am-noon & 4.30-6.30pm) This basilica-style 5th-century Byzantine church has notable mosaics and frescoes. The name, meaning 'made without hands', refers to a miraculous 12th-century appearance of an icon of the Virgin.

Monastery of Vlatadon   MONASTERY
(cnr Eptapyrgiou & Agathangelou; ☺7.30am-5pm & 5.30-8pm, museum 10am-noon Sun) Near Ano Poli's Byzantine Walls, this relaxing place in a leafy, secluded location has a small museum and gift shop. Founded by the pious brothers Vlatades (1360), it was important during the Hesychast spiritual movement, as attested by a fresco of St Gregory Palamas, Hesychasm's spiritual leader. Other remarkable frescoes date from 1360–80.

A now-lost imperial *chrysobull* (gold-sealed decree) of the Byzantine Empress indicates Anna Paleologina endowed Vlatadon, which still preserves a rich archive of documents dating to the 15th century.

Church of Osios David   CHURCH
(Vlatadon 1; ☺9am-noon & 4-6pm Mon-Sat) This little 5th-century church allegedly commemorated the baptism site of the anti-Christian Galerius' daughter, Theodora, a ceremony conducted secretly while her father was away on business. It contains well-preserved

mosaics and rare 12th-century frescoes depicting the baptism of Christ.

Church of Nikolaos Orfanos CHURCH

(☏ 2310 213 627; Irodotou 20; ⊙ 8.30am-2.30pm Tue-Sun) This 4th-century church has superb (though age-darkened) frescoes. To preserve them, candles are only lit during Sunday-morning mass.

Archaeological Museum MUSEUM

(☏ 2310 830 538; www.amth.gr; Manoli Andronikou 6; adult/student/child €6/3/free; ⊙ 8am-3pm) Macedonia's major prehistoric, ancient Macedonian and Hellenistic finds are here, except for Vergina's gold tomb finds, which are exhibited in Vergina. The **Derveni Crater** (330–320 BC) is a huge, ornate Hellenistic bronze-and-tin vase. Used for mixing wine and water, and later as a funerary urn, it's marked by intricate relief carvings of Dionysos, with mythical figures, animals and ivy vines.

The **Derveni Treasure** contains Greece's oldest surviving papyrus piece (250–320 BC). The ground-floor exhibit, Pre-Historic Thessaloniki, boasts the **Petralona Hoard** of prehistoric implements from the Petralona Cave north of Halkidiki, plus Neolithic and Bronze Age daggers, pottery and tools.

A compound ticket (€8) grants admission to the Byzantine Museum too.

Museum of Byzantine Culture MUSEUM

(☏ 2313 306 400; www.mbp.gr; Leof Stratou 2; €4; ⊙ 8am-8pm Tue-Sun) With ambient lighting and running wall-placard text, this cool museum explains more than 3000 Byzantine objects, including frescoes, mosaics, embroidery, ceramics, inscriptions and some early-Christianity to late-Byzantine icons. Free admittance on certain annual Greek or European holidays.

Museum of the Macedonian Struggle MUSEUM

(☏ 2310 229 778; www.imma.edu.gr; Proxenou Koromila 23; ⊙ 9am-2pm Tue-Fri, 10am-2pm Sat) FREE Ground zero for Greek nationalism, this museum recounts how heroic Hellenes wrested Macedonia from both Turks and Bulgarians. Housed in Greece's former Ottoman consulate, the museum has hard-to-find maps, old firearms, photos, uniforms and more.

Thessaloniki Museum of Photography MUSEUM

(☏ 2310 566 716; www.thmphoto.gr; Warehouse A, Port; €2; ⊙ 11am-7pm Tue-Sun) In a former

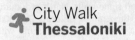

City Walk
Thessaloniki

START KASTRA/BYZANTINE WALLS
FINISH PORT
DISTANCE 4.5KM
DURATION THREE TO FOUR HOURS

Go early (around 9am) – many churches close by noon. Avoid Mondays, when most sites are closed.

From the Kastra, head for the ❶ **viewing platform**. For panoramic views, enter the recently opened *pyrgos* (tower) at the easternmost end of the walls surrounding the inner citadel or Eptapyrgio. Follow the walls west on the main road (also called Eptapyrgio); after Agathangelou, to see the church and museum at leafy ❷ **Monastery of Vlatadon** (p243).

Continue west along Eptapyrgio, turn left down the stairs on Sthenonos and veer right along Dimitriou Poliorkitou. Further left, a narrow stairway doubles backwards; follow it down and turn left on Parodos Kassianis to the 5th-century ❸ **Church of Osios David** (p243), with rare 12th-century frescoes of Christ's baptism, and holy water from an ancient spring.

From here, wander labyrinthine Ano Poli eastwards along the small streets. The most direct route follows Fotiou across Akropolitis and straight on Krispou, then along Arolou, back up on Moreas, and right on Amfitryonos before turning left on Irodotou for the 4th-century ❹ **Church of Nikolaos Orfanos** (p244), with exquisite 14th-century frescoes. The friendly English-speaking caretaker can explain the church's history and art.

Returning to Moreas, go south, crossing Olymbiados to Kassandrou. Walk several blocks west and turn south on Agiou Nikolaou. On your right, ❺ **Yeni Hamam** (p246) is a restored 17th-century Turkish bath, also called Aigli. This voluminous, atmospheric structure hosts concerts.

Just below it, the enormous ❻ **Church of Agios Dimitrios** (p243) occupies its own square. See the saint's relics, the 8th-century mosaics near the altar, and the otherworldly, subterranean crypt, where St Dimitrios was martyred.

Continue south on Agnostou Stratiotou across Olympou, for the ❼ **Roman Agora**

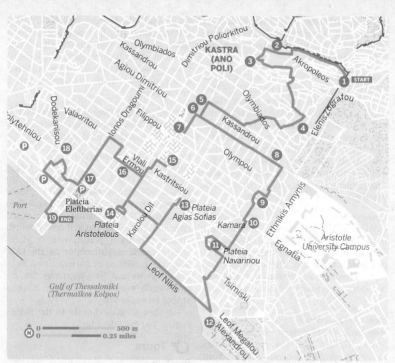

(p243). The marked entrance leads to a helpful explanatory board. Return to Agiou Dimitriou and proceed east nine blocks to **⑧ Atatürk's House** (p246) on your left, inside the Turkish consulate.

A block further east on Agiou Dimitriou, turn right on Dimitriou Gounari for the **⑨ Rotunda of Galerius** (p243). Gape at its grandeur inside and inspect the ruins behind. Continue downhill to the photogenic, statue-studded **⑩ Arch of Galerius** at Kamara. Crossing Egnatia, continue downhill. Roman ruins on this pedestrianised street culminate at the **⑪ Palace of Galerius** (p242).

Continue downhill, cross Tsimiski and, at Plateia Fanarioton, arc left down Pavlou Mela for the beloved **⑫ White Tower** (p239) and its hip multimedia museum. Continue west for a seaside stroll.

Leave the water by crossing Leof Nikis at Agias Sofias. See the **⑬ Church of Agia Sofia** (p243) by walking up until Plateia Agias Sofias, or proceed west on Tsimiski, with fashionable shops. You'll hit Aristotelous, with cafes, unique architecture and lively **⑭ Plateia Aristotelous**.

Continue up Aristotelous' western side and cross Egnatia for the atmospheric **⑮ Bey Hamam** (p246), a restored Turkish bathhouse that hosts art and photography exhibitions. Return to Aristotelous, proceed downhill and turn right on Ermou. Veer into **⑯ Modiano Market**, full of fish on ice and trays of olives and cheese.

Continue through Modiani, cross Venizelou and turn towards the water on Ionos Dragoumi, through the former florists' market, the Louloudadika district, now containing clothes shops, bars and restaurants. Continue down Ionos Dragoumi. At the Tsimiski intersection, note the splendid **⑰ National Bank of Greece** (p246) building; after it, turn right onto Mitropoleos, immediately left on Katouni and right on Aigyptou. Here begins the **⑱ Ladadika district**, once comprising olive-oil warehouses and now home to atmospheric restaurants and bars.

The tour ends across Kountouriotou, at the newly beautified port. Enter the gate and, on the eastern jetty, sink into a big, soft couch at the **⑲ Kitchen Bar** (p249) for a relaxing drink.

portside warehouse, this museum displays historic and contemporary Greek photography, plus dynamic temporary exhibitions, with a waterfront cafe.

Atatürk's House
HISTORIC BUILDING

(☑2310 248 452; Apostolou Pavlou 75; ☺9am-5pm) **FREE** In 1881, modern Turkey's illustrious founder, the dashing Mustafa Kemal was born here, in today's Turkish consulate (bring your identity card or passport). Recently renovated, it's more popular than ever. Along with numerous original furnishings and memorabilia, you'll see other Atatürk paraphernalia such as dapper suits, white gloves and a cane. Sporting!

Eptapyrgion
HISTORIC BUILDING

(Ano Poli) **FREE** A prison from Ottoman times until 1989, the Eptapyrgion, or Yediküle in Turkish (in both languages, 'Seven Towers'), is a grim reminder of Thessaloniki's penal past, recounted in *rembetika* (old Greek blues) songs. Behind the Byzantine Walls.

Yeni Hamam
HISTORIC BUILDING

(Aigli; cnr Kassandrou & Agiou Nikolaou) An atmospheric 17th-century structure, this former Turkish bath has great acoustics, making it ideal for concerts – and it hosts contemporary art exhibitions.

Bey Hamam
HISTORIC BUILDING

(Paradeisos Baths; cnr Egnatia & Plateia Dikastirion; ☺9am-9pm Mon-Fri, 8.30am-3pm Sat & Sun) **FREE** Thessaloniki's oldest Turkish bath (1444), Bey Hamam hosts art exhibitions inside its labyrinthine interior.

Jewish Museum of Thessaloniki
MUSEUM

(☑2310 250 406; www.jmth.gr; Agiou Mina 13; ☺11am-2pm Tue, Fri & Sun, 11am-2pm & 5-8pm Wed & Thu) **FREE** This touching museum traces Thessaloniki's Jewish heritage from 140 BC to the 15th-century Sephardic immigrations, until the Holocaust. Remains from the Nazi-vandalised Jewish cemetery are displayed.

Synagogues
SYNAGOGUES

Monastirioton Synagogue (☑2310 524 968; Syngrou 35) is Thessaloniki's only surviving synagogue. However, services are held at the small **Yad Lazikaron** (☑2310 275 701; Vassiliou Irakliou 24), on Mitropolios, in the former Jewish district.

Jewish Mansions
HISTORIC BUILDINGS

Two east-side 19th-century mansions attest to the bygone wealth and prominence of Thessaloniki's Jews: the **Villa Allatini** (Ol-

gas 98) and **Villa Mordoch** (Olgas 162). It's a fifteen-minute trip by bus along Leoforos Vasillissis Olgas. Incidentally, Olgas (the street on which both mansions are located) crosses Saadi Levi, named for the publisher of one of Thessaloniki's 35 erstwhile Jewish newspapers.

National Bank of Greece
HISTORIC BUILDING

(Tsimiski 11) This Neoclassical structure has considerable architectural grandeur.

Noesis Science Center & Technology Museum
MUSEUM

(☑2310 483 000; www.noesis.edu.gr; 6th km Thessaloniki-Thermi Rd; adult/child €7/5; ☺10am-2.30pm Tue-Fri, 6-10pm Sat-Sun) Although 6km east of town, this fascinating museum of science and technology, old and new, is worth visiting. There's a planetarium, a giant-screen cinema and simulator for the kids, while the exhibition of ancient Greek technology shows just how ingenious the ancients really were. Out of summer, it opens at 1pm on weekends.

City bus 66 goes directly to the Noesis stop, or you can take a taxi.

Tours

Bus Tour
BUS

(White Tower; €3; ☺hourly 8am-9pm Jun-Sep, 9am-4pm Oct-May) While our walking tour (p244) is the best way to see Thessaloniki's sights, those preferring the easy way can take the city-sponsored bus tour. It leaves from the White Tower, heading in zigzag fashion uphill past various sites, finishing in Ano Poli. Jump on, jump off, or walk between sites. The tourism office has leaflets detailing the route and sights covered.

Festivals & Events

HelExpo (www.helexpo.gr) hosts trade fairs, the biggest, in autumn. The **International Trade Fair** is followed by a **cultural festival**, which includes film screenings and musical performances, culminating with St Dimitrios' Day on 26 October and Ohi Day on 28 October.

Autumn sees festivals like September's **Reworks International Music Festival** (www.reworks.gr), for electronic music. The **Thessaloniki International Film Festival** (☑2310 378 400; www.filmfestival.gr) in November shows 150 or so high-quality international films, from experimental and obscure to well-known directors' works. The **Thes-**

saloniki Documentary Festival (www.film-festival.gr) is in mid-March.

The new city-sponsored **Urban Picnic** (www.urbanpicnic.gr) attracts more than 3000 summertime visitors for impromptu food, drink, free concerts and cinema in the Roman Agora.

The Office of Tourism Directorate (p254) provides cultural events info.

🛏 Sleeping

Finally, good-quality hostels, apartments and midrange hotels have arrived. In general, rates rise during autumn convention season at **HelExpo** (www.helexpo.gr) and other fairs.

Little Big House   HOSTEL $
(☑2313 014 323; www.littlebighouse.gr; Andokidou 24, Ano Poli; dm/d from €17/48; ※ 🛜) This clean and cosy new hostel, up in quiet Ano Poli, is an ideal base for taking a walking tour. It's run by the uproarious Vicky and her brother, Haris. Between the self-catering dorms and one private room, there are only 22 beds, so book ahead. Free coffee and tea are available all day, and tasty tavernas exist nearby.

From the train station, take bus 23 to the Agios Pavlos stop. Another local landmark is Plateia Kallithea, just below Andokidou.

Hostel Arabas   HOSTEL $
(☑6973817188; www.hostelarabas.gr; Sahtouri 28; dm/s/d €11/25/34; ※ 🛜) Up a hill, hard to find, with warm welcomes and a washing machine – here's hostelling as it used to be. Brothers Kostas and Dimitris Pappas oversee this simple place on a sidestreet above Egnatia, with spartan dorms, and singles and doubles with private baths. There's a relaxing front garden for coffee (and sometimes parties) plus free luggage storage. The hostel is a 15-minute walk northeast from the train station – see the website for the exact route.

Colors Rooms & Apartments   APARTMENTS $
(☑2310 502 280; www.colors.com.gr; Valaoritou 21; s/d/ste €45/55/65; ※ 🛜) Valaoritou party people, you finally have somewhere nice to crash. These 15 sparkling new apartments rival more expensive hotel rooms, with cool lighting, minimalist decor and mod cons including iPhone docks with radio. Four of the apartments are self-catering. A pastry breakfast (€5 extra) is brought to your room, or you can eat in the first-floor reception/coffee area.

Rent Rooms Thessaloniki   HOSTEL $
(☑2310 204 080; www.rentrooms-thessaloniki.com; Konstantinou Melenikou 9, near Kamara; dm/s/d/tr/q incl breakfast €19/38/49/67/82; ※ 🛜) This well-kept Kamara-area hostel has a relaxing back-garden cafe with Rotunda views, where breakfast and drinks are served. Some dorms and rooms have minikitchens; all have en-suites. The friendly staff provides local info and can assist with bike rental.

Hotel Aegeon   HOTEL $
(☑2310 522 921; www.aegeon-hotel.gr; Egnatia 19; s/d incl breakfast €45/60; ※ 🛜) Although rooms are simple and somewhat cramped, the Aegeon is a budget godsend by west-Egnatia standards, surrounded as it is by pricey chain hotels and sordid dens of iniquity. The train station's a five- to 10-minute walk, and the popular Valaoritou bars are just behind Egnatia opposite.

★ Colors Central
Ladadika   BOUTIQUE HOTEL $$
(☑2316 007676; www.colorscentral.gr; Oplopoiou 1, Ladadika; s/d/ste €55/65/75; ※ 🛜) This stylish boutique hotel, opened in summer 2013, occupies a grand heritage house with 12 uniquely decorated rooms. There's an eclectic combination of old and new, with modern pop-art decor and vibrant tones, plus a traditional Thessaloniki music corner, and even vending machines with various 'travel packs'. Enthusiastic owner Christina Drakopoulou provides info on current local events.

Met Hotel   LUXURY HOTEL $$
(☑2310 017 000; www.themethotel.gr; 26 Oktovriou 48; s/d incl breakfast from €70/100; ※ 🛜 ※) Nearer to the port and train stations, the Met is a posh, minimalist hotel with sleek modern bathrooms, spa centre and outdoor pool, next to Thessaloniki's best rooftop bar. Amenities include designer soaps, flat-screen TVs and some seriously comfortable mattresses. Recent price cuts have made it more tempting, and it's relatively close to eating and drinking hotspots, too.

Le Palace Art Hotel   HOTEL $$
(☑2310 257 400; www.lepalace.gr; Tsimiski 23; s/d/tr incl breakfast from €50/60/75; ※ 🛜) On busy Tsimiski, Le Palace occupies a renovated Neoclassical building. Its modern rooms have high ceilings and subtle decor. Soundproofed (mostly) windows keep out street noise. The buffet breakfast has varied offerings.

City Hotel
BUSINESS HOTEL **$$**

(✆ 2310 269 421; www.cityhotel.gr; Komninon 11; d/tr/ste incl breakfast from €80/110/130; ❊@?) This sleek four-star place near Plateia Eleftherias, east of Ladadika, has handsome rooms (some wheelchair-friendly) with subdued elegance. There's a big American-style breakfast and spa centre.

Tourist Hotel
HOTEL **$$**

(✆ 2310 270 501; www.touristhotel.gr; Mitropoleos 21; s/d/tr incl breakfast €55/70/90; ❊?) This classic place (built 1925), has a gated lift leading to renovated rooms with sound-proofed windows and elegant decor. The breakast is good, but service can be gruff.

Electra Palace Hotel
LUXURY HOTEL **$$$**

(✆ 2310 294 000; www.electrahotels.gr; Plateia Aristotelous 9; d from €150; ❊?≋) Even if just coming to gaze on the harbour from the rooftop garden cafe, you can't miss the appeal of this five-star city landmark, standing splendidly over Plateia Aristotelous. The renovated rooms are spacious, with ornate furnishings and all amenities. There's a mosaic-tiled indoor pool, rooftop outdoor pool and *hammam*.

Egnatia Palace Hotel
HOTEL **$$$**

(✆ 2310 222 900; www.egnatia-hotel.gr; Egnatia 61; s/d/ste €90/120/140; ❊?≋) This four-star hotel, well-situated above Plateia Aristotelous, offers bright, individually decorated rooms and suites. It's slightly overpriced, though the 'wellness' facilities include pool, gym, *hammam*, sauna and massage.

✖ Eating

From sweets and souvlaki to seafood and international delicacies, Thessaloniki has it covered. Greece's economic downturn has prompted restaurants to offer a '€10 Tuesday' fixed-menu option. See www.tavernoxoros.gr for more listings.

★ Paparouna
MODERN GREEK **$**

(✆ 2310 510 852; www.paparouna.com; cnr Pangaiou 4 & Doxis; mains €7-11; ?10am-2am) The ever-popular Paparouna spills onto the pavement in its new Ladadika location, having brought with it its vibrant colours, checkerboard floor, cheerful staff and an intriguing menu which changes seasonally. Try the sauteed pork with mustard cream and fresh mushrooms, or baked bream with sauteed grue. Charismatic chef and owner Antonis Ladas plays Latin, soul and jazz inside, enhancing the youthful vibe.

I Nea Follia
GREEK **$**

(✆ 2310 960 383; cnr Aristomenous & Haritos; mains €7-11; ?1.30pm-1am Sep-Jul) This is the kind of place Anthony Bourdain would pretend to discover. A bare-bones taverna opened in 1966 on a nondescript northside alley, it was recently commandeered by three young chefs serving classic Greek fare with a contemporary twist.

The menu changes daily, so it's hard to augur what they'll do next, but it's very vegie-friendly and there's a stunning range of cheeses. Good meat dishes include pork with apricot sauce. Closed August.

I Giannoula
GREEK **$**

(✆ 2310 263 928; Kassandrou 50; mains €4-6; ?10am-11pm Sep-Jun) Although kindly Kyria Giannoula may be a step slower at age 80, she still does much of the cooking at this tiny taverna she established in 1974, north of the Roman Agora. Try her tasty spinach salad and the *kotopoulo gemisto* (chicken stuffed with cheese). And hey, she may surprise you with something not even on the menu. Closed July and August.

Myrsini
CRETAN **$**

(✆ 2310 228 300; Tsopela 2; mains €8-12; ?lunch & dinner Sep-Jun) Down near the White Tower, Thessaloniki's original Cretan restaurant serves a delicious array of representative dishes, from *dakos* (rusks topped with tomato and olive oil) and wild *horta* (greens) to roast rabbit and *myzithropitakia* (flaky filo triangles with sweet sheep's milk cheese). The worn wooden floors and traditional decor is enhanced by violin-driven Cretan music. Usually closed July to August.

To Etsi
SOUVLAKI **$**

(✆ 2310 222 469; Nikoforos Fokas 2; grills €2.80-4; ?11am-1am) This bawdily decorated, iconic eatery near the White Tower is a local institution offering refreshingly light souvlaki and *soutzoukakia* (meat rissoles in tomato sauce) with vegetable dips, in Cypriot-style pitta bread. Look for the neon sign.

Sebriko
GREEK **$**

(✆ 2310 557 513; Frangon 2; mains €7-11; ?9am-1am Tue-Fri, 2pm-1am Sat-Sun) A new restaurant near the western Byzantine walls, Sebriko became a hit after opening in 2012. It doesn't overlook the walls, but is a friendly place with simple taverna-style decor, good salads and grills, and even *Sfakiani pita* from Crete (Cretan pitta served with honey).

Fri

MEZEDHES $

(☑2310 222 008; Doxis 4 & Salaminos, Ladadika; mezedhes €6-8; ⊗12pm-12am Mon-Fri, to 1am Sat-Sun) This trendy new Ladadika eatery, popular with young Greeks, specialises in healthy mezedhes (appetisers) such as seaweed with feta cheese and cherry tomatoes, tasty fried shrimp and 'black' risotto, darkened by squid ink. Plenty of *tsipouro* (distilled spirit similar to ouzo but usually stronger) and wines are on hand, too.

Ergon

MODERN GREEK $

(☑2310 284 224; www.ergonproducts.gr; Kouskoura 3-5; mezedhes €6-10; ⊗9am-1am) With an adjoining, eponymous shop, Ergon is dedicated to the trendy 'locally sourced' concept, using recipes and ingredients from specific parts of Greece. While it's a bit precious and the portions small, there's no denying that itinerant celebrity chef Dimitris Skarmoutsos (a 'MasterChef Greece' TV judge) knows his stuff. Try the aubergine with prosciutto, sizzling egg and cheese croquettes.

Omikron

GREEK $

(☑2310 532 774; Oplopiou 3, Ladadika; mains €7-10; ⊗12pm-1am) This neat and tidy new Ladadika taverna does excellent fresh fish and inventive grills (try the beef *soutzoukakia* on risotto with yoghurt). Ask owner Haris to decipher the colourful daily special's chalkboard behind the door.

Athivoli

CRETAN $

(☑2310 508 509; www.athivoli.gr; Katouni 15, Ladadika; mezedhes €5-8; ⊗lunch & dinner) Look for the neon outline of Crete to find Ladadika's Cretan restaurant, which has good traditional music playing in the background. The food's tasty, though portions are small, and the all-important *myzithropitakia* (flaky cheese pies with sweet myzithra cheese) aren't as sweet as purists might expect.

To Inglis

GREEK $

(Irodotou 32; mains €6-10; ⊗12pm-2am) Up in Ano Poli near Plateia Kallithea, this local favourite has standard fare including good meatballs and fresh salads. The *lahmacan*, however, bears only a passing resemblance to the Turkish original. Come on Tuesdays or Wednesdays for live *rembetika*.

Extra Blatt

INTERNATIONAL $

(☑2310 256 900; Svolou 46; mains €7-11; ⊗9am-2am) East of Plateia Navarinou, this long-established lunch spot and bar serves Continental pub grub accompanied by numerous European beers.

Pizza Poselli

PIZZA $

(Vilara 1; pizza slice €2.30; ⊗12pm-4am) This busy shop set improbably in an ornate parlour under a ballroom chandelier does a roaring trade with the late-night Valaoritou bar crowds, offering a variety of tasty thin-crust pizzas by the slice.

Punto.ES

GREEK $$

(☑2310 532 503; Frangon 4; mains €9-15; ⊗8am-2am Tue-Sun) On a warm summer's evening, it's hard to beat the ambience here. Tables are set on a pebbled back courtyard, tucked into a flowery section of Thessaloniki's long-forgotten western Byzantine walls. Try the smoked salmon and bruschetta appetisers, and the pungent chicken with Chian Mastello cheese. The atmosphere's completed by wafting jazz.

Kitchen Bar

INTERNATIONAL $$

(☑2310 502 241; www.kitchenbar.com.gr; Warehouse B, Port; mains €11-17; ⊗9am-12am) Out on the port, this cafe-meets-restaurant is a perennial favourite. Housed in a big renovated warehouse, it has outdoor waterfront tables too. The salads and risotto are as bright as the flames in the open kitchen, where the chefs, like the style-conscious clientele, are on display. Good burgers, but avoid the 'Mexican' offerings.

Agioli

INTERNATIONAL $$

(www.agioli.gr; cnr Leof Nikis & Ploutarhou; mains €7-15; ⊗9.30am-1am) The waterfront Agioli serves gourmet burgers, light pastas and salads on its ground floor, with somewhat fancier fare (such as the sea bass with lemon risotto and mushrooms) served on the upper floor. Sea views can be had from both, but the kids' set course (€11) is only available upstairs.

Dore Zythos

TAVERNA $$

(☑2310 279 010; Tsirogianni 7; mains €10-18; ⊗lunch & dinner) Grab an outside table when the weather's warm, and watch the White Tower while savouring imaginative Mediterranean cuisine.

Panellinion

TAVERNA $$

(☑2310 567 220; Salaminos 1, Ladadika; mains €8-16; ⊗lunch & dinner) This Ladadika taverna has classic wood floors, and walls lined with olive-oil bottles and tins of produce. Offerings include numerous ouzos, cheeses and delicious seafood mezedhes.

SWEET INDULGENCES

For a quick breakfast or sinful dessert, Thessaloniki's *zaharoplasteia* (patisseries) are unbeatable. Although classics such as baklava or chocolate profiterole are available throughout Greece, Thessaloniki's historic ties with the Ottoman East have bequeathed it with an especially rich tradition of sweets – and a discerning local population to enjoy them. The following well-polished *zaharoplasteia* are particularly famous. Most prices are by the kilo (cakes are around €2 to €4 per piece).

Just above the Rotunda, the classic **Kokkinos Fournos** (Apostolou Pavlou 1, Rotunda) bakery does Thessaloniki's best *koulourakia vanilias* – crunchy, slightly sweet, golden cookies, a breakfast staple perfect for dipping in honey or Greek coffee. Another breakfast favourite, *tzoureki* (a brioche-style bread flavoured with mastic and mahlepi), is particularly associated with **Turkenlis** (Aristotelous 4; sweets €1-3), which has an array of sweet-scented confections on Plateia Aristotelous.

Then there's the legendary **Hatzis** (☑ 2310 968 400; Egnatia 119; sweets €1.40-3). First opened back in 1908, when Thessaloniki was still Ottoman, it preserves the tastes of old Constantinople. After Hatzis, you'll never ask for a simple 'baklava' again. The veritable symphony of sweets served here includes *vezir parmak* (*politika* syrup cake with cream filling), *hanoum bourek* (handmade pastry with raisins, peanuts and cream) and *malempi mastiha* (cream from milk and rice porridge, flavoured with *mastiha*, a sweet liquor from Chios, and served with rose syrup).

A newer local favourite, **Ble** (☑ 2310 231 200; www.ble.com.gr; cnr Agias Sofias 19 & Georgiou Stavrou; cakes €2-5; ⊘ 24hr), is a chic emporium of treats sweet and savoury – the chocolate profiterole and various fruity concoctions are all delicious. The giant funnel-like obelisk towards the back is an oven, which ownership claims to be the biggest anywhere, at a towering 12 metres.

Finally, **Trigona Elenidis** (☑ 2310 257 510; cnr Dimitriou Gounari & Tsimiski; trigones from €1.40), a veritable institution since 1960, is a very rare thing in today's world: a shop specialising in only one product. Its sweet, flaky triangular cones filled with cool and unbelievably tasty cream are legendary; locals emerge with 2kg boxes, but one large triangle will certainly fill you up.

Draft GREEK $$

(☑ 2310 555 518; cnr Lykourgou 3 & Salaminos, Ladadika; mains €10-19; ⊘ 10am-1am) This classic three-level brick-and-wood restaurant with pub has a vintage jukebox, well-shone rails and long bar. It serves designer pub fare, though upstairs cultivates a more after-hours lounge-bar effect, with dimmed lights and Latin and jazz.

Krikelas GREEK $$$

(☑ 2310 501 600; Salaminos 6, Ladadika; mains €16-25; ⊘ Mon-Sat, lunch & dinner) Good old Krikelas is somewhat touristy (and thus a bit dearer than other Ladadika places) but does offer an extensive wine list to match its unique cuisine, which includes wild game, Cretan snails and other local specialities.

Drinking & Nightlife

What financial crisis? Thessaloniki's irrepressible drinking scene rumbles on undaunted. If anything, Greece's economic downturn has benefitted the scene, forcing more creativity, competition and better live music. The following lists some of the best bars, cafes and clubs by location.

Valaoritou

After five years of solid success, gritty, graffiti-strewn Valaoritou is still the alternative fave, though more mainstream and Greek places have arrived too.

★ La Doze BAR

(Vilara 1; ⊘ 8pm-4am) La Doze is probably Thessaloniki's only bar where the skateboarding unemployed and owners of sports cars mingle – the crowd is so diverse and unpretentious in this happy little aquarium of sparkling light and freestyle-DJ action that no one even notices when the bartenders crack open a €500 bottle of tequila (one of 50 varieties here).

Indeed, La Doze is famous citywide for its 150 expertly made cocktails. Musically, no two nights are the same. The owner (art dealer and world traveller George Tsiridis) loves travellers – throw your backpack in the locked storeroom in the upper art gallery (for free), and he'll even welcome you to Thessaloniki with a complimentary beer.

Gambrinus
BAR

(☎ 6987151489; Vilara 2; ⏱ noon-late) Although it's not immediately distinguishable from its neighbours, you'll soon discern the rock pumping out of the darkness within, where the enthusiastic Czech owners serve an excellent range of beers from the homeland. There are tasty snacks, sausages and...free popcorn! Closed Sundays.

Fragile
BAR

(☎ 2310 547 443; Valaoritou 29; ⏱ 11pm-5am Apr-Oct) High above Valaoritou, Fragile is an open-air rooftop bar. Surrounded as it is by the neighbourhood's other dark and derelict office blocks and rundown shops, the views are more Gotham City than postcard-pretty, but no matter – it's a fun spot that broadcasts an eclectic mix of pop, indie and electronica into the night. Tip: locals also call it Taratsa.

Partizan Bar
BAR

(☎ 6947945492; Valaoritou 29; ⏱ 8am-3am Mon-Thu, 8am-5am Fri-Sat, noon-3am Sun) Bohemian Partizan was Valaoritou's first bar and almost a decade on it's still popular. Unlike most other places here, it's open for coffee by day, though it's busiest late.

Elvis
BAR, CLUB

(☎ 2310 556 828; cnr Valaoritou 31 & Syngrou) Once a waterfront bar, Elvis has left the building and is now domiciled up on Valaoritou, where its slick interior and chilled-out DJ parties have preserved its bar-cum-club feel.

Coo
BAR

(☎ 2311 274 752; coobarcafe@gmail.com; Vasileos Irakliou 4; ⏱ 6pm-3am) What started as a venue to promote the musical creations of a few friends has become an alternative bar. Beneath lies a musty cellar for experimental theatre, photo exhibits and summer concerts. There's a Coo internet radio station too, involving DJs in various countries.

Collectiva Alternativa
BAR

(☎ 6977228195; Katholikon 1 & Typou; ⏱ 9pm-3am) This grungy side-street bar has gained a certain following since opening in 2012 and sometimes has live acts in its narrow standing-room-only contours.

Enola
BAR

(www.enola.gr; Valaoritou 19, 2nd floor; ⏱ 10pm-3am) Despite lingering hard feelings between the Pride movement and the church, Thessaloniki's most popular gay bar is amusingly enough housed above an ecclesiastical supplies shop, in an underpass from Egnatia. Enter from the Valaoritou side and take the elevator to the second floor. '80s and dance music are generally well represented, though Thursday is Greek night.

🍺 Ladadika & Around

Somewhere in the foggy past, Ladadika's brothels were patronised by visiting seamen; by the '90s, its renovated warehouses had become tasty tavernas. Ladadika somehow lost its mojo after that, but competition from Valaoritou's upstarts has inspired a recent comeback.

★ Rover
LIVE MUSIC

(☎ 2310 544 304; Salaminos 6, Ladadika) Rover is excellent for live music, especially rock and blues. The high-beamed, wood-and-brick interior includes a well-lit corner stage and a long upper balcony offering great views of the action, making it feel like an intimate concert hall. But the depth of the interior means there are also upstairs nooks for quieter conversation away from the packed front.

Cocktail Bar
BAR

(☎ 2310 524 242; Polytehneiou 17; ⏱ 8.30pm-3.30am) Among Thessaloniki's most popular new places, Cocktail Bar attracts the beautiful people. As Thessaloniki's only self-service cocktail bar, the bartenders follow your precise instructions – or, just concoct delicious recipes that will keep you ordering (despite the relatively high prices).

Sinatra
BAR

(☎ 2310 223 739; cnr Mitropoleos 20 & Komninon; ⏱ 7am-4am) Espresso bar by day, wine bar by night – the latest offering of budding bar-mogul Filippos Apostolidis has a substantial stock of Greek wines (85 and counting). A 30-something crowd predominates at Sinatra; it plays jazzy numbers of which Frank himself would no doubt approve.

Kismet
BAR

(☎ 2310 548 490; Katouni 11, Ladadika; ⏱ 10pm-4am) Set smack between Ladadika's restaurants, Kismet is a fine, though cramped spot for live bands, ranging from rock and pop to Greece's most popular *rembetika* (Greek blues) acts.

Froyd's Cocktail Bar
BAR

(✆ 6942464672; Kalapothaki 3; ⊙ 7pm-3am) Set in a quieter spot on little Kalapothaki, this new place offers creative sweet cocktails and DJ parties on weekends.

White Tower & Waterfront

West of the White Tower and along the waterfront was modern Thessaloniki's first nightlife hotspot – what remains are mostly glossy and uniform seafront bars, but there are some interesting places too.

★ Kafeneion Giasemi
CAFE

(✆ 2315 316 300; Tsopela 4; ⊙ 11am-2am) This is a beautiful place. The cosy interior cheerfully blends classic countryside Greece and colourful retro, with space for just a few tables. Kind young owner Ioanna plays swing and big band. Along with coffees and drinks, Giasemi offers small mezedhes (the menu entries are carefully handwritten in pencil). Sometimes there's live music in summer.

Thermaïkos
BAR

(✆ 2310 239 842; www.thermaikos.net; Leof Nikis 23; ⊙ 10am-4am) Bars come and go, but Thermaïkos will be here forever. This waterfront bar-club is best in the cooler months, when the weather forces people indoors. Then you appreciate its mottled marble columns, subdued lanterns, elliptical corners and mirrors – an accidental architectural masterpiece, enlivened by late-night hipsters and the DJ's deep-house beats.

Loxias
CAFE

(✆ 2310 233 925; Isavron 7; ⊙ 6pm-2am) This evenings-only cafe off Plateia Navarinou is an old-time *steki* (hang-out) for educated Greeks, who grapple with philosophy, politics or literature over ouzo or snacks. It's decorated with wine casks, bursting bookshelves and historic photos and prints. Romantics can duck the commotion on the back balcony's table for two, overlooking Roman ruins.

On The Road
BAR

(✆ 2310 271 240; Leof Nikis 61; ⊙ 10am-3am) This fun waterfront bar is packed with students and older folks, and its Latin music and lack of glitz make it more interesting than other Nikis neighbours.

Kafenai
CAFE

(✆ 2310 220 310; cnr Ethnikis Amynis & Tsopela; ⊙ 9am-2am) This classic *kafeneio* exudes old Salonica, with its 1950s-style Greek decor and lofty ceilings supported by columns. It's popular with local students, artists and musicians.

Kafe Nikis 35
CAFE

(✆ 2310 230 449; Leof Nikis 35) Set on the waterfront, this snug cafe sits just under street level. It's perfect for a Sunday-morning espresso – get a window table and feel the dappled sunlight dancing through the blinds.

Boat Bars
BAR

(Waterfront; ⊙ 6pm-1am) For partiers preferring an aqueous environment, take a booze cruise. Boat bars, moored on the waterfront south of the White Tower, by Alexander the Great's statue, have slightly different decorations and themes, with music from pop to reggae to R&B.

These cruisers leave every 20 minutes for a half-hour chug around the Thermaikos Kolpos; there's no admission charge and you can stay on board whether docked or adrift, for the whole evening – just keep drinking!

Berlin
BAR

(Hrysostomou Smyrnis 10; ⊙ 2am-7am) The afterbar to beat all after-bars, Berlin has operated since 1979, and still has a dedicated crowd of bleary-eyed partiers looking to keep the fun going till dawn. The music is varied, like the clientele.

North of Egnatia

Quieter and more residential, the area above Egnatia has less nightlife, though interesting places do exist.

Cantina Tropicana
BAR

(✆ 2310 539 727; Egnatia 31; ⊙ 10pm-4am) Just above Egnatia, Cantina Tropicana has music (sometimes live) wafting from the western side, across an underpass where tables stand outside and within the narrow bar. There are tropical drinks in this dive bar, albeit no tropical atmosphere. Nevertheless, it's a laid-back place and fun late.

I Prinkipos
CAFE

(Apostolou Pavlou 22) This big old *kafeneio* beside the Turkish consulate, where students play backgammon, does good Greek coffee.

Bate Skyli ROCK BAR
(Olympou 61; ⊙3pm-3am) Thessaloniki's bare-bones punk and metal dive bar has friendly folks, but hey, what's with the noose?

Freidirikos Agapi Mou CAFE, BAR
(☑2310 238 532; Olympou 87; ⊙10am-2am) This offbeat corner cafe – named for the owners' dog – attracts people, often with their dogs, for coffee. It offers inexpensive cocktails by night but stays fairly subdued.

☆ Entertainment

The **National Theatre of Northern Greece** (☑2310 288 000; www.ntng.gr; Ethnikis Amynis 2) offers opera, classical Greek drama and modern theatre.

Additionally, these cinemas operate:

Aristotelion (☑2310 262 051; Ethnikis Amynis 2)

Cinema Pallas (☑2310 278 515; Leoforos Nikis 73)

Olympion (☑2310 277 113; Plateia Aristotelous)

Plateia Alpha Odeon (☑2310 290 100; cnr Tsimiski & Plateia Aristotelous)

🛍 Shopping

West Egnatia has bargain-basement shopping, and Tsimiski, more upscale items. The big malls are out of town. January sees incredible sales.

Georgiadis HANDICRAFTS
(Egnatia 107; icons from €15; ⊙9am-2pm, 5-9pm) This crammed Kamara-area place has purveyed handcrafted Orthodox icons (from €15) since 1902. You can commission a specific one with advance notice.

Ergon Products FOOD
(☑2310 223 550; www.ergonproducts.gr; Kouskoura 5; ⊙9am-7pm) Beside the eponymous restaurant, this shop sells several hundred Ergon-branded delicacies from across Greece, such as olive oils, traditional seasonings, sauces and honey. Their provenance, qualities, organic-ness and everything else is proudly noted.

Beerstore BEER
(☑2310 233 438; www.beer.gr; Kalapothaki 6; ⊙noon-2am) This unexpected shop sells more than 200 brews, covering everywhere from Crete to California (with Belgium and Central Europe especially well represented). You can drink there (and in the evening, some do); prices are about €2 higher for consumption on the premises.

Rihardos MUSICAL INSTRUMENTS
(☑2310 860 254; www.rihardos.gr; Konstantinopoleos 27) Who knew there were so many different kinds of bouzouki? Rihardos is among Greece's biggest traditional instruments dealers, with an array of Greek (and Western) instruments, including guitars and basses. Friendly owner Rihardos and his English-speaking son, Joseph, will happily explain (as well as test out) the national instruments.

Take bus 31 from Egnatia east to Faliro stop (five to 10 minutes); cross the intersection with Paraskeopoulos, turn left and Rihardos is opposite.

Travel Bookstore Traveller BOOKS
(☑2310 275 215; www.traveler.gr; Proxenou Koromila 41) Sells maps, plus Lonely Planet and other travel titles.

ℹ Information

EMERGENCY
Whenever closed, Thessaloniki pharmacies must list nearby working pharmacies. On west Egnatia, **Farmakeio Sofia Tympanidou** (☑2310 522 155; Egnatia 9) is well-stocked and owner Sofia can get hard-to-find medicines quickly. In Ano Poli, **Farmakeio Gouva-Peraki** (☑2310 205 544; Agias Sofias 110, Ano Poli; ⚑) also has experienced staff.

Some 2km east of centre, **Ippokration** (☑2310 837 921; Papanastasiou 50) is Thessaloniki's largest public hospital. Minor emergency-room treatment is usually free.

INTERNET ACCESS
Free wi-fi zones and internet cafes abound.

MONEY
Except for Ano Poli, banks and ATMs are widespread. Commission-hungry exchange offices line western Egnatia.

PERMITS
Mt Athos Pilgrims' Bureau (☑2310 252 575; www.agioritikiestia.gr; Egnatia 109; ⊙9am-4pm Mon-Sat) Issues permits for the Mt Athos monasteries.

POST
Post Office Aristotelous (Aristotelous 26; ⊙7.30am-8pm Mon-Fri, 7.30am-2.15pm Sat, 9am-1.30pm Sun); Koundouriotou (Koundouriotou 6; ⊙7.30am-2pm) The latter's by the port. The train station has a post window.

TOURIST INFORMATION
For local happenings and other info, visit the frequently updated **www.enjoythessaloniki.com** website, run by young local enthusiasts.

Office of Tourism Directorate (☎ 2310 221 100; www.visitgreece.gr; Tsimiski 136; ◷ 9am-3pm Mon-Fri) The tourism office, near the White Tower, has well-informed staff speaking English and German.

TRAVEL AGENCY

Remember Travel (☎ 2310 246 026; remembertravel@mail.gr; Egnatia 119) Just off Kamara. Sells tickets and has good customer service.

❶ Getting There & Away

AIR

Besides Greece's **Aegean Airlines** (☎ 2310 280 050; El Venizelou 2), many foreign carriers use Thessaloniki for domestic and international flights. Prices and routes are fluid, so ascertain which companies are currently flying from the airport website. Then visit a travel agent or book online.

The **Makedonia Airport** (www.thessaloniki airport.com), 16km southeast of town, is served by local bus 78; a taxi costs around €15 to €25.

BOAT

The poor ferry connections of Greece's second-largest city is disappointing. At time of research, **Nel Lines** (www.nel.gr) boats were going only once weekly to the Northeast Aegean islands of Limnos (€20, eight hours), Lesvos (€30, 14 hours), Chios (€32, 19 hours) and Samos (€40, 20 hours); the old Sporades ferry remained scuttled. Double-check with port-area travel agencies such as **Karacharisis Travel & Shipping Agency** (☎ 2310 513 005; b_karachari@ tincewind_techpath.gr; Navarhou Koundourioti 8; ◷ 8am-8.30pm).

BUS
Domestic

Thessaloniki's **main bus station** (☎ 2310 595 408; www.ktelmacedonia.gr; Monastiriou 319), KTEL Makedonia, is 3km west of centre. Each destination has its own specific ticket counter. However, for Athens only, avoid the trip by going to **Monastiriou Bus Station** (☎ 2310 500 111; Monastiriou 69) – an easy-to-miss office opposite the train station – where all Athens-bound buses start before calling in at KTEL Makedonia. Additional discounts to regular fares apply for kids, students, special-needs travellers, retirees and soldiers (well, Greek ones, anyway).

For **Halkidiki**, first reach the eastern Thessaloniki **Halkidiki bus terminal** (☎ 2310 316 555; www.ktel-chalkidikis.gr; Karakasi 68) via city buses 45A or 45B, which from the main bus station stop en route at the train station, Plateia Aristotelous and Kamara. With waiting and traffic, this 'express' service can take over an hour. Then there's the trip to Halkidiki itself. The whole

production can take three to six hours; it's much wiser to rent a car.

International

KTEL offers twice-daily international services to Sofia (five hours, €26) and Tirana (nine hours, €30).

Currently, small bus companies opposite the courthouse (Dikastirion), serve Skopje, İstanbul, Tirana, Sofia and Bucharest. Here, try **Simeonidis Tours** (☎ 2310 540 970; www.simeonidis-tours.gr; 26 Oktovriou 14; ◷ 9am-9pm Mon-Fri, to 2pm Sat). From the Kolomvou bus stop on Egnatia, walk west and then down to the left on 26th Oktovriou.

Also, **Crazy Holidays** (www.crazy-holidays.gr) operates buses to İstanbul (via Kavala, Xanthi, Komotini and Alexandroupoli), departing at 7am and 11pm. They have offices on Aristotelous, and by the train station, though all buses leave from near KTEL Makedonia, at Anagnostaki and Konstantinoupoleos; to get there, take city buses 8 or 3 along Egnatia to the end. Crazy Holidays also serves Tirana, Sofia, Skopje and Belgrade.

Bus Services from Thessaloniki's Main Bus Station (KTEL)

DESTINATION	TIME	FARE	FREQUENCY
Alexandroupoli	3¾hr	€34	8 daily
Athens	6¼hr	€42	11 daily
Drama	2hr	€15	20 daily
Didymotiho	5½hr	€39	8 daily
Edessa	2hr	€9	11 daily
Florina	2¾hr	€17	6 daily
Igoumenitsa	4hr	€43	2 daily
Ioannina	3½hr	€32	6 daily
Kastoria	2½hr	€19	9 daily
Kavala	2¼hr	€17	11 daily
Komotini	2¾hr	€28	7 daily
Litohoro	1¼hr	€9	12 daily
Orestiada	6hr	€45	8 daily
Pella	45min	€4	12 daily
Serres	1¼hr	€11	12 daily
Veria	1hr	€8	13 daily
Volos	4hr	€21	8 daily
Xanthi	2½hr	€22	9 daily

TRAIN

At time of research, Greece's international trains were still suspended indefinitely, and domestic routes were still restricted. The situation is fluid, so check ahead at Thessaloniki **train station** (☎ 2310 599 421; www.trainose.gr; Monastiriou) or consult the OSE website (www.trainose.gr).

Trains are regular or intercity (IC or ICE). Nice trains now operate from Thessaloniki–Larisa and Thessaloniki–Edessa. Prices here are for regular trains. If possible, book a day ahead, as long lines are common.

Trains serve Athens (€36, 6¾ hours, 10 daily), via Litohoro (€7, one hour), Larisa (€10, two hours) and Volos (€14, 4½ hours). Intercity trains to Athens (€48, 5½ hours) are more expensive, but not significantly faster.

Several daily trains serve Veria, Edessa and Florina; only two daily trains now serve Xanthi, Komotini and Alexandroupoli in Thrace.

Thessaloniki's train station has ill-kept downstairs toilets, ATMs, post office, card phones and small modern eateries, plus an Orthodox chapel. Self-serve luggage storage lockers start from €3. Additionally, a staffed luggage storage room (€3 per item per day) operates until 10pm daily – you need to show your train ticket when depositing luggage.

Getting Around

TO/FROM THE AIRPORT
Bus 78 runs half-hourly from the airport west to the main bus station via the train station (€0.80). Taxis to the airport cost €15 to €25, even more from midnight until 5am.

BUS
Dependable city buses have electronic rolling signs listing the next destination, accompanied by a recording repeating this in Greek and English. Screens above most bus stops also note how many minutes until the next buses. Bus 1 connects the bus station and the train station, while buses 45A and 45B stop at both (plus Plateia Aristotelous and Kamara) en route to the Halkidiki bus station. From the train station, major points on Egnatia are constantly served by buses such as the 10 and 14.

Buy tickets at *periptera* (street kiosks) for €0.80, or from on-board blue ticket machines (€0.90). Validate the former, in the orange machines. You can switch buses on the same ticket within a total 90-minute time span.

Alternatively, buy a 24-hour unlimited usage ticket (€3). The blue machine neither gives change nor accepts bills, so if you don't have a ticket when boarding, have the right change, and buy and validate your ticket immediately. Thessaloniki's ticket police pounce at any sign of confusion – foreigners are especially easy targets. If they nab you, you'll pay €30 on the spot, or you can go with one of them to plead your case to the police.

CAR
For roadside assistance, call **ELPA** (Greek Automobile Club; ☑ 2310 426 319; Vasilissis Olgas 228). **Budget Rent a Car** (☑ 2310 229 519;

Angelaki 15) and **Euro Rent** (☑ 2310 826 333; Georgiou Papandreou 5) rent vehicles. If driving, avoid Ano Poli's steep and narrow streets.

If you can't find free parking, try either the ferry passenger terminal lot (per hour €2), or Parking XANTH (the Greek abbreviation for the nearby YMCA), which is near the White Tower, Tsimiski and Office of Tourism Directorate. Entrances are on both Tsimiski and Nikolaou Germanou, around the corner. Prices are €4.50 for the first hour, €3.50 for the second and €2.50 per hour after that.

TAXI
Thessaloniki's blue-and-white taxis carry multiple passengers, and only take you if you're going their way. Stand in the direction in which you hope to go, flag one down, yell out your destination and anticipate the driver's upwards eyebrow roll of denial – good luck! The minimum fare is €3.40. A more expensive 'night rate' takes effect from midnight until 5am.

Around Thessaloniki

Just 25km south of Thessaloniki, Epanomi village has the nearest swimmable beaches, good fish tavernas and two 19th-century churches, both with lavish icons. The must-see winery here, Ktima Gerovassiliou (☑ 23920 44567; www.gerovassiliou.gr; Epanomi village), enjoys a spectacular setting, overlooking the sea from a high bluff (even Mt Olympos is visible on clear days). While touring the facilities and sampling the wines, see the fascinating wine museum, which includes Mycenaean and Byzantine amphorae, antique coopers' tools, handmade 18th- to 20th-century wine presses, colourful 16th- to 20th-century bottles, and an eclectic collection of historic corkscrews.

Sandy Faros Beach and adjoining Potamos Beach, 3km from Epanomi, have clear waters and cafes, and in summer there is beach volleyball and live music. The well-maintained Hotel Camping Akti Retzika (☑ 6937456551; www.retzikas.gr; Potamos Beach, Epanomi; camp sites per person/tent €5/5, r from €35; ☺ May-Oct), has extensive campgrounds, modern rooms, and a restaurant and snack bar.

Nearby, birdwatchers will particularly enjoy the 5½ sq km Fanari protected wetlands, which host rare flora and fauna, including migratory birds. You can get more information from the winery or from camping staff.

Halkidiki Χαλκιδική

The popular **Halkidiki Peninsula** can be roughly understood thus: **Kassandra** has the nightlife, **Sithonia** has the beaches and **Athos** has the monks.

Being closest to Thessaloniki, Kassandra is more built-up (though it has good beaches too), while the more subdued Sithonia has campgrounds, hidden coves and clear waters. Both are popular with Greek and foreign holidaymakers (most from Eastern and Central Europe). Much of the easternmost peninsula belongs to the Mt Athos monastic community. Active for well over 1000 years, it's accessible by boat and open to male pilgrims (with advance reservations).

Kassandra and Sithonia are mostly populated along the coasts, the interiors of both being rugged, with thick pine forests. The main roads, therefore, hug the coasts. Many Halkidiki beach villages were settled by refugees during the 1923 population exchanges with Turkey; while the government gave the 'useless' coastal land to these newcomers, their descendants would have the last laugh when beach tourism took off in the 1970s.

In high summer, traffic can be exasperating and finding accommodation tough. However, today's economic crisis has hit the area hard, keeping domatia rates down. Additionally, more than 30 high-quality campgrounds exist. For beach-bar parties and nightclubs, July and August are best, while families and solitude-seekers will prefer September, when waters are warmest and the crowds disappear.

Kassandra Peninsula
Χερσόνησος Κασσάνδρας

Half of Thessaloniki pours into built-up Kassandra on summer weekends and its beach towns are popular with European package tourists. It has Halkidiki's best nightlife and accommodation is slightly cheaper than in Sithonia.

Built-up **Kallithea** has fleshed-out discos and bars, and a long, crowded beach. For self-catering rooms ask at Kallithea Market, beside the bus stop, or at **Manita Tours** (☑ 23740 24036), which also does day trips, including boat tours (€30) to Sithonian beaches.

A few kilometres further east, **Polyhrono** is a quieter, family-oriented budget beach destination, popular with travellers from

former Yugoslav states. Try **Hotel Odysseas** (☑ 23720 51923; www.odysseas.net; d/tr €56/64; P ✳ ᗅ 🏊), with clean, spacious rooms and a nice garden and pool, 70m from the beach. By the beach, posher **Akrogiali Boutique Hotel** (☑ 23740 51500; www.hotelakrogiali.com; d/tr €60/80; P ✳ ᗅ) is a well-designed, romantic place with attached restaurant. Waterfront tavernas include **Flegra Traditional Taverna** (☑ 6989585960; Waterfront; ⊙ 9am-midnight Apr-Oct), with many Greek dishes, seafood specials and kid-friendly fare. Nearby **Ice Therapy** (Waterfront; ⊙ 9am-midnight, May-Sep) offers sweets and iced coffees on the beach.

Kassandra's good campgrounds include **Posidi**, where the Greek National Tourist Organisation runs **Camping Kalandra** (☑ 23740 41123; ⊙ May-Sep; P). Big **Camping Anemi Beach** (☑ 23740 71276; ⊙ May-Sep; P) is at **Nea Skioni** on the quieter western shore.

For **island camping** excursions, contact ethnomusicologist, traveller and former hostel owner **Grigoris Delihristou** (☑ 6979773905; gd065@hotmail.com). For €100 per person, Greg takes small groups on four-day camping trips to tiny islets between Kassandra and Sithonia. You can bliss out on the beach, swim or go spearfishing. Prices includes van and boat transport, plus all food and drinks.

ⓘ Getting There & Away

Buses from Thessaloniki's Halkidiki bus terminal serve Kallithea (€8.80, 1½ hours, 13 daily), Pefkohori (€11.80, two hours, 10 daily) and Polyhrono (€11, 2¼ hours, 10 daily) on the east coast, via Kryopigi and Hanioti (€11.50, 2½ hours). Buses also reach Paliouri (€12, two hours, seven daily) on the southern tip. Discounts apply for 15-day open-return tickets.

SithonianPeninsula
Χερσόνησος Σιθωνίας

People come to Sithonia (particularly, the east) for superb beaches, laid-back nightlife and an escapist feel. Although it's no longer 'undiscovered', you can find hidden coves by venturing down dirt roads or exploring by boat. After August, things quieten down.

The coast road loops around Sithonia, skirting wide bays, climbing into pine-forested hills and dipping down to a few small resorts. However, buses from Thessaloniki sometimes operate different lines for eastern and western coastal destinations – if you're on the wrong bus, you may have to change at Nikiti, at Sithonia's northern base.

WEST COAST

The entry to Sithonia, where the coast roads diverge, is **Nikiti** – beyond here on the west coast are beaches like **Paradisos**, **Kalogria Beach** and **Lagomandra Beach**. Further, **Neos Marmaras** is Sithonia's largest resort, with a crowded beach but many domatia and good seafood tavernas.

From Neos Marmaras the road climbs into the hills, before descending to more beaches and campgrounds. **Toroni** and **Porto Koufos**, two subdued southwestern resorts, offer relaxing beaches and a yacht harbour sheltered in a deep bay, with domatia and fish tavernas.

Kalamitsi is the last major stop on the bus' west-coast route. Its gorgeous beach has brought much development, though it does have boat hire and diving excursions (€50) and courses (from €80) through the **North Aegean Diving Centre** (☑ 23750 41338).

Porto Camping (☑ 23750 41346; camp sites per adult/tent €3.80/4.50), on Kalamitsi's main beach, and the pricier **Camping Kalamitsi** (☑ 23750 41411; camp sites per adult/ tent €6.50/7.20; ☺ May-Sep) around the headland, are both good. The best rooms are **O Giorgakis** (☑ 23750 41338; studios €75), above the eponymous restaurant opposite the beach. The studios sleep five and are fully equipped. The quieter **Souzana Rooms** (☑ 23750 41786; apt €50) has a spacious garden and good-sized apartments.

EAST COAST

Starting from northern Nikiti, Halkidiki's most fabled and exotic beaches extend southwards, separated by steep, wooded cliffs. The first miniresort, **Vourvourou**, has a pretty, boat-lined harbour and the lovely nearby **Karydi Beach**. On the town waterfront, **Paris Restaurant** (☑ 23750 91312; www.parisrestaurant.gr; waterfront; mains €8-11; ☺ 10am-2am May-Oct) is a sprawling place run by the friendly Grigorios Tolios and family, with good grills, fresh fish and excellent service.

Just inland, **Hotel Vergos** (☑ 23750 91379; www.halkidiki.com/vergos; Vourvourou village; s/d/ studio/apt incl breakfast €65/77/90/120; ☒) has well-furnished rooms, a pool and a big lawn for kids. Somewhat pricier but more sublime is **Ekies All Senses Resort** (☑ 23750 91000; www.ekies.gr; Vourvourou; s/d/ste €140/200/260; ☒ ☎). The resort offers elegant rooms and

suites in soft tones, plus spa, a restaurant, and an outdoor bar with palm-frond loungers over its own private beach, 300m from Karydi Beach. A less expensive option here is **Karidi Beach Apartments** (☑ 23750 91102; www.karidibeach.gr; Vourvourou village; apt from €80; ☒ ☒), a family-run place offering simple but renovated apartments with spacious lawns, 50m from the beach.

South from Vourvourou, the terrain becomes wilder, leading to campgrounds on secluded coves. Look out for the sign pointing down a (1.8km) dirt road to **Akti Zografou**, two sandy beaches separated by cliffs covered in scrub pine. The left-hand fork leads to the signposted **Porto Elea Camping** (☑ 6984625587; www.portoelea.com; Akti Zografou; adult/child €7/4, tents from €5.50; ☺ May-Oct), while the right-hand one leads to a curving sandy stretch and the former 'Bahia' beach bar (at time of research, popular Thessaloniki restaurant Paparouna was operating it). The campground rents canoes and it's also easy to swim between the two coves.

Further south down the main road, and 20km before the final east-coast village of Sarti, the large and very popular **Camping Armenistis** (☑ 23750 91487; www.armenistis. com.gr; Sarti village; camp sites per person/tent €7.20/8.30; ☺ May-Oct; ☒) enjoys a fantastic setting between forest and beach. Services here run from market, restaurant and crêperie to cinema, sports grounds and medical centre. Summer sees frequent concerts and DJ parties. Additionally, a sort of 'tent hostel' sleeps eight (€15 per bed) and has a BBQ and fridge.

For a little civilisation (and an ATM machine) continue to **Sarti**, probably Sithonia's best base. Kids will like its long, sandy beach with playground, the restaurants are good and there's memorable nightlife. Essentially three streets and a beach, Sarti somehow still has the vaguely 1972 vibe that once made it an escapist haven. Indeed, 6km north the **Kavourotrypes** (Crab Holes) beaches are still nudist-friendly.

For sleeping, scour local domatia or visit **Sithon Travel** (☑ 23750 94066; www.sarti.gr; Sarti; ☺ 9am-9pm), which owns the majority of local rooms anyway. Expect to pay from €40 to €60 per room. **Iliadis House** (☑ 23750 94290; www.sarti-iliadis.gr; s/d €40/50; ☺ May-Oct), near the bus stop and two blocks from the waterfront, has simple, clean rooms with balconies. Friendly owner Sokratis is

NORTHERN GREECE HALKIDIKI

keen to inform on local attractions. Alternatively, **Sarti Vista Bed & Breakfast Resort** (☑ 23750 94651; www.sartivista.com; Sarti village; apt from €80; P ✳ ☞ ☲) has great sea views from its hillside location behind town. It offers modern self-catering apartments, an outdoor barbecue area, an infinity pool and gardens.

Towards the waterfront's northern edge, **Kivotos** (Noah's Ark; ☑ 23750 94143; waterfront; mains €5-9; ☉ 10am-1am May-Oct) has to be among Halkidiki's best seafood restaurants. Empathetic owner Daniel (a dead-ringer for Richard Gere) and his staff offer excellent service at this colourful place with tables on the sand. Try the baked aubergine mezes and the great grilled fish (choose from the day's catch). The nearby **Orange Cafe Beach Bar** (waterfront; ☉ 9am-2am) has big couches under gauze curtains and palm fronds, many drinks on offer and free wi-fi.

One street inland from the waterfront, **Peponaki** (☉ 9am-3am) is a fun and laid-back bar decked out in reggae tones, with ice cream next door. One street further back is **George's Pub** (☑ 23750 94157; george.pub@ gmail.com; ☉ 9pm-3am), a place that has to be seen to be believed. Local icon and musician George has been on the Sarti bar scene since the '70s, as the cobwebs on the vintage vinyl record collection and worn wood furnishings attest. George plays music ranging from rock to reggae and jazz, sometimes accompanying it on his trumpet. Finally, some 3km beyond Sarti, the famous **Goa Beach Bar** (3km north of Sarti; ☉ 24hr) works day and night, with occasional DJ parties.

If driving, explore less-visited beaches further south, or visit the (thoroughly untouristed) **Sykia**. Other Sithonians call this village 'Little Texas' for its independent streak.

❶ Getting There & Away

Driving is the best way to do Halkidiki, saving considerable transit time and letting you explore the best beaches. Otherwise, there's no better way to feel like a miserable tourist than to go by bus.

First you'll need to take a Thessaloniki city bus (45A or 45B, running from the main bus station to the train station, Plateia Aristotelous and Kamara), to the east-side **Halkidiki Bus Station** (☑ 2310 316 555; www.ktel-chalkidikis.gr; Ethniki Odos, Thessaloniki), filled with chatting locals and confused, perspiring tourists. Counting the time lost waiting and in heavy traffic, it can take

an incomprehensible three to six hours to actually arrive at Halkidiki from Thessaloniki.

Buses serve Vourvourou (€12.20, 1¾ hours, four daily), Akti Zografou (€15.50, 3 hours, four daily), Camping Armenistis (€17, 3¼ hours, four daily), and Sarti (€18.30, 3½ hours, four daily). However, some east-coast buses reach Camping Armenistis and then turn back, neglecting Sarti. Nevertheless, Sarti buses cross the southwestern tip when returning to Thessaloniki. The discounted return ticket is valid for 15 days.

Crossing to Sithonia from Kassandra by bus requires changing at Nea Moudania, at Kassandra's northern foot. Halkidiki's buses do not go east to Kavala (or anywhere else); it's back to Thessaloniki for everyone.

Athos Peninsula (Secular Athos)
Χερσόνησος του Άθω

The Athos peninsula has family-friendly beaches on its northernmost part; south of Ouranoupoli is the Mt Athos monastic community. Land entry is prohibited between the two. At the northeastern, secular edge, **Ierissos** once had ferries to the monasteries but is currently infamous for its proposed Canadian gold-mining project, which the cash-strapped Greek government approved in 2012 despite local protests. At time of research, protests from locals (and the monks) on environmental grounds continued to delay the gold-diggers.

Just off Athos' northwestern coast, **Ammouliani** is a small island with fine beaches, pensions, camping, tavernas and 600 year-round inhabitants. Five daily ferries travel here from **Trypiti** and Ouranoupoli. Excursion boats from Sithonia also visit. The kiosk above the dock has local maps, with contact details and locations of everything on Ammouliani; it's opposite **Restaurant Janis** (☑ 23770 51322; Ammouliani; fish €6-12; ☉ 9am-11pm May-Oct), which has nice waterfront views and delicious fresh fish.

Ammouliani's best beach, **Alykes**, is a 20-minute stroll westward. Walking to more distant beaches and accommodation can take over an hour, and the shadeless island has no taxis, so call ahead for a free lift if staying overnight.

Southwestern **Ouranoupoli** is Athos' major village, with ferries to the monasteries, and some excellent beaches. Also, daily sightseeing **Athos boat cruises** give otherwise banned females the chance to see west-

Athos Peninsula

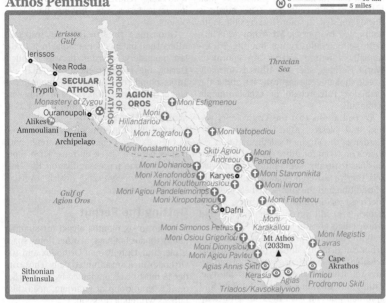

Athos Peninsula — **0** — 10 km / **0** — 5 miles

coast monasteries from 500m away. Boat hire (€40) accesses the sandy **Drenia archipelago**, 1.9km offshore, east of Ammouliani.

Ouranoupoli's **Pyrgos Prosforeiou** (Prosforeiou Tower; ☎23770 71651; adult/student & child €2/1; ◷9am-6pm Tue-Sun), a restored 14th-century Byzantine tower, exhibits ancient and Byzantine artefacts, and honours the Locks, an Australian couple who inhabited it in the 1920s. Large maps and detailed images highlight local sites. These include the ruined 11th-century **Monastery of Zygou**, east of town on the border of monastic Athos; women can visit it.

🛏 Sleeping & Eating

Except for high summer, simple and inexpensive domatia are easily available.

Xenios Zeus   PENSION $
(☎23770 71274; www.ouranoupoli.com/zeus; Ouranoupoli; s/d/tr €40/55/65; ❋) Near the tower, Xenios Zeus is a bit old-fashioned but has clean and comfortable rooms with balconies. Breakfasts are ample and fresh. Like other places, it will hold unnecessary luggage for monastic pilgrims. Members of the Britain-based Friends of Mt Athos get a discount.

Camping Ouranoupoli   CAMPGROUND $
(☎23770 71171; www.camping-ouranoupoli.gr; camp sites per adult/tent €9/9; ◷late May–Oct) A decent, though pricey, campground on Ouranoupoli's northern beach side.

Lazaros Andonakis Rooms   PENSION $
(☎23770 71366; s/d €45/55; ❋🐾🛜) These airy, pine-furnished rooms, some with harbour views, are 50m from the Pilgrims' Office.

Kritikos   SEAFOOD $$
(☎23770 71222; www.okritikos.com; Ouranoupoli; fish per kilo €45/60; ◷lunch & dinner) Whether you're looking to celebrate a 'last supper' before visiting food-deprived Mt Athos or just want somewhere for a leisurely dinner, this bright place on a central side street offers Ouranoupoli's best fresh fish. Landlubbers can try the inventive pastas and salads.

Mt Athos (Agion Oros)
Αγιον Ορος

If you're lucky enough to be able to visit Mt Athos, do it – it's an experience you won't forget. For over a millennium, unbroken spiritual activity has survived on this isolated peninsula, in a semi-autonomous monastic republic following the Julian calendar. Athos has 20 working monasteries, and *skites* (monastic dependencies), plus *kelli* (ascetic hermitages). The north is thickly forested, the more inaccessible south dominated by soaring **Mt Athos** (2033m). With neither industry nor hunting, it's essentially a nature reserve. An enormous World Heritage site, Mt Athos is formally Greek, though ecclesiastically it's under the Orthodox Patriarchate of Constantinople (İstanbul).

Legend attests that the Virgin Mary visited and blessed Athos; considered the Garden of the Virgin, it's dedicated to her – there's no room for other women. Although this has frustrated some Eurocrats in Brussels, they've proven no match for 1000 years of tradition and the gold-sealed *chrysobulls* (decrees) of Byzantine emperors, whose names are still invoked in prayers and whose edicts are still respected.

With advance preparations, male pilgrims can visit for four days (with extensions possible). The experience is peaceful and tiring. You usually follow the monks' lifestyle, eating and attending services (at 3am and 3pm daily, but on feast days sometimes up to 10 hours standing). When you traipse the quiet Athonite forest paths and marvel at the monastic architecture and art treasures, the uniqueness of the place registers; whether or not you're religious, the experience will leave a strong impression.

History

Mid-Byzantine ascetics gravitated towards rugged, inaccessible Athos. Emperor Basil I's AD-885 *chrysobull* confirmed its status, and in 943 its territory was mapped. In 963 the Holy Mountain was formally dedicated, when Emperor Nikoforos II Fokas funded Megistis Lavras, which is still Athos' biggest monastery.

Athos flourished under imperial patronage, but growing commercial involvement sparked protests from conservative monks who feared old-school traditions were being diluted. Corrective imperial edicts reaffirmed prior ones: most famously, in 1060 Constantine IX Monomahos banned women, female domestic animals, beardless persons and eunuchs. Today women are still banned, hens are tolerated for their eggs, beards are no longer mandatory and eunuchs are not readily available.

After a glorious 11th century, pirates, Catalans and Crusaders (in 1204) pillaged intermittently. Nevertheless, the Holy Mountain was always reborn; founding and subsidising monasteries was very prestigious for donors.

Ottomans arrived in 1430, but respected Athos' semi-independent status. In 1542 the last monastery, Stavronikita, was founded. During the Independence War (1821–29), Turks plundered and burned monasteries and their libraries. In perhaps his only wise decision, Hitler spared Athos during Germany's WWII occupation.

Athos' 1924 Constitution was guaranteed in Greece's 1975 Constitution. Foreign-born monks become Greek citizens. Each monastery has one representative on the Holy Council *(Iera Synaxis)*, which oversees Athos' 1600 monks.

Getting the Permit

Book up to six months ahead for summer and Orthodox holidays; at other times, space is plentiful. Only 10 non-Orthodox and 100 Orthodox men are admitted daily. Those under 18 must be accompanied by their father or, if with a group or guardian, need their father's written permission.

Email or fax your preferred visit dates and passport copy to the Thessaloniki-based Mt Athos Pilgrims' Bureau (p253) and they will inform you when you can pick up your permit. Otherwise, if not passing through Thessaloniki, print the confirmation email/fax. Clergymen need written permission from the **Ecumenical Patriarchate of Constantinople** (☑ in Turkey 90 21253 49037; İstanbul). Next, phone the monasteries to reserve specific nights; some get rather crotchety if you show up unannounced. Finally, take your written/printed confirmation and luggage to Ouranoupoli for the *diamonitirion* (final permit).

Entering Athos

Ouranoupoli's small **Pilgrims' Office** (☑ 23770 71422; fax 23770 71450; Ouranoupoli; ⊙ 8.10am-2pm), marked by a black-and-yellow Byzantine flag, is on the side street towards the water, by the Jet Oil station. Go well before boat departure time to avoid long lines. Show your passport and booking confirmation to get the three-night (four-day) *diamonitirion*: students pay €10, Orthodox believers €25, everyone else €30. Free entry is granted on a case-by-case basis to the poor, the sick and so on. There's a parking lot (per day €7.50) on Ouranoupoli's south side, though street parking is free.

ATHOS DAY TRIPS BY BOAT

If you can't visit Mt Athos or simply don't have time, regular **boat trips** from Oura-noupoli trace the southern peninsula, passing Athos' most spectacular clifftop monas-teries and wild nature.

Athos Sea Cruises (☑ 23770 71071; www.athos-cruises.gr; Ouranoupoli) runs a three-hour trip (adult/child under six €18/free) on the 300-seat *Kapetan Fotis* (10.30am and 1.45pm daily, from Easter through October). It passes nine major west-coast monaster-ies with good views of Athos' peak. The boat cruises 500m from shore (the legal dis-tance), allowing photo opportunities, while running commentary is provided in English, German and Greek. There's a cold buffet, icon shopping and Athos-related videos too.

If you're based on Halkidiki's Sithonian Peninsula, similar tours run from Ormos Panagias or Sarti (€25 or €30). These cruises depart around 9am and return by 5pm. A lunch stopover at Ammouliani island is often included.

From Ouranoupoli, the *Agia Anna* leaves for Athos' port of Dafni at 8am and 11am Monday to Saturday, and 8.30am Sunday (€8). The *Axion Esti* leaves at 9.45am (€6). Nearby to the **ticket office** (☑ 23770 71248; Ouranoupoli) on the far waterfront, you can get *bougatsa* (creamy semolina pudding wrapped in a pastry envelope and baked) and coffee.

The ferry stops at several monasteries before reaching **Dafni** (two hours total). There, a bus serves **Karyes**, the administra-tive capital (€2.60). Otherwise, for monas-teries further down the coast, change boats at Dafni.

Monasteries offer free accommodation and food, generally for one night. The *dia-monitirion* can be extended in Karyes for another two days. However, a friendly mon-astery may let you stay longer without the administrative hassle.

Exploring Athos

While monastic vehicles, buses and boats operate, walking is ideal for experiencing Athos' serenity. Centuries-old paths criss-cross tranquil forests, enlivened by the rustling of leaves, chirping of birds and occa-sional passing monk, rhythmically reciting his prayers. Spring, when the flowers come out, is an especially beautiful time to visit.

Twice-daily boats from Dafni (around €2.50) serve west-coast monasteries like Di-onysiou, Simonas Petras, Agiou Pavlou and Agias Triados/Kavsokalyvion.

Karyes hosts the 10th-century **Protaton** (the basilican church opposite the Holy Epistasia), with artwork by Panselinos, mas-ter of the 'Macedonian School' of painting.

◉ Sights

KARYES TO THE SOUTHEAST COAST MONASTERIES & MT ATHOS

From Karyes, walk southeast through the **Kapsala** woods to coastal **Moni Stavroni-kita** (☑ tel/fax 23770 23255; ◷ noon-2pm) or, just under it, **Moni Iviron** (☑ 23770 23643; fax 23770 23248; ◷ noon-2pm). This Georgian-founded monastery contains more than 2000 manuscripts, including 100 rare Georgian-language parchments.

From Iviron, coastal paths reach hospita-ble **Moni Filotheou** (☑ 23770 23256; fax 23770 23674), also accessible from Karyes along a shady path with spring water (3½ hours). Beyond **Moni Karakallou** (☑ 23770 23225; fax 23770 23746), the Byzantine-era path be-comes a road leading (after 5½ hours) to Moni Megistis Lavras. Alternatively, buses from Karyes go there.

Magnificent **Moni Megistis Lavras** (☑ 23770 23754; fax 23770 23013) is Athos' big-gest monastery and the only one never dam-aged by fire. Treasures include Theophanes of Crete's frescoes and founder St Athana-sios' tomb.

From here, a small boat sometimes serves the hospitable west-coast **Agias Annis Skiti** (☑ 23770 23320). For real adventure, hike the tough trail around the peninsula's southern tip; it passes the Romanian **Timiou Pro-dromou Skiti**, then coastal **Agias Triados/ Kavsokalyvion** (☑ 23770 23319). Definitely call ahead for stays at this ornery place, known for its icon-painting tradition.

Next is **Kerasia** (☑ 23770 23318). Kerasia and Agias Annis Skiti are both good bases for the difficult ascent to **Mt Athos** (2033m). Below the summit, at the Panagia (Virgin

NORTHERN GREECE HALKIDIKI

Mary) Chapel, enjoy fresh spring water. Boats from Agias Annis serve Dafni.

KARYES TO THE SOUTHWEST COAST MONASTERIES

If heading southwest from Karyes you will first encounter leafy, hospitable **Moni Koutloumousiou** (☑ 23770 23226; fax 23770 23731). Further west, coastal **Moni Xiropotamou** (☑ 23770 23251; fax 23770 23733; ◷ 12.30-2.30pm), has comfortable, oil-lit guest rooms. Pilgrims here dine separately from the monks. The path southward accesses Dafni; either walk the coastal path or take the boat, which leaves at 12.30pm, calling at Simonos Petras, Osiou Grigoriou, Dionysiou, Agiou Pavlou, Agias Annis and Agias Triados/Kavsokalyvion. Alternatively, wooded paths in the peninsula's centre, accessible from Moni Koutlomousiou or Moni Filotheou, reach Simonos Petras.

Spectacular **Moni Simonos Petras** (Simopetra; ☑ 23770 23254; fax 23770 23707; ◷ 1-3pm), fronted by wooden balconies over a cliff, is Athos' most-photographed monastery. Here and at the other cliff monasteries, standing in the dark under a sky teeming with stars, with the sound of the sea below, is almost a religious experience in itself. From here the coastal path branches off towards the *arsanas* (monastery port/dock) at a small shrine, accessing **Moni Osiou Grigoriou** (☑ 23770 23668; fax 23770 23671), a seafront monastery with a comfortable guesthouse.

The hilly coastal path south reaches **Moni Dionysiou** (☑ 23770 23687; fax 23770 23686) another tranquil cliff-hanging monastery. Dionysiou's *katholikon* (principal church) contains a unique wax-and-mastic icon of the Virgin and Child. In the year 626, as Persian and Avar forces besieged Constantinople, the patriarch carried the icon round the walls; miraculously, the enemy armies melted away. Athos' oldest icon, its features are barely visible, though the dark shape resonates with a strange power in its ornate silver case.

After Dionysiou, the coastal path continues to the architecturally magnificent **Moni Agiou Pavlou** (☑ 23770 23741; fax 23770 23355) and Agias Annis Skiti.

KARYES TO THE NORTHERN MONASTERIES

Northwards from Karyes, the road passes sprawling **Skiti Agiou Andreou** (☑ 23770 23810). This enormous former Russian place is still being renovated (it was largely abandoned during Soviet times). Happily, a new band of icon-painting brothers now dwell here (see the gift shop's unique works).

The main route continues to coastal **Moni Pandokratoros** (☑ 23770 23880; fax 23770 23685); alternatively, a two-hour forest path reaches the coastal **Moni Vatopediou** (☑ 23770 41488; fax 23770 41462; ◷ 9am-1pm); the wealthiest Athonite monastery (there's even wi-fi), Vatopediou follows the modern Gregorian calendar. Its sumptuous church has a jaw-dropping collection of treasures.

From Vatopediou, a coastal path leads to **Moni Esfigmenou** (☑ 23770 23229), technically schismatic over ecumenical matters, but friendly. Further is **Moni Hilandariou** (☑ 23770 23797; fax 23770 23108), a very hospitable Serbian monastery (also accessible from Dafni by south-coast boat, and then a connecting bus ride). The UK-based Friends of Mt Athos donated towards rebuilding structures here that were destroyed in a 2004 fire. The humble, pretty **Moni Konstamonitou** (☑ tel/fax 23770 23228) is worth visiting, as is the Bulgarian **Moni Zografou** (☑ tel/fax 23770 23247) further north. Its name, meaning 'painter,' comes from a miraculous icon not painted by human hands. The northernmost west-coast monastery, **Moni Dohiariou** (☑ tel/fax 23770 23245), slopes towards the sea and boasts remarkable architecture.

Next down the coastal path, venerable **Moni Xenofondos** (☑ 23770 23633; fax 23770 23631) was first mentioned in 998, but probably dates to the 6th century. Although loot-seeking pirates often plundered it, impressive mid-Byzantine marble and wood-carved iconostases still survive in its 10th-century *katholikon;* its newer one, from 1838, is Athos' largest. Finally, **Moni Agiou Panteleimonos** (☑ tel/fax 23770 23252; ◷ 10am-noon), further on, is a typically grand and friendly Russian monastery.

🛏 Sleeping & Eating

Athos' two nonmonastic guesthouses, a nameless **guesthouse** (☑ 23770 23362) and the **Ilarion Guest House** (☑ 23770 23243) are in Karyes. Karyes and Dafni have rudimentary bakeries, food shops and a cafe.

If you're staying in a monastery where pilgrims dine alongside the monks, the meal concludes when the simultaneous spiritually edifying reading ends – so eat up!

ℹ️ Information

Dafni has a port authority, police, customs, post office, gift shops and card phones. Karyes has an ATM, post office, OTE card phone, a **Community Clinic** (☑ 23770 23217; Karyes) and a **Civil Administration Office** (☑ 23770 23314; Karyes), for permit extensions. All Greek mobile-phone networks operate.

ℹ️ Getting There & Away

The Ouranoupoli bus leaves Halkidiki Bus Station (p258) in Thessaloniki (€12.40, 3½ hours, seven daily). Either take the first bus (5.30am) from Thessaloniki on the date you'll enter Athos, or stay over the night before in Ouranoupoli. Get your *diamonitirion* and ticket before the next morning's 9.45am boat. Staying overnight in Ouranoupoli lets you rest, buy supplies and store unnecessary luggage.

The Athos–Ouranoupoli ferry leaves Dafni at noon, after a customs check to prevent antiquities theft. The morning boat from monasteries south of Dafni is timed to catch this ferry, which also collects passengers from the coastal monasteries north of Dafni.

The last Ouranoupoli–Thessaloniki bus leaves at 5.45pm. Unfortunately, you can't continue from Ouranoupoli to eastern Macedonia or Thrace by bus.

Kavala   Καβάλα

POP 54.027

Palm-fronted Kavala appeals with its hill-top castle and colourful Panagia old quarter. A ferry hub for the Northeastern Aegean Islands (especially Thasos), it gets many one-night visitors. However, it deserves further inspection; the aqueduct of Ottoman Sultan Süleyman the Magnificent (r 1520–66), a Byzantine fortress and atmospheric cafes repay the visit.

Modern Kavala was once ancient Philippi's port. More infamously, Ottoman Pasha Mehmet Ali (1769–1849), eventual founder of Egypt's last royal dynasty, ruled here. This genocidal Ottoman ordered his Egyptian Muslim fleet to slaughter tens of thousands of Christian Greeks on islands like Kassos and Psara, during Greece's independence struggle (islanders still commemorate these events annually). Somewhat ironically, Ali's former home has become an ultra-luxurious boutique hotel.

👁 Sights & Activities

Archaeological Museum   MUSEUM
(☑ 25102 22335; Erythrou Stavrou 17; adult €2; ☉ 8am-3pm Tue-Sun) On Ethnikis Antistasis' western end, this museum displays sculpture, jewellery, grave stelae, terracotta figurines and vases from ancient Amfipoli, a gold-digging Athenian colony that mined Mt Pangaeum.

Municipal Museum of Kavala   MUSEUM
(☑ 25102 22706; Filippou 4; ☉ 8am-2pm Mon-Sat) **FREE** This contemporary and folk-art museum contains costumes, jewellery, handicrafts, household items and tools.

Panagia Quarter   HISTORIC AREA
Panagia's narrow, tangled streets are lined by pretty pastel houses. It's good for evening strolls or atmospheric dining. Now a hotel, the huge, 18-domed **Imaret** (1817) here was Pasha Mehmet Ali's hostel for Islamic theology students.

Beaches   BEACH
Rapsani Beach, 2km west of town, is popular for swimming, though **Batis Beach** further west is better.

🛏 Sleeping

Kavala's hotels remain business-oriented. For €1, the tourist office can arrange accommodation for you, sometimes getting discounts and saving you from aimless wandering in the heat.

Galaxy Hotel   HOTEL $
(☑ 25102 24812; www.airotel.gr; Eleftheriou Venizelou 27; s/d €40/50; ✳ 🛜) Opposite the tourist office, the Galaxy has ordinary, old-style rooms, some with port views.

Oceanis Kavala Hotel   HOTEL $
(☑ 25102 21981; Leof Erythrou Stavrou 32; s/d incl breakfast €68/82; ✳ 🛜) This old business hotel behind the western waterfront has comfortable, well-maintained rooms with balconies.

Batis Beach Camping   CAMPGROUND $
(☑ 25102 45918; camp sites per adult/tent €6/4.90) A small, decent campground 3km west of town, Batis occupies Kavala's best beach.

Imaret   BOUTIQUE HOTEL $$$
(☑ 25106 20151; www.imaret.gr; Poulidou 6; s/d/ste incl breakfast €250/360/500; ✳ 🛜 🏊) Posh and pricey Imaret complements the original stone architecture devised by Kavala's most famous villain, Pasha Mehmet Ali, with modern luxuries and elegant lighting. The huge rooms have vaulted ceilings, harbour views and large fireplaces. Try the restored Turkish *hammam* and candlelit indoor pool.

✕ Eating & Drinking

Limonidis Bougatsa BAKERY $
(📞25108 32526; cnr Ionos Dragoumi & Megas Alexandrou; bougatsa €3.20; ⊙6am-2pm) Behind the tourist information centre, Limonodis does Kavala's best *bougatsa*, plus coffees.

Psarotaverna Panos Zafira SEAFOOD $$
(📞 25102 27978; cnr Plateia Karaoli Dimitriou; fish €9-15; ⊙10am-1am) Since 1965, this friendly eastern waterfront taverna has been serving fresh fish dishes and good grills.

Psarotaverna Nikiforos SEAFOOD $$
(📞25102 28167; Plateia Karaoli 44; fish €9-17; ⊙11am-1am) Nikiforos has a wide selection of fresh fish and good harbour views.

Glaros BAR
(📞25125 10514; Poulidou Theodorou 19; ⊙11am-4am) Among Kavala's oldest cafe-bars, Glaros has a great Panagia setting. It switches into rock mode by night.

Omilos CAFE
(port; ⊙10am-late) You can watch the bobbing boats from the draped blue-and-white-striped couches at this smooth western port cafe.

Katinara CAFE
(📞25108 34208; Nyremvergis 17; ⊙9am-3am) Decked out in weathered wood and lipstick-red decor, Katinara's a fun cafe with character, named after Kavala's most admired whore of yesteryear.

Nouvelle Vague BAR
(📞25102 20744; Erythrou Stavrou 18; ⊙9am-1am) This chic new waterfront place has eclectic decorations, playing up its 'theatrical' and vaguely French attraction.

❶ Information

Alkyon Travel Service (📞25102 31096; alkyon-trv@ticketcom.gr; Eleftheriou Venizelou 37; ⊙9am-6pm) Friendly travel agency in a central upstairs office books ferry tickets to Limnos, Lesvos and Samos.
Port Authority (📞25102 23716; cnr Ethnikis Andistasis & Averof)
Post Office (cnr Hrysostomou Kavalas & Erythrou Stavrou)
Tourist Office (📞25102 31011; detaktic@ otenet.gr; Plateia Eleftherias; ⊙8am-9pm Mon-Fri) Helpful English- and German-speaking staff provide maps, plus transport and events information and hotel bookings.

❶ Getting There & Away

AIR
Kavala shares Alexander the Great Airport, near Hrysoupoli (29km), with Xanthi. **Aegean Airlines** (📞25210 29000; Erythrou Stavrou 1) offers three daily Athens flights (€60). Island flights go via Athens or Thessaloniki.

BOAT
From the western port (near the bus station), summer hydrofoils (sometimes) serve Limenas in Thasos. Buy tickets on board.

More dependable ferries serve Skala Prinou in Thasos, from the eastern waterfront. From the bus station, it's a brisk 15-minute walk along the waterfront to get here. Ferries to Lesvos and beyond are here too. A small building on the left sells tickets for Thasos; tickets for the other islands are sold by Alkyon Travel Service (p264), **Euro Kosmos Travel Agency** (📞25102 21960; www.eurokosmos.gr; Erythrou Stavrou 1) or **Maritime Agency Miliadis** (📞25102 26147; www.miliadou.gr; Karaoli-Dimitriou 36).

BUS
Kavala bus station (📞25102 22294; www.ktelkavalas.gr; cnr Filikis Eterias & Hrysostomou Kavalas) serves Athens (€55, 8¾ hours, two daily), Xanthi (€5.40, one hour, half-hourly), Keramoti (€4.20, one hour, hourly), Serres (€9.30, two hours, four daily), Alexandroupoli (€15, two hours, seven daily) and Thessaloniki (€15, 2¼ hours, 11 daily). The *apothiki* (storeroom) stores luggage.

❶ Getting Around
Airport taxis (€45) wait near the bus station.
Alkyon Travel Service (📞25102 31096; alkyon-trv@ticketcom.gr; Eleftheriou Venizelou 37) rents cars from €40.

Litohoro & Plaka Litohorou
Λιτόχωρο & Πλάκα Λιτοχώρου
POP 6995 / ELEV 305M

Atmospheric, relaxing **Litohoro** (lih-*to*-ho-ro) is a village of cobbled upper streets and wood-balconied houses. Best known for being close to Mt Olympus and ancient Dion, it's an agreeable place in its own right, with cozy lodgings and excellent restaurants.

Litohoro's extensive beach area, the nearby **Plaka Litohorou**, is the site not only of hotels and swimming holes but also Litohoro's train and bus stations (on the Athens–Thessaloniki line). The general area is known as Pieria, and beaches of the 'Pierian

Riviera' such as **Gritsa**, **Leptokarya** and **Skotina** are very popular with Greek and foreign tourists.

Litohoro and Plaka Litohorou also make an excellent base for seeing the monasteries at Meteora. In August, enjoy the **Festival Olympou** (www.festivalolympou.gr). It's held in town and at nearby historic sites such as ancient Dion and the Castle of Platamonas, and includes concerts, plays and other cultural happenings.

🤸 Activities

EOS   MOUNTAIN CLIMBING
(Greek Alpine Club; ☑23520 84544; ☉9.30am-12.30pm & 6-8pm Mon-Sat Jun-Sep) Below the public parking lot; EOS distributes pamphlets with general and Olympus hiking information. Take Ithakisiou from the square; turn left after 100m. The EOS runs three mountain refuges.

SEO   MOUNTAIN CLIMBING
(Association of Greek Climbers; ☑23520 84200; ☉6-10pm) This place is informative and runs an Olympus refuge. Walk down Ithakiou, turn left and then left again.

🛏 Sleeping

Litohoro village has atmospheric rustic digs, and the lengthy beaches around Plaka Litohorou have both full-serve campgrounds and a few excellent hotels.

**★Cavo Olympo Luxury
Resort & Spa**   RESORT $$$
(☑23520 22222; www.cavoolympo.gr; Plaka Litohorou; r/ste incl breakfast from €190/280; ℙ❋@🛜🏊) On Plaka Litohorou's seafront, this minimalist masterpiece consists of 49 rooms and suites overlooking either Olympos or the sea, some with spas or private pool. All are airy, spacious and relaxing, with big balconies. The hotel's centrepiece – an enormous 'infinity pool' sloping towards the bluff overlooking the water – must be among Greece's largest.

Cavo Olympo also has a refined restaurant and spa centre (with indoor heated pool). It's 2.5km south of the train station on the coast road.

Xenonas Papanikolaou   GUESTHOUSE $
(☑23520 81236; www.xenonas-papanikolaou.gr; Nikolaou Episkopou Kitrous 1; s/d incl breakfast €45/60; ℙ❋@) This romantic guesthouse in a flowery back-street garden has spacious self-catering rooms, with nice views

of Litohoro's traditional terracotta rooftops. The downstairs lounge has fireplace and couches. From the square, take 28 Oktovriou uphill and turn left on Nikolaou Episkopou Kitrous.

Hotel Olympus Mediterranean   HOTEL $$
(☑23520 81831; www.olympusmed.gr; Dionysou 5; d/tr incl breakfast €70/90, luxury ste €100; ❋@🏊) This four-star hotel occupies a neoclassical building with ornate balconies, and has 20 luxurious rooms and three suites, plus an indoor pool, a mosaic-tiled jacuzzi pool and sauna. Some rooms have fireplace and spa.

Olympios Zeus   CAMPGROUND $
(☑23520 22115; www.olympios-zeus.gr; Plaka Litohorou; camp sites per adult/tent €7/3.50) This Plaka Litohorou beachfront campground is solid, though somewhat ramshackle.

Olympos Beach   CAMPGROUND $
(☑23520 22112; www.olympos-beach.gr; Plaka Litohorou; camp sites per adult €7, tent €5-7) This leafy, well-run camping option on the Plaka Litohorou strand has a lively nightclub.

🍴 Eating & Drinking

★Gastrodromio   FINE DINING $$
(☑23520 21300; Plateia Eleftherias; mains €7-13; ☉10am-11pm) If Gastrodromio was around in Olympian times, Zeus and Co would have eaten here. Litohoro's most inventive restaurant serves flavourful dishes such as octopus with peppercorn, cumin, garlic, hot pepper and wine; or rabbit cooked in wine and glazed with almonds, cinnamon and nutmeg. The wine list is 21 pages long.

Damaskinia   TAVERNA $
(☑23520 81247; Vasileos Konstandinou 4; mains €6-11; ☉10am-11pm) A popular upper-town taverna, Damaskinia does tasty *mousakas* and *kokoretsi* (spit-roasted lamb offal, wrapped in intestines).

Mylos Beach Bar   BAR
(Plaka Litohorou; ☉9am-3am) Plaka Litohorou's most popular beach bar by day and night, Mylos also serves food.

ℹ Information

Plateia Eleftheria has ATMs.
Medical Centre (☑23520 22222; Plaka Litohorou) About 5km away, at the Litohoro turn-off from the main coastal highway.
Municipal Website (www.litohoro.gr)

Police (☑23520 81100; cnr Ithakisiou & Agiou Nikolaou)

Post Office (28 Oktovriou 11)

Tourist Information Booth (Nikolaou; ⊙9am-6pm) In a white building with wooden eaves, just before Ithakiou.

ℹ Getting There & Away

From the **bus station** (☑23520 81271; Agiou Nikolaou), buses serve Katerini (€2.30, 25 minutes, 13 daily), Thessaloniki (€8.50, 1¼ hours, 13 daily) and Athens (€33, 5½ hours, three daily via Katerini). Buses from Thessaloniki to Volos/Athens leave you on the highway to catch a Katerini–Litohoro bus.

Litohoro's train station, 9km away at Plaka Litohorou, is on the Athens–Volos–Thessaloniki line.

Around Litohoro

Mt Olympus   MOUNTAIN

The cloud-covered lair of the Ancient Greek pantheon, awe-inspiring Mt Olympus (Ορος Ολυμπος), fires the visitor's imagination today, just as it did for the ancients who venerated it. Greece's highest mountain, Olympus hosts 1700 plant species, some rare and endemic. Its slopes are thickly forested with different deciduous, conifer and pine trees, its peaks often shrouded in fog.

The first known mortals to reach **Mytikas** (2918m), Olympus' highest peak, were Litohoro local Christos Kakalos and Swiss climbers Frederic Boissonas and Daniel Baud-Bovy, in August 1913. Olympus became Greece's first national park in 1937.

Although you can drive up Olympus, most people walk; consult the Litohoro-based hiking associations for maps and current conditions, or check online with the grandly named **Management Agency of Olympus National Park** (www.olympusfd.gr), which also lists the hiking routes and the regulations for visitors. Both provide info on the mountain's 15 refuges, where hikers can sleep.

Ancient Dion   ANCIENT SITE

(Δίον; ☑23510 53484; Dion Archaeological Park; adult/student €6/2; ⊙8am-8pm) North of Litohoro, **Dion** was sacred for ancient Macedonians worshipping the Olympian gods, especially Zeus. Before his epic eastern adventures, Alexander the Great made sacrifices here. Dion has 14 clearly marked ruins, attesting to its evolution over centuries.

A fertility earth goddess was worshipped here. The related ruins of the 6th-century-BC **Sanctuary of Demeter** are the first you'll see and the site's oldest.

Further along is the leafy **Sanctuary of Zeus Hypsistos**, with copies of statues and column bases (the originals are in the on-site museum). Other replicas adorn the remnants of Dion's (usually flooded) **Sanctuary to Isis**, across a small bridge. As elsewhere in the Hellenistic world, worship of this Egyptian goddess was merged with that of Artemis and Aphrodite.

Other ruins attest to Dion's urban structure. Note the wide central avenue and dwellings; one **ruined villa** has a well-preserved mosaic floor (AD 200) depicting the Dionysos Triumphal Epiphany. Later constructions include 4th-century AD Christian **basilica ruins** and **public baths** once paved with mosaics.

During the Festival Olympou (p265) in August, Dion's reconstructed theatre hosts performances.

Taxis from Litohoro cost €15.

Castle of Platamonas   CASTLE

(Κάστρο του Πλαταμώνα; ☑23250 42775; Platamonas; adults/children €2/free; ⊙8am-3pm daily) Looming from a coastal bluff near Platamonas village, 20km south of Plaka Litohorou, this well-preserved 11th-century castle was once defended by brave Byzantines, safeguarding trade routes and scanning for pirates. Today, however, the only *stratiotes* (soldiers) you're likely to see are handymen with weed whackers and the occasional lumbering turtle in his own defensive suit of armour.

From the parking area, pass the (unmanned) booth and take the hilly path 150m to the castle and ticket booth. From here, follow the walls counter-clockwise to understand the fortress' development over time. English-language placards provide some explanation (a book is also on sale for €8).

The first small tower on the right dates from the 6th-century Emperor Justinian, predating much of the existing structure. A placard nearby describes the ruined, Byzantine **Church B**, rebuilt in the 17th century.

Following the walls, peek over for great sea views before reaching the more extensive **Church A** ruins, protected by a wooden enclosure. Built over a 2nd-century-AD Hellenistic warehouse, it has faint fresco remains. At the castle's nearby northeastern edge, scale the narrow stair for magnificent views of sandy **Skotinas Beach** below and Mt Olympus behind.

Skeletal outlines of medieval dwellings (*oikous*) and shops are signposted further down the walls. The final upwards turn into the archway leads to the **acropolis**, where the castle's deep **cistern** lies, under a grate. This well-protected space contains the castle's most magnificent tower, the **pyrgos**; unfortunately closed, it dates from the 14th century, and the last Byzantine (Palaeologan) dynasty.

Archaeologists believe that Late Antique Herakleion was originally here. Sadly, funding is currently lacking to continue excavations. As at Dion, the castle hosts concerts during the Festival Olympou (p265).

Veria βέροια

POP 48,306

Around 75km west of Thessaloniki on the Vergina road, Veria might seem unremarkable at first. However, its atmospheric old quarters, cool museums and Byzantine churches make it worth a peek. While nearby agricultural interests make it primarily a business destination, Veria also has good eating and nightlife.

◎ Sights & Activities

Barbouta HISTORIC AREA
Veria's evocative former Jewish Quarter, Barbouta is reached from Plateia Andoniou down Vasileos Konstandinou, old Veria's commercial street, with shops and *kafeneia*. The huge, ancient plane tree here is where the Turks hanged Archbishop Arsenios in 1430, after taking Veria. Opposite, the decapitated minaret on the dilapidated 12th-century **cathedral** indicates Ottoman interference.

Archaeological Museum MUSEUM
(☑ 23310 24972; Leof Anixeos 45; ⊘ 8.30am-3pm Tue-Sun) FREE This museum, at Anixeos' northern end, contains Vergina tomb finds. Funerary items, ancient vases, silver, gold and a lovely statue of 'Aphrodite taking off her sandals' also impress.

Byzantine Museum MUSEUM
(☑ 23310 25847; Thomaidou 26; €2; ⊘ 8am-3pm Tue-Sun) Up the hill across town, this chic museum presents priceless icons and other Byzantine antiquities such as 5th-century floor mosaics, marble epigraphy and ornate sarcophagi in a sumptuously lit, three-floor space complemented by explanatory wall placards.

Church of the Resurrection of Christ CHURCH
(⊘ 8.30am-3.30pm Tue-Sun) Veria has dozens of **Byzantine churches**; few are open, but this fresco-rich, 14th-century central church usually is.

Mt Vermio SKIING
(☑ 23310 49226) Some 22km west of town, Mt Vermio has eight slopes and three lifts – good for beginners.

⌂ Sleeping

Hotel Macedonia HOTEL $$
(☑ 23310 66902; www.makedoniahotel.gr; Kontogiorgaki 50; s/d €69/75; P ❋ ☎) The renovated Macedonia has handsome, well-furnished rooms, and a rooftop terrace.

Hotel Villa Elia HOTEL $$
(☑ 23310 26800; eliaver@otenet.gr; Elias 16; s/d €55/70; ❋) This central business hotel has large, comfortable rooms.

Hotel En Eari HOTEL $$
(☑ 23310 75788; www.eneari.gr; Leof Anixeos 82; s/d/tr €50/70/120; P ❋ ☎) Price cuts have made the business-class En Eari more attractive. If the wi-fi doesn't work in the room, try down on the cafe floor.

✗ Eating & Drinking

Mezedopolio Elias Gi FINE DINING $$
(☑ 23310 23053; Anixeos 65, cnr Koundouriotou; mains €8-16) Excellent home-cooked Macedonian fare including veal cutlet in quince sauce, or *hasapiko zygouri* (aged lamb). Other unusual dishes include dried beef liver with apple. Prices are cheaper at lunch hours.

Vergiotiko FINE DINING $
(☑ 23310 74133; Thomaidou 2; mains €5-11; ⊘ lunch & dinner) This grotto-like traditional restaurant is literally carved from Veria's old Byzantine walls, and serves hearty portions. Try the pork with aubergines, or pungent mushrooms. It's up a hill, where the road forks left to Vergina.

Sta Kala Kathoumena Katafygio TAVERNA $
(☑ 6986855941; Kontogeorgaki 18; mains €6-9) Formerly known as To Katafygio, this restaurant occupies a restored old building and serves solid traditional cuisine, including pork or chicken *tigania* (fried cubes).

La Grange BAR
(Patriarch Ioakim 7; ⊘ 9pm-late) Old-school rock devotees patronise this simple wood-and-stone old-town bar, which sometimes hosts live bands.

DON'T MISS

TRACES OF ANCIENT MACEDON: VERGINA & PELLA

While significant sites associated with the ancient Macedonian dynasty are sprinkled across the Balkans and Mediterranean, Greece loudly boasts two of the greatest. Vergina (ver-yee-nah), 11km southeast of Veria, was the royal burial site and had the first capital (ancient Aigai). While nearer to Edessa, ancient Pella was Alexander the Great's birthplace.

Vergina is also where King Philip II was assassinated, at his daughter Cleopatra's wedding, in 336BC. This World Heritage–listed site is also called the Royal Tombs. Enter the major *tholos* (beehive-shaped tomb) to see the four individual tombs. Tomb I, 'Persephone's Tomb,' alludes to an intact mural depicting Hades' rape of Persephone. Tomb II, discovered in 1977, probably belonged to Philip II himself. It contained a gold larnax (ossuary) with bones; the 16-pointed star of the royal Macedonian family on the larnax lid and damage to the skull identical with descriptions of an injury Philip sustained, identified the king. Philip's larnax and that of his presumed concubine or wife, plus some exquisite gold-leaf diadems, are displayed. Tomb III was probably designated for Alexander IV, son of Alexander the Great. Tomb IV was looted in antiquity.

About 400m past the Royal Tombs lie extensive **palace ruins** of 3rd-century-BC King Antigonos Gonatas. Its large Doric peristyle is surrounded by pebble-mosaic floors, the most beautiful with geometric floral design.

Pella became famous when King Archelaos (r 413–399 BC) made it the capital, though Aigai remained the royal cemetery. Its phenomenanal mosaics, created with naturally coloured, subtly contrasting stones, depict mythological scenes. The ruins of the ancient structures remain in situ or in the museum. Six re-erected columns and a courtyard decorated with a black-and-white geometric mosaic are on the northern side.

On the southern side, the **museum** has one room with ancient house wall reconstruction, and a circular table inlaid with intricate floral and abstract designs, plus a second with more mosaics.

Thessaloniki buses serve Pella (€2.90, 40 minutes, every 45 minutes) between 6am and 10pm. To visit both sites in one day, first see Pella, then take a Thessaloniki-bound bus to Halkidona, and a Vergina bus from there.

Fournos
BAR

(☑ 23310 29829; Ellis 14; ⊙ 10am-2am) One of several cafes clustered along Ellis, studenty Fournos has expansive indoor seating and a few curbside tables.

Vatrahos
CAFE

(☑ 23310 20282; Karakosti 13) You can smell the rich coffee brewing at this little place near the new church, tucked neatly into the buildings. By night it's a bar, with an intriguing foreign-beer selection.

ℹ Information

ATM-equipped banks line Venizelou and Mitropoleos.

Police (☑ 23310 22391; Mitropoleos)
Post Office (Dionysiou Solomou 4)

ℹ Getting There & Away

BUS

Veria's two central adjoining stations serve Thessaloniki (€6.80, one hour, half-hourly), Athens (€35, 6½ hours, three daily), Edessa (€4.70, one hour, four daily) and Vergina (€1.60, 20 minutes, eight daily).

Another station, 2km west of town in a small restaurant/shop at Pieron 155, serves Kastoria (€12, two hours, six daily), Ioannina (€27.10, five daily), Igoumenitsa (€26.60, two daily), Preveza (€29.30, two daily) and in summer Kerkyra/Corfu (€30.20, one daily).

TRAIN

The **train station** (☑ 23310 24444), north of town, has trains for both Thessaloniki and Florina.

ℹ Getting Around

Veria is walkable and has **taxis** (☑ 23310 63394).

Edessa
Εδεσσα

POP 18,229

Verdant Edessa (*edh*-eh-sah) is best known for its great waterfalls that keep the air moist and refreshing. Its attractive (though dilapidated) old quarter, little streams, shaded parks and a Byzantine bridge are other sights in this town, perched on a ledge overlooking a long agricultural plain.

Until the 1977 discovery of Vergina's royal tombs, Edessa was thought to have been ancient Macedonian Aigai. With the government's Hellenisation project following the 1923 Greek–Turkish population exchanges, the town's long-existing Slavic name, Voden ('place of water'), was replaced with the archaic Edessa.

◉ Sights

Edessa's **waterfalls** emerge east of its expansive park. The biggest thunders dramatically down a cliff, filling the air with moisture. Enter the **observation deck** inside this waterfall and breathe in the mist from the crashing waters. Also enter the small nearby **cave**, inside the cliff mass.

A winding path downwards accesses a second, less impressive waterfall. Further right, the **Water Museum** (adult €2; ⏱11am-4pm Wed-Mon) exhibits various water-industry equipment and a small **aquarium**, with various species of fish, amphibians, snapping turtles and snakes.

Varosi, Edessa's old quarter, is further south, between the ridge and centre. It features cobbled streets, chapels, traditional houses and a colourful **Folkloric Museum** (adult €2; ⏱10am-5pm Tue-Sun). Opposite the waterfalls through the park is Edessa's pretty **Byzantine bridge**, once on the ancient Via Egnatia.

🛏 Sleeping

★ Varosi Four Seasons   BOUTIQUE HOTEL $$
(☎23810 51440; www.varosi4seasons.gr; Arhiereos Meletiou; s/d incl breakfast €70/90; 🅿❄🤖) This boutique hotel is 50m from the related pension, Varosi. Six of the 10 rooms overlook the outstretched Edessa plain (as does the outdoor verandah cafe). Rooms are pristine and sumptuously decorated, and service is friendly. The wood-and-glass floor reveals part of Edessa's ancient walls.

Varosi   PENSION $$
(☎23810 21865; www.varosi.gr; Arhiereos Meletiou 45-47; s/d incl breakfast €55/70; 🅿❄🤖) This atmospheric pension in the eponymous old quarter occupies a restored traditional Macedonian wood-and-stone house. Rooms have double-wood doors, fine linen, colourful embroidery and antique brass beds. In winter a fireplace heats the lounge rooms, while the flower-filled balcony is nice for a relaxing coffee in summer.

Hagiati   PENSION $
(☎23810 51500; www.hagiati.gr; Makedonomahon 40; s/d incl breakfast €50/60; 🅿❄🤖) The first guesthouse visible on entering the Varosi quarter, the colourful Hagiati features a lovely open courtyard and peaceful setting. It operates year-round.

🍴 Eating

★ Tsipouradiko Ousies   GREEK $
(☎23815 02414; 25th Martiou 4; mains €5-8; ⏱12pm-1am) A hit since opening in 2012, Ousies serves mezedhes such as dolmadhes and fish to mains such as the house chicken, wrapped in bacon and stuffed with yellow cheese and peppers. It's all accompanied by fiery *tsipouro*, the best being from the local grape varietal, *opsimo*. The rustic decor, including historic photos and hanging instruments, is enhanced by wistful *rembetika* music.

Raeti   TAVERNA $
(☎23810 28769; 18 Oktovriou 20; mezedhes €3-5, mains €5.50-8) Try the well-prepared mezedhes and filling meat dishes here.

Katarraktes Edessas   TAVERNA $
(☎23810 27810; Kapetan Gareti-Perdika 1; mains €5-9) Publicly owned Katarraktes Edessas, before the falls, has standard but dependable fare.

ℹ Information

ATM-equipped banks line Dimokratias.
Police (☎23810 23333; Iroön Polytehniou)
Post Office (Dimokratias 26)
Tourist Information Office (☎23810 23101; www.edessacity.gr; ⏱10am-8pm) Kiosk before the waterfalls; provides maps of Edessa and nearby attractions.

ℹ Getting There & Around

From **Edessa Bus Station** (KTEL Pellas; ☎23810 23511; www.ktelpellas.gr; Pavlou Mela 13) buses serve Thessaloniki (€12, two hours, hourly), Veria (€4.70, one hour, five daily) and Athens (€45.60, eight hours, three daily). The bus to Florina (€8.10, 1½ hours, three daily) departs from 30m away.

The **train station** (☎23810 23510; Leoforos Nikis) is on the Thessaloniki–Athens line and also serves Florina.

Florina   Φλώρινα

POP 16,771

Nestled between mountains in a verdant valley, Florina (*flo*-rih-nah) is famous for its sweet red peppers. It's a small student town, with buzzing cafes on its central pedestrian street. In the evening, the small river is good for a leisurely stroll.

Florina accesses the Prespa Lakes to the west and is 40km south of lively Bitola in the Former Yugoslav Republic of Macedonia (FYROM). On the Prespa road (15km west of Florina) is the small Vigla ski resort.

Florina was the northernmost town occupied and annexed by Greek troops during the Balkan Wars of 1912–13; being just south of the mountains kept it near the front in subsequent wars. The existence of Greece's (Slavic) Macedonian minority, denied outright by the government and Greece's latter-day fascists, has always been sensitive in the Florina, Edessa and Prespa regions, where the Macedonian language is spoken by the Greek population. Heavy, though subtle, pressure from Greek society, media and government has suppressed it, but if you have sharp ears, you'll still hear Macedonian spoken, though mostly by older people.

⊙ Sights

Archaeological Museum   MUSEUM
(✆23850 28206; Sidirodromikou Stathmou 3; €2; ⊙8.30am-3pm Tue-Sun) Near the train station, this museum contains ancient finds, including objects from the Hellenistic City site on Agios Panteleimonos hill.

Museum of Modern Art   MUSEUM
(✆23850 29444; Leof Eleftherias 103; ⊙6-8pm Tue-Sat, 10am-1pm Sun) FREE Straddling both riverbanks, Old Florina contains attractive Turkish houses and neoclassical mansions; a restored one hosts this museum of contemporary Greek art. Walk down 25 Martiou, cross the bridge and turn right; the museum is 200m further.

Folk Museum   MUSEUM
(Karavitou 2; ⊙6-8pm Mon, Wed & Sat) FREE Near the courthouse, the Folk Museum has unique photographs and folk costumes.

⌔ Sleeping

★**Hotel Lingos Tottis**   HOTEL $
(✆23850 28322; www.hotel-lingos.gr; Tagmatarhou Naoum 1; s/d incl breakfast €40/50; P❋ 🖥) Steep price cuts have made this Best Western-owned business hotel Florina's best option, considering its ideal location just north of Plateia Georgiou Modi and by the pedestrian strip. It offers sharp rooms, a roof garden and helpful staff.

Pleiades   BOUTIQUE HOTEL $$
(✆23850 44070; www.pleiadesflorina.gr; Papathanasiou; s/d/tr €80/90/100; P❋ 🖥) This self-enclosed stone village of cottages and suites fuses traditional Macedonian architecture with modern amenities including a spa and indoor and outdoor pools (and an outdoor skating rink in winter). It's 2km north of town.

Hotel Hellinis   HOTEL $
(✆23850 22671; www.hotel-hellinis.gr; Pavlou Mela 31; s/d €35/40; 🖥) This central budget option is dated but has clean, modern rooms and friendly staff. It's two minutes west of the train station and a three-minute walk from the bus station.

Hotel Veltsi   HOTEL $
(✆23850 46555; www.hotel-veltsi.gr; Km 6 Florina-Prespes Rd; s/d €30/40; P❋ 🖥 ♨) This new hotel 6km west of town has stylish, well-furnished rooms and an outdoor pool. It's also good in winter (Mt Vigla ski resort is 15km farther).

✖ Eating & Drinking

★**Psarotaverna O Giorgos**   SEAFOOD $
(✆23850 23622; Grevenon 16; fish €5-9; ⊙8pm-1am Mon-Sat, 12pm-6pm Sun) Up in the backstreets, Georgios Hasos has long maintained Florina's only fish restaurant. Try the Aegean or freshwater fish (grilled trout only €6) accompanied by a local sparkling lemonade, along with vintage '50s Greek music. Open after 9pm in summer.

Mezedopoleon Koukoutsi   GREEK $
(✆23850 46010; Stoa Spyraki 6; mezedhes €3-6; ⊙11am-1am) Opened in 2012 on a west-end shopping alley above the river, Koukoutsi serves refreshing mezedhes and is good for vegetarians; try the seasonal wild greens, grilled mushrooms and famous Florina sweet red peppers with garlic and tomato. There are also some light meats, such as *keftedakia* (meatballs) and sausages.

Prespa   TAVERNA $
(✆23850 23973; Tyrnovou 12; mains €5-8; ⊙dinner) This simple, central taverna has good grills.

GREECE'S FORGOTTEN WATERWAYS: THE PRESPA LAKES

West of Florina, the twin **Prespa Lakes** (collectively called Prespes by Greeks) are rich in nature, history and sheer tranquility. Although it takes some effort to get there, a sojourn along the lakes is revitalising and educational.

Megali Prespa and **Mikri Prespa** (Great Prespa and Small Prespa) are separated by a narrow strip of land. Greece shares the former with the Former Yugoslav Republic of Macedonia (FYROM) to the north and Albania to the west, and the latter with Albania. Nevertheless, on all shores the inhabitants are ethnically (Slavic) Macedonian, which has meant occasional political friction in all three countries. To compound things, the Greek bus system keeps locals isolated: there's only one bus from Florina to Prespes, on Wednesdays at 7am. Alternatively, drive or take an expensive taxi from Florina (€60 to €80).

A tectonic lake at least one million years old, Megali Prespa is among Europe's oldest, feeding the equally old (but much larger) Lake Ohrid to the northwest through underground springs. On the Greek side, much of the shoreline is precipitous rock, rising dramatically from the chilly blue water.

Polished **Agios Germanos**, filled with wonderful stone houses and Byzantine sites, is Prespes' main town and, though inland, offers the most atmospheric accommodation. There's also good eating and hill trails. Here see **Agios Athanasios** and 11th-century **Agios Germanos**, two extraordinary works of ecclesiastic mid-Byzantine architecture. The latter is a cosy, domed brick structure with vivid frescoes.

Out on Lake Megali Prespa's promontory, **Psarades** is a gusty, slightly disoriented village of old stone houses, populated by friendly, mostly elderly Macedonians; as with the inscription on the local 1893 **Church of Kimisis Theotokou**, many of them call the village by its original Macedonian-language name, Nivitsi (a kind of small local fish). Colourful caïques line Psarades' lakefront, where unique, endemic miniature cows spar in the grass. The upper streets are totally authentic, filled with stone houses, jutting wood beams and drying blankets. You'll hear the Macedonian language spoken widely here.

Village fishermen offer **boat trips** to Megali Prespa's isolated Byzantine *askitiria* (hermitages). These include the 13th-century **Metamorfosi**, where scant remnants survive of paintings and two sections from a wood-carved *temblon* (votive screen), the 15th-century **Mikri Analipsi** and the equally old rock **Church of Panagia Eleousa**, tucked above a ravine and boasting beautiful frescoes. Climb the stairs for great lake views. More religious rock paintings visible opposite Psarades include **Panagia Vlahernitisa** (1455–56) and **Panagia Dexiokratousa** (1373).

Prespa's main attraction, however, is on the reedy smaller lake: the semidetached **island of Agios Ahillios**. The grand, concave outer wall of the ruined **Basilica of Agios Ahillios** stands on its eastern shore, with some half-toppled walls, columns and a stone floor. It's a legacy of the 10th-century Bulgarian Tsar Samuel, who expanded his empire across much of the southern Balkans, chronically sparring with Byzantium.

The island's name derives from the church, which itself references Samuel's invasion of Thessaly; while conquering Larissa in 983, he 'borrowed' the sacred relics of 4th-century Saint Ahillios, an avid opponent of heretics who had miraculously coaxed oil to ooze from a rock to make his theological point. To celebrate his conquest, Samuel dedicated the new church to the abducted saint.

To get here from Agios Germanos, cross the connecting strip between the two lakes and turn immediately left; from Psarades, just keep going straight south instead of turning onto the interlake strip. After parking, walk across a 1km-long floating pontoon bridge. Off the bridge, the signposted path going slightly left hugs the east coast and leads to the basilica and other church ruins. Alternatively, turn right off the bridge for the shop and restaurant.

Agios Ahillios is sparsely inhabited, though August's **Prespes Festival** features a headlining concert in the amphitheatre-like basilica – magically transformed into a stage, with audiences of up to 5000-strong watching from the hill above, sometimes clutching candles.

Taverna Petrino
TAVERNA $

(📞 23850 22560; Pavlou Mela 2; mains €5-8; ⏲ 10am-11pm) If you're waiting for a train, this big taverna on the crossroads above the station has standard Greek fare.

Olympion Café
CAFE

(cnr Pavlou Mela & Papathanasiou; ⏲ 9am-2am) Halfway up pedestrianised Pavlou Mela, this student cafe offers 10% off drinks on Tuesdays.

Art Café
CAFE

(📞 23850 26535; Pavlou Mela 106; ⏲ 9am-2am) Outdoors on Pavlou Mela's western end, this has colourful retro couches.

ℹ Information

ATM-equipped banks are near the square, on Stefan Dragoumi.

InFlorina (📞 23850 44144; www.inflorina.gr; Plateia Giorgiou Modi 13) Private agency with local tourism information.

Police (📞 23850 22222; Sangariou 24) Around 500m west of Plateia Giorgiou Modi.

Post Office (Kalergi 22) Left of Stefanou Dragoumi when approaching the bus station.

ℹ Getting There & Away

BUS
Domestic

Florina Bus Station (KTEL Florinas; 📞 23850 22430; www.ktelflorinas.gr; Makedonomahon 10) serves Athens (€50.50, nine hours, two daily) and Thessaloniki (€14, 2¾ hours, eight daily). Four serve Thessaloniki direct via the Egnatia Odos; the other (slightly slower) four go meso Edessas (through Edessa).

For Prespa, buses now leave only on Wednesdays at 7am, returning at 2pm, to Agios Germanos; continue by taxi to Psarades. For Kastoria, go to Amyntaio (€3.70, 30 minutes, eight daily) and change buses there. Amyntaio has three daily buses for Kastoria. Twice-weekly Florina buses also reach Ioannina (€30).

International

During the school year, two daily buses go near the FYROM border, for Niki; otherwise, it's only on Wednesdays (€1.80, 30 minutes). The Greece–Albania border crossing at Krystallopigi (€5.40, one hour) is served once-weekly.

TAXI

A taxi to Bitola (40km) in the FYROM costs €45 one-way or €60 return (including two hours for shopping and sightseeing). Florina cabbies also drive to the Prespa Lakes villages; Agios Germanos is €60, Psarades €80.

TRAIN

Florina's **train station** (📞 23850 22404) connects with Edessa and Thessaloniki.

Kastoria
Καστοριά

POP 16,958

Sprawled out along a forested promontory in **Lake Orestiada**, Kastoria (kah-stor-*yah*) is among Greece's more inscrutable towns. Its compact centre sprawls north to south across a narrow but hilly strip, which widens out eastward into the old quarter, Doltso, and then spreads further east into an unpopulated wooded stretch above the lake – from above, the whole enterprise looks like a giant, bludgeoned manta ray.

Historically, the fur trade made Kastoria rich, as evidenced by the stately 17th- and 18th-century *arhontika* (mansions) of erstwhile fur barons in Doltso. While today the fur may be imported, the craftsmanship tradition continues. Kastoria's former glory is also attested by more than 50 lavishly decorated Byzantine and post-Byzantine churches (most are closed).

Kastoria has been considered salubrious since Byzantine times, when its remarkable lack of humidity attracted tuberculosis patients. Most recently, Kastoria made Greeks proud when the women's and men's rowing teams took silver and bronze medals, respectively, in London's 2012 Olympics – some Kastorians were on these teams, which train on the lake. You can stroll or cycle around it (9km total) – if you're lucky, you might spot a reclusive otter, in the more remote stretches.

⊙ Sights & Activities

Taxiarhia of the Metropolis
CHURCH

(Plateia Pavlou Mela) South of Plateia Omonias, note the 13th-century **fresco of the Madonna and Child** above this church's entrance. It contains the sacrosanct **tomb of Pavlos Melas**, leader of the 1904–08 'Macedonian Struggle' against the Ottomans.

Byzantine Museum
MUSEUM

(📞 24670 26781; Plateia Dexamenis; ⏲ 8.30am-3pm Tue-Sun) FREE This museum houses outstanding local icons.

Arhontika
HISTORIC BUILDINGS

(Doltso) Doltso's *arhontika* include the **Emmanouil, Basara, Natzi, Skoutari, Papia** and **Papaterpou**, mansions all named after their former resident families.

Kastorian Museum of Folklore
MUSEUM

(✔ 24670 28603; Kapetan Lazou; adult/child €2/ free; ⊗ 8.30am-2pm Tue-Sun) In the Nerantzis Aïvazis family's former 530-year-old mansion, the museum displays ornaments, utensils and tools.

O Podilatis
CYCLING

(✔ 24670 23834; www.yellowbike.gr; Megas Alexandrou 119; ⊗ 9am-8pm) This southern waterfront shop rents mountain bikes, regular bicycles and tandem fun bikes. The English- and Italian-speaking staff can explain local routes and arrange guided mountain biking trips. Bike prices are €3 for first hour, or €8 for full-day rental.

Festivals & Events

Ragkountsaria Festival
DANCE, CULTURE

(⊗ 6-10 Jan) This winter festival (with likely pagan roots), features traditional dancing, costumed merrymaking and much eating and drinking.

Nestorio River Festival
MUSIC, ARTS

(www.riverparty.gr; ⊗ Jul) This popular six-day party each July features Greek singers and DJs. Around 10,000 youngsters camp along the river. Distractions include paintball, archery, sports and art. The website has info on performances, camping accommodation and ticket vendors; in Thessaloniki, try **Ticket House** (✔ 2310 253 630; cnr Ethnikis Amynis & Tsimiski). KTEL Kastoria runs special festival buses to Nestorio.

Sleeping

★ Dhiston
APARTMENTS $$

(✔ 24670 22250; Leof Megalou Alexandrou 91; s/d/tr €50/60/75) Some of these spacious suites have lake views. The French- and English-speaking manager provides local information. From the bus station it's a five-minute walk, above a waterfront cafe.

Esperos Palace Hotel
SPA HOTEL $$

(✔ 24670 24670; www.esperospalacekastoria.gr; Fountoukli; s/d/tr from €60/80/100; ❄ 🛜 🏊) If you don't mind a short drive to the quiet northwestern coast, the Esperos represents phenomenal value: spacious, gleaming rooms, spa centre with pool and *hammam*, fine dining, bars, hairdressers and more.

Arhondiko tou Vergoula
B&B $$

(✔ 24670 23415; www.vergoulas.gr; Aidistras 14; s/d/tr incl breakfast €55/75/100; 🛜) This restored 150-year-old Doltso mansion has lake views and evocative traditional rooms, plus a cosy breakfast/dinner salon.

Katerina Suites
SUITES $$

(✔ 24670 24645; www.katerina-suites.gr; Leof Megalou Alexandrou 127; s/d €70/80) A 20-minute walk from the bus station eastward on the waterfront, these spacious, modern suites with lake views can accommodate five people each.

Eating & Drinking

Kratergo
TAVERNA $

(✔ 24670 22981; Orestion 19, Psaradika; mains €6-9; ⊗ 8pm-2am) This north-side lakefront taverna is worth the 20-minute drive. Featuring well-prepared Greek specialities, it has impressive stone arches, ambient lighting, lake views and wistful *rembetika*.

★ Grada
BISTRO $$

(✔ 24670 29615; www.grada-bistro.gr; Oresteion 37; mains €8-17; ⊗ 1-5pm & 8pm-12am Tue-Sun) This trendy, northwest waterfront bistro has style, with bright decor, cool jazz, 1950s-style diner seats and some of Macedonia's most inventive cuisine. Try the risotto with strawberries and dark chocolate, or bon filet with wild mushrooms. Salads and pastas are excellent too. Note the odd opening hours.

Ta Kymata Psaradika
FISH TAVERNA $$

(✔ 24670 28887; Psaradika; fish €9-13; ⊗ 9am-12am) Since 1953, this colourful taverna on the north-side lakefront has been serving excellent Aegean and freshwater fish. Try grilled river trout or *barbounia* (red mullet), and sample creative appetisers such as *mydopilafi* (mussels with rice) or *tsirosalata* (smoked mackerel). Local lake fish (120kg catfish, anyone?) are available, except during May's temporary fishing suspension.

Doltso
TAVERNA $$

(✔ 24670 24670; Plateia Doltso; mains €9-13) Near the eponymous square, this restored *arhontika* taverna has excellent local dishes and more than 70 wines. Try the *berdama* (aubergine baked with tomato, bacon and pepper, all topped with melted cheese). Meat portions are generous. Wild boar (€13) is available November through March.

★ Vatrahos
BAR

(✔ 24675 03375; Thomaidos 11; ⊗ 11am-late) This unpretentious north-waterfront bar behind gauze curtains is popular with locals and foreigners. Good for coffee by day, it gets lively at night and plays more varied music than most Kastoria bars.

Zaza
BAR

(☑ 24670 24016; Megas Alexandrou 61; ⊘ 10am-3am) Amidst the south coast's cafe row, Zaza is as weirdly shaped as Kastoria itself, with curvy bars, a deep interior and twinkling lights. It has good cocktails and is packed on weekends.

A Rock Tale
BAR

(Tsoutou Barda 6; ⊘ 9am-late) On a hilly central street halfway between the north and south coasts, this almost-dive bar is reserved for Kastoria's ageing rockers. Live bands sometimes perform (September through March).

Lago Cafe Tip Bar
BAR

(Megas Alexandrou 53; ⊘ 10am-late) This trendy southern-waterfront bar is sleek and club-like, with unusual decor such as bicycles, skeletons and Uncle Sam in mural. Its owners also run the **Nautical Hall**, a summer-only outdoor club on the northeastern coast, near the rowing club.

ⓘ Information

Municipal Tourist Office (☑ 24670 26777; www.kastoria.gr; ⊘ 8am-3pm Mon-Fri) Brochures, maps and information; in the lakeside park.

Police Station (☑ 24670 83214; Grammou) Near the bus station.

Post Office (Leof Megalou Alexandrou)

ⓘ Getting There & Away

Kastoria's **Aristotelis airport** (☑ 24670 42515) is 10km south. **Sky Express** (www.skyexpress. gr) serves Athens (€79.10, two weekly).

Kastoria Bus Station (KTEL Kastorias; ☑ 24670 83455; www.ktel-kastorias.gr; Athanasiou Diakou) is on the southern waterfront, near the roundabout and centre. Buses serve Thessaloniki (€17.60, 2½ hours, six daily), Ioannina (€19.60, 3½ hours, four weekly), Athens (€48.50, nine hours, two daily) and Veria (€12, two hours, two daily). For Florina (€3.80, 30 minutes, eight daily), take the Amyntaio bus and another from there.

Taxis (☑ 24670 82100) are available.

THRACE
ΘΡΑΚΗ

Diverse, dusty and still somewhat mysterious, Thrace (thr-*aaa*-kih) is among Greece's most striking but least-visited areas. Once home to a powerful, non-Greek ancient Thracian civilisation, the region has been dramatically affected by other neighbouring peoples; geographically, it's shared with Bulgaria and Turkey.

Thrace's agricultural traditions are attested today by tobacco crops, rolling wheat fields and vivid plains of sunflowers. Its unique Muslim minorities have roots in Ottoman times, and pockets of Thrace are indeed dotted with mosques, Turkish-style houses, and traditional sweet shops – among Greece's best.

Other Thracian attractions include unique expanses of wilderness. In the north, the rolling Rhodopi Mountains demarcate the Bulgarian border, and contain pristine forests and animal life; Thrace's eastern reaches, nearer to Turkey, host significant migratory bird populations at the Dadia Forest Reserve and the Evros Delta on the Aegean. The largest town, Alexandroupoli, is also the jumping-off point for ferries to Samothraki.

History

The ancient Thracians spoke a now-lost language. Greek-language sources, myth and supposition depict them as warlike sorts, devoted to mystery religions like the Great Gods cult, which influenced Greek pagan religion too. At the Thracians' supreme temple on Samothraki island, ancient Macedonian, Roman and Egyptian rulers were initiated. Secret rituals were associated with Orpheus, the mythical, tragic Thracian father of music.

During the 7th century BC, powerful Greek city-states vied with the Persians for Thrace's coast. Athens prevailed at the Battle of Plataea, though Philip II of Macedon took over in 346 BC. Later, with the Roman Empire's 395 AD division, Thrace's strategic positioning on the Via Egnatia trade route made it important. Eastern Thrace's significant wheat production also gave it the nickname 'the breadbasket of Constantinople'.

Constantinople's defensive zone was the Thracian plain, though its flatness made it vulnerable to marauding Goths, Huns, Vandals, Bulgars, Pechenegs, Cumans and poorly behaved Latin Crusaders – relatively few historic structures thus remain predating the Ottomans' 14th-century invasion.

In the 19th century, Thrace's turbulent past reawakened. The 1877 Russo–Turkish War, the 1912–13 Balkan Wars, WWI and finally Greece's failed 1922 invasion of Anatolia saw

Thrace

the territory change hands frequently. A mess of treaties and tragedies resulted in its final tripartite division.

Along with the Greeks of Constantinople/İstanbul and Imvros (Gökçeada) and Tenedos (Bozcaada) islands, the Turks of Greek Thrace were exempt during the 1923 population exchanges. But while İstanbul's Greek population was largely expelled after a 1955 pogrom, the Turks of Greek Thrace remain.

Xanthi   Ξάνθη

POP 63,083

Atmospheric Xanthi is famous for its old quarter, where traditional Ottoman houses cluster on steep, winding streets. Once wealthy from tobacco, Xanthi boasts refined 'tobacco baron' mansions. Indeed, the weed (and other agriculture) still sustains what is now a university town with ever-improving restaurants and bars.

To the south, the ports of Keramoti and Kavala have ferries to Thasos and other islands. North, the rippling Rhodopi Mountains offer forest hikes and thermal baths, while the western Nestos River has kayaking and birdwatching opportunities.

◉ Sights

Old Xanthi   HISTORIC AREA
On a serene hillside above town, Old Xanthi features pastel-coloured, timber-framed **houses** on narrow, winding lanes, and grand neoclassical **mansions** once inhabited by tobacco barons. The somewhat forlorn, faded grandeur has been enlivened by a vibrant nightlife scene (on Orfeas).

Folk Museum   MUSEUM
(☏ 25410 25421; Antika 5-7; ⊗ 8.30am-2.30pm Wed-Fri, 10.30am-3pm Sat & Sun) **FREE** Occupying the adjacent mansions of the Kougioumtzoglu brothers (erstwhile tobacco millionaires), this museum has original ceilings, wall paintings and folk items.

Open Market   MARKET
(⊗ Sat) Xanthi's Saturday market, east of Plateia Dimokratias, sells clothes, jewellery, fruit and vegetables.

✷ Festivals & Events

Winter Carnival   MUSIC, CULTURE
(www.carnivalx.gr) This nationally famous pre-Lenten celebration features colourful floats accompanied by music and masked merrymaking.

Xanthi Old Town
Festival   PERFORMING ARTS, MUSIC
(⊗ late Aug–early Sep) Festival features theatre, music and art exhibits.

🛏 Sleeping

Hotel Paris   HOTEL $
(☏ 25410 20531; www.parishotel.gr; Dimokritou 12; s/d €35/45; ❄ @) Near the bus station, Paris has good firm beds and some large balconies. However, there's street noise and the centre's a 15-minute uphill walk.

Hotel Xanthippion   HOTEL $
(☏ 25410 77061; 28 Oktovriou 212; s/d/tr €50/60/70; ❄ ☎) Some 500m south of Plateia Dimokratias, Xanthippion has well-kept, clean budget rooms near the old town. It's also 500m from the train station.

Hotel Dimokritos   HOTEL $
(☏ 25410 25111; www.hoteldimokritos.gr; 28 Oktovriou 41; s/d €40/55; ❄ @) About 100m south of Plateia Dimokratias, Dimokritos has clean, but smallish rooms.

★ Hotel Elisso   BOUTIQUE HOTEL $$$
(☏ 25410 84400; www.hotelelisso.gr; Vas Sofias 9; s/d/ste €80/120/160; ❄ @ ☎) This chic old-town boutique hotel has double rooms (and two suites), some equipped for people with a disability. Decor is minimalist yet bright and cheerful, characterised by geometric patternwork and big comfy beds.

🍴 Eating & Drinking

★ Ermis   MEZEDHES $
(Orfeas 37-39; mezedhes €2-5; ⊗ 10am-3am) This friendly bar in a restored old-town mansion has a fun vibe, old *avli* (back courtyard) with secluded tables and colourful upstairs for winter. The owners, friendly siblings Theodota and Georgios, serve homemade Greeks-meets-international mezedhes; there's no menu, but it's all healthy (Theodota's a professional nutritionist). Both the food and admirably varied drinks are astonishingly inexpensive.

Taverna To Perasma   TAVERNA $
(☏ 25410 78014; Ikoniou 16; mezedhes €2.50-4, mains €5-9) On a side street near the bus station, To Perasma serves huge portions. Try the *roka* (rocket) salad with tomato and cucumber, *melitzanes* 'special' (oven-cooked aubergines with cheese), *sykoti krasato* (liver with wine) and *yiaourtlou* kebab (spicy

beef kebabs with yoghurt on fried pitta with salsa); it'll cost about €20 and feed four.

Restaurant Palia Poli TAVERNA $
(☑ 25410 68685; Hasirtzoglou 7; mains €7-9) More inventive than other old-town places, this wood-and-brick taverna offers quail, roast pork with plum sauce and orange duck.

Embargo CAFE, BAR
(Vasilissis Sofias 5; ◎ 9am-3am) Above a sturdy stone embankment near the old town, Embargo has pretty people, outdoor seating and a neat circular interior.

Café Antica CAFE
(☑ 25410 62193; Vasileos Konstantinou 86; ◎ 9am-2am) This two-level, central cafe has long wooden rafters, soft couches and wall-bound antique implements. Try wine in summer, or a tasty hot chocolate in winter.

ℹ Information

The bus station is 800m southeast of the square (Plateia Dimokratias), and the train station 2km south of it. Dimokritou (later Karaoli) leads to Plateia Dimokratias from the bus station, as does 28 Oktovriou from the train station.

ATM-equipped banks, restaurants and shops line Plateia Dimokratias and Plateia Antiko.

Police Station (☑ 25410 23333; cnr Nestou & Lykourgou Thrakis)

Post Office (A Georgiou 16)

ℹ Getting There & Away

AIR

Xanthi shares **Alexander the Great Airport** (40km southwest, near Hrysoupoli) with coastal Kavala.

BUS

Xanthi Bus Station (KTEL Xanthis; ☑ 25410 27200; www.ktelxanthis.gr; Dimokritou 6) serves Komotini (€5, one hour, 14 daily), Thessaloniki (€19, 2½ hours, 10 daily) and Athens (€61, nine hours, one daily). Thessaloniki buses go via Kavala (€6, one hour). For Alexandroupoli (€8, one hour, every 45 minutes), change at Komotini. Buses also serve Pomakohoria villages (€3.80, 1½ hours, two daily) and Stavroupoli to the west.

For Bulgaria, buses leave daily at 9.30am and 5.30pm, for Svilengrad, Harmanli, Haskovo and Plovdiv (Philippopouli in Greek).

TRAIN

Xanthi's **train station** (☑ 25410 22581; Terma Kondyli) connects Alexandroupoli and Komotini with Thessaloniki twice daily.

ℹ Getting Around

Only **taxis** (€35) serve the airport. Alternatively, Kavala-bound buses serve Hrysoupoli (from there, take a taxi 12km to the airport).

Around Xanthi

North of Xanthi, the fascinating **Pomakohoria** (Pomak villages) lies tucked into the forested Rhodopi Mountains, near Bulgaria. These 25-or-so villages are inhabited by Muslims speaking Greek, Bulgarian and Turkish. Spread across the borders, their ethnic identity is a subject of some uncertainty (even to themselves). In Greece, they are officially classified as 'Greek Muslims'. During the Cold War, this border area was off-limits, and tourists are still rare.

Along with unspoiled nature, some Pomak villages offer activities, such as the **hot mineral baths** of **Thermes**, 43km north of Xanthi. The main bath, in a building opposite the church, costs money; the outdoor bath (100m to the right-hand side of the village shop, and below the entry road) is free. The baths are relaxing and therapeutic, so enjoy, but don't forget that this is a conservative area and the baths are no place for debauchery, shouting or gleeful nudity.

Enjoy rustic country salad and spit-roasted goat or lamb at Thermes' shop-restaurant, **Kafe Psistaria O Kalemtzi** (Thermes village; lunches €7). Owner Kemal Kalemtzi, rents basic rooms at **Enoikiazomena Domatia Kalemtzi Kemal** (☑ 25540 22474, 6977597500; Thermes village; d €25) next door. His son Hassan speaks English.

Some 35km northwest of Xanthi, **Stavropouli** is relatively unvisited by foreigners, but is well-situated on the **Nestos River**. Not as cold as other northern rivers, but just as enchanting, the Nestos runs from the Rodhopi Mountains into an Aegean delta. Kayaking and rafting are organised by **Riverland Outdoor Activities** (☑ 25410 62488; www.riverland.gr; Toxotes village), based in **Toxotes** village, southwest of Xanthi. Riverland also offers horseback riding and Nestos delta birdwatching tours.

ℹ Getting There & Away

The Xanthi–Thermes bus (€3.80, 90 minutes) departs at 6.30am daily and returns at 3.30pm. A later bus runs at 2.10pm, meaning you must stay overnight in Thermes. Other buses serve Stavroupoli and Toxotes.

Komotini Κομοτηνή

POP 60,648

Komotini (ko-mo-tih-*nee*), 52km east of Xanthi, is the Rhodopi prefecture's capital. It's a backwater, but has several intriguing museums and historic buildings. It's enlivened by university students who fill the cafes on the square (Plateia Irinis). Roughly half the population of Komotini are Turkish, a higher percentage than any other major Greek town.

Attractions reflect Komotini's mixed heritage, with Byzantine churches, Ottoman mosques and neoclassical mansions. Its street markets, old quarter and Turkish sweets create an authentic Thracian feel.

◉ Sights

Byzantine Fortress   RUINS
Komotini's 4th-century-AD Byzantine Fortress was built by Emperor Theodosius, near today's Plateia Irinis. Remnants include one of 16 original towers.

Church of the Assumption of Mary   CHURCH
(Ekklisia Kimiseos Theotokou; ☑25310 22827; Eleftheriou Venizelou; ◔8am-7pm) Built in 1800 on a Byzantine shrine site, the church contains 16th-century icons and wood carvings.

Archaeological Museum   MUSEUM
(☑25310 22411; Simeonidi 4; ◔8.30am-5pm) FREE Significant archaeological finds, accompanied by English-language wall texts, detail ancient Thracian history. Also see the Roman coins, clay figurines, delicate gold wreaths and Byzantine glazed ceramics. A detailed map showing Thracian and eastern Macedonian sites is available.

Ecclesiastical Museum   MUSEUM
(Imaret; ☑25310 34177; Xenofontos 8; €3; ◔10.30am-1.30pm Tue-Sun, 5-8pm Wed-Fri) This museum occupies Komotini's early Ottoman almshouse (*ptohokomeio* in Greek), inside a courtyard. The structure's brickwork and design resemble a Byzantine church. Ottoman conqueror Gazi Ervinoz Bey built it around 1363. It exhibits post-Byzantine icons, 500-year-old printed gospels, silver ceremonial crosses, gold embroidery and 18th-century Hebrew scrolls.

Turkish Quarter   HISTORIC AREA
Just behind Plateia Irinis, Komotini's relaxing Turkish quarter has old houses, barber shops and teahouses. Sights include the 1884 Clock Tower (Orologio), Yeni Camii ('New Mosque' in Turkish) and Eski Camii ('Old Mosque' from 1608), still operational.

🛌 Sleeping

Orpheus Hotel   HOTEL $
(☑25310 23663; www.hotelorpheus.g; Parassiou 1; s/d/tr €40/50/60; ﹡) Well-positioned on the *plateia*, Orpheus has renovated soundproofed modern rooms.

Anatolia Hotel   HOTEL $$
(☑25310 36242; www.anatoliahotel.gr; Anchialou 56; s/d €50/70; ﹡🛜) The minimalist Anatolia combines comfy rooms with smooth decor. It's in northeastern Komotini, behind the sports hall.

Hotel Astoria   HOTEL $$
(☑25310 22707; www.astoriakomotini.gr; Plateia Irinis 28; d €60; ﹡@) Slightly concealed by the square's side cafes, Astoria has attractive rooms with small balconies overlooking the square.

✖ Eating & Drinking

Nedim   SWEETS $
(☑25310 22036; cnr Leof Orfeos & Syntagmatos Kriton; sweets €2-4) Nedim has been serving perhaps the best baklava this side of İstanbul since 1950. Try *saray kataïfi*, the Ottoman palace's preferred treat, and *samali*, an almond cake flavoured by Chios mastic. The monstrous, sausage-shaped *soutzouk loukoumi* is thick Turkish delight dusted with confectioner's sugar.

To Sokaki tis Lakokolas   TAVERNA $
(☑25310 81800; Parasiou 5; mains €5-7; ◔noon-midnight) In an underpass opposite Emboriki Bank, this lively taverna has simple, nourishing grills.

Klimis   SWEETS $
(☑25310 33177; Orfeos 8; ◔8am-11pm) While other sweet shops are better known, some locals swear by this unassuming little shop between the square and the mosque. The kindly owner offers *soutzouk loukoumi* and and myriad dried fruits and nuts.

Kouti   TAVERNA $
(☑25310 25774; Orfeos 45; mains €5-9) This slightly upscale central restaurant has Greek and international fare.

Petrino   OUZERIE $
(☑25310 73650; Serron 25; mains €7-9) Petrino features lovely rustic decor and great Thracian dishes to complement numerous ouzos.

El Clasico CAFE, BAR
(☑ 25310 70007; www.el-clasico.gr; Zoidi 52-54; ⊙ 7.30am-2am) Near the bus station, this new cafe has coffees, frozen yoghurts and drinks, plus light eats. The odd cavernous interior contrasts wood-and-brick walls with inlaid TVs, whiplashed by neon-green squiggly lines, all overlooked by ventilation grates and bisected by wrap-around couches. There's no real concept, but students like it.

Café Bel Air CAFE
(Plateia Irinis 55; ⊙ 10am-3am) Cafes and bars line Plateia Irinis; Bel Air gets the early-30s crowd.

Theatro CAFE
(Plateia Irinis) On the *plateia*, Theatro is a student fave.

ℹ Information

Hospital (☑ 25310 24601; Sismanoglou 45) 900m southeast of Plateia Irinis.

ℹ Getting There & Away

BUS
From **Komotini Bus Station** (KTEL Rodopis; ☑ 25310 22912; www.ktelrodopis.gr) buses serve Xanthi (€5.30, one hour, nine daily) and Alexandroupoli (€4.80, one hour, 14 daily). Buses also serve Thessaloniki (€25.30, 2½ hours, eight daily) and Athens (€63, 8¾ hours, one daily). The station offers free luggage storage; keys are in the *apothiki* (storeroom). It is a five-minute walk northeast up to Plateia Irinis and ATMs.

TRAIN
The **train station** (☑ 25310 22650) connects Orestiada and Alexandroupoli with Xanthi, Thessaloniki and Athens twice daily. It is 1km southwest of town on Panagi Tsaldari.

ℹ Getting Around

Komotini sprawls, but is walkable. There are **taxis** (☑ 25310 37777) and **Evros Car Rental** (☑ 25310 32905; evroscar@hol.gr; Tountzas 1) has cars (from €45) and jeeps (€60).

Alexandroupoli
Αλεξανδρούπολη

POP 61,702

Alexandroupoli (ah-lex-an-*dhroo*-po-lih) is eastern Thrace's largest and most appealing town. The axis of regional travel, this port serves visitors heading to or from Turkey, Bulgaria, and in summer, Samothraki island. Alexandroupoli has two marvellous museums, a pretty lighthouse, some good seafood restaurants and nightlife.

◉ Sights

Ethnological Museum of Thrace MUSEUM
(☑ 25510 36663; www.emthrace.com; 14 Maiou 63; adult/child €3/free; ⊙ 10am-2pm & 6-9pm Tue-Sat, 10am-2pm Sun) Housed in an 1899 mansion, this museum with backyard cafe exhibits traditional costumes, musical instruments, oil presses, a dye-room and sweets-making equipment. You'll learn how many silkworms are needed to make 25g of silk and which Greek sweet is made by slamming the ingredients against the wall.

Ecclesiastical Art Museum of Alexandroupoli MUSEUM
(☑ 25510 26359; Plateia Agiou Nikolaou; adult/child €3/free; ⊙ 9am-2pm Tue-Fri, 10am-2pm Sat) The museum contains priceless icons, many brought by refugees in 1923, plus early printed Greek books.

Cathedral of Agios Nikolaos CHURCH
(Plateia Agiou Nikolaou) This cathedral houses the miracle-working 13th-century **icon of the Panagia Trifotissa**, from Aenos (Enez in Turkish) across the Evros River. Villagers with eyes damaged by the reflected glare of the sun on the salt marshes around Aenos had their vision restored by praying before it.

Demirali & Agia Paraskevi Beaches BEACHES
Just 4km west of Alexandroupoli, sandy **Demirali Beach** is popular for swimming and has good eats. **Agia Paraskevi Beach**, 6km further west, is even better, with beach bars and clubs.

⌷ Sleeping

Hotel Erika HOTEL $
(☑ 25510 34115; www.hotel-erika.gr; Dimitriou Karaoli 110; s/d €40/50; ❄) Opposite the port, 100m from Alexandroupoli's lighthouse, Erika has tasteful, if dated rooms and waterfront views.

Camping Alexandroupoli CAMPGROUND $
(☑ 25510 28735; www.ditea.gr; Leof Makris 1; camp sites per adult/tent €7/5.50; ⊙ Apr-Oct; P ❄) This large, well-run campground has water sports and beach volleyball, plus basketball and tennis courts. It's 2km west (take local bus 7 from Plateia Eleftherias).

Astir Egnatia Alexandroupolis RESORT $$

(☑ 25510 38000; www.classicalhotels.com/astir-egnatia; Egnatia Park; s/d €90/150; P ❄ @ 🖤 🛋) Although it bills itself as 'the megaresort of the north', this 200-room Grecotel on the sea, just west of town, isn't completely opulent. The resort does have friendly staff, several pools, a fitness and massage centre, restaurants and babysitting services.

Apartment Hotel Athina HOTEL $

(☑ 25510 34492; Konstantinou Paleologou 53; s/d €50/60; ❄) Essentially a budget hotel, the central Athina offers clean and simple rooms, some with balconies. First child (under age four) stays free.

✗ Eating

Psarotaverna tis Kyra Dimitras SEAFOOD $

(☑ 25510 34434; cnr Kountourioti & Dikastirion; fish €6-13) Venerable old Kyra Dimitra is still overseeing this seafood restaurant, in the family since 1915. Choose from the daily catch, set out on ice; *tsipoura* (sea bream) is tasty and only €20 per kilo, and the mussels are good too.

Ai Giorgis TAVERNA $

(☑ 25510 71777; Demirali Beach; fish €7-12; ☉ 10am-1am) On Demirali Beach, Ai Giorgi has smooth wooden floors and candlelit tables. Everything is good, from varied salads and stuffed mushrooms to fish dishes.

I Love Gelato ICE CREAM $

(☑ 25510 24832; cnr Megas Alexandrou & Karaiskaki; gelato €2; ☉ 10am-midnight) An Italy-trained gelato-maker runs this ice-cream parlour, opposite the lighthouse.

To Nisiotiko SEAFOOD $$

(☑ 25510 20990; Zarifi 1; fish €8-16) This somewhat pricy west-side fish taverna has ambience, with light, eclectic decor and expertly prepared seafood.

🍷 Drinking

NOA BAR

(Naftikos Omilos Alexandroupoleos; ☑ 25510 53226; port; ☉ 9am-2am) On the central ferry pier, Alexandroupoli's 'yacht club' bar is a classy bar, and also does snacks and international fare.

Sparrow Vinoteca WINE BAR

(☑ 25510 23302; cnr Mesolongiou 1 and Megas Alexandros; ☉ 8am-3am) A nicely done rockin' new wine bar, Sparrow is on the waterfront, opposite the lighthouse.

Muziq Bar BAR

(☑ 25510 32438; Koleti 5) This fun bar-club in town specialises in funk, jazz and R&B.

🔒 Shopping

Myrsini HANDICRAFTS

(☑ 25510 31205; www.silkyhouse.gr; Plateia Polytehniou) Come for original Soufli silks, from table runners (€15 to €100) and ornate scarves (€20) to enormous silk spreads embellished with Byzantine double-headed eagles and floral motifs (€807).

ℹ Information

Leof Dimokratias has ATM-equipped banks.

Leon Tours (☑ 25510 27754; www.leontours.gr; 14 Maiou 51; ☉ 9am-3pm & 6-9.30pm Mon-Sat) Led by the helpful Maria Karakampatzaki, this central travel agency sells bus tickets to İstanbul and ferry tickets for Samothraki. They offer international tours, such as a combo trip to Cannakale and Ayvalik (in Turkey) and Lesvos island.

Kassapidis Exchange (☑ 25510 80910; Leof Dimokratias 209; ☉ 8am-9.30pm Mon-Sat, 10am-2pm Sun) Changes 87 currencies, including Balkan currencies, plus Western Union transfers.

ℹ Getting There & Away

AIR

Alexandroupoli's Dimokritos Airport is 7km east, near Loutra. **Aegean Airlines** (☑ 25510 89150; www.aegeanair.com; Dimokritos Airport), based at the airport, serves Athens. **Sky Express** (www.skyexpress.gr) serves Sitia in Crete. Charter flights from Russia operate in summer.

BOAT

Ferries serve Samothraki (€14.50, two hours) only. There is usually one daily boat, but schedules and times can change suddenly; always check locally, at the portside SAOS kiosk, or travel agencies such as Leon Tours (p280).

BUS
Domestic

From **Alexandroupoli Bus Station** (KTEL Evrou; ☑ 25510 26479; www.ktelevrou.gr; Eleftheriou Venizelou 36) frequent buses ply the northeastern line to Feres (€2.30, 30 minutes), Soufli (€6, 1½ hours), Didymotiho (€8.60, 1½ hours) and Orestiada (€10.60, two hours); some continue to Kastanies, for the border crossing with Turkey. Another bus terminates at Kipi, the main Turkish border crossing (€3.90, 35 minutes, five daily), east of Alexandroupoli.

Buses serve Athens (€63, 10 hours, one daily) and Thessaloniki (€29, 3¾ hours, nine daily).

For Kavala (€19, two hours, 14 daily), they go via Komotini (€6.30, 70 minutes) and Xanthi (€10.60, 1¾ hours).

International
The railway company's international bus and train services remain suspended. For İstanbul, a **bus** (€18 one-way, €33 return) that's run by Thessaloniki-based Crazy Holidays (p254) leaves twice daily from portside.

TRAIN
The **train station** (☑ 25510 26395) connects Alexandroupoli with Thessaloniki via Komotini and Xanthi twice daily.

ℹ Getting Around

Only the campground, beach resorts or further beaches require bus or taxi. For the airport, take a Loutra-bound bus from Plateia Eleftherias, or a **taxi** (☑ 25510 28358; €12). Some buses plying the Alexandroupoli–Orestiada route transit the airport.

Evros Delta   Δέλτα Εβρού

If you can tell your glossy ibis from your slender-billed curlew (apparently, one of the world's rarest birds), you'll love the **Evros Delta**. Just 20km southeast of Alexandroupoli, it's among Europe's most important **wetlands**, comprising 188 sq km of coastal lakes, lagoons, interior rivers, sand dunes, swamps and reed beds. This birdwatcher's paradise hosts 316 of Greece's 422 known bird species, and sundry fish, amphibians, reptiles and mammals. And hey, there's also the sheer thrill of snapping pictures in a heavily militarised border zone.

Consult the **Evros Delta visitor centre** (☑ tel/fax 25510 61000; www.evros-delta.gr; ☉ 8am-4pm), 14km east of Alexandroupoli. The delta's western segment is always open, though motorised transport is restricted along the southern littoral. The most fascinating eastern section, near Turkey, requires a police and army **permit**, arranged for free by the visitor's centre: just fax or email them 14 days ahead with your full name, date of birth, passport number and expiry date. The centre provides maps and conducts guided tours (€10 per person) and minibus and boat trips.

Alexandroupoli to Soufli
Αλεξανδρούπολη προς Σουφλί

Three roads run northwards from Alexandroupoli to Didymotiho and Orestiada. The westernmost, country route runs through unvisited Esymi, Megalo Derio and Mikro Derio; some 10km west of the latter is **Roussa**, and its 9th-century-BC **megalithic Thracian tombs**, decorated with mysterious rock carvings.

The middle route from Alexandroupoli is the faster, 'new' road heading straight north; the older, third road east of it accompanies the train line along the Evros River, by the Turkish border. The rolling hills here are punctuated by storks' nests on phone poles and great fields of wheat and sunflowers.

Frequent bus (and some train) connections from Alexandroupoli are possible.

Feres   Φέρες

On the eastern river route 29km northeast of Alexandroupoli, Feres boasts the frescoed **Church of Panagia Kosmosotira** (1152), built by Byzantine royal Isaac Komnenos. Feres has a small **tourist office** (☑ 25550 24310).

Tyhero   Τυχερό

Beyond Feres, little Tyhero offers the family-friendly **Thrassa Eco-Tourism Guesthouse** (☑ 25540 20080; www.thrassa.gr; s/d/ste €45/65/95; ℗ ❋ ☎). Along an 800m-long lake, it has big, breezy rooms and numerous hanging plants and vines. Friendly owner and tennis coach Sofia Hajisavva organises sports, boat and pony rides for kids, who can also run on the lawns and antagonise ducks, fish and turtles. While mosquitoes vex, the rooms and buildings have screens.

If arriving via river-road bus, ask for Tyhero's Gymnasio stop; 200m opposite it stands Thrassa. It has a cafe, but Tyhero's centre has the tavernas. **O Thomas** (☑ 25540 41259; Tyhero; mains €5-8), an old favourite, also delivers to Thrassa.

Dadia Forest Reserve
Δάσος της Δαδιάς

Further north, off the central main road (30km from Feres), a left-hand turn-off leads 7km west to **Dadia Forest Reserve**, situated on one of Europe's two main bird migration routes. It's home to 36 of the 38 European raptors (birds of prey) species, some rare. Dadia has a protected inner zone (73 sq km) and buffer zone (352 sq km). Local slaughterhouses donate some 1000kg of meat a week to keep the birds satiated.

Almost as entertaining as watching the birds frolic on their carrion through long-lens telescopes is observing the most zealous birdwatchers argue about which bird it is they're actually seeing.

It's best in May, before migration begins, or in July, when baby vultures hop curiously out of their nests. The **Ecotourist Centre** (☑ 25540 32202; www.dadia-np.gr; Dadia; ◷ 10am-4pm Dec-Jan, 9am-7pm Mar-May & Sep-Nov, 8.30am-8.30pm Jun-Aug) has detailed bilingual wall displays, an educational film and minibus service to the Alamo-like bird hide (€3). Alternatively, hike one hour up the trail – it's marked orange heading up and yellow coming down. The hide contains binoculars, telescopes and a tripod for photography buffs. For still more details, find the itinerant World Wildlife Foundation scientist, whose office adjoins the Ecotourist Centre.

The on-site **Ecotourist Hostel of Dadia** (☑ 25540 32263; www.ecoclub.com/dadia; Dadia; s/d/tr/qd €30/43/50/55) has simple but clean en-suite private rooms. There's an adjoining cafe. Otherwise, try **Traditional Family Taverna** (☑ 25540 32481; mains €4-6), near the church in Dadia village (1km).

Soufli   Σουφλί

Soufli, 38km north of Alexandroupoli, has been producing silk since Alexander the Great's time; today, the silkworms are still munching on its mulberry trees. However, the industry suffered after 1923 when farmers lost groves to the new Turkish state. More recently, mulberry groves have been chopped to create more arable land. While small-scale production continues, people whisper of cheap Chinese imports passed off as Soufli-made: ensure you're buying the real thing.

The **Art of Silk Museum** (☑ 25540 22371; www.silkmuseum.gr; Vasilis Georgiou 199; ◷ 9am-8pm) and shop, in a restored silk-producing mansion, documents Soufli silk production past and present through displays, films and interactive, multilingual audio guides. For overnights, try the atmospheric **Koukouli Inn** (☑ 25540 22400; Olorou 14; s/d incl breakfast €45/55), in a former 19th-century silkworm harvesting factory.

Soufli has ATMs and services, as well as perhaps Greece's smallest old-school bus station.

Orestiada   Ορεστιάδα
POP 23,584

The largest town beyond Alexandroupoli, Orestiada has shopping, social life and surprisingly fine dining. Perhaps because they don't get many tourists, Orestiada locals are friendly, down-to-earth, proud of their town and Evros in general. It's a good base for Evros day trips, and a jumping-off point for Bulgaria and Turkey – the latter is accessible from nearby Kastanies village, which hosts the summertime **Ardas River Festival**.

WORTH A TRIP

DIDYMOTIHO: WHERE BYZANTINE MEETS OTTOMAN

Didymotiho (dih-dih-mo-tih-ho), a military outpost north of Soufli, is a sleepy place; however, its strategic borderland nature has endowed it with intriguing historical monuments worth seeing when passing through Evros.

It was founded in the late 8th century as a hinterland fort defending Constantinople. Didymotiho's name derives from its once-magnificent double walls (didymo 'twin', tihos 'wall'); remnants of these **Byzantine Walls** stand in the upper town, near the icon-rich **Church of Agios Athanasios**. Along the inner walls, look out for the engraved symbol of Byzantine noble Tarhaniotis. Strange, catacomb-like side structures lurk nearby.

Numerous eminent Byzantines were born in Didymotiho and, in 1341, Emperor John Kantakouzenis was crowned here. However, 20 years later Turkish Sultan Murad I conquered Didymotiho and it became the Ottoman capital until the capital was relocated to Adrianoupoli (Edirne, Turkey) in 1365. Nevertheless, Murad's work was not done, as is attested by the huge, pyramid-roofed and derelict mosque on Didymotiho's square. Ordained by Murad and finished in 1368 by his son Bayezit, it's known as **Bayezit's Mosque**. It was Europe's first, and the biggest the Ottomans would build there.

Hourly Alexandroupoli–Orestiada buses transit Didymotiho. Its bus station has no left luggage service, however.

Orestiada was built for the 1923 population exchanges. Unlike the many ragged refugees dispersed throughout Greece, Orestiada's dignified founders collectively resettled across the river here.

◉ Sights & Activities

Folk Museum   MUSEUM
(☑ 25520 28080; www.musorest.gr; Agion Theodoron 103; €2; ☺ 10am-1pm & 7-9pm Tue-Sun) This museum exhibits Thracian furniture, costumes, old weaponry and, intriguingly, a fragment from the original Lausanne Treaty, which stipulated the Greek–Turkish population exchange.

**Metropolitan Church of
the Saints Theodoros**   CHURCH
(cnr Konstantinopoleos & Orfeas) West of the *plateia,* this unusual red-brick structure contains beautiful icons.

Cataract Water Park   SWIMMING
(☑ 25520 28922) Almost 3km from Orestiada on the Didymotiho road, Cataract has various pools and slides for beating the summer heat, a disco, a bar and a *bouzoukia.*

🛏 Sleeping

★ Hotel Elektra   HOTEL $
(☑ 25520 28922; www.hotelelectra.gr; Athanasiou Pantazidou 52; s/d €40/58; P ❋ 🛜) This friendly and well-kept hotel in a restored neoclassical mansion is just off the square, near the best restaurants and cafes. Ask the helpful Ismini or Manya for info on nearby sights.

Hotel Alexandros   HOTEL $$
(☑ 25520 27000; Vasileos Konstantinou 10; s/d/tr €50/60/70; P ❋ @) Located near the train station, the Alexandros has breezy rooms with balconies.

🍴 Eating & Drinking

Orestiada's cafe-bars line Emmanouel Riga, between Konstantinopoleos and Athanasiou Pantazidou by the square. Popular places include **Bel Air** and **Social**.

Safran   TAVERNA $
(☑ 25520 29088; Vasileos Konstantinou; mains €5-7) Longtime favourite Safran does international-style taverna cuisine.

★ Sapore Cucine Italiana   ITALIAN $$
(☑ 6932385040; cnr Athanasiou Pantazidou & Emmanouil Rlga; mains €8-13; ☺ 10am-11pm) An unexpected delight in deepest Thrace, this new Italian restaurant features a short but excellent seasonal menu. Try the tasty bruschetta, and lasagna with goat cheese or ravioli in wine sauce, accompanied by rich local wines (from Ormenio).

Friendly owner Ioannis is an innovator, as attested by the 'Venetian' tiramisu and chocolate soufflé with toffee. Soft music and candlelight enhance the atmosphere in this classic wood-and-brick place with lofty ceilings.

ℹ Information

ATM-equipped banks hug the newly refurbished square.

Hatzigiannis Tours (☑ 25520 28333; cnr Konstantinoupoleos & Emmanouel Riga) Sells plane, boat and train tickets.

Post Office (☑ 25520 22435; Athanasiou Pantazidou)

ℹ Getting There & Around

From Orestiada's **bus station** (☑ 25520 22550), buses serve Didymotiho (€1.80, 20 minutes, hourly), with many of them continuing to Alexandroupoli (€10.60, 1¼ hours). Other buses go northwards to Dikea (€5.70, 45 minutes, four daily) and Ormenio (€5.50, 40 minutes, two daily) for Bulgaria. The Turkish border crossing at Kastanies is also served (€1.80, 20 minutes, six daily).

The **train station** (☑ 25520 22328) connects Orestiada with Thessaloniki, via Alexandroupoli. International trains remained suspended at the time of research.

Around Orestiada

Some 18km southeast on the old road following the Evros River and railroad, the **Byzantine Castle of Pythio** (Pythio village; ☺ daylight) **FREE** guards a tall bluff above **Pythio** village (Empython, in Byzantine times), overlooking the Thracian plain and river's dark treeline. Built in 1347 by Emperor John Kantakouzenos, during a turbulent period of civil wars and Turkish invasions, it's Thrace's only surviving example of Byzantine defensive architecture. Renovations continue. Ask the *fylakos* (guard) for the key. Even if you don't get in, you can appreciate the castle's grandeur.

If driving, a circular **northern Evros day trip** from Orestiada accesses intriguing, unvisited sights. Drive west through Valtos for **Mikri Doxipara**, where a 1st-century-AD Roman tomb was discovered, with five interred funerary carts with horses and harnesses. From here, turn north towards **Kyprinos** village and its **Church of Agiou Georgiou**, with icons and a very ancient baptistery. Watch out for Father Nikolaos, a transplanted Cretan who may spontaneously leap into heel-slapping Cretan dance.

If it's a weekend, stop further north at **Pendalofos** village's game restaurant, **Evrothirama** (☑ 25560 61202; mains €7-10), for pheasant, venison or wild boar. Otherwise, you'll find other tavernas here and there. After Pendalofos, continue to **Petrota**, northwestern Evros' last village before Bulgaria, with vineyards and traditional stone houses. The border road continues eastward through **Ormenio** (famous for its wines) and Dikea, before looping south back to Orestiada.

Some 19km north of Orestiada near **Kastanies**, the **Ardas River Festival** (☑ 25520 81140; www.ardas.gr) occurs each July, drawing several thousand youngsters. Top Greek singers, Turkish and Bulgarian groups, and Greek and foreign DJs perform. Besides music, there's beach volleyball, minisoccer, motocross, theatre and water-park trips.

Kastanies itself is a sleepy hamlet, and Greece's northernmost Turkish border crossing; evocative **Edirne** (Adrianoupoli in Greek) is just 9km east. If you're feeling limber and travelling light, turn at Aegean Petrol's *benzinadiko* (petrol station), walk east 500m to the border police checkpoint, and continue a couple of kilometres over the river and through the woods into Turkey. Sometimes there are minibuses here heading into Edirne or its bus station.

If you are attempting the same feat from the opposite direction, note that the last Kastanies–Orestiada bus (€1.60) departs at 7pm. Aegean Petrol has tickets.

EPIROS ΗΠΕΙΡΟΣ

Northern Greece's most dramatic terrain lies in Epiros, a place that will (literally) take your breath away, in the sprawling, impenetrable Pindos Mountains. Bisecting the Pindos is the magnificent 12km-long Vikos Gorge – probably the world's deepest (900m) – a national park filled with forests, waterfalls and ice-cold mountain lakes, surrounded by the Zagorohoria's immaculate stone-and-slate villages.

South of these mountains, Ioannina is a fun, studenty city with character, unfolding around a placid lake. Straight west, the Ionian coast features long sandy beaches punctuated by archaeological sites. As with the Ionian Islands opposite, a Venetian legacy has flavoured the so-called 'Epirot Riviera,' especially at photogenic Parga. Further north, Igoumenitsa's ferries provide access to Italy.

Reaching Epiros is an event in itself. The road from Kalambaka in Thessaly winds over the Pindos Mountains; from Macedonia, the marvellous Egnatia Odos highway cuts straight through them, into massive tunnels. Note that this highway is infested with toll booths and bereft of rest stops.

History

The Dorian invasion (1100–1000 BC) left three main Greek-speaking tribes: the Thesproti, the Chaones and the dominant Molossi. The marriage of Molossi princess Olympias to powerful Macedonian king Philip II brought conflict with emerging Rome. King Pyrrhus (319–272 BC) famously defeated the Romans at Ausculum, at a heavy cost; hence the concept of a 'Pyrrhic victory.'

The Roman Empire's split in AD 395 left Epiros Byzantium's westernmost province. Centuries later, it became important after the 1204 Latin sack of Constantinople; Byzantine nobles escaping here established a key successor state. Eminent Byzantines again fled to Epiros' mountain fastnesses after the Ottomans conquered Constantinople in 1453.

Infamously linked with Epiros is 18th-century Albanian despot Ali Pasha, who kept a harem of 400 women. Ali ransacked much of Albania and western Greece, while wheeling-and-dealing with Turks, Brits and even Napoleon, before Ottoman troops finally killed him in 1822, on Ioannina's lake island. Nevertheless, Ali had tacitly aided Greek freedom fighters elsewhere by wearing down and distracting the Turks.

Epiros was divided after 1912 when newly created Albania got a northern chunk of the region. Mussolini's 1940 invasion was repelled in Epiros, which became a communist resistance stronghold, first against the Nazis and then against the right-wing army in the Greek Civil War (1946–49). Although the communists lost, Epiros remains generally leftist.

Ioannina Ιωάννινα

POP 80.371

Hip Ioannina (pronounced 'ih-o-*ah*-nih-nah' or '*yah*-nih-nah') is a bustling little city, although slightly melancholic (it rains nine months a year). The 20,000 university students based here faithfully support the excellent eating and nightlife scene. Ioannina faces sheer mountains erupting behind Lake Pamvotis; you'll have the best views from Kastro, an old quarter interspersed with narrow lanes and Byzantine and Ottoman architecture.

History

Byzantine Emperor Justinian founded Ioannina in the 6th century, and it became an important commercial and cultural outpost. In 1204, when Latin Crusaders sacked Constantinople and dismembered Byzantium, Ioannina became capital of Michael I Komnenos Doukas' Byzantine successor state. Ottomans conquered in 1430, but made Ioannina, a leading cultural and artistic centre, with a Sephardic Jewish population arriving after 1492. Ioannina was (and is) known for its silver craftsmanship and, through the 16th and 17th centuries, an 'Epirot School' of religious painting also blossomed.

Epiros

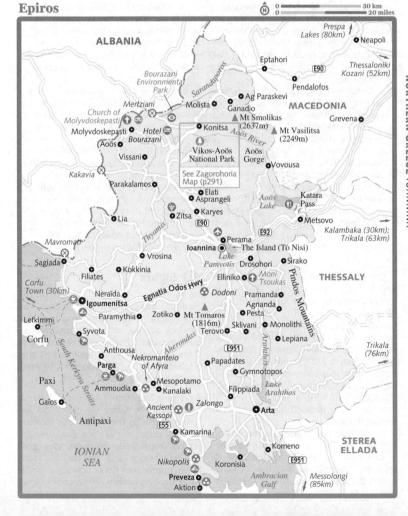

WORTH A TRIP

METSOVO

South of the magnificent Katara Pass, idyllic Metsovo (*met*-so-vo) clings to a mountainside at 1156m. It's best-known for its skiing, traditional architecture, cheeses and hospitable locals – mostly Vlachs, descendants of a nomadic sheep-herding people who spoke the Arromanian language. Since it derives from Latin, some believe Vlachs descend from Roman soldiers stationed in these mountains.

Metsovo's shepherds were enriched by the Ottomans, who rewarded them for guarding the Katara Pass (1705m), the only route across the Pindos Mountains. However, in 1795 Ali Pasha abolished Metsovo's privileges. In 1854 Ottoman troops caused considerable damage.

Nevertheless, Metsovo succeeded through commerce, industry and other non-sheep-related enterprises. Local luminaries Georgios Averof (1815–99) and Mihail Tositsas (1885–1950) donated heavily towards restoring Metsovo's former glory. Today, the Tositsas Mansion houses the fascinating **folk museum** (☑ 26560 41084; adult/student €3/2; ☺ 9am-1.30pm & 4-6pm Fri-Wed), and the **Averof Gallery** (☑ 26560 41210; adult/student €3/2; ☺ 10am-6.30pm Wed-Mon) exhibits 19th- and 20th-century works of Greek painters and sculptors. Other old Metsovo houses have become hotels and twee tourist shops. Traipsing the old town and breathing in the mountain air is wonderfully relaxing.

In winter, try Metsovo's **ski centre** (☑ 26560 41211; ☺ 9.30am-3.45pm), which has an 82-seat ski lift, two downhill runs and a 5km cross-country run, plus taverna. Rent skis in Metsovo.

Metsovo's numerous refurbished stone mansions line the steep entrance road and square. **Hotel Asteri** (☑ 26560 42222; www.asterimetsovo.com; s/d €40/50), set prominently atop Metsovo, has 40 cheerful rooms, some with fireplaces and a nourishing restaurant. **Hotel Bitouni** (☑ 26560 41217; www.hotelbitouni.com; d/ste €60/80; Ⓟ @), with its sauna and traditional wood fixtures, has a ski-lodge feel, with 24 doubles, and seven suites (two with spas). Finally, **Hotel Egnatia** (☑ 26560 41900; Tositsa 19; d/studios incl breakfast €60/80) – to the right of the square – offers doubles and spacious studios with superb mountain views.

Metsovo's rustic country cooking is famous nationwide. Central **To Koutouki tou Nikola** (☑ 26560 41732; mains €7-10) serves hearty traditional dishes, from *pites* (savoury pies) to roast lamb and *gida vrasti* (boiled goat soup). Another traditional place, strong on meats but with good vegetarian options, is **Paradosiako** (mains €8-11).

Buses serve Ioannina (€10, 1½ hours, four daily). For a Thessaloniki bus (€27, 1½ hours), reach the main road and wave down the bus coming from Ioannina.

Crafty opportunists like Albanian warlord Ali Pasha (1741–1822) capitalised on Ottoman decline to vie for Ioannina. In 1789, Ali made it the capital of his far-ranging fiefdom. Despite a penchant for cruelty that sickened pious philhellene Lord Byron, Ali enforced the law, and Ioannina flourished. Nevertheless, in 1822, trapped at the Agios Panteleimon monastery on the Island (To Nisi) in Lake Pamvotis, octogenarian Ali was finally liquidated by some very irritated Ottomans, who paraded his severed head around İstanbul.

Greeks liberated Ioannina in the 1912–13 Balkan Wars. The 1923 population exchanges saw Turks replaced by Anatolian Greek refugees. Tragically, in 1943 the Nazis deported the Jewish population to concentration camps.

◉ Sights

Its Kale
CITADEL

(Kastro; ☺ 8am-5pm & 8-10pm Tue-Sun) Kastro's sublime citadel rises over a long bluff overlooking lake and mountain. It holds the **Tomb of Ali Pasha** and restored **Fetiye Cami** (Victory Mosque), built in 1611 after a failed Greek uprising that saw Christians expelled from the citadel.

Byzantine Museum
MUSEUM

(☑ 26510 25989; Kastro; €3; ☺ 8am-5pm Tue-Sun) Adjacent to the citadel, this museum presents early Christian and Byzantine art, pottery, coins and silverware, plus post-Byzantine icons and manuscripts, early Venetian-produced Greek books and ornate silver jewellery boxes with cloisonné enamel.

Textual accompaniments detail Ioannina's history from the 4th to the 17th century.

Municipal Ethnographic Museum   MUSEUM
(🖉 26510 26356; Kastro; adult/student €3/1.50; ⏾ 8am-8pm) The erstwhile **Aslan Pasha Mosque** (1619) exhibits local costumes and period photographs, along with tapestries and prayer shawls from Ioannina's former **synagogue** (Ioustinianou 16).

Folklore Museum   MUSEUM
(🖉 26510 23566; Mihail Angelou 42-44; adult/student €2/1; ⏾ 9am-2pm Tue, Thu & Fri, 9am-2pm & 5.30-8pm Wed & Sat) Exhibits ethnographic and folk items, like embroidery and cooking utensils.

Archaeological Museum   MUSEUM
(🖉 26510 33357; www.amio.gr; Plateia 25 Martiou 6; €2, Sun free; ⏾ 8.30am-3pm Tue-Sun) This top-notch museum contains more than 3000 Epirot finds, including neolithic items and antiquities from Dodoni, Vitsa and Efira.

🏃 Activities

The relaxing one-hour **lake cruise** (🖉 6944470280; €5; ⏾ 10am-midnight daily summer, Sat & Sun winter) departs from near the ferry quay.

For Anavasi's *Pindus-Zagori* 1:50,000 hiking map (€8), inquire at local *periptera* (kiosks) or **Papasotiriou Bookstore** (🖉 26510 64000; Mihail Angelou 6). Hikers should consult EOS about mountain conditions.

🛏 Sleeping

Kastro has atmospheric, quieter options.

★ Filyra   BOUTIQUE HOTEL $
(🖉 6932601240; www.hotelfilyra.gr; Andronikou Paleologou 18, Kastro; s/d €45/55; P ❋) This flower-bedecked boutique hotel is a perennial favourite, with five spacious self-catering suites on a quiet side street. At time of research, the friendly owners were opening additional well-renovated rooms nearby.

Limnopoula Camping   CAMPGROUND $
(🖉 26510 25265; Kanari 10; campsites per tent/adult €4/8; ⏾ Apr-Oct) This breezy lakeside campground 2km from centre has kitchen, laundry and restaurant. Don't swim, but do bring mosquito repellent. Open April to October.

Hotel Kastro   PENSION $$
(🖉 26510 22866; www.hotelkastro.gr; Andronikou Paleologou 57; s/d incl breakfast €50/65; P ❋) This friendly, restored Kastro mansion overlooking Its Kale has great atmosphere: antique brass beds, stained-glass windows and a tranquil courtyard create a secluded feel.

Dafni Traditional Hotel   BOUTIQUE HOTEL $$
(🖉 6932601240; www.hotelfilyra.gr; Ioustinianou 12, Kastro; s/d €45/65; P ❋) Set discreetly inside the Kastro's enormous outer walls. Dafni offers rooms combining traditional and modern amenities. There's one grand, well-decorated family room (€90). Reception is at nearby sister establishment, Filyra (p287).

Olympic   HOTEL $$
(🖉 26510 22233; www.hotelolymp.gr; Melanidhis 2; s/d €90/110; P ❋ @) Ioannina's poshest hotel has fine rooms with lake views. It's in a noisy central spot, but has a piano bar.

Politeia   HOTEL $$
(🖉 26510 22235; www.etip.gr; Anexartisias 109; s/d/ste incl breakfast €65/75/90; P ❋ 🛜) Around a quiet inner courtyard, Politeia offers tastefully decorated studios with kitchenettes.

🍴 Eating

Ioannina's best places only open for dinner.

Ippotes   ITALIAN $
(🖉 6983884076; Soutsou 7; mains €7-11; ⏾ 7pm-2am) This nice new place, with stone walls, pastel tones and relaxing backyard, combines wine bar with Italian food.

Es Aei   FINE DINING $
(🖉 26510 34571; Koundouriotou 50; mains €8-12; ⏾ 8pm-1am) The glass-roofed courtyard dining room here is as unique as the food, which includes mezedhes made from organic ingredients and Ioannina specials such as grilled pork sausages.

Mystagogia   TAVERNA $
(🖉 26510 34571; Koundouriotou 44; mains €6; ⏾ dinner) A popular late-night *tsipouradhiko (ouzerie)*, Mystagogia has nourishing mezedhes and good beef *keftedhes* (rissoles).

Pasta Fresca   ITALIAN $
(Apsaki 48; mains €7-10; ⏾ 7pm-12am Tue-Sun) A hardworking mother-daughter team run this tiny new place known for its handmade pastas.

Seirios   GREEK $$
(🖉 26510 77070; www.seirioskouzina.gr; Patriarhou Evangelidi 1; mains €8-12; ⏾ noon-11pm) Locally recommended Seirios has excellent and

Ioannina

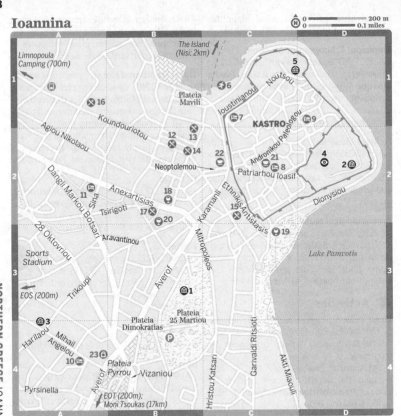

imaginative specials. Try the stuffed mushrooms in oil-and-lemon sauce and *yiaourtlou konstaninoupolitiko* (sausage in a spicy Greek yoghurt sauce on pitta).

Stoa Louli   FINE DINING **$$**
(☑26510 71322; Anexartisias 78; mains €7-12) Built in 1875, Stoa Louli has been an inn, trade centre for Jewish leather merchants and Ottoman Bank. Fronted by grand arches, it serves Greek favourites with a contemporary twist.

🍷 Drinking & Nightlife

Popular student bars are in Skala, opposite the castle's southern stretches. Off Anexartisias, check out Stoa Liabei, an arched laneway with a checkerboard pavement packed with bars.

★ Golfy's Bar   BAR
(☑26510 39217; Stoa Liabei 19; ⊙10pm-4am) Down Stoa Liabei, Golfy's is a cosy, two-room affair frequented by students and older folks too. With 20 years on the scene, easygoing Lefteris Pexomadis is considered Ioannina's best resident DJ.

Denouar   BAR
(☑6984766894; Anexertasias 40-42, Stoa Liabei; ⊙7pm-4am) This bar occupies a beautifully arching 200-year-old former *agora* (market), with friendly people, twinkling lights, strange curvy stairs and an interesting musical mix.

Mouselimi Café   CAFE
(☑26510 44217; Andronikou Palaeologou 8, Kastro; ⊙10am-11pm) This colourful new corner cafe is a jazzy spot good for coffees, teas and homemade sweets.

Fournos   BAR
(cnr Ethnikis Antistaseos; ⊙9am-late) One of Skala's only bars operating year-round, Fournos spreads out under big canopies and gets busy late.

Ioannina

Sights
1	Archaeological Museum	B3
2	Byzantine Museum	D2
3	Folklore Museum	A4
4	Its Kale	D2
5	Municipal Ethnographic Museum	C1

Activities, Courses & Tours
6	Lake Cruise	C1

Sleeping
7	Dafni Traditional Hotel	C1
8	Filyra	C2
9	Hotel Kastro	D1
10	Olympic	A4
11	Politeia	A2

Eating
12	Es Aei	B2
13	Ippotes	B2
14	Mystagogia	B2
15	Pasta Fresca	C2
16	Seirios	A1
17	Stoa Louli	B2

Drinking & Nightlife
	Byzantine Museum Cafe	(see 2)
18	Denouar	B2
19	Fournos	C3
20	Golfy's Bar	B2
21	Mouselimi Café	C2
22	Synnefia 9	C2

Shopping
23	Papasotiriou Bookstore	A4

Byzantine Museum Cafe CAFE
(☑ 26510 64206; Its Kale; ⊙ 9pm-midnight) On Its Kale, this big and busy museum cafe offers coffees, waffles with ice cream and other snacks.

Synnefia 9 CAFE
(☑ 26510 33131; Neoptolemou 9; ⊙ 9am-11pm Sep-Jun) Although kindly owner Miltos Miltiadis has turned his former restaurant into a cafe, he has retained the relaxing old-world decor and warm feel here ('Cloud Nine' in Greek)

🛍 Shopping

★ **Centre of Traditional Handcraft of Ioannina** HANDICRAFTS, JEWELLERY
(www.kepavi.gr; Arhiepiskopou Makariou 1; ⊙ 9.30am-2.30pm & 5.30-8.30pm) Savour Ioannina's centuries-old silverwork tradition at this collective artisans' workshop and store; it has Ioannina's best quality and prices. Creations run from earrings and necklaces (€15) to elaborate silver dining sets (€2000). Even if you don't like jewellery, you probably know someone who does, and with global silver prices rising this is a canny investment.

ℹ Information

Plateia Pyrrou and Averof have banks and ATMs.
EOS (Greek Alpine Club; ☑ 26510 22138; Smyrnis 15; ⊙ 7-9pm Mon-Fri)
EOT (Greek National Tourist Organisation; ☑ 26510 41142; Dodonis 39; ⊙ 7.30am-2.30pm Mon-Fri) General info and hiking updates for the Zagorohoria and Vikos Gorge.
Post Office Post offices are on Georgiou Papandreou and 28 Oktovriou 3.

ℹ Getting There & Away

AIR
Aegean Airlines (☑ 26510 64444) serves Athens. The airport is 5km northwest of town.

BUS
Ioannina Bus Station (KTEL Ioanninon; ☑ 26510 25014; www.ktelioannina.gr; Georgiou Papandreou 45) serves Athens (€39, 6½ hours, nine daily), Konitsa (€6.20, 1¼ hours, seven daily), Thessaloniki (€32, 3½ hours, six daily) and Metsovo (€5.80, one hour, four daily). Summer buses sometimes serve Parga (€12, 1½ hours), otherwise, go via Igoumenitsa (€9.80, 1¼ hours, eight daily) or Preveza (€10.40, two hours, six daily). Buses also serve Dodoni (€2, 20 minutes). Zagorohoria buses are irregular, so check.

Buses from Ioannina serve Albanian border-post Kakavia (€6, one hour, nine daily).

ℹ Getting Around

For the airport (5km northwest, on the Perama road) take Bus 7 from the clock tower (every 20 minutes). **Budget Rent a Car** (☑ 26510 43901; Dodonis 109) and **Auto Union Car Rental** (☑ 25610 67751; Dodonis 66) are at the airport.

Taxis (☑ 26510 46777) wait near Plateia Pyrrou and the lake.

Around Ioannina

The Island ISLAND
(Το Νησί; To Nisi) lies opposite Ioannina, amidst woods and wildflowers in Lake Pamvotis. In the 17th-century, refugees from Peloponnesian Mani built its portside village, where around 300 people still live.

The island's secluded monasteries are significant for their unusual frescoes and book collections, while the laneways with old, white-plastered houses lend atmosphere.

Here unfolded the last act in despot Ali Pasha's grand drama. After years of duplicitous double-dealing and brazen challenges the Ottomans decided to eliminate the 82-year-old 'Lion of Ioannina' in 1822. Perfidiously assured of a pardon, Ali withdrew with his guard to the island's Moni Panteleimon. There he was trapped and Ottoman soldiers shot him; note the fatal bullet hole in the floorboards at the **Ali Pasha Museum** (The Island; adult €1; ⊗8am-10pm summer, 9am-9pm winter). An English-language narrrative recounts Ali's last days, and exhibits personal effects and etchings of the portly pasha in full repose, sitting fat and happy with consort, beard and hookah. To get there, take the main street left from above the port.

The 13th-century **Moni Filanthropinon** (Μονή Φιλανθρωπινών; The Island; ⊗9am-6pm) **FREE**, on the western side, was built by the Filanthropini, a leading Constantinopolitan family fleeing the 1204 Crusader conquest. Its 16th-century frescoes of pagan Greek philosophers Plato, Aristotle and Plutarch sit alongside more suitably Christian personalities. The expressive pathos of the paintings, characteristic of the 'Epirot School', has excited art historians. In Ottoman times, it was also a secret school for Christians.

Restaurant Kyra Vasiliki (☑26510 81681; The Island; mains €6-8), under a plane tree by the ferry dock, serves grills and some fish. **Propodes** (☑26510 81214; The Island; fish €4-6), under an awning on the Moni Panteleimon path, is fronted by tanks filled with wriggling eels, hopping frogs and crayfish waiting for the kettle. For a quiet drink, walk just downhill from the square to the new **Kafeteria Ta Bakakakia** (☑6947135096; The Island; ⊗9am-9pm daily May-Sep, Sat-Sun Oct-Apr), which has juices, milkshakes and more, plus lovely views across the lake to the mountains.

Ioannina's **ferry quay** has ferries (€2, 10 minutes) from 7am to 11.30pm in summer, and 7am to 10pm in winter. Summer services are every 15 minutes; in winter, only hourly.

Perama Cave
CAVE

(Σπήλαιο Περάματος; ☑26510 81521; www.spilaio-perama.gr; adult/student €6/3; ⊗8am-8pm) Stalactite-rich Perama Cave (4km from Ioannina) is among Greece's largest and most impressive. The enormous 1100m-long cave has three storeys of chambers and passageways. There is an hour-long tour.

Buses 8 and 16 from Ioannina's clocktower run every 20 minutes to Perama, 250m south of the cave.

Moni Tsoukas
MONASTERY

(Μονή Τσούκας; ☑26510 89223; Elliniko village; ⊗9am-6pm) **FREE** Some 17km southeast of Ioannina, clifftop Moni Tsoukas overlooks the Arahthos Gorge. Its name derives from the Slavonic *chouka* (peak). The views of gorge, river and mountains are stunning. Byzantine Emperor Isaakios Angelos built this walled monastery in 1190. The church has a sumptuous interior and impressive art (most important, the **Panagia icon**, venerated on 8 September).

This working monastery is often encircled with thin, stringy candles – on feast days, the whole church gets cocooned by these testaments to individual wishes and prayers.

From Ioannina, drive south through Elliniko and up to the parking (20 to 30 minutes total). A taxi from Ioannina costs €30.

Dodoni
ANCIENT SITE

(Δωδώνη; ☑26510 82287; adult €2; ⊗8am-5pm) The colossal, 3rd-century-BC Theatre of Dodoni, 21km southwest of Ioannina, is Epiros' best ancient site. From around 2000 BC, the earth goddess worshipped here spoke through Greece's oldest oracle. By the 13th century BC, Zeus was speaking here too, through a sacred oak tree's rustling leaves. Today, foundations and a few columns remain from his temple.

King Pyrrhus' restored **theatre** now hosts Ioannina's summertime Festival of Ancient Drama. The north-side **acropolis** has wall remnants. East of the theatre are **bouleuterion** (council house) foundations and the small **Temple of Aphrodite**. Nearby once stood Zeus' sanctuary and sacred talking tree.

Buses from Ioannina serve Dodoni twice daily. A taxi costs €35 return plus €3 per hour for waiting.

The Zagorohoria
Τα Ζαγοροχώρια

The Zagorohoria's 46 traditional stone-and-slate villages, tucked into the Pindos range, offer atmospheric accommodation, crisp alpine air, sublime views and myriad local legends. Once connected only by mountain paths and stone bridges, they're now connected by paved roads, some of which enjoy spectacular twists and turns.

Although time and emigration have depopulated many villages, boutique and environmental tourism have allowed savvy locals to prosper by converting *arhontika* (mansions) and smaller traditional homes into inviting guesthouses. Hikers also come for the immediate proximity to the Vikos Gorge and other mountain routes.

After Constantinople was conquered (first by the Crusaders in 1204, later by the Turks in 1453), noble Byzantine families fled here, safeguarding Greek culture and traditions. The Ottomans also gave the Zagorohorians privileges and autonomy in exchange for guarding the mountain passes. The locals thus became quite wealthy and also worldly, creating a cultured diaspora in centres of learning and commerce in Early Modern Europe.

Vikos-Aoös National Park
Εθνικός Δρυμός Βίκου-Αώου

The Vikos-Aoös National Park bursts with pristine rivers and forests, flowering meadows and shimmering lakes reflecting jagged mountains and endless blue sky. Almost one-third of Greece's flora (some endemic) lives here, along with native fish, foxes and chamois, rare hawks, otters and bears. The park's Tymfi Massif contains numerous ear-popping peaks including **Mt Trapezitsa** (2022m), **Mt Astraka** (2436m) and **Mt Gamila** (2497m). Beneath them, the 12km-long Vikos Gorge may be the world's deepest.

While hikers comprise the majority of visitors to Vikos-Aoös National Park, semi-nomadic Vlach and Sarakatsani shepherds still take their flocks up to high grazing ground in summer, returning to the valleys in autumn.

NORTHERN GREECE THE ZAGOROHORIA

Zagorohoria

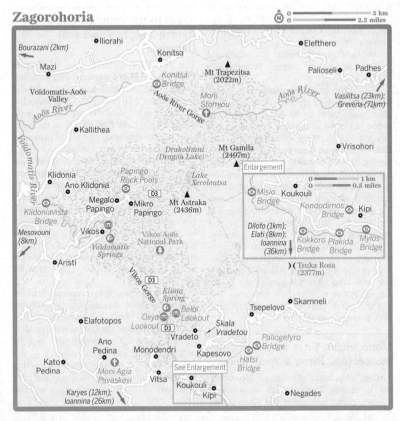

Dilofo &Negades
Δίλοφο & Νεγάδες

Just 32km northeast of Ioannina, enchanting **Dilofo** (population seven) is for both romantics and hikers. It's tranquil and totally authentic, a jumble of slate-roofed houses tucked into a mountainside. It's also a lesser-known entry point for the Vikos Gorge, allowing the longest hike.

Dilofo gazes across the valley at another tranquil village, **Koukouli**. It's intimately associated with the enormous, 13.5m-high **Loumidi Mansion**, on the left-hand side when entering Dilofo. The story goes that after a Koukouli girl married a Dilofo man, she became so homesick that she threatened to leave. The groom's patient father instead built a mansion tall enough for her to wave to mum and dad over in Koukouli – problem solved.

Dilofo's small *plateia* features an enormous, 400-year-old plane tree, a usually dysfunctional card phone, a taverna and one of Zagorohoria's best guesthouses. In Dilofo's upper part, the **Church of Kimiseos Theotokou** (Dormition of the Virgin) has an intricate, hand-carved wooden iconostasis and icons (village doctor Giorgos Triandafilidis has the key).

Just 13km east, **Negades** is a stone-housed village with little tourism. The 20-minute drive involves superb views of **stone bridges** spanning cliffsides and wooded valleys. Negades' impressive 1792 **Church of Agios Georgios** is sumptuously decorated with exquisite icons and a gilded, hand-carved wood iconostasis. Its wall-to-wall frescoes include rare paintings of pagan philosophers Aristotle and Plutarch. Women once attended mass behind a grill in the back; note here the persuasive frescoes – apparently created for moral edification, they include a depiction of Judas being devoured by a sea monster, and a scrawny demon riding and beating a bedded husband and wife who were too lazy to get up for church. Whoops.

The church isn't always open; consult with Ioannina's EOT (p289).

Monodendri, Vitsa & Ano Pedina
Μονοδένδρι, Βίτσα & Ανω Πεδινά

Around 38km north of Ioannina, **Monodendri** is among Zagorohoria's most-visited villages, partly because of the Vikos Gorge.

Check out the square's **Rizareion Idryma** (Monodendri; ⊘8am-4pm Wed-Mon), a cultural centre which exhibits historic photos and artworks. It sells lavish coffee-table books depicting Zagori history through photos and text (€20).

Moni Agia Paraskevi has spectacular gorge views. According to legend, Lord Mihalis Voevodas Therianos founded it in 1413 to thank God for healing his daughter of an incurable illness. The church's frescoes partially date to the 15th century. Also see the cross-domed, 17th-century **Church of Agios Minas** near the square.

South of Monodendri, the less-visited Vitsa (Byzantine Vizitsini) also has a cross-domed, 17th-century shrine, the **Church of Agios Nikolaos**. Between Monodendri and Vitsa lie **ancient Molossi settlement ruins** (9th- to 4th-century BC).

From Vitsa, drive 7.2km west–northwest to **Ano Pedina**, more touristy but a good base for exploring.

Aristi to the Papingo Villages
Αρίστη προς τα χωριά του Πάπιγκου

The ribboning northern road to **Megalo Papingo** and **Mikro Papingo** offers Zagorohoria's most breathtaking views. If driving from Vitsa or Ano Pedina, look for where the secondary road joins the main road. Head west through **Kato Pedina**, follow the main road northwards and, when it branches after 4.1km, turn right for Papingo.

Aristi, the last village before Papingo, features the lovely **Monastery of Panagia Spiliotissa** (1665); this arched, frescoed church stands aside a boulder by the Voïdomatis River. After Aristi, the paved road hugs the river and opens onto increasingly spectacular views. It's all white-knuckle driving as you navigate a tight succession of 15 hairpin turns upwards to the **Papingo villages**, set under hulking Mt Astraka. Look right for the Vikos Gorge.

Touristy Megalo (big) Papingo features enormous stone formations, the 'towers'. Mikro (small) Papingo is quieter, with a **WWF information centre** (www.wwf.gr; Mikro Papingo; ⊘11am-5.30pm Fri-Wed) with exhibits on local wildlife and fauna.

The Papingo villages have refreshing **rock pools**, good for a revitalising dip after a hot day of hiking. They're down a 300m path from a bend in the road connecting the villages.

Vikos Gorge   Χαράδρα του Βίκου

The 12km-long, 900m-deep **Vikos Gorge**, bisecting the Zaorogoria, is the world's deepest, according to Guinness. It begins south of Monodendri, running north until the Papingo villages.

Ioannina's EOS (p289) advises on weather conditions and provides maps and information. You'll need water, stout walking boots and some endurance for the almost seven-hour hike.

Monodendri is a popular starting point. Survey the gorge from the 15th-century **Moni Agia Paraskevi**. A steep, marked path into the gorge begins the four-hour walk; at canyon's end a right-hand trail leads to Mikro Papingo (2½ hours). Megalo Papingo is a further 2km west, but the track splits at the hike's base. The only water is at **Klima Spring**, halfway along the gorge.

If you stop hiking at **Vikos**, south of Papingo, the square's *kafeneio* owner will drive you to Monodendri for €40 (taxis cost double). Vikos, 5km northeast of Aristi, has accommodation and excellent views.

Oxya Lookout, 5km beyond Monodendri on a good dirt road, has fantastic gorge views, as does **Beloi Lookout** opposite. To get there, drive 9km on a winding road or go to **Vradeto** (from the signposted turn-off near Kapesovo), and hike 1.5km along a marked trail after the dirt road (it's a bumpy drive). Vradeto is set along striated limestone cliffs. For the Beloi Lookout, climb the rock stairway, **Skala Vradetou**, signposted outside **Tsepelovo**, another relaxing base for hiking northern Zagorohoria sites like the **Drakolimni** (Dragon Lake). It has a post office, card phone, and good accommodation and eating options.

🏃 Activities

In Kato Pedina, **Compass Adventures** (☑ 26530 71770; info@compassadventures.gr; Kato Pedina) organises hiking, skiing and mountain-biking. In winter, Compass offers a ski school and leads off-piste skiing on virgin terrain.

In Aristi, **Rafting Athletic Center** (☑ 6942015143, 26530 41888; info@rafting-athletic-center.gr; Aristi) offers rafting, kayaking, hiking and even archery and paintball.

🛏 Sleeping

Arhontiko Dilofo   GUESTHOUSE **$**
(☑ 26530 22455; www.dilofo.com; Dilofo; d incl breakfast from €50; **P**) One of Zagorohoria's finest guesthouses, this 480-year-old restored mansion in placid Dilofo is ideal for anyone seeking peace and natural harmony. Rooms feature traditional carpets, furnishings and ornate painted window shutters that, when closed, make you feel you're inside the hold of a grand seafaring vessel. There's a charming courtyard and views over Dilofo's cluttered slate rooftops.

At time of research, the friendly and immensely knowledgeable owner, Georgios Kontaxis, was preparing an exhibit of the amazing antiques he discovered while renovating the 1633 mansion. Greek, English, German and Italian are spoken here.

Archontiko Zarkada   PENSION **$**
(☑ 26530 71305; www.monodendri.com; Monodendri; s/d incl breakfast €40/60; **P**) Gaze on the gorge from your balcony at this lovely old stone house with clean, snug rooms. Some rooms have spa baths.

Xenonas Dias   GUESTHOUSE **$**
(☑ 26530 41257; www.diaspapigo.gr; Mikro Papingo; s/d incl breakfast €40/55) In quiet Mikro Papingo, this rustic pension has 12 rooms and a restaurant. Similar, but smaller, is the nearby **Xenonas Mikro Papingo 1700** (☑ 26530 41179; Mikro Papingo; s/d €45/60; **P**), offering five handsomely appointed, atmospheric rooms.

Papaevangelou   GUESTHOUSE **$$**
(☑ 26530 41135; www.hotelpapaevangelou.gr; Megalo Papingo; d/studio incl breakfast from €75/120) This popular Papingo guesthouse has nice stone rooms, spectacular views and hearty homemade breakfasts served in the rustic tavern/bar. At the central square, turn left on the unpaved road to find it. If it's full, try the similarly restored **Hotel Agriogido** (☑ 6945364484, 26530 42055; georgio@papingo.gr; Megalo Papingo; s/d/tr incl breakfast €60/80/100; **P**), at the village entrance.

To Arhontiko tis Aristi   B&B **$$**
(☑ 6945676261, 26530 42210; www.arhontiko-aristis.gr; Aristi; s/d/tr €100/120/140; **P**) In an 1800 stone mansion, this Aristi guesthouse offers spectacular views, and combines classic stone-and-wood decor with amenities such as spas. It has billiards too.

Porfyron B&B $$
(📞26530 71579; Ano Pedina; s/d €55/70; P) This red-painted 19th-century mansion has rooms with antique furnishings and soft-coloured walls, complementing the wood-panelled ceilings. Some rooms have fireplaces too.

Primula B&B $$
(📞26530 71133; Ano Pedina; d from €70; P) This central Ano Pedina guesthouse has uniquely designed rooms. The walls of some are stone, while others are painted in mottled pastel tones.

Mikri Arktos B&B $$
(Little Bear; 📞26530 81128; kittasth@otenet.gr; Tsepelovo; d from €80; P) This cosy guesthouse on Tsepelovo's *plateia* is a friendly place. Sleep in the shade of a plane tree, try the specials at the downstairs taverna, or cook in the vividly painted rooms' kitchenettes.

Xenos Vikos PENSION $$
(📞26530 71370; Monodendri; d €50-70; ⏱Mar-Dec; P) Only 400m from the Vikos Gorge at Monodendri's lower square, this lively guesthouse has a leafy breakfast courtyard, communal kitchen and lounge.

✗ Eating

Restaurant H Tsoumanis TAVERNA $
(📞26530 42170; www.tsoumanisnikos.gr; Vikos; mains €6-9; ⏱lunch & dinner) Gorge yourself near the gorge at this iconic Vikos taverna, with excellent meats (including seasonal wild game). Above it is a nice guesthouse.

Spiros Tsoumanis TAVERNA $
(📞26530 42108; Megalo Papingo; mains €8-13) At village's end, this classic taverna specialises in local *pites* (pies), roast lamb and *sti gastra* (chickpea stew), with *horta* (salads).

O Dionysos TAVERNA $
(📞26530 71366; Monodendri; pites €5-6) Along upper Monodendri's main street, Dionysos serves tasty *fakopita* (lentil pie) among other traditional Epirot pies.

Sopotseli TAVERNA $
(📞26530 22629; mains €5-7) Dilofo's little taverna serves hearty grills and fresh salads.

Ta Soudena TAVERNA $
(📞26530 71209; Ano Pedina; mains €5-8) Greek vegetable mezedhes, *pites* and grilled meats are served at this popular place.

★ Sta Riza GREEK $$
(📞26530 71550; Elati village; mains €9-13; ⏱12.30-11pm daily 15 Jul–15 Aug, Fri-Tue, 15 Aug–15 Jul) It's hard to disagree with the locals – Sta Riza, overlooking rolling hills, is the place for hearty country cooking with a gourmet flair. Friendly owners Dionyssos 'Saki' Kevasso and his wife, Vassiliki prepare excellent specials such as *manitaria fournitsa* (baked mushrooms in red wine, tomato, feta and herbs) and *arnakia vlahika* (soft baked lamb with yoghurt).

Elati is in the southernmost Zagorohoria; from Ioannina, turn right for Metamorphosi, and at the crossroads where multiple villages are signposted, follow the signs to Elati; it's a very narrow village, so park 30m before the restaurant.

❶ Getting There & Away

To really see Zagorohoria, drive. Otherwise, (limited) bus services from Ioannina operate.

For Dilofo (€3.80, 40 minutes) **buses** go at 6am and 1.30pm on Monday, Wednesday and Friday, continuing to Tsepelovo (€4.40, 1½ hours). Other buses leave for Megalo Papingo and Mikro Papingo (€5.10, two hours) at 5am and 3pm on Monday, Wednesday and Friday; the Wednesday bus hits Vikos (€4.80, 1¾ hours) in summer. Buses to Monodendri (€4.30, one hour) leave at 5.30am and 1pm on Monday, Wednesday and Friday. All buses return to Ioannina immediately.

Taxis from Ioannina to various villages cost from €20 to €55; try negotiating.

Konitsa Κόνιτσα
POP 2942

Carved into a hillside under blue skies 64km north of Ioannina, Konitsa (*ko-nit-sah*) is where kayakers, hikers and river explorers circle their wagons at night. Greek hunters also use Konitsa as a sort of cowboy depot. It's near the Mertziani border crossing with Albania.

Beyond Konitsa, the old road arcs northeast magnificently between the Grammas and Smolikas Mountains to Kastoria. While still passable, this road can be dangerous, especially at night, since it suffers from a lack of upkeep.

➶ Activities

From Konitsa's southern entrance begins a 4.5km **river hike** along the Aoös River Gorge to 15th-century **Moni Stomiou**, originally built on Mt Trapezitsa. The 20m-high, 40m-long single-arched stone **Konitsa Bridge**, dating from 1870, straddles the rushing river. After it, a signposted trail becomes a narrow path between the water and a steep bank, and turns upwards through thick forests. Enjoy the views over the Aoös River canyon and the spring water.

In Konitsa, **No Limits** (☑ 26550 23777; www.nolimits.com.gr; Konitsa) provides equipment and experienced guides for kayaking, horse riding, rafting, climbing and mountain biking.

🛏 Sleeping & Eating

To Dendro Guesthouse   PENSION $
(☑ 26550 22055; d/tr €40/55; P) A moustachioed man clad in leather and answering to the name 'Johnny Dendro', who trims his hedges with a hunting knife, Yiannis Mourehidis has been a Konitsa legend for over 35 years. His guesthouse offers clean and comfortable rooms. For fancier digs, try his **Grand Hotel Dendro** (☑ 26550 29365; www.grandhoteldentro.gr; d/tr/ste €60/75/100; P ❄), which has spacious rooms with hydromassage showers and fireplace.

Yiannis also serves wild boar in wine, pot-roasted lamb and lake trout at the popular **To Dendro Restaurant** (☑ 26550 22055; mains €5-8). Entering town, look for the UN-like display of flags.

Konitsa Mountain Hotel   HOTEL $$
(☑ 26550 29390; www.konitsahotel.gr; s/d/tr/ste incl breakfast €70/90/120/150; P ❄) This excellent hotel on the hill behind town offers spacious rooms, combining smooth marble and beautifully seasoned wooden floors. Some rooms have large spas and fireplaces. The hotel has a sauna, Turkish baths and gym. Take the road behind the centre uphill for 2km. Taxis go from the *plateia* (about €3).

❶ Information

Konitsa's square has pharmacies, post office and ATM-equipped banks. The bus station is a short walk downhill. There's also a small first-aid clinic.

❶ Getting There & Away

Konitsa Bus Station (☑ 26550 22214) serves Ioannina (€6.20, two hours, seven daily), but not Kastoria.

Buses reach Mertziani (€1.60, 30 minutes, three daily) for Albania.

Preveza   Πρέβεζα

POP 20,795

Occupying a peninsula between the Ionian Sea and the Ambracian (Amvrakikos) Gulf, Preveza (*preh*-veh-zah) has a yacht-lined harbour and colourful back-street houses. Despite its small student population and some holidaying Greeks, it's more business than pleasure-oriented. However, locals believe that with expected Russian and Arab hotel investments on the nearby coast, Preveza is set to take off. Indeed, seeking to promote tourism, authorities now allow yachts free mooring at the central waterfront.

🏃 Activities

Eco Cruising   CRUISE
(☑ 26820 41992; www.eco-cruising.gr; Akragantos 5; cruises from €20) On the central waterfront, Eco Cruising offers sailboat cruises on the Amvrakikos Gulf and to the islands. Tours can be single-day or multiday and include sunset cruises, dolphin-spotting, and bird-watching trips in protected wetlands.

🛏 Sleeping

Hotel Dioni   BOUTIQUE HOTEL $$
(☑ 26820 27381; www.masthotels.gr/boutique-hoteldioni; Kalou 4; s/d/ste from €70/80/110; ☎) 📍 This totally renovated central hotel offers sumptuous rooms loaded with amenities and friendly service.

Rooms O Kaixis   PENSION $
(☑ 6947899404; Parthenagogiou 7; s/d €20/30) Above the eponymous taverna near the waterfront, this solid budget pension has simple but clean rooms, and a knowledgeable owner.

Camping Kalamitsi   CAMPGROUND $
(☑ 26820 22192; www.campingkalamitsi.com; Kalamitsi; camp sites per adult/tent €6.50/5; P ☎ ❄) Large and well-outfitted beach campground, 4km along the Preveza–Parga road. It has a pool and a restaurant.

🍴 Eating

O Kaixis   SEAFOOD $
(☑ 6947899404; Parthenagogiou 7; fish €5-9) The friendly 'mermaid' taverna on a side street near the water prepares excellent fresh fish dishes and grills.

Amvrosios   SEAFOOD $$
(☑ 26820 27192; Grigoriou tou Pemptou 9; fish €7-11) Amvrosios is a good, but relatively pricey

fish taverna spilling onto a flowering side lane by the waterfront.

Information

Leof Irinis, two blocks up from the waterfront, has banks and ATMs.

An underwater **car tunnel** (€3) 2.5km west of Preveza links it with Aktion; no passenger ferry exists. However, the tunnel management is legally obliged to transport cyclists and pedestrians through, for free.

On a southern-waterfront alley, **Karyatis Travel** (📞 6949225729; www.karyatis-travel. gr; cnr Salaminos 1 & Venizelou; ⏰ 9am-2pm & 5-8pm) sells ferry and plane tickets. Ebullient owner Tzeni Nota speaks Greek, English, Thai and Arabic.

 Getting There & Away

AIR

Preveza airport (7km south; sometimes called Lefkada or Aktion) is a European summer

---

SAILING TO ITALY: IGOUMENITSA CONNECTIONS

If you're heading to Italy by ferry, you'll have to pass through **Igoumenitsa** (ih-goo-meh-nit-sah), in Epiros' far northwest. This dull, characterless port also serves Ionian islands such as Corfu (Kerkrya) and Paxos.

Ferries leave from three adjacent quays on the waterfront. Ferries for Ancona and Venice depart from the southern port; those for Brindisi and Bari use the old port, by the shipping offices; and north of the new port are ferries for Corfu (Kerkyra) and Paxos.

Just show up in Igoumenitsa to buy deck-class passenger tickets to Italian ports; book ahead for car tickets or sleeping cabins. Be at the port two hours before departure, and check at the shipping agent's office for your boarding pass. On-board 'camping' is allowable for those with campervans (bring your own oxygen).

At time of research, passenger deck-class tickets cost €58 to Brindisi (six to 9½ hours), €61 to Bari (8½ to 10½ hours), €72 to Ancona (15 hours), and €83 to Venice (23 hours). A passenger ticket in a four-bed cabin with shower is generally twice as expensive. Vehicle prices for Bari and Brindisi start from €57, and from €90 to €112 for Ancona and Venice. Each destination has from two to four sailings per day.

The different ferry companies charge similar prices; check with their local offices or websites. They include **Agoudimos Lines** (📞 26650 21175; www.agoudimos-lines.com; Agion Apostolon 147), **ANEK Lines** (📞 26650 22104; www.anek.gr; Revis Travel Tourism & Shipping, Ethnikis Andistasis 34), **Endeavor Lines** (📞 26650 26833; www.endeavor-lines. com/en/schedules; Eleni Pantazi General Tourism Agency, Ioniou Pelagous), **Minoan Lines** (📞 26650 22952; www.minoan.gr; Ethnikis Andistasis 58a), **Superfast Ferries** (📞 26650 29200; www.superfast.com; Pitoulis & Co Ltd, Agion Apostolon 147) and **Ventouris Ferries** (📞 26650 23565; www.ventouris.gr; Milano Travel, Agion Apostolon 11b). The central **Milano Travel** (📞 26650 23565; milantvl@otenet.gr; Agion Apostolon 11b; ⏰ 9am-7pm) also sells tickets. If you're planning ahead from Preveza, Karyatis Travel (p296) can find hidden discounts and cabin upgrades. If in Parga, try International Travel Services (p299).

For Corfu ferry information, call the **English-speaking operator** (📞 26650 99460).

There's no reason to stay over, but if you do, the **Angelika Pallas Hotel** (📞 26650 26100; www.angelikapallas.gr; Agion Apostolon 145; s/d/tr incl breakfast from €65/75/90; ❄️🛜) is Igoumenitsa's best, located on the central waterfront near the Corfu boat terminal. It offers clean, modern rooms (some, disabled-friendly) and a nourishing restaurant. Slightly cheaper but less attractive places line the waterfront, the best being **Jolly Hotel** (📞 26650 23971; jollyigm@otenet.gr; Ethnikis Andistasis 44; s/d incl breakfast €40/60; @). For a more memorable experience, head for the Nea Selefkia upper neighbourhood, where the luxurious **Hotel Seleykos Palace** (📞 26650 27157; www.selefkos.gr; Nea Selefkia; s/d/tr incl breakfast €60/70/80; 🅿️❄️🛜🛁) offers fantastic views from its roof garden, a restaurant, swimming pool and beauty salon.

From **Igoumenitsa Bus Station** (KTEL Thesprotias; 📞 26650 22309; www.ktel-thesprotias.gr; Arhillohou), two blocks behind the Corfu ferry docks, buses serve Ioannina (€11, two hours, nine daily), Parga (€7.10, one hour, four daily), Athens (€48, eight hours, five daily), Preveza (€12, 2½ hours, two daily) and Thessaloniki (€42, eight hours, one daily). Buses are less frequent from October to May.

charter-flight hub, with numerous destinations. Domestically, **Sky Express** (www.skyexpress. gr) serves Sitia in Crete and several Ionian islands. Taxis cost €12.

BUS

Preveza's bus station is 2km from town; taxi drivers charge €4 or more to the centre. Buses serve Ioannina (€10.40, two hours, nine daily), Parga (€5.50, two hours, five daily), Igoumenitsa (€13.30, 2½ hours, two daily), Thessaloniki (€39.30, eight hours, two daily) and Athens (€37.30, six hours, five daily).

Nikopoli   Νικόπολη

In 31 BC Octavian (later, Emperor Augustus) defeated Mark Antony and Cleopatra in the naval Battle of Actium (present-day Aktion). **Nikopoli** (City of Victory; ☑ 26820 41336; adult/child €2/free; ☉ 8.30am-3pm) was built to commemmorate this. After 5th- and 6th-century barbarian raids, Emperor Justinian rebuilt it. But the 11th-century Bulgarians sacked it for good.

Scant **Roman walls**, and better-preserved **Byzantine walls** and a **theatre** are visible, as are remains of a **Temple of Ares**, a **Temple of Poseidon**, an **aqueduct**, **Roman baths** and a restored **Roman odeum**. The enormous site sprawls across the Preveza–Arta road and buses stop here. At the time of research, the site was closed for further excavations and reconstruction; check locally.

Nikopoli's **Archaeological Museum** (☑ 26820 41336; adult/child €4/free; ☉ 8.30am-3pm) has ancient finds (others are in Ioannina's Archaeological Museum).

Parga   Πάργα

POP 2415

Crowned by a Venetian castle, pretty Parga overlooks a curving bay with sandy beach and little island opposite. The streets of its old quarter are white-plastered and flowery, with historic chapels and intriguing museums tucked within. Long sandy beaches lie outside of town, and in high season Parga's waterfront bars are packed. Nevertheless, it's never truly hectic and little kids can scamper about freely.

The hospitable locals in this former Venetian possession indeed have a certain Italian resemblance. Parga is a great base for local beaches, historic sites and excursions to Ionian islands.

◎ Sights

In the old quarter, a permanent **photography exhibition** of historic images was about to open at time of research. Here, don't miss the small, austere **Church of the Dodeka Apostoli** (1780) and **Church of Agios Dimitrios** (1850).

Venetian Castle CASTLE
(To Kastro) ᴳᴿᴱᴱ The clifftop Castle of St Andreas offers superb views of coast and town from its ramparts. The renovated central area has intact cannons and a cafe (☑ 26840 31150; ☉ 11am-late) in the former French armoury. The ramparts are partially unfenced, so mind the kids.

Beaches BEACHES
The central waterfront's **Kryoneri Beach** is sandy, with shallow waters, opposite the island. A 15-minute walk over the castle hill leads to the 2km-long **Valtos Beach**, with loungers (€4 to €6). Alternatively, 2km south of Parga, **Lyhnos Beach** is more relaxed, with a small, shady campground and clear waters. There's a taverna and villa accommodation on the steep, winding entry road.

Paragaea Olive Oil Museum MUSEUM
(☑ 26840 32889; www.paragaea.gr; Tzavella 19; €3.50; ☉ 10am-11pm) This fascinating old-town museum opened in 2013, in Parga's erstwhile olive-oil factory, operational from 1929 until 1974. The wooden building, filled with original machinery and even documents found during renovations, attests to Parga's major pre-tourism industry. A guided tour comes with the ticket. It covers the local industry, technology and what working here was like. Finally, there's a scrumptious sampling of bread and local olive oils (some with intriguing flavours such as lemon or orange). Buy more oils in the museum shop.

⚘ Activities

Across from the bus stop, long-established International Travel Services (p299) books trips to the Nekromanteio of Afyra (€42), cruises on the Aherondas River (€25) or to Paxos and Antipaxos (€20).

Parga Tour Train (www.tour-train.parga.com; waterfront) offers an edifying, child-friendly two-hour diversion. Starting from the waterfront at 9.30am, this open-sided fun train chugs up the coast road, veers into shady olive groves and stops at **Anthousa** village's forested **Watermill Museum**. Here, kindly

Vassilis Nakas explains the antiquated machinery once used to grind flour. Next is a waterfall walk (or, rest at the watermill's cafe). The evening train instead visits Anthousa village (800m up from the watermill) and its ruined **Castle of Ali Pasha.**

🛏 Sleeping

★ Acropol Hotel   HOTEL $$
(📲 26840 31239; www.acropol.biz; Agion Apostolon 4; s/d €60/90; ❄) In Parga's old quarter, the refined Acropol (built 1884) offers 10 luxurious rooms with king-sized beds, hydromassage showers and handmade Italian furniture. Some balconies face the Venetian castle. It is well-signposted within the quarter. The Acropol also hosts the discerning Castello Restaurant (p298).

★ Salvator Villas & Spa Hotel   HOTEL $$$
(📲 26840 31833; www.sansalvator.com; Kyperi; deluxe apt/villa incl breakfast €200/700; P ❄ 🛜 🛁) The friendly, luxurious Salvator overlooks Parga and the coast from the main road, 1km south of town. Villas have two bedrooms, kitchenette and terrace, and some have private pools (there's also a central outdoor pool). The buffet breakfast and restaurant are excellent, and a spa centre operates. Free shuttle buses go into town throughout the day.

Bella Vista Studios & Apartments   APARTMENTS $$
(📲 26840 31457, 26840 31833; www.bellavista.com.gr; Lihnos Beach; studio/apt €80/100; P ❄ 🛜 🛁) Above Lihnos Beach, these modern studios and apartments encircle an inviting pool set amidst citrus trees. The apartments sleep up to five, and the upper rooms have large balconies overlooking the beach and hills. It's a steep downhill walk to the beach, but the management also offers discounted car hire.

Enjoy Lihnos Beach Camping   CAMPGROUND $
(📲 26840 31171; www.enjoy-lichnos.net; Lihnos Beach; camp sites per adult/tent €6/4, d €55; P) Lihnos Beach's relaxed campground occupies a shaded spot with beach volleyballs, free umbrellas, minimarket and restaurant. Studios are also available.

Valtos Camping   CAMPGROUND $
(📲 26840 31287; www.campingvaltos.com; Valtos Beach; camp sites per adult/tent €6.50/6; P) This campground set amidst orange trees on busy Valtos Beach has a restaurant and bungalows with kitchenette and air-con. It's

a steep 15-minute walk from Parga centre (or five-minute drive).

Hotel Paradise   HOTEL $$
(📲 26840 31229; Spyrou Livada 23; s/d €60/75; ❄ @ 🛁) The friendly, central Hotel Paradise has airy modern rooms, pool and downstairs bar.

🍴 Eating & Drinking

★ Castello Restaurant   FINE DINING $$
(📲 26840 31833; www.castello-restaurant.com; Hotel Acropol, Agion Apostolon 4; mains €8-14; ⊙12pm-1am) Longtime favourite Castello offers a creative fusion of French, Italian and Greek cuisine. Service is excellent, and the elegant, romantic feel is accentuated by the relaxing jazz music and soft tones. Note the well-stocked wine cellar, visible through a glass panel beneath your feet.

Motley Coffeesweet   SWEETS $
(📲 26840 32115; waterfront; sweets €3-5; ⊙8am-2am) This glossy new cafe and sweet shop, overlooking Parga beach, opened in 2013. It has a delicious variety of homemade desserts, plus ice cream.

O Arkoudas   SEAFOOD $$
(📲 26840 32553; fish €8-15; ⊙12pm-1am) 'The Bear' has tasty fresh fish dishes and great waterfront views.

Taverna to Souli   TAVERNA $
(📲 26840 31658; Anexartisias 45; mezedhes €4-6, mains €6-11; ⊙12pm-1am) Local mezedhes such as *feta Souli* (grilled feta cheese with tomatoes and herbs) are well-done here, as are Epirot specialities like the *kleftiko* (oven-baked lamb or goat).

Symposium   TAVERNA $$
(📲 26840 32177; waterfront; mains €9-13; ⊙10am-11pm) Overlooking the water, Symposium offers traditional Greek fare, seafood and views.

Sugar Bar   BAR
(www.sugarbar.gr; waterfront; ⊙10am-late) The secret weapon of this ever-popular waterfront bar? Some 100-plus different cocktails. The loyal following, like the music, is both Greek and international.

Antico   BAR
(📲 26840 32713; Anexartasies 4; ⊙10am-3am) On an old-town side street, Parga's classic rock bar gets busy late.

ⓘ Information

The Preveza–Igoumenitsa road passes above Parga; the southeast-side entrance accesses the beach and waterfront, the northwestern one, the bus stop and the centre (down Spyrou Livada). Another road further west accesses Valtos Beach.

Pargas has ATM-equipped banks and a small medical centre. For emergencies, **Dr Spiros Radiotis** (☑ 6944162261, 26840 32450; Alexandrou Baga 1; ⊙ 24hr), by the Emnoriki Trapeza, is on call 24 hours a day.

International Travel Services (ITS; ☑ 26840 31833; www.parga.net; Spyrou Livada 4) By the bus station, the long-established and helpful ITS finds accommodation, books local tours, arranges travel tickets and provides general information. A Budget Rent a Car office is within.

Post Office (Alexandrou Baga 18)

ⓘ Getting There & Away

BUS

Parga Bus Station (☑ 26840 31218) serves Igoumenitsa (€5.90, one hour, five daily), Preveza (€7.10, two hours, four daily), Thessaloniki (€45.70, seven hours, one daily) and Athens (€41.20, seven hours, three daily).

CAR

Hire a car (from €40 per day) at **Europcar** (☑ 26840 32777; Spyrou Livada 19) or **Budget Rent a Car**, located at ITS.

WATER TAXI

Water taxis serve Valtos Beach (€4) from 9.30am to 6pm; Lihnos Beach (€7) from 11am to 5pm; and Sarakiniko (€8) from 10am to 5pm.

Nekromanteio of Afyra
Νεκρομαντείο της Αφύρας

The ancients feared it as the gate of Hades, god of the underworld; for visitors today the Nekromanteio of Afyra (☑ 26840 41206; adult/child €2/free; ⊙ 8.30am-3pm) is just the labyrinthine ruin at the end of a beautiful boat ride up the Aherondas River. However, at time of research it was closed – to be fully reconstructed, in all its morbid glory – so check locally.

The Nekromanteio was an oracle: ancient Greek pilgrims offered up milk, honey and the blood of sacrificial animals, and the itinerant priests would duly arrange a conference call with their dead ancestors. The ferrymen who transported pilgrims down the river made an absolute killing and, so the legend goes, would throw the penniless overboard to drown. The wily priests' intense show-ritual involved much mumbo-jumbo, hallucinogenic substances, leading questions and lowering pilgrims into a dark, dank underground vault for two days. No wonder, then, that it was like a religious experience when they were blinded by sunlight from a hidden aperture during the dramatic finale.

This cottage industry flourished for centuries before dying out when Christianity became prominent. However, the existence of a **graveyard** (located near the ruined Byzantine **Monastery of Agios Ioannis Prodromos**) indicates that the site's macabre identity outlived it.

Nekromanteio tours, sometimes packaged with other sites, cost about €40. Make sure you confirm that the Nekromanteio has reopened before booking, or you may be taken to a less interesting 'replacement' attraction instead. If you're driving, head south towards Mesopotamo (19km), and take the Nekromanteio turn-off (1km before Mesopotamo).

Saronic Gulf Islands

Best Places to Eat

➡ Sunset (p313)

➡ Elia (p304)

➡ Aspros Gatos (p308)

➡ Akrogialia (p317)

➡ Four Seasons (p314)

Best Places to Stay

➡ Poseidonion Grand Hotel (p317)

➡ Hydra Hotel (p311)

➡ Rosy's Little Village (p306)

➡ Hotel Miranda (p311)

➡ Orloff Resort (p317)

Why Go?

The Saronic Gulf Islands (Νησιά του Σαρωνικού) dot the waters nearest Athens and offer a fast track to Greek island life. As with all Greek islands, each of the Saronics has a unique feel and culture so you can hop between classical heritage, resort beaches, exquisite architecture and remote escapism.

Aegina is home to a spectacular Doric temple and ruined Byzantine village, while nearby pine-clad Angistri feels protected and peaceful outside of the booming midsummer months. Further south, Poros, with its forested hinterland, curves only a few hundred metres from the Peloponnese. The Saronic showpiece, Hydra, is a gorgeous car-free island with a port of carefully preserved stone houses rising from a chic history-charged harbour. Deepest south of all, pine-scented Spetses also has a vibrant nautical history and pretty town architecture plus myriad aqua coves only minutes from the Peloponnese.

When to Go
Hydra

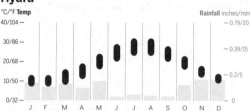

May The islands awaken after winter; come for flower-filled Easter.

Jun Celebrate Miaoulia in Hydra with sparkling waters and warm weather.

Sep The best-kept secret: clear skies, thinning crowds, and Spetses' Armata celebration.

ATTICA

Gulf of
Megara

Corinth
(20km)

Diaporioi

Ypsili

Salamina
Paloukia
Straits of
Salamina
Salamina

Perama
Piraeus

Saronic
Gulf

Aegina
Town
Souvala
Temple of
Aphaia
Agia Marina

Mylos
Skala
Perdika
Paleohora
Aegina

Kira

Angistri
Moni

Nafplio
(25km)

Gulf of
Epidavros

Epidavros

Methana

AEGEAN
SEA

Poros

Poros Town
Galatas

PELOPONNESE

Cape Spathi

Argolic
Gulf

Kranidi
Ermioni
Kapari
Island
Dokos

Gulf
of Hydra

Cape
Zourvas

Porto
Heli
Kosta

Hydra Town
Hydra

Spetses
Town
Spetses
Trikeri

MYRTOÖN
SEA

Spetsopoula

MEDITERRANEAN
SEA

N   0   20 km
    0   12 miles

Saronic Gulf Islands Highlights

1 Bounce between **Hydra's** (p309) gorgeous port – with its excellent museums and chic scene – and the island's deserted trails and ubiquitous swimming rocks.

2 Delve into Aegina's ancient history at the **Temple of Aphaia** (p305) and **Byzantine Paleohora** (p305).

3 Taste test your way through **Spetses'** (p315) top restaurants, trace the region's history in Spetses Town museums, or ride the island's ring road to dip into sparkling bays.

4 Get away from it all in sleepy **Angistri** (p306) in the low season, when the beaches are most tranquil.

5 Explore the peaceful interior of **Poros** (p307).

AEGINA   ΑΙΓΙΝΑ

POP 13,190

Beyond its bustling port, Aegina (*eh*-yi-nah) has the seductive, easygoing character of a typical Greek island but with the added bonus of more than its fair share of prestigious ancient sites. Weekending Athenians spice up the mix of laidback locals and commuters who use the island like an Athens suburb. Unique Aegina treats include a special, and delicious, pistachio nut, the splendid 5th-century Temple of Aphaia and the magical Byzantine ruins called Paleohora.

Aegina was the leading maritime power of the Saronic Gulf during the 7th century BC, when it grew wealthy through trade and political ascendancy. The island made a major contribution to the Greek victory over the Persian fleet at the Battle of Salamis in 480 BC. Despite this solidarity with the Athenian state, the latter invaded in 459 BC out of jealousy of Aegina's wealth and status and of its liaison with Sparta. Aegina never regained its glory, although in the early 19th century it played a bold part in the defeat of the Turks and was the temporary capital of a partly liberated Greece from 1827 to 1829.

Aegina & Angistri

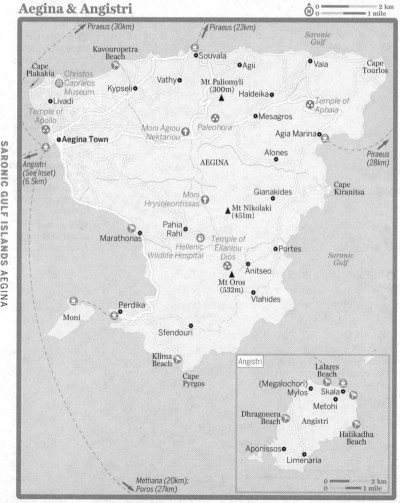

BOAT SERVICES FROM AEGINA

DESTINATION	PORT	TIME	FARE	FREQUENCY
Angistri (Skala)	Aegina Town	20min	€2.50	1 daily
Angistri (Skala)*	Aegina Town	10min	€5.20	6 daily
Methana	Aegina Town	40min	€5.70	2-3 daily
Piraeus	Aegina Town	1hr 10min	€9.50	hourly
Piraeus*	Aegina Town	40min	€13.50	hourly
Piraeus	Agia Marina	1hr	€9.50	3-4 daily, summer
Piraeus	Souvala	1hr 35min	€9.50	3-4 daily, summer
Poros	Aegina Town	1hr 50min	€8.50	2-3 daily

*high-speed service

❶ Getting There & Away

Aegina's main port, Aegina Town, has ferries operated by **Hellenic Seaways** (☎ 22970 22945), **Nova Ferries** (☎ 22970 24200) and **Agios Nektarios** (☎ Aegina 22970 25625, Piraeus 21042 25625; www.anes.gr) and high-speed ferries operated by **Hellenic Seaways** (☎ 22970 26777) and **Aegean Flying Dolphins** (☎ 22970 25800) to/from Piraeus and Angistri. Some ferries continue on to Methana (Peloponnese) and Poros. Ferries dock at the large outer quay, hydrofoils at the smaller inner quay.

Alexandros (☎ 210 482 1006; www.alexcruises.gr) serves Aegina's smaller ports, Agia Marina and Souvala, and Piraeus in high season only.

Even in winter, high-speed ferries from Piraeus get fully booked for weekends: book ahead.

Angistri Express (☎ 6947118863) several daily in high season to Skala and Milos on Angistri (€5, 20 minutes). Departs from midway along Aegina harbour, where timetables are displayed.

Water taxis (☎ 69722 29720, 22970 91387) to Angistri cost €45 one way, regardless of the number of people.

❶ Getting Around

BUS

Buses from Aegina Town run frequently around the island (departure times are displayed outside the ticket office on Plateia Ethnegersias; you must buy tickets there).

Agia Marina (€2, 30 minutes), via Paleohora (€1.40, 15 minutes) and Temple of Aphaia (€1.70, 25 minutes)

Perdika (€1.80, 15 minutes)

Souvala (€1.40, 20 minutes)

CAR, MOTORCYCLE & BICYCLE

Numerous outfits hire out vehicles; prices start from €30 per day for cars, €15 for a 50cc motorcycle and €8 for bicycles.

Sklavenas Rent A Car For cars, jeeps, scooters, quads and bikes. Branches in **Aegina Town** (☎ 22970 22892; Kazantzaki 5), located on the road towards the Temple of Apollo, and in **Agia Marina** (☎ 22970 32871).

Karagiannis Travel (☎ 22970 28780; Kanari 2, Aegina Town)

TAXI

Taxi (☎ 22970 22010)

Aegina Town   Αίγινα

POP 8905

The sparkling harbour of Aegina Town is backed by a buzzing promenade of people, motorbikes, cafes and restaurants. As you wander back into the narrow town streets, with kids riding bikes and laundry strung from balconies, small-town Greek life takes over again.

The parallel streets Irioti and Rodi backing the harbour are crammed with shops of every kind, and a few 19th-century neoclassical buildings intermix with whitewashed houses. Ancient Greece is represented by the impressive ruins of the Temple of Apollo, just north of the harbour.

❶ ISLAND HOPPING

No direct ferries connect Aegina and Angistri with Hydra and Spetses; go via Piraeus or Poros. For day trips, take an Aegina–Poros–Hydra **cruise boat** (www.athensonedaycruise.com). Pegasus Cruises (p142) goes from Nafplio to Spetses and Hydra.

⊙ Sights

Temple of Apollo RUINS
(☑22970 22637; adult/child €3/2; ⊙8.30am-2.30pm Tue-Sun) Northwest of the port, ruined walls, cisterns and broken pillars in honey-coloured stone are lorded over by a solitary surviving column. It's all that's left of a 5th-century-BC temple that was once part of an ancient acropolis (built on a prehistoric site). The informative **Sanctuary Museum** has translations in English and German.

Folklore Museum MUSEUM
(☑22970 26401; S Rodi; ⊙8.30am-2.30pm Wed-Fri, 10am-1pm Sat & Sun, also 5.30-8.30pm Fri & Sat) FREE Peruse historic clothing, housewares and artwork recreating the mood of old-time island life.

✿ Festivals & Events

Aegina Fistiki Fest FOOD
(www.aeginafistikifest.gr; ⊙September) *Fistiki* means pistachio and this three-day brouhaha celebrates Aegina's famous PDO (Protected Designation of Origin) pistachio (*fistiki aeginis*) through music, art and culinary contests.

🛏 Sleeping

Book ahead at weekends.

Aeginitiko Archontiko PENSION $
(☑22970 24968; www.aeginitikoarchontiko.gr; cnr Ag Nikolaou & Thomaiados; s/d/tr incl breakfast €50/55/60; ✳🗢) The rich character of this centrally located old mansion translates through period 19th-century features, a charming salon and courtyard and a splendid breakfast. Rooms, however, are a bit cramped and worn, and bathrooms are basic. Sea views from the rooftop terrace.

Electra Pension PENSION $
(☑22970 26715; www.aegina-electra.gr; s/d €40/45; ✳🗢) There are no views from this small whitewashed pension, but rooms are impeccable and comfy in a quiet corner of the town centre. It outclasses nearby hotels by a long way.

Marianna Studios PENSION $
(☑22970 25650; www.aeginastudiosmarianna.com; Kiverniou 16-18; s/d €30/35; ✳) Simple, very basic rooms and very friendly owners create a top-notch budget choice. Some rooms have balconies or overlook a quiet, leafy garden alongside the interior courtyard. One has a kitchen (double/triple €40/45).

Hotel Rastoni HOTEL $$
(☑22970 27039; www.rastoni.gr; Odos Stratigou Dimitri Petriti 31; d/tr incl breakfast €80/110; P✳@🗢) Spacious rooms have balconies overlooking the lovely garden and the Temple of Apollo. Generous breakfasts and friendly staff round out the experience. Find it in a residential neighbourhood a few minutes north of the harbour.

Fistikies Holiday Apartments APARTMENTS $$
(☑22970 23783; www.fistikies.gr; Logiotatidou 1; studio €90, 4-person apt €120; P✳🗢⛱) This complex of tidy, family-friendly apartments was built in 2007 on the southern edge of town, inland from the football field. Spacious apartments have DVD players and terraces overlooking the pool.

✗ Eating

The harbourfront restaurants make for lazy world-watching but are not particularly good, unless you hit the unvarnished *ouzeries*.

Aegina's pistachio nuts are on sale everywhere (from €6 for 500g, depending on quality).

★ Elia MEDITERRANEAN $
(☑22975 00205; Koumoundourou 4; mains €6-9; ⊙lunch & dinner, winter hrs reduced) Burrow into the backstreets to find this excellent eatery popular with locals. Imaginative, fresh specialities include the pistachio pesto and pitas of the day.

ONLINE RESOURCES

Monthly **Saronic Magazine** (www.saronicmagazine.com), available on all the main islands, has partial coverage of what's on. Island websites have links to houses for rent, usually a good deal for larger groups.

Aegina www.aeginagreece.com

Poros www.poros.gr

Hydra www.hydra.com.gr, www.hydra-direct.com, www.hydraislandgreece.com, www.hydraview.gr

Spetses www.spetsesdirect.com, www.spetses.gr, www.spetses.wordpress.com/english

Gelladakis
MEZEDHES $

(☎ 22970 27308; Pan Irioti 45; dishes €7-12; ⊙ lunch & dinner) Ensconced behind the noisy mid-harbour fish market, this vibrant joint and its immediate neighbour are always thronging with people tucking into hell-fired octopus or sardines, plus other classic mezedhes.

Tsias
TAVERNA $

(☎ 22970 23529; Dimokratias 47; mains €7-10; ⊙ lunch & dinner) Harbour-side eating at its best. Try shrimps with tomatoes and feta, or one of the daily specials.

Bakalogatos
MEZEDHES $$

(☎ 22970 23818; Pan Irioti & Neoptolemou; mains €7-13; ⊙ lunch & dinner Tue-Sun) Mezedhes in an elegant setting, with faux finished tables and traditional products on the walls.

🍷 Drinking & Nightlife

Music bars and cafes line the harbour.

Remvi
CAFE, BAR

(Dimokratias 51; 🛜) Popular music cafe-bar hops day and night.

International Corner
BAR

(S Rodi) Get off the main strip. The gregarious owner takes requests, from Top 40 to fantastic Greek music. In a character-filled, wood-panelled bar-room.

Avli
BAR

(☎ 22970 26458; Pan Irioti 17) Bubbles with activity in a covered garden; tunes from '60s to Greek. Vartan, across the road, chics it up.

ℹ Information

Aegina has no tourist office. Check Karagiannis Travel (p303) for car hire, tours and non-Aegina boats. Harbourfront banks have ATMs.
Hospital (☎ 22970 24489)
Port Authority (☎ 22970 22328) At the entrance to the ferry quays.
Tourist Police (☎ 22970 27777; Leonardou Lada) Up a lane opposite the hydrofoil dock.

Around Aegina Town

Aegina is lush and wildflower laden in spring, and year-round offers some of the best archaic sites in the Saronic Gulf. The interior hills and mountains add drama to the small island, but beaches are not its strongest suit. The east-coast town of **Agia Marina** is the island's main package resort. It has a shallow-water beach that is ideal for families, but it's backed by a fairly crowded main drag. A few thin, sandy beaches line the roadside between Aegina Town and Perdika, such as **Marathonas**.

⭐ Temple of Aphaia
TEMPLE

(☎ 22970 32398; adult/child €4/free; ⊙ 8am-3pm) The well-preserved remains of this impressive temple stand proudly on a pine-covered hill with far-reaching views over the Saronic Gulf. Built in 480 BC, it celebrates a local deity of pre-Hellenic times. The temple's pediments were originally decorated with splendid Trojan War sculptures, most of which were stolen in the 19th century and now decorate Munich's Glyptothek. Panels throughout the site also have information in English.

Aphaia is 10km east of Aegina Town. Infrequent buses to Agia Marina stop (20 minutes); taxis cost about €12 one way.

⭐ Paleohora
CHURCHES, RUINS

(Παλαιοχώρα) FREE This enchanting remote hillside is dotted with the remains of a Byzantine village. More than 30 surviving **churches** punctuate the rocky heights of the original citadel, and several have been refurbished. They are linked by a network of paths, carpeted with wildflowers in spring. The ancient town of Paleohora was Aegina's capital from the 9th century through the medieval period and was only abandoned during the 1820s.

Paleohora is 6.5km east of Aegina Town near enormous modern church Moni Agiou Nektariou. Buses from Aegina Town to Agia Marina stop at the turn-off to Paleohora (10 minutes); taxis cost €8 one way.

Christos Capralos Museum
MUSEUM

(☎ 22970 22001; Livadi; admission €2; ⊙ 10am-2pm & 6-8pm Tue-Sun Jun-Oct, 10am-2pm Fri-Sun Nov-May) The home and studio of acclaimed sculptor Christos Capralos (1909–93), on the seacoast near Livadi, 1.5km north of Aegina Town, has been made into a museum displaying many of his fluid, powerful works. Monumental sculptures include the 40m-long Pindus Frieze.

Perdika & Around Πέρδικα

The quaint fishing village of Perdika lies about 9km south of Aegina Town on the southern tip of the west coast and makes for a relaxed sojourn.

Perdika's harbour is very shallow so, for the best swimming, catch one of the regular caïques (little boats, €4) to the small island of **Moni**, a few minutes offshore. A **nature reserve,** it has a tree-lined beach and **summertime cafe.**

Tavernas line Perdika's raised harbourfront terrace, and sultry sunset relaxation makes way for summertime buzzing nightlife when late-night music bars rev into gear.

Sleeping & Eating

Villa Rodanthos   STUDIOS **$**
(22970 61400; www.wix.com/villarodanthos/perdika; Perdika; studios from €45; ❄ ✿ ⊛) A gem of a place, not least because of its charming owner. Each room has its own colourful decor and a kitchen.

Angie Studios   HOTEL, APARTMENTS **$$**
(22970 61445; www.antzistudios.gr; Perdika; studios €60-120; P ✿ ⊛ ❄) A range of rooms and apartments overlook a central pool. Top-floor apartments in the newer building have some sea views.

O Thanasis   TAVERNA, SEAFOOD **$**
(22970 31348; Portes; mains €7-8; ⊘ lunch & dinner, winter hrs reduced) In Portes. A charming family welcomes you to a seafront terrace festooned with flower pots.

Miltos   SEAFOOD, TAVERNA **$$**
(22970 61051; Perdika; mains €12-15; ⊘ lunch & dinner) The most locally popular of Perdika's seafood tavernas; known for the highest-quality seafood and no-nonsense Greek staples.

ANGISTRI   ΑΓΚΙΣΤΡΙ
POP 1,120

Tiny Angistri lies a few kilometres off the west coast of Aegina and out of high season makes a rewarding day trip or a worthwhile longer escape. Visit www.agistri.com.gr for island information.

Getting There & Away

Fast hydrofoils and car ferries come from Piraeus (hydrofoil/ferry 55min/90min, €13.50/10.50) via Aegina (hydrofoils 10min, €5.20, 6 daily; ferry 20min, €2.50, 1 daily). Angistri Express (p303) serves Aegina several times daily, Mon-Sat.

Water taxis (p303) costs €45 one way between Aegina and Angistri.

Getting Around

Several buses a day during summer run from Skala and Mylos to Limenaria and Dhragonera Beach. It's worth hiring a scooter (€15) or sturdy bike (€6) to explore the coastline road.

You can also follow tracks from Metohi overland through cool pine forest to reach Dhragonera Beach. Take a compass; tracks divide often and route-finding can be frustrating.
Kostas Bike Hire (22970 91021; Skala)
Takis Rent A Bike & Bicycles (22970 91001; Mylos)

Skala & Around   Σκάλα

The port-resort village of Skala is crammed with small hotels, apartments, tavernas and cafes but life, in general, still ticks along gently. A right turn from the quay leads to the small harbour beach and then to a church on a low headland. Beyond lies the best beach on the island, but it disappears beneath sun loungers and broiling bodies in July and August. Turning left from the quay at Skala takes you south along a dirt path through the pine trees to the pebbly and clothing-optional **Halikadha Beach.**

About 1km west from Skala, Angistri's other port, **Mylos** (Megalochori), has an appealing traditional character, rooms and tavernas, but no beach.

Aponissos has turquoise waters, a small offshore island, and a reliably tasty taverna. **Limenaria** has deeper green waters. The island as a whole gets super-sleepy in low season.

Sleeping & Eating

Book ahead, especially for August and summer weekends. A board on Skala's quay lists accommodation.

★ **Rosy's Little Village**   PENSION **$$**
(22970 91610; www.rosyslittlevillage.com; s/d/tr/q €52/65/75/100, restaurant mains €6-10; ⊘ restaurant lunch & dinner; ❄ ✿) A complex of Cycladic-style cubes steps gently down to the sea, a short way east of Skala's quay. Full of light and colour, with built-in couches and tiny balconies with sea views, Rosy's also offers mountain bikes, summertime courses, weekly picnics and live-music evenings. Their **restaurant** emphasises organics.

★ **Alkyoni Inn**   PENSION, TAVERNA **$**
(22970 91378; www.alkyoni-agistri.com; s/d/maisonette from €30/40/75, mains €6-10; ⊘ break-

SARONIC GULF ISLANDS SKALA & AROUND

fast, lunch & dinner Easter-Sep; ❄ 📶 🏠) The welcoming family-run Alkyoni is a 10-minute stroll southeast of Skala's quay. The popular taverna dishes up well-prepared fish and meat while the hotel offers some sea-facing rooms with fabulous, unobstructed views. Two-storey family maisonettes sleep four.

ℹ️ Information

There's a bank with ATM in Skala's main street.

POROS ΠΟΡΟΣ

POP 4010

Poros is separated from the mountainous Peloponnese by a narrow sea channel, and its protected setting makes the main settlement of Poros Town seem like a cheery lakeside resort. Its pastel-hued houses stack up the hillside to a clock tower and make a vibrant first impression.

Poros is made up of two land masses connected by a tiny isthmus: **Sferia**, which is occupied mainly by the town of Poros, and the much larger and mainly forested **Kalavria**, which has the island's beaches and seasonal hotels scattered along its southern shore. Poros still maintains a sense of remoteness in its sparsely populated, forested interior.

The Peloponnesian town of **Galatas** lies on the opposite shore, making Poros a useful base from which to explore the ancient sites of the Peloponnese. For example, the exquisite ancient theatre of **Epidavros** (p146) is within reach by car or taxi (☑ in Galatas 22980 42888).

ℹ️ Getting There & Away

Daily ferries connect Piraeus to Poros in summer (reduced timetable in winter). High-speed ferries continue south to Hydra, Spetses, Ermioni and Porto Heli. Conventional ferries connect Aegina

Poros

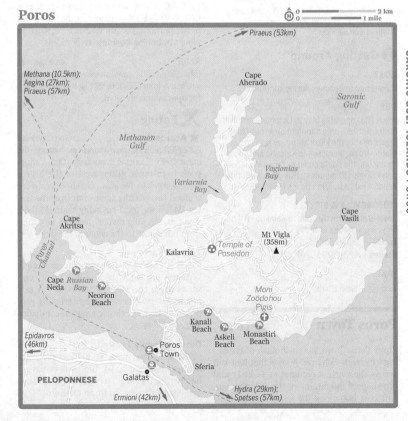

to Poros and Methana on the mainland. Travel agents (p309) sell tickets.

Caïques shuttle constantly between Poros and Galatas (€0.80, five minutes). They leave from the quay opposite Plateia Iroön, the triangular plaza near the main ferry dock in Poros Town. Hydrofoils dock about 50m north of here and car ferries to Galatas (person/car €0.89/5.60) leave from the dock several hundred metres north again, on the road to Kalavria.

You can also do a one-way rental between branches of **Pop's Car** (☑ in Galatas 22980 42910; www.popscarrental.com) at Athens airport and Galatas (or Ermioni).

Galatas has a **bus station** (☑ 22980 42480).

Boat Services from Poros

DESTINATION	TIME	FARE	FREQUENCY
Aegina	1¼hr	€8.30	2-3 daily
Hydra*	30min	€12.50	5-6 daily
Methana	30min	€4.50	2-3 daily
Piraeus	2½hr	€12.80	2-3 daily
Piraeus*	1hr	€22.50	5-6 daily
Spetses*	1½hr	€14.50	3-4 daily

*high-speed services

ⓘ Getting Around

BOAT
Caïques go to beaches during summer.

BUS
A bus (€3) operates May to October every half hour from 7am until midnight on a route that starts next to the kiosk at the eastern end of Plateia Iroön. It crosses to Kalavria and goes east along the south coast as far as Moni Zoödohou Pigis (10 minutes), then turns around and heads west to Neorion Beach (15 minutes).

MOTORCYCLE & BICYCLE
Several places on the road to Kalavria rent out bicycles/scooters (per day €15/4)
Fotis (☑ 22980 25873)
Stelios (☑ 22980 23026)

TAXI
Taxi (☑ 22980 23003)

Poros Town   Πόρος
POP 4102

Zippy Poros Town is a mishmash of charming ice cream–coloured houses that look out across the narrow channel at Galatas and the shapely mountains of the Peloponnese. Sailboats bob along the lengthy quay while ferries glide through the channel and smaller vessels scurry to and fro. Behind the harbour, *plateïes* (squares) and tavernas hide from view and a rocky bluff rises steeply to a crowning clock tower.

🛏 Sleeping

Seven Brothers Hotel   HOTEL $
(☑ 22980 23412; www.7brothers.gr; s/d/tr €40/45/55; ❄ 🛜) Conveniently close to the hydrofoil quay, this modern hotel has bright, comfy rooms with super-duper bathrooms. Some have small balconies, some sea views.

Georgia Mellou Rooms   PENSION $
(☑ 22980 22309; http://porosnet.gr/gmellou; Plateia Georgiou; d/tr €30/40; ❄) Simple, old-fashioned rooms are tucked into the heart of old town, next to the cathedral, high above the harbour. The charming owner keeps everything ship-shape. Book ahead for fantastic views from west-side rooms.

Hotel Manessi   BUSINESS HOTEL $
(☑ 22980 22273; www.manessi.com; Paralia; d €40-50; ❄ @ 🛜) Well placed at the mid-point of the harbour, the Manessi is a bit worn in places but offers business-style rooms.

Roloi   APARTMENTS $$
(☑ 22980 25808; www.storoloi-poros.gr; studio/apt/house from €55/100/150; ❄) Good source for apartments in town.

🍴 Eating

★ Aspros Gatos   SEAFOOD, TAVERNA $
(☑ 22980 25650; www.whitecat.gr; Labraki 49; mains €6-15; ☺ lunch & dinner Easter-Oct) A short walk from town, 400m west of the bridge on the road to Neorion Beach, Poros' best seafood taverna sits smack out over the water. Watch the local kayaking team do their thing as the jolly owner provides anything from bolognese to the catch of the day.

Taverna Karavolos   TAVERNA $
(☑ 22980 26158; www.karavolos.com; mains €6-9; ☺ dinner) Karavolos means 'big snail', and snails are a speciality of the house at this quaint eatery on a backstreet. Friendly proprietors also offer classic Greek meat dishes and some fish.

Dimitris Family Taverna   TAVERNA $
(☑ 22980 23709; mains €6-10; ☺ dinner) Renowned for their meat, the owners have a butchering business, so cuts of pork, lamb and chicken are of the finest quality.

Oasis TAVERNA **$**
(☑22980 22955; mains €6-12; ☉lunch & dinner)
Harbourside home-cooked Greek staples
and seafood.

❶ Information

Poros has no tourist office. Harbourfront agencies arrange accommodation, car hire, tours and cruises. Banks on Plateia Iroön have ATMs.

Askeli Travel (☑22980 25857; www.askeli-travel.com)

Family Tours (☑22980 23743; www.family-tours.gr) Sells conventional-ferry tickets.

Marinos Tours (☑22980 23423; www.marinostours.gr) Across from the hydrofoil quay; sells hydrofoil tickets.

Tourist Police (☑22980 22256; Dimosthenous 10) Behind the high school.

Around Poros

Poros' best beaches include the pebbly **Kanali Beach**, on Kalavria 1km east of the bridge, and the long, sandy **Askeli Beach**, about 500m further east. Askeli has a few year-round seafront tavernas and **Hotel New Aegli** (☑22980 22372; www.newaegli.com; d €50-90; ❃@🕸🏊), a decent resort-style hotel, with all the expected amenities and sea views.

The 18th-century monastery **Moni Zoödohou Pigis**, well signposted 4km east of Poros Town, has a beautiful gilded iconostasis from Asia Minor. Nearby, **Sirene Blue Resort** (☑22980 22741; www.sirenblueresort.gr; Monastiri Beach; d incl breakfast €120-155; ❃🕸🏊) offers a deluxe seaside vacation.

From the road below the monastery head inland to reach the 6th-century **Temple of Poseidon**. There's very little left of the temple, but the **walk** gives superb views of the Saronic Gulf and the Peloponnese. From the ruins you can continue along the road and circle back to the bridge onto Sferia. It's about 6km in total.

Neorion Beach, 3km west of the bridge, has **water skiing** and **banana-boat** and **air-chair rides**. The best beach is at **Russian Bay**, 1.5km past Neorion.

HYDRA ΥΔΡΑ

POP 3044

Hydra (*ee-dhr-ah*) is truly the gem of the Saronic Gulf and stands alone among Greek islands as the one free of wheeled vehicles. No cars or scooters, just tiny marble-cobbled lanes, donkeys, rocks and sea. Artists (Brice Marden, Nikos Chatzikyriakos-Ghikas, Panayiotis Tetsis), musicians (Leonard Cohen),

Hydra

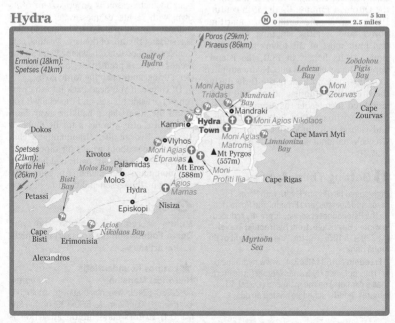

actors and celebrities (Melina Mercouri, Sophia Loren) and travellers (you) have all been drawn to Hydra over the years. So in addition to the island's exquisitely preserved stone architecture, criss-crossing rural paths and clear, deep waters, you can find a good cappuccino along the people-watching harbour.

The mules and donkeys are the main means of heavy transport and they, along with the rustic aspects of life on the island, give Hydra its two faces: chic and earthy.

History

Hydra was sparsely populated in ancient times and is just mentioned in passing by Herodotus. The most significant evidence of settlement dates from Mycenaen times. But, in the 16th century, Hydra became a refuge for people fleeing the skirmishes between the Venetians and the Ottomans. Many hailed from the area of modern-day Albania.

By the mid-1700s the settlers began building boats and took to the thin line between maritime commerce and piracy with enthusiasm. They travelled as far as Egypt and the Black Sea and ran the British blockade during the Napoleonic Wars (1805–15). As a result of steady tax paying, the island experienced only light interference under the Ottoman Empire. By the 19th century, Hydra had become a full-blown maritime power, and wealthy shipping merchants had built most of the town's grand mansions. At its height in 1821, the island's population reached 28,000. Hydra supplied 130 ships for a blockade of the Turks during the Greek War of Independence and the island bred such leaders as Admiral Andreas Miaoulis, who commanded the Greek fleet, and Georgios Koundouriotis, president of Greece's national assembly from 1822 to 1827.

🛈 Getting There & Away

High-speed ferries link Hydra with Poros, Piraeus and Spetses, and Ermioni and Porto Heli on the Peloponnese; service is greatly reduced in winter. Buy tickets from **Hydreoniki Travel** (🖰 22980 54007), up the lane to the right of the Alpha Bank.

Freedom (🖰 69442 42141; www.hydralines. gr) runs between Hydra and Metohi (little more than a car park) on the mainland (€6.50, 10 minutes, hourly, schedule posted on quay).

Boat Services from Hydra

DESTINATION	TIME	FARE	FREQUENCY
Ermioni*	20-40min	€9.50	3-4 daily
Piraeus*	1-2hr	€25.50	6-8 daily
Poros*	30min	€12.50	5-6 daily
Porto Heli*	1hr	€15	3 daily
Spetses*	40min	€10.50	5-6 daily

*high-speed services

🛈 Getting Around

Generally, people get around Hydra by walking.

In summer, caïques from Hydra Town go to the island's beaches. **Water taxi** (🖰 22980 53690) fares are posted on the quay (Kamini costs €10, Vlyhos €14).

Donkey owners clustered around the port charge €10 to €15 to transport your bags to your hotel. Quick donkey rides around the port cost about €10 per person.

Hydra Town   Ύδρα
POP 1980

Life in Hydra centres around the gorgeous port. Whether you sail or ferry in, the sparkling boat-filled harbour and the bright light striking the tiers of carefully preserved stone houses make a lasting impression. The harbour in high season is an ecosystem of its own, with yachts, caïques, water taxis and sailboats zipping in and out. The marble quay is a surging rhythm of donkeys, visitors, cafe denizens and boat-taxi hawkers. By night the scene becomes a promenade: grab a chair, order a drink, and watch the world go by.

Of course, if you head back into the warren of port-side houses, and especially if you climb the steep slopes banking away from the town centre, you get a totally different view on Hydriot life. Grandmothers chat in quiet lanes about what's for dinner, and roads peter out into dirt paths that head into the mountains, ever-changing in colour, depending on the season and the time of day.

🔘 Sights

Melina Mercouri Exhibition Hall and **Deste Foundation** (www.deste.gr) host high-season art shows.

★ Lazaros Koundouriotis Historical Mansion   MUSEUM
(🖰 22980 52421; www.nhmuseum.gr; adult/child €4/free; ⊙10am-2pm & 5.30-8.30pm Tue-Sun Mar-Oct) Hydra's star cultural attraction is

this handsome ochre-coloured *arhontiko* (stone mansion) high above the harbour. It was the home of one of the major players in the Greek independence struggle and is an exquisite example of late-18th-century traditional architecture. It features original furnishings, folk costumes, handicrafts and a painting exhibition.

★**Historical Archives
Museum of Hydra**   MUSEUM
(☑22980 52355; www.iamy.gr; adult/child €5/3; ☉9am-4pm) This fine harbourfront museum houses an extensive collection of portraits and naval artefacts, with an emphasis on the island's role in the War of Independence. It hosts temporary exhibitions in summer, and concerts on the rooftop terrace.

Kimisis Tis Theotokou   CHURCH, MUSEUM
Housed in the peaceful monastery complex on the harbour, the cathedral dates from the 17th century and has a Tinian marble bell-tower. Its **Ecclesiastical Museum** (☑22980 54071; adult/child €2/free; ☉10am-2pm Tue-Sun Apr-Oct) contains a collection of icons.

☆⚝ **Festivals & Events**

Easter   RELIGION
Week-long extravaganza including a famous parade of a flower-festooned epitaph into the harbour at Kamini.

Miaoulia Festival   HISTORY
(☉approximately 3rd weekend of Jun) Celebration of Admiral Miaoulis and the Hydriot contribution to the War of Independence with a spectacular boat burning (with fireworks) in Hydra harbour.

🛏 **Sleeping**

Accommodation in Hydra is of a high standard, but you pay accordingly. Most owners will meet you at the harbour and organise luggage transfer.

Nereids   PENSION $
(☑22980 52875; www.nereids-hydra.com; Kouloura; d €60; ❋ 🛜) This carefully restored stone house contains lovely rooms of exceptional value and quality. Spacious, peaceful and with beautiful decor, rooms have open views to Hydra's rocky heights and top-floor rooms have sea views.

Pension Erofili   PENSION $
(☑22980 54049; www.pensionerofili.gr; Tombazi; s/d/tr €45/50/70; ❋ 🛜) Tucked in the inner town, these pleasant, unassuming rooms are

a decent deal for Hydra. Also has a studio with kitchen.

Kirki   PENSION $
(☑22980 53181; www.kirkihotel.com; Miaouli; d €50; ❋ 🛜) Basic, tidy, central rooms have views into the rooftops and trees.

Glaros   PENSION $
(☑6942523338, 22980 53679; www.hydra.com.gr/glaros; d €55; ❋ 🛜) Simple, well-kept rooms in a convenient spot just back from the harbour.

★**Hydra Hotel**   BOUTIQUE STUDIOS $$
(☑6972868161, 22980 53420; www.hydra-hotel.gr; Petrou Voulgari 8; studio incl breakfast €100-185, maisonette €230; ❋ 🛜) Climb high on the south side of the port to swishy, top-of-the-line apartments in an impeccably renovated ancient mansion with kitchenettes and sweeping views. Get room 202 for a tiny balcony with panoramas to die for.

★**Hotel Miranda**   HOTEL $$
(☑22980 52230; www.mirandahotel.gr; Miaouli; s/d incl breakfast from €120/140; ☉Mar-Oct; ❋) Pretend you're a 19th-century sea captain in this antique-laden jewel. Public spaces are decked out in antique prints, carved woodwork and rotating exhibitions. Gaze at your inlaid ceilings or, in the higher-end rooms, from your balcony.

Hotel Sophia   BOUTIQUE HOTEL $$
(☑22980 52313; www.hotelsophia.gr; Harbour Front; d incl breakfast €80-120; ☉Apr-Oct; ❋ 🛜) Gorgeous, small rooms sit right on the harbour and some have balconies. Each has been painstakingly outfitted with all the mod cons, bathrooms are luscious marble, and some are two storeys.

Cotommatae   BOUTIQUE HOTEL $$
(☑22980 53873; www.cotommatae.gr; d/ste incl breakfast from €120/190) This recently renovated mansion has retained the character and some of the memorabilia of the original family while adding impeccable modern touches. Some suites have private terraces or a jacuzzi.

Piteoussa   PENSION $$
(☑22980 52810; www.piteoussa.com; Kouloura; d €65-75; ❋ 🛜) Jolly owners maintain beautiful rooms in two buildings on a quiet, pine tree–lined street. Rooms in the restored corner mansion drip with period character and modern amenities, while the smaller rooms in the second building were renovated in 2010 and have a mod feel.

Hydra Town

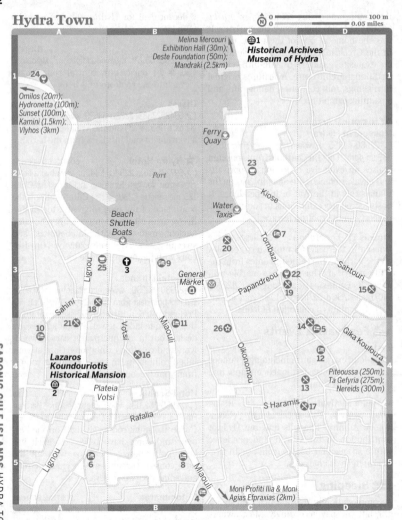

Angelica Hotel BOUTIQUE HOTEL **$$**

(☎ 22980 53202; www.angelica.gr; Miaouli; d incl breakfast €110-150, tr/q €180/240; ❄ 🛜) An attractive boutique hotel in a quiet location, the Angelica is popular for its comfortable, luxurious rooms and spacious, impeccable bathrooms. Superior rooms have balconies. Relax in the jacuzzi or courtyard.

✗ Eating

Pirate (p313) cafe-bar does scrummy breakfasts and lunches. **Flora's** (Votsi) sweet shop on inland Plateia Votsi makes *galaktoboure-ko* (custard pie), rice pudding and ice cream from local goats' milk.

Ostria TAVERNA **$**

(Stathis & Tassoula; ☎ 22980 54077; mains €5-8; ⊙ lunch & dinner) Often referred to by just the gregarious owners' names, this year-round taverna serves only what's fresh. Throw out the menu and ask: perhaps chicken cutlets, or fava or zucchini balls. Stathis catches his own calamari, sweet and delicious.

Psarapoula TAVERNA **$**

(☎ 22980 52630; www.psaropoula.com; harbour; mains €7-12; ⊙ lunch & dinner) Don't be fooled

Hydra Town

by the port-side location: it's not a tourist trap. Visitors and locals alike dig into daily specials at this historic eatery that was established in 1911. They have a higher-end location above the main bakery.

Ta Gefyria TAVERNA $
(☎22980 29677; Kouloura; mains €5-10; ☺lunch & dinner) On a quiet, tree-lined street in the rear of town. Friendly owners make consistently yummy grilled meats and mezedhes.

★**Sunset** MEDITERRANEAN $$
(☎22980 52067; mains €9-22; ☺lunch & dinner Easter-Oct) Famed for its splendid panoramic spot near the cannons to the west of the harbour, Sunset also has fine, fresh cuisine. Tasty salads, inventive pastas and local fish are prepared with flair and a hint of elegance.

★**Barba Dimas** ITALIAN $$
(☎22980 52967; Tombazi; mains €11-20; ☺dinner) Authentic Italian food like Pietro's Neapolitan grandmother used to make. Menus change daily. Reserve in high season.

Paradosiako TAVERNA $$
(☎22980 54155; Tombazi; mains €7-14; ☺lunch & dinner Easter-Nov) This little streetside spot is traditional Greek personified. Sit on the corner terrace to watch the people-parade as you dig into classic mezedhes such as beetroot salad with garlic dip or meats and seafood, like fresh, filleted and grilled sardines.

Caprice ITALIAN $$
(☎22980 52454; Sahtouri; mains €9-15; ☺dinner Apr-Oct) A chance for romantic candlelit din-

ing with a solid repertoire of Italian dishes, some using fresh-made pasta.

Bratsera MEDITERRANEAN $$
(☎22980 52794, 22980 53971; www.bratsera hotel.com; Tombazi; mains €9-20; ☺breakfast, lunch & dinner Apr-Oct) The in-house restaurant by the pool (no day-use) of the Bratsera Hotel offers the chance to have a higher-end meal in blissful peace. Breakfast buffet (€14) is decadent.

Gitoniko TAVERNA $$
(Christina & Manolis; ☎22980 53615; Haramis; mains €7-15; ☺lunch & dinner Easter-Oct) Usually referred to by its owners' names, Christina and Manolis, Gitoniko offers a broad range of Greek fare, but it is known for its (pricey) fish.

Veranda MEDITERRANEAN $$
(☎22980 52259; Lignou; mains €7-15; ☺dinner Apr-Oct) Cheerful brothers run this dreamy terrace restaurant with views looking out across the port and mountains.

🍷 Drinking & Nightlife

Prices are high, but lively people-watching comes with your coffee or cocktail. The harbour revs up after midnight.

★**Pirate** CAFE, BAR
(☎22980 52711) Friendly Wendy and Takis and their kids Zara and Zeus run this daytime cafe with first-rate coffees, breakfasts and home-cooked lunches, and morph it

into a raging party-place at night. Music changes with the crowd and the mood.

★ Hydronetta
CAFE, BAR

(☎ 22980 54160) You can't beat this gorgeous waterfront location on the swimming rocks to the far west of the harbour. Brothers Andreas and Elias provide snazzy cocktails and lunch (high season only) with a smile.

Isalos
CAFE

(☎ 22980 53845) Isalos makes exceptional coffees and a solid run of sandwiches and pastas.

Amalour
COCKTAIL BAR

(www.amalour.com; Tombazi) A lively line in cocktails, relaxed outdoor seating and dancing inside after midnight.

Omilos
CLUB

(☎ 22980 53800; www.omilos-hydra.com) Chic waterside restaurant (good lunch and dinner fixed-price specials) that turns into a night-time dance venue.

☆ Entertainment

Cinema Club of Hydra
CINEMA, THEATRE

(☎ 22980 53105; http://cineclubhydras.blogspot.com; Oikonomou) In July and August the open-air cinema screens blockbusters and indie flicks. It also organises excursions to plays at the ancient theatre of **Epidavros**.

❶ Information

There's no tourist office on Hydra. ATMs are at harbourfront banks.

Hospital (☎ 22980 53150; Votsi)

Tourist Police (☎ 22980 52205) Shares an office with regular police.

Around Hydra

Hydra's mountainous, arid interior makes a robust but peaceful contrast to the clamour of the quayside. A useful map for walkers is Anavasi's *Hydra* map. A map is posted on the quay, and several marked trails extend across the island. Once you leave Hydra/Kamini/Vlyhos there are no services. Take plenty of water.

An unbeatable experience is the long haul up to **Moni Profiti Ilia**. The wonderful **monastery complex** contains beautiful icons, and boasts super views. It's a solid hour or more through zigzags and pine trees to panoramic bliss on top.

The smaller monastery, **Moni Agias Efpraxias** sits just below Profiti Ilia and is run by nuns.

Other paths lead to **Mt Eros** (588m), the island's highest point, and along the island spine to east and west, but you need advanced route-finding skills or reliable directions from knowledgeable locals.

The coastal road turns into a simple, beautiful trail about a 1.5km walk west of the port, after **Kamini**. Kamini has a tiny **fishing port**, several good tavernas, **swimming rocks** and a small pebble **beach**. In fact, Hydra's shortcoming – or blessing – is its lack of sandy beaches to draw the crowds. People usually swim off the rocks, but if you go as far as **Vlyhos**, 1.5km after Kamini, this last little hamlet before the mountains offers two slightly larger pebble beaches (one called Vlyhos and the other the more pristine **Plakes**), tavernas and a restored 19th-century stone bridge.

The coastal road leads 2.5km east from the port to a pebble beach at **Mandraki** where trampoline-and-music beach resort Miramare offers occasional watercraft rentals.

Boats run from the harbour to all of these places, but you certainly need them to reach **Bisti Bay** or **Agios Nikolaos Bay**, on the island's southwest, with their remote but umbrella-laden pebble beaches and green waters.

🍴 Sleeping & Eating

★ Christina
TAVERNA $

(☎ 22980 53516; Kamini; mains €6-12; ⊗ lunch & dinner Thu-Tue) Just inland from the port in Kamini, Mrs Christina and her kids dish out some of the island's best Greek dishes and fresh fish.

To Pefkaki
SEAFOOD, MEZEDHES $

(☎ 6974406287; Kamini; mains €5-10; ⊗ lunch & dinner Thu-Tue Easter-Oct) Worth the short walk along the coast to Kamini for a laid-back lunch of mezedhes and fresh seafood (delicious fried anchovies).

★ Four Seasons
TAVERNA, PENSION $$

(☎ 22980 53698; www.fourseasonshydra.gr; Plakes; mains €6-12; ⊗ lunch & dinner Easter-Oct; 🛜) This scrummy seaside taverna offers a different face of Hydra: the sound of the breeze and the waves instead of the portside buzz. Don't miss the *taramasalata* (fish roe dip) with bread and whatever else tickles your fancy. It also has handsome suites (€220 incl breakfast).

Pirofani INTERNATIONAL $$

(☑ 22980 53175; www.pirofani.com; Kamini; mains €12-16; ☉ dinner Wed-Sun) Gregarious Theo creates an eclectic range of dishes, from a beef fillet with rose-pepper sauce to a spicy Asian curry.

Enalion TAVERNA $$

(☑ 22980 53455; www.enalion-hydra.gr; Vlyhos; mains €6-12; ☉ lunch & dinner Easter-Oct) Perhaps the best seaside option at Vlyhos beach.

SPETSES ΣΠΕΤΣΕΣ

POP 4070

Spetses stands proudly just a few kilometres from the mainland Peloponnese, but there is a stronger sense of carefree island Greece here than in other Saronic Gulf destinations. The lively, historic old town is the only village on the island; the rest, ringed by a simple road, is rolling hills and crystal-clear coves. Relaxed-feeling Spetses has great nightlife, some of the Saronic's best restaurants and easily-accessible, gorgeous swimming spots.

History

In Spetses Town there's evidence of early Helladic settlement near the Old Harbour and at Dapia. Roman and Byzantine remains have been found in the area behind Moni Agios Nikolaos, halfway between the two.

From the 10th century, Spetses is thought to have been uninhabited for almost 600 years, until the arrival of Albanian refugees fleeing the fighting between Turks and Venetians in the 16th century.

Spetses, like Hydra, grew wealthy from shipbuilding. Island captains busted the British blockade during the Napoleonic Wars and refitted their ships to join the Greek fleet during the War of Independence. In the process they immortalised one local woman, albeit originally from Hydra, the formidable Laskarina Bouboulina, ship's commander and fearless fighter.

The island's forests of Aleppo pine, a legacy of the far-sighted philanthropist Sotirios Anargyros, have been devastated by fires several times in the past 20 years. The trees are slowly recovering.

❶ Getting There & Away

Highspeed ferries link Spetses with Hydra, Poros and Piraeus, and Ermioni and Porto Heli in the Peloponnese. In summer, caïques (€2 per person) and a car ferry (€1.50) go from the harbour to Kosta on the mainland.

SARONIC GULF ISLANDS SPETSES

Spetses

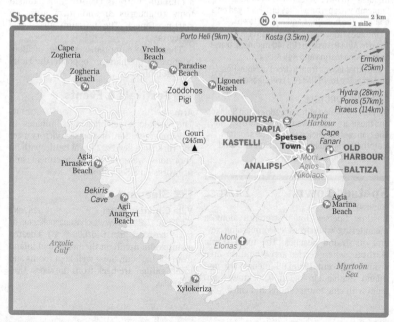

Bardakos Tours (📞 22980 73141; Dapia Harbour)

Mimoza Travel (📞 22980 75170)

Boat Services from Spetses

DESTINATION	TIME	FARE	FREQUENCY
Hydra*	40min	€10.50	5-6 daily
Ermioni*	20-30min	€7.50	2 daily
Piraeus*	2hr 10min	€35	5-6 daily
Poros*	1½hr	€14.50	3-4 daily
Porto Heli*	15min	€5.50	3 daily

*high-speed services

ℹ️ Getting Around

BICYCLE

Bike Center (📞 22980 72209; ⏰ 10am-3.30pm & 5.30-10pm) behind the fish market rents out bikes (€6 per day), including baby seats.

BOAT

In summer, caïques serve the island's beaches (€10 return). **Water taxi** (📞 22980 72072; Dapia Harbour) fares are displayed on a board. All leave from the quay opposite Bardakos Tours.

BUS

Two routes start over Easter and increase in frequency to three or four daily from June to September. Departure times are displayed on a board by the bus stops and around town.

One goes from Plateia Agiou Mama in Spetses Town to Agia Paraskevi (€6, 40 minutes), travelling via Agia Marina and Agii Anargyri.

The other leaves from in front of Hotel Poseidonion going to Vrellos (€4) via Ligoneri.

CAR & MOTORCYCLE

Only locally owned autos are allowed on Spetses, and those are not allowed in the centre of town. The transport of choice tends to be scooters. Motorbike- and quad-bike-hire shops abound (€15 to €25 per day).

Spetses Town   Σπέτσες

POP 3550

Bustling Spetses Town stretches along a meandering waterfront encompassing several quays and beaches. The main **Dapia Harbour,** where ferries arrive, and the area around adjacent Plateia Limenarhiou and inland Plateia Orologiou (Clocktower Sq) teem with chic tourist shops and cafes.

As you head further inland on the quieter lanes or go left along the harbour-front road of Sotiriou Anargyriou, past the town beach and Plateia Agiou Mama, impressive *arhontika* (old mansions) illustrate Spetses' historic wealth.

Passing the church of **Moni Agios Nikolaos** you arrive at the attractive **Old Harbour** (Palio Limani), and the interesting **Baltiza** yacht anchorage and boatbuilding area.

From the north side of Dapia Harbour a promenade and road lead through the seafront **Kounoupitsa** area.

◉ Sights

Spetses Museum   MUSEUM
(📞 22980 72994; adult/child €3/2; ⏰ 8.30am-2pm Tue-Sun) Small, fascinating collections are housed in the old mansion of Hatzigiannis Mexis (1754–1844), a shipowner who became the island's first governor. They include island artefacts, traditional costumes and portraits of the island's founding fathers.

Bouboulina's Museum   MUSEUM
(📞 22980 72416; www.bouboulinamuseum-spetses.gr; adult/child €6/free; ⏰ several tours daily Apr-Oct) The mansion of Spetses' famous daughter, the 19th-century seagoer Laskarina Bouboulina, has been converted into a museum. Entry is via 40-minute guided tours (billboards around town advertise starting times). The museum also hosts concerts.

There's an impressive **statue** of Bouboulina on the harbour opposite the Hotel Poseidonion.

🎎 Festivals & Events

Armata   CULTURE
The week-long celebration culminates in a commemoration of Spetses' victory over the Turks in a key 1822 naval battle, with an enormous water-borne re-enactment and fireworks on 8 September.

🛏️ Sleeping

Villa Christina Hotel   PENSION $
(📞 22980 72218; www.villachristinahotel.com; d/tr incl breakfast from €45/60; ❄️🛜) Located about 200m uphill on the main road inland from the harbour, these well-kept rooms and lovely garden are back from the worst traffic noise.

Hotel Kamelia
PENSION $

(☎ 69390 95513; http://hotelkamelia.gr; s/d €35/40; ☺ Easter-Oct; ❄ 🛜) Good-value airy rooms are tucked away from the busy seafront with a bougainvillea-draped terrace.

Villa Marina
PENSION $

(☎ 22980 72646; www.villamarinaspetses.com; d €45; ❄ 🛜) Super-basic rooms have refrigerators and there is a well-equipped communal kitchen downstairs. Just to the right of Plateia Agiou Mama.

Kastro
APARTMENTS $$

(☎ 22980 75319; www.kastro-margarita.com; studio/apt incl breakfast €100/150; ❄ 🛜 🏊) A private, quiet complex encloses these studios and apartments close to the centre of town. Low-key decor and modern amenities combine with extensive terraces.

Klimis Hotel
HOTEL $$

(☎ 22980 73725; www.klimishotel.gr; Dapia; s/d from €65/80; ❄ 🛜) Serviceable rooms, some with seafront balconies, at this standard hotel sit above a ground floor cafe-bar and patisserie.

★ Poseidonion Grand Hotel
LUXURY HOTEL $$$

(☎ 22980 74553; www.poseidonion.com; Dapia; d incl breakfast €220-361, 4-person ste €562; ❄ 🛜 🏊) Here's your chance to live like a wealthy dame or gent in the roaring '20s. This venerable old hotel has been totally renovated and every inch, from the chic rooms to the gracious lobby bar and luxurious pool, drips with luxury. Oh, and it also has two of the island's best restaurants.

Orloff Resort
LUXURY PENSION $$$

(☎ 22980 75444; www.orloffresort.com; d incl breakfast €140-160; ☺ Mar-Oct; ❄ 🛜 🏊) On the edge of town along the road to Agia Marina and near the old port, the pristine Orloff hides behind high white walls. Enjoy stylish rooms and a crystal-clear pool.

Zoe's Club
APARTMENTS $$$

(☎ 22980 74447; www.zoesclub.gr; studio from €165; ❄ 🛜 🏊) Freestanding spacious apartments surround a decadent pool and courtyard. It's behind a high stone wall in the central part of town, close to the Spetses Museum.

✗ Eating

The Poseidonion Grand Hotel and Nissia Hotel have outstanding restaurants.

★ Akrogialia
SEAFOOD, TAVERNA $$

(☎ 22980 74749; Kounoupitsa; mains €9-17; ☺ 10.30am-midnight) This superb restaurant is on the Kounoupitsa seafront and matches its delicious food with friendly service and a bright setting. Tasty options include oven-baked *melidzana rolos* (eggplant with creamy cheese and walnuts). Enjoy terrific fish risotto or settle for a choice steak; all are accompanied by a thoughtful selection of Greek wines.

Patrali
SEAFOOD $$

(☎ 22980 75380; Kounoupitsa; mains €7-15; ☺ lunch & dinner Jan-Oct) Operating for more than 70 years and known island-wide for its outstanding seafood, Patrali is located smack on the seafront in the Kounoupitsa neighbourhood.

To Nero tis Agapis
MEDITERRANEAN $$

(☎ 22980 74009; Kounoupitsa; mains €12-19; ☺ lunch & dinner) The sweetly named 'Water of Love' is a sister restaurant to Tarsanas but offers meat as well as fish dishes. The crayfish tagliatelle is worth every bite, as is the *zarzuela* (fish stew). There's a selection of creative salads.

Orloff
MEDITERRANEAN $$

(☎ 22980 75255; Old Harbour; mains €13-19; ☺ dinner) Fresh fish and super specialities such as seafood linguini or pork fillet with aubergine puree are hallmarks of the popular Orloff. The terrace sits above the water at a bend in the road just before the old harbour.

La Scala
ITALIAN $$

(☎ 22980 73207; Old Harbour; mains €10-20; ☺ dinner) Sup on Italian specialties like fresh-made pasta and delicious, beautifully presented seafood and meat, on a terrace in the old harbour.

Spetsiotiko
TAVERNA $$

(Agiou Mama; mains €15-20; ☺ lunch & dinner) Dine overlooking the water on the freshest Greek staples. The owners never scrimp and the food is always lovely.

Tarsanas
SEAFOOD $$$

(☎ 22980 74490; Old Harbour; mains €17-26; ☺ lunch & dinner) A hugely popular *psarotaverna* (fish taverna), this family-run place deals almost exclusively in fish dishes. It can be pricey, but the fish soup (€6) alone is a delight and other starters such as anchovies marinated with lemon start at €6.

Drinking & Nightlife

Spetses' lively nightlife is concentrated in the Old Harbour–Baltiza area. **La Luz** has live music, and **Mourayo** plays Greek pop. Dance venues include **Stavento Club**.

Bar Spetsa   BAR
(✆22980 74131; www.barspetsa.org; ⏰8pm-late) One of life's great little bars, this Spetses institution never loses its easygoing atmosphere. Find it 50m beyond Plateia Agiou Mama on the road to the right of the kiosk.

Ariston Brasserie   CAFE
(✆22980 73803; Dapia) A touch of class on the waterfront.

Roussos   CAFE
(Dapia; ⏰9am-late) Old-time Spetsiot coffee house with pastries, on the harbour.

ℹ Information

Banks at Dapia Harbour have ATMs.
Mimoza Travel (✆22980 75170; mimozakent@aig.forthnet.gr) On the harbour; helps with accommodation and other services.
Municipal Kiosk (⏰10am-9pm May-Sep) On the quay, seasonal staff provide answers to general questions about the island.
Port Authority (✆22980 72245) Just inland from the cafe-terrace overlooking Dapia Harbour.
Tourist Police (✆22980 73100; ⏰mid-May–Sep) Just inland from the cafe-terrace overlooking Dapia Harbour; housed with the port authority.

Around Spetses

Spetses' gorgeous coastline undulates with pebbly coves and small pine-shaded beaches. A 26km surfaced road skirts the entire coastline, so a scooter, quad or bicycle are ideal for exploring. A detailed map is a must for inland explorers: download (http://spetsesdiadromes.wordpress.com) or buy the detailed map (€3.50 at newsstands).

Tiny, tranquil **Xylokeriza** on the southwest coast has a souvlaki kiosk with yummy, fresh salads and delicious oven potatoes.

Further along, the popular, long, pebbly **Agia Paraskevi** and the sandier **Agii Anargyri** have picturesque, albeit crowded, beaches. Both have tavernas and water sports of every description and are served by boats and buses in summer. At the north end of Anargyri, you can follow a small path to submerged, swimmable **Bekiris Cave**.

Other beautiful spots include **Vrellos** and **Zogheria** beaches.

Closer to town, **Agia Marina** is a small resort with a beach that gets packed. The beach at **Ligoneri**, about 2.5km northwest of Spetses Town, is easily reached by bus.

The small island of **Spetsopoula**, off the southern coast, is owned by the Niarchos family and not open to the public.

Cyclades

Includes ➡

Best Places to Eat

➡ Levantis (p347)

➡ 1500bc (p384)

➡ The Nest (p375)

➡ Thalassaki (p328)

➡ Archondoula (p401)

Best Places to Stay

➡ Petros Place & Yialos Beach Hotel (p374)

➡ Aroma Suites (p381)

➡ Salt (p401)

➡ Petali Village Hotel (p405)

➡ Carbonaki Hotel (p339)

Why Go?

Ringed with cinnamon sand and ink blue sea, the Cyclades (kih-*klah*-dez; Κυκλάδες) are natural magnets. Throw in stunning, sugar-cube villages, a good dose of sophistication and a stylish culture that seems to have bounced its way down from Athens, and you do have the best of both worlds.

These dramatic islands, with ochre hills and plunging coastlines, have drawn artists throughout the ages. Sculptors have chiselled away at the marble of Paros and Naxos since ancient times, while Santorini and Amorgos are home to modern galleries. Cuisine and wine making also reach artistic highs here and archaeological sights abound; the infamous spectacle of Delos and the more recently excavated Ancient Akrotiri are accompanied by smaller yet impressive ruins and museums scattered throughout the islands.

Each island has a personality of its own: from hedonistic Mykonos and Ios to flashy Santorini and the relaxed charm of Paros and Naxos. A little further afield at Amorgos or Sifinos you'll feel a slow inhale of happy tranquillity.

When to Go
Mykonos Town

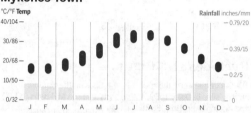

Apr & May Catch early-season sun without overheating and early boats without overcrowding.

Jun–Aug Sun, sea and sand, balmy nights and lively company.

Sep & Oct Quieter beaches, open spaces, the sweet scent of herbs and great walks on island hills.

Cyclades Highlights

① Get immersed in the spellbinding sites of **Delos** (p396) and **Ancient Akrotiri** (p388)

② Savour the scrumptious cuisine on **Santorini** (p377), **Paros** (p343) and **Ios** (p372)

③ Slip away to serenity on the remote-feel islands of **Kythnos** (p409) or **Sikinos** (p391)

④ Soak up the glamour and party away on **Mykonos** (p335)

⑤ Explore quaint, artistic villages and recline on the white sand of **Naxos** (p352)

⑥ Amble along ancient footpaths through the deep valleys of **Andros** (p322)

⑦ Marvel in the dazzling

monastery above the crashing waves on **Amorgos** (p367)

⑧ Make a pilgrimage to **Tinos** (p325) with its famous icon and marble ornamented villages

⑨ Join in the holiday atmosphere on idyllic **Sifnos** (p402)

⑩ Be mesmerised by the dramatic, volcanic coastline of **Milos** (p398)

History

The Cyclades are said to have been inhabited since at least 7000 BC. Around 3000 BC there emerged a cohesive Cycladic civilisation that was bound together by seagoing commerce and exchange. During the Early Cycladic period (3000–2000 BC) the tiny but distinctive Cycladic marble figurines, mainly stylised representations of the naked female form, were sculpted. Recent discoveries on Keros, an uninhabited island near Koufonisia in the Little Cyclades, indicate that the island was a possible pilgrimage site where figurines that had been broken up as part of rituals were deposited.

In the Middle Cycladic period (2000–1500 BC) many of the islands were occupied by the Minoans, who probably colonised from Crete. At Akrotiri, on Santorini, a Minoan town has been excavated and artefacts from the site have all the distinctive beauty of those from Crete's Minoan palaces. At the beginning of the Late Cycladic period (1500–1100 BC) the archipelago came under the influence of the Mycenaeans of the Peloponnese, who were supplanted by northern Dorians in the 8th century BC.

By the mid-5th century BC the Cyclades were part of a fully fledged Athenian empire. In the Hellenistic era (323–146 BC) they were governed by Egypt's Ptolemaic dynasties and later by the Macedonians. In 146 BC the islands became a Roman province and lucrative trade links were established with many parts of the Mediterranean.

The division of the Roman Empire in AD 395 resulted in the Cyclades being ruled from Byzantium (Constantinople), but after the fall of Byzantium in 1204 they came under a Venetian governance that doled out the islands to opportunistic aristocrats. The most powerful of these was Marco Sanudo (the self-styled Venetian Duke of Naxos), who acquired Naxos, Paros, Ios, Santorini, Anafi, Sifnos, Milos, Amorgos and Folegandros, introducing a Venetian gloss that survives to this day in island architecture.

The Cyclades came under Turkish rule in 1537, although the empire had difficulty in managing, let alone protecting, such scattered dependencies. Cycladic coastal settlements suffered frequent pirate raids, a scourge that led to many villages being relocated to hidden inland sites. They survive as the 'Horas' (capitals) that are such an attractive feature of the islands today. Ottoman neglect, piracy and shortages of food and water often led to wholesale depopulation of more remote islands, and in 1563 only five islands were still inhabited. The Cyclades played a minimal part in the Greek War of Independence, but became havens for people fleeing from other islands where insurrections against the Turks had led to massacres and persecution. Italian forces occupied the Cyclades during WWII. After the war, the islands emerged more economically deprived than ever. Many islanders lived in deep poverty; many more gave up the struggle and headed to the mainland, or to America and Australia, in search of work.

The tourism boom that began in the 1970s revived the fortunes of the Cyclades. The challenge remains, however, of finding alternative and sustainable economies that will not mar the beauty and appeal of these remarkable islands.

CYCLADES

ⓘ CYCLADES ISLAND HOPPING

Part of the trick of sculpting an itinerary through the islands is learning which ferries go where, and when. *And beware, in low season services are reduced or nonexistent on some routes.* In high season, a host of companies offer connections throughout the Cyclades. Check schedules at www.greekferries.gr or www.openseas.gr. Buy tickets online, directly from the company, or at local ticket agencies (though agents often represent only some of the companies...ask around). For example:

➡ **NEL Lines** (p737) and **Blue Star Ferries** (p737) Have a host of crisscrossing seasonal routes.

➡ **Hellenic Seaways** (☏ 210 419 9000; www.hsw.gr) Has summer high-speed services.

➡ **Sea Jets** (p737) Routes go Rafina–Tinos–Mykonos–Paros or Iraklio–Santorini–Ios–Naxos–Paros–Mykonos.

➡ **Zante Ferries** (p737) Route goes Piraeus–Kythnos–Serifos–Sifnos–Milos–Kimolos.

ANDROS ΑΝΔΡΟΣ

POP 9170

Andros, the second-largest of the Cyclades, is a walker's paradise. Its wild mountains are cleaved by fecund valleys with trilling streams and ancient stone mills. On this lush island, springs tend to be a feature of each village and waterfalls cascade down hillsides most of the year. It's worth renting a car to get out to the footpaths, many of them stepped and cobbled, that will lead you through these majestic landscapes and among its copious wildflowers and fascinating archaeological remnants. The handsome main town of Hora, also known as Andros, is a ship owners' enclave packed with neoclassical mansions.

ⓘ Getting There & Away

Reach Andros from the mainland port of Rafina (66km, two hours) or via regular high-season ferries running south to Tinos, Syros and Mykonos, from where onward links can be made. Buy tickets at **Ploes Travel** (☑ 22820 29220; Empirikou) in Hora or Kyklades Travel (p322) in Gavrio. The **port authority** (☑ 22820 22250) has schedule information.

Boat Services from Andros

DESTINATION	TIME	FARE	FREQUENCY
Kea (Tzia)	6hr 20min	€10	2 weekly
Kythnos	5hr 10min	€14	1 weekly
Mykonos	2hr 20min	€14	3 daily
Rafina	2½hr	€16	4-8 daily
Syros	2hr 50min	€9	2 weekly
Tinos	1hr 35min	€12	5 daily

ⓘ Getting Around

KTEL Andros (☑ 22820 22316) has nine buses daily (fewer on weekends) linking Gavrio and Hora (€4, 55 minutes) via Batsi (€2, 15 minutes). Schedules are posted at the bus stops in Gavrio and Hora. Low-season buses are usually timed to meet Rafina ferries.

Taxis (☑ Batsi 22820 41081, Gavrio 22820 71561, Hora 22820 22171) from Gavrio to Batsi cost about €10 and to Hora €35.

Roads can be rough and narrow, but many walking paths and sights are only accessible by car (about €35 in August, €25 in low season).

Dino's Rent-a-Bike (☑ 22820 41003) In Batsi, scooters €16 to €19 per day.

Euro Rent A Car (☑ 22820 72440; www.renta-careuro.com) Opposite the Gavrio ferry quay.

Gavrio Γαύριο

POP 1199

Sleepy Gavrio on the west coast is the main port of Andros.

🛏 Sleeping & Eating

Standard tavernas line Gavrio's waterfront.

Ostria Hotel and Apartments APARTMENT $
(☑ 22820 71551; www.ostria-studios.gr; s/d/apt €30/40/50; P ❋ @) Spacious, simple rooms 300m from Gavrio along the Batsi road.

Andros Camping CAMPGROUND $
(☑ 22820 71444; www.campingandros.gr; per adult/tent €6.50/3.50; P ❋) Set up among tiny olive trees about 400m along a winding road behind the harbour.

Perrakis HOTEL $$
(☑ 22820 71456; www.hotelperrakis.com; Chrissi Ammos; d incl breakfast from €100; ⊙ year-round; P ❋ 🛜 ❋) Across the road from the sweep of Golden Beach, south of Gavrio, are super views and swell rooms.

Giannoulis TAVERNA $
(☑ 22820 71385; Agios Petros Beach; mains €6-10; ⊙ lunch & dinner Jun-Sep, lunch only May & Oct) Tuck into traditional Greek fare on the waterfront at Agios Petros Beach, between Gavrio and Batsi.

ⓘ Information

Buses stop at the ferry quay. There are ATMs and a post office. Check www.andros.gr for island information.

Kyklades Travel (☑ 22820 72363) Opposite the ferry quay. Sells ferry tickets and arranges accommodation.

Batsi Μπατσί

POP 957

Worn little Batsi lies 7km southeast of Gavrio on the overbuilt shores of a handsome bay with a long beige-sand beach. The island's main resort, it revs up through July and August.

🛏 Sleeping & Eating

Book ahead for July and August and weekends in June and September.

Cavo D'ora Pension PENSION $
(☑ 22820 41766; www.andros-cavodoro.gr; s/d €30/45) Located above a pizzeria across

Andros

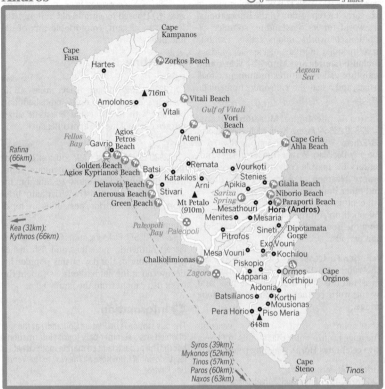

0 ─────── 10 km
0 ─────── 5 miles

Cape Kampanos
Cape Fasa
Hartes
Zorkos Beach
Aegean Sea
▲716m
Amolohos
Vitali Beach
Vitali
Gulf of Vitali
Vori Beach
Agios Petros Beach
Fellos Bay
Gavrio
Ateni
Andros
Cape Gria
Ahla Beach
Rafina (66km)
Golden Beach
Agios Kyprianos Beach
Remata
Vourkoti
Delavoia Beach
Batsi
Katakilos
Arni
Stenies
Apikia
Gialia Beach
Anerousa Beach
Stivari
Sariza Spring
Niborio Beach
Green Beach
Mt Petalo (910m)
Mesathouri
Paraporti Beach
Kea (31km); Kythnos (66km)
Menites
Mesaria
Hora (Andros)
Paleopoli Bay
Paleopoli
Pitrofos
Sineti
Dipotamata Gorge
Mesa Vouni
Exo Vouni
Kochilou
Chalkolimionas
Piskopio
Zagora
Kapparia
Ormos Korthiou
Cape Orginos
Aidonia
Batsilianos
Korthi
Pera Horio
Mousionas
Piso Meria
648m
Syros (39km);
Mykonos (52km);
Tinos (57km);
Paros (60km);
Naxos (63km)
Cape Steno
Tinos

from the beach, the handful of pleasant rooms are good value.

Krinos Suites Hotel   BOUTIQUE HOTEL $$$
(☑ 22820 42038; www.krinoshotel.com; Batsi; ste from €180; ☺ Apr-Oct) One of Andros' high-end entries is decked out with organic toiletries and mattresses. Some rooms have sea-view balconies.

Stamatis Taverna   TAVERNA $$
(☑ 22820 41283; mains €6-18; ☺ lunch & dinner) Sup above the harbour on starters such as *pikandiko* (feta, tomato, green pepper, oregano and spices baked in a pot) and delicious soups.

❶ Information

Greek Sun Holidays (☑ 22820 41198; www.andros-greece.com) Helps with accommodation, car hire, ferry tickets and island walks and excursions.

Hora (Andros)
Χώρα (Ανδρος)

POP 1801

Hora perches dramatically on a rocky promontory and has surprising views through the neoclassical mansions to two vibrant bays on either side: Niborio and Paraporti. The peninsula is tipped by the remains of a Venetian fortress, and the town itself owes its grand mansions and squares to both the Venetian settlement and the shipowners who came to inhabit it. Hora's cultural pedigree is burnished by its Museum of Contemporary Art, an impressive archaeological museum and several important churches.

◉ Sights & Activities

★ **Museum of Contemporary Art**   MUSEUM
(☑ 22820 22444; www.moca-andros.gr; adult/student Jun-Sep €6/3, Oct-May €3/1.50; ☺ 10am-2pm

& 6-8pm Wed-Sat & Mon, 10am-2pm Sun Jun-Sep, reduced hours Oct-May) This venerable museum has earned a reputation in the international art world for its outstanding summer exhibitions of world-famous artists. Exhibits have included the likes of Picasso, Matisse, Toulouse-Lautrec and Miró. The year-round sculpture gallery features prominent Greek artists, and a sea-view cafe offers homemade sweets.

Andros Archaeological Museum MUSEUM
(☑ 22820 23664; Plateia Kaïri; adult/child/student €3/2/free; ☉ 9am-4pm Tue-Sun Apr-Nov, Fri & Sun only Dec-Mar) Peruse the exquisite 2nd-century BC marble copy of the 4th-century bronze **Hermes of Andros** by Praxiteles, and other impressive finds from the 9th- to 5th-century BC settlements of Zagora and Paleopoli on Andros' west coast, as well as from the Roman, Byzantine and early Christian periods.

Venetian Fortress RUIN
The ruins of a Venetian fortress stand on an island linked to the tip of the headland by the worn remnants of an arched stone bridge.

Afanis Naftis MONUMENT
The huge bronze sailor that stands in Plateia Riva celebrates Hora's seagoing traditions.

Kidonieos Foundation ARTS CENTRE
(☑ 22820 24598; Empirikou; ☉ high season) FREE
Hosts a summer program of art, theatre and music.

🛏 Sleeping

Prices rise on weekends.

Karaoulanis Rooms & Apartments PENSION, APARTMENT $
(☑ 22820 24412; www.androsrooms.gr; d/apt €50/100; P ❋ 🛜) Self-catering apartments on the inland edge of Hora and a guesthouse with rooms in Niborio both have comfortable furnishings. Scooter and boat hire also.

Micra Anglia BOUTIQUE HOTEL $$
(☑ 22820 22207; www.micra-anglia.gr; Goulandri 13; d incl breakfast from €100; ☉ May-Oct; ❋ 🛜) Hora's luxury offering, with all the amenities. Discounts online.

Archontiko Eleni BOUTIQUE HOTEL $$
(☑ 22820 22270; www.archontikoeleni.gr; Empirikou 9; d from €75; ❋ 🛜) Snuggle into comfy beds in this neoclassical mansion.

Hotel Egli HOTEL $$
(☑ 22820 22060; www.eglihotel.gr; d from €65; ❋ @ 🛜) Housed in a grand old building, the Egli is an elegant, comfortable mix of old and new.

✗ Eating

Parea TAVERNA $
(☑ 22820 23721; Plateia Kaïri; mains €6-10; ☉ lunch & dinner; ☑) Long-established and popular with locals, Parea boasts a super terrace overlooking Paraporti Beach.

Skalakia TAVERNA $
(☑ 22820 22822; mains €7-9; ☉ dinner Mon-Sat) Tables spill down the eponymous stairs from this buttercup-yellow restaurant. Inside feels more like a bistro with quaint bric-a-brac and the Andriot specialities are tops!

Nonna's SEAFOOD $
(☑ 22820 23577; Plakoura; mains €6-10; ☉ lunch & dinner) Authentic mezedhes and fish dishes are the order of the day at this popular little taverna at the old harbour. Ask about the fresh fish caught from the family boat.

ⓘ Information

The bus station is on Plateia Goulandri at the top of which sits a summer-only tourist information booth. The pedestrianised marble main street leads downhill from here all the way to the Venetian *kastro*.

Around Andros

It's worth renting a car to explore Andros' vast mountains and sprinkling of villages as well as to reach its footpaths and beaches.

The north of the island, with the lush watershed around **Arni**, gives way to raw windswept hills as the road zigzags to **Vourkoti** and **Agios Nikolaou** with its sweeping views.

Paleopoli, 7km south of Batsi on the coast road, is the site of Ancient Andros and its sunken harbour. Only rubble remains but the small **Archaeological Museum of Paleopoli** (☑ 22829 41985; ☉ 9am-4pm Tue, Thu & Fri) FREE displays finds.

The island is cleaved by a sweeping agricultural valley and loads of small villages with springs, often marked by marble lions' heads and the like, surround Hora. The road winds through **Sariza**, **Stenies**, **Mesathouri**, **Strapouries** and **Menites** – all fun to explore.

In the south, visit quaint agricultural villages like Livadia, Kochilou, Piskopio and Aidonia, which has ruined tower houses. The area's charming landscape of fields and cypresses encircle Ormos Korthiou, an uninspiring bay-side village.

Activities

Footpaths
WALKING

Andros is crisscrossed by trails. For example, hike up the dramatic Dipotamata Gorge, signposted as you drive inland, after Sineti. The trail, cobbled part of the way, leads past ancient bridges and water mills and through vivid foliage, water burbling below. Many paths are difficult to locate, so get hold of the newly published *Hiking in Andros* guide, free from the city, or an excellent map (Anavasi's *Andros* map; www. anavasi.gr). Better yet, book a guided walk with Trekking Andros (6937236362; www. trekkingandros.gr), or the highly informed Andros Routes (6977334334; www.andros-routes.gr) which combines walking with cultural history.

Beaches
BEACH

Between Gavrio and Paleopoli Bay pleasant beaches include Golden Beach (Xrisi Ammos); Delavoia, half of which is naturist; Anerousa; and Green Beach. Spectacular Chalkolimionas with tawny sand and a tiny church sits 2km down a stone-terraced valley near the junction for Hora. Many of the best beaches, such as Ahla, Vori and Vitali, are best reached with a 4WD or by boat.

Riva Boats
BOAT HIRE

(6974460330, 22820 24412; Niborio; per day about €80) Hire a boat to reach the west and north coasts' excellent beaches. No licence is required; boats are available in Hora or Batsi.

Sleeping & Eating

Onar Residence
COTTAGES $$$

(210 625 1052, 6932563707; www.onar-andros.gr; Ahla Beach; 3-/5-/7-person cottages €210/350/650; May-Oct; P✹☎) Eco-friendly, unique and luxurious secluded cottages on the beach; also has an organic restaurant.

★ Stou Zozef
TAVERNA $

(22820 51050; Pitrofos; mains €6-10; lunch & dinner) Gregarious Katerina Remoundou welcomes you to her sitting room or her tree-lined courtyard, like a long-lost auntie.

She'll show you what she's cooked and chat with locals and visitors alike as they sup on true Andriot fare such as stewed kid, or fresh local cheeses such as rich, creamy *tsinomizithra*. Call ahead.

★ Balkoni Tou Ageiou
TAVERNA $

(22820 41020; Ano Aprovatou; mains €7-8; lunch & dinner Jun-Aug, Sat & Sun Sep-May) The owners of this traditional taverna also operate a cheese factory, so sample their wares before tucking into Andriot dishes like *fourtalia,* an insanely huge omelette packed with succulent potatoes and local sausage. Views sweep the coast. Find it signposted south of Batsi, about 3km off the main road.

TINOS
ΤΗΝΟΣ

POP 8590

Tinos is one of those sleeper hit islands. It's known widely for its sacred Greek Orthodox pilgrimage site: the Church of Panagia Evangelistria, in the port and main town, Hora. The imposing church is home to the sacred icon of the Holy Virgin Megalochari where pilgrims pray for healing, not unlike Catholics do in Lourdes, France. But as soon as you leave the throngs in town, Tinos is a wonderland of natural beauty, dotted with over 40 marble-ornamented villages, in hidden bays, on terraced hillsides and atop misty mountains. Also scattered across the brindled countryside are countless ornate dovecotes, a legacy of the Venetians. There is a strong artistic tradition on Tinos, especially for marble sculpting, as in the sculptors' village of Pyrgos in the north, near the marble quarries. The food, made from local produce (cheeses, sausage, wild artichokes), is some of the best you will find in Greece.

❶ Getting There & Away

Year-round ferries serve the mainland ports of Rafina and Piraeus and the islands Syros, Andros and Mykonos. Hellenic Seaways (p737) sometimes offers summer high-speed services. Get tickets at Malliaris Travel (22830 24241; www.malliaristravel.gr/; Harbourfront).

Hora has two ferry departure quays: the New or Outer Port (300m to the north of the main harbour) serves conventional and larger fast ferries. The Old or Inner Port (at the north end of the town's main harbour) serves smaller fast ferries. Check which quay your ferry is leaving from.

Boat Services from Tinos

DESTINA-TION	TIME	FARE	FREQUENCY
Andros	1hr 35min	€12	5 daily
Lavrio	5½hr	€18	1 weekly
Mykonos	30-40min	€7	5 daily
Paros	55min	€33	1 weekly
Piraeus	4½hr	€32	1 daily
Rafina	3hr 50min	€23	4 daily
Syros	30min	€7.50	1-3 daily

❶ Getting Around

Buses (☑ 22830 22440) run frequently from June to September from Hora to Porto and Kionia (€1.60, 10 minutes) and to Panormos (€4.50, one hour, several daily) via Kambos (€1.60, 15 minutes) and Pyrgos (€3.70, 50 minutes). The Hora bus station is on the harbour near the Poseidon Hotel. Buy tickets on board.

Hire motorcycles (€15 to €20 per day) and cars (€40 per weekday, €60 on weekends in high season) along the Hora waterfront. You can also try **Vidalis Rent a Car & Bike** (☑ 22830 23400; www.vidalis-rentacar.gr).

Phone for a **taxi** (☑ 22830 22470).

Hora (Tinos) Χώρα (Τήνος)

POP 3990

Hora, also known as Tinos, is the island's welcoming capital and port. Though the harbourfront is lined with cafes and hotels and the narrow back streets are packed with restaurants and tavernas, Hora's crowning glory is its Church of Panagia Evangelistria, perhaps the most important pilgrimage site for the Greek Orthodox religion. The streets leading up to the church are lined with shops and stalls crammed with souvenirs and religious wares. On one side of Leoforos Megalocharis you'll see a rubberised strip used by pilgrims crawling towards the church and pushing long candles before them. Religion certainly takes centre stage in Hora (woe betide the tourist looking for a room on one of the high holy days), but the town still hums with the vibrancy of a low-key island port

⦿ Sights

★ **Church of Panagia Evangelistria**   CHURCH
(☑ 22830 22256; www.panagiatinou.gr; ⊙ 8am-8pm) FREE Tinos' highly revered religious focus is the neoclassical Church of the Annunciation and its sacred icon of the Virgin Mary. The hallowed icon was found in 1822 on land where the church now stands after a nun in Tinos, now St Pelagia, was visited by visions from the Virgin instructing her where to find the icon. From the start, the icon was said to have healing powers, thus encouraging mass pilgrimage. Our Lady of Tinos became the patron saint of the Greek nation.

As you enter the church, the icon is on the left of the aisle, and is totally draped in jewels. The church, which is built of marble from the island's Panormos quarries, lies within a pleasant courtyard flanked by cool arcades. The complex has sweeping views all around and three excellent **museums** (⊙ 8am-4pm Tue-Fri, 9am-5pm Sat, 10am-2pm Sun) FREE which house religious artefacts, icons and secular art.

Cultural Foundation of Tinos   GALLERY
(☑ 22830 29070; www.itip.gr; adult/child & student €3/free; ⊙ 10am-3pm Mon, Wed-Sat, also Sun in summer) This excellent cultural centre in a handsome neoclassical building on the southern waterfront houses a superb permanent collection of the work of famous Tinian sculptor Yannoulis Chalepas. A second gallery has rotating exhibitions. Musical events are staged in summer. There's a shop and harbourfront cafe.

Archaeological Museum   MUSEUM
(☑ 22830 22670; Leoforos Megalocharis; admission €2; ⊙ 8am-3pm Tue-Sun) Near the church, this museum has a collection that includes impressive clay *pithoi* (Minoan storage jars).

✦ Festivals & Events

Assumption of the Virgin Mary   RELIGIOUS
On 15 August the town is beyond full for the Virgin's feast day.

⊨ Sleeping

Hora is overcrowded on 25 March (Annunciation), Greek Easter, 15 August (Feast of the Assumption) and 15 November (Advent).

---

❶ **CHURCH ETIQUETTE**

While there are not necessarily bouncers at the door, church-goers and priests prefer respectful garb: long pants or skirts and covered shoulders.

Tinos

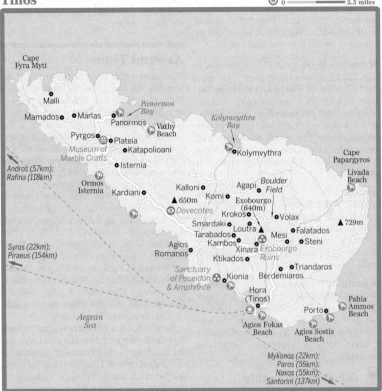

Cape
Fyra Myti

Malli
Mamados○ ○Marlas
Pyrgos○ ○Panormos
Museum of   ○Plateia
Marble Crafts ○Katapolioani
Andros (57km);
Rafina (118km)
Ormos   ○Isternia
Isternia Kardiani○
Panormos
Bay
Vathy
Beach
Kolymvythra
Bay
Kolymvythra
Cape
Papargyros
Livada
Beach

Kalloni○   Agapi○ Boulder
Komi○   Field
▲650m   Exobourgo
Dovecotes Krokos○ (640m)
Smardaki○ Loutra○ ▲ Volax
Tarabados○ Mesi○ ○Falatados
Agios   Kambos○ ○Steni
Romanos○ Xinara Exobourgo
Ktikados○ Ruins
Sanctuary
of Poseidon ○Kionia Berdemiaros
& Amphitrite Triandaros
Hora
(Tinos)
Porto○
Agios Fokas
Beach
Agios Sostis
Beach
Pahia
Ammos
Beach
▲729m

Aegean
Sea

Syros (22km);
Piraeus (154km)

Mykonos (22km);
Paros (55km);
Naxos (55km);
Santorini (137km)

Book months ahead or join devotees sleeping in the street.

Favie Suzanne   HOTEL $
(☎22830 22693; www.faviesuzanne.gr; Antoniou Sohou 22; s/d/tr from €40/50/65; ☉mid-Apr–Oct; ❋☎❋) A bit inland and with a pool, rooms in the new wing are bigger.

Hotel Poseidonio   HOTEL $
(☎22830 23123; www.poseidonio.gr; Paralia 4; s/d/tr incl breakfast from €35/50/75; ❋☎) Decent rooms mid-waterfront.

Nikoleta   PENSION $
(☎22830 24719; www.nikoletarooms.gr; Kapodistriou 11; s/d from €30/40; ❋☎) Little Nikoleta is a fair walk inland from the more industrial south end of town, but it's one of the best value. There is a lovely garden and some rooms have kitchens.

★Tinion Hotel   HISTORIC HOTEL $$
(☎22830 22261; www.tinionhotel.gr; Eleftherias Sq; d/tr incl breakfast €70/84; ❋☎) This old-school central hotel has a broad verandah and sweeping stairs leading to comfortable antique-filled rooms, some with balconies and sea views.

Altana Hotel   BOUTIQUE HOTEL $$
(☎22830 25102; www.altanahotel.gr; s/d/ste incl breakfast from €80/90/100; ☉May-Oct; P❋@☎) Located about 700m north of town, this engaging hotel has a modernist Cycladic style, all snowy white walls and cool interiors incorporating distinctive Tinian motifs.

✗ Eating

Tinian food tends to be fresh and creative, using local products. Beer lovers should look for Tinos' own **Nissos** (www.nissosbeer.com).

★ **Mesklies**　CAFE $

(☑22830 22151; www.mesklies.gr; Harbourfront; ⊙9am-late) Delectable sweets of all sorts from homemade ice cream to *liknaraki* (sweet cheese cupcakes).

★ **Itan Ena Mikro Karavi**　MEDITERRANEAN $$

(☑22830 22818; www.mikrokaravi.gr; Trion Ierarchon; mains €10-18; ⊙lunch & dinner Easter-Oct, dinner Fri, lunch Sat & Sun Jan-Easter) Elegant Greek fair with Mediterranean flair is served in a relaxing courtyard with a grapevine pergola. Dishes like ravioli with shrimp or lentils with octopus and wild pickled greens are also available in half-portions so you can sample more.

Tarsanas　SEAFOOD $$

(☑22830 24667; Harbour; mezedhes €6-10, fish by kg; ⊙noon-midnight) The owner grills out front of this friendly spot at the eastern end of the harbour, specialising in seafood mezedhes. The smoked fish dip is out of this world.

To Koutouki Tis Elenis　TAVERNA $$

(☑22830 24857; G Gagou 5; mains €9-15; ⊙lunch & dinner) This rustic little place is on the narrow taverna-packed lane veering off the bottom of Evangelistria. Try fresh local cheeses or rabbit stew with pearl onions. Occasional live music.

 Drinking & Nightlife

In the back lanes opposite the Middle Port a clutch of dance bars churn out clubby standards, or try **Koursaros** (☑22830 23963; Akti Ellis 1) at the southern end of the harbour.

> **DON'T MISS**
>
> ## MARVELLOUS MARBLE
>
> On the slopes above Pyrgos is the superb **Museum of Marble Crafts** (☑22830 31290; www.piop.gr; adult/child €3/1.50; ⊙10am-6pm Wed-Mon Mar–mid-Oct, 10am-5pm mid-Oct–Mar). This outstanding, modern museum completely explains quarrying and sculpting techniques. It is extremely well curated and includes films and beautifully illustrated displays and animations with English translations, along with top examples of artefacts and architectural features shaped from Tinian marble. The films of some of the last living quarry-men plying their trade are fascinating.

ⓘ Information

Port Police (☑22830 22348; Kionion) Opposite the Outer Port.

Around Tinos

Tinos countryside is a glorious mix of broad terraced hillsides, mountaintops crowned with crags, unspoiled villages, fine beaches and fascinating architecture including picturesque **dovecotes**. Rent a car to see it all.

Kionia, 3km northwest of Hora, has several small beaches and the scant remains of the 4th-century BC **Sanctuary of Poseidon and Amphitrite** (admission €2), a once enormous complex that drew pilgrims.

First along the way north of town, beautiful Ktikados perches in a hanging valley and has a matched set of blue-topped church and campanile. **Drosia** (☑22830 41387; Ktikados; mains €6-10; ⊙lunch & dinner) is tops for local lunches and magnificent views.

Kambos is home to the **Costas Tsoclis Museum** (☑22830 51009; www.tsoclismuseum. gr; Kambos; ⊙10am-1.30pm & 6-9pm Wed-Mon Jun-Sep) FREE and sits on the top of a sublime hill surrounded by fields.

Tarabados is a fun maze of small streets decorated with marble sculptures and leading to a breezy valley lined with dovecotes.

Lovely **Kardiani**, 17km northwest of Hora, perches on a steep cliff slope enclosed by greenery. Narrow lanes wind around the village; the view towards Syros is exhilarating.

Go to **Ormos Isternia**, a stony beach set among plunging hills, if only to eat at **Thalassaki** (☑22830 31366; tothalassaki@gmail. com; Ormos Isternia; seafood €10-14; ⊙lunch & dinner Easter-Oct, weekends only Apr–Easter), for perhaps the best meal in Greece. The seafront taverna crafts local cheese, sausage, wild artichokes and the like into veritable works of art and has outstanding seafood. Book ahead in high season.

Pyrgos is a handsome village where even the **cemetery** is a feast of carved marble. During the late 19th and early 20th centuries Pyrgos was the centre of a remarkable sculpture enclave sustained by the supply of excellent local marble.

The fascinating **Museum House of Yannoulis Halepas** (adult/child €5/2.50; ⊙10.30am-2.30pm & 5-8pm Apr–mid-Oct) preserves the sculptor's humble rooms and workshop. An adjoining gallery has splendid examples of the work of local sculptors.

About 12km north of Hora on the north coast is emerald **Kolymvythra Bay**, where **Tinos Surf Lessons** (http://tinossurflessons.com) takes advantage of the breaks at two excellent, sandy beaches.

A worthwhile detour inland takes you to **Agapi**, in a lush valley of dovecotes. Ethereal and romantic, it lives up to its name.

Pass eye-catching **Krokos** with its **Evangelismou tis Panagias**, an enormous Catholic church, to reach **Volax**, about 6km directly north of Hora. This hamlet sits at the heart of an amphitheatre of low hills festooned with hundreds of enormous, multicoloured boulders. The taverna **Volax** (☑ 22830 41021; mains €6-9; ☺ lunch & dinner) serves reliable Tinian favourites like wild artichokes with lemon.

The ruins of the Venetian fortress of **Exobourgo** lie 2km south of Volax, on top of a mighty 640m rock outcropping.

The northeast coast beach at **Livada** is spectacular, but the ones east of Hora, such as **Porto** and **Pahia Ammos**, can seem comparatively built up.

SYROS ΣΥΡΟΣ

POP 21,390

Endearing Syros merges traditional and modern Greece. One of the smallest islands of the Cyclades and relatively rural outside of the capital, it has the highest population since it is the legal and administrative centre of the entire archipelago. It is also the ferry hub of the northern islands and home to Ermoupoli, the grandest of all Cycladic towns, with an unusual history. It buzzes with life year-round, boasts great eateries, and showcases the best of everyday Greek life.

History

Excavations of an Early Cycladic fortified settlement and burial ground at Kastri in the island's northeast date from the Neolithic era (2800–2300 BC).

During the 17th and 18th centuries Capuchin monks and Jesuits settled on the island. Becoming overwhelmingly Catholic, Syros even called upon France for help during Turkish rule.

During the War of Independence, thousands of Orthodox refugees from islands ravaged by the Turks, such as Chios, fled to Syros. They brought an infusion of Greek Orthodoxy and a fresh entrepreneurial drive that made Syros the commercial, naval and cultural centre of Greece during the 19th

DON'T MISS

ANO SYROS

Originally a medieval Catholic settlement, Ano Syros boasts narrow lanes and whitewashed houses that tower above Ermoupoli.

From the bus terminus, head into the delightful maze and search out the finest of the Catholic churches, the 13th-century **Agios Georgios Cathedral**, with its star-fretted barrel roof and baroque capitals (under renovation at the time of research). Continue past stunning viewpoints to reach the main street, sweet **Our Lady of Mt Carmel**, the **Vamvakaris Museum** (☺ 10am-2pm & 6-11pm Jul & Aug) **FREE**, celebrating locally born partriarch of *rembetika* (blues) Markos Vamvakaris, and the **monasteries** of the Jesuits and the Capuchins.

century. Syros' position declined in the 20th century, but you still see shipyards, textile manufacturing, thriving horticulture, a sizeable administrative sector and a continuing Catholic population.

🛈 Getting There & Away

AIR

Olympic Air flies daily from Athens (€70, 45 minutes) to **Syros Airport** (JSY; ☑ 22810 81900), 5km south of Ermoupoli.

BOAT SERVICES FROM SYROS

Year-round ferries serve the mainland ports of Piraeus and Rafina and neighbouring islands. Buy tickets at Teamwork Holidays (p334) or **Vassilikos** (☑ 22810 84444; www.vassilikos.gr; Akti Papagou 10) in Ermoupoli.
Port Authority (☑ 22810 82690; Plateia Laïkis Kyriarchias) On the eastern side of the port.

🛈 Getting Around

Regular buses loop from Ermoupoli bus station to Galissas (€1.60, 20 minutes) and Vari (€1.60, 30 minutes), and back to Ermoupoli (half-hourly June to September, hourly rest of the year). About five buses go to Kini (€1.60, 35 minutes) or to Ano Syros (€1.60, 15 minutes) every day except Sunday. Schedules are posted at the waterfront bus station.

A free bus traverses the harbour between the car parks at the north and south ends of town (half-hourly 7am to 10pm Monday to Friday, to 4pm Saturday and Sunday).

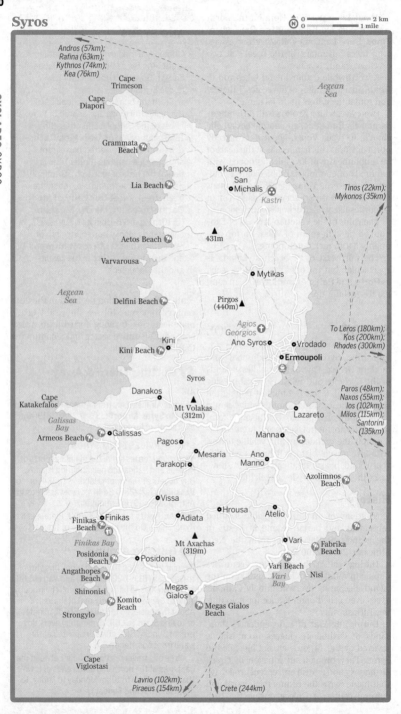

Syros

Andros (57km);
Rafina (63km);
Kythnos (74km);
Kea (76km)

Cape
Trimeson

Cape
Diapori

*Aegean
Sea*

Grammata
Beach

Kampos

Lia Beach

San
Michalis

Kastri

Tinos (22km);
Mykonos (35km)

Aetos Beach

▲
431m

Varvarousa

*Aegean
Sea*

Mytikas

Delfini Beach

Pirgos
(440m) ▲

*Agios
Georgios*

To Leros (180km);
Kos (200km);
Rhodes (300km)

Kini

Ano Syros

Vrodado

Ermoupoli

Kini Beach

Syros

Danakos

▲
Mt Volakas
(312m)

Paros (48km);
Naxos (55km);
Ios (102km);
Milos (115km);
Santorini
(135km)

Cape
Katakefalos

*Galissas
Bay*

Lazareto

Armeos Beach

Galissas

Pagos

Mesaria

Manna

Parakopi

Ano
Manno

Azolimnos
Beach

Vissa

Hrousa

Atelio

Finikas
Beach

Finikas

Adiata

Vari

Fabrika
Beach

Finikas Bay

Posidonia
Beach

▲
Mt Axachas
(319m)

Posidonia

Vari Beach

*Vari
Bay*

Nisi

Angathopes
Beach

Shinonisi

Megas
Gialos

Komito
Beach

Megas Gialos
Beach

Strongylo

Cape
Viglostasi

Lavrio (102km);
Piraeus (154km)

Crete (244km)

You can hire cars (€40 per day) and scooters (from €15 per) at agencies on the waterfront, such as Vassilikos (p329). Avoid driving in central Ermoupoli; there are mostly stairs or pedestrianised ways.

Taxis (☑ 22810 86222) charge €4 to Ano Syros from the port, €11 to Galissas and €11 to Vari.

Ermoupoli   Ερμούπολη

POP 9,016

As you sail into Ermoupoli, named after Hermes, its peaked hilltops emerge, each topped by a dazzling church. The Catholic settlers built on high, and the 19th-century Orthodox newcomers built from below. Now buildings spread in a pink-and-white cascade over it all, and the centre is a fun maze of stairways, pedestrianised shopping streets and neoclassical mansions all radiating out from the grand Plateia Miaouli with its impressive town hall.

Catholic **Ano Syros** and Greek Orthodox **Vrodado** spill down from high hilltops to the northwest and northeast of town, with even taller hills rising behind.

◉ Sights

Take a stroll around the **Vaporia** district for elegant shipowners' mansions and palm-lined squares.

★**Plateia Miaouli**   SQUARE

This great square is perhaps the finest urban space in the Cyclades. Once situated immediately upon the seahore, today it sits well inland and is dominated by the dignified neoclassical **town hall**, designed by Ernst Ziller. Flanked by palm trees and lined along its south side with cafes and bars, the square and accompanying statue are named for Hydriot naval hero Andreas Miaoulis.

The town's small **archaeological museum** (☑ 22810 88487; Benaki; admission €3; ◷ 8.30am-3pm Tue-Sun) is housed in the rear of the hall.

BOAT SERVICES FROM SYROS

DESTINATION	TIME	FARE	FREQUENCY
Anafi	9hr 35min	€19	2-3 weekly
Andros	2hr 50min	€9	1 weekly
Astypalea	6¼hr	€25.50	3 weekly
Donousa	7hr	€19	2 weekly
Folegandros	5hr 20min	€14	1 weekly
Ios	3½hr*7hr	€17	1 weekly
Iraklia	4hr 20min	€18	3-4 weekly
Kea (Tzia)	3hr 40min	€12	2 weekly
Kimolos	3¾hr	€14	3 weekly
Kos	6hr 20min	€39	3 weekly
Koufonisia	5½hr	€19.50	4 weekly
Kythnos	2hr 10min	€9	4 weekly
Lavrio	4hr 25min	€18	3 weekly
Leros	4hr 35min	€34	3 weekly
Milos	5hr	€14	4 weekly
Mykonos	1hr 20min	€7-11	2 daily
Naxos	2hr 10min	€14.50	1 daily
Paros	55min	€8-11.50	1-3 daily
Patmos	3hr 25min	€32	3 weekly
Piraeus	4hr	€29.50	1-3 daily
Rhodes	9hr 25min	€46	3 weekly
Serifos	4hr	€9	1 weekly
Tinos	30min	€7.50	1-3 daily

Ermoupoli

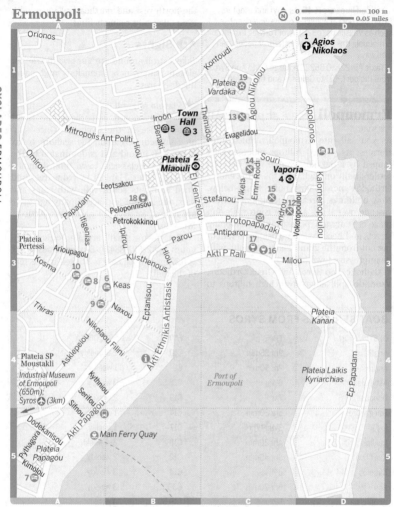

★ **Industrial Museum of Ermoupoli**   MUSEUM

(☎ 22810 84762; www.hermoupolis.gr; George Papandreou 11; adult/concession €2./1.50; ☉ 10am-2pm & 6-9pm Thu-Sun, 10am-2pm Mon & Wed) This excellent chronicle of Syros' industrial and shipbuilding traditions occupies a restored factory packed with over 300 well-labelled items relating to sewing, printing, spinning, engines, ships and more. Ask if the Aneroussis lead shot factory is open - it's fascinating. You will find the musuem about 1km south of the centre.

★ **Agios Nikolaos**   CHURCH

(Vaporia District) All the shipowners' wealth is evident in this grand church loaded with fine murals, icons, gilt and chandeliers.

🏃 Activities

Cyclades Sailing   SAILING

(☎ 22810 82501; www.cyclades-sailing.gr) Charters yachts.

Syros Windsurf   WINDSURFING

(☎ 6946771400; http://syroswindsurf.gr) This operator can arrange windsurfing at Komito Beach.

Ermoupoli

◉ Top Sights
1 Agios Nikolaos D1
2 Plateia Miaouli B2
3 Town Hall B2
4 Vaporia C2

◉ Sights
5 Archaeological Museum B2

▦ Sleeping
6 Aegli Hotel B3
7 Diogenis Hotel A5
8 Ethrion A3
9 Hermoupolis Rooms A3
10 Lila Guesthouse A3
11 Ploes Hotel D2

✪ Eating
12 Kouzina C2
13 Oneiro C1
14 Stis Ninettas C2
15 To Petrino C2

◉ Drinking & Nightlife
Cafe Ploes .... (see 11)
16 Liquid Bar C3
17 Ponente C3
18 Scritto B2
Severo .... (see 16)

✪ Entertainment
19 Apollo Theatre C1

⬥ Courses

Omilo LANGUAGE COURSE
(www.omilo.com) Offers Greek language courses in Andros and Syros.

☞ Tours

Coach Trips COACH TOUR
Teamwork Holidays (p334) offers island
coach trips. The cost for adult/child is €20/
free.

🛏 Sleeping

Most budget options cluster above the ferry
quay, while boutique hotels in renovated
mansions, like **Ploes Hotel** (☎ 22810 79360;
www.hotelploes.gr; Apollonos 2; d from €200), dot
the Vaporia district. Much accommodation
opens year-round, with discounts in low
season.

Ethrion HOTEL $
(☎ 22810 89066; www.ethrion.gr; Kosma 24; d/tr
€40/45; ❄ @ 🛜) Set back in a small courtyard, several of Ethrion's clean, comfortable
rooms boast views over the sea and town.

Hermoupolis Rooms PENSION $
(☎ 22810 87475; www.hermoupolis-rooms.gr;
Naxou; s/d/tr from €35/40/50; ❄ 🛜) There's
a cheerful welcome at these well-kept self-
catering rooms, a short climb from the
waterfront. Front rooms open onto tiny,
bougainvillea-cloaked balconies.

★ Lila Guesthouse PENSION $$
(☎ 22810 82738; www.guesthouse.gr; Kosma, cnr
Filikis Eterias; s/d/tr incl breakfast €80/100/120,
ste from €140; ❄ 🛜) In the former French
consulate, these elegantly renovated rooms
and suites are kitted out with impeccable

modern decor and top-notch bathrooms.
Suites are spacious with dining tables and
antiques. A bodacious breakfast is served by
the genial proprietors in the airy common
area. Port pick-up available.

Diogenis Hotel HOTEL $$
(☎ 22810 86301; www.diogenishotel.gr; Plateia
Papagou; s/d/tr incl breakfast from €50/60/70;
❄ 🛜) Completely renovated in 2013 with
double-pane windows and modern everything, Diogenis is tops for business-class
quality. Some rooms at this well-run waterfront hotel have sea views.

Aegli Hotel HOTEL $$
(☎ 22810 79279; www.lux-hotels.com/aegli; Klis-
thenous 14; s/d/tr incl breakfast from €55/72/90;
❄ @ 🛜) This attractive hotel on a quiet side
street has a marble lobby with an air of ex-
clusivity, and comfy rooms. A roof garden
has panoramic views.

✗ Eating

Standard restaurants and cafes throng the
waterfront, especially along Akti Petrou Ral-
li and the southern edge of Plateia Miaouli.

To Petrino MEZEDHES $
(☎ 22810 87427; Stefanou 9; dishes €4-10; ⏱ lunch
& dinner) Swathes of bougainvillea bedeck
the pretty enclave of Stefanou, and popular
To Petrino serves mezedhes such as squid
stuffed with feta.

Stis Ninettas CAFE $
(☎ 22810 87119; Emmanuel Roidi 11; snacks €3.50-
9; ⏱ 10am-late) Something different in style
and personality, this cafe and its charm-
ing owner offer sandwiches, salads and
desserts.

WORTH A TRIP

SAN MICHALIS

If you have your own wheels, don't miss the drive to the northern village of San Michalis, along the spine of the island, with spectacular views of unspoilt valleys and neighbouring islands on either side. Famous for its cheese, San Michalis is now a small hamlet of stone houses and vineyards. Walk the winding rock path to the hilltop church, and get Syran food at its best at **Plakostroto** (☑6973980248; mains €7-11; ◷lunch & dinner Easter-Oct, Fri-Sun Nov-Easter). They've got that local cheese plus rooster, lamb or rabbit grilled on the open wood fire. Views sweep down the hillside to Kea, Kythnos and beyond.

★ **Kouzina**   MEDITERRANEAN **$$**
(☑22810 93150; www.kouzinasyros.gr; Androu 5; mains €8-18; ◷dinner Jun-Sep, lunch & dinner Tue-Sun Oct-May) Reserve ahead for a seat in this colourfully lit, intimate dining room where fresh, local ingredients are the building blocks of creative Mediterranean cuisine. Save room for desserts like chocolate pie with pistachios and cream.

Oneiro   MEDITERRANEAN **$$**
(☑22810 79416; Theatre Sq; mains €10-15; ◷dinner Tue-Sun Jun-Aug, lunch & dinner Sep-May) One of Syros' finest for local produce prepared with flair. The refined, glass-fronted dining room lets onto a warmly lit large courtyard that turns into a thriving bar scene after hours in high season.

🍷 Drinking & Nightlife

Music bars such as **Liquid Bar** (☑22810 82284; Akti Petrou Ralli), **Severo** (☑22810 88243; Akti Petrou Ralli) and **Ponente** (Akti Petrou Ralli) line the waterfront. **Cafe Ploes** (Apollonos 2) offers dramatic sea views with frilly cocktails.

Scritto   BAR
(Hiou) For perfect retro, drop in to Scritto, a great cafe-bar where classic rock rules, and posters and album covers represent Hendrix to Jagger.

☆ Entertainment

Apollo Theatre   THEATRE
(☑22810 85192; ◷box office 10am-2pm & 6.30-9pm) Built from 1862 to 1864 this venerable theatre was partly modelled on La Scala in Milan.

ℹ Information

Check www.syros.gr for island information.

EMERGENCY
Hospital (☑22810 96500; Papandreou)
Police Station (☑22810 96100; Plateia Vardaka)

TOURIST INFORMATION
Information Booth (☑22810 80485) Run by the Syros Hotels' Association on the waterfront; opening times vary.

TRAVEL AGENCIES
Enjoy Your Holidays (☑22810 87070; Akti Papagou 2) Sells ferry tickets and advises on accommodation.
Teamwork Holidays (☑28810 83400; www.teamwork.gr; Akti Papagou 18) Sells ferry tickets; arranges accommodation, excursions and car hire.

Around Syros

Outside of Ermoupoli, Syros comprises a series of hills and valleys folding down to small bays and beaches, most well served by buses. The old resort town **Galissas** has seen better days. It does have one choice restaurant, **Iliovasilema** (☑22810 43325; mains €9-13; ◷lunch & dinner Jan-Nov), with fresh seafood and a welcoming ambience.

The beaches south of Galissas all have domatia and some have hotels. **Finikas** has a small, lively harbour. Between the thin beach at **Posidonia Beach** and the sleepy harbour of **Angathopes** find the simple **Possidonion Hotel** (☑22810 42100; d from €40 incl breakfast; ◷May-Sep), or get rooms at **Krinakia Agathopes** (☑22810 42375; ◷May-Sep). Nearby, low-key **Komito Beach** is surrounded by hillsides and clear, blue water.

Inland, the town of **Posidonia** (Delagrazia) was the historic shipowners' vacation spot; keep your eyes open for many grand villas.

The south coast town of **Megas Gialos** has a couple of roadside beaches, but gorgeous **Vari Bay**, further east, is the better bet with its light grey sandy beach and hills, though the waterfront and tavernas get packed in high season.

If you're at **Azolimnos**, stop for delicious mezedhes at **Tis Filomilas** (☑22810 62088; dishes €5-10; ◷lunch & dinner May-Oct, Fri-Sun

Nov-Apr), overlooking the bay and the broad, sandy beach.

Kini Beach, on the west coast, has a long, thin stretch of beach and is developing into a popular resort. Tops for eats is **Allou Yialou** (☑ 22810 71196; mains €6-15; ⊙ lunch & dinner May-Sep) with excellent fish stew and other seafood. Just north, **Delfini Beach** is known for its shimmering sand.

MYKONOS ΜΥΚΟΝΟΣ

POP 10,190

Mykonos is the great glamour island of the Cyclades and it happily flaunts its sizzling style and reputation. The high-season mix of good-time holidaymakers, cruise-ship crowds which can reach as many as 15,000 a day, and posturing fashionistas throngs through Mykonos town, a traditional Cycladic maze, delighting in its authentic cubist charms and its pricey cafe, bar and shopping scene.

In high season, you should come only if you are bankrolled and intent on joining the jostling street crowds, the oiled-up lounger lifestyle at the island's packed main beaches, and the relentless party. Out of season, devoid of gloss, glitter and preening celebrities, you will find a more subdued local life, the occasional soft-pink pelican wandering the empty streets, and beaches backed by banging clubs which have gone silent for the winter.

Mykonos is also the jumping-off point for the splendid archaeological site of the nearby island of Delos.

❶ Getting There & Away

AIR

Mykonos Airport (JMK; ☑ 22890 22490), 3km southeast of the town centre, has flights year-round to Athens (€57 to €200, 50 minutes, three to seven daily) with Olympic Air and **Aegean Airlines** (A3; www.aegeanair.com). Astra Airlines (p631) serves Thessaloniki. Approximately May to mid-September direct international flights include easyJet to London and Air Berlin to Germany.

BOAT

Year-round ferries serve mainland ports Piraeus and Rafina (sometimes quicker if you are coming directly from Athens airport), and nearby islands, Tinos and Andros. In the high season, Mykonos is well connected with all neighbouring islands, including Paros and Santorini. Hora is

loaded with ticket agents; turn to p342 for more information.

Mykonos has two ferry quays: the **Old Port**, 400m north of town, where some conventional ferries and smaller fast ferries dock, and the **New Port**, 2km north of town, where the bigger fast ferries and some conventional ferries dock. When buying outgoing tickets double-check which quay your ferry leaves from.

Port Authority (☑ 22890 22218; Akti Kambani) Midway along the waterfront.

DESTINATION	TIME	FARE	FREQUENCY
Andros	2hr 20min	€14	3 daily
Ios*	1hr 40min	€48.50	2 daily
Iraklio*	6hr 35min	€68	1-2 daily
Naxos	2hr 25min	€9	1 weekly
Naxos*	45min	€29.50	2 daily
Paros*	1hr	€29.50	2 daily
Piraeus	4¾hr	€35	1-2 daily
Rafina	4½hr	€25	2-3 daily
Rafina*	2hr 10min	€49	2 daily
Santorini (Thira)*	2½hr	€56.50	2 daily
Syros	1hr 20min	€7-11	2 daily
Tinos	30min	€7	5 daily

*high-speed services

❶ Getting Around

TO/FROM THE AIRPORT

Buses from the southern bus station serve Mykonos' airport (€1.60). Arrange airport transfer with your accommodation (around €7) or take a taxi to town (€9).

BOAT

Caïque (little boat) services go from Platys Gialos or Ornos to Paradise (round-trip €5), Super Paradise (€6), Agrari (€7) and Elia (€7) Beaches from Easter to mid-October.

BUS

The Mykonos **bus network** (☑ 22890 23360, 22890 26797) has two main bus stations plus a pick-up point at the New Port. Low season services are much reduced.

Northern bus station (Remezzo), behind the OTE office, has frequent high-season services to Agios Stefanos via Tourlos (€1.60), Ano Mera (€1.60), Elia Beach (€1.90) and Kalafatis Beach (€2.10). Trips range from 20 minutes to 40 minutes. Two buses daily serve Kalo Livadi Beach (€1.70). Buses for the New Port, Tourlos and Agios Stefanos stop at the Old Port.

Southern bus station (Fabrika Sq (Plateia Yialos)) serves Agios Ioannis Beach, Ornos,

Mykonos

5 km
2.5 miles

Syros (35km);
Rafina (133km);
Piraeus (174km);

Delos

Renia

Excursion Boat

Cape
Alogomandra

Nea
Mykonos

Kapari
Beach
Kapari

Agios
Ioannis
Beach

Korfos

Psarou
Beach

Ornos

Platys
Gialos
Beach

Platys
Gialos

Paraga
Beach

Psarou

VriSsi

Hora
(Mykonos Town)

Old Port

Vothonas

New Port

Tourlos
Beach

Tourlos

Agios
Stefanos
Beach

Agios
Stefanos

Houlakia
Beach

Cape
Armenistis

372m ▲

Marathi

Lake
Marathi

Moni
Panagias
Tourlianis

Ano Mera

Panormos
Beach

Agios Sostis
Beach

Panormos Bay

Mersini
Beach

Cape
Mavros

Mersini Bay

Ftelia
Beach

275m ▲

Platys
Gialos

Super
Paradise
Beach

Paradise
Beach

Agrari
Beach

Elia

Elia
Beach

Excursion Boats

Kalo
Livadi
Beach

Cape
Mavrokefalas

Fokos
Beach

Merchias Bay

Profitis Ilias
Anomeritis
(351m) ▲

Cape
Evros

Cape
Goni

Lia Beach

Kalafatis Beach

Cape
Kalafatis

Kalafatis

AEGEAN
SEA

Dragonisi

↑ *Naxos (46km); Paros (54km);*
Ios (70km); Santorini (128km)

Donousa (75km);
Amorgos (96km)

Platys Gialos, Paraga and Paradise Beaches (each €1.60).

Buy tickets (at machines, street kiosks, mini-markets and tourist shops) before boarding (remember to get return tickets) and validate on board. Night buses (12.15am to 6am) in high season cost €2.

CAR & MOTORCYCLE

Cars start at €45 per day in high season; €35 in low season. Scooters/quads are €20/40 high season; €15/30 low season. Avis and Sixt are among the agencies at the airport. You can rent from Mykonos Accommodation Centre (p342), **OK Rent A Car** (☑ 22890 23761; www. okmykonos.com; Agios Stefanos; ☺May-Oct) near New Port, and **Apollon** (☑ 22890 24136; www.apollonrentacar.com; ☺year-round), one of several agencies near Hora's southern bus station.

TAXI

Taxis (☑ 22400 23700, airport 22400 22400) queue at Hora's Plateia Manto Mavrogenous (Taxi Sq), bus stations and ports, but waits can be long in high season. All have meters and minimum fare is €3.30 (plus €0.38 per bag, €3 for phone booking). Fares include from Hora to: New Port (€8), Agios Stefanos (€9), Ornos (€8.50), Platys Gialos (€9.50), Paradise (€10), Kalafatis (€16) and Elia (€16).

Hora (Mykonos)

Χώρα (Μύκονος)

POP 6467

Hora (also known as Mykonos), the island's well-preserved port and capital, is a warren of narrow alleyways and white-walled buildings overlooked by the town's famous **wind-mills**. In the heart of the waterfront **Little Venice** quarter (Venetia), which is spectacular at sunset, tiny flower-bedecked churches jostle with trendy boutiques, and there's a cascade of bougainvillea around every corner. High-season streets are crowded with chic boutiques, cool galleries, jangling jewellers and both languid and loud music bars – plus a catwalk cast of thousands.

◉ Sights

★**Panagia Paraportiani**　　CHURCH
(☺variable, usually open mornings) FREE
Mykonos' most famous church, the rocklike Panagia Paraportiani, comprises four small chapels plus another on an upper storey reached by an exterior staircase.

ℹ **NAVIGATING HORA**

Without question, you will soon pass the same junction twice. It's entertaining at first, but can become frustrating amid throngs of equally lost people and fast-moving locals. For quick-fix navigation, familiarise yourself with **Plateia Manto** and the three main streets of **Matogianni**, **Enoplon Dynameon** and **Mitropoleos**, which form a horseshoe behind the waterfront.

★**Archaeological Museum**　　MUSEUM
(☑ 22890 22325; Agiou Stefanou; adult/concession €2/1; ☺9am-4pm Tue-Sun) Peruse pottery from Delos and grave *stelae* (pillars) and jewellery from the island of Renia (Delos' necropolis). Chief exhibits include a statue of Hercules in Parian marble.

Aegean Maritime Museum　　MUSEUM
(☑ 22890 22700; Enoplon Dynameon 10, ground fl; adult/concession €4/1.50; ☺10.30am-1pm & 6.30-9pm Apr-Oct) Fascinating nautical paraphernalia includes detailed models of local boats and an enormous Fresnel lighthouse lantern in its sunny interior courtyard.

Lena's House　　MUSEUM
(☑ 22890 22591; Tria Pigadia; ☺6.30-9.30pm Mon-Sat May–mid-Oct) FREE This charming late-19th-century, middle-class Mykonian house (with furnishings intact) takes its name from its last owner, Lena Skrivanou.

Mykonos Folklore Museum　　MUSEUM
(☑ 6932178330; Paraportianis; ☺5.30-8.30pm Mon-Sat May–mid-Oct) FREE This folklore museum, housed in an 18th-century sea captain's house, features a large collection of furnishings and other artefacts, including old musical instruments.

☞ Tours

Mykonos Accommodation Centre (p342) organises guided tours: Delos (adult/child €40/30) including entrance fee and guide; Tinos (adult/child €59/38); Mykonos bus tour (adult/child €33/22); and island cruise (adult/child €43/21.50). It also arranges private charters, including gay-only boat cruises.

🛏 Sleeping

Mykonos' myriad accommodation options are generally pricey in high season, and

Hora (Mykonos)

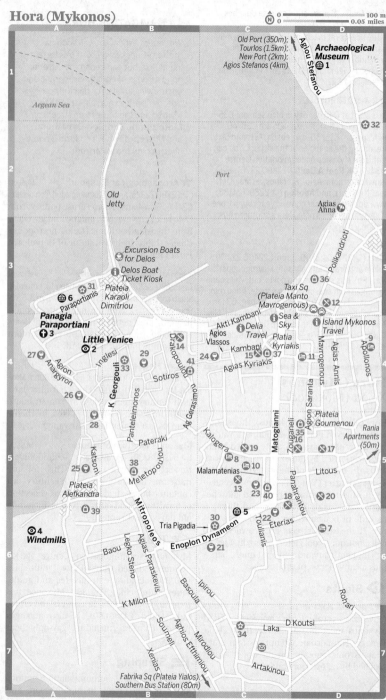

Aegean Sea

Old Port (350m);
Tourlos (1.5km);
New Port (2km);
Agios Stefanos (4km)

Agiou Stefanou

**Archaeological
Museum**
1

32

Port

Old
Jetty

Agias
Anna

Polikandrioti

Excursion Boats
for Delos

Delos Boat
Ticket Kiosk

36

Plateia
Karaoli
Dimitriou

Taxi Sq
(Plateia Manto
Mavrogenous)

12

31

6

Paraportianis

**Panagia
Paraportiani**
3

Little Venice
2

Agion Anargyron

Inglesi

K Georgouli

33

29

Sotiros

Drakopoulou

14

41

Ag Gerasimou

24

Akti Kambani
Agios
Vlassos

Delia
Travel

Kambani

15

Aglas Kyriakis

Sea &
Sky

Platia
Kyriakis

37

Island Mykonos
Travel

11

9

Apollonos

Agias Annis

Mavrogenous

27

26

28

Panteleimonos

Pateraki

Kalogera

Matogianni

Agion Saranta

Zouganeli

35

16

Plateia
Goumenou

Rania
Apartments
(50m)

25

38

Meletopoulou

19

8

Malamatenias

10

13

23

40

17

Litous

Panahrantiou

20

Plateia
Alefkandra

39

Windmills
4

30

Tria Pigadia

5

Enoplon Dynameon

22

18

Eterias

Touliani

7

Katsoni

Mitropoleos

Agias Paraskevis

Legko Steno

Baou

21

K Milon

Basoula

Ipirou

Mirodiou

Aghios Efthimiou

Xenias

Soumeli

Fabrika Sq (Plateia Yialos),
Southern Bus Station (80m)

34

Laka

D Koutsi

Artakinou

Rohari

Hora (Mykonos)

those on main streets are noisy. If you arrive without a reservation between July and September consult **Hoteliers Association of Mykonos** (☎22890 24540; www.mha.gr; ⊙9.30am-4pm Apr-Oct), Building 1 in the row of buildings at the old port and at a **desk** (☎22890 25770; ⊙9am-10pm) at the airport, or **Association of Rooms, Studios and Apartments** (☎22890 24860; fax 22890 26860; ⊙9am-5pm Apr-Oct) in Building 2 at the Old Port.

During late July and early August some hotels require minimum three-night stays.

★**Carbonaki Hotel** BOUTIQUE HOTEL **$$**
(☎2289024124;www.carbonaki.gr;23Panahrantou; s/d/tr/q €110/122/170/196; ✳🛜) This family-run boutique hotel in central Mykonos is a delightful oasis with bright, comfortable rooms, relaxing public balconies and sunny central courtyards. Chill out in the Jacuzzi and small sauna. Some wheelchair access and great low-season discounts.

Manto Hotel HOTEL **$$**
(☎22890 22330; www.manto-mykonos.gr; Evagelistrias 1; s/d incl breakfast €55/80; ⊙year-round; ✳🛜) Buried in the heart of town, cheerful Manto is an excellent affordable option (for

Mykonos), with well-kept colourful rooms, some with balconies, an inviting breakfast room and friendly owners.

Rania Apartments APARTMENT **$$**
(☎22890 22315; www.rania-mykonos.gr; Leondiou Boni 2; s/d/tr/apt from €65/85/145/235; ✳🛜🛆) In a lovely garden setting, these charming self-catering apartments are well appointed and quiet. The location high above the harbour means an uphill walk from town.

Hotel Philippi PENSION **$$**
(☎22890 22294; www.philippihotel.com; Kalogera 25; s/d from €70/90; ⊙Apr-Oct; ✳🛜) A verdant courtyard-garden makes this a welcome choice in the heart of Hora. Bright, clean rooms open onto a railed verandah overlooking the garden.

Hotel Lefteris PENSION **$$**
(☎22890 23128; www.lefterishotel.gr; Apollonas 9; d/tr/apt from €65/112/152; ✳@🛜) A colourful entranceway and owner set the tone for this international meeting place tucked away from the crowds. Simple bright, comfy rooms have fans or air-con, and apartments are well equipped. Guests share a kitchen and roof terrace.

Hotel Elysium
BOUTIQUE HOTEL **$$$**

(📞 22890 23952; www.elysiumhotel.com; s/d/tr/q from €200/250/380/456; ☺ Apr-Oct; [P][✱][🛜][⛱]) High above the main town, this stylish gay hotel (nongays are also welcome) has cool decor, and frills include personal computers in deluxe rooms, a rockin' pool bar, spa and high-camp entertainment.

Fresh Hotel
BOUTIQUE HOTEL **$$$**

(📞 22890 24670; www.hotelfreshmykonos.com; Kalogera 31; d incl breakfast €190; [✱][@][🛜]) In the heart of town with a leafy central garden, stylish breakfast room, bar and Jacuzzi, rooms have wood floors and minimalist slate-and-white decor.

🍴 Eating

High prices don't necessarily reflect high quality in Mykonos. Cafes line the waterfront; you'll find good food and coffee drinks at **Kadena** (📞 22890 29290; mains €10-20; ☺ 8am-late; 🛜). Souvlaki shops dot Enoplon Dynameon and Fabrika Sq (Plateia Yialos). For the party-sated, get delivery from the extensive menu at **Oregano** (📞 22890 27410; www.oregano-mykonos.com; mains €8-16; ☺ lunch & dinner). Most places stay open late during high season.

Suisse Cafe
CAFE **$**

(📞 22890 27462; Matoyani; snacks €4-6; ☺ 9am-late; 🛜) Top-notch breakfasts, crepes and people-watching.

L'île Bistro-Cafe
BISTRO **$**

(Kambani; snacks €4-6; ☺ 7am-1am) Relax at tables with red-checked tablecloths under a bougainvillea while tucking into homemade quiches, sandwiches and salads.

Antonini
TAVERNA **$$**

(📞 22890 22319; www.antoninimykonos.com; Plateia Manto; mains €8-22; ☺ lunch & dinner) A long-standing local hang-out with standard, but reliable, Greek food and a view of all of Mykonos passing by.

Nautilus
GREEK **$$**

(📞 22890 27100; www.nautilus-mykonos.gr; Kalogera 6; mains €11-16; ☺ 7pm-1am Mar-Nov) The whitewashed terrace spills out onto the street and Greek fusion dishes incorporate top ingredients.

To Maereio
GREEK **$$**

(📞 22890 28825; Kalogera 16; dishes €14-21) A small but selective menu of Mykonian favourites keeps this cosy place popular, though service can be spotty.

★ M-Eating
MEDITERRANEAN **$$$**

(📞 22890 78550; www.m-eating.gr; Kalogera 10; mains €15-26; ☺ dinner) Attentive service and relaxed luxury are the hallmarks of this creative restaurant specialising in fresh Greek products prepared with flair. Sample anything from tenderloin stuffed with Metsovo cheese to shrimp ravioli with crayfish sauce. Don't miss the Mykonian honey pie or, for beer lovers, the Volcano microbrew from Santorini.

Uno Con Carne
STEAKHOUSE **$$$**

(📞 22890 24020; www.unoconcarne.gr; mains €19-70; ☺ dinner Jun-Oct) Sup on prime steaks and fine wines on a beautifully lit verandah. The

---

GAY LIFE

Mykonos is one of the world's liveliest and most famous gay-friendly destinations. The many gay-centric bars and hang-outs fill with late-night crowds spilling onto the streets, and most welcome a mixed crowd too. The waterfront area, between the Old Harbour and the Church of Paraportiani is a focus for the late night gay scene. In addition to those below, the **Sunset pool bar** at the Hotel Elysium (p340) gets hopping.

Kastro (Agion Anargyron) Less relentlessly trendy, this is a good place to start the night with cocktails as the sun sets on Little Venice.

Porta (📞 22890 27807; Ioanni Voinovich) Porta's cruisey ambience fills small-scale rooms where things get crowded and close towards midnight.

Jackie O' (📞 22890 17968; www.jackieomykonos.com; Old Harbour) Jackie O' is one of Mykonos' main gathering points for gay and straight alike. Throngs circulate from the retro-chic interior to the harbourfront, starting in early evening. There is a new outpost at Super Paradise Beach.

Babylon (📞 22890 25152; Old Harbour) Gay-friendly masses party pier-side next to Jackie O'.

kitchen closes at 2am but you can party on in this fine setting. Signposted one block uphill from Panahrantou, near Litous.

Avra GREEK $$$
(✆22890 22298; www.avra-mykonos.com; Kalogera 27; mains €15-30; ⊙dinner Apr-Oct) Top Greek and fusion eats in a golden-lit courtyard perfect for romance.

🍷 Drinking & Nightlife

Folks come to Mykonos to party. Each major beach has at least one beach bar which gets going during the day. Night action in town starts around 11pm and warms up by 1am, and revellers often relocate from Hora to Cavo Paradiso (p343) in the wee hours. Hora offers an action-packed bar hop: from cool sunset cocktails to sweaty trance dancing. Wherever you go, bring a bankroll (cover alone runs around €20) – the high life doesn't come cheap.

Hora's Little Venice quarter puts the Mediterranean at your feet and is tops for rosy sunsets, windmill views and a swathe of colourful bars. A top spot is **Caprice** (✆22890 24541; Lambrou Katsoni 8), a long-standing favourite for both sunset drinks and parties into the night. **Galleraki** (✆22890 27188) turns out superb cocktails while **La Scarpa** (✆22890 23294) lets you lean back on its comfy sea-front cushions. Further north, **Katerina's Bar** (✆22890 23084; Agion Anargyron) has a cool balcony and eases you into the evening's action with chilled-out sounds.

Deeper into town, faithfully stylish **Aroma** (✆22890 27148; Enoplon Dynameon; ⊙9am-late) sits on a strategic corner, providing the evening catwalk view. It's great for breakfast and coffee as well. Just across the way, down an alleyway, is **Bolero Bar** (Malamatenias 1), a Mykonos mainstay frequented in its time by such celebs as Keith Richards.

Further down Enoplon Dynameon superfashionable **Astra** (✆22890 24767; Enoplon Dynameon), with modernist Mykonos decor at its best, hosts Athens' top DJs who spin rock, funk, house and drum and bass. Cocktail-cool **Aigli** (✆22890 27265; Enoplon Dynameon) has another useful terrace for people-watching.

Bubbles Bar (✆22890 78122; Agios Vlassis) is a champagne bar that also serves cocktails and Leonidas Belgian chocolates.

Scandinavian Bar (✆22890 22669; Ioanni Voinovich 9) supplies mainstream mayhem with ground-floor bars and an upstairs space for close-quarters moving to retro dance hits. Drinks tend to be a hair cheaper than elsewhere.

For big action into the dawn, enormous **Space** (✆22890 24100; Laka) is the place. They spin techno, house and progressive, but some say the scene's too hectic. **Remezzo** (Polikandrioti) features lounge and dance for a more relaxing vibe but has strict face control.

🛍 Shopping

Fashion boutiques and art galleries vie for attention throughout Hora's streets. The full gamut of name-brands (Lacoste, Dolce & Gabbana, Diesel) have set up shop, but so have many excellent Greek designers. Most shops close in low season.

Parthenis CLOTHING
(✆22890 22448; http://profile.orsalia-parthenis.gr; Plateia Alefkandra) For something special, find the work of Athens designer and long-time Mykonos resident, Dimitris Parthenis and his daughter Orsalia.

Scala Shop Gallery ARTS & CRAFTS
(www.scalagallery.gr; Matogianni 48) Changing displays of fine art; also sells contemporary jewellery and ceramics.

Art Studio Gallery ARTS & CRAFTS
(✆22890 22796; www.artstudiogallery.gr; Agion Saranta 22) Exhibits accomplished Greek painters and sculptors.

The Room Art Shop CLOTHING, ACCESSORIES
(✆22890 78098; Drakopoulou 23) Handmade T-shirts, knit goods and other creative bits.

Kampanas SHOES
(✆22890 22638; Mitropoleos 3; ⊙mid-Apr–Oct) Locally made sandals and handbags.

Ilias Lalaounis JEWELLERY
(✆22890 22444; www.lalaounis.gr; Polikandrioti 14) Mouth-wateringly fine jewellery from the Greek designer.

International Press BOOKS
(Kambani 5) International newspapers, magazines and books.

ℹ Information

Mykonos has no tourist office. Visit travel agencies instead.

EMERGENCY

Police Station (✆22890 22716) On the road to the airport.
Tourist Police (✆22890 22482) At the airport.

MEDICAL SERVICES

First Aid Clinic (☎22890 22274; Agiou Ioannou)
Hospital (☎22890 23994) About 1km along
the road to Ano Mera.

MONEY

Alphabank (Matogianni)
Eurobank (Matogianni)
Eurochange (Plateia Manto)

TRAVEL AGENCIES

Mykonos Accommodation Centre (☎22890
23408; www.mykonos-accommodation.com;
Enoplon Dynameon 10, 1st fl) Very helpful for all
things Mykonos (accommodation, guided tours,
island info), including gay-related aspects.

Around Mykonos

⊙ Sights

Mykonos is synonomous with parties and
beaches. If you want to dip into a bit of culture, rent wheels and cruise the back roads
through rocky valleys and small villages.
Nondescript Ano Mera has a peaceful **monastery** (Ano Mera; ⊗10am-1pm & 3.30-7pm)
with a carved marble facade and bell tower.

⊙ Beaches

Mykonos' golden-sand beaches in their
formerly unspoilt state were the pride of
Greece. Now most are jammed with umbrellas and backed by beach bars, but they
do make for a hopping scene. Moods range
from the simply hectic to the outright snob-
by, and nudity levels vary. You will find an
excellent guide to island beaches and their
clientele on www.mykonos-accommodation.
com. Catch caïques from Ornos and Platys
Gialos to further beaches, or call for a **sea
taxi** (☎6944374983).

About 4km south of Hora are family-
oriented **Agios Ioannis** and **Kapari**. The
nearby packed and noisy **Ornos** and the
package-holiday resort of **Platys Gialos**
have boats for the glitzier beaches to the
east. Nearby, sweet **Agia Anna** has a couple
of tavernas and a mellower feel.

Approximately 1km south of Platys Gialos you'll find brown-sand **Paraga Beach**,
which has a small gay section.

Party people should head about 1km east
to famous **Paradise**, which is not a recognised gay beach, but has a lively younger
scene. **Super Paradise** (aka Plintri or Super
P) has a fully gay section and a huge chic club.

Mixed and gay-friendly **Elia** is the last
caïque stop, and then just a few minutes' walk
from here is the secluded **Agrari**. Nudity is
fairly commonplace on all of these beaches.

North-coast beaches can be exposed to
the *meltemi* (north wind), but **Panormos**
and **Agios Sostis** with their golden sand
are fairly sheltered and less busy than the
south-coast beaches.

For out-of-the-way beaches you'll need
tough wheels to reach the likes of little **Lia**
in the southeast, or even smaller white-sand
Fokos and **Mersini** in the northeast.

The nearest beaches to Hora, Malaliamos
and Tourlos, 2km to the north of town, were
overtaken by the New Port. That leaves little **Agios Stefanos** (4km), within sight of
docking cruise ships.

🏃 Activities

Dive Adventures   DIVING
(☎22890 26539; www.diveadventures.gr; Paradise
Beach) Offers a full range of diving courses
with multilingual instructors: from single
dive (€55) to PADI certification (€290).
Snorkelling costs €45.

Planet Windsailing   WINDSURFING
(☎22890 72345; www.pezi-huber.com; Kalafatis
Beach) One-hour or one-day windsurfing
(€30/70), or a two-hour beginner's course for
two people (€80), at great Kalafatis Beach.

Kalafati Dive Center   DIVING
(☎22890 71677; www.mykonos-diving.com; Kalafatis
Beach) Full range of diving courses and pack-
ages from a 'discover scuba diving' session
(€63) to 10 boat dives with full gear (€385).

🛏 Sleeping

Mykonos Camping   CAMPGROUND, HOSTEL $
(☎22890 225915; www.mycamp.gr; Paraga Beach;
camp sites per adult/child/tent €10/5/10, dm €20,
bungalow per person €15-30; P🛜❄) Basic
camping with laundry and cooking area.
Bungalows and apartments sleep two to six.
Offers port and airport transfers.

San Giorgio Hotel   BOUTIQUE HOTEL $$$
(☎22890 27474; www.sangiorgio-mykonos.com;
Paradise Beach; d incl breakfast from €250; ⊗May-
mid-Oct) Right at the glammest of the beaches.
Guests get VIP service at Paradise Club.

🍴 Eating

Ahinaioi   TAVERNA $$
(☎22890 23467; Agia Anna (Paraga); mains €8-
15; ⊗lunch & dinner May-Sep) Tidy tables fill a

tree-filled courtyard and spill onto the sea road. Beachfront seafood eating at its best.

Christos
SEAFOOD **$$**

(Agios Ioannis Beach; mains €6-18) Fisherman, chef and sculptor Christos runs his beachside eatery with unassuming style, serving the best fish and seafood, not least unbeatable *astakos* (crayfish or spiny lobster).

🍷 Drinking & Nightlife

Cavo Paradiso
CLUB

(☏22890 27205; www.cavoparadiso.gr) When dawn gleams over the horizon, hard-core bar hoppers move from Hora to Cavo Paradiso, the open-air megaclub that's featured top world DJs at Paradise Beach since 1993.

Paradise Club
CLUB

(☏6940794879; www.paradiseclubmykonos.com; Paradise Beach) White-on-white decor backing Paradise Beach sets off all that bronzed skin.

PAROS ΠΑΡΟΣ

POP 12,853

Paros rests nonchalantly in the shadows of the limelight. Long tagged as primarily a ferry hub, its stylish, beautiful capital, trendy resort towns and culturally plump mountain villages are all the more charming for their lack of crowds or tourist kudos. Geologically speaking, Paros has long been a Greek star; white marble drawn from the island's mountainous interior made the island prosperous

BOAT SERVICES FROM PAROS

DESTINATION	TIME	FARE	FREQUENCY
Amorgos	4hr	€16	1-2 daily
Anafi	6½-8¾hr	€17	3-4 weekly
Antiparos	10min	€2	23 daily
Astypalea	4hr 50min	€30	5 weekly
Donousa	2½hr	€14	1-3 daily
Folegandros	3½hr	€9	5 weekly
Ios	2½hr	€11	2 daily
Iraklia	2hr	€13.50	1-2 daily
Iraklio*	3hr 40min	€75.50	1 daily
Kea (Tzia)	7hr 50min	€18	2 weekly
Kimolos	5hr 35min	€24	2 weekly
Koufonisia	3hr	€16	1-2 daily
Kythnos	6hr 50min	€16	2 weekly
Milos	6¾hr	€14	4 weekly
Mykonos*	1hr	€27.50	3 daily
Naxos	1hr	€8	5 daily
Naxos*	35min	€15.50	2 daily
Piraeus	4¾hr	€32.50	6 daily
Piraeus*	2½hr	€48.50	4 daily
Rafina*	3hr 10min	€52.80	1 daily
Santorini (Thira)	3-4hr	€18.50	5 daily
Santorini (Thira)*	2¼hr	€45	2-3 daily
Schinousa	2hr 20min	€10.50	1-2 daily
Serifos	3¾hr	€10	2 weekly
Sifnos	4¾hr	€5	3 weekly
Sikinos	4hr 25min	€9	3-4 weekly
Syros*	45min	€8.50	3 daily
Tinos	1¼hr	€32.70	1 daily

*high-speed services

Paros & Antiparos

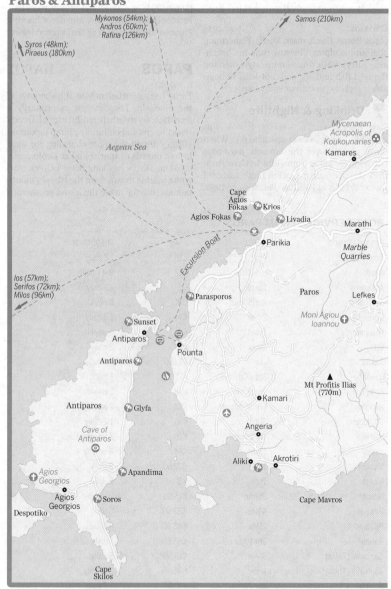

Mykonos (54km);
Andros (60km);
Rafina (126km)

Samos (210km)

Syros (48km);
Piraeus (180km)

Aegean Sea

Ios (57km);
Serifos (72km);
Milos (96km)

Mycenaean
Acropolis of
Koukounaries

Kamares

Cape
Agios
Fokas

Krios

Agios Fokas

Livadia

Marathi

Parikia

Marble
Quarries

Excursion Boat

Parasporos

Paros

Lefkes

Moni Agiou
Ioannou

Sunset

Antiparos

Pounta

Antiparos

Mt Profitis Ilias
(770m)

Antiparos

Glyfa

Kamari

Cave of
Antiparos

Angeria

Agios
Georgios

Apandima

Aliki

Akrotiri

Agios
Georgios

Soros

Despotiko

Cape Mavros

Cape
Skilos

from the Early Cycladic period onwards. Most famously, the *Venus de Milo* was carved from Parian marble, as was Napoleon's tomb.

The smaller island of Antiparos, 1km southwest of Paros, is easily reached by car ferry or excursion boat.

Getting There & Away

Paros is the main ferry hub for onward travel to other islands in the Aegean. It is thus well-served by regular ferries from Piraeus and by connections to most of the other islands of the

ℹ️ Getting Around

BOAT

Water taxis leave from the quay for beaches around Parikia. Tickets range from €8 to €15 and are available on board.

BUS

About 12 buses daily link Parikia and Naoussa (€1.60) directly, and there are seven buses daily from Parikia to Naoussa via Dryos (€2.60), Lefkes (€1.60) and Piso Livadi (€2.20). There are 10 buses to Pounta (for Antiparos; €1.60) and six to Aliki (via the airport; €1.60).

CAR, MOTORCYCLE & BICYCLE

There are rental outlets along the waterfront in Parikia and all around the island. A good outfit is **Acropolis** (☑ 22840 21830). Minimum hire per day in August for a car is about €45; for a motorbike it's €20.

TAXI

Taxis (☑ 22840 21500) gather beside the roundabout in Parikia. Fares include the airport (€17), Naoussa (€13), Pounta (€12), Lefkes (€13) and Piso Livadi (€22). Add €1 if going from the port. There are extra charges of €2 if you book ahead more than 20 minutes beforehand, €3 if less than 20 minutes. More than two pieces of luggage are charged at €1 each.

Parikia   Παροικία

POP 5812

For its small size, Parikia packs a punch. Its labyrinthine old town is pristine and filled with boutique shops, trendy cafes and some of the Cyclades top restaurants. You'll also find a handful of impressive archaeological sites, a waterfront crammed with tavernas and bars and a sandy stretch of beach.

⊙ Sights

Panagia Ekatondapyliani   CHURCH
(Parikia; ⊘ 7.30am-9.30pm) The Panagia Ekatondapyliani, which dates from AD 326, is one of the finest churches in the Cyclades. The building is three distinct churches: Agios Nikolaos, the largest, with superb columns of Parian marble and a carved iconastasis in the east of the compound; the ornate Church of Our Lady; and the ancient Baptistery. The name translates as Our Lady of the Hundred Gates, though this is a wishful rounding-up of a still-impressive number of doorways. The **Byzantine Museum** (admission €1.50; ⊘ 9.30am-2pm & 6-9pm), within the compound, has a collection of icons and other artefacts.

Cyclades, and also to Thessaloniki, Crete and the Dodecanese.

There is one flight daily from Athens to Paros (€70, 45 minutes).

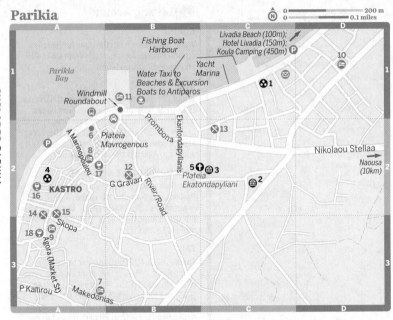

Parikia

Archaeological Museum   MUSEUM
(☏22840 21231; admission €2; ⊗8am-3pm Tue-Sun) Tucked behind the Panagia Ekatondapyliani, this museum offers a cool escape into the island's past. It harbours some marvellous pieces, including a 5th-century Nike on the point of alighting, as well as a 6th-century Gorgon also barely in touch with the surly earth. Some earlier examples of splendid pottery include the *Fat Lady of Saliagos,* while a major exhibit is a fragment slab of the 4th-century **Parian Chronicle**, which lists the most outstanding artistic achievements of ancient

Greece. It was discovered in the 17th century. (Two other slabs ended up in the Ashmolean Museum, in Oxford, England.)

Ancient Cemetery   RUIN
North along the waterfront is a fenced ancient cemetery dating from the 7th century BC. It was excavated in 1983 to discover Roman graves, burial pots and sarcophagi, all now floodlit at night.

Frankish Kastro   RUIN
Check out the outer walls of this fortress, built by the Venetian Duke Marco Sanudo of Naxos in AD 1260. Built with the stones

from ancient buildings that once stood on this site, you can find remnants from the arc temple of Athena and an Ionic temple from the 5th century BC.

Tours

Santorineos Travel Services
SIGHTSEEING TOURS
(22840 24245; www.traveltoparos.gr; D Vasileou) This company can book bus tours of Paros (€35), boat trips to Mykonos and Delos (adult/child €45/23), to Santorini including a bus tour of the island (adult/child €55/30), to Naxos (adult/child €10/5) and to Iraklio and Koufonisia (adult/child €40/20).

Sleeping

In August the **Rooms Association** (22840 22722, after hours 22840 22220), located on the quay, has information on domatia; otherwise, owners meet ferries. The **Hotel Association** (22840 51207) has information about hotels on Paros and Antiparos. All campgrounds have minibuses that meet ferries.

Koula Camping
CAMPGROUND $
(22840 22801; www.campingkoula.gr; campsites per tent/person €4/8, tent rental €7; Apr–Oct;) With plenty of trees, and just footsteps from the sea, this is a decent place to pitch your tent. It's at the north end of the Parikia waterfront and there are free transfers to and from town. There's also an on-site restaurant, shop and laundry.

Pension Sofia
PENSION $$
(22840 22085; www.sofiapension-paros.com; Parikia; d/tr €70/85;) Tucked a couple of blocks in from the waterfront, Sofia's lovingly tended garden alone makes it worth the stay. Swings, shade, trees, flowers and plenty of benches create a quiet oasis. Rooms are clean and airy and the charming owners are a wealth of knowledge. Breakfast is available for €8. You'll find Sofia 400m east of the ferry quay.

Angie's Studios
APARTMENT $$
(22840 26977, 22840 23909; www.angies-studios.gr; Makedonias; d €68; Apr–Oct;) Located just south beyond the Old Town, Angie's is worth seeking out. Spacious, immaculate rooms with flagstone floors and lots of local touches are set within a garden glowing with bougainvillea. Each room has a private balcony and a kitchenette, and the staff are warm and lovely. You'll quickly start calling this home. Call ahead

and they will come to collect you from the dock.

Hotel Dina
HOTEL $$
(22840 21325; www.hoteldina.com; Agora (Market St); s/d €55/65) These eight rooms in the heart of the Old Town are a find. With white-washed walls and wrought-iron beds, they're spotless, comfortable and uncramped. Each has a small balcony looking out over Market St, with shared courtyards and verandahs in the traditional building's centre. The hostess is goodnatured and helpful.

Hotel Argonauta
HOTEL $$
(22840 21440; www.argonauta.gr; Plateia Mavrogenous; s/d/tr €70/90/110; Apr–mid-Oct;) Overlooking Plateia Mavrogenous, the Argonauta has a peaceful ambience. Splashes of blue and green, marble floors and wooden ceilings make these rooms inviting. Small balconies and family-style service make it all the more appealing. There's also a popular, on-site restaurant.

Hotel Livadia
HOTEL $$
(22840 21597; www.paroslivadiahotel.com; d/tr €70/80) The beach beckons from the balconies of these bright, clean rooms. Robin-egg blue shutters and a friendly family welcome you, while the home-cooked meals at the cool on-site restaurant may keep you lingering all day. You'll find the Livadia east of the town centre directly across from the sea.

Eating

Micro Café
CAFE $
(Agora; dishes €4-7;) Tiny and popular, this cafe spills out onto Market St. Breakfasts, filling salads, snacks and sandwiches fill your belly while plenty of lively conversation and music fills the air until the early hours.

Cafe Distrato
CAFE $
(22840 25175; G Gravari; mains €3-10; breakfast, lunch & dinner) Tucked down a small alley in the Old Town, this casual restaurant exudes wholesomeness. Attached to a shop selling local products, the food is straightforward and fresh, comprising crepes, sandwiches, burgers, pastas and salads. Also has a long smoothie and cocktail list. Dine outside under a canopy of trees.

Levantis
GREEK $$
(22840 23613; levantisrest@yahoo.gr; Agora, Kastro; dishes €14-22) A vine-covered courtyard and simple, whitewashed interior with splashes of modern art create an unhurried,

polished setting for some of the Cyclades' finest contemporary Greek cuisine. The menu makes for hungry reading – choose from dishes like slowly braised honey-spiced lamb or perfumed couscous with roast veg and figs. For dessert, how about 'one hell of a pear' in orange, cointreau and cinnamon and served with local yoghurt. The service is stellar, as is the house wine.

Ephessus GREEK $$
(☑22840 22520; dishes €6-15) Come here for a lively Greek experience. Dig into a dish of home-cooked souvlaki, grills and seafood and you'll quickly understand why this traditional family restaurant is so popular. It's all cooked in a traditional wood oven and washed down with a decent house wine. There are plenty of vegetarian options as well. It's tucked on a side road between the harbour and Panagia Eatondalpyliani.

Drinking & Nightlife

The southwestern harbour is heavily peppered with bars, popular with both locals and visitors.

★Koukoutoi BAR
(Plateia Mavrogenous) On the edge of the main square yet slightly out of view, this local hangout is a total gem. Small and lively, with walls covered in posters and wooden benches filled with cushions, come here to nibble on mezedhes and sip juices, coffees, beer or a shot of ouzo.

Evinos BAR
Perched atop a set of stairs across from the water next to the Kastro, this multi-level bar draws a weekend crowd with soul and funk tunes. Sip cocktails on the terrace at candle-lit tables and soak up the ambience.

Pirate BAR
Ultracool and cavelike, Pirate is an ideal refuge within the Old Town. Head all the way down the main pedestrian street, near Market St, and keep your ears tuned for funky rock.

Information

On the waterfront, Santorineos Travel Services (p347) sells ferry tickets, can advise on accommodation and car hire, and has a luggage store (€1 per hour). You can also book various tours here.

Health Centre (☑22840 22500; Prombona; ⊙9am-1.30pm Mon-Fri) Also has a dentist.

Parosweb (www.parosweb.com) Comprehensive and useful information on Paros and Antiparos.
Police Station (☑22840 23333; Plateia Mavrogenous)
Port Police (☑22840 21240) Back from the northern waterfront, near the post office.
Post Office (☑tel, info 22840 21236) Located 400m east of the ferry quay.

Naoussa Ναούσα
POP 3027
Heading north to Naoussa takes you through lush farmland where cows lazily munch grass in the valley. Naoussa itself has been transformed from a quiet fishing village into an increasingly stylish resort. Perched on the shores of the large Plastira Bay, there are pleasant beaches nearby, excellent restaurants and an ever-expanding number of stylish beach-side cafes and bars. Behind the waterfront is a maze of narrow whitewashed streets, peppered with cafes, smart boutiques and souvenir shops.

Sights & Activities

The best beaches in the area are Kolimbythres and Monastiri, which has some good snorkelling. Low-key Lageri is also worth seeking out. Santa Maria, on the other side of the eastern headland, is ideal for windsurfing. These beaches can all be reached by road, but caïques go from Naoussa to each of them during July and August.

The Erkyna Travel (p350) office can help with various excursions including an island bus tour, water sports and boat trips to other islands.

Byzantine Museum MUSEUM
(admission €2; ⊙10am-1pm & 6-9pm Aug) Naoussa's Byzantine museum is housed in the blue-domed church, about 200m uphill from the central square on the main road to Parikia. The inside glitters with over a hundred icons from the 15th to 19th centuries.

Moraitis Winery WINERY
(☑22840 51350; www.moraitiswines.gr; ⊙10am-3.30pm Mon-Sat) Pressing grapes since 1910, the Moraitis family has got it down to a fine art. Tour the original stone cellars and consider early contraptions and equipment before sitting down for a taste. The white Meltemi is particularly good. The winery is an easy walk southeast of the centre.

Folklore Museum
MUSEUM
(☑22840 52284; admission €1.80; ☺9am-1pm & 7-9pm May-Sep) Housed in a traditional home, this small museum offers an eyeful of traditional dress and old island photos. It's inland from the main square, behind the church.

Kokou Riding Centre
HORSE RIDING
(☑22840 51818; www.kokou.gr) The well-established Kokou has 2½-hour morning rides (€50), where you get to venture on horseback into the sea, and 1½-hour evening rides (€35). They'll collect you from Naoussa's main square for €3.

Tao's Center
MEDITATION
(☑22840 28882; www.taos-greece.com; Ambelas) Tao's is a retreat and meditation centre located in splendid seclusion on a hilltop east of Naoussa. The centre offers workshops and courses in meditation, qi gong, yoga and dance, as well as massage therapies, all in sympathetic surroundings and with stylish facilities. It also organises activities for youngsters. It has strong green credentials and runs a popular Asian restaurant. The centre can be reached by turning off the main road to Ambelas and then following conspicuous signs along a mainly surfaced track.

🛏 Sleeping

Young Inn
HOSTEL $
(☑6976415232; www.young-inn.com; dm/d €20/60; P✳🤖) With basic dorm rooms and an activity-packed calendar, this is Naoussa's international backpackers hub. It's located to the east of the harbour, beyond Naoussa's cathedral.

Hotel Kalypso
HOTEL $$
(☑22840 51488; www.kalypso.gr; Agi Aargiri Beach; s/d incl breakfast €80/120; P✳@🤖) Right on the beach, this older complex has been given a makeover and has a surprisingly chic lounge, simple, spotless rooms with homey touches and plenty of ocean views.

Hotel Galini
HOTEL $$
(☑22840 53382; www.hotelgaliniparos.com; incl breakfast d with/without balcony €70/85, tr €95; ✳🤖) Run by a local family for three generations, this little hotel has comfortable, clean rooms. Ask for a balcony and a sea view. Galini is opposite the blue-domed local church (Byzantine Museum), on the main road into town from Parikia.

Katerina Mare
APARTMENT $$$
(☑22840 51642; www.katerinamare.com; incl breakfast d €125, ste €175-215; P✳🤖) In a word, this place is lovely. Recently renovated rooms are classy and pristine, with wooden furniture and crisp linens. Each room has phenomenal views and every convenience, including a first-rate kitchenette. Service is stellar.

Lilly Residence
BOUTIQUE HOTEL $$$
(☑22840 51716; www.lillyresidence.gr; d/ste incl breakfast €210/400; P✳🤖) This is quite easily Naoussa's most stylish hotel. Stone, wood and wicker make the rooms aesthetically pleasing and calm. Just back from the water, all rooms have sea views and suites sleep four. The pool is a narrow slice of blue and the verandah is a peaceful escape. Service is discreet.

🍴 Eating & Drinking

Beyond the harbour, there's a beachfront line of cafes and music bars with cool lounge decor worthy of Mykonos. Places like **Fotis** and **Briki** spill out onto little beaches and play a mix of classical strands by day and jazzier, funkier sounds by night.

⭐ Glafkos
MEDITERRANEAN $
(☑22840 52100; mains €6-13; ☺lunch & dinner) With tables practically on top of the ocean, it's not surprising that this place specialises in seafood. Try steamed mussels and grilled calamari, or dig into orzo pasta with shrimp or black risotto with cuttlefish. The wine list is almost as novel.

La Piazza
ITALIAN $$
(☑22840 52657; www.lapiazza.com.gr; mains €8-14) This menu will inspire your appetite. Haddock stuffed with tomato and herbs, crispy bread with eggplant salad and pastas, pizza and risottos with a Greek slant are all as good as they sound. The atmosphere is casual with a good dose of class. You'll find it just off the main square.

Sousouro
CAFE $
(☑6976904498; www.barphilosophy.com; ☺9am-3am) Occupying a small corner in the Old Town, this cafe is big on flavour. Come for breakfast to try kiwi and basil smoothies, almond butter banana milkshakes; fresh bread with local cheese, strawberries, pistachio and honey; or quinoa granola with fig jam. At night, the wholesomeness makes way for cocktails.

Xamilothoris Patisserie
CAFE $

(☑ 22840 51240; Main Sq; pastries €3-5; 🛜) Pretend you've come for the coffee (which is, in fact, excellent) but really indulge in the cakes, tarts and crepes. The homemade ice cream is divine – try fig or pistachio. Here since 1967, this place is a fixture on the main square.

To Takimi
BAR

(Music Cafe; ☑ 22840 55095) Just south of the main square, this is where locals come to drink beer or ouzo and listen to live music, often played on the traditional string instruments waiting on the walls. Everything from *rembetika* to rock goes down here.

🛍 Shopping

Paria Lexis
BOOKS

(☑ 22840 51121) Travel books, maps and novels in English.

ℹ Information

The bus from Parikia terminates some way up from the main square just in from the waterfront. The main street of Naoussa lies on the left of the riverbed. If arriving by car, be warned: parking in certain areas is banned from June to September and fines are hefty.

To find the heart of the Old Town, take the pedestrian street to the left of Xamilothoris Patisserie. The post office is a tedious uphill walk from the main square. There are several banks with ATMs around the main square.

Erkyna Travel (☑ 22840 22654; www.erkynatravel.com) On the river road. Sells ferry tickets and can help with accommodation, car hire and excursions.

Naoussa Information (☑ 22840 52158; 🕙 10am-midnight Jul & Aug, 11am-1pm & 6-10pm mid-Jun–Jul) Local information and help with accommodation. Based in a booth by the main square.

Lefkes
Λεύκες

POP 494

Lovely Lefkes clings to a natural amphitheatre amid hills whose summits are dotted with old windmills. Siesta is taken seriously here and the village has a general air of serenity. Just 9km southeast of Parikia, it was the capital of Paros during the Middle Ages. The village's main attraction is wandering through its pristine alleyways, past beautiful architecture. The Cathedral of Agia Triada is an impressive structure, shaded by olive trees.

Around Paros

Down on the southeast coast is the attractive harbour and low-key resort of Piso Livadi, where there is a pleasant beach. Perantinos Travel and Tourism (☑ 22840 41135; www.perantinostravel.gr) can arrange accommodation, car hire and boat trips to other islands, and also arranges money exchange. There is an ATM next to Perantinos.

👁 Sights & Activities

Paros is a hot favourite for windsurfing and kiteboarding, while the clear waters round the island make for excellent diving.

Down the coast at Pounta are Eurodivers Club (☑ 22840 92071; www.eurodivers.gr) and Paros Kite Pro Center (☑ 22840 92229; www.paroskite-procenter.com).

There is a fair scattering of beaches around the island's coastline, including Paros' top beach, Hrysi Akti (Golden Beach), on the southeast coast, with good sand and several tavernas. The area is popular with windsurfers. This is where Aegean Diving College (☑ 6932289649, 22840 43347; www.aegeandiving.gr) runs a range of dives of archaeological and ecological interest, and Octopus Sea Trips (☑ 6932757123; www.octopuseatrips.com) runs snorkel diving, excursions and marine environmental courses. Also at Golden Beach, Force7 Surf Centre (☑ 22840 42189; www.force7paros.gr; Hrysi Akti) runs windsurfing, diving, kayaking and wake-boarding sessions.

ANTIPAROS ΑΝΤΙΠΑΡΟΣ

POP 1037

Antiparos lies dreamily offshore from Paros. As soon as your ferry docks, you feel a distinct slowing down in the pace of things. The main village and port (also called Antiparos) are relaxed. There's a touristy gloss around the waterfront and main streets, but the village runs deep inland to quiet squares and alleyways giving way suddenly to open fields.

The rest of the island runs to the south of the main settlement through quiet countryside. There are several decent beaches, especially at Glyfa and Soros on the east coast.

👁 Sights & Activities

Castle of Antiparos
FORT

From the top of the pedestrianised main street, head for the distinctive, giant plane tree of Plateia Agios Nikolaou. From here, a narrow lane leads to the intriguing remnants of the Venetian Castle of Antiparos, entered through an archway. The castle dates from the 13th to the 16th centuries. The surrounding wall boasts external quirky staircases and balconies while the remains of the central keep is crowned by a stone water tower and clasped round by gnomic churches. There's a small **Folk Museum** here also.

Cave of Antiparos   CAVE
(admission €3.60; ⊙10.45am-3.45pm summer) About 8km south of the port, this atmospheric cave remains impressive despite much looting of stalactites and stalagmites in the past. Descending the 400-plus steps into the cave can be a dank and gloomy affair. Follow the coast road south until you reach a signed turn-off into the hills. From the port there are hourly buses to the cave (one way €1.60).

Blue Island Divers   DIVING
(☑ 6983159452, 22840 61767; www.blueisland-divers.gr) Halfway up the main street is a diving and beach gear shop where you can get information about Blue Island Divers and its wide range of dive options. A four-day PADI open-water course is €395 and a 'discover scuba-diving' course is €50. Trips can be tailored to suit individual wishes.

☞ Tours

MS Alexandros   SIGHTSEEING TOURS
(☑ 6972026585, 22840 61273) Runs boat tours around the island daily, stopping at several beaches. Prices range from €35 to €45 per adult (less for children), and cover barbecue and drinks; you can book at local travel agencies.

🛏 Sleeping & Eating

Camping Antiparos   CAMPGROUND $
(☑ 22840 61221; www.camping-antiparos.gr; camp sites per adult/child/tent €8/4/5) This beachside campground is planted with bamboo 'compartments' and cedars and is 1.5km north of the port. It has a minimarket, bar and restaurant. A site bus picks up from the port.

Hotel Mantalena   HOTEL $$
(☑ 6977352363,2284061206;www.hotelmantalena .gr; s/d/tr €72/80/96; ✲ @ ☎) The Mantalena has bright, clean rooms and sits across from the sea, a short distance to the north of the

main harbour quay. Balconies look over the garden or out to the ocean. There's a spacious harbour-view terrace where you can have breakfast or cocktails.

Margarita's   GREEK $
(Agora; mains €8-20; ⊙breakfast, lunch & dinner) Halfway up the main street, this bright and colourful little eatery will satisfy you with big salads and other delicious modern Greek dishes like tasty seafood pasta.

The waterfront and main street of Antiparos have several cafes and tavernas serving Greek staples and fish dishes. You'll also find supermarkets and a bakery in the main street.

☕ Drinking & Nightlife

There are a couple of stylish cafe-bars at the top of the village where they'll happily rustle up a cocktail and Greek-style 'tapas' to a lively playlist.

ℹ Information

Go right from the ferry quay along the waterfront. The main street, Agora, heads inland just by the Anarghyros Restaurant. Halfway up the main street are an Emporiki Bank and National Bank of Greece (next to each other and both with ATMs). The post office is also here. To reach the central square turn left at the top of the main street and then right.

There are several tour and travel agencies, including **Oliaris Tours** (☑ 22840 61231; oliaros@ par.forthnet.gr).

ℹ Getting There & Away

In summer, frequent excursion boats depart for Antiparos from Parikia (€5). There is also a half-hourly car ferry that runs from Pounta on the west coast of Paros to Antiparos (one way €1.10, per scooter €1.90, per car €6.10, 10 minutes); the first ferry departs from Pounta about 7.15am and the last boat returning to Pounta leaves Antiparos at about 12.30am.

ℹ Getting Around

The only bus service on Antiparos runs, in summer, to the cave in the centre of the island (€5). The bus continues to Soros and Agios Georgios.

Cars, scooters and bicycles can be hired from **Aggelos** (☑22840 61027, 22840 61626), which is the first office as you come from the ferry quay. Cars start at about €40 per day (high season), scooters are €15 per day and bicycles are €5 per day.

NAXOS ΝΑΞΟΣ

POP 12.089

The largest island of the Cyclades, Naxos packs a lot of bang for its buck. Its main city of Hora is a web of steep cobbled alleys, filled with the hubbub of tourism and shopping. Yet you needn't travel far to find isolated beaches, atmospheric villages and ancient sites.

It was on Naxos that an ungrateful Theseus is said to have abandoned Ariadne after she helped him escape the Cretan labyrinth. She didn't pine long, and was soon entwined with Dionysos, the god of wine and ecstasy and the island's favourite deity. Naxian wine has long been considered a useful antidote to a broken heart.

Naxos was a cultural centre of classical Greece and of Byzantium, while Venetian and Frankish influences have left their mark. It is more fertile than most of the other Cyclades islands and produces olives, grapes, figs, citrus fruit, corn and potatoes. Mt Zeus (1004m; also known as Mt Zas) is the Cyclades' highest peak and is the central focus of the island's interior where you will find such enchanting villages as Halki and Apiranthos. The island also draws outdoor enthusiasts, with kiteboarding off the sandy southern beaches, and traditional footpaths to follow between villages, churches and other sights. Walking guides and maps are available from local bookshops.

ℹ️ Getting There & Away

Like Paros, Naxos is something of a ferry hub of the Cyclades, with a similar number of conventional and fast ferries making regular calls to and from Piraeus and weekly links to and from the mainland ports of Lavrio and Rafina via the Northern Cyclades.

There is a daily flight to and from Athens (€98, 45 minutes).

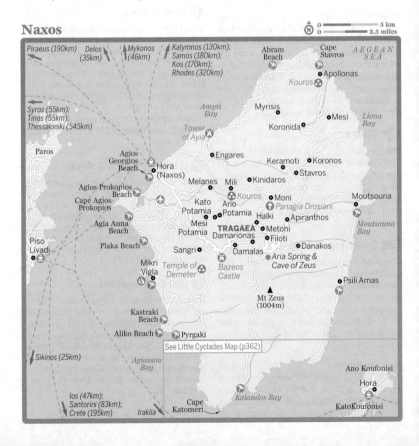

Naxos

BOAT SERVICES FROM NAXOS

DESTINATION	TIME	FARE	FREQUENCY
Amorgos	2¾hr	€14.50	2-3 daily
Amorgos*	1hr 15min	€24.20	3 daily
Anafi	5½hr	€14	1 weekly
Astypalea	3hr 55min	€24.50	5 weekly
Donousa	1-4hr	€7.60	1-3 daily
Folegandros	5¾hr	€11	5 weekly
Folegandros*	4hr	€37.40	6 weekly
Ios	2hr 50min	€10	1-3 daily
Ios*	50min	€25.50	1-2 daily
Iraklia	1hr	€7.50	2-3 daily
Kalymnos	8hr 40min	€21	2 weekly
Kea (Tzia)	8hr 35min	€19	1 weekly
Kimolos	4hr 40min	€15	2 weekly
Kos	9hr 50min	€24.50	2 weekly
Koufonisia	2hr	€9.50	2 daily
Kythnos	7¾hr	€18	1 weekly
Lavrio	9hr 25min	€23	1 weekly
Milos	5hr	€56.20	4 weekly
Mykonos	2hr 25min	€12	1 weekly
Mykonos*	45min	€26.50	2 daily
Paros	1hr	€8	5 daily
Paros*	35min	€15.50	3 daily
Piraeus	4¾hr	€31	4-5 daily
Piraeus*	3¾hr	€48	4 daily
Rafina*	3hr	€52.50	1 daily
Santorini (Thira)	2hr	€16.50	5 daily
Santorini (Thira)*	1hr 35min	€37	2-3 daily
Schinousa	1hr 20min	€7	1-2 daily
Sikinos	2¼hr	€8	3-4 weekly
Syros	2h 10min	€10	1 daily
Tilos	13hr	€24.50	2 weekly
Tinos	1hr	€26.50	1 daily

*high-speed services

ⓘ Getting Around

TO/FROM THE AIRPORT

The airport is 3km south of Hora. There is no shuttle bus, but buses to Agios Prokopios Beach and Agia Anna pass close by. A taxi costs €10 to €15 depending on luggage amounts, the time of day and if booked. All taxis are now metered and should give a receipt.

BUS

Frequent buses run to Agia Anna (€2) from Hora. Five buses daily serve Filoti (€2.30) via Halki (€2); four serve Apiranthos (€3.10) via Filoti and Halki; and at least three serve Apollonas (€6.20), Pyrgaki (€2.30) and Melanes (€1.60). There are less frequent departures to other villages.

Buses leave from the end of the ferry quay in Hora; timetables are posted outside the **bus information office** (☑ 22850 22291; www.naxos-destinations.com), diagonally left and across the road from the bus stop. You have to buy tickets from the office or from the machine outside.

CAR & MOTORCYCLE

August rates for hire cars range from about €45 to €65 per day, and quad bikes from €30. There are a number of rental agencies along Hora's waterfront; try **Rental Center** (22850 23395; Plateia Evripeou), **Auto Tour** (22850 25480; www.naxosrentacar.com) or **Fun Car** (22850 26084; www.funcarnaxos.com).

Hora (Naxos) Χώρα (Νάξος)

POP 6727

Hora has the colour and bustle you'd expect of the island's port and capital. Settled on the west coast, the old town is a tangle of steep footpaths and is divided into two historic Venetian neighbourhoods: Bourgos, where the Greeks lived; and the hilltop Kastro, where the Roman Catholics lived. Despite being fairly large, Hora can still be easily managed on foot.

◉ Sights

It's almost impossible not to get lost in the old town and maps are of little use. To see the **Bourgos** area, head into the winding backstreets behind the northern end of Paralia. The most alluring part of Hora is the residential **Kastro**. Marco Sanudo made the town the capital of his duchy in 1207. Several Venetian mansions survive in the centre of Kastro, and you can see the outside of his castle, the **Tower of Sanoudos**, that was once surrounded by marble balconies. Take a stroll around the Kastro during siesta to experience its hushed, timeless atmosphere. If you lose your bearings, remember that roads that go up eventually lead to Kastro and roads heading downwards will take you back to the sea.

Mitropolis Museum   MUSEUM

(22850 24151; Kondyli; ⊙8am-3pm Tue-Sun) FREE A short distance behind the northern end of the waterfront are several churches and chapels, and the Mitropolis Museum. The museum features fragments of a Mycenaean city of the 13th to 11th centuries BC that was abandoned because of the threat of flooding by the sea. It's a haunting place where glass panels underfoot reveal ancient foundations and larger areas of excavated buildings.

Archaeological Museum   MUSEUM

(admission €3; ⊙8am-3pm Tue-Sun) This museum is located in the Kastro, housed in the former Jesuit school where novelist Nikos Kazantzakis was briefly a pupil. It's slightly musty but items are well labelled and contain fascinating finds from the Ionic and Doric eras. Watch for the oversized statue of Antonius, the Roman General.

Della Rocca-Barozzi
Venetian Museum   MUSEUM

(22850 22387; guided tours adult/student €5/3; ⊙10am-2.40pm & 6.30-9.30pm mid-May–Oct) This atmospheric museum is housed in a handsome old tower house of the 13th century. If it feels as if someone still lives here but has just stepped out, it's because it's true; the owners (direct decendents of the original Italian aristocrat owners) continue to live here a few months of each winter. Wander through their rooms to see what they wore, how the table was laid and how they furnished their rooms throughout the centuries.

It's worth taking the tour, as guides have huge amounts of knowledge. The museum is within the Kastro ramparts (by the northwest gate). There are changing art exhibitions in the vaults. Evening concerts and other events are staged in the grounds of the museum.

Folk Museum   MUSEUM

(22850 25561; www.naxosfolkmuseum.com; Old Market St; admission €3; ⊙10am-2pm & 7-10pm) This small but well-maintained museum has managed to fit in farming implements, bee keeping, bread making, clothing, wine making, cheese production and history without leaving you feeling overwhelmed.

🏃 Activities

Flisvos Sport Club   WINDSURFING

(22850 24308; www.flisvos-sportclub.com; Agios Georgios) Well organised and offering a range of windsurfing courses, walking trips in the mountains, and bike tours.

Naxos Bike   CYCLING

(22850 26612; www.naxosbikes.com) Get all of your equipment here, from trekking bikes to children's seats. They'll also set you up with maps to get you out exploring. Cycle rental starts from €8 per day. Located next to Mitropolis Museum.

Naxos Horse Riding   HORSE RIDING

(6948809142; www.naxoshorseriding.com) Offers daily morning, afternoon and evening horse rides inland and on beaches (€50 per person). You can book a ride up until 6pm the day before and can arrange pick-up and return to and from the stables. Beginners, young children and advanced riders are catered for.

Tours

There are frequent excursion boats to Delos and Mykonos (adult/child €45/23), Santorini, including a bus tour (adult/child €55/30), Paros and Naoussa (adult/child €20/10), and Iraklia and Koufonisia (adult/child €40/20); book through travel agents.

🛌 Sleeping

Hora has plenty of accommodation options. If you settle for an offer at the port from a persistent hawker, establish with certainty the true distance of the rooms from the centre of town. In high season there may be booths on the quay dispensing information about hotels and rooms.

There are several campgrounds near Hora, and all have decent facilities. Minibuses meet the ferries. The sites are all handy to beaches.

Despina's Rooms PENSION $
(✆ 22850 22356; www.despinarooms.gr; Kastro; d €45; ✳) These decent rooms are a steal. Tucked away in the heart of Kastro, some have sea views. Rooms on the roof terrace are popular despite their small size. There's a communal kitchen.

Camping Maragas CAMPGROUND $
(✆ 22850 42552; www.maragascamping.gr; camp sites €9, d €45, studio €70) Located at Agia Anna Beach, south of Hora.

Naxos Camping CAMPGROUND $
(✆ 22850 23500; www.naxos-camping.gr; camp site per person €9; ✳) Situated about 1km south of Agios Georgios Beach.

Plaka Camping CAMPGROUND $
(✆ 22850 42700; www.plakacamping.gr; camp site per person €9; ✳) Down at Plaka Beach, 6km south of town.

Hotel Grotta HOTEL $$
(✆ 22850 22215; www.hotelgrotta.gr; s/d incl breakfast €70/85; P✳@✆✳) On high ground overlooking the Kastro and main town, this excellent hotel has comfortable, immaculate rooms, great sea views from the front, spacious public areas and a Jacuzzi. Even better, it has a cheerful, attentive atmosphere.

Xenia Hotel HOTEL $$
(✆ 22850 25068; www.hotel-xenia.gr; d/tr incl breakfast €90/100) Sleek and minimalist, this brand-new hotel is right in the old town scene. Balconies overlook the bustle of the streets but thick glass keeps the noise out when you decide to call it a night. It's just steps from the harbour.

Hotel Glaros BOUTIQUE HOTEL $$
(✆ 22850 23101; www.hotelglaros.com; Agios Georgios Beach; d €115-125, ste €145; ✳@✆) Edgy yet homy, simple yet plush, this well-run and immaculate hotel has a seaside feel with light blues and whites and handpainted wooden furnishings. Service is efficient and thoughtful and the beach is only a few steps away. Breakfast is €7.

Chateau Zevgoli HOTEL $$
(✆ 22850 26123; www.apollonhotel-naxos.gr; Kastro; s/d/ste €85/95/105; ✳✆) Tucked away in the heart of Kastro, this family-run, well-loved hotel has a leafy garden setting to go with the traditional Naxian style of rooms and furnishings.

Adriani Hotel HOTEL $$
(✆ 22850 23079; www.adriani.gr; d incl breakfast €60-90) Open year-round, this lovely hotel has fresh-feeling, comfortable rooms. The best are at the back, where it's quieter. Rooms at the top are recently renovated and colourful and share a spacious verandah with views of the old town. You'll find it on the edge of town, on the main road heading east.

Golden Beach Studios HOTEL $$
(✆ 22850 24657; goldenbeachstudios@hotmail. com; d €50-60; ✳) This place is a bargain. Well located for Agios Georgios, the spacious, well-kept rooms have a distinct old-school Bavarian feel and all have kitchenettes and balconies. The very friendly owner could have been your mum in another life.

Hotel Galini HOTEL $$
(✆ 22850 2214; www.hotelgalini.com; d incl breakfast €80; ✳✆) A serious nautical theme lends this place lots of character. Updated, spacious rooms have small balconies and wrought-iron beds with breezy canopies. The location is great, just blocks from the beach and the Old Town, and the breakfast is hearty.

🍴 Eating

Naxos town has a fantastic dining. For the freshest seafood, head to the tavernas on the waterfront where the fishermen hang out, and sample their catch.

Hora (Naxos)

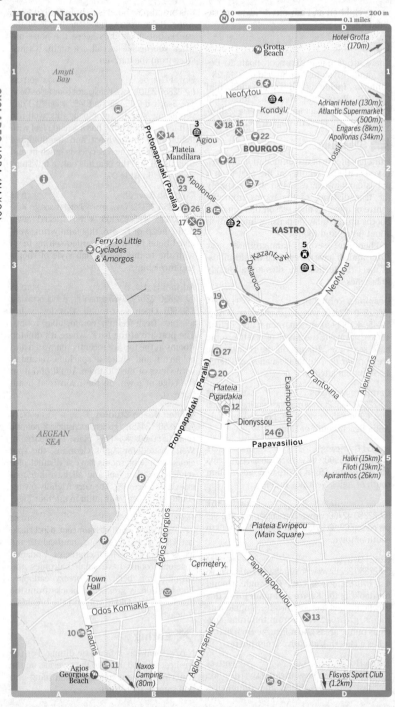

Hora (Naxos)

The cheapest supermarkets are **Atlantic** and **Vidalis**, both a little way out of town on the ring road.

Meze 2   SEAFOOD $
(☑ 22850 26401; Paralia; mains €6-13) It would be easy to dismiss this waterfront restaurant as a tourist trap, but don't. Its Cretan and Naxian menu and fantastic service make it stand out from the bunch. The seafood is superb; try stuffed squid, grilled sardines, fisherman's *saganaki* (seafood baked with tomato sauce and feta) or mussels in ouzo and garlic. The salads are creative and filling, particularly the Naxian potato salad. Yum!

There is another Meze at Plaka Beach during July and August.

Anna's Garden Café   BISTRO $
(Paparrigopoulou; dishes €5-10; ☑ ⌨) Entirely earthy feeling and 100% organic, Anna creates two international, vegetarian dishes daily, depending on the local produce that's in season. Breakfasts are €4 to €6 (think homemade museli and yoghurt) and for lunch you can build your own sandwich. Anna also supplies picnic baskets if ordered a day in advance. This place is very child-friendly.

Irini's   TAVERNA $
(☑ 22850 26780; Paralia; mains €6-15) Watch the bobbing boats and dine on beef in wine with lemon sauce, shrimps and mussels with

saffron rice and more traditional fare like stuffed veggies and *saganaki*.

★**L'Osteria**   ITALIAN $$
(☑ 22850 24080; mains €10-15; ⊙ dinner) Follow your nose to this authentic Italian eatery, in a small alley uphill from the harbour and tucked beneath the Kastro walls. Plunk yourself down in the relaxed courtyard and prepare to be gastronomically wowed. The daily menu conjures up dishes like cabernet braised beef, salmon lasagne and breaded sausage with orange. The ravioli is homemade. Need we say more?

Labyrinth   GREEK $$
(☑ 22850 22253; mains €8-13) It's a toss-up as to which is more welcoming: the warm interior and private, pretty courtyard of this restaurant or the wafts of fabulous smells from the kitchen. Consider it as you munch through marinated veggies with grilled *manouri,* swordfish with herbs, or seafood risotto with ouzo sauce and red saffron. The salads are entirely satisfying; think chicken, spinach, rocket, crabapples and yoghurt. Located in the northern part of the old town called Bourgos, it's easiest to find if you enter the winding alleys from the north.

O Apostolis   GREEK $$
(Old Market; mains €9-13) Right at the heart of labyrinthine Bourgos, O Apostolis serves up tasty dishes in its atmospheric flagstone coutyard. Try mussels in garlic butter and

parsley, and *bekri mezes,* a popular Cretan dish of casserole beef. The *kleftiko* (lamb wrapped in filo pastry), with sautéed vegetables and feta cheese, is delicious.

 Drinking & Nightlife

There are a few large, louder clubs at the southern end of the waterfront. Bossa and Ocean have been carrying the party scene for years and draw young, sparkling crowds.

520 BAR

With a deck overlooking the harbour, this cool, comfortable bar whips up divine cocktails. Read a newspaper or party – it's all possible in this chic, cushioned interior.

La Vigne WINE BAR

For a relaxed take on Naxian nightlife, head for this cheerful wine bar just behind Plateia Mandilara. It's run by two French expats who know more than a thing or two about fine wines and good conversation. French wines take pride of place and to soak it up, they serve mezedhes-style dishes (€4 to €8), such as aubergine bruschetta with Greek cheese and codfish with garlic and lemon.

Naxos Cafe BAR

(☑22850 26343; Old Market St) If you want to drink but don't fancy the club scene, here's your answer. This atmospheric, traditional bar is small and candlelit and spills into the cobbled street. Drink Naxian wine with the locals.

Citron Cafe CAFE

(Protopapadaki) You can begin your day on a sofa here, drinking a coffee with a harbour view, and end it with a glass local wine or *kitron* (a liqueur made from the leaves of the citron tree) from Halki's distillery. Black and white photos of a long-ago Hora add a bit of atmosphere.

Dacosta CLUB

Right behind the port police, this sleek club brings well-known guest DJs from Athens to play dance music into the wee hours. All white and wood and chic, it has a loungy feel which gives you somewhere to relax while you contemplate the well-stocked bar.

 Entertainment

Della Rocca-Barozzi Venetian Museum CLASSICAL MUSIC

(☑22850 22387; Kastro; events admission €15-20; ☺8pm Apr-Oct) Special evening cultural events are held at the museum, and com-

prise traditional music and dance concerts, and classical and contemporary music recitals. Prices depend on seat position.

 Shopping

Papyrus BOOKS

(☑22850 23039) What began as a box of books left by a traveller has turned into a shockingly organised collection of over 10,000 secondhand books. Covering over 10 languages and genres ranging from sci-fi to westerns to religion and travel, you'll be hard-pressed to not find something you want to read. Shop or exchange. You'll find it uphill from the port, behind Meze 2.

Kiriakos Tziblakis HOMEWARES

(Papavasiliou) The pungent smell will bowl you over as soon as you get through the door. This cavelike shop is where locals come to buy bulk spices, capers and traditional cheese. It's crammed with a fascinating array of local produce and goods, from pots and brushes to soaps, wine, *raki* (Cretan firewater) and olive oil.

Zoom BOOKS

(☑22850 23675; Paralia) A large, well-stocked newsagent and bookshop that has most international newspapers the day after publication and perhaps the best collection of postcards in Greece.

Promponas FOOD

(☑22850 22258; Protopapadaki) The shelves of this waterfront shop are filled with sweets, nougat and all kinds of local liqueurs, including the local *raki* spiced with cinnamon and cloves.

ℹ Information

There is no official tourist information office on Naxos. Travel agencies can deal with most queries.

Agricultural Bank of Greece (Paralia) Has an ATM.

Alpha Bank (cnr Paralia & Papavasiliou) Has an ATM.

Hospital (☑22853 60500; Prantouna)

National Bank of Greece (Paralia) Has an ATM.

Naxos Tours (☑22850 22095; www.naxostours.gr; Paralia) Sells ferry tickets and organises accommodation, tours and car hire.

OTE (Organismos Tilepikoinonion Ellados; Paralia) Has several phone kiosks in an alleyway.

Police Station (☑22850 22100; Paparrigopoulou) Southeast of Plateia Protodikiou.

Port Police (☎22850 22300) Just south of the quay.

Post Office (Agios Georgios) Go past the OTE, across Papavasiliou, then turn left at the forked road.

Zas Travel (☎22850 23330; Paralia) Sells ferry tickets and organises accommodation, tours and car hire.

Around Naxos

Conveniently just south of the town's waterfront is sandy **Agios Georgios**, Naxos' town beach. It's backed by hotels and tavernas at the town end where it can get crowded, but it runs for some way to the south where you can spread out a little, and its shallow waters make it great for families.

The next beach south of Agios Georgios is **Agios Prokopios**, which is also sandy and shallow, in a sheltered bay to the south of the headland of Cape Mougkri. It merges with **Agia Anna**, a stretch of shiny white sand, quite narrow but long enough to feel uncrowded at its southern end. Development is fairly solid at Prokopios and the northern end of Agia Anna. If you can't drag yourself away, **Santana** (☎22850 41007; www.santana beach.gr; d/tr €60/75) is right on the beach with a big, shaded, style-conscious deck and simple, clean rooms with seaview decks.

Sandy beaches continue as far as **Pyrgaki**, passing the beautiful turquoise waters of **Plaka Beach** and gorgeous sandy bays punctuated with rocky outcrops. You'll find plenty of restaurants, rooms and bus stops along this coast.

One of the best of the southern beaches is **Mikri Vigla**, where golden granite slabs and boulders divide the beach into two. This beach is becoming increasingly big fish on the kitesurfing scene. **Flisvos** (Kite Centre; ☎22850 75490; www.flisvos-kitescentre. com) offers classes and rents equipment to certified surfers. It also offers mountain bike trips and rents windsurfing equipment. You can stay next door at **Orkos Beach Hotel** (www.orkosbeach.gr; d/t/apt incl breakfast €105/155/170), where rooms are comfortable, but will hardly see you as you'll be too busy on the beach.

Tragaea   Τραγαία

The Tragaea region is a vast plain of olive groves and unspoilt villages, beneath the central mountains with **Mt Zeus** (1004m; also known as Mt Zas) dominating overall.

Filoti, situated on the slopes of Mt Zeus, is the region's largest village. It has an ATM booth just down from the main bus stop. On the outskirts of the village (coming from Hora), an asphalt road leads off right to the isolated hamlets of **Damarionas** and **Damalas**.

From Filoti, you can also reach the **Cave of Zeus**, a large, natural cavern at the foot of a cliff on the slopes of Mt Zeus. There's a junction signposted Aria Spring and Zas Cave, about 800m south of Filoti. If travelling by bus, ask to be dropped off here. The side road ends in 1.2km. From the road-end parking, follow a walled path past the **Aria Spring**, a fountain and picnic area, and on to a very rough track uphill to reach the cave. The path leads on from here steeply to the summit of Zas. From beyond the fountain area, it's a stiff hike of several kilometres; it's essential to have good walking shoes, water and sunscreen, and to have some hill-climbing experience. A good way to return to Filoti from the top of Zas is to follow the path that leads northeast from the summit and then to head north at a junction to reach the little chapel of Aghia Marina on the road to Danakos. This is about 4km. From the chapel a mix of road walking and stepped paths then leads, in another few kilometres, to Filoti. This route can be done in reverse or as a way there and back to the top of Zas. Either way is no mere stroll.

The area between Melanes and Kinidaros has been the island's **marble quarry** since ancient times. Marble is still collected from this region today and you will see the sides of the mountains sliced open and looking like huge slabs of feta. At Flerio, near Mili, is an area of ancient marble working and there remain two striking examples of a **kouros** (youth) – large marble statues of the 6th and 7th centuries BC. Each *kouros* measures about 5.5m and both are in a broken state (the theory being that they were damaged during transportation or were simply left unfinished by dissatisfied sculptors). The first *kouros* you come to is lying on its back under a tree; its sheer size and the absurdness of it just being left there takes you by surprise. There is also a **cult sanctuary** here, believed to be associated with the archaic marble quarrying, along with an **aqueduct** and **ancient beehives**. The site has interpretive boards.

Halki   Χάλκη

To visit Naxos and not visit Halki would be a crime. This historic village is a vivid reflection of historic Naxos, with the handsome facades of old villas and tower houses, a legacy of its wealthy past as the island's long-ago capital. Today it is home to a fascinating collection of shops and galleries, drawing artists and culinary wizards. Halki lies at the heart of the Tragaea mountainous region, approximately 20 minutes' drive from Hora.

The main road skirts Halki. In summer it is not permitted to park on the main road; there is parking to the right in the dried-up riverbed, reached just after the bridge coming from Hora, along with parking (summer only) in the schoolyard at the top of the village. Lanes lead off the main road to the picturesque square at the heart of Halki.

Paths and lanes radiate from Halki through peaceful olive groves and flower-filled meadows. The atmospheric 11th-century **Church of St Georgios Diasorites** lies a short distance to the north of the village. It contains some splendid frescoes.

◉ Sights & Activities

★ **Vallindras Distillery**   DISTILLERY
(☑ 22850 31220; ☉ 10am-11pm Jul-Aug, 10am-6pm May-Jun & Sep-Oct) The Vallindras Distillery in Halki's main square still distills *kitron* the old-fashioned way. There are free tours of the old distillery's atmospheric rooms, which contain ancient jars and copper stills. *Kitron* tastings round off the trip.

Fish & Olive   GALLERY
(www.fish-olive-creations.com) This gallery displays the exquisite work of Naxian potter Katharina Bolesch and her partner, artist and craftsman Alexander Reichardt. Each piece of work reflects ancient Mediterranean themes of fish and olives, motifs that frame the edges of shining plates, tumble down the sides of elegant jugs and bowls and dart across platters. The artists' work has been exhibited both nationally and internationally, at the UN Headquarters in New York and the Design Museum of Helsinki. The gallery also hosts exhibitions by other local and international artists.

Phos Gallery   GALLERY
(☑ 22850 31118; www.phosgallery.gr; ☉ May-Oct) See the island through the lens of talented photographer Dimitris Gavalas. Stunning landscapes – most of Naxos – grace the walls of this gallery, along with a handful of conceptual prints.

✗ Eating

Yianni's Taverna   TAVERNA $
(☑ 22850 31214; dishes €4-9; ☉ lunch & dinner) With tables filling Halki's central square, Yianni's Taverna is well known for its savoury pies, village sausage, Naxian cheeses and fresh salads.

Dolce Vita   BAKERY $
(☑ 6981194819; snacks €3-7; ☉ breakfast, lunch & dinner) Cool and inviting with dark wood and a gramophone daring to be wound, this is the place to lounge over homemade baking, coffees and ice creams. If you're missing a sweet tooth, they also have savoury pies to snack on.

El Basilico   ITALIAN $$
(☑ 22859 31140; mains €9-24) Near the entrance to Halki coming from Hora, this lively restaurant offers an excellent changing menu and sources ingredients daily. The garden patio and colourful tiles add to the atmosphere (as do the well-sourced Italian wines!).

🛍 Shopping

Era   FOOD
(☑ 22859 31009; eraproducts@mail.gr) A visit to this shop will give you a peek into the open workshop where more than 20kg of delicious marmalade, jam and spoon desserts are made every day. This stuff is only sold on the island; make sure you taste it while you can!

L'Olivier   CERAMICS, JEWELLERY
(☑ 22850 32829; www.fish-olive-creations.com; Halki) L'Olivier is both a gallery and shop selling beautiful pieces of stoneware ceramics and jewellery by Naxian potter Katharina Bolesch and her partner, artist and craftsman Alexander Reichardt.

Penelope   ARTS & CRAFTS
The know-how has been passed down to Penelope through at least four generations, and her fingers and feet fly on the loom. Watch her creating traditional designs which she turns into hats, scarves, bags and tablecloths that make fab souvenirs. You'll notice a lot of red and blue – the traditional colours of Naxos.

LOCAL LIQUEUR

Since the late 19th century Halki has had strong connections with the production of *kitron*, a strong liqueur made from the leaves of the citron fruit. The citron *(Citrus medica)* was introduced to the Mediterranean area in about 300 BC and thrived on Naxos for centuries. The fruit is barely edible in its raw state, but its rind is very flavoursome when preserved in syrup as a *ghlika kutalyu* (spoon sweet). *Kitroraki, a raki*, can be distilled from grape skins and citron leaves, and by the late 19th century the preserved fruit and a sweet version of *kitroraki*, known as *kitron*, were being exported in large amounts from Naxos.

The Vallindras Distillery (p360) has been distilling *kitron* in the same way since 1896, passing from one generation to the next. Producing over 10,000 litres a year, it sells the liqueur which is no longer exported from the island. Leaves are collected from October to February, then dried, dampened and distilled up to three times with water and sugar. Dye is then added to mark its strength: yellow is the strongest and green is the lightest and sweetest. White is somewhere in the middle. Visit the distillery to sample all three.

Panagia Drosiani
Παναγία Δροσιανή

The **Panagia Drosiani** (⊙10am-7pm May–mid-Oct) evokes an immediate sense of awe in visitors. Located just below Moni and 2.5km north of Halki, it is one of the oldest and most revered churches in Greece. Inside is a warren of cavelike chapels. In the darkest chapels, monks and nuns secretly taught Greek language and religion to local children during the Turkish occupation. Several of the frescoes still grace the walls and date back to the 7th century. Look for the depiction of Mary in the eastern chapter; the clarity and expression will take your breath away. Donations are appreciated.

Sangri
Σαγκρί

The handsome towerlike building of **Bazeos Castle** (☑22850 31402; ⊙10am-5pm & 6-9pm) stands prominently in the landscape about 2km east of the village of Sangri. The castle was built in its original 17th-century form as the Monastery of Timios Stavros (True Cross). It was later bought by the Bazeos family, who refurbished the building, and it now functions as a cultural centre which stages art exhibitions and the annual **Naxos Festival** during July and August, when concerts, plays and literary readings are held.

About 1.5km south of Sangri is the impressive **Temple of Demeter** (Dimitra's Temple; ☑22850 22725; ⊙8.30am-3pm Tue-Sun). The ruins and reconstructions are not large, but they are historically fascinating. There is a site **museum** with some fine reconstructions of temple features. Signs point the way from Sangri.

Apiranthos
Απείρανθος

Apiranthos seems to grow out of the stony flanks of the rugged Mt Fanari (883m). The village's unadorned stone houses and marble-paved streets reflect a rugged individualism that is matched by the villagers themselves. Many of them are descendants of refugees who migrated from Crete, and today the village's distinctive form of Greek language has echoes of the 'Great Island'. Apiranthos people have always been noted for their spirited politics and populism and the village has produced a remarkable number of academics. These days, the village is peppered with wonderful, quirky shops, galleries and cafes, and it's a lovely place to spend an afternoon wandering.

On the main road, to the right of the free parking lot and bus stop, is the **Museum of Natural History** (admission €3; ⊙8.30am-2pm Tue-Sun). The **Geology Museum** (admission €3; ⊙8.30am-2pm Tue-Sun) and the **Archaeology Museum** (⊙8.30am-2pm Tue-Sun) FREE are partway along the main street. The latter has a marvellous collection of small Cycladean artefacts. The museums are notionally open from 7pm to 10pm in summer, but these hours are 'flexible'.

Check out the **Apiranthos Women's Association**, a small shop selling handmade embroidery and traditional woven goods and run entirely by local women who sit and stitch while you browse. Also visit **Apiranthos Art**, the gallery and workshop of local sculptor Narkissos, who creates glazed objects from local materials.

✖️ Eating

Taverna o Platanos GREEK $
(☎ 22850 61192; mains €6-10; ⏰ lunch & dinner)
Set beneath the shade of its namesake tree,
this family restaurant serves up everything
from yoghurt to grilled local meat to homemade cheeses. Hearty and popular, it's a
lively place to dine.

Lefteris GREEK $
(☎ 22850 61333; snacks €2-6; ⏰ breakfast, lunch
& dinner) With a deck taking in a phenomenal view, this place has the look and feel
of an old country kitchen, complete with
a well-filled hat stand, preserves and local
baking. Treat yourself to traditional snacks
and treats.

Apollonas Απόλλωνας
POP 107

Heading north, the roads wind and twist
like spaghetti, eventually taking you to the
seaside village of Apollonas. In an ancient
quarry on the hillside above the village is a
collosal 7th-century-BC **kouros**. There is no
real parking and it's not well signposted, but
you'll know it when you see it.

Apollonas' beach isn't great but its seafood is. Tavernas line the waterfront and
serve the freshest of fish.

With your own transport you can return
to Hora via the west-coast road, passing
through wild and sparsely populated country with awe-inspiring sea views. En route,
stop for a look at the **Tower of Ayia**, the
magestic ruins of a castle with a spectacular
ocean backdrop.

LITTLE CYCLADES
ΜΙΚΡΕΣ ΚΥΚΛΑΔΕΣ

The medley of tiny islands that lies between
Naxos and Amorgos are like miniature outposts of calm. In the days of antiquity, all
were densely populated, revealed by the
large number of ancient graves that have
been uncovered. During the Middle Ages,
only wild goats and even wilder pirates inhabited these islands. Post-independence,
intrepid souls from Naxos and Amorgos recolonised the Little Cyclades, and today four
have permanent populations – Donousa,
Ano Koufonisia, Iraklia and Schinousa. More
recently, the islands have welcomed a growing number of independent-minded tourists.

Donousa is the northernmost of the group
and the furthest from Naxos. The others are
clustered near the southeast coast of Naxos.
Each has a public telephone and post agency

Little Cyclades

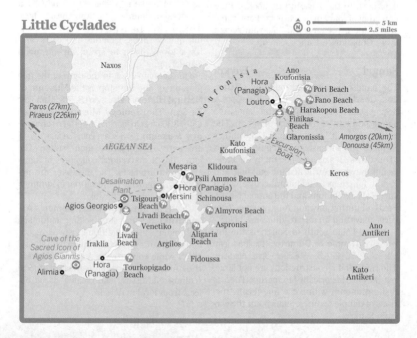

and there are ATMs on all islands, although you should still bring a decent amount of ready cash with you. A handy source of info is www.smallcyclades.com.

ⓘ Getting There & Away

There are several connections a week between Piraeus and the Little Cyclades via Naxos, and daily connections to and from Naxos. Make sure you have plenty of time before committing yourself – these islands are not meant for last-minute or one-night visits.

Blue Star ferries serve the Little Cyclades throughout the year but the sturdy little ferry **Express Scopelitis** (☑ 22850 71519, 22850 71256; Katapola, Amorgos) is the mainstay service (weather permitting in winter), except for its annual refit layoff, usually in January. The *Scopelitis* leaves from Naxos in the afternoon Monday to Saturday, and calls at the Little Cyclades and Amorgos. It returns to Naxos early the following morning. Each of the small islands has at least one small tour boat. From June to September you may be able to negotiate one-way travel between the islands with these boats, although it will be more costly than the regular ferries.

Boat Services from Iraklia

DESTINATION	TIME	FARE	FREQUENCY
Amorgos	1¾hr	€8.50	2-3 daily
Donousa	2hr 20min	€7	1-2 daily
Koufonisia	1hr	€5	2-3 daily
Naxos	1hr	€7.50	2-3 daily
Paros	2¼hr	€12.50	1-2 daily
Piraeus	7hr 20min	€30	1-2 daily
Schinousa	15min	€4.50	2-3 daily
Syros	3hr 35min	€22.70	4 weekly

Boat Services from Schinousa

DESTINATION	TIME	FARE	FREQUENCY
Amorgos	1hr 40min	€8-10.50	2-3 daily
Donousa	2hr	€13.50	1-2 daily
Iraklia	15min	€4.50	2-3 daily
Koufonisia	40min	€4.60	2-3 daily
Naxos	1hr 20min	€6.70	1-2 daily
Paros	2hr 20min	€10	1-2 daily
Piraeus	7½hr	€31	1-2 daily
Syros	5½hr	€13	4 weekly

Boat Services from Koufonisia

DESTINATION	TIME	FARE	FREQUENCY
Amorgos	1hr 5min	€7.50	3 daily
Donousa	1¼hr	€5.50	1-2 daily
Folegandros*	3hr	€56.20	1 daily
Iraklia	1hr	€5	2-3 daily
Milos*	4¼hr	€56.20	1 daily
Naxos	2hr	€9.50	1-2 daily
Paros	3hr	€16	1-2 daily
Piraeus	8hr	€31	2-3 weekly
Piraeus*	7hr 20min	€57.20	1 daily
Schinousa	40min	€4.50	2-3 daily
Syros	5½hr	€13	4 weekly

*high-speed services

Boat Services from Donousa

DESTINATION	DURATION	FARE	FREQUENCY
Amorgos	1hr 50min	€7	1-2 daily
Astypalea	2hr 20min	€17	5 weekly
Iraklia	2hr 20min-4hr	€7-14.40	1-2 daily
Koufonisia	1¼hr	€6.50	1-2 daily
Naxos	1hr 10min-4hr	€7.60	2-3 daily
Paros	2½hr-6hr	€14	1-3 daily
Piraeus	7hr 10min	€31	4 weekly
Schinousa	2hr	€7	1-2 daily
Syros	7hr	€14	4 weekly

Iraklia   Ηρακλεία

POP 151

Iraklia is only 19 sq km in area, a little Aegean gem dozing in the sun. Dump the party gear and spurn the nightlife, the sightseeing and the souvenir shops. Instead, brace yourself for a serene and quiet life and Iraklia will not disappoint. Only in July and August will you have to share the idyll with like-minded others.

The island now boasts the first offshore **desalination plant** in Greece. *And* it's driven by solar panels and windpower. You pass it as you enter the harbour.

The port and main village of Iraklia is Agios Georgios. It has an attractive cove-like harbour, complete with a sandy beach. Turn right at the end of the ferry quay and then left for the well-supplied general store,

Perigiali Supermarket. Further uphill is a smaller store and *kafeneio* called Melissa's, which is also the ferry ticket office and postal agency. There are card phones outside Perigiali Supermarket and Melissa's, and there is an ATM just up from the harbour. A medical centre is next to Perigiali Supermarket. The island's website is www.iraklia.gr.

◉ Sights & Activities

A surfaced road leads off to the left of the ferry quay, and after about 1km you'll reach Livadi, the island's best beach. A steep 2.5km further on is Hora (Panagia). Where the road forks at the village entrance, keep to the right for the main street. From here, a surfaced road carries on to Tourkopigado Beach.

The island's major 'sight' is the Cave of the Sacred Icon of Agios Giannis, which can be reached on foot from Panagia in a four-hour return trip. The path starts just beyond the church at a signpost on the right and is very rocky and steep in places; boots or walking shoes are essential and you should take plenty of water. At the site there is a large open cave on the left. On the right, white-painted rocks surround the tiny entrance to the main sequence of caves. A torch is useful and the initial scramble along a low-roofed tunnel is worth it, leading as it does to caves full of stalactites and stalagmites. On 28 August, the eve of the death of John the Baptist, crowds of local people assemble at the cave and crawl inside to hold a candlelit service.

Beyond the cave the path leads to the beach at Alimia, which is also served by boat from Agios Georgios in summer, offering a shortcut to the cave.

During July and August, a local boat ferries people to island beaches and also runs day trips to nearby Schinousa. Enquire at Perigiali Supermarket.

⌂ Sleeping & Eating

Domatia and tavernas are concentrated in and around Agios Georgios, although a few open on the beach at Livadi in summer. Domatia owners meet the boats, but in high season it's advisable to book.

There are a few tavernas in Agios Georgios. All serve fresh fish dishes and other Greek standards.

Anna's Place PENSION $
(☑ 22850 71145; s/tr €40/85, d €50-70; ✸) Located on high ground above the port, these airy, comfortable rooms have front balconies with sweeping views. There's a big communal kitchen and outside eating area.

Agnadema APARTMENT $
(☑ 6978048789, 22850 71484; studio s/d €40/50; ✸) There's a great choice at this peaceful, family-owned property on the hillside above Agios Georgios harbour. Agnadema's rooms are big, bright and immaculate. Agnadema means 'great view', which you'll soon see is no exaggeration.

Perigiali TAVERNA $
(☑ 22850 71118; dishes €4-8) This popular place has standard, consistent fare that's served to you at a large marble table encircling an old pine tree.

Taverna to Steki TAVERNA $
(☑ 22850 71579; dishes €4-8) Based in Hora, this classic village eatery is well known for its locally sourced ingredients and traditional food.

Schinousa Σχοινούσα

POP 206

Like its neighbours, Schinousa, has an easygoing pace and a rare sense of timelessness, although high season can be realtively lively. The island has a gentle landscape and the major settlement Hora (Panagia) has a long, narrow main street lying along the breezy crest of the island. There are several beaches scattered round the low-lying coast.

Ferries dock at the fishing harbour of Mersini. Hora is a hot 1km uphill. Domatia owners, with transport, meet ferries from about May onwards and will always meet booked guests.

In Hora, Paralos Travel (☑ 22850 71160; fax 22850 71957) is halfway along the main street. It sells ferry tickets for vessels other than the *Scopelitis* and also doubles as the post office and newsagent in season. Grispos Travel (☑ 22850 29329), down at the Grispos Hotel and Restaurant at Tsigouri Beach and at an office at the far end of the village, sells all ferry tickets plus those for the *Express Scopelitis*.

There's a public telephone in Hora's main square and an ATM nearby. A useful website is www.schinousa.com.

◉ Sights & Activities

On the way down to Tsigouri beach is a little folk museum that features a reconstructed bread oven. Opening hours go with the flow of island life.

Dirt tracks lead from Hora to beaches around the coast. The nearest are sandy **Tsigouri** and **Livadi**, both uncrowded outside August. Haul a little further to decent beaches at **Almyros** with its shallow water and the three small bays of **Aligaria**. With the exception of Tsigouri, there are no shops or tavernas at the beaches, so take food and water.

From mid-June to September, the tour boat **Aeolia** (☑6979618233) runs various trips daily, including to Iraklia and Koufonisia. Prices range from about €15 to €30. Private trips can also be arranged.

🛏 Sleeping

There are a few rooms down at Mersini and around the island, but Hora makes an ideal base.

Iliovasilema   HOTEL $
(☑22850 71948; www.iliovasilemahotel.gr; Hora; s/d/tr/q €45/55/60/65; ❄🛜) Near the village centre, with king-of-the-castle sunset views, rooms here are slightly dated, but clean. The views from the balconies are fab and the service is warm.

Galini   PENSION $
(☑22850 71983; d/tr €50/60) Most rooms at this well-positioned pension have fabulous views. It stands quietly in its own grounds, just beyond Hora. Rooms are bright and clean and pleasantly quaint. There's no air-conditioning, but the rooms have sturdy ceiling fans.

Grispos Villas   APARTMENT $$
(☑22850 71930; www.grisposvillas.com; incl breakfast d €85-95, tr €105-115; ❄@) Down a rough track from Hora, the Grispos complex stands in an enviable location above Tsigouri Beach. Rooms are average and come in a variety of forms with varying views. Have a look at a couple before you choose. There's also an on-site restaruant.

🍴 Eating

Akbar   CAFE $
(dishes €3-6.50) A colourful little cafe in the main street, Akbar has mezedhes and fresh salads, as well as breakfast (€7 to €12). It does sandwiches as well as sweet crepes and ice cream.

Deli Restaurant and Sweet Bar   GREEK $$
(☑22850 74278; mains €17-25; ☺dinner) At the heart of village life, Deli belies the simple life of Schinousa. Its gourmet menu includes dishes like local veal seasoned with cinnamon and orange, and fried feta cheese wrapped in a crunchy filo dough with honey and local sesame. Ingredients are sourced as locally as possible; they even make their own bread from grain from the family farm.

The upper floor houses the sea-view restaurant, the ground floor is a very cool cafebar and downstairs there's a sweet section that will seduce you. The wine list is trim, but excellent, with some fine Greek vintages.

Koufonisia   Κουφονήσια

POP 366

Koufonisia is made up of three main islands, however, the populated **Ano Koufonisia** is where you'll arrive. Excellent beaches make this low-lying island one of the most visited of the Little Cyclades; it sees a flash flood of tourism each summer season and has the infrastructure to prove it. Still, the island retains its low-key charm, and a substantial fishing fleet sustains a thriving local community outside the fleeting summer season.

The flat profile of **Kato Koufonisia** is just to its south and a short caïque ride away. Kato Koufonisia has some beautiful beaches and a lovely church.

East of here is the dramatic **Keros**, a rugged mountain of an island with dramatic cliffs. Archaeological digs on Keros have uncovered more than 100 Early Cycladic figurines, including the famous harpist and flautist now on display in Athens' National Archaeological Museum. In recent years, archaeologists discovered hoards of deliberately broken figurines, dating from the period 2500 BC to 2000 BC. It is theorised they were broken for ritualistic purposes rather than due to vandalism or by accident and may have been deposited on Keros because the island was an important centre of Cycladean ritual.

⊙ Sights

An easy 2km walk along the sandy coast road to the east of the port leads to **Finikas**, **Harakopou** and **Fano Beaches**. All tend to become swamped with grilling bodies in July and August and nudity becomes more overt the further you go.

Beyond Fano a path leads to several rocky swimming places, and then continues to the great bay at **Pori**, where a long crescent of sand slides effortlessly into the ultimate Greek-island-dream sea. Pori can also be reached by an inland road from Hora.

☞ Tours

Koufonissia Tours BOAT TRIPS
(☑ 22850 71671; www.koufonissiatours.gr) Based at Villa Ostria hotel, Koufonissia organises caïque trips to Keros, Kato Koufonisia and other islands of the Little Cyclades and can help organise ferry tickets.

Marigo BOAT TRIPS
(☑ 6945042548, 22859 71438) Hop on this boat to transfer to and from various beaches. It runs every two hours from 10am for about €5.

🛏 Sleeping

Anna's Rooms PENSION $$
(☑ 22850 71697; annavillas.gr; s/d €50/60; ❇ 🖥) In a quiet location just back from the beach, these fresh, bright rooms are charming. All have verandahs overlooking the old harbour and small kitchenettes.

Ermis APARTMENT $$
(☑ 22850 71693; fax 22850 74214; s/d €60/70; ❇ 🖥) These immaculate rooms are in a quiet location behind the post office. They have fresh, pastel colour schemes and are bounded by a lovingly kept garden. The upper rooms at the back have big balconies with sea views.

Villa Ostria HOTEL $$
(☑ 22850 71671; www.koufonissiatours.gr; s €60-70, d €70-80, studios €90-110; ❇ 🖥) Among several hotels on the high ground east of the beach, Ostria has attractive rooms and studios with some quirky decor. A kettle and a toaster enhance the smaller rooms and there are full cooking facilities in the studios. Ceiling fans and the absence of TVs are something of a plus.

🍴 Eating & Drinking

Capetan Nikolas SEAFOOD $
(☑ 22850 71690; mains €4.50-14) One of the best seafood places around, this cheerful family-run restaurant overlooks the harbour at Loutro. The lobster salad is famous and the seafood pasta delicious. Locally caught fish, such as red mullet and sea bream, are priced by the kilo.

Karnagio MEZEDHES $
(mains €4.50-12) Don't miss this tiny *ouzerie* at Loutro where the tables skirt the harbour. The prawn *saganaki* is delicious as are the homemade pies such as cheese and sun-dried tomato.

Kalamia Café CAFE $
(snacks €2.50-7; 🖥) A friendly gathering point. As well as snacks there's a range of breakfast fare from €4 to €6. At night Kalamia becomes a very sociable bar.

Scholio BAR
(☑ 22850 71837; ◷ 7pm-3.30am; 🖥) A cosy bar and creperie, Scholio plays to the crowd with jazz, blues or rock. It's at the western end of the main street above Loutro. The owners are accomplished photographers and often have exhibitions of their work on show.

ℹ Information

Koufonisia's only settlement spreads out behind the ferry quay. On one side of the quay is the yacht marina; on the other side is a wide bay filled with moored fishing boats. A large beach of flat, hard sand gives a great sense of space to the waterfront. Its inner edge is used as a road. The older part of town, the hora, sprawls along a low hill above the harbour and is one long main street, often strewn with fallen leaves of bougainvillea.

There are a couple of supermarkets along the road that leads inland from the beach to link with the main street, and there's a ticket agency, **Prasinos** (☑ 22850 71438), halfway along the main street. The post office is along the first road that leads sharply left as you reach the road leading inland from the seafront. There is an ATM outside the post office.

DONOUSA ΔΟΝΟΥΣΑ
POP 163

Donousa is the out-on-a-limb island where you stop bothering about which day it might be. In late July and August the island can be swamped by holidaymaking Greeks and sun-seeking northern Europeans, but out of season be prepared to linger – quietly.

Agios Stavros is Donousa's main settlement and port, a cluster of whitewashed buildings around a handsome church, overlooking a small, sandy bay. Little has changed here over the years. There's an excellent **beach**, which also serves as a thoroughfare for infrequent vehicles and foot traffic to a clutch of homes, rental rooms and a taverna across the bay.

Kendros, 1.25km to the southeast of Agios Stavros along a surfaced road or stepped track, is a sandy and secluded beach with a seasonal taverna. Livadi, a 1km hike further east, sees even fewer visitors. Both Kendros and Livadi are popular with naturists.

Bulldozed, unsurfaced roads have marred Donousa in places, but there are still paths and tracks that lead into the hills to timeless little hamlets such as Mersini.

Sleeping & Eating

You should book ahead for stays in July and August, and even early September.

The hub of Agios Stavros village life is Kafeneio To Kyma, located by the quay, where things liven up late into the night in summer.

Prassinos Studios APARTMENT $
(☑ 6979299113, 22850 51579; prassinosstudios@gmail.com; s/d €40/45, studios/apt €80/95) In a lofty position on the high ground on the far side of the beach, this charming place has peaceful, well-kept rooms and studios, most with kitchenettes.

Skopelitis Studios APARTMENT $
(☑ 22850 52296; skopelitis@gmx.net; s/d €40/50) These cheerful rooms with verandahs and kitchenettes have imaginative decor and a friendly vibe. They lie just behind the beach in a remarkable flower-filled garden with hefty bottle palms.

Captain Giorgis TAVERNA $
(☑ 22850 51867; mains €4.50-9) Sturdy traditional food, such as baked goat with potatoes and tomatoes, served on a terrace, just above the harbour and with good views across the bay.

❶ Information

Sigalis Travel (☑ 6942269219, 22850 51570) is the ticket agency for all ferries and has an office just inland from the harbour road and a second office in the To Iliovasilema restaurant complex. It opens every evening and 40 minutes before ferry arrivals.

There is an ATM next to a small gift shop on the harbour road (it's sometimes hidden behind a blue shutter for protection from blown sand), but be sure to bring sufficient cash in high season. There is a public telephone up a steep hill above the waterfront; it's hidden behind a tree.

There is a **medical centre** (☑ 22850 51506) and postal agency just below the church.

AMORGOS ΑΜΟΡΓΟΣ
POP 1859

Dramatic Amorgos lies on the distant, southeastern arc of the Cyclades, pointing the way towards the Dodecanese. As you approach by sea, its long ridge of mountains appears to stretch ever skyward, the high summits often scarfed with plump purple clouds.

Amorgos is just 30km from tip to toe but reaches over 800m at its highest point. The southeast coast is unrelentingly steep and boasts an extraordinary monastery built into the base of a soaring cliff. The opposite coast is just as spectacular, but softens a little at the narrow inlets where the main port and town of Katapola and the second port of Aegiali lie. The enchanting Hora (also known as Amorgos) lies amid a rocky landscape high above Katapola.

Amorgos is much more about archaeology and activities than beaching – there's a great walking, scuba diving and a burgeoning rock-climbing scene.

❶ Getting There & Away

Connections between Amorgos and Naxos are very good with the small ferry, *Express Scopelitis*, running each day and connecting the Little Cyclades and Amorgos, as well as the big Blue Star ferries running to and from Piraeus, Santorini, Astypalea and Rhodes. Buy your tickets from the small booth in Katapola harbour, opposite where the ferries dock or at N Synodinos (p370).

❶ Getting Around

Buses go regularly from Katapola to Hora (Amorgos; €1.60, 15 minutes), to Moni Hozoviotissis (€1.80, 15 minutes), to Agia Anna Beach (€1.80, 20 minutes) and less often to Aegiali (€2.70, 30 minutes). Weekends see fewer services. There are also buses from Aegiali to the picturesque village of Langada. Schedules are posted at the main stop in each village.

Cars and motorcycles are available for hire from **Hermes** (☑ 22850 72065; info@pension-sofia.gr; Katapola). Expect to pay about €50 per day for a small car in August.

Katapola Κατάπολα
POP 485

Tiny Katapola straggles round the curving, yacht-filled shoreline of a picturesque bay in the most verdant part of the island. The remains of the ancient city of Minoa, as well as a Mycenaean cemetery, lie above the port and can be reached by footpath or a steep,

Amorgos

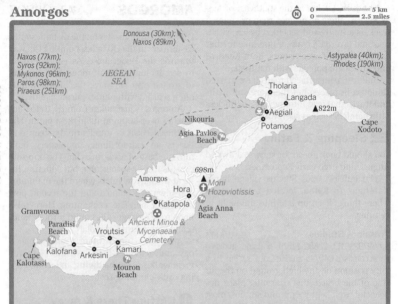

surfaced road. Amorgos has also yielded many Cycladic finds; the largest figurine in the National Archaeological Museum in Athens was found in the vicinity of Katapola.

🛏 Sleeping

Minoa Hotel   HOTEL $

(📞228550 74055, 22850 71480; www.hotelminoa.gr; Katapola; s/d/tr €50/55/65; ❄🔊) This place couldn't be more convenient for early morning ferries. Service is friendly and the simple rooms have revamped bathrooms and balconies overlooking a tree- and bird-filled garden, making you feel miles away from town. The modern lobby shares space with a cafe and patisserie, handy for breakfasts or late-night treats.

Pension Sofia   APARTMENT $

(📞22850 71494; www.pensionsofia.gr; d/tr €55/80; ❄🔊) Just back from the waterfront, Sofia's rooms are clean and airy, with kitchen facilities and sea views. There's also a shared garden that offers plenty of scope for relaxation.

Villa Katapoliani   HOTEL $$

(📞6947810407, 22850 71664; www.villakatapoliani.gr; Katapola; d/tr/ste €60/70/85; ❄🔊) These simple rooms have been given a lot of TLC with painted wooden furniture and plenty of local artistic touches. The lovely balconies look over a garden filled with begonias and the scattered ruins of the ancient temple of Apollo. Or scoot upstairs to the rooftop terrace for views of the sea. Suites sleep up to four with kitchen facilities and you're just 50m from the port.

Diosmarini   HOTEL $$

(📞tel, info 22850 71636; www.diosmarini.com/; d €70) High on the northeastern side of the harbour, 1km north from the ferry quay, these simple rooms are spotless and colourful with great big views of the sea from their balconies. All have basic kitchenettes. Your hostess is both welcoming and helpful.

🍴 Eating

★**Karamel**   MEDITERRANEAN $

(📞22850 71516; dishes €3-8; ⏲lunch & dinner) Pass the beach and follow the narrow strip of road over to the eastern side of the harbour to find this fantastic bistro. Inside it feels homy and French or you can opt to sip wine from the tables on the beach. Daily dishes include grilled local veggies and shrimp, gaspacho or pork with sage. Try the divine homemade iced tea and scoff bread served with olive paste and tzatziki.

Mouragio
SEAFOOD **$**

(tel 22850 71011; dishes €6-10; ☻ dinner) They don't do anything fancy here. They don't need to. Big plates of superfresh prawns, fish and octopus are enough to draw nightly crowds to this harbourside restaurant. Stick to seafood for your main meal, nicely rounded off with stuffed tomatoes or local salads.

★ Captain Dimos
GREEK **$$**

(Katapola; mains €6-15; ☻ lunch & dinner) 'I respect tradition but add my own ideas,' the captain explains as he whips up mouthwatering modern Greek dishes to serve on his colourful harbourside patio. Mussels in olive oil and oregano; lamb in ouzo and honey; and pork with orange and mint all crowd the tempting menu. Try the *bugiurdi* (three cheeses, tomato sauce, eggplant and herbs) or choose from the list of creative pastas and pizzas.

Honey & Cinnamon
BAKERY **$**

(22850 71485; Katapola) Look for the bright red window shutters and follow your nose to the aroma of Christmas. This tiny patisserie, just back from the waterfront, bakes up cakes, pastries and lots of local cookies. Try the ones made with the local liquor, *amoraki*. If you can't wait to dig in, plunk yourself down at a table and order an excellent coffee.

Drinking & Nightlife

Teloneio
BAR

(Katapola) It's questionable if the customs officer would be pleased with the present incarnation of his former office. Now a small, busy bar, its weekend DJs play to the crowd while the bartendar pours mainly Greek beer and spirits.

Shopping

Amorgos Art Gallery
ARTS & CRAFTS

(☎ 6970198686; www.amorgosphotoart.gr; Katapola) Stella Spanou's paintings of local scenes, photography and creations fill this small gallery. Lemons and pomegranates decorate light (as in, easy-on-the-luggage-allowance) bamboo bowls and containers, T-shirts and even magnets. Shopping here lets you support a talented local artist as well as score some great souvenirs.

Amorgos' Music & Book Store
BOOKS

(☎ 22850 771831; Katapola) Trade in your novel for some fresh reading material and pick

BOAT SERVICES FROM AMORGOS

DESTINATION	TIME	FARE	FREQUENCY
Aegiali	50min	€4.70	1-2 daily
Donousa	2hr 20min	€6.50	1-2 daily
Folegandros*	2hr 25min	€56.20	1 daily
Ios	5hr 20min	€11.50	1 weekly
Iraklia	1¾hr-5hr	€12	2-3 daily
Kos	5hr	€24.50	2 weekly
Koufonisia	1hr 5min	€7.50	2-3 daily
Leros	3hr 10min	€21.50	2 weekly
Milos*	3hr 25min	€56.20	1 daily
Naxos	1-4hr	€7.50	1-3 daily
Paros	4hr	€16	1-2 daily
Patmos	2hr	€19.50	2 weekly
Piraeus	9hr	€31	4 weekly
Piraeus*	7hr 25min	€57	1 daily
Rhodes	8hr	€27	2 weekly
Schinousa	1hr 40min	€8-10.50	2-3 daily
Santorini (Thira)*	1¼hr	€32	1 daily
Syros	5¼hr	€29.80	4 weekly

*high-speed services
All services leave from Katapola.

up maps, history books and local walking guides, all stocked in English.

ℹ Information

Boats dock right on the waterfront. The bus station is to the left along the main waterfront, on the eastern shore of the bay.

A bank (with ATM) is mid-waterfront and there's an ATM next to N Synodinos. There is a postal agency next to the Hotel Minoa on the central square.

A useful and informative website is www. amorgos-island-magazine.com.

N Synodinos (☑ 22850 71201; synodinos@nax. forthnet.gr) Sells ferry tickets and has a money exchange.

Port Police (☑ 22850 71259) On the central square.

Hora (Amorgos)
Χώρα (Αμοργός)

POP 414

The old capital of Hora sparkles like a snow-drift across its rocky ridge. It's capped by a 13th-century *kastro* and guarded by wind-mills that stand like sentinels on the surrounding cliffs. There's a distinct veneer of sophistication, not least in the handful of trendy bars and shops that enhance Hora's appeal without eroding its timelessness. The main activity here is wandering, amply rewarded with beautiful village settings around each corner.

The bus stop is on a small square at the edge of town where there's also car parking. There's an ATM next to a minimarket right at the entrance to Hora and the village also has a post office and **police station** (☑ 22850 71210) on the main road. Hora's **archaeology collection** (⊙ 9am-1pm & 6-8.30pm Tue-Sun) is on the main pedestrian thoroughfare.

🛏 Sleeping & Eating

Pension Ilias PENSION **$**
(☑ 22850 71277; www.kastanis.com.gr; s/tr €45/65, d €50-60, apt €80-90; ※ 🛜) Tucked away amid a jumble of traditional houses just down from the bus stop is this friendly family-run place with pleasant, comfortable rooms.

Emprostiada GUESTHOUSE **$$**
(☑ 6932248867, 22850 71814; www.amorgos-studios.amorgos.net; Hora; d €100, ste €130-140; P ※ 🛜) Built in a peaceful garden, these very private, characterful suites are housed in a lovely traditional merchant's home. Attentive

service and a quiet location at the back of the village make it a near oasis. Choose from doubles, maisonettes and suites.

Triporto CAFE **$**
(☑ 6942027112; breakfast €8, snacks €3-5) Once the village bakery, this cafe has a strong traditional feel, plumped up with some colourful, hip decor. This is the kind of place where you could easily while away an afternoon, snug in a cushioned nook on the rooftop terrace. Come for breakfast to create an omelette from ingredients like olive sauce and hot paprika cream, or snack on salads, sandwiches and sweets. The friendly owner is a virtual encylopaedia of local knowledge.

Jazzmin CAFE **$**
(☑ 22850 74017; snacks €3-6) 🍴 Down a set of stairs from the main pedestrian street, this cafe is spread throughout the numerous floors and cosy rooms of a traditional home. Choose a magazine and perch in a window seat or lounge on the view-filled deck. Many of the herbs for the teas and juices are picked straight from the garden.

Try the fresh lemon and mint juice, the banana and chai smoothie and the rusk sandwich with tomatoes, olives and feta. The long list of cocktails hints at the impressively stocked bar.

To Xyma GREEK **$**
(mains €3-5) With tables lining the main pedestrian thoroughfare, it's tricky to miss the colourful To Xyma. The quaint interior is filled with local art, books, photos and traditional instruments, while the menu is brimming with traditional fare like sausage, aubergine *saganaki* and meatballs.

Pizza Petrino PIZZERIA **$**
(☑ 22850 71507; pizzas €8-10) Sit outside beneath the shade of the tree or inside by the giant stone fireplace. You'll also find friendly service and traditional pizzas along with inspired alternatives like chicken with local herbs. It's on the main pedestrian street.

Moni Hozoviotissis
Μονή της Χοζοβιώτισσας

As you round the bend and first catch sight of this iconic **monastery** (⊙ 8am-1pm & 5-7pm), seemingly embedded into the cliff face high above the sea, you'll quickly forget the zillions of stairs you've climbed to reach it. This is scenery at its most dramatic. Built on the precipitous east coast below Hora, the monastery contains a miraculous icon that was found in the sea below the cliff. Enter through a green, hobbit-sized door to discover the secrets of the monastery. Entrance is free, but donations are appreciated.

The dress code is modest and strict. No shorts, no mini-skirts, no bare shoulders and no women in trousers. No exceptions.

From about mid-May to October there's a daily bus service to the monastery from Katapola, Hora and Aegiali.

Aegiali   Αιγιάλη

POP 487

Aegiali is Amorgos' second port and sees fewer yachts and a bit more of the holiday-maker scene. A sweep of sand lines the inner edge of the bay on which the village stands while steep slopes and impressive crags lie above.

🏃 Activities

Ask at travel agencies about boat trips around the island (€30) and to the Little Cyclades (€40).

Amorgos Diving Center   DIVING
(☑6932249538, 22850 73611; www.amorgos-diving.gr) Enthusiastic and friendly instruction can be had at this diving centre whose office also stocks climbing, walking and angling gear. Dives (with equipment) start at €50, with night dives, wreck dives and PADI courses available. It also offers a Bubblemaker class for kids aged eight to 10 and climbing classes and excursions.

👉 Tours

Special-Interest-Holidays   WALKING TOURS
(☑6939820828; www.amorgos.dial.pipex.com) Based at Langada, this outfit organises walking holidays with very experienced and knowledgeable guides.

🛏 Sleeping

Aegiali Camping   CAMPGROUND $
(☑22850 73500; www.aegialicamping.gr; camp sites per adult/child/tent €4/2.20/3) Very basic facilities with tents under the vines and the majority of guests out diving with the on-site dive centre. Rent a tent for €5.

★**Yperia**   HOTEL $$
(☑22850 73084; www.yperia.com; d with garden/sea view incl breakfast €95/00; ❄🎧🛏) Built in

the style of a traditional island estate, these modern rooms have warm, artsy touches, handmade wood and iron furnishings, big bathrooms and excellent sea views. The pool overlooks the ocean and the hotel is just a block from the beach. There's also a family suite available for €150. Staff are friendly and accommodating.

Apollon Studios   APARTMENT $$
(☑22850 73297; www.apollon-amorgos.com; studios €55-85; ❄🎧) With a nautically themed lobby, this hotel is in the heart of the village and has studios with well-equipped kitchens and harbour-view balconies. Rooms aren't fussy, but they're comfortable, and brick and stone work add a bit of character. The owners go the extra mile in hosting you and this place draws lots of repeat guests and families.

🍴 Eating

For drinks and coffee, the steps leading up from the eastern end of the waterfront boast several cafe-bars. **Maestro** is a cool spot that starts with breakfast (€4.50 to €6.50) and keeps going until late into the night.

To Limani   TAVERNA $
(☑22850 73269; www.limani.amorgos.net; dishes €4-7; ⊙breakfast, lunch & dinner) This popular restaurant carries its traditional atmosphere comfortably. Using home-grown produce, they whip up an amazing fish soup, black-eyed bean salad, village sausage and chicken with feta. And definitely save room for some homemade orange pie.

Restaurant Lakki   GREEK $
(☑22850 73253; mains €4-9) A beach and garden setting makes the restaurant of Lakki village a relaxing place to enjoy well-prepared Greek dishes.

Askas Taverna   TAVERNA $
(mains €4.50-8) Next to Aegiali Camping and Pension Askas, this friendly taverna offers Greek food with many of the ingredients locally sourced (the family olive groves are right next door). The Amorgian lamb baked with potatoes and chopped tomatoes is a traditional favourite. They stage *rembetika* (blues) evenings four times a week in July and August.

ℹ Information

Amorgos Travel (☑22850 73401; www.amorgostravel.gr), above the central supermarket on the waterfront, can help with a host of travel needs including ferry tickets, accommodation and island tours. Check it out for diving and walking possibilities also. Long-established **Aegialis Tours** (22850 73107; www.aegialis-tours.com) sells ferry tickets and can organise accommodation, tours and vehicle hire.

There's a postal agency about 100m uphill from Aegialis Tours.

Around Amorgos

Heading south of Hora, the road hugs the plunging east coast. You'll soon reach the turning for Agia Anna Beach, popular for its starring role in the French film *Le Grand Bleu*. It's dramatic, but tiny and rocky; the car park is bigger. It's a similar story with the rest of the beaches along this coast. At the far southwestern tip of the island is the grounded ship that also featured in the film and draws French tourists in droves. A history of drugs and insurance scams is less romantic than the movie version.

Heading northeast from Hora along the spine of the island offers arresting views back over the white village and Katapola. The lovely villages of Langada and Tholaria nestle amid the craggy slopes above Aegiali. The two are linked to each other, and to Aegiali, by a signposted circular path that takes about four hours to walk. Regular buses run between the villages and Aegiali.

In Langada, the Pagali Hotel (22850 73310; www.pagalihotel-amorgos.com; s/d €58/65, ste €98-120; ❄ ☎) is tucked away in the lower village with superb views. Rooms and studios are very comfortable and the hotel offers alternative activities like grape or olive harvesting, climbing courses and yoga sessions.

Just outside Tholaria, the Aegialis Hotel & Spa (22850 73393; wwwamorgos-aegialis.com; d incl breakfast €159) has sleek rooms with fabulous views over Aegiali's harbour. If you've been hiking, the spa is the place to revive your weary feet with everything from hydrotherapy to massage and an indoor saltwater pool. There's also an on-site restaurant.

IOS   ΙΟΣ

POP 1838

On Ios, you can have your cake and eat it too – quite literally. Spend days exploring the winding footpaths of the traditional hilltop old town or ensconced on a sandy beach. Discover the isolated interior and then return to town in time for the party. Or visit in the shoulder season for a quieter pace, when Ios

draws families and more mature travellers. In July and August, it's still the much-loved stomping ground of youth and hedonism.

While Ios is a popular destination, there's a special magic at work here. You won't feel pressured or hassled; instead, the islanders take pride in working together to keep their visitors smiling – and returning.

ⓘ Getting There & Away

Ios lies conveniently on the Mikonos–Santorini ferry axis and has regular connections with Pireaus. Purchase tickets at Acteon Travel (p376) in Ormos.

Boat Services from Ios

DESTINATION	TIME	FARE	FREQUENCY
Amorgos	50min	€4.50	1-2 daily
Anafi	3½hr	€9	5 weekly
Folegandros	1hr 5min	€7	1-2 daily
Kimolos	5½hr	€11	1-2 weekly
Kythnos	10½hr	€20	2 weekly
Lavrio	12hr 10min	€25	2 weekly
Milos	3½hr	€17	1-2 weekly
Mykonos	1hr 40min	€36	3-4 daily
Naxos*	45min	€25.50	1-2 daily
Paros	3½hr	€11	2 daily
Piraeus	7hr	€32.50	4-5 daily
Piraeus*	3hr 20min	€53-56	3 daily
Santorini (Thira)	1hr 20min	€8	5 daily
Santorini (Thira)*	40min	€18	3 daily
Sikinos	25min	€5	1-4 daily
Syros	3½hr	€16	4 weekly

*high-speed services

ⓘ Getting Around

In summer crowded buses run between Ormos, Hora (€1.60) and Mylopotas Beach (€1.60) about every 15 minutes. Schedules are posted at the main village bus stops or check online at www.ktel-ios.gr. From June to August private excursion buses go to Manganari Beach (one way €3.50) and Agia Theodoti Beach (one way €3). Buses leave at 11am and return at 4pm. For taxis call **Ios Taxi Service** (6977760570).

Caïques travelling from Ormos to Manganari cost €12 per person for a return trip (departing 11am daily). Ormos, Hora and Mylopotas Beach all have car and motorcycle hire. You can book through Acteon Travel (p376).

Ios

Hora, Ormos & Mylopotas
Χώρα, Ορμος & Μυλοπότας

Ios' four main centres sit nearly on top of one another on the west coast. The port, Ormos, is lined with tavernas and cafes, and stretches out into sandy Gialos Beach, backed by beachside bars. Just 2km uphill (or 1.2km up a stone staircase), sits the capital of Hora, a stunning traditional village and the nightlife hub. From here, the road winds south to the brown sugar sand of Mylopotas Beach, with upscale and backpacker-style resorts. You'll find places to eat, sleep, drink and dance in all three settlements. Banks and grocery stores are in Ormos and Hora.

The bus terminal in Ormos is straight ahead from the ferry quay on Plateia Emirou. If you don't mind stairs, it's a fairly easy walk from the port to Hora; follow the signs off the main road out of town.

In Hora there is a seasonal information kiosk at the bus stop, across the road from the big cathedral. Hora's central square is Plateia Valeta, buried deep in the old town. The road straight ahead from Hora's bus stop leads to Mylopotas Beach.

◉ Sights

Hora is a charming Cycladic village with a labyrinth of narrow lanes and cubist houses. Visit during the day and wander from the main streets into the quiet residential quarters to get a glimpse of village life that carries on behind the tourist hype scene.

Skarkos   ARCHAEOLOGICAL SITE
('The Snail'; admission €2; ⊙8am-3pm Mon-Fri, closed Oct-May) Crowning a low hill in a picturesque plain just outside Hora, this Early to Late Bronze Age settlement has restored walled terraces and the low ruins of several Cycladic-style buildings for you to explore.

A small visitor centre and interpretation boards in Greek and English clue you in to what you're looking at. To drive here, take the turning between Ormos and Hora. To walk, follow the traditional stone footpath from the back of Hora, passing goats and farmhouses. (You will feel lost more than once but fear not.) The walk takes around 15 minutes.

Archaeological Museum MUSEUM
(22860 91246; Hora; admission €2, EU students free; ⊙ 9am-4pm Tue-Sun) Finds from Skarkos are displayed at this thorough, if slightly dry, museum in the town hall next to the bus stop in Hora. There are also exhibits from island excavations in general.

🏃 Activities

Yialos Watersports WATER SPORTS
(⌂ 6974290990, 22860 92463; www.yialoswatersports.com; Gialos Beach) With everything from dive trips and boat hire to water striders, banana rides (€12), canoe hire (per hour €9) and windsurfing equipment (per hour €17), Yialos Watersports can get you afloat. You can also hire mountain bikes (per day €10), use the floodlit volleyball court or join a kayaking excursion to Theodoti Beach.

Mylopotas Water Sports & Dive Center WATER SPORTS, DIVING
(⌂ 22860 91622, 22860 92340; www.ios-sports.gr; Mylopotas) Try a PADI 'discover scuba-diving' session (€55) or more intensive PADI courses from €290. There are also wreck dives from €180 and deep-sea dives from €65. Join a snorkelling trip for €20 or rent windsurfing gear, pedal boats (per hour €15) and kayaks (per hour single/double €8/12, per day €20/25). Waterskiing (per session €30), banana rides (€12 to €15), tube rides (€10 to €25) and sailing (per hour/day €25/70) are also available. Beach volleyball and soccer rental is from €3 to €15. There is also a speedboat taxi available for hire (€10 to €30).

Meltemi Water Sports & Dive Center WATERSPORTS, DIVING
(⌂ 22860 91680; www.meltemiwatersports.com; Mylopotas) Rent a windsurfer (per hour/day €15/40), canoe or pedalos straight off the beach here or at Manganari Beach. They offer diving, including a two-hour 'Try Scuba' for €55, PADI courses from €200 and wreck, cave, photography and night dives. Hop on their water taxi from Mylopotas to other beaches (€15 to €25).

🛏 Sleeping

🛏 Ormos

The port has several good sleeping options, reasonable eating places, a couple of handy beaches, and regular bus connections to Hora and other beaches.

Petros Place & Yialos Beach Hotel HOTEL $$
(⌂ 22860 91421; www.thegreektravel.com/ios/petros-place; Ormos; d €80; ❄ 🛜 ⛵) Just a block up from the beach, this newly restored, 200-year-old stone building feels like the home you wish you had. Crisp, characterful rooms, wooden beamed ceilings, traditional beds and a flower-filled poolside give it the edge. The owners are attentive and the breakfast room is just like your Greek grandma's kitchen.

To Corali HOTEL $$
(⌂ 22860 91272; www.coralihotelios.gr; d/tr incl breakfast €95/105, apt €120; P ❄ @ 🛜 ⛵) These standard rooms are in a good position right opposite the beach, some with balconies opening to the sea, There's a poolside pizza restaurant, gregarious owners and a colourful garden.

Hotel Helena HOTEL $$
(⌂ 22860 91276; www.hotelhelena.gr; s/d €42/60, apt €75-100; ❄ @ 🛜 ⛵) Down a short, quiet lane from the beach, this small hotel has clean, no-fuss rooms and well-equipped apartments. Be sure to request a sea-view balcony.

🛏 Hora

Avanti Hotel HOTEL $$
(⌂ 22860 91165; www.avanti-hotelios.com; s/d/tr €80/95/120; P ❄ @ 🛜 ⛵) A short stroll out of Hora, but far enough away to offer a little peace, are these fresh, sparkling rooms. Private balconies and a beautiful pool are the icing on the cake. The owner, Margarita, is an encyclopaedia of local knowledge and very welcoming, but doesn't crowd your space.

Liostasi BOUTIQUE HOTEL $$$
(⌂ 22860 92140; www.liostasi.gr; Hora; d €174-196, ste €265-315; P ❄ @ 🛜 ⛵) Just step into the lobby of this place and you won't want to leave. A contemporary Scandinavian feel blends chic and comfy in just the right proportions. The on-site spa and restaurant are

top quality while the rooms are crisp with splashes of colour, gorgeous sea views and the niceties of home.

Pavezzo   GUESTHOUSE $$
(☑ 6977946091; www.iospavezzo.com; Hora; d & ste €70-100) This place is just steps from Hora but away from the night-time noise, on a quiet side road to Kolitsani Beach. The seven rooms are a steal; they are clean and comfortable with country-style decor and private, sea-view patios. Suites have well-stocked kitchens and your hosts are welcoming and attentive.

Francesco's   HOSTEL $$
(☑ 22860 91223; www.francescos.net; dm €20, s/d/ tr €58/70/105; ✳@☎☀) One-time backpackers are now sending their own 18-year-olds to Francesco's, which is still going strong. Staying here is like being welcomed into the family. Rooms are spotless, views of the harbour are dreamy and it's within stumbling distance of Hora's nightlife. Mingle on the terrace bar, take a dip in the pool and eat like a king at the breakfast table (€5; conveniently served until 2.30pm). To find it, head towards the main square and turn left down Odos Scholarhiou for 200m. Or ask anyone.

Hermes   HOTEL $$
(☑ 22860 91471; www.hermesios.com; Hora; s/d/ tr €68/80/95; P✳☎☀) Halfway along the road between Hora and Mylopotas Beach, Hermes offers basic, spotless rooms with sparkling sea views. What ups its ante is the resortlike extras on offer – Thai massage on the sundeck, barbecues at the pool bar, hammocks and double sunbeds. This place is young and friendly and feels like a community unto itself.

Mylopotas

Far Out Camping & Beach Club   HOSTEL, CAMPGROUND $
(☑ 22860 91468; www.faroutclub.com; camp sites per person €12, bungalows €15-22, studios €100; P@☎☀) Nearly on top of the beach is this backpackers party haven with poolside bars, restaurants and everything from laundry to tattooing. They even have payphones to call home. The 'bungalows' range from small tent-sized affairs to little 'roundhouses' with single and double beds. Studios are in a separate location with all mod cons.

✕ Eating

✕ Ormos

La Randa   ITALIAN $
(☑ 22860 92448; www.larandaios.altervista.org; Ormos; mains €8-11; ☎) Right on the port, this place is the bomb for Italian food. The owner has carted an authentic oven over from Italy and crafts drool-worthy pizzas and pastas dripping in homemade tomato sauce.

✕ Hora

In addition to Hora's raft of restaurants, there are fast-food outlets sellig *gyros* (rotisserie meat with pitta bread), crepes and kebabs until the wee hours near the main square.

★ The Nest   GREEK $
(☑ 22860 91778; Hora; mains €6-10) The Nest feel authentic right down to the *rembetika* music and the tables of older men deep in discussion over rounds of *raki*. This is where local families dine, and with good reason. Local garlic sausage, chicken souvlaki, stuffed eggplant and lamb *keftiko* are served with bowls of tzatziki, olives and fresh bread. Wine is served by the jug and the veggies come from the owner's garden.

Elia   GREEK $
(☑ 698 3192650; Hora; mains €7-10; ☺ dinner) Elia exudes wholesomeness. With a smattering of photos on the walls, it has a classy, country farmhouse feel. Small enough to be intimate, it will wow you with modern Greek meals like tenderloin with plums and figs, shrimp *saganaki* with white cheese, cured beef pies and salads sprinkled with Parmesan and cranberries. To find Elia, head towards the main square and take the first turning to the right.

Thai Smile   THAI $
(☑ 22860 91925; mains €7-9; ☺ dinner) Ignore the international dishes and go for the authentic Thai food. This hole-in-the-wall has plenty of atmosphere and serves plates overflowing with phad king, musaman curry and jasmine rice.

Ali Baba's   THAI $
(Hora; dishes €7-12; ☺ dinner) As popular for its upbeat atmosphere as for its food, this friendly, long-standing restaurant dishes up Thai food and cocktails served in fishbowls.

Opt for the garden courtyard. It's on the same street as the Emporiki bank.

★ Katogi
MEZEDHES $$

(☏ 6983440900; mains €6-12; ☺ dinner) This place is full of life. Stepping into it is like being welcomed into a party in someone's living room, where bright, homy decor flows into a gorgeous garden. And the food is divine. Try pork bites in honey sauce, spicy shrimp and marinated anchovies, tortilla rolls stuffed with slow-cooked beef or pasta purses with cheese and pear.

Lord Byron
MEDITERRANEAN $$

(☏ 22860 92125; dishes €7-14; ☺ dinner; 🛜) An explosion of colour and quirky decor, this laid-back, lively restaurant is as pleasing to the stomach as it is to the eye. Enjoy huge portions of creative salads and mains, with specials like pasta with smoked salmon and creamy dill sauce or beetroot salad with feta bruschetta. Order wine by the glass or ouzo by the gram. Service gets five stars.

Arhondiko
MEDITERRANEAN $$

(☏ 22860 92558; dishes €10-15; ☺ lunch & dinner) The traditional stone and wood interior is as enticing as the contemporary menu. Local products are used to create mezes, salads and tasty mains. Dishes change regularly; watch for the watermelon salad with feta, pistachio and mint and the grilled haloumi with tomato. Spread over two floors, Arhondiko is just off the main square and crowned by a fabulous roof garden with panoramic views.

Mylopotas

Cantina del Mar
CAFE $

(☏ 22860 91016; Mylopotas; dishes €4-6; ☺ breakfast, lunch & dinner) Chill out next to the beach over brunches, sandwiches and wraps. Choose from a huge number of smoothies named Grandma's Garden, Bloody Carrot or Sunset Crush. The hangover smoothies are sworn by; and they've got alco-smoothies for when you're feeling well again.

Drinking & Nightlife

Nightlife at the heart of Hora is full on and radiates from the tiny main square, where it gets so crowded by midnight that you won't be able to fall down, even if you need to. Be young and carefree – but also be careful.

With everything from jazz bars to frantic backpacker bars that dole out cheap shoot-ers, venues open and close and change in popularity regularly. Look for **Blue Note** and **Liquid** but follow the crowds, find a place that suits your mood and spread the love.

Foiniki Music Cafe
BAR

(☏ 22860 92247; Hora) Settle into this funky little bar, with its rich colours, wooden beams, stacks of magazines and handcrafted beer from around Greece. Tucked behind Lord Byron, it's a great spot for a predinner tipple.

Crazy Cake Hole
CAFE

(☏ 6977826649; Hora; 🛜) Head towards the fairy lights, down the narrow alley just behind the cathedral. In the evening and wee hours of the morning, the outdoor tables are a relaxed spot to sip cocktails or scoff crème brûlée. During the day, hole up in this cosy nook for wraps, baguettes, waffles and smoothies. Cupcakes served all day.

Smiles
BAR

(☏ 6972723603; www.iosparty.gr; Hora) Venture past the main square to find this oasis of cool. Multilevel outdoor patios are filled with sofas, lanterns, twinkling trees and fantastic drinks from the impressive cocktail menu. It's at once chilled out and classy.

🛍 Shopping

Mirabello
ARTS & CRAFTS

(mirabello_ios@yahoo.com; Hora) With very cool hand-painted T-shirts, posters, paintings, prints and music, this overflowing shop is a cacophony of colour and sound. The artist is a local painter and musician who first opened his doors over 40 years ago.

ℹ Information

There's an ATM right by the information kiosks at the ferry quay. In Hora, the National Bank of Greece, behind the church, and the Commercial Bank, nearby, both have ATMs.

The post office in Hora is a block behind the main road on the narrow road that leads off right by the final bend as you enter Hora coming uphill from Ormos.

Acteon Travel (☏ 22860 91343; www.acteon. gr) On the square near the quay, and in Hora and Mylopotas.

Hospital (☏ 22860 91227) On the way to Gialos, 250m northwest of the quay; there are several doctors in Hora. For emergencies, contact the 24-hour on-call doctor (☏ 6932420200).

Port Police (☏ 22860 91264) At the southern end of the Ormos waterfront.

Around Ios

It's easy to escape the crowds on Ios; simply rent a car and venture into the seemingly isolated countryside with its goat farms, honey boxes and dramatic views. Head to Cape Gero Angeli, at the northernmost tip of the island and 12km from Hora, to the believed site of **Homer's Grave**. There's nothing much to see here but the panoramic sea views are fabulous.

En route to Psathi is **Paleokastro**, the remains of a Byzantine castle perched atop a seaside cliff. Follow the stone pathway from the roadside; it'll likely just be you and the goats here. Also on the road to Psathi is the island's formidable **cheese factory**. If it's open, you can pop in for a gander and buy some of the lip-smacking wares. There's also an outlet in Ormos.

Ios is well known for its beaches. Vying with Mylopotas for first place is **Manganari**, a long swathe of fine white sand on the south coast, reached by bus or by caïque in summer. **Agia Theodoti** has the bluest of blue water and is favoured by Greek families in the summer. Nearby **Psathi** is quieter, with a popular taverna and is an ace windsurfing venue.

SANTORINI (THIRA)
ΣΑΝΤΟΡΙΝΗ (ΘΗΡΑ)

POP 12,440

Santorini may well have conquered a corner of your imagination before you've even set eyes on it. With multicoloured cliffs soaring over 300m from a sea-drowned caldera, it rests in the middle of the indigo Aegean, looking like a giant slab of layered cake. The island spoons the vast crater left by one of the biggest volcanic eruptions in history.

Smaller islands curl around the fragmented western edge of the caldera, but it is the main island of Thira that will take your breath away with its snow drift of white Cycladic houses lining the cliff tops and, in places, spilling like icy cornices down the terraced rock. When the sun sets, the reflection on the buildings and the glow of the orange and red in the cliffs is spectacular.

Santorini is no secret and draws crowds for most of the year, yet it wears its tourism well and its offerings make it worth the bustle. The island's intrigue reaches deep into the past, with the fascinating Minoan site of Akrotiri and the gorgeous traditional hilltop village of Oia. It also glides effortlessly into the future with accomplished artists, excellent wineries, a unique brewery, and some of the Cyclades finest dining experiences. The sandy, multicoloured beaches are simply the icing on the cake.

History

Minor eruptions have been the norm in Greece's earthquake-prone history, but Santorini continually bucked this trend – eruptions were genuinely earth-shattering, and so wrenching they changed the shape of the island several times.

Dorians, Venetians and Turks occupied Santorini, but its most influential early inhabitants were Minoans. They came from Crete between 2000 BC and 1600 BC, and the settlement at Akrotiri dates from the peak years of their great civilisation.

The island was circular then and was called Strongili (Round One). Thousands of years ago a colossal volcanic eruption caused the centre of Strongili to sink, leaving a caldera with towering cliffs along the east side. The latest theory, based on carbon dating of olive-oil samples from Akrotiri, places the event 10 years either side of 1613 BC.

A BENT FOR CYCLADIC TRAVEL

Long before the hip lotus eaters of the 1960s discovered their dream world in the Greek islands, a redoubtable pair of travellers had been thoroughly 'doing' the Cyclades during the late 19th century. James Theodore Bent and his wife, Mabel, travelled extensively throughout the Aegean, 'researching' the cultural life of the islands as much as their archaeology. J Theodore's 1885 island-by-island book, *The Cyclades, Or Life Among the Insular Greeks*, is a quirky masterpiece that describes the sights and cultural realities of the islands in the late-19th century – along with Bent's often eccentric reflections. A full edition is published by **Archaeopress** (www.archaeopress.com). An abridged edition, published by **Anagnosis** (www.anagnosis.gr), may sometimes be found in bookshops on bigger islands such as Santorini.

Santorini (Thira)

0 ___ 5 km
0 ___ 2.5 miles

Ios (41km); Naxos (87km);
Paros (105km); Mykonos (128km);
Syros (135km); Piraeus (240km);
Thessaloniki (627km)

Kalymnos (155km);
Kos (165km)

Baxedes

Paradise Beach

AEGEAN SEA

Sifnos (105km);
Serifos (120km);
Milos (131km)

Sigalas Winery

Pori Beach

Ammoudi

Oia

Finikia

Cape Riva

Armeni Beach

Potamos Beach

Santorini (Thira)

Karpathos (160km);
Rhodes (230km)

Potamos

Imerovigli

Vourvoulos

Gialos Beach

Agrilla

Manolas

Firostefani

Fira

Karterados Beach

Thirasia

Fira Skala

Karterados

Monolithos

Monolithos Beach

Nea Kameni

Messaria

Volcan Wine Museum

Cape Trypiti

Hot Springs

Vothonas

Exo Gonia

Art Space & Argyros Canava Winery

Palia Kameni

Santo Wines

Santoríni Brewery

Athinios

Pyrgos

Aspronisi

Megalohori

Hatzidakis Winery

Canava Roussos Winery

Kamari

Crete (128km)

Boutari Winery

Mt Profitis Ilias (567m)▲

Kamari Beach

Moni Profiti Ilia

Ancient Thira

Cape Akrotiri

Akrotiri

Emporio

Perissa

567m ▲

Ancient Akrotiri

Black Beach

White Beach

Red Beach

Akrotiri Beach

Cape Mesa Vouno

Vlihada Beach

Perivolos Beach

Agios Georgios Beach

Anafi (56km)

Cape Evo Mytis

Santorini was recolonised during the 3rd century BC, but for the next 2000 years sporadic volcanic activity created further physical changes that included the formation of the volcanic islands of Palia Kameni and Nea Kameni at the centre of the caldera. As recently as 1956 a major earthquake devastated Oia and Fira, yet by the 1970s the islanders had embraced tourism as tourists embraced the island, and today Santorini is a destination of truly spectacular appeal.

🛈 Getting There & Away

There are several flights a day to and from Athens (€85, 45 minutes). There are also a good number of ferries each day to and from Piraeus and many of Santorini's neighbouring islands.

Thira's main port, Athinios, stands on a cramped shelf of land at the base of sphinxlike cliffs and is a scene of marvellous chaos that always seems to work itself out when ferries arrive. Buses (and taxis) meet all ferries and then cart passengers up the towering cliffs through an ever-rising series of S-bends to Fira.

ⓘ Getting Around

TO/FROM THE AIRPORT

There are frequent bus connections in summer between Fira's bus station and the airport, located southwest of Monolithos Beach. The first leaves Fira at 7am and the last departs at 7pm. Enthusiastic hotel and domatia staff meet flights, and some also return guests to the airport. A taxi to the airport costs €12.

BUS

In summer buses leave Fira at least once an hour for Oia (€1.60). There are also numerous daily departures for Akrotiri (€1.80), plenty to Kamari (€1.60) and Perivolos Beach (€2.20), and a few to Monolithos (€1.60).

Buses leave Fira, Kamari and Perissa for the port of Athinios (€2.20, 30 minutes) an hour to 1½ hours before most of the ferry departures, but it's wise to check well in advance. Buses for Fira meet all ferries, even late at night.

BOAT SERVICES FROM SANTORINI (THIRA)

DESTINATION	TIME	FARE	FREQUENCY
Amorgos*	1¼hr	€32	1 daily
Anafi	1hr 10min	€8	5 weekly
Folegandros	2½hr	€9	1-2 daily
Folegandros*	30min	€29.50	1 daily
Ios	40min	€18	2-3 daily
Ios	1hr 35min	€8	4 weekly
Iraklio	4½hr	€51.50	1-2 daily
Kalymnos	5½hr	€30	2-4 weekly
Karpathos	11hr 55min	€28	2-3 weekly
Kasos	10hr, *14hr	€28	2-3 weekly
Kimolos	5½hr	€11	2 weekly
Kos	5hr	€30	2 weekly
Kythnos	12hr	€24	2 weekly
Lavrio	1¾hr	€29	2 weekly
Milos	3½hr	€17	2 weekly
Milos*	2hr	€39.60	1 daily
Mykonos*	2½hr	€50	2-3 daily
Naxos	2hr	€16.50	5 daily
Naxos*	1½hr	€37	2-3 daily
Nisyros	8hr	€30	2-3 weekly
Paros	3-4hr	€18.50	5 daily
Paros*	2¼hr	€45	2-3 daily
Piraeus	9hr	€33.50	4-5 daily
Piraeus*	5¼hr	€58-61.50	3 daily
Rafina*	4¾hr	€58-62	1 daily
Rhodes	13½hr	€30	1-2 daily
Sikinos	2¾hr	€14.10	1-4 daily
Sikinos*	2¼hr	€8	1 weekly
Sitia (Crete)	7hr 25min	€25	2 weekly
Syros	8¼hr	€21	2 weekly
Tilos	9½hr	€30	2-3 weekly

*high-speed services

CABLE CAR & DONKEY

A **cable car** (☏ 22860 22977; M Nomikou) runs (every 20 minutes 6.30am to 10pm June to August) between Fira and the small port below, known as Fira Skala, from where volcanic island cruises leave. One-way cable car tickets cost €4/2 per adult/child and luggage is €2. Less frequent services operate outside the peak season. You can make a more leisurely, and aromatic, upward trip by donkey (about €5).

CAR & MOTORCYCLE

A car is the best way to explore the island during high season, when buses are intolerably overcrowded and you'll be lucky to get on one at all. Be very patient and cautious when driving – the narrow roads, especially in Fira, can be a nightmare. Note that Oia has no petrol station, the nearest being just outside Fira.

Two very good local hire outfits are **Damigos Rent a Car** (☏ 6979968192, 22860 22048) and, for scooters, **Zerbakis** (☏ 6944531992, 22860 33329).

TAXI

Fira's **taxi stand** (☏ 22860 22555, 22860 23951) is on Dekigala just around the corner from the bus station. A taxi from the port of Athinios to Fira costs between €10 to €14 and a trip from Fira to Oia about €12 to €15. Expect to add €1 to €2 if the taxi is booked ahead or if you have luggage. A taxi to Kamari is about €12, to Perissa €16, and to Ancient Thira about €25 one way.

Fira   Φήρα

POP 2291

Santorini's main town of Fira is a vibrant, bustling place, its caldera edge layered with hotels, cave apartments, infinity pools and swish restaurants, all backed by a warren of narrow streets full of shops and even more bars and restaurants. A multitude of fellow admirers cannot diminish the impact of Fira's stupendous landscape. Views over the multicoloured cliffs are breathtaking, and at night the caldera edge is a frozen cascade of lights.

◉ Sights & Activities

Archaeological Museum   MUSEUM
(☏ 22860 22217; M Nomikou; adult/student €3/2; ⊙ 8.30am-3pm Tue-Sun) Near the cable-car station, this museum houses impressive finds from Akrotiri and Ancient Thira, along with some Cycladic figurines, and beautiful Hellenistic and Roman sculptures. The con-

tent is strong, however the museum itself is in need of a little TLC.

Museum of Prehistoric Thira   MUSEUM
(Mitropoleos; admission €3; ⊙ 8.30am-3pm Tue-Sun) On the southern edge of town, this museum houses extraordinary finds excavated from Akrotiri and is all the more impressive when you realise just how old they are. Most impressive is the glowing gold ibex figurine, dating from the 17th century BC and in amazingly mint condition. Also look for fossilised olive tree leaves from within the caldera from 60,000 BC.

Megaro Gyzi Museum   MUSEUM
(Erythrou Stavrou; admission €3.50; ⊙ 10.30am-1.30pm & 5-8pm Mon-Sat, 10.30am-4.30pm Sun) Come to this quiet escape in the north of town to take in fascinating photographs of Fira before and immediately after the 1956 earthquake, along with a collection of engravings, paintings and 15th-century manuscripts.

**Petros M Nomikos
Conference Centre**   MUSEUM
(☏ 22860 23016; www.therafoundation.org; adult/child €4/free; ⊙ 10am-7pm May-Oct) The centre is run by the Thera Foundation and hosts major conferences, but also stages the fascinating 'Wall Paintings of Thera' exhibition, a collection of three-dimensional life-size reproductions of the finest Akrotiri wall paintings.

⮕ Tours

Tour companies operate various trips to and across the caldera. Options include a tour to the volcanic island of Nea Kameni (€15), to the volcano and hot springs (including swimming) of Palia Kameni (€20), full-day boat tours to the volcanic islets, Thirasia and Oia (€28), a sunset boat tour (€35) and a bus tour including wine tasting (€25). Book at travel agencies.

The *Thalassa,* an exact copy of an 18th-century schooner, scoots around the caldera every afternoon on a sunset buffet dinner tour (€50, from May to October), stopping for sightseeing on Nea Kameni and for ouzo on Thirasia. Most travel agencies sell tickets.

Santorini's lauded wines are its crisp, clear dry whites, such as the delectable *asyrtiko,* and the amber-coloured, unfortified dessert wine Vinsanto. Most local vineyards hold tastings and tours. You can also join a half-day tasting tour with **WIS** (Wine In

Santorini; ✆ 22860 7161; www.wineinsantorini.com; per person €70). Guides are knowledgeable and ensure you get some food along the way.

A worthwhile visit is to **Santo Wines** (✆ 22860 22596; www.santowines.gr; Pyrgos) where you can sample a range of wines and browse a shop full of choice vintages as well as local products including fava beans, tomatoes, capers and preserves.

One of the most entertaining venues is the **Volcan Wine Museum** (✆ 22860 31322; www.volcanwines.gr; admission €7; ⊗ noon-8pm), housed in a traditional *canava* (winery) on the way to Kamari. Admission includes an audio guide and three wine tastings.

Also worth visiting is the **Santorini Brewery** (✆ 22860 30268; www.santorinibrewingcompany.gr; ⊗ Mon-Sat). You'll have seen their beer, with its bright donkey logos. Unfiltered and fresh, 300L are produced here each day. Take a tour and sample the lager, ale and Greece's first IPA (otherwise known as Crazy Donkey).

Other wineries that are worth a visit include **Boutari** (✆ 22860 81011; www.boutari.gr; Megalohori), **Canava Roussos** (✆ 22860 31278; www.canavaroussos.gr; Mesa Gonia), **Hatzidakis** (✆ 22860 32552; www.hatzidakiswines.gr; Pyrgos) and **Sigalas** (✆ 22860 71644; www.sigalas-wine.com; Oia). All of these should be contacted before visiting.

🛏 Sleeping

Few of Fira's sleeping options are cheap. For a caldera view, expect to pay a much higher price. Some domatia touts at the port may claim that their rooms are in town, when they're actually a long way out; ask to see a map showing the exact location. Many hotels on the caldera rim cannot be reached by vehicle and may well involve several flights of steps leading to your accommodation. Most budget and midrange places offer free transfer to port or airport; other hotels may charge anything from €10 upwards for a transfer.

Santorini Camping   HOSTEL, CAMPGROUND **$**
(✆ 22860 22944; www.santorinicamping.gr; Fira; dm/d/q €15/50/70, camp sites per person €12.50; ⊗ Mar-Nov; [P][@][≋]) Located on the eastern outskirts of town, this hostel and campground has some shade and decent facilities. You get what you pay for with the rooms, which are fairly clean but nothing special. There's a self-service restaurant, minimarket and pool.

SANTORINI'S SWALLOWS

You'll quickly notice the popularity of swallows as decoration on Santorini's ancient pottery. In particular, pots from Akrotiri are seemingly alive with these small black birds swooping and darting across them. Long ago, the island was a huge nesting ground for swallows and, even fairly recently, the caldera cliff came alive each spring with them. Sadly, construction has interfered with their nesting area and fewer and fewer shack up here every year. Nevertheless, many current artists are rekindling the symbolism of the swallows, which indicate new life and springtime.

Villa Soula   HOTEL **$$**
(✆ 22860 23473; www.santorini-villasoula.gr; s/d €60/80; [❄][🛜][≋]) Cheerful and spotless, this hotel is a great deal. Rooms aren't large but are freshly renovated with small, breezy balconies. Colourful public areas and a small, well-maintained pool give you room to spread out a little. The breakfast room is a tad dark, but you can opt to take it on your balcony. It's a short walk from the town centre.

Karterados Caveland Hostel   HOSTEL **$$**
(✆ 22860 22122; www.cave-land.com; Karterados; incl breakfast dm €15-21, d with/without bathroom €70/50, apt €120; [P][❄][🛜][≋]) This new facility, opened in 2011, is based in a fascinating old winery complex in Karterados about 1km from central Fira. It was once a local tennis club and the courts are available to guests. Accommodation is in the old wine caves, all of them with creative and colourful decor and good facilities. The surrounding garden and public areas are peaceful and relaxing. There are yoga classes on offer for €7 to €35.

Villa Roussa   HOTEL **$$**
(✆ 22860 23220; www.villaroussa.gr; Dekigala; s/d/tr €60/80/95; [P][❄][🛜][≋]) This place is all about location. Footsteps from the caldera (without the prices to match) and seconds from the bus station (but thankfully out of earshot), it has fresh, immaculate rooms and warm, helpful staff.

Hotel Sofia   HOTEL **$$**
(✆ 22860 22802; www.sofiahotelsantorini.com; Firostefani; d €70-80; [❄][🛜][≋]) Comfortable, with a touch of character, these rooms at

Fira

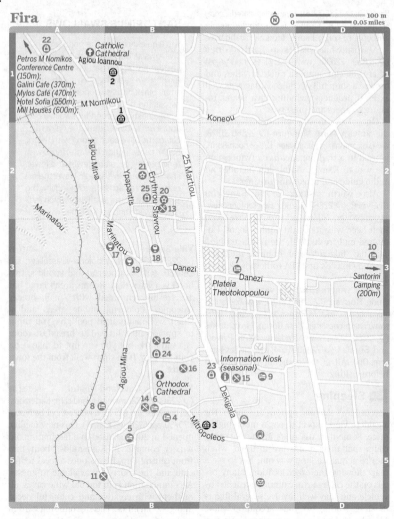

the heart of Firostefani are a great alternative to the bustle of Fira. With caldera views, they're a near steal and the small, lovely pool and verandahs are perfect for a lazy afternoon. Fira's centre is about 1.5km south, along a lovely caldera-edge walkway.

Pelican Hotel   HOTEL **$$**
(☎ 22860 23113; www.pelicanhotel.gr; Danezi; s/d/tr incl breakfast €68/78/95; ❄ @ ☎) There's no caldera view, but strong wooden furnishings and traditional carpets give this long-standing hotel a homy feel. It's just metres from the centre of town.

Aroma Suites   BOUTIQUE HOTEL **$$$**
(☎ 6945026038, 22860 24112; www.aromasuites.com; Agiou Mina; d €160-270; ❄ @ ☎) Overlooking the caldera at the quieter southern end of Fira, and more accessible than similar places, this boutique hotel has charming service and plush, beautiful rooms. Built into the side of the caldera, the traditional interiors are made all the more lovely with strong colour touches and individual touches like canopied beds, local art, books and stereos.Balconies offer a feeling of complete seclusion.

Fira

Hotel Atlantis HOTEL $$$
(☑ 22860 22232; www.atlantishotel.gr; Fira; d incl breakfast €205-315; P ❄ @ 🕿 ☒) The Atlantis is a regal building that overlooks the widest section of the caldera-edge promenade. It's full of cool, relaxing lounges and flower-filled terraces, and the bright, airy bedrooms are quiet and very well equipped. Front rooms have caldera views.

Aressana Spa Hotel BOUTIQUE HOTEL $$$
(☑ 22860 23900; www.aressana.gr; d €270; P ❄ @ 🕿 ☒) When you're greeted with a refreshing lemongrass cloth, you know you're in for some pampering. Rooms at this rockstar joint are simple and modern, with all the niceties that give it the edge of luxury. The pool with its waterfall and private patio cabanas make the lack of a caldera view more than tolerable. The spa and the huge breakfast seal the deal.

Mill Houses BOUTIQUE HOTEL $$$
(☑ 22860 27117; www.millhouses.gr; Firostefani; studio/ste incl breakfast €240/290; ❄ @ 🕿 ☒) Built right into the side of the caldera at Firostefani, these superb studios are chic and plush. Lots of white linen and whitewashed walls fill them with light. King-sized beds, slippers and very private patios looking out over the Aegean are just a few of the lavish touches.

Porto Fira Suites HOTEL $$$
(☑ 22860 22849; www.portofira.com; Agiou Mina; 2-/4-person ste incl breakfast €270/400; ❄ 🕿) If you're staying here, your day of luxury begins with not just breakfast, but breakfast in bed. Ultramodern rooms are white, crisp and cool in more ways than one, yet retain their traditional, caldera cave ambience.

✗ Eating

Overpriced, indifferent food geared towards tourists is still an unfortunate feature of summertime Fira; thankfully, there are many excellent exceptions. In general, there's a price hike for a caldera view.

Ouzeri MEZEDHES $
(☑ 22860 21566; Fabrika Shopping Centre; dishes €6-12) Extremely central and verging on classy, this terrace restaurant has surprisingly reasonable prices. It's a longstanding favourite with locals and tourist alike, with top traditional dishes like mussel *saganaki,* baked feta and stuffed tomatoes.

Mama's House GREEK $
(mains €7-14; ☺ breakfast, lunch & dinner) Down steps just before the main square is this 'institution' famed for its mega breakfasts (€6 to €8.50), hearty Greek dishes and creative salads, all enjoyed on a big, lively terrace. The mezedhes menu is vast, with items like stuffed peppers with cheese and spicy sauce, and eggplant rolls with feta.

Galini Cafe CAFE $$
(☑ 22860 22095; www.galinicafesantorini.com; mains €6-14; ☺ breakfast, lunch & dinner) Just as you reach Firostefani, this breezy cafe welcomes you with brightly coloured flower pots and a handcrafted school of fish swimming overhead. Chilled and friendly, with unparalleled caldera views, it's a great place for breakfast or a light meal and a cocktail at

A LITTLE FISHY

At first you may be a little perplexed to see weary shoppers with their feet in ground-level aquariums. Fish spas have become all the rage on Santorini. Look closely and you'll see hundreds of tiny garra rufa fish crowded around the clients' feet, looking like they're nibbling away. Exactly: these toothless critters suck away at your dry skin to stimulate blood flow. Test it out by dipping your feet for 10 minutes for around €10 or dive in for a full-body, hour-long plunge for around €70.

sunset. Full breakfasts, savoury crepes, well-stuffed sandwiches and truly tasty salads are carefully prepared. (The one with figs and pomegranate is especially nice.)

Assyrtico Wine Restaurant
GREEK $$

(☑ 22860 22463; www.assyrtico-restaurant.com; mains €13-21; ☺ lunch & dinner; ☎) Settle in on this verandah above the main drag for carefully prepared food accompanied by caldera views. Start with the rocket salad with caramalised walnuts and then try the seafood pappardelle with saffron and limoncello. Service is relaxed and friendly.

Camille Stefani
GREEK $$

(☑ 22860 22762; www.camillestefani.com; mains €8-15; ☺ lunch & dinner) Going strong since the late '70s, this rooftop restaurant has views across to the east coast. Its authentic, traditional atmosphere matches its meals. Dig into countless mezes like *saganaki* cheese and stuffed vine leaves or opt for *mousakas,* stuffed chicken or pasta with local herbs. This place is as popular with locals as it is with tourists.

Mylos Café
CAFE $$

(Firostefani; lunch €9-17, dinner €15-30; ☺ lunch & dinner; ☎) Located in a converted windmill on the caldera edge, this uberstylish venue has upscale food like quail with molasses or smoked eel with mandarin basil sauce.

★1500bc
SEAFOOD $$$

(☑ 22860 21331; www.1500bc.gr; mains €30-45; ☺ dinner) With top views south across the caldera, this peaceful, elegant patio serves truly divine food. Ravioli stuffed with shrimp and eggplant, caramalised octopus, and grilled lobster with oregano are just a few of the choices. Service is impeccable – they'll debone the fish at your table and bring you a shawl if you're chilly – and the wine list will leave you feeling spoiled.

Koukoumavlos
GREEK $$$

(☑ 22860 23860, 22860 23807; mains €28-36; ☺ dinner) Just to the side of the hustle and bustle, this terrace is filled with nearly gleeful diners partaking of fresh, modern, Aegean cuisine. The creative chefs here are not afraid of combining unusual flavours. Try risotto with lamb and smoked feta mousse or pumpkin soup with saffron, chestnut and wild mushrooms. Look for the pink building and wooden doorway or simply follow your nose.

🍷 Drinking & Nightlife

After midnight Erythrou Stavrou fires up as the clubbing caldera of Fira.

Kira Thira
BAR

(☑ 22860 22770; Erythrou Stavrou) The oldest bar in Fira and one of the best. Dark wood and vaulted ceilings give it an intimate atmosphere with smooth beer and smoother jazz. It also sees the occassional live band.

Tropical
BAR

(☑ 22860 23089; Marinatou; ☎) Nicely perched just before the caldera edge, Tropical draws a vibrant crowd with well-made cocktails, a relaxed atmosphere and a steady mix of rock, soul and occasional jazz, plus unbeatable balcony views.

Franco's Bar
COCKTAIL BAR

(☑ 22860 24428; www.francos.gr; Marinatou) The classical music is a hint that this is more of a place to absorb the views and sip champagne cocktails than to party.

Enigma
CLUB

(☑ 22860 22466; Erythrou Stavrou) A Fira top spot with three bars and a big dance space, this is the catwalk clientele's favourite spot amid cool decor and full-on sounds from house to mainstream hits.

Koo Club
CLUB

(☑ 22860 22025; www.kooclub.gr; Erythrou Stavrou) Multi-tiered outdoor balconies with sofas to lounge on while hanging out with new friends, sipping cocktails to live DJs.

🔒 Shopping

In Fira you can get everything from Armani and Versace to Timberland and Reef –

alongside souvenir shops selling dancing donkeys and olive-wood utensils. You'll also find more unique galleries and boutiques. You'll be spoiled for choice but the prices run high.

Mati Art Gallery   ARTS & CRAFTS, JEWELLERY
(☑ 22860 23814; www.matiartgallery.com; Cathedral Plateau) The outside instillation art will intrigue you before you even step inside this gallery. You'll be spellbound by the gold and silver and the glass and metal highlighted by turquoises and deep oranges. This is the main exhibition space of Yorgos Kypris, an internationally celebrated artist who takes much of his inspiration from the chunk of time he spends annually on Santorini.

Take in his larger sculptures and pieces and then consider home items, pendants and jewellery that are hard to resist.

New Art   CLOTHING
(☑ 22860 23770; Erythrou Stavrou & Fabrika Shopping Centre) Forget the standard painted-on T-shirts. If you want quality to take back home, the subtle colours and motifs of designer Werner Hampel's tees have real style.

Art of the Loom   ARTS & CRAFTS
(☑ 22860 21190; www.artoftheloom.gr) Tucked behind the cathedral, this gallery is filled with diverse pieces from the island's top artists. Silver jewellery, paintings, glasswork and ceramics make for interesting eye candy.

Books & Style   BOOKS
(Dekigala) An excellent range of books in various languages. There's a great selection of volumes on Greece as well as travel guides, children's books and novels.

❶ Information

Fira doesn't have an EOT (Greek National Tourist Organisation) or tourist police.

Toilets are north of Plateia Theotokopoulou near the port police building. You may need to brace yourself (they're of squat vintage). Bring your own paper.

EMERGENCY
Hospital (☑ 22860 22237) On the road to Kamari. A new hospital at Karterados was nearing completion at the time of writing.
Police Station (☑ 22860 22649; Karterados) About 2km from Fira.
Port Police (☑ 22860 22239; 25 Martiou) North of the square.

MONEY
There are numerous ATMs scattered around town.

Alpha Bank (Plateia Theotokopoulou) Represents American Express and has an ATM.
National Bank of Greece (Dekigala) South of Plateia Theotokopoulou, on the caldera side of the road. Has an ATM.

POST
Post Office (Dekigala)

TRAVEL AGENCIES
Dakoutros Travel (☑ 22860 22958; www.dakoutrostravel.gr; ☺ 8.30am-10pm) Main street, just before Plateia Theotokopoulou.

Oia   Οία
POP 962

Perched on the northern tip of the island, the village of Oia (ee-ah) reflects the renaissance of Santorini following the devastating earthquake of 1956. Restoration work has whipped up beauty and you will struggle to find a more stunning Cyclades village. Built on a steep slope of the caldera, many of its dwellings nestle in niches hewn into the volcanic rock. A magical way to reach the village is along a cliff edge walkway that rambles north from Fira through a series of linked settlements. If you travel by road, you'll pass through sage green slopes splattered with wildflowers, rich red- and coffee-coloured earth and views of blue, blue sea.

Not surprisingly, Oia draws enormous crowds and overcrowding is the price it pays for its good looks. Try to visit in the morning or spend the night here; afternoons and evenings often bring busloads from the cruise ships moored in the bay.

◉ Sights & Activities

Maritime Museum   MUSEUM
(☑ 22860 71156; adult/student €3/1.50; ☺ 10am-2pm & 5-8pm Wed-Mon) This museum is located along a narrow lane that leads off right from Nikolaou Nomikou. It's housed in an old mansion and has endearing displays on Santorini's maritime history.

Ammoudi   PORT
This tiny port of colourful fishing boats lies 300 steps below Oia. It's a hot haul down and up again but well worth it for the views of the blood-red cliffs, the harbour and back up to Oia. Once you're down there, have lunch at one of the excellent tavernas right on the water's edge; try Katina or Dimitris. In summer, boats and tours go from Ammoudi to Thirasia daily; check with travel agencies in Fira for departure times.

YORGOS KYPRIS – SANTORINI'S INSPIRATIONAL SIDE

Although his studio is in Athens, it was only natural for Yorgos to become a citizen of an island and of Santorini in particular, and it's in Fira that he chooses to have his gallery. Yorgos passed much of his childhood near the sea and first came to the island when he was still a teenager. He immediately felt it was something special, and unlike any other island he had experienced. He quickly became 'entrapped in the nets of Santorini'.

Santorini has been an inspiration to much of Yorgos' art work. Much of it focuses on fish, which he uses as a tool to analyse the cruelty of human bheaviour, taking his starting point from overfishing and killing. But his work is far from hostile. Instead, he strives to evoke sentiments of opposing cruelty – the beauty of the fish and the life in the movement and rhythm of the fish.

Here's a peek at the artist's list of Santorini's most inspirational locations. Head to any of them to let the island work its magic.

→ Walk up the steps of Pyrgos and check out the 360-degree views of the islands.

→ Sit and observe the caldera from Fira's plateau (p380). Settlements have been built here since antiquity to be on the lookout for pirates. You'll still see the older population just sitting and watching. You'll almost feel that you can control the sea.

→ Visit the theatre in Ancient Thira (p388). Just the walk to it offers fantastic views south to the sea. Once you're there, soak up the history.

→ Spend a day at the excavated town of Akrotiri (p388) and get a feel for the Minoan people, a fascinatingly advanced civilisation. Many speculate that this was once the centre of Minoan culture.

→ Escape to Sigalas (p381) winery in the north, where you can relax on the verandah between tasting the grapes.

Museum of Ancient Greek Music   MUSEUM
(☑ 22860 31812; Nikolaou Nomikou; admission €2; ☉ 10am-2pm May-Sep) This narrow room is filled with Christodoylos Halaris' fascinating collection of over 80 instruments from as far back as 2800 BC. It's run by the collector, himself a prominent musician, and hours are somewhat irregular.

🛏 Sleeping

Oia Youth Hostel   HOSTEL $
(☑ 22860 71465; www.santorinihostel.gr; dm incl breakfast €16; ☉ May–mid-Oct; @🛜) Welcoming and clean, this is one of the best-run hostels you'll hope to find. Dorms have eight to 12 beds per room but you're likely to spend more time at the little bar or on the lovely rooftop terrace with great views. To find the hostel, keep straight on from the bus terminus for about 100m.

Chelidonia Traditional Villas   APARTMENT $$$
(☑ 22860 71287; www.chelidonia.com; Nikolaou Nomikou; studios €180, villas €210-280; ❄@🛜) Traditional cliff-side dwellings that have been in the owner's family for generations and offer a grand mix of old and new. Modern niceties are balanced with traditional

wooden furniture, and private patios offer uninterrupted caldera views.

Zoe Houses   BOUTIQUE HOTEL $$$
(☑ 22860 71466; www.zoe-aegeas.gr; ste €260) Traditional houses built into the caldera's edge with all the comforts of home. Classy decor, amazing views and unrivalled hospitality mean that this place gets a lot of returning guests. Book ahead. Each suite is entirely different from the others and sleeps up to four.

🍴 Eating

⭐**Lotlita's Gelato**   ICE CREAM $
(☑ 22860 71279; cones €3-6) The sign outside says, 'Taste our ice-ceam. Feel the love in it.' One bite, and you do. Near the bus station, Lotlita's sells scoopfuls of homemade heaven. With a gelato machine brought from Italy, they use fresh milk, fruit and nuts, and come up with original flavours such as a gelato made from a local wine. It's not to be missed.

Melenio   BAKERY $
(☑ 22860 71149; Nikolaou Nomikou; snacks €2-5; ☉ breakfast & lunch) Head downstairs to this breezy little bakery, filled with traditional

treats, ice cream and croissants. The tiled floor and views out to sea make it a lovely spot for breakfast or a coffee break.

Skala
GREEK $
(Nikolaou Nomikou; dishes €9-15) Watch life pass up and down to Ammoudi from the high ground of Skala's relaxed terrace. Traditional dishes like souvlaki, baked eggplant or cheese pies with pine nuts fill the popular menu.

Karma
GREEK $$
(22860 71404; www.karma.bz; mains €9-17; ☉dinner) With fountains, flickering candles, golden-coloured walls and deep wine cushions, this courtyard restaurant feels rather royal and august. And the comtemporary food follows suit. Start with fava with caramelised onions and capers, and then try grilled octopus sautéed with ouzo and fresh thyme. There's also *soutzoukakia,* a dish of ground meat kebabs bathed in red wine and tomato sauce and traditionally served as an aphrodisiac.

1800
GREEK $$$
(22860 71485; www.oia-1800.com; Nikolaou Nomikou; dishes €13-35) Housed in a restored sea captain's mansion, the artistically prepared modern Greek cuisine has won this restaurant accolades for years. Sea bass with an aromatic spell of quinoa, artichoke and fennel purée or grilled lamb with sweet-and-sour green applesauce give you a glimpse at the creative menu. Dine inside or on the caldera-view rooftop.

Ambrosia
GREEK $$$
(22860 71413; www.ambrosia-nectar.com; mains €21-30; ☎) On a stone deck overlooking the sea, Ambrosia serves truly tasty meals among flickering candlelight and white tablecloths. Savour modern Greek dishes like grilled shrimp with mango and sweet wine sauce or duck with whild cherry.

🛍 Shopping

★ Atlantis Books
BOOKS
(22860 72346; www.atlantisbooks.org; Nikolaou Nomikou) This amazing little bookstore is a destination in itself. Follow quotes and words that wind their way down the stairs into a hobbit hole that appears to be held up by row upon row of books. Look for unusual (and often small, light) publications along with stationery-style keepsakes such as locally bound notebooks and diaries.

Staff are friendly and knowledgeable, and musicians and other events are hosted on the rooftop.

Iatis
JEWELLERY, CERAMICS
(22860 72127; Nikolaou Nomikou) With his studio at the back of the gallery, Papageorgiou Christos wows passers-by with his contemporary designs. Stunning silver and gold jewellery is professionally crafted and shimmers next to the artist's striking pottery.

ℹ Information

From the bus terminal, head left and uphill to reach the rather stark central square and the main street, Nikolaou Nomikou, which skirts the caldera.

ATMS can be found on Nikolaou Nomikou and also by the bus terminus.

NSTravel (22860 71199; www.nst-santorin-itravel.com) In the bus terminal square; sells ferry tickets and can arrange accommodation and car hire.

Around Santorini

Santorini is not all about the caldera edge. The island slopes gently down to sea level on its eastern and southern sides and here you'll find dark-coloured beaches of volcanic sand at popular resorts such as Kamari and Perissa. Inland lie charming traditional villages such as Vourvoulos, to the north of Fira, and Megalohori and Pyrgos to its south. Pyrgos, in particular, is worth visiting and a good alternative to Oia, with shops, fabulous restaurants and stunning views. Ancient Thira, above Kamari, is a major, worthwhile site while the Minoan site of Akrotiri is truly gob-smacking.

DISAPPEARING ACT

No one knows what happened to the Minoan people of Akrotiri. No human remains have been found at the site. Some believe the people fled the city following the earthquake that took place two or three weeks before the volanic eruption and are buried elsewhere on the island, beneath tonnes of ash. Others speculate that they recognised signs of impending doom and fled by boat towards Crete.

◉ Sights

The best beaches are on the east and south coasts.

One of the main beaches is the long stretch at Perissa, a popular destination in summer. Perivolos and Agios Georgios, further south, are long stretches of black sand, pebbles and pumice stones. While they're backed by bars, tavernas, hotels and shops, they remain fairly relaxed. Red Beach, near Ancient Akrotiri, has impressive red cliffs and smooth, hand-sized pebbles submerged under clear water. It's a bit of a trek over uneven rock to reach it. Vlihada, also on the south coast, is a pleasant venue.

Kamari (population 1351) is 10km from Fira and is Santorini's best-developed resort. It has a long beach of black sand, with the rugged limestone cliffs of Cape Mesa Vouno framing its southern end and the site of Ancient Thira on its summit. The beachfront road is dense with restaurants and bars, and things get extremely busy in high season.

At times, Santorini's black-sand beaches become so hot that a sun lounge or mat is essential.

★ **Ancient Akrotiri**   ARCHAEOLOGICAL SITE
(☑ 22860 81366; admission €5; ⊙ 8am-3pm Tue-Sun) In 1967, excavations began at the site of Akrotiri. What they uncovered was phenomenal: an ancient Minoan city buried deep beneath volcanic ash from the catastrophic eruption of 1613 BC. Today, the site retains a strong sense of place and reverent awe. Housed within a cool, protective structure, wooden walkways allow you to pass through various parts of the city.

Peek inside three-storey buildings that survived, and see roads, drainage systems and stashes of pottery. The vibe of excitement still courses through the site, with continued excavations and discoveries.

Ancient Thira   ARCHAEOLOGICAL SITE
(admission €4; ⊙ 8am-2.30pm Tue-Sun) First settled by the Dorians in the 9th century BC, Ancient Thira consists of Hellenistic, Roman and Byzantine ruins and is an atmospheric and rewarding site to visit. The ruins include temples, houses with mosaics, an *agora* (market), a theatre and a gymnasium. There are splendid views from the site. From March to October Ancient Thira Tours (☑ 22860 32474; Kamari) runs a bus every hour from 9am until 2pm, except on Monday, from Kamari to the site. If driv-

ing, take the surfaced but narrow, winding road from Kamari for just over 1km. From Perissa, on the other side of the mountain, a hot hike up a dusty path on sometimes rocky, difficult ground takes a bit over an hour to the site.

Art Space   GALLERY
(☑ 22860 32774; www.artspace-santorini.com; Exo Gonia) This unmissable, atmospheric gallery is just outside Kamari, in Argyros Canava, one of the oldest wineries on the island. The atmospheric old wine caverns are hung with superb artworks, while sculptures transform lost corners and niches. The collection is curated by the owner and features some of Greece's finest modern artists. Winemaking is still in the owner's blood, and part of the complex is given over to producing some stellar vintages. A tasting of Vinsanto greatly enhances the whole experience.

🛏 Sleeping

The main concentration of rooms can be found in and around Kamari and Perissa.

Stelios Place   HOTEL $
(☑ 22860 81860; www.steliosplace.com; Kamari; d/tr/q €55//70/90; ᴘ ✱ ☏ ☀) This hotel has a great position set back from the main drag but barely a minute from the beach. Rooms sparkle with cleanliness, not character. Ask for a seaward balcony.

Narkissos Hotel   HOTEL $
(☑ 22860 34205; Kamari; s/d incl breakfast €45/55; ✱ ☏) A decent option with well-kept rooms, friendly service and a good breakfast to set you off. The Narkissos is at the southern end of town.

Aegean View Hotel   HOTEL $$
(☑ 22860 32790; www.aegeanview-santorini.com; Kamari; studios/apt/ste incl breakfast €130/150/170; ᴘ ✱ @ ☏ ☀) Tucked below the limestone cliffs high above Kamari, this outstanding hotel has spacious studios and apartments superbly laid out and with first-class facilities, including small kitchen areas. There's a lift to some rooms.

Hotel Drossos   HOTEL $$
(☑ 22860 81639; www.familydrossos.gr; Perissa; s/d/tr incl breakfast €102/112/132, apt €165; ᴘ ✱ @ ☏ ☀) Behind the simple facade of this fine hotel lies a lovely complex of rooms and studios with stylish decor and furnishings.

The same management has other decent hotels in the area.

Hotel Matina HOTEL $$
(☑ 22860 31491; www.hotel-matina.com; Kamari; s/d/tr/apt incl breakfast €108/116/144/172; ✴ @ 🛜 🛋) A very well-run, independent hotel, the Matina has spacious, brightly decorated rooms and is set back from the road in quiet grounds.

🍴 Eating

Most beaches have a range of tavernas and cafes.

Kasteli GREEK, ITALIAN $$
(Pyrgos; mains €9-20; ⊙ dinner) Near the centre of the village, over-the-top chandeliers are juxtaposed with traditional whitewashed walls. The food is tasty – chicken with wild cherry or seafood pizza – and made fresh. Sit on the rooftop for amazing views all the way to Oia.

Nichteri SEAFOOD $$
(☑ 22860 33480; www.nichteri.gr; Kamari; mains €10-15; ⊙ lunch & dinner) With a bit of class, a relaxed atmosphere and a unique menu, this restaurant has an edge on the endless stream of restaurants along Kamari's seafront. Try steamed mussels with wine and ginger sauce or salmon risotto with asparagus, fennel and lime.

Selene MODERN EUROPEAN $$$
(☑ 22860 22249; www.selene.gr; Pyrgos; mains €20-30) Meals here aren't just meals – they're a culinary experience. When a menu contains phrases like 'scented Jerusalem artichoke veloute', you know it's not going to be run-of-the-mill. The chef uses local products wherever possible and is continually introducing new dishes.

Building on its success over the past two decades, you'll now find a museum here along with a wine and meze bar, and you can sign up for full-day cooking classes. See the website for details.

ℹ Information

Lisos Tours (☑ 22860 33765; lisostours@san.forthnet.gr) is especially helpful and has an office on the main road into Kamari, and another just inland from the centre of the beach. It sells ferry tickets and can organise accommodation and car hire. All kinds of tours can be arranged and there's internet access and a bureau de change.

Thirasia & Volcanic Islets
Θηρασία & Ηφαιστειακές Νησίδες

Unspoilt Thirasia (population 268) was separated from Santorini by an eruption in 236 BC. The cliff-top *hora* (main town), Manolas, has tavernas and domatia. It's an attractive place, noticeably more relaxed and reflective than Fira could ever be. Thirasia is a stop on a couple of main ferry routes to and from Athinios a few times a week (€2, 20 minutes).

The unpopulated islets of Palia Kameni and Nea Kameni are still volcanically active and can be visited on various boat excursions from Fira Skala and Athinios. A day's excursion taking in Nea Kameni, the hot springs on Palia Kameni, Thirasia and Oia is about €28.

ANAFI ΑΝΑΦΗ
POP 273

Anafi is situated a mere 19km east of Santorini, a tiny island perched on a distant horizon somewhere with a slow-paced traditional lifestyle and striking Cycladic landscapes. There are few other visitors outside high summer, which is a big part of its charm.

ℹ Getting There & Away

Anafi may be out on a limb and you can still face a challenge getting there out of season, but in summer the island has reasonable connections to Piraeus, Santorini, Sikinos, Folegandros, Naxos, Paros and even Syros.

ℹ Getting Around

A small bus takes passengers from the port up to Hora. Caïques serve various beaches and nearby islands.

⊙ Sights

There are several lovely beaches near Agios Nikolaos. Palm-lined Klissidi, a 1.5km walk to the port, is the closest and most popular.

Anafi's main sight is the monastery of Moni Kalamiotissas, 9km by road from Hora or reached by a more appealing 6km walk along a path. It's in the extreme east of the island, near the meagre remains of a Sanctuary to Apollo and below the summit of the 470m Monastery Rock, which is

BOAT SERVICES FROM ANAFI

DESTINATION	TIME	FARE	FREQUENCY
Folegandros	4hr 20min	€12	5 weekly
Ios	3hr 25min	€9	5 weekly
Karpathos	6¼hr	€18	5 weekly
Kea (Tzia)	14hr 10min	€28	2 weekly
Kythnos	13hr 10min	€25	2 weekly
Naxos	5½hr	€14.30	5 weekly
Paros	6hr 35min–9hr	€17	3-4 weekly
Piraeus	11hr 20min	€31	3 weekly
Rhodes	12hr	€25	5 weekly
Santorini (Thira)	1½hr	€8	5 weekly
Sikinos	4hr	€10	4 weekly
Syros	9hr 35min	€19	4 weekly

the highest rock formation in the Mediterranean Sea, outstripping even Gibraltar. The walk to the monastery is a rewarding expedition, but it's a fairly tough trip in places and is a day's outing there and back. There is also a ruined Venetian *kastro* at **Kastelli**, east of Hora.

🛏 Sleeping

Many of the rooms in Hora have good views across Anafi's rolling hills to the sea and to the great summit of Monastery Rock.

Domatia owners prefer long stays in high season, so if you're only staying one night you should take whatever you can get (and book ahead).

Apollon Village Hotel   APARTMENT **$$**
(☑ 22860 28739; www.apollonvilla.gr; s/d/apt €70/95/115; ☺ May-Sep; ❄ @) Rising in tiers above Klissidi Beach, these lovely individual rooms and studios with glorious views are each named after a Greek god and remain outstanding value. The Blue Cafe-Bar is a cool adjunct to the hotel with homemade sweets and pastries.

Margarita's Rooms   PENSION **$$**
(☑ 22860 61237; anafi1@hotmail.com; s/d €50/60) Right by the beach and next to Margarita's cafe, these pleasant little rooms hark back to the Greek island life of quieter times.

Villa Galini   PENSION **$$**
(☑ 22869 61279; www.villagalini-anafi.com; d/ studio €60/75) Comfortable rooms in a quiet position below the main village. Each has a spacious, private verandah with sea views and studios have kitchenettes.

🍴 Eating

There are several tavernas in Hora, all of which are on the main street.

Liotrivi   TAVERNA **$**
(☑ 22860 61209; mains €4-9) Fresh fish is brought in from the family's boat while just about everything else, from eggs to vegetables and honey, comes from their garden.

Armenaki   TAVERNA **$**
(mains €5-6.50) Greek traditional food at this very traditional taverna is enhanced by an airy terrace and the pleasure of live bouzouki music on summer evenings.

Margarita's   TAVERNA **$**
(Klissidi; mains €6-10.50) A sunny little terrace overlooking the bay at Klissidi makes for a pleasant dining experience. The pork with mushrooms in a lemon sauce is particularly tasty. Breakfasts are €3 to €5.

ℹ Information

The island's port is Agios Nikolaos. From here, the main village, Hora, is a 10-minute bus ride up a winding road, or a 1km hike up a less winding but steep walkway. In summer a bus runs every two hours from about 9am to 11pm and usually meets boats. Hora's main pedestrian thoroughfare leads uphill from the first bus stop and has most of the domatia, restaurants and minimarkets.

There is an ATM in a kiosk just past a public telephone halfway along the harbour front, on the left.

There is a postal agency that opens occasionally, next to Panorama at the entrance to Hora.

You can buy ferry tickets at the **travel agency** (☑ 22860 61408) in Hora's main street next to Roussou minimarket or at an office on the harbour front before ferries are due.

SIKINOS ΣΙΚΙΝΟΣ

POP 238

It's tempting to keep Sikinos a secret. A stone's throw from Santorini, it's really worlds away. Quiet and remote, this is the place to come if you want to experience traditional island life at its least commercial. With a staggeringly stunning old town, a few worthwhile sights and terraced hills that sweep down to sandy beaches, Sikinos offers a true escape.

The main clusters of habitation are the port of Alopronia, and the linked inland villages of Hora and Kastro. The latter are reached by a 3.4km road winding up from the port. There's a post office at the entrance to Kastro, and an ATM in the central square of Kastro. The medical centre is next door to the ATM. In summer, you can hire scooters in Alopronia for around €20.

❶ Getting There & Around

The local bus meets all ferry arrivals and runs between Alopronia and Hora/Kastro (€1.60, 20 minutes) every half-hour in August, but less frequently at other times of the year. A timetable is sometimes posted near the minimarket. It's wise to be in good time at the departure point. Ferry

Sikinos

Sikinos map. Scale: 0–5 km / 0–2.5 miles (N)

AEGEAN SEA · Moni Zoödohou Pigis · Malta Beach · Kastro · Agios Georgios Beach · Manalis Wine Factory · Hora · ▲552m · Agios Nikolaos Beach · Moni Episkopis · Alopronia · Sikinos · ▲432m · Kalogeri · Karra Beach · Kardiotissa · Santorini (56km); Ios (65km)

Folegandros (19km); Naxos (30km); Paros (30km); Sifnos (55km); Milos (75km); Syros (85km); Piraeus (250km)

tickets can be bought at the port at **Koundouris Travel** (☑ 6936621946, 22860 51168). Note that outside of high season, boat services are skeletal.

Boat Services from Sikinos

DESTINATION	TIME	FARE	FREQUENCY
Anafi	4hr	€10	4 weekly
Folegandros	40min	€5	1-3 daily
Ios	20min	€5	1-4 daily
Kea (Tzia)	11hr	€24	2 weekly
Kythnos	10¼hr	€18	2 weekly
Naxos	2¼hr	€8	4 weekly
Paros*	3hr 10min	€15.10	1-2 daily
Piraeus	8hr 25min	€31	4 weekly
Santorini (Thira)	1¾hr	€8	4 weekly
Syros	7hr	€13	1-3 daily

*high-speed services

◉ Sights

A Venetian fortress that stood here in the 13th century gave **Kastro** its name. Today it is a truly charming, lived-in place, with winding alleyways between brilliant white houses. At its heart is the main square and the **Church of Pantanassa**. Check out the buildings surrounding the church which were homes to the town's weathy merchants; two-storey affairs with remnants of ornate stonework around the windows.

The shells of old windmills cling to the plunging cliffside on the northern side of Kastro. Also to the north, a flight of whitewashed steps leads to the once-fortified monastery of **Moni Zoödohou Pigis**, high above the town. Originally built as a women's monastery in 1690, this is where the villagers would hide during pirate attacks. You can still see the cells where the nuns lived along with their household items and farming tools.

Just west of Kastro, above steeply terraced fields and reached by another flight of steps, is the reclusive, beautiful **Hora**. Still home to 15 residents, it's a patchwork of derelict and well-tended houses and is definitely worth a wander.

From the saddle between Kastro and Hora, a surfaced road leads southwest to **Moni Episkopis** (⊙ 6.30pm-8.30pm) FREE. The remains here are believed to be those of a 3rd-century AD Roman mausoleum that was transformed into a church in the 7th century and a monastery 10 centuries later. From here you can climb to a little **church** and **ancient ruins** perched on a precipice to the south, from where the views are spectacular.

En route to Episkopis, it's worth stopping at the **Manalis Wine Factory** (22860 51281; www.manaliswinery.gr), where wine is produced using self-sustaining, traditional methods. You can easily spend a day here nibbling on snacks and sipping wine on the view-filled patio.

The beach at Alopronia is small but sandy with some shade and a children's playground. A narrow, dramatic bay with a small sandy patch, **Agios Nikolaos Beach** is a 20-minute walk through the countryside from the port. The water here is shallow and clear but rocky. To find it, follow signs to Dialiskari. Caïques (about €6) run to good beaches at **Agios Georgios**, **Malta** (which boasts ancient ruins on the hill above) and **Karra**. Buses run to these beaches from Alopronia in summer.

🛏️ Sleeping & Eating

You can opt to stay near the port and the beach, but Hora is a more atmospheric place to stay.

🏨 Alopronia

Lucas Rooms PENSION $

(22860 51076; www.sikinoslucas.gr; Alopronia; d/studios €55/85; ✱ 🛜) These rooms are lovingly decorated with bed frames and mirrors handcrafted from local branches or traditional stone floors and blossoms stencilled on the walls. Rooms are on the hillside, 500m from the port, while studios are on the far side of the bay from the ferry quay. All have sea-view balconies and plenty of peace.

Porto Sikinos HOTEL $$

(22860 51220; www.portosikinos.gr; Alopronia; s/d/tr incl breakfast €107/135/177; ✱ 🛜) Rooms here are traditional tile and marble affairs with waterside balconies. This is the closest thing to a standard hotel on Sikinos and slightly pricey because of it.

Lucas Taverna TAVERNA $$

(Alopronia; dishes €8-13) Prime location with a large deck built right on the beach, this is the place to come for well-prepared Greek standards without frills, including fish by the kilo.

🏨 Kastro

Stegadi APARTMENT $$

(22860 51271; www.stegadi.com; Kastro) Near the heart of Kastro, these four traditional apartments are each individually decorated with modern furnishings and splashes of vibrant colour. The balconies are small oases with views across the white village to the sea.

Persefoni's Rooms PENSION $$

(6974181331, 22860 51229; Kastro; s/d/tr €40/60/70) Clean, well-kept studios not far from the square and run by a welcoming family.

Anemelo CAFE $

(22860 51216; Kastro; mains €4-6; ⊙ breakfast, lunch & dinner) With rich colours, exposed rock and swinging lanterns, this is Kastro's most atmospheric place to grab a local tea, a beer or a simple crepe and salad lunch. Locals yabber at the tables over chess games or lounge over breakfast at the tables outside.

Hilaxtida CAFE $

(22860 51095; Kastro; snacks €3-6; ⊙ lunch & dinner) Head to this patio on the western edge of town to fill up on nibbles and a great big view over the Aegean.

Kzumataria GREEK $$

(22860 51065; Kastro; mains €8-13; ⊙ lunch & dinner; 🛜) Filling, fresh food, local wine and beaming service greets you on the main road into the village. Start with buns still warm from the oven and indulge in chicken stuffed with soft cheese, *galeus saganaki* with lemon, local sausage or platters heaped with mixed grills.

FOLEGANDROS
ΦΟΛΕΓΑΝΔΡΟΣ

POP 667

Folegandros lies on the southern edge of the Cyclades with the Sea of Crete sweeping away to its south. The island has a bewitching beauty that's amplified by its alluring cliff-top Hora, one of the most appealing villages in the Cyclades. Folegandros is barely 12km by 4km but shoulders a somewhat dark past. The remoteness and ruggedness of the island made it a place of exile

Folegandros

for political prisoners from Roman times to the 20th century, and as late as the military dictatorship of 1967–74. Today, the seductive charm of Folegandros has left its grim history behind.

Boats dock at the little harbour of Karavostasis, on the east coast. The only other settlement of any size is Ano Meria, 4km northwest of Hora. There are several good beaches, but be prepared for strenuous walking to reach some of them.

❶ Getting There & Away

Once poorly served by ferries, Folegandros (at least in summer) has good connections with Piraeus through the western Cyclades route. It even has connections to Santorini and as far as Amorgos in the high season.

❶ Getting Around

The local bus meets all ferry arrivals and takes passengers to Hora (€1.50). From Hora there are buses to the port one hour before all ferry departures. Buses from Hora run hourly in summer to Ano Meria (€1.80) and divert to Angali Beach (€2). The bus stop for Ano Meria is on the western edge of Hora.

There is a **taxi service** (☑ 6944693957, 22860 41048) on Folegandros. Fares to the port

are about €6 to €9, to Ano Meria €10 and to Angali Beach €9 to €13.

You can hire cars from a number of outlets in high season for about €60 per day, and motorbikes from about €25 per day. Rates can drop by half outside high season.

In summer, small boats ply between beaches.

Karavostasis Καραβοστάσις

POP 55

Folegandros' port is a sunny place with a pleasant pebble beach. Within a kilometre north and south of Karavostasis lies a series of beaches, all enjoyable and easily reached by short walks. In high season, boats leave Karavostasis for beaches further afield.

🛏 Sleeping & Eating

There are a couple of tavernas at the port serving fairly standard dishes, and a couple of good beachside bars. For enduring character, **Evangelos** is right on the beach and is the place for relaxed drinks, snacks and great conversation.

Aeolos Beach Hotel HOTEL **$$**
(☑ 22860 41205; www.aeolos-folegandros.gr; incl breakfast s €50, d €85-95; ❋ ⑤) Settle in just across from the beach in a peaceful garden.

BOAT SERVICES FROM FOLEGANDROS

DESTINATION	TIME	FARE	FREQUENCY
Amorgos*	3hr 20min	€59.60	1 daily
Anafi	4¾hr	€13	5 weekly
Ios	1hr 5min	€8	1-2 daily
Kea (Tzia)	10hr 10min	€22	2 weekly
Kimolos	1hr 20min	€7	5 weekly
Koufonisia*	3½hr	€56.20	1 daily
Kythnos	7¼hr	€19	2 weekly
Milos	2½hr	€9	5 weekly
Milos*	1¼hr	€29.60	4 weekly
Naxos	5hr 35min	€39.70	4 weekly
Piraeus	13hr	€32	4 weekly
Piraeus*	4hr	€54-59.60	1-3 daily
Paros	4-6hr	€10	5 weekly
Santorini (Thira)	2½hr	€9	1-3 daily
Santorini (Thira)*	30min	€29.50	1 daily
Serifos	7hr 40min	€19	5 weekly
Sifnos	4½hr	€17	1-3 daily
Sifnos*	1hr	€20	4 weekly
Sikinos	40min	€6	1-3 daily
Syros	5hr 10min	€15	4 weekly

*high-speed services

Rooms have a sea or mountain view and are each unique with varying degrees of character; check out a few if you can.

Anemi　　　　　　　　　　LUXURY HOTEL **$$$**
(☎22860 41610; www.anemihotels.com; incl breakfast d €290-370, ste €450-590; P ❄ @ ☲) Oh so modern and entirely luxurious, this is a place for pampering. Rooms are plush but sleek, brought to life by modern artwork used as headboards. The pool is a large sheet of blue that seems to stretch to the sea and some of the suites even have their own private pools.

Kalia Kardi　　　　　　　　　TAVERNA **$**
(mains €5-10; ☉breakfast, lunch & dinner) The 'Good Heart' is an excellent traditional taverna on the upper terrace of the harbour road. Try the tasty spinach pies or fish soup.

Hora (Folegandros) Χώρα (Φολέγανδρος)

POP 374

A major feature of Hora is its medieval *kastro* with its attractive main street flanked by traditional houses. The meandering main street winds happily from leafy square to leafy square. The village proper starts at Plateia Pounta; on its north side, it stands on the edge of a formidable cliff.

◉ Sights

Hora is a pleasure to wander through. The medieval **kastro**, a tangle of narrow streets spanned by low archways, dates from when Marco Sanudo ruled the island in the 13th century. The wooden balconies of the houses blaze with bougainvillea and hibiscus.

The extended village, outside the *kastro*, is just as attractive. From Plateia Pounta and the bus turnaround, a steep zigzag path leads up to the large church of the Virgin, **Panagia** (☉6pm-8pm), which sits perched on a dramatic cliff top above the town.

☞ Tours

Boat trips around the island (per adult/child including lunch €28/10) and to nearby Sikinos (per adult/child €22/11) can be booked through Diaplous Travel (p395) and Sottovento Tourism Office (p395).

🛏 Sleeping

In July and August most domatia and hotels will be full, so book well in advance.

Aegeo HOTEL **$$**
(☑ 22860 41468; www.aegeohotel.com; s/d/tr €80/95/120; ❄ @ 🛜) On the outskirts of town, these simple rooms are immaculate and bright, with wooden furnishings and private balconies.

Anemomylos Apartments HOTEL **$$$**
(☑ 22860 41309; www.anemomilosapartments. com; d with partial/full sea view €200-250, ste €300; ❄ @ 🛜 ⬚) A prime cliff-top location, with awesome views from the seaward-facing rooms of this stylish complex and its lovely terraces. Rooms are elegant and embellished with fine antiques. The pool is simply divine.

🍴 Eating

Pounta TAVERNA **$**
(☑ 22860 41063; Plateia Pounta; dishes €6-12; ⊙ breakfast, lunch & dinner) Relax in Pounta's beautiful garden over some truly tasty food. The restaurant has been in the family for years and the current Danish chef follows traditional recipes with a lighter touch. It's all served on her lovely handmade crockery. Definitely try the watermelon cake!

Eva's Garden GREEK **$$**
(mains €9-25) Eva's brings a modern flair to Folegandros cuisine. Starters include fava-bean purée with onion and parsley, while mains include crayfish and saffron risotto and pork fillet in smoked cheese sauce with potato purée. The wine list includes Argiros vintages from Santorini. Keep right beyond Plateia Kontarini.

Il Caffe dei Viaggiatori ITALIAN **$$**
(☑ 22860 41444; mains €8-15) On the small verandah of a traditional Venetian home on the main square, Italians whip up home-made pasta, focaccia and pizza. Add some Italian cured meats and certainly accompany it with limoncello (also homemade!).

🍷 Drinking & Nightlife

Folegandros has some stylish cafe-bars such as **Caffé de Viaggiatori**, next door to Sottovento Tourism Office and offering Italian wines and finger food. Deeper into Hora is **To Mikro**, a good place for coffee, crepes and cakes by day and cocktails at night.

At Hora's very own 'West End' is a clutch of colourful music bars playing everything from lounge music to rock, reggae and Greek disco.

ℹ Information

Folegandros does not have an official tourism office. A good source of information is the Sottovento Tourism Office and its website.

There's an ATM on the far side of Plateia Dounavi, next to the community offices. The post office is on the port road, 200m downhill from the bus turnaround.

Diaplous Travel (☑ 22860 41158; www. diaploustravel.gr; Plateia Pounta) Helpful and efficient agency – sells ferry tickets, exchanges money and arranges boat trips. Internet access available. There is also an office at Karavostasis.

Maraki Travel (☑ 22860 41273; fax 22860 41149; Plateia Dounavi; ⊙ 10.30am-noon & 5-9pm) Sells ferry tickets and exchanges money. There is also an office at Karavostasis.

Medical Centre (☑ 22860 41222; Plateia Pounta)

Police Station (☑ 22860 41249) Straight on from Plateia Maraki.

Sottovento Tourism Office (☑ 22860 41444; www.folegandrosisland.com) On Plateia Pounta; doubles as the Italian consulate and is very helpful on all tourism matters, including accommodation, international and domestic flights, and boat trips.

Ano Meria   Ανω Μεριά
POP 293

The settlement of Ano Meria is a scattered community of small farms and dwellings that stretches for several kilometres. This is traditional Folegandros where tourism makes no intrusive mark and life happily wanders off sideways.

The **folklore museum** (admission €1.50; ⊙ 5pm-8pm) is on the eastern outskirts of the village. Ask the bus driver to drop you off nearby.

There are a couple of colourful traditional tavernas in Ano Meria, including **I Synantisi** (☑ 22860 41208; dishes €4-8), also known as Maria's, and **Mimi's** (☑ 22860 41377; dishes €4). The speciality is *pastitsio* (lamb with macaroni and tomatoes).

Around Folegandros

For **Livadi Beach**, 1.2km southeast of Karavostasis, take the 'bypass' road just past the Anemi Hotel and follow it around the coast.

SANCTUARIES OF THE FOREIGN GODS

Delos was a place of worship for many beyond the Greeks, and these temples are concentrated in the area called the **Sanctuaries of the Foreign Gods**. At the **Shrine to the Samothracian Great Gods**, people worshipped the Kabeiroi (twins Dardanos and Aeton). At the **Sanctuary of the Syrian Gods** there are remains of a **theatre** used for mystical rites (some say ritual orgies). The **Shrine to the Egyptian Gods** honoured deities including Serapis and Isis.

Katergo Beach is on the southeastern tip of the island and is best reached by boat from Karavostasis.

The sandy and pebbled **Angali** beach, opposite Hora, is a popular spot. There are some rooms here and reasonable tavernas.

About 750m west of Angali over the hill along a footpath is **Agios Nikolaos**, a clothes-optional beach. A number of beaches can be reached from where the road ends beyond Ano Meria. **Livadaki Beach** is a 1.5km hike from the bus stop near the church of Agios Andreas at Ano Meria. Boats connect these west-coast beaches in high season. **Agios Georgios Beach** is north of Ano Meria and requires another demanding walk. Have tough footwear, sun protection and, because most beaches have no shops or tavernas, make sure you take food and water.

In July and August, weather permitting, excursion boats make separate round trips from Karavostasis to Katergo (€8), from Angali to Agios Nikolaos (€4), and from Angali to Livadaki Beach (€8), every half-hour between 11am and 7pm.

DELOS   ΔΗΛΟΣ

The Cyclades fulfil their collective name (*kyklos* – circle) by encircling the sacred island of **Delos** (☑ 22890 22259; museum & sites adult/concession €5/3; ⊙ 8.30am-3pm Tue-Sun). The mythical birthplace of twins Apollo and Artemis, splendid Ancient Delos was a shrine turned sacred treasury and commercial centre. This Unesco World Heritage Site is one of the most important archaeological sites in Greece. Cast your imagination wide to transform this sprawling ruin into the magnificent city it once was.

While many significant finds from Delos are in the National Archaeological Museum in Athens, the site's museum retains an interesting collection, including lions from the Terrace of the Lions (those on the terrace itself are plaster-cast replicas).

The island, just 5km long and 1300m wide, has no permanent population, so offers a soothing contrast to Mykonos (though in highest summer many visitors throng to the island). Overnight stays are forbidden and boat schedules allow a maximum of four hours at Delos. Bring water and food; wear a hat, sunscreen and walking shoes.

The ticket office sells detailed Delos guidebooks, and Mykonos bookshops sell some with reconstructions which are helpful for picturing the ruins as they were in their heyday.

History

Delos won early acclaim as the mythical birthplace of the twins Apollo and Artemis and was first inhabited in the 3rd millennium BC. From the 8th century BC it became a shrine to Apollo, and the oldest temples on the island date from this era. The dominant Athenians had full control of Delos – and thus the Aegean – by the 5th century BC.

In 478 BC Athens established an alliance known as the Delian League, which maintained its treasury on Delos. A cynical decree ensured that no one could be born or die on Delos, thus strengthening Athens' control over the island by expelling the native population.

Delos reached the height of its power in Hellenistic times, becoming one of the three most important religious centres in Greece and a flourishing centre of commerce. Many of its inhabitants were wealthy merchants, mariners and bankers from as far away as Egypt and Syria. They built temples to their homeland gods, but Apollo remained the principal deity.

The Romans made Delos a duty-free port in 167 BC. This brought even greater prosperity, due largely to a lucrative slave market that sold up to 10,000 people a day. During the following century, as ancient religions diminished and trade routes shifted, Delos began a long decline. By the 3rd century AD there was only a small Christian settlement on the island, and in the

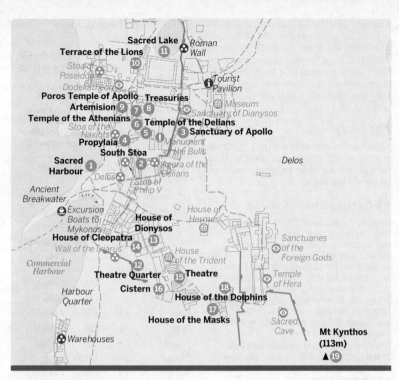

Site Tour
Ancient Delos

LENGTH THREE HOURS

Excursion boats dock on a bay south of the tranquil **1 Sacred Harbour**. The narrow spit dividing the two bays was man-made.

Pass the ruins of the **2 South Stoa**, built after the mid-3rd century BC with 28 Doric columns, and used to house shops and workshops, to reach the **3 Sanctuary of Apollo**, northeast of the harbour. The Sacred Way entered the complex through the **4 Propylaia**, to a compound of magnificent temples and treasuries. Three were dedicated to Apollo: **5 Temple of the Delians** (or Great Temple), **6 Temple of the Athenians** and **7 Poros Temple of Apollo**. The Sanctuary also housed the Classical **8 treasuries** and the **9 Artemision**, a sanctuary of Artemis.

North of the Sanctuary is the much-photographed **10 Terrace of the Lions**. These marble beasts (originally thought to number 16) were offerings from the people of Naxos, presented to Delos in the 7th century

BC to guard the sacred area. To the northeast, the **11 Sacred Lake** (drained in 1925 to prevent malarial mosquito-breeding) is where Leto gave birth to Apollo and Artemis.

Head south to the **12 Theatre Quarter**, where the wealthiest inhabitants lived. These houses had peristyle courtyards, with intricate, colourful mosaics. The most lavish were the **13 House of Dionysos**, named after a mosaic depicting the wine god riding a panther, and the **14 House of Cleopatra**. The **15 theatre** dates from 300 BC; its large **16 cistern** supplied much of the town's water.

The **17 House of the Masks** also has a mosaic of Dionysos resplendently astride a panther between two centaurs. The extraordinary mosaic at the **18 House of the Dolphins** incorporates lions, griffins and dolphins.

19 Mt Kynthos (113m) rises to the southeast of the harbour. It's worth the steep climb: on clear days there are terrific views of the encircling islands. It also has monuments such as the Sanctuaries of Zeus Kynthios and Athena Kynthia and the Temple of Hera.

following centuries the ancient site was a hideout for pirates and looted of many of its antiquities. It was not until the Renaissance that its antiquarian value was recognised. Every now and then fresh discoveries are unearthed: in recent years a gold workshop was uncovered alongside the Terrace of the Lions.

☞ Tours

Mykonos Accommodation Centre (p342) organises multilingual guided tours to Delos (adult/child €40/30) including boat, entrance fee and guide.

❶ Getting There & Away

Boats for Delos (return €17, 30 minutes) leave Hora (Mykonos) three times daily in high season starting at about 9am, with the last outward boat about 11am. Boats return between 12.30pm and 1pm. Departure/return times are posted at the ticket **kiosk** at the foot of the jetty at the south end of the old harbour. When buying tickets, establish which boat you can return on. There are fewer boats outside July and August. No boats go Mondays, when the site is closed.

In Hora buy tickets at the kiosk or at **Delia Travel** (☎ 22890 22322; www.mykonos-delia. com; Akti Kambani), Sea & Sky or Mykonos Accommodation Centre.

MILOS ΜΗΛΟΣ

POP 4960

Volcanic Milos arches around a central caldera and is ringed with dramatic coastal landscapes of colourful and surreal rock formations. The island's most celebrated export, the iconic *Venus de Milo*, is far away in the Louvre but hot springs, the most beaches of any Cycladic island and a series of quaint villages populated by friendly people add to its current, compelling, attractions.

Capital Plaka and stunning Klima are just two of the little villages worth visiting and Filakopi, an ancient Minoan city in the island's northeast, was one of the earliest settlements in the Cyclades.

The island has a fascinating history of mineral extraction dating from the Neolithic period when obsidian was exported to the Minoan world of Crete. Today Milos is the biggest bentonite and perlite centre in the EU.

Visit www.mymilos.gr and www.milos.gr for more island information.

❶ Getting There & Away

AIR

Milos Airport (MLO; ☎ 22870 22381) Olympic Air has two flights daily to/from Athens (€65, 40 minutes).

BOAT

Milos is on the same Western Cyclades ferry routes as Serifos. Buy tickets at **Riva Travel** (☎ 22870 24024; www.rivatravel.gr) or **Milos Travel** (☎ 22870 22000; www.milostravel.gr) in Adamas.

Port Authority (☎ 22870 22100) On the waterfront.

DESTINATION	TIME	FARE	FREQUENCY
Amorgos*	3½hr	€65	1 daily
Folegandros*	1¼hr	€27.50	4 weekly
Ios*	3hr	€42	5-6 weekly
Iraklio	9hr 25min	€22	3 weekly
Kimolos	1hr	€5	3 weekly
Mykonos	5hr	€65	1 daily
Naxos	4½hr	€53.50	4 weekly
Paros	6hr	€14	2 weekly
Piraeus	8hr	€33	1-2 daily
Piraeus*	3-4hr	€57.50	1 daily
Santorini (Thira)	4hr	€18	2 weekly
Santorini (Thira)*	2hr	€42	1 daily
Sifnos	2½hr	€7	1-2 daily
Sifnos*	35min	€15.50	1 daily
Serifos	3hr	€8	1-2 daily
Serifos*	1½hr	€16	1 daily
Syros	5hr	€14	4 weekly

*high-speed services

❶ Getting Around

No buses serve the airport. Taxis to Adamas cost about €11, plus €0.30 per suitcase.

Buses leave Adamas for Plaka and Trypiti about every hour. Buses run to Pollonia (four Monday to Saturday, two in low season), Paleohori (three daily), Provatas (three daily) and Achivadolimni (Milos) Camping, east of Adamas (three daily). All fares are €1.60.

Hire cars, motorcycles and mopeds along the waterfront, at Riva Travel (p398), or at **Europcar** (☎ 22870 41473; www.milosrent.gr) at the airport or Pollonia. **Giourgas Rent a Car** (☎ 6937757066, 22870 22352; www.milos-giourgas.gr), 250m from the port, will pick up.

Taxis (☑ 6945689966, 6942590951, Adamas 22870 22219) from Adamas to Plaka are €9 and to Pollonia about €13; add €1 at night.

Adamas   Αδάμας

POP 1347

Fishermen sell their wares in the early morning at the lively port of Adamas (also Adamantas). Loaded with accommodation, shops and general services, the modern village also has a diverting waterfront scene.

◉ Sights

Milos Mining Museum   MUSEUM
(☑ 22870 22481; www.milosminingmuseum.gr; adult/concession €3/1.50; ⊙ 10am-2pm & 5.30-9.30pm Jun-Sep, reduced hours in low season) This excellent small museum details Milos' mining history, about 600m east of the ferry quay.

Ecclesiastical Museum of Milos   MUSEUM
(☑ 22870 23956; www.ecclesiasticalmuseum.org; ⊙ 9.15am-1.15pm & 6.15-10.15pm) FREE Tucked in where the waterfront road turns inland, this intriguing collection in the Church of the Holy Trinity boasts fine icons and artefacts.

⊨ Sleeping

In summer, lists of available domatia are distributed at the quay-side tourist office.

Terry's Rooms   APARTMENT $
(☑ 22870 22640; http://terrysmilostravel.com; d €40, apt €60-75; ✳ 🛜) Lovely rooms and apartments above the harbour.

Hotel Delfini   HOTEL $
(☑ 22870 22001; www.delfinimilos.gr; s/d/tr €30/40/55; ⊙ Apr-Oct; ✳ @ 🛜) A comfortable hotel with a lovely terrace and warm ambience. West of the quay behind the Lagada Beach Hotel, which unfortunately blocks the view.

Studios Helios   APARTMENT $$
(☑ 22870 22258; www.milos-island.gr; studio €70; ⊙ May-Oct; ✳) Rising high above the port, these stylish, self-catering studios are neat as a pin, and have sea-view balconies.

✖ Eating & Drinking

Music bars rock out just above the port during July and August. Stylish **Akri** (☑ 22870 22064) has a splendid terrace overlooking the port.

O Hamos   TAVERNA $
(☑ 22870 21672; www.ohamos-milos.gr; mains €6-11; ⊙ lunch & dinner Easter-Oct; 🛜) Eat seafood, salads and creative taverna fare southwest of town, across the road from Papakinou Beach.

Flisvos   TAVERNA $
(☑ 22870 22275; dishes €7-9; ⊙ lunch & dinner; 🛜) Choose from fish by the kilogram or Greek specialities, such as lamb in lemon sauce and tasty cheese and mushroom pies, at this busy waterfront taverna.

Barko   MEZEDHES $
(☑ 22870 22660; dishes €5-13; ⊙ lunch & dinner) This classic *mezedhopoleio* on the road to Plaka, near the outskirts of town, serves local dishes such as Milos cheese pie and octopus in wine.

❶ Information

The port has free wi-fi.

Municipal Tourist Office (☑ 22870 22445; ⊙ 9am-midnight mid-Jun–mid-Sep) Opposite the quay.

Police Station (☑ 22870 21378) On the main square, next to the bus stop.

Terry's Travel Services (☑ 22870 22640; www.terrysmilostravel.com) Arranges accommodation, car hire, kayaking, sailing, diving and more. Left of the ferry quay, and just past bend in the road, go right up a lane.

Plaka & Trypiti   Πλάκα & Τρυπητή

Supercharming Plaka (population 877), 5km uphill from Adamas, embodies the Cycladic ideal with its white houses and labyrinthine lanes perching along the edge of an escarpment. Plaka was built on the site of Ancient Milos, which was destroyed by the Athenians and rebuilt by the Romans. It meanders straight into the settlement to the south, Trypiti (population 489), and they both rise above several villages converging to the southwest. Plaka's **main church courtyard** has spectacular views and gets packed out for sunset in high season.

◉ Sights & Activities

Archaeology Museum   MUSEUM
(☑ 22870 28026; Plaka; adult/child €3/free; ⊙ 8am-3pm Tue-Sun Jun-Sep, by appointment Oct-May) This handsome old building contains some riveting exhibits, including a plaster

(sidebar) CYCLADES ADAMAS

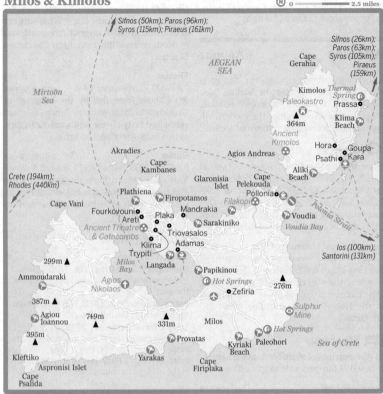

cast of *Venus de Milo* made by Louvre craftsmen. A perky little herd of tiny bull figurines dates from the Late Cycladic period.

Milos Folk and History Museum MUSEUM
(☑ 22870 21292; Plaka; adult/child €3/1.50; ☺ 10am-2pm Tue-Sat Jun-Aug, to 1pm Tue-Sun Sep) Peruse traditional costumes, woven goods and household artefacts in a series of traditionally furnished rooms.

Frankish Kastro FORT
FREE Signs mark the path climbing to the hilltop fortress, built on the ancient acropolis and offering panoramic views of the island. The 13th-century church, **Thalassitras**, lies inside the walls.

Catacombs RUIN
(☑ 22870 21625; adult/child €3/2; ☺ 8.30am-2pm Tue-Sun) Greece's only Christian catacombs, the Roman ruins near Trypiti, date from the 1st century and were the burial site for early

believers. Get off the Trypiti bus at the T-junction with a signpost indicating the way.

Walks WALKING
Off the road to the Catacombs, a dirt track leads to the somehow thrilling spot where a farmer found the **Venus de Milo** (a 4th-century BC statue of Aphrodite) in 1820; it's marked by a sign. A bit further along, the well-preserved **Roman theatre** hosts the **Milos Festival** each summer, and footpaths lead down to Klima or onto the promontory with ancient stone walls and two small churches.

🛏 Sleeping

Studios Betty APARTMENT **$**
(☑ 22870 21538; www.studiosbetty-milos.com; Plaka; d €35-50, tr €40-60; ❋ 🐾) In the more expensive studios you get sunset views as glorious as Santorini's from this welcoming family house at Plaka's cliff edge.

Archondoula Studios
APARTMENT $$

(☑22870 23820; www.archondoula-studios.gr; Plaka; studio/apt €70/90; ☺Mar-Nov; ❋☎) Cheerful Stavros runs efficient, sleek studios which sleep two to four. Take in spectacular caldera and sunset views from the top floor.

Mimallis
APARTMENT $$

(☑6972808758, 22870 21094; www.mimallis.gr; Plaka & Klima; apt from €80; ☺Apr-Oct; ❋☎) Three small houses in Plaka, and one in precious Klima, are each different, comfortable and packed with amenities.

Windmill of Karamitsos
APARTMENT $$

(☑6945568086, 22870 21921; www.milos-island. gr/windmill/karamitsos; Trypiti; windmill €150; ☺Apr-Oct; ℗) Bed down in a unique converted windmill that sleeps four. On a hilltop with panoramic views.

✖ Eating

★Archondoula
MEZEDHES $

(☑22870 21384; Plaka; dishes €4-12; ☺lunch & dinner; ☎✎) The whole cheerful family is involved at this top-notch *mezedhopoleio*. Classic Greek dishes have a creative flare and range from fresh salads to beef with honey sauce. Vegetarians will love the grilled vegetables with *manouri* (soft cheese from the north) or the heavenly eggplant salad.

Ergina
TAVERNA $$

(☑22870 22524; Trypiti; mains €8-12; ☺lunch & dinner Jun-Sep) Friendly owners prepare fantastic Greek eats with sweeping views to match.

Pollonia   Πολλώνια

Pollonia, on the north coast, is a low-key fishing village with azure waters that transforms into a summer resort. Surrounded by beaches it is a good warm-weather base and is also the jumping-off point for Kimolos. It's sometimes mapped as Apollonia.

🛏 Sleeping & Eating

Pollonia has loads of domatia, excellent seafood tavernas and portside cafes.

Nefeli Sunset Studios
PENSION, APARTMENT $$

(☑22870 41466; www.milos-nefelistudios.gr; d/ studio/ste €80/130/160; ℗❋☎) Whitewashed cubes combine modern design with traditional touches, bay-front on the northwest edge of the village.

★Salt
BOUTIQUE HOTEL $$$

(☑22870 41110; www.salt-milos.com; d/ste from €130/150; ℗❋☎) Sparklingly minimal with all the luxuries and views to the sea. Suites have Jacuzzis.

★Armenaki
SEAFOOD $$

(☑22870 41061; www.armenaki.gr; dishes €4-12, fish by kg; ☺lunch & dinner Apr-Oct) Seafood is cooked to perfection and starters are accompanied by homemade sourdough bread with organic olive oil. The emphasis is on organics and local products, and the sommelier pairs everything with excellent wine.

Gialos
SEAFOOD $$

(☑22870 41208; mains €7-15; ☺lunch & dinner Easter-Oct; ☎) Watch port life while digging into fresh seafood and yummy pastas.

Around Milos

Milos and its offshore islets are rimmed by splendid beaches in different coloured sands and stone. Rent wheels or hire a boat to compare! Plathiena is a fine sandy beach north of Plaka, and on the way you can visit fishing villages Areti and Fourkovouni. Sarakiniko is a must, with its snow-white rock formations and natural terraces.

On the south coast, small, golden-sanded Provatas feels remote but has a couple of tavernas. Kyriaki is backed by otherworldy grey, rose and rust-coloured hills and has soft, grey sand. The long taupe arch of Paleohori is backed by banded cliffs and has hot springs.

> **DON'T MISS**
>
> ### KLIMA
>
> Tiny Klima clings to the beach-front cliff face below Trypiti. It is the best example of Milos' *syrmata*, the traditional fishermen's encampments, where the downstairs, with brightly painted doors, are used for rough-weather boat storage, and the upstairs for family life. In Klima, which was orignally the port of Ancient Milos, the homes, most still in use today, are incorporated into the rocks. Be sure to walk all the way around the southern point to find the hidden dock.

◉ Sights & Activities

Filakopi
RUIN

(☉8am-3pm) **FREE** This ancient Minoan city in the island's northeast was one of the earliest settlements in the Cyclades. Now it's not much more than rubble, but the seaside setting is spectacular with cavelike rock formations all around.

Milos Diving Center
DIVING

(☑22870 41296; www.milosdiving.gr) Dives (from €35) and courses, based at Pollonia.

Kayak Milos
KAYAKING

(☑22870 23597; www.seakayakgreece.com) Organises day trips (€65 per person) and longer expeditions.

☞ Tours

Milos Cruises
BOAT TOURS

Cruise on wooden-hulled **Captain Yiangos** (☑6944375799; cruise €30; ☉May-Sep) departing daily at 9am, stopping at beaches around the island and Kimolos for lunch. Buy tickets on the waterfront. **Thalassitra** (☑6947276590, 22870 23570; www.thalassitra. com) offers sailboat tours.

🛏 Sleeping & Eating

Achivadolimni (Milos)

Camping
CAMPGROUND $

(☑22870 31410; www.miloscamping.gr; Achivadolimni; camp sites per couple €17, bungalows €45-74; **P** 🛜 ☒) Excellent facilities include a restaurant, bar and bike hire. It's 4.5km east of Adamas. Does pick-ups.

Scirocco
TAVERNA $

(☑22870 31201; Paleohori Beach; mains €7-12; ☉lunch & dinner Apr-Oct; **P** 🛜) Sky-blue-and-white eatery smack-bang on the shore.

KIMOLOS
ΚΙΜΩΛΟΣ

POP 920

Exquisite Kimolos, perched off the northeast tip of Milos, feels like a step back in time. Barely a trickle of visitors get the chance to take in its fantastical sienna-coloured walls hand-hewn of volcanic stones, or its sparkling bays.

The boat docks at **Psathi**, from where it's 1.5km to the pretty capital, **Hora**. Wander the maze of streets to reach Hora's central cafes and a medieval **kastro**. The kastro's semi-crumbling labyrinth holds the entirely intact Church of the Nativity and the fascinating **Folk and Maritime Museum of Kimolos** (☑22870 51118).

Caïques from Psathi buzz out to **beaches**. Use four-wheel drive to reach the fortress of **Paleokastro** on the 364m-high cliff in the island's centre.

Domatia (€35/55 per single/double), tavernas, cafes and bars pepper Hora and Psathi. Domatia owners meet ferries. **Meltemi Rooms** (☑22870 51360; http://kimolos-meltemi. gr; d incl breakfast €45; ❄🛜), on the edge of Hora, has sea views and one room with a kitchen. The **Windmill Hotel** (☑22870 51554; www.kimoloshotel.com; d/q from €95/160) offers boutique living in a renovated windmill above Psathi.

The taverna **To Kyma** (☑22870 51001; dishes €5-14; ☉lunch & dinner), on the beach at Psathi, is excellent for seafood and locally sourced vegetarian dishes. **H Kali Kardia** (Vohoris; ☑22870 51495; mains €4.50-6.50; ☉lunch & dinner) in Hora dishes up simple, tasty eats.

There's an ATM at the port and one petrol station near Psathi. Find island information at www.kimolos.gr.

❶ Getting There & Away

Some Milos long-distance ferries stop at Kimolos. **Kimolos Travel** (☑22870 51219; Hora) sells tickets. A small **car ferry** (☑6948308758, 22870 51184; www.kimolos-link.gr; person/car €2/8.30; ☉30 minutes) connects Pollonia, Milos with Psathi, Kimolos seven times daily in high season, three times in low.

❶ Getting Around

Buses connect Psathi and Hora in high season only.

Phone for a **taxi** (☑6945464093).

SIFNOS
ΣΙΦΝΟΣ

POP 2570

Sifnos has an exquisite dreamlike quality. A string of three whitewashed villages, anchored by the capital Apollonia, sit like pearls along the crest of the island. The changing light kisses the landscape and as you explore the flanking slopes of the central mountains you'll discover abundant terraced olive groves, almond trees, oleander and aromatic herbs. Each of the island's bays harbours a spectrum of aqua waters, and offers breathtaking vistas.

Unspoiled footpaths link villages, such as the one encircling tiny hilltop Kastro. Get Anavasi map series *Topo 25/10.25 Aegean Cyclades/Sifnos* for footpath details.

During the Archaic period (from about the 8th century BC), Sifnos was enriched by its gold and silver deposits, but by the 5th century BC the mines were exhausted. Sifnos is now known for pottery, basket weaving and cookery. The island hibernates October to Easter (most hotels and restaurants close) and in high season it attracts the chic set (book ahead). Visit www.sifnos.gr for island information.

ℹ Getting There & Away

Sifnos is on the Piraeus–Western Cyclades ferry route with summer connections to Serifos, Milos, Folegandros, Santorini and Amorgos. NEL Lines serves Paros in high season only. Get tickets at **Xidis Travel** (☑ Apollonia 22840 32373, Kamares 22840 31895; www.xidis.com.gr) or the tourist office (p404).

Boat Services from Sifnos

DESTINA-TION	DURATION	FARE	FREQUENCY
Andros	7hr	€14	1 weekly
Folegan-dros	2hr	€7	1 weekly
Kimolos	1hr	€7	5 weekly
Milos	2½hr	€7	1-2 daily
Milos*	35min	€15.50	1 daily
Paros	3½hr	€5	2 weekly
Piraeus	5¼hr	€31	2 daily
Piraeus*	2hr 40min	€39-48	1-2 daily
Santorini (Thira)	7hr 20min	€13.50	2 weekly
Serifos	50min	€7	1-2 daily
Serifos*	25min	€14	1-2 daily
Syros	5hr 20min	€10	2 weekly

*high-speed services

ℹ Getting Around

Frequent buses connect Kamares with Apollonia (€1.60); some continue to Artemonas, Kastro, Vathy, Faros and Platys Gialos.

Car rental costs about €40 per day.

Taxis (☑ 22840 31347) hover around the port and Apollonia's main junction. Fares from Kamares: Apollonia €7, Platys Gialos €16, Vathy €18.

Apollo Rent a Car (☑ 22840 33333; www.automotoapollo.gr; Apollonia)

Sifnos

Moto Car Rental (☑ 22840 33791; www.protomotocar.gr; Kamares)

Kamares   Καμάρες

POP 245

The port of Kamares always seems to have a holiday atmosphere with its large beach and waterfront cafes, tavernas and shops. But the real action is up near Apollonia or at more idyllic bays.

🛏 Sleeping & Eating

Domatia owners rarely meet boats; book ahead in high season.

Camping Makis   CAMPGROUND $
(☑ 6945946339, 22840 32366; www.makiscamping.gr; camp sites per adult/child €7/4, apt €70-210; ☉ Apr-Nov; 🅿 ❇ 🛜) Pitch your tent behind the beach in a basic lot with attractive olive trees. There are well-equipped apartments, an outdoor cafe, barbecue, communal kitchen, minimarket and laundry.

Simeon   APARTMENT $
(☑ 22840 31652; www.simeon-sifnos.gr; d/tr €50/60, apt €95; ☉ Apr-Oct; ❇ 🛜) High above the port, the front balconies on four- to five-person apartments have stunning views across the bay to soaring mountains beyond.

Stavros Hotel
HOTEL $

(✉ 22840 33383; www.sifnostravel.com; s/d/tr
€45/55/50; ❄ 🛜) Main street's Stavros has
bright and comfy rooms with sea views. Arranges car hire. The same family owns Hotel Kamari (✉ 22840 33383; d/tr €50/55) on
the outskirts of town.

Hotel Afroditi
PENSION $$

(✉ 22840 31704; www.hotel-afroditi.gr; s/d/tr incl
breakfast €70/91/114; P ❄ 🛜) The welcoming,
family-run Afroditi has decent-sized rooms
across the road from the beach. Breakfast
on the verandah is a definite plus. There are
sea views to the front and mountain views
to the rear.

Café Stavros
CAFE $

(snacks €2.50-5.50) Overlooking the water
halfway along the main street and ideal for
people-watching, it does filling breakfasts
(€4.50 to €10).

ℹ️ Information

Municipal Tourist Office (✉ 22840 31975,
22840 31977; www.sifnos.gr) Very helpful with
ferry tickets, accommodation and bus time-
tables. Opposite the bus stop. Opening times
vary with boat arrivals. Luggage storage per
item €1.

Apollonia
Απολλωνία

POP 1070

Apollonia comes alive in high season with
its parade of well-dressed Athenians strut-
ting their stuff along the Steno (Odos
Prokou, known as Steno because of its nar-
rowness). Cafes, bars, clubs, shops and
eateries buzz with life.

Quirky Museum of Popular Art (✉ 22840
31341; admission €1; ⊙ 7-11pm, but hours are er-
ratic) at the central junction contains a fun
confusion of old costumes, textiles and
photographs.

The main vehicular road cuts right
through the centre of town, but park at the
large free car park downhill from the vil-
lage and walk up and into the warren of
streets.

🛏️ Sleeping & Eating

Mrs Dina Rooms
PENSION $

(✉ 6945513318, 22840 31125; d/tr/q €40/50/55;
❄) This pleasant little complex of rooms
bedecked with flowers has a cheerful atmos-
phere and sits above the road 200m south

towards Vathy with views across to Kastro.
Kitchen available.

Patriarca
BOUTIQUE HOTEL $$

(✉ 22840 32400; www.patriarca.gr; d €60-120;
⊙ Jun-Sep) Promenade straight down the
Steno to this design hotel where rooms may
be small, but they sure are tricked out.

Kafeneion O Drakakis
CAFE $

(✉ 22840 31233; mains €9-11; ⊙ Mar-Oct; 🛜)
This old-school *kafeneio* (coffee house)
sits smack in the centre of the Steno, with
Greek music emanating from its quaint interior. Sit out front under bougainvillea sipping coffee or tucking into excellent daily
specials.

Apostoli to Koutouki
TAVERNA $$

(✉ 22840 33186; mains €9-14; ⊙ lunch & dinner
Easter-Sep) Signature dishes such as beef
baked in a clay pot with tomatoes, auber-
gine, cheese and wine complement fish
by the kilo at this long-established Steno
favourite.

🍷 Drinking

Among the array of bars from which to see
and be seen on the Steno, is Batsi, with soft
mood lighting and delicious drinks.

🛍️ Shopping

Browse your heart away along the Steno.
Favourites include Oasis for women's sum-
mer clothes, and the Kykladon Horos, a
cool complex of shops, restaurants and bars.

Ano Petali & Artemonas

After crossing the main road from Apollon-
ia, the string of houses continues north into
Ano Petali and reaches Artemonas with its
grand mansions. Walk the pedestrian-only
streets to take it all in.

Artemonas has a central square off the
winding main road as well, with a bus stop,
municipal wi-fi and a great little bakery
specialising in *kritsinia* (sesame-coated
breadsticks).

🛏️ Sleeping & Eating

Hotel Artemon
HOTEL $

(✉ 22840 31303; www.hotel-artemon.com; Arte-
monas; s/d/tr €35/40/60; P ❄ 🛜) Large, basic
hotel but front rooms overlook the main
road.

★ Petali Village Hotel HOTEL **$$**
(☎ 22840 33024; www.petalihotel.gr; Ano Petali; d incl breakfast from €120; ❋ 🐾 ☎) Suspended on a walking street between Apollonia and Artemonas, this terraced array of rooms has sweeping views to Kastro and the sea. They can pick up from the port.

Smaragdi BOUTIQUE HOTEL **$$**
(☎ 22840 33901; www.smaragdi.gr; Artemonas; s/d/tr/q from €84/95/110/145; ❋ 🐾) Fronted by a broad verandah as you enter Artemonas' main square, Smaragdi maintains cute, clean rooms.

Margarita MEZEDHES **$**
(☎ 22840 33074; Artemonas; dishes €3.50-4.50; ⊙ lunch & dinner) Delicious, simple small plates like chickpea dumplings are served on a patio under trees on Artemonas' central square.

Mamma Mia ITALIAN **$$**
(☎ 22840 33086; www.mammamiasifnos.com; Ano Petali; mains €8-15; ⊙ lunch & dinner) Real Italians cook real Italian specialities, with gregarious smiles.

Around Sifnos

Not to be missed is the walled cliff-top village of **Kastro**, 3km from Apollonia. The former capital is a magical place of buttressed alleyways and whitewashed houses surrounded by valleys and sea. It has a modest **archaeological museum** (☎ 22840 31022; ⊙ 8.30am-3pm Tue-Sun) **FREE**, and the small port **Seralia** is nestled below.

On the southeast coast, the little fishing hamlet of **Faros** has a couple of nice beaches nearby, including **Fasolou**, reached up steps and over the headland from the bus stop.

The handsome whitewashed monastery of **Chrysopigi** perches on an islet connected to the shore by a tiny footbridge and is abutted by spectacular beaches with clear, azure waters. Footpaths rim the headlands.

Platys Gialos, 10km south of Apollonia, has a big, generous beach entirely backed by tavernas, domatia and shops.

Vathy, on the southwest coast, is a super-low-key village on an almost circular bay of aquamarine beauty.

In the north, wild barren cliffs drop to the sea and small, bedraggled **Heronisos** sits on a protected bay 15km from Apollonia. Excellent **Vroulidia Beach** requires four-wheel drive or a boat.

◉ Sights & Activities

Acropolis of Agios Andreas RUIN
(☎ 22840 31488; admission €2; ⊙ 8am-3pm Tue-Sun) At the heart of the island, about 2km south of Apollonia, this well-excavated hilltop acropolis dates from the Mycenaean period (13th century BC). Take in extensive views of interior valleys and neighbouring Paros from the intact defensive wall. There is a small museum. The adjacent **Church of Agios Andreas** dates from about 1700.

Footpaths WALKING
Sifnos is crisscrossed by footpaths. For example, old paved pathways between Kastro and Apollonia start 20m to the right (Vathy road) of the T-junction in Apollonia. Another path, with extraordinary views, circumnavigates Kastro. A trail also connects Kastro to **Poulati** with its postcard-perfect monastery above a rocky cove.

🛏 Sleeping & Eating

🏠 Kastro

Loungey cafes like **Dolci** (☎ 22840 32311; snacks €5-10; ⊙ 9am-late Easter-Sep) make cocktails, coffee and crepes as you enter town.

Antonis Rooms PENSION **$**
(☎ 22840 33708; http://sifnosholidays.gr; d €45; ❋ 🐾) Just as you enter Kastro, find these simple, inviting rooms overlooking the bay. Communal kitchen.

Aris & Maria
Traditional Houses APARTMENT **$$**
(☎ 6946874360, 22840 31161; www.arismaria-traditional.com; studio €65-80; ❋) For an authentic Kastro experience, these family-run apartments at the heart of the village are in traditional Sifniot houses. Some have sea views.

★ Leonidas TAVERNA **$$**
(☎ 22840 31153; mains €6-15; ⊙ lunch & dinner Easter-Sep) With superb views, this popular place offers tasty local dishes, from chickpea croquettes to *mastelo* (grilled cheese).

Astron TAVERNA **$$**
(☎ 22840 31476; mains €7-14; ⊙ lunch & dinner Jun-Sep) Sup on octopus with olives or aubergine with lobster in the heart of Kastro.

🏠 Chrysopigi

Roubina Rooms APARTMENT **$**
(☎ 22840 31416; d/tr €50/55; 🅿 ❋) Simple self-catering apartments with unbeatable views over Chrysopigi.

Apokofto TAVERNA **$**
(☑ 22840 71272; mains €8-9; ☺ lunch & dinner
Easter-Oct) One of two equally excellent tavernas at Chrysopigi, smack on the beach.
Also has rooms to let.

Platys Gialos

Hotel Efrosini HOTEL **$$**
(☑ 22840 71353; www.hotel-efrosini.gr; d/tr incl
breakfast €75/90; ☺ Easter-Sep; ✳ 🛜) This well-
kept hotel is one of the best on the Platys
Gialos strip. Small balconies overlook a leafy
courtyard with the sea lapping just in front.

Hotel Verina BOUTIQUE HOTEL **$$$**
(☑ 22840 71525; www.verina.gr; d/apt in Platys
Gialos from €160/180) This set of chic hotels
and apartments has outposts in Platys Gialos, Ano Petali and above Poulati, plus rents
full villas.

Mamma Mia ITALIAN **$$**
(☑ 22840 71219; www.mammamiasifnos.com;
Platys Gialos; mains €8-15; ☺ lunch & dinner May-
Oct) Marco and Luca run this beachfront
Italian eatery with an emphasis on seafood.

Ariadne Restaurant GREEK **$$**
(☑ 22840 71277; mains €6-16; ☺ lunch & dinner
Jun-Sep) Care sourcing and preparation lead
to simple but delicious modern Greek dishes
like wild caper salad, lamb in red-wine sauce
and seafood risotto.

Vathy

Vathy has an array of beachfront tavernas,
such as **Oceanida** and **Manolis**, offering reliable Greek dishes.

Studios Nikos APARTMENT **$$**
(☑ 22840 71512; www.sifnosrooms.com; apt €75-
120; ☺ Apr-Oct; 🅿 ✳) These welcoming well-
equipped studios (with kitchenettes) sit at a
sparkling corner of Vathy Bay.

Areti Studios APARTMENT **$$**
(☑ 22840 71191; d/apt €60/100; 🅿 ✳) Just in
from the beach amid olive groves and a lovely garden, rooms here are clean and bright
and some have cooking facilities.

SERIFOS ΣΕΡΙΦΟΣ

POP 1480

Serifos has a raw, rugged beauty with steep
mountains plunging to broad ultramarine
bays. Relatively deserted outside of the
quaint hilltop capital of Hora or the dusty,
Wild West–feeling port of Livadi down below, the island feels like it's gone beautifully
feral. All that you find are the occasional
remnants of past mining enterprises (rust-
ing tracks, cranes), the whoosh of the wind
(which can be fierce), and the flitting of
butterflies. Rent wheels to make the most
of it.

In Greek mythology, Serifos is where Perseus grew up and where the Cyclops were
said to live. Now, there is some fine walking on Serifos: Anavasi's map *Topo 25/10.26
Aegean Cyclades/Serifos* is useful.

❶ Getting There & Away

Serifos is on the Piraeus–Western Cyclades
ferry route and has good summer connections
south. Buy tickets at **Kondilis** (☑ 22810 52340)
on Livadi's waterfront.

Boat Services from Serifos

DESTINATION	TIME	FARE	FREQUENCY
Andros	4hr 50min	€12	2 weekly
Folegandros	4½hr	€19	1 weekly
Kythnos	1hr 20min	€9	1-2 daily
Milos	3hr	€8	1-2 daily
Milos*	35min	€16	1 daily
Paros	2½hr	€10	2 weekly
Piraeus	5hr	€24	1-2 daily
Piraeus*	2¼hr	€30-43	1-2 daily
Santorini (Thira)	6½hr	€19	2 weekly
Sifnos	50min	€7	1-2 daily
Sifnos*	25min	€14	1-2 daily
Syros	4hr	€9	1 weekly
Tinos	3½hr	€14	2 weekly

*high-speed services

❶ Getting Around

Buses connect Livadi and Hora (€1.60, 15 minutes, hourly); the timetable is posted at bus stop
by yacht quay. Other buses are very infrequent.

Rent cars (per day €40), scooters (€22)
and quads (€28) at **Poseidon Rent A Car**
(☑ 6974789706, 22810 52030) which will pick
up/drop off, or **Krinas Travel** (☑ 22810 51488;
www.serifos-travel.gr) on the waterfront.

Taxis (☑ 6932431114, 6944473044) to Hora
cost €7, Psili Ammos €7, Sykamia €20, Vagia €11
and Megalo Livadi €20.

Serifos

AEGEAN SEA

Platys
Gialos
Bay
Moni
Taxiarhon
Sykamia
Beach
Galani
Kendarhos
Panagia
Pirgos
Psili
582m
Agios
Ammos
Avessalos
Ioannis
Beach
Agios
Beach
Georgios
Hora
Megalo
502m
Livadi
Koutalas
Livadi
Lia Beach
Livadakia
Ganema
Beach
Paros
(72km)
Vagia
Karavi
Kalo
Beach
Kythnos (52km);
Ambeli
Cape
Piraeus (135km)
Katano
Beach

Sifnos (24km);
Kimolos (41km);
Milos (55km); Ios (83km);
Santorini (120km)

Livadi   Λιβάδι

POP 600

The picturesque port town of Serifos is a fairly low-key place where, in spite of growing popularity, there's still a reassuring feeling that the modern world has not entirely taken over. Just over the headland that rises from the ferry quay lies the fine, tamarisk-fringed beach at **Livadakia**. Further south over the next headland, **Karavi** is the unofficial clothing-optional beach.

🛌 Sleeping & Eating

Much of the accommodation clusters at Livadakia Beach. Most hoteliers can pick up at the port by arrangement.

⭐ Coralli Camping & Bungalows   CAMPGROUND, APARTMENT $

(☑ 22810 51500; www.coralli.gr; Livadakia Beach; camp sites per adult/child/tent €8/4/6, bungalows & apt €65-110; 🅿 🛜 🏊) Right behind Livadakia Beach, this very well-equipped and well-run eucalyptus-shaded campground also has excellent bungalows with mountain or sea views. The complex includes a cool pool and bar, a **restaurant** (mains €5-10), minimarket, kitchen and barbecue. Nearby self-catering apartments are of an equally high standard.

Alexandros-Vassilia   APARTMENT $

(☑ 22810 51119; www.alexandros-vassilia.gr; Livadakia Beach; d/apt incl breakfast €60/80; ☉ Easter-Sep; ❄ 🛜) Most well known for its beachfront **taverna** (mains €6 to €10) in a rose-fragrant garden, this compound also has clean, simple rooms and well-equipped apartments.

Medousa   PENSION, APARTMENT $

(☑ 22810 51128; www.medousaserifos.com; Livadakia Beach; d/tr €50/60; 🅿 ❄ 🛜) A short jaunt up from the beach, comfy rooms above a lovely garden have views of nearby Livadakia Bay; some have cooking facilities.

⭐ Studios Niovi   APARTMENT $$

(☑ 22810 51900; www.studiosniovi.gr; Livadi; apt incl breakfast from €70) On the furthest eastern curve of Livadi's bay, these immaculate apartments look at the broad changing expanse of the water, bustling Livadi, towering Hora, and the mountains beyond. The owner is a gem and makes a super breakfast spread.

Kali's   SEAFOOD $

(☑ 22810 52301; Harbourfront; mains €8-12; ☉ lunch & dinner; 🛜) White tables on the water's edge with gregarious waiters and delicious home-cooking, including mezedhes.

Takis   TAVERNA $

(☑ 22810 51559; Harbourfront; mains €5-12; ☉ lunch & dinner; 🛜) Reliable Greek fare and seafood.

Passaggio   CAFE $

(Harbourfront; mains €7-14; ☉ 9am-late; 🛜) All-day restaurant and cafe with good international dishes.

Metalleio   GREEK $$

(☑ 22810 51755; Livadi; mains €10-15; ☉ 8.30pm-late) Located on the road behind the waterfront, Metalleio dishes up quality cuisine from various Cycladic islands, such as *matsata,* a dish of Folegandran pasta with smoked pork, tomatoes and *graviera* (a type of yellow cheese). It doubles as the island's main music venue.

> ℹ **DRINKING WATER**
>
> Serifos is one of the few islands where locals drink the water.

Drinking & Nightlife

Livadi's waterfront comes alive with several music bars such as Karnayio, which pumps classic rock. Metalleio is the top music venue and occasionally has live bands.

Anemos Café   CAFE
(☎) Above Krinas Travel, Anemos' broad verandah offers top views of the marina and distant Hora. The proprietors are friendly, snacks and coffees are good and cheap, and it gets hopping around boat arrivals.

Yacht Club Serifos   BAR
(☉7am-3am) This classic waterfront cafe-bar has a cheerful buzz. It plays lounge music by day for coffee drinkers and mainstream rock, disco and funk late into the night for other tipplers.

ℹ Information

Useful websites include www.e-serifos.com and www.serifos-island.com. The two ATMs on the waterfront are the only ones on the island.
Port Authority (☎22810 51470) Up steps beside Krinas Travel.

Hora (Serifos)
Χώρα (Σέριφος)

The *hora* of Serifos spills across the summit of a rocky hill above Livadi and is one of the most striking of the Cycladic capitals.

Hora's bus terminus and main car park are located on its upper side, near a series of windmills, as is its teeny archaeological collection (☎22810 51138; admission €2; ☉8.30am-4pm Tue-Sun) which displays fragments of mainly Hellenic and Roman sculpture excavated from the *kastro*. From there steps climb into the maze of Hora proper and lead to the charming main square, watched over by the lovely little neoclassical town hall.

From the square, narrow alleys and more steps lead ever upwards to small churches like Agios Ioannis Theologos, carved into the rock and built on the site of an ancient temple to Athena, and the remnants of the ruined 15th-century Venetian Kastro from where the views are spectacular. As the village cascades down the slope, the alleyways lead to a bright blue domed church, near which is another car park.

🛏 Sleeping

I Apanemia   PENSION $
(☎6971891106, 22810 51517; d €40; ✱) This excellent-value family-run place has decent, well-equipped rooms with front balcony views to the distant sea and side views towards Hora.

Anemoessa Studios   APARTMENT $$
(☎22810 51132; www.serifos-anemoessa.gr; apt €80-100; ✱☎) Pretty, contemporary apartments sleep four in whitewashed Cycladic splendour.

🍴 Eating & Drinking

⭐ Stou Stratou   CAFE $
(☎22810 52566; Plateia Ag Athanasiou; dishes €4-14; ☉9am-late Easter-Oct; ☎) Charming Stou Stratou, in the pretty main square, serves breakfast (€3 to €8) and light snacks such as fennel pie or a mixed plate of smoked meats, stuffed vine leaves, feta, tomatoes and egg. Cocktails and coffee, too!

Petros   TAVERNA $
(☎22810 51302; mains €6-9; ☉2pm-midnight Easter-Sep) Hora's best for Greek classics, on the windmill square with views to the mountains.

Aloni   MEDITERRANEAN $$
(☎22810 52603; mains €8-15; ☉dinner May-Sep) Halfway up the hill between Livadi and Hora, signposted on the right, Aloni gives amazing views and an upscale feel, with delicious food to match.

Aerino   BAR
Just off the windmill square, Aerino offers great chilling out with super views.

Around Serifos

About 1.5km north of Livadi pretty, little Psili Ammos Beach offers the best swimming close to Livadi, and has two excellent tavernas.

A footpath from Hora heads north for about 4km to the village of Kendarhos (also known as Kallitsos), from where you can continue by a very winding road for another 3km to the 17th-century fortified Moni Taxiarhon, which has impressive 18th-century frescoes. Take food and water, as there are no facilities in Kendarhos.

Platys Gialos Beach in the north has a good summer-only taverna.

Sykamia is one of the best beaches on the island, with an incredible approach along a steep, windy road through terrraced hills and dovecotes. The beach itself is grey-brown sand full of stones. Bitos (mains €6-9; ⊙ lunch & dinner summer only), one of the only signs of development, serves good food. To reach Sykamia you will pass through the quaint village of Panagia.

Megalo Livadi, on the southwest coast, is a fun visit for its sparkling bay, neoclassical buildings (remnants of the mining era) and excellent seafront Kyklopas (☑ 22810 51009; mains €5-12; ⊙ lunch & dinner Easter-Sep) taverna. The cave where the Cyclops was said to dwell is near here.

The best beaches on the south coast tend to be broad and sandy, on exquisite bays, and deserted out of high season. Try Ganema, Vagia and Kalo Ambeli.

KYTHNOS ΚΥΘΝΟΣ
POP 1310

Kythnos is a series of folding hills and sere crenellations punctuated by stone huts and ancient walls, vibrant green valleys and unspoilt beaches. An agricultural island mostly, life is still simple. Port life in Merihas and village life in beautiful Hora and Dryopida remain easy-going. Islanders accept friendly visitors who adapt to Kythnos' gentle rhythms.

ⓘ Getting There & Away

Ferries serve Piraeus and Lavrio on the mainland, Kea to the north, and in high season, islands to the south. Out of season it's hard to connect south. In Merihas buy tickets at **Anerousa Travel** (☑ 22810 32372) or Larentzakis Travel Agency (p410).

ⓘ Getting Around

In high summer buses go from Merihas to Dryopida (€1.60), continuing to Kanala (€2.80) or Hora (€1.60). Less regular services run to Loutra (€2.80). Usually buses leave Merihas from the turn-off to Hora. During term-time the only buses tend to be school buses.

The best way to see the island is by car or scooter. Rent at Larentzakis Travel Agency (p410): about €30 a day, scooters start at €15.

Taxis (☑ 69442 71609, 22810 32883) cost about €9 to Hora and €7 to Dryopida. A **taxi-boat** (☑ 6944906568) to/from beaches in summer costs about €10 return.

Merihas Μέριχας
POP 289

Tiny Merihas is home to much of the island's low-season life. Cafes and restaurants line the small harbour, and rooms for let dot its hills. The best beaches within walking distance are north of the quay at Episkopi and Apokrousi. There is free wi-fi in the port.

🛏 Sleeping & Eating

Domatia owners usually meet boats. Book ahead for July and August. When eating, make sure you check what was made fresh that day.

Kontseta   APARTMENT **$**
(☑ 22810 33024; www.kontseta.gr; d €50; ⊙ Apr-Oct; ❄) High above the ferry-quay side of the harbour, with sunset views, these modern apartments are a cut above.

Kythnos

Syros (74km);
Tinos (81km);
Mykonos (98km) / Cape Kefalos
Kea (Tzia) (39km); Lavrio (48km)
AEGEAN SEA
297m
Loutra ○ ⊙ Thermal Baths
Kolona Beach Apokrousi Beach
308m
● Hora (Kythnos)
Episkopi Beach
Piraeus (96km)
● Merihas
● Dryopida   Cape Tzoulis
302m ▲
Flambouria Beach
Kanala ○
Skylou Beach
Gaidouromantra Beach
Dimitrios Beach
Cape Berou
Kimolos (41km); Serifos (52km);
Sifnos (63km); Milos (85km);
Santorini (155km)

0 —— 5 km
0 —— 2.5 miles

BOAT SERVICES FROM KYTHNOS

DESTINATION	TIME	FARE	FREQUENCY
Andros	5hr 40min	€14	1 weekly
Kea	1hr 20min	€7	3 weekly
Kimolos	5-11hr	€18	2 weekly
Lavrio	2hr	€10	2 daily
Piraeus	3hr 10min	€23	1-2 daily
Serifos	1hr 20min	€9	1-2 daily
Syros	2hr 10min	€9	4 weekly

Studios Maria Gonidi   APARTMENT **$**
(☑ 22810 32324; d €40; ✳) Located on the far side of the bay, this place offers lofty views. Sparkling rooms have full self-catering facilities.

Ioanna's Rooms   APARTMENT **$**
(☑ 22810 32858; www.kithnosisland.gr/ioannas; d from €40; @) This is another good bet on the far side of the harbour. The rooms come with balconies.

Taverna to Kandouni   TAVERNA **$**
(☑ 22810 32220; mains €6-14; ☺ lunch & dinner) On the southern bend of the waterfront, Kandouni specialises in grilled meat dishes and souvlaki (cubes of meat on skewers).

Molos   SOUVLAKI **$**
(gyros €2; ☺ lunch & dinner) Scrummy souvlaki just where the ferries dock.

Ostria   SEAFOOD **$$**
(☑ 22810 32263; mains €6-15; ☺ lunch & dinner) Ostria is the place for fish (fish soup or anchovies are favourites) and mezedhes.

🍷 Drinking & Nightlife

Cruise the waterfront to pick from a series of cafe-bars.

Rock Castle   BAR
High above the harbour, with unbeatable views, Rock Castle serves a super selection of cocktails and beers, including Greek microbrews. Sounds range from jazz to reggae and rock, occasionally live.

ℹ Information

Larentzakis Travel Agency (☑ 6944906568, 22810 32104) Sells ferry tickets, arranges accommodation and hires cars.
Port Authority (☑ 22810 32290) On the waterfront.

Hora (Kythnos)
Χώρα (Κύθνος)

The distinctively charming capital, Hora (also known as Kythnos or Messaria) nestles in the lap of rolling agricultural fields and perseveres an inherent Greek character. Small, colourful cafes and shops light up the traditional village lanes, still populated by grannies hanging out the wash.

The long main street makes for a pleasant stroll through a cute central square to a series of cafes, restaurants, ceramicists and sweet shops. Find excellent apartments with kitchens at **Filoxenia** (☑ 22810 31644; www.filoxenia-kythnos.gr; d/tr €60/70; ☺ year-round; **P** ✳). Tavernas **To Steki** and **Messaria** serve good island cuisine. **Koursaros** is fun for a drink and people-watching. An ATM and the island's **police station** (☑ 22810 31201) are at the car park where you enter from Merihas.

Around Kythnos

Low-key resort and fishing village, **Loutra**, 3km north of Hora, sits on a windy bay with **thermal baths**. **Porto Klaras** (☑ 22810 31276; www.porto-klaras.gr; d €75-90, 4-person apt €120; ☺ Apr-Oct; ✳ ☎) has impeccable studios with kitchens. Among the port-front seafood tavernas, the best bet is **Araxovoli** (☑ 22810 31082; fish from €10 per kg; ☺ lunch & dinner). **Koutsiko** (☑ 22810 31185; mains €6-12; ☺ lunch & dinner), just as you enter the village, has excellent grilled meat.

Dryopida, a picturesque town of red-tiled roofs and winding streets clustered steeply on either side of a ravine, is connected to Hora by a footpath.

The island's most famous beach is the double-bay of **Kolona**, a thin strip of sand, like a peninsula, leading to an offshore is-let. Low season it is amazing and a favoured anchorage for yachts. It's best to reach it by boat since the roads to it are poor. It has a high-season taverna.

Find other good beaches at **Flambouria** about 2.5km south of Merihas, or at remote **Skylou** and **Gaidouromantra**.

Kanala on the southeast coast has an interesting monastery, **Panagia Kanala**, on the point, but the beach is so-so.

KEA (TZIA)

POP 2420

Kea (*kay*-a), although naturally beautiful with craggy cliffs, spectacular coastline and fecund hillsides, has been overrun by vacation homes. Being the island closest to Attica, it's just too easy to reach. Rent wheels to get off the beaten path and find its charms: rocky spires, verdant valleys filled with orchards, olive groves and almond and oak trees, farmers loading donkeys with water from wells. The main settlements are the port of Korissia and the attractive capital, Ioulida, situated about 5km inland. Local people call the island Tzia.

ℹ️ Getting There & Away

Kea's only mainland service is to Lavrio. Connections to other islands are few. Weekend boats are packed. Book ahead with ticket agents for **Marmari Express** (☑ Kea 22880 21435, Lavrio 22920 26200), or the **agent** (☑ Kea 22880 21920, Lavrio 22920 69380) for **Makedon**, **NEL Lines** and **Artemis**. There is a ticket kiosk on the Korissia waterfront.

ℹ️ Getting Around

In July and August regular buses, in theory, go from Korissia to Vourkari, Otzias, Ioulida and Piosses Beach. A **taxi** (☑ 6936660251, 22880 21228, 22880 21021) may be a better bet: to Ioulida €7, Otzias €6 and Piosses €22.

Leon Rent A Car (☑ 6937185053, 22880 21898) is located mid-harbourfront: scooters cost per day from €17 and cars from €45.

Korissia   Κορησσία

POP 881

The fairly bland port of Korissia has enough tavernas and cafes to pass the time. The north-facing beach tends to catch the wind.

🛏️ Sleeping & Eating

Domatia owners don't meet ferries. Book ahead in high season and at weekends.

United Europe   APARTMENT **$**
(☑ 22880 21362; www.uekeastudios.gr; d €40; ❄️🛜) Big, airy self-catering rooms make this quiet place an excellent option. Since it's about 200m along the river road behind the beach, owners can pick up from the port.

Hotel Karthea   HOTEL **$$**
(☑ 22880 21204; www.hotelkarthea.gr; d €75; ⊙ Easter-Oct) This central, straightforward hotel has good, basic rooms with spacious bathrooms and some seafront balconies.

Odale   CAFE **$**
(☑ 22880 29060; www.odale.gr; snacks €5-10; ⊙ 9am-late Apr-Oct) Fresh, innovative and great for breakfast, sandwiches and pastries. Find it where the road curves inland.

Magazes   MEDITERRANEAN **$$**
(☑ 22880 21104; www.magazes.gr; mains €8-13; ⊙ lunch & dinner; 🛜) Mid-harbourfront, Magazes is in a restored warehouse. Recommended for its seafood, signature dishes include mussel risotto with fresh fennel and peppers.

BOAT SERVICES FROM KEA (TZIA)

DESTINATION	TIME	FARE	FREQUENCY
Andros	6hr 20min	€10	2 weekly
Kythnos	1hr 20min	€7	3 weekly
Lavrio	1hr	€10	4 daily
Milos	12hr 20min	€14	2 weekly
Paros	6hr 20min	€18	2 weekly
Syros	3hr 40min	€12	2 weekly
Tinos	5hr	€13	4 weekly

Lagoudera TAVERNA $$
(☑ 22880 21977; mains €7-12; ☺ lunch & dinner; �) Tops for tasty Greek dishes such as mushroom pie and pork with celery.

ℹ️ Information

Free wi-fi is in the port. Useful websites include www.kea-tzia.gr and www.kea.gr.

Tourist Information Office (☑ 22880 22651) Opposite the ferry quay, has lists of domatia in Greek, but not much more.

Ioulida   Ιουλίδα

POP 1536

Ioulida (ee-oo-lee-tha) is Kea's gem. Its pretty scramble of narrow alleyways and interesting buildings drapes across two hilltops. Once a substantial settlement of ancient Greece it now has a distinctly cosmopolitan feel at weekends.

The bus turnaround is on a square just at the edge of town, from where an archway leads into the village. (Park in the car park below the square.) Beyond the archway, turn right and uphill along Ioulida's main street for its shops and cafes and to reach the famed Kea Lion.

THE RED TRACTOR FARM

Kea's **Red Tractor Farm** (☑ 22880 21346; www.redtractorfarm.com; d €90, studios €130-180; 🅿 ❄ @ 🛜) lies inland from Korissia within a serene world of its own amid organic vineyards and olive groves. Kostis Maroulis and Marcie Mayer operate this sustainable, creative agro-tourism farm with beautiful Cycladic buildings combining tradition and excellent modern style and comfort. Kostis and Marcie also produce olive oil, wine, marmalade and chutney.

⦿ Sights

★ **Kea Lion** MONUMENT

The enigmatic Kea Lion, chiselled from slate in the 6th century BC, lies across a small valley beyond the last of Ioulida's houses. The walk itself is fantastic. Follow wooden signs reading Αρχαίος Λέων from the top of the main street until the path leads you out of town (you'll see the lion if you look closely, across the valley). The footpath curves past a cemetery and the lion, with its smooth-worn haunches and Cheshire cat smile, is reached through a gate on the left.

The path continues to Otzias.

Archaeological Museum MUSEUM

(☑ 22880 22079; adult/child €2/free; ☺ 8am-3pm Tue-Sat Jun-Sep) Find intriguing artefacts, including some superb terracotta figurines, mostly from Agia Irini. Just before the post office on the main thoroughfare.

🛏️ Sleeping & Eating

Ask about rooms at tavernas. The best spot to eat by far is **Estiatorio I Piatsa** (☑ 22880 22195; mains €7.50-9; ☺ lunch & dinner) just inside the archway where packed tables full of gregarious locals sup on grilled meat, shrimp and taverna favourites.

Around Kea

The beach road from Korissia leads past **Gialiskari Beach** for 2.5km to tiny **Vourkari**, a favourite with yachties, where the waterfront is lined with sailboats and cafes. **H Strofi tou Mimi** (☑ 22880 21480; mains €6-9; ☺ lunch & dinner, weekends only in winter), on the far side of the bay, is one of the best seafood tavernas on the island.

Otzias has a sandy beach and great family-friendly apartments 50m inland at **Anemousa** (☑ 22880 21355; www.anemousa.

gr; studio/apt from €80/100; P ✳ 🛜 🏊). A spectacular coastal road continues 5km to the breathtakingly situated 18th-century Moni Panagias Kastrianis, high on a rock top. If you're circling back to Ioulida, the road from here is equally gorgeous, along the crest of hills with grove-covered valleys plunging to either side, and rural villages.

Eight kilometres southwest of Ioulida, Piosses, the island's best beach, is backed by verdant orchards, olive groves and rugged hills. Well-kept Camping Kea (🖉 22880 31302; campingkea@yahoo.gr; camp sites per adult/tent/car €5.50/5.50/4, bungalows €40; ☺ May-Sep; P 🛜), under thick eucalyptus, has a shop and cafe. The beach's taverna, Christoforos (🖉 22880 31308; mains €6-10; ☺ Mar-Oct), has great fish dishes.

Inland Kato Meria is known for its meat and mezedhes restaurant, H Taverna tou Simou (🖉 22880 24280; mains €6-15; ☺ lunch & dinner high season).

Crete

Best Places to Eat

Best Places to Stay

Why Go?

Crete (Κρήτη) is in many respects the culmination of the Greek experience. Nature here has been prolific, creating a dramatic quilt of big-shouldered mountains, stunning beaches and undulating hillsides blanketed in olive groves, vineyards and wildflowers. There are deep chiselled gorges, including one of Europe's longest, and crystal-clear lagoons and palm-tree-lined beaches that conjure up the Caribbean.

Crete's natural beauty is equalled only by the richness of a history that spans millennia. The Palace of Knossos is but one of many vestiges of the mysterious Minoan civilisation. Venetian fortresses, Turkish mosques and Byzantine churches bring history alive all over the island, but nowhere more so than in charismatic Hania and Rethymno.

Ultimately, though, it's humans – not stones – that create the most vivid memories. Crete's hospitable and spirited people uphold their unique culture and customs, and traditions remain a dynamic part of the island's soul.

When to Go
Crete (Iraklio)

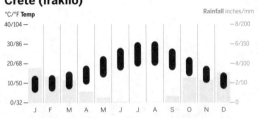

Apr A painter's palette of wildflowers blankets the island as locals prepare for Easter.

Jun Hit the beaches before they get crowded and rejoice in the bounty of local produce.

Oct Warm seas, blue skies and thinning crowds as the grape harvest gets under way.

History

Although inhabited since neolithic times (7000–3000 BC), Crete is most famous for being the cradle of Europe's first advanced civilisation, the Minoans. Traces of this enigmatic society were only uncovered in the early 20th century, when British archaeologist Sir Arthur Evans discovered the palace at Knossos and named the civilisation after its ruler, the mythical King Minos.

Minoans migrated to Crete in the 3rd millennium BC. Their extraordinary artistic, architectural and cultural achievements culminated in the construction of huge palace complexes at Knossos, Phaestos, Malia and Zakros, which were all levelled by an earthquake around 1700 BC. Undeterred, the Minoans built bigger and better ones over the ruins, while settling more widely across Crete. Around 1450 BC, the palaces were mysteriously destroyed again, possibly by a tsunami triggered by a volcanic eruption on Santorini (Thira). Knossos, the only palace saved, finally burned down around 1400 BC.

Archaeological evidence shows that the Minoans lingered on for a few centuries in small, isolated settlements before disappearing as mysteriously as they had come. They were followed by the Mycenaeans and the Dorians (around 1100 BC). By the 5th century BC, Crete was divided into city-states but did not benefit from the cultural glories of mainland Greece; in fact, it was bypassed by Persian invaders and the Macedonian conqueror Alexander the Great.

By 67 BC Crete had become the Roman province of Cyrenaica, with Gortyna its capital. After the Roman Empire's division in AD 395, Crete fell under the jurisdiction of Greek-speaking Constantinople – the emerging Byzantine Empire. Things went more or less fine until AD 824, when Arabs appropriated the island. In AD 961, though, Byzantine general emperor Nikiforas Fokas (AD 912–69) won Crete back following a nine-month siege of Iraklio (then called El Khandak by the Arabs). Crete flourished under Byzantine rule, but with the infamous Fourth Crusade of 1204 the maritime power of Venice received Crete as part of its 'payment' for supplying the Crusaders' fleet.

Much of Crete's most impressive surviving architecture dates from the Venetian period, which lasted until 1669 when Iraklio (then called Candia) became the last domino to fall after a 21-year Ottoman siege. Turkish rule brought new administrative organisation, Islamic culture and Muslim settlers. Cretan resistance was strongest in the mountain strongholds but all revolts were put down brutally, and it was only with the Ottoman Empire's disintegration in the late 19th century that Europe's great powers expedited Crete's sovereign aspirations.

Thus in 1898, with Russian and French consent, Crete became a British protectorate. However, the banner under which future Greek Prime Minister Eleftherios Venizelos and other Cretan rebels were fighting was *Enosis i Thanatos* (Unity or Death) – unity with Greece, not mere independence from Turkey. Yet it would take the Greek army's successes in the Balkan Wars (1912–13) to turn Crete's de facto inclusion in the country into reality, with the 1913 Treaty of Bucharest.

Crete suffered tremendously during WWII, due to being coveted by Hitler for its strategic location. On 20 May 1941 a huge flock of German parachutists quickly overwhelmed the Cretan defenders. The Battle of Crete, as it would become known, raged for 10 days between German and Allied troops from Britain, Australia, New Zealand and Greece. For two days the battle hung in the balance until the Germans captured the Maleme Airfield, near Hania. The Allied forces fought a valiant rearguard action, enabling the British Navy to evacuate 18,000 of the 32,000 Allied troops. The harsh German occupation lasted throughout WWII, with many mountain villages bombed or burnt down and their occupants executed en masse.

🛈 Getting There & Away

AIR

Most travellers arrive in Crete by air, usually with a change in Athens. Iraklio's Nikos Kazantzakis Airport is Crete's busiest airport, although **Hania** (www.chania-airport.com) is convenient for travellers heading to western Crete. Sitia only receives a handful of domestic flights.

Between May and October, European low-cost carriers and charter airlines such as easyJet, Germanwings, AirBerlin, Fly Thomas Cook and Jet2 operate direct flights to Crete, mostly from UK and German airports. Aegean Airlines operates direct flights to Iraklio from several European cities, including Brussels, Frankfurt, Paris and St Petersburg; coming from another destination requires connecting in Athens. Travellers from North America need to connect via a European gateway city such as Paris, Amsterdam or Frankfurt and sometimes again in Athens.

CRETE

To Piraeus

To Piraeus

To Antikythira;
Gythio; Kythira;
Piraeus

SEA OF
CRETE

Rodopos
Peninsula

Gramvousa
Peninsula

Balos

Stavros

Akrotiri
Peninsula

Gulf of Hania

Souda
Bay

Cape Drepano

Bali

Panormo

Perama

Bay of
Kissamos

Spilia

Hania

Souda

Falasarna

Kissamos

Kalyviani

HANIA

Fournes

Adele

Rethymno

Moni
Arkadiou

Anogia

Polyrrina

Meskla

Lakki

Vryses

Georgioupolis

Milia

Theriso

Episkopi

Agia Irini

Omalos

Mt Volakias
(2116m)

Kournas
Lake

RETHYMNO

Mt
Psiloritis
(2456m)

Xyloskalo

Pachnes
(2454m)

Myrthios

Amari

Elafonisi

Samaria
Gorge

Aradena

Imbros

Selia

Lefkogia

Spili

Amari
Valley

Paleohora

Sougia

Anopoli

Komitades

Plakias

Elafonisi
Islet

Lissos

Agia
Roumeli

Loutro

Marmara
Beach

Hora
Sfakion

Moni
Preveli
& Preveli
Beach

Mt Kedros
(1777m)

Agios
Pavlos

Agia
Galini

Agia Triada

Vori

Mire

Frangokastello

Triopetra

Tymbaki

Phaestos

Matala

Mesara Gulf

Gavdopoula

Paximadia
Islands

Cape
Lithino

Sarakiniko
Beach

Karabe

Gavdos

Crete Highlights

① Make a date with King
Minos at the **Palace of
Knossos** (p425)

② Follow up a pilgrimage to
Moni Preveli (p437) with a

swim on palm-studded **Preveli
Beach** (p438)

③ Explore Minoan ruins
and sample the local tipple in
Iraklio Wine Country (p428)

④ Embark on an aimless
wander around the evocative
historic quarter of **Hania**
(p439)

⑤ Find out why **Moni
Arkadiou** (p435) occupies

To the Cyclades

To Santorini

**To Kasos;
Karpathos;
Rhodes;
Halki**

20 km
12 miles

SEA OF CRETE

Cape
Stavros

Dia

Cape
Sideros

Fodele

Iraklio
Bay

Iraklio

Gournes

Hersonisos

Cape Agios
Ioannis

Plaka

Spinalonga Island

Moni
Toplou

Vaï

Tylisos

❶ Palace of
Knossos

Skalani

Myrtia

Malia

Malia

Elounda

Kolokytha
Peninsula

Palekastro

Sitia

❸

Arhanes

Peza

Neapoli

Agios
Nikolaos

Gulf of
Mirabello

Mohlos

Zakros
Palace

Iraklio Wine
Country

Alagni

Tzermiado

Lato

Kri-Kri

Zakros

Kato
Zakros

Rouvas
Gorge

Psyhro

❼ Lasithi
Plateau

Kritsa

Istron

LASITHI

Zaros

Agia Varvara

Dikteon
Cave

Agios Georgios

Gournia

IRAKLIO

Mt Dikti
(2148m)

Kalamafka

Koutsouras

Gortyna

Ano
Viannos

Myrtos

❺ Ierapetra

Koufonisi

Pyrgos

Arvi

Lendas

Gaïdouronisi
(Hrysi)

LIBYAN SEA

---

such an important spot in the
Cretan soul

❻ Feel the poignant history
of the former leper colony on
Spinalonga Island (p457)

❼ Cycle among windmills on
the **Lasithi Plateau** (p463)

❽ Revel in isolated **Elafonisi**
(p452), one of Crete's most
magical beaches

❾ Get lost in the charismatic
jumble of buildings in
Rethymno's old quarter (p433)

❿ Hike the **Samaria Gorge**
(p449), one of Europe's
longest canyons

To reach Crete by air from other Greek islands also requires changing in Athens, except for the following flights operated by the Crete-based airline **Sky Express** (www.skyexpress.gr).

Domestic Flights from Crete

DESTINATION	AIRPORT	TIME	FREQUENCY
Alexandroupoli	Sitia	1½hr	3 weekly
Athens	Iraklio	1hr	3 weekly
Ikaria	Iraklio	50min	4 weekly
Kos	Iraklio	45min	3 weekly
Kythira	Iraklio	1hr	3 weekly
Preveza	Sitia	1¾hr	3 weekly
Rhodes	Iraklio	50min	daily
Santorini (Thira)	Iraklio	30min	daily

BOAT

Crete is well served by ferry with at least one daily departure from Piraeus (near Athens) to Iraklio and Hania year-round and several per day in summer. There are also slower ferries once or twice a week to Sitia in the east and the western port of Kissamos. Services are considerably curtailed from November to April. Timetables change from season to season, and ferries are subject to delays and cancellations at short notice due to bad weather, strikes or mechanical problems.

Ferry companies operating from Crete are **Anek Lines** (www.anek.gr), **Hellenic Seaways** (www.hellenicseaways.gr), **Lane Sea Lines** (www.lane-kithira.com), **Minoan Lines** (www.minoan.gr) and **SeaJets** (www.seajets.gr).

The following table should be used as a guideline only since actual schedules and prices fluctuate frequently. Prices quoted are for deck seating. For current routes and timetables or to buy tickets, consult the ferry company's website or go to www.ferries.gr or www.greekislands.gr.

ⓘ Getting Around

The extensive **KTEL** (www.bus-service-crete-ktel.com) bus network makes it relatively easy to travel around Crete, although the frequency of service changes seasonally and is often curtailed (or nonexistent) at weekends. The website has the latest timetable.

Taxis are widely available except in remote villages. Large towns have taxi stands that post a list of prices, otherwise you pay what's on the meter. If a taxi has no meter, settle on a price before driving off.

CENTRAL CRETE

Central Crete comprises the Iraklio prefecture, named after the island's burgeoning capital, and the Rethymno prefecture, named after its lovely Venetian port town. Along with its dynamic urban life and Venetian remnants, the region is home to the island's top-rated tourist attraction, the Palace of Knossos, as well as other major and minor Minoan sites. Even if the coastal stretch east of the city of Iraklio is one continuous band of hotels and resorts, just a little bit inland villages sweetly lost in time provide pleasing contrast. Taste the increasingly sophisticated tipple produced in the Iraklio Wine Country, walk in the footsteps of Nikos Kazantzakis and revel in the rustic grandeur of the mountain village of Zaros.

Rethymno is a fascinating quilt of bubbly resorts, centuries-old villages and energising towns. Away from the northern coast, you'll quickly find yourself immersed in endless tranquillity and natural beauty as you drift through such villages as Anogia, where locals cherish their timeless traditions. The south coast is a different animal altogether – a wild beauty with steep gorges and bewitching beaches in seductive isolation, along with the relaxed resort of Plakias and the old hippie hang-out of Matala.

Iraklio   Ηράκλειο

POP 174,000

Crete's capital city, Iraklio (ee-*rah*-klee-oh, also called Heraklion), is Greece's fifth-largest city and the island's economic and administrative hub. It's a somewhat hectic place, roaring with motorbikes throttling in unison at traffic lights and aeroplanes thrusting off into the sky over a long waterfront lined with the remnants of Venetian arsenals, fortresses and shrines.

Though not pretty in a conventional way, Iraklio can grow on you if you take the time to explore its nuances and wander its backstreets. A revitalised waterfront invites strolling and the newly pedestrianised historic centre is punctuated by bustling squares rimmed by buildings from the time when Columbus set sail.

Iraklio has a certain urban sophistication, with a thriving cafe and restaurant scene, the island's best shopping and lively nightlife. Of course, don't miss its blockbuster sights either, like the amazing archaeological museum and the Palace of Knossos, both fascinating windows into Minoan culture.

◉ Sights

Iraklio's main sights are wedged within the historic town, hemmed in by the waterfront and the old city walls. Many of the finest buildings line up along the main thorough-fare, 25 Avgoustou, which skirts the lovely central square, Plateia Venizelou (Venizelou Sq, also called Lion Sq after its landmark Morosini Fountain). East of here, Koraï is the hub of Iraklio's cafe scene, leading to the sprawling Plateia Eleftherias (Eleftherias Sq) with the archaeological museum nearby.

★ **Iraklio Archaeological Museum** MUSEUM
(☑ 2810 279000; http://odysseus.culture.gr; Xan-thoudidou 2; adult/concession €4/2, incl Knossos €10/5; ⊙ 8am-8pm Tue-Sat, 8am-3pm Sun, 1-8pm Mon Apr-Oct, reduced hours Nov-Mar) This out-standing museum is one of the largest and most important in Greece. There are arte-facts spanning 5500 years from neolithic to Roman times, but it's rightly most famous for its extensive Minoan collection. The treasure trove includes pottery, jewellery, figurines and sarcophagi, plus some famous frescoes. The most exciting finds come from the sites of Knossos, Phaestos, Zakros, Malia and Agia Triada. A visit here will greatly en-hance your understanding and appreciation of Crete's history and culture. Don't skip it.

While the main museum building was closed for a six-year restoration, key exhibits could be admired in a nearby annex entered from Hatzidakis St. However, in 2012 some of these moved back into the north wing of

CRETE IRAKLIO

BOAT SERVICES FROM CRETE

DESTINATION	PORT	TIME	FARE	FREQUENCY
Anafi	Iraklio	4hr	€18	1 weekly
Anafi	Sitia	8hr	€19	1 weekly
Antikythira	Kissamos	2hr	€10	2 weekly
Gythio	Kissamos	7hr	€23	2 weekly
Halki	Iraklio	11¼hr	€21	1 weekly
Ios	Iraklio	3hr	€57	1 daily
Kalamata	Kissamos	9½hr	€25	3 weekly
Karpathos	Iraklio	7¾hr	€18	2 weekly
Karpathos	Sitia	4½hr	€18	2 weekly
Kasos	Iraklio	6hr	€20	2 weekly
Kasos	Sitia	2½hr	€11	2 weekly
Kythira	Kissamos	4hr	€20	up to 2 daily
Milos	Iraklio	10½hr	€22	1 weekly
Milos	Sitia	14½hr	€23	1 weekly
Monemvasia	Kissamos	6½hr	€20	1 weekly
Mykonos	Iraklio	4¾hr	€68	1 daily
Naxos	Iraklio	3½hr	€65	2 weekly
Paros	Iraklio	4hr	€65	1 daily
Piraeus	Hania	9hr	€28-35	2 daily
Piraeus	Iraklio	8½hr	€36-39	2 daily
Piraeus	Kissamos	11½hr	€24	2 weekly
Piraeus	Sitia	19½hr	€39	2 weekly
Rhodes	Iraklio	13½hr	€28	2 weekly
Rhodes	Sitia	10¼hr	€26	2 weekly
Santorini (Thira)	Iraklio	6hr	€24	1 weekly
Santorini (Thira)	Sitia	10hr	€26	1 weekly
Santorini (fast boat)	Iraklio	2hr	€56	1 daily

Iraklio

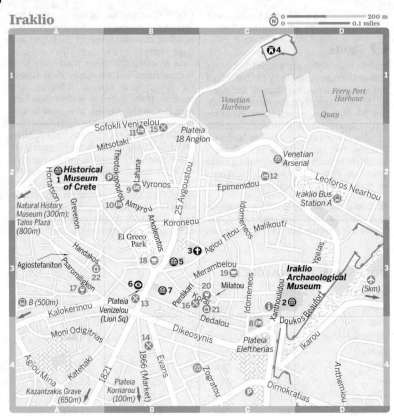

0 — 200 m
0 — 0.1 miles

the revamped structure with more sections expected to open in 2013 and 2014. Upon completion, there will be 23 chronologically organised rooms.

The ground floor of the revamped main museum building is dedicated to 1000 years of classical sculpture, including the monumental pieces from the Archaic-Classical period and statues of Roman gods and statesmen. Upstairs is the Gallery of the Minoan Frescoes with the famous original wall-paintings from the Palace of Knossos. Highlights include the Procession Fresco, the Griffin Fresco (from the Throne Room), the Dolphin Fresco (from the Queen's Room), the Parisienne and the elegant Prince of the Lilies.

Standouts still in the annex at the time of writing include the Minoan Gold Bee (case 7), found in Malia, which depicts two bees dropping honey into a comb. Among

the pottery objects, pay special attention to the Harvester Vase (case 16), found at Agia Triada and decorated with a relief of farm workers returning from olive picking. Even more striking is black-stone Bull's Head (case 13), a libation vessel with a fine head of curls, gold horns and painted crystal eyes. The fascinating figurines of a bare-breasted snake goddess found in a Knossos shrine are in the next case (14). Also from Knossos, in case 10, are Linear A and B tablets. From Phaestos, the most prized find is the mysterious Phaestos Disk (case 18), a 16cm circular clay tablet inscribed with (still undeciphered) pictographic symbols. Considered one of the greatest achievements in Minoan art is the Sarcophagus of Agia Triada, which depicts scenes associated with worship, death and the afterlife.

Over time, all these objects will be transferred to the restored main building.

Iraklio

★ **Historical Museum of Crete** MUSEUM
(☑ 2810 283219; www.historical-museum.gr; Sofokli Venizelou 27; adult/concession €5/3; ☉ 9am-5pm Mon-Sat) Exhibits at this engagingly curated museum shine the spotlight on aspects of Cretan history spanning from the Byzantine to the Venetian and Turkish periods and culminating in WWII. Excellent English labelling, interactive stations throughout, as well as an audio guide (€3), greatly enhance the experience.

First-floor highlights include a newly reorganised coin collection and the only two El Greco paintings in Crete, 13th- and 14th-century frescoes, exquisite Venetian gold jewellery and embroidered vestments. The most interesting rooms on the 2nd floor are the recreated study of *Zorba the Greek* author Nikos Kazantzakis and others dramatically detailing aspects of the WWII Battle of Crete in May 1941, including the Cretan resistance and the role of Allied secret services. The top floor features an outstanding folklore collection.

Natural History Museum MUSEUM
(☑ 2810 282740; www.nhmc.uoc.gr; Sofokli Venizelou; adult/concession €6/4; ☉ 9am-9pm, shorter hours Oct-May) In a cleverly recycled power station, this museum introduces visitors to regional fauna and flora, but gets special kudos for its hands-on Discovery Centre, living zoo and earthquake simulator. The star exhibit, though, is the life-size representation of the elephant-like *Deinotherium gigantum*, the world's third-largest land mammal known to have existed, standing 5m tall. The museum is on the waterfront, about a 10-minute walk west of the Venetian Harbour.

Koules Venetian Fortress FORTRESS
(Venetian Harbour) Iraklio's landmark, this squat 16th-century fortress at the beginning of the Venetian Harbour breakwater was called Rocca al Mare under the Venetians. It stopped the Turks for 21 years and later became a Turkish prison for Cretan rebels. It's closed for renovation for the foreseeable future.

Morosini Fountain FOUNTAIN
(Plateia Venizelou) Named for its architect but better known as 'Lion Fountain', this beloved Venetian vestige spurts water from four lions' jaws into curved marble troughs. The centrepiece marble statue of Poseidon was destroyed during the Turkish occupation.

Municipal Art Gallery ART GALLERY
(☑ 2810 399228; 25 Avgoustou; ☉ 9am-1.30pm Mon-Fri) **FREE** Originally built in 1239, the Basilica of Agios Markos (St Mark's) served as an archbishop's seat under the Venetians and was later turned into a mosque by the Turks. Today it houses changing art exhibits that may feature works by such Cretan creatives as Maria Fiorakis, Lefteris Kanakakis and Thomas Fanourakis.

Loggia HISTORIC BUILDING
(25 Avgoustou) Built by Francesco Morosini, Iraklio's town hall is housed in this stately 17th-century palazzo, which was originally a Venetian version of a gentleman's club, where the male aristocracy gathered for drinks and gossip.

Church of Agios Titos CHURCH
(Plateia Agiou Titou; ☉ 7.30am-1pm & 4.30-7.30pm) This majestic church has Byzantine origins in AD 961, morphed into a Catholic church

DON'T MISS

IRAKLIO MARKET

An Iraklio institution just south of the Morosini Fountain, narrow **Odos 1866** (1866 St) is part market, part bazaar and, despite being increasingly tourist-oriented, a fun place to browse and stock up on picnic supplies or souvenirs. Fruit and vegetable stands alternate with butchers and vendors selling local cheeses, honey, olives, herbs and mountain tea. There's also a good supply of leather goods, hats, jewellery and beach gear. Cap off a spree with lunch at **Giakoumis** (€6-9; ⊙ lunch & dinner) or continue north to the fish section with its own cluster of small taverns. The lane culminates at Plateia Kornarou (Kornarou Sq), where the **Turkish Sebil** (pump house, now a cafe) is an eyecatcher, as is the **Bembo Fountain**, which was cobbled together in the 16th century from an ancient Roman sarcophagus and headless alabaster statue.

under the Venetians and a mosque by the Ottomans before being consecrated as an Orthodox church in 1925. Paintings on the side walls show scenes from the life of St Titus, a compatriot of St Peter who became Crete's first bishop in AD 59. His much-revered skull is housed in a small room off to the left of the entrance.

🛌 Sleeping

Iraklio Youth Hostel HOSTEL $
(☑ info 2810 286281; heraklioyouthhostel@yahoo.gr; Vyronos 5; €10) In a nice old building in a quiet but central side street, this hostel is a no-frills but clean affair. It's rarely busy and handy if you're just stopping over for the night. Most rooms have balconies. Free linen and towels.

Kronos Hotel HOTEL $
(☑ 2810 282240; www.kronoshotel.gr; Sofokli Venizelou 2; s/d €44/57; ❄@🛜) This top budget pick has inviting public areas that transition well to recently overhauled rooms with balconies (some sea-facing), although noisy traffic may not invite lingering. Double-glazed windows, though, ensure you'll have a good night's sleep. Breakfast is €5.

★ **Lato Boutique Hotel** BOUTIQUE HOTEL $$
(☑ 2810 228103; www.lato.gr; Epimenidou 15; d incl breakfast €89-136; P ❄@🛜) Iraklio goes Hollywood – with all the sass but without the attitude – at this mod boutique hotel in a lofty perch above the Venetian Harbour. A recent overhaul has resulted in an added wing, rooms brimming with colourful lacquered furniture, updated bathrooms and a rooftop restaurant with killer views.

Kastro Hotel HOTEL $$
(☑ 2810 284185; www.kastro-hotel.gr; Theotokopoulou 22; s/d incl breakfast €60/75; ❄@🛜) Offering standout value for money, the smartly renovated Kastro gets a big thumbs up for its smiley staff, generous breakfast buffet, spacious rooftop terrace and central location. Most rooms are sheathed in natural tones, but coolhunters might prefer the all-white retreats with designer bathrooms.

Capsis Astoria HOTEL $$
(☑ 2810 343080; www.capsishotel.gr; Plateia Eleftherias 11; s/d incl breakfast €77/100; P ❄@🛜🏊) The hulking Capsis is a class act all the way from the generous lobby to the rooftop pool (summer only). Rooms sport soothing neutral tones and ultracomfy mattresses and are decorated with historic black-and-white photographs of Heraklion. Wonderful breakfast buffet. Buses to Knossos, the beach and the airport leave from out front.

🍴 Eating

Paralia GREEK $
(☑ 2810 282475; www.paraliacrete.gr; Sofokli Venizelou 5; mains €5.50-12; ⊙ noon-midnight; 🛜) At first glance there aren't many menu surprises at this breezy, contemporary restaurant. But it's the punctilious preparation and appealing presentation that makes it a standout among several others down by the waterfront.

Fyllo...Sofies CAFE $
(☑ 2810 284774; www.fillosofies.gr; Plateia Venizelou 33; bougatsa €2.70-4.50; ⊙ 5am-late; 🛜) With a terrace spilling towards the Morosini Fountain, this been-here-forever cafe is *the* go-to place for *bougatsa*: a traditional pastry filled with cream or *myzithra* (sheep's milk cheese) and sometimes served with ice cream or sprinkled with honey and nuts.

Ippokambos SEAFOOD $
(☑ 2810 280240; Sofokli Venizelou 3; mains €6-13; ⊙ noon-midnight; 🛜) This traditional waterfront eatery usually buzzes with clued-in lo-

cals here for the fish – freshly caught, simply but expertly prepared and sold at fair prices. An above-average appetiser selection and the fresh and crunchy bread also put the place above the competition.

★ Herb's Garden
CRETAN **$$**

(Brillant; ☑ 2810 228103; www.brillantrestaurant.gr; Epimenidou 15; mains €10-22; ☼ lunch & dinner; 🛜) It's hard to decide what's more stunning about Lato Hotel's rooftop alfresco eatery: the harbour views or the global mix-and-match menu that gives old-time recipes a modern workout and eye-candy presentation. Typical palate teasers: vine-leaf-wrapped lamb or slow-cooked kid goat finished with grape-must. From November to April, the restaurant moves indoors and downstairs and renames itself Brillant.

Peri Orexeos
GREEK **$$**

(☑ 2810 222679; Koraï 10; mains €7-13; 🛜) This artsy, tunnel-shaped outpost of modern Hellenic cuisine scores with its prime ingredients, friendly staff and consistent quality. The chicken with cream and kataïfi (angel-hair pastry) is a menu standout, while raki gives the humble burger an innovative twist. Come early to score a table in the small courtyard.

🍷 Drinking & Nightlife

The see-and-be-seen scene sprawls around Koraï, Perdikari and El Greco Park. West of here, Handakos, Agiostefaniton and Psaromiligkon have more alternative-flavoured hang-outs. High-energy hipster joints clus-

ter on the waterfront around Talos Plaza, along about 1km west of the Venetian Harbour.

★ Bar Blow-Up
BAR

(http://barblowup.blogspot.de; Psaromiligkon 1; ☼ 1.30pm-late; 🛜) This funky party lair draws unpretentious types for beer, beats and bands. There's an alchemy of electro, funk and new wave on the turntable and Greek indie bands on the stage for the occasional live concert.

Fix
CAFE, BAR

(☑ 2810 289023; cnr Mirabello & Aretousa; ☼ 10am-late; 🛜) This tree-shaded cafe, backed by graffiti that would have done the Berlin Wall proud, draws chatty types for coffee, beer and cocktails.

Hallabro
BAR

(Milatou 10; ☼ 10am-late; 🛜) This stylish open-air bar is a smashing summertime hangout, even if prices are a little high by local standards (cocktails €10, wine from €5).

Central Park
CAFE, LOUNGE

(☑ 2810 346500; Arkoleontos 19; ☼ 8am-2am; 🛜) Any time is a good time to drop by Central Park, easily Iraklio's most popular outdoor cafe. Bask in a cacophony of conversation while sipping a Freddo Delight and checking out the all-ages crowd.

Envy
CAFE, BAR

(☑ 2810 372763; Sofokli Venizelou, nr Minoos, opposite Talos Plaza; ☼ 9am-late; 🛜) This is the unofficial club house of Iraklio's young, hip

---

NIKOS KAZANTZAKIS – CRETE'S LITERARY LION

Crete's most famous modern writer, Nikos Kazantzakis was born in Turkish-dominated Iraklio in 1883 in the ferment of revolution that finally broke out in 1897 and forced him to leave for studies in Naxos, Athens and Paris. His self-professed greatest work is the *Odyssey*, a modern-day epic loosely based on the trails and travels of the ancient Ulysses. The work that brought him international renown, though, was the 1946 *Life and Adventures of Alexis Zorbas* (later renamed *Zorba the Greek*), which gave rise to the image of the free-spirited Greek male as immortalised by Anthony Quinn in the 1964 *Zorba the Greek* movie.

Cretans are fiercely proud of their home boy, as you can gather when your plane touches down at the Nikos Kazantzakis Airport in Iraklio. Places to pay homage to the man include the well-curated **Nikos Kazantzakis Museum** (☑ 2810 741689; www.kazantzakis-museum.gr; adult/child €3/1; ☼ 9am-5pm Mar-Oct, 10am-3pm Sun Nov-Feb) in Myrtia, some 15km southeast of Iraklio, past Knossos. To see a **recreation of his office**, visit the Historical Museum of Crete (p421) in Iraklio, then swing by his **grave** (Martinengo Bastion) atop Martinengo Bastion, which is part of Iraklio's well-preserved Venetian town wall. The epitaph on his grave reads: 'I hope for nothing, fear nothing, I am free.'

and fashionable – a huge indoor/outdoor space right on the waterfront. A breezy summer vibe rules, especially around the pool where you can relax in (free) sun chairs or get down on the dance floor during hot-stepping pool parties.

Shopping

Aerakis Music
MUSIC

(2810 225758; www.aerakis.net; Koraï Sq 14) Specialises in Cretan traditional music.

Roadside Travel
BOOKS, MAPS

(2810 344610; Handakos 29; ⊙9am-2pm & 5.30-9pm) Great selection of maps and guidebooks.

ℹ Information

Iraklio's two hospitals are far from the centre and work alternate days – call first to find out where to go. Banks with ATMs are ubiquitous, especially along 25 Avgoustou. For online information, try www.heraklion-city.gr.

Main Post Office (Plateia Daskalogianni; ⊙7.30am-8pm Mon-Fri, 7.30am-2pm Sat)

Tourist Office (2810 228225; Xanthoulidou 1; ⊙9am-3pm Mon-Fri)

University Hospital (2810 392111) At Voutes, 5km south of Iraklio.

Venizelio Hospital (2810 368000) On the road to Knossos, 4km south of Iraklio.

ℹ Getting There & Away

AIR

Crete's biggest airport is about 5km east of the city centre. Infrastructure includes a well-stocked duty-free shop.

BOAT

Iraklio's **ferry port** (2810 244956) is located 500m east of the Venetian Harbour and has boats to Piraeus, Santorini (Thira), Ios, Paros and Mykonos, Karpathos, Kasos, Rhodes, Milos and Anafi. Buy tickets from agencies lining the upper end of 25 Avgoustou; **Paleologos** (2810 346185; 25 Avgoustou 5; ⊙9am-8pm Mon-Fri, 9am-4pm Sat) is recommended.

BUS

Iraklio has two major bus stations. **Bus Station A**, near the waterfront, serves eastern and western Crete (including Knossos), has a left-luggage office that's open from 6.30am to 8pm and charges €2 per piece per day. Local buses also stop here.

Bus Station B, just beyond Hania Gate west of the centre, serves Anogia, Phaestos, Agia Galini and Matala. See KTEL (www.bus-service-crete-ktel.com) for the current timetable.

Bus Services from Iraklio – Bus Station A

DESTINATION	TIME	FARE	FREQUENCY
Agios Nikolaos	1½hr	€7.10	up to 21 daily
Arhanes	30min	€1.70	up to 14 daily
Hania	3hr	€13.80	up to 16 daily
Hersonisos	40min	€3	at least half-hourly
Ierapetra	2½hr	€11	up to 6 daily
Kastelli	1hr	€3.70	up to five daily
Knossos	20min	€1.50	3 hourly
Lasithi Plateau	2hr	€6.50	1 daily
Malia	1hr	€3.80	at least half-hourly
Rethymno	1½hr	€7.60	up to 21 daily
Sitia	3¼hr	€14.70	up to 5 daily

Bus Services from Iraklio – Bus Station B

DESTINATION	TIME	FARE	FREQUENCY
Agia Galini	2hr	€8	up to 4 daily
Anogia	1hr	€3.80	up to 3 daily
Matala	2hr	€7.80	up to 3 daily
Phaestos	1½hr	€6.50	up to 5 daily

ℹ Getting Around

TO/FROM THE AIRPORT

The airport is just off the E75 motorway. Bus 1 connects it with the city centre every 10 minutes between 6.15am and 10.45pm (€1.10). Handy in-town stops are Bus Station A and Plateia Eleftherias. A taxi into town costs around €10. Handy in-town stops are Bus Station A and the stop on the east side of Plateia Eleftherias.

CAR & MOTORCYCLE

Iraklio's streets are narrow and chaotic, so it's best to drop your vehicle in a car park (per day €4 to €7) and explore on foot.

All the international car- and scooter-hire companies have branches at the airport. Local outlets on 25 Avgoustou include **Sun Rise** (2810 221609; www.sunrise-cars-bikes.gr; 25 Avgoustou 46; per day cars from €30, scooters from €12) and **Motor Club** (2810 222408; www.motorclub.gr; Plateia 18 Anglon; per day car from €40, scooters from €28).

TAXI

Central taxi ranks are at Bus Station A, on Plateia Eleftherias and on Plateia Kornarou. Or order one by **phone** (☏ 2810 210102).

Around Iraklio

Knossos   Κνωσσός

Crete's must-see historical attraction is the Minoan **Palace of Knossos** (☏ 2810 231940; adult/concession €6/3; ☺ 8am-8pm Jun-Sep, 8am-5pm Oct-May), the capital of Minoan Crete and only 5km south of Iraklio. To beat the crowds and avoid the heat, get there before 9am or after 3pm. Guided tours (in English, €10) last about 90 minutes and leave from the kiosk past the ticket booth. Budget at least two hours for your visit.

History

Knossos' first palace (1900 BC) was destroyed by an earthquake around 1700 BC, rebuilt to a grander and more sophisticated design, partially destroyed again between 1500 and 1450 BC and inhabited for another 50 years before finally burning down. The complex comprised royal domestic quarters, public reception rooms, shrines, workshops, treasuries and storerooms, all orbiting a central court.

The ruins of Knossos were unearthed in 1900 by the British archaeologist Sir Arthur Evans (1851–1941). Evans was so enthralled by his discovery that he spent 35 years and £250,000 of his own money excavating and reconstructing sections of the palace. Although controversial in expert circles, his reconstructions help casual visitors tremendously in visualising what the palace might have looked like in its heyday.

◉ Sights

Evans' reconstruction brings to life the palace's most significant parts, including the columns that are painted deep brown-red with gold-trimmed black capitals and taper gracefully at the bottom. Vibrant frescoes add dramatic flourishes. The advanced drainage system and a clever floorplan that kept rooms cool in summer and warm in winter are further evidence of Minoan advanced living standards.

There's no prescribed route to explore the palace, but the following tour takes in the key highlights. Entering from the **West Court**, you'll see a trio of circular pits on your left – called **kouloures**, they were once used for grain storage. Turn left past the pits and walk along the palace's western wall

Palace of Knossos

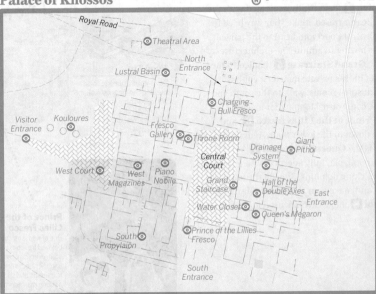

Palace of Knossos

THE HIGHLIGHTS IN TWO HOURS

The Palace of Knossos is Crete's busiest tourist attraction, and for good reason. A spin around the partially reconstructed complex delivers an eye-opening peek into the remarkably sophisticated society of the Minoans, who dominated southern Europe some 4000 years ago.

From the ticket booth, follow the marked trail to the **North Entrance 1** where the Charging Bull fresco gives you a first taste of Minoan artistry. Continue to the Central Court and join the queue waiting to glimpse the mystical **Throne Room 2**, which probably hosted religious rituals. Turn right as you exit and follow the stairs up to the so-called Piano Nobile, where replicas of the palace's most famous artworks conveniently cluster in the **Fresco Room 3**. Walk the length of the Piano Nobile, pausing to look at the clay storage vessels in the West Magazines, to a staircase descending to the **South Portico 4**, beautifully decorated with the Cup Bearer fresco. Make your way back to the Central Court and head to the palace's eastern wing to admire the architecture of the **Grand Staircase 5** that led to the royal family's private quarters. For a closer look at some rooms, walk to the south end of the courtyard, stopping for a peek at the **Prince of the Lilies fresco 6**, and head down to the lower floor. A highlight here is the **Queen's Megaron 7** (bedroom), playfully adorned with a fresco of frolicking dolphins. Stay on the lower level and make your way to the **Giant Pithoi 8**, huge clay jars used for storage.

ANDREA SCHULTE-PEEVERS ©

ANDREA SCHULTE-PEEVERS ©

South Portico
Fine frescoes, most famously the Cup Bearer, embellish this palace entrance anchored by a massive open staircase leading to the Piano Nobile. The Horns of Consecration recreated nearby once topped the entire south facade.

Fresco Room
Take in sweeping views of the palace grounds from the west wing's upper floor, the Piano Nobile, before studying copies of the palace's most famous art works in its Fresco Room.

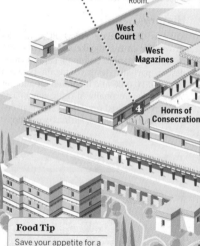

West Court

West Magazines

Horns of Consecration

Food Tip
Save your appetite for a meal in the nearby Iraklio Wine Country, amid sunbaked slopes and lush valleys. It's just south of Knossos.

ANDREA SCHULTE-PEEVERS ©

Prince of the Lilies Fresco
One of Knossos' most beloved frescoes was controversially cobbled together from various fragments and shows a young man adorned in lilies and peacock feathers.

Planning

To beat the crowds and avoid the heat, arrive before 10am. Budget several hours to explore the site thoroughly.

Throne Room

Sir Arthur Evans who discovered the Palace of Knossos in 1900, imagined the mythical King Minos himself holding court seated on the alabaster throne of this beautifully proportioned room. However, the lustral basin and griffin frescoes suggest a religious purpose, possibly under a priestess.

North Entrance

Bulls held a special status in Minoan society as evidenced by the famous relief fresco of a charging beast gracing the columned west bastion of the north palace, which harboured workshops and storage rooms.

Grand Staircase

The royal apartments in the eastern wing were accessed via this monumental staircase sporting four flights of gypsum steps supported by columns. The lower two flights are original. It's closed to the public.

Piano Nobile

3

1

2

5

Central Court

Royal Apartments

8

6

7

Queen's Megaron

The queen's bedroom is among the prettiest in the residential eastern wing thanks to the playful Dolphin Fresco. The adjacent bathroom (with clay tub) and toilet are evidence of a sophisticated drainage system.

Giant Pithoi

These massive clay jars are rare remnants from the Old Palace period and were used to store wine, oil and grain. The jars were transported by slinging ropes through a series of handles.

towards the theatral area, then turn right past the lustral basin (in a square building), then right again to enter the palace itself via the North Entrance. Stop to admire the Charging Bull Fresco before continuing to the vast Central Court.

Grouped around the central court are the palace's most important rooms, including the Throne Room on your right. Peering through security glass, you can make out a simple, beautifully proportioned alabaster throne and walls decorated with frescoes of griffins, regarded as sacred by Minoans. Past the Throne Room a staircase leads to the upper floor (called Piano Nobile by Evans) where the reception and staterooms may have been located. On its north end, above the Throne Room, the restored Fresco Room houses replicas of the most famous frescoes found at Knossos, including the Bull-Leaper, the Ladies in Blue and the Blue Bird. The originals are in the Iraklio Archaeological Museum. At the far east end of the Piano Nobile, past the west magazines (storage rooms), steps lead down to the South Propylaion adorned with the Cup Bearer fresco.

Make your way back to the central court, briefly popping by the Prince of the Lillies fresco on the south flank, then crossing diagonally to get to the impressive Grand Staircase once leading down to the royal apartments. Study the residential wing's layout from above before heading down for close-ups of the Dolphin Fresco in the Queen's Megaron (room) and the adjacent bathroom. The king resided next door in the Hall of the Double Axes, which takes its name from the double axe marks (*labrys*) on its light well, a sacred symbol to the Minoans and the origin of the word 'labyrinth'.

In sections further north you'll see parts of the palace's sophisticated drainage system and giant pithoi before returning to the central court.

❶ Getting There & Away

There's no shortage of signs directing drivers to Knossos, but with parking at a premium in summer, it may be better to take bus 2 from Bus Station A or from just outside the Hotel Capsis Astoria on Plateia Eleftherias (€1.50, every 20 minutes).

Iraklio Wine Country

About 70% of wine produced in Crete comes from the Iraklio Wine Country, which starts just south of Knossos and is headquartered in Peza. Almost two dozen wineries are embedded in a harmonious landscape of shapely hills, sunbaked slopes and lush valleys. Winemakers cultivate many indigenous Cretan grape varietals, such as Kotsifali, Mandilari and Malvasia; many estates now offer tours, wine museums and wine tastings. Here are three of our faves, but do check www.winesofcrete.gr for more options and look for the burgundy-red road signs directing you to local wineries.

◉ Sights

Boutari   WINERY
(☑ 2810 731617; www.boutari.gr; Skalani; ☺ 9am-5pm Mon-Fri year-round, on weekends by appointment) In Skalani, just south of Knossos, Boutari is a sleek, modern operation that offers tours as well as sampling sessions in a vast tasting room that overlooks the vineyards.

Lyrarakis   WINERY
(☑ 2810 284501; www.lyrarakis.gr; Alagni; ☺ 11am-8pm Mon-Fri, 1-6pm Sat Apr-Oct) In Alagni, about 25km south of Iraklio, this award-winning winery is famous for resuscitating two nearly extinct white Cretan grape varieties called Dafni and Plyto.

Minos-Miliarikis   WINERY
(☑ 2810 741213; www.minoswines.gr; Peza; ☺ 9am-4pm Mon-Fri, 10am-3pm Sat) Right on the Peza main street, massive Minos was the first winery to bottle its product in Crete in 1952. Worth trying: a full-bodied single-vineyard organic red and a fragrant Blanc de Noirs.

✖ Eating

Elia & Diosmos   CRETAN
(☑ 2810 731283; www.olive-mint.gr; Skalani; mains €10-19; ☺ lunch & dinner Tue-Sun) Among the many fine restaurants in the wine country, Elia & Diosmos in Skalani is a veritable foodie playground and a good lunch spot if you're visiting Knossos.

Cretaquarium

The massive Cretaquarium (☑ 2810 337788; www.cretaquarium.gr; adult/concession €9/6; ☺ 9.30am-9pm May-Sep, 9.30am-5pm Oct-Apr) at Gournes, 15km east of Iraklio, is a vast high-tech indoor sea on the grounds of a former US Air Force base. Inhabited by some 2500 Mediterranean and tropical aquatic critters, this huge aquarium will likely bring smiles

OTHER MINOAN PALACES

Besides Knossos, central Crete has a trio of key Minoan sites that were not reconstructed and thus provide a glimpse into this ancient society without Evans' interpretations.

Phaestos
Φαιστός

Some 63km southwest of Iraklio near Matala, **Phaestos** (☑ 28920 42315; adult/concession/under 18 & EU students €4/2/free, incl Agia Triada €6/3/free; ⊗ 8am-7.30pm Jun-Oct, to 5pm Nov-Apr) was Crete's second-most-important Minoan palace-city after Knossos and enjoys an awe-inspiring setting with panoramic views of the Mesara Plain and Mt Psiloritis. The celebrated Phaestos Disk, now in the Iraklio Archaeological Museum, was found just northwest of the palace.

Like Knossos, Phaestos (fes-*tos*) was built atop a previously destroyed older palace and laid out around a central court. In contrast to its bigger cousin, though, this site had fewer frescoes as walls were apparently covered with white gypsum only.

Past the ticket booth, you'll first come across the **Upper Court**, which may have been a market square. From here, stairs lead down to the **West Court** with the **Theatral Area** off to the right and a sweeping **Grand Staircase** to the left. This once led to the **Propylae**, the main palace entrance, of which only the pillar bases survive. Past a series of storage rooms lies the vast **Central Court** with the royal living quarters in the north wing (turn left). These include the **queen's and the king's megaron** (under cover) and the **Peristyle Court**, an elegant inner courtyard.

Phaestos is served by KTEL (p418) buses up to five times daily from Iraklio (€6.50, 1½ hours), twice from Matala (€1.80, 30 minutes) and three times from Agia Galini (€2.10, 45 minutes).

Agia Triada
Αγία Τριάδα

In an enchanting spot 3km west of Phaestos, **Agia Triada** (☑ 27230 22448; adult/concession/under 18 & EU students €3/1.50/free, incl Phaestos €6/3/free; ⊗ 10am-4.30pm Apr-Oct, 10am-3pm Nov-Mar) encompasses vestiges of an L-shaped royal villa, a ramp once leading out to sea and a village with residences and stores. Built around 1550 BC, Agia Triada (ah-*yee*-ah trih-*ah*-dha) succumbed to fire around 1400 BC but was never looted. This accounts for the many Minoan masterpieces found here, most famously the **Agia Triada Sarcophagus**, now a star exhibit at the Iraklio Archaeological Museum.

The signposted turn-off to Agia Triada is about 500m past Phaestos on the Matala road. There's no direct public transport to the site, so either walk or hitch a ride from Phaestos.

Malia
Μάλια

On the north coast, about 35km east of Iraklio, near the eponymous coastal resort, the **Palace of Malia** (☑ 28970 31597; adult/seniors & EU students/under 18 €4/2/free; ⊗ 8.30am-3pm Tue-Sun) is a relatively easy site to comprehend thanks to a free map, an exhibition hall and labelling throughout.

Enter from the **West Court**, turn right and walk south along a series of **storage rooms** to eight circular pits believed to have been grain silos. Continue past the silos and enter the palace's **Central Court** from the south. On your left, in the ground, is the **Kernos Stone**, a disc with 24 holes around its edge that may have had a religious function. Just beyond here are the palace's most important rooms, including the **Pillar Crypt** behind a stone-paved vestibule, the **Grand Staircase** and the elevated **Loggia**, most likely used for ceremonial purposes. Still further were the **royal apartments**, while buildings north of the central court held **workshops** and **storage rooms**.

Buses leave from Iraklio's Bus Station A several times hourly for Malia with a stop at the palace (€3.80, one hour).

to even the most Playstation-jaded youngster. Interactive multimedia help explain the mysteries of this rich and diverse underwater world.

Half-hourly buses en route to Malia (€1.70, 30 minutes) from Iraklio's Bus Station A can drop you on the main road; from there it's a 10-minute walk.

WORTH A TRIP

GORTYNA
ΓΟΡΤΥΝΑ

En route to Matala, build in a stop in **Gortyna** (☑28920 31144; adult/concession/under 18 & EC students €4/2/free; ☺8.30am-8pm Jul & Aug, shorter hours rest of year), which was once a subject town of powerful Phaestos (p429) but later became the capital of Roman Crete. At its peak, as many as 100,000 people may have milled around its streets.

There are two sections to Gortyna, with the best-preserved relics in the fenced area on the north side of the road. These include the 6th-century Byzantine **Church of Agios Titos**, the finest early Christian church in Crete and, even more importantly, the massive stone tablets inscribed with the 6th-century-BC **Laws of Gortyna**, the oldest law code in the Greek world. In mythology, the evergreen **plane tree** just north of here was Zeus and Europa's 'love nest'.

Most of the major Roman structures are spread over a vast area south of the highway and are therefore not as easy to locate. Look for road signs pointing to the **Temple of Apollo**, the main sanctuary of pre-Roman Gortyna. East of here is the 2nd-century-AD **Praetorium**, which was the Roman governor's residence, a **Nymphaeum** (public bath) and an amphitheatre.

Gortyna is 46km southwest of Iraklio and 15km east of Phaestos. Buses between Iraklio and Matala can drop you off.

Zaros
Ζαρός

POP 3370

At the bottom of the mighty Rouvas Gorge in the Mt Psiloritis foothills, the rustic mountain village of Zaros is famous for its natural spring water, which is bottled and sold all over Crete. Clued-in foodies flock here for the fresh farm-raised trout, which can be enjoyed in numerous tavernas around town and on emerald-green Lake Votomos.

Zaros also lures outdoor-lovers with its easy to moderate 5km hike through the **Rouvas Gorge**. The trail starts near the Limni taverna but doesn't enter the gorge for another 1km, just past Moni Agios Nikolaos, a modern monastery that wraps around a historic church rife with icons and fresco fragments. The path first weaves through fire-damaged forest but soon the vegetation becomes increasingly lush with oak trees, lilies, orchids, sage and other mountain flora. At the end is a little chapel of Agios Ioannis where benches and tables invite a leisurely picnic.

🛏 Sleeping & Eating

Eleonas Cottages
COTTAGES $$

(☑6976670002, 28940 312389; www.eleonas.gr; Zaros; studio/cottage incl breakfast from €85/98; ❄@🛜🏊) This is an attractive mountain retreat set among the olive groves in a terraced hillside overlooking a valley. Smartly appointed units have cooking facilities and owners can arrange a slew of activities – horse riding, archery, mountain bikes and guided walking tours.

★Vegera
CRETAN $

(☑28940 31730; www.vegerazaros.gr; Main St; four-course meal €12; ☺breakfast, lunch & dinner; ☑) The vivacious Vivi has a knack for turning farm-fresh local produce into amazingly flavourful and creative dishes based on traditional recipes. A full meal with fresh bread, a garden salad, cheese and olives, a cooked main course, pastries and *raki* is just €12.

Limni
FISH, CRETAN $$

(☑28940 31338; Zaros; mains €7-17; ☺9am-late) Right on Lake Votomos, this taverna is a peaceful oasis serving fresh grilled trout and Cretan specialities. The basket of starters that comes out with the bread adds a nice touch.

❶ Getting There & Away

Zaros is about 46km southwest of Iraklio. From Iraklio's Bus Station B, one bus daily stops in Zaros en route to Kamares (€4.70; one hour). Check KTEL (www.bus-service-crete-ktel.com) for timings.

Matala
Μάταλα

POP 300

In mythology Matala (*ma*-ta-la) is the place where Zeus swam ashore with the kidnapped Europa on his back before dragging her off to Gortyna and getting her pregnant with the future King Minos. In more recent times, Matala earned legacy status thanks to the scores of hippies flocking here in the late 1960s to take up rent-free residence in cliffside caves. Joni Mitchell famously immortalised the era in her song 'Carey'. Since 2011, tens of thousands of revelers come in July to celebrate the peace and love spirit during the Matala Beach Festival (www.matalabeachfestival.com). On normal summer days, though, the village feels anything but peaceful thanks to coachloads of day trippers. Stay overnight or visit in the off-season, though, and it's still possible to discern the Matala magic: the setting along a crescent-shaped bay flanked by headlands is simply spectacular.

◎ Sights & Activities

Matala's sightseeing credentials are limited to the famous 'hippie' caves (admission €2; ◎10am-5pm Apr-Sep) that actually date back to neolithic times and were used as tombs by the Romans. To escape the main beach crowds in summer, embark on a 30-minute scramble over the rocks to clothing-optional Red Beach (bring snacks and water) or head to Kommos Beach about 2km north of Matala, home to two tavernas.

🛏 Sleeping

'Hotel Row' runs perpendicular to the main drag opposite Hotel Zafiria (en route to Red Beach). There's also a scruffy, sometimes-open campground above the main beach.

Matala Valley Village RESORT $
(🖉28920 45776; www.valleyvillage.gr; s/d/bungalow €40/50/85; ◎May-Oct; P✳🛜≋) This family-friendly garden resort, located at the eastern village entrance, consists of low-lying buildings with fairly basic rooms and two-dozen spiffier whitewashed bungalows with Jacuzzi tubs and a separate shower. Frolicking grounds include a lawn, small playground and big pool.

Hotel Nikos HOTEL $
(🖉28920 45375; www.matala-nikos.com; Hotel Row; r €40-45; ✳🛜) A standout on hotel row, family-run Nikos has 17 rooms, many with small kitchens and a terrace, on two floors flanking a flower-filled courtyard, the nicest being the top-floor No 24 with cave views. Breakfast is €6.

✕ Eating

Gianni's GREEK $
(🖉6983619233; mains €5.50-13.50; ◎noon-4pm & 6pm-midnight) No waterfront views but honest-to-goodness grilled meats and fish are the ammo at this been-there-forever family tavern with the cheerfully blue chairs just past the central square.

Bunga Bunga GREEK $
(Kommos Beach; mains €5-10; ◎breakfast, lunch & dinner) One of two tavernas at Kommos Beach, about 2km north of Matala, the Caribbean-style Bunga Bunga serves tasty, fresh, organic fare.

Scala Fish Tavern SEAFOOD, GREEK $$
(🖉28920 45489; mains €7-15; ◎lunch & dinner; 🛜) Maria's place, past all the bars on the east end of the cove, gets top marks for its fresh fish, superior service and romantic sunset views of the caves.

Mystical View GREEK $$
(🖉6944139164; Kommos Beach; mains €7-13; ◎lunch & dinner; 🛜) Views are truly stunning from this clifftop outpost overlooking Kommos Beach, especially at sunset. Look for the signpost at the roundabout about 2km outside of Matala.

ⓘ Getting There & Away

Up to three KTEL (www.bus-service-crete-ktel.com) buses daily leave Iraklio's Bus Station B for

---

WORTH A TRIP

MUSEUM OF CRETAN ETHNOLOGY

This museum (🖉28920 91110; www.cretanethnologymuseum.gr; Voroi Pirgiotissis, Vori; admission €3; ◎11am-5pm Apr-Oct, by appointment in winter) is the best of its kind in Crete and worth a quick detour to Vori for fascinating insight into traditional Cretan culture. The English-labelled exhibits are organised around such themes as rural life, food production, war, customs, architecture and music. Although most of the items are rather ordinary – hoes, olive presses, baskets, clothing, instruments etc – they're all engagingly displayed in darkened rooms accented with spotlights. It's well signposted from the main Mires–Tymbaki road.

Matala (€7.80, two hours). There's free roadside parking and a beach parking lot that charges €2.

Rethymno Ρέθυμνο

POP 54,900

Basking between the commanding bastions of its 15th-century fortress and the glittering Med, Rethymno (*reth*-im-no) is one of Crete's most delightful towns. Its Venetian-Ottoman quarter is a lyrical maze of lanes draped in flowers and punctuated by wood-balconied houses; minarets add an exotic flourish. While architectural similarities invite comparison to Hania, Rethymno has a character all of its own, thanks in large part to a sizeable student population. Crete's third-largest town has lively nightlife, some excellent restaurants and even a decent beach right in town. The busier beaches, with their requisite resorts, stretch almost without interruption all the way to Panormo, some 22km east.

⊙ Sights

Rethymno is fairly compact, with most sights, accommodation and tavernas wedged within the largely pedestrianised Old Quarter off the Venetian Harbour. The long sandy beach starts just east of the harbour.

Fortezza   FORTRESS

(Venetian Fortress; Paleokastro Hill; adult/senior/family €4/3/10; ⊙8am-8pm Jun-Oct, 10am-5pm Nov-May) Looming over Rethymno, the massive Venetian fortress cuts an impressive figure with its massive walls and imposing bastions, but was still unable to stave off the Turks in 1646. Over time, an entire village took shape on the grounds, most of which was destroyed in WWII. Views are fabulous from up here and it's fun to poke around the ramparts, palm trees and remaining buildings, most notably the Sultan Bin Imbrahim Mosque with its huge dome.

Rethymno

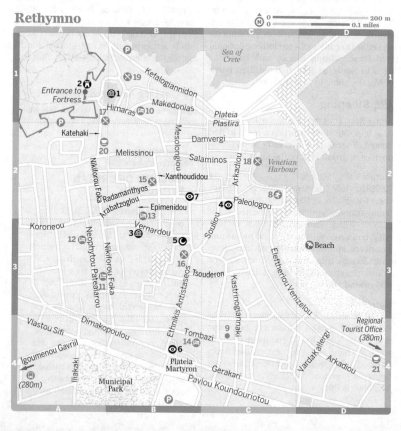

Archaeological Museum MUSEUM
(☎28310 54668; adult/concession €3/2; ⏱9am-3pm Tue-Sun) In a Turkish-era building that served as a prison until the 1960s, this small museum showcases treasures from neolithic to Roman times, including bronze tools, Minoan pottery, Mycenaean figurines, Roman oil lamps and a 1st-century-AD sculpture of Aphrodite.

Old Quarter NEIGHBOURHOOD
Pride of place among Rethymno's many Venetian vestiges goes to the **Rimondi Fountain** (cnr Paleologou & Petihaki Sq), with its spouting lion heads and Corinthian capitals, and the nearby **Loggia**, which was once a meeting house for nobility and is now a gift shop. South of here, the **Porta Guora** (Great Gate; cnr Ethnikis Antistaseos & Dimakopoulou) is the only remnant of the Venetian defensive wall.

Among the few remaining Ottoman structures, the most important is the triple-domed **Neratzes Mosque** (Vernardou), which was converted from a Franciscan church in 1657 and is now used as a music conservatory and concert venue.

Rethymno

Sights

1	Archaeological Museum	B1
2	Fortezza	A1
3	Historical & Folk Art Museum	B3
4	Loggia	C2
5	Neratzes Mosque	B3
6	Porta Guora	B4
7	Rimondi Fountain	B2

Activities, Courses & Tours

8	Dolphin Cruises	C2
9	Happy Walker	C4

Sleeping

10	Atelier	B1
	Avli Lounge Apartments	(see 15)
11	Casa dei Delfini	A3
12	Casa Vitae	A3
13	Hotel Veneto	B2
14	Rethymno Youth Hostel	B4

Eating

15	Avli	B2
16	Lemonokipos	B3
17	Soul Kitchen	A1
18	Taverna Knossos	C2
19	Thalassografia	B1

Drinking & Nightlife

20	Chalikouti	A2
21	Livingroom	D4

On the same street, the five-room **Historical & Folk Art Museum** (☎28310 23398; Vernardou 26-28; adult/student €4/2; ⏱9.30am-2.30pm Mon-Sat), in a lovely Venetian mansion, documents traditional rural life with displays of clothing, baskets, weavings and farming tools.

Activities

Dolphin Cruises BOAT TOUR
(☎28310 57666; www.dolphin-cruises.com; Venetian Harbour; cruises €18-35) Dolphin runs cruises to pirate caves and the seaside resorts of Panormo and Bali, as well as fishing trips.

Happy Walker HIKING
(☎28310 52920; www.happywalker.com; Tombazi 56; day walks €32) Happy Walker runs single- and multi-day hikes through gorges, along ancient donkey trails and to traditional villages in Crete's lush hinterland.

Sleeping

Atelier PENSION $
(☎28310 24440; www.frosso-bora.com; Himaras 25; d €45-55; ❄📶) With their exposed stone walls and Venetian architectural features, these four rooms attached to a pottery workshop near the fortress are an excellent budget pick. Both are run by local ceramicist Frosso Bora.

Rethymno Youth Hostel HOSTEL $
(☎28310 22848; www.yhrethymno.com; Tombazi 41; dm €10; 📶) Friendly, well run and central, this hostel sleeps six to eight people in clean and functional dorms and features a patio and bar conducive to making friends out of strangers. Breakfast and snacks are available too. The reception is staffed from 8am to 1pm and 5pm to 11pm. Sheets are €1.

★ **Hotel Veneto** BOUTIQUE HOTEL $$
(☎28310 56634; www.veneto.gr; Epimenidou 4; s/d €70/110; ❄📶) This Venetian-era charmer encapsulates everything Rethymno has to offer: history, beauty, art and great food (in the onsite restaurant). Each of the 10 rooms tells a story, such as No 101, which used to be a monk's cell, or No 106, which was once a *hammam* (Turkish bath). Optional breakfast is €6.

Casa dei Delfini BOUTIQUE HOTEL $$
(☎6937254857, 28310 55120; www.casadeidelfini.com; Nikiforou Foka 66-68; studio/maisonette €70/110; ❄📶) The four rooms in this el-

egant guesthouse orbit a small courtyard with a dolphin mosaic and brim with historic character. In one, the bathroom used to be a *hammam*; in another, the bed is tucked into an arched stone alcove. All have kitchenettes. The two-storey maisonette comes with a large private terrace.

Casa Vitae
BOUTIQUE HOTEL **$$**

(☑6973237897, 28310 35058; www.casa-vitae.gr; Neophytou Patealarou 3; r €80-143; ❄ 🤖) This charismatic Venetian-era hotel has 11 quietly elegant rooms mixing stone and wood and wrapping around a fountain-anchored courtyard where home-cooked breakfast is served beneath the vine-covered pergola. Those in an annex across the lane are cheaper but just as lovely.

Avli Lounge Apartments
BOUTIQUE HOTEL **$$$**

(☑28310 58250; www.avli.gr; Xanthoudidou 22, cnr Radamanthyos; r incl breakfast €140-270; ❄ 🤖) Luxury is taken very seriously at this hushed retreat, where you'll be ensconced in warmly furnished studios sporting stone walls, beamed ceilings and Jacuzzi tubs. Retire to plush beds after a first-rate dinner in Avli's romantic courtyard garden restaurant.

✗ Eating

Taverna Knossos
GREEK **$**

(www.knosos-rethymno.com; Old Venetian Harbour; mains €6-12, set menu for two €30; 🤖) Most tout-fronted tavernas in the Venetian Harbour focus more on ambience than on food quality. Owned by the Stavroulaki family for half a century, Knossos is a happy exception. Dishes are loaded with flavour, the fish is outstanding and the service swift and gracious.

Soul Kitchen
VEGETARIAN **$**

(☑28310 30553; cnr Katehaki & Himaras; dishes €4-9; ⊙10am-11pm; 🤖🍴) At this plant-based restaurant only organic, local and seasonal ingredients make it into the daily changing roster of tasty homemade soups, salads and casseroles. Service is...mellow.

★ Prima Plora
SEAFOOD **$$**

(☑28310 56990; www.primaplora.gr; Akrotiriou 4; mains €7.50-22; ⊙lunch & dinner; 🤖) If you want seaside dining without the faux folklore of the harbour tavernas, head 2km west of the Fortezza where Prima Plora delivers romance by the bucket amid a contemporary nautical vibe. Take in views of bay and castle while finding your favourites on the globally inspired menu.

Thalassografia
MEDITERRANEAN **$$**

(☑28310 52569; Kefalogiannidon 33; mains €5-20; ⊙lunch & dinner May-Oct; 🤖) If it's not too windy, friendly service, superb fortress and sea views, and eclectic Mediterranean cuisine invite lingering in this artist-owned cafe with its breezy cascading terraces.

Lemonokipos
CRETAN **$$**

(☑28310 57087; www.lemontreegarden.com; Ethnikis Antistaseos 100; mains €7-24; 🤖) Candles, wine and a table for two in an enchanted courtyard are the hallmarks of a romantic night out. But even if your date doesn't make you swoon, the creative Cretan classics served beneath the lemon trees should still ensure an unforgettable evening.

Avli
CRETAN **$$$**

(☑28310 58250; www.avli.com; Xanthoudidou 22, cnr Radamanthyos; mains €11.50-27; 🤖) This well-established Venetian garden villa serves creative Cretan food with a side of romance. Farm-fresh fare steers the menu resulting in dishes with bold flavour pairings: kid goat meets honey and thyme, sea bass cuddles up with lemon saffron sauce, and octopus teams up with caramelised onions.

🍷 Drinking & Nightlife

Rethymno's young and restless are mostly drawn to the cafe-bars along Eleftheriou Venizelou, while the area around the Rimondi Fountain tends to be more popular with tourists.

Livingroom
CAFE, BAR

(www.livingroom.gr; Eleftheriou Venizelou 5; ⊙9am-3am; 🤖) The sleekest bar on the waterfront strip wows with its eclectic decor (big mirrors, velvet chairs, stylish lamps) and live DJ sets.

Chalikouti
CAFE, BAR

(☑28310 42632; Katehaki 3; ⊙9am-1am; 🤖) In the artsy quarter below the Fortezza, this cafe collective draws talkative locals who appreciate the coffee from Mexican Zapatistas, sugar from landless workers in Brazil and raki from a Cretan women's cooperative.

ℹ Information

There are free public wi-fi hotspots at the town hall, Plateia Iroon (Iroon Sq), the Venetian Harbour and the Municipal Garden, all within the Old Town.

Hospital (☑28210 27491; Triandalydou 17; ⊙24hr)

Post Office (Moatsou 21; ☺7am-7pm Mon-Fri)
Regional Tourist Office (☎28310 29148; www.rethymnon.gr; Sofokli Venizelou; ☺8am-2pm Mon-Fri)

❶ Getting There & Away

BUS

The **bus station** (cnr Igoumenou Gavriil & Kefalogiannidon) is on the western edge of the centre. Check KTEL (www.bus-service-crete-ktel.com) for the current schedule.

Bus Services from Rethymno

DESTINATION	TIME	FARE	FREQUENCY
Agia Galini	1½hr	€6.20	up to 4 daily
Anogia	1¼hr	€5.50	2 Mon-Fri
Hania	1hr	€6.20	hourly
Hora Sfakion	2hr	€7.30	2 daily
Iraklio	1½hr	€7.60	hourly
Moni Arkadiou	40min	€2.80	up to 3 daily
Omalos (Samaria Gorge)	1¾hr	€15	1 daily
Plakias	1hr	€4.50	up to 5 daily
Preveli	1¼hr	€4.50	2 daily

❶ Getting Around

Auto Moto Sports (☎28310 24858; www.automotosport.com.gr; Sofoklis Venizelou 48; per day from €32; ☺10am-7pm) rents cars and motorbikes, or ask your hotel to make a referral or booking. Bike rentals are available from **Nature & Adventure** (☎28310 29508, 6977541550; www.nat-adv.gr; Sofokli Venizelou 4a; per day from €10; ☺10am-7pm).

Moni Arkadiou
Μονή Αρκαδίου

The 16th-century **Moni Arkadiou** (Arkadi Monastery; ☎28310 83136; www.arkadimonastery.gr; admission €2.50; ☺9am-8pm Jun-Sep, shorter hours rest of year), some 23km southeast of Rethymno, has deep significance for Cretans as a stark and potent symbol of resistance in the struggle towards freedom from Turkish occupation.

In November 1866 massive Ottoman forces arrived to crush island-wide revolts. Hundreds of Cretan men, women and children fled their villages to find shelter at Arkadiou. However, far from being a safe haven, the monastery was soon besieged by 2000 Turkish soldiers. Rather than surrender, the entrapped locals blew up stored gunpowder kegs, killing everyone, Turks included. One small girl miraculously survived and lived to a ripe old age in a village nearby. A bust of this woman and another of the abbot who lit the gunpowder are outside the monastery not far from the old windmill – now an **ossuary** with skulls and bones of the 1866 victims neatly arranged in a glass cabinet.

Arkadiou's impressive **Venetian church** (1587) has a striking Renaissance facade topped by an ornate triple-belled tower. Grounds include a small museum and the old wine cellar where the gunpowder was stored.

Three buses daily arrive here (two on weekends) from Rethymno (€2.80, 40 minutes).

Anogia
Ανώγεια
POP 2400

Perched aside Mt Psiloritis, 37km southwest of Iraklio, Anogia is known for its rebellious spirit and determination to express its undiluted Cretan character. During WWII, it was a centre of resistance and suffered heavily for it. The Nazis burned down the town and massacred all the men in retaliation for their role in sheltering Allied troops and aiding in the kidnapping of a Nazi general.

Anogia is also famous for its stirring music and has spawned many of Crete's best-known musicians such as Nikos Xylouris, whose home is now a small museum. Locals cling to time-honoured traditions and it's not rare to see men gossiping in the kafenia dressed in traditional black shirts with baggy pants tucked into black boots. Elderly women, meanwhile, keep busy flogging traditional woven blankets and embroidered textiles. Though beautiful and well-priced, not all are actually produced locally, so *caveat emptor*.

🛏 Sleeping & Eating

Hotel Aristea HOTEL $
(☎28340 31459; www.hotelaristea.gr; s/d incl breakfast €35/42, apt €70-110; P🅿🛜) Run by the chatty and charming Aristea, this small inn offers sweeping valley views from balconies attached to fairly basic but spotless and comfortable enough rooms. The split-level apartments in a next-door annex are more modern. Don't skip the home-cooked breakfast.

Arodamos CRETAN $

(☑28340 31100; www.arodamos.gr; mains €6-10; ⊙lunch & dinner) This big restaurant in a modern stone house in the upper village is held in high regard for its perky Cretan fare and gracious hospitality. Local specialities include the flame-teased lamb or goat (*ofto*) and spaghetti cooked in stock and topped with local cheese.

Ta Skalomata CRETAN $

(☑28340 31316; www.skalomata.gr; mains €4-9; ⊙lunch & dinner; ⑤) In the upper village, Skalomata has provided sustenance to locals and travellers for about 40 years with great grilled meats (the roast lamb is especially good), homemade wine and bread, and even tasty meatless fare such as zucchini with cheese and eggplant.

❶ Getting There & Away

There are up to three buses daily from Iraklio (€3.80, one hour) and two buses Monday to Friday from Rethymno (€5.50, 1¼ hours).

Mt Psiloritis
Ορος Ψηλορείτης

At 2456m, Mt Psiloritis, also known as Mt Idi, is Crete's highest mountain. At its eastern base is the **Nida Plateau** (1400m), a wide, fertile expanse reached via a paved 21km-long road from Anogia past several *mitata* (round, stone shepherd's huts) and the turnoff to the highly regarded **Skinakas Observatory** (www.skinakas.org.gr; ⊙full moon summer weekends). At the top, a simple taverna offers refreshment and spartan rooms (€25). It gets chilly up here, even in summer, so bring a sweater or light jacket.

From the parking lot, it's a 1km uphill walk to the **Ideon Cave**. Although just a huge and fairly featureless hole in the ground, Ideon has sacred importance in mythology as the place where Zeus was reared by his mother Rhea, protected from the clutches of his child-devouring father Cronos.

Back on the plateau itself, you can make out a sprawling landscape sculpture called **Andartis – Partisan of Peace** that looks like an angel when seen from above and commemorates Cretan WWII resistance fighters.

Spili
Σπίλι

POP 700

Spili (*spee-lee*) is a pretty mountain village and shutterbug favourite thanks to its cobbled streets, big old plane trees and flower-festooned whitewashed houses. A convenient lunch stop on coast-to-coast trips, its surrounding mountains are also a haven for hikers. In town, a restored **Venetian Fountain** spurts (potable) water from 25 stone lion heads into a long trough. Minor attractions include a teensy church museum, a folklore museum and the vast modern monastery complex at the north end of town.

🛌 Sleeping & Eating

Heracles PENSION $

(☑6973667495, 28320 22111; heraclespapadakis@hotmail.com; Main Rd; s/d €30/40; ❋⑤) The five balconied rooms here are quiet, spotless and handily furnished, but it's Heracles himself who makes the place memorable. A retired geologist, he's intimately familiar with the area and can put you on the right hiking trail, birdwatching site or hidden beach. Breakfast starts at €3.85.

Yianni's GREEK $

(☑28320 22707; Main Rd; mains €4-11; ⊙lunch & dinner) Past the Venetian Fountain, this friendly taverna has a big roadside terrace, reliably good traditional cooking and a decent house red.

Panorama CRETAN $$

(☑28320 22555; mains €6-13; ⊙dinner daily, lunch Sun; ⑤) Enjoy superb views from the terrace of this fine traditional taverna on the eastern outskirts of Spili while munching on homemade bread, toothsome mezedhes and such tantalising mains as succulent kid goat with *horta* (mountain greens).

❶ Information

There are two ATMs and a post office on the main street.

❶ Getting There & Away

Spili is on the Rethymno–Agia Galini bus route, which has up to five services daily. See KTEL (www.bus-service-crete-ktel.com) for the schedule.

Plakias
Πλακιάς

POP 200

Set beside a sweeping sandy crescent and accessed via two scenic gorges – Kotsifou and Kourtaliotiko – Plakias gets swarmed with package tourists in summer (when it can get very windy), but otherwise remains a laid-back indie travellers' favourite. There's good swimming and diving here (two operators run shore and boat excursions) and excellent coastal and mountain hikes. In summer, the owner of the Smerna Bar runs daily boat trips to Preveli Beach (p438).

🛏 Sleeping

A handy lodging website is www.plakias-filoxenia.gr. There's also good lodging in pretty Myrthios above Plakias.

Morpheas Apartments APARTMENTS $
(☑ 6974654958, 28320 31583; www.morpheas-apartments-plakias-crete-greece.com; d €45-67; ❄ 🖥) These nicely decked-out rooms and apartments are run with professionalism and panache by Olga and Manolis Koumentaki. The supermarket right below comes in handy since most units have well-equipped kitchens, along with sea views, to enjoy with meals.

Plakias Youth Hostel HOSTEL $
(☑ 28320 32118; www.yhplakias.com; dm €10; ❄ Easter-Oct; 🅿 @ 🖥) Set around a lawn amid olive groves about 500m from the waterfront, this indie hostel has six bungalows with dorms sleeping eight people in bunks. Each has a fan. Low-cost breakfast and beverages are available. It's very popular, so book ahead if possible. Reception is staffed 9am to noon and 5pm to 8.30pm.

★ Plakias Suites APARTMENTS $$
(☑ 6975811559, 28320 31680; www.plakiassuites.com; studios €90-130; ❄ Apr-Oct; 🅿 ❄ 🖥) Run by a young couple, the six stylish two- and three-room units are within a whisker of the best stretch of local beach. They're spacious and have modernist yet warm aesthetics and nifty touches such as large LCD TVs, rainforest showers and chic kitchenettes.

🍴 Eating & Drinking

Taverna Scirocco CRETAN $
(mains €5-12; ❄ 11am-midnight; 🖥) A short walk west of town, en route to Souda, this waterfront taverna gets high scores for its congenial service and original and flavour-packed dishes, including some interesting salads.

Taverna Christos CRETAN $$
(☑ 28320 31472; mains €5-16.50; ❄ lunch & dinner; 🖥) Sit next to the waves on a tamarisk-shaded terrace and tuck into a daily changing roster of dishes you won't find everywhere, including home-smoked sea bass or lamb cooked in egg-lemon stock.

FRIDAY FROLIC

Local or not, everybody loves a good party, which is why **Taverna Panorama** (☑ 28320 31450; Myrthios; mains €5-12; ❄ 9am-late; 🖥) in pretty Myrthios, right above Plakias, bursts at the seams on Friday, when a Greek band strikes up traditional tunes and the crowd gets more raucous with each carafe of wine. It's well worth the 2km uphill walk, which begins just before the youth hostel (or take a cab).

Joe's Bar BAR
(Nufaro; ❄ 9am-late; 🖥) Officially called Nufaro but better known as Joe's, this rocking joint has cheap beer and UK and German soccer on the big screen.

ℹ Information

Plakias has two ATMs on the central waterfront. The post office is on the first side street coming from the east.

ℹ Getting There & Around

Up to five KTEL (www.bus-service-crete-ktel.com) buses daily link Plakias with Rethymno (€4.50, one hour); one goes to Preveli (€2.30, 30 minutes). **Cars Alianthos** (☑ 28320 31851; www.alianthos-group.com; per day from €36; ❄ 24hr) is a reliable car-hire outlet.

Around Plakias

About 11km east of Plakias, the historic **Moni Preveli** (Μονή Πρέβελη; ☑ 28320 31246; www.preveli.org; admission €2.50; ❄ 9am-7pm mid-Mar–May, 9am-1.30pm & 3.30-6.30pm Jun-Oct) cuts an imposing silhouette high above the Libyan Sea. Like most Cretan monasteries, it was a centre of resistance during the Turkish occupation and also played a key role in WWII when hiding trapped Allied soldiers from the Nazis until they could escape to Egypt by submarine.

On the road to the monastery, a **memorial** showing a gun-toting abbot and an Allied British soldier commemorates this heroic act, as does a **fountain** on the right as you enter the monastery. To the left is a small **museum** with some exquisite icons, richly embroidered vestments and two silver candelabra presented by grateful soldiers after the war.

In summer, there are two daily buses from Rethymno (€4.50, 1¼ hours) and one from Plakias (€2.30, 30 minutes).

Beaches Between Plakias & Agia Galini

Preveli Beach
BEACH

(Παραλία Πρέβελη; Palm Beach) A collage of natural beauty, Preveli Beach is like an exclamation mark idling at the mouth of the Megalopotamos River at the end of its meander through the rugged Kourtaliotiko Gorge. Where the canyon meets the beach, the stream's chilly water tumbles through a jungle of oleander endemic palm trees into a lagoon hemmed in by soft sand and the shimmering Med. Its stunning setting makes Preveli one of Crete's most celebrated strands.

A steep 1km path leads down to the beach from a car park (€2), 1km before Moni Preveli. Alternatively, drive 5km along a signposted dirt road from a stone bridge and the excellent Taverna Gefyra off the Moni Preveli main road. It dead ends at Amoudi Beach from where Preveli Beach is about a 1km walk over the headland. There's a snack bar for cold drinks and snacks.

Triopetra
BEACH

(Τριόπετρα) Triopetra is a big beach named after three giant rocks jutting out of the sea. A headland divides the sandy strip into 'Little Triopetra' and 'Big Triopetra'. The former is home to Pavlos Place (mains €5-12, rooms d/tr/q €36/40/45; ⊙ Apr-Oct), which has fabulously fresh fish caught by the owner himself as well as inspired salads and vegetable sides prepared with home-grown organic produce. There are also a few simple but comfortable rooms that are often booked up by yoga workshop participants.

Because of submerged sand shelves, Little Triopetra is not ideal for swimming, so head to the 'big' beach for that. There are two more tavernas with rooms along here.

Triopetra can be reached from Agios Pavlos (about 300m is drivable dirt road) or via a 12km winding asphalt road from the village of Akoumia on the Rethymno–Agia Galini road.

Agios Pavlos
BEACH

(Αγιος Παύλος) Cradled by cliffs, Agios Pavlos is little more than a couple of small tavernas with rooms and a beach bar set around a picture-perfect crescent with dark, course sand with the distinctive silhouette of Paximadia Islands looming offshore. A steep staircase on the bay's western end leads up Cape Melissa to some intricately pleated and colourful rock formations.

The bay gets busy in summer when excursion boats arrive from Agia Galini, but it's possible to escape the crowds by heading to the beaches behind the headland to the west. Beware that getting there involves a scramble down (and up) a steep sand dune. Bring water and snacks.

Agios Pavlos Hotel (☑ 28320 71104; www.agiospavloshotel.gr; d €28-40, apt €45-60; ⊙ Apr-Oct; ❋) has waterfront rooms above its taverna and super-nice modern apartments up on the hill.

To get to Agios Pavlos, look for the turnoff to Saktouria on the Rethymno–Agia Galini road and follow the winding asphalt about 13km down to the sea.

Agia Galini   Αγια Γαλήνη

POP 923

Agia Galini (a-ya ga-*lee*-nee) is an erstwhile picturesque fishing village where package tourism and overdevelopment have diluted much of the original charm. With ageing hotels and restaurants clinging densely to a steep hillside and hemmed in by cliffs, small beaches and a busy harbour, the town can feel claustrophobic in high season but definitely has its charms at other times. It's a convenient base for visits to Phaestos, Agia Triada and the remote beaches west of here. The town all but shuts down in winter.

🛏 Sleeping

Adonis
HOTEL $

(☑ 28320 91333; www.agia-galini.com; r €45, studio €50-60, apt €80-120; P ❋ @ 🕸 🛋) It takes a healthy ego to decorate the reception with a supersized poster of oneself in strapping, hairy-chested 1970s glory. It also tells you that the proprietor is a bit of a character. Adonis still presides over his sprawling 75-room complex, with the nicest rooms being in the pool-adjacent newer building. It's in the upper part of the village, just off the main street. Turn uphill next to the Pallada Hotel.

Palazzo Greco
BOUTIQUE HOTEL $$

(☑ 28320 91187; www.palazzogreco.com; d €80-120; P ❋ 🕸 🛋) Match your mood to the wall colour – green, blue or red – in fine-looking rooms with flat-screen TVs, fridges and circular marble sinks in the bathrooms. The top-floor two-bedroom suite (€180) sleeps up to seven. On the main road.

✕ Eating

Taverna Stohos   GREEK $
(www.stochos.gr; Main Beach; mains €4.50-13; ⊙8am-midnight; 🛜) Locals swear by this beachfront taverna with attached apartments (€45). Sit on the trellised terrace decorated with gourds and anticipate heaping portions of succulent lamb, chicken or rabbit slow-cooked in the *kleftiko*, a traditional Cretan stone oven.

Faros   SEAFOOD $$
(✉28320 91346; Shopping St; mains €7-13, fish €30-55 per kg; ⊙lunch & dinner) This no-frills family-run fish taverna is usually packed to the gills, and for good reason: the owner himself drops his nets into the Med, so you know what's on the plate that night was still swimming in the sea in the morning. Squid cooked in their own ink, lobster spaghetti and fish soup are specialities.

ℹ Information

Cafe Zanzibar (✉28320 91142; www.kapi-crete .com; free wifi, internet per 20min €1; ⊙9am-1am; 🛜), on the main street down near the port, has internet terminals and free wi-fi. The post office and ATMs are nearby. For web information try www.agia-galini.com.

ℹ Getting There & Away

Buses stop in front of Cafe Zanzibar on the main street down near the port. In peak season there are up to four buses daily to Iraklio (€8, two hours) and Rethymno (€6.20, 1½ hours), up to three to Phaestos (€2.10, 30 minutes) and two to Matala (€3.30, 45 minutes).

NORTHWEST CRETE

Crete's northwestern coastline is anchored by the preening port city of Hania, once a jewel of a capital and full of arty boutique hotels, galleries and great eateries. Nearby, the ethereal Balos lagoon and the sweeping beach at Falasarna beckon as urban antidotes. Hania is also the gateway to Samaria, one of Europe's grandest gorges, tucked in among steep mountains that ripple all the way down to the southern shores.

Hania   Χανιά
POP 53,910

Hania (hahn-*yah;* also spelled Chania) is Crete's most evocative city, with its pretty Venetian quarter, criss-crossed by narrow lanes, culminating at a magnificent harbour. Remnants of Venetian and Turkish architecture abound, with many old townhouses now transformed into atmospheric restaurants and boutique hotels.

Although all this beauty means the Old Town is deluged with tourists in summer, it's still a great place to unwind. The Venetian Harbour is a good place for a stroll and a coffee. There's great shopping in charming indie boutiques and an entire lane (Skrydlof) dedicated to leather products. All throughout, roofless Venetian buildings have been turned into outdoor restaurants.

◉ Sights

From Plateia 1866 (1866 Sq), the Venetian Harbour is a short walk north up Halidon. Zambeliou, once Hania's main thoroughfare, is lined with craft shops, small hotels and tavernas. The slightly bohemian Splantzia quarter, running from Plateia 1821 (1821 Sq) between Daskalogianni and Halidon, has leafy restaurants and cafes, boutique hotels and traditional shopping. The headland near the lighthouse separates the Venetian Harbour from the crowded town beach in the modern Nea Hora quarter.

Venetian Harbour   HISTORIC SITE
A stroll around here is a must for any visitor to Hania. The restored **Venetian lighthouse** at the harbour entrance is reached along a 1.5km walk around the sea wall. On the inner harbour's eastern side, the prominent **Mosque of Kioutsouk Hasan** (also called Mosque of Janissaries) occasionally hosts art exhibitions. Further east, the well-restored Venetian Grand Arsenal houses the **Centre for Mediterranean Architecture**, which presents events and exhibits.

★**Hania Archaeological Museum** MUSEUM
(✉28210 90334; Halidon 21; admission €2/1, incl Byzantine & post-Byzantine Collection €3/2; ⊙8.30am-3pm Tue-Sun) The setting alone in the beautifully restored 16th-century Venetian Church of San Francisco is reason to visit this fine collection of artefacts from neolithic to Roman times. Late-Minoan sarcophagi catch the eye as much as a large glass case with an entire herd of clay bulls

Hania

CRETE HANIA

Nea Hora
Beach (500m)

P Firkas
Fortress

3
Ritsou

8

16
28
Angelou

Venetian
Harbour

15

Pireos

14   12
Theotokopoulou

Theofanous

13

9

Apostolidou

Moshon

Zambeliou

Akti Koundourioti

Sourmeli

Lithinon

Akti Tombazi

Patriarhou Ioanikiou

Portou

Douka

Skoufou

Kondylaki

Zambeliou

Plateia
Venizelou

Katre

Potie

Karaoli Dimitriou

Isodion

Agion Deka

Hrys Episkopou

NEA
HORA

21

6

18

Hania
Archaeological
Museum

Patriarhou Gerasimou

26   19

1

Orthodox
Cathedral

Portou

Piga

11

Halidon

Betolo

Skrydlof

Plateia
Hortatson

Mousouron

Pireos

Kyrilou

Giannari

Skalidi

Plateia
1866

Kriari

P Kalaidi

Zymvrakidon

Koraka

Mylonogiannini

Karaiskaki

Kydonias

Hania Bus
Station

0   200 m
0   0.1 miles

Akti Defkaliona

10

Ikarou

Sarpidona

P

27

Epimenidou

Grand
Arsenal

4 Plateia
Katehaki

22

Arholeon

Venetian
Shipyards
(Neoria)

Kalergon

Akti Maouli

Arholeon

Kalistou

Agiou Markou

Kanevaro

Sifaka

Sifaka

Minoos

Kyprou

Gavaladon

Vourdouba

Plateia 1821   5

Melidoniou

Sarpaki

24

20

Kalistou

Nikiforou Episkopou

23

Daskalogiannii

SPLANTZIA   25

17

Daliani

Nikiforou Foka

Tsouderon

Plateia
Markopoulou
P

Agora

2

El Venizelou

Buses to
Souda

Giannari

Thalassino Ageri
(2km)

Anek

Stadium

Apokoronou

Plastira

Voloudakidon

Tzanakaki

Boniali

Andrea Papandreou

Trikoupi

Kydonias

Peridou

Stakion

Public
Garden

Greek Mountaineering
Association (125m)

Hania

(used to worship Poseidon). Other standouts include three Roman floor mosaics, Hellenistic gold jewellery, clay tablets with Linear A and Linear B script, and a marble sculpture of Roman emperor Hadrian.

Permanent Collection of Ancient & Traditional Shipbuilding   MUSEUM

(☑ 28210 91875; Neorio Moro, Akti Defkaliona; admission €2; ☉ 9am-5pm Mon-Sat, 10am-4pm Sun) The *Minoa*, a painstaking replica of a Minoan ship that sailed from Crete to Athens for the 2004 Olympics ceremonies, now permanently docks in a converted Venetian shipyard *(neoria)*. Tools used in its mak-

ing and photographs from the epic journey bring to life this amazing feat.

Church of Agios Nikolaos   CHURCH

(Plateia 1821; ☉ 7am-noon & 4-7pm) One of Hania's most intriguing buildings is this Venetian-era church with both a belltower and minaret – the latter was added during its stint as a mosque under Turkish rule. Inside, the massive bronze chandeliers dangling from a barrel-vaulted coffered ceiling will likely draw your attention.

Maritime Museum of Crete   MUSEUM

(☑ 28210 91875; www.mar-mus-crete.gr; Akti Koundourioti; adult/concession €3/2; ☉ 9am-5pm Mon-Sat, 10am-6pm Sun) Part of the hulking Venetian-built Firkas Fortress at the port entrance, this museum celebrates Crete's nautical tradition with model ships, naval instruments, paintings, photographs, maps and memorabilia. One room is dedicated to historical sea battles while upstairs there's a thorough documentation on the WWII-era Battle of Crete. The gate to the fortress itself is open from 8am to 2pm.

Etz Hayyim Synagogue   SYNAGOGUE

(☑ 28210 86286; www.etz-hayyim-hania.org; Parodos Kondylaki; welcome donation €2; ☉ 10am-6pm Mon-Fri) Crete's only remaining synagogue was badly damaged in WWII and reopened in 1999. It sports a *mikve* (ritual bath), tombs of rabbis and a memorial to the local Jews killed by the Nazis. Today it serves a congregation of seven and it is open to visitors.

Byzantine & Postbyzantine Collection   MUSEUM

(☑ 28210 96046; Theotokopoulou 82; adult/concession €2/1, incl Archaeological Museum €3/2; ☉ 8.30am-3pm Tue-Sun) In an impressively restored Venetian church, this well-edited collection consists of artefacts, icons, jewellery and coins spanning the period from AD 62 to 1913. Standouts include a fine mosaic floor, evocative mural fragments from a late-12th-century church and icons from the Cretan school.

Agora   MARKET

(www.chaniamarket.com; ☉ 7am-5pm Mon & Sat, 7am-9pm Tue-Fri) Hania's cross-shaped market hall bustles mostly with souvenir-hunting tourists, although a few authentic produce, meat and cheese stands – along with cafes – are still part of the mix.

Activities

Nea Hora Beach
BEACH

(Akti Papanikoli) Hania's in-town beach is only a 10-minute walk west of the Venetian Harbour. The half-kilometre-long yellow-sand strip is backed by tavernas, small markets and holiday apartment rentals. Fairly shallow, it's good for kids and popular with locals on weekends. For sustenance, try Akrogiali (p444).

Greek Mountaineering Association
HIKING

(EOS; ☑ 28210 44647; www.eoshanion.gr; Tzanakaki 90; ⊙ 8.30am-6pm) Visit the local EOS branch to get the scoop on various outdoor sports, including serious climbing in the Lefka Ori, mountain refuges and the E4 trail. EOS also runs regular weekend excursions.

Limnoupolis
WATERPARK

(☑ 28210 33246; www.limnoupolis.gr; Varypetro; day pass adult/child 3-12 €23/17, afternoon pass €16/13; ⊙ 10am-7pm mid-May–Sep) Eight kilometres south of town, near Varypetro, this giant waterpark has enough pools, slides and rides to keep kids' tempers cool, along with cafes and pool bars for adults. Buses leave regularly from the bus station.

🛏 Sleeping

Pension Theresa
PENSION $

(☑ 28210 92798; www.pensiontheresa.gr; Angelou 8; r €40-50; ☀) Part of the Venetian fortifications, this creaky old house with a steep (and narrow!) spiral staircase and antique furniture delivers snug rooms with character aplenty. Views are stunning from the rooftop terrace with a communal kitchen.

Vranas Studios
APARTMENT $

(☑ 28210 58618; www.vranas.gr; Agion Deka 10; studio €40-70; ☀ 🕱) Tucked into an Old Town alley, this popular place has large, uncluttered and immaculately maintained studios with kitchenettes. Some have such extra flourishes as four-poster beds and narrow French balconies. There are additional units on Plateia Mitropolis (Mitropolis Sq).

Splanzia Hotel
BOUTIQUE HOTEL $$

(☑ 28210 45313; www.splanzia.com; Daskalogianni 20; d/tr incl breakfast €115/138; ☀ @ 🕱) This smart designer hotel in an Ottoman building has eight stylish rooms, some decorated with four-poster beds and drapery. The back rooms overlook a lovely courtyard with cheerful bougainvillea and one of Hania's few remaining Turkish wells.

Amphora Hotel
HOTEL $$

(☑ 28210 93224; www.amphora.gr; Parodos Theotokopoulou 20; s €95, d €110-130; ☀ 🕱) Most of the elegantly decorated rooms at this immaculately restored Venetian mansion wrap around a courtyard, with a few more in a connected wing. Those on the top floors have harbour views, but front rooms can be noisy in the summer. Breakfast is €10.

Madonna Studios & Apartments
APARTMENTS $$

(☑ 28210 94747; madonnastudios@yahoo.co.uk; Gamba 33; studio €85-110; ☀ 🕱) This charming small hotel has five attractive and traditionally furnished studios and a lovely flower-filled courtyard. The front top room has a superb balcony, while a courtyard room features the original stone wash trough.

★ Casa Leone
BOUTIQUE HOTEL $$$

(☑ 28210 76762; www.casa-leone.com; Parodos Theotokopoulou 18; ste incl breakfast €135-175; ☀ 🕱) This Venetian residence combines the elegance of your rich uncle's mansion with the cheerful warmth of your parents' home. Each of the five suites is classically furnished with rich woods and textiles and comes with a balcony overlooking the Venetian Harbour.

Casa Delfino
BOUTIQUE HOTEL $$$

(☑ 28210 87400; www.casadelfino.com; Theofanous 9; ste & apt incl buffet breakfast €190-350; ☀ 🕱) Luxury is taken very seriously at this elegant 17th-century mansion in the Venetian quarter. The 24 suites come in various sizes but are all richly trimmed in bespoke furniture, marble floors and romantic flourishes. Days start with breakfast in the pebble-mosaic courtyard while the Turkish spa and the rooftop terrace are perfect end-of-day unwinding spots.

🍴 Eating

Hania has some of the finest restaurants in Crete, often housed in roofless Venetian ruins. Skip the waterfront tavernas.

★ Portes
CRETAN $

(☑ 28210 76261; Portou 48; mains €7-9.50; ⊙ noon-late; 🕱) Fine dining without the pretence. Both tourists and neighbourhood old-timers give this place top marks for its creative Cretan fare that veers toward modernity without straying from simplicity. You can't go wrong ordering from the specials board.

CRETE HANIA

Kouzina E.P.E.
GREEK $

(☑28210 42391; Daskalogianni 25; mains €6-9.50; ☺noon-7.30pm; ☜) This cheery lunch spot gets contemporary designer flair from the cement floor, country-white tables and dangling silver origami boats. It's a local favourite away from the crowds, serving blackboard-listed *mayirefta* (ready-cooked meals) that can be inspected in the open kitchen.

Well of the Turk
MIDDLE EASTERN $$

(☑28210 54547; www.welloftheturk.com; Sarpaki 1-3; mains €8-15; ☺dinner Wed-Mon) In an age-old stone building flanking a quiet square, this artsy taverna specialises in richly textured dishes inspired by North Africa, the Middle East and Turkey, yet all prepared with the finest Cretan ingredients. The cheesecake with rosewater and orange makes a great culinary coda.

To Karnagio
GREEK $$

(☑28210 53366; Plateia Katehaki 8; mains €5-18; ☺noon-midnight May-Oct; ☜) Tucked into a quiet square behind the Grand Arsenal, this locally popular place delivers fresh fish along with authentic Cretan comfort food, including perfectly flaky *boureki* (stuffed pastry).

Akrogiali
SEAFOOD $$

(☑28210 71110; Akti Papanikoli 20; mains €6.50-12; ☺lunch & dinner; ☜) This airy white-and-blue space on Nea Hora Beach does fabulously fresh fish and seafood, including some inspired stuffed-squid varieties.

Ela
CRETAN $$

(☑28210 74128; www.ela-chania.gr; Kondylaki 47; mains €7-16; ☺noon-1am; ☜) Built as a soap factory in 1650, Ela has also seen incarnations as a school, distillery and cheese-processing plant and is now a charismatic roofless lair serving upscale Cretan specialities. The tacky board outside tells you it's in every guidebook, but the accolades are not undeserved.

Vineria 36
MODERN GREEK $$

(☑28210 57590; Sarpaki 36; mains €8-15; ☺dinner; ☜) The chic-rustic decor, unusual menu and friendly service blend together perfectly at this deli-cum-dining room on a lovely Old Town square. As the name suggests, special attention is paid to good wine to match the made-from-scratch dishes.

★ Thalassino Ageri
SEAFOOD $$$

(☑28210 51136; www.thalasino-ageri.gr; Vivilaki 35; fish per kg €55; ☺from 7.30pm late-Mar–mid-Oct) Tucked away in a tiny port among the ruins of old tanneries, this fish taverna is one of Crete's top eateries. The day's catch dictates the menu but most dishes hum with creativity, including the fisherman's salad. It's about 2km east of the centre via Venizelou.

🍷 Drinking & Nightlife

The cafe-bars around the Venetian Harbour are nice places to sit, but charge top euro. For a more local vibe, head to Plateia 1821 or to alt-flavoured Sarpidona on the eastern end of the harbour.

Sinagogi
BAR

(☑28210 95242; Kondylaki 15; ☺8pm-late June-Sep; ☜) In a roofless Venetian building and former synagogue, this popular lounge is great for relaxing beneath the stone arches.

Kibar
BAR

(☑28210 50172; Daliani 22; ☺2pm-late; ☜) Beautifully set in the courtyard of a 16th-century monastery turned art centre (Monastiri Tou Karolou), this cafe has a vibrant ambience and lots of international bottled beer.

Ta Duo Lux
CAFE, BAR

(☑28210 52519; Sarpidona 8; ☺10am-late; ☜) Further along the harbour, this arty cafe-bar is a perennial favourite among wrinkle-free alternative types and is popular day and night. Nearby **Bororo** and **Hippopotamos** are also popular hang-outs.

Fagotto Jazz Bar
BAR

(☑28210 71877; Angelou 16; ☺7pm-2am) This Hania institution in a Venetian building offers smooth jazz, soft rock and blues (sometimes live) in a setting brimming with jazz paraphernalia, including a saxophone beer tap. The action picks up after 10pm.

❶ Information

Banks cluster around Plateia Markopoulou (Markopoulou Sq) in the new city, but there are also some ATMs in the Old Town on Halidon.

Hospital (☑28210 22000; www.chania hospital.gr; Mournies)

Local Tourist Office (☑28210 41665; tourism @chania.gr; Milonogianni 53; ☺9am-2pm)

Post Office (Peridou 10; ☺7.30am-8pm Mon-Fri, 7.30am-2pm Sat)

Tellus Travel (☑28210 91500; www.tellus travel.gr; Halidon 108; ☺8am-11pm)

❶ Getting There & Away

AIR

Hania's **airport** (www.chaniaairport.com) is 14km east of town on the Akrotiri Peninsula and is served seasonally from throughout Europe.

BOAT

Hania's port is at Souda, 7km southeast of town and has one daily overnight ferry run by **Anek** (☑ 28210 27500, ext 4; www.anek.gr) to Piraeus. The port is linked to town by bus (€1.50) and taxi (€9). Buy tickets online or at the port.

BUS

Hania's **bus station** (☑ 28210 93052; Kydonias 73-77) has a left-luggage service (per day, per piece €2). Check KTEL (www.bus-service-crete-ktel.com) for the current schedule.

Bus Services from Hania

DESTINATION	TIME	FARE	FREQUENCY
Elafonisi	2hr	€10	1 daily
Falasarna	1½hr	€7.60	5 daily
Gramvousa	1hr	€6.20	1 daily
Hora Sfakion	1hr 40min	€7.60	2 daily
Iraklio	2¾hr	€13.80	17 daily
Kissamos	45min	€4.70	up to 15 daily
Omalos (for Samaria Gorge)	45min	€6.90	3 daily
Paleohora	1½hr	€7.60	5 daily
Rethymno	1hr	€6.20	17 daily
Sougia	2hr	€7.10	1 or 2 daily
Stavros	30min	€2.10	up to 5 Mon-Sat

❶ Getting Around

TO/FROM THE AIRPORT

KTEL (www.bus-service-crete-ktel.com) buses link the airport with central Hania up to 20 times daily (€2.30, 30 minutes). A taxi to or from the airport costs €20 (plus €2 per bag).

BUS

A handily central stop for Souda, Halepa, Nea Hora and other local destinations is on **Giannari**, near the Agora market hall.

CAR

Most of the Old Town is pedestrianised. There's free parking just west of Firkas Fortress and along the waterfront towards Nea Hora beach.

Akrotiri Peninsula
Χερσόνησος Ακρωτήρι

The Akrotiri Peninsula, to the northeast of Hania, is a barren, hilly stretch of rock covered with scrub. It has a few coastal resorts, Hania's airport and a massive NATO naval base on Souda Bay. Buses travel out here, but if you're driving, the poorly signposted roads can make it a difficult region to explore. Near Akrotiri's northern tip, sandy **Stavros Beach** is good for a dip and is famous as the backdrop for the final dancing scene in *Zorba the Greek*. Five buses Monday to Friday and three on Saturday travel out to Stavros (€2.10, 30 minutes). A taxi should be about €25.

Kissamos   Κίσσαμος
POP 10,800

About 40km west of Hania, Kissamos exudes an unpolished, almost gritty, air compared to other north-coast towns. This is not a place given entirely over to tourism. There are two beaches in town, separated by a waterfront promenade: the sandy **Mavros Molos** in the west and the pebbly **Telonio beach** to the east.

Kissamos was the harbour of the Dorian city-state of Polyrrina and reached its heyday during Roman times, from which many vestiges have been dug up and are now displayed in the local museum and the archaeological museums of Hania and Iraklio.

◉ Sights

Archaeological Museum of Kissamos   MUSEUM

(☑ 28220 83308; Plateia Tzanakaki; adult/concession €2/1; ⊘ 8.30am-3pm Tue-Sun) In an imposing two-level Venetian-Turkish building on the main square, this museum presents locally excavated treasure, including statues, jewellery, coins and a large mosaic floor from a Kissamos villa. Most items are from the Hellenistic and Roman eras, though there are also some Minoan objects.

🛏 Sleeping & Eating

⭐ **Stavroula Palace**   HOTEL $$

(☑ 28220 23620; www.varouchakis.gr/stavroula palace; s/d/tr incl breakfast €50/65/80; ❄ 🐾 🛜) Run by the warm and gracious Stavroula and her family, this cheery and good-value waterfront hotel has breezy, modern rooms with balconies fronting a large swimming pool and immaculately kept garden where breakfast is served. Tavernas, cafes, the town centre and a nice beach are all a short walk away. There's even a small children's recreation area out the back.

Taverna Sunset
GREEK $

(☎ 28220 41627; Paraliaki; mains €4-12; ⏱ lunch & dinner; ☜) Locals mix with in-the-know visitors at this quintessential family taverna presided over by Giannis, who's usually ensconced behind the grill coaxing meat and fish into succulent perfection. It's right on the waterfront.

ⓘ Information

The main commercial drag, Iroön Polytechniou, has supermarkets, banks with ATMs, the post office and the bus stop.

ⓘ Getting There & Away

BOAT

From the port 3km west of town, **Lane** (☎ 27360 37055; www.lane-kithira.com) operates ferries to Piraeus via Antikythira, Kythira and Gythio. In summer, a bus meets ferries; otherwise taxis into town cost around €5. For tickets, try **Chalkiadaki Travel** (☎ 28220 22009; Skalidi 49).

BUS

Buses leave from the KTEL (www.bus-service-crete-ktel.com) office at Iroön Polytechniou 77, opposite the EKO gas station. Check the website for timings.

Bus Services from Kissamos

DESTINATION	PRICE	TIME	FREQUENCY
Elafonisi	€6.30	1¼hr	1 daily
Falasarna	€3.50	20min	3 daily
Hania	€4.70	45min	13 daily
Hora Sfakion (via Hania)	€11.90	3hr	2 daily
Paleohora	€7.20	1¼hr	3 daily

Around Kissamos

Falasarna
Φαλάσαρνα

Some 16km west of Kissamos, Falasarna is little more than a long sandy beach – but what a beach! This broad sweep opens up from the road coming in from Kissamos and is considered among Crete's finest, even though views are somewhat marred by greenhouses set among the olive groves. Spread your towel on the Big Beach (Megali Paralia) at the south end or pick a spot in one of the coves separated by rocky spits further north.

Falasarna was a 4th-century-BC Cretan city-state and trading centre with its own harbour. Today you can wander among the ancient ruins, reached via a 2km dirt road which starts where the paved road ends. The entrance is just past the 'stone throne'. Admission is free.

Falasarna has no centre as such, although there are several tavernas, bars and small supermarkets. Lodging options include Sunset Taverna & Apartments (r/apt incl breakfast €40/65, mains €7-8; 🅿 ☜), which has a terrace with fig trees and wonderful views, its own natural spring and beach access, along with simple but comfortable rooms.

There are three buses daily from Kissamos (€3.50, 20 minutes) and five daily buses from Hania (€7.60, 1½ hours).

Gramvousa Peninsula
Χερσόνησος Γραμβούσα

Northwest of Kissamos, the wild and remote Gramvousa Peninsula cradles the lagoon-like white powdery beach of Balos off its western tip. Its shallow, shimmering turquoise waters will bring a giggle to your holiday-hungry throat. The beach overlooks two islets, the larger one (Imeri) crowned by the ruins of a huge Venetian fortress built to keep pirates at (and out of the) bay. Excursion boats from Kissamos make a two-hour stop here before continuing on to Balos.

It's thanks to these cruise boats (with up to four daily summertime departures) that the lagoon feels far from idyllic between 11am and 4pm in the peak season. The only way to avoid the crowds is to get there by car before or after the boats arrive. The 12km dirt road picks up near the village of Kalyviani and ends at a parking lot with snack bar from where a 1.2km trail leads down to the lagoon. Umbrellas and sunbeds rent for about €7. Nondrivers could try hitching a ride or walk, although you'll be eating a lot of dust from passing vehicles.

Cruise boats are operated by Gramvousa Balos Cruises (☎ 28220 24344; www.gramvousa .com; adult/child €25/12) and leave from Kissamos port around 10am, returning around 6pm with two two-hour stops each on Imeri and at Balos. Book online for discounted tickets. Reasonably priced food and drink is available on board.

SOUTHWEST COAST

The stark and muscular Lefka Ori (White Mountains) meet the sea along Crete's corrugated southwestern coast indented with a handful of laid-back beach communities, some of them accessible only by boat and therefore completely untouched by mass tourism. You can walk to perfectly isolated little beaches or soak up the majestic scenery and fragrant air on a scramble through wildy romantic gorges away from the busy Samaria Gorge, which ends in Agia Roumeli.

ⓘ Getting There & Around

Anendyk (☑ 28210 95511; www.anendyk.gr) operates ferries between Hora Sfakion and Paleohora on a seasonally changing schedule, also stopping in Loutro, Agia Roumeli and Sougia. Boats make extended stops in Agia Roumeli to accommodate Samaria Gorge hikers. Ferries may be cancelled in bad weather, so be careful not to get stuck in landlocked Agia Roumeli or Loutro. Some ferries carry vehicles (from €15, reservation required). There are also ferries to Gavdos Island from Hora Sfakion and Paleohora.

KTEL (www.bus-service-crete-ktel.com) buses travel daily to Paleohora, Hora Sfakion and Sougia from Hania and Rethymno.

Frangokastello
Φραγγοκαστέλλο
POP 150

Dominated by a magnificent 14th-century fortress, Frangokastello is a low-key resort with a fabulous wide and sandy beach that slopes gradually into shallow warm water, making it ideal for kids. There's no actual village, just a few tavernas, small markets and low-rise holiday apartments scattered along the main street to the fortress, which was built by the Venetians to guard against pirates and feisty Sfakian rebels. On 17 May 1828, during the War of Independence, many Cretan fighters were killed here by the Turks. According to legend their ghosts – the *drosoulites* – can be seen marching past the fortress in the early dawn on the battle's anniversary.

Among the tavernas, **Oasis** (☑ 28250 92136; www.oasisrooms.com; mains €6-9; 🛜) does well-executed Cretan specials and also rents spacious self-catering apartments (€50 to €60).

Frangokastello is some 70km southwest of Hania and 30km west of Plakias. There's one daily bus to Hania (€8.40, 2½ hours).

Hora Sfakion
Χώρα Σφακίων
POP 300

The more bullet holes you see in the passing road signs, the closer you are to Hora Sfakion (*ho*-ra sfa-*kee*-on, commonly called

Sfakia), whose residents are long renowned in Cretan history for their rebellious streak. But don't worry, the pintsize fishing village is an amiable, if eccentric, place that caters well enough to today's foreign visitors – many of whom are Samaria Gorge hikers stumbling off the Agia Roumeli boat on their way back to Hania. Most pause only long enough to catch the next bus out, but the village also offers access to some attractive beaches and other hikes.

🏃 Activities

In the village, unfold your towel on **Vrissi Beach**, a pretty cove on the western village end. Further west is lovely **Sweetwater Beach**, which is accessible by a small daily ferry (May to October, per person €4), by taxi boat (one-way/return €20/30) or on foot via a stony and partly vertiginous one-hour coastal path starting at the first hairpin turn of the Anopoli road. A small cafe rents umbrellas and sun chairs.

There's decent diving around Hora Sfakion. PADI-certified dive centre **Notos Mare** (☑ 6947270106; www.notosmare.com; from €39) offers the gamut of shore and boat dives as well as certification courses.

🛌 Sleeping & Eating

The tavernas along the harbour all offer similar fare and thus vociferously compete for your business. Most also rent rooms. Try the Sfakian pita – a pancake filled with sweet *myzithra* cheese and flecked with honey.

Hotel Stavris　　　　　　　　HOTEL $
(☑ 28250 91220; www.hotel-stavris-chora-sfakion. com; s/d/tr from €28/33/38; ❄🛜) This long-running place, owned by the Perrakis family, has clean, basic rooms with harbour-facing balconies. It's well worth spending a few more euros for one in the renovated main building.

Xenia Hotel　　　　　　　　HOTEL $
(☑ 28250 91490; www.sfakia-xenia-hotel.gr; d €33-38; ❄🛜) For best value and location look no further than this refurbished hotel on the western waterfront; swimmers can climb down a ladder into the sea.

The Three Brothers　　　　　　GREEK $
(above Vrissi Beach; mains €5-12; ⊗ 8am-midnight; 🛜) The menu features all the staples, but it's the location overlooking Vrissi Beach that sets this taverna apart from the others in the

SAMARIA GORGE   ΦΑΡΑΓΓΙ ΤΗΣ ΣΑΜΑΡΙΑΣ

Hiking the **Samaria Gorge** (28210 45570; www.samariagorge.eu; adult/child €5/2.50; 7am-sunset May–late-Oct) (sah-mah-rih-*ah*) is considered one of the 'must do' experiences in Crete, which is why you'll never be without company. In peak season, up to 3000 people per day tackle the stony 16km-long trail, and even in spring and autumn, it's rarely fewer than 1000 hikers. The vast majority arrive on organised coach excursions from the big northern resorts. You'll encounter a mix of serious trekkers as well as less experienced types attempting the trail in flip-flops.

Nevertheless, there's an undeniable raw beauty to Samaria, whose vertical walls soar up to 500m high and are just 3m apart at the narrowest point. The hike begins at an elevation of 1250m just below the Omalos Plateau and ends in the coastal village of Agia Roumeli. It's especially scenic in April and May when wildflowers brighten the trail. Samaria is also home to the *kri-kri*, a rarely seen endangered wild goat.

Hiking the Gorge

The trail begins at **Xyloskalo**, a steep and serpentine stone path that descends some 600m into the canyon to arrive at the simple cypress-framed Agios Nikolaos chapel. Beyond here the gorge is wide and open for the next 6km until you reach the abandoned settlement of **Samaria** whose inhabitants were relocated when the gorge became a national park. Just south of the village is a 14th-century chapel dedicated to St Maria of Egypt, after whom the gorge is named.

Further on, the gorge narrows and becomes more dramatic until, at the 11km mark, the walls are only 3.5m apart. These are the famous **Sideroporta** (Iron Gates), where a rickety wooden pathway leads hikers the 20m or so across the water.

The gorge ends at the 12.5km mark just north of the almost abandoned village of Palea (Old) Agia Roumeli. From here it's a further uninteresting 2km hike to the seaside village of **Agia Roumeli**, whose fine pebble beach and sparkling water are a most welcome sight. Few people miss taking a refreshing dip or at least bathing sore and aching feet. The entire trek takes from about four hours for the sprinters to six hours for the strollers.

The Low-Down

➡ An early start (before 8am) helps to put you ahead of the crowds.

➡ Hikers starting after 3pm are only allowed to walk a distance of 2km from either end.

➡ There's a 1200m elevation drop going north to south. Wear sturdy shoes and take sunscreen, sunglasses, some food, a hat and a water bottle, which you can refill from taps with potable water along the way. Drink plenty!

➡ There are several rest stops with toilets, water, trash bins and benches along the trail.

---

harbour. It's especially crowded when Giannis fires up the barbecue. Great at sunset.

ℹ Information

Hora Sfakion has two ATMs, a post office and an internet cafe. For pretrip planning, try www.chora-sfakion.com.

ℹ Getting There & Away

Hora Sfakion is about 60km south of Hania via a winding road through the magnificent Lefka Ori (White Mountains). Gas up before you leave.

BOAT

The ferry harbour is a 10-minute walk east of the main village, past the ticket kiosk.

Ferry Services from Hora Sfakion

DESTINATION	TIME	FARE	FREQUENCY
Agia Roumeli	1hr	€10	up to 3 daily
Gavdos	2½hr	€16	up to 6 weekly
Loutro	20 min	€4.50	up to 5 daily

BUS

In summer, there are up to three buses daily to Hania (€7.60, two hours) and to Rethymno (with a change in Vryses, €7.30, two hours). The last bus at 6.15pm waits for the boat from Agia Roumeli.

➡ Falling rocks occasionally lead to injuries but generally it's the heat that's a far bigger problem. Check ahead as park officials may close the gorge on rainy or exceptionally hot days.

➡ Early in the season it's sometimes necessary to wade through the stream. Later, as the flow drops, the stream-bed rocks become stepping stones.

➡ If the idea of a 16km-hike does not appeal, get a taste of Samaria by doing it 'the Lazy Way', ie starting in Agia Roumeli and heading north for as long as you feel like before doubling back. The Sideroporta, for instance, can be reached in about an hour.

Sleeping & Eating

Overnighting in Omalos and getting an early lift from there allows you to get your toe on the line for the starting gun. There's nowhere to spend the night in the gorge, although there are tavernas and lodging in Agia Roumeli.

Artemis Studios (☎ 6972237384, 28250 91377; www.agiaroumeli.com; Agia Roumeli; s/d/tr €35/45/60; ❄ 🛜) Blissfully set away from the trail and just 50m from the beach in Agia Roumeli, the family-run Artemis has 12 self-catering studios accommodating up to four people.

Hotel Neos Omalos (☎ 28210 67269; www.neos-omalos.gr; Omalos; s/d/tr incl breakfast €33/43/54 ; P 🛜) A rustic mountain feel pervades this comfortable and contemporary hotel where views from your balcony will get you in the mood for hiking. The owners are a fount of information on local hikes and other outdoor activities and can also shuttle you to the Samaria Gorge.

Getting There & Away

Most people hike the gorge one way going north–south on an organised day trip but, with some planning, it's also possible to do the trek on your own. There are daily early-morning public buses to Omalos from Hania (€6.90, 45 minutes) and Rethymno (€15, 1¾ hours) as well as thrice-weekly service from Sougia (€4.20, one hour) and Paleohora (€6.40, one hour). At the end of the trail, in Agia Roumeli, ferries take you back to Sougia and Hora Sfakion where they are met by public buses. From Hora Sfakion, buses go to both Rethymno (€7.30, two hours) and Hania (€7.60, 1¾ hours), while from Sougia there's only service to Hania (€7.10, two hours).

Organised bus tours can be booked in every sizable town and resort in Crete. Note that prices listed usually don't include the €5 admission to the gorge or the €10 boat ride from Agia Roumeli to Sougia or Hora Sfakion.

Loutro   Λουτρό

A crescent of flower-festooned white-and-blue buildings hugging a narrow pebbly beach, the pintsized fishing village of Loutro lies between Agia Roumeli and Hora Sfakion and is only accessible by boat and on foot. It's the departure point for several coastal walks to isolated beaches, such as Finix, Marmara Bay and Sweetwater. Ask locally for directions or get here by canoe, available for hire from the Hotel Porto Loutro for €16 per day.

For overnights, try **Sifis Hotel** (☎ 6942413109, 28250 91346; www.sifishotel-loutro.com; d €50-70; ❄ 🛜), which has squeaky clean rooms with sea-facing balconies (Nos 5 and 10 are best). Don't leave without trying owner Cristina's famous cheesecake. Breakfast is €5. Recommended taverns include **Ilios** (☎ 28250 91197; www.ilios.loutro.gr; mains €5-15; ⊙ 8am-midnight) for some excellent *mayirefta* (ready-cooked meals) and fish, and **Pavlos** (☎ 28250 91336; www.pavlos.loutro.gr; mains €6-10) for grilled meats.

Note that there is no ATM in Loutro.

Up to five boats daily make the 20-minute trip from Hora Sfakion (€4.50) en route to Agia Roumeli.

IMBROS GORGE   ΦΑΡΑΓΓΙ ΙΜΠΡΟΥ

Half the length of its illustrious sister at Samaria, the 8km-long Imbros Gorge (admission €2; ⊙ year-round), 57km south of Hania, is no less beautiful and a lot less busy, especially in the afternoon. The hike takes you past 300m-high walls buttressed by cypresses, holm oaks, fig and almond trees and redolent sage. Landmarks include a giant arch at the 2km mark (coming from the south) and the narrowest point of the ravine (near the 4.5km mark), which is just 2m wide.

Most people begin the walk in the mountain village of Imbros and hike south to the village of Komitades. Doing it the other way around provides a bit more of a workout as you'll be walking up a gentle grade the entire time. The trail is rocky (wear sturdy shoes) but easy to follow as it traces the stream bed past rockslides and caves. There are tavernas at both ends.

Hora Sfakion–Hania buses can drop you on the main road about 2km from Komitades and also in Imbros. A taxi between the two costs about €20 and can be arranged by any taverna. From Komitades it's about a 5km walk or €10 taxi ride to Hora Sfakion.

Sougia   Σούγια
POP 100

Sougia (*soo*-yah), 67km south of Hania and on the Hora Sfakion–Paleohora ferry route, is one of the most laid-back and refreshingly undeveloped southern beach resorts. Cafes, bars and tavernas line a tamarisk-shaded waterfront promenade while most lodging options enjoy a quieter inland setting.

🏃 Activities

Sougia has a lovely 1km-long grey sand-and-pebble beach. Like most south coast villages, it's also great hiking territory. A taxi to the Samaria Gorge trailhead is €60, but with a day or two advance notice, staff at the taxi kiosk can put together a pool of hikers to share the cost.

If you don't like the Samaria crowds, head for the Agia Irini Gorge (admission €1.50; ⊙ all year) instead, which cuts deep through the mountains some 14km north of Sougia. The bus to Hania can drop you off near the trailhead in the eponymous village, from where a 7km mostly shaded hike (with a 500m elevation drop) takes you down to the excellent Taverna Oasis (⊘28230 51121). From here, it's another 7km walk via a quiet, paved road (or a €15 taxi ride) back to Sougia. Of course, it's also possible to do the hike in reverse.

🛏 Sleeping

Aretousa Studios & Rooms   APARTMENT $
(⊘28230 51178; s/d/studio €35/40/45; ⊙ Apr-Oct; P ❄ 🛜) This lovely 12-room hotel on the road to Hania, 200m from the sea, has cheerfully decorated and newly spiffed rooms and studios with a balcony and (mostly) kitchenettes. Kids can romp around the garden and playground out the back.

Syia Hotel   HOTEL $$$
(⊘28230 51174; www.syiahotel.gr; studio incl breakfast €60-80, apt incl breakfast €80-100; P ❄ 🛜) This professionally run family hotel is as fancy as things get in laid-back Sougia. Set in a quiet garden environment, units have plenty of elbow room along with a balcony, contemporary furnishings and full kitchens with upmarket appliances.

🍴 Eating

Polyfimos   GREEK $
(⊘28230 51343; mains €5-8; ⊙ dinner; 🛜 🐾) Tucked off the Hania road behind the police station, ex-hippie Yianni makes his own oil, wine and *raki* that go well with the finger-lickin' charcoal-grilled meats and a rich *tsigaristo* (cubes of lamb sauteed with wine and spices). There's also a fair selection of meat-free dishes.

★Omikron   INTERNATIONAL $$
(⊘28230 51492; mains €5-13.50; ⊙ 8am-late; 🛜 🐾) At this elegantly rustic lair, Jean-Luc Delfosse has forged his own culinary path in a refreshing change from taverna staples. Mushroom crêpes to *Flammekuche* (French-style pizza), seafood pasta to peppersteak – it's all fresh, creative and delicious.

ⓘ Information

There's an ATM next to Taverna Galini. For pre-trip planning, check out www.sougia.info.

Internet Lotos (☑28230 51191; per hr €3; ⊙7am-late) on the beach promenade can get you online.

ⓘ Getting There & Away

Two buses (one on Saturday) operate between Hania and Sougia (€7.10, two hours) with a stop in Agia Irini to drop off gorge hikers. The 6.15pm bus waits for the Agia Roumeli boat.

Boats leave in the morning for Agia Roumeli (€6.30, 40 minutes) with onward service to Loutro (€12, 1½ hours) and Hora Sfakion (€13, 1¾ hours). There's also an afternoon service west to Paleohora (€8, 40 minutes).

Paleohora   Παλαιόχωρα

POP 2200

Appealing, laid-back and full of character, Paleohora (pal-ee-*oh*-hor-a) lies on a narrow peninsula flanked by a long, curving tamarisk-shaded sandy beach (Pahia Ammos) and a pebbly beach (Halikia). Shallow waters and general quietude also make the resort a good choice for families with small children. The most picturesque part of Paleohora is the maze of narrow streets around the castle. Tavernas spill out onto the pavement and occasional cultural happenings, as well as Cretan and international music, inject a lively ambience. In spring and autumn, Paleohora attracts many walkers.

⊙ Sights

Venetian Castle   CASTLE

FREE It's worth clambering up the ruins of the 13th-century Venetian castle for the splendid view of the sea and mountains.

🛏 Sleeping

Most accommodation options close in the low season.

Homestay Anonymous   PENSION $
(☑28230 42098; www.anonymoushomestay.com; s/d/tr €23/30/32; ❄🔊) A fine choice for wallet-watching nomads, this simple pension has seven smallish but clean and tastefully furnished rooms in two buildings around a central garden. Owner Manolis is welcoming and is a mine of information for local things to do and see.

★ Joanna's   APARTMENTS $
(☑6978583503, 28230 41801; www.joannas-paleochora.com; studio €45-55; ⊙Apr-Nov; 🅿❄🔊) This charmer sits in a quiet spot across from a small beach at the southeastern tip of the peninsula. Spacious and spotless studios are outfitted with locally made furniture, and there's a kitchenette for preparing breakfast to enjoy on your balcony.

Hotel Rea   HOTEL $$
(s/d incl breakfast €50/60; ❄🔊) All the comforts and amenities are accounted for in the rooms of this friendly hotel, where breakfast is served on a garden-enclosed courtyard. There are also self-catering studios in a building across the street.

✕ Eating & Drinking

★ Methexis   GREEK $
(☑28230 41431; www.methexistaverna.com; mains €3.50-10; ⊙noon-1am; 🔊) It's well worth the short saunter to the peninsula's southeastern tip to sample the authentic comfort food and warm hospitality at this locally adored taverna with its own small beach. All the classics are here along with such menu surprises as the meat-free chestnut *stifado* (stew), salt cod with garlic sauce and the Methexis salad drizzled with delicious 'mystery sauce'.

Third Eye   VEGETARIAN $
(☑28230 41234; www.thethirdeye-paleochora.com; mains €6-7; ⊙8.30am-late; 🔊🍴) Both airy and intimate, this local institution just in from the sandy Pahia Ammos is a cheerful herbivore haven that dishes up an eclectic daily menu of curries, salads and pastas, as well as Greek and Asian dishes. There's occasional live music in the garden and basic rooms upstairs (€25 to €30).

Skala   BAR
(www.skalabar.gr; mains €2.50-7; ⊙7am-late; 🔊) This rocking portside pub is packed from breakfast time until the last tippler staggers out in the wee hours. Their big burgers are great for restoring balance to the brain.

ⓘ Information

Three ATMs are on Eleftheriou Venizelou, while the post office is at Pahia Ammos' northern end. In summer, a tourist information booth may be open in the harbour. **Selino Travel** (☑28230 42272; selino2@otenet.gr) sells boat tickets and excursions, including to the gorges of Samaria (€32) and Agia Irini (€27).

ⓘ Getting There & Away

BOAT

Boats leave from the old harbour at the pebbly beach's southern end. There is a daily morning ferry from Paleohora to Sougia (€8, 40 minutes) and Agia Roumeli (€14, 1½ hours) where the boats stops for 90 minutes before continuing to Loutro (€15, 40 minutes) and Hora Sfakion (€16, one hour). In summer, there's also thrice-weekly service to Gavdos Island (€19, 4 hours) and a daily ferry to Elafonisi (return €16, one hour).

BUS

KTEL (www.bus-service-crete-ktel.com) runs four daily buses to Hania (€7.60, 1½ hours) and a thrice-weekly service leaving at 6.15am to Omalos (€6.40, one hour) for the Samaria Gorge.

Elafonisi   Ελαφονήσι

If much of life in Crete is like a beach, remote Elafonisi *is* a beach and a stunning one at that. Tucked into Crete's southwest corner, this symphony of fine pinkish-white sand, turquoise water and gentle dunes looks as though it's lifted from the Caribbean. Off the long, wide strand lies Elafonisi Islet, easily reached by wading through 50m of knee-deep water. The entire area is part of Natura 2000, the environmental protection program of the European Union.

Alas, this natural gem is hardly a secret and less than idyllic in summer when hundreds of umbrellas and lounge chairs (€7) clog the beach. The invasion puts enormous pressure on this delicate ecosystem and on the minimal infrastructure, especially the toilets. Come early or late in the day or, better yet, stay overnight to truly sample Elafonisi's magic.

🛏 Sleeping & Eating

Elafonisi Resort   HOTEL **$**
(☑ 28250 61274; www.elafonisi-resort.com; s/d €35/45; 🌫 🛜) This grandly named cluster of five white-washed buildings among the olive trees offers nicely appointed rooms, some of them with a view of the beach, as well as apartments with kitchens. Don't expect culinary flights of fancy from the attached taverna.

Innahorion   CRETAN **$**
(☑ 28250 61111; mains €4-7, r €30-40; 🌫 🛜) About 2.5km before reaching Elafonisi beach, this taverna is considered the best in the area, serving good Cretan food with panoramic views. Owners also rent basic rooms.

❶ Getting There & Away

Elafonisi is about 75km southwest of Hania. There is one daily boat to Paleohora (€8, one hour), roughly from mid-May through September and one daily bus to Hania (€10, two hours) and Kissamos (€6.30, 1¼ hours), which returns in the afternoon.

Gavdos Island
Νησί της Γαύδου
POP 45

Europe's most southerly point, Gavdos lies 45km south of Hora Sfakion in the Libyan Sea. There's little to do here except to swim, walk and relax. The island is surprisingly green, with almost 65% covered in low-lying pine and cedar trees and vegetation. With only a smattering of rooms and tavernas, it's a blissful spot with several unspoilt beaches – some accessible only by boat. The island attracts campers, nudists and free spirits happy to trade the trappings of civilisation for an unspoiled nature experience.

◉ Sights & Activities

Boats land at **Karabe** on the east side of the island, while the capital Kastri is in the centre. The biggest beach community at **Sarakiniko**, in the northeast, has a wide swathe of sand and about a dozen tavernas. West of here, stunning **Agios Ioannis** beach is popular with campers and has three tavernas and a public shower. Lavrakas, Potamos and Pyrgos are even more remote but gorgeous beaches on the north coast (no facilities).

South of Karave, **Korfos** has a pebbly beach and a couple of tavernas with rooms. From here a 3.5km trail leads down via near-unpopulated Vatsiana to **Tripiti** – the southernmost tip of Europe.

🛏 Sleeping & Eating

Camping is tolerated in most places and especially popular in Agios Ioannis. There's only one small shop in Sarakiniko. The folks running the website at www.gavdos-online.com can help with reservations. Recommended options include **Consolas Gavdos Studios** (☑ 28230 42182; www.gavdosstudios.gr; d/tr studio incl breakfast €50/70; 🌫 🛜) and **Sarakiniko Gavdos** (☑ 28230 41103; http://gavdos-crete.com; r/studio €40/45), in Sarakiniko.

❶ Getting Around

Bike, scooter and car hire are available in Karave and Sarakiniko. Enquire about boat taxis to take you to remote beaches. From Karave, it takes about 30 minutes to walk to Sarakiniko, one hour to Korfos and 90 minutes to Agios Ioannis.

ⓘ Getting There & Away

In high season, Anendyk (www.anendyk.gr) serves Gavdos thrice weekly from Paleohora (€19, four hours) and four times weekly from Hora Sfakion (€16, 2½ hours), with some boats picking up passengers in Loutro, Agia Roumeli and Sougia.

EASTERN CRETE

Head east from Iraklio past the rocking package-tourist resorts of Hersonisos and Malia and you enter the island's easternmost prefecture of Lasithi, a more relaxed Cretan world that is never short of surprises. Looking for a charming resort town with a hot-stepping after-dark vibe? None better than Lasithi's main tourist draw of Agios Nikolaos. Ancient sites and culture? Lasithi has Minoan and Mycenean sites aplenty. The fertile Lasithi Plateau, tucked into the Mt Dikti ranges, offers cycling opportunities through tranquil villages and the Dikteon Cave where Zeus himself was born. Outdoor types can also look forward to walking the dramatic Valley of the Dead at Kato Zakros.

Added value comes with such unique attractions as the historic monastery of Toplou and Vaï's famous palm-backed beach. Scores of smaller towns and villages, meanwhile, maintain a rich undertow of Cretan history and spirit. All of this diversity is underpinned by a choice of accommodation and some of Crete's finest tavernas and restaurants.

Agios Nikolaos
Άγιος Νικόλαος

POP 27,100

Lasithi's capital, Agios Nikolaos (ah-yee-os nih-ko-laos) has an enviable location on hilly terrain overlooking the shores of the sensuously curving Mirabello Bay. It may feel less Cretan than other towns, partly because of its resort-style flair, tree-lined avenues and largely modern architecture. However, there's also a strong local character to Agios Nikolaos that makes it a charming and friendly place. A narrow channel separates the atttractive harbour from the circular Voulismeni Lake, whose pedestrianised shore is lined with tourist cafes and restaurants. At night a decidedly chic ambience descends on the harbour as lounge-bars fill

with stylish young Greeks and holidaymakers from the nearby resorts.

⊙ Sights

Archaeological Museum MUSEUM
(☑28410 24943; Paleologou Konstantinou 74) Crete's most significant Minoan collection (after the Iraklio Archaeological Museum) includes clay coffins, ceramic musical instruments and gold from Mohlos. Following an extended renovation, it is expected to reopen in 2014.

Folk Museum MUSEUM
(☑28410 25093; Paleologou Konstantinou 4; admission €3; ⊙10am-2pm Tue-Sun) This small museum provides a window on traditional, rural life but also features precious icons, fine silk needlework and historic guns.

🏃 Activities

Within town, sandy **Ammos Beach** and pebbly **Kytroplatia Beach** are fairly small and can get crowded, but they are convenient for a quick dip. About 1km north and south respectively, **Ammoudi Beach** and **Almyros Beach** are also busy but much longer, with better sand. All have snack bars, cafes and umbrella and sun-chair rentals.

🛏 Sleeping

Pergola Hotel HOTEL $
(☑28410 28152; Sarolidi 20; s/d €35/40; ✳🛜) An old-school family hotel, the Pergola has a homey feel, comfortable rooms with sea views, and a rooftop terrace with lounge chairs on which to relax or have a cold beer. The furniture is not the newest, but at these prices you know you're not getting the Ritz. Breakfast is €5.

★**Villa Olga** APARTMENTS $$
(☑28410 25913; www.villa-olga.gr; Anapafseos 18, Ellinika; apt €80-95; ✳🛜🌊) Olga has poured her heart and cash into these delightful self-catering apartments sleeping two to six in Ellinika, about midway between Agios Nikolaos and Elounda. Set in a well-tended terraced garden with a small swimming pool, they are well equipped and have traditional furniture, scattered artefacts and glorious bay views.

Hotel Creta APARTMENTS $$
(☑28410 28893; www.agiosnikalaos-hotels.gr/creta; Sarolidi 22; s/d/tr €55/65/75; ✳🛜) A major renovation has catapulted this great-value

Agios Nikolaos

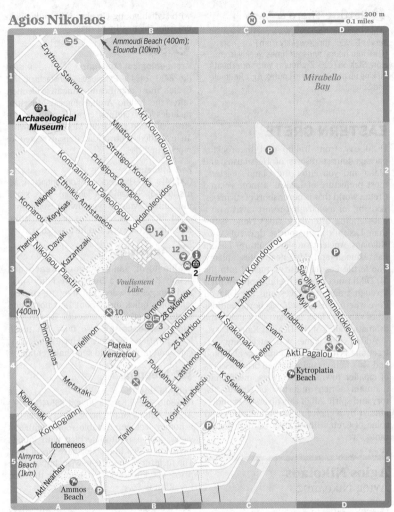

CRETE AGIOS NIKOLAOS

property into the 21st century. The 23 apartments with modern kitchens are in a quiet street yet close to the action. A lift takes you to the upper rooms with views of the bay and the little Agii Pantes island. Breakfast is €5.

Du Lac Hotel HOTEL **$$**
(☎28410 22711; www.dulachotel.gr; 28 Oktovriou 17; s/d/studio with lakeview €45/60/80; ✷ ⚏) Smack dab in the centre, this popular hotel has fine views over Voulismeni Lake from its decent rooms and spacious, fully fitted-out studios. Both have stylish contemporary

furnishings, a balcony and nice bathrooms. Street-facing units are about €10 less.

Minos Beach Art Hotel BOUTIQUE HOTEL **$$$**
(☎28410 22345; www.minosbeach.com; Akti Ilia Sotirchou; r incl breakfast from €280; P ✷ ⚏ ⚊) A short drive out of town, this mod luxury boutique hotel is a class act all throughout and comes with its own art gallery, Ayurvedic spa and dive centre. Even the smallest rooms are blissfully spacious and have a balcony or terrace – perfect for daydreaming about ditching the rat race.

Agios Nikolaos

✕ Eating

Away from lakeside tourist tavernas, there's great eating to be done around town.

★ Chrisofyllis
CRETAN $

(📞28410 22705; Akti Pagalou; mezedhes €4-8; ⊙12.30pm-12.30am; ☎) Locals swear by this hip mezedhes place near Kitroplatia beach. Sitting among eclectic decor that includes a bicycle and oversized silverware, you can build a meal with a selection from about 40 flavour-maximising dishes, including a creamy leek risotto and lamb filet with honey and sundried tomatoes.

Itanos
CRETAN $

(📞28410 25340; Kyprou 1; mains €6-12; ⊙noon-midnight; ☎) This friendly taverna with beamed ceilings and stucco walls is well-regarded locally for its home-style Cretan cooking. Pick your favourite from the trays of straightforward but excellent *mayirefta* (ready-cooked meals), such as goat with artichokes or lamb fricassee.

Pelagos
MEDITERRANEAN $$

(📞28410 25737; cnr Koraka & Katehaki; mains €7-23; ⊙lunch & dinner; ☎) Pelagos is not for the indecisive. First you must choose whether to sit in the elegantly rustic historic house or in the enchanting, lantern-festooned garden. Tough one, but perhaps not as tough as finding your top menu pick from the big selection of fresh fish, grilled meats, inventive salads and homemade pastas.

Amalthea
CRETAN $$

(📞28410 21801; Akti Pagalou 17; mains €6.50-15; ⊙noon-midnight; ☎) Market-fresh ingredients find their destiny in beautiful and crisp takes on classic recipes that keep regulars coming back for more. White tables and old kitchen equipment form a fresh backdrop.

Migomis
MEDITERRANEAN $$$

(📞28410 24353; www.migomis.com; Nikolaou Plastira 20; mains €12-38; ⊙lunch & dinner Apr-Oct; ☎) Dining in Agios Nikolaos doesn't get any fancier than in this hushed dining room with live piano music and superb views from high above Voulismeni Lake. The menu is ostensibly Italian yet laced with plenty of other influences that should please even the most discerning palates. For the same sublime views without the price tag, grab a coffee at the **Ano Kato Cafe** next door.

🍷 Drinking & Nightlife

The chic harbour-facing lounge-bars along Akti Koundourou are busy from mid-morning until the wee hours. About half-a-dozen dance clubs cluster on the lower end of 25 Martiou, just up from the harbour.

Alexandros Roof Garden
BAR

(Kondylaki; ⊙noon-late; ☎) This local institution gets you into party mood with its killer views, colourful cocktails, dance hits from the '70s to the '00s and funky, almost tropical decor.

Peripou Cafe
CAFE

(28 Otkovriou 13; ⊙9.30am-2am; ☎) Appealing to more of an arty, intellectual crowd, this cafe-bar has a narrow balcony with lake views and occasionally hosts singer-songwriters.

🛍 Shopping

Atelier Ceramica
CERAMICS

(📞28410 24075; Konstantinou Paleologou 28; ⊙9.30am-9pm) Watch artist and master restorer Nic Gabriel in his shop/workshop combo as he handmakes stunningly precise copies of antique vases, vessels and other artefacts, down to the knicks and cracks of the original. Prices are reasonable considering the artistry and amount of time that go into each piece, most of them one-of-a-kind.

ℹ️ Information

Most banks, ATMs, travel agencies and shops are on Koundourou and the parallel 28 Oktovriou.

Hospital (☑ 28410 66000; Konstantinou Paleologou) Behind the Archaeological Museum.

Post Office (28 Oktovriou 9; ⊘ 7.30am-2pm Mon-Fri)

Tourist Office (☑ 28410 22357; www.agios nikolaos.gr; ⊘ 8am-10pm Apr-Nov) At the bridge separating the harbour and the lake.

ℹ️ Getting There & Away

The **main bus station** is on Epimenidou. The bus to Elounda makes several other stops in town. Check the KTEL (www.bus-service-crete-ktel. com) website for the current schedule.

Bus Services from Agios Nikolaos

DESTINATION	TIME	FARE	FREQUENCY
Elounda	20min	€1.70	up to 14 daily
Ierapetra	1hr	€3.80	up to 7 daily
Iraklio	1½hr	€7.10	up to 21 daily
Kritsa	15min	€1.60	up to 11 daily
Sitia	1¾hr	€7.30	up to 5 daily

ℹ️ Getting Around

A new local bus links the main bus station with the harbour and the two in-town beaches (€1). **Manolis Bikes** (☑ 28410 24940; 25 Martiou 12) has a huge range of scooters, motorcycles and quad bikes. For car rentals, try **Club Cars** (☑ 28410 25868; www.clubcars.net; per day from €40). The most central **taxi rank** is behind the tourist office.

Around Agios Nikolaos

Elounda   Ελούντα

POP 2185

There are fine mountain and sea views along the 11km road north from Agios Nikolaos to Elounda (el-*oon*-da), which is centred on a handsome fishing harbour. The backdrop is standard resort, but there is also a refreshing down-to-earth feel to the village, along with some excellent waterfront eateries. The pleasant but unremarkable town beach, a short walk north of the harbour, can get very crowded. On the south side of Elounda a causeway leads to the Kolokytha Peninsula.

🛏️ Sleeping

Olive Grove Apartments   APARTMENTS **$$**
(☑ 28410 41448; www.olivegrove-apts.com; Naksou 2; apt €55; P ✳ 🕸 🏊) One short block off the main square, this modern complex is run by a charming family and has 14 large and spotless units wrapped around a large pool with a bar.

Corali Studios   APARTMENTS **$$**
(☑ 28410 41712; www.coralistudios.com; Akti Poseidonos; r €45-75; P ✳ 🕸 🏊) On the road to Plaka, these self-catering studios in an immaculately kept building have balconies overlooking the municipal beach and a large swimming pool with bar out the back. The same family also runs the adjacent Portobello Apartments, whose units can accommodate up to four people.

🍴 Eating

Arodamos   GREEK **$**
(☑ 28410 41122; Naksou 6; mains €4-9; ⊘ 11am-late; 🕸) Andriani and Dimitris' charismatic eatery occupies a century-old house fronted by a sweet little garden. The inspired mezedhes are a great overture to the succulent roast chicken or authentic *kondosouvli* (roasted liver wrapped in intestines) from the outdoor rotisserie. It's one block from the main square.

Kaaren's   CAFE **$**
(☑ 28410 41709; Akti Poseidonos 47; mains €4.50-6.50; ⊘ 9am-6pm; 🕸 🍴) This daytime-only cafe makes great breakfasts and light meals. On Fridays, homesick Brits practically mob the place for newspaper-wrapped fish 'n' chips.

★ **Lotus Eaters**   MEDITERRANEAN **$$**
(☑ 28410 41538; www.lotus-eaters.com; mains €7.50-26.50; ⊘ lunch & dinner; 🕸) In an enviable location at the end of the waterfront restaurant row, this taverna has a smart, contemporary feel that goes well with the fresh and intricately flavoured cuisine from around the Med. A great wine list is another reason why it's at the top of many a foodie's fave list.

Poulis   GREEK **$$**
(☑ 28410 41451; waterfront restaurant row; mains €7-15; ⊘ 10am-late; 🕸) Although not as slick as

some of the other fish restaurants in town, Poulis is often packed to the gills thanks to its wonderful owners, soulful seafood and richly nuanced mezedhes and vegetable dishes.

ℹ️ Information

The post office and ATMs are on Elounda's main square, which doubles as a car park and overlooks the harbour. From June to October, a **tourist information kiosk** (📞 28410 42464; ⊙ 8am-8pm Jun-Oct) may be open here, but if not Lynn at the **Eklektos** (📞 28410 42086) bookshop (great selection of English-language novels) is a generous fount of useful information.

ℹ️ Getting There & Around

From Agios Nikolaos, up to 14 daily buses serve Elounda (€1.70, 20 minutes), stopping in the main square. See KTEL (www.bus-service-crete-ktel.com) for the schedule. A taxi is about €13. Boats to Spinalonga leave every half-hour (adult/child €10/5) between 9am and 5pm.

Spinalonga Island
Νήσος Σπιναλόγκα

Known as the 'leper island', Spinalonga (admission €2; ⊙ 9am-6pm) was catapulted into pop-cultural consciousness by Virginia Hislop's 2005 bestselling novel *The Island* and the subsequent Greek TV series spin-off *To Nisi*. Sitting pretty off the northern tip of the Kolokytha Peninsula (confusingly also known as Spinalonga Peninsula), its massive fortress was built by the Venetians in 1579 to protect the bays of Elounda and Mirabello, and fell under Ottoman control in 1715.

In 1903, the island began its most notorious period as a leper colony. Also known as Hansen's Disease, the condition causes skin lesions, nerve damage and muscle weakness and has been around since ancient times. Then believed to be highly contagious, sufferers were stigmatised and isolated, including as many as 1000 Greeks quarantined on Spinalonga, initially under squalid and miserable living conditions. This changed in 1936 with the arrival of Epaminondas Remoundakis, a law student who had contracted leprosy at age 21, and who fought passionately for better medical care and infrastructure on the island. A cure for leprosy was finally discovered in 1948 and the last person left Spinalonga in 1957.

Thanks to Hislop's tale about her own family's connection to the island, interest in Spinalonga has skyrocketed and you're unlikely to feel lonely when visiting the island. A 1km trail starts at Dante's Gate, the 20m-long tunnel through which patients arrived, and takes you past such 'sights' (mostly ruined) as a church, the disinfection room, the hospital and the cemetery. Since there's little descriptive panelling, the illustrated booklet (€6) sold at the ticket kiosk may be worthwhile for a more indepth experience.

Ferries to Spinalonga depart half-hourly from Elounda (€10) and Plaka (€5), giving you an hour on the island (though you can stay longer and return on a different boat). There's also one daily boat from Agios Nikolaos (€25).

Kritsa
Κριτσά

The fine traditions of the old mountain village of Kritsa (krit-sah), 11km southwest of Agios Nikolaos, are a touch blurred by the often insistent techniques of sellers of embroidered goods. The upper village, however, beneath rugged crags, is redolent with romantic decay and the ghosts of the past. Note that tour coaches pile into Kritsa from late morning until late afternoon.

About 1km before Kritsa is the turnoff to the photogenic 13th-century Church of Panagia Kera (📞 28410 51806; admission €3; ⊙ 8.30am-3pm Tue-Sun), which contains some of the finest Byzantine frescoes in Crete.

There are hourly buses here from Agios Nikolaos (€1.60, 15 minutes). A taxi costs about €13.

Lato
Λατώ

About 4km north of Kritsa, the 7th-century-BC Dorian city of Ancient Lato (admission €2; ⊙ 8.30am-3pm Tue-Sun) is one of Crete's few non-Minoan ancient sites. Lato (lah-to), once a powerful city state, sprawls over two acropolises in a lonely mountain setting overlooking the Gulf of Mirabello. It was named after Leto, the mother of Artemis and Apollo.

There are no buses to Lato. If you're driving, look for the signposted turnoff as you approach to Kritsa. A taxi from Agios Nikolaos costs about €16.

Gournia
Γουρνιά

The Minoan settlement of Gournia (admission €3; ⊙ 8.30am-3pm Tue-Sun) (goor-nyah) lies 19km southeast of Agios Nikolaos. Made up

LOCAL KNOWLEDGE

ISTRON'S DREAMY BEACHES

A short drive southeast of Agios Nikolaos, the highway enters a superbly panoramic stretch where the raw beauty of the coastal mountains spills down to a craggy coastline indented with coves shimmering softly in myriad shades of blue and green. Tourism development has been kept at bay for now, in part because of archaeological excavations near the village of Istron, which is also home to a trio of stunning, well-organised beaches.

First up is **Karavostasi**, a half-kilometre-long strip of fine sand, where a snack bar serves refreshments. A footpath around a big rock leads to the second beach of **St Panteleimon**, named for a small chapel built into the hill above it. Tamarisk and olive trees provide some shade along with umbrellas and sun chairs (€7).

Top billing, though, goes to **Vulisme** beach, aka Golden Beach, a clean, sweeping crescent whose tepid, shallow waters and white sand exude a distinct Caribbean feel. Unfortunately, it can get awfully busy in summer. A concession stand rents jet skis and paddleboats and there's a cafeteria as well.

Up to 14 buses daily travel from Agios Nikolaos to Istron (€1.60, 30 minutes).

of a small palace and residential areas, it was built between 1600 and 1500 BC, destroyed in 1450 BC and reoccupied from 1375 to 1200 BC. There are streets, stairways and houses with walls up to 2m high. Domestic, trade and agricultural implements discovered here indicate that Gournia was fairly prosperous.

When exploring the site, study the overview map just past the entrance, then follow a narrow ancient road as it curves uphill to the palace ruins, skirting **workshops** and **storage rooms**, including one where a clay wine press was found. The trail ends at the palace's central courtyard with steps on your right indicating the main entrance. On the opposite (west) side of the courtyard, smaller stairs lead down to an upright slab considered a 'sacred stone'. There are 10 explanatory panels scattered around the site as well as a booklet for sale at the ticket kiosk (€5).

Sitia and Ierapetra buses from Agios Nikolaos can drop you at the site.

Mohlos   Μόχλος

POP 90

At the end of a narrow road winding past massive quarries, tranquil Mohlos (*mohlos*) is an off-the-radar gem along Crete's northern shore. In this authentic fishing village time moves as gently as the waves lapping onto the pebble-and-grey-sand beach. There's little to do but relax and soak in the peacefulness.

Mohlos was once a thriving Early Minoan community and connected to the small is-

land that is now 200m offshore. Swimmers should be wary of strong currents.

🛏 Sleeping & Eating

Bellavista Apartments   APARTMENTS $
(☑6976578655; apt €35-40; P ✳ 🛜) Splashed in fresh colours and decorated with original paintings by the mother of charismatic owner Katia, these spacious studios are a wonderful find. All have full kitchens and balcony views of Mohlos Island.

Mohlos Mare   APARTMENTS $$
(☑28430 94005; www.mochlos-mare.com; apt €50-80; P ✳ 🛜) These spacious and well-appointed apartments are bright and airy and the top rooms have great views from the big balconies. There's a vineyard and garden out the front with hundreds of roses, and a communal outdoor kitchen and barbecue.

Ta Kochilia   GREEK $$
(☑28430 94432; mains €4.50-16; ⊙ lunch & dinner; 🛜) The oldest among several waterfront restaurants (since 1902), this family-run taverna is known for its fresh fish served at wallet-friendly prices. Meals start with a basket of delicious bread with tapenade and tomato coulis and conclude with owner Giorgos' homemade *raki*. In summer, the sea-urchin salad gets top marks.

ⓘ Getting There & Away

Buses running between Agios Nikolaos and Sitia can drop you at the turn-off for Mohlos from where you can try hitching a ride down or embark on a 5km walk.

Sitia   Σητεία

POP 9900

Sitia (si-*tee*-ah) is an attractive seaside town with a fishing harbour hemmed by a wide promenade lined with tavernas and cafes. Its white-washed houses cling to the hillside bisected by steep staircases. It's a friendly place where tourism is fairly low key and agriculture is the mainstay of the local economy. A long, sandy beach skirts a wide bay to the east of town.

⊙ Sights

Palm-tree studded Plateia Iroön Polytechniou is Sitia's main square.

Sitia Archaeological Museum   MUSEUM
(☑ 28430 23917; Piskokefalou; adult/concession €2/1; ⊙ 8.30am-3pm Tue-Sun) This showcase of archaeological finds from eastern Crete has objects spanning the arc from neolithic to Roman times, with an emphasis on Minoan artefacts. Pride of place goes to the *Palekastro Kouros* – a statue carved from hippopotamus tusks that was once fully covered in gold leaf. Finds from the palace at Zakros include a wine press, a bronze saw and cult objects scorched by the fire that destroyed the palace.

Venetian Fort   FORT
(⊙ 8.30am-3pm) **FREE** Strategically perched atop a hill, this structure is locally called *kazarma* (from the Venetian *casa di arma*) and was built as a garrison by the Venetians. These are the only remains of the fortifications that once protected the town. The site is now used as an open-air venue.

🛏 Sleeping

Plenty of reasonably priced three-star city hotels but no fancy resorts.

Sitia Bay Hotel   HOTEL **$$**
(☑ 28430 24800; www.sitiabay.com; s/d €105/120; P ❋ ⎈ ⛱) There's plenty to like about this modern hotel, which caters to both couples and families with three room sizes, all with a spacious bathroom, kitchenette and a balcony to let in the sea breezes. The swimming pool is nonchlorinated and has soothing massage jets. Breakfast is €7.

Hotel Flisvos   HOTEL **$$**
(☑ 28430 27135; www.flisvos-sitia.com; Karamanli 4; s/d incl breakfast €50/60; P ❋ ⎈) This mod-

ern and well-kept property along the southern waterfront has harbour views from its (balconied) front rooms and a flowery courtyard for breakfast and post-lunch chilling in the shade. The furniture is standard-issue but comfortable enough.

🍴 Eating & Drinking

The tourist-geared waterfront tavernas offer standard fare at normal prices. North of the main square, the promenade is lined with cafes, bars and music clubs, ranging in style from drab to fab.

To Steki   GREEK **$**
(☑ 28430 23857; Papandreou 10; mains €6-9; ⊙ 11am-11pm; ⎈) Empty wine bottles and retro wall clocks create a quaint setting in this locally adored taverna, which churns out a changing roster of honest-to-goodness *mayirefta* (ready-cooked meals) and tasty grills. It's especially busy at lunchtime.

Oinodeion   GREEK **$**
(El Venizelou 157; mains €6-9; ⊙ lunch & dinner; ⎈) Sporting a wall decorated with old-fashioned kitchen utensils, this local place sits quietly alongside more glitzy cafes on the main waterfront. There's a good range of mezedhes, such as snails in vinegar sauce, and meat and fish standards.

Balcony   FUSION **$$**
(☑ 28430 25084; www.balcony-restaurant.com; Foundalidou 19; mains €13-20; ⊙ lunch & dinner; ⎈) On the 1st floor of a yellow house with shutters painted a cheerful purple, this country-chic restaurant is headed by Tonya Karandinou, who has a knack for infusing Cretan cuisine with Mexican and Asian influences for mash-ups that pack a flavour punch. Fine Greek wines complement the dishes.

ℹ Information

There are several banks with ATMs in the centre of town. You may want to cash up here if you're headed further east, as there is only one other ATM in Palekastro.

Post Office (Dimokritou; ⊙ 7.30am-3pm) Inland, the first left off Venizelou.

Tourist Office (☑ 28430 28300; Karamanli; ⊙ 9.30am-2.30pm & 5-8.30pm Mon-Fri, 9.30am-2.30pm Sat summer only) In summer, an information kiosk operates on the promenade.

ⓘ Getting There & Away

AIR

Sitia's airport is about 1.5km north of town and receives only domestic flights. A taxi into town costs about €8.

BOAT

Ferries dock 600m north of Plateia Iroön Polytechniou. Sitia is on the Piraeus–Rhodes route operated by Aegeon Pelagos, a subsidiary of Anek (www.anek.gr), with stops in Karpathos, Iraklio, Santorini and Milos. **Akasti Travel** (☑ 28430 20400; www.akasti.gr; Kornarou 93; ☺ 9am-9pm Mon-Sat, 9am-5pm Sun) can help with tickets.

BUS

The bus station is on Papanastasiou, near Missonos. See KTEL (www.bus-service-crete-ktel.com) for the current timetable.

Bus Services from Sitia

DESTINATION	TIME	FARE	FREQUENCY
Agios Nikolaos	1¾hr	€7.30	up to 5 daily
Ierapetra	1½hr	€6.30	up to 4 daily
Iraklio	3¼hr	€14.70	up to 5 daily
Palekastro	45min	€2.60	3 Mon-Fri
Vaï	1hr	€3.60	4 daily May-Oct
Zakros	1hr	€4.10	2 Mon, Tue & Fri

Around Sitia

Moni Toplou   Μονή Τοπλού

Perched in splendid isolation on a windswept bluff above the sea, **Moni Toplou** (☑ 28430 61226; admission €3; ☺ 10am-5pm Apr-Oct, Fri only Nov-Mar) is one of the most historically significant monasteries in Crete, whose defences were tested by all, from pirates to crusading knights and the Turks. It is also one of the wealthiest, owning vast sweeps of land, including the beach at Vaï, and producing excellent wine and olive oil.

Its most prized possession is the stunningly intricate **Megas i Kyrie** (Lord Thou Art Great) icon by celebrated Cretan artist Ioannis Kornaros. Dozens of stories from the Old and New Testaments are depicted here; see if you can find Noah's Ark, Jonah and the Whale or Moses parting the Red Sea. Other rooms hold more icons, copper engravings and a WWII memorial exhibit.

The monastery is about 18km east of Sitia. Buses can drop you off at the junction on the Sitia–Palekastro road from where it's a 3km walk.

Vaï   Βάι

The beach at Vaï, 24km east of Sitia, is famous for its large grove of Phoenix theophrastii **palms**. With calm, clear waters, it is one of Crete's most popular strands, whose rows of umbrellas and sunbeds (€8) often get filled by 10am in July and August. Jet skis kick into gear shortly thereafter. In other words, come early or after 5pm to appreciate Vaï's natural beauty in tranquillity.

If you want a nice beach without the crowds (or the palms), take the 1km scramble east over the rocky headland; there are no facilities, so pack everything you need. The trail starts just past the gazebo lookout reached via stone steps leading up from the reasonably priced **taverna** (mains €5-9; ☺ 11.30am-10pm).

There are four buses daily to Vaï from Sitia (€3.60, one hour) from May to October. Parking is €3.

Zakros & Kato Zakros
Ζάκρος & Κάτω Ζάκρος
POP 912

Zakros (zah-kros), 45km southeast of Sitia, is the starting point for the trail through the Zakros Gorge, known as the Valley of the Dead on account of the ancient burial sites in the caves that honeycomb the canyon walls. Zakros, however, is a mere prelude to coastal Kato Zakros, 7km down a winding road through rugged terrain. Halfway down, it loops left to reveal a vast curtain of mountains and the red jaws of the Zakros Gorge breaching the cliffs. Behind Kato Zakros' pebbly beach and its huddle of tavernas, the remarkable ruins of the Minoan Zakros Palace are clearly defined.

⊙ Sights & Activities

Zakros Palace   ARCHAEOLOGICAL SITE
(☑ 28410 22462; Kato Zakros; adult/concession €3/2; ☺ 8am-3pm, extended summer hours possible) Ancient Zakros, the smallest of Crete's four Minoan palatial complexes, was a major port, trading with Egypt, Syria, Anatolia

and Cyprus. The palace comprised royal apartments, storerooms and workshops flanking a central courtyard. The exquisite rock-crystal vase and stone bull's head now in Iraklio's Archaeological Museum were among the treasure trove of antiquities found at Zakros. While the ruins are sparse, the wildness and remoteness of the setting make it an attractive place to explore.

Zakros Gorge   WALKING

This easy 8km walk starts from just below Zakros village and winds it way through a narrow and (at times) soaring canyon with a riot of vegetation and wild herbs before emerging close to Zakros Palace, 200m from the beach. For a shorter walk, pick up the trailhead about 3km down the road to Kato Zakros. A taxi back to Zakros costs about €6.

🛏 Sleeping & Eating

★ Stella's Traditional Apartments   APARTMENTS $$

(28430 23739; www.stelapts.com; Kato Zakros; studios €60-80; P ✳ 🛜) Close to the wooded mouth of the Zakros Gorge, these charming self-contained studios sport distinctive wooden furniture and artefacts made by co-owner Elias Pagiannides. There are hammocks under the trees, barbecues and an outdoor kitchen with an honour system for supplies. Elias has excellent knowledge and experience of hiking trails and other outdoor activities around the area.

Kato Zakros Palace   APARTMENTS $$

(28430 29550; www.katozakros-apts.gr; Kato Zakros; r/studio €50/60; P ✳ 🛜) High on the slopes above Kato Zakros beach, these rooms and studios have cooking facilities and a guests laundry room. Views are predictably stunning.

Akrogiali Taverna   CRETAN $

(28430 26893; Kato Zakros; mains €5-10; 🛜) The food gods have been smiling upon Kato Zakros' oldest taverna, which does a brisk business in fresh fish and Cretan classics, all prepared with locally sourced ingredients. The beachfront setting adds another notch to its appeal.

❶ Getting There & Away

Every Monday, Tuesday and Friday, two buses make the trip out here from Sitia via Palekastro (€4.10, one hour). In summer, these continue to Kato Zakros.

Ierapetra   Ιεράπετρα
POP 27,600

Ierapetra (yeh-*rah*-pet-rah) is a laid-back seafront town and the commercial centre of southeastern Crete's substantial greenhouse-based agribusiness. Hot and dusty in summer, it offers a low-key, authentic Cretan experience and is also the jumping-off point to the semitropical Gaïdouronisi Island (also called Hrysi). The local grey-sand beaches are extensive and backed by tavernas and cafes where the nightlife is busy in summer.

Though little is left, Ierapetra has an impressive history with interludes as a Roman port for conquering Egypt and a Venetian stronghold based on the still-standing harbour fortress. The narrow alleyways of the Turkish quarter recall its Ottoman past.

◉ Sights & Activities

Ierapetra's main town beach is near the harbour, while a second beach stretches east from Patriarhou Metaxaki. Both have coarse grey sand, but the main beach has more shade.

Ierapetra Archaeological Museum   MUSEUM

(28420 28721; Adrianou 2; admission €2; ⊗8.30am-3pm Tue-Sun) Ierapetra's small but worthwhile archaeological collection occupies a former school from the Ottoman period. A standout among the mostly headless classical statuary is an intact 2nd-century-AD sculpture of the goddess Persephone. Another splendid piece is a Minoan larnax (clay coffin) from 1300 BC and decorated with 12 painted panels showing hunting scenes, an octopus and a chariot procession.

Kales Fortress   FORTRESS

(⊗8.30am-3pm Tue-Sun) FREE South along the waterfront, this rectangular fortress was built in the early years of Venetian rule and strengthened by Francesco Morosini in 1626. It's open to visitors but there's not much to see, although views to the eastern mountains from above are pretty grand.

🛏 Sleeping

Popy Apartments   APARTMENTS $

(28420 24289; Kazantzaki 27; apt €40; ✳ 🛜) Run by a fall-over-backwards-friendly family, these good-sized self-catering apartments have balconies overlooking a garden and won't take a big bite out of your wallet.

Cretan Villa Hotel HOTEL **$**

(☑ 28420 28522; www.cretan-villa.com; Lakerda 16; s/d €45/50; ❄ ☎) This well-maintained 18th-century house manages to create a charming, almost rural, character in the heart of town. Rooms have stone walls, traditional dark-wood furnishings and cluster round a peaceful courtyard. It's only a few minutes' walk from the bus station.

✗ Eating & Drinking

In addition to choices listed below, the waterfront is lined with cafes and tavernas, many of them quite good, authentic and reasonably priced. Nightclubs line up along Kyvra.

I Kalitexnes GREEK, ARABIC **$**

(☑ 28430 28547; Kyprou 26; mains €5-9; ☺ closed Sun; ☎) There's no fixed menu at this quirky little place, but instead you decide how to fill your tummy after taking a peek into the big pots in the open kitchen. No matter what it is, it'll be fresh, delicious and organic. With one day's notice, the Egyptian owner can also whip up authentic couscous with lamb or chicken.

Napoleon CRETAN **$$**

(☑ 28420 22410; Stratigou Samouil 26; mains €6-12; ☎ ☑) At the southern end of the waterfront, this is one of the oldest and most popular establishments in town. A mixed fish plate is a good choice, as is *kakavia* (fish soup). Good selection of meatless fare as well.

Veterano CAFE

(☑ 28420 26136; Plateia Eleftherias; ☺ 7.30am-11.30pm; ☎) Incredible cakes, baklava and ice cream.

Ntoukiani BAR

(Ethnikis Antistaseos 19; ☺ 8pm-late; ☎) Ierapetra has a long tradition of *rakadika*, relaxed evening hang-outs where a carafe of *raki* or wine comes with half a dozen or more tasty tidbits, making it a good-value slow dining experience. This place has an especially authentic vibe and excellent traditional music.

Odeion CAFE, BAR

(Lasthenous 18; ☺ 7pm-late; ☎) The sprawling courtyard garden of this neoclassical villa is always abuzz with the sounds of clinking glasses and animated conversation. Pick from a selection of mezedhes to go with your wine.

ℹ Information

Look for banks and ATMs around Plateia Eleftherias and along Lasthenous. The **post office** (Giannakou 1; ☺ 7.30am-2pm) is a few steps west of Plateia Venizelou.

ℹ Getting There & Away

The bus station is on Lasthenous, just north of Plateia Plastira (Plastira Sq). Check the schedule with KTEL (www.bus-service-crete-ktel.com).

Bus Services from Ierapetra

DESTINATION	TIME	FARE	FREQUENCY
Agios Nikolaos	1hr	€3.80	up to 7 daily
Iraklio	2½hr	€11	7 daily
Myrtos	30min	€2.20	up to 5 Mon-Sat
Sitia	1½ hr	€6.30	up to 4 daily

Gaïdouronisi (Hrysi)
Γαϊδουρονήσι (Χρυσή)

About 5km long and 1.5km wide, tranquil and protected Gaïdouronisi (Donkey Island), marketed as Hrysi (Golden Island), has nice sandy beaches, a couple of tavernas and Lebanon cedars – the only such stand in Europe. It can get very crowded when the tour boats are in, but you can usually find a quiet spot.

In summer, up to seven **excursion boats** depart for the 45-minute journey from the quay in Ierapetra every morning, returning in the afternoon. All travel agents in town sell tickets (about €20).

Myrtos Μύρτος
POP 622

Myrtos (*myr*-tos) lies 14km west of Ierapetra. It has a devoted clientele who swear by the area's easygoing and creative vibe. No big resort-style hotels mar the long stretch of fairly narrow grey pebble-and-sand beach flanked by a paved promenade with cafes and shops.

🛏 Sleeping & Eating

Big Blue APARTMENTS **$**

(☑ 28420 51094; www.big-blue.gr; d/apt €45/85, studio €50-70; ❄ ☎) For overnight stays, Big Blue has large airy studios with sea views and cheaper ground-floor rooms, all with cooking facilities. Breakfast starts at €6.

Kastro APARTMENTS $
(☑ 28420 51444; www.kastromyrtos.gr; studio €40-55; P ✳ 🛜 🌊) Kastro's modern and spotless studios and apartments are set in a dreamy garden wrapped around a huge pool with a bar.

★**Katerina** CRETAN $$
(☑ 6948325739; mains €5.50-19.50; ☺ lunch & dinner) Your tastebuds will do somersaults at Katerina, where Yiannis is the kind of chef that puts a creative mark on even the most classic dishes. Don't overdose on the homemade bread that accompanies the free appetiser to enjoy such flavour-bombs as the aromatic lamb *kleftiko*, the ouzo-flambeed saganaki (fried cheese) and the gooey chocolate cake. Foodies might also be interested in Yiannis' herb-collecting tours and cooking courses.

Platanos CRETAN $
(mains €5-12; ☺ 11am-late; 🛜) Beneath a giant plane tree, tourist-geared Platanos is a focus of village social life and has live music on many summer evenings. It offers reliable Cretan staples.

ⓘ Getting There & Away

Seven daily buses go from Ierapetra to Myrtos (€2.20, 20 minutes).

Lasithi Plateau
Οροπέδιο Λασιθίου

The tranquil Lasithi Plateau, 900m above sea level, is a vast expanse of green fields interspersed with almond trees and orchards. It's really more of a plain than a plateau, sitting as it does in a huge depression amid the rock-studded mountains of the Dikti range. Lasithi would have been a stunning sight in the 17th century when it was dotted with some 20,000 windmills with white canvas sails, which the Venetians built for irrigation purposes. The few that remain are an iconic (and much photographed) sight.

Tzermiado
Τζερμιάδο

The largest of Lasithi's 20 villages, Tzermiado (dzer-mee-ah-do) is still a bucolic place. Taverna Kourites (www.kourites.eu; mains €7.50-10.50) does a brisk lunchtime business with coaches full of day-trippers. At other times, it's a large and peaceful spot where menu options include top-notch lamb and suckling pig roasted in a wood-fired oven. There are clean and simple rooms above the taverna and in a nearby small hotel (☑ 28440 22054; www.kourites.net; s/d €35/40, breakfast €5). Guests can make use of free (old) bicycles. For a more upscale rural retreat, head to Argoulias (☑ 28440 22754; www.argoulias.gr; d incl breakfast €55-80; ✳), a set of studios in stone houses built into the hillside high above the main village (views!).

Tzermiado has two ATMs, two gas stations and a post office.

Agios Georgios
Αγιος Γεώργιος

For such a quiet little village, Agios Georgios (*agh*-ios ye-*or*-gios) is quite a fruitful sightseeing stop, largely because of the intriguing Folklore Museum (☑ 28440 31462; adult/concession €3/2; ☺ 10am-4pm Apr-Oct), whose eclectic exhibits include farming tools, traditional workshops, carved wooden furniture, faded black-and-white photographs and WWI relics. A separate building houses a rather turgid exhibit on political legend Eleftherios Venizelos.

On the outskirts of town, the Lasinthos Eco-Park (☑ 28440 89100; www.lasinthos.gr; admission €4; ☺ 10am-7pm late-Mar–mid-Nov) is a recreated village that celebrates rural traditions. Watch a wood carver and a ceramicist at work, meet barnyard animals and learn how honey, wine and *raki* are produced, before stocking up on the same in the large shop.

For eats, try Taverna Rea (mains €7-8), a bright artefact-filled place on the main street. The rooms above the taverna can be rented for €30.

Psyhro & the Dikteon Cave
Ψυχρό& Δικταίον Αντρον

Psyhro (psi-*hro*) is the closest village to the Dikteon Cave (☑ 28440 31316; admission €4; ☺ 10am-2.30pm, extended hours possible Jul-Aug) and is often clogged with tour buses. According to legend, Rhea hid in this cave to give birth to Zeus, far from the clutches of his offspring-gobbling father Cronos. From the entrance a staircase descends steeply to the more partly illuminated lower cave with some evocatively shaped formations.

Numerous votives discovered here indicate cult worship since ancient times.

It is a steep 15-minute (800m) walk up to the cave entrance, either via a rocky natural trail or a more comfortable paved track. Donkey rides are available for €15 (€20 return). Parking is €2.

There are numerous tourist taverns in town and snack stands in the parking lot. A more authentic **taverna** (mains €5-8; ⊙ 8am-6pm Apr-Oct, extended hours in summer) sits halfway up the road to the cave where Joanna turns her husband's farm products into no-nonsense Greek classics, including a richly nuanced *mousaka*.

ⓘ Getting There & Away

The Lasithi Plateau is the domain of tour buses and poorly served by public ones. In fact, there's only one bus daily from Iraklio to Psyhro (€6.50, 2 hours). By car, the main approach is by turning south off the coastal highway near Stalida, just past Hersonisos. The best approach from Agios Nikolaos is via Neapoli.

Dodecanese

Why Go?

Ever pined for old Greece, where you can still catch a sense of that authentic magic? Enter the remote Dodecanese (Δωδεκάνησα; do-de-*ka*-ni-sa) Islands in the southeastern Aegean. The footprints of the Byzantine and Ottoman Empires, Italian occupation and medieval knights are all found here, and beyond better-known Rhodes and Kos there are enigmatic islands begging you to explore them.

Hikers, naturalists and botanists flock to Tilos, while climbers scale the limestone cliffs in Kalymnos; divers have underwater caves and ancient wrecks to explore, while kitesurfers visit southern Karpathos for its legendary winds. Archaeologists and history buffs have a bevy of ancient sites to let their imaginations loose, and sybarites can find myriad beaches, free of the package crowds, to worship Helios.

Best Places to Eat

➡ Barbarossa (p515)

➡ Taverna Mylos (p524)

➡ Marco Polo Mansion (p477)

➡ Meraklis (p497)

Best Places to Stay

➡ Marco Polo Mansion (p475)

➡ Melenos (p480)

➡ To Archontiko Angelou (p526)

➡ Villa Melina (p519)

When to Go
Rhodes

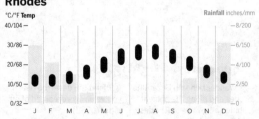

Apr & May Prices are low, there are few tourists and the sea is warming up.

Jul & Aug Peak season for accommodation and visitors – book ahead.

Sep The best time to go: beaches are empty, the sea warm and hotel prices have dropped again.

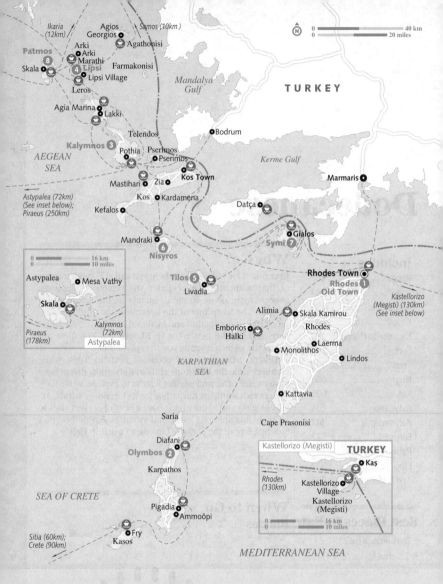

Dodecanese Highlights

1 Wander beneath Byzantine arches and along the ancient cobbled alleyways of **Rhodes Old Town** (p470)

2 Follow the winding road up to the traditional mountaintop village of **Olymbos** (p489)

3 Test your mettle diving for wrecks or climbing limestone cliffs on **Kalymnos** (p517)

4 Find the deserted beach you've always dreamed of on **Lipsi** (p532)

5 Go hiking or birding on postcard-perfect **Tilos** (p498)

6 Enter the fabled volcano of **Nisyros** (p501), home to an imprisoned Titan

7 Feel your pulse quicken as your boat pulls into **Symi's** (p494) gorgeous Italianate harbour

8 Make a pilgrimage to **Patmos** (p527), where St John wrote his 'Revelations'

History

The Dodecanese islands have been inhabited since pre-Minoan times. Following Alexander the Great's death in 323 BC, Ptolemy I of Egypt ruled the Dodecanese.

The Dodecanese islanders were the first Greeks to become Christians. This was through the tireless efforts of St Paul, who made two journeys to the archipelago during the 1st century, and through St John, who was banished to Patmos where he had his revelation and added a chapter to the Bible.

The early Byzantine era saw the islands prosper, but by the 7th century AD they were plundered by a string of invaders. The Knights of St John of Jerusalem (Knights Hospitaller) arrived in the 14th century and eventually became rulers of almost all the Dodecanese, building mighty fortifications strong enough to withstand time but not sufficient to keep out the Turks in 1522.

The Turks were themselves ousted by the Italians in 1912. The latter, inspired by Mussolini's vision of a vast Mediterranean empire, made Italian the official language of the Dodecanese and prohibited the practice of Orthodoxy. They also constructed grandiose public buildings in the fascist style, which was the antithesis of archetypal Greek architecture. More beneficially, they excavated and restored many archaeological monuments.

After the Italian surrender of 1943, the islands (particularly Leros) became a battleground for British and German forces, with much suffering inflicted upon the population. The Dodecanese were formally returned to Greece in 1947.

RHODES ΡΟΔΟΣ

The largest of the Dodecanese Islands, Rhodes (*ro*-dos) is abundant in beaches, wooded valleys and ancient history. Whether you seek the buzz of nightlife and beaches, diving in crystal-clear water or a culture-vulture journey through past civilisations, it's all here. The atmospheric old town of Rhodes is a maze of cobbled streets spiriting you back to the days of the Byzantine Empire and beyond. Further south is the picture-perfect town of Lindos, a weave-world of sugarcube houses spilling down to a turquoise bay.

History

The Minoans and Mycenaeans were among the first to have outposts on the islands, but it wasn't until the Dorians arrived in 1100 BC – settling in Kamiros, Ialysos and Lindos – that Rhodes began to exert power.

Switching alliances like a pendulum, it was first allied to Athens in the Battle of Marathon (490 BC), in which the Persians were defeated, but shifted to the Persian side by the time of the Battle of Salamis (480 BC). After the unexpected Athenian victory at Salamis, Rhodes hastily became an ally of Athens again, joining the Delian League in 477 BC. Following the disastrous Sicilian Expedition (416–412 BC), Rhodes revolted against Athens and formed an alliance with Sparta, which it aided in the Peloponnesian Wars.

In 408 BC the cities of Kamiros, Ialysos and Lindos consolidated their powers, co-founding the city of Rhodes. Rhodes became Athens' ally again, and together they defeated Sparta at the Battle of Knidos (394 BC). Rhodes then joined forces with Persia in a battle against Alexander the Great but, when Alexander proved invincible, quickly allied itself with him.

In 305 BC Antigonus, one of Ptolemy's rivals, sent his son, the formidable Demetrius Poliorketes (the Besieger of Cities), to conquer Rhodes. The city managed to repel Demetrius after a long siege. To celebrate this victory, the 32m-high bronze statue of Helios Apollo (Colossus of Rhodes), one of the Seven Wonders of the Ancient World, was built.

After the defeat of Demetrius, Rhodes knew no bounds. It built the biggest navy in the Aegean and its port became a principal Mediterranean trading centre. The arts also flourished. When Greece became the battleground upon which Roman generals fought for leadership of the empire, Rhodes allied itself with Julius Caesar. After Caesar's assassination in 44 BC, Cassius besieged Rhodes, destroying its ships and stripping the city of its artworks, which were then taken to Rome. This marked the beginning of Rhodes' decline, and in AD 70 Rhodes became part of the Roman Empire.

When the Roman Empire split, Rhodes joined the Byzantine province of the Dodecanese. It was granted independence when the Crusaders seized Constantinople. Later, the Genoese gained control. The Knights of St John arrived in Rhodes in 1309 and ruled for

Rhodes

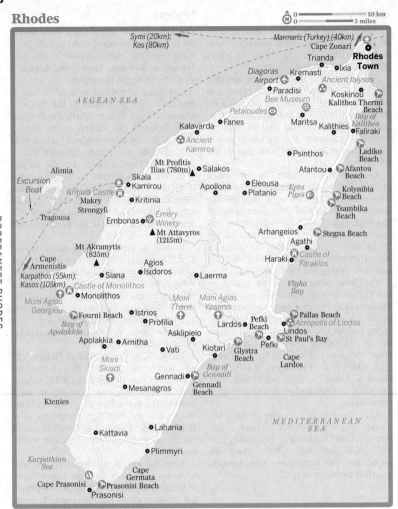

213 years until they were ousted by the Ottomans, who were in turn kicked out by the Italians nearly four centuries later. In 1947, after 35 years of Italian occupation, Rhodes became part of Greece along with the other Dodecanese islands.

ℹ Getting There & Away

AIR

Olympic Air (☎22410 24571; www.olympicair.com; Ierou Lohou 9) has flights across Greece and the Dodecanese while **Aegean Airlines** (☎22410 98345; www.aegeanair.com; Diagoras

airport) offers flights to Athens, most of Europe and to the US.

BOAT

Rhodes is the main port in the Dodecanese and offers a complex timetable of departures to Piraeus, Sitia, Thessaloniki and many stops in between. **Dodekanisos Seaways** (Map p474; ☎22410 70590; Afstralias 3) runs daily catamarans up and down the Dodecanese, as do **Blue Star Ferries** (☎0030 210 891 9800; www.bluestarferries.com), which are slower but cheaper. Tickets are available from the kiosk at the dock. In Rhodes Town you'll also find the Sea Star ticket booth for ferries to Tilos and the

ANES ticket booth for long-distance ferries to Athens (also services by Blue Star).

The EOT (Greek National Tourist Organisation) in Rhodes Town can provide you with current schedules. Tickets are also available from Skevos' Travel Agency (p479).

There is a daily car-carrying caïque (small boat) between Skala Kamirou, on Rhodes' west coast, and Halki (€10, 1¼ hours). From Skala Kamirou services depart at 9am, and from Halki at 4pm. There are also excursion boats to Symi (€25 return) daily in summer, leaving Mandraki Harbour at 9am and returning at 6pm. You can buy tickets at most travel agencies, but it's better to buy them at the harbour, where you can check out the boats personally.

Two local ferries, the *Nissos Halki* and *Nikos Express*, run five times per week between Halki and Skala Kamirou (€10, approximately 30 minutes), including a daily car-carrying caïque.

International

A daily catamaran from Rhodes' Commercial Harbour to Marmaris, Turkey (50 minutes, return ticket €65), departs at 8am and 4.30pm from June to September. In winter, there are sailings twice weekly at 2pm. Tickets cost €31 one-way plus €12 Turkish port tax. Same-day return tickets are €51. There is also a car-ferry service on this same route (one-way/return €95/175 excluding taxes, 1¼ hours), running four or five times a week in summer and less often in winter. Book online at www.rhodes.marmarisinfo.com or contact Triton Holidays (p479).

ⓘ Getting Around

TO/FROM THE AIRPORT

The Diagoras airport is 16km southwest of Rhodes Town, near Paradisi. Buses depart regularly between the airport and Rhodes Town's

BOAT SERVICES FROM RHODES

DESTINATION	DURATION	FARE	FREQUENCY
Astypalea	10hr	€35	1 weekly
Halki	2hr	€9	3 weekly
Halki*	1¼hr	€16	3 weekly
Kalymnos	4½hr	€23	3 weekly
Kalymnos*	3hr	€38	1 daily
Karpathos	5hr	€20	3 weekly
Kasos	8hr	€24	3 weekly
Kastellorizo	4hr 40min	€22	1 weekly
Kastellorizo*	2hr	€36	1 weekly
Kos	3hr	€23	1 daily
Kos*	2½hr	€30	1 daily
Leros	5hr	€31	4 weekly
Leros*	3½hr	€41	1 daily
Lipsi	8hr	€25	1 weekly
Lipsi*	5½hr	€45	1 daily
Nisyros	4½hr	€13	2 weekly
Nisyros*	2¾hr	€28	2 weekly
Patmos	6hr	€35	3 weekly
Patmos*	5hr	€46	1 daily
Piraeus	13hr	€59	almost daily
Sitia	10hr	€26	2 weekly
Symi**	2hr	€20	1 daily
Symi*	50min	€25	1 daily
Thessaloniki	21hr	€65	1 weekly
Tilos	2½hr	€14	2 weekly
Tilos*	2hr	€25	2 weekly

*high-speed services
**leaves from Mandraki. All other services leave from Commercial Harbour.

THE COLOSSUS OF RHODES

One of the Seven Wonders of the Ancient World, the bronze statue of Helios was apparently so vast that high-masted *triremes* (warships) could pass into the harbour through his legs. Built in 292 BC, it took 12 years to build, stood 33m high and fell a few decades later when an earthquake struck in 226 BC. For almost a millennium it lay in ruins until it was broken into pieces and sold by invading Arabs to a Syrian Jew in AD 654, then allegedly transported abroad on the backs of 900 camels.

Eastern Bus Terminal from 6.30am to 11.15pm (€2.20, 25 minutes). On Sunday, buses stop running at around 11.45am.

BICYCLE

A range of bicycles is available for hire at **Bicycle Centre** (22410 28315; Griva 39; per day €5).

BOAT

There are excursion boats to Lindos and Symi (€25 return) daily in summer, leaving Mandraki Harbour at 9am and returning at 6pm.

BUS

Rhodes Town has two island bus terminals located a block away from one another. Each services half of the island. There is regular transport across the island all week, with fewer services on Saturday and only a few on Sunday. You can pick up schedules from the kiosks at either terminal or from the EOT office.

From the Eastern Bus Terminal there are regular services to the airport (€2.20), Kalithea Thermi (€2.20), Salakos (€4.30), Ancient Kamiros (€5) and Monolithos (€6). From the Western Bus Terminal there are services to Faliraki (€2.20), Tsambika Beach (€3.50), Stegna Beach (€4) and Lindos (€5).

CAR & MOTORCYCLE

There are numerous car- and motorcycle-hire outlets in Rhodes Town. Shop around and bargain because the competition is fierce. You can also book through Triton Holidays.

The following agencies will deliver vehicles to you:

Drive Rent A Car (22410 81011, 22410 68243; www.driverentacar.gr; airport) Sturdier, newer scooters and cars.

Orion Rent A Car (22410 22137)

Rent A Moto Thomas (22410 30806) Offers the best prices on scooters, but check the exhausts are solid.

TAXI

Rhodes Town's main taxi rank is east of Plateia Rimini. There are two zones on the island for taxi meters: Zone One is Rhodes Town and Zone Two (slightly higher) is everywhere else. Rates are double between midnight and 5am.

Taxis prefer to use set-fare rates which are posted at the rank. Sample fares are as follows: airport €22, Faliraki €17, Kalithea €9 and Lindos €55. Phone for **taxis** (22410 27666, 22410 64712, in Rhodes Town 22410 69800, outside Rhodes Town 22410 69600) or **disabled-access taxis** (22410 77079).

Rhodes Town   Ρόδος

POP 58,984

Nowhere else in the Dodecanese are so many layers of architectural history piled upon one another as in the fortified Old Town; be it classical, medieval and Byzantine or Ottoman and Italian periods. A *volta* (stroll) down its hauntingly pretty cobbled streets is evocative, as black-clad octogenarians loom from doorways, the scent of leather shops competing with bougainvillea. Half the fun is letting yourself get lost.

The New Town, to the north, boasts upscale shops and waterfront bars servicing the package crowd, while in the backstreets are hidden bistros and boho bars worth seeking out. It's also where you'll find the city's best beach. The Commercial (large ferries) and Kolona (catamarans) harbours lie to the east of the Old Town. Excursion boats, small ferries, hydrofoils and private yachts use Mandraki Harbour, further north.

Sights

Old Town

A mesh of Byzantine, Turkish and Latin architecture, the Old Town is divided into the Kollakio (the Knights' Quarter, where the Knights of St John lived during medieval times), the Hora and the Jewish Quarter. The Knights' Quarter contains most of the medieval historical sights while the Hora, often referred to as the Turkish Quarter, is primarily Rhodes Town's commercial sector with shops and restaurants.

The Old Town is accessible by nine *pyles* (main gates) and two rampart-access portals. The 12m-thick city walls are closed to the public, but you can take a pleasant walk around the imposing walls of the Old Town via the wide, pedestrian moat walk.

Knights' Quarter   NEIGHBOURHOOD

Begin your tour of the Knights' Quarter at Liberty Gate, crossing the small bridge into the Old Town. In a medieval building is the original site of the Museum of Modern Greek Art (Map p474; www.mgamuseum/gr; 2 Plateia Symis; 3 sites €3; ⊙ 8am-2pm Tue-Sat). Inside you'll find maps and carvings. The main exhibition is at the New Art Gallery (Map p474; Plateia G Charitou; €3) with an impressive collection of painting, engraving and sculpture from some of Greece's most popular 20th-century artists, including Gaitis Giannis, Vasiliou Spiros and Katraki Vaso. For the museum's temporary exhibits, head to the Centre of Modern Art (Map p474; 179 Sokratous St; admission €3). All three galleries keep the same hours and one ticket gains you entrance to all three.

Across the pebbled street from the Museum of Modern Greek Art, take in the remains of the 3rd-century-BC Temple of Aphrodite (Map p474), one of the few ancient ruins in the Old Town.

Continuing down Platonos, the Museum of the Decorative Arts (Map p474; ☑ 22410 72674; Plateia Argyrokastrou; admission €3; ⊙ 8.30am-2.40pm Tue-Sun) houses an eclectic array of artefacts from around the Dodecanese. It's chock-a-block with instruments, pottery, carvings, clothing and spinning wheels and gives a colourful view into the past. Captions are sparse; pick up explanatory notes at the door.

In the atmospheric 15th-century knights' hospital down the road is the Museum of Archaeology (Plateia Mousiou; admission €5; ⊙ 8am-4pm Tue-Sun). Its biggest draw is the exquisite *Aphrodite Bathing,* a 1st-century-BC marble statue recovered from the local seabed.

Wander up the Avenue of the Knights (Ippoton) that was once home to the knights themselves. They were divided into seven 'tongues' or languages, according to their place of origin – England, France, Germany, Italy, Aragon, Auvergne and Provence – and each group was responsible for protecting a section of the bastion. The Grand Master, who was in charge, lived in the palace. To this day the street exudes a noble, forbidding aura.

First on the right, if you begin at the eastern end of the Avenue of the Knights, is the 1519 Inn of the Order of the Tongue of Italy (Map p474; Ippoton). Next door is the Palace of Villiers de l'Isle Adam (Map p474; Ippoton). Next along is the Inn of France (Map p474; Ippoton), the most ornate and distinctive of all the inns.

Further along is the Chapelle Française (Chapel of the Tongue of France; Map p474; Ippo-

DODECANESE RHODES TOWN

A DODECANESE GUIDE TO MYTHOLOGY

References to the Dodecanese Islands are scattered throughout Greek mythology.

Rhodes Rhodes was owned by Helios, the god of the sun. The Colossus of Rhodes, one of the Seven Wonders of the Ancient World, was made in his likeness.

Leros Leros was once at the bottom of the sea. Artemis (the goddess of hunting) and Selene (the goddess of the moon) persuaded Apollo (the god of light) to help them raise it to the air.

Karpathos This island was once home to the mighty giants known as the Titans, whom Zeus had to defeat before establishing his pantheon on Mount Olympus.

Nisyros Today's volcano on Nisyros is said to be the interred Titan Polyvotis, whom Poseidon managed to bury with a chunk of rock he ripped off Kos.

Lipsi Homer's hero, Odysseus, was distracted by the considerable charms of the nymph Calypso for seven years en route home from the Trojan War. This is her island, described in the 'Odyssey' as Ogygia.

Symi Glaucos, son of Poseidon and a sea god in his own right, endowed his islander descendants with his merman skills of deep diving and holding his breath for lengthy periods – pretty handy attributes for a sponge-diving island.

Kalymnos Supposedly named after the mighty Titan Kalydnos – son of Gaea (the earth) and Uranus (the heavens) – who lived here.

Kos According to legend this is the sacred land of Asclepius, the god of healing. No wonder Hippocrates, the father of modern medicine, based himself and the world's first hospital here.

Rhodes Town

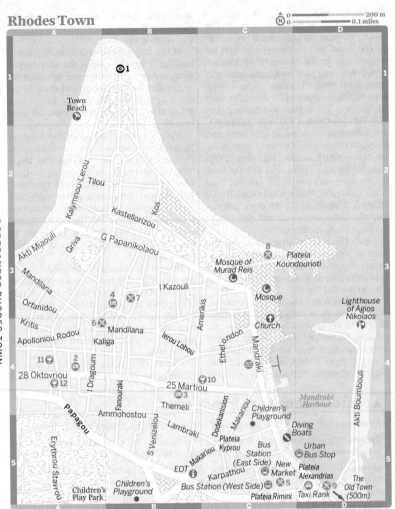

ton), embellished with a statue of the Virgin and Child. Next door is the residence of the Chaplain of the Tongue of France. Across the alleyway is the Inn of Provence (Map p474; Ippoton), with four coats of arms forming the shape of a cross, and opposite is the Inn of Spain (Map p474; Ippoton). Near the end of the avenue, St John of the Collachio (Map p474; St John of the Collachio) was originally a knights' church with an underground passage linking it to the palace across the road.

On the right is the truly magnificent 14th-century Palace of the Grand Masters (Map p474; 22410 23359; admission €6; 8.30am-3pm Tue-Sun); severely damaged by the Turkish siege and then destroyed by an explosion in the mid-1800s, the Italians rebuilt it, introducing a grandiose, lavish interior. Only 24 of the 158 rooms can be visited; inside you'll find antique furnishing, sculptures, frescoes and mosaic floors.

From the palace, walk through D'Amboise Gate, the most atmospheric of the gates, which takes you across the moat. When the palace is open, you can also gain access to the walkway along the top of the wall from here, affording great views into the Old Town and across to the sea. Another

Rhodes Town

⊙ Sights
1 Cret Aquarium..................................... B1

⊜ Sleeping
2 Hotel Anastasia................................... A4
3 Lydia Hotel... B4
4 New Village Inn.................................... B3

⊗ Eating
5 Indigo.. C5
6 Koykos.. A4
7 Niohori.. B3
8 To Meltemi... C3
9 Yachting Club Cafe D5

⊜ Drinking & Nightlife
10 Casa La Femme C4
11 Christo's Garden.................................. A4
12 Methexi.. A4

option is to follow the peaceful **Moat Walkway**, which you can access next to **St Anthony's Gate**.

Hora   NEIGHBOURHOOD
Bearing traces of its Ottoman past is the Hora. During Turkish times, churches were converted to mosques, the most important of which is the colourful, pink-domed **Mosque of Süleyman** (Map p474), at the top of Sokratous. Currently closed to the public, it was built in 1522 to commemorate the Ottoman victory against the knights. Opposite is the 18th-century **Muslim Library** (Map p474; Sokratous; ⊙9.30am-4pm Mon-Sat) FREE. Founded in 1794 by Turkish Rhodian Ahmed Hasuf, it houses a small number of Persian and Arabic manuscripts and a collection of Korans handwritten on parchment.

Continuing through the winding pedestrian streets will bring you to the municipal **Hammam Turkish Baths** (Map p474; Plateia Arionis; ⊙10am-5pm Mon-Fri, 8am-5pm Sat). Closed when we passed, it may be open by the time you read this.

Jewish Quarter   NEIGHBOURHOOD
(Map p474) The Jewish Quarter is an almost forgotten sector of Rhodes Old Town, where life continues at an unhurried pace. This area of quiet streets and sometimes dilapidated houses was once home to a thriving Jewish community.

Built in 1577, **Kahal Shalom Synagogue** (Map p474; Polydorou 5) is Greece's oldest synagogue and the only one surviving on Rhodes. The Jewish quarter, in the 1920s,

had a population of 4000. Have a look in the **Jewish Synagogue Museum** (Map p474; ✑22410 22364; www.rhodesjewishmuseum.org; Dosiadou; ⊙10am-3pm Sun-Fri, closed winter). Exhibits include early 20th-century photos, intricately decorated documents and displays about the 1673 Jews deported from Rhodes to Auschwitz in 1944. Only 151 of them survived.

Close by you will also find **Plateia Evreon Martyron** (Square of the Jewish Martyrs; Map p474).

Old Town Aquarium   AQUARIUM
(Map p474; ✑22470 86700; Agiou Fanouriou, Old Town; adult/child €5/3; ⊙9am-11pm) Hidden in the backstreets just off Sokratous, this new aquarium is packed with marine life – stingrays, octopuses, eels, cuttlefish, starfish and more.

⊙ New Town
The **Acropolis of Rhodes**, southwest of the Old Town on Monte Smith, was the site of the ancient Hellenistic city of Rhodes. The restored 2nd-century-AD tree-lined **stadium** once staged competitions in preparation for the Olympic Games. The adjacent **theatre** is a reconstruction of one used for lectures by the Rhodes School of Rhetoric, while steps above here lead to the **Temple of Pythian Apollo**. A small exhibition between the stadium and the road details the history of the site and the reconstruction. This unenclosed site can be reached on city bus 5.

North of Mandraki Harbour, at the eastern end of G Papanikolaou, is the graceful **Mosque of Murad Reis** (Map p472). In its grounds are a Turkish cemetery and the Villa Cleobolus, where Lawrence Durrell lived in the 1940s, writing *Reflections on a Marine Venus*.

The modest **Cret Aquarium** (Map p472; ✑22410 27308; www.hcmr.gr; Kos 1; adult/child €5/€2.50; ⊙9am-8.30pm Apr-Oct, 9am-4.30pm Nov-Mar) is an art deco building constructed by the Italians in the 1930s. Check out the taxidermic tiger and thresher sharks.

The town **beach**, beginning north of Mandraki Harbour, stretches around the island's northernmost point and down the west side of the New Town. The best spots tend to be on the east side, where there's usually calmer water and more sand and facilities.

Rhodes Old Town

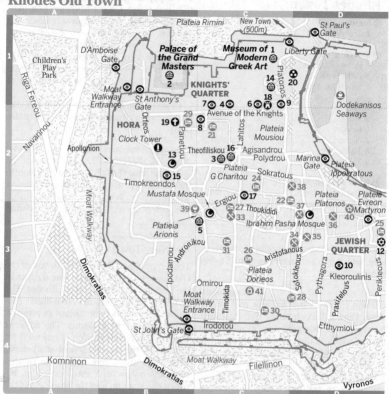

Activities

A number of diving schools operate out of Mandraki, offering a range of courses, including a 'One Day Try Dive' for €75 and three-day PADI open-water certification for €350 to €390. You can get information from their boats at Mandraki Harbour.

Waterhoppers Diving Centre DIVING
(☎ 6972500971, 22410 38146; www.waterhoppers. com) Established for over 15 years, Waterhoppers Diving Centre offers a range of diving courses, including two- and three-day PADI open-water certifications. Choose from night, wreck and cave dives if you're an advanced diver. You can get information at Mandraki Harbour.

Scuba Diving Trident School DIVING
(☎ tel/fax 22410 29160) Scuba Diving Trident School offers a range of diving courses. You can get information at Mandraki Harbour.

They also do beginner classes and two- and three-day PADI certified courses.

Sleeping

During the summer, finding an affordable bed in the Old Town is possible *if* you book ahead. In winter, most budget places close. For more atmosphere, definitely stay in the Old Town.

Domus Rodos Hotel PENSION $
(Map p474; ☎ 22410 25965; info@domusrodoshotel. gr; Platonos; s/d €40/75; ⊙ year-round; ❄ @ 🛜) En suite rooms are compact and clean with armoire, TV and desk. There's a welcoming breakfast room and self-catering kitchen, and the place is in a great location facing a peaceful square, but it's the sheer warmth of the staff that keeps visitors returning.

New Village Inn PENSION $
(Map p472; ☎ 6976475917, 22410 34937; www.new villageinn.gr; Konstantopedos 10; d €40; ❄) You'll

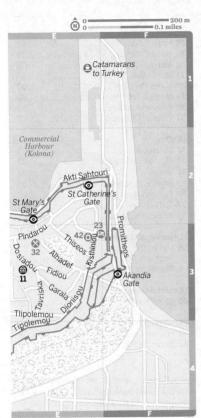

Map labels:
- Catamarans to Turkey
- Commercial Harbour (Kolona)
- Akti Sahtouri
- St Catherine's Gate
- St Mary's Gate
- Pindarou
- Thiseos
- Alhadef
- Dosiadou
- Fidiou
- Garala
- Tavriska
- Dionisou
- Tlipolemou
- Tipolemou
- Promitheos
- Kisthiniou
- Akandia Gate
- 23
- 42
- 32
- 11

DODECANESE RHODES TOWN

nishings and TV, fridge and en suite. Some rooms enjoy balconies. There's also an inviting breakfast bar in the lush garden.

Pension Olympos
PENSION $

(Map p474; ☑ 22410 33567; www.pension-olympos. com; Agiou Fanouriou 56; s/d/tr €40/50/60; ❄ ☎) Delicious bijou rooms, finished in shades of blue, green and orange, with iron beds, en suites, fridges and, outside, an Edenic little garden eclectically stocked with gods. The corridors are crammed with more statuary than the Acropolis!

Mango Rooms
PENSION $

(Map p474; ☑ 22410 24877; www.mango.gr; Plateia Dorieos 3, Old Town; s/d/tr €44/58/66; ❄ @ ☎) Set in an old square, these are spotless en suite rooms with safety deposit box, fridge and en suite. Downstairs is a lovely restaurant turning out locally sourced food.

★ Marco Polo Mansion
BOUTIQUE HOTEL $$

(Map p474; ☑ 22410 25562; www.marcopolo mansion.gr; Agiou Fanouriou 40, Old Town; d incl breakfast €90-180; ❄ ☎) We love the vivid style in this 15th-century former Ottoman official's house; with its heavy antique furniture and eastern rugs, and stained-glass windows washing the oxblood walls in blue light. The rooms are spectacularly romantic with huge beds, and tasteful furnishings. Try the split-level ex-harem bedroom.

Outside, the shaded courtyard is lovely for breakfast and dinner, and rings with laughter and bohemian flair.

Pension Andreas
PENSION $$

(Map p474; ☑ 22410 34156; www.hotelandreas. com; Omirou 28d; s €45-55, d/tr/dm €75/85/95; ☺ year-round; ❄ @ ☎) This former Ottoman house has seven individual rooms to choose from ranging from basic to lavish. Our favourite is at the top of the house with a raised captain's bed. The communal verandah and bar with its sea views and bougainvillea-crowned ceiling is magical.

There's also a new sun-dappled deck to chill on.

Hotel Cava d'Oro
PENSION $$

(Map p474; ☑ 22410 36980; www.cavadoro.com; Kisthiniou 15; s/d/tr incl breakfast €65/85/120; P ❄ ☎) A former storage building of the Knights of St John, it has plenty of appeal with a cool cafe, sunny terrace and stone-walled rooms with high-beamed ceilings. There's also a private section of the ancient wall that you can walk on if you stay here.

find a pleasant, leafy courtyard ornamented with icons and four whitewashed, en suite rooms in this downtown pension. Two rooms enjoy private balconies. Down a quiet street.

Hotel Isole
PENSION $

(Map p474; ☑ 6937580814, 22410 20682; www. hotelisoles.com; Evdoxou 35; s/d/ste incl breakfast €50/55/85; ❄ @ ☎) Painted Aegean blue and white, this delightful guesthouse in a 700-year-old former harem has seven delightful rooms opening out onto a breakfast area hung with mermaids and curios. Doubles vary from small to spacious, however the best room is at the top of the house with its own magical roof terrace.

Hotel Anastasia
PENSION $

(Map p472; ☑ 22410 28007; www.anastasia-hotel. com; 28 Oktovriou 46; s/d/tr €40/55/65; ❄ @ ☎) Handsomely set back from the road this lovely white villa has charming ochre rooms, wood shutters, tiled floors, traditional fur-

Rhodes Old Town

◎ **Top Sights**
1 Museum of Modern Greek Art C1
2 Palace of the Grand Masters B1

◎ **Sights**
3 Centre of Modern Art C2
4 Chapelle Française C1
5 Hammam Turkish Baths C3
6 Inn of France C1
7 Inn of Provence C1
8 Inn of Spain C2
9 Inn of the Order of the Tongue of
   Italy C1
10 Jewish Quarter D3
11 Jewish Synagogue Museum E3
12 Kahal Shalom Synagogue D3
13 Mosque of Süleyman B2
14 Museum of the Decorative Arts C1
15 Muslim Library B2
16 New Art Gallery C2
17 Old Town Aquarium C2
18 Palace of Villiers de l'Isle Adam C1
19 St John of the Collachio B2
20 Temple of Aphrodite D1

◎ **Sleeping**
21 Avalon Boutique Hotel C2
22 Domus Rodos Hotel C2
23 Hotel Cava d'Oro E3

24 Hotel Isole C2
25 Hotel Spot D3
26 Mango Rooms C3
27 Marco Polo Mansion C3
28 Minos Pension D3
29 Nikos & Takis Hotel B2
30 Pension Andreas C4
31 Pension Olympos C3

◎ **Eating**
32 Hatzikelis E3
33 Marco Polo Mansion C3
34 Nireas D3
35 Romios Restaurant D3
36 Taverna Mystagoyia D3
37 To Megiston D3
38 Yanni's Restaurant D2

◎ **Drinking & Nightlife**
39 Macao Bar B3
   Rock and Roll .... (see 39)
   Rogmitou Chronou .... (see 39)

◎ **Entertainment**
40 Cafe Chantant D3

◎ **Shopping**
41 Antique Gallery C3
42 Byzantine Iconography E3

Hotel Spot   PENSION $$
(Map p474; ☑ 22410 34737; www.spothotelrhodes.gr; Perikleous 21; s/d/tr incl breakfast €70/110/130; ✳ @ 🖔) Silk curtains billow from antique-accented, stone wall rooms, there's a mellow courtyard to read in, a secondhand library, inviting breakfast area and a breezy roof garden. By the time you read this there will also be a yoga room, and spa for reiki and massage treatments.

Lydia Hotel   PENSION $$
(Map p472; ☑ 22410 22871; www.lydiahotel.com; 25 Martiou; s/d/f €120/145/160; ✳ @ 🖔) In the heart of the New Town close to the beach, Lydia has a classy international feel, despite the odd cat wandering through the lobby. Stylish rooms have chocolate-hued walls, cosy quilts, cable TV, fridge and private balconies.

Minos Pension   PENSION $$
(Map p474; ☑ 22410 36980; www.minospension.com; cnr Omirou & Sofokleous; r €50-80; ✳ @ 🖔) Offering the best Old Town views thanks to its rooftop cafe, family-run Minos has well-appointed studio rooms with gleaming kitchenettes, cable TV and fridge. Down-

stairs there's a cosy communal lounge, flat-screen TV and book exchange. In a nice spot opposite an old windmill.

★ **Nikos & Takis Hotel**   BOUTIQUE HOTEL $$$
(Map p474; ☑ 22410 70773; www.nikostakishotel.com; Panetiou 29; ste €170-400; P ✳ @ 🖔) Soaked in shades of ochre and green, this hilltop eyrie abounds in eclectic style; a melange of Moorish and Indian influences – check out its Rajasthan wall hangings – illustrated arched doors, as well as a gorgeous pebble mosaic courtyard. Its eight individually designed suites are fit for a vizier with four posters, silk drapes, traditional wooden ceilings and tangerine-hued walls.

Avalon Boutique Hotel   BOUTIQUE HOTEL $$$
(Map p474; ☑ 22410 31438; www.avalonrhodes.gr; Charitos 9; d €240-320; ✳ @ 🖔) Housed in the former house of an Ottoman official, Avalon glitters with stylish suites boasting huge beds, plunge baths, flat-screen TVs, fine furniture and soothing peach walls. There's also a riad-style courtyard that's perfect for reading and lowering the pulse.

Eating

Old Town

The most flavoursome food and inviting tavernas are in the backstreets.

★Nireas
TAVERNA $

(Map p474; ☎ 22410 31741; Sofokleous 45-47; mains €8-16; ❄) With a pretty, vine-shaded canopy, this fresh restaurant features calamari, octopus salad, whitebait, grilled prawns and Symi shrimp to name but a few. Inside are candlelit lemon-walled stone alcoves. Pure romance.

To Megiston
TAVERNA $

(Map p474; ☎ 29127; Sofokelous; mains €10-15; ❄ 10.30am-late) We like it for its lively Greek soundtrack and earthy cuisine. People-watch alfresco, as you feast on a menu of *mousakas* (baked layers of eggplant or zucchini, minced meat and potatoes topped with cheese sauce), swordfish, souvlakia (cubes of meat on skewers), pasta and lamb *kleftiko* (slow oven-baked).

Yanni's Restaurant
TAVERNA $

(Map p474; ☎ 22410 36535; Platonos; mains €8; ❄ noon-midnight; ❄ ❄ ❄) The Karpathian matriarch dressed in colourful rustic garb dispenses wise smiles and sesame-coated biscuits, while the walls are daubed in marine frescoes, the air dancing with aromas of *stifadho* (meat, game or seafood cooked with onions in a tomato puree) and seafood souvlakia. Hidden but well worth the search.

★Marco Polo Mansion
MEDITERRANEAN $$

(Map p474; www.marcopolomansion.gr; Agiou Fanouriou 40-42; mains €15; ❄ 10am-midnight) ⌀ A passion for food combined with the quintessence of *filoxenia* (hospitality) are the ingredients of Rhodes' finest restaurant. That and an ever-changing menu of shrimps *saganaki,* tuna in sesame marinated with orange, lamb souvlakia on a bed of risotto and Greek wine sauce with yoghurt...

Come wind or balm this courtyard haven, choking on olive trees and flowers, is deservedly packed to the gills with aesthetes and food lovers.

★Hatzikelis
RESTAURANT $$

(Map p474; ☎ 22410 27215; Alhadef 9; mains €20-30) Favoured by famous actors, Hatzikelis is class with velvet curtains, candelabra and white walls. Indulge your sea genes on Poseidon-rich treasures like freshly harpooned grouper, swordfish, snapper – red, silver and royal (filleted in front of you) – as well as calamari, octopus and lobster.

Taverna Mystagoyia
TAVERNA $$

(Map p474; Themistokleus; mains €17; ❄ 9am-midnight; ❄) Secreted down a sun-dappled street, Mystagoyia offers locally sourced organic food – fish, calamari, salads, homemade pasta dishes, as well as the catch of the day. All food is prepped by Zorba the Greek lookalike, Philippos.

Romios Restaurant
TAVERNA $$

(Map p474; ☎ 22410 25549; Sofokleous; mains €15; ❄ 11am-midnight) In the arbour of an enormous fig tree in a garden packed with wood sculptures, Romios occupies a romantic, relaxing spot. Bouzouki music flows over a classically Rhodian menu of squid risotto, stuffed eggplant, shrimp *saganaki,* grilled octopus and souvlakia.

New Town

To Meltemi
TAVERNA $

(Map p472; Kountourioti 8; mains €10-15; P ❄ ❄) With widescreen views of the sea and just yards from the beach, this breezy taverna has a cosy, nautically themed interior, or you can dine out on the semi-alfresco terrace. Staff are charming and the menu swimming in feisty salads, salted mackerel, dolmadhes (vine leaves stuffed with rice and sometimes meat), calamari and octopus.

Koykos
GREEK $

(Map p472; Mandilana 20-26; mains €3-8; ❄ ❄ ❄) The first thing that hits you here is the bouquet of freshly baked pastries drifting on to the street. Koykos is perfect for a coffee or retsina pit stop accompanied by one of their celebrated homemade pies. There's also sandwiches, salads and seafood dishes.

Niohori
TAVERNA $

(Map p472; ☎ 22410 35116; I Kazouli 29; mains €7; ❄ 1pm-midnight) This authentic taverna delivers with a meat-accented menu – the owner is also a butcher, so he selects the best cuts. Tuck into veal liver with oil and oregano, *stifadho,* steak, and meatballs seasoned with organ music from the nearby church. Great value.

Yachting Club Cafe
BRASSERIE $

(Map p472; Plateia Alexandrias; snacks €6; ❄ 7am-1am) Looking out on glittering yachts and distant stag-topped pillars where the Colossus of Rhodes once stood, this Balaeric-style cafe bubbles with a young crowd. Eat a midday snack – pie, pizza or brioche – or pop in for a coffee or sundowner cocktail.

Indigo TAVERNA $
(Map p472; ☑ 69726 63100; New Market 105-106; mains €9; ☺ dinner; ☎) Sitting beside an old watchmaker's, Indigo makes for a haven of blue calm in the bustling market. Experience their specials like calamari risotto, or octopus with fava beans, as well as regulars like halloumi, and Greek salad.

Drinking & Nightlife

Take your pick between the Old Town's chic, chillsome bars and nautical dens that look as if they've been spewed up from the seabed. Most Greeks don't go out until *midnight*.

Old Town

The majority of nightlife happens around Platonos and Ippokratous squares.

Rock and Roll BAR
(Map p474; Plateia Arionos; ☎🍴) Cool diner-style haunt with metro-tiled walls and '50s songs playing as you plant yourself at the bar, fix your quiff in the mirror and tuck into a burger. Great balls of fire!

Rogmitou Chronou BAR
(Map p474; www.rogmitouxronou.gr; Plateia Arionos; ☺10pm-5am; ☎) Otherwise known as the Music Bar, this cosy wood-and-exposed-stone watering hole has a down and dirty appeal. Dark enough to please a goth and lively enough to keep you awake till dawn, Friday night there's live rock, while on Monday there's an acoustic set.

Macao Bar BAR
(Map p474; ☺9.30pm-3am) Uberstylish bar hidden in the Old Town down a back alley; expect moody, low-lit ambience, buffed cement floors, the stars in panorama above the decked terrace, and a well-heeled crowd of fashionistas. Mojitos (€7).

New Town

Locals hang out along the bar-lined I Dragoum, while the tourist haunts are found along Akti Miaouli, Orfanidou and Griva.

★Methexi BAR
(Map p472; 28 Oktovriou, cnr Griva; ☎) If Leonard Cohen was a bar he'd look something like this bohemian, jazz-infused joint. Candelabra, antique mirrors, indie film posters and vintage typewriters are part of its charm. There's a lively sun terrace out front which has partial shade. Coffees and spirits.

Christo's Garden BAR
(Map p472; Griva; ☺10pm-late) With its grotto-like bar and a pebble mosaic courtyard abloom with flowers, a visit to Christo's is a flight into tranquillity. Come dark the fairy lights twinkle. Perfect for a romantic drink.

Casa La Femme BAR
(Map p472; 25 Martiou, cnr Amerikis; ☺8am-midnight; ☎) Heavenly white and decked in chic contemporary furniture and faux industrial piping, La Femme has easy tunes and a large sun terrace. Snacks, pasta and salads. Park yourself at the bar for a dry Martini (€7).

Entertainment

★Cafe Chantant LIVE MUSIC
(Map p474; ☑ 32277; Dimokratou 3; ☺11pm-late Fri & Sat) Locals sit at long wooden tables here, listening to live traditional music while drinking ouzo or beer. It's dark inside and you won't find snacks or nibbles, but the atmosphere is palpable and the band is lively.

Shopping

The New Town is useful for household brands, while the Old Town is better for icons, classical busts, leather sandals and jewellery. Release your inner magpie.

Byzantine Iconography ARTS & CRAFTS
(Map p474; ☑ 22410 74127; Kisthiniou 42) Visit artisan Basilios Per Sirimis in his cramped studio, the walls shimmering with gold and the air thick with resin and paint. Paintings go for €210 to €2000.

Antique Gallery ARTS & CRAFTS
(Map p474; Omirou 45; ☺9am-8pm) Best viewed by night, this Aladdin's cave conjures up *Arabian Nights,* with its eastern mosaic lights glowing like clusters of fireflies.

❶ Information

INTERNET ACCESS
Mango Cafe Bar (www.mango.gr; Plateia Dorieos 3; per hr €5; ☺9.30am-midnight) Located in the Old Town, free internet for customers.

Walk Inn (Plateia Dorieos 1; per hr €2; ☺10am-11pm) In the Old Town.

INTERNET RESOURCES

www.rhodesguide.com What's on, where to stay and where to hang out in Rhodes.

www.rodos.gr Upcoming events, links and background for Rhodes.

MEDICAL SERVICES

Emergencies & Ambulance (☑166)

General Hospital (☑22410 80000; Andreas Papandreou) State-of-the-art hospital.

Krito Private Clinic (☑22410 30020; Ioannou Metaxa 3; ☺24hr)

MONEY

You'll find plenty of ATMs throughout Rhodes Town and at the following banks. You'll also find a handy ATM at the international ferry quay.

Alpha Credit Bank (Plateia Kyprou) In the New Town.

Commercial Bank of Greece (Plateia Symis) There is also an ATM near where the boats leave for Turkey on the east side of Commercial Harbour.

National Bank of Greece New Town (Plateia Kyprou, New Town); Old Town (Plateia Mousiou, Old Town)

POLICE

Port Police (☑22410 22220; Mandraki)

Tourist Police (☑22410 27423; ☺24hr) Next door to the EOT.

POST

Main Post Office (Map p472) At Mandraki Harbour.

TOURIST INFORMATION

EOT (Greek National Tourist Organisation; Map p472; ☑22410 35226; www.ando.gr; cnr Makariou & Papagou; ☺8.30am-3pm Mon-Fri) Supplies brochures, city maps and the *Rodos News*, a free English-language newspaper. As well as museum info and ferry times.

TRAVEL AGENCIES

Rodos Sun Service (☑22410 26400; 14 New Market) Books flights and boat tickets.

Skevos' Travel Agency (☑22410 22461; skeos@rho.forthnet.gr; 111 Amerikis) Books flights and boat tickets throughout Greece. Speak to helpful Charoula.

Triton Holidays (☑22410 21690; www.triton dmc.gr; Plastira 9, Mandraki) Air and sea travel, hire cars, accommodation and tours throughout the Dodecanese. It also sells tickets to Turkey.

ⓘ Getting Around

Local buses leave from the **urban bus stop** (Map p472; Mandraki) on Mandraki Harbour. Bus 11 does a circuit around the coast, up past the aquar-

ium and on to the Acropolis. Hopping on for a loop is a good way to get your bearings. Bus 2 goes to Analipsi, bus 3 to Rodini, bus 4 to Agios Dimitrios and bus 5 to the Acropolis. Buy tickets on board.

Eastern Rhodes

The majority of Rhodes' sandy beaches are along its east coast, home to its summer resorts filled with package-holidaymakers and endless strips of tourist bars. From Rhodes Town, there are frequent buses to Lindos, but some of the more deserted beaches en route are a bit of a hike from the road.

Restored to its former glory, **Kalithea Thermi** (☑22410 65691; www.kallitheasprings. gr; Kalithea; admission €2.50; ☺8am-8pm Apr-Oct, 8am-5pm Nov-Mar) was originally an Italian-built spa, 9km from Rhodes Town. With grand buildings, colonnades and countless archways delivering stunning sea views, it's worth a wander. You'll also find a cafe and a small sandy beach for swimming.

Ladiko Beach, touted locally as 'Anthony Quinn Beach', is in fact two back-to-back coves with a pebbly beach on the north side and volcanic rock platforms on the south. The swimming is good, the water noticeably colder.

Further down the coast, a right turn at Kolymbia takes you to the **Epta Piges** (Seven Springs), 4km away. The springs bubble into a river, which flows into a shaded lake, home to turtles. Reach the lake by following a footpath or by walking through a narrow, dark tunnel that's ankle deep with fast-flowing river water. If you're claustrophobic opt for the path. There's a cafe next to the springs and a children's playground. There are no buses to Epta Piges; take a Lindos bus and get off at the turn-off.

Back on the coast, the beaches of **Kolymbia** and **Tsambika** are sandy but can get crowded in summer. Further up the road is a turn-off to sandy, idyllic **Stegna Beach**. Another 4km along is a turning for Haraki from where you'll find a path up to the ruins of the 15th-century **Castle of Faraklos**. Once a prison for recalcitrant knights and the island's last stronghold to fall to the Turks, it offers great views. Nearby is the sandy cove of **Agathi**.

Lindos   Λίνδος

POP 1090

Unbelievably pretty, your first glimpse of Lindos from the elevated road will steal your breath; the towering acropolis radiant on the cypress-silvered hill, below it the sugarcube houses of the whitewashed town tumbling down to an aquamarine bay. The town itself is a magical warren of hidden alleys, packed with boutiques, effervescent bars and cafes set in old sea captain's houses with carved relief facades. Pick your way past donkeys as you coax your calves up to the acropolis and one of the best views in Greece.

Ancient Lindos was founded by the Dorians around 2000 BC thanks to its excellent harbour and vantage point. It's overlaid with a conglomeration of Byzantine, Frankish and Turkish remains.

◉ Sights & Activities

Acropolis of Lindos   ARCHAEOLOGICAL SITE
(admission €6; ⊙ 8am-6pm Tue-Sun Jun-Aug, to 2pm Sep-May) An alluring mix of Byzantine architecture on the outside, insulating 2nd-century-BC Doric architecture, this beautifully preserved Acropolis is worth the climb up the 116m-high rock, thanks to its partial reconstruction allowing you a glimpse of its former greatness. Look out for the 20-columned Hellenistic stoa (200 BC) and the Byzantine Church of Agios Ioannis, with its ancient frescoes, to the right. The wide stairway behind the stoa leads to a 5th-century-BC propylaeum, beyond which is the 4th-century Temple to Athena. Athena was worshipped at Lindos as early as the 10th century BC; this temple has replaced earlier ones on the site.

Donkey rides to the Acropolis cost €5 one way, but to get here under your own steam, head straight into the village from the main square, turn left at the church and follow the signs. There's no shade at the top so pack a hat and some water.

Beaches   BEACH
Main Beach, to the east of the Acropolis, is sandy with shallow water, making it a perfect swimming spot for kids. You can follow a path north to the western tip of the bay to the smaller, taverna-fringed Pallas Beach, beyond which are some rocks you can bathe on if it gets too crowded. Avoid swimming near the jetty as it's home to sea urchins. A 10-minute walk from town, on the western side of the Acropolis, is sheltered St Paul's Bay. Its turquoise water will make your heart ache.

🛏 Sleeping

Accommodation in Lindos is limited and usually reserved so be sure to call ahead.

Anastasia Studio   APARTMENT $
(☑ 6972703362, 22440 31751; www.lindos-studios. gr; d/tr €45/50; P ❄ 🤶) On the eastern side of town, these six split-level apartments based around a geranium-filled courtyard enjoy soaring acropolis views and have tiled floors, TV, sofa bed, a well-equipped kitchen and separate bedroom. Room 6 has its own private balcony.

Electra   PENSION $
(☑ 22440 31266; www.electra-studios.gr; s/d/tr €30/40/45; ❄) Delightful whitewashed rooms, varnished wooden beds, fridges and fresh blankets. Some rooms have balconies and there's a lovely communal roof terrace overlooking a lemon grove and the sea.

Filoxenia Guest House   PENSION $$
(☑ 22440 32080; www.lindos-filoxenia.com; d/ste incl breakfast €115/140; ❄ @) This enclosed courtyard accommodation bursting with flowers has beautifully finished rooms with modern furniture, wood-beamed ceilings and traditionally raised-platform beds. All rooms have fridge and kitchenette, and family rooms are also available. It's next to the police station.

★ Melenos   BOUTIQUE HOTEL $$$
(☑ 22440 32222; www.melenoslindos.com; ste incl breakfast from €261; ❄ @ 🤶) 🕊 This Moorish-style palace is magical – think bougainvillea walkways, mosaic pebble floors, verandahs festooned in lanterns and an eclectica of glass bauble lights casting glows on Ottoman furniture. Staff glide discreetly around you as you drink up the stunning bay view. Rooms are lovingly recreated in traditional Lyndian style with raised beds, wooden ceilings and private balconies.

🍴 Eating & Drinking

★ Captain's House   CAFE $
(snacks €6; ⊙ 8am-midnight; 🤶) Soaked in Lyndian atmosphere this nautically themed, 16th-century sea captain's house is perfect for a juice on your way down from the acropolis. Grab a pew in the pebble mosaic courtyard.

Eklekton   CAFE $
(mains €5; ⊙ 9am-1pm; 🤶) This cosy hole-in-the-wall has pebble floors, bougainvil-

lea snaking up the whitewashed walls and a pretty vine-shaded canopy to enjoy their breakfast, *gyros* (meat slithers cooked on a vertical rotisserie; usually eaten with pitta bread), salads, wraps and tasty baklava (filo pastry with walnut filling).

Village Cafe
DELI $

(mains €8; ⊙8.30am-7pm; ▣📶) On the donkey route close to Elektra guesthouse, this white-walled bakery/cafe has a mouthwatering array of cheese cakes, cherry pies, salads, wraps, ice cream and freshly prepared sandwiches. Try their delectable *bougatsa* (vanilla custard pie).

Mare Mare
CAFE $

(mains €9; 📶📶) Fronting Pallas beach, chic Mare Mare has a menu featuring steaks, breakfasts, souvlakia and succulent calamari. Head here early or late afternoon to miss the crowds.

Kalypso
TAVERNA $$

(mains €10-12; ▣📶) Admire the sea captain's facade as you tuck into sea bream, swordfish and calamari. Plenty of children's options and vegie dishes too. Take the second right off the main drag to find it.

★Melenos
GREEK $$$

(mains €24; ⊙8am-midnight; 📶) Melenos' roof restaurant menu is a conoisseur's dream of salmon marinated in ouzo, grilled sea bream with olive oil and homegrown herbs, and grilled beef fillet with spicy sauce, quince and caramelised onions. You won't want to wash your taste buds clean!

❶ Information

The village is totally pedestrianised. All vehicular traffic terminates on the central square of Plateia Eleftherias, from where the main drag, Acropolis, begins. The donkey terminus for rides up to the Acropolis itself is a little way along here. Turn right at the donkey terminus to reach the post office after 50m.

By the donkey terminus is the Commercial Bank of Greece, with an ATM. The National Bank of Greece, located on the street opposite the Church of Agia Panagia, also has an ATM.

Try www.lindos-holiday.com, a handy private website with a number of alternative villa accommodation options.

24hr Self Service (internet per hr €3) Open daily this hole-in-the-wall also sells sweets and drinks. Close to the main town square.

Doctor Fish (Acropolis; €10 per 15min) Hundreds of tiny surgeon fish nibble away at the dead skin on your soles as you immerse your feet in a tank of water. East off the main drag.

Island Of The Sun Travel (☑22440 31264; Acropolis) Organises local excursions, hire cars and accommodation.

Medical Clinic (☑22440 31224, 22440 31401; ⊙8am-12.30pm Mon-Fri) Located behind the Amphitheatre Club 500m out of town heading towards Rhodes. Ask for Dr Nikos.

Waterhoppers (☑6981270341; Plateia Eleftherias) Find it near the car park behind Main Beach. Cave and wreck dives available at €80 per day. Three-day open-water Padi course €390.

Western Rhodes & the Interior

Western Rhodes is redolent with the scent of pine, its hillsides shimmering with forests. More exposed than the east side, it's also windier – a boon for kite- and windsurfers – so the sea tends to be rough and the beaches mostly pebbled. If you're cycling or have a scooter or a car, the east–west roads that cross the interior have great scenery and are worth exploring.

Ancient Ialysos   Αρχαία Ιαλυσός

The Doric city of **Ialysos** (adult €4; ⊙8.30am-3pm Tue-Sun) was built on Filerimos Hill and has attracted successive invaders throughout the centuries. Over time, it became a hotchpotch of Doric, Byzantine and medieval remains. As you enter, stairs lead to the ancient remains of a 3rd-century-BC temple and the restored 14th-century **Chapel of Agios Georgios** and **Monastery of Our Lady**. All that's left of the temple are the foundations, but the chapel is a peaceful retreat.

Take the path left from the entrance to a 12th-century **chapel** (looking like a bunker) filled with frescoes.

Outside the entrance you'll find a small kiosk, a whole lot of peacocks and a popular tree-lined path with the **Stations of the Cross**. There are also ruins of a **Byzantine church** below the car park. Ialysos is 10km from Rhodes, with buses running every half-hour.

Ialysos to Petaloudes   Ιαλυσός προς Πεταλούδες

Heading south from Ialysos, visit the **Bee Museum** (www.mel.gr; adult/child €2/1;

⊗ 8.30am-3pm), where you'll learn about honey making and the history of beekeeping on Rhodes. See bees at work, watch demonstrations of making honey and stock up on honey rum, soap and sweets in the gift shop. To reach the museum, join the super-smooth Tsairi Airport motorway towards Kalithies; it's on the right, just past Pastida.

From here it's a short trip to Maritsa from where the scenic road takes you up over pine-forested hills to Psinthos, where you'll find a lively square lined with lunch spots. To Stolidi Tis Psinthoy (mains €7-9) has a country feel with wooden beams, checked tablecloths and family photos on the walls. Try the spicy pork, dolmadhes and freshly baked country bread.

Petaloudes Πεταλούδες

Northwest of Psinthos, Petaloudes (adult €6; ⊗ 8am-2.30pm) is better known as the Valley of the Butterflies. Visit in June, July or August when these colourful creatures mature and you'll quickly see why. They're actually moths *(Callimorpha quadripunctarea)* drawn to the gorge by the scent of the resin exuded by the storax trees. In summer it's choking with tour buses, but come out of season and you'll have the gorgeous forest path, streams and pools to yourself (though sadly, no butterflies).

Ancient Kamiros
Αρχαία Κάμειρος

The extensive ruins of the Doric city of Kamiros stand on a hillside above the west coast, 34km south of Rhodes Town. The ancient city, known for its figs, oil and wine, reached the height of its powers in the 7th century BC. By the 4th century BC it had been superseded by Rhodes. Most of the city was destroyed by earthquakes in 226 and 142 BC, leaving only a discernible layout. Ruins include a Doric temple, with one column still standing, Hellenistic houses, a Temple to Athena and a 3rd-century great stoa. It's best visited in the afternoon when there are few people to break the spell cast on your imagination.

Ancient Kamiros to Monolithos
Αρχαία Κάμειρος προς Μονόλιθο

Picturesque Skala Kamirou, 13.5km south of ancient Kamiros, serves as the access port

for travellers heading to and from the island of Halki.

Just south of the harbour, before the town of Skala, is a turning for Kritinia. This will lead you to the ruined 16th-century Kritinia Castle with awe-inspiring views along the coast and across to Halki. It's a magical setting where you expect to come across Romeo or Rapunzel.

The road south from here to Monolithos has some stunning scenery. From Skala Kamirou the road winds uphill, with a turning left for the wine-making area of Embonas about 5km further on. The main road continues for another 9km to Siana, a picturesque village below Mt Akramytis (825m).

The village of Monolithos, 5km beyond Siana, has the spectacularly sited 15th-century Castle of Monolithos perched on a sheer 240m-high rock and reached via a dirt track. To enter, climb through the hole in the wall. Continuing along this track, bear right at the fork for Moni Agiou Georgiou, or left for the very pleasant shingled Fourni Beach.

Wine Country

From Salakos, head inland to Embonas on the slopes of Mt Attavyros (1215m), the island's highest mountain. Embonas is the wine capital of Rhodes and produces some of the island's best tipples. The red Cava Emery or Zacosta and white Villare are good choices. You can taste and buy them at Emery Winery (www.emery.gr; Embonas; ⊗ 9.30am-4.30pm April-Oct) FREE, which offers tours of its cottage production. You'll find it on the eastern edge of town.

Detour around Mt Attavyros to Agios Isidoros, 14km south of Embonas, a prettier and still unspoilt wine-producing village en route to Siana.

Southern Rhodes

South of Lindos along the east coast, the island takes on a windswept appearance and enjoys less tourist traffic; the villages here seem to have a slower pace. Just 2km south of Lindos, sandy Pefki Beach is deservedly popular. If it's too crowded, try Glystra Beach, just down the road and a great spot for swimming.

The flourishing village of Laerma is 12km northwest of Lardos.

Gennadi Γεννάδι

POP 655

This sleepy one-street town has a few *kafeneia* (coffee houses), friendly locals and a cluster of whitewashed buildings set back a few hundred metres from the pebbled beach. You'll find a fruit market, bakery, supermarket, internet cafe, car hire and a couple of tavernas.

Flanked by an 800-year-old mulberry tree, **Effie's Dreams Apartments** (☑22440 43410; www.effiesdreams.com; s/d/f €50/55/60; ✳ @ 🛜) have lovely sea views and balconies from which to enjoy them. There's also a welcoming piazza to read in, and a natty cafe with wi-fi, snacks and cocktails. A 10-minute walk from the beach.

A mythically muralled eatery, principally serving up pizzas, **Mama's Kitchen** (mains €7-10) also has a grilled section including tasty lamb chops and souvlakia.

Gennadi to Prasonisi
Γεννάδι προς Πρασονήσι

From Gennadi an almost uninterrupted beach of pebbles and sand dunes extends down to **Plimmyri**, 11km south.

Watch for a signposted turning to **Lahania**, 2km off the main highway, and head downhill into the old town to find a village of winding alleyways and traditional buildings.

If a rural holiday takes your fancy but you want to do it in comfort, stay at the **Four Elements** (☑6939450014; www.thefourelements. be; studio & apt per week €510-725; P ✳ @ 🛜 ⊠) with its exceptionally homey and spacious apartments. All have full kitchens and there's a divine pool, kid's pool, outdoor grill and garden. One of the apartments is wheelchair accessible.

While in Lahania, stop for lunch at **Taverna Platanos** (mains €5-7) tucked behind the church in the main square. With traditional decor and a flower-filled patio, it's a great place to take a break.

The main coastal road continues south past countless chapels to **Kattavia**, Rhodes' most southerly village. It's a friendly place that doesn't see a lot of tourists. Stop at **Penelope's** (mains €7-12) in the main square for fresh fish and handmade chips.

From Kattavia, a windswept 10km road snakes south to remote **Cape Prasonisi**, the island's southernmost point. Joined to Rhodes by a narrow sandy isthmus in the summer months, come winter higher water levels completely isolate it. Thanks to the Karpathian meeting the Mediterranean here, wind conditions are favourable for kitesurfing and there are a couple of outfits kitted out to help you, including **Pro Center Kristof Kirschner** (☑22400 91045; www.prasonisi.com). If you're looking for lunch or a bed, there's a resort here that caters to windsurfers and has surfer-dude-style restaurants and hostels. Outside of the summer season it's totally shut.

Kattavia to Monolithos
Κατταβιά προς Μονόλιθο

Lonely and exposed, Rhodes' southwest coast doesn't see many visitors. If you have time it's a beautiful place to visit with an edge-of-the-earth feeling. About 10km north of Kattavia, a turn-off to the right leads to the serene 18th-century **Moni Skiadi**, with terrific views down to the coast. Monolithos itself is a whitewashed amphitheatre of houses crouched beneath the pine-shrouded *kastro* (castle) far above on the hill.

HALKI ΧΑΛΚΗ

POP 310

Arriving on Halki is like stepping into a composite of everything Greek; an old fisherman shelling prawns under a fig tree, an Orthodox priest flitting down a narrow alley, while boats bob colourfully at the dock. All the limited action of this former sponge-diving island is based around its neoclassical harbour of Emborios. For the most part the island is rocky, but there are some temptingly quiet beaches wrapped in aquamarine water to sun yourself. And keep your eyes peeled – there are 14 types of butterfly, and over 40 kinds of birds.

🛈 Getting There & Away

There is a daily boat (€10) from Skala Kamirou on Rhodes with a connecting bus to Rhodes Town every day except Saturday and Sunday. Walk 150m from the Skala Kamirou ferry quay to the main road to find the bus stop. **Stelios Kazantzidis** (☑6944434429) also runs an independent ferry service to Skala Kamirou.

Ferries also connect Halki with Karpathos, Kolona, Piraeus, Santorini, Sitia in Crete, and Tylos. Tickets are available from Zifos Travel in Emborios. Two local ferries, the *Nissos Halki* and *Nikos Express*, run daily between Halki and Skala Kamirou (€10, 30 minutes).

Boat Services from Halki

DESTINATION	TIME	FARE	FREQUENCY
Karpathos	3hr	€12	3 weekly
Piraeus	19hr	€39	2 weekly
Rhodes	2hr	€9	5 weekly
Rhodes*	1¼hr	€16	2 weekly
Santorini (Thira)	15hr	€27	2 weekly

*high-speed services

🛈 Getting Around

The majority of people get around the island on foot. In summer, a minibus runs hourly between Emborios and Moni Agiou Ioanni (€5). Prices and telephone numbers are posted at kiosks. There's also a water taxi that serves the main beaches and you can find excursion boats to the uninhabited island of Alimia (€30), with fields of wild herbs. Call **Kiristanis Cruises** (📞 6988155630).

Emborios   Εμπορειός

POP 50

Emborios ticks all the Greek island fantasy boxes with its turquoise bay and distinctive crayon-coloured Italianate mansions, once the homes of 16th-century sea captains. Venetian-style shuttered windows grace facades of ochre and cream, below them cats yawn on the wharf-side, while old-timers flick worry beads. There's a bunch of enticing tavernas to relax in before bronzing yourself on nearby Ftenagia Beach.

◉ Sights

The old mansions that festoon the harbour are a visual feast, and many have been restored to their former glory, while others rest in a complete state of disrepair.

The impressive stone clock tower at the southern side of the harbour is a gift from the expat Halki community in Florida.

The Church of Agios Nikolaos has the tallest belfry in the Dodecanese and boasts an impressive pebbled courtyard on the east side. The Traditional House (📞 22460 45284; adult €3; ⊙ 11am-3pm & 6-8pm Mon-Fri) offers a glimpse into the past in this recreation of an island cottage. Follow the road up the hill past the bakery.

🛏 Sleeping

There are few accommodation options open to the ad hoc traveller so book ahead in the busier months. Zifos Travel, opposite the bakery, can help you find a room.

Captain's House   PENSION $
(📞 6932511762, 22460 45201; capt50@otenet.gr; d €40; ❄ 🛜) This former resistance fighter's house has three lovely rooms with original 19th-century high ceilings and wood floors, and features antique clocks and pictures of old schooners. There's also a terrific sun terrace with great harbour views, plus a courtyard to chill in.

St Nicolas Boutique Hotel   BOUTIQUE HOTEL $$
(📞 22460 45208; www.stnicolas.com; d/ste incl breakfast €150/170; 🅿 ❄ 🛜) This former sponge factory has 20 refined rooms with chic furniture and private balconies, and there's a palatial marbled lobby and contemporary restaurant. A few yards away on the old loading pier are steps leading into the sea for swimming.

🍴 Eating

Maria's Taverna   TAVERNA $
(mains €9) On the watefront in the corner by the post office, Maria's sits under the shade of a fig tree and has fresh fish, langoustine, lamb stew, *mousakas* and traditional homemade Halki spaghetti.

Black Sea   TAVERNA $
(mains €7; 🛜) 🌿 Sitting peacefully on its own to the left side of the harbour, and metres from bobbing boats, this brightly coloured haunt has scorpionfish, snapper, live lobster, lamb *kleftiko*, souvlakia and shrimp. Run by a charming Georgian family.

Dimitri's Bakery   BAKERY $
(mains €2) 🌿 Deservedly popular for its spinach and apple pies, croissants, cheese flans and, in the evening, slices of pizza. Get here at dawn for fresh pastries.

🛈 Information

Boats arrive at the centre of Emborios' harbour and most services and accommodation are within easy walking distance. The free quarterly *Halki Visitor* is a good source of local information.

When we passed, the ATM at the information booth on the harbour – the island's only source of withdrawal – was no longer working and due for replacement, so bring plenty of spare cash.

A good website with suggestions on things to do and places to eat is www.halki-travel-guide.com.
Clinic (📞 22460 45206; ⊙ 9am-2pm & 6-8pm Mon-Fri) Weekend numbers are posted on the

door of Zifos Travel. A larger clinic is currently being built.

Police and Port Police (☎22460 45220) On the harbour.

Post Office (⊙9am-1.30pm Mon-Fri) On the harbour.

Twelve Islands Bank ATM Near Zifos Travel and opposite the ferry quay.

Zifos Travel (☎22460 45082; zifostravel.gr; ⊙10am-8pm daily) Run by Jane, Zifos helps with accommodation, travel, excursions and currency exchange.

Around Halki

In the next bay south, sandy **Podamos Beach** is a dreamy strip of pebbles lapped by turquoise waves and goats nibbling at its grassy slopes. Just up from it, **Podamos Beach Taverna** (mains €8; ⊙lunch & dinner) has a seafood-accented menu. Only 1km from Emborios in the direction of Horio, it has shallow water ideal for children. You'll find a basic taverna and loungers and umbrellas for hire. Pebbly **Ftenagia Beach**, past the headland and 500m to the south of Emborios, looks out onto achingly clear water. The **Ftenagia Beach Taverna** (mains €9; ⊙8am-8pm) is a cosy waterside eatery (try their mouth-watering calamari).

Horio, a 30-minute walk (3km) along Tarpon Springs Blvd from Emborios, was once a thriving community of 3000 people, but it's now almost completely derelict. The **church** contains beautiful frescoes but is only unlocked for festivals. On 14 August the entire island climbs up here for a ceremony devoted to the Virgin Mary, the church's icon. A barely perceptible path leads from Horio's churchyard up to the **Knights of St John Castle**. It's a steep 15-minute walk with spectacular views.

Moni Agiou Ioanni is a two-hour, unshaded 8km walk along a broad concrete road from Horio. You can sometimes stay in the church's simple rooms in exchange for a donation.

KARPATHOS ΚΑΡΠΑΘΟΣ

POP 6080

This rugged island, celebrated for its wild mountains and gas-blue coves, is one of the most authentic places in Greece. Legend has it Prometheus and his titans were born here, and with its cloud-wrapped villages and

Karpathos

craggy beauty, there is something primal about the place.

The south of the island is popular with adrenaline junkies and is in the spotlight each summer when it hosts an international kitesurfing competition. Meanwhile, the fierce wind that lifts the spray from the turquoise waves blows its way to the mountainous north, battering pine trees and howling past sugarcube houses. Karpathian women at this end of the island still wear traditional garb, especially in the magical village eyrie of Olymbos, perched on the ridge of a mountain.

ℹ Getting There & Away

Karpathos has a large airport with daily links to Athens (€98), Kasos (€44) and Sitia (€67), and a five flights per week to Rhodes (€45). Buy tickets from Possi Travel (p487) in Pigadia.

Scheduled ferries service Agios Nikolaos, Kasos, Milos, Piraeus, Rhodes, Santorini and Sitia. Buy tickets from Possi Travel. A small local caïque also runs three times weekly between Finiki (Karpathos) and Fry (Kasos).

Boat Services from Karpathos

DESTINATION	TIME	FARE	FREQUENCY
Halki*	2hr	€12	3 weekly
Kasos	1½hr	€8	3 weekly
Milos	16hr	€36	1 weekly
Piraeus	17hr	€39	2 weekly
Rhodes	5hr	€20	3 weekly
Santorini (Thira)	11hr	€25	2 weekly
Sitia	4hr	€18	2 weekly

*leaves from Diafani port

ℹ Getting Around

TO/FROM THE AIRPORT

Frustratingly, there is no airport bus. Hop in a taxi to get to Pigadia (€25) and beyond.

BOAT

From May to September there are daily excursion boats from Pigadia to Diafani with a bus transfer to Olymbos (€25). Boats depart Pigadia at 8.30am. There are also frequent boats to the beaches of Kyra Panagia and Apella (€20). Tickets can be bought at the quay.

From Diafani, excursion boats go to nearby beaches and occasionally to the uninhabited islet of Saria, where there are some Byzantine remains.

BUS

Pigadia is the transport hub of the island; a schedule is posted at the **bus terminus** (☑ 22450 22338; M Mattheou) and the tourist info kiosk. Buses (€2, July and August only, daily except Sunday) serve most of the settlements in southern Karpathos, including the west coast beaches. There is no bus between Pigadia and Olymbos or Diafani.

CAR, MOTORCYCLE & BICYCLE

On the eastern side of Pigadia, **Rent A Car** (☑ 22450 22690/911; 28 Oktovriou) hires cars and motorcycles from €30. The best scooters are at **Pegasus Motorbikes** (☑ 6979794727; from €18.50 per day; ☺ 9am-1pm & 5-8pm). Motorcycle hire requires a motorbike permit on your driving licence.

TAXI

Pigadia's **taxi rank** (☑ 22450 22705; Dimokratias) is close to the centre of town where you'll find current rates posted. A taxi to Ammoöpi costs €10, the airport €20, Arkasa and Pyles €22, Kyra Panagia €25 and Spoa €30.

Pigadia   Πηγάδια
POP 1690

Pigadia lacks the photogenic good looks and geometrically pleasing whitewashed houses of other islands. Give it a little time though as you wander its harbour, waterfront bars, tavernas and backstreets bakeries, and the place may grow on you. Determinedly Greek, it barely looks up from its afternoon retsina to acknowledge your arrival. But isn't that what we sometimes long for?

You will find plenty of ATMs and minimarkets here.

⊙ Sights

Archaeological Museum of Karpathos   MUSEUM
(☺ 9am-1pm & 6-8.30pm Tue, Thu & Sat, 8.30am-3pm Wed, Fri & Sun) FREE Looking down over the town from a small seaside bluff, the Archaeological Museum of Karpathos houses local artefacts including coins, an early baptismal font and ceramics.

⊨ Sleeping

Pigadia has lots of budget options.

Hotel Karpathos   HOTEL $
(☑ 22450 22248; www.karpathoshotel.gr; d/tr €40/50; ❇ 🛜) Run by a friendly lady, these are smart, central digs with sunshine-filled rooms enjoying en suite, TV, private balcony, fridge and sea views.

Rose's Studios   APARTMENT $
(☑ 6974725427, 22450 22284; www.rosesstudios.com; r €30; ❇ 🛜) Worth the trudge up the hill these are simple, very fresh rooms with clean en suite, large balconies with sea views and decent fittings. There's also TV, plus kitchenette.

Hotel Titania
HOTEL $

(☑22450 22144; www.titaniakarpathos.gr; d/tr €50/60; ❄☎) From its '70s throwback lobby to the clean and functional rooms, with TV and en suite, everything here has a retro feel. Opt for a room at the back to avoid noisy traffic. Come breakfast eat in the shaded garden.

Oceanis Hotel
HOTEL $$

(☑22450 22975; r from €55; P❄☎) This '80s hotel screams kitsch from the moment you enter its mirrored lobby and gold-trim bar. Upstairs there are decent white-walled rooms with tasteful furniture, TV, balcony and sea views. There's also a terrace for sundowners.

✗ Eating

Conveniently, most of the bakeries, bars and tavernas are based on the waterfront or just behind it. Watch for the local speciality, *makarounes* (homemade pasta cooked with cheese and onions).

★ To Helenikon
TAVERNA $

(Apodimon Karpathion; mains €7; ⊙year-round; ❄☎) With its wood rafters and walls decorated with images of Greek gods and philosophers, this stylish taverna may well be the best on the island. Try their rib-eye steak, flame-grilled pork chops and veal, and don't miss their Karapthian speciality *makarounes*.

Pastry Shop
BAKERY $

(Dimokratias; sweets €1-4) This traditional patisserie peddles a treasure trove of biscuits, Karpathian baklava, eclairs, spinach pies, brownies and ice cream and drinks.

Posidon Taverna
TAVERNA $

(waterfront; mains €9) If it's freshly caught seafood you have a hankering for, look no further than this wharf-side taverna decked out with blue tables and chairs. Grilled prawns, swordfish, souvlakia, Karpathian sardines and, of course, calamari. A favourite with passing fishermen, try the dolmadhes washed down with an afternoon ouzo.

Akropolis
BRASSERIE $$

(Apodimon Karpathion; mains €15-25) At this welcoming harbour-side cafe, with Sinatra drifting over the wicker terrace, the menu boasts a selection of steaks: entrecôte, T-bone, fillet, sirloin and rib-eye, as well as the delectable *chateau briand* (€50). Plus there's breakfast, salads and pasta.

▾ Drinking & Nightlife

Beneath the museum you'll find a new open-air **theatre** where music and cultural events are often hosted in summer. For an evening drink, head to the seaside, which is lined with bars and cafes, particularly west of the info kiosk. Try waterfront **En Plo** (cocktails €6; ⊙8am-late) to sample a huge list of cocktails and coffee in a low-lit interior. If you're looking for somewhere to boogie, **Heaven Club** and **Fever** (⊙until 1am nightly, Fri & Sat only in winter), both out of town, offer a free bus which roams the streets from 1pm and will take you there.

❶ Information

The ferry quay is at the northeastern end of the wide harbour. It's a short walk to the centre of Pigadia, which is punctuated by the main street, Apodimon Karpathion. This in turn leads west to the central square of Plateia 5 Oktovriou. For the sandy beach, head west 300m to Pigadia Bay.

The website www.inkarpathos.com is locally maintained and has articles, news and info.

Cyber Games (seafront; internet per hr €2; ⊙9am-1am)

National Bank of Greece (Apodimon Karpathion) Has an ATM.

Police (☑22450 22224) Near the hospital at the western end of town.

Possi Travel (☑22450 22235; www.possi-holidays.gr; ⊙8am-1pm & 5.30-8.30pm) The main travel agency for ferry and air tickets, excursions and accommodation. The staff here are very helpful and speak excellent English.

Post Office (Ethnikis Andistasis) Near the hospital.

Tourist Information Office (☑22450 23835; ⊙Jul-Aug) In a kiosk in the middle of the seafront.

Southern Karpathos

The south of the island is more geared towards tourists and has some sandy beaches and quiet towns to relax in. Scenic walking tracks crisscross the land; pick up a map in Pigadia.

Menetes
Μενετές

Tiny Menetes sits high up in cliffs buffeted by mountain gales. Climb to its church before exploring its narrow whitewashed streets and **museum** (⊙on request) FREE. For a snapshot of mountain life with locals tucking into *mousakas, stifadho* and calamari, head to **Taverna Manolis** (☑22450

81103; mains €5-7). Alternatively, **Dionysos Fiesta** (22450 81269; mains €5-7) is good for local dishes, including an artichoke omelette and Karpathian sausages. Down the hill on the road, **Taverna Perdiga** (mains €6) is patronised by rebellious octogenarians, and chimes with chequers and politics; sample their squid, *gyros,* sardines and lamb chops, and wash it all down with some woody retsina.

Arkasa   Αρκάσα

Once a traditional Karpathian village, Arkasa is now a low-key resort. The village itself sits up from the water, 9km from Menetes, with its beachside resort below.

Follow a turn-off from the bottom of the village for 500m to the remains of the 5th-century **Basilica of Agia Sophia**, where two chapels stand amid mosaic fragments and columns. Below it you can walk along the coast to an ancient **acropolis**. Just south across the headland from here is **Agios Nikolaos Beach**. About 600m off the main road, it's small and sandy. Kip out on the water's edge at **Glaros Studios** (22450 61015; glaros@greekhotel.com; Agios Nikolaos; studios €50-55; P 🛜), where rooms are decorated in traditional Karpathian style. There's a relaxed adjoining restaurant.

On the road to Finiki, **Eleni Studios** (22450 61248; www.elenikarpathos.gr; Arkasa; r €50; P ❄🛜🏊) has white-and-blue, well-spaced apartments looking out to the nearby sea. There's also a welcoming **cafe** finished in French greys and candelabra. For something a little plusher, try **Arkasa Bay Hotel** (22450 61410; www.arkasabay.com; apt €100; ❄🛜🏊) for its rugged views of the pounding surf. The rooms are palatial and well equipped with kitchenettes. The family pool is a further boon if you've got little ones.

Finiki   Φοινίκι

Picturesque Finiki lies 2km north of Arkasa. Typically Aegean with its white-and-blue houses fronting a small pebbled beach and sleepy harbour, there's a peppering of tavernas here. The best local swimming is at **Agios Georgios Beach**, between Arkasa and Finiki. **Kamarakia Beach**, signposted before Agios Georgios, is a narrow cove with strong currents.

Just above the village, **Finiki View Hotel** (22450 61400; www.finikiview.gr; r €60, apt €80; ❄🛜🏊) has dramatic views of the beach and harbour below. There's a fresh, homey feel to the place and all studios and apartments have kitchenettes, pine green furniture, white walls and sea views. Some have traditional raised beds. It's five minutes' walk from the harbour.

Overlooking the gentle turquoise bay, **Marina Taverna** (mains €4-7) is metres from the water, and has a seafood-accented menu of squid, crab and grilled meats. Eating outside on the terrace is relaxing.

Nestled in a verdant garden some 9km north of Finiki are the **Pine Tree Studios** (6977369948; www.pinetree-karpathos.gr; Adia; d €35, apt €50-70; ❄). Rooms and apartments are comfortable and spacious with kitchenettes and views over to Kasos. The restaurant serves fresh fruit and vegetables from the garden.

Walkers can head up the **Flaskia Gorge**, or, as an easier option, hike to the nearby **Iliondas Beach**.

Lefkos   Λευκός
POP 120

You'll find the summer resort of Lefkos 2km down towards the sea from the main coastal road.

Archaeology buffs explore the underground remains of a **Roman cistern**, reached by heading up the approach road and looking for a sign on the left to the 'catacombs'. Drive to the very end of the rough road and then strike out along trail K16.

If you decide to stay in this neck of the woods, try **Le Grand Bleu** (22450 71400; www.legrandbleu-lefkos.gr; studio/apt €85/120; P ❄@🛜) for a well-equipped apartment overlooking the curving Gialou Horafi middle beach in Lefkos. You'll also find an excellent, shady **taverna** (mains €7-12) on-site with mezedhes (appetisers) like garlic mushrooms and *imam baïldi* (aubergine in oil with herbs).

There are daily buses to Lefkos; a taxi from Pigadia costs €24. **Lefkos Rent A Car** (22450 71057; www.lefkosrentacar.com) is a reliable outlet that will deliver vehicles, free of charge, to anywhere in southern Karpathos.

Northern Karpathos

The beautiful mountain road winding north takes you so high you think you're scaling Mount Olympus; certainly you pass through the odd cloud! The road suffers occasional rock falls in some sections after heavy rains, so avoid driving here in bad weather. That said, 98% of it is sealed and navigable and the village eyrie of Olympos must *not* be missed. Many hop on a boat to get to Diafani from where you catch a connecting bus to take you to Olympos. There's also excellent trekking to be had in the north and the pebbly beaches boast especially transparent water.

Diafani   Διαφάνι

POP 250

Diafani is an intimate, wind-blasted huddle of white houses fronted by cobalt blue water, back-dropped by a mountain. Bar the crash of the waves and old men playing backgammon, nothing else stirs. Most people only pass through Diafani, though if you do stay you'll likely have the beaches and trails to yourself.

🏃 Activities

Join an excursion trip on the *Captain Manolis* to the otherwise inaccessible reaches of Karpathos and to the satellite island of **Saria**. Boats leave from the jetty in the centre of town at around 10am, returning at 5pm. It costs around €20.

Walkers should pick up the Road Editions *1:60,000 Karpathos-Kasos* map (available in Pigadia) or visit the Environment Management office near Diafani's seafront. Walks are signposted with red or blue markers or stone cairns. Follow a half-hour coastal track for 4km north through the pines to **Vananda Beach**. A more strenuous two-hour walk takes you 11km northwest to the Hellenistic site of **Vroukounda**. En route you'll pass the agricultural village of **Avlona**. Take all your food and water with you as there are no facilities.

🛏 Sleeping & Eating

Head to **Balaskas Hotel** (☑ 22450 51320; www.balaskashotel.com; s/d €30/40; ❄ 🛜) where 19 fresh rooms have tiled floors, colourful bedspreads, satellite TV and wi-fi, as well as a hotel boat which can take you to neighbouring islands for a mere €10 per person. It's two minutes' walk from the beach.

At the northern end of the bay, **Dolphin Studios** (☑ 22450 51301; apt €35; ❄) has homey studios with large en suite, basic cooking facilities, fine views, sugar-white walls and an attractive sun terrace. Turn left at La Gorgona taverna.

The waterfront is lined with restaurants. **Rahati** (☑ 22450 51200; mains €8) attracts locals for its souvlakia, octopus, zucchini, *mousakas, gyros* and calamari. While at **La Gorgona** (☑ 22450 51509; mains €7; ⊗ 8am-late) instead of turning to stone you may turn to jelly; with fine sea views, and even finer Italian cuisine. The homemade spaghetti is delicious (try the carbonara), as are the local shrimps, bruschetta and *saganaki*.

ℹ Information

You can exchange currency at the **Orfanos Travel Agency** (☑ 6974990394; ⊗ 8am-1pm & 5.30-8.30pm), as well as organising ferry and air tickets. There's no bank, post office, gas station or ATM in town, so bring cash and fuel with you. For local info, check out www.diafani.com.

ℹ Getting There & Away

Scheduled ferries call at the wharf and a summertime excursion boat arrives daily from Pigadia, to be met by buses that transport visitors to Olympos. Otherwise, scheduled buses leave for Olympos daily at 8am, 2.30pm and 5pm year-round. A boat to Pigadia leaves at 8am and returns at 3pm, three times a week.

Olympos   Ολυμπος

POP 330

This mist-blown eyrie of pastel-coloured houses clings precariously to the summit of Mt Profitis Ilias (716m) as if flung there by a titan's paw. Wander the wind-buffeted alleyways past old ladies sporting vividly coloured garb, and it's easy to feel as if you've stepped onto a film set. This is about as traditional as it gets, for locals still speak with a dialect containing traces of ancient Dorian Greek. There are a few shops selling soaps, rugs and traditional headscarves and some cosy tavernas to take in the jaw-dropping views. Try to get here late afternoon or early morning – when the day-trippers have gone – as locals take to their violins.

🛏 Sleeping & Eating

To the left of the church **Hotel Aphrodite** (☑ 22450 51307; filippasfilipakkis@yahoo.gr; d €35) has four elegant, white-walled, tile floored rooms and the best sea views in the village. Meanwhile, **Mike's** (☑ 22450 51304; r €25-30), at the southern edge of town, has four fresh rooms with bathrooms and kitchenettes and a kindly Cerberus in the form of elderly owner, Sofia. The colourful *kafeneio* below does traditional dishes like *stifadho* and dolmadhes (mains €7).

DODECANESE NORTHERN KARPATHOS

Traditional **Hotel Olymbos** (☎22450 51009; r €25-35) ✆ has terrific views from rooms with raised beds, thick blankets and a great restaurant upstairs featuring meatballs, stewed goat and *makarounes*. Ask to see their Romany caravan-style shop selling dolls and painted crockery. **Irene's House** (☎6944636327; per night €60, per week €300) is a newly renovated house and sleeps four.

Head for the **Parthenon Restaurant** (mains €4-8) in the square for walls decked in instruments, a wood ceiling, antique photos and a traditional menu featuring *soutzoukakia* (meatballs in wine and tomato sauce) and souvlakia.

And finally, **Eden Garden** (mains €4-8), south of the church, is a simple taverna with mountain views, check-cloth tables and a menu of homemade sausage, local goat *stifadho*, pizzas and salads.

KASOS ΚΑΣΟΣ

POP 980

Battered by severe winds and imprisoned by huge turquoise waves, isolated Kasos looks like the Greece that time forgot. Most of its visitors are rare seabirds; 90% of the human returnees are Kasiots on fleeting visits, having left in droves years ago to seek employment. But get here and you'll discover a tumbledown charm to the Dodecanese' southernmost island.

In 1820, the Turkish-ruled island had 11,000 inhabitants and a large mercantile fleet. Tragically, Mohammad Ali, the Turkish governor of Egypt, regarded this fleet as an impediment to his plan to establish a base in Crete and on 7 June 1824 his men landed on Kasos and killed around 7000 inhabitants. This massacre is commemorated annually and Kasiots return from around the world to participate.

ⓘ Getting There & Away

There are daily flights to Karpathos (€21, 10 minutes), Sitia (€38, 40 minutes) and Rhodes (€34, one hour) with **Olympic Air** (☎22450 41555; Kritis Airport).

Boat Services from Kasos

DESTINATION	TIME	FARE	FREQUENCY
Heraklion	5½hr	€20	2 weekly
Karpathos	1½hr	€8	3 weekly
Piraeus	19hr	€39	3 weekly
Rhodes	7hr	€24	3 weekly
Santorini	10hr	€25	2 weekly
Sitia	2½hr	€11	3 weekly

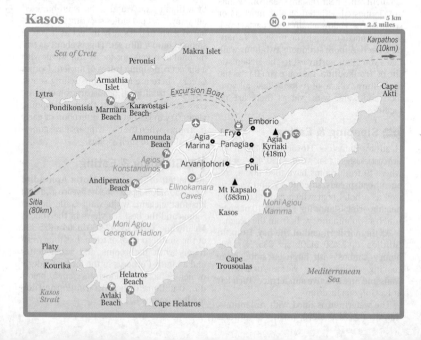

Kasos

ℹ Getting Around

The local bus was broken when we called in but usually serves all the island villages with a dozen or so scheduled runs; tickets are €1. There are two **taxis** (☑ 6973244371, 6977944371) on the island. Scooters or cars can be hired from **Oasis – Rent-a-Car & Bikes** (☑ 22450 41746) in Fry.

Fry   Φρυ

POP 270

Pretty white houses, with typical navy blue doors and window frames, line the harbour of Fry (*free*), the island's capital and port. Several cafes sit waiting for customers while barnacled fishermen fiddle with their orange nets on the impossibly photogenic quay of Bouka. As late as June this is still a ghost town of peeling facades and wind-pocked streets.

◉ Sights & Activities

Archaeological Museum   MUSEUM
(☉ 9am-3pm, summer only) **FREE** Fry's Archaeological Museum displays objects pulled from ancient shipwrecks, a collection of ancient oil lamps and finds from Polis such as inscribed Hellenistic stone slabs.

Athina Excursion Boat   BOAT TRIP
(☑ 6977911209, 22450 41047; return €15) The Athina excursion boat travels daily in summer to the uninhabited Armathia Islet, departing Fry harbour at 3pm and returning at 7pm. The speck of an island has superb sandy beaches, but you'll need to bring all of your own supplies.

⊨ Sleeping

Hotel Anagennissis   HOTEL $
(☑ 22450 41323; s/d €35/45; ✱) Slap bang on the waterfront in the village centre, this fresh midranger has quality rooms with comfy beds, fridges, TV and nice decor. If no one's at reception, head to the Kasos Maritime Tourist Agency next door (with the same owners).

Evita Village   PENSION $
(☑ 22450 41695, 6972703950; evitavillage@mail.gr; s/d incl breakfast €30/35; ✱) Meticulously equipped studios are spacious and tasteful. They sport every kitchen appliance imaginable, along with a TV and DVD player, and sleep up to three people. It's 300m from the centre.

✕ Eating & Drinking

Retro Cafe   CAFE $
(Plateia Iroön Kasou; mains €3; ✱ 🛜) Retro has tomato-red walls and a pleasant alfresco area with swallow-you-up cushions to eat your sandwich (from its tempting deli). Great breakfasts, waffles, pies and juices conjured with a smile from owner Polly.

O Mylos   TAVERNA $
(Plateia Iroön Kasou; mains €7; 🛜 ☑) Overlooking the port, this homey taverna has unbroken sea views and a reliable menu of souvlakia, shrimp, *mousakas*, pot roast rabbit stew and various seafood.

Apangio   CAFE $
(Bouka; mezedhes €4; ☉ 9am-late; ✱ 🛜) This sugarcube house fronting beautiful Bouka harbour has a chic, nautical feel with a cloud-frescoed ceiling, stone walls and friendly service. Mainly a stop for coffee and mezedhes, they also serve breakfast and juice.

ℹ Information

The large harbour complex abuts the port village right next to its main square, Plateia Iroön Kasou. Fry's main street is Kritis. The airport is 1km west along the coast road. Turn left from the harbour to get to Emborio.

A stand-alone Commercial Bank ATM is next to the port entrance, while there's a Co-operative Bank of the Dodecanese branch with an ATM on Plateia Iroön Kasou.

An informative website in Greek and English is www.kasos.gr.

Farmacy (☑ 22450 41164) For all medicinal needs.

Health Centre (☑ 22450 41333) Often unattended; you may need to call ahead.

Kasos Maritime & Travel Agency (☑ 22450 41495; www.kassos-island.gr; Plateia Iroön Kasou) For all travel tickets. Run by Fotini.

Police (☑ 22450 41222) On a narrow paved street running south from Kritis.

Port Police (☑ 22450 41288) Behind the Agios Spyridon Church.

Post Office (☉ 7.30am-2pm Mon-Fri) Diagonally opposite from the police.

Retro Cafe (☉ 8am-late) Offers free wi-fi.

Around Kasos

Tiny Emborio is a satellite port of Fry used for pleasure craft and fishing boats. With a sandy beach and clear water, it's the nearest place to Fry for a quick dip.

The island's best beach is the isolated pebbled cove of Helatros, near Moni Agiou Georgiou Hadion, 11km southwest of Fry along a paved road. The beach has no facilities and you'll need your own transport to reach it. Avlaki is another decent yet small beach here, reached along a track from the monastery. None of Kasos' beaches offer shade.

Agia Marina, 1km southwest of Fry, is a pretty village with a gleaming white-and-blue church. On 17 July the Festival of Agia Marina is celebrated here. From Agia Marina, the road continues to verdant Arvanitohori, with abundant fig and pomegranate trees. Poli, 3km southeast of Fry, is the former capital, built on the ancient acropolis. Panagia, between Fry and Poli, now has fewer than 50 inhabitants; its once-grand sea captains' and many ship owners' mansions are either standing derelict or under repair.

KASTELLORIZO (MEGISTI)
ΚΑΣΤΕΛΛΟΡΙΖΟ (ΜΕΓΙΣΤΗ)
POP 430

So close to the Turkish coast (2km away from Kaş) it can almost taste the East, far-flung Kastellorizo is insanely pretty, with cobbled alleys and brightly coloured neoclassical houses with tiled roofs and wrought-iron balconies reflecting in the horseshoe bay. The island enjoys an enviable 320 days of sunshine per year, and the quality of the light here – the barren rock, the bright shades of the houses contrasted with the aquamarine-green of the sea – is stunningly photogenic. And while it may lack powder-fine beaches the island lays claim to the fabulous Blue Cave.

With only a few ferries and flights per week, Kastellorizo is not an easy place to get to, but those who do make the effort are rewarded with tranquillity, simple accommodation and a few nice restaurants.

History

Thanks to its harbour – allegedly the best between Beirut and Piraeus – Kastellorizo was once a thriving trade port serving Dorians, Romans, Crusaders, Egyptians, Turks and Venetians. It came under Ottoman control in 1552 and its cargo fleet became the largest in the Dodecanese. Kastellorizo lost all strategic and economic importance after the 1923 Greece–Turkey population exchange and in 1928 it was ceded to the Italians, who severely oppressed the islanders. Many emigrated to Australia, where approximately 30,000 continue to live.

During WWII Kastellorizo suffered bombardment and English commanders ordered the few remaining inhabitants to abandon the island. Most fled to Cyprus, Palestine and Egypt. When they returned they found their houses in ruins, and many re-emigrated. While the island has never fully recovered from this population loss, in recent years returnees have brought a period of resurgence and resettlement.

❶ Getting There & Away

You can hop on a flight to Rhodes or wait for a ferry or catamaran, although boat services from the island are often tenuous and always infrequent.

AIR

Olympic has four flights per week to Rhodes (€47, 20 minutes) from where you can get connections to Athens. For flight and ferry tickets, visit **Papoutsis Travel** (☑ 6937212530, 22460 70630; www.kastelorizo.gr) in Kastellorizo Village.

Boat Services from Kastellorizo (Megisti)

DESTINATION	TIME	FARE	FREQUENCY
Piraeus	23hr	€81	1 weekly
Rhodes	4¾hr	€22	2 weekly
Rhodes*	2½hr	€36	1 weekly

*high-speed services

❶ Getting Around

To reach the airport, take the sole island **taxi** (☑ 6938739178) from the port (€5) or the local community bus (€1.50). The bus leaves the square by the port 1½ hours prior to each flight departure.

Kastellorizo Village
Καστελλόριζο
POP 275

Besides Mandraki, the satellite neighbourhood over the hill, Kastellorizo Village is the main settlement on the island. Its waterfront is skirted by vibrantly coloured three-storey mansions that sit directly on the turquoise water. The labyrinthine backstreets are slowly being restored and rebuilt. The village has a strong Aussie presence of returned expats, adding an upbeat cosmo energy to the community.

◎ Sights

Follow a rickety metal staircase up to the **Knights of St John Castle** for splendid views of Turkey. Below the castle stands the **museum** (⏰7am-2pm Tue-Sun) FREE with a collection of archaeological finds, costumes and photos. Beyond the museum, steps lead down to a coastal pathway from where more steps go up the cliff to a rock-hewn **Lycian tomb** with an impressive Doric facade dating back as far as the 4th century BC. There are several along the Anatolian coast in Turkey, but they are very rare in Greece.

Moni Agiou Stefanou, on the north coast, is the setting for one of the island's most important celebrations, the feast of Agios Stefanos on 1 August. The path to the little white monastery begins behind the post office. From the monastery, a path leads to a bay where you can swim.

Paleokastro was the island's ancient capital. Within the old city's Hellenistic walls are an ancient tower, a water cistern and three churches. To reach it (1km), follow the concrete steps just beyond a soldier's sentry box on the airport road.

🏃 Activities

Excursion boats go from Kastellorizo harbour to the spectacular **Blue Cave (Parasta)**, famous for its brilliant, mirrorlike blue water, produced by refracted sunlight. Visitors are transferred from a larger caïque to a small motorised dingy in order to enter the very low cave entrance – claustrophobics be warned. Inside, the cave reaches up 35m and sometimes you may see seals. Visitors are usually allowed a quick dip. The excursion costs about €15; look for Georgos Karagiannis who runs the *Varvara* and *Agios Georgios* daily from the harbour. Boats leave at 9am and return around 1pm.

You can also take day trips to the islets of Ro and Strongyli for swims and picnics. The trips cost about €20 and boats depart around 9am from the harbour.

Join islanders on one of their frequent shopping trips to Kaş in Turkey. A day trip costs about €20 and is available from boats along the middle waterfront. Passports are required by the police 24 hours beforehand.

🛏 Sleeping

Many hotels stay open year-round.

★ Mediterraneo
PENSION **$$**

(☑22460 49007; www.mediterraneo-kastelorizo.com; r €80-170; 🛜) This mustard-hued gem is bursting with élan – mint-fresh, fan-only rooms with white bedspreads, icon-dotted walls, shabby chic touches and fresh flowers at every turn. Right on the water, with loungers outside your door, the hotel is at the far western tip of the harbour.

Megisti Hotel
HOTEL **$$**

(www.megistihotel.gr; ste/d €220/140; ❄@🛜🏊) Located on the edge of Kastellorizo harbour (a two-minute walk from the main square), newly renovated Megisti has four suites and 15 rooms with cable TV, rain showers, DVD players, safety deposit boxes, fridges and fresh towels daily. It's also in a safe spot for swimming.

Damien & Monika's
PENSION **$$**

(☑6978066375, 22460 49028; www.kastellorizo.de; r €60; ❄@🛜) These comfy rooms in the centre of town are tastefully finished with traditional furnishings, fridge, and lots of windows to let in that special Kastellorizo light. You'll also find a book exchange and heaps of local info. Considerable discounts outside of peak season.

Poseidon
APARTMENT **$$**

(☑6945710603, 22460 49257; www.kastelorizo-poseidon.gr; s/d €50/60; ❄🛜🏊) Poseidon's two restored houses offer large rooms with private verandahs and big sea views. There's also a lovely roof terrace. It's on the west side of the harbour, one block back from the waterfront. As a further bonus, Poseidon allows you to bring your pet!

🍴 Eating & Drinking

Tables spill out onto the narrow harbour and by night the atmosphere is special – just don't tip into the nearby water! Keep an eye out for traditional sweets, *katoumari* and *strava*.

Lazarakis
SEAFOOD **$**

(☑22460 49370; mains €9, 3-course dinner incl wine €35; ⏰breakfast, lunch & dinner) This Aegean white and blue restaurant occupies a tasteful spot in which to work through a seafood-heavy offering of fresh lobster, squid, octopus and Symi shrimp, all fired up on the grill. By the jetty in the middle of the harbour.

Radio Cafe

CAFE $

(breakfast & snacks €7; ❄ 🛜) Other than internet access, this cafe makes a mean coffee and dishes up filling breakfasts, light snacks and pizzas as classical music plays. Sunset views are thrown in for free and it's run by a welcoming couple.

Mediteraneo

TAVERNA $

(🕙 breakfast, lunch & dinner; ❄ 🛜 🍴) Up the hill in the midst of Kastellorizo village, this spacious restaurant is open from June through September and makes for a peaceful spot to enjoy *stifadho* octopus, cabbage leaf dolmadhes and an ever-changing menu of specials to keep your taste buds on their toes.

Faros Bar

BAR

(🕙 9am-late; 🛜) In an enviable position by the old lighthouse, this is a great spot to swim in the turquoise shallows then take breakfast, drinking up wide-screen views of Turkey and Kastellorizo village. Salads and snacks throughout the day and come 6pm, tapas.

ℹ Information

The quay is at the southern side of the bay. The central square, Plateia Ethelondon Kastellorizou, abuts the waterfront almost halfway round the bay, next to the yachting jetty. The settlements of Horafia and Mandraki are reached by ascending the wide steps at the east side of the bay.

First Aid (☎ 22460 45206) For emergencies and basic health needs. There's also a new pharmacy next to the ferry stop.

National Bank of Greece (☎ 22460 49054) ATM.

Papoutsis Travel (☎ 22460 49356, 22460 70630; papoutsistravel@galileo.gr) For air and sea tickets.

Police Station (☎ 22460 49333) On the bay's western side.

Port Police (☎ 22460 49333) At eastern tip of the bay.

Post Office Next to the police station.

Radio Cafe (internet per hr €3)

SYMI

ΣΥΜΗ

POP 2610

Thrumming with day-trippers, beautiful Symi (*see*-me) evokes *oohs* and *aahs* from ferry passengers before they've even got off the boat! For sailing into the Italianate harbour of Gialos with its biscuit- and wine-coloured houses is a sight for sore eyes. Indeed if the Greek isles were models, Symi would be the dainty diva, drawing as she does regular visits from Hollywood A listers. Gialos (the capital) must surely have one of the prettiest ports in the Dodecanese (thanks to Italian colonisation) with its neoclassical facades. Above it rising steeply up the mountainside is the village of Horio, to which it is connected by the Kali Strata, a steep cobbled stairway winding through sea captains' houses and crumbling remains.

This magical island aglitter with crystal-clear water so transparent in places the boats look as if they're floating on thin air, has plenty of blue coves and beaches to explore, as well as walking tour operators.

History

Symi has a long tradition of sponge diving and shipbuilding, and is mentioned in the 'Iliad' as sending three ships to assist Agamemnon's siege of Troy. In Ottoman times it was granted the right to fish for sponges in Turkish waters. In return, Symi supplied the sultan with first-class boat builders. This exchange brought prosperity to the island, gracious mansions were built and culture and education flourished. By the beginning of the 20th century, the population was 22,500 and the island was launching some 500 ships a year. But the Italian occupation, the introduction of the steamship and Kalymnos' rise as the Aegean's principal sponge producer put an end to Symi's prosperity.

ℹ Getting There & Away

Catamarans, excursion boats and **ANES** (☎ 22460 71444; www.anek.gr) run regular boats between Symi and Rhodes, as well as to islands further north and to Kastellorizo. One service calls in at Panormitis on the south side of the island. Symi Tours runs Saturday excursions from Gialos to Datça in Turkey (including Turkish port taxes; €40).

BOAT

In summer, daily excursion boats run between Symi and Rhodes (€15). The Symi-based *Symi I* and *Symi II* usually go via Panormitis.

Boat Services from Symi

DESTINATION	TIME	FARE	FREQUENCY
Kalymnos*	2hr	€31	5 weekly
Kos*	1½hr	€22	5 weekly
Leros*	3hr	€40	5 weekly
Patmos*	4hr	€44	5 weekly
Piraeus	15hr	€51	2 weekly
Rhodes	2hr	€13	2 weekly
Rhodes*	50min	€16	1 daily
Tilos	2hr	€8	1 weekly

*high-speed services

Symi

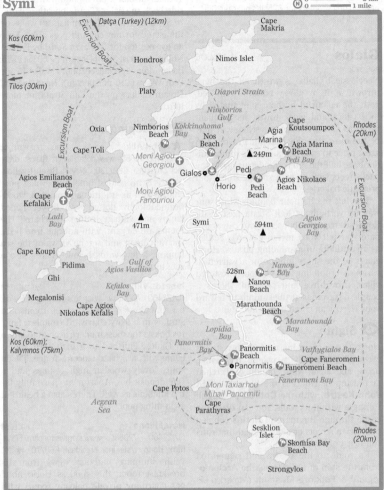

Datça (Turkey) (12km)

Kos (60km)

Tilos (30km)

Cape Makria

Hondros

Nimos Islet

Platy

Diapori Straits

Nimborios Gulf

Oxia

Nimborios Beach

Kokkinohoma Bay

Nos Beach

Agia Marina

Cape Koutsoumpos

Rhodes (20km)

Cape Toli

Moni Agiou Georgiou

Gialos

Pedi

▲249m

Agia Marina Beach

Pedi Bay

Agios Emilianos Beach

Cape Kefalaki

Moni Agiou Fanouriou

Horio

Pedi Beach

Agios Nikolaos Beach

Ladi Bay

▲471m

Symi

594m ▲

Agios Georgios Bay

Cape Koupi

Pidima

Ghi

Gulf of Agios Vasilios

528m ▲

Nanou Beach

Nanou Bay

Megalonisi

Cape Agios Nikolaos Kefalis

Kefalos Bay

Marathounda Beach

Marathounda Bay

Kos (60km); Kalymnos (75km)

Lopidia Bay

Panormitis Bay

Panormitis Beach

Panormitis

Vathygialos Bay

Cape Faneromeni

Faneromeni Beach

Faneromeni Bay

Cape Potos

Moni Taxiarhou Mihail Panormiti

Cape Parathyras

Aegean Sea

Sesklion Islet

Skomisa Bay Beach

Rhodes (20km)

Strongylos

DODECANESE SYMI

ℹ️ Getting Around

BOAT

Several excursion boats do trips from Gialos Harbour to Moni Taxiarhou Mihail Panormiti (€25), and Sesklion Islet (€25), where there's a shady beach. Check the boards for the best-value tickets. There are also boats to Agios Emilianos beach, on the far west side of Symi.

The small **water taxis** (☎ 22460 71423) *Konstantinos* and *Irini* go to many of the island's beaches (€12 to €16), leaving at 10.15am and 11.15am respectively.

BUS & TAXI

The bus stop and taxi rank are on the south side of the harbour in Gialos. The bumble-bee-coloured **minibus** (☎ 6945316284) makes hourly runs between Gialos and Pedi Beach (via Horio; flat fare €1). The turquoise **minibus** (☎ 22460 71311) departs Gialos at 10am and 3pm daily for Panormitis (€6 return). Taxis depart from a rank 100m west of the bus stop and cost €25 (each way) to Panormitis.

CAR

Glaros (☎ 6948362079, 22460 71926; www. glarosrentacar.gr; Gialos; scooters/cars

€25/45) hires cars for around €45 and very new-looking scooters for €25. It's near the Gialos clock tower.

Gialos Γιαλός

POP 2200

Neoclassical Gialos is worth all the hype thrown at it by glossy editorials. Indeed, with the colourful harbour punctuated by its basilica and clock tower, its excellent tavernas and crayon-colour scheme, it may be the most stunning harbour in Greece. A great place to spot famous actors hiding under hats, half the fun is wandering about the backstreets spilling with sponge stores and aromatic bakeries.

Leaving the harbour behind, wind your way up vertiginous Kali Strata past traditional sea captains' houses – your calves will hate you but your memory won't. Settled as an antidote to marauding pirates, Horio clings to the sheer hillside in a warren of variously crumbling and gloriously restored villas. Crowd-free and peaceful, there's a couple of tavernas at the summit to reward your Herculean climb up the 500 steps.

◎ Sights

Horio (Χωριό) is a maze of narrow streets zigzagging through a palette of sienna, ochre and sugar-white buildings. Perched at the top of Horio is the **Knights of St John Kastro**, with the **Church of Megali Panagia** within its walls. You can reach the castle through the maze of Horio's cobbled pedestrian streets or along a road that runs southeast of Gialos.

En route to the *kastro* and signposted from the stop of Kali Strata, the **Archaeological & Folklore Museum** (admission €2; ◑10am-2pm Tue-Sun) has Hellenistic, Byzantine and Roman exhibits, as well as some folkloric material. The nearby **Chatziagapitos House** is a restored 18th-century mansion that you can look around when the museum is open.

Behind the **children's playground** in the port of Gialos, the **Nautical Museum** (admission €2; ◑11am-4pm Tue-Sun) details Symi's shipbuilding history and has wooden models of ships and other naval memorabilia.

🏃 Activities

Symi Tours (☑22460 71307) has multilingual guided walks (€12) around the island (every Tuesday at 8am), often ending with a boat ride back to Gialos. The publication *Walks in Symi* by Lance Chiltern lists 20 walks on the island for novices and pros alike. Keep an eye out too for *Walks in Symi* by Francis Noble Tsavaris. **Symi Dream** (☑69364 21715; Horio) offers specialised photo walks in the Pedi Valley (€10 per person). Head to Symi Dream Gallery on the Kali Strata for more info.

🛏 Sleeping

★**Hotel Aliki**   BOUTIQUE HOTEL **$$**
(☑22460 71655; www.hotelaliki.gr; Gialos; d/ste incl breakfast €60/130; ❇🗢) Biscuit-yellow Aliki is Symi's oldest hotel and evokes pure charm with its traditionally painted, wood-beamed lobby, dotted with flower-shaded lamps and vintage leather armchairs. The rooms are elegant, with antique iron beds, fragrant linen and serene views of the sea lapping a few yards below. There's also a roof terrace.

Iapetos Village   APARTMENT **$$**
(☑22460 72777; www.iapetos-village.gr; Gialos; d & apt €135; ❇@🗢▧) With 29 rooms and studios in a leafy courtyard complex, Iapetos boasts the most modern accommodation in Gialos. Finished to a high spec, rooms come with a private balcony, fridge, TV, en suite, lovely wooden high ceilings and a safe deposit box. Apartments have fully fitted kitchens as well. There's also a beautiful swimming pool.

Hotel Fiona   HOTEL **$$**
(☑22460 72088; www.symivisitor.com/Fiona. htm; Horio; r/ste incl breakfast €60/70; ❇🗢) With stunning harbour views from its breakfast room, this spotless Horio hotel has charming private balcony rooms with fresh-painted turquoise furniture, chocolate bedspreads and white walls. To reach Fiona, turn left at the top of Kali Strata and walk a further 30m.

Hotel Garden   PENSION **$$**
(☑22460 72429; www.symitop5.gr; Gialos; d €60-80; ❇🗢▧) This pension is enchanting with its blue, green and biscuit exterior, and raised beds. Family apartments have separate bedrooms for the kids and a communal kitchen with tasteful old furniture, as well as fridges and TV. It's mmaculate throughout, and there's a lovely garden courtyard to chill in.

✗ Eating

In Gialos, eateries line the harbour; in Horio, they tend to be clustered at the top of Kali Strata.

✗ Gialos

★ Meraklis   SEAFOOD $
(mains €8-10; 🛜) This magical backstreet taverna has Santorini-blue walls decked out with vintage diving photos, antique mirrors and a menu straight from the table of Poseidon. Feast on fresh octopus, sea bream, Symi shrimp and swordfish. The souvlakia, meatballs and roast lamb are all exceptionally tasty. Why not try a mixed seafood dish for two (€30)?

★ Manos Fish Restaurant   SEAFOOD $
(mains €8-10; ✳ 🍴) Festooned in nets and nautical lanterns, its walls astir with lobsters in tanks, Manos is arguably the best-loved seafood restaurant in the Dodecanese – certainly it packs in more Hollywood demigods than a tin of sardines. Octopus cooked in wine, mixed seafood saganaki, shark fillet, crab claws and sea snails are a few of its treasures.

Nikolas Patisserie   BAKERY $
(sweets €3-4) Hidden behind the harbour this aromatic patisserie is a wonderland of éclairs, tarts, cheesecake, baklava, cookies and homemade ice cream. A place to forget your diet – sit in the shade and indulge!

La Vaporetta   SEAFOOD $$
(lunch mains €10, dinner mains €14-25; ⊙ noon-5pm & 7pm-midnight; 🛜🍴) With its orange painted floor, giant net billowing across the ceiling and walls finished in old black-and-white photos, this is a romantic spot for dinner (especially outside by the sea). The menu excels with carpaccio of swordfish, steak, pasta dishes and Adriatic sea prawns with rosemary. Finish off with one of their delicious sorbets.

✗ Horio

Olive Tree   CAFE $
(Horio; light meals €2-5; ⊙ 8.30am-3.30pm year-round; 🛜🍴) 🚭 This place is newly relocated to a fantastic vantage point looking down over Gialos. Sit yourself down beneath the vine-shaded terrace (with smoking and non-smoking sections), as you tuck into smoothies, juices, cakes, quiche, locally sourced

salads, homemade cheese and snacks. You'll find it near the top of Kali Strata.

Giorgos   TAVERNA $
(mains €10) Boasting a great view of the bay, Giorgos is traditional from its pebble mosaic terrace to its no-frills menu of Symi lamb, rabbit stew, dolmadhes and sea urchin salad.

🍷 Drinking & Nightlife

Eva   BAR
(Gialos harbour) This popular harbourfront bar with exposed stone walls, Edwardian velvet couches and chillsome vibes invokes a cool atmosphere with a 30-something crowd. Head here for a sunset cocktail.

Harani Bar   BAR
(Gialos harbour; ⊙ 8am-late) Locals head to Harani for its no-nonsense interior and alfresco position on the left-hand corner of the harbour. Happy hour is usually from 6.30pm to 8pm.

ℹ Information

Arriving ferries, hydrofoils and catamarans dock just to the left of the quay's clock tower; excursion boats dock a little further along. Ferries can depart from either side of the harbour so check when you buy your ticket. The harbour and the promenade running southwest from its centre are the hub of Gialos activity. Kali Strata, a broad stairway, leads from here to hilltop Horio.

There is no official tourist office here but Kalodoukas Holidays is a great source of info.

The website www.symivisitor.com is a useful source of island information with an accommodation-booking service.

Cafe Platia (internet per hr €1.60; ⊙ 8am-11pm) On the right side of the harbour has wi-fi and internet access.

Kalodoukas Holidays (🖉 22460 71077; www.kalodoukas.gr) At the beginning of Kali Strata; rents houses, organises excursions and offers yachting services. Recommended.

National Bank of Greece (🖉 22460 72294) On the western side of the harbour; with an ATM. There's a second ATM at the Co-operative Bank across the harbour.

Police (🖉 22460 71111) By the ferry quay.

Port Police (🖉 22460 71205) By the ferry quay.

Post Office By the ferry quay.

Symi Tours (🖉 22460 71307; www.symitours.com) Half a block back from the east side of the harbour. Does excursions, including to Datça in Turkey, provides yachting services and is also the agent for Blue Star and Dodekanisos Seaways.

Around Symi

Pedi is a fishing village and busy mini holiday resort in a fertile valley 2km downhill from Horio. There are some sandy stretches on its narrow beach and private rooms and studios to rent, plus hotels and tavernas. The Pedi Beach Hotel (☏22460 71981; www. blueseahotel.gr; Pedi; d €100; ❋) has simple rooms that open on to the beach. Walking tracks down both sides of Pedi Bay lead to Agia Marina beach in the north and Agios Nikolaos in the south. Both are sandy, gently shelving beaches, good for kids.

Nos is the closest beach to Gialos. It's a 500m walk north of the clock tower at Panormitis Bay. There's a taverna, bar and sun beds. Nimborios is a long, pebbled beach 3km west of Gialos – take the road by the east side of the central square and go straight ahead bearing left after the church and following the stone trail. Here you can stay at Niriides Apartments (☏22460 71784; www.niriideshotel.com; apt €70-80), with excellent views and yards from the beach.

Moni Taxiarhou Mihail Panormiti MONASTERY (Μονή Ταξιαρχού Μιχαήλ Πανορμίτη | Monastery of Archangel Michael of Panormitis; ☉dawnsunset) FREE A winding road leads through scented pine forests, before dipping spectacularly down to Panormitis Bay, and Symi's biggest attraction.

A monastery was first built here in the 5th or 6th century, however, the present building dates from the 18th century. The principal church contains an intricately carved wooden iconostasis, frescoes, and an icon of St Michael that supposedly appeared miraculously where the monastery now stands. St Michael is the patron saint of Symi and protector of sailors. When pilgrims and worshippers ask the saint for a favour, it's tradition to leave an offering; you'll see piles of these, plus prayers in bottles, that have been dropped off boats and found their own way into the harbour.

The large monastery complex comprises a Byzantine museum and folkloric museum, a bakery with excellent bread and a basic restaurant-cafe to the north side. Accommodation is available at the fairly basic guesthouse (☏22460 72414; s/d €20/32), where bookings in July and August are mandatory. The monastery is a magnet for day-trippers, who commonly arrive at around 10.30am on excursion boats; it's a good idea to visit early or after they have left. Some ferries call in to the monastery and there is a minibus from Gialos. A taxi here from Gialos costs €45. Dress modestly to enter the monastery.

TILOS ΤΗΛΟΣ

POP 530

If you're looking for a green adventure on a lost island, Tilos is the place, with mountains turning russet gold in the afternoon, and fishing boats bobbing in Livadia's pretty harbour. Unlike some of its barren neighbours, the island is abloom with a variety of vivid wildflowers and home to a beguiling biodiversity, which draws birdwatchers and wildlife buffs from across the globe. If you're a nature lover, there are miles of trails through meadows, mountains and green valleys to work up a sweat before flopping onto one of many deserted beaches. The azure waters here also play host to monk seals and sea turtles. Check out the blog at http://octopus-in-my-ouzo.blogspot.com.

History

The bones of mastodons (midget elephants that became extinct around 4600 BC) were found in a cave here in 1974. It's believed that over 6 million years ago the island was attached to Asia Minor and when the disconnection occurred the elephants, with no natural predators, no longer had to be so large and shrunk in size. The Harkadio Cave (closed) is signposted from the Livadia–Megalo Horio road; it's brilliantly illuminated at night.

❶ Getting There & Away

The Tilos-owned Sea Star (☏22460 44000) connects the island with Rhodes. Mainland ferries erratically link Tilos to Piraeus, Rhodes and nearby islands in the Dodecanese. Tickets are sold at Tilos Travel in Livadia.

Boat Services from Tilos

DESTINATION	TIME	FARE	FREQUENCY
Kos	3hr	€10	2 weekly
Kos*	1½hr	€22	2 weekly
Nisyros	1hr	€7	6 weekly
Nisyros*	40min	€13	2 weekly
Piraeus	19½hr	€51	2 weekly
Rhodes	2½hr	€13	4 weekly
Rhodes*	1½hr	€24	6 weekly
Symi	2hr	€9	2 weekly

*high-speed services

Tilos

ⓘ Getting Around

A bus plies the island's main road seven times daily, with the first departure from Livadia at 8am and the last return from Megalo Horio at 10.15pm. The timetable is posted at the bus stop in the square in Livadia. Stops include Megalo Horio (€1.50), Eristos Beach (€1.50) and Agios Andonis (€1.50). On Sunday there is a special excursion bus to Moni Agiou Panteleimona (€5 return), leaving Livadia at 11am with one hour at the monastery. There is currently no taxi running.

During summer there are various excursions offered from Livadia to isolated beaches. Look for posters around Livadia for more information.

Livadia   Λιβαδειά

POP 470

Picture-perfect Livadia is low-key, white-washed and inviting, its little square hugged by cafes, an Italianate police station, and tavernas with old boys sipping retsina. Its port is the first thing you'll see of the island and welcomes a cosmo cast of artists, yachties and earthy locals. It's a great base from which to hire a scooter to explore the island, or simply relax on its beach, a 2km arc of red, volcanic sand. You might not believe it, but somnolent Livadia is actually the main pulse of the island.

◉ Sights & Activities

Mikro Horio   ARCHAEOLOGICAL SITE

Not far from Livadia, Tilos' original, ancient settlement was built inland as protection from pirates. The last inhabitants left in the 1960s, mainly due to water scarcity. Wandering around is fascinating – and if you're here as the light fades, faintly eerie – with houses in various states of abandonment.

Walks   WALKING

Tilos is riddled with terraced landscapes and trails once used by farmers to reach distant crops; today, these provide perfect paths for keen walkers. A 3km walk heads north of Livadia to **Lethra Beach**, an undeveloped pebble-and-sand cove with limited shade. The trail starts at the far north side of the port; follow the tarmac behind Ilidi Rock Hotel to the start of the footpath. The path is well maintained and very scenic. Returning via the picturesque **Potami Gorge** brings you to the main island highway.

A second walk is a longer return track to the small abandoned settlement of **Yera** and its accompanying beach at **Despoti Nero**. From Livadia, follow the road south around Agios Stefanos Bay, past the Church of Agios Ioannis on the east side of the bay, and keep walking. Allow half a day for this 6km-long hike.

BIRDWATCHERS' PARADISE

Remote Tilos, thanks to its fertile valleys and low density population, plays host to a number of rare bird species. Keep your eyes peeled for the Bonelli's eagle, long-legged buzzard, Sardinian warbler, Scops owl, peregrine falcon and Mediterranean black shag. In a recent study, 155 species of birds – 46 of them threatened – were identified. Some are residential, others migratory. The useful Tilos Park Association can help you spot and identify them, and also lead half day treks (€15).

Tilos Heritage Tours (✆6974912412) run by Charlie are a useful outfit for finding out more about the island, as are **Tilos Trails** (✆6946054593, 22460 44128; www.tilostrails. com; per person €25). Both are licensed guides. Finally, **Tilos Park Association** (✆22460 70883; www.tilos-park.org.gr; half-day trek to abandoned settlement per person €15; ⊙9am-2.30pm), run by Felicien, are the people to go to for wildlife-infused walks.

🛏 Sleeping

Apollo Studios APARTMENT $
(✆22460 44379; www.apollostudios.gr; d/apt €50/80; ❄☎) Run by a pleasant couple, these are fresh, well-appointed studios with spotless kitchenettes, fridge, modern en suites, private balconies and a great communal roof terrace. The apartments are roomy with tiled floors, flat-screen TVs and sofa bed – try for number 3. A few streets back from the harbour.

★**Ilidi Rock Hotel** HOTEL $$
(✆22460 44293; www.tilosholidays.gr; incl breakfast studio/apt €80/90, ste €110-140; ❄@☎☀) Ilidi looks out to sea with unbroken views from its whitewashed eyrie. You'll have to walk like Sisyphus up a steep hill to reach it (only five minutes!), however their cosy studios merit the effort. Rooms are spotless with four-posters, self catering facilities, and private balconies. Beyond the chic communal lobby there's also a stylish cafe bar.

Livadia Beach Apartments APARTMENT $$
(✆22460 44324, 22460 44397; www.tilosisland. com; apt €140; P❄@☎) On the beach in a courtyard of sugarcube houses, these apartments are bursting with sunshine, gerani-

ums and taste, with tiled bathrooms, kitchenettes, TVs and comfy sofas. There's also a pleasant cafe with sea views through the tamarisk trees.

🍴 Eating

For picnics and self-catering, there are three grocery stores in Livadia with lots of fresh local produce.

★**Omonoia Cafe** TAVERNA $
(✆22460 44287; mains €6-9; ☎☎) If the elderly owners were any friendlier you'd stick them in your bag and smuggle them home. Omonoia's tables are shaded by a mature fig tree and make a perfect spot for breakfast, light lunch or dinner. The menu is replete with grilled meats, seafood and salads. Beware waistlines – their sponge cake is dangerously tasty.

To Mikro Kafé CAFE $
(snacks €5-7, mains €5-12; ⊙6.30pm-late Mon-Fri, 4pm-late Sat & Sun; ❄☎☎🍴) Micro in size, yet there's nothing diminutive about this cosy nook's appeal. With its exposed stone walls and peppering of nautical eclectica, Micro is great for the kids, with porthole windows, board games and little corners to play in, while you nurse a sundowner on the terrace facing the beach. Salads, seafood, pies, mezedhes and sandwiches.

Taverna Trata TAVERNA $$
(✆22460 44364; mains €12; ☎) 🌿 Lantern-lit Trata has a delightful terrace shaded by mature carob and fig trees. Their menu boasts locally sourced octopus, calamari, lobster, veal chop and goat in tomato sauce, all grilled on the fire before you. Follow your nose up from the seafront, 100m past the square.

🍷 Drinking & Nightlife

Cafe Bar Georges BAR
(⊙7am-late) Georges is a stone building on the square where all the old boys gather. Inside it's refreshingly blue with glass-topped tables, walls bedecked in old fisherman pictures and coffee strong enough to wake the dead.

Spitico CAFE
(snacks €2-3) Overlooking the square, this cosy cafe makes great coffee, cheese pies, baklava and local sweets. The sign is in Greek but everybody knows the place.

ℹ Information

All arrivals are at Livadia. The small port is 300m southeast of the village centre. Tilos has no official tourist bureau. The Bank of the Dodecanese has a branch and an ATM in Livadia. The post office is on the central square.

Clinic (☎22460 44171; ⊙noon-5pm) Behind the church.

Police (☎22460 44222) In the white Italianate building at the quay.

Port Police (☎22460 44350) On the harbour.

Remetzo (internet per hr €1) Next to the ferry dock. Play pool or nibble at the deli while waiting for one of two computers.

Tilos Travel (☎22460 44360; www.tilos-travel.co.uk; ⊙9am-10pm) Also known as Stefanakis Travel, this helpful agency is at the port. Credit card withdrawals and currency exchange are available, as well as book exchange and car (€32) and mountain-bike hire.

ℹ Getting There & Away

Drive Rent A Car (☎22460 44173) Just up from Tilos Park Association. Reliable scooters (€20 per day) and cars (€40 per day).

Sea Star (☎22460 44000; sea-star@otenet.gr; ⊙9am-4.30pm) Sells tickets for the *Sea Star* catamaran.

Megalo Horio
Μεγάλο Χωριό

POP 50

Megalo Horio, the island's tiny capital, hugs the hillside with narrow streets teeming with battle-scarred cats and sun-blasted cubic houses. The little **museum** (⊙8.30am-2.30pm, summer only) **FREE** on the main street has mastodon bones. From Megalo Horio you can also visit the **Knight's Castle**, a taxing one-hour uphill walk from the north end of the village. On the way you'll pass the **ancient settlement** of Tilos, which once overlooked Megalo Horio.

Close to the supermarket, **Miliou Studios** (☎6932086094, 22460 44204; d €33-45; ❄) has comfortable rooms with self-catering facilities, homely furniture and balconies boasting amazing sea views. Dine at the **Kastro Cafe** (mains €5-6.50) with beautiful bay views. On the menu are organic goat, locally raised pork, calamari and whitebait. Among whitewashed houses you'll find **Palio Meraki Kafenion** (Megalo Horio; ⊙breakfast & lunch), a stone-floored, turquoise and white affair by the church (above the museum). Come here for a simple breakfast.

Megalo Horio's bus station is at the bottom of town.

Around Megalo Horio

Just before Megalo Horio, a turn-off to the left leads 2.5km to pebbly **Eristos Beach**, fringed by tamarisk trees that cast shadows over its sapphire-hued waters. Pretty deserted but for the odd local line-fishing, you may have it to yourself off-season.

Just off the beach is **Eristos Beach Hotel** (☎22460 44025; www.eristosbeachhotel.gr; d/ste €50/80; ℗❄❖❄), situated in lush gardens crowded with hibiscus, orchids and lemon trees. Fresh rooms with tiled floors look out from balconies to the sea beyond. Studios have kitchenettes and sleep four. There is also an on-site restaurant, a bar and lovely adult and kid's pool.

En Plo (mains €7) is a traditional taverna a few hundred metres back from Eristos Beach. The menu spans delicious squid *saganaki* to pasta dishes and salads. The goat in tomato sauce is lovely washed down with a glass of retsina. They also have rooms to rent.

A signposted turn-off leads to the quiet settlement of **Agios Antonios**. A further 3km west is the undeveloped, pretty **Plaka Beach**. It's situated in a cove where the water is slightly warmer and has natural shade in the afternoon. Once you wade in a little, the rock shelves are good for snorkelling.

NISYROS ΝΙΣΥΡΟΣ

POP 950

Intimate and photogenic, Nisyros is eclipsed by nearby Kos – good news for the independent traveller. It's most famous for the otherworldly 'Stefanos' caldera (volcano crater), which gives rise to the island's fertility; drawing botanists and gardeners from around the world to see its unique flora. Today, it sits like an abandoned Star Trek set.

Nisyros' main town of Mandraki is a languid maze of whitewashed alleys radiating from the aquamarine harbour, vividly strung with drying octopus. The black and volcanic beaches are nothing spectacular; this is more a place for exploring dazzling hilltop villages like Nikea and Emborios, hiking a little and sampling the local produce.

Keep an eye out for *koukouzina,* a drink produced from grapes and figs.

Nisyros

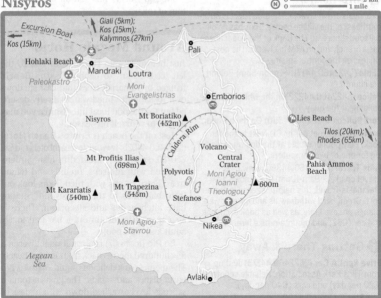

Getting There & Away

BOAT

Nisyros is linked by regular ferries to Rhodes, Kos and Piraeus. The *Dodekanisos Pride* catamaran calls in with connections to neighbouring Dodecanese islands. The small local ferry *Agios Konstantinos* links Mandraki with Kardamena on Kos (€8, two hours, daily), while the larger *Panagia Spyliani* links Nisyros with Kos Town (€8, daily). Check with the harbour office or Enetikon Travel for up-to-date schedules.

Boat Services from Nisyros

DESTINATION	TIME	FARE	FREQUENCY
Kalymnos	2½hr	€10	2 weekly
Kos	1¼hr	€10	2 weekly
Kos*	45min	€15	2 weekly
Piraeus	18hr	€51	2 weekly
Rhodes	4½hr	€14	2 weekly
Rhodes*	2¾hr	€28	2 weekly

*high-speed services

Getting Around

BOAT

In July and August there are excursion boats (return €8) to the pumice-stone islet of Giali, where there's a relaxing, sandy beach.

BUS

In summer, bus companies run up to 10 excursion buses daily between 9.30am and 3pm (€8 return) that give you about 40 minutes at the volcano. In addition, three daily buses travel to Nikea (free) via Pali. The bus stop is located at Mandraki's port.

CAR, MOTORCYCLE & TAXI

Manos Rentals (☑ 22420 31029) on the quay is the most handy for motorbikes and cars (motorbikes €10 to €20, cars €20 per day). For cars, also try **Diakomihalis** (☑ 6977735229, 22420 31459) in town. For a cab call **Irini** (☑ 22420 31474). A taxi from Mandraki to the volcano costs €20 return, to Nikea €11 and to Pali €10.

Mandraki   Μανδράκι

POP 660

Lapped by gentle waters, this pretty, white-washed port spreads itself elegantly across the hillside climbing up to the ruins of the impressive *kastro*. Its winding backstreets dotted with black-garbed pensioners flicking worry beads, fruit spilling colourfully from grocers' shop fronts and a host of seafood joints and aromatic tavernas will leave you spellbound. By night the place drips with charm, the church beneath the castle lighting up like a candle.

⊙ Sights

Towering over Mandraki is the 14th-century cliff-top **Moni Panagias Spilianis** (Virgin of the Cave; admission by donation; ⊙10.30am-3pm). The views from the top are worth the climb. Turn right at the end of the main street to reach the signposted stairs up to the monastery. On the way up, you'll pass the **Cultural Museum** (admission €3; ⊙10am-3pm May-Sep), which has traditional objects like a bed, grinding tools and clothing.

Near the seafront and beneath the original cave of the monastery lies the **Church Museum** (⊙10am-3pm May-Sep) FREE, with glittering ecclesiastic objects from churches around the island. Altars, cups, fonts and objects dating back as far as the 1st century AD are crammed in here.

In town, the brand-new **Archaeological Museum** (admission €3; ⊙10am-3pm May-Sep) has an interesting collection of Hellenistic and Roman pottery and sculpture, as well as a short film about the island's history.

Above Mandraki, **Paleokastro** (Old Kastro), the impressive Mycenaean-era acropolis, has restored 4th-century Cyclopean walls built from massive blocks of volcanic rock that you can perch atop for breathtaking views. There are good explanatory notes in English throughout the site. Follow the route signposted '*kastro*', heading southwest from the monastery steps. You can drive here too.

Hohlaki is a black-stone beach on the western side of Moni Panagias Spilianis, and is reached by a paved footpath around the headland. Don't attempt this walk in bad weather. The small sandy **Mandraki beach**, halfway between the port and the village centre, is popular for swimming but sometimes covered in seaweed.

🛏 Sleeping

★ Hotel Porfyris   HOTEL $
(☎22420 31376; diethnes@otenet.gr; r incl breakfast €50-60; ❋ 🛜 ☀) This elegant hillside dame looks towards Kos, the fragrance of a nearby citrus grove wafting through her marble lobby, sumptuous lounge and sparkling swimming pool. Expect simple, cosy rooms with verandah, en suite, comfy beds and decent furniture. Near Plateia Ilikiomenis, five minutes' walk from the harbour.

Three Brothers Hotel   APARTMENT $
(☎22420 31344; iiibrothers@kos.forthnet.gr; d/studio €45/70; ❋ 🛜) Cosy, vanilla-coloured Three Brothers is superfresh, port-facing and has studios and rooms with marble floors, kitchenettes, TV, fridges, stylish burgundy drapes and mocha-hued bedspreads. The sea views from the verandahs are hypnotic. There's also a decent **cafe**. Open year-round.

Hotel Romantzo   PENSION $
(☎22420 31340; r incl breakfast €45; ❋ 🛜) Handy for early ferry starts, Romantzo is just up from the jetty, and has sunny, spotless rooms with marble floors and bijou en suites, plus a great communal sun trap of a terrace. Fridges, flat-screen TVs, wi-fi and breakfast also make Nisyros' oldest hotel a good-value option.

🍴 Eating

The backstreets and waterfront are strung with cafes and tavernas. Ask for the island speciality, *pitties* (chickpea and onion patties), and wash them down with a refreshing *soumada*, a nonalcoholic local beverage made from almond extract.

★ Cleanthis Taverna   SEAFOOD $
(mains €8-12; 🛜) Look for the octopus drying in the sun like an art installation, then follow your nose to this lovely taverna. Apart from the live lobster gazing nostalgically back at the nearby sea, there's an ocean of choice from shrimp souvlakia to fried cuttlefish, cod and octopus.

The calamari is caught locally and so perfectly chewy your jaw will ache with mastication.

Restaurant Irini   CAFE $
(Plateia Ilikiomenis; mains €7; ❋ 🛜 🅿 🚻) Homely Irini sits in a pebble mosaic square beneath the shade of a carob tree, and with its earthy menu of Greek salads, *saganaki,* pizza, *mousakas,* squid and octopus, it's easy to see why it's so popular. The salads are generous and fresh, but it was the souvlakia that stole our hearts.

Taverna Panorama   TAVERNA $
(grills €7; 🅿) Heading towards Hotel Porfyris, this hilltop taverna pipes out delicious aromas of homemade meatballs, dolmadhes, pasta, squid and fresh fish, as well as *mousakas,* stuffed tomatoes and *seftelies* (Cypriot-style herb-laced sausages). Look out for the blue-checked tables outside.

Bakery Pali   BAKERY $
(snacks €1-3) A block up from the waterfront, this bakery alchemises traditional Nisirian

bread and cakes, as well as croissants, cheese pies, Thessaloniki buns, sweet bread and doughnuts. Look for the biscuit-coloured door.

Drinking & Nightlife

Plateia Ilikiomenis is lined with cafes and bars, as is the waterfront.

Enallax Music Bar BAR
(seafront, Mandraki; ☺7pm-late; 🛜) This nocturnal haunt glows with Moorish lanterns. Sit outside on the sea-facing terrace, or prop up the bar peppered with vintage photography. Great world music, coffee, cocktails and *masticha* (made from tree sap).

Shopping

Yadez JEWELLERY
(waterfront, Mandraki) Follow your magpie inclinations to this delightful shop with a sign of a mermaid outside; and lose yourself in its Kahloesque nook of homemade jewellery, icons and objets d'art.

Information

The port is 500m northeast of the centre of Mandraki. Take the road right from the port and you will hit the town centre. A couple of blocks up, you'll come to a Y-junction. Head left to reach the tree-shaded Plateia Ilikiomenis, Mandraki's focal point. Head right along the main drag for signs for the monastery and castle.

The Co-operative Bank of the Dodecanese has an ATM at the harbour and a branch in Mandraki. There's also an ATM at the post office on the road up to the Porfyris Hotel.

The website www.nisyros.co.uk is excellent; it details beaches, things to do, accommodation and eating in Nisyros. Or try www.nisyros.gr for info on sights, history and the environment.

Diakomihalis (☑22420 31015; diakomihalis@kos.forthnet.gr; Mandraki) Sells ferry tickets and hires cars.

Enetikon Travel (☑22420 31180; agiosnis@otenet.gr) Run by the ever helpful Michelle, Enetikon dispenses free advice, sells tickets and owns the small tourist boat that goes to Kos every morning (€8). It also runs bus trips to the crater (€8, leaves 10.30am). A hundred metres from the quay towards Mandraki.

Police (☑22420 31201) Opposite the quay.

Port Police (☑22420 31222) Opposite the quay.

Post Office Opposite the quay.

Proveza Internet Cafe (per 30min €1.40) Catch up on your email over a frappé by the sea in this chillsome cafe. It makes great snacks and coffee and has internet and wi-fi.

Around Nisyros

The Volcano Το Ηφαίστειο

Nisyros sits on a volcanic fault line. The island originally culminated in a mountain of 850m, but the centre collapsed 30,000 to 40,000 years ago after three violent eruptions. Their legacy are the white-and-orange pumice stones that can still be seen on the northern, eastern and southern flanks of the island, and the large lava flow that covers the whole southwest, around Nikea village.

The islanders call the volcano Polyvotis after the eponymous Titan who was imprisoned under the rock of Nisyros. Legend has it that during the battle between the gods and Titans, Poseidon ripped a chunk off Kos and used it to trap the giant in the bowels of the earth; today's volcano is his angered voice.

Descending into the **caldera** (admission €2.50; ☺9am-8pm) is other-worldly. Cows graze near the craters amid sci-fi-set rocks. A path descends into the largest of the five craters, **Stefanos**, where you can examine the multicoloured 100°C fumaroles, listen to their hissing and smell the sulphurous vapours. The surface is soft and hot, making sturdy footwear essential. Don't stray too far out as the ground is unstable and can collapse. Another unsignposted but more obvious track leads to **Polyvotis**, which is smaller and wilder looking but doesn't allow access to the caldera itself. The fumaroles are around the edge here so be very careful.

You can reach the volcano by bus, car or along a 3km-long trail from Nikea. Get there before 11am and you may have the place to yourself.

Emborios & Nikea
Εμπορειός & Νίκαια

Nikea, like some geometrical sugarcube miracle, clings to the rim of the caldera with wide-screen views of the depression below. Emborio, just a few kilometres away, is equally pretty with whitewashed streets punctuated by crimson bougainvillea and yawning cats. It too sits on the caldera's edge.

Ampia Taverna (☑22420 31377; Emborios; mains €6-12; 🛜☑), behind the church, has tasteful burgundy-and-mustard walls and a chillout area to work in. Its menu excels with souvlakia, octopus, meatballs and stuffed peppers, and wood-fired goat; eat upstairs for Olympian drama. Just opposite, overlooking the caldera, is the heavily aromatic **Balcony Restaurant** (Emborios, Nisyros; mains €9; ⊘ 9am-10pm), firing up mouth-watering chops and steaks.

Nikea has dazzling white houses with vibrant gardens and a lovely mosaic-tiled central square. The bus terminates on Plateia Nikolaou Hartofyli from where Nikea's main street links the two squares. At the edge of town is the **Volcanological Museum** (admission €2; ⊘ 11am-3pm May-Sep) detailing the history of the volcano and its effects on the island. In the village's main square, divinely pretty with its pebble mosaic, **Kafenion Forta** (mains €7.50) has tables and chairs outside to enjoy the mountain view over a cool drink, toastie, juice or beer.

The steep path down to the volcano begins from Plateia Nikolaou Hartofyli. It takes about 40 minutes to walk it one way. Near the beginning you can detour to the signposted **Moni Agiou Ioanni Theologou**, where there is an annual feast on 25 and 26 September.

Pali   Πάλοι

This tiny, wind-buffeted village sits by the sea and has a few sun-beaten buildings following the line of the marina. You can eat at a few sleepy tavernas, rent a scooter and explore the nearby beach of **Lies**, Nisyros' most usable beach, about 5.5km around the coast. You can also walk an extra kilometre from the end of the road along an occasionally precarious coastal track to **Pahia Ammos**, a broad expanse of gravelly volcanic sand. Bring your own shade.

In Pali, **Mammis' Apartments** (☑ 22420 31824, 22420 31453; www.mammis.com; d €70; ⊘ year-round; ❋ ☏) is set in gardens rioting with flowers, and has imaginatively decorated rooms with kitchenettes and private balconies with sea views; as well as a separate room with a sofa bed for kids. **The Captain's House** (mains €8; ⊘ 8am-midnight), attracting yachties and wizened fishermen alike, is festooned with yellow nets and so close to the harbour you can taste the salt. Its menu is packed to the gills with octopus, calamari, baby shark and cuttlefish.

KOS   ΚΩΣ

POP 19,872

Soaked in history and ruins, after a few hours wandering Kos town's fortress and the Asklepion (Hippocrates' ancient sanatorium), you become almost blasé at sidestepping millenia-old Corinthian columns gathering weeds at the roadside. Indeed the past and present converge magically on this island (the second-largest in the Dodecanese) of varied treasures: from vernal valleys and peacock-blue coves, to sylvan hillsides and rocky stretches – one moment you find yourself in a rustic mountain taverna the next in a busy cosmopolitan cafe. There really is something for everyone here.

History

So many people lived in fertile Kos by Mycenaean times that it was rich enough to send 30 ships to the Trojan War. In 477 BC, after suffering an earthquake and subjugation to the Persians, it joined the Delian League and again flourished.

Hippocrates (460–377 BC), the Ancient Greek physician known as the founder of medicine, was born and lived on the island. After his death, the Sanctuary of Asclepius and a medical school were built, which perpetuated his teachings and made Kos famous throughout the Greek world.

Ptolemy II of Egypt was born on Kos, thus securing it the protection of Egypt, under which it became a prosperous trading centre. In 130 BC Kos fell under Roman domination and in the 1st century AD it was administered by Rhodes, with which it has since shared the same ups and downs of fortune, including the influential tourist trade of the present day.

ⓘ Getting There & Away

AIR

Olympic Air has two daily flights to Athens (€84, 55 minutes) and three weekly to Rhodes (€61, 20 minutes), Leros (€61, 15 minutes) and Astypalea (€68, one hour). Buy tickets from **Kos Travel** (☑ 22420 22359; kostravel@otenet.gr; Akti Koundourioti, Kos Town) on the harbour.

BOAT

Kos has services to Piraeus and all islands in the Dodecanese, the Cyclades, Samos and Thessaloniki, run by three ferry companies: **Blue Star Ferries** (☑ 22420 28914), **Anek Lines** (☑ 22420 28545) and **ANE Kalymnou**

Kos & Pserimos

N 0 — 10 km
0 — 5 miles

Leros (15km);
Lipsi (35km);
Petmos (50km)

TURKEY

Bodrum
(Turkey)
(5km)

Kalymnos

Pothia

Pserimos

Platy

Pserimos

Cape
Ammoudia

Lambi

Kos Town

Psalidi

Cape
Louros

Leros (15km);
Patmos (45km)

Tingaki

Platanos

Cape
Fokas

Aegean Sea

Marmari

Zipari

Asklipieion

Ferry

Mastihari
Beach

Mastihari

Pyli

Lagoudi

Agios
Dimitrios

Agios Fokas

Kos

Pyli
Castle

Zia

Asfendiou

Therma
Loutra

Antimahia

Antimahia
Castle

Mt Díkeos
(843m)

Limnionas
Beach

Plaka
Forest

Kardamena

Cape
Drepano

Kefalos

2

4 5 6 7

3

8

Cape Agios
Nikolaos

Agios
Theologos
Beach

1

Kefalos
Bay

9

1	Kamari Beach
2	Agios Stefanos Beach
3	Camel Beach
4	Paradise Beach
5	Banana Beach
6	Markos Beach
7	Sunny Beach
8	Magic Beach
9	Exotic Beach

Astypalea

Moni Agiou
Ioanni

Moni Agiou
Theologou

Excursion Boat

Giali

Excursion Boat

Nisyros (5km)

Nisyros
(5km)

Nisyros
(5km)

Rhodes
(65km)

(☎ 22420 29900). Catamarans are run by Dodekanisos Seaways at the inter-island ferry quay. Local passenger and car ferries run to Pothia on Kalymnos from Mastihari. For tickets, visit **Fanos Travel & Shipping** (☎ 22420 20035; www.kostravel.gr; 11 Akti Kountourioti, Kos Town) on the harbour. It also runs a hydrofoil to Bodrum (return €25), Nisyros (return €25), Patmos (return €40), Rhodes (return €50) and Symi (return €40).

In summer, daily excursion boats leave at 8.30am from Kos Town to Bodrum in Turkey (return €25, one hour), and return at 4pm.

Getting Around

TO/FROM THE AIRPORT

The **airport** (☎ 22420 51229) is 24km southwest of Kos Town. Kefalos-bound buses stop at the big roundabout near the airport entrance. An airport bus leaves from the town's bus station (€3.20) several times per day. A taxi from the airport to Kos Town costs around €30.

BOAT

From Kos Town, lining the southern arm of Akti Koundourioti, there are half a dozen boats that make excursions around Kos and to other islands. Return fares to Kalymnos, Pserimos and Platy are €40, including lunch. The boats vary in age and appeal but keep an eye out for the bonniest babe in the bay, **Eva** (☎ 694369300; Akti Koundourioti, Kos Town) a 110-year-old caïque with a finely crafted crow's nest and gunwhales. There's also a daily excursion boat from Mastihari to Kalymnos (€6).

BUS

Bus station (☎ 22420 22292; Kleopatras 7, Kos Town) Buses regularly serve all parts of the island, as well as the all-important beaches on the south side of Kos. A bus to the beaches will cost around €3 to €3.20.

CAR, MOTORCYCLE & BICYCLE

There are numerous car, motorcycle and mopedhire outlets; always ask at your hotel as many have special deals with hire companies. Cycling is very popular in Kos and you'll be tripping over bicycles for hire; prices range from €5 per day for a boneshaker to €15 for a half-decent mountain bike. In Kos Town try **George's Bikes** (☑ 22420 24157; Spetson 48; cycle/scooter per day €4/15) for decent bikes at reasonable prices.

Kos Town   Κως
POP 14,750

Scattered with ruins from the Hellenistic, Roman and Byzantine periods, this handsome, stylish town is a mix of the original old town – what remains of it after the 1933 earthquake, with its gauntlet of boutiques and close-knit tavernas – and modern streets and parks bursting with palms and bougainvillea. The town retains its dignity with a sedate pace and friendly locals. The harbour is especially pretty with the Castle of the Knights picturesquely perched at its centre, and like some coastal Amsterdam, everybody here gets about on bikes (there are bike lanes at every turn).

◉ Sights & Activities

Archaeological Museum   MUSEUM
(Plateia Eleftherias; admission €3; ⊙ 8am-2.30pm Tue-Sun) The archaeological museum is based in an old Italianate building and hosts local sculptures from the Hellenistic to late Roman eras. The most renowned statue is that of Hippocrates; there's also a 3rd-century-AD mosaic in the vestibule that's worth seeing.

Castle of the Knights   CASTLE
(☑ 22420 27927; admission €3; ⊙ 8am-2.30pm Tue-Sun) You can now reach the once impregnable Castle of the Knights by crossing a bridge over Finikon from Plateia Platanou. The castle, which had massive outer walls and an inner keep, was built in the 14th century and separated from the town by a moat (now Finikon). Damaged by an earthquake in 1495 and restored in the 16th century, it was the knights' most stalwart defence against the encroaching Ottomans.

Archaeological Sites   ARCHAEOLOGICAL SITE
The **ancient agora** is an open site south of the castle. A massive 3rd-century-BC stoa, with some reconstructed columns, stands on its western side. On the north side are the ruins of a **Shrine of Aphrodite**, **Temple of Hercules** and a 5th-century **Christian basilica**.

North of the agora is the lovely cobblestone Plateia Platanou, where you can sit in a cafe while paying respects to the once-magnificent **Hippocrates Plane Tree** (Plateia Platanou), under which Hippocrates is said to have taught his pupils. Beneath it is an old sarcophagus converted by the Turks into a fountain. Opposite the tree is the boarded-up 18th-century **Mosque of Gazi Hassan Pasha**.

On the other side of town is the **western excavation site**. Two wooden shelters at the back of the site protect the 3rd-century **mosaics of the House of Europa**. The best-preserved mosaic depicts Europa's

DODECANESE KOS TOWN

BOAT SERVICES FROM KOS

DESTINATION	TIME	FARE	FREQUENCY
Leros	3hr	€14	3 weekly
Leros*	1hr 40min	€22	1 daily
Kalymnos	1hr	€8	3 daily
Kalymnos*	30min	€15	1 daily
Nisyros	1hr 20min	€9	2 weekly
Nisyros*	45min	€16	1 daily
Patmos	4hr	€19	3 weekly
Patmos*	2½hr	€29	6 weekly
Piraeus	10hr	€51	1 daily
Rhodes	3hr	€24	1 daily
Rhodes*	2½hr	€30	1 daily
Samos	5½hr	€40	1 daily
Symi*	1½hr	€22	1 daily

*high-speed services

Kos Town

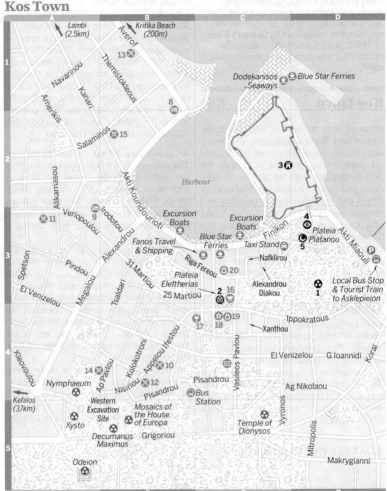

Lambi (2.5km)

Kritika Beach (200m)

Averof

Themistokleous

Navarinou

Kanari

Amerikis

Salaminos

Alikarnasou

Veriopoulou

Irodotou

Akti Koundourioti

Alexandrou

Spetson

Pindou

Megalou

31 Martiou

Tsaldari

El Venizelou

Kleovoullou

Nymphaeum

Ap Pavlou

Kolokotroni

Nisiriou

Appelou Ifestou

Pisandrou

Riga Fereou

25 Martiou

Dodekanisos Seaways

Blue Star Ferries

Harbour

Excursion Boats

Excursion Boats

Blue Star Ferries

Finikon

Taxi Stand

Fanos Travel & Shipping

Nafkliriou

Plateia Eleftherias

Alexandrou Diakou

Plateia Platanou

Akti Miaouli

Local Bus Stop & Tourist Train to Asklepieion

Ippokratous

Xanthou

Vasileos Pavlou

El Venizelou

G Ioannidi

Korai

Pisandrou

Bus Station

Ag Nikolaou

Vyronos

Mitropolis

Kefalos (37km)

Western Excavation Site

Xysto

Decumanus Maximus

Mosaics of the House of Europa

Grigoriou

Temple of Dionysos

Makrygianni

Odeion

abduction by Zeus in the guise of a bull. In front of here is an exposed section of the **Decumanus Maximus** (the Roman city's main thoroughfare), which runs parallel to the modern road then turns right towards the **nymphaeum**, which consisted of once-lavish latrines, and the **xysto**, a large Hellenistic gymnasium with restored columns. A short distance to the east, the **Temple of Dionysos** is overgrown with oleander but has a few evocative ruins.

On the opposite side of Grigoriou is the impressive 2nd-century **odeion**. It was initially a venue for the senate and musical competitions and was restored during the Italian occupation when it was discovered, filled with sculptures (many now in the Archaeological Museum).

Beaches   BEACH

On the east side of town, **Kos Town Beach** has a thin strip of sand and deep water for swimming. It tends to be dominated by the restaurants and hotels along this stretch. West of town, **Kritika Beach** is a long sandy stretch that's polka-dotted with umbrellas in the summer. It gets crowded but is within easy walking distance from the town centre.

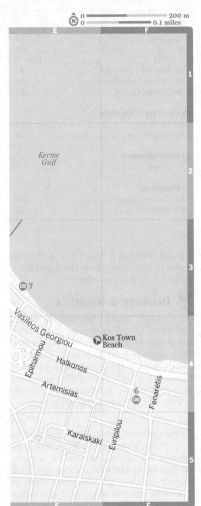

er hotels in Kos but none with the special soul of this fine, family-run establishment.

Hotel Sonia   HOTEL $$
(☑ 22420 28798; www.hotelsonia.gr; Irodotou 9; s/d/tr €45/60/75; ✳ @ 🛜) On a peaceful street, this pension has sparkling rooms with par- quet floors, flat-screen TVs, fridges, chic bathrooms and an extra bed if you need it. There's a relaxing communal verandah with wrought-iron chairs, spacious private balco- nies, and a decent library. Room 4 has the best sea view.

Kosta Palace   HOTEL $$
(☑ 22420 22855; www.kosta-palace.com; cnr Akti Kountourioti & Averof; s/d/apt €65/85/110; ⊙ year-round; ✳ @ 🛜 ▣) This swanky port- side edifice facing the Castle of St John has 160 rooms with kitchenette, cable TV and private balcony. Apartments have separate rooms. There's also a kids' and adult's pool and snack bar on the roof. Clean and func- tional but lacks character.

Kos Aktis Hotel   HOTEL $$$
(☑ 22420 47200; www.kosaktis.gr; Vasileos Geor- giou 7; s/d from €148/188; ✳ @ 🛜 ▣) Rectan- gular and glass-accented, the soundtrack to this chic option is the lap of the waves. By night from its plush bedrooms – with granite floors and bathrooms too perfect to insult with your presence – you can see Bod- rum lit up like a chandelier. Rooms also have balconies and flat-screen TV, and beyond there's a gym and inviting pool.

✗ Eating

★ Elia   MEDITERRANEAN $
(Appelou Ifestou 27; mains €6.50; ✳ 🛜 🍷 🍴) 🌿 This side-street restaurant exudes authentic- ity, with stone walls, wood floors and walls frescoed with Greek gods (see how many you can name with your kids). The menu features seasonal vegetables, myriad Greek wines, lamb in tomato with cinnamon, beef with cheese, stuffed meatball with feta, rus- tic sausage and drunken pork (in wine).

The aftertaste is so sweet you won't want to brush your teeth.

Zorba's   GREEK $
(Plateia Diagora; mains €8; ⊙ lunch & dinner; ✳ 🛜 🍷) Attractively Aegean with blue and white trim, Zorba's serves up fresh salads, souvlakia, steaks, *gyros, kleftiko, stifadho* and stewed beef; as well as plenty of veggie options like fried zucchini. Service is friend- ly and the owner benign.

🛏 Sleeping

★ Hotel Afendoulis   HOTEL $
(☑ 22420 25321; www.afendoulishotel.com; Evripi- lou 1; s/d €30/50; ⊙ Mar-Nov; ✳ @ 🛜) Peaceful Afendoulis has unfailingly friendly staff and sparkling rooms with adobe white walls, small balconies, flat-screen TV, hairdryer, and spotless en suite. Downstairs there's an open breafast room and flowery terrace with wrought iron tables and chairs. Breakfast is a feast of homemade jams and marmalades.

Like stepping into the pages of a Durrell novel, once you've visited you'll be a returning character. There may be more modern, plush-

Kos Town

H2O
CAFE $

(☑ 22420 47200; Vasileos Georgiou 7; mains €15-20, snacks €9-17; ❋🏠🍴) The city's glitziest salt-lick is patronised by urbanites and fashionistas and makes for a great stop for a healthy lunch or dinner, out on the decked terrace facing Bodrum. Choose from bruschetta, grilled veg, battered shrimp, chicken risotto, or simply plump for a sundowner mojito (€7.50).

Bittersweet
CREPERIE $

(Apellou Ifestou; mains €6; ⊙ 9am-1pm; ❋🏠) Take a break from the jewellery gauntlet of Apellou Ifestou and step into this grotto-like oasis, taking a crepe, ice cream or cocktail. The interior features shadowy nooks, lanterns festooned from the ceiling and lounge music as sugary as your dessert.

Nick the Fisherman
SEAFOOD $$

(Averof 21; mains €10-14) This side-street seafood taverna is bedecked with nets and dangerous-looking fish on the walls. Try their sardines, red snapper, striped mullet and grouper. Live mussels are kept in an aquarium.

Petrino Meze Restaurant
MEZEDHES $$

(Plateia Theologou; mains €15-20; ⊙ lunch & dinner; ❋🏠) Peaceful and balmy, this graceful restaurant has a leafy terrace shaded by bougainvillea. An upscale menu features octopus, lobster, *saganaki*, red snapper, and carnivore's delight of steak, rack of lamb and various souvlakia. Overlooking the ancient *agora* (marketplace).

If you're self-catering, head to the well-stocked **Co-op** (Verriopoulou). **Pikoilas Bakery** (cnr Salaminos & Kanari) has a dizzying choice of doughnuts, pies, cinnamon buns, baklava and chocolate cake.

🍸 Drinking & Nightlife

On weekends locals congregate at Plateia Eleftherias (Freedom Sq) to drink coffee and gossip in the many cafes. Kos' nightlife geared for partying tourists is centred a block south of the harbour, along Diakou. There's also a plethora of similar bars along the waterfront on Kritika Beach. If you're looking for clubs, just follow the crowds.

Aenaos
CAFE

(Plateia Eleftherias; sweets €3.50; 🏠) Next to an exquisite mosque, this lovely cafe with wrought-iron chairs and shade is a pleasant stop for an iced coffee or espresso. Treat yourself to their delectable spectrum of chocoloate (try the forest fruit and strawberry €3.50). They also serve juices, cake and brownies.

Global Cafe
BAR

(Ioannidi; ⊙ 8.30am-late; 🏠) Chiming with the sound of youths playing backgammon, this courtyard bar is fresh, with stone walls, canvas sail canopies, shabby chic furniture and an easy soundtrack. Read, work, drink a beer, fruit juice or cocktail, and then grab a sandwich.

☆ Entertainment

Orfeas
CINEMA

(www.cine-orfeas.gr; Plateia Eleftherias; tickets adult/child €7/5; 🎬) If you're suffering movie withdrawal, this cinema shows English-speaking blockbusters with Greek subtitles along with some local flicks. There are three shows per day, at 5pm, 7.30pm and 10pm, the earliest of which is usually a kids' film. In high summer their open-air cinema is open.

 Shopping

For high-street–style shops head to the eastern end of Ioannidi and the pedestrian streets south of Ippokratous. **Dimoiki Dorag** (Plateia Eleftherias) is a bijou bazaar where you can buy anything from herbs, fresh cherries, olive oil and indigenous honey to mythological curios and Kalymnian sponges.

News Stand   BOOKS
(☑ 22420 30110; Riga Fereou 2) Sells foreign-language newspapers and publications, as well as guides to Kos.

 Information

EMERGENCY
Police (☑ 22420 22222; Eparhio Bldg, Akti Koundourioti) Shares the Municipality Building with the tourist police.
Port Police (cnr Akti Koundourioti & Megalou Alexandrou)
Tourist Police (☑ 22420 22444)

INTERNET ACCESS
Del Mare (Megalou Alexandrou 4; per hr €2.50; ⊙8.30am-midnight) This newly refurbished cafe has wood floors and free wi-fi. Use their complimentary tablet to hook up to your emails.
e-global (cnr Artemisias & Korai; per hr €2; ⊙24hr)

INTERNET RESOURCES
www.travel-to-kos.com Comprehensive guide to most of Kos' attractions.
www.kos.gr Official site of tourism of the Municipality of Kos.

MEDICAL SERVICES
Hospital (☑ 22420 22300; Ippokratous 32)

MONEY
Alpha Bank (El Venizelou) Has a 24-hour ATM.
National Bank of Greece (Riga Fereou) Has an ATM.

POST
Post Office (Vasileos Pavlou)

TRAVEL AGENCIES
Fanos Travel & Shipping (☑ 22420 20035; www.kostravel.gr; 11 Akti Koundourioti) Runs the hydrofoil service to Bodrum, sells boat tickets, rents cars, and offers yachting services.

 Getting Around

BUS
Urban buses depart from Akti Miaouli and have two ticket prices: Zone A (€1.10) and Zone B (€1.50). Tickets from vending machines are slightly cheaper than those bought on board. You'll find one in front of the Blue Star Ferries office on the harbour. For schedules, check the local bus office.

TAXI
Taxis congregate at a stand on the south side of the port.

TOURIST TRAIN
In summer, a good way to get your bearings is to hop on the city's Tourist Train city tour (€5, 20 minutes), which runs from 10am to 2pm and 6pm to 10pm, starting from the bus station on Akti Kountouriotou. You can also take a train to the Asklipieion and back (€5), departing on the hour from 10am to 5pm Tuesday to Sunday, from the bus stop on Akti Miaouli.

Around Kos

The nearest decent beach to Kos Town is the crowded **Lambi Beach**, 4km to the northwest. Further round the coast is a long, pale-sand stretch of beach, divided into **Tingaki**, 10km from Kos Town, and **Marmari Beach**, 14km west and slightly less crowded. Windsurfing is popular at all three beaches. In summer there are boats from Marmari to the island of Pserimos.

Vasileos Georgiou in Kos Town leads to the three busy beaches of **Psalidi**, 3km from Kos Town, **Agios Fokas** (8km) and **Therma Loutra** (12km). The latter has hot mineral springs that warm the sea.

Asklipieion   Ασκληπιείον

The island's most important ancient site is the **Asklipieion** (☑ 22420 28763; adult/student €4/3; ⊙8am-7.30pm Tue-Sun), built on a pine-covered hill 3km southwest of Kos Town, with lovely views of the town and Turkey. The Asklipieion consisted of a religious sanctuary devoted to Asclepius (the god of healing), a healing centre and a school of medicine, where training followed the teachings of Hippocrates, the daddy of modern medicine. Until AD 554, when an earthquake destroyed the sanatorium, people came from far and wide for treatment.

The ruins occupy three levels. The **propylaea** (approach to the main gate), Roman-era public **baths** and remains of guest rooms are on the first level. On the 2nd level is a 4th-century-BC **altar of Kyparissios Apollo**. West of this is the **first Temple of Asclepius**, built in the 4th century BC. To the east is the 1st-century-BC **Temple to Apollo**. On the 3rd level are the remains of the once magnificent 2nd-century-BC **Temple of Asclepius**.

The hourly bus 3 and the Kos Town Tourist Train go to the site. It's also a pleasant cycle or walk.

Mastihari   Μαστιχάρι

This quiet town might not be architecturally photogenic but its powder-fine beach dotted with tamarisk trees, clutch of studio accommodation and tasty waterfront eateries make it a nice place to reside or stop for lunch. In the summer months there are excursion boats that run to Pserimos. Mastihari is also an arrival/departure point for ferries to Pothia on Kalymnos.

A block back from the seafront, **Athina Studios** (☑22420 59030; www.athinas-studios.gr; d/tr €30/60) has superfresh studio rooms with blue Aegean trim and spotless kitchenettes, as well as private balconies, TV, fridge and an extra bed for the kids. One of the rooms has bunk beds, double bed and a large balcony. There's also a roof garden. Opposite on the same street, **Studios Diana** (☑22420 59116; apt €45) has clean and basic studios with private balconies and dated kitchens.

The beachfront is lined with restaurants and cafes, many offering children's menus. Right on the harbour, **Kali Kardia Restaurant** (fish €9-12) is atmospheric with a wood interior patronised by older folk staring out to sea, and a kitchen piping aromas of squid, shrimp, cuttlefish and oysters. The beachside taverna **El Greco** (mains €7) pleases with fresh salads, zucchini, souvlakia, and lamb with rosemary sauce; as well as all-day breakfasts.

Mountain Villages

The villages scattered on the green northern slopes of the Dikeos mountain range are a great place for exploring. At **Zipari**, 10km from the capital, a road to the southeast leads to **Asfendiou**. En route, 3km past Zipari, stop in at **Taverna Panorama** (mains €6-10; ⊙lunch & dinner) for coastal views, traditional cuisine and good mezedhes.

From Asfendiou, a turn-off to the right leads to the pretty village of **Zia**, essentially a one-street affair with a gauntlet of souvenir shops and enticing tavernas. Take a right through the market and head up the hill to **The Watermill** (mains €6) for spectacular views. In the house of an old mill this whitewashed eyrie has a serene vine-covered arbour and restful patio and makes delicious crepes, fruit salads, juices, omelettes and pasta dishes. If you're thirsty, try their moreish homemade lemonade.

The **Village Tavern** (mains €7; ⊙8.30am-11pm), festooned in flags, pipes out chirpy bouzouki music across its blue-and-white decor and turns out salads, tzatziki (sauce of grated cucumber, yoghurt and garlic), zucchini balls, mixed mezedhes and sausages. Also worth a visit is **Taverna Oromedon** (☑22420 69983; mains €9; ⊙8am-midnight), popular for its vine-laced sun terrace, unbroken sea views and traditional Greek menu of shrimp *saganaki*, dolmadhes, *stifadho* and souvlakia.

Returning north from Zia, follow signs for **Pyli**. Just before the village, a left turn leads to the extensive ruins of the medieval village of **Old Pyli** where a well-marked trail leads up to **Pyli Castle**. This magical area of towering rocks carpeted in pine trees and crowned by the ruinous castle is so wild you half expect Pan to pop up. Equally delightful is **Oria Taverna** (mains €7; ⊙9am-9pm) on the opposite hillside. Instead of walking left for the fort, head up the steps. The taverna sits on a hill with possibly the best view on the island – a 1000-year-old ruined fort. Tuck into their seasonal, locally sourced menu of steaks, meatballs, zucchini and tzatziki.

Buses leave Kos for Pyli (€2) four times per day.

Kamari & Kefalos Bay   Καμάρι & Κέφαλος

Southwest from Mastihari is the huge Kefalos Bay, fringed by a 12km stretch of incredible sand. Don't be put off by the tacky tourist shops, restaurants and hotels behind on the main road; these divine beaches are idyllic, backed by green hills and lapped by warm water. Each is clearly signposted from the main road. The most popular is **Paradise Beach**, while the most undeveloped is **Exotic Beach**. **Banana Beach** (also known as Langada Beach) is a good compromise.

Agios Stefanos Beach, at the far western end, is reached along a short turn-off from the main road and worth a visit to see the island of **Agios Stefanos**. Within swimming distance, this tiny island is home to the ruins of two 5th-century basilicas and to another lovely, sandy beach.

Further down the road, you'll reach **Kamari Beach**, a resort strip packed with restaurants, accommodation and shops. You'll find a small tourism office next to the beachside bus stop and an ATM on the top road. Excursion boats leave from here for Nisyros (€16) two or three times weekly. There are also daily boats to Paradise Beach in the summer, departing from Kamari at 10.30am and returning at 5.30pm.

About 150m north of the Kamari seafront bus stop you'll find accommodation at **Anthoula Studios** (☑ 22420 71904; studios €40), a spotless set of airy, roomy studios surrounded by a vegetable garden.

Small, authentic **Kefalos** barely stirs from its afternoon retsina as you pass. **Kafenion Agiatrida** (snacks €3) behind the church is a homey turquoise-and-white-walled, wood-raftered cafe, perfect for a mid-afternoon frappé. The central square, where the bus from Kos Town terminates, has a post office and bank with an ATM.

The southern peninsula has the island's most rugged scenery. Rewardingly miles away from resort land, **Agios Theologos Beach** is backed by meadow bluffs carpeted in olive groves. You'll find the water here unusually clear and the waves invigoratingly large. Above the beach the seasonal **Restaurant Agios Theologos** (mains €7-15) enjoys the best sunsets in Kos. The menu includes homemade feta, olives, the bread and goat. Their mezedhes are fantastic.

ASTYPALEA
ΑΣΤΥΠΑΛΑΙΑ

POP 1240

When the only sound to break your thoughts is the solitary coo of a wood pigeon, you know you've discovered a place under the tourist radar. Swathed in silk aquamarine waters, far-flung, butterfly-shaped Astypalea is richly rewarding for walkers, campers and history buffs. An island hunter's ultimate escape; think mountainous meadows straight from the pages of Homer, and rugged beaches fringed in gas-blue turquoise. Chance of sighting a mermaid: fair.

The main settlement is hilltop Hora, which cascades amphitheatrically down to the fishing port of Skala in a tumble of Persil-white houses. Windblown and remote, there's an undeveloped tourist infrastructure here, and 90% of visitors are Greek, the remainder being French and Italian. Fed up with the package crowd and fish and chips? You've come to the right place then.

❶ Getting There & Away

AIR

Olympic Air has three flights per week to Leros (€61, 20 minutes), Kos (€68, one hour) and Rhodes (€68, 1½ hours) and five per week to Athens (€75, one hour). Astypalea Tours in Skala is the agent for Olympic Air.

BOAT

Astypalea has ferry services to Piraeus and Rhodes with various stops along the way. Services dock at the rather isolated small port of Agios Andreas, 6.5km north of Skala. A bus is scheduled to meet all arriving ferries, but don't bank on it. The Kalymnos-based ferry F/B *Nissos Kalymnos* links the island with Kalymnos and islands further north in the Dodecanese (four times per week), and docks, conveniently, at Skala. Ferry tickets are available from Paradise Travel Agency (p515) or from Astypalea Tours (p515), both in Skala.

Boat Services from Astypalea

DESTINATION	TIME	FARE	FREQUENCY
Kalymnos	2½hr	€13	4 weekly
Kalymnos*	2¾hr	€11	3 weekly
Kos	3½hr	€18	1 weekly
Naxos	3½hr	€27	4 weekly
Paros	5hr	€34	4 weekly
Piraeus	10hr	€35	5 weekly
Rhodes	9hr	€32	1 weekly

* leaves from Skala

❶ Getting Around

The airport is 8km northeast of Skala. Flights from Athens and Rhodes are usually met by the local bus, though a taxi (€10) is a more reliable option. June through September a bus leaves Hora for the airport before flights. In summer, buses run half-hourly from Skala to Hora and Livadi (€2), and hourly from Hora and Skala to Analipsi (Maltezana, €2) via Marmari Beach. Services are scaled back the rest of the year. There are only three taxis on the island and as many car- and scooter-hire agencies. **Vergoulis** (☑ 22430 61351; scooters per day €15, cars €40-60) in Skala is a reputable agency with feisty scooters.

Astypalea

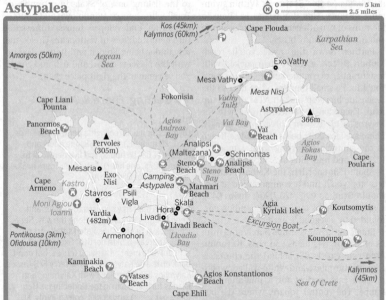

From July to August, you can hop on **Thalassopouli** (☑ 6974436338) for boat excursions to the remote western beaches of Agios Ioannis, Kaminakia and Vatses, or to the islets of Koutsomytis (with ethereal, emerald-green water) or Kounoupa. When the weather is good, longer round-island excursions are offered. Tickets (€25 to €30) can be bought on the boat.

Skala & Hora
Σκάλα & Χώρα

We might delight in Hora's waterfall of white houses crowned by its impressive *kastro*, but for the original inhabitants of Scala down the hill, the upward migration came about due to the constant threat of marauding pirates in the 14th and 15th centuries. These days you can wander round the hushed warren of streets and visit the fort. It's a pretty settlement with dramatic views and photogenic locals who mark time in a clutch of inviting *kafeneia* and tavernas by the Cycladic-style windmills.

Skala meanwhile is the waterfront village strewn with nets, aromatic odours drifting from the local bakery and a little sand-and-pebble beach where locals bathe. There are a few tavernas peppered with old seadogs, and some decent accommodation.

◉ Sights

Kastro   CASTLE
(☺ dawn-dusk) **FREE** During the 14th century, Astypalea was occupied by the Venetian Quirini family who built the imposing castle, adding to and renovating it throughout their 300-year rule. In the Middle Ages the population lived within the castle walls to escape pirate attacks. The last inhabitants left in 1953, following a devastating earthquake in which the stone houses collapsed. Above the tunnel-like entrance is the **Church of The Virgin of the Castle** and within the walls is the magical **Church of Agios Georgios**.

Archaeological Museum   MUSEUM
(☑ 22430 61206; ☺ 9am-1pm & 6-8pm Tue-Sun) **FREE** Skala is home to a small archaeological museum with treasures found across the island, from the prehistoric Mycenaean period to the Middle Ages. Highlights include grave offerings from two Mycenaean chamber tombs and a little bronze Roman statue of Aphrodite. The museum is at the beginning of the Skala–Hora road.

⌴ Sleeping

It's essential to make reservations in July and August.

Hotel Paradissos
HOTEL **$**

(✆ 22430 61224; www.astypalea-paradissos.com; Skala; d/tr €55/65; ❈ 🛜) Twelve sea-view rooms so close to the harbour you can taste salt on your lips. Stately and peaceful, Paradissos is clean and stylish with mint-green rooms with desks, en suites, cupboards, TV, fridge and private balconies. There's also a great cafe and attached travel agency.

Avra Studios
APARTMENT **$**

(✆ 6972134971, 22430 61363; Skala; d €50; ❈) This place sits on the beach – you can literally fall out of bed onto the sand. Modern, superfresh rooms enjoy plenty of space, French-green kitchens, tiled floors, cosy decor and private balconies.

Kaith Rooms
PENSION **$**

(✆ 22430 61131; Hora; s/apt €50/60; ❈ 🛜) Just off the road leading down to Hora, Kaith has decent rooms with large beds, TV, fridge, kitchenette and tasteful furnishings; as well as terrific views of the harbour from the communal balcony. The end apartment has its own private sun trap.

★ Studio Kilindra
BOUTIQUE HOTEL **$$$**

(✆ 22430 61131; www.astipalea.com.gr; Hora; d/apt incl breakfast €100/120; ❈ @ 🛜 ☀) ✐ Just below the *kastro*, this magical boutique hotel has a lush pool to float in as you gaze at the mouthwash-green bay below. Their lobby is brilliantly eclectic, scattered in antiques and a grand piano, while rooms fuse contemporary and traditional, with split level floors, raised beds, sofas, kitchenettes and a sense of home.

Stone massage treatments, reiki and acupuncture therapies (€20) are also available.

Thalassa Hotel
BOUTIQUE HOTEL **$$$**

(✆ 22430 59840; www.stampalia.gr; Hora; r incl breakfast €120; ❈ @ 🛜) Thalassa's 12 rooms boast incredible views of the harbour and bay from their spacious roof terraces. The rooms are marble floored with four-poster beds, Caribbean-blue fittings and floral bedspreads. That said, despite the free airport transfer it seems a little overpriced.

✗ Eating

There are some tempting eating options in Hora and Skala and a string of chichi restaurants in Livadi.

★ Barbarossa
TAVERNA **$**

(Hora; mains €9; ❈ 🛜 ✐) ✐ Food with soul, this is the island's best restaurant. Inside are exposed stone walls covered with antique Greek poster girls, plus amazing views from the back window. Meanwhile outside, there's a buzzing little terrace close to the town hall. Barbarossa's menu of mussels *saganaki,* grilled shrimps, souvlakia and pork fillet with mushrooms will leave your taste buds aglow.

Agonigrmi
TAVERNA **$**

(Hora; mains €6; ⊘ 2pm-midnight) This pizzeria and kebab house has a whitewashed interior stippled with stone flags and lit with red pendant lights. Outside on the terrace explore a raft of pizzas and pasta dishes. Close to the windmills.

Maïstrali
TAVERNA **$**

(✆ 22430 61691; Skala; mains €8-12; ⊘ 10am-late; ❈ 🛜 ✐) One street back from the harbour, this stylish restaurant dishes up everything from zucchini balls, lamb chops and eggplant salad, to grilled shrimp *saganaki* and rabbit in tomato sauce.

Restaurant Aitherio
TAVERNA **$**

(Skala; mains €9; ⊘ 1pm-late; 🛜 ✐) This bijou taverna has a shaded terrace looking onto the harbour below (look out for the blue tables and chairs). The menu features delicacies like shrimps in hot honey sauce, squid stuffed with cheese, Astypalea sausage and pork fillet wth blue cheese. Original and fresh.

🛍 Shopping

Just up the street from Hotel Paradissos, **Koursaros** (Skala) is an eclectic cave of jewellery, hats, icons, pashminas, bags and boho blouses. Look out for the sign of the pirate.

❶ Information

For history, pictures, facilities and sights go to www.astypalaia.com.

Astypalea Tours (✆ 22430 61571; Skala; ⊘ 6-9pm) For air tickets.

Commercial Bank (✆ 22430 61402; Skala) Has an ATM on the waterfront, the island's only bank.

Municipal Tourist Office (✆ 22430 61412; Hora; ⊘ 10am-noon & 6-9pm) In a restored windmill.

Paradise Travel Agency (✆ 22430 59808, 22430 61224; paradisostravel@yahoo.gr) Books ferry tickets.

Police (✆ 22430 61207; Skala) In an Italianate building on the waterfront.

Port Police (☑22430 61208; Skala) Shares premises with the police.

Post Office (Hora) At the top of the Skala–Hora road.

ℹ Getting Around

Taxi (☑6976256461, 6975706365) There are two taxis on the island.

Livadi Λειβάδι

Head directly to Livadi Beach (2km from Hora) for a string of funky restaurants and bars. Compared to the rest of the island, this buzzing gauntlet seems as if it's been transplanted from the pages of a fashion magazine. On the seafront, Hotel Manganas (☑22430 61468; astyroom@otenet.gr; studios €60; ✳ 🅿 🛜) offers eight sea-facing rooms with homely kitchens, tables to eat in or out, and even washing machines and cable TV. For something really special though, head to the boutique dream of Fildisi Hotel (☑22430 62060; www.fildisi.net; studios €140-260; ✳ 🛜 🅿). Split into terraces, its centrepiece is an infinity pool accompanied by a juice bar and marvellous view of the sea. The breakfast/chill room is chic, while the ubercool rooms enjoy balconies, kitchenettes, flat-screen TVs and sea views.

Trapezakia Exo (☑22430 61083; mains €5-9) at the western end of the beach serves fresh sandwiches from its deli. Take away or eat steak, Armenian sausage, mussels, meatballs and shrimp at their stylish beachside terrace. Nearby Astropelos (☑22430 61473; mains €9; ☺8am-midnight; 🛜 🅿) has a decked verandah with chic white tables and a menu of octopus salad, breaded crab's pincers and lobster. French lounge tunes under the shade of tamarisk trees accompany the view of distant Hora.

West of Skala

Heading west of Skala you hit the Astypalea outback – gnarled, bare rolling hills, perfect for a Cyclops, with scarcely a sealed road to speak of. It's just about driveable. The road eventually leads to the Kastro ruins and Moni Agiou Ioanni, situated next to each other above the coast. From here, the strictly fit may venture downwards on foot to Agios Ioannis beach. An equally rough road leads to Panormos Beach which you'll likely have to yourself.

On the south coast, a rough track winds through mountainous meadows then drops to Kaminakia Beach, Astypalea's best altar to sun-worshipping. Bookended by granite boulders, the water is so clear you can see the pebbles through the turquoise. There's also a good seasonal restaurant, Sti Linda (☑6932610050; mains €4-7; ☺Jul-Sep), serving hearty fish soups, oven-baked goat and homemade bread. If your nerves aren't shattered, detour to the pretty, tree-shaded Agios Konstantinos Beach on the south side of Livadi Bay.

East of Skala

Marmari, 2km northeast of Skala, has three bays with pebble and sand beaches and is home to Camping Astypalea (☑22430 61900; camp sites per adult/tent €8/2; ☺Jun-Sep). This tamarisk tree-shaded and bamboo-protected campground is right next to the beach (which unfortunately is right next to the road) and has 24-hour hot water, a kitchen, cafe and minimarket. Steno Beach, 2km further along, is one of the better but least frequented beaches on the island. It's sandy, conveniently shallow for the kids, shady and well protected. The island is just 2km wide here.

Analipsi (also known as Maltezana) is 7km up the road in a fertile valley on the isthmus. A former Maltese pirates' lair, it's a scattered, pleasantly laid-back settlement. On its outskirts are remains of the Tallaras Roman baths with mosaics. Analipsi Beach is southeast of town and is a long beach, with sand, pebbles, shade and clean, shallow water.

For accommodation in Analipsi, head to Villa Barbara (☑22430 61448; s/d €40-45; ✳). Instantly appealing with its flowering gardens and sugar-white facade, Barbara's rooms are fresh with separate kitchenettes, tiled floors, TVs and balconies aimed towards the beach (100m away). Hotel Maltezana Beach (☑22430 61558; www.maltezanabeach.gr; s/d incl breakfast €100/130; 🅿 ✳ 🛜 🅿) next door is plush with manicured gardens huddled around a fine pool and restaurant. Rooms are fresh and spacious with fridge and balcony. On the seafront the Analipsi Taverna serves up traditional fare (it's near the jetty).

Continuing east, remote Mesa Vathy hamlet is an indolent yacht harbour in a sheltered bay and home to only half a dozen families. The swimming isn't good, but you can fish for your lunch or dine at the laid-back **Galini Cafe** (☑ 22430 61201; mains €3-5; ☺ Jun-Oct), which offers meat and fish grills and oven-baked specials.

KALYMNOS ΚΑΛΥΜΝΟΣ

POP 8,586

Vibrantly Greek, this rugged place of vertical cliffs (drawing hardy climbers from all over the world) and turquoise bays is soaked in the sea; indeed from the mermaid on the point and statue of Poseidon in the harbour, to its rich history of sponge diving, Kalymnos is tied to the deep. There are a lot of damaged old lungs in town but the islanders are proud of their tenacity as hardy sponge divers. Even today, scattered about the capital of Pothia, you'll find old sponge warehouses stacked to the gills with these unearthly marine treasures.

Unlike some of its neighbours, Kalymnos is comparatively green, its roads lined with pink oleanders contrasting with brilliantly blue water. Local gastronomic treats include octopus in ouzo, and *spinialo* (devilfish and urchins in sea water).

Kalymnos is the third-largest island in the Dodecanese and to do it justice you'll need three days and wheels.

❶ Getting There & Away

AIR

Kalymnos is linked by Olympic Air with a daily flight to Athens (€90, 20 minutes). Tickets can be bought at Kapellas Travel (p520). The airport is 3.5km northwest of Pothia and the seaplane terminal is 1.5km east.

BOAT

Kalymnos is linked to Rhodes, Piraeus and the islands in between via car-ferries, hydrofoils and catamarans. Services are provided by local boats and **Blue Star Ferries** (☑ 22430 26000), **Anek Lines** (☑ 22430 23700), **Dodecanese Seaways** (☑ 22430 28777; Pothia quay) and **ANE Kalymnou** (☑ 22430 29612). Tickets can be bought from Magos Travel (p520). Small local car and passenger ferries leave six times daily from Pothia to Mastihari (€8) on Kos. The fast Lipsi-based *Anna Express* links Pothia with Leros and Lipsi three times weekly. A daily boat leaves Pothia for Pserimos (€5 each way) at 9.30am and returns at 5pm. There's also a daily caïque from Myrties to Xirokambos (€10) on Leros. A

caïque runs between Myrties and Telendos Islet (€2) throughout the day.

Boat Services from Kalymnos

DESTINATION	TIME	FARE	FREQUENCY
Astypalea	3½hr	€12	3 weekly
Kos	50min	€6	3 daily
Kos*	35min	€14	1 daily
Leros	1½hr	€9	4 weekly
Leros*	50min	€20	1 daily
Lipsi*	1hr 20min	€20	1 daily
Patmos	4hr	€12	4 weekly
Patmos*	1hr 40min	€26	6 weekly
Piraeus	13hr	€48	3 weekly
Rhodes*	3hr	€38	1 daily
Rhodes	4½hr	€23	3 weekly

*high-speed services

❶ Getting Around

BOAT

In summer there is a daily excursion boat from Myrties to Emborios (€8), leaving at 10am and returning at 4pm. Day trips to **Kefalas Cave** (€20), impressive for its 103m corridor filled with stalactites and stalagmites, run from both Pothia and Myrties. There are also regular boats from Pothia to Pserimos, with its big, sandy beach and tavernas. The large sailboat **Katerina** (☑ 6938325612) does regular excursions around Kalymnos.

BUS

Buses regularly leave Pothia for Emporio (€2) starting from 9am, with the last one returning at 3.50pm. For Vathys (€2) buses leave every two hours, with the first leaving at 6.30am and the last returning at 5.30pm. Buy tickets from the Municipality of Kalymnos ticket office by the bus stop in Pothia.

CAR & MOTORCYCLE

There are plenty of vehicle-hire companies on the island, mainly concentrated in Pothia. Try **Rent-a-Bike** (☑ 6937980591; scooter/car €8/20) or **Automarket Rental** (☑ 6927834628, 22430 51780). Expect to pay €8 to €15 for a scooter and €20 to €40 for a car for one day's hire.

TAXI

Shared taxi services cost a little more than buses and run from the Pothia **taxi stand** (☑ 22430 50300; Plateia Kyprou) to Masouri. The taxis can also be flagged down en route. A regular taxi costs €9 to Myrties, €15 to Vathys and €10 to the airport. To the port costs €5.

Kalymnos

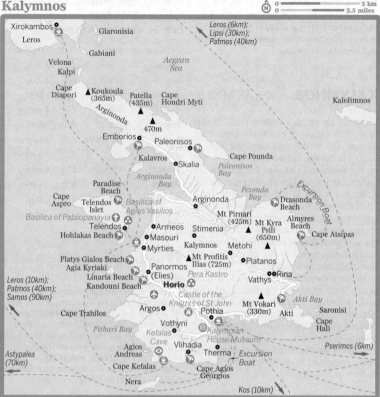

Pothia

Πόθια

POP 10.500

Crouching below brooding mountains, Pothia is rich with Greek vignettes: nut-brown fishermen mending nets, veteran divers with fantastically photogenic faces nursing retsinas between gazing nostalgically out to sea; and young islanders blithely marking time in the garland of wharf-side *kafenia*. And while Pothia's whitewashed alleys might seem little different from other towns, what makes it special is its past as Greece's sponge diving capital; imagine the feats of bravery undertaken by these people time and again at the bottom of the sea, to feed their families.

◉ Sights

Archaeological Museum MUSEUM
(☑ 22430 23113; adult/student €5/3; ☉ 10am-1pm Mon, Wed & Fri) The Archaeological Museum is packed with a vast array of artefacts dating back as far as 2500 BC and found as recently as 2001. One of the most striking pieces is an arresting bronze statue of a woman in a detailed chiton from the 2nd century BC, found off the coast of Kalymnos. Behind the main building is the **mansion of Nicklas Vouvalis**, a wealthy 19th-century sponge trader who was the island benefactor. Inside, rooms appear as they did when he lived here.

Nautical & Folklore Museum MUSEUM
(☑ 22430 51361; admission €3; ☉ 10am-1pm Mon, Wed & Fri, May-Sep) In the centre of the waterfront, this museum has displays on traditional regional dress and the history of sponge diving. For an even bigger eyeful of sponge, visit the **exporting factory** of NS Papachatzis, overflowing with sponges of every conceivable shape and size.

🏃 Activities

Rock Climbing

In recent years Kalymnos has become Greece's climbing mecca with 50 different climbing sites and over 2000 bolted routes. Every October the **North Face Kalymnos Climbing Festival** (www.kalymnosclimbingfestival.com) draws more than 300 climbers from 20 different countries. The newly expanded **Kalymnos Adventure Centre & Climber's Nest** (☑ 22480 48160, 6984933327; www.climbkalymnos.com; Masouri; half-day beginner's climbing course €40) in Masouri, is where you'll find equipment, maps, guidebooks and experienced guides. Beginner half-day courses cost €40.

The Official Climbing Info desk is based at the Municipal Tourist office at the entrance to the harbour. Also check out www.climbkalymnos.com for more information.

Scuba Diving

The annual **Kalymnos Skandalopetra Diving Festival** held in summer offers participants the chance to compete in underwater target shooting, cliff diving, scuba diving through wrecks and even hunting for lost treasure. See the municipality's website (www.kalymnos-isl.gr) for further details. **Kalymnos Scuba Diving Club** (☑ 6974646413, 22430 47253; www.kalymnosdiving.com; 1-day dive €50, 3-day open water PADI €350) offers one-day dives to wrecks, underwater volcanoes, reefs and caves. Owner Dimitris runs one-day boat trips explaining the history of sponge diving, and can demonstrate the ancient art of *skandalopetra* (stone and rope free-diving).

Hiking

There are 10 established hiking routes scattered around the island and detailed on the excellent 1:25,000 *Kalymnos Hiking Map* published by **Anavasi** (www.mountains.gr; Stoa Arsakiou 6a, Athens). A popular hike is the Vathys-Pothia B1 4.25km 'Italian Road', a stone pathway built by the Italians at the beginning of the 20th century.

The newly revamped Kalymnos Adventure Centre (p519) in Masouri, also arranges organised treks.

🛏 Sleeping

★**Villa Melina**   BOUTIQUE HOTEL **$**
(☑ 22430 22682; antoniosantonoglu@yahoo.de; r incl breakfast €55-65; ❄ 🛜 ✉) This 1930s Italian villa exudes old-world style from the moment one of their cats brushes your leg and invites you to follow it down wood-panelled corridors ornamented with gilt-framed nautical oils and Persian rugs. The antique-accented rooms are achingly pretty, featuring stucco ceilings, lilac walls, mahogany armoires and huge beds.

And we haven't even got to the sparkling pool, the garden dripping with flowers or Antonios, the fabulous owner.

Greek House   PENSION **$**
(☑ 6972747494, 22430 23752; s/d/apt €20/30/40) Hidden up a side street running from the left-hand corner of the harbour, this excellent budget option has four wood-panelled, split-level rooms with kitchen facilities and plenty of beds (some with as many as eight!). There's also a communal balcony. Follow the yellow signs to Paorama Hotel and you'll find it en route.

Arhodeko Hotel   PENSION **$**
(☑ 22430 24051; s/d €30/35; ⊙ year-round; ❄) Located on the harbour, this neoclassical gem has pleasant rooms with harbour views, tiled floors, Persian rugs, TV, fridge and balconies. There's bags of atmosphere, from the moment you step through its elegant facade and under the original stone archways. Great value.

Hotel Panorama   HOTEL **$**
(☑ 22430 23138; www.panorama-kalymnos.gr; s/d incl breakfast €30/40; ⊙ year-round; P ❄ 🛜) Panorama earns its moniker with breathtaking rooftop views from a hilltop eyrie. The 13 rooms are fresh with TVs, private balconies, contemporary furniture and a communal sun terrace. Book ahead for this bijou belle, and ask for free pick-up from the ferry.

Evanik Hotel   HOTEL **$**
(☑ 22430 22037, 22430 23125; s/d/tr incl breakfast €35/50/65; ❄ 🛜) This imposing yet intimate hotel, a few blocks up from the harbour, has plush rooms of varying sizes, with tiled floors, Ikea-style furniture, reading lamps, fridge, TV and immaculate en suite. Downstairs there's a pleasant breakfast area. Ask for a quieter room at the back.

Olympic Hotel   HOTEL **$**
(☑ 22430 51710; Martiou, Pothia; s/d/tr €35/45/55; ❄ 🛜) The 42-room Olympic sits on the harbour and has a smart lobby but forgettable rooms; with desks, private balconies, en suite, TV and fridge.

✗ Eating

Rebetiko Taverna GREEK $
(mains €7; ⊘10am-midnight; ✸ 🛜 🍴) Eat on the alfresco terrace close to the harbour (more romantic), or inside at this appealingly fresh taverna with cream tables and chairs. Choose from a menu rich in carbonara, bolognese, swordfish, shrimps and souvlakia.

Barba Yiannis GREEK $
(Harbour, Pothia; mains €8; ⊘9am-midnight) Yiannis is smart, mercifully breezy and has fine harbour views. It's a great spot to head to for traditional Greek fare like *stifadho*, lobster, fresh fish and souvlakia, and has a pretty decked terrace.

Mania's SEAFOOD $
(mains €9; ⊘8am-midnight; ✸ 🛜) Commanding views of the harbour, this taverna is run by the grandson of a famous free-diver and boasts a catch of shrimps, octopus, cod, whitebait, sea urchin salad and calamari. Most of the seafood is netted by their own boat. Traditional instruments are played some evenings.

Pandelis Restaurant GREEK $
(🗐22430 51508; mains €9; ⊘9am-midnight; 🛜🍴) The specialities at this homey eatery are goat in red-wine sauce and homemade dolmadhes. Worth a mention too are the prawns in pasta and charcoal-grilled meat cuts. Good wine selection.

If you're self-catering, head for **Vidhalis Market**, a well-stocked supermarket (great for fresh fruit) on the waterfront or **Anash's Bakery** at the back of town for baked goods like olive bread, cookies, pies, croissants and sponge cake.

🍷 Drinking & Nightlife

Sirroco Bar BAR
(Harbour, next to Automarket; ⊘7pm-1.30am) This traditional nautical bar feels like stepping into yesteryear with its old brass clocks, portholes, cosy wood booths and ships' wheels stuck on the wall. Hang out with the seadogs and swap maritime yarns. Look for the boat outside to find it.

ℹ Information

Pothia's quay is at the southern side of the port. Most activity, however, is centred on the waterfront square, Plateia Eleftherias. The main commercial centre is on Venizelou. Stay constantly alert while walking around Pothia; traffic hurtles up and down its narrow footpath-less roads.

The Commercial, National and Ionian banks, all with ATMs, are close to the waterfront.

Alter Holidays (🗐6946596030, 22430 47398; www.alterholiday.gr) Tailor-made holidays for diving, walking and climbing, Alter also arranges accommodation, with a focus on alternative, authentic destinations. The one-month pass entitles you to dramatic discounts on diving, hotels, and tours at wholesale prices. Look out for their apps, soon to cover all the best of the Dodecanese.

Kapellas Travel (🗐22430 29265; kapellas travel@gallileo.gr; Patriarhou Maximou 12) For air tickets.

Magos Travel (🗐22430 28777; www.magos tours.gr) Hydrofoil and catamaran tickets, including a day's excursion to Bodrum (€25), as well as flights and bus excursions. There's a 24-hour ticket machine outside.

Main Post Office A 10-minute walk northwest of Plateia Eleftherias. There is a more convenient agency south of Plateia Ethnikis Andistasis.

Municipal Tourist Information (🗐22430 29299; george@kalymnos.gr; 25 Martiou; ⊘7.30am-3pm Mon-Fri) By the edge of the harbour and run by George, this is an excellent, well-organised source of info for buses, climbing, diving and ferries.

Neon Internet C@fe (🗐22430 48318; internet per hr €3; ⊘9.30am-midnight) Teen haunt with internet, gaming, free wi-fi and bowling!

Police (🗐22430 22100; Venizelou)

Port Police (🗐22430 24444; 25 Martiou)

www.kalymnos-isl.gr Informative site hosted by the municipality of Kalymnos.

Around Pothia

South of Pothia, the road to Moni Agiou Savra takes you past **Kalymnian House Museum** (admission €3; ⊘9am-2pm & 4-8pm May-Sep), a small traditional home where you'll learn about local customs through guided tours in English. Running northwards from the port is a busy valley with a series of settlements. The ruined **Castle of the Knights of St John** (Kastro Hrysoherias) looms to the left of the Pothia–Horio road with a small **church** inside its battlements.

On the east side of the valley, **Pera Kastro** was a pirate-proof village inhabited until the 18th century. Within the crumbling walls are the ruins of stone houses and six tiny 15th-century churches. Check out the few remaining frescoes in the Church of Transfiguration. Steps lead up to Pera Kastro from the end of the main road in **Horio**; it's an unshaded climb with incredible views.

A tree-lined road continues from Horio to **Panormos**, a pretty village 5km from Pothia. The beaches of **Kandouni** and **Linaria** are a stone's throw from one another and within walking distance of Panormos. Kandouni is a particularly pretty cove surrounded by mountains, with cafes, bars and hotels overlooking the water and a small sandy beach. You can also rock climb from here and there is an annual cliff-diving competition.

For dining and sleeping, Linaria is slightly quieter. **Giorgio's Family Restaurant** (mains €6-12), at the northern end of Linaria beach, has creative salads, fresh fish and seafood. Try the chilli feta, *saganaki* shrimp. Nearby **Kafes Alati** (mains €8-15; ⊙noon-midnight; ❄️ 🔊) has a cream interior, fine sea views and delicious grilled aromas drifting from its open range. Eat in or outside on the terrace. **Sevasti Studio** (☑ 22430 48779; d/apt €40/50; ❄️) has cheerful apartments and a verandah with gorgeous sea views.

Up the road, **Platys Gialos** is a bit more of a trek from Panormos. The beach here is less developed and pebbly.

Myrties, Masouri & Armeos
Μυρτιές, Μασούρι & Αρμεός

From Panormos the road continues to the west coast, with stunning views of Telendos Islet. **Myrties**, **Masouri** and **Armeos** are low-key resorts and essentially one long street with restaurants, bars, souvenir shops and minimarkets. But of the two, Masouri has more of a buzz thanks to the excellent Kalymnos Adventure Centre & Climber's Nest (p519), a magnet for adventurers and the op-centre of everything adrenalin-laced. Choose from climbing, caving, hiking, biking, horse riding and via ferrata.

An extinct volcano plug divides the beach here into two sections: Myrties beach with Melitsahas harbour and the marginally better Masouri and Armeos beaches to the north.

Spread throughout all three centres are currency-exchange bureaus, a Dodecanet ATM and car and motorcycle hire outlets like the reliable **Avis Rental** (☑ 22430 47145; Myrties). To get online, visit **Babis Bar** (Myrties; per hr €2).

Of the three towns, Myrties is the quietest place to stay. As sun-dappled as a Monet, **Acroyali** (☑ 22430 47521; www.acroyali-kalymnos.gr; Myrties; d/tr €50/60; ❄️ 🔊) is bursting

with vegetation by the turquoise sea. The village-style studios have colourful touches and private balconies. **Hotel Atlantis** (☑ 22430 47497; AtlantisStudios@hotmail.com; d/tr €35/40; ❄️), up from the sea, has amazing views and a lobby decked in mythological reliefs. The rooms are sparkling with great balconies, comfy beds, kitchenettes and pleasant furnishings.

Take the first turning to the left to find the seafront **Smuggler's Restaurant** (Myrties; mains €8; ⊙8am-late; ❄️🍴). Shipwrecked by the lapping water close to the jetty this lovely taverna looks like the inside of a boat. Perfect then for nautical appetites looking to devour swordfish, mussels, shrimps and calamari.

From Myrties there are regular small boats to Telendos Islet (€2).

Telendos Islet
Νήσος Τέλενδος

Only 10 minutes by caïque from the Myrties quay, thanks to its traffic-free roads Telendos feels remote and touched with Aegean magic. Crowned by its rocky mountain, most activity centres on its pretty harbour of tavernas and whitewashed guesthouses. It was once the capital of Kalymnos until an earthquake in AD 554 set it adrift and cast the ruins to the seabed.

Head right for the ruins of the early Christian **basilica of Agios Vasilios**. From here you can also follow a footpath to the **basilica of Palaiopanayia**. Further along the coast, there are several small pebble-and-sand beaches including **Paradise Beach** (sometimes popular with nudists). Heading left from the quay and turning right just before Zorba's will bring you to the windswept, fine-pebbled **Hohlakas Beach**.

Telendos is a popular climbing destination; pop into Cafe Naytikos for oodles of info. The small **Katerina** (☑ 6944919073) taxis climbers from Myrties to sites on Telendos (€30 per boat load, up to five people), departing at 7am and returning at 2pm.

Hotels, rooms and restaurants are spread alongside the quay and on the eastern side of the island. Turn right from the quay to **On the Rocks Rooms** (☑ 6932978142, 22430 48260; www.otr.telendos.com; s/d/tr €40/50/60; ❄️ @ 🔊). It has a great open bar and terrace strung with nautical eclectica, and attracts climbers thanks to its for spacious studios with kitchenettes, private balconies, foot massage and washing machines, TV and CD players. Airport transfers available too.

A little further along, classically lined **Hotel Porto Potha** (☑ 22430 47321; portopotha@ klm.forthnet.gr; d incl breakfast €52; ❄ ⚡ ⚠) sits at an elevation and has comfortable rooms, gorgeous views, an inviting swimming pool and a very friendly owner.

At the left of the pier, **Zorba's** (☑ 22430 48660; mains €3-8, r €30; ❄ ⚡) is traditional and has great sea views. The owner fishes for the seafood himself (if you're a guest you can go with him), bringing up squid, octopus, tuna and swordfish. They also have three small but pleasant pink-walled rooms with pine furniture.

Beneath the shade of a tamarisk tree, **Cafe Naytikos** (☉ year-round) is popular with early morning climbers seeking zestful coffee, breakfasts and snacks. Their helpful signpost at the end of the jetty gives you valuable distances and directions to popular climbs. Meanwhile, next door **Cafe Rita** (mains €8) is decked out in blue chairs and check-cloth tables and has a menu of omelettes, breakfasts, salads, sandwiches, baklava and a raft of seafood.

There's also a local crafts shop and secondhand bookshop.

Caïques for Telendos depart regularly from the Myrties quay between 8am and 1am (one way €2).

Emborios Εμπορειός

The scenic west coast road, bordered in oleander, winds a further 11.5km from Masouri to sleepy Emborios; a clutch of sugar-white houses huddled around a small pebble beach with crystal-clear water. Laid-back **Artistico Cafe** (☑ 22430 40115; mains €7; ☉ 9am-late) faces the beach and is shaded by tamarisk trees. Some nights they have impromptu jam sessions. Either way the menu is tasty with *stifadho,* breakfasts, lamb stew, calamari, souvlakia and steaks. Try the giant prawn *saganaki.*

One of the island's favourites, **Harry's Paradise** (☑ 22430 40062; www.harrys-paradise .gr; Emborios; standard/f apt €48/90; ❄ @) sits in an Edenic garden of jasmine, roses, aromatic herbs and hibiscus. The food is divine; locally sourced, quintessentially Kalymnian but with a modern twist. Think prawns, cheese and parsley rolled in filo pastry, or grilled rabbit with wine potatoes and garlic. The apartments are no less tasteful with shabby chic elements, rocking chairs, kitchenettes and large balconies with sea views. Book ahead!

Vathys & Rina Βαθύς & Ρίνα

Vathys, set in a fertile valley on the east coast of Kalymnos, is one of the most beautiful parts of the island. Narrow roads wind between citrus orchards, bordered by high stone walls called *koumoula.*

Rina, Vathys' little harbour, feels as if it's on a fjord, for the teal-green sea snakes around a rocky bend before opening out into the ocean. But for the click of old timers playing backgammon there's little movement here. **Water taxis** (☑ 6947082912, 22430 31316) take tourists to quiet coves, such as the nearby **Almyres** and **Drasonda** bays. There are a number of churches you can hike to from Pina, including **Hosti** with 11th-century frescoes, found on the western slope of the harbour. An **annual cliff-diving competition** also takes place at Vathys as part of the International Diving Festival.

The colourful harbour is lined with restaurants. Stop for lunch at **Galini Taverna** (mains €9; ☉ 9am-late; P ❄ ⚡). With its checked tablecloths, friendly manager, bougainvillea ceiling and fine view of the harbour it's a peaceful spot for salads, seafood and grilled meat. The dolmadhes are full of flavour.

Vathys is 13km northeast of Pothia. From here, a blustery new road winds through the mountains from Emborios, making it a speedier way of reaching the north than via the west coast.

LEROS ΛΕΡΟΣ

POP 8210

It was said Artemis lived here, and like the Goddess of The Hunt there's something alluringly wild and beautiful about Leros; scattered with beautiful orthodox churches, dazzling blue coves and whitewashed villages. Capital Platanos, with its striking fort and windmills towering above, is divinely pretty, while below, the picturesque harbour of Agia Marina – the heart of the island – pulses with Itailianate bakeries, cafes and nautical-themed bars. Leros is less about chasing activities and more about worshipping Helios, seeking out your favourite

Leros

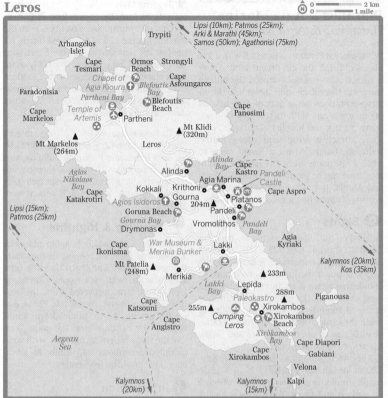

beach and letting the magic of the place slowly unwind you.

ⓘ Getting There & Away

AIR

There are daily flights to Athens (€76) and thrice-weekly flights to Rhodes (€70), Kos (€61) and Astypalea (€61). **Olympic Air** (☏ 22470 22777) at the airport will sell you tickets.

BOAT

Leros is on the main north–south route for ferries between Rhodes and Piraeus, with daily departures from Lakki. Buy tickets at **Blue Star Ferries** (☏ 222470 26000; Lakki) in Lakki. In summer, hydrofoils and catamarans arrive daily in Agia Marina and depart from Lakki, on their trip through the Dodecanese, with tickets available on the quays. Note that if the weather is inclement, catamarans leave from Agia Marina harbour. The comfortable **Anna Express** (☏ 6976244125, 22479 41215) departs from Agia Marina and links Leros with Kalymnos

(€17), Lipsi (€10) and Arki (€10) three times per week, as well as Agathonisi (€12) four times a week. The caïque *Katerina* leaves Xirokambos each morning for Myrties on Kalymnos (€10). Day-tripper boats to Bodrum (€65), via Kos, leave Lakki on Thursday at 5am, returning at 10.30pm.

ⓘ Getting Around

The **airport** (☏ 22470 22777) is near Partheni in the north. There is no airport bus. A taxi from the airport to Alinda will cost €10.

The hub for Leros' buses is Platanos. There are three buses daily to Partheni via Alinda and four buses to Xirokambos via Lakki (€4 flat fare). Flag these green-and-beige-striped buses down and they usually stop for you.

Car-, motorcycle- and bicycle-hire outlets are mainly on the Alinda tourist strip. **Motoland** (☏ 22470 24584; scooter per day €10) offers bikes and scooters. Phone for a **taxi** (☏ 22470 22550/23070/23340).

Platanos & Agia Marina
Πλάτανος & Αγια Μαρίνα

POP 3500

Whitewashed Platanos is peaceful with a few places to drink and eat decent food. Above it rises the imposing *kastro* on the hill. To the north the village spills down into the effervescent, photogenic port of Agia Marina (ay-*i*-a ma-*ri*-na). With its bakeries, chic waterfront cafes and jewellery boutiques, plus some attractive ochre- and wine-coloured Italianate buildings, it's a lovely place to while a few hours away. The nearest accommodation can be found in Pandeli, Krithoni and Alinda. If you're arriving by ferry this is probably your first glimpse of the island.

◉ Sights

Perched on the hill overlooking the harbour, **Pandeli Castle** (☏22470 23211; admission castle €2, castle & museum €3; ⊘8am-12.30pm & 4-8pm) is worth visiting for its breathtaking 360-degree views from the ramparts. Running south from the castle is a picturesque string of recently renovated **windmills**. To reach the castle, you can drive from Platanos or walk east of the main square and follow the arrows to the staircase.

The **Archaeological Museum** (⊘8am-2.30pm Tue-Sun May-Sep) FREE is in a 19th-century building and has artefacts collected on and around Leros. You'll pass it on the edge of Agia Marina, en route up the hill to Platanos.

✕ Eating

Smoked mackerel and thyme honey are specialities of Leros.

★**Taverna Mylos** SEAFOOD $
(Agia Marina; mains €9; ⊘year-round; ❄ 🤶 🖊 🖳)
🍴 Lapped by turquoise waves beside an old windmill at the end of a pebbled beach, it's not just the view that steals your heart, your taste buds will get romantic too. O Mylos infuses classic seafood recipes with a modern twist – think octopus carpaccio, or spaghetti and prawns in white sauce. Great for sunset dinners on its stylish terrace.

★**To Paradosiakon** BAKERY $
(Agia Marina; mains €2; ⊘7am-11.30pm; ❄ 🤶) 🍴
Set in a handsome Italianate building, this bakery is packed with baklava, cheesecakes, strawberry tarts, croissants, spinach pies and locally made ice cream. If heaven were a bakery...

🍷 Drinking & Nightlife

Enallaktiko Cafe (p525) is a hip place for a drink and game of pool, while nautically themed **Meltemi Bar** (Agios Marina; ⊘6pmlate), strewn with sea ropes, hurricane lamps and urns recovered from the seabed, is atmospheric. Meanwhile **Faros Bar** (⊘10.30pm-late; 🤶), a tumbledown haunt beneath the lighthouse on the point, feels like the shipwreck of an old boat, with wallmounted accordions and dimly lit ambience. Live music on weekends.

ⓘ Information

The focal point of Platanos is the central square, Plateia N Roussou. From here, Harami leads down to Agia Marina. The Platanos bus station and taxi rank are both about 50m in the other direction, along the Platanos–Lakki road. In Agia Marina, taxis wait at the quay.

BOAT SERVICES FROM LEROS

DESTINATION	PORT	TIME	FARE	FREQUENCY
Kalymnos	Lakki	1hr 40min	€10	1 weekly
Kalymnos*	Lakki	50min	€20	1 daily
Kos	Lakki	3¼hr	€14	4 weekly
Kos*	Agia Marina	1hr	€22	1 daily
Lipsi*	Agia Marina	20min	€14	1 daily
Patmos*	Agia Marina	45min	€16	1 daily
Piraeus	Lakki	8hr	€39	3 weekly
Rhodes	Lakki	3½hr	€30	3 weekly
Rhodes*	Agia Marina	4hr	€41	3 weekly

*high-speed services

The National Bank of Greece is on Platanos' central square. There are two ATMs at Agia Marina, including a handy one at the port itself.

Go to www.leros.org.uk for info on local history and facilities.

Enallaktiko Cafe (internet per hr €2; ⊙10am-midnight) Opposite the quay, an uberchic lounge bar with free wi-fi and terminals.

Laskarina Tours (☑22470 24550; fax 22470 24551) In Platanos; ferry tickets and island cruises.

Police (☑22470 22222) In Agia Marina.

Post Office West of the quay in Agia Marina.

Pandeli   Παντελή

South of Platanos, Pandeli is a picture postcard village with a sand and shingle beach bookended by white windmills and white houses tumbling into the bay.

On the east side of the bay, **Rooms to Rent Kavos** (☑22470 23247, 22470 25020; d €50; 🖘) is super fresh and close to the water. Comfy rooms have balconies, stone flooring, fridges, desks and kitchenettes. **Panteli Beach Hotel** (☑22470 26400; www.panteli-beach.r; Pandeli; studio/apt €100/140) is plusher with pretty studios with fresh white walls, nice duvets, sparkling kitchenettes, flat-screen TVs, wi-fi and a communal cafe bar.

Pension Happiness (☑22470 23498; www.studios-happiness-leros.com; d/studio/apt €45/55/70; ✱) has great sea views from its vibrant white and blue studios with kitchenettes, twin beds and private balconies. Rooms vary in size and are spotless throughout. For lunch, head to **Taverna Psaropoula** (☑22470 25200; mains €9; ⊙lunch & dinner). Right on the beach and bluer than a mermaid's iris, this taverna dishes up grilled meats, salads, braised lamb, rabbit stew, calamari, octopus and mezedhes. Try the prawn souvlakia.

Vromolithos   Βρωμόλιθος

As you stand upon the cliff looking down onto Vromolithos beach it's easy to imagine the myths taking place here; the water a perfect shade of Aegean blue scattered with turquoise.

Up on the hill, **Pension Rodon** (☑22470 22075; s/d €40/45; ⊙year-round) has clean and welcoming rooms with stupendous sea views of distant Turkey, balconies, kitchenettes and TVs. Next door, **Bald Dimitris**

(☑22470 25626; mezedhes €3-7; ⊙noon-4pm & 6pm-late) is a hilltop eyrie with a pretty terrace. Bouzouki music washes over a wonderful menu of sea urchin salad, whitebait, meatballs, octopus carpaccio, steamed mussels and hearty portions of calamari. Recommended.

What strikes you first about the eminently languid cliff-top lounge bar **Cafe Del Mar** (☑22470 24766; www.leroscafedelmar.com; snacks €3-8; ⊙9am-late) is the paradisaical view of the bay through the trees. It boasts cool tunes, regular guest DJs spinning the decks by night, comfy deckchairs and chillsome Balaeric-style patios in pine-shaded spots, as well as sandwiches, salads and pasta dishes. Perfect for sunset mojitos, if Circe was a bar this might be it.

Lakki   Λακκί
POP 2370

Between 1912 and 1948 Lakki was a significant naval base for the Italians and its footprint can be clearly seen in the art deco buildings along the dock. These days it barely has a pulse. A few cafes line the waterfront attracting trade from the yachtie crowd who moor at the nearby marina.

Hotel Miramare (☑22470 22469; georvirv@otenet.gr; d €30; P✱🖘) is shadowy and dated, with comfy rooms with thick blankets, TV, fridge and retro radios. It's a block back from Diva Club. **Petrino** (mains €10; ⊙7am-11pm), a popular restaurant with a shaded terrace, is the preferred choice on the island for carnivores. Apart from delicious steaks, there's octopus salad, stewed rabbit and beef in lemon sauce.

The port has internet access and wi-fi at the quayside **Diva Club** (☑22470 2259; per hr €3; mains €7) which also does decent coffee, breakfasts, salads, ice cream and juices. There are a number of ATMs throughout the town. The island's largest grocery store is on the road to Platanos.

Even if you're not a history buff, it's worth detouring to the engrossing **War Museum** (☑22470 25520; admission €3; ⊙9.30am-1.30pm), a short drive west towards Merikia. Who knew that such a decisive WWII battle took place on this wee island? When the Germans captured Leros from the Italians and British in 1943, locals hid in bunkers, which are now home to countless war-time objects.

Xirokambos Ξηρόκαμπος

Southern Xirokambos Bay has a restaurant alongside a few village homes. The beach is pebble and sand with some good spots for snorkelling. En route to Xirokambos a signposted path leads up to the ruined fortress of Paleokastro for pretty views.

Xirokambos' Camping Leros (☑944238490, 22470 23372; camp sites adult/ tent €6.50/4; ☺Jun-Sep) is set in a 400-year-old olive grove with a welcoming cafe with barbecues in the evening. The campground is 500m from the beach and 3km from Lakki.

Ten minutes' walk from the beach, Villa Alexandros (☑6972914552, 22470 22202; d €50; ❄☎) has wood-accented apartments with tiled floors, large kitchen and plenty of space. The apartments upstairs have balconies overlooking a flowery garden. Right on the beach, To Aloni (☑22470 26048; mains €9) is bordered by tamarisk trees and makes its own vegetables and olive oil. Try the tasty *bourekia* (soft cheese and bacon in filo pastry) between mouthfuls of zucchini, octopus, lobster and swordfish.

Krithoni & Alinda
Κριθώνι & Αλιντα

Krithoni and Alinda sit next to each other on Alinda Bay, running parallel to the beach and bordered by a few *kafeneia* and restaurants.

Leros' longest beach is at Alinda – although narrow, it's shaded and sandy with clean, shallow water. Alinta Seasport (☑22470 24584) hires out row boats, canoes and motor boats. On the bay, the Historic & Folklore Museum (admission €3; ☺9am-12.30pm & 6.30-9pm Tue-Sun) is in what was once a stately home and houses arachaeological finds from the Neolithic and Bronze ages as well as WWII exhibits.

On Krithoni's waterfront there is a poignant war cemetery. After the Italians surrendered in WWII, Leros saw fierce fighting between German and British forces.

For the best sun-worshipping round here, head through Krithoni and Alinda to Dio Liskaria Beach (a few minutes' scooter ride away); bookended by rocks and backdropped by a taverna, it's caressed by aquamarine water.

🛏 Sleeping

Hotel Alinda HOTEL $
(☑22470 23266; Alinda; s/d €35/50; ❄☎) Lovely rooms with private balconies looking out across its leafy garden to the bay. Rooms vary in size but all are spotless with comfy beds, armoire, TV and desk. There's also an excellent Greek restaurant here too. Charming owner.

★ To Archontiko Angelou HOTEL $$
(☑22470 22749; www.hotel-angelou-leros.com; Alinda; r incl breakfast €60-160; 🅿❄☎) ✈ Spilling with oleander and jacaranda, this incurably romantic, 19th-century rosé-coloured villa is like stepping into a vintage Italian film; think wood floors, Viennese frescoes, antique beds and old-world style rooms. Breakfast on the sun-dappled terrace is an event, the owner playing Aphrodite in the kitchen to produce mouth-watering homemade bread, jams and marmalades.

One of the finest hotels in the Dodecanese.

Nefeli Hotel APARTMENT $$
(☑22470 24611; www.nefelihotels.com; studio €85, apt €100-150; 🅿❄☎) Vividly coloured in lavender and pink these sugar-white apartments are beautifully finished with stone floors, gleaming kitchens, flat-screen TVs, moulded-stone couches and swallow-you-up beds. All have private balconies and there's a tempting cafe in the herb-fragrant courtyard.

🍴 Eating & Drinking

Alinda is lined with lots of stylish cafes and restaurants.

Head towards Krithoni for a drink at Nemesis (☑22470 22070). With Cuban jazz playing and the light swimming through suspended glass bottles, nurse an ouzo and watch the sunset on the terrace.

O Lampros Restaurant TAVERNA $
(☑22470 24154; Alinda; mains €8.50-10; ☺6am-late) Patronised by gnarled elderly gents flicking worry beads, O Lampros offers breakfast, snacks and traditional cuisine like tzatziki, mezedhes, Greek salads, swordfish and octopus. Treat yourself to shrimp *saganaki*.

Fanari GREEK $
(☑6984135216; mains €8-10; ❄☎) At shabby-chic Fanari you can eat on the patio or by the waves. The menu spans breakfast, mezedhes

and lamb *stifadho* to pasta dishes. But you can also try combo dishes for two (€20) which gives you meatballs, halloumi, tzatziki and green peppers.

Northern Leros

The north of the island is dotted with small fishing communities, beehives and rugged terrain. Just west of the airport, the **Temple of Artemis** (the island's ancient patroness) dates from the 4th century BC but has yet to be excavated.

East of here, **Blefoutis Beach** is a narrow stretch of sand and pebble on a pretty enclosed bay.

PATMOS ΠΑΤΜΟΣ

POP 3040

In AD 95 St John the Divine received a vision in a cave and wrote the sinister Book of Revelations here. Exuding a bewitching spirituality, Patmos is special. No, really, David Bowie thinks so, as do the thousands of pilgrims who annually travel to the white-washed sanctity of hilltop Hora; scattered with crow-black pensioners, galleries, fine boutiques and tavernas.

As one free-diver commented: 'The island either rejects you or holds on to you.' And from the moment you enter Hora's 10th-century monastery with its diabolical friezes of demons and hell, you'll either be creeped or enraptured. Patmos also has more than its fair share of gas-blue coves, green mountains and fine-pebble beaches, while its stylish harbour of Skala buzzes and is full of tasteful boutiques.

History

In AD 95, St John the Divine was banished to Patmos by the pagan Roman Emperor Domitian. While residing in a cave on the island, St John heard the voice of God from a cleft in the rock, and wrote the Book of Revelations. In 1088 the Blessed Christodoulos, an abbot, obtained permission from the Byzantine Emperor Alexis I Komninos to build a monastery in Patmos to commemorate St John. Pirate raids necessitated powerful fortifications, so the monastery looks like a mighty castle.

Under the Duke of Naxos, Patmos became a semi-autonomous monastic state and achieved such wealth and influence that it was able to resist Turkish oppression.

ⓘ Getting There & Away

BOAT

Patmos is connected with Piraeus, Rhodes and a number of islands in between through mainline services with Blue Star Ferries and Anek Lines. The F/B *Nissos Kalymnos* and *Anna Express* provide additional links to Lipsi and Leros three times per week. The local **Patmos Star** (☑ 6977601633) serves Lipsi and Leros (€8), while *Lambi II* goes to Marathi and Arki (€7). Hydrofoils and catamarans also link Patmos with Samos and the rest of the Dodecanese. Boat tickets are sold by Apollon Travel (p530) in Skala.

BOAT SERVICES FROM PATMOS

DESTINATION	TIME	FARE	FREQUENCY
Agathonisi	55min	€8	4 weekly
Kalymnos*	1hr 40min	€26	6 weekly
Kos*	3hr	€29	6 weekly
Leros	2hr	€11	4 weekly
Leros*	40min	€16	6 weekly
Lipsi*	25min	€13	6 weekly
Piraeus	7hr	€36	3 weekly
Rhodes	6hr	€37	4 weekly
Rhodes*	5hr	€47	6 weekly
Samos	5hr	€9	4 weekly
Symi*	4hr	€44	3 weekly

*high-speed services

Patmos

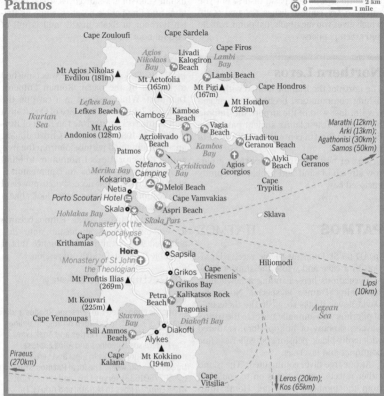

N 0 ———— 2 km
0 ———— 1 mile

Patmos map labels:

Cape Zouloufi
Cape Sardela
Cape Firos
Agios Nikolaos Bay
Livadi Kalogiron Beach
Lambi Bay
Lambi Beach
Mt Agios Nikolas Evdilou (181m)
Mt Aetofolia (165m)
Mt Pigi (167m)
Cape Hondros
Lefkes Bay
Lefkes Beach
Kambos
Kambos Beach
Vagia Beach
Mt Hondro (228m)
Ikarian Sea
Mt Agios Andonios (128m)
Agriolivado Beach
Kambos Bay
Livadi tou Geranou Beach
Patmos
Agriolivado Bay
Agios Georgios
Alyki Beach
Cape Geranos
Merika Bay
Stefanos Camping
Kokarina
Netia
Meloï Beach
Cape Trypitis
Porto Scoutari Hotel
Skala
Cape Vamvakias
Hohlakas Bay
Aspri Beach
Skala Port
Sklava
Monastery of the Apocalypse
Cape Krithamias
Hora
Sapsila
Hiliomodi
Monastery of St John the Theologian
Grikos
Cape Hesmenis
Mt Profitis Ilias (269m)
Grikos Bay
Lipsi (10km)
Kalikatsos Rock
Mt Kouvari (225m)
Petra Beach
Tragonisi
Aegean Sea
Cape Yennoupas
Stavros Bay
Diakofti Bay
Psili Ammos Beach
Alykes
Diakofti
Piraeus (270km)
Cape Kalana
Mt Kokkino (194m)
Cape Vitsilia
Marathi (12km);
Arki (13km);
Agathonisi (30km);
Samos (50km)
Leros (20km);
Kos (65km)

ⓘ Getting Around

BOAT

Excursion boats go to Psili Ammos Beach from Skala, departing around 10am and returning about 4pm.

BUS

From Skala, there are eight return buses daily to Hora and four to Grikos and Kambos. Fares are a standard €1.50.

CAR & MOTORCYCLE

There are several car- and motorcycle-hire outlets in Skala including **Avis** (☑ 22470 33025). The best scooter shop, **Moto Rent Faros** (☑ 22470 29330), is behind Skala harbour on the road to Hora, and has quick, regularly serviced bikes.

TAXI

You can catch a **taxi** (☑ 22470 31225) from Skala's taxi rank opposite the police station.

Skala   Σκάλα

Photogenic Skala hugs the dock with white-washed houses rising amphitheatrically up the hill, and is threaded with boutiques, shadowy bars, guesthouses and aromatic tavernas in its web of backstreets. Periodically quiet then suddenly busy with throngs of pilgrims disgorged from cruise ships, it's a great place to meet locals over a frappé.

⦿ Sights & Activities

Skala has a couple of religious sites, including the place where St John first baptised the locals in AD 96, just north of the beach. To find out more and to see religious objects from across the island, visit the **Orthodox Culture & Information Centre** (⊙ 9am-1pm Thu-Tue & 6-9pm Mon, Tue, Thu & Fri) in the harbour-side church.

If you feel like a workout, climb up to the remains of an ancient acropolis on the hillside to the west of town. The route is not well signposted; head for the prominent chapel then follow the dirt trail across the fields full of wildflowers and lizards. The views from the top are stunning.

🛏 Sleeping

Hotel and studio owners often meet boats at the port, but it's best to call ahead and arrange a pick-up.

Pension Maria Pascalidis   PENSION $
(☑ 22470 32152; s/d/tr €20/35/45; 🛜) This garden complex of 10 rooms feels like a slice of home. Twin, single and double rooms, most of which have an en suite, all enjoy a communal kitchen. The garden, blooming with flowers, is a restful place to read. It's on the road leading to Hora.

Hotel Chris   HOTEL $$
(☑ 22470 31001; www.patmoschrishotel.gr; d back €40, sea view €70-80; 🅿 ❄ 🛜) Enjoying a recent revamp, rooms here have private sea-facing balconies, tiled floors, TV, dark-wood furniture, four posters and modern en suites. Get a room out back to avoid road noise.

Captain's House   HOTEL $$
(☑ 22470 31793; www.captains-house.gr; d/apt incl breakfast €70/80; ❄ 🛜 ❄ ♨) These delightful wharf-side digs have high spec rooms and apartments with en suite, flat-screen TVs and desks, as well as balconies overlooking the nearby sea, fridges and a lovely swimming pool out back with sun loungers. There's also a great breakfast terrace. Perfect family option.

Delfini Hotel   HOTEL $$
(☑ 22470 32060; www.delfini-patmos.gr; s/d €30/45; ❄ 🛜) Portside Delfini, next to the Captain's House, is colourful and fresh with sea- and Hora-facing rooms with fridge, tiled floors, tangerine-hued bedspreads and clean en suites. Plus there's no extra charge for an additional kid's bed.

Kalderimi Apartments   BOUTIQUE HOTEL $$
(☑ 22470 33008; www.kalderimi.com; apt incl breakfast from €110; ❄ 🛜) Whitewashed and abundant with palms, bougainvillea and Moorish lanterns in its shaded courtyard, apartments here have a traditional feel with wooden beams and stone walls, plus sparkling kitchen, safety deposit box and fridge. At the foot of the path up to the monastery.

Blue Bay Hotel   HOTEL $$
(☑ 22470 31165; www.bluebaypatmos.gr; s/d/tr incl breakfast €85/100/145; ❄ @ 🛜) Just south of the harbour, these are appealing rooms with powder-blue bedspreads, large bathrooms, flat-screen TV, contemporary furniture and balconies with sea views. There's also a breakfast buffet.

🍴 Eating

Meltemi   CAFE $
(full breakfast €5; ⏲ 9am-late; 🛜) This attractive nautical-style bar has portholes and low-lit ambience. Toasted sandwiches, fruit salad, breakfasts, milkshakes, quiche and coffee, while the waves lap at your toes.

Tzivaeri   SEAFOOD $
(mains €9; ⏲ dinner) With its walls beshacked in shells, sponges and black-and-white photos and the air thick with bouzouki, this is a memorable stop for calamari, shrimp, octopus and plenty more seafood.

Loukas Grill House   TAVERNA $
(mains €8; ⏲ dinner; ❄) Redolent of old Greece, and thick with grilled aromas, cavernous Loukas has a carnivorous menu of skewered pork sausage, veal steak and spit roast pork, as well as rabbit *stifadho* and goat in red sauce. Toward the back of the maze behind the harbour.

Ostria   TAVERNA $
(mains €8-12; ⏲ lunch & dinner; ❄) Right on the harbour, this Aegean blue and white belle is fresh, breezy and great for a romantic dinner as the sun drops. Mussels, sea urchins, shrimps, souvlakia, zucchini balls and mezedhes are but a few of its treasures. For groceries, head to **AB Food Market**, a well-stocked store 100m along the Hora road in Skala.

🍷 Drinking & Nightlife

⭐ **Koukoumavia**   BAR
(⏲ 10am-late; 🛜) 🎨 Imagine the lovechild of Tim Burton and Frida Kahlo opening a coffee house and you're getting close; interesting art spattered across green and orange walls, cool tunes, cocktails and excellent coffee. There's also a little garden terrace.

Mostra Cafe   CAFE
(mains €3.50; ⊘7.30am-midnight; 🛜) Follow
the backstreets radiating from the harbour
to this dinky, New England–style white and
blue cafe. Fruit salads, cakes, smoothies,
juices and ice cream.

Arion   BAR
(🛜) Over a hundred years old, shadowy,
high-raftered Arion is popular with locals
and travellers who sit outside and people-
watch. Wi-fi plugs you back into the 21st
century. On the harbour.

🔒 Shopping

Koukoumavla (www.patmos-island.com/kouk-
oumavia) has funky handmade T-shirts, bags,
handmade jewellery, original art, lamps and
badges. On the harbour, **Selene** (Harbour;
⊘9am-1pm & 3-11pm) is a real curiosity shop
of contemporary sculptures, puppets, ceramics, icons and jewellery.

In the warren of streets behind the central square, **Apyos News Agent** sells international papers, novels and maps.

ℹ️ Information

All transport arrives at the centre of the quay in
the middle of Skala. To the right the road leads to
a narrow, sandy beach, the yacht port and on to
the north of the island. To the left the road leads
to the south side of the island. From a roundabout near the ferry terminal, a road heads inland
and up to Hora. The bus terminal and taxi rank
are at the quay and all main services are within
100m.

There are three ATM-equipped banks in Skala:
the National Bank of Greece, the Emporiki Bank
and the Commercial Bank.

The website www.patmos-island.com has lots
of local listings and info. And there's www.
patmosweb.gr for history, listings and photos.
Apollon Travel (📋22470 31324; apollontravel
@stratas.gr) Ticketing for flights and ferries as
well as advice on accommodation.
Dodoni Gelateria (internet per hr €4; ⊘9am-
9pm; 🛜) Get online while scoffing homemade
ice cream.
Hospital (📋22470 31211) Two kilometres along
the road to Hora.
Municipal Tourist Office (📋22470 31666;
⊘summer) Shares the same building as the
post office and police station. Open from June.
Police (📋22470 31303) On the main waterfront.
Port Police (📋22470 31231) Behind the quay's
passenger-transit building.

Hora (Patmos)
Χώρα (Πάτμος)

Visit hilltop Hora and its centrepiece monastery of St John, and you cannot help but
pick up its rarefied vibe. By night it's ghostly,
sanctified and creaking in the wind. Revelations, that curiously frightening book,
was written in a cave nearby and some of
its Boschian spectres seem to scuttle invis-
ibly behind as you wander the 17th-century
maze of streets.

The immense **Monastery of St John
the Theologian** (admission €4 incl museum entrance; ⊘8am-1.30pm daily & 4-6pm Tue, Thu, Wed
& Sat) crowns the island of Patmos. Attending a service here, with plumes of incense,
religious chants and devoted worshippers, is
unforgettable. To reach it, many people walk
up the Byzantine path which starts from a
signposted spot along the Skala–Hora road.

Some 200m along this path, a dirt trail
to the left leads through pine trees to the
Monastery of the Apocalypse (treasury
€2; ⊘8am-1.30pm daily, plus 4-6pm Tue, Thu &
Sun), built around the cave where St John
received his revelation. You can see the rock
the saint used as a pillow and the triple fissure in the roof from where the voice of God
issued. Grab a pew and try not to think of
The Omen!

A five-minute walk west of St John's Monastery, the **Holy Monastery of Zoodohos
Pigi** (⊘8am-noon & 5-7pm Sun-Fri) FREE is a
women's convent with incredibly impressive
frescoes. On Good Friday, a beautiful candlelit ceremony takes place here.

Just east of St John's Monastery, Andreas
Kalatzis is a Byzantine icon artist who lives
and works in a 1740s traditional home. Inside, you'll find an interesting mix of pottery, jewellery and paintings by local artists.
Seek out **Patmos Gallery** (run by Kalatzis)
for an eclectic range of abstract and figura-
tive paintings, jewellery and illuminated
sculptures.

★**Archontariki** (📋22470 29368; www.
archontariki-patmos.gr; ste incl breakfast €220-
400; ✳️🛜) is a 400-year-old building with
four gorgeous suites equipped with every
convenience, traditional furnishings and
plush touches. Relaxing under the fruit trees
in the cool and quiet garden, you'll wonder
why the hotel isn't named Paradise.

Up in the seat of the gods, looking down
on the white-cube cluster of Skala, mint-

ST JOHN THE DIVINE & THE APOCALYPSE

Patmos' Hora is home to the Cave of the Apocalypse, where St John the Divine was allegedly visited by God and instructed to write the Book of Revelations. He is often believed to be John the Apostle of Jesus or John the Evangelist, though many would dispute this due to his exile in AD 95 by the Roman Emperor Domitian. The Book of Revelations describes the end of the world – involving the final rebellion by Satan at Armageddon, God's final defeat of Satan and the restoration of peace to the world. Due to its heavy, dark symbolism some critics have suggested that it was the work of a deranged man. Whatever you choose to believe, it's worth visiting the cave where it all supposedly took place.

fresh **Pantheon** (mains €6-12) dishes up grilled octopus, meatballs, fried cheese, juices and homemade yoghurt. A few metres further up, **Jimmy's Balcony** (Hora; mains €6-9; ⊘10am-11pm; 🛜🍴) has regal views and a terrace to enjoy their delicious salads, breakfast, *mousakas* or one of their veggie options. It's also the only spot to pick up clear wi-fi.

At the **Vangelis Taverna** (mains €10) there are jaw-dropping views from under their carob tree out back, plus a menu of roast rabbit and onion, fresh Patmos goat and octopus *macarounes*. For a drink, sorbets and homemade sweets, head to **Stoa Cafe**, a hip oasis with wi-fi across the square.

North of Skala

The narrow, tree-shaded **Meloï Beach** is just 2km northeast of Skala. If you've brought your tent, head for pine-shaded **Stefanos Camping** (📞22470 31821; camp sites per person/tent €7/2; ⊘May-Oct). It's clean and well equipped with bamboo-enclosed and tree-shaded sites, a minimarket and cafe-bar.

Just north of Skala on the road to Kambos is the plush **Porto Scoutari Hotel** (📞22470 33123; www.portoscoutari.com; incl breakfast d €90-190, tr €145-215; 🅿️❄️@🛜🏊). Backed by a lavish swimming pool and spa centre, this elegant hotel has amazing sea views and palatial-sized rooms with nautical frescoes, sofas, flat-screen TV, spotless en suite, private balconies and antique beds.

Further up the road is the inland village of **Kambos**, from where the road descends to the relatively wide and sandy **Kambos Beach**, perhaps the most popular and easily accessible beach on the island.

Superchilled **George's Place** (snacks €8; ⊘breakfast, lunch & dinner; 🅿️❄️🛜🏄) 🍴 sits by the peacock-blue bay with an enticingly shaded sun-dappled terrace, easy tunes and wi-fi; plus a simple menu of salads, homemade pies, chocolate cake and pastries to keep you happy. Just opposite is a **water sports** outfit that can take you wakeboarding and water-skiing and where you can hire sunbeds.

The main road forks left to **Lambi**, 9km from Skala, where you wind down green hills to an impressive beach of multicoloured pebbles. High above, **Leonidas** (mains €9; 🅿️❄️🍴) 🍴 has roast lamb, souvlakia, calf's liver, lobster (€85 per kilo) and octopus. Eat in the garden or homely interior. On the beach itself, lulled by the nearby waves, **Lambi Fish Tavern** (mains €7-14; ⊘10am-late; 🅿️❄️🏄) is a tranquil setting to enjoy meatballs, salted mackerel, stuffed vine leaves, souvlakia and octopus cooked in wine.

Under the protected lee of the north arm of the island are several more beaches, including **Vagia Beach**. Overlooking the beach **Cafe Vagia** (mains €3-5; ⊘9am-7pm) is a real gem, its hillside garden enjoying turquoise views and fragrant with fresh-baked pies alchemised in the kitchen.

Further east is the shaded **Livadi tou Geranou Beach**, with a small church-crowned island opposite. Remote with heavenly sea views, **Livadi Geranou Taverna** (mains €9; ⊘10am-late) is backdropped by heather-clad hills and has a menu of souvlakia, whitebait and octopus.

South of Skala

Small, tree-filled valleys and picturesque beaches fill the south of Patmos. Closest to Skala is the tiny, peaceful settlement of **Sapsila**. **Mathios Studios** (📞22470 32583; www.mathiosapartments.gr; studio/apt €70/80; ❄️@)

has the most appealing midrange studios on the island; check-cloth tables, comfy beds, driftwood sculptures, books to read and great kitchens with sea views. Dine nearby at Benetos (Sapsila; mains €7-14; ⊘ dinner Tue-Sun; 🖍) 🖊, a working boutique farmhouse restaurant that specialises in Mediterranean fusion dishes with an occasional Japanese kick. Try zucchini blossoms stuffed with mushrooms and cheese. Open in July onwards.

Grikos, 1km further along over the hill, has a long, sandy beach lined with tavernas, and the chapel of Agios Ioannis Theologos where many believe St John baptised islanders. Overlooking Petra Beach is Flivos Restaurant (mains €7.50), with traditional decor and a terrific seafood menu including swordfish and shrimps with garlic sauce.

Want to eat sushi on an elegant boat moored in the moonlight? You can on Spartan (🖉 6972119206), a 14m-long caïque run by friendly Reiko. She also skippers the craft to Arki, Lipsi and Marathi, sailing from Grikos harbour for the day. On board you can buy some of her exquisite one-off pieces of jewellery. Look for the boat with the mermaid in Grikos harbour.

Just south, Petra Beach is very peaceful with plenty of shade. A spit leads out to the startling Kalikatsos Rock. A rough coastal track leads from here to Diakofti, the last settlement in the south. (You can also get here by a longer sealed road from Hora.) From here you can follow a half-hour walking track to the island's best spit of sand; tree-shaded Psili Ammos Beach, where there's a seasonal taverna.

LIPSI ΛΕΙΨΟΙ

POP 700

The 8km-long Lipsi might be small, but what a powerful presence it evokes on the traveller; its low-slung harbour bunched with crayon-yellow nets, its whitewashed, church-crowned village of Lipsi climbing up the hill behind. If it's rugged hills, serene blue coves and deserted beaches you seek, then you may have just found heaven.

In Homer's 'Odyssey', Lipsi was home to the nymph Calypso who waylaid the hero Odysseus for several years. Abandon yourself to sun-worshipping and wandering the backstreets of Lipsi Village, and you may fare the same. Within the blue-domed church of Panagia tou Harou there's a unique icon inside whose glass cabinet miraculously bloom unwatered lilies every 23 August.

Check out too the local speciality *mzithra* cheese, made from goat's milk and sea water, and pick up a jar of distinctive thyme honey.

❶ Getting There & Away

Sea connections with Lipsi are tenuous, although it is linked with Piraeus through long-haul ferries and neighbouring islands via catamaran, a Kalymnos-based ferry and the larger *Patmos Star*. The local **Anna Express** (🖉 22479 41382) connects with Agathonisi, Arki, Kalymnos and Leros.

BOAT SERVICES FROM LIPSI

DESTINATION	TIME	FARE	FREQUENCY
Agathonisi	3hr	€7	4 weekly
Agathonisi*	40min	€12.50	1 weekly
Kalymnos	1½hr	€9	1 daily
Kalymnos*	20min	€20	1 daily
Kos*	5hr 50min	€29	6 weekly
Leros	1hr	€6.50	6 weekly
Leros*	20min	€14	1 daily
Patmos	25min	€6	1 daily
Patmos*	10min	€12.50	1 daily
Rhodes*	5½hr	€45	6 weekly

*high-speed services

Lipsi

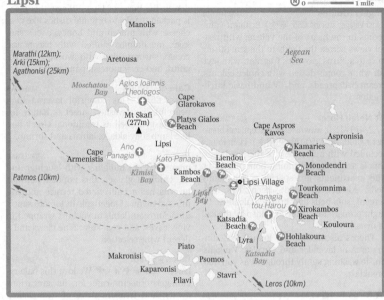

ⓘ Getting Around

Stretching 8km end to end, Lipsi is small. In summer, a minibus departs Lipsi Village hourly to the beaches of Platys Gialos, Katsadia and Hohlakoura (each €1.50) between 10.30am and 6pm. Two **taxis** (📞6942409679/7) operate on the island; you'll find them roaming around Lipsi Village. Hire scooters in Lipsi Village from **Marcos Maria Rent A Bike** (📞22479 41130).

Lipsi Village   Λειψοί

POP 600

Hugging the deep harbour, Lipsi Village – the only community on the island – is a cosy, intimate affair with an atmospheric old town of blue-shuttered houses radiating up the hill in a web of backstreets. The harbour is the hub of Lipsi's action; there's everything you need here from an ATM and a great bakery, to delectable seafood restaurants. And don't forget to visit the beautiful church of Panagia tou Harou (p533).

🏃 Activities

Liendou Beach is on the edge of the village, with a narrow strip of sand and shallow, calm water. It's just north of the ferry port over a small headland. Around 40 min-

utes' walk from Lipsi Village, rugged **Gialos Beach** rings with goats' bells, and shelves gently into Evian-clear water.

Rena and Margarita offer **boat trips** (per person €20) to Lipsi's offshore islands such as exquisite Aspronisia and Macronisi (with their sapphire waters and weird rock formations) for a picnic and swim. Both excursion boats can be found at Lipsi's smaller jetty and depart at around 10am daily. A five-island tour of local idylls can also be organised through Lipsi Bookings and costs as little as €15.

🎉 Festivals & Events

Panagia tou Harou   RELIGIOUS

This annual religious festival takes place on the 23 August, when the island fills up with visitors who come to pay homage to the famous icon of the Virgin, and witness the miraculous flowering of the rootless lilies. Following a procession, expect all-night revelry in the lower village square.

Wine Festival   FOOD

This Dionysian festival takes place for three days during August with dancing and free wine. Check locally for the exact dates.

🛏 Sleeping

Angela Studios   APARTMENT $

(Lipsi Village; studios €55; ❄ 🛜) Brilliant-value rooms in the heart of the village, with restful views across the fields to the sea. Sitting next to a citrus grove it's fragrant, with stylish white rooms dotted with choice colours, cream bedspreads, and TV and basic kitchenettes.

⭐ Nefeli Hotel   APARTMENT $$

(📞 22470 41120; www.nefelihotels.com; incl breakfast r €100, apt €150-170; P ❄ 🛜) Deliciously secluded with a fine view of the bay below, this is a stylish, welcoming boutique hotel. The apartments are spacious with comfy beds, kitchenettes, flat-screen TVs, silk screens, sofa beds and private balconies; by night prepare to be lulled to sleep by the call of owls.

There's also a Moorish lounge and dining area of lavender and purples, Vangelis' music washing subtly through it as you take breakfast.

⭐ Rizos Studios   APARTMENT $$

(📞 6976244125; www.annaexpress-lipsi.services.officelive.com/rizos.aspx; d €70; ❄ 🛜) These are superior rooms with interior flair; think lavender-blue fittings, private balconies with sea views, stone-flag floors, and kitchenettes with a wealth of cooking utensils. It's 10 minutes' walk from the dock up a hill, so phone ahead for a lift from the port.

Aphroditi Hotel   HOTEL $$

(📞 22470 41000; www.hotel-aphroditi.com; s/d/apt incl breakfast €60/70/110; ❄) Spearmint-fresh Aphroditi, just behind Liendou Beach, has a swish cafe as well as 28 rooms and studios, with additional sofa beds, tiled floors, bureaus, TVs, kitchenettes, balconies and a contemporary feel.

Apartments Poseidon   APARTMENT $$

(📞 22470 41130; www.lipsi-poseidon.gr; d incl breakfast €70; ❄) On your left as you walk from the boat to town, rooms here are spacious and cool, with tiled floors, silk curtains, private balconies with sea views, and kitchenettes. The family-sized apartments have additional sofa beds, washing machines and a larger kitchen with a cooker.

🍴 Eating

⭐ Manolis Tastes   TAVERNA $

(📞 6980534452; mains €8-10; ⊙ noon-4pm & 5.30pm-late; 🛜) 🖉 Chef Manolis only cooks with food whose origin he can trace. Hidden in the maze of Lipsi Village, this place is packed thanks to original dishes like goat cheese with museli and honey, chef's sausage, mushrooms stuffed with bacon and cream, shrimp salad with avocado and yoghurt, and *very* moreish pannacotta.

Cafe de Moulin   TAVERNA $

(mains €6.50) This colourful taverna in a peaceful, whitewashed street is handy for breakfasts as well as traditional Greek fare like lamb souvlakia, calamari and shrimp.

Pefko   TAVERNA $

(mains €7-8; 🛜) Bubbling with laughter and the chink of glasses, this popular harbour taverna has a multi-tiered terrace and traditional menu of meatballs in tomato sauce, *ambelourgou* (lamb in yoghurt wrapped in vine leaves) and goat stew. Fine views and a decent wine selection.

Bakery Shop   BAKERY $

(sweets €1-3; ❄ 🛜 🏀) 🖉 We love this bakery-cum-gelateria-cum-cafe for its gregarious owner, and treasure trove of fresh baked cookies, croissants, sausage rolls, pies, bespoke baguette sandwiches, cakes, baklava and alcohol to enjoy on their terrace or indoors. If you've got kids it's right by the playground.

ℹ Information

All boats dock at Lipsi Port, where there are two quays. Ferries, hydrofoils and catamarans all dock at the larger outer jetty, while excursion boats dock at a smaller jetty nearer the centre of Lipsi Village. The *Anna Express* docks close to the large main church in the inner port.

The post office is opposite the church on the upper central square in the old town. The lower harbour-side square is home to a **tourist office** (⊙ summer only), which opens for most ferry arrivals, along with a shaded children's playground. The Co-operative Bank of the Dodecanese on the port changes money and has an ATM.

The website www.lipsi-island.gr is a useful resource about the island.

Cafe Kabos (per hr €2) Close to the ferry landing.

Doctor (📞 22470 41204; ⊙ 9am-1.30pm Mon-Fri) There's a small medical clinic in the village.

Lipsi Bookings (📞 22470 41382; www.lipsibookings.com) Run by the ever-helpful Sarah, Lipsi issues tickets for the *Anna Express* and organises excursions, accommodation and specialist photography walking tours. She also acts as an estate agent.

Police (22470 41222) In the port.

Port Police (22470 41133) In the port.

Ticket Office (22470 41250; 30min prior to departures) A small office on the outer jetty issuing boat tickets.

Around Lipsi

Getting to Lipsi's villages makes for pleasant walks through countryside dotted with olive groves, cypress trees and endless views. The minibus services the main beaches.

Just 1km beyond Lipsi Village, **Kambos Beach** offers some shade and is narrower but sandier than its neighbour, Liendou. The water is also deeper and rockier underfoot.

From here, a further 2.5km (40 minutes' walk) brings you to shallow and child-friendly **Platys Gialos**, the best beach on the island for turquoise water. Above the beach is **Kostas Restaurant** (6944963303; grills €9; 8am-6pm Jul-Aug), for fish and grill dishes.

Just 2km south from Lipsi Village, sandy **Katsadia Beach** is wilder, especially if it's windy. Tamarisk trees offer some shade and on the beach is the **Dilaila Cafe Restaurant** (22470 41041; mains €9; Jun-Sep), with an easy vibe. Open late as a bar, the seafood is also great.

Beaches on the east coast are more difficult to reach. Due to rough roads, neither taxis nor buses come here.

ARKI & MARATHI
ΑΡΚΟΙ & ΜΑΡΑΘΙ

Arki and Marathi, just north of Patmos and Lipsi, are the most peaceful islets in this chain. The former is home to only 50 inhabitants who make a living from farming, goat breeding and fishing. The turquoise-ometer of the water? Off the scale! Expect an eclectic mix of yachties, artists and the occasional

backpacker. There are neither cars nor motorbikes – just calmness. Pack your bathers, books and iPod and leave the chaos behind.

ⓘ Getting There & Away

The F/B *Nissos Kalymnos* calls in up to four times weekly as it shuttles between Patmos and Samos on its vital milk run. The Lipsi-based, speedy *Anna Express* links Arki with Lipsi (15 minutes) twice weekly. In summer, Lipsi-based excursion boats and Patmos-based caïques do frequent day trips (return €20) to Arki and Marathi. A local caïque runs between Marathi and Arki (1¼ hours).

Arki   Αρκοί
POP 50

Only 5km north of Lipsi, tiny Arki has rolling hills and secluded, sandy beaches. Its only settlement is the little west-coast port, also called Arki. Away from the village, the island seems almost mystical in its peace and stillness.

There is no post office or police on the island, but there is one cardphone. The **Church of Metamorfosis** stands on a hill behind the settlement. Several **sandy coves** can be reached along a path skirting the north side of the bay.

Tiganakia Bay, on the southeast coast, has a good sandy beach. To walk there from Arki village, follow the road heading south and then the network of goat tracks down to the water. Keep an eye out for dolphins.

Arki has a few tavernas with comfortable, well-maintained rooms; bookings are necessary in July and August. To the right of the quay, **O Trypas Taverna & Rooms** (22470 32230; tripas@12net.gr; d €35; mains €5-7) has simple rooms and serves excellent *fasolia mavromatika* (black-eyed beans) and *pastos tou Trypa* (salted fish). Nearby, **Taverna Nikolaos Rooms** (22470 32477; d €45; mains €8; ❋) dishes up potatoes au gratin, stuffed peppers with cheese or the local goat cheese called *sfina*, which is like a mild form of feta. Rooms have sunset views.

DODECANESE AROUND LIPSI

BOAT SERVICES FROM ARKI & MARATHI

DESTINATION	PORT	TIME	FREQUENCY
Patmos	Arki/Marathi	–	4 weekly
Samos	Arki/Marathi	–	4 weekly
Lipsi	Arki	15min	2 weekly
Arki	Marathi	1¼hr	1 daily

Marathi　　　Μαράθι

Marathi is the largest of Arki's satellite islets, with a superb sandy beach. Before WWII it had a dozen or so inhabitants, but now it has only two families. The old settlement, with an immaculate little church, stands on a hill above the harbour. There are two tavernas on the island, both of which rent rooms. Taverna Mihalis (☑22470 31580; d €40; mains €4-6) is the more laid-back and cheaper of the two, while Taverna Pandelis (☑22470 32609; d €40; mains €8) at the top end of the beach is a tad plusher.

AGATHONISI　ΑΓΑΘΟΝΗΣΙ

POP 160

Arriving in Agathonisi's harbour – enclosed by a fjordlike formation and the buildings so few you could count them in a breath – is pure magic. So far off the tourist radar its neighbours barely acknowledge it, Agathonisi is quiet enough to hear a distant Cyclops break wind. There's little to do here but read, swim, explore the island's caves (once used by islanders to hide from pirates) and then restart the formula. Accommodation is mainly in the harbour village of Agios Georgios.

Keep an eye out too for the *Klidonas* ritual of jumping through fire to cleanse your spirit.

ℹ Getting There & Away

Agathonisi has regular ferry links with Samos and Patmos. A hydrofoil also links the island with Samos and destinations further south. Ferry agent Savvas Kamitsis (☑22470 29003) is spectacularly grumpy but sells tickets at the harbour prior to departures and from the kiosk at Mary's Rooms guesthouse.

ℹ Getting Around

There is no local transport. It's a steep and sweaty 1.5km uphill walk from Agios Georgios to the main settlement of Megalo Horio; somewhat less to Mikro Horio. From Megalo Horio, the island's eastern beaches are all within a 3km walk.

Agios Georgios
Άγιος Γεώργιος

The village of Agios Georgios (*agh*-ios ye-*or*-yi-os) is the island's primary settlement and has a few tavernas and simple sugarcube pensions. The highpoint of the day is sitting on the harbour beach pondering the turquoise and watching the fishermen roll in with their catch. Spilia Beach, 900m southwest around the headland, is quieter and better for swimming; a track around the far side of the bay will take you there. A further 1km walk will bring you to Gaïdouravlakos, a small bay and beach where water from one of the island's few springs meets the sea.

🛏 Sleeping & Eating

In the middle of the waterfront, Mary's Rooms (☑6932575121, 22470 29004; s/d €35/45) are houseproud digs with kitchenettes, balconies with sea views, desks and fridges. Nearby on the left side of the harbour, Studios Theologia (☑22470 29005; d/tr €40/50; ✳@) has simple waterfront rooms with hip retro furniture, TVs, fridges and baclonies.

Follow your nose to Glaros Restaurant (☑22470 29062; mains €9; 🛜☑) and its heavenly aromas – souvlakia, octopus and lamb chops. The menu is simple but the predominantly organic produce is cooked with love. If this place is full, try George's Taverna (mains €7; 🛜) near the boat landing for tasty zucchini balls, beef *stifadho*, rabbit stew and mezedhes.

BOAT SERVICES FROM AGATHONISI

DESTINATION	TIME	FARE	FREQUENCY
Arki	45min	€8	2 weekly
Kalymnos*	2hr	€26	1 weekly
Lipsi	1hr	€7	2 weekly
Patmos	2hr	€8	4 weekly
Rhodes*	5hr	€46	1 weekly
Samos	1hr	€7.50	4 weekly

*high-speed services

ℹ Information

Boats dock at Agios Georgios, from where roads ascend right to Megalo Horio and left to Mikro Horio. There is no tourist information, but there is an ATM at the post office in Megalo Horio. The police are in a prominently marked white building at the beginning of the Megalo Horio road.

Around Agathonisi

A hard trek up the hill from the harbour brings you to the tiny hamlet of Megalo Horio. It's worth the view from the cliff. It doesn't stir until June. Later still, the annual religious festivals of Agiou Panteleimonos (26 July), Sotiros (6 August) and Panagias (22 August), when the village celebrates with abundant food, music and dancing, are all worth attending. To the east of Megalo Horio there's a series of accessible beaches: Tsangari Beach, Tholos Beach, Poros Beach and Tholos (Agios Nikolaos) Beach, close to the eponymous church. All are within easy walking distance although Poros Beach is the only sandy option. If you're after a very quiet stay, Studios Ageliki (☑ 22470 29085; s/d €35/45; ❄) in Megalo Horio has four basic but comfortable studios with kitchenettes and stunning views over a small vineyard and down to the port. Eating in the village is limited to Restaurant I Irini (☑ 22470 29054; mains €7) on the central square, which makes great lamb stew and *stifadho,* or Nico's Taverna (mains €7), serving mezedhes washed down by *raki,* ouzo and woody retsina.

Northeastern Aegean Islands

Best Places to Eat

➡ Hotzas (p561)

➡ Thea (p547)

➡ Taverna Angelos (p574)

➡ Artemis (p586)

➡ Mandouvala (p548)

➡ Soulatso (p576)

Best Places to Stay

➡ Rooms Dionysos (p545)

➡ Archipelagos Hotel (p548)

➡ Chios Rooms (p576)

➡ Ino Village Hotel (p552)

➡ Nassos Guest House (p573)

➡ Alkaios Rooms (p571)

Why Go?

The wildly varied northeastern Aegean Islands (Τα Νησιά του Βορειοανατολικού Αιγαίου) invite travellers to experience old-fashioned island cuisine, traditional village culture and dramatic celebrations.

Eccentric Ikaria is marked by jagged landscapes, pristine beaches and a famously long-lived, left-leaning population. Nearby Chios, an ecotourism paradise, is fertile ground for the planet's only gum-producing mastic trees. The islands range from rambling Lesvos, Greece's third-largest island and producer of half the world's ouzo, to midsize islands such as semitropical Samos and workaday Limnos, and bright specks in the sea such as Inousses and Psara. Samothraki is home to the ancient Thracian Sanctuary of the Great Gods, while northernmost Thasos seems nearly an extension of the mainland. In fact, both Thasos and Samothraki are mostly accessible from Northern Greece ports. Lesvos, Chios and Samos offer easy connections to Turkey.

When to Go
Vathy (Samos)

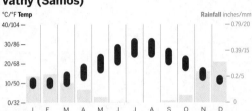

Apr & May Wild red poppies adorn the back roads and Greek Easter livens up every village.

Jul & Aug Succulent apricots are in season, perfect for a picnic at the beach.

Oct & Nov Summer crowds evaporate, and hearty soups return to the tavernas.

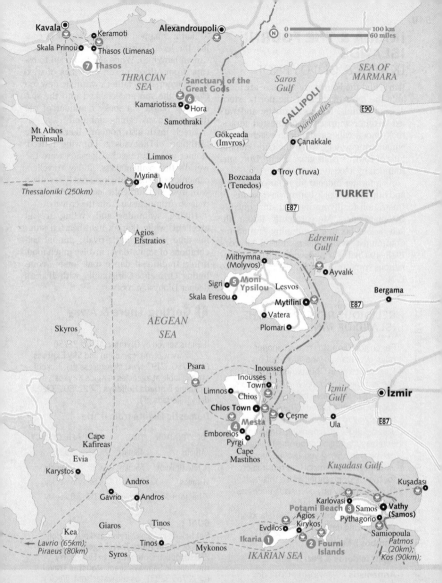

Northeastern Aegean Islands Highlights

1 Challenge your brain cells at Ikaria's annual **international chess tournament** (p542)

2 Enjoy the Aegean's best lobster from a waterfront taverna while the sun sets over the **Fourni Islands** (p548)

3 Wade through the river to wooded waterfalls in northwest Samos, followed by a swim and a drink on chilled-out **Potami Beach** (p557)

4 Wander along the winding medieval alleyways of **Mesta** (p563) in southern Chios

5 Gaze out over Lesvos from the elevated Byzantine monastery of **Moni Ypsilou** (p575), home of medieval manuscripts and ecclesiastical treasures

6 Contemplate the mysteries of the 10th-century-BC **Sanctuary of the Great Gods** (p586) on Samothraki

7 Cycle through lush old-growth forests at Thasos' annual **international mountain biking race** (p591)

IKARIA & THE FOURNI ISLANDS

ΙΚΑΡΙΑ & ΟΙ ΦΟΥΡΝΟΙ

Ikaria and the Fourni archipelago are arguably the most magical of the northeastern Aegean Islands. Ikaria's dramatic and varied terrain comprises deep, forested gorges, rocky moonscapes and hidden beaches with aquamarine waters, while the bare, sloping hills of Fourni's islets graze the horizon, surrounded by a lobster-rich sea.

As a former hideout for nefarious pirates and other scallywags, Fourni was a source of frustration for Byzantine and subsequently Ottoman rulers. More recently, Ikaria (ih-kah-*ree*-ah) became a dumping ground for Communist sympathisers during Greece's 1946–49 Civil War and again during the infamous 'time of the colonels' from 1967 to 1974.

Ikaria is named for Icarus, son of Daedalus, the legendary architect of King Minos' Cretan labyrinth. When the two tried to escape from Minos' prison on wings of wax, Icarus ignored his father's warning, flew too close to the sun and crashed into the sea, creating Ikaria – a rocky reminder of the dangers of overweening ambition.

Greek myth also honours Ikaria as the birthplace of Dionysos, god of wine; indeed, Homer attested that the Ikarians were the world's first winemakers. Today travellers can enjoy the signature local red here, along with fresh and authentic local dishes in a serene environment far from the crowds.

Hiking, swimming and cycling are all excellent, while Ikaria's light-hearted summertime *panigyria* (festivals; annual celebrations of saints' days) involve much food, drink, traditional dance and song – combining Orthodox Christianity with Ikaria's deeper Dionysian roots.

RELIGIOUS REVELRY ON THE ISLAND OF WINE

Pagan god Dionysos may no longer reign over Ikaria's vineyards, but his legacy lives on in Christianised form in the summertime *panigyria* (festivals; all-night celebrations held on saints' days across the island). There's no better way to dive headfirst into Greek island culture than drinking, dancing and feasting while honouring a village's patron saint. Bring your wallet, however: *panigyria* are important fundraisers for the local community. Use this fact to explain away any overindulgences as well-intended philanthropy.

Panigyria occur across the island on the following dates:

Kambos 5 May

Agios Isidoros & Pezi 14 May

Armenistis 40 days after Orthodox Easter

Platani 29 June

Karavostamo 1 July

Agios Kirykos & Ikarian Independence Day 17 July

Hristos Rahes & Dafne 6 August

Akamatra 15 August

Evdilos 15–20 August

Agios Sofia 17 September

ⓘ Getting There & Away

AIR

Ikaria is served by **Olympic Air** (☑ 22750 22214; www.olympicair.com) and **Sky Express** (☑ 22750 32197; www.skyexpress.gr). Tickets are available at agencies in Agios Kirykos, including **Ikariada Holidays** (☑ 22750 23322; depy@ikariada.gr).

Domestic Flights from Ikaria

DESTINATION	TIME	FARE	FREQUENCY
Athens	45min	€73	2 daily
Crete (Iraklio)	55min	€95	6 weekly
Limnos	25min	€50	6 weekly
Thessaloniki	60min	€111	6 weekly

BOAT

Get tickets in Agios Kirykos at Ikariada Holidays or **Dolihi Tours Travel Agency** (☑ 22750 23230; dolichi@otenet.gr). In Evdilos, try the Hellenic Seaways agent, **Roustas Travel** (☑ 22750 32931), on the waterfront. Weekly day-trip excursion boats to Fourni depart from Agios Kirykos and Evdilos (€25), and from Agios Kirykos to Patmos (55 minutes, one to two per week, €50), 20km south.

ⓘ Getting Around

BOAT

In summer, daily water taxis go from Agios Kirykos to Therma (€5 return). Heading the other way, a summertime caïque (small boat) travels most days (depending on weather) between

Agios Kirykos and Karkinagri and Manganitis (€10 return), two southwest coastal fishing villages. The boat stops first at Maganitis and the idyllic Seychelles Beach, then goes to Karkinagri. The boat captain usually hangs around and sells sodas from a cooler, returning you to Agios Kirykos later in the afternoon.

BUS & TAXI

A daily bus makes the winding route from Agios Kirykos to Hrisos Rahes (€9), via Evdilos (€6) and Armenistis (€9). A local bus makes the 10-minute trip to Therma every half hour (€1). A taxi between Agios Kirykos (or the airport) and Evdilos costs around €55.

CAR & MOTORCYCLE

It is a good idea to hire a car or scooter for travel beyond the main towns (though hitchhiking is very common and considered safe by locals). Try Dolihi Tours Travel Agency or **Ikariada Travel** (☑ 22750 23322; www.ikariada.gr) in Agios Kirykos and Evdilos; **Mav Cars** (☑ 22750 31036; mav-cars@hol.gr) in Evdilos, and **Aventura Car & Bike Rental** (☑ 22750 31140; aventura@otenet.gr) in Evdilos and Armenistis. Most car-hire offices can arrange for airport pick-up or drop-off too. You can also rent good motorbikes from **Pamfilis Bikes** (☑ 6979757539), next to Alpha Bank in Agios Kirykos.

Agios Kirykos
Αγιος Κήρυκος

POP 1880

Ikaria's capital is an easy-going and dependable Greek port, with clustered old streets, tasty restaurants, hotels and domatia, along with a lively waterfront cafe scene. Xylosyrtis Beach (4km southwest) is the best of several nearby pebble beaches, and the re-

❶ BUSSING IT

Taking a bus on Ikaria is to be part of a travelling village. Passengers call the driver by first name and chat as friends and neighbours get on and off along the way. If you're travelling, for instance, between the port towns of Agios Kirykos and Evdilos, you'll begin your holiday with a friendly introduction to the island. And, if you intend to rent a car during your stay, you can generally return it to the airport at no extra charge, regardless of where you pick it up.

nowned radioactive hot springs attract aching bodies from around the region.

🏃 Activities

Radioactive Springs   SPRING
(Asklipios Bathhouse; ☑ 22750 50400; admission €5; ⊙ 7am-2.30pm & 5-9pm Jun-Oct) There are a few radioactive saltwater springs in and around Agios Kirykos. In terms of safety, the waters, which contain minute levels of radiation, are carefully monitored (for mineral content as well) and supervised by health authorities.

You can sample their salutary effects in town at Asklipios Bathhouse, named for the mythical Greek god of healing. At this simple facility, hot water is piped in from a spring in the sea. Drop-in visitors are welcome. An average bath takes about 30 minutes, by which time you should be able to melt back into the landscape. Ikaria's radioactive hot springs are famed for their beneficial effects on health issues, such as arthritis and rheumatism.

BOAT SERVICES FROM IKARIA

DESTINATION	TIME	FARE	FREQUENCY
Chios	5hr	€14	1 weekly
Fourni	1hr	€7	2-3 daily
Kavala	24hr	€38	1 weekly
Lesvos (Mytilini Town)	9hr	€21	1 weekly
Mykonos*	3hr	€18	6 weekly
Piraeus	9½hr	€29	3 weekly
Piraeus*	8½hr	€29	3 weekly
Samos (Karlovasi)	2½hr	€7	3 weekly
Samos (Vathy)	3hr	€9	3 weekly

* leaves from Evdilos

Ikaria & the Fourni Islands

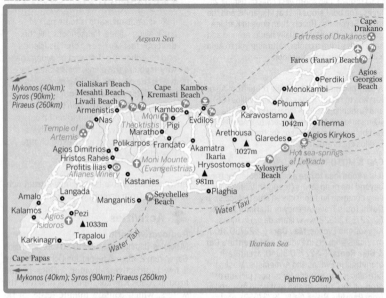

Aegean Sea

Cape Drakano

Fortress of Drakanos

Faros (Fanari) Beach

Mykonos (40km); Syros (90km); Piraeus (260km)

Gialiskari Beach
Mesahti Beach
Livadi Beach
Armenistis
Nas
Temple of Artemis
Theoktistis
Polikarpos
Agios Dimitrios
Hristos Rahes
Profitis Ilias
Afianes Winery
Kastanies

Cape Kambos
Kremasti Beach
Kambos
Pigi
Maratho
Frandato
Moni Mounte
(Evangelistria)

Agios Georgios Beach
Perdiki
Monokambi
Ploumari
Karavostamo ▲1042m
Evdilos
Arethousa
Akamatra ▲1027m
Ikaria
Hrysostomos ▲981m

Therma
Agios Kirykos
Glaredes
Hot sea-springs of Lefkada
Xylosyrtis Beach

Amalo
Kalamos
Agios Isidoros
Karkinagri

Langada
Pezi
▲1033m
Trapalou

Manganitis
Seychelles Beach
Plaghia

Water Taxi

Ikarian Sea

Cape Papas

Mykonos (40km); Syros (90km); Piraeus (260km)

Patmos (50km)

Other radioactive springs near Agios Kirykos are at **Therma**, and the natural outdoor sea spring at **Lefkada**, where the environment is less about healing and more about enjoying a hot soak.

★ Festivals & Events

In late July and August, Ikaria is host to several island-wide festivals.

Ikaria International Chess Tournament
CHESS

(☏ 6955475693; www.ikariachess.blogspot.com; ☉ Jul) This small annual event, organised by local chess aficionado Kosmas Kefalos, draws chess players of all types from around Europe and beyond. The tournament has been held for more than 30 years and has a distinct local flavour. This battle of wits takes place each July, with several cash prizes allotted to the best players.

Icarus Festival for Dialogue Between Cultures
MULTICULTURAL

(☏ 6979783201, 22940 76745; www.icarusfestival.gr; per event €10; ☉ performances from 9.30pm Jun-Aug) This summer-long, island-wide series of concerts, new cinema, dramatic works and music workshops pulls in prominent Greek and international artists. Events

are scattered around the island and buses are organised for festival-goers.

Frikaria Music Festival
MUSIC

(www.frikariafestival.tk; ☉ late Jul/early Aug) **FREE** The hip Frikaria Music Festival attracts music freaks and free spirits alike to various locations, usually above Evdilos. The three-day event, held in late July or early August, features Greek rock bands and DJ sets. Programs are available from cafes in Evdilos (try Rififi) and Agios Kyrikos.

Dionysos Theatre Festival
THEATRE

(www.aegean-exodus.gr; €10) This festival features classical Greek plays, complete with masks, performed in open-air theatres around the island.

🛏 Sleeping

Hotel Akti
HOTEL **$**

(☏ 22750 23905; www.pensionakti.gr; s/d €35/60; ❄ ☎) A fine budget choice in a prime spot, Akti has cosy and attractive modern rooms with fridge, TV, overhead fans and mosquito netting, plus friendly, English-speaking owners. A cafe-bar overlooks the sea and port below. Follow the steps just right of Alpha Bank.

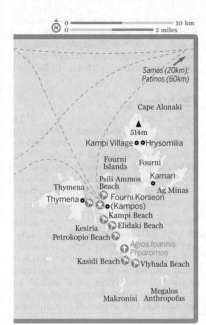

Samos (20km);
Patmos (60km)

Cape Alonaki

▲ 514m
Kampi Village ● ● Hrysomilia

Fourni Islands · Fourni
Psili Ammos · Kamari
Thymena · Beach · Ag Minas
Thymena ● · Fourni Korseon
● (Kampos)
Kampi Beach
Kesiria · Elidaki Beach
Petrokopio Beach
Agios Ioannis Prodromos
Kasidi Beach · Vlyhada Beach
Megalos
Makronisi · Anthropofas

Pension Maria-Elena   HOTEL $

(☑ 22750 22835; www.island-ikaria.com/hotels/mariaelena.asp; s/d €35/50; ❄ 🛜) This small pension, some 500m from the port near the hospital, is open year-round. It enjoys a garden setting and offers 16 simple but clean rooms with balconies overlooking the sea, plus a few suites.

Isabella Hotel   HOTEL $

(☑ 6977196515, 22750 22839; s/d from €30/35) This small pension-style family hotel on the waterfront has tidy rooms, airy and sunlit bathrooms, and double-glazed windows to keep it quiet. Friendly owners Alex and Isabella provide sweet service.

Hotel Kastro   HOTEL $

(☑ 22750 23480; www.island-ikaria.com/hotels/kastro.asp; d €50; ❄ 🛜 🏊) This well-appointed hotel has handsome rooms with balconies and all mod cons. There's a bar and even a rooftop pool. You'll find it 30m to the left once atop the stairs leading from Alpha Bank.

✖ Eating & Drinking

Filoti   TAVERNA $

(mains €4-6.50) This tasty eatery 30m from the square offers Agios Kirykos' best-value meals (including decent pizzas).

Taverna Klimataria   TAVERNA $

(mains €6-10) An inviting back-street taverna, behind the national bank, with a lovely shaded courtyard. Strong on grilled meats and *pastitsio* (layers of buttery macaroni and seasoned minced lamb).

Tzivaeri   QUICK EATS $

(☑ 22750 22850; food €2-4) Best pitta souvlakia, gyros at the port. Next to Klimataria Taverna.

Restaurant Tsouris   TAVERNA $

(mains €7-10) Beside the square and Agios Nikolaos church, this busy eatery serves tasty *mayirefta* (ready-cooked meals) and fresh fish (priced by weight).

Kazino Cafe   CAFE

(☑ 22750 23290; coffee & snacks €1.50-4; ⏱ 8am-midnight) This waterfront standby, set in an 1850-era building, serves up traditional Greek coffee, espresso, fresh juices and a variety of daily goodies, from made-to-order chocolate milkshakes to fresh *tyropita* (cheese pie) snacks. A charming old-fashioned Greek cafe, managed by the philosophical Manolis.

ℹ Information

Banks with ATMs are at the *plateia*. The post office is left of it.

Dolihi Tours Travel Agency (☑ 22750 23230) Helpful full-service agency; located next to Alpha Bank.

Hospital (☑ 22753 50200)

Ikariada Travel (☑ 22750 23322; www.ikariada.gr) Waterfront agency sells ferry and plane tickets; arranges accommodation.

Island Ikaria (www.island-ikaria.com) Online guide to Ikaria.

Police (☑ 22750 22222) Above Alpha Bank.

Port Police (☑ 22750 22207)

Around Agios Kirykos

The **hot sea-springs of Lefkada**, 2km north of Agios Kirykos, are free, therapeutic and relaxing. This is a designated radioactive saltwater spring, but in truth, it's just a beautiful spot on the beach, identifiable by an irregular circle of rocks. You'll know you're in the right spot when you feel the now-it's-hot-now-it's-not intermingling of spring and seawater. To find the springs, drive 2km north and look for a small blue and white sign (saying 'hot springs') next to a path leading to the rocky beach below.

Ikaria's eastern tip boasts the 2km-long **Faros (Fanari) Beach**, 10km north along the coast road, and the 4th-century BC **Fortress of Drakanos** (☺8.30am-3pm Tue-Sat) `FREE`, which sponsored religious rites dedicated to Eilythia, a fertility deity. A 13m lookout tower anchors the site, which features informative signboards and two helpful English-speaking volunteers. A path from a small chapel here leads to tiny **Agios Georgios Beach**.

Less than 100m from Faros Beach, the friendly Greek-Australian Evon Plakidas at **Evon's Rooms** (☑6977139208, 22750 32580; www.evonsrooms.com; Faros; ste from €40-110; P✳@🛜) rents high-quality suites, some with spiral stairs, all with kitchenettes. The studios hold up to six people. The adjoining cafe serves breakfast, delicious crepes, sweet *loukoumadhes* (ball-shaped doughnuts served with honey and cinnamon) and fresh juices and salads.

In the village of **Therma**, just east of Agios Kyrikos, time seems to have stopped. There are traditional **hot springs** (☑22750 22665), along with an enjoyable cave-like natural sauna, **Spilio Baths** (To Spilio; ☑22750 24048; €3-4.50; ☺daily until dusk), and an exceedingly charming lodging, **Agriolykos Pension** (☑22750 22433; www.island-ikaria.com/hotels/agriolykos.asp), with stairs to the small bay which it overlooks. Worth a stop if you're driving is **Taverna Arodou** (☑22750 22700), an excellent traditonal eatery overlooking the sea, 5km southwest of Agios Kirykos.

Evdilos   Εύδηλος

POP 460

Evdilos, Ikaria's second port, is 41km northwest of Agios Kirykos; they're connected by Ikaria's two main roads. The memorable trip takes in high mountain ridges, striking sea views and slate-roof villages. Evdilos itself skirts a small semicircular bay and rises in tiers up a hillside. It features stately old houses on winding streets and a relaxed and appealing waterfront with a small free car-park to one side.

🛏 Sleeping

Hotel Atheras   HOTEL $
(☑22750 31434; www.atheras-kerame.gr; s/d €50/60; ✳🛜✱) The friendly and modern Atheras has an almost Cycladic feel due to its bright white decor contrasting with the blue Aegean beyond. There's an outdoor bar by the pool and the hotel is in the backstreets, 200m from the port.

Kerame Studios   APARTMENTS $
(☑22750 31434; www.atheras-kerame.gr; studio/apt from €70/90; ✳🛜✱) These diverse and well-managed studios and apartments (1km before Evdilos) are the sister establishment of Hotel Atheras. Prices are as variable as the quarters, which feature kitchens and spacious decks with views. The restaurant is built into a windmill.

Rooms-for-Rent   PENSION $
(☑22750 31518; s/d €40/50) Otherwise known as Anna's place, these simple and spotless rooms above Alpha Bank overlook the port and have overhead fans.

🍴 Eating & Drinking

Restaurant Koralli   TAVERNA $
(Plateia Evdilou; mains €4-9) The best of the waterfront tavernas, Koralli specialises in fresh fish and chips, excellent meat grills, vegie salads and *mayirefta* dishes.

Tsakonitis Cafe   OUZERIE $
(Plateia Evdilou; mezedhes €4-7) This *ouzerie* (place that serves ouzo and light snacks) on

---

MOUNTAIN WALKS & MONKS' SKULLS

With its solitude and rugged natural beauty, Ikaria's perfect for mountain walks. One that's invigorating, but not too hard on the bones, is the one-day circular walk along dirt roads from **Kambos** south through **Dafni**, the remains of the 10th-century **Byzantine Castle of Koskinas**, and picturesque **Frandato** and **Maratho** villages.

When you reach **Pigi**, look for the Frandato sign; continue past it for the unusual little Byzantine **Chapel of Theoskepasti**, tucked into overhanging granite. You must clamber upwards to get to it, and duck to get inside. Provided the row of old monks' skulls don't give you the creeps, the chapel makes for a wonderfully peaceful visit and is near **Moni Theoktistis**, with frescoes dating from 1686. The nearby *kafeneio* (coffee house) is good for a relaxed coffee or juice with Maria, the kindly owner.

the waterfront is a local favourite known for its homemade Greek yoghurt.

Café-Bar Rififi
CAFE

(Plateia Evdilou; snacks €2-5) This snappy portside bar with great pitta snacks, draft beer and good coffee owes its name to the bank next door, with which it shares a common interior wall. Rififi in Greek is a nickname for bank robber, and the servers love to point out where the serious money is stashed.

❶ Information

The waterfront has two ATMs and the ticket agency for **Hellenic Seaways** (☑ 22750 32931).

Aventura (☑ 22750 31140) Rents cars and motorbikes.

Mav Cars (☑ 22750 31036) Rents cars and motorbikes.

Medical Center (☑ 22750 32922, 22750 33030) Located 2km east of Evdilos; English-speaking doctor.

Police (☑ 22750 31222)

West of Evdilos

Kambos
Κάμπος

POP 250

Kambos, 3km west of Evdilos, was once mighty Oinoe (derived from the Greek word for wine), Ikaria's capital. Traces of this ancient glory remain, compliments of a ruined Byzantine palace, Ikaria's oldest church and a small museum. Kambos' other main attractions are its sand-and-pebble beach and scenic hill walks.

◉ Sights

On the right-hand side when entering Kambos from Evdilos stand the modest ruins of a **Byzantine palace**. Other sights around Kambos include the small archaeological museum and Ikaria's oldest surviving Byzantine church.

Agia Irini Church
CHURCH

Built on the site of a 4th-century basilica, this 12th-century church contains some columns from this original. Alas, many of Agia Irini's frescoes remain covered with protective whitewash because there are no funds to pay for their removal.

Archaeological Museum
MUSEUM

(☑ 22750 31300) **FREE** Kambos' small museum displays neolithic tools, geometric vases, classical sculpture fragments, figurines and ivory trinkets. If it's closed, ask Vasilis Kambouris (at Rooms Dionysos) to open it.

🛏 Sleeping & Eating

★ Rooms Dionysos
PENSION $

(☑ 6944153437, 22750 31300; www.ikaria-dionysos rooms.com; d/tr incl breakfast €45/55; ☐ ⊚) The many happy guests who return every year attest to the magical atmosphere of this pension run by the charismatic Vasilis 'Dionysos' Kambouris, his Australian-born wife Demetra and Italian-speaking brother Yiannis. Rooms are simple but well maintained, with private bathrooms, while the rooftop terrace beds are a summer steal at €10. Breakfast is served on a shaded patio overlooking nearby Kambos Beach and guests can enjoy the relaxed conviviality of the place over an evening glass of wine. There's even a book exchange.

Partheni
TAVERNA $

(mains €6-8) On Kambos Beach, the Partheni serves simple but tasty Greek food, and great *kalamari* (fried squid). It also does nourishing *mayirefta*, and makes a relaxing place to eat after a swim at the 'virgins' beach'. Partheni means virgin and the beach was once reserved for young women in long swimming dresses.

Popi's
TAVERNA $

(Kambos; mains €5-8.50; ⊚ dinner) Very traditional setting on the road between Kambos and Evdilos. Excellent taverna fare, cooked and happily served by Popi.

❶ Information

Kambos is fairly self-explanatory but for insider info, track down long-time local tourism provider Vasilis Kambouris. He can usually be found catering to guests at his Rooms Dionysos. Vasilis can also help organise taxis, car hire and ferry tickets.

Kambos to the Southwest Coast

From Kambos, two roads head west: the main road, which hugs the northern coast until Armenistis, and then becomes a secondary road continuing down the northwestern coast; and another secondary road, half of which is a good dirt track, which winds its way southwest through stunning moonscapes to remote Karkinagri on the southern coast.

The road through central Ikaria accesses **Moni Theoktistis** and the tiny **Chapel of**

Theoskepasti, just northwest of Pigi. From Pigi, continue south to Maratho, then west for the impressive Moni Mounte, also called Moni Evangelistrias. Some 500m beyond it lies a tiny dam with goldfish and croaking frogs.

Another fork leads to popular Hristos Rahes, an eclectic hillside village and good hiking base, known for its late-night shopping and cafe scene. Stop in at the Women's Cooperative (☏ 22750 41076; Hristos Raches) for local jams, herbs and sweet treats. Along with various traditional products, there's a useful walking map, *The Round of Rahes on Foot* (€4), sold at most shops; proceeds go to maintaining the trails (www.hikingikaria. blogspot.com).

Just above Hristos Rahes, the excellent Afianes Winery (☏ 6977893731, 22750 40008; www.afianeswines.gr; ⊘noon-8pm Thu-Tue) FREE offers daily tours and free tastings. An exhibition room features vintage equipment and 19th-century wedding dresses.

After Hristos Rahes, the road south finds rustic Profitis Ilias, and then the sign-posted village of Pezi. The landscape now becomes even more rugged and extreme, with wind-whipped thick green trees clinging to bleak boulders, and wild goats a common sight. The road finally reaches tiny Karkinagri, which has a few tavernas, rooms and a nearby beach.

In summer this fishing village also has daily boat service to Agios Kirykos. This highly recommended voyage follows Ikaria's rugged and partially inaccessible southern coast. The boat calls in at Manganitis village; nearby (2.5km) is a secluded stretch of white pebbles and crystal-clear waters – the appropriately named Seychelles Beach tucked within a protected cove.

Alternatively, if coming to Seychelles Beach by car along the coastal road connecting Manganitis with Evdilos and Agios Kirykos, you'll see an unmarked parking area on the right-hand side, about 125m after the tunnel; from here, clamber down the path (10 to 15 minutes) to the beach.

🛏 Sleeping & Eating

Fakaros Rooms
PENSION $
(☏ 22750 41269; Hristos Rahes; s/d €20/30) Modest domatia (room, usually in a private home; cheap accommodation option), a few metres from the plateia at Hristos Rahes, attractive, comfortable, and managed by the English-speaking Fakaros family.

O Karakas
TAVERNA $
(Karkinagri; mains €6-9) On a bamboo-roofed seafront patio, this excellent family-run taverna does good fresh fish and salads. Try Ikaria's speciality *soufiko*, a tasty vegetable stew. Domatia available should you linger.

Armenistis to Nas
Αρμενιστής προς Να

Armenistis, 15km west of Evdilos, is Ikaria's humble version of a resort. It boasts two long, sandy beaches separated by a narrow headland, a fishing harbour and a web of hilly streets to explore on foot. Cafes and tavernas line the beach. Moderate nightlife livens up Armenistis in summer with a mix of locals and Greek and foreign tourists.

⊙ Sights & Activities

Livadi Beach
BEACH
Just 500m east of Armenistis is Livadi Beach, where currents are strong enough to warrant a lifeguard service and waves are sometimes big enough for surfing. Beyond Livadi are two other popular beaches, Mesahti and Gialiskari.

Nas Beach
BEACH
Westward 3.5km from Armenistis lies the pebbled beach of Nas, located far below the road and a few tavernas. This nudist-friendly beach has an impressive location at the mouth of a forested river, behind the ruins of an ancient Temple of Artemis, easily viewed from Taverna O Nas.

🛏 Sleeping

Armenistis has its share of package pensions and touristy eateries. Try these exceptions for a change of pace.

★ Pension Astaxi
PENSION $
(☏ 22750 71318; www.island-ikaria.com/hotels/PensionAstaxi.asp; Armenistis; d/tr from €35/50; ☞@☎) This excellent budget choice is tucked back 30m from the main road, just above the Carte Postal cafe. The welcoming owner, Maria, has created a comfortable and attractive lodging, with a dozen brightly outfitted rooms with fans and balcony views to the sea.

Hotel Daidalos
HOTEL $
(☏ 22750 71390; www.daidaloshotel.gr; Armenistis; s/d incl breakfast from €40/50; ⊘May-Oct; ☞❄☎☀) You can't miss the traditional blue-and-white island colour scheme at this

attractive and well-managed mid-sized hotel (25 rooms). Rooms are large and cheerful, most with sea views. It's 200m west of the small bridge.

Atsachas Rooms HOTEL $
(☎22750 71226; www.atsachas.gr; Livadi Beach; d from €60) Right on Livadi Beach, the Atsachas has clean, well-furnished rooms, some with sophisticated kitchens and most have breezy, sea-view balconies. The cafe spills down to the lovely garden, where a stairway descends to the beach.

Armenistis View HOTEL $
(☎697621806, 22750 71529; www.armenistis.eu; d/apt from €40/60) You could easily miss these five studio apartments below the road about 30m before the bridge, with kitchenettes and roomy sea-view verandas.

Villa Dimitri APARTMENTS $
(☎22750 71310; www.villa-dimitri.de; Armenistis; 2-person studios & apt with private patio €50-70; ⏲Mar-Oct; ❄@📶) This assortment of six secluded apartments, each one blue and white with wood and stone touches, and set on a cliff amid colourful flowers, is managed by a welcoming Greek-German couple. It's 800m west of Armenistis and requires a minimum stay of one week.

Eating & Drinking

★Pashalia Taverna TAVERNA $
(☎6975562415, 22750 71302; Armenistis; mains from €5; ⏲Jun-Nov) Meat dishes such as *katsikaki* (kid goat) or veal in a clay pot are specialities at this, the first taverna along the Armenistis harbour road. The father-and-son owners, Haris and Vasilis, also have three apartments above the taverna.

★Thea TAVERNA $
(Nas; mains €5-9) One of several fine tavernas in Nas, Thea's serves up excellent mezedhes, meat grills and a perfect vegie *mousakas* (baked layers of eggplant or zucchini, minced meat and potatoes topped with cheese sauce). Good barrel wine and local *tsipouro* (distilled spirit similar to ouzo but usually stronger) complete the deal. An outdoor patio overlooks the sea. Thea (aka Dorothy) also has five bright and cosy rooms above the restaurant, with breakfast.

Taverna Baido TAVERNA $
(☎6982331539; Armenistis; mains €4.50-8) Past the bridge towards Nas, this interesting taverna is the work of Marianthi, who serves well-priced dishes using local products, fresh fish, and Ikarian wine. Exceptional Turkish meat balls (*soutzoukakia*), and *taramasalata* (a thick pink or white purée of fish roe, potato, oil and lemon juice).

Kialaris Ouzerie TAVERNA $
(☎22750 71227; Gialiskari; mains €6-11) Kelari serves its own fresh-caught fish, along with midday *mayirefta* dishes from the oven. Look for the landmark church on the point, 2km east of Armenistis.

Carte Postale CAFE, BAR
(Armenistis; drinks, small plates €2-7; ⏲10am-2am) This arty cafe-bar 100m west of the church sits high over the bay. Snacks range from small pizzas and salads, to breakfast omelettes and evening risotto. There's a hip ambience, signalled by an eclectic musical mix from world beat to Greek fusion.

Karnayo CAFE, BAR
(☎22750 71240; Gialiskari) Cool bar with eclectic music mix, midway among several good *ouzeries* strung together above the beach at Gialiskari.

ℹ Information

Aventura (☎22750 71117; Armenistis) Travel agency by the patisserie, just before the bridge. Offers car hire, jeep tours of eastern Ikaria, along with ferry and plane tickets.

Dolihi Tours & Lemy Rent-a-Car (☎22750 71122, 6983418878; Armenistis) Efficient travel agency next to the village market. It rents out cars, organises walking tours and jeep safaris.

Around Evdilos

Karavostamo Καραβόσταμο

POP 550

One of Ikaria's largest and most beautiful coastal villages is Karavostamo, 6km east of Evdilos. From the main road, the village cascades down winding paths scattered with flowering gardens, village churches, vegie patches, chickens and goats, finally reaching a cosy *plateia* (square) and small fishing harbour. Here, you'll find nothing more than a bakery, small general store, a few domatia, tavernas and *kafeneia* (coffee houses) where the villagers congregate each evening to chat, argue, eat, play backgammon, drink and tell stories. To reach the *plateia*, take the signed road off the main

A LESSON FROM BREAD

In the village of Karavostamo, on Ikaria's north coast, everything you need to know about island values can probably be found at **To Yefiri** ('the bridge'), the village bakery, where Petros Pavlos bakes long loaves of bread in his wood oven, along with crunchy *paximadia* (rusks) and sweet *koulouria* (fresh pretzel-style bread).

Once the baking is done, the bread is put out on the counter in wicker baskets and the day's work is done. The baker leaves, but he also leaves the door to the bakery open.

Village regulars, or kids doing errands for their parents, stop by during the day, pick out a loaf or two, and leave money in an open container. The system has worked for years, another reason perhaps why Ikarians don't get too excited about fluctuations in the global price of oil. Olive oil maybe.

road. Accommodation is available near the village square at **Despina Rooms** (☎ 21066 14371, 6973050505; Karavostamo; r from €40-60; P ❀ ☎), and the seafront taverna **Mandouvala** (☎ 22750 61204; mains €7-12; ☉ lunch & dinner) excels, while the little *ouzerie* **To Steki** (☉ lunch & dinner) caters to the regulars who gather nightly.

Arethousa, 3km above Karavostamo, is the village home of the **Ikarian Centre** (www.greekingreece.gr), a Greek language school which runs intensive one-week residential courses.

The Fourni Islands
Οι Φούρνοι

POP 1500

The Fourni archipelago is one of Greece's great unknown island gems. Its low-lying vegetation clings to gracefully rounded hills that overlap, forming intricate bays of sandy beaches and little ports. This former pirates' lair is especially beautiful at dusk, when the setting sun turns the terrain shades of pink, violet and black – the effect is especially dramatic when viewed from an elevated point.

In centuries past, Fourni's remoteness and quietude attracted pirates seeking refuge, though today those headed here are travellers seeking a cool getaway – and some of the Aegean's best seafood.

A clue to the area's swashbuckling past can be found in the name of the archipelago's capital, Fourni Korseon. The Corsairs were French privateers with a reputation for audacity, and their name became applied generically to all pirates and rogues then roaming the Eastern Aegean.

Nowadays, Fourni Korseon offers most of the accommodation and services, plus several beaches. Other settlements include little Hrysomilia and Kamari to the north, plus another fishing hamlet on the islet of Thymena. In the south of the main island, the monastery of Agios Ioannis Prodromos stands serene over the far coast.

◉ Sights & Activities

The island's rolling hills are ideal for **hiking**, and trails inevitably find a beach. The nearest to Fourni Korseon, **Psili Ammos Beach**, waits 600m north on the coast road, with umbrellas and a beach bar that hums all night.

Along the coast road heading south, **Kampi Beach** is excellent. Further along about 2km, **Elidaki Beach** has a gentle sandy bottom, followed by the small-pebbled **Petrokopeio Beach**.

Near Fourni's southernmost tip, near the **Monastery of Agios Ioannis Thermastis**, the fine, sandy **Vlyhada Beach** lies before the more secluded **Kasidi Beach**.

Fourni's other main settlements, **Hrysomilia** and **Kamari**, are 17km and 10km from Fourni Korseon respectively (approximately a 30-minute drive on winding upland roads). Both are tranquil fishing settlements with beaches, but limited services. The trip from Fourni Korseon to these villages is spectacular, opening onto myriad views of sloping hills and hidden coves.

☞ Sleeping

Most accommodation is in Fourni Korseon, though sleeping in the smaller settlements is possible, as is free beach camping.

★ **Archipelagos Hotel**   HOTEL **$$**
(☎ 22750 51250; www.archipelagoshotel.gr; Fourni Korseon; s/d/tr from €40/50/60; P ❀ ☎) This elegant small hotel on the harbour's northern edge comprises Fourni's most sophisticated lodgings. From the patio restaurant, set under flowering stone arches, to the well-appointed rooms, the Archipelagos

combines traditional yet imaginative Greek architecture with modern luxuries.

Studios Nektaria APARTMENTS $
(☑ 22750 51148; studiosnektaria@yahoo.gr; Fourni Korseon; d/tr €35/45; ❄ ☎) On the harbour's far side, a Fourni bargain with small, clean rooms, three of which overlook a small beach.

Toula Rooms-to-let PENSION $
(☑ 6976537948, 22750 51332; info@fournitoula studio.gr; waterfront; s/d €40/50) Look for the Aegean blue balconies at this seafront standby near shops and tavernas. It has clean and simple rooms with fans.

✗ Eating & Drinking

Fourni is famous for seafood, especially *astakomakaronadha* (lobster with pasta).

Psarotaverna O Miltos SEAFOOD $
(Fourni Korseon; mains €7-10) Excellent lobster and fresh fish are expertly prepared at this iconic waterfront taverna.

Psarotaverna Nikos SEAFOOD $
(Fourni Korseon; mains €7-10) Next door to O Miltos, this is a great seafood option.

Taverna Kali Kardia TAVERNA $
(Fourni Korseon; mains €5-8) Hearty Kali Karida on the *plateia* does excellent grilled meats, and is enlivened by animated old locals. With luck, you may find *ameletita*, a rare speciality that a male lamb can only provide two of.

Taverna Almyra TAVERNA $
(Kamari village; fish €5-9) Up in Kamari, this relaxing fish taverna on the waterfront has subtle charm and plenty of fresh fish and lobster.

Cafe Meltemi CAFE, BAR
Popular wi-fi cafe with coffee and drinks till the wee hours.

❶ Information

Perpendicular to the central waterfront, the main street of Fourni Korseon runs inland to the *plateia*; this nameless thoroughfare hosts the National Bank of Greece with ATM, travel agency, post office and village **pharmacy** (☑ 22750 51188).

Health Centre (☑ 22750 51202)
Karla Irini Travel (☑ 22750 51481; Fourni Korseon)
Port Police (☑ 22750 51207)

❶ Getting There & Away

Fourni is connected to Ikaria (Agios Kyrikos) and Samos by ferry and hydrofoil services. **Fourni Island Tours** (☑ 22750 51540; www.fourni island.ssn.gr; Fourni Korseon) provides information and sells tickets.

Boat Services from Fourni

DESTINATION	TIME	FARE	FREQUENCY
Ikaria (Agios Kirykos)	35min-1hr	€7	1-2 daily
Piraeus	11hr	€33	3 weekly
Samos (Karlovasi)	1½hr	€5	6 weekly
Samos (Vathy)	2hr	€8	6 weekly

❶ Getting Around

Gleaming new asphalt roads, all 20km of them, connect Fourni Korseon with Hrysomilia and Kamari; however, enjoying these Fourni freeways requires befriending a local, renting a motorbike, hitching or taking the island's lone **taxi** (☑ 6977370471, 22750 51223), commandeered by the ebullient Manolis Papaioannou.

Until rental cars find Fourni, hire a scooter at **Escape Rent a Motorbike** (☑ 22750 51514; gbikes@hotmail.com) on the waterfront.

Alternatively, go by **boat**. Two weekly caïques serve Hrysomilia, while another three go to Thymena year-round.

SAMOS ΣΑΜΟΣ

POP 32,820

Lying seductively just off the Turkish coast, semitropical Samos is one of the northeastern Aegean Islands' best-known destinations. Yet beyond the low-key resorts and the lively capital, Vathy, there are numerous off-the-beaten-track beaches and quiet spots in the cool, forested inland mountains, where traditional life continues.

Famous for its sweet local wine, Samos is also historically significant. It was the legendary birthplace of Hera, and the sprawling ruins of her ancient sanctuary, the Ireon, are impressive. Both the great mathematician Pythagoras and the hedonistic father of atomic theory, the 4th-century BC philosopher Epicurus, were born here. Samos' scientific genius is also affirmed by the astonishing Evpalinos Tunnel (524 BC), a spectacular feat of ancient engineering that stretches for 1034m deep underground.

❶ Getting There & Away

AIR

Samos' airport is 4km west of Pythagorio. There are no airline offices on Samos. Contact the following airlines, all of which serve Samos, or any local travel agency.

Aegean Airlines (www.aegeanair.com)
Olympic Air (www.olympicair.com)
Sky Express (www.skyexpress.gr)

Domestic Flights from Samos

DESTINATION	TIME	FARE	FREQUENCY
Athens	45min	€83	2-3 daily
Chios	30min	€40	2 weekly
Limnos	2½hr	€50	2 weekly
Lesvos	1½hr	€50	2 weekly
Rhodes	1hr	€50	2 weekly
Thessaloniki	50min	€55	4-5 weekly

BOAT

A new ferry terminal in Vathy (Samos) for ferries to Greece-only destinations is at the southeast end of the harbour, 1.7km from the old ferry terminal which is only for boats to Turkey. A taxi between the terminals is €5.

ITSA Travel (☎ 22730 23605; www.itsatravel samos.gr; Themistokleous Sofouli), directly opposite Vathy's old ferry terminal provides detailed information, offers free luggage storage and sells tickets, including to Turkey. The helpful staff here will also pick you up at the new terminal for free.

In Pythagorio, check ferry and hydrofoil schedules with the **tourist office** (☎ 22730 61389), the **port police** (☎ 22730 61225) or By Ship Travel (p555).

For boat services, see also the table on p553.

❶ Getting Around

TO/FROM THE AIRPORT

Buses run to and from and the airport nine times daily (€2); taxis from the airport cost an extortionate €25 to €30 to Vathy (Samos) or €6 to Pythagorio, from where there are local buses to Vathy.

BOAT

Summer excursion boats travel twice weekly (Monday and Friday) from Pythagorio to Patmos (return €5), leaving at 8am. Daily excursion boats go from Pythagorio to Samiopoula islet (including lunch, €25).

BUS

From Vathy **bus station** (☎ 22730 27262; www.samospublicusses.gr; Themistokli Sofouli), frequent daily buses serve Kokkari (€1.50, 20 minutes), Pythagorio (€1.70, 25 minutes), Agios Konstantinos (€2.20, 40 minutes), Karlovasi (€4, one hour), the Ireon (€2.50, 25 minutes) and Mytilinii (€1.60, 20 minutes).

Samos

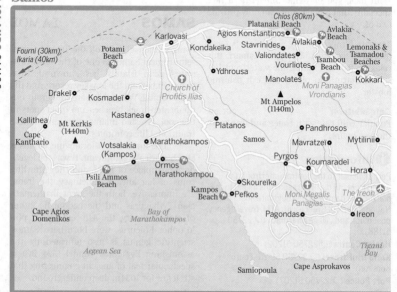

Additionally, from Pythagorio itself, five daily buses reach the Ireon (€1.60, 15 minutes) while four serve Mytilinii (€1.90, 20 minutes). Buy tickets on the buses. Services are reduced on weekends.

CAR & MOTORCYCLE

Opposite the port entrance in Vathy, **Pegasus Rent a Car** (☑ 6972017092, 22730 24470; pegasussamos@hotmail.com; Themistokli Sofouli 5) offers the best rates on car, jeep and motorcycle hire. Another option is **Auto Union** (☑ 22730 29744; Themistokli Sofouli 79).

In Pythagorio, try **John's Rentals** (☑ 22730 61405; www.johns-rent-a-car.gr; Lykourgou Logotheti).

TAXI

The **taxi rank** (☑ 22730 28404) in Vathy is by the National Bank of Greece. In Pythagorio the **taxi rank** (☑ 22730 61450) is on the waterfront on Lykourgou Logotheti.

Vathy (Samos) Βαθύ (Σάμος)

POP 2025

Vathy (also called Samos) is the island's capital and enjoys a striking setting within the fold of a deep bay, a curving waterfront lined with bars, cafes and restaurants. However, the historic quarter of Ano Vathy, filled with steep, narrow streets and red-tiled 19th-century hillside houses brims with atmosphere. The town centre boasts two engaging museums and a striking century-old church.

Vathy also has two pebble beaches, the best being Gagos Beach, about 500m north from the old quay. Along the way, you'll pass a string of cool night bars clinging to the town's northeastern cliff.

◉ Sights & Activities

Vathy's attractions include the Ano Vathy old quarter (inland 1km via Sofouli), relaxing municipal gardens and Roditzes and Gagos Beaches, as well as a first-rate archaeological museum and the splendid church of **Agios Spyridonas** (Plateia Dimarheiou; ⊙ 7.30-11am & 6.30-7.30pm). About 15km east of Vathy is one of the island's best and least crowded beaches, at the fishing hamlet of **Agia Paraskevi**.

Archaeological Museum   MUSEUM
(adult/student €3/2, free Sun; ⊙ 8am-3pm Tue-Sun, last entry 2.45pm) One of the best in the islands, this museum contains finds starting from the rule of Polycrates (6th century BC), the most famous being the imposing *kouros* (male statue of the Archaic period), plucked from the Ireon (Sanctuary of Hera) near Pythagorio. At a height of 5.5m it's the largest standing *kouros* known.

Ecclesiastical (Byzantine) Museum MUSEUM
(28 Oktovriou; adult/student €3/2, free Sun; ⊙ 8.30am-3pm Tue-Sun) Houses rare manuscripts, liturgical objects of silver and gold, as well as striking icons dating from the 13th century. Samos owes some of this holy loot to its status as a bishopric (administering also Ikaria and Fourni).

Museum of Samos Wines   WINERY
(☑ 22730 87551; ⊙ 8am-8pm Mon-Sat) FREE
Look for this handsome stone building oppposite the new ferry quay to find one of Samos' best vintners. Winery tours usually take place when you show up, and conveniently include free tasting, with several wines for sale.

🛏 Sleeping & Eating

★**Pythagoras Hotel**   HOTEL $
(☑ 22730 28601; www.pythagorashotel.com; Kallistratou 12; s/d/tr incl breakfast €20/35/45; ⊙ Feb-Nov; ❄@🖥) This budget gem, just up from the port, owes its efficient charm to the hospitality of owner Stelios Mihalakis. Many rooms have breezy, sea-facing balconies and all have large fans. A pebbled beach lies

Kuşadası (Turkey) (15km)

Cape Kotsikas

Livadaki Beach

Agia Paraskevi

Vathy Bay

Moni Zoödohos Pigis

Cape Praso

Kamara

Myrtia Beach

Vathy (Samos)

Paleokastro

Kervelis Beach

Cape Katsouni

Psili Ammos Beach

Klima Beach

Posidonio

Potami Beach

Evpalinos Tunnel

Pythagorio

Kuşadası (Turkey) (15km)

Mihale Straits

TURKEY

Patmos (20km);
Leros (30km);
Kalymnos (60km)

Vathy (Samos)

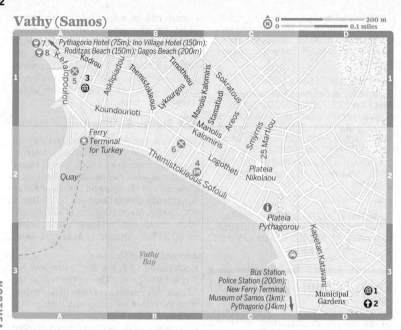

Vathy (Samos)

Sights
1 Archaeological Museum	D3
2 Church of Agios Spyridonas	D3
3 Ecclesiastical (Byzantine) Museum	A1

Sleeping
4 Hotel Medousa	B2

Eating
5 Taverna Artemis	A1
6 To Steki	B2

Drinking & Nightlife
7 Ble	A1
8 Escape Music Bar	A1

below the shaded breakfast patio. Ring ahead for free pick-up from the ferry or bus station.

Hotel Medousa HOTEL $
(☑ 6976559972, 22730 23501; waterfront; s/d €25/35) Basic digs are clean, friendly and appealing especially for the six sea-view rooms with quieter glazed windows overlooking the waterfront, and the handy ice-cream shop downstairs.

⭐ Ino Village Hotel & Restaurant HOTEL $$
(☑ 22730 23241; www.inovillagehotel.com; Kalami; s/d/tr incl breakfast €58/72/92; P✱❖☎) With its courtyard pool flanked by ivy-clad, balconied white buildings, Ino Village, just 1km above Vathy, feels remote and elegant. While this miniresort is sometimes booked by small tour groups, walk-in travellers can expect very reasonable rates. The hotel also boasts the popular Elea restaurant and cocktail bar, which includes fine Samian wines.

⭐ Taverna Artemis TAVERNA $
(Kefalopoulou 4; mains €5-9) The Vathy Greek crowd relies on Artemis for fresh fish and well-prepared *mayirefta* dishes, though they are best known for *sardeles pandremenos*. In Greek *pandremenos* means married, and the sardines are served open-faced, in pairs, like a couple. Open year-round.

To Steki TAVERNA $
(Aogotheti 61; mains €4.50-7.50; ☺ lunch & dinner) An unpretentious and welcoming back-alley eatery with generous grills, *gavros* (marinated small fish), salads and homemade soups.

🍷 Drinking & Nightlife

The nightlife in Vathy is more Hellenic than it is in Pythagorio, where the bars tend to be frequented by Northern Europeans. While most cafes and bars cling to the waterfront, the coolest ones, such as Escape Music Bar (☑ 22730 28345; Kefalopoulou 9; ☺ 10pm-6am) and Ble (Kefalopoulou 7; ☺ 11am-4am), hang over the water along Kefalopoulou 100m beyond the quay. Music and dancing is usually in full swing by midnight.

ℹ Information

Banks with ATMS line Plateia Pythagora and the waterfront. There is free wi-fi at Plateia Pythogorou and at nearly all the waterfront cafes and bars.

Police (☑ 22730 27404; Presveos Dim Nikolareïzi 2)

Port Police (☑ 22730 27890) One block north of the quay.

Post Office (Plateia Nikolaou; ☺ 7.30am-2pm)

Samos General Hospital (☑ 22730 27407) Efficient regional hospital, opposite Pythagoras Hotel.

Pythagorio   Πυθαγόρειο

POP 1330

On the southeastern coast, opposite Turkey, pretty Pythagorio has a yacht-lined harbour, and Samos' main archaeological finds. All boats departing south from Samos leave from Pythagorio, including day trips to Samiopoula islet. A 1.5km walk west of Pythagorio brings you to a pristinely clean beach with umbrellas, toilets and decent swimming.

◉ Sights

Evpalinos Tunnel   ARCHAEOLOGICAL SITE
(Pythagorio; adult/student €4/2; ☺ 8am-8pm Tue-Sun) Back in 524 BC, when Pythagorio (then called Samos) was the island's capital and a bustling metropolis of 80,000, securing sources of drinking water became crucial. To solve the problem, ruler Polycrates put his dictatorial whims to good use, ordering labourers to dig into a mountainside according to the exacting plan of his ingenious engineer, Evpalinos; many workers died during this dangerous dig. The result was the 1034m-long Evpalinos Tunnel. In medieval times locals used it to hide from pirates.

The Evpalinos Tunnel is actually two tunnels: a service tunnel and a lower water conduit visible from the walkway. You enter the tunnel via a narrow stair, and it's single file from there. Not much more than 100m of tunnel is accessible, but it's enough to be impressed by this golden-age engineering feat.

Castle of Lykourgos Logothetis   CASTLE
(☺ 9am-dusk Tue-Sun) Samians took the lead locally in the 1821 War of Independence, and this castle, built in 1824 by resistance leader Logothetis, is the major relic of that turbulent time. It's situated on a hill at the southern end of Metamorfosis Sotiros, near the car park. The city walls once extended from here to the Evpalinos Tunnel.

Archaeological Museum of Pythagorio   MUSEUM
(☑ 22730 62813; Polykratous; €4; ☺ 8am-8pm Tue-Sun) This sparkling and recently renovated

BOAT SERVICES FROM SAMOS

DESTINATION	PORT	TIME	FARE	FREQUENCY
Chios	Karlovasi	3hr	€13	3 weekly
Fourni	Vathy	2½hr	€8	3 weekly
Ikaria (Agios Kirykos)**	Vathy	3½hr	€10	3 weekly
Ikaria (Evdilos)**	Vathy	4hr	€9	3 weekly
Kalymnos	Pythagorio	6hr	€20	3-4 weekly
Kavala	V/K*	21hr	€38	2 weekly
Lesvos (Mytilini)	V/K*	7hr	€18	3 weekly
Limnos	V/K*	11hr	€28	3 weekly
Mykonos	Vathy	7hr	€18	3 weekly
Piraeus	Vathy	12hr	€32	3 weekly
Syros	Vathy	8hr	€29	3 weekly

*Vathy or Karlovasi
**via Fourni

museum contains well-displayed finds from the 6th-century-BC Ireon, with museum labels in Greek, English and German.

Moni Panagias Spilianis
MONASTERY

(Monastery of the Virgin of the Grotto; ☑ 22730 61361; ☺ 9am-8pm) FREE About 1.5km northwest of Pythagorio, the road forks right past traces of an ancient theatre, before reaching this grotto monastery. The walk meanders up through old olive groves and, despite tourist kiosks, is a welcome respite from the summer heat, with clear views to the Turkish coast.

🏃 Activities

Along with swimming and sunbathing, try scuba diving with **Samos Dive Center** (☑ 6972997645; www.samosdiving.com; harbour) or **Aegean Scuba** (☑ 22730 23006; www. aegeanscuba.gr; Pythagorio marina). Professional instructors lead dives in search of moray eels, sea stars, octopuses, lobsters and other critters lurking in the sponge-covered crevices around Pythagorio. A two-dive half-day for beginners costs €35. Snorkelling (€20) is also offered.

🛏 Sleeping

Pension Despina
PENSION $

(☑ 22730 61677; www.samosrooms.gr/despina; A Nikolaou; d €35; ❋ 🤶) A clean, quiet pension on Plateia Irinis, the Despina offers simple studios and rooms with balconies (some have kitchenettes), plus a relaxing back garden.

Philoxenia Pension
PENSION $

(☑ 22730 61055, 6973768371; www.pensionphilo xeniasamos.blogspot.com; ❋ @ 🤶) Opposite the archaeological museum, look for the small flower-filled courtyard. Rooms are spotless and comfortable, with overhead fans, common kitchen and laundry. The owner's family lives in an adjacent apartment, so help is never far off.

Polyxeni Hotel & Cafe
HOTEL $

(☑ 22730 61590; www.polyxenihotel.com; s/d/tr incl breakfast €40/55/70) In the middle of the port, turn left from the main road to find this well-managed seafront lodging, with several balcony harbour-view rooms (with overhead fans and double-glazed windows), a popular lobby cocktail bar and cheerful staff.

TURKISH CONNECTIONS

Visiting the main resorts and historical sites of Turkey's Aegean coast from Samos, Chios and Lesvos is easy. Visas aren't necessary for day trips. But where required, they are issued on the Turkish side. While boat itineraries, prices and even companies change often, the following explains how things generally work.

From **Samos**, boats leave twice daily from Vathy (Samos) for the 90-minute trip to **Kuşadası**, a cool resort near **ancient Ephesus** (Efes). The Greek *Samos Star* leaves at 8.30am, and the Turkish-flagged *Kudasi Express* departs at 5pm. Additionally, from Pythagorio, a boat serves Kuşadası one to two times per week. From April through October, two ferries go weekly from Vathy. Tickets cost around €45 open return and €35 one way (plus €10 for Turkish port taxes). Daily excursions run from May through October, with the option to also visit Ephesus (€25 extra). For tickets and information, contact ITSA Travel (p116), opposite the old ferry terminal for boats to Turkey.

From **Chios**, boats depart year-round from Chios Town for **Çeşme**, a port near bustling **İzmir**, though they're most frequent in summer. From May through October, the Turkish ferry **Erturk** (www.ertruk.com.tr) leaves daily to Çeşme at 8.30am, returning at 6.30pm; on Sunday, however, it returns at 5pm (50 minutes; one-way/return €20/35). A popular package day-tour to Izmir runs from €30 to €35. Get information and tickets from **Hatzelenis Tours** (☑ 22710 20002; mano2@otenet.gr; Leoforos Aigaiou 2) or Sunrise Tours (p566).

From **Lesvos**, boats leave Mytilini Town for **Ayvalik**. Two Turkish companies, Turyol and Jale, leave Mytilini Town daily in summer (May through October) at 9am, returning at 6pm (€25 return). Thursday boats are popular for market day in Ayvalik, while the Tuesday and Saturday trips offer a day-tour of **ancient Pergamon** (Bergama) for €45.

Most Mytilini Town travel agencies sell Turkish tours; try Olive Groove Travel (p573) or Mitilene Tours (p572).

✕ Eating & Drinking

Faros
TAVERNA $

(mezedhes €4-6, mains €6.50-10; ⊙11am-midnight) This eastern harbour eatery doesn't disappoint. A tad pricey, Faros is a minimalist, contemporary Mediterranean bistro overlooking the bay. Think *mesklo* cheese or *dolmadhakia* for meze and *exohiko* (stuffed lamb) for main.

Robinson
QUICK EATS $

(pitta gyros €2-4; ⊙11am-11pm) Excellent pit stop for juicy pitta souvlakia and *gyros* (meat slithers cooked on a vertical rotisserie; usually eaten with pitta bread). At main junction of Pythagorio, a few doors towards the port.

Elia Taverna
GREEK $

(☑22730 61436; mains €5.50-9; ⊙lunch-dinner) At the far northeast corner of the port, Elia ('olive') serves excellent *mayirefta* dishes such as *yemista* (stuffed tomatoes), and *kleftiko* (slow oven-baked lamb) in a shaded outdoor setting.

Kafeneio To Mouragio
CAFE $

(mezedhes €3-6; ⊙8am-midnight) The warm ambience and predominantly Greek clientele hint towards the fact that this place delivers the goods with snacks such as chickpea croquettes and meatballs, plus iced ouzo, wine and beer. You can also leave your luggage for free if you are a customer.

Notos
BAR

From the main road, turn right (south) at the port to find this popular late-night music bar and taverna, situated opposite a public car park. Live music most Tuesdays and Saturdays.

ℹ Information

There are several ATMs along the main streets. Most cafes and restaurants offer free wi-fi. Taxis gather on Egeou Pelagous next to the harbour.

By Ship Travel (☑22730 62285; www.byship travel.gr) Helpful full-service travel agency, car hire, accommodations, air and ferry tickets. At main town junction.

Port Police (☑22730 61225)

Post Office (Lykourgou Logotheti)

Tourist Office (☑22730 61389; deap5@ otenet.gr; Lykourgou Logotheti; ⊙8am-9.30pm)

Tourist Police (☑22730 61100; Lykourgou Logotheti)

Around Pythagorio

The Ireon
Το Ηραίον

Ireon, the resort village beyond the archaeological site, is smaller and lower key than Pythagorio. It has a variety of nightlife and bathing options and is popular for moonrise watching.

◉ Sights

Ireon
RUINS

(☑22730 95277; adult/student €4/2; ⊙8am-dusk Tue-Sun) From the scattered ruins of the Ireon, one can't imagine the former magnificence of this ancient sanctuary of the goddess Hera, located 8km west of Pythagorio. The 'Sacred Way', once flanked by thousands of marble statues, led from the city to this World Heritage–listed site, built at Hera's legendary birthplace. However, enough survives to provide a glimpse of a sanctuary that was four times larger than the Parthenon.

Built in the 6th century BC, the Ireon was constructed over an earlier Mycenaean temple. Plundering and earthquakes have left only one column standing, though extensive foundations remain. Other remains include a stoa (long colonnaded building), a 5th-century Christian basilica, and the headless, and deeplly disturbing, statues of a family, the Geneleos Group. Deep trenches mark where archaeologists continue to unearth treasures.

🛏 Sleeping & Eating

Hotel Restaurant Cohyli
TAVERNA $

(☑22730 95282; www.hotel-cohyli.com; Ireon; s/d/tr incl breakfast from €35/42/55; 🅿 ❊ 🛜) You will sleep and eat well at this welcoming hotel-taverna gem. Rooms are cosy and clean, with fridges and fans. When you are hungry just relocate to the shaded courtyard

A MATTER OF MEASUREMENTS

While the obsession with the 'proper pint' may seem modern, the ancient Greeks too fixated on measuring their alcohol. Pythagoras, that great Samian mathematician (and, presumably, drinker) created an invention that ensured party hosts and publicans could not be deceived by guests aspiring to inebriation. His creation was dubbed the *dikia-koupa tou Pythagora* (Just Cup of Pythagoras). This mysterious, multiholed drinking vessel holds its contents perfectly, unless filled past the engraved line – at which point the glass drains completely from the bottom, punishing the glutton!

Today faithful reproduction, made of colourful, glazed ceramic, are sold in Samos gift shops, tangible reminders of the Apollan Mean: 'Everything in moderation'.

next door to sample excellent mezedhes and *saganaki* (fried cheese).

Restaurant Glaros SEAFOOD $
(📞 22730 95457; Ireon; mains €4-7; ⊙ 11am-11pm) Fish prices here are reasonable and the fish are fished and eaten, not frozen and consumed. Try the fish soup and finger-wrapped dolmadhes. Savour all on a rustic, vine-covered veranda facing a topaz-blue sea.

Psili Ammos   Ψιλή Άμμος

Sandy **Psili Ammos Beach**, 11km east of Pythagorio, is the best of the southeastern beaches, a lovely cove facing Turkey. It's bordered by shady trees and has shallow kid-friendly waters. Several good fish tavernas compete for the best bay view. Sleep the sea and sardines off at the classy **Apartments Elena** (📞 22730 23645; www.elenaapartments. gr; Psili Ammos; s/d €45/60; P ✴ 🕯) where the rooms are spacious and comfy.

Southwestern Samos

Pythagorio to Drakeï
Πυθαγόρειο προς Δρακαίους

The drive west from Pythagorio traverses spectacular mountain scenery with stunning views of the south coast. This route also features many little signposted huts, where beekeepers sell superlative but inexpensive Samian honey.

Along the way, around the village of **Pyrgos** you'll be treated to magnificent views of mountain, sky and sea before reaching **Ormos Marathokambou** (Bay of Marathokampos). Another 4km west is **Votsalakia Beach** (often called Kambos), with its long, sandy beach. To escape the midsummer mob, however, head 3km further west

to more tranquil **Psili Ammos Beach**, stay the night in domatia here, and sample the fresh fish at the beach tavernas.

Hikers keen on exploring the flanks of **Mt Kerkis**, or even reaching its peak (1434m), should enquire in Votsalakia for the trail head, which passes the **convent** of Evange-listrias on the way.

Past Kambos, the rugged western route, undeveloped and tranquil, skirts Mt Kerkis until reaching the villages of **Kallithea** and **Drakeï**, where the road abruptly ends. A walking trail is the only link between this point and Potami on the north coast.

Northern Samos

Vathy to Karlovasi
Βαθύ προς Καρλοβάσι

From Vathy (Samos), the coast road west passes a number of beaches and resorts. The first, **Kokkari** (10km from Vathy), was once a fishing village, but has become something of a package resort. Windsurfing from its long pebble beach is good when the wind's up in summer. The popular nearby beaches of **Lemonaki**, **Tsamadou**, **Tsambou** and **Livadhaki** are the most accessible for Kokkari-based travellers.

Continuing west, the landscape becomes more forested and mountainous. Take the left-hand turn-off after 5km to reach the lovely mountain village of **Vourliotes**. The village's multicoloured, shuttered houses cluster on and above a *plateia*. Walkers can alternatively take a good *monopati* (footpath) from Kokkari.

Back on the coast road, look for the signposted turn-off for another fragrant village, **Manolates**, 5km further up the lower slopes of Mt Ambelos (1153m). Set amidst thick pine and deciduous forests, and boasting gorgeous traditional houses, Manolates is nearly encircled by mountains and offers a cooler alternative to the sweltering coast.

The shops of both Vourliotes and Manolates sell handmade ceramic art and icons, along with the Cup of Pythagoras. Good tavernas are plentiful and, despite the touristy patina, both villages are worth visiting for a glimpse of old Samos.

Back on the coast heading west, the road continues through Agios Konstantinos – a flower-filled village with a rather bleak seafront – before coming to workaday Karlovasi, Samos' third port.

Just 3km beyond Karlovassi lies the sand-and-pebble Potami Beach, blessed with good swimming and a reggae beach bar. It's complemented by nearby forest waterfalls; head west 50m from the beach and they're signposted on the left. Entering the forest you'll first encounter the centuries-old Metamorfosis Sotiros chapel, where the devout light candles. Continuing about 1.5km through the wooded trail along the river brings you to a river channel where you must wade or swim before enjoying a splash under the 2m-high waterfalls.

Find Terrain Editions (www.terrainmaps.gr) map of Samos for exploring the region, available from Lexis Bookstore (☑22730 92271) in Kokkari, which also carries foreign books, magazines and newspapers.

🛏 Sleeping

Studio Angela   APARTMENTS **$**
(☑21050 59708, 22730 94478; Manolates; d €35; ❋) A great budget choice, these five studios near the church in Manolates, built into a hillside overlooking the sea, have modern rooms and kitchenettes, views to the sea, and the hospitality of owner Angela.

Kokkari Beach Hotel   HOTEL **$$**
(☑22730 92238; www.kokkaribeach.com; Kokkari; d incl breakfast €75; P❋🛜⛱) This striking, upmarket establishment 1km west of the bus stop is set back from the road in a mauve and green building, just opposite the beach. The airy and cool rooms are equally colourful.

🍴 Eating & Drinking

Café Bar Cavos   CAFE **$**
(Kokkari; mains €6-12; ⏲9am-midnight; 🛜) It's easy to hang out in this cool harbour bar, whether you're after a good breakfast, afternoon snack or evening cocktail. Prices are

good and there's free wi-fi and PC terminals. Ask for Uli's homemade cake of the day.

Pizzeria Tarsanas   PIZZA **$**
(Kokkari; mains €6-12; ⏲7pm-12am; 🛜) This popular eatery is in fact an authentic old-style Greek taverna that happens to do great pizzas. It also does excellent *mousakas*, rolls out luscious dolmadhes and pours its own homemade wine.

Galazio Pigadi   TAVERNA **$**
(Proödou, Vourliotes; mains €5-8; ⏲9am-11pm) Just past the *plateia* in Vourliotes this atmospheric place has a variety of mezedhes including *revythokeftedhes* (chickpea rissoles) and *bourekakia* (crunchy cheese-in-filo pastries). Worthy local wine on hand.

Pera Vrysi   TAVERNA **$**
(Vourliotes; mains €6-9; ⏲10am-12am, closed Mon) This old-style Samian taverna by the spring at Vourliotes' entrance offers exceptional village cuisine in ample portions and homemade barrel wine.

Loukas Taverna   TAVERNA **$**
(mains €5-8; ⏲lunch & dinner) Upon entering Manolates, you'll see signs, one after the other, pointing the way to this traditional eatery above the village. Follow them. Proud owner Manolis serves up excellent and hearty taverna standards along with his own top-notch wines.

Kallisti Taverna   TAVERNA **$**
(Manolates; mains €5-7) This intriguing taverna located on the square has numerous excellent dishes including *kleftiko* (lamb with vegetables), and unusual desserts, such as a tasty orange pie.

Despina Taverna   TAVERNA **$**
(Manolates; mains €5-9) Under the shade of a wooden pergola and next to a running spring, this little taverna, halfway up the village in Manolates, serves grills and fine *mayirefta*.

Hippys Restaurant Café   TAVERNA **$**
(www.hippys.gr; Potami Beach; ⏲9am-late) This cool open cafe-bar on Potami Beach combines Greek and South Seas decor with Brazilian jazz, reggae, good omelettes and pasta.

ℹ Information

EOT (Greek National Tourist Organisation; ☑22730 92217; Kokkari; ⏲9am-1pm, Mon-Sat; 🛜) Helpful English-speaking office, 10m east of the church by the bus stop.

CHIOS ΧΙΟΣ

POP 53,820 / AREA 859 SQ KM

Likeable Chios (*hee*-os) is one of Greece's bigger islands, and is significant in national history, along with the tiny neighbouring island of Inousses, as the ancestral home of shipping barons. Its varied terrain ranges from lonesome mountain crags in the north to the citrus-grove estates of Kampos, near the island's port capital in the centre, to the fertile Mastihohoria in the south – the only place in the world where mastic trees are commercially productive.

Chians are a hospitable lot who take great pride in their history, traditions and livelihood. For the visitor, this translates into excellent opportunities for hands-on interaction with Chian culture, ranging from art and history to hiking and eco-activities.

Chios enjoys good regular boat connections throughout the northeastern Aegean Islands, and has an airport. Between them, the ports of Chios Town in the east and Mesta in the southwest offer regular ferries to the intriguing, little-visited satellite islands of Psara and Inousses, which share Chios' legacy of maritime greatness, and to the lively Turkish coastal resorts just across the water.

History

Similarly to Samos and Lesvos, geographic proximity to Turkey brought Chios both great success and great tragedy. Under the Ottoman rule, Chios' monopolistic production of mastic (which was the sultan's favourite gum) brought Chians wealth and special privileges. However, during the 1821–29 War of Independence, thousands of Chians were slaughtered by Ottoman troops.

In 1922, a military campaign launched from Chios to reclaim lands with Greek-majority populations in Asia Minor, ended disastrously, as waves of refugees from Asia Minor (Anatolia) flooded Chios and neighbouring islands. The following year saw the 'population exchange' in which two million ethnic Greeks and Turks were forced to return to the homelands of their ancestors.

ⓘ Getting There & Away

AIR

The airport is 4km from Chios Town. There's no shuttle bus; an airport taxi to/from the town costs €8. Tickets are available from Hatzelenis Tours.

Domestic Flights from Chios

DESTINATION	TIME	FARE	FREQUENCY
Athens	45min	€90-100	3 daily
Lesvos	30min	€46	2 weekly
Limnos	90min	€57	2 weekly
Rhodes	90min	€68	2 weekly
Samos	30min	€47	1 weekly
Thessaloniki	55min	€72	1 daily

BOAT

Buy tickets from Hatzelenis Tours (p562), or from **NEL Lines** (☑ 22710 23971; Leoforos Egeou 16) in Chios Town.

BOAT SERVICES FROM CHIOS

DESTINATION	PORT	TIME	FARE	FREQUENCY
Ikaria (Agios Kirykos)	Chios	4½hr	€14	1 weekly
Inousses	Chios	1hr	€5	1 daily
Kavala	Chios	15hr	€32	2 weekly
Lavrio (via Psara)	Mesta	8hr	€26	3 weekly
Lesvos (Mytilini Town)	Chios	3hr	€113-20	2 daily
Limnos	Chios	11hr	€22	3 weekly
Piraeus	Chios	6-9hr	€32	6 weekly
Psara	Chios	3½hr	€8-15*	1 weekly
Psara	Mesta	1¼hr	€7-14*	1 weekly
Samos (Karlovasi)	Chios	3hr	€10	1 weekly
Samos (Vathy)	Chios	3½hr	€13	3 weekly
Thessaloniki	Chios	12hr	€36	1-2 weekly

*round-trip

Chios

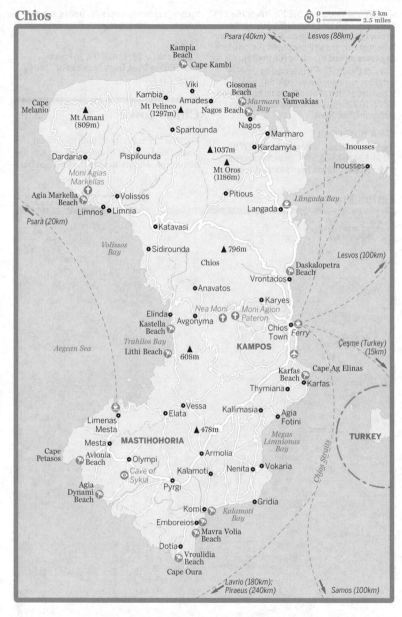

There are daily **water taxis** (☑ 6944168104) that operate between Langada and Inousses (the cost is €65, shared between up to eight passengers).

ℹ️ Getting Around

BUS

From the waterfront's **long-distance bus station** (☑ 22710 27507; www.ktelchios.gr; waterfront) in Chios Town, daily green buses serve Pyrgi (€2.80), Mesta (€3.90), Lithi Beach

(€2.80), and Kardamyla (€3.10), Nagos (€3.80), Kambia (€5.40) via Langada (€1.80). Thrice-weekly buses serve Volissos (€4.50). From June to September, this well-organised station offers **day-tours** around the island (€8 to €15).

Karfas Beach (€1.60) is served by the blue (city) bus company (on Vounaki Sq), with schedules posted at both the **local bus station** (☎ 22710 22079) and the long-distance bus station in Chios Town.

CAR & MOTORCYCLE

The reliable **Chandris Rent a Car** (☎ 22710 27194, 6944972051; info@chandrisrentacar. gr; Porfyra 5) is Chios Town's longest-running agency, and owner Kostas Chandris gladly provides island information.

TAXI

A **taxi rank** (☎ 22710 41111) is on Plateia Vounakiou in Chios Town. Taxis can be hired by the hour (€25).

Chios Town   Χίος

POP 23,780

The island's main port and capital on the central east coast is home to almost half the island's inhabitants. Behind the long and busy

Chios Town

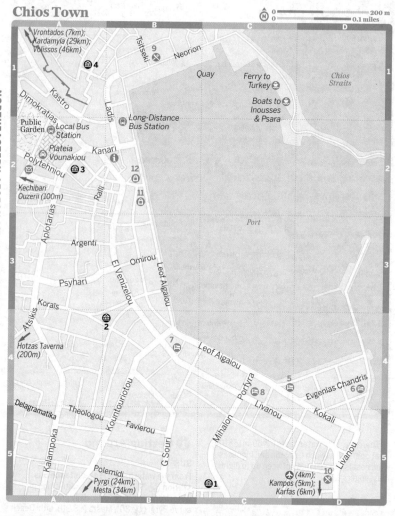

waterfront lies a quieter, intriguing old quarter, where some lingering traditional Turkish houses stand around a Genoese castle and city walls. There's also a busy market area behind the waterfront, and spacious public gardens (Vounaki) where an open-air cinema (€6) operates on summer evenings. The nearest decent beach is popular Karfas, 6km south.

◉ Sights

Argentis Museum & Korais Library   MUSEUM
(Korai; admission €2; ◎8am-2pm Mon-Fri, 5-7.30pm Fri, 8am-12.30pm Sat) On the upper floor of the **Korais Library**, the Filippos Argenti Folkloric Museum contains displays of embroideries, traditional costumes and portraits of the wealthy Argentis family. Born in Marseilles in 1891, Argentis devoted his life to researching Chian history.

Archaeological Museum   MUSEUM
(☑22710 44239; Mihalon 10; admission €2; ◎8am-3pm Tue-Sun) Along with prehistoric and Archaic treasures from the excavations of the British School at Emporios, there are impressive neolithic and classical finds (coins, sculptures, pottery) from Agios Galas and Fana.

Byzantine Museum   MUSEUM
(☑22710 26866; Plateia Vounaki; €2; ◎8am-3pm Tue-Sun) The museum, in a 19th-century mosque, the Medjitie Djami, has relics from the Byzantine, post-Byzantine, Genoese and Islamic periods, including old canons, fine icons and Jewish and Muslim tombstones.

Giustiniani Palace Museum   MUSEUM
(☑22710 22819; admission €2; ◎9am-3pm Tue-Sun) Near the Kastro's main gate, the tiny museum (or 'Palataki'), still looks like the 15th-century fortress it once was. Of particular interest are 12 Byzantine frescoes of the prophets, dating from the 13th century, along with an 18th-century full-length icon of the Archangel Michael.

⌂ Sleeping

★ Chios Rooms   PENSION $
(☑22710 20198; www.chiosrooms.gr; Leoforos Egeou 110; s/d/tr from €25/30/40; ☏) An eclectic, hostel-like neoclassical house on the waterfront, Chios Rooms is the inspiration of its owner, native New Zealander Don. Marked by handsome vintage furnishings, traditional rugs and lofty ceilings, the place has character to spare. Most rooms have private bathrooms; other rooms share.

Rooms Alex   PENSION $
(☑6979535256; roomsalex@hotmail.gr; Livanou 29; s/d €30/45) Host Alex Stoupas was a sea captain for 21 years and his handmade model ships decorate each of the simple but clean rooms. The *kapetanios*, "100% helpful" as he'll happily tell you, picks guests up from the ferry, and speaks English, French and Spanish.

Ionia Rooms   PENSION $
(☑6932467821, 22710 82979; www.ioniarooms.gr; s/d/tr incl breakfast from €25/35/45; ❀☏) A short block from the busy waterfront brings you to this attractive, clean and efficient seven-room domatia, with minifridge and mosquito screens.

Hotel Kyma   HOTEL $$
(☑22710 44500; www.hotelkyma.com; Evgenias Handris 1; s/d/tr incl breakfast €70/90/110; ❀☏) Aside from the sea-view balconies and stately decor of this converted mansion, what makes the Kyma more than just another period hotel is its service; owner Theodoros Spordylis solves problems in English, Italian and German.

✕ Eating

★ Hotzas Taverna   TAVERNA $
(☑22710 42787; Kondyli 3; mains €5.50-9; ◎dinner Mon-Sat) Superb and traditional taverna above Chios Town. This attractive and welcoming spot serves fine Greek standards such as rooster in wine sauce, locally made sausages and *dolmadakia* with lemon.

There is a variety of great vegie dishes, including risotto, and white beans in a light tomato sauce. Everything is *herisia* (handmade), from pasta to dessert.

★**Kechibari Ouzerie** OUZERIE $
(Agion Anargyron 7; mains €4-7; ⊗lunch Jun-Sep) This cosy gem of an *ouzerie*, a 10-minute walk up from the waterfront, serves a variety of small plates in addition to excellent fish, including mussels, baked potatoes and small salads. Snappy service and reasonable prices. Opposite the church.

To Tavernaki tou Tassou TAVERNA $
(✷22710 27542; Livanou 8; mains €6-8; ⊛) Family-friendly eatery near the sea and Hotel Kyma. It offers classic taverna fare, Chios' own Kambos lemonade and an adjoining kids' play area.

Ouzeri Tzivaeri TAVERNA $
(✷22710 43559; Neoreion 13; mezedhes €3-8) Busy portside eatery touts oil-drenched sundried tomatoes, grilled cod strips and traditional Chios sausages, and always has fresh *gavros* and good grills.

🛍 Shopping

Mastihashop BEAUTY
(✷22710 81600; www.mastihashop.com; Leoforos Egeou 36) This place has a range of mastic-based products such as lotions, toothpaste, soaps and condiments.

Sarandis Tourist Shop SOUVENIRS, BOOKS
(✷22710 24224; www.saranti.gr; cnr Leoforos Aigaiou & Roïdi) Rambling Sarandis sells mastic-style products such as lotions, soaps and condiments, along with good island maps.

ℹ Information

Banks with ATMS can be found along the waterfront and in the *plateia*. Free wi-fi is common at waterfront cafes.

Chios General Hospital (✷22710 44302; El Venizelou 7) Just 2km north of the centre.

Chios Tourist Office (✷22710 44344; infochio @otenet.gr; Kanari 18; ⊗7am-3pm & 6-10pm Jul-Aug) This friendly and resourceful office has information on accommodation, car hire, bus and boat schedules, plus a useful free booklet *Cultural Routes of Chios*.

Hatzelenis Tours (✷22710 20002; mano2@ otenet.gr; Leoforos Aigaiou 2) Opposite the port, this dependable full-service travel agency arranges ferry and air tickets, excursions, accommodation and car hire.

Police (✷22710 44427; cnr Polemidi 1 & Koundouriotou)
Post Office (✷22710 44350; Plateia Vounaki; ⊗7.30am-7pm)
Tourist Police (✷22710 44427; Neorion)

Central Chios

North of Chios Town about 2km, **Vrontados** is the site of Homer's legendary stone chair, the **Daskalopetra** (in Greek, teacher's stone), a rock pinnacle close to the sea, an obvious choice for holding class.

Immediately south of Chios Town is **Kampos**, a lush area with citrus trees, where wealthy Genoese and Greek merchant families summered from the 14th century onwards. You can see elaborate gardens and high-walled mansions, some restored, others crumbling. The handsome **Citrus Memories Museum** (✷22710 31513; www.citrus-chios.gr; Kambos; ⊗10am-10pm Jun-Sep) **FREE** documents the agricultural base of this community with summer concerts and art exhibits.

At the island's centre is **Nea Moni** (New Monastery; ⊗8am-1pm & 4-8pm) **FREE**, a World Heritage–listed 11th-century Byzantine monastery. Once one of Greece's richest monasteries, Nea Moni attracted pre-eminent Byzantine artists to create the mosaics in its *katholikon* (principal church). Disastrously, during the Greek War of Independence, the Turks torched the monastery and massacred its monks. Another catastrophe occurred in an 1881 earthquake that demolished the *katholikon* dome. Nea Moni is now a nunnery.

Another solemn site lies 10km northwest, at the end of a silent road. **Anavatos**, filled with abandoned grey-stone houses and narrow stepped pathways, was built on a precipitous cliff over which villagers hurled themselves to avoid capture during Turkish reprisals in 1822. Nowadays, it's referred to as the 'ghost village'.

Of the quieter central-west-coast beaches, picturesque **Lithi** is most popular.

🛏 Sleeping

Spiti Elaionas STUDIO $
(✷22710 20002; mano2@otenet.gr; Kambos; d from €40) Two traditional and beautifully decorated stone houses, 300m from Karfas Beach in a quiet hillside setting, with great views across to the Turkish coast.

Perleas Mansion HISTORIC HOTEL **$$**
(☑ 22710 32217; www.perleas.gr; Vitiadou, Kampos; d/tr incl breakfast from €100/120; P ✳ 🛜) The restored Perleas mansion offers seven well-appointed apartments. This relaxing estate, built in 1640, exemplifies high Genoese architecture. The restaurant serves traditional Greek cuisine.

Northern Chios

The craggy peaks of Mt Pelineo, Mt Oros and Mt Amani mark the drive north from Chios Town along the east coast, an astonishing trip through bizarre, boulder-strewn slopes that seem from another planet.

After the small coastal settlements of Vrontados and Langada are the main villages of Marmaro and Kardamyla, ancestral homes of many wealthy ship-owning families. About 5km further west is the fishing village of Nagos, where the road continues northwest, skirting Mt Pelineo (1297m), then winding and twisting its way through Kambia, high up on a ridge overlooking the sea.

The central road will lead you south via Diefha to Volissos, Homer's legendary birthplace, with its impressive Genoese fort. Some 5km beyond Volissos' working port of Limnia, you will reach the Agia Markella Monastery, named for the island's patron saint. From Volissos the coastal road continues south until Elinda, then returns eastwards to Chios Town.

Worth the trip to Volissos by itself is the excellent restaurant (and domatia), Taverna Fabrika (☑ 6976255829, 22740 22045; www.chiosfabrika.gr; mains €6-8.50; ⊙ lunch & dinner; P). The best sleeping option in Marmoro is Hotel Kardamyla (☑ 22720 23353; www.hotelkyma.com; Marmaro; s/d/tr incl breakfast €70/100/120; P ✳ 🛜).

Southern Chios

Unique southern Chios is arguably the island's best destination. Though it grows elsewhere in the Aegean, the gum-producing mastic tree of Chios has for centuries been the sole commercial producer of mastic gum. The tree thrives in a fertile, reddish territory known as the Mastihohoria (Mastic villages). This region of rolling hills, crisscrossed with elaborate stone walls running through olive and mastic groves, is highly atmospheric.

The Ottoman rulers' penchant for mastic made the Mastihohoria wealthy for centuries. Some architectural wonders remain in the villages of Pyrgi and Mesta. The former features houses decorated in unusual colourful patterns, while the latter is a car-free, walled fortress settlement built by the Genoese in the 14th century.

Pyrgi   Πυργί
POP 1040

Located 24km southwest of Chios Town, Pyrgi (peer-*ghi*), the Mastihohoria's largest village, juxtaposes traditional and modern architecture, with facades decorated in intricate grey-and-white patterns, some geometric and others based on flowers, leaves and animals. The technique, called *xysta,* uses equal amounts of cement, volcanic sand and lime as well as bent forks and a fine eye.

Pyrgi's central square is flanked by tavernas, shops and the little 12th-century Church of Agios Apostolos (⊙ 10am-1pm Tue-Thu & Sat). East of the square, note the house with a plaque attesting to its former occupant – one Christopher Columbus, also a fan of mastic gum, though he apparently preferred it as a sealant in boat construction.

Six kilometres southeast of Pyrgi, Emboreios was the Mastihohoria's port back when the mastic producers were high-rollers. Today it's much quieter, though it does boast Mavra Volia Beach, named for its black volcanic pebbles. You can stay the night here in domatia and eat in a couple of shaded tavernas.

Mesta   Μεστά

Mesta (mest-*aah*) is a truly memorable village and one of Greece's most unusual. Here, appealing stone alleyways, intertwined with flowers and intricate balconies, are completely enclosed by thick defensive walls – the work of Chios' former Genoese rulers, who built this fortress town in the 14th century to keep pirates and would-be invaders out.

Mesta is an ingenious example of medieval defensive architecture, featuring a double set of walls, four gates and a pentagonal structure. Since the rooftops are interconnected, with the right guide you can actually walk across the entire town. In medieval times, mastic was a hot commodity, prized for its medicinal powers, meaning Mesta had to be especially well fortified.

As a car-free village, it's a relaxing, romantic place where children can run around safely. Mesta also makes a good base for hill walking, exploring southern beaches and caves, and participating in cultural and eco-tourism activities.

Village life converges on the central square with its small cafes and restaurants, and, nearby, the enormous Church of the Taxiarhes. Along the tranquil, secluded lanes, rooms for rent are almost indistinguishable from the attached residences.

◉ Sights

Churches of the Taxiarhes   CHURCH
There are two Churches of the Taxiarhes (Archangels). The older and smaller one dates from Byzantine times and features a magnificent 17th-century iconostasis. The larger, 19th-century church was built entirely from the townspeople's donations and labour.

🏃 Activities

**Masticulture Ecotourism
Activities**   ECOTOUR
(☑ 6976113007, 22710 76084; www.masticulture.com; Plateia Taxiarhon) To get your hands dirty and participate in traditional cultural activities, including Chian farming, contact Vasilis and Roula. This helpful couple provide unique ecotourism opportunities that introduce visitors to the local community, its history and culture. Some activities (from €18) include mastic cultivation tours, stargazing, plus bicycle and sea-kayak outings. They can help find area accommodation, and arrange trips to nearby Psara.

Chios Underwater   DIVING
(☑ 6906062901;   www.medi-sea.blogspot.com; Mesta) Provides certified diving and sea-kayaking.

Sleeping & Eating

Masticulture Ecotourism Activities can help arrange rooms in Mesta, Olympi or Pygi. Also ask at the small *plateia* cafe or retaurant for the proprietors listed here.

★Dhimitris Pipidhis Rooms   PENSION $
(☑ 6937829450, 22710 76029; www.pippidisrooms.gr, in Greek; Mesta; house €60-70; ❋) The friendly, English-speaking Dhimitris and Koula Pipidhis (aka Popi) rent two traditional houses in Mesta. Each is well-appointed, with two bedrooms, a *pounti* (Mesta-styled

atrium), kitchen and washing machine. Excellent value; book ahead in summer.

Lida Mary Rooms   HOTEL $
(☑ 6976629668, 22710 76217; www.lidamary.gr/en; r from €42) Another lovely and well-managed option in the village. A few rooms overlook the *plateia*.

**Despina Karabela Traditional
Apartments**   APARTMENTS $
(☑ 22710 76065; karabela@chi.forthnet.gr; s/d €40/50; ❋🗟) A short walk from the village square, these lovely apartments are cosy and tastefully decorated. Exposed stone highlights the interior, while the loft 'bedroom' is a raised platform.

Anna Floradis Rooms   PENSION $
(☑ 22710 76455; www.floradi.gr; s/d €40/50; ❋🗟) The friendly Anna Floradis, who speaks French and some English, has rooms, studios and kitchenette suites throughout Mesta.

★Meseonas   TAVERNA $
(Plateia Taxiarhon; mains €5-10) With tables spread across Plateia Taxiarhon, this venerable old favourite appeals to locals and tourists alike, and serves hearty portions of *mayirefta*, beef *keftedhes* (rissoles) and grills. Everything is local, right down to the *souma* (mastic-flavoured firewater).

❶ Getting Around

Mesta is a walking-only town; there are regular buses to Chios Town. English-speaking **Dimitris Kokkinos** (☑ 6972543543) provides a taxi service. Sample fares from Mesta include: Limenas Mesta €7; Olympi €5; Pyrgi €20; and Chios Town €50.

Around Mesta

Mesta's workaday west-coast port of Lime-nas Meston (also called Limenas) offers a shorter exit to the Greek mainland via Psara to Lavrio. There are a couple of decent tavernas to feed travellers and transients, including the fish taverna **Limani Meston**.

For swimming, head to **Agia Dynami Beach** (7km south of Olympi), a curving, sandy cove where the water is a stunning turquoise, backed by two tamarisk shade trees and a popular canteen.

Some 3km southeast of Mesta is **Olympi** – like Mesta and Pyrgi, a mastic-producing village characterised by its defensive architecture. A well-maintained 3km trail connects Oympi and Mesta.

A popular side-trip takes you 5km south to the splendid **Cave of Sykia Olymbi** (☑ 22710 93364; admission €5; ◷ 11am-6pm Tue-Sun), signposted at Olympi as 'Olympi Cave', a 150-million-year-old cavern discovered accidentally in 1985. The cave is some 57m deep and is filled with multicoloured stalactites and other rock formations with whimsical names such as the Pipe Organ, Cacti and the Jellyfish. Floodlights light it up, and a series of platforms and staircases with handrails connect it all – be prepared for some climbing. The cave maintains a steady temperature of 18°C and humidity is a moist 95%. Guided tours are mandatory and run every 30 minutes.

INOUSSES   ΟΙΝΟΥΣΣΕΣ

POP 375 / AREA 14 SQ KM

Just northwest of Chios, placid Inousses is the ancestral home to nearly a third of Greece's shipping barons (the *arhontes*), whose wealthy descendents return here annually for summer vacations from their homes in London, Paris or New York.

Inousses was settled in 1750 by ship-owning families from Kardamyla in northeastern Chios, and some amassed huge fortunes during the 19th and early 20th centuries; traces of this history linger in Inousses' grand mansions and ornate family mausoleums high above the sea.

Although Inousses is little-visited, it does get lively in high season, with an open-air cinema, cafes and night-time beach parties. Nevertheless, it has retained its serenity and remains an escapist destination, with only a few rooms and studios for rent.

The island's port attests to its seafaring identity. Arriving by ferry, you'll see a small, green sculpted mermaid watching over the harbour – this is the Mitera Inoussiotissa (Mother of Inoussa), protector of mariners. Inousses also boasts a merchant marine academy.

◉ Sights & Activities

Inousses has numerous hill-walking opportunities and pristine beaches. Just a 10-minute walk from the port, you'll find pretty and swimmable **Kakopetria Beach**. Another five to 10 minutes will bring you to **Bilali Beach**, set on a tranquil bay with a not-quite-tranquil beach cantina that buzzes all night in summer.

ⓘ NAUTICAL DILEMMA

The **Nautical Museum of Inousses** (☑ 22710 55182) and the ferry schedules don't mix well. For one-night visitors, the ferry arrives after the museum's daily 2pm closing, and departs before it opens the next day at 10am. But worry not, as the gracious manager-curator, Eleni Achlipta, promises to open up for anyone who calls ahead.

Orthodox pilgrims visit the **Evangelismou Theotokou Monastery** at the western end of the island.

Nautical Museum   MUSEUM
(☑ 22710 44139; Stefanou Tsouri 20; admission €1.50; ◷ 10am-2pm) Created in 1965, this little museum showcases the collection of local shipping magnate Antonis Lemos. Many of the models on display (some half-completed, then set flush against a mirror so that you 'see' the whole vessel) were made by French prisoners-of-war around the time of the Napoleonic Wars. There's also a swashbuckling collection of 18th-century muskets and sabres, a WWII-era US Navy diving helmet, a hand-cranked lighthouse made in 1864 and paintings of Nazi submarines attacking Greek sailing vessels.

Mausoleum of Inousses   CEMETERY
In the leafy courtyard of the Church of Agia Paraskevi stands the Nekrotafion Inousson (Mausoleum of Inousses), where the island's ship-owning dynasties have endowed the tombs of their greats with huge chambers, marble sculptures and miniature churches. It's a melancholy, moving place and speaks volumes about the worldly achievements and self-perception of the extraordinary natives of these tiny islands.

Perhaps more touching is the elegant Platia tis Naftosynis (**Seamanship Square**) near the port, with nothing more than a proud statue, backed by a commemorative panel with the names of sailors who have died at sea, with still room for more.

🛏 Sleeping

Rooms Bilali   APARTMENTS $
(☑ 6944677882; d from €45-70; ✳) Contact Kostas at Bilali Beach Bar for information on well-appointed one- and two-bedroom apartments in the upper village.

Rooms Tsouri ACCOMMODATION SERVICES $$
(☑6946286791; ✳) For help in finding village rooms, contact the resourceful Despina Tsouri. Doubles about €75.

✗ Eating & Drinking

To Pateroniso TAVERNA $
(mains €5-8) This reliable taverna near the *plateia* serves Greek grills, salads and seafood, including the Inousses/Chios speciality of *atherinopita*, a scrumptious heads-and-all pan-fry of onions and fresh anchovies.

Taverna Glaros TAVERNA $
(mains €7-12; ☙ lunch & dinner) Glaros ('seagull'), perched on the waterfront, serves excellent, if expensive, taverna standards including fresh fish and appetisers.

Naftikos Omilos Inousson BAR, RESTAURANT
(Yacht club; ☑22720 55596; ☙ 9am-3am; 🔊) At the waterfront's end, the Inousses Yacht Club's long bar and outdoor patio are filled mostly with young Greeks and their vacationing diaspora relatives.

Bilali Beach Bar BAR
Cool spot on a small and shallow swimming bay, with shady tables and thumping music which can seem almost mellow given the serene setting. This is where the young locals hang.

☆ Entertainment

A summertime open-air cinema (tickets €3) near the central waterfront brings Hollywood hits to Inousses, nightly at 9.30pm.

ⓘ Information

The bank (but no **ATM**) and post office are next to the Nautical Museum. Wi-fi is available in the waterfront cafes.
Dimarhio (Town Hall; ☑22710 55326) Can help with rooms; next to port.
Doctor (☑22710 55300)
Police (☑22710 55222)

ⓘ Getting There & Away

The little *Oinoussa III* (€5 one way, one hour, daily) leaves from Chios in the afternoon and returns from Inousses the next morning, warranting overnight stays. Purchase tickets onboard or from **Sunrise Tours** (☑22710 41390; www.sunrisetours.gr; Kanari 28) in Chios Town. There are weekly summertime day excursions (€20).

Daily **water taxis** (☑6944168104) travel to/from Langada (20 minutes), 15km north of Chios Town. The one-way fare is a hefty €60, but split among up to eight passengers.

ⓘ Getting Around

Inousses has neither buses nor car hire; ask at the port for its one semitaxi. You can also bring a bicycle or scooter on the ferry from Chios.

PSARA ΨΑΡΑ

POP 420 / AREA 45 SQ KM

Celebrated Psara (psah-*rah*), is one of maritime Greece's true oddities. A tiny speck in the sea two hours northwest of Chios, this island of scrub vegetation, wandering goats and weird red rock formations has one settlement (also called Psara), a remote monastery and pristine beaches.

Little Psara looms inordinately large in modern lore. The Psariot clans became wealthy through shipping, and their participation in the 1821–29 War of Independence is etched into modern Greek history, particularly the daring exploits of Konstantinos Kanaris (1793–1877) whose heroic stature propelled him, six times, to the position of prime minister.

Kanaris' most famous operation occurred on the night of 6 June 1822. In revenge for Turkish massacres on Chios, the Psariots destroyed the Turkish admiral's flagship while the unsuspecting enemy was holding a post-massacre celebration. Kanaris' forces detonated the ship's powder keg, blowing up 2000 sailors and the admiral himself. However, as in Chios, their involvement sparked a brutal Ottoman reprisal, with help from Egyptian and French mercenaries, that decimated the island in 1824.

Over the next century, many Psariots resettled in America and other foreign lands. Their descendents still return every summer, so don't be surprised if the first Greek you meet speaks English with a Brooklyn accent.

◉ Sights & Activities

Psara village is tucked within a long bay on the island's southwest. When you disembark from the ferry, you can't miss the jagged *Mavri Rachi*, or 'Black Shoulder' – the rock from which thousands of Psariots are said to have hurled themselves during the 1824 Ottoman assault.

Psara's main cultural attraction, the **Monastery of Kimisis Theotokou** (Dormition of the Virgin), 12km north of town, is a smallish chapel surrounded by protective walls, and containing rare hieratric scripts from Mt Athos and a sacred icon which is paraded through the village on the night of 4 August.

In the centre of Psara village is the **Konstantinos Kanaris Monument**, where Greeks honour their national hero who is actually buried in Athens while his heart is kept in the Naval Museum in Piraeus.

Flag

Throughout town, you will notice Psara's memorable red-and-white flag waving proudly in the breeze. Emblazoned with the revolutionary slogan *Eleftheria i Thanatos* (Freedom or Death), it features a red cross at its centre, with an upturned spear jutting from one side, while on the other is an anchor apparently impaling a green snake. And as if the reference to the Islamic rule of the Turks wasn't apparent enough, there's an upside-down crescent moon and star under these items for good measure. The yellow dove of freedom flutters, patiently, to one side.

Hiking

Visitors should take the splendid introductory walk along the **Black Shoulder** (aka Black Rock) to the little chapel of **Agios Ioannis** and the **lookout memorial**. The views are impressive from up top – especially at sunset.

A further three relatively short and documented hiking trails can also be tackled. The first one takes you to the **cannon emplacements** at the northwestern tip of Psara (2km each way); the second takes you to remote **Limnonaria Beach** (900m each way) on the south coast and the third is a circular route (3km) taking in **Adami** and **Kanalos Bays**. All three hikes are detailed on the **Terrain Maps** (www.terrainmaps.gr) map of Psara.

Beaches

There are a number of clean pebble-and-sand beaches stretched out along Psara's jagged edges. The closest are the village beaches of **Kato Gialos** and **Katsouni**. The former is on the west side of the headland and is pebbled, while the latter is a short

walk north of the harbour and is sandy with shallow water, ideal for kids. Both have tavernas.

Further afield and just over 1km northeast are the twin beaches of **Lazareta** and **Megali Ammos** consisting of fine pebbles. **Lakka Beach**, 2.5km up the west coast, is the next option, followed by **Agios Dimitrios**, 3.5km from Psara.

🛏 Sleeping

Village accommodation consists primarily of rooms and studios. Masticulture Ecotourism (p564) in Mesta can book ahead for rooms.

Kato Gialos Apartments   APARTMENTS $
(☑ 6945755321, 22740 61178; s/d/apt €40/50/70; ❄) Spyros Giannakos rents out clean, bright rooms and kitchenette apartments overlooking Kato Gialos Beach.

✖ Eating & Drinking

Spitalia   TAVERNA $
(Katsounis Beach; mains €5-8; ⊙ 11am-1am) Formerly an Ottoman quarantine station, this excellent eatery is great for a lazy beachside lunch or dinner, with stuffed goat the signature dish. Steps lead from the restaurant patio directly to the sea.

Ta Delfinia   SEAFOOD $
(fish €7-12; ⊙ 7am-1am) Island native Manolis Thirianos offers some of Psara's best seafood at this *psarotaverna* (fish taverna) on the central waterfront.

Idrahos   CAFE, BAR
(snacks €2-4; ⊙ 10am-midnight) Snappy waterfront cafe open all day, with all variety of drinks, plus grilled cheese sandwiches.

ℹ Information

National Bank of Greece with **ATM** is on the waterfront square. There's an island **doctor** (Medical Centre; ☑ 22740 61277) and **police** (☑ 22740 61222) for emergencies. Free **public wi-fi** is in the main square.

For tourist information, **Diana Katakouzinou** (☑ 6932528489) of Psara Travel is ever-helpful. There's also a summer Tourist Kiosk.

ℹ Getting There & Away

In Chios Town, buy tickets to Psara from Hatzelenis Tours (p562); in Mesta, contact Masticulture Ecotourism Activities (p564). Ferries reach Psara from both Chios Town (€12 return, three

NORTHEASTERN AEGEAN ISLANDS PSARA

hours, six weekly) and from Mesta (€7, 1½ hours, three weekly).

ⓘ Getting Around

Neither car nor motorbike hire is available on Psara, and no taxi either, so you may want to consider bringing your own transport with you, or ferrying a hire car or motorbike from Chios. Hitchhiking is common on the island.

LESVOS (MYTILINI)
ΛΕΣΒΟΣ (ΜΥΤΙΛΗΝΗ)

POP 95,330 / AREA 1637 SQ KM

Greece's third-largest island, after Crete and Evia, Lesvos is marked by long sweeps of rugged, desert-like western plains that give way to sandy beaches and salt marshes in the centre of the island. Further east are thickly forested mountains and dense olive

groves (some 11 million olive trees are cultivated here).

The island's port and capital, Mytilini Town, is a lively place year-round filled with exemplary *ouzeries* and good accommodation, while the north-coast town of Molyvos (aka Mythimna) is an aesthetic treat, with old stone houses clustered on winding lanes overlooking the sea.

Along with hiking and cycling, Lesvos is a mecca for birdwatching (more than 279 species, ranging from raptors to waders, are often sighted). The island boasts therapeutic hot springs that gush with some of the warmest mineral waters in Europe.

Despite its undeniable tourist appeal, hard-working Lesvos makes its livelihood firstly from agriculture. Olive oil is a highly regarded local product, as is ouzo; indeed, the island's farmers produce around half of the aniseed-flavoured firewater sold worldwide.

Lesvos (Mytilini)

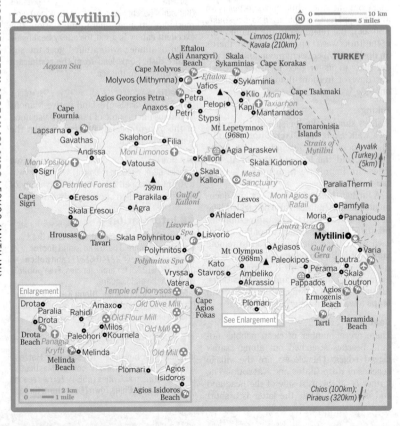

Lesvos' great cultural legacy stretches from the 7th-century-BC musical composer Terpander to 20th-century figures such as Nobel Prize–winning poet Odysseus Elytis and primitive painter Theofilos. The ancient philosophers Aristotle and Epicurus also led a philosophical academy here. Most famous, however, is Sappho, one of ancient Greece's greatest poets. Her sensuous, passionate poetry has fuelled a modern-day following that draws lesbians from around the world to Skala Eresou, the west Lesvos beach village where she was born (c 630 BC).

ℹ Getting There & Away

AIR

The airport is 8km south of Mytilini Town; a taxi costs €10; a bus to town costs €1.60.

Olympic Air (☑ 22510 61590; www.olympic air.com), **Aegean Air** (☑ 22510 61120; www. aegeanair.com) and **Sky Express** (☑ 28102 23500; www.skyexpress.gr) have offices at the airport. Mytilini Town travel agents sell tickets as well.

Domestic Flights from Lesvos (Mytilini)

DESTINATION	TIME	FARE	FREQUENCY
Athens	40min	€77	4-5 daily
Chios	30min	€49	2 weekly
Crete (Iraklio)	50min	€98	5 weekly
Limnos	30min	€59	5 weekly
Rhodes	70min	€78	5 weekly
Samos	40min	€59	2 weekly
Thessaloniki	35min	€79	3-4 daily

BOAT

In Mytilini Town, buy ferry tickets from Mitilene Tours (p572) and Olive Groove Travel (p573).

Boat Services from Lesvos (Mytilini)

DESTINATION	TIME	FARE	FREQUENCY
Chios	3hr	€14-20	1-2 daily
Ikaria	8½hr	€21	1 weekly
Kavala	11hr	€28	2 weekly
Limnos	6hr	€18	3 weekly
Piraeus	11-12hr	€41	1 daily
Samos (Karlovasi)	7½hr	€23	1 weekly
Samos (Vathy)	8hr	€18	2 weekly
Thessaloniki	13½hr	€36	1 weekly

ℹ Getting Around

BUS

From Mytilini's **long-distance bus station** (☑ 22510 28873; El Venizelou), near Agias Irinis Park, one to two daily buses serve Skala Eresou (€10.90, 2½ hours) via Eresos; two to three serve Molyvos (Mithymna; €6.90, 1¾ hours) via Petra (€6.40, 1½ hours); and one reaches Sigri (€10.40, 2½ hours). Three daily buses serve Plomari (€4.50, 1¼ hours), three serve Agiasos (€2.90, 45 minutes) and three end at Vatera (€7, 1½ hours), the latter via Polyhnitos. Travelling between these smaller places often requires changing in Kalloni, which receives three daily buses from Mytilini (€4.50, one hour). Also, five daily buses go north from Mytilini Town to Moni Taxiarhon (€4.10, one hour). Mytilini's **local bus station** (Pavlou Kountourioti), near Plateia Sapphou, serves in-town destinations and nearby Loutra, Skala Loutron and Tahiarhis.

CAR & MOTORCYCLE

Two local companies, **Discover Rent-a-Car** (☑ 6936057676; Venezi 3; ⊙ 7:30am-10pm) and **Billy's Rentals** (☑ 6944759716; waterfront; ⊙ 7:30am-10pm) have good new cars and flexible service. For scooters and motorcycles, check along Pavlou Kountourioti.

Mytilini Town   Μυτιλήνη

POP 29,650

Lesvos' port and major town, Mytilini, is a lively student town with great eating and drinking options, plus eclectic churches and grand 19th-century mansions and museums. Indeed, the remarkable Teriade Museum boasts paintings by Picasso, Chagall and Matisse, along with home-grown Theofilos. In fact, the island is known in equal parts for its poets and painters, its olive oil and ouzo.

Ferries dock at the northeastern end of the curving waterfront thoroughfare, Pavlou Kountourioti, where most of the action is centred. Handmade ceramics, jewellery and traditional products are sold on and around the main shopping street, Ermou, and there are many fine *ouzeries* and student-fuelled bars to enjoy.

⊙ Sights & Activities

Fortress   FORTRESS
(adult/student €2/1; ⊙ 8.30am-2.30pm Tue-Sun) Mytilini's imposing early Byzantine fortress was renovated in the 14th century by Genoese overlord Francisco Gatelouzo, and

Mytilini Town

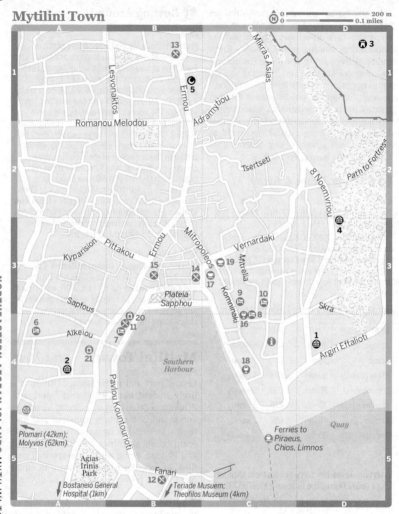

then the Turks enlarged it again. It's popular for a stroll and is flanked by pine forests.

Archaeological Museum
MUSEUM

(Old Archaeological Museum; adult/child €3/2; ⊙8.30am-3pm Tue-Sun) Located one block north of the quay, this museum contains impressive finds from neolithic to Roman times, including ceramic somersaulting female figurines and gold jewellery. The ticket also grants entry to the New Archaeological Museum.

New Archaeological Museum
MUSEUM

(⏴Noemvriou 22510 40223; adult/child €3/2; ⊙8.30am-3pm Tue-Sun) The new museum, 400m from the original museum, portrays island life from the 2nd century BC to the 3rd century AD, including striking floor mosaics under glass.

Church of Agios Therapon
CHURCH

(Arionos; ⊙9am-1pm Mon-Sat) The bulbous dome of this church crowns Mytilini's skyline. Its ornate interior boasts a huge chandelier, an intricately carved iconostasis, a priest's throne and a frescoed dome. Within

Mytilini Town

Sights
1	Archaeological Museum	D4
2	Byzantine Museum	A4
	Church of Agios Therapon	(see 2)
3	Fortress	D1
4	New Archaeological Museum	D3
5	Yeni Tzami	B1

Sleeping
6	Alkaios Rooms	A4
7	Hotel Lesvion	B4
8	Iren Rooms	C4
9	Porto Lesvos Hotel	C3
10	Theofilos Paradise Boutique Hotel	C3

Eating
11	Averoff Restaurant	B4
12	Jimmy's Hodros	B5
13	O Ermis	B1
14	Ouzeri P	B3
15	Taverna Kalderimi	B3

Drinking & Nightlife
16	Bobiras	C4
17	Briki	C3
18	Hotspot	C4
19	Mousiko Kafenio	C3

Shopping
20	North Aegean Shop	B4
21	Sfetoudi Bookshop	A4

the church courtyard, you'll find the icon-rich **Byzantine Museum** (☑ 22510 28916; www.immyt.net/museum; adult/student €2/1).

Yeni Tzami　　　　　　　　　　MOSQUE
This early 19th-century Turkish mosque with crumbling atmosphere to spare, is near the end of Ermou Str, where a Turkish market used to thrive.

Teriade Museum　　　　　　　　MUSEUM
(☑ 22510 23372; admission €2; ⊙ 8.30am-2pm & 5-8pm Tue-Sun) Varia, 4km south of Mytilini, is the unlikely host of the Teriade Museum with its astonishing collection of paintings by artists such as Picasso, Chagall, Miro, Le Corbusier and Matisse. The museum honours the Lesvos-born artist and critic Stratis Eleftheriadis, who brought the work of primitive painter and fellow Lesvos native Theophilos to international attention.

Theophilos Museum　　　　　　MUSEUM
(admission €2; ⊙ 10am-4pm Tue-Sun) Several prestigious Greek museums and galleries display paintings by so-called primitive painter Theophilos, a folk hero among Greek literati, though he barely scratched out an existence, moving frequently and painting coffee-house walls for his daily bread.

Courses

Hellenic Culture Centre　　LANGUAGE COURSE
(☑ 6944105484, 22510 91660, in Athens 210 523 8149; www.hcc.edu.gr; Varia; 2-week course €750) The well-organised Hellenic Culture Centre conducts intensive summer Greek–language courses in Varia, 3km south of Mytilini Town. At time of research, the school was

relocating. Contact them for exact location and summer schedule.

Sleeping

★**Alkaios Rooms**　　　　　　　PENSION $
(☑ 6945507089, 22510 47737; www.alkaiosrooms. gr; Alkaiou 16 & 30; s/d/tr incl breakfast €35/45/55; ❋ ☞) This collection of 30 clean, well-kept rooms nestled discreetly in several renovated traditional buildings is Mytilini's most attractive budget option. It's a two-minute walk up from Paradosiaka Bougatsa Mytilinis on the waterfront.

Hotel Lesvion　　　　　　　　HOTEL $
(☑ 22510 28177; www.lesvion.gr; waterfront; s/d/tr from €45/60/70; ❋ ☞) The well-positioned Lesvion is the newest addition to the harbour, a well-managed lodging with attractive modern rooms and friendly service.

Iren Rooms　　　　　　　　　PENSION $
(☑ 22510 22787; cnr Komninaki & Imvrou; s/d/tr €35/45/55; ❋ ☞) Welcoming Iren has reasonably priced and spotless rooms, up the stairs from a small inviting lobby. It's the sister establishment of Alkaios Rooms, though a closer walk if coming from the ferry dock, and next to an internet cafe.

Theofilos Paradise Boutique Hotel　　　BOUTIQUE HOTEL $$
(☑ 22510 43300; www.theofilosparadise.gr; Skra 4; s/d/tr/ste incl breakfast from €70/100/125/145; ▣ ❋ @ ☞ ❋) This smartly restored 100-year-old mansion is elegant, cheerful and good value, with modern amenities, along with a traditional *hammam* (Turkish bath). The 22 rooms are spread among three adjacent buildings surrounding a courtyard.

Porto Lesvos Hotel
HOTEL $

(☑ 22510 41771; www.portolesvos.gr; Komninaki 21; s/d/tr incl breakfast €35/50/60; ❄ 🛜) Behind the far end of the waterfront, this efficient and friendly lodging is good value. Rooms are a tad snug but clean and comfortable. Upper rooms have sea or castle views.

🍴 Eating

O Ermis
TAVERNA $

(cnr Kornarou & Ermou; mezedhes €5-9) This very good no-frills taverna began life in 1800 as a cafe in the Turkish quarter, as the intriguing traditional decor within reveals in faded bits and pieces. Good Macedonian and Limnos wines are offered, and the bread is warm and fresh.

Ouzeri P
OUZERIE $

(mains €2-7; ⊘ 11am-3am) This hip back-alley *ouzerie* draws a young crowd for its unusual and well-priced small plates, eclectic music mix and all-around cool atmosphere. Stuffed peppers with feta, tomato and bacon, plus a draft beer is €5.

Taverna Kalderimi
TAVERNA $

(cnr Ermou & Thason; mains €5-10; ⊘ Mon-Sat) This pleasant alleyway cafe is between Ermou and the waterfront, with everything from *gavros* and grilled pork chops to *mayirefta* and seasonal salads. A mezedhes plate which serves four is a reasonable €15.

Averoff Restaurant
RESTAURANT $

(☑ 22510 22180; waterfront; ⊘ 10am-10pm) No-frills eatery in the middle of the waterfront, next to Hotel Lesvion, specialising in generous *mayirefta* plates, such as chicken and potatoes, stuffed tomatoes and *briam* (mixed vegies).

Jimmy's Hodros
TAVERNA $

(☑ 22510 42614; Fanari St) At this place, best translated as 'Fat Jimmy's', look for excellent grills and fresh fish, along with low-key mandolin and guitar duo performing on summer weekends.

⭐ Taverna Efkaliptos
FISH TAVERNA $

(☑ 22510 32727; old harbour; mains €6-9; ⊘ lunch & dinner) You might be sitting closer to the fishing boats than the kitchen at this first-class fish taverna in Panagiouda, 4km north of Mytilini. Excellent mezedhes and well-priced fresh fish, great service, and white wine from nearby Limnos.

🍷 Drinking & Nightlife

Mytilini's loud waterfront cafes are inevitably busy, though the best watering holes are found in the backstreets.

⭐ Mousiko Kafenio
CAFE

(cnr Mitropoleos & Vernardaki; ⊘ 7.30am-2am) This hip student favourite is filled with eclectic paintings, old mirrors and well-worn wooden fixtures giving it a relaxed, arty vibe. Mix in the great music, and it's one of the most fun places in town. It offers great drinks, fresh juices and coffees, and even homemade iced tea on hot summer days.

Bobiras
OUZERIE

(Komninaki str) Bobiras fills up as the night goes on. Great small plates, ouzo and atmosphere to spare.

Hotspot
BAR

(waterfront; ⊘ 10am-3am) Along the far end of the waterfront where the big bars dominate, little Hotspot stands out for its cosy interior and great mix of sounds.

Briki
CAFE, BAR

(⊘ 11am-2am) Briki is the name of the little brass pot for making Greek and Turkish coffee, but this friendly hole-in-the-wall serves a bit of everything.

🛍 Shopping

North Aegean Shop
FOOD, DRINK

(☑ 22510 26918; Pavlou Kountourioti 21) Next to Paradosiaka Bougatsa Mytilinis, this shop sells traditional products such as Greek sweets, with unusual varieties involving watermelon, olive and nuts.

Sfetoudi Bookshop
BOOKS

(☑ 22510 22287; Ermou 51) Sells good maps from Greece's leading Terrain and Anavasi map-makers. Also stocks books on Lesvos.

ℹ Information

The long-distance bus station is beside Irinis Park, near the domed church. The local bus station is opposite Plateia Sapphou. The airport is 8km south along the coast. ATMs line the southern waterfront. Free wi-fi is in most cafe-bars.

Bostaneio General Hospital (☑ 22510 57700; E Vostani 48)

EOT (☑ 22510 42512; Aristarhou 6; ⊘ 9am-1pm Mon-Fri)

Mitilene Tours (☑ 22510 54261; www.mitilene-tours.gr; Kountourioti 87) Full service agency which handles trips and tours to Turkey.

Olive Groove Travel (☎22510 37533; www.olive-groove.gr; 11 Pavlou Kountourioti; ☺7.30am-10pm) Friendly, all-purpose travel agency on the central waterfront; sells air and ferry tickets, including to Turkey.

Port Authority (☎22510 40827)

Port Police (☎22510 28827; waterfront)

Post Office (Vournasson)

South of Mytilini

The small, olive-groved peninsula south of Mytilini has several unique attractions. Following the coast road 7km south, opposite the airport, you'll find the long pebbled Neapoli Beach hosting a few chilled-out beach bars, popular with swimsuited students and usually pulsating with reggae and Greek sounds.

In Skala Loutron, the Museum of the Memorial of the Refugees of 1922 (☎22510 91086; ☺5-8pm & by request) FREE honours Anatolia's lost Greek culture, abruptly ended after 2000 years by the Greek-Turkish population exchanges of 1923.

Some 9km south, the peninsula wraps around to the popular sand-and-pebble Agios Ermogenis Beach and Haramida Beach, which has toilets and showers under pine trees on the bluff above the beach. A campground is located near the lovably eccentric Karpouzi Kantina (☎69779 46809), a drinks-and-snacks wagon named after its mascot – an old skiff, painted like a giant watermelon. Enthusiastic owner Fanis also oversees the campground.

Northern Lesvos

With rolling hills covered in pine and olive trees, peaceful beaches and the aesthetically harmonious town of Molyvos (also called Mithymna), northern Lesvos offers both solitude and low-key resort action. Seaside hot springs and intriguing Byzantine monasteries round out the region's offerings.

Mantamados MONASTERY
(Μανταμάδος| Monastery of Taxiarhon; Mantamados village; ☺8am-dusk) FREE Some 36km north of Mytilini Town, near Mantamados village, stands one of Lesvos' most important pilgrimage sites: an axis of Orthodoxy, myth and militarism, the grand 17th-century Moni Taxiarhon is pretty full-on – note the fighter plane parked out front, reminding

thee faithful that the Archangel Michael is the patron saint of the Hellenic Air Force.

While at the monastery, visit the shop of the Agricultural Co-op of Mandamados (☎22530 61096), which sells numerous natural products from local farmers, such as the unique hard cheese, *ladotyri*, made from sheep's milk.

Molyvos (Mithymna)
Μόλυβος (Μήθυμνα)

POP 1500

Molyvos, also known as Mithymna, is a well-preserved Ottoman-era town of narrow cobbled lanes and stone houses with jutting wooden balconies, wreathed in flowers, overlooking a sparkling pebble beach below. Its grand 14th-century Byzantine castle, good nearby beaches and north-central island location combine to make Molyvos a good spot to explore Lesvos.

◉ Sights & Activities

Beach-lovers can take an excursion boat at 10.30am daily for Skala Sykaminias and Eftalou (from €20). Sunset cruises are also available. Enquire with the portside Faonas Travel (☎22530 71630; tekes@otenet.gr), in the Sea Horse Hotel, or Lesvorama (☎22530 72291; info@lesvorama.gr; ☺9am-10pm) on the main road.

Additionally, a popular yoga retreat organised by Angela Farmer (www.angela-victor.com/work.html; Molyvos) is based in Molyvos at the Yoga Hall. Workshop dates vary through the year.

Byzantine-Genoese Castle CASTLE
(admission €2; ☺8.30am-dusk Tue-Sun) This handsome 14th-century castle stands guard above Molyvos; the steep climb is repaid by sweeping views over the town, sea and even Turkey shimmering on the horizon. In summer the castle hosts several festivals (enquire at the tourist office).

🛏 Sleeping

More than 50 registered, good-quality domatia are available in Molyvos. Ask at the municipal tourist office, near the National Bank.

★Nassos Guest House GUESTHOUSE $
(☎22530 71432; www.nassosguesthouse.com; Arionis; d/tr €20/35; 🖨) Head up to the old town's only blue house to reach one of Lesvos'

ALL ABOUT OLIVES

With nearly 12 million olive trees on the island, it's no wonder two museums are devoted to the endeavour.

In Agia Paraskavi, south of Molyvos, the **Museum of Industrial Olive Oil Production** (☑ 22530 32300; www.piop. gr; Agia Paraskavi; admission €3; ⊙ 10am-6pm Mar-Oct, closed Tue) is a handsomely restored oil mill, full of polished equipment and well-signed displays.

And modestly tucked away in the village of Papados between Mytilini and south-coast Ploumari, the little **Vrana Olive-Press Museum** (☑ 22510 82007; Papados; admission €1; ⊙ 9am-7pm, closed Mon) showcases old presses and vintage paintings of a bygone era. It also occupies a bit Greek literary history; it was built by Nicholas Vranas, grandfather of Greek Nobel prize winning poet Odysseas Elytis.

best sleeping spots. This refurbished Turkish mansion with a small enclosed garden feels like home. One room has a private bathroom and there's a full kitchen too. Friendly Dutch manager Tom provides local information. Check ahead for availability.

Lela Studios-for-Rent APARTMENTS $
(☑ 6942928224, 22530 71285; www.eftalouolive grove.com; studio €40; ❄ 🛜) This recent addition to the Molyvos sleep scene is a bargain. There are two studios set in a courtyard of roses and geraniums, with inviting and spotless rooms that sleep two, plus a kitchenette and a sliver of seaview.

Marina's House PENSION $
(☑ 22530 71470; waterfront; s/d from €35/40; ❄ 🛜) Look for the overflowing geraniums on the steps of this well-managed pension, on the main road, 50m from the port. Marina's husband, Kostas, paints icons.

Amfitriti Hotel HOTEL $$
(☑ 22530 71741; www.amfitriti-hotel.com; s/d/tr incl breakfast €54/74/92; ❄ 🛜 ⛱) Just 50m from the beach, this well-managed traditional stone hotel has modern, tiled rooms and a large garden pool. Staff are friendly and helpful, and the hotel's quiet location is a plus.

Sea Horse Hotel HOTEL $
(☑ 22530 71630; www.seahorse-hotel.com; harbour; s/d/tr incl breakfast €55/65/75; ❄ 🛜) Located in the heart of the port area, this waterfront lodging has spacious modern rooms (all overlooking the harbour), along with the family's restaurant and travel agency.

Molyvos Hotel HOTEL $$
(☑ 22530 71496; www.molyvos-hotels.com; waterfront; d incl breakfast from €65; ❄ 🛜) Another package-tour favourite, this handsome waterfront hotel is also a good choice for independent travellers, with well-kept rooms opposite a narrow tree-shaded beach, friendly service and a good breakfast spread.

Municipal Camping Mithymna CAMPGROUND $
(☑ 22530 71169; www.campinglesvos.gr; camp sites per adult/tent €5/2; ⊙ Jun-Sep) Well-managed publicly run campground occupies an excellent shady site 1.5km from town, signposted from near the municipal tourist office.

🍴 Eating & Drinking

⭐**Taverna Angelos** GREEK $
(mains €4-8.50; ⊙ lunch & dinner) Look for the yellow awning, just past the tourist office, for this exceptional no-frills taverna serving great salads, vegie briam, and stifado. *Mayirefta* dishes such as *yemista* (tomatoes stuffed with rice) and fresh fish are excellent, prices are reasonable and service charming.

Betty's TAVERNA $
(☑ 22530 71421; 17 Noemvriou; mains €3-10; ⊙ 8.30am-11pm) This restored Turkish pasha's residence on the upper street offers a tasty variety of excellent *mayirefta* dishes such as baked eggplant with cheese, lamb souvlaki and *kotyropitakia* (small cheese pies), plus tasty breakfast specials. Betty also has two spacious and well-appointed apartments near the restaurant.

To Hani TAVERNA $
(☑ 22530 71618; agora; mains €5.50-9; ⊙ lunch & dinner) Snappy family taverna on the *agora* above the waterfront; great for well-priced fresh fish, grills, plus stellar views of the sea.

Alonia TAVERNA $
(mains €4.50-7; ⊙ lunch & dinner) Locals swear by this unpretentious place just outside of town, on the road to Eftalou Beach. Convivial atmosphere and fresh fish.

Friends   QUICK EATS $
(mains €1.60-2.50; ⊙10am-midnight) Between
the national bank and the town parking, this
quick-stop eatery is tops for pitta souvlaki,
kebabs and small vegie plates.

Molly's Bar   BAR
(⊙6pm-late) With its thickly painted walls
and blue stars, beaded curtains and bottled
Guinness, this whimsical British-run bar on
the waterfront's far eastern side is always in
ship-shape condition. Molly's caters to an
older, lively international crowd.

Sunset   CAFE
(waterfront; ⊙8am-1am) On the waterfront,
close to the Molyvos Hotel, this friendly all-
day cafe has a great selection of coffees and
attentive service.

ℹ Information

Banks with ATMs are centrally located. Wi-fi is
widely available.
Com.travel (☑22530 71900; www.comtravel.
gr) Efficient full-service agency on the main
road.
Kosmos Rent-a-Car (☑22530 71710; info@
lesvosrentals.com) Reliable agency opposite
the National Bank.
Medical Centre (☑22530 71333)
Municipal Tourist Office (☑22530 71347;
www.visitmolivos.com) This busy office next to
the National Bank provides a wealth of information, and can help with accommodation, maps
and excursions.
Post Office (Kastrou)

Petra   Πέτρα

This well-known destination is a mostly
overrated beach village 5km south of Molyvos. Petra's one cultural site, situated above
the giant overhanging rock for which the
village was named, is the 18th-century **Panagia Glykofilousa** (Church of the Sweet-
kissing Virgin), accessible on foot up 114
rock-hewn steps.

While Petra has accommodation, the village itself is barely a strip of souvenir shops
and some restaurants. It's far nicer to stay in
Molyvos or nearby Eftalou Beach.

Eftalou Beach   Παραλία Εφταλού

The place for solitude-seekers, Eftalou
Beach (also called Agii Anargyri Beach) is
2km northeast of Petra.

Backed by a cliff, the narrow, pebbled
and serene Eftalou Beach has pristine waters and also boasts the charming **Mineral
Baths of Eftalou** (☑22530 72200; Eftalou; old
common/new private bathhouse €4/5; ⊙old bathhouse 6am-9pm), with clear, cathartic 46.5°C
water. Nearby, the hot mineral water filters
into the cool sea. A vintage bathhouse has
a pebbled floor; the new, and comparatively sterile one offers private bathtubs. The
springs are said to treat various ailments
from arthritis to hypertension. Professional
massage is offered by **Elefteria Vamvoukou**
and there are Greek dance events as well.

Beyond the baths, the beachfront **Hrysi
Akti** (☑22530 71879; Eftalou Beach; s/d €35/45)
offers simple rooms with bathrooms in an
idyllic pebbled cove, complete with the
friendly owners' small **restaurant** (☑22530
71947; mains from €4.50) overlooking the sea.

Western Lesvos

Western Lesvos was formed by massive,
primeval volcanic eruptions that fossilised
trees and all other living things, making it
an intriguing site for prehistoric-treasure
hunters. The striking, bare landscape, broken only by craggy boulders and the occasional olive tree, is dramatically different to
that in the rest of Lesvos.

Further to the southwest, however, a
grassier landscape emerges, leading to the
coastal village of Skala Eresou, birthplace to
one of Greece's most famous lyric poets, Sappho, dubbed the tenth muse by Plato.

The sensuous, erotic nature of Sappho's
surviving poems – and the fact that she
taught and inspired an inner circle of female
devotees – has made her into a latter-day lesbian icon.

Kalloni to Sigri
Καλλονή προς Σίγρι

After driving 34km west from Kalloni, stop
for a coffee or lunch break in **Andissa**, a jovial, rustic village of narrow streets kept cool
by the two enormous plane trees that stand
over its *plateia*. Listen to the crickets and
the banter of old-timers over a Greek coffee
or frappé, while farmers hawk watermelons
and oranges from the back of their pickups.

Some 9km west of Andissa, the Byzantine
Moni Ypsilou (Monastery of Ypsilou; ⊙8am-
8pm) **FREE** stands atop a solitary peak

surrounded by volcanic plains. Founded in the 8th century, this storied place includes a flowering arched courtyard and a small but spectacular museum with antique icons and Byzantine manuscripts dating back to the 10th century. From the top of the monastery walls, you can gaze out over the desolate ochre plains stretched out against the sea.

Some 4km beyond the monastery, a signposted left-hand road leads, after another 4.9km, to Lesvos' celebrated **petrified forest** (www.petrifiedforest.gr; admission €2; ⊙9am-8pm). More realistically, it's a petrified desert; the 20-million-year-old stumps in this baking, shadeless valley are few and far between.

The best specimens are in the **Natural History Museum of the Lesvos Petrified Forest** (☑22530 54434; Sigri; admission €5; ⊙9am-8pm 1 Jul-30 Sep, to 5pm Tue-Sun 1 Oct-30 Jun) in Sigri, a coastal village 7km west. This engaging modern museum manages to make old rocks and dusty fossils interesting.

Sleepy **Sigri** is a fishing port with a sometimes operational ferry port. The village has beautiful sea views, especially at sunset, and there are idyllic, little-visited beaches just southwest.

Skala Eresou   Σκάλα Ερεσού

POP 1560

The once-quiet fishing village of Skala Eresou has learned to profit from its history. This bohemian beach town, where passionate poet Sappho was born in 630 BC, is supposedly ground zero for the lesbian international. The town's essential appeal derives from its 2km-long beach, good seafood, and low-key nightlife, all enhanced by shiatsu, fruit smoothies, healing arts and wi-fied cafes.

Near the town market, the remains of the early Christian Basilica of Agios Andreas include partially intact 5th-century mosaics.

✦✦ Festivals & Events

The town livens up every September, as the **International Eressos Women's Festival** (www.womensfestival.eu) marks the apogee of the season for lesbians. This international event with a local feel rambles on for two weeks of partying and activities ranging from live music and open-air cinema to Greek dancing and beach volleyball. There are water sports, yoga, poetry and meditation, all in a gay-friendly atmosphere under the sun and stars.

🛏 Sleeping

Skala Eresou has reasonable domatia options, as well as (fairly pricey) hotels. Most former women-only places have gone unisex.

★Kouitou Hotel   HOTEL $

(☑22530 53311; koutiou.hotel@gmail.com; s/d €25/45; P@奈) Managed by the energetic team of Vasso and Alejandro, the Kouitou is a delightful and rambling lodging of clean and quirky rooms, each with different hand-painted decor, plus a fan. It's a five-minute walk to the seaside, visible from the roof bar. Vasso's family offers a home-cooked meal each day, always with all-natural local ingredients.

Heliotopos   APARTMENTS $

(☑6977146229; www.heliotoposeressos.com; apt €45-70; P❄奈) This lovely garden spot, a 10- to 15-minute walk from the village, features five studios for one to two people, and three two-bedroom apartments, all with kitchens. The owners, UK-transplants Debby and Patrick, make it a habit to have fresh fruit and vegies on hand, and also lead nearby birdwatching excursions. Free bikes are available for peddling around.

Hotel Gallini   HOTEL $

(s/d incl breakfast from €30/45; P❄奈) This budget gem, about 80m back from the waterfront, has tile floors and small balconies overlooking the hillside. Breakfast, with homemade jams and cheeses, is served on the flowery veranda.

Sappho the Eresia   HOTEL $

(Sappho Hotel; ☑22530 53233; www.sappho-hotel.com; waterfront; s/d from €35-55) In laid-back Skala Eresou, the friendly Sappho is what passes for a big hotel. But its modest position on the quieter west end of the beach is appealing, along with overhead fans and a cafe-bar. The best rooms overlook the sea and island of Psara.

✕ Eating

Skala Eresou's restaurants and bars line the beach, as do *amariki* (salt trees). Fresh fish is a speciality. Look for the hanging squid and octopus. On clear days Chios emerges on the horizon.

★Soulatso   TAVERNA $

(fish €6-13; ⊙lunch & dinner) This busy beachfront *ouzerie* with large outdoor patio specialises in fresh fish and is known for the best mezedhes in the village. Good service and worthy wines.

★ Neval Kebap
TURKISH $

(☑ 22530 53893; plateia; mains €2-5; ☺ lunch & dinner) Outstanding Turkish eatery worth a visit just for the copper fixtures. Handmade pitta and perfect kebabs, salads and tea. A tasty and filling lunch plate is €4.50.

Aigaio
TAVERNA $

(mains €3.50-8.50) Owner Theodoris spends most mornings fishing to provide the evening's fresh fish. There are also very good *mayirefta* dishes, and traditional Greek music in the background.

Taverna Karavogiannos
TAVERNA $

(mains €5-9) Another fine seaside taverna, with fresh fish, several vegie dishes and salads.

Sam's Café-Restaurant
TAVERNA $

(Eressos; mains €4-8) This excellent Lebanese-Greek patio taverna is worth the 5km drive up the hill to Eressos, for a change of fare and a taste of Sam and Niki's home cooking.

🍷 Drinking & Nightlife

Skala Eresou's low-key nightlife consists of a contiguous series of small cafe-bars strung along the eastern waterfront.

Parasol
BEACH BAR

(☑ 22530 52050) With its orange lanterns and super-eclectic music mix, little Parasol does cocktails that match its South Seas decor.

Zorba the Buddha
BAR

(☑ 22530 53777; waterfront; snacks & juices €2-5; ☺ 9am-1am) The place furthest down on the eastern waterfront is a popular old standby that's full till late. It has fresh juices, great pies and pasta.

Notia Jazz Bar
BAR

(Plateia; cocktails from €5) Come for the drinks, stay for the jazz at this hip music bar. Live jazz on summer weekends. Good cocktails, Greek wine, draft beer, plus Miles and Monk.

Margaritari
CAFE, BAR

(waterfront) By day, an inviting cafe with great homemade sweets and cakes, and by night a cool bar scene with mellow music.

Portokali
CAFE, BAR

(drinks & snacks €2-4) Tiny and convivial cafe-bar 3km up the hill in Eressos. It's the village favourite for coffee and conversation.

🛍 Shopping

Thalassaki
ARTS & CRAFTS

(☑ 6973525421; waterfront; ☺ 11am-11pm) Despina Iossifelli makes the handmade ceramics and jewellery at this bright and inviting waterfront gift shop.

Technis Malama
JEWELLERY

(Malama's Art) Sells unusual and handmade jewellery.

ℹ Information

The central square of Plateia Anthis faces the waterfront, where most cafes offer free wi-fi. Behind the *plateia* is the Church of Agias Andreas. Further west along Gyrinnis are the major services and ATMs. There's also a **doctor** (☑ 22530 53947; ☺ 24hr) and **pharmacy** (☑ 22530 53844).

Full-service **Sappho Travel** (☑ 22530 52130; www.sapphotravel.com) does car hire, accommodations and provides information about the International Eressos Women's Festival.

Southern Lesvos

Interspersed groves of olive and pine trees mark southern Lesvos, from the flanks of Mt Olympus (968m), the area's highest peak, right down to the sea, where the best beaches lie. This is a hot, intensely agricultural place where the vital olive oil, wine and ouzo industries overshadow tourism.

Just south of the Mytilini–Polyhtinos road, **Agiasos** is the first point of interest. On the northern side of Mt Olympus, it's a quirky, well-kept traditional hamlet where village elders sip Greek coffees in the local *kafeneia*, and local ceramic artisans hawk their wares. It's a relaxing, leafy place and boasts the exceptional **Church of the Panagia Vrefokratousa**.

The road south along the western shore of the Gulf of Gera reaches **Plomari**, the centre of Lesvos' ouzo industry. It's an attractive, if busy, seaside village with a large, palm-lined *plateia* and waterfront tavernas. It also has the **Varvagianni Ouzo Museum** (☑ 22520 32741; ☺ 9am-4pm Mon-Fri, by appointment Sat & Sun) where the family has made ouzo for five generations, and where you're invited to compare different ouzo tastes. The popular beach settlement of **Agios Isidoros**, 3km east, absorbs most of Plomari's summertime guests. But **Tarti**, a bit further east, is less crowded. West of Plomari, **Melinda** is a tranquil fishing village with beach, tavernas and domatia.

Melinda to Vatera
Μελίντα προς Βατερά

From Melinda, the road less taken to the beach resort of Vatera passes through tranquil mountain villages, richly forested hills and steep gorges.

Driving north, you'll past the picturesque villages of **Paleohori**, **Akrassi** and **Ambeliko**, from where a signposted, rental-car-friendly dirt road descends through serene olive and pine forests with great views to the coast. The total driving time from Melinda to Vatera is about an hour.

Hikers here can enjoy southern Lesvos' **olive trails**, which comprise paths and old local roads threading inland from Plomari and Melinda. The **Melinda–Paleohori trail** (1.2km, 30 minutes) follows the Selandas River for 200m before ascending to Paleohori, passing a spring with potable water along the way. The trail ends at the village's olive press.

Another appealing trail leads to **Panagia Kryfti**, a cave church near a **hot spring** (built for two) and the nearby **Drota Beach**, or take the **Paleohori–Rahidi trail** (1km, 30 minutes), which is paved with white stone and passes springs and vineyards. Rahidi, which was only connected to electricity in 2001, has charming old houses and a *kafeneio*.

ℹ Information

Other, more complicated hiking trails can get you directly from Melinda to Vatera; consult the **EOT** (☑ 22510 42511; Aristarhou 6; ☺ 9am-1pm Mon-Fri) or the **tourist office** (☑ 22530 71347), both in Mytilini Town.

Vatera & Polyhnitos
Βατερά & Πολυχνίτος

Despite its 9km-long sandy beach, Vatera (vah-ter-*ah*), remains a low-key getaway destination, with only a few small hotels and domatia operating, and even fewer bars.

On its western edge, at Cape Agios Fokas, the sparse ruins of an ancient **Temple of Dionysos** occupy a headland overlooking the sea. In the cove between the beach and the cape, evidence indicates an ancient military encampment; indeed, some historians believe this is the place Homer was referring

to in the *Iliad* as the resting point for Greek armies besieging Troy.

Vatera's most ancient history has attracted international attention. Fossils have been found here dating back 5.5 million years, including remains of a tortoise as big as a Volkswagen Bug, though possibly faster, and fossils of a gigantic horse and gazelle. The small and inviting **Vrisa Natural History Museum** (☑ 22520 61890; http://vrisa.geol.uoa.gr; Vryssa; admission €1; ☺ 9.30am-3pm & 4-8pm Jun-Sep, 9.30am-3.30pm Wed-Sun Oct-May) located in Vryssa's old schoolhouse, displays these and other significant remains.

Agricultural **Polyhnitos**, 10km north of Vatera on the road back to Mytilini town, is known for its two nearby **hot springs**, one just to the southeast and the other 5km north, outside Lisvorio village. The former, known as the **Polyhnitos Spa** (☑ 22520 41229; www.hotsprings.gr; adult/child €4/3, private bath €5.50; ☺ 2am-8pm Mon-Sat, 10am-8pm Sun) is in a pretty, renovated Byzantine building, and has some of Europe's hottest bath temperatures, at 31°C (87.6°F). Rheumatism, arthritis, skin diseases and gynaecological problems are treated here.

Some 5km northwest of Polyhnitos, the fishing port of **Skala Polyhnitou** lies on the Gulf of Kalloni. It's a relaxing, if unremarkable place, where caïques bob at the docks and fishermen untangle their nets, and is great for low-key seafood dinners at sunset.

🍴 Sleeping & Eating

★**Hotel Vatera Beach** HOTEL $
(☑ 22520 61212; www.vaterabeach.com; Vatera; s/d €60/90; P ❋ @ ☎) This peaceful beachfront hotel regards its guests, many of whom return annually, as dear old friends. The congenial Takis Ballis provides free multilingual newspapers, and the hotel's excellent restaurant gets most of its ingredients from the owners' organic farm.

Agiasos Hotel HOTEL $
(☑ 22520 22242; Agiasos; s/d/tr €20/25/30) Next to the Church of Panagia in Agiasos, this friendly place has simple, clean rooms near the centre of the action.

Stratis Kazatzis Rooms HOTEL $
(☑ 22520 22539; Agiasos; s/d/tr €20/25/30) Right at the entrance of Agiasos, these handsome rooms are also good value for money. Like the Agiasos Hotel, it's a small place so book ahead.

★**Psarotaverna O Stratos** FISH TAVERNA $
(Skala Polyhnitou; fish €6-9; ⊙10am-1am) Look
for the fishing boats moored beside this
popular fish taverna on Skala Polyhnitou's
waterfront, with inexpensive fresh seafood,
plus salads such as *vlita* (wild greens) and
tasty mezedhes such as *taramasalata* (a
thick pink or white purée of fish roe, potato,
oil and lemon juice).

LIMNOS   ΛΗΜΝΟΣ

POP 16,992 / AREA 482 SQ KM

Isolated Limnos, all alone in the northeastern Aegean, save for neighbouring Agios Efstratios, appeals to those looking for Greek
island life relatively unaffected by modern
tourism. Its capital, Myrina, has retained
its classic Greek fishing harbour feel, while
a grand Genoese castle provides a dramatic
backdrop.

The island's eastern lakes are visited by
spectacular flocks of flamingoes and the
austere central plain is filled with spring
wildflowers. Superb sandy beaches lie near
the capital, as well as in more distant corners of the island.

Limnos is perhaps best known as being
the central command post of the Hellenic Air

Force – a strategic decision, as Limnos is in
an ideal position for monitoring the Straits
of the Dardanelles leading into İstanbul. For
this very reason the island was used as the
operational base for the failed Gallipoli campaign in WWI; a moving military cemetery
for fallen Commonwealth soldiers remains
near Moudros, where the Allied ships were
based. A small town in Victoria, Ausralia,
bears the name Lemnos to this day.

🛈 Getting There & Away

AIR

The airport is 22km east of Myrina; taxis cost
about €25. Both **Olympic Air** (www.olympicair.
com) and **Sky Express** (www.skyexpress.gr) are
located at the airport.

Domestic Flights from Limnos

DESTINATION	TIME	FARE	FREQUENCY
Athens	50min	€90	1-2 daily
Chios	30min	€61	2 weekly
Ikaria	40min	€55	6 weekly
Lesvos	30min	€61	6 weekly
Rhodes	3hr	€110	5 weekly
Samos	30-45min	€61	2 weekly
Thessaloniki	30min	€79	6 weekly

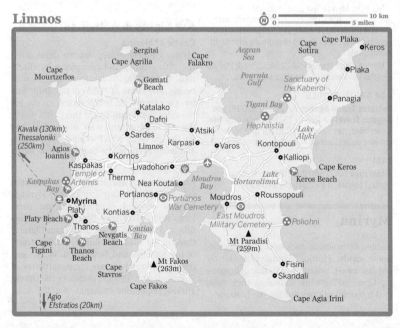

Limnos

BOAT SERVICES FROM LIMNOS

DESTINATION	TIME	FARE	FREQUENCY
Agios Efstratios	2hr	€7	6 weekly
Chios	10½hr	€22	3 weekly
Ikaria (Agios Kirykos)	15½hr	€30	2 weekly
Kavala	4½hr	€16	5 weekly
Lavrio	10hr	€30	4 weekly
Lesvos (Mytilini)	6hr	€19	3-4 weekly
Piraeus	24hr	€43	1-2 weekly
Samos (Karlovasi)	14½hr	€30	1-2 weekly
Samos (Vathy)	14hr	€28	1 weekly
Thessaloniki	7hr	€23	1-2 weekly

BOAT

Buy ferry tickets at Petrides Travel Agency, Aegean Travel, or Atzamis Travel.

❶ Getting Around

BUS

Limnos' bus service has one diabolical purpose: to bring villagers to town for their morning shopping and to get them home by lunch. Going and returning by bus in the same day is only possible to four destinations, by no means the most interesting ones, either. For example, buses serve Plaka, Skandali, Katalako and Kontias, but only return the next day.

But from Myrina, five daily buses serve Moudros, via the airport (€3, 30 minutes), with the last return bus leaving at 12.15pm. However, note that the buses do not coordinate with flight departures.

Myrina's **bus station** (☑ 22540 22464; Plateia Eleftheriou Venizelou) displays schedules.

CAR & MOTORCYCLE

Petrides Travel Agency (☑ 22540 22039) and **Aegean Travel** (☑ 22540 23280), both near the waterfront, hire cars from €30 per day. Motorcycle-hire outlets are on Kyda-Karatza.

TAXI

A **taxi rank** (☑ 22540 23820) is on Myrina's central square. It's €20 to the airport.

Myrina   Μύρινα

POP 5110

Backed by volcanic rock and a craggy Genoese castle, Limnos' capital is strikingly old-fashioned, where you'll see fishermen sip Greek coffee while unfolding their nets, and colourful caïques dotting the harbour.

In summer Myrina comes to life, with shops selling traditional foods, handicrafts and more in its bustling *agora*. Its white-washed stone houses, old-fashioned barber shops and *kafeneia* amid weather-worn neoclassical mansions create a relaxed old-world charm.

The town (and Limnos in general) is mostly frequented by Greek tourists, lending a distinct Hellenic flavour to its water-front nightlife. Above the town on the castle's overgrown slopes, it's a different story, where shy, fleet-footed deer dart after dark, even venturing down to the *agora* on winter nights.

◎ Sights & Activities

Castle of Myrina   CASTLE

Myrina's lonely hilltop *kastro* dates from the 13th century and occupies a headland that divides the town from its popular beach. The ruins of the Venetian-built fortress are imposing, but deserted, except for the deer that roam freely there. It's worth the 20- to 25-minute walk up the hill, just for the sea views which extend to Mt Athos, and come evening, the twinkling cafe lights below.

Archaeological Museum   MUSEUM

(admission €2; ◎ 8.30am-3pm Tue-Sun) Myrina's fine neoclassical mansion-museum overlooks Romeïkos Gialos Beach, and contains 8th- and 7th-century-BC finds from Limnos' three major sites of Poliohni, the Sanctuary of the Kabeiroi and Hephaistia. Worth seeing are the earthenware lamp-statuettes of Sirens, along with vivid details of the Greek-Turkish population exchange of 1923.

Beaches
BEACH

The town's beaches include the wide and sandy **Rea Maditos**, and the superior **Romeïkos Gialos**, beyond the harbour; further on, it becomes **Riha Nera** (shallow water), named for its gently shelving seafloor. Waterfront cafes and restaurants stay open late through summer.

Five minutes south on the road towards Thanos Beach, **Platy Beach** is a shallow, sandy crescent with cantinas and tavernas.

Boat Tour
BOAT TOUR

From June to September, Petrides Travel Agency (p582) organises round-the-island boat trips (half-/full-day €20/35), with stops for swimming and lunch, usually ending at sunset.

🛏 Sleeping

Apollo Pavillion
HOTEL $

(☑ 22540 23712; www.apollopavilion.gr; studios incl breakfast from €50; P ❉ 🛜) Tucked behind the port in a neoclassical house with charm to spare, plus large rooms, each with kitchenette and balcony. On Garoufalidhou, 150m above the port, near the police station.

Hotel Lemnos
HOTEL $

(☑ 22540 22153; s/d/tr €30/40/50; ❉ 🛜) The middle-of-the-waterfront Lemnos is a good budget choice with friendly staff and modern, if smallish, rooms, plus balconies overlooking the harbour or castle.

Villa Victoria
APARTMENTS $

(☑ 6942906120, 22540 29077; www.villa-victoria.gr; s/d/apt from €50/60/75; P ❉ 🛜 🅿) These attractive stone buildings are just a stone's throw from the beach, set on a rambling kid-friendly green with pool. Smart wood-and-stone motif, with kitchenettes. Several two-floor apartments can sleep four.

Paradise Apartments
APARTMENTS $

(☑ 6945443455, 22540 26200; nzafei@gmail.com; Platy Beach; r from €45) A sparkling white block with blue doors, set 150m back from the beach with palm trees and rose bushes. Rooms are bright and spotless, all with kitchenette.

To Arhontiko
HOTEL $$

(☑ 22540 29800; www.arxontikohotel.gr; cnr Sahtouri & Filellinon; s/d/tr incl breakfast from €45/65/75; P ❉ 🛜) This restored mansion dating from 1851 impresses with swank boutique rooms, helpful staff, classic charm throughout and a breakfast to last the day.

On a quiet alleyway near the *plateia* of Romeikos Gialos.

🍴 Eating

★ Ouzeri To 11
SEAFOOD $

(Plateia KTEL; seafood mezedhes €4.50-8.50) This unassuming little *ouzerie* by the bus depot is the local favourite for seafood. From *kydonia* (mussels with garlic and Venus clams) to sea urchins, crayfish and more, 'To *En*-dhe-ka' (as it's pronounced) serves all the strange stuff, along with plenty of ouzo to make you forget what you're eating.

O Platanos Restaurant
TAVERNA $

(main street; mains €5-8) Homemade pasta, good Limni wine, and excellent *mayirefta* with an emphasis on meats are served at this iconic place under two majestic plane trees, halfway along the *agora*'s main street, Kyda-Karatza.

Ouzerie Venetia
TAVERNA $

(waterfront; seafood mezedhes €3-7) The first of several eateries towards the end of the waterfront, snappy Venetia specialises in small plates, big salads and no frills.

To Limanaki
TAVERNA $

(waterfront; mains €6-9.50) Near the end of the waterfront, just before Taverna Glaros, with fresh well-priced seafood and cheery service, along with late-night meat grills and good Limnos wine.

Kosmos
TAVERNA $

(Romeikos Gialos; mains €6-9; ⏲ lunch & dinner) Waterfront favourite known for well-prepared fresh fish at decent per-kilo prices. It also has postcard-sunset views across the sea to Mt Athos.

O Sozos
TAVERNA $

(Platy village; mains €5-8) In Platy, 2km east of Myrina, O Sozos excels in traditional Greek fare. Specialities include *kokkaras flomaria* (rooster served with pasta), lamb and dolmadhes.

🍷 Drinking & Nightlife

Myrina's summer nightlife is mostly centred around the bars above Romeïkos Gialos beach.

Karagiozis
BAR

(Romeïkos Gialos beach; drinks €4-6; ⏲ 9am-5am) On a leafy terrace near the sea, Karagiozis morphs from snazzy frappé-cafe by day, to a

NORTHEASTERN AEGEAN ISLANDS MYRINA

drink-till-you drop bar under the stars. Good mixed drinks.

Cafe Naftilos   CAFE
(☑22540 23621; waterfront; crepes €2-4) Great crepes, cheesy snacks and coffees in the morning; drinks in the evening.

❶ Information

There are three ATMs around Myrina's central square, Plateia Eleftheriou Venizelou, which sits midway along the main thoroughfare of Kyda-Karatza (aka the *agora*). Another ATM is on the quay. Most waterfront cafes have free wi-fi.

Aegean Travel (☑22540 25936; www.aegean travel.eu; waterfront) Arranges car hire and island excursions.

Atzamis Travel (☑22540 25690; atzamisk@ otenet.gr; waterfront) Arranges ferry and air tickets, accommodations, excursions and bicycle rentals.

Myrina Travel (☑22540 22900, 22540 22460; hrissa5a@otenet.gr; waterfront) Specialises in trips to Agios Efstatios island.

Petrides Travel (☑22540 22039; www. petridestravel.gr; Kyda-Karatza 116) Arranges sightseeing tours, car hire, transfers and accommodation.

Police Station (☑22540 22201; Nikolaou Garoufallidou)

Port Police (☑22540 22225)

Post Office (Nikolaou Garoufallidou)

Western Limnos

North of Myrina, the road left after **Kaspakas** village accesses the appealing **Agios Ioannis Beach**, with a few tavernas and beach houses set nicely beneath an overhanging volcanic slab.

From Kaspakas continue east 2km to the junction for Kornos and Therma. The swank and state-of-the-art **Therma Spa** (☑22540 62062; www.thermaspa.gr; Therma), a lavishly restored Ottoman-era bath, is 1km south of the junction.

Further east, the road turns south at **Livadohori**, passing barren, tawny hills and modest farmlands until reaching charming **Kontias**, with traditional stone houses and vintage windmills. It then swings southwest back to Myrina, on the way passing the exceptional and popular, **Agios Pavlos Beach** and **Thanos Beach**, only a 10-minute drive from Myrina.

Central Limnos

Central Limnos' flat plateaus are dotted with wheat fields, small vineyards and sheep – plus the Greek Air Force's central command (large parts are thus off-limits to tourists). Limnos' second-largest town, **Moudros**, occupies the eastern side of muddy Moudros Bay, famous for its role as the principal base for the ill-fated Gallipoli campaign in February 1915, and home to Winston Churchill's secret wartime headquarters.

The **East Moudros Allied Military Cemetery**, with the graves of Commonwealth soldiers from the Gallipoli campaign, is 1km east of Moudros on the Roussopouli road. Here you can read a short history of the Gallipoli campaign. A second Commonwealth cemetery, **Portianos Military Cemetery** (6km south of Livadohori on the road to Thanos Beach and Myrina) is the area's other sombre attraction.

Eastern Limnos

Historical remnants and remote beaches draw visitors to eastern Limnos. Its three archaeological sites (◷8am-dusk) **FREE** include Poliohni, the Sanctuary of the Kaberioi and Hephaistia. Contact Myrina's Petrides Travel (p582) for tour information.

Poliohni, on the southeast coast, considered the first prehistoric settlement in the Aegean, has the remains of four ancient settlements – the most significant being a pre-Mycenaean city that predated Troy VI (1800–1275 BC). The site, with a tiny and free museum, is fascinating, but remains are few.

The **Sanctuary of the Kabeiroi** (Ta Kaviria), lies at the northern tip of remote Tigani Bay. The worship of the Kabeiroi gods here actually predates that which took place on nearby Samothraki. The major attraction is a **Hellenistic sanctuary** with 11 partial columns. Nearby, the legendary **Cave of Philoctetes** is supposedly where that Trojan War hero was abandoned while his gangrenous, snake-bitten leg healed. A marked path from the site leads to the sea cave.

Once Limnos' main city, **Hephaistia** (Ta Ifestia) is where Hephaestus, god of fire and metallurgy, was hurled down from Mt Olympus by Zeus. Little remains, however, other than low walls and a partially excavated theatre.

NORTHEASTERN AEGEAN ISLANDS WESTERN LIMNOS

Limnos' northeastern tip has some rustic, little-visited villages, plus remote **Keros Beach**, popular with windsurfers. Flocks of flamingoes sometimes strut on the coastal salt lagoon, **Lake Alyki**, and the nearby salt marsh, **Lake Hortarolimni**. From Cape Plaka, at Limnos' northeastern tip, Samothraki and Imvros (Gökçeada in Turkish) are visible. These three islands were historically considered as forming a strategic triangle for the defence of the Dardanelles, and thus İstanbul (Constantinople); this was Turkey's case for clinging to Imvros in 1923, even after Greece had won back most of its other islands a decade earlier.

AGIOS EFSTRATIOS
ΑΓΙΟΣ ΕΥΣΤΡΑΤΙΟΣ

POP 370

Little-visited Agios Efstratios lies isolated in the Aegean, south of Limnos. Abbreviated by locals as 'Aï-Stratis', it attracts a few curious visitors drawn by the island's fine, remote beaches and generally escapist feel. They certainly don't come for the architecture: a 1968 earthquake destroyed most of the port village's classic buildings, a bad situation made worse by Greece's military junta which hired crooked contractors to manage the reconstruction. Nevertheless, this sparsely populated place has domatia, good seafood tavernas, relaxing hill walks and fine beaches.

During the 'time of the colonels', as Greeks refer to the military dictatorship that ruled from 1967–74, many dissidents and suspected communists were exiled here, including renowned composer Mikis Theodorakis and poets Kostas Varnalis and Giannis Ritsos.

Sights include the **village beach**, which has dark volcanic sand and warm waters. You'll find few vehicles on Agios Efstratios and fewer roads. The island's two best beaches, **Agios Dimitrios**, 5km south, and **Ftelio**, 8km south, are best reached by local boat, jeep or motorbike. Enquire with Mr Aris at **Taverna Artemonas** (✆22540 93333; ⏱9am to midnight), near Agios Nikolas church.

Most travellers book rooms for Agios Efstratios when they purchase ferry tickets. In Limnos, contact **Myrina Travel** (✆22540 22460), or else find domatia upon arrival; try **Rooms-to-Let** (Rooms Kakali; ✆6973061585;

s/d €30/35). The island is popular in summer, though all 50 rooms seldom fill up at once. The island's single *kafeneio* and two tavernas offer inexpensive and fresh seafood.

A small ferry, the *Aeolis*, runs between Limnos and little Agios Efstratios six times per week (Monday to Saturday, two hours, €7 each way). Buy tickets at Myrina Travel in Myrina on Limnos, and plan to stay overnight; the ferry leaves Limnos at 3pm, and returns from Agios Efstratios at 6.30am. Day trips are not available.

There are also four ferries (NEL lines) per week from both mainland Lavrio (eight hours, €25), and Kavala (seven hours, €21). Day trips are seldom available.

SAMOTHRAKI
ΣΑΜΟΘΡΑΚΗ

POP 2860 / AREA 176 SQ KM

Lush Samothraki sits alone in the northeastern Aegean, halfway between the mainland port of Alexandroupoli and Limnos to the south. This thickly forested island is rarely visited out of high season, but it boasts one of the most important archaeological sites in Greece: the ancient Thracian Sanctuary of the Great Gods. Also here stands the Aegean's loftiest peak, Mt Fengari (1611m), from where Homer recounts that Poseidon, god of the sea, watched the Trojan War unfold.

Samothraki's mountainous interior is bursting with massive gnarled oak and plane trees, making it ideal for hiking and mountain biking. And the island's waterfalls, which plunge into deep, glassy pools, provide cool relief on hot summer days. Remote southeastern beaches are pristine, while the west offers hot baths at Loutra (Therma). Inland from the main fishing port of sleepy Kamariotissa lies the former capital, Hora, bursting with flowers and handsome homes, all overlooking the distant sea.

The island's remoteness and poor public transport mean that it's often forgotten by island-hoppers, but devotees of ancient archaeology, or those pursuing hiking and canyoning will find it worth the effort it takes to get here. (Hikers should look for the Terrain Map, *Samothrace*; and Anavasi Maps' booklet, *Canyoning in Samothraki*).

Samothraki

ℹ Getting There & Away

Somewhat unpredictable SAOS ferries (p737) connect Samothraki with Alexandroupoli – they may be twice daily in summer, less frequent out of season, and vary in price (€9.50 to €14.50, two hours). Purchase tickets from Niki Tours (p585) in Kamariotissa or at the port kiosk.

ℹ Getting Around

BOAT

In summer the tour boat **Theodora** (☑ 25510 42266) embarks on circular day trips of the island, departing from Therma at 12pm and returning by 6pm. The boat passes the Byzantine Castle of Fonias, the Panias rock formations and Kremasto Waterfall, and stops midway at Vatos Beach for swimming. Snacks are available on board and (sometimes) a beach BBQ is offered. To participate call the boat operator or inquire at Kamariotissa's Samothraki Travel (p585).

BUS

In summer, daily buses run from Kamariotissa **bus station** (☑ 25513 41533) to Hora and Palaeopolis (€1.50); and to Therma, the campgrounds and Profitis Ilias (each €2.20), the last via Alonia and Lakoma.

CAR & MOTORCYCLE

Kyrkos Rent-a-Car (☑ 6972839231, 25510 41620) rents cars and small Jeeps, while motorcycles and scooters are offered by **Rent-a-Motor-Bike** (☑ 25510 41057). Both are opposite the ferry quay in Kamariotissa.

TAXI

The friendly cabbie, **Evdohia Brahiolia Taxi** (☑ 6976991271, 6976991270), serves most destinations from Kamariotissa, including Hora

(€6), Profitis Ilias (€11), Sanctuary of the Great Gods (€7), Loutra (Therma; €14), Fonias River (€12), and Kipos Beach (€17).

Kamariotissa Καμαριώτισσα

POP 960

Samothraki's port, largest town and transport hub, Kamariotissa has the island's main services and a nearby pebble beach with bars and decent swimming. While most visitors don't linger, it's a likeable and attractive port filled with flowers and fish tavernas.

✷ Festivals & Events

Although not technically a festival, the August **full moon hike** to the summit of Mt Fengari, organised by the Hellenic Trekking Association, is a beloved annual event that sees scores of enthusiastic young hikers climb to an open field at 1200m on the day of the full moon, drink in the sight of it during a nighttime party, and continue to the summit (1611m) the next morning. Since the association is not terribly organised, unless you know a member you should enquire ahead.

✦ Activities

With its beaches, craggy peaks, lush jungle rivers and waterfalls, Samothraki is ideal for outdoor adventure activities. However, paths are poorly marked and rushing mountain waters can turn torrential, making a good guide essential. Kamariotissa's Samothraki Travel (p585) offers guided trekking

(€15) on hard-to-find mountain trails, as well as canyoning (from €40) along 10 spectacular routes. Both are guided by experienced Iorgos Andreas, usually in August and September. Trips can be tailored for kids as young as 12.

The same agency offers **scuba-diving** trips that include equipment and a PADI-certified instructor (€50 for two).

Although not held every year, June sometimes sees a fun **Capoeira Camp** (a Brazilian martial art/dance). Check ahead with Haris Hatzigiannakoudis of Niki Tours.

🛏 Sleeping

Most domatia and hotels are out of town, and unlike many Greek isles, you won't find locals hawking rooms to arriving ferry passengers.

Niki Beach Hotel HOTEL $
(☑ 25510 41545; s/d €40/65; ❄ 🤶 ☒) This handsome and well-managed hotel with large, modern rooms is just opposite the town beach. Balconies face the sea, and there is a lovely garden of flowers and poplar trees.

Hotel Aeolos HOTEL $
(☑ 25510 41595; s/d incl breakfast €60/80; ❄ 🤶 ☒) Up behind Niki Beach Hotel, the comfortable Aeolos stands on a hill overlooking the sea. Front rooms face a swimming pool and garden, while back rooms overlook Mt Fengari.

🍴 Eating & Drinking

I Synantisi OUZERIE $
(fish €6-10) Since the owner is also a spear diver, you can count on a fresh catch at this hard-working outdoor *ouzerie* on the central waterfront.

Kosmikon OUZERIE $
(☉ lunch & dinner) Popular waterfront cafe-*ouzerie*, with tasty mixed fish plates and salads.

Klimitaria Restaurant TAVERNA $
(mains from €6) This waterfront eatery serves the unusual *gianiotiko*, an oven-baked dish of diced pork, potatoes, egg and more, along with excellent *mousakas* and other *mayirefta* standbys.

Petrinos Kipos CAFE, BAR
(☉ 8am-midnight) Laid back all-day cafe, with live traditional music on summer nights.

ℹ Information

Exiting the ferry, turn left 50m for the tourist information booth (open July and August) and local bus station. The adjacent waterfront is host to the village's cafes, restaurants, travel and rent-a-car agencies, an ATM and a supermarket. Kamariotissa's small beach is 100m further east.

Samothraki Travel (☑ 6984908254, 25510 89444; www.samothrakitravel.gr) Excellent tour and travel operation, run by the helpful Ioannis Glinias and Katerina Mihalentzaki. It offers information on lodging and outdoor adventures, from diving to trekking and canyoning.

Niki Tours (☑ 25510 41465; niki_tours@hotmail.com) For ferry tickets and accommodation. Opposite buses on the port road.

Port Police (☑ 25510 41305)

Tourist Information Kiosk (☑ 25510 89242)

Hora (Samothraki)
Χώρα (Σαμοθράκη)

Set within a natural fortress of two sheer cliffs, and with a commanding view of the sea, Hora (also called Samothraki) was the obvious choice for the island's capital. In the 10th century the Byzantines built a castle on its northwestern peak, though today's substantial remains mostly date from the 15th-century Genoese rule.

Marked by cobbled streets wreathed in flowers, and crumbling traditional houses with terracotta roofs, Hora is perfect for enjoying a leisurely lunch or coffee. The great views and interplay of angles, shadows and colour make it fun for photographers, and on summer evenings, there's easy-going nightlife in the small lanes and rooftop bars.

At time of research, the long-closed Byzantine castle ruins were planned to be open to the public in summer 2014, with a previously unseen Byzantine wall section now unearthed. The *pyrgos* (tower) is a 10-minute walk from Hora centre and contains a display of medieval artifacts.

🛏 Sleeping

Hora has several domatia, though the one with the best value is **Hotel Axieros** (☑ 6972771515, 25510 41294; www.axieros.gr; d from €25; ❄ 🤶), in the heart of the village. Friendly and welcoming, these handsomely furnished traditional rooms feature well-equipped kitchenettes, and views of the village.

✖ Eating & Drinking

Cafes and tavernas are found higher on the street, where there's a small fountain with mountain-spring water.

★ O Lefkos Pyrgos
SWEETS $

(desserts €4-6; ⊙9am-3am Jul-Aug) The summer-only Lefkos Pyrgos is an excellent and inventive sweets shop run by master confectioner Georgios Stergiou and wife Dafni. Try lemonade with honey and cinnamon, or Greek yoghurt with bitter almond. Exotic teas, coffees and mixed drinks are also served with all-natural ingredients.

Café-Ouzeri 1900
TAVERNA $

(mains €5-9) This flower-filled taverna offers friendly service and great mezedhes. Start the day here with yoghurt and honey, or sample the house *tzigerosarmades* (goat with onion, dill and spearmint). The large, colourful menu, printed to look like a newspaper, is a take-home memento.

O Pyrgos
QUICK EATS $

(snacks ; ⊙11am-11pm)   Great views from the castle, good coffee, snacks and sweets.

★ Lydia
BAR

Unique both for its exotic cocktails and for being Hora's only year-round bar, Lydia is Hora's liveliest nightspot, playing ambient music for a fun crowd.

ℹ Information

Buses and taxis stop in the square, below the village. Walk upwards along the main street to find the OTE (Organismos Tilepikoinonion Ellados; Greece's major telecommunications carrier), Agricultural Bank, post office and **police station** (☑ 25510 41203).

Sanctuary of the Great Gods
Το Ιερό των Μεγάλων Θεών

Some 6km northeast of Kamariotissa, the **Sanctuary of the Great Gods** (☑ 25510 41474; combination site & museum adult/student €3/2; ⊙9am-4pm Tue-Sun summer, 8.30am-3pm Tue-Sun winter) is one of Greece's most mysterious archaeological sites. The Thracians built this temple to their fertility deities around 1000 BC. By the 5th century BC, the secret rites and sacrifices associated with the cult had attracted famous pilgrims, including Egyptian Queen Arsinou, Philip II of Macedon (father of Alexander the Great)

and Greek historian Herodotus. Remarkably, the Sanctuary operated until paganism was forbidden in the 4th century AD.

The principal deity, the Alceros Cybele (Great Mother), was a fertility goddess; when the original Thracian religion became integrated with the state religion, she was merged with the Olympian female deities Demeter, Aphrodite and Hecate. The last of these was a goddess associated with darkness, the underworld and witchcraft. Other deities worshipped here were the Great Mother's consort, the virile young Kadmilos (god of the phallus), later integrated with the Olympian god Hermes; and the demonic Kabeiroi twins, Dardanos and Aeton, the sons of Zeus and Leda. Samothraki's Great Gods were venerated for their immense power; in comparison, the bickering Olympian gods were considered frivolous.

Little is known about what actually transpired here, though archaeological evidence points to two initiations, a lower and a higher. In the first, the Great Gods were invoked to grant the initiate a spiritual rebirth; in the second, the candidate was absolved of transgressions. This second confessional rite took place at the prominent **Hieron**, whose remaining columns are easily the most photographed ruin of the sanctuary.

For all its mystery, the rituals at the sanctuary were open to all – men, women, citizens, servants and slaves; and since death was the penalty for revealing the secrets of the sanctuary, the main requirements seem to have been showing up and keeping quiet.

Sights

Although the site is well-labelled, visiting the **museum** (☑ 25510 41474; free with site ticket; ⊙8.30am-3pm Tue-Sun) first helps to get an overview of the sanctuary. Museum **exhibits** include a striking marble frieze of dancing women, terracotta figurines and amphora, jewellery and clay lamps, indicative of the nocturnal nature of the rituals. A plaster cast stands in for the celebrated Winged Victory of Samothrace (now in the Louvre), found in 1863 by French diplomat and amateur archaeologist Champoiseau.

A good map of the site is available upon entrance, and the paths are well marked. Excavation is on-going at the sanctuary.

About 75m south of the museum and entrance stands the **Arisinoeion** (rotunda), a gift from Queen Arsinou of Egypt; the sanctuary's original rock altar was discovered nearby. Pilgrims assembled at the adjacent and rectangular **Anaktoron** for their first initiation. The second took place at the sacred **Hieron**, followed by a celebratory feast in the adjacent hall, the **Temenos**. Opposite the Hieron stand remnants of a **theatre**. Nearby, a path ascends to the **Nike monument** where once stood the magnificent Winged Victory of Samothrace (*nike* means 'victory' in Greek), which faced northward overlooking the sea – appropriate since it was likely dedicated to the gods following a victorious naval battle. The ruins of a massive **stoa** or portico that sheltered pilgrims lie to the northwest. Initiates' names were recorded on its walls.

Loutra (Therma)
Λουτρά(Θερμά)

Loutra (also called Therma), 14km east of Kamariotissa near the coast, is Samothraki's most popular place to stay. This relaxing village of plane and horse-chestnut trees, dense greenery and gurgling creeks comes to life at night when people of all ages gather in its outdoor cafes.

◎ Sights & Activities

Thermal Bath   SPRING, BATHHOUSE
(admission €3; ⊙ 7-10.45am & 4-7.45pm Jun-Sep) The village's synonymous name, Therma, refers to its warm therapeutic, mineral-rich springs, reportedly curing everything from skin problems to infertility. The prominent white building by the bus stop houses the official bath; however, bathing for **free** is possible at two small outdoor baths about 75m up the hill. From here, a challenging trail continues to the peak of Mt Fengari, a five-hour trek.

Paradeisos Waterfalls   WATERFALL
Some 500m past Kafeneion Ta Therma, a lush wooded path (100m) leads to a series of rock pools and waterfalls, the most impressive being 30m in height. This is gorgeous, Lord-of-the-Rings-like terrain, where gnarled, 600-year-old plane trees covered in moss loom out of fog over a forest floor of giant ferns and brackish boulders. Although the trail is narrow, it is accessible for children and allows for an ice-cold dip on a hot summer's day.

Ghria Vathra Canyon   HIKING
Running roughly parallel with the Paradeisos Waterfalls, but further east along the coast road, this lush canyon is known for its shimmering series of rock pools and waterfalls, and is an easy and enjoyable hike-and-splash if going inland from the waterfront road.

For a more challenging semicircular nine-hour hike which traces the canyon but requires a guide and professional canyoning equipment, ask at Samothraki Travel (p585) in Kamariotissa.

🛏 Sleeping

⭐**Hotel Samothraki Village**   HOTEL **$**
(☑ 25510 42300; www.samothrakivillage.gr; Paleopolis; s/d/tr/ste €50/60/70/110; ✱ 🛜 ≋) Located 4km east of Kamariotissa on the coast road, and 1km before the Sanctuary of the Great Gods, this excellent lodging consists of spacious modern rooms with sea-view balconies. There are two outdoor pools (and a miniplayground for kids), plus a small fitness centre, *hammam* and massage services. Book ahead for free pick-up.

Studios Ktima Holoway   HOTEL **$$**
(☑ 6945947182, 25510 98335; www.ktimaholoway.com; d/tr €70/80) Located 16km east of Kamariotissa, this relaxing getaway has very modern, two-room self-catering studios set on a grassy lawn 50m from the beach, and a miniplayground for kids. The price also includes a free hire car.

Aleka Studios   APARTMENTS
(☑ 25510 98272; www.alekastudos.com; d from €30) High quality private rooms and bungalows in a flower-filled garden setting. Rooms are spacious and striking with splendid sea or mountain views.

Hotel Orfeas   HOTEL **$**
(☑ 25510 98233; Therma; s/d incl breakfast from €40/50; ✱ 🛜) Just across the lane from the local stream, the new Orfeas is simple, comfortable and friendly. The best rooms have balconies overlooking the stream.

Mariva Bungalows   VILLAS **$$**
(☑ 25510 98230; d incl breakfast €80; ✱) These secluded bungalows, with breezy modern rooms, sit on a lush hillside near a waterfall. To reach them, turn from the coast road inland towards Loutra, and then take the first left. Follow the signs to the bungalows (600m further on).

✖ Eating

Loutra (Therma) has decent and quick gyros and souvlaki spots, though **Paradisos Restaurant** (mains €5-8) has good sit-down fare.

★**Kafeneio Ta Therma**   CAFE $
(✆ 6984994856; ⊗ 8am-2am) Run by the jovial Iordanis Iordaninis for more than 20 years, this is the centre of the action in Therma, with live music, impromptu vendors, artists and dancers in the open areas around, plus coffee, beer and sweets. It is near the baths and several trails.

Fonias River   Ποτάμι Φονιάς

After Loutra on the northeast coast is the Fonias River, and the famous **Fonias rock pools** (€1). The walk starts at the bridge 4.7km east of Loutra, by the (summer-only) ticket booths. The first 40 minutes are an easy well-marked track leading to a large and swimmable rock pool fed by a dramatic 12m-high waterfall. The river is known as the 'Murderer', and in winter rains can transform the waters into a raging torrent. The real danger, however, is getting lost: though there are six waterfalls, marked paths only run to the first two. For hiking here and near Mt Fengari, consult Samothraki Travel (p585) in Kamariotissa.

Beaches

The 800m-long **Pahia Ammos Beach** is a superb sandy beach along an 8km winding road from Lakoma on the south coast. In summer, caïques from Kamariotissa visit. The boat tour from Loutra (Therma) stops around the headland at the equally superb, nudist-friendly **Vatos Beach**.

The formerly Greek-inhabited island of Imvros (Gökçeada) – ceded to Turkey under the Treaty of Lausanne in 1923 – is sometimes visible from Pahia Ammos.

Pebbled **Kipos Beach** on the southeast coast, accessed via the road skirting the north coast, is pretty but shadeless; it's reached in summer by caïque or excursion boat.

Other Villages

The small villages of **Profitis Ilias**, **Lakoma** and **Xiropotamos** in the southwest are all serene and seldom visited, though they're easily accessible. The hillside Profitis Ilias has several tavernas: **Vrahos** (✆ 25510 95264) and **Paradisos** (✆ 25510 95264) are both renowned for their roast goat, and nearby **Taverna Akrogiali** (✆ 25510 95123; Lakkoma Beach) for fresh fish.

THASOS   ΘΑΣΟΣ

POP 14,900

One of Greece's greenest and most gentle islands, Thasos lies 10km from mainland Kavala. While similar climate and vegetation give the feeling that the island is an extension of northern Greece, it boasts enviable sandy beaches and a forested mountain interior. It's quite inexpensive by Greek island standards and is popular with families and young people from neighbouring Bulgaria and the ex-Yugoslav republics. Frequent ferries from the mainland allow independent travellers crossing northern Greece to get here quickly, and the excellent bus network makes getting around easy.

Over its long history, Thasos has benefitted from its natural wealth. The Parians who founded the ancient city of Thasos (Limenas) in 700 BC struck gold at Mt Pangaion, creating an export trade lucrative enough to subsidise a naval fleet. While the gold is long gone, Thasos' white marble is still being exploited, though scarring a mountainside in the process.

For visitors today, however, the island's main sources of wealth are its natural beauty and historic attractions. The excellent archaeological museum in the capital, Thasos (Limenas), is complemented by the Byzantine Monastery of Arhangelou, with its stunning clifftop setting, and the ancient Greek temple on the serene southern beach of Alyki.

While some of Thasos' best beaches are filled from mid-July to mid-August, untouched spots remain on this 'emerald isle', especially outside the short high season. Only the capital, Limenas, has functioning hotels in winter.

❶ Getting There & Away

Thasos is only accessible from the mainland ports of Keramoti and Kavala. There are hourly ferries between Keramoti and Limenas (€3, 45 minutes). There are two to three per day

Thasos

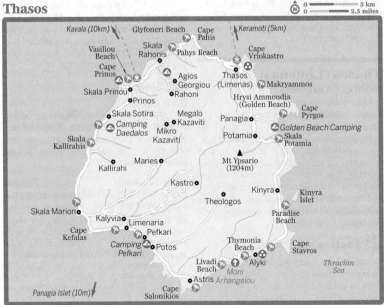

N 0 ——————— 5 km
   0 ——————— 2.5 miles

Kavala (10km)
Glyfoneri Beach
Cape Pahis
Keramoti (5km)
Vasiliou Beach
Skala Rahonis
Pahys Beach
Cape Vriokastro
Cape Prinos
Agios Georgiou
Thasos (Limenas)
Makryammos
Skala Prinou
Rahoni
Hrysi Ammoudia (Golden Beach)
Prinos
Cape Pyrgos
Skala Sotira
Megalo Kazaviti
Panagia
Golden Beach Camping
Camping Daedalos
Mikro Kazaviti
Potamia
Skala Potamia
Skala Kallirahis
Maries
Mt Ypsario (1204m)
Kallirahi
Kastro
Kinyra
Kinyra Islet
Theologos
Skala Marion
Paradise Beach
Kalyvia
Limenaria
Pefkari
Cape Kefalas
Thymonia Beach
Cape Stavros
Camping Pefkari
Potos
Livadi Beach
Alyki
Thracian Sea
Panagia Islet (10m)
Astris
Moni Arhangelou
Cape Salonikios

between Kavala and Skala Prinou (€4.70, 1¼ hours).

Get ferry schedules at the **ferry ticket booths** (☑ 25930 22318) in Thasos (Limenas) and the port police (p591) at Skala Prinou.

ⓘ Getting Around

BICYCLE

Basic bikes can be hired in Thasos (Limenas), but top-of-the-line models and detailed route information are available in Potos on the southwest coast from **Yiannis Raizis** (☑ 6946955704, 25930 52459; www.mtb-thassos.com; regular/used/new mountain bikes €10/15/20 per day).

BOAT

The **Victoria excursion boat** (☑ 6977336114; day trip €27) makes full-day trips around Thasos, with stops for swimming and lunch. The boat departs the old harbour at 10am. Water taxis run regularly to Hrysi Ammoudia (Golden Beach) and Makryammos Beach from the old harbour. Excursion boats of varying sizes and alcohol content also set sail regularly from the coastal resorts. Enquire at Billias Travel (p591).

BUS

Frequent buses serve the entire island coast and inland villages too. Buses meet arriving ferries at Skala Prinou and Thasos (Limenas), the island's transport hub. The two port towns are connected by eight daily buses (€1.70).

Daily buses run throughout the day from Thasos (Limenas) to **west-coast** villages such as Skala Marion (€3.80), Limenaria (€4.50), Potos (€4.70) and Theologos (€5.90). Buses from Limenas also reach the **east-coast** destinations of Hrysi Ammoudia (Golden Beach; €1.60), Skala Potamia (€1.70) via Panagia (€1.50) and Potamia (€1.80), Paradise Beach (€2.90), Alyki and nearby Moni Arhangelou (€4.10).

A full circular tour (about 100km) runs six times daily (€10.60, 3½ hours), three clockwise and three counter-clockwise. This round-the-island ticket is valid all day, so you can jump on and off without paying extra. The **bus station** (☑ 25930 22162) on the Thasos (Limenas) waterfront provides timetables.

CAR & MOTORCYCLE

Potos Car Rentals (☑ 25930 52071; Limenas) is reliable and reasonable; and **Avis Rent-a-Car** (☑ 25930 22535; Limenas) in Thasos, Potamia, and Skala Prinou is widespread.

Mike's Bikes (☑ 25930 71820), 1km from the old harbour in Thasos (Limenas), and **2 Wheels** (☑ 25930 23267), on the Prinos road, offer bike and motorcycle hire.

TAXI

The Thasos (Limenas) **taxi rank** (☑ 69441 70373, 25930 22394) is on the waterfront, next to the main bus stop. (Skala Prinos €20; Panagia €11; Skala Potamia €18; Aliki €40; Potos €50).

In Potos, a taxi rank with listed prices is beside the main road's bus stop.

Thasos (Limenas)
Θάσος (Λιμένας)

POP 2610 / AREA 375 SQ KM

Thasos (also known as Limenas), has the island's main services and year-round activity, along with a picturesque fishing harbour, sandy beach, shopping, a few ancient ruins and an archaeological museum. Considering the relatively expensive accommodation and restaurant offerings here, and the superior beaches, mountain forests and nightlife further on, lingering isn't necessary.

✨ Festivals & Events

In late July and August, the lively **Philippi Thasos Festival** (www.philippifestival.gr) takes place in both mainland Kavala and Thasos. Classical drama, painting exhibitions and contemporary Greek music are featured. Programs are available at hotels, cafes and tourist agencies. Both the Kavala EOT and the Thasos tourist police have ticket information.

⊙ Sights

Archaeological Museum   MUSEUM
(☑25930 22180; admission €2; ⊙8.30am-3pm Tue-Sun) The museum displays neolithic utensils from a mysterious central Thasos tomb, plus Ancient Greek art, including a 5m-tall 6th-century-BC *kouros* (male statue of the Archaic period) carrying a ram.

Ancient Agora   RUINS
Next to the archaeological museum stand the ruins of the ancient *agora*, the commercial centre in ancient Greek and Roman times. The foundations of stoas, shops and dwellings remain. About 100m east of the agora, the **ancient theatre** stages performances of ancient dramas and comedies during the Philippi Thasos Festival. The theatre is signposted from the small harbour.

A path connects the *agora* to the **acropolis**, where substantial remains of a medieval fortress stand, complete with commanding views of the coast. Carved rock steps descend to the foundations of the ancient town.

If you're exploring the eastern side of town, note the signpost for historical sites after Restaurant Alexandra. From that point, it's a 5-minute walk up a shaded trail to the lovely **chapel** of Agioi Apostoli, with great views over the seafront.

🛏 Sleeping

Hotel Angelica   HOTEL $
(☑25930 22387; www.hotel-angelica.gr; old harbour; s/d incl breakfast €40/60; ❉ 🛜) Old harbour views, large modern bathrooms and cheerful service make this a top budget choice in Thasos.

Hotel Timoleon   HOTEL $
(☑25930 22177; www.hotel-timoleon.gr; old harbour; s/d €60/80; ❉ 🛜) Located next to the Hotel Possidon, the three-star Timoleon has 30 rooms (15 with sea view); each well-appointed, spotless and spacious. The manager, Chrysoula, is helpful and welcoming.

Hotel Possidon   HOTEL $
(☑25930 22739; www.thassos-possidon.com; old harbour; s/d €40/50; ❉ 🛜) This friendly waterfront hotel's renovated lobby bar straddles the harbour and main shopping street of 18 Oktovriou. Rooms are modern, many with comfortable sea-view balconies.

Hotel Galini   HOTEL $
(☑25930 22195; Theageneou; s/d €44/50; ❉) This small, slightly worn place, a block inland from the waterfront, has 16 simple but clean rooms and a flowery back garden.

🍴 Eating & Drinking

Taverna To Karanti   TAVERNA $
(Miaouli) An outdoor *ouzerie* on the old harbour, frequented by locals and tourists alike, Taverna To Karanti has a picturesque setting overlooking fishing boats, complemented by its traditional music and tasty mezedhes.

Simi   TAVERNA $
(☑25930 22517; old harbour; mains €7-10) At first glance, Simi looks like all the other old harbour tavernas with touting waiters; however, locals agree that it serves Limenas' best fish, along with good taverna fare.

Island Beach Bar   BAR $
(Miaouli) Next to Karanti, this swank outdoor bar has free wi-fi, good breakfasts, decent drinks and hip music throughout the day and evening.

Taverna Tarsanas TAVERNA $

(☑ 25930 23933; mezedhes €4, mains €10-15) Located 1km west of Thasos, Tarsanas offers great fish and unique seafood mezedhes.

Karnagio BAR

(☑ 25930 23170) Stroll past the old harbour for a quiet sunset drink here, with outdoor seating straddling a rocky promontory lapped by waves. You can also clamber up the rocks to a small, candlelit chapel.

ℹ Information

ATMs can be found near the central square.

Billias Travel Service (☑ 25930 24003; www. billias-travel-service.gr; Gallikis Arheologikis Scholis 2) Full-service travel agency.

EOT (☑ 25102 22425) In Kavala. Also has information and tickets for the Philippi Thasos Festival.

Port Police (☑ 25930 22106)

Thassos Island Nature (www.gothassos.com) Useful online resource.

Tourist Police (☑ 25930 23111)

West Coast

Thasos' west coast has been assailed by package tours for years, though there are still a few idyllic spots and quiet sandy beaches. Better still, the inland mountain villages preserve a traditional pace of life and fine stone architecture.

⊙ Sights

Following the coast west from Thasos (Limenas), two sandy beaches emerge, decent **Glyfoneri** and the superior **Pahys Beach**.

Continuing west, the port of **Skala Prinou** has ferries to Kavala (€4.70), though little else to warrant a stop. But 6km inland, past the town of Prinos, the hillside villages of **Mikros Kazaviti** and **Megalo Kazaviti** (aka the Prinou villages) offer a lush break from the touristed coast, with undeniable character and a few places to stay and eat. An easy-to-follow trail network branches off from the pretty *plateia* of Megalo Kazaviti, with a sign marking the routes.

The next real point of interest lies further south, the whimsical fishing port of **Skala Marion**. Its few canopied tavernas overlooking the sea are faithfully populated by village elders shuffling backgammon chips, while children scamper about. The village features a few domatia, a bakery and an in-

ternet cafe on the northern jetty. On the village's feast day (24 June), church services are followed by folk dancing around the square.

The coast road south passes more beaches until reaching **Limenaria**, Thasos' second-largest town, followed quickly by **Potos** and **Pefkari**, two fishing-villages-turned-package-resorts, both with long sandy beaches lined with cafes and tavernas.

Two interior villages warrant a day trip. Inland about 6km from Skala Marion, forested **Maries** rewards visitors with cool upland air and a handsome monsastery, **Agios Taxiarchis**. Although technically nowhere near the west coast, Thasos' medieval and Ottoman capital, **Theologos**, is only accessible from Potos, where the road leads inland to this forested hamlet of 400 souls, notable for its whitewashed slate-roofed houses. Find the **Church of Agios Dimitrios** (1803), distinguished by its grand slate roof and white-plastered clock tower.

From the Theologos-Potos corner of the main road, head southeast round the coast for views of stunning bays. The last southwestern settlement, **Astris**, has a good beach with tavernas and domatia including **Menir Luxury Apartments** (☑ 25930 58270; www. menir-thassos.gr; s/d incl breakfast from €50/80).

🏃 Activities

Despite its touristy feel, Thasos' west coast offers worthwhile outdoor activities such as scuba diving, mountain biking, birdwatching and more.

Birdwatching Boat Trips BIRDWATCHING, BOATING
The rocky, uninhabited **Panagia Islet**, southwest of Potos, is home to Greece's largest sea cormorant colony (www.yrefail.net/ Thasos/habitats.htm); local environmentalist Yiannis Markianos at Aldebran Pension arranges birdwatching boat trips.

International Mountain Biking Race CYCLING
(Potos; ☺ last Sun in Apr) This popular amateur event draws more than 200 contestants to Potos, who race across the island's wooded interior, scaling Mt Ypsario (1204m) and returning through scenic Kastro village. Incredibly, the entry fee (only €20) also includes three nights' hotel accommodation. Yiannis Raizis (p589), who hires out high-quality mountain bikes year-round from his domatio in Potos, organises this event and

also runs guided biking and hiking tours to Mt Ypsilariou.

Pine Tree Paddock
HORSE RIDING

(☑ 6945118961; Rahoni; ☉ 10am-2pm & 5pm-sunset) Further north, inland Rahoni hosts the Pine Tree Paddock, offering mountain ponies and horses (€20 per hour). There are also guided trail rides (€25 per hour). Advance reservations are required.

Diving Club Vasiliadis
DIVING

(☑ 6944542974; www.scuba-vas.gr; Potos) Scuba-diving for both beginners and experienced divers is offered in Potos by Vasilis Vasiliadis, including coastal Alyki's submerged and interesting ancient marble quarry.

🛌 Sleeping

⭐ Aldebran Pension
PENSION $

(☑ 6973209576, 25930 52494; www.thasos.eu; Potos; d from €40; ✱ 🛱) Aldebaran is still the best in town, with friendly and well-informed owners, plus a leafy courtyard and table tennis. It boasts recently redone baths, a communal kitchen, and all-day coffee and tea. Resident ornithology expert Giannis does tours and provides info on birdwatching and hiking in Thasos. It's one street inland from the central waterfront.

Domatia Filaktaki
PENSION $

(☑ 6977413789, 25930 52634; Skala Marion; r from €35; ✱ 🛱) These simple but air-conditioned rooms are situated above the home of the kind Maria Filaktaki and family in Skala Marion. It's the first place you'll reach when descending to the waterfront from the bus stop.

Camping Pefkari
CAMPGROUND $

(☑ 25930 51190; www.camping-pefkari.gr; camp sites per adult/tent €5/5; ☉ Jun-Sep) This appealing campground on a wooded spot above Pefkari Beach is popular with families and has spotless bathrooms, a laundry, and cooking and BBQ facilities.

Camping Daedalos
CAMPGROUND $

(☑ 25930 58252; tseltha@otenet.gr; camp sites per adult/tent €6/4) This beach-front campground north of Skala Sotira includes a minimarket and restaurant. Sailing, windsurfing and water-skiing lessons are offered as well.

🍴 Eating & Drinking

⭐ Armeno
TAVERNA $

(Skala Marion; mains €5-9) This relaxing waterfront taverna in offbeat Skala Marion

has tasty fish, plus a full taverna menu. The organic produce is from the gardens of the friendly Filaktaki family, who also rent rooms and can help with local information and car hire.

Piatsa Michalis
TAVERNA $

(Potos; mains €6-10) Potos' 50-year-old beach-front taverna started working well before mass tourism came to town, and sticks to the recipe with specialities such as stewed rabbit and octopus in red-wine sauce, plus a full menu of taverna fare.

O Georgios
TAVERNA $

(Potos; mains €4.50-7) This traditional Greek grillhouse set in a pebbled rose garden is a local favourite away from the tourist strip on Potos' main road, offering friendly service and portions big enough to share.

Cafe Margarita
CAFE, BAR

(☑ 25930 51576; ☉ 9am-1pm) Fun and friendly cafe-bar on northern edge of the waterfront, open morning until late for coffee, snacks and drinks. It also rents rooms above the cafe (single/double €40/50).

Kafeneio Tsiknas
CAFE $

(Theologos) At the beginning of Theologos, right before the church, this charming cafe has balcony seating, coffees and snacks.

ℹ️ Information

There are ATMs in Skala Prinou, Limenaria and Potos; all large villages with numerous services.

East Coast

Thasos' east-coast beaches can fill up in summer, though less so than the more developed west coast. The dramatic coastal landscape features thick forests that run down from mountains to the sea. There are fewer organised activities here, along with a more relaxed feel, and the warm, shallow waters are excellent for families with small children.

👁️ Sights

Panagia & Potamia
CHURCH, MUSEUM

These inland villages, just south of Thasos (Limenas) are nothing if not photogenic. Their characteristic architecture includes Panagia's stone-and-slate rooftops and the elegant blue-and-white domed and icon-rich **Church of the Kimisis tou Theotokou** (Church of the Dormition of the Virgin). To reach this peaceful quarter, follow the sound of rushing spring water upwards along a stone path heading inland.

Less-picturesque Potamia boasts the **Polygnotos Vagis Museum** (admission €3; ☺8.30am-noon & 6-8pm Tue-Sat, to noon Sun & holidays), devoted to Greek-American artist Polygnotos Vagis (born here in 1894). It's beside the main church.

Beaches   BEACH

Panagia and Potamia are 4km west of the east coast's most popular beaches: sandy and sand-duned **Hrysi Ammoudia (Golden Beach)**, tucked inside a long, curving bay, and gentle **Skala Potamia**, on its southern end. A bus between the two (€1.30) runs every couple of hours. Both have accommodation, restaurants and a bit of nightlife.

Further south of Skala Potamia is the deservedly popular and nudist-friendly **Paradise Beach**, 2km after tiny **Kinyra** village.

Alyki   RUINS

This village is Thasos' best place to unwind by the beach – and get some culture, too. This escapist destination features two fine sandy coves, with small snack shops and a taverna. The beaches are separated by a little olive grove dotted with ancient ruins comprising the **archaeological site of Alyki**. This inscrutable but well-signed site lies alluringly above the southeastern beach and includes the remains of an **ancient temple** where the gods were once invoked to protect sailors. A now-submerged nearby **marble quarry** operated from the 6th century BC to the 6th century AD.

West of Alyki   BEACH, MONASTERY

Continuing west from Alyki, you'll pass **Thymonia Beach** before rising upwards to the clifftop **Moni Arhangelou** (☺9am-5pm) **FREE**, an Athonite dependency and working nunnery, notable for its 400-year-old church (with some ungainly modern touches) and stunning views of the sea. Those improperly attired will get shawled up for entry.

Heading west from here, watch out for the small dirt road to the left which leads to **Livadi Beach**, one of Thasos' most beautiful, with aquamarine waters ringed by cliffs and forests, with just a few umbrellas set in the sand.

Mt Ypsario   HIKING

Potamia makes a good jumping-off point for climbing Thasos' highest peak, Mt Ypsario (1204m). A tractor trail west from Potamia continues to the valley's end, after which arrows and cairns point the way along a steep path upwards. The three-hour Ypsario hike is classified as moderately difficult. You can sleep at the Ypsario Mountain Shelter by contacting Leftheris of the **Thasos Mountaineering Club** (☑6972198032) to book and get the key. The shelter has fireplaces and spring water, but no electricity.

🛏 Sleeping & Eating

There's less accommodation at Kinyra and Alyki than at Hrysi Ammoudia (Golden Beach) and Skala Potamia, and there's no accommodation on Paradise Beach.

★**Domatia Vasso**   PENSION **$**
(☑25930 31534, 6946524706; Alyki; r €50; P ❋) Just east of Alyki's bus stop on the main road, look for the big burst of flowers and sign pointing up the drive to this relaxing set of eight self-catering domatia run by friendly Vasso Gemetzi and daughter Aleka. There's a relaxing outdoor patio with tables and cooking space. Kids stay free. A minimum two-night stay is required.

Thassos Inn   HOTEL **$**
(☑25930 61612; www.thassosinn.gr; Panagia; s/d from €40/60) Just follow the sound of rushing spring water to this rambling and traditionally renovated hotel by the church, with great views of Panagia's slate-roofed houses. The welcoming owners Toula and Tasos are full of information about the area. It's also a good choice for hikers who want to be close to the trailhead leading into the mountains.

★**Hotel Kamelia**   HOTEL **$**
(☑25930 61463; www.hotel-kamelia.gr; Skala Potamia; s/d incl breakfast €40/60; P ❋ 🛜) This beach-front gem is the best in town, understated, with cool jazz in the garden bar and friendly service throughout. It serves a good breakfast overlooking the sea. It is a short walk just north of the main beach, over a very small bridge section of the road.

Golden Beach Camping   CAMPGROUND **$**
(☑25930 61472; Hrysi Ammoudia; camp sites per adult/tent €5/4; P) A party-feel pervades Golden Beach Camping, with its minimarket, bar, beach volleyball, and many young people from Greece, Serbia, Bulgaria and beyond. It's a fun place on the beach's best spot.

★ Arhontissa Alyki
RESTAURANT **$**

(🗐 25930 31552; Alyki; mains €5-10; ⊙lunch & dinner) The friendly Anastasios Kuzis and family run this tranquil taverna with great sea views, off on its own about 800m east of the village carpark. It's signposted up a steep drive and serves excellent fare, fresh fish and mezedhes among the star offerings.

Taverna Grill Elena
TAVERNA **$**

(🗐 25930 61709; Panagia; mains €8-11; ⊙10am-midnight) This classic taverna under a shady patio off the square, run by the ebullient Georgios, specialises in spit-roasted lamb and goat. For appetisers, try the *papoutsakia* (stuffed aubergine with minced beef and béchamel sauce), or *bougloundi* (baked feta with tomatoes and chilli).

Taverna En Plo
TAVERNA **$**

(Skala Potamia; mains €5-8) The combo taverna-domatia is great for a frosty frappé under red umbrellas in a garden setting, wi-fi included. It also has a few small but attractive rooms, each with kitchenette and balcony.

Restaurant Koralli
TAVERNA **$**

(Skala Potamia; mains €7-11) Bring your appetite to this rambling taverna where the generous dishes range from baked eggplant and sirloin steaks, to carpaccio and zucchinis stuffed with fresh crab.

DAVID BEATTY/ROBERT HARDING WORLD IMAGERY/CORBIS ®

Cultural Legacy

Expressions of the Greek passion for life can be seen throughout the country, woven into the culture and built into the landscape. From building massive sacred temples to acoustically perfect theatres, from whipping up delicately spiced desserts to throwing wild, showy festivals, Greeks continue to live creatively.

Contents

Above: Greek women in traditional dress

The Feast

You might wonder what conquests and invasions have to do with food; in the case of Greece, everything. The Turkish rule left tantalising spices and syrupy sweets while Italians imparted thick-sauced pastas and thin crusted pizzas. The Greeks have taken all of this into their kitchens and added their own flavourful slant. Meanwhile, they keep whipping up traditional dishes with unique, local ingredients – everywhere you go offers something new to try.

1. Mousakas
Greece's signature dish involves layers of baked eggplant, minced meat and potatoes, topped with cheese and béchamel sauce.

2. Yemista
Hollowed-out tomatoes and peppers are stuffed with herbed rice and baked with cheese to create this delicious summer favourite.

3. Souvlaki
Although it may arrive at your table in various guises, souvlaki is essentially grilled meat wrapped in a pitta or served on a skewer, kebab-style.

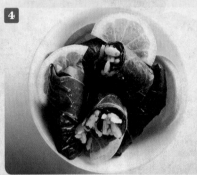

4. Dolmadhes
Soft parcels of spiced rice, often meat free, are wrapped in vine leaves.

5. Revythokeftedhes
These fritters made from chickpeas and fresh herbs are often served with cheese.

6. Seafood Saganaki
Mussels or prawns served with a rich tomato sauce and local cheese.

7. Stifadho
This sweet stew of rabbit or beef is cooked with tomato and onions.

8. Pastitsio
A thick pasta and meat bake that is often eaten during the winter.

9. Psarosoupa
This soup is made with local fish, such as red mullet or whitebait, and simmered with vegetables and spices.

10. Horiatiki
The ubiquitous Greek salad includes a bright mix of tomatoes, cucumber, onions, feta, olives and often local *horta* (wild greens).

11. Lokoumadhes
These ball-shaped doughnuts are served with honey and cinnamon.

12. Ghlika Kutalyu
Also known as 'spoon sweets', these syrupy desserts are often served over yoghurt or ice-cream.

Monumental Highs

Breathtaking for their size, age and beauty, Greece's colossal monuments are nothing short of awesome. Standing before them, it's clear why this is a land of enduring myths, powerful gods and daring goddesses – it's the perfect setting. The ancient Greeks built countless temples, monuments and churches to honour those they worshiped.

Monuments & Temples

Visiting Greece's ruins is like being given the chance to time travel. As you wander through ancient sites, it's impossible not to try to imagine life here thousands of years ago and to wonder at the might and determination of those who built these majestic, often mammoth temples.

Sitting like an august crown atop the capital, the **Acropolis** is undoubtedly Greece's most iconic sight. Built in the 5th century BC, this city of temples showcases Doric architecture with graceful, fluted columns and finely detailed friezes. Although ancient Greeks had been living at the site since neolithic times, the monuments that remain standing are not Greece's oldest.

A short distance across the deep blue Aegean, the Greeks started chipping away at the temples of **Delos** in the 8th century BC. The glorious sun-bleached ruins on this tiny sacred island, including ancient temples and elaborate mosaics, continue to attest to the ancients' need to appease the gods and, in the process, demonstrate their superior design and architectural ability. Similar temples, on smaller scales and in varying degrees of ruin, are peppered heavily across Greece. These remarkable ruins stand stoic yet

1. Moni Agias Varvaras Rousanou (p222), Meteora **2.** Erechtheion (p76), Acropolis, Athens **3.** Temple of Apollo (p191), Ancient Delphi

abandoned beneath the blazing sun, in silent harmony with their surroundings.

The ruins of **Delphi**, dating from the 6th century BC, rest on the gentle slopes of Mt Parnassos. It almost feels like the setting was designed for the temples rather than the other way around. Delphi, once believed to be the centre of the world, was the site of a famous oracle who gave advice to kings and warriors. Today its remaining temples are strangely intact and, together with the charming setting, conjure an atmosphere of wonder.

Churches

Christian houses of worship speckle the land, often perching on hilltops. A visit is worth the climb. Many of these buildings are filled with glitzy icons that belie the stark whitewashed or simple stone exteriors. Byzantine churches, often tiny oases overflowing with intriguing histories, are particularly atmospheric. Most of these churches are still in use, with plumes of incense, flickering candlelight and devoted monks and nuns passing through the cloisters.

If you're on Patmos, visit the **Monastery of St John the Theologian**. If you're on Naxos, head to **Panagia Drosiani**. In Thessaloniki, don't miss the **Church of Agia Sofia**. The options for church-going in Greece are endless. However, the unmissable stop is **Meteora**. This place will leave you soaring. Built atop seemingly inaccessible pinnacles of rock, Meteora's seven churches were hideouts for hermit monks in the 14th century. The engineering feat of building and reaching the churches is staggering. Stepping inside the cloisters will only increase your awe.

STEVEN MIRIC/GETTY IMAGES ©

1. Orthodox Easter eggs 2. Patras Carnival (p180) 3. Easter at Monastery of St John the Theologian (p530), Hora (Patmos)
4. Saint's day celebrations, Ikaria (p540)

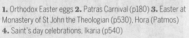

MICHAEL ANHAEUSER/ DPA / CORBIS ©

Festival Laden

Greeks seem up for celebrating almost everything. This is the country where you get two birthdays – the day of your birth and the official day of the saint you are named after. From sombre to downright riotous, you are never far from a festival.

Carnival

More of a season than a single festival, this is Greece's most colourful event and culminates in a weekend street party with floats, dancing and costumes. Each region has its own take on it; head to Patra for the biggest and wildest celebrations, or Skyros to see entire towns dressed as goats, copper bells and all.

Orthodox Easter

While many restaurants hold feasts, this is a great time to get invited to a local home for dinner. Huge amounts of feasting eventually succumbs to traditional dancing and drinking. Fireworks are thrown and red-dyed eggs are everywhere. As an important place of Christian pilgrimage, Patmos has one of the largest celebrations.

August Moon Festival

Considered the brightest and most beautiful moon of the year, the August moon inspires towns across the country to host special nighttime events and parties. In Athens historical venues open for free moonlit performances of theatre and dance.

Name Days

The Greek church calendar is chock-a-block with days designated to particular saints. Most Greeks are named after one of these saints and celebrate their namesake each year. A bigger splash than birthdays, name days are honoured with sweets, presents and parties.

Odeon of Herodes Atticus (p78), Ather

Theatre-Goers

Watching a Greek drama unfold beneath starlight, perched on the stone seats worn smooth by audiences who have been coming here since the 4th century BC, is an atmospheric and almost eerie experience. The ancient Greeks built theatres to hold up to 20,000 spectators and would host plays during festivals and games such as the Olympics.

There were originally three genres of drama: tragedy, which dealt with themes such as love and loss, pride and compassion; comedy, which mocked the powerful for their vanity and foolishness; and satyr plays, which were short and more surreal and dealt with mythology in a comic way. Actors wore masks with exaggerated expressions that were designed to amplify their voice and,

through the ages, the original cast of just three grew to accommodate more complex plots and themes.

The 4th-century-BC theatre at **Ancient Delphi** is particularly well preserved. Plays were performed here during the Pythian festival, held every four years. The views from the top row of seating remain as dramatic as anything once performed on stage. The **Theatre of Epidavros** was built in the 3rd century and is one of Greece's best-preserved Classical structures. Its acoustics are phenomenal – hear for yourself at one of the summer performances. In Athens, the carefully restored **Odeon of Herodes Atticus** sits dramatically beneath the Acropolis and hosts both modern and classical events throughout the Athens Festival.

Evia & the Sporades

Best Places to Eat

➡ Dina's Amfilirion Restaurant (p607)

➡ Taverna-Ouzerie Kabourelia (p612)

➡ Nastas Ouzerie (p616)

➡ Hayati (p622)

➡ Taverna Mouries (p628)

Best Places to Stay

➡ Hotel Nefeli (p625)

➡ Atrium Hotel (p614)

➡ Pension Sotos (p616)

➡ Liadromia Hotel (p620)

➡ Perigiali Hotel & Studios (p626)

Why Go?

Evia (Εύβοια) and the four Sporades islands (Οι Σποράδες) remain largely off the beaten island path, though two bridges at Halkida join Evia to the mainland. But away from its commercial hub of Halkida, the pace slows as the landscape stretches out, dotted by hilltop monasteries, small farms, vineyards and not a few curious goats.

The Sporades ('scattered ones') seem like extensions of the forested Pelion Peninsula, and, in fact, they were joined in prehistoric times. Skiathos, easily the most developed of the group, claims the sandiest beaches in the Aegean. Low-key Skopelos kicks back with a postcard-worthy harbour and forest meadows. Remote Alonnisos anchors the National Marine Park of the Northern Sporades. Skyros, the southernmost of the chain, is known for its culinary and artistic traditions that date from Byzantine times when these islands were home to rogues and pirates.

When to Go
Skíathos Town

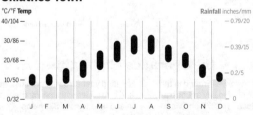

Feb & Mar Carnival season keeps things warm with plenty of merry-making.

Apr & May Spring is in the air and Easter festivities linger long into the night.

Jun & Sep Perfect temperatures and clear skies – ideal hiking conditions.

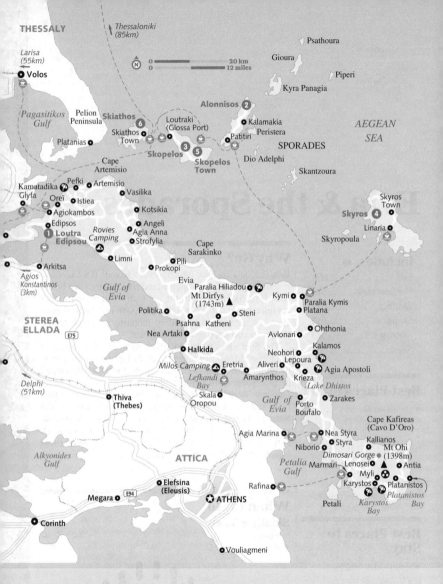

Evia & the Sporades Highlights

1 Swim year-round in the thermal-fed bay at **Loutra Edipsou** (p607), on Evia

2 Watch for dolphins and falcons while sailing around Greece's only national marine park at **Alonnisos** (p620)

3 Find your favourite orchids and butterflies while hiking the inland meadows of **Skopelos** (p614)

4 Nuzzle up with the gentle and rare Skyrian horse on **Skyros** (p623)

5 Hear great bouzouki music after midnight above the *kastro* overlooking **Skopelos Town** (p615)

6 Sample the monks' wine at Moni Evangelistrias on **Skiathos** (p610), where Greek independence was declared in 1807

EVIA   ΕΥΒΟΙΑ

Evia (*eh*-vih-ah), Greece's second-largest island after Crete, offers glorious mountain roads, challenging treks, major archaeological finds and many uncrowded beaches. A north–south mountainous spine divides the island's eastern cliffs from the gentler and resort-friendly west coast. Ferries link the island to the mainland, along with two bridges at Halkida; one is a sliding drawbridge over the narrow Evripos Channel which reverses direction about seven times daily, an event whose full explanation has eluded observers since Aristotle.

ℹ Getting There & Away

There are regular buses between Halkida and Athens (€7, 1¼ hours, half-hourly), Ioannina (€39, seven hours, four to six daily) and Thessaloniki (€40, 6¼ hours, eight to 10 daily). There is also a regular train service between Halkida and Athens and an express service between Halkida and Thessaloniki. Five ports on Evia serve the mainland, and one serves the island of Skyros.

Central Evia

From Halkida, the road veers south, following the coastline to Eretria, a bustling resort and archaeological site. Further on, a string of hamlets and fishing villages dot the route until the junction at Lepoura, where the road forks north towards Kymi. A rough dirt road winds west from Kymi to the beach at Paralia Hiliadou.

Halkida   Χαλκίδα

POP 69,940

Mentioned in the 'Iliad', Halkida (aka Halkis) was a powerful city state in the 7th century BC. The name derives from the bronze that was manufactured here in antiquity. Today, it's a gateway to Evia and is a lively commercial centre. As evening approaches, the waterfront promenade by the Old Bridge comes to life.

To glimpse Halkida's interesting religious history, head up Kotsou towards the *kastro* (castle) to find a striking 15th-century **mosque** and 19th-century **synagogue**, adjacent to Plateia Tzami. About 150m south is the Byzantine **church** of Agia Paraskevi. An **Archaeological Museum** (Leoforos Venizelou 13; admission €2; ⊙8am-3pm Tue-Sun) displays marble and bone figurines from the Early Bronze Age.

🍴 Sleeping & Eating

Best Western Lucy Hotel   HOTEL $$
(✉22210 23831; www.lucy-hotel.gr; Voudouri 10; s/d/tr/ste incl breakfast €60/80/110/130; P❄@🛜) Rooms at the well-managed Lucy are on the modern side, with stylish furnishings and long desks. The multilingual staff can clue you in to the adjacent boardwalk cafe scene.

Pantheon 1900   TAPAS $
(Voudouri; tapas €3-7; ⊙lunch & dinner) Nestled in a handsome waterfront neoclassical building, this smart tapas bar features great Greek wines, along with tasty small plates and snappy service.

ℹ Information

Several ATMs cluster near the corner of Venizelou and Voudouri.
Hospital (✉22210 21902; cnr Gazepi & Hatzopoulou)
Post Office (cnr Karamourtzouni & Kriezotou; ⊙8am-2pm Mon-Fri)
Tourist Police (✉22210 77777)

ℹ Getting There & Away

From Halkida, buses serve Athens, Ioannina and Thessaloniki. Regular trains also connect

BOAT SERVICES FROM EVIA

DESTINATION	PORT	TIME	FARE	FREQUENCY
Agia Marina	Nea Styra	45min	€3.50	9-12 daily
Arkitsa	Loutra Edipsou	40min	€3.40	8-14 daily
Glyfa	Agiokambos	20min	€2.30	5-8 daily
Rafina	Marmari	1hr	€7	4-6 daily
Skala Oropou	Eretria	25min	€2	half-hourly
Skyros	Paralia Kymis	1¾hr	€9	1-2 daily

Halkida with Athens, and an express service with Thessaloniki.

From **Halkida KTEL bus station** (☑ 22210 22640; cnr Styron & Arethousis), 3km east of the Old Bridge, buses also connect to the following destinations on Evia:

DESTINATION	FARE	TIME	FREQUENCY
Eretria	€2	25min	hourly
Karystos	€11.70	3hr	3 daily
Kymi Town & Paralia Kymis	€8.50	2hr	hourly
Limni	€7.90	2hr	3 daily
Loutra Edipsou	€12	2hr	1 daily
Steni	€3	1hr	4 daily

Eretria   Ερέτρια

POP 3220

From Halkida, the first place of interest for travellers is Eretria, which has a small harbour and a lively boardwalk of fish tavernas, cafes and beach bars.

⊙ Sights

West of the **ancient acropolis** are the remains of a theatre with a subterranean passage once used by actors to reach the stage. Close by, the **Archaeological Museum of Eretria** (admission €2; ⊙ 8.30am-3pm Tue-Sun) includes the fascinating **House of Mosaics**, dating from the 4th century BC and the 8th-century BC **Sanctuary of Apollo**.

🛏 Sleeping & Eating

Milos Camping   CAMPGROUND $
(☑ 22290 60420; www.camping-in-evia.gr; camp sites per adult/tent €6.20/4.40) This well-managed, shaded campground 1km northwest of Eretria has a small restaurant, bar and a 200m-long pebble beach.

Villa Belmar Apartments   APARTMENT $$
(☑ 6971588424; www.villabelmar.gr; s/d/f incl breakfast from €50/70/95; P ❄ @ 🛜) Just 100m southwest of the port, these stylish apartments, Eretria's smartest digs, are managed by welcoming sisters Lina and Renia. You can climb into the sea from the waterfront deck.

Taverna Cubana   TAVERNA $
(Arheou Theatrou 44; mains €5-11) Just past the supermarket, and known for well-priced fresh fish, late-night grills and tasty seafood appetisers.

ⓘ Getting There & Away

Ferries travel daily between Eretria and Skala Oropou. Purchase tickets from the dock kiosks.

Steni   Στενή

POP 1080

From Halkida, it's 31km to the lovely mountain village of Steni, with its gurgling springs and shady plane trees.

Steni is the starting point for **hiking** up **Mt Dirfys** (1743m), Evia's highest mountain. The **Dirfys Refuge** (☑ 22280 25655; per person €12), at 1120m, can be reached along a 9km dirt road. From there, it's a steep 7km to the summit. Experienced hikers should allow about six hours from Steni to the summit. For lodging information at the refuge, contact **Minas Patsourakis** (☑ 6940687312, 6974057517, 22210 85760) and the EOS-affiliated **Halkida Alpine Club** (☑ 22210 25230; www.eoschalkidas.gr; Angeli Gouviou 22, Halkida). See Anavasi's detailed topo map, *Mt Dirfys*.

A twisting road continues from Steni to **Paralia Hiliadou** on the north coast, where a grove of maple and chestnut trees borders a fine pebble-and-sand beach, along with a few domatia (private rooms) and tavernas.

🛏 Sleeping & Eating

Hotel Dirfys   HOTEL $
(☑ 22280 51370; s/d incl breakfast €35/45; P 🛜) This is the most appealing of Steni's three hotels. All rooms have balcony views of the surrounding forest, sparkling bathrooms, and the hotel taverna draws locals come evening.

Taverna Kissos   TAVERNA $
(mains €7-12) 🌿 One of a cluster of attractive brook-side eateries, with hearty meat grills, *mayirefta* (ready-cooked meals) and generous salads prepared from locally grown greens.

Kymi & Paralia Kymis
Κύμη & Παραλία Κύμης

POP 3040

The workaday town of Kymi perks up at dusk when the town square comes to life. The port of Paralia Kymis, 4km downhill, is the departure point for ferries to Skyros, Alonnisos and Skopelos.

The **Folklore Museum** (☑ 22220 22011; admission €1.50; ⊙ 10.30am-1pm Wed, 10.30am-2pm Sat & Sun), 30m downhill from the main square, includes a display honouring Kymi-born Dr George Papanikolaou, inventor of the Pap smear test.

Kymi is home to **Figs of Kymi** (🖉22220 31722; figkimi@otenet.gr; ⊘9am-9pm Sep-Nov & by appointment), a lively agricultural co-op supporting local fig farmers and sustainable production. Preservative-free figs and jams are on sale in the shop.

🛏 Sleeping & Eating

In Paralia Kymis, the reliable **Hotel Beis** (🖉22220 22604; www.hotel-beis.gr; s/d/tr incl breakfast €40/60/70; P❋🞈) is opposite the ferry dock for Skyros. A string of tavernas and *ouzeries* (places serving ouzo and light snacks) lines the waterfront. Just 3km south in tiny Platana, check out the exceptional fish taverna **Koutelos** (🖉22220 71272; mains €7-11; ⊘lunch & dinner).

Northern Evia

From Halkida a road heads north to **Psahna**, the gateway to the highly scenic mountainous interior of northern Evia. A good road climbs and twists 60km through pine forests to the woodsy village of **Prokopi**, home of the pilgrimage church of **St John the Russian**. At Strofylia, the road heads southwest to picturesque **Limni**, then north to quaint **Loutra Edipsou** and the ferry port at **Agiokambos**.

Loutra Edipsou   Λουτρά Αιδηψού

POP 3600

The classic spa resort of Loutra Edipsou has therapeutic sulphur waters, celebrated since antiquity. Famous skinny-dippers have included Aristotle, Plutarch and Sylla. Today, the town has Greece's most up-to-date hydrotherapy and physiotherapy centres. The town beach (Paralia Loutron) heats up year-round thanks to the thermal waters that spill into the bay.

🏃 Activities

Most hotels offer various **spa treatments**, from simple hot baths (€5) to four-hand massages (€160).

The more affordable of the resort's two big spas is the welcoming **EOT Hydrotherapy-Physiotherapy Centre** (🖉22260 23501; 25 March St 37; ⊘7am-1pm & 5-7pm 1 Jun-31 Oct), speckled with palm trees and a large outdoor pool that mixes mineral and sea water. Hydromassage bath treatments start at €8.

Ultra-posh **Thermae Sylla Hotel & Spa** (🖉22260 60100; www.thermaesylla.gr; Posidonos 2), with a late-Roman ambience befitting its name, offers assorted health and beauty treatments, from thermal mud baths to seaweed body wraps.

🛏 Sleeping & Eating

Three snappy waterfront eateries worth a taste are **Ouzerie Ta Kohilia** (🖉22260 23478; 28 October; mains €4-7; ⊘lunch & dinner) for mezedhes (appetisers), **Alli Yefsi** (🖉6984460759; mains €2-4; ⊘lunch & dinner) for skewered grills and **Captain Cook Self-Service** (mains €3-7; ⊘lunch & dinner) for everything else.

★ Hotel Kentrikon   HOTEL $
(🖉22260 22302; www.kentrikonhotel.com; 25 Martiou 14; s/d/tr incl breakfast €40/50/60; ❋@🞈🏊) Managed by Greek-Irish Konstantinos and Una, the Kentrikon is equal parts kitsch and old-world charm. Rooms are spacious and bright, with modern bathrooms and balcony views. An inviting free thermal pool awaits, along with professional massage therapist, **Vicky Kavartziki** (🖉6945146374).

Hotel Istiaia   HOTEL $
(🖉22260 22309; www.istiaiahotel.com; 28 Octovriou 2; s/d/tr incl breakfast from €35/45/65; ❋@🞈) The vintage Istiaia has an old-world feel with high-ceiling rooms and a grand staircase. A cafe-wine bar faces the sea.

Thermae Sylla Hotel & Spa   LUXURY HOTEL $$$
(🖉22260 60100; www.thermaesylla.gr; Posidonos 2; s/d/ste incl breakfast from €110/160/250; P❋@🞈🏊) This posh in-your-mud-masked-face seaside resort offers elegant luxury accommodation along with countless beauty treatments. Day visitors can sample the outdoor thermal pool (€27).

★ Dina's Amfilirion Restaurant   GREEK $
(28 Octovriou 26; mains €7-10) Daily specials, *sans* menu, await at this modest eatery. A tasty grilled cod with oven potatoes, tomato-cucumber salad and wine costs about €12. Look for the small wooden sign with green letters, 20m north of the ferry dock.

ℹ Information

Free wi-fi is available on the waterfront. For medical needs, contact English-speaking **Dr Symeonides** (🖉22260 23220; Omirou 17).

EVIA & THE SPORADES NORTHERN EVIA

ⓘ Getting There & Away

BOAT

Regular ferries run between Loutra Edipsou and mainland Arkitsa, and also between nearby Agiokambos and mainland Glyfa. Purchase tickets at the dock kiosks.

BUS

From the **KTEL bus station** (☑ 22260 22250; Thermopotamou), 200m from the port, buses run to Halkida (€14, four hours, once daily at 5.30am), Athens (€14, three hours, three daily via Arkitsa) and Thessaloniki (€25, four hours, daily at 10am via Glyfa).

Limni   Λίμνη

POP 2120

Picturesque Limni's maze of whitewashed houses and narrow lanes spill onto a cosy harbour speckled with cafes and tavernas. The town's old-fashioned folk **museum** (☑ 22270 31335; admission €2; ☺ 9am-1pm Mon-Sat, 10.30am-1pm Sun) is located 50m from the waterfront.

The 16th-century **Convent of Galataki** (☺ 9am-noon & 5-8pm), 9km southeast of Limni above a narrow coastal road, is home to a coterie of six nuns and a fine fresco in its *katholikon* (principal church), the *Entry of the Righteous into Paradise.*

🛏 Sleeping & Eating

Home Graegos   APARTMENT $
(☑ 22270 31117; www.graegos.com; apt from €55; 𝐏 ❋ 🛜) Opposite the southern end of the waterfront, the well-managed Graegos has four apartments with modern kitchenettes and verandah sea views.

Zaniakos Domatia   PENSION $
(☑ 6973667200, 22270 32445; www.zaniakos.gr; r €35; 𝐏 ❋) English may be in short supply at this tidy domatia 200m above the waterfront, but the welcoming owners go out of their way to be helpful.

Rovies Camping   CAMPGROUND $
(☑ 22270 71120; www.campingevia.com; camp sites per adult/tent €6.50/6; 🛜) Attractive and shaded Rovies sits just above a pebble beach, 12km northwest of Limni.

Ouzerie Fiki   MEZEDHES $
(mezedhes €2-5) Pick an outside table at this waterfront stand-by and enjoy well-prepared mezedhes like grilled octopus and *taramasalata* (purée of fish roe, potato, oil and lemon juice).

Southern Evia

East of Eretria, the road branches at Lepoura: the left fork leads north to Kymi, the right south to Karystos. A turn-off at Krieza, 3km from the junction, leads to Lake Dhistos, a shallow lake bed favoured by migrating egrets. Heading south, you'll pass high-tech windmills and catch views of both coasts as the island narrows before reaching Karystos Bay.

Karystos   Κάρυστος

POP 5130

Set on wide Karystos Bay below Mt Ohi and flanked by two sandy beaches, this low-key coastal resort is the starting point for treks to Mt Ohi and Dimosari Gorge. The town's lively Plateia Amalias faces the harbour.

◉ Sights

Karystos, mentioned in Homer's 'Iliad', was a powerful city-state during the Peloponnesian Wars. The displays at **Karystos Museum** (admission €2; ☺ 9am-3pm Tue-Sun) range from tiny neolithic clay lamps to an exhibit of the 6th-century BC *drakospita* (dragon houses) of Mt Ohi and Styra. The museum sits opposite a 14th-century Venetian castle, the **Bourtzi** (admission free; ☺ year-round).

☞ Tours

South Evia Tours   CRUISE, HIKING
(☑ 22240 26200; www.eviatravel.gr; Plateia Amalias) can help with accommodation and ferry tickets, and organise excursions to the *drakospita* near Styra, bicycle and kayak rentals, as well as cruises around the Petali Islands (€35). Owner Nikos and staff can also arrange transport for hikes to the summit of Mt Ohi and back, and four-hour guided walks through Dimosari Gorge (€25).

BikeGreece   MOUNTAIN BIKING
(☑ 6944618565; www.bikegreece.com) Find out what mountain bikes are really for with BikeGreece. Its week-long bicycle tours of the wild south Evian landscape explore the slopes of Mt Ohi, the Dimosari Gorge, and include beach bonfires and even the occasional village wine tasting. Rates include vehicle support, food and lodging. Semi-expat James Brown organises the show with a deep appreciation of the local landscape and culture.

✿ Festivals & Events

Wine & Cultural Festival   CULTURAL

Karystos hosts a summer Wine & Cultural Festival during the last week of August, including theatre performances, traditional dancing to the tune of local musicians, and exhibits by local artists. The summer merry-making features local wines, free for the tasting.

🛏 Sleeping & Eating

Hotel Karystion   HOTEL **$**

(☑ 22240 22391; www.karystion.gr; Kriezotou 3; s/d incl breakfast from €38/45; P❄🙝) The handsome Karystion sits above the beach just beyond Bourtzi castle, and features modern, well-appointed rooms and a helpful multilingual staff. A stairway leads to a sandy beach, great for swimming.

Hotel Galaxy   HOTEL **$**

(☑ 22240 22600; www.galaxyhotelkaristos.com; s/d incl breakfast from €35/50; ❄@🙝) About 100m south of the *plateia* (square), the bright and airy Galaxy is a Karystos stand-by with a woody motif and welcoming atmosphere. Upper rooms have harbour views, and breakfast eggs come from the owners' farm.

★ Cavo d'Oro   TAVERNA **$**

(mains €5-8) 🖉 Join the locals in this cheery alleyway restaurant off the main square for well-prepared Greek mainstays and country salads featuring local produce and olive oil. The genial owner, Kyriakos, is a regular at the summer wine festival, bouzouki in hand.

🍷 Drinking & Nightlife

Aeriko   BAR

(☑ 22240 22365; 🙝) Aeriko is the pick of the harbour beach bars, with live music on summer weekends, sunbeds, decent drinks and a copasetic all-ages clientele.

ℹ Information

An Alpha Bank ATM is on the main square.

ℹ Getting There & Away

BOAT

There is regular ferry service from Marmari (10km west of Karystos) to Rafina, and from Nea Styra (35km north of Karystos) to Agia Marina.

Purchase tickets from either the dock kiosk or from South Evia Tours (p608) in Karystos.

WORTH A TRIP

WHISTLING VILLAGE OF ANTIA

East of Karystos and overlooking the sea, the 'whistling village' of Antia is famous for its linguistically talented villagers who speak a whistling language, devised during Byzantine times to warn of danger and invasion. Today, it's mostly the old-timers who still put their lips together and blow, unfortunately not quite as well as they once did before many of them were obliged to wear false teeth.

BUS

From the **Karystos KTEL bus station** (☑ 22240 26303) opposite Agios Nikolaos church, buses run to Halkida (€11.70, three hours), Athens (€18.60, three hours) and Marmari (€1.80, 20 minutes). A taxi to Marmari is €15.

Around Karystos

Explore the villages and chestnut forests nestling in the foothills between Mt Ohi and the coast. The ruins of **Castello Rosso** (Red Castle), a 13th-century Frankish fortress, are a short walk from Myli. Another 4km above Myli, there is an ancient **Roman quarry** (Kylindroi) scattered with massive columns of Karystian *cipollino* marble, abandoned since the time of Caesar.

🏃 Activities

Hiking

Day hikers will swoon over **Dimosari Gorge**, where a beautiful and well-maintained 10km trail can be covered in about four hours (including time for a swim). Much of this stunning trek follows a cobbled path, splashing through shady creeks and forest before ending at Kallianos.

From Myli, a delightful, well-watered village 4km inland from Karystos, it's a three-to four-hour hike to the summit of **Mt Ohi** (1398m), overlooking the sea. The summit (Profitis Ilias peak) is home to the ancient and mysterious *drakospita,* or dragon houses, a group of Stonehenge-like dwellings or temples dating from the 7th century BC. They were hewn from rocks weighing up to several tonnes and joined without mortar. Smaller examples near the road to Styra (30km north of Karystos) are equally fascinating. It's also possible arrange a shuttle bus to a shelter-refuge at 1000m, overnight it and then hike up to catch the sunrise.

Contact Nikos at South Evia Tours (p608) for route and transport suggestions, both for Mt Ohi and Dimosari Gorge.

THE SPORADES

Skiathos   Σκιάθος

POP 6110

Blessed with some of the Aegean's most beautiful beaches, it's little wonder that in July and August Skiathos can fill up with sun-starved northern European travellers, as prices soar and rooms dwindle.

Skiathos Town, the island's major settlement and port, lies on the southeast coast. The rest of the south coast is interspersed with walled-in holiday villas and pine-fringed sandy beaches.

❶ Getting There & Away

AIR

During summer there is one flight daily to/from Athens (€88), in addition to numerous charter flights from northern Europe. **Olympic Air** (☑ 24270 22200; www.olympicair.com) has an office at the airport.

BOAT

Skiathos' main port is Skiathos Town, with links to Volos and Agios Konstantinos (on the mainland), and Skopelos and Alonnisos.

Tickets can be purchased from either **Hellenic Seaways** (☑ 24270 22209; fax 24270 22750) at the bottom of Papadiamanti or from **NEL Lines** (☑ 24270 22018) on the waterfront.

❶ Getting Around

BOAT

Water taxis depart hourly from the old port for Achladies Bay (€2.50, 15 minutes), Kanapitsa (€3, 20 minutes) and Koukounaries (€5, 30 minutes).

BUS

Buses leave Skiathos Town for Koukounaries Beach (€2, 30 minutes, every half-hour between 7.30am and 11pm). The buses stop at 26 numbered access points to the beaches along the south coast.

CAR & MOTORCYCLE

Reliable motorbike and car-hire outlets in Skiathos Town include **Europcar/Creator Tours** (☑ 24270 22385), which also has bicycles, and **Heliotropio Tourism & Travel** (☑ 24270 22430), both on the new port.

TAXI

The **taxi stand** (☑ 24270 21460) is opposite the ferry dock. A taxi to/from the airport costs €6.

Skiathos Town   Σκιάθος

The town is a major tourist centre, with hotels, souvenir shops, galleries, travel agents, tavernas and bars spread along the waterfront and narrow pedestrian thoroughfare, Papadiamanti. Opposite the waterfront via a short causeway lies tiny and inviting **Bourtzi Islet**.

BOAT SERVICES FROM SKIATHOS

DESTINATION	TIME	FARE	FREQUENCY
Agios Konstantinos	2½hr	€30	1 daily
Agios Konstantinos*	1¾hr	€37	1-2 daily
Alonnisos	2½hr	€11	1-2 daily
Alonnisos*	1½hr	€17	2-3 daily
Skopelos (Glossa)	40min	€6	4 weekly
Skopelos (Glossa)*	20min	€10	2-3 daily
Skopelos (Skopelos Town)	1¼hr	€9.50	1-2 daily
Skopelos (Skopelos Town)*	40min	€17	3-4 daily
Volos	2½hr	€23	1-2 daily
Volos*	1½hr	€38	2-3 daily

*hydrofoil services

Skiathos

N 0 ——————— 2 km
0 ——————— 1 miles

Kastronisia
Cape Kastro
Lalaria Beach
Kastro
Cape Ag Sozon
Agios Haralambos
AEGEAN SEA
Moni Evangelistrias
Agios Apostolis
Cape Kefala
Kehrias Bay
Kehria Beach
Mikros Aselinos Beach
Panorama Pizza
Skiathos
Cape Gournes
Aspronisos
Moni Panagias Kounistras
Skiathos Town
Ring Rd
Skiathos Bay
Villa Helidonia
Cape Ag Elenis
Megali Amos Beach
Siferi Bay
Cape Plakes
Cape Pounta
Arko
Agia Eleni Beach
Wetland
Camping Koukounaries
Achladies Apartments
Water Taxi
Maragos
Little Banana
Salt & Pepper Restaurant
Atrium Hotel
Achladies Bay
Koukounaries Beach
Big Banana
Cape Tourkovigia
Troulos Beach
Troulos
Paraskevi Beach
Kolios
Kolios Beach
Kanapitsa
Water Taxi
Cape Tsimokokalo
Vromolimnos Beach
Cape Kalamaki
Skopelos (10km); Alonnisos (25km)
Water Taxi
Volos (45km); Agios Konstantinos (57km)
Tsougriaki
Tsougria
Tsougriaki

EVIA & THE SPORADES SKIATHOS

⊙ Sights

Skiathos was the birthplace of famous 19th-century Greek novelist and short-story writer Alexandros Papadiamanti, whose writings draw upon the hard lives of the islanders he grew up with. His humble 1860 house is now a charming **museum** (Plateia Papadiamanti; admission €1; ⊙ 9.30am-1.30pm & 5-8.30pm Tue-Sun) with books, paintings and old photos.

⚐ Tours

Excursion boats make half- and full-day trips around the island (€15 to €25), and usually visit Cape Kastro, Lalaria Beach and the three *spilies* (caves) of Halkini, Skotini and Galazia. Other boats visit the nearby islets of Tsougria and Tsougriaki for swimming and snorkelling; you can take one boat over and return on another for €10. Check out the signboards in front of each boat at the old port.

For a splendid **sailing tour** of the island waters between Skiathos and Alonnisos, climb aboard the **Argo III** (☑ 6932325167; www.argosailing.com; per person €65), managed by husband-and-wife team George and Dina.

⌂ Sleeping

In busy July and August, there's also a helpful quayside kiosk with prices, pictures and pitches.

★ **Gisela's Rooms-in-Town** PENSION **$**
(☑ 6945686542, 24270 21370; gisbaunach@hotmail.com; r €45; ❄ ☎) Cosy and quiet on a back street off Papadiamanti, this well-managed budget choice has two rooms, two twin beds in each, overhead fans, mosquito screens, table, plus a flowery verandah. The owner also manages the secluded seaside **Villa Helidonia** (Swallows Villa; ☑ 6945686542, 24270 21370; gisbaunach@hotmail.com; apt €75-95; 🅿 @ ☎).

Lena's Rooms
PENSION $

(☑ 24270 22009; Bouboulinas; r from €35; ✳ @ 🛜) These six double rooms over the owner's flower shop are airy and spotless, each with mini-fridge, balcony, a well-equipped common kitchen and shady, flower-filled verandah.

Hotel Meltemi
HOTEL $

(☑ 24270 22493; meltemi@skiathos.gr; s/d/f €45/55/80; ✳ @ 🛜) You could easily miss the friendly Meltemi, set back in a shady courtyard at the new port, but its old-fashioned charm is appealing, from antique-filled hallways to super-tidy rooms.

Hotel Bourtzi
BOUTIQUE HOTEL $$

(☑ 24270 21304; www.hotelbourtzi.gr; s/d/tr incl breakfast €70/100/125; ᴘ ✳ 🛜 🏊) On upper Papadiamanti, the swank Bourtzi escapes much of the town noise and features austere modern rooms and an inviting garden and pool.

✖ Eating

Skiathos has its share of overpriced touristy eateries with *etsi-ketsi* (so-so) food. Explore the narrow lanes around the old port to find exceptions like those described below.

★ Taverna-Ouzerie Kabourelia
TAVERNA $

(mains €4-9) Poke your nose into the open kitchen to glimpse the day's catch at the only year-round eatery at the old port, with perfect fish grills at moderate prices. Grilled octopus and *taramasalata* are just two of several standout mezedhes.

Taverna Hellinikon
TAVERNA $

(mains €7-10; ⏲ lunch & dinner) Opposite the church above the old port, little Hellinikon is a mother-and-daughter affair, with well-prepared taverna standards such as slow-roasted lamb with potatoes and lemon. Good house wines, along with live Greek music summer evenings.

Lo & La
ITALIAN $

(☑ 6972408465; mains €7.50-12) Perched above the old port, Lo & La shows off an Italian-Greek couple's kitchen favourites. Pastas are handmade, and the risotto with local mushrooms excels.

Grill House Aura
GREEK $

(Chicken George; mains €5-9) Locals call this popular old-port eatery Chicken George. You'll find generous portions of chicken, lamb and pork on-the-spit, with everything from *gyros* (meat slithers cooked on a vertical rotisserie) to chops.

No Name Fast Food
QUICK EATS $

(Simionos; mains €2) It's actually not too fast, and his name is Aris. Best *gyros* in town.

Medousa Pizza
PIZZA $

(☑ 24270 23923; Club St; mains €6-8) Refuel here after sampling the drink-till-you-drop waterfront clubs.

🍷 Drinking & Nightlife

The drink-till-you-drop scene heats up after midnight along the club strip past the new harbour.

Kentavros
BAR

(☑ 24270 22980) Handsome Kentavros, opposite Plateia Papadiamanti, promises rock, jazz and blues, and gets the thumbs-up from locals and expats for its mellow ambience, artwork and sturdy drinks.

Main Street
BAR

(Papadiamanti) Convivial cafe-bar, with good sounds, on mid-Papadiamanti.

Rock & Roll Bar
BAR

(☑ 24270 22944) Huge beanbags have long replaced many of the pillows lining the wide steps outside this trendy bar on the steps by the old port, resulting in fewer customers rolling off as the night rolls on. Solid drinks, fair prices.

☆ Entertainment

For clubbing, the best DJs are at **Club Pure** (☑ 6979773854), **Kahlua** (☑ 24270 23205) and **BBC** (☑ 24270 21190), open till dawn.

Cinema Attikon
CINEMA

(☑ 24720 22352; tickets €7) Catch current English-language movies at this open-air cinema, sip a beer and practise speed-reading your Greek subtitles.

🔒 Shopping

Loupos & His Dolphins
ANTIQUES

(☑ 24270 23777; Plateia Papadiamanti; ⏲ 10am-1.30pm & 6-11.30pm) Find delicate hand-painted icons, handsome ceramics, and gold and silver jewellery at this high-end gallery shop, in the courtyard by Papadiamanti Museum.

Galerie Varsakis
ANTIQUES

(Plateia Trion Ierarhon; ⏲ 10am-2pm & 6-11pm) Browse for unusual antiques such as 19th-century spinning sticks made by grooms for their intended brides. The collection rivals the best Greek folklore museums.

Olive Tree Skiathos GIFTS
(Papadiamanti 28) Small and inviting shop features hand-crafted bowls, jewellery and more, all made from olive wood.

ℹ Information

The bus terminus is at the northern end of the new harbour. You'll find free wi-fi all along the port and in most cafes on Papadiamanti. Numerous ATMs are on Papadiamanti and the waterfront.

Health Centre Hospital (☑ 24270 22222; above Old Port)

Port Police (☑ 24270 22017; Quay)

Tourist Police (☑ 24270 23172; Ring Rd; ⊙ 8am-9pm)

ℹ Getting There & Away

The bus terminus is at the northern end of the new harbour.

Around Skiathos

◉ Sights

With some 65 beaches to choose from, beach-hopping on Skiathos can become a full-time occupation. Buses ply the south coast, stopping at 26 numbered beach access points. The first long stretch of sand worth getting hopping off for is the pine-fringed Vromolimnos Beach. The road continues to Koukounaries Beach, backed by pine trees and a small wetland, and touted as the best beach in Greece. But come midsummer, it's best viewed at a distance, from where the 1200m long sweep of pale gold sand does indeed sparkle.

West of Koukounaries, Big Banana Beach, known for its curving shape, soft white sand and beach-bar buzz, lies across a narrow headland. Skinny-dippers prefer to hang at equally frenetic Little Banana Beach (also popular with gay and lesbian sunbathers) around the rocky corner.

About 400m north, elegant Agia Eleni Beach is a favourite with windsurfers. Sandy Mandraki Beach, a 1.5km walk along a pine-shaded path, is just far enough to keep it clear of the masses, and sports a good taverna. From Troulos, it's 4km to Megalos Aselinos Beach, a lovely long stretch of sand, with tiny Mikros Aselinos and secluded Kehria Beach a few kilometres further on.

The northwest coast's beaches are less crowded but are subject to summer *meltemi* (northeasterly winds). Lalaria Beach is a tranquil strand of pale grey, egg-shaped pebbles on the northern coast, but be only reached by excursion boat from Skiathos Town.

Kastro LOOKOUT
Kastro, perched dramatically on a rocky headland above the north coast, was the fortified pirate-proof capital of the island from 1540 to 1829. An old cannon remains at the northern end, along with four restored churches, including Christos, home to several fine frescoes. Excursion boats come to the beach below Kastro, from where it's an easy clamber up to the ruins.

Moni Evangelistrias MONASTERY
(Monastery of the Annunciation; museum admission €2; ⊙ 10am-dusk) The most famous of the island's monasteries was a hilltop refuge for freedom fighters during the War of Independence, and the Greek flag was first raised here, in 1807. Today, two monks do the chores, which include wine making. You can sample the tasty results in the museum shop. An adjacent shed of vintage olive and wine presses recalls an earlier era, long before the satellite dish was installed above the courtyard.

Moni Panagias Kounistras MONASTERY
(Monastery of the Holy Virgin; ⊙ morning-dusk) From Troulos (bus stop 20), a road heads 4km north to the serene 17th-century Moni Panagias Kounistras, worth a visit for the fine frescoes adorning its *katholikon*.

🏃 Activities

Diving

The small islets off the south shore of Skiathos make for great diving. Rates average €40 to €50 for half-day dives, equipment included.

The dive instructor team Theofanis and Eva of Octopus Diving Centre (☑ 6944168958, 24270 24549; www.odc-skiathos.com; New Harbour) lead dives around Tsougria and Tsougriaki islets for beginners and experts alike. Call or enquire at their boat on the new port.

Skiathos Diving Centre (☑ 6977081444; www.skiathosdiving.gr; Papadiamanti) is also popular for first-time divers.

Hiking

A 6km-long hiking route begins at Moni Evangelistrias, eventually reaching **Cape Kastro** before circling back through Agios Apostolis. Kastro is a spring mecca for **bird-watchers**, who may spot long-necked Mediterranean shags or blue rock-thrushes skimming the waves.

Sleeping & Eating

Achladies Apartments APARTMENT $
(☑ 24270 22486; https://sites.google.com/site/achladiesapartments; Achladies Bay; d/tr/f incl breakfast €45/60/75; P �🛜) This welcoming gem, 5km south of Skiathos Town, in addition to kitchenette rooms (two-night minimum stay) with ceiling fans, features an eco-friendly tortoise sanctuary and rambling succulent garden winding down to a sandy beach. From here, water taxis connect with Skiathos Town and Koukounaries Beach.

Camping Koukounaries CAMPGROUND $
(☑ 24270 49250; camp sites per adult/tent €11/free; P ☎) Shaded by fig and mulberry trees opposite Koukounaries Beach, with spotless bathroom and cooking facilities, a mini-market and taverna.

★ **Atrium Hotel** LUXURY HOTEL $$$
(☑ 24270 49345; www.atriumhotel.gr; Paraskevi Beach; s/d/ste incl breakfast from €120/160/200; P ✳ @ 🛜 🏊) Traditional architecture and modern touches make this hillside perch the best in its class. Rooms are low-key elegant, with basin sinks and private balconies. Amenities include sauna, children's pool, billiards, ping-pong and a lavish breakfast buffet to start the day.

Panorama Pizza PIZZA $
(pizzas €7-10; ⏱ noon-4pm & 7pm-late) Hilltop retreat off the ring road for brick-oven pizza and killer views.

Salt & Pepper INTERNATIONAL $$
(☑ 2427049329; mains €8-14) This upscale addition to the Skiathos food scene features innovative fish and meat grills and a variety of traditional salad-vegie dishes. A full bar anchors the outdoor garden. Opposite the Troulos turn-off (bus stop 18).

Skopelos Σκόπελος

POP 5400

Skopelos is a handsome island of pine forests, vineyards, olive groves and orchards of plums and almonds, which find their way into many local dishes.

Like Skiathos, the high cliffs of the northwest coast are exposed, while the sheltered southeast coast harbours several sand-and-pebble beaches. There are two settlements: the capital and main port of Skopelos Town on the east coast and the northwest village of Glossa, 2km north of Loutraki, the island's second port (but referred to in ferry timetables as 'Glossa').

❶ Getting There & Away

BOAT

Skopelos has two ports, Skopelos Town and Glossa (aka Loutraki), both with links to Volos,

BOAT SERVICES FROM SKOPELOS

DESTINATION	PORT	TIME	FARE	FREQUENCY
Agios Konstantinos*	Glossa	3½hr	€38	1 daily
Agios Konstantinos**	Skopelos Town	2½hr	€50	1 daily
Alonnisos	Skopelos Town	40min	€6	1 daily
Alonnisos**	Skopelos Town	20min	€9	2-3 daily
Skiathos	Skopelos Town	1hr	€10	2-3 daily
Skiathos*	Skopelos Town	45min	€16	2 daily
Skiathos**	Glossa	30min	€10	2 daily
Evia (Paralia Kymis)	Skopelos Town	7hr	€30	3 weekly
Volos	Skopelos Town	3¾hr	€28	2 daily
Volos**	Glossa	2½hr	€40	1 daily
Volos*	Skopelos Town	3hr	€48	2-3 daily

*fast-ferry services
**hydrofoil services

Skopelos

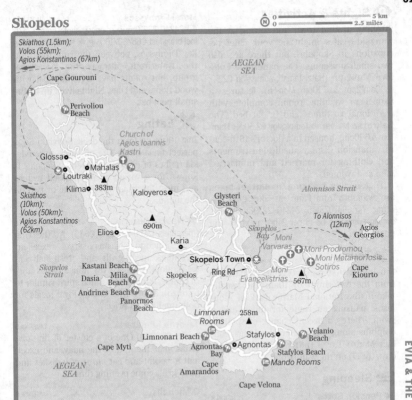

Skiathos (1.5km);
Volos (55km);
Agios Konstantinos (67km)

AEGEAN SEA

Cape Gourouni

Perivoliou Beach

Church of Agios Ioannis Kastri

Glossa

Mahalas

Loutraki

Klima   383m

Kaloyeros

Glysteri Beach

Alonnisos Strait

Skiathos (10km);
Volos (50km);
Agios Konstantinos (62km)

690m

Elios

Karia

Skopelos Bay

Moni Narvaras

To Alonnisos (12km)

Agios Georgios

Skopelos Town

Moni Prodromou

Moni Metamorfosis Sotiros

Cape Kiourto

Kastani Beach

Milia Beach

Dasia

Skopelos

Ring Rd

Moni Evangelistrias   567m

Andrines Beach

Panormos Beach

Limnonari Rooms

258m

Limnonari Beach

Stafylos

Velanio Beach

Cape Myti

Agnontas Bay

Agnontas

Stafylos Beach

Mando Rooms

AEGEAN SEA

Cape Amarandos

Cape Velona

Skopelos Strait

EVIA & THE SPORADES SKOPELOS

Agios Konstantinos, and the islands of Skiathos, Alonnisos and Skyros.

Tickets are available from **Hellenic Seaways** (24240 22767; fax 24240 23608) in Skopelos Town and the port of Glossa (Loutraki); Madro Travel (p617) also handles tickets for Volos, Agios Konstantinos and Thessaloniki. In Glossa, **Lemonis Travel** (24240 23608; waterfront) handles tickets for Skyros.

ⓘ Getting Around

BOAT

A water taxi departs Skopelos Town late morning for Glysteri Beach (€5 each way).

BUS

In summer, there are six buses per day from Skopelos Town to Glossa/Loutraki (€5, one hour) and Elios (€3.80, 45 minutes); and three more that go only as far as Panormos (€2.80, 25 minutes), Milia (€3.50, 35 minutes), Agnontas (€1.60, 15 minutes) and Stafylos (€1.60, 15 minutes).

CAR & MOTORCYCLE

Car- and motorcycle-hire outlets line the eastern end of the waterfront near the ring road, including **Motor Tours** (24240 22986; fax 24240 22602) and **Magic Cars** (6973790936, 24240 23250).

TAXI

Taxis wait by the bus stop. A taxi to Stafylos is €7.50, to Limnonari €13 and to Glossa €30.

Skopelos Town   Σκόπελος

Skopelos Town skirts a semicircular bay and rises in tiers up a hillside of dazzling white houses with bright shutters and flower-adorned balconies, ending at an old fortress and a cluster of four churches.

The town's waterfront is flanked by two quays. The old quay wraps around the western end of the harbour; the new quay at the eastern end is used by all ferries and hydrofoils.

◉ Sights & Activities

Strolling around town and sitting at the waterside cafes might be your chief occupations in Skopelos, but there are also two small museums. The handsome **Folklore Museum** (Hatzistamati; admission €2.50; ⊙10am-2pm & 7-10pm Mon-Fri) features a Skopelean wedding room, complete with traditional costumes and bridal bed. The **Bakratsa Museum** (admission €2.50; ⊙ 11am-1pm & 6-10pm), housed in a doctor's 18th-century mansion, displays medical instruments and clothing for married and unmarried men and women.

High-quality **trekking/mountain bikes** are available from Panos at **Skopelos Cycling** (☑6947023145, 24240 22398; skopeloscycling@yahoo.gr; €8-18 per 24hr), next to the post office.

⟲ Tours

Day-long **cruise boats** (€20 to €40) depart from the waterfront by 10am and usually take in the National Marine Park of Alonnisos, pausing en route for lunch and a swim. There's a decent chance of spotting dolphins along the way. For bookings, contact Madro Travel (p617) or Thalpos Holidays (p617) on the waterfront.

🛌 Sleeping

★ Pension Sotos   PENSION $
(☑24240 22549; www.skopelos.net/sotos; s/d from €30/45; ❄ 🛜) The pine-floored rooms at this charming waterfront pension are each a bit different; an old brick oven serves as a handy shelf in one. There's a relaxing interior courtyard, flowery terrace and communal kitchen, all managed by the welcoming and resourceful Alexandra.

Hotel Agnanti   HOTEL $
(☑6978713252, 24240 22722; www.skopelos.net/agnanti; s/d/tr from €40/50/70; P ❄ @ 🛜) Theo and Eleni run the show at this rustic 12-room oasis on the old quay, with ceiling fans, period furniture, ceramic decorations, plus a paperback lending library.

Lina's Guest House   PENSION $
(☑24240 23976; r €30-40; ❄ 🛜) Tucked above the family's waterfront gift shop are four simple rooms, with wooden floors and homey decorations. Two rooms overlook the harbour, and two face the quieter back street.

Hotel Dionyssos   HOTEL $$
(☑24240 23210; www.dionyssoshotel.com; s/d/tr incl breakfast €65/80/100; P ❄ 🛜 ⊠) The low-key Dionyssos, between the ring road and the waterfront, attracts the occasional group, but rooms have a homey feel with wood floors and rugs. Nights liven up by the small pool bar.

✗ Eating

Just 100m up from the dock, Souvlaki Sq is perfect for a quick bite of *gyros* or souvlakia (cubes of meat on skewers). Skopelos is known for a variety of plum-based recipes and most tavernas will have one or two on the menu.

★ Nastas Ouzerie   GREEK $
(mezedhes €2.50-5, mains €6-10) At the ring road junction, Nastas serves excellent mezedhes, meat grills and fresh fish entrees, along with worthy house wines and, of course, *tsipouro* (distilled spirit similar to to ouzo). A favourite among loyal locals for both quality and price.

Taverna Klimataria   TAVERNA $
(mains €5.50-10) One of a cluster of fine tavernas near the end of the quay, and excellent for point-and-eat *mayirefta* dishes and good grills come evening time.

O Michalis   CAFE $
(snacks €3-5) The red door gives away this snappy hole-in-the-wall about 50m behind Sotos Pension. Mihalis' *tyropita* (cheese pie) is superb, and at night the place morphs into a mellow wine bar.

To Perivoli Restaurant   GREEK $$
(☑24240 23758; mains €7-14) Just beyond Souvlaki Sq, To Perivoli delivers excellent Greek cuisine in an elegant courtyard setting. Specialities include rolled pork with *koromila* (local plums) in wine sauce, plus fine Greek wines.

Anna's Restaurant   GREEK $$
(☑24240 24734; Gifthorema; mains €7-19) A lone palm tree marks this handsome and upscale alleyway bistro, serving authentic Skopelos dishes like sautéed veal with plums.

🍷 Drinking & Nightlife

Away from the waterfront, try mellow standby **Oionos Blue Bar** (☑6942406136), and the newer **Hidden Door**.

Platanos Jazz Bar   BAR
(☑ 24240 23661) Near the end of the old quay, this leafy cafe-bar is open for morning coffee and late-night drinks.

Bardon   BAR
(☑ 24240 24494; www.bardonskopelos.com) Set in the courtyard of a renovated olive factory. Live music on most summer weekends.

Mercurios Music Cafe-Bar   BAR
(☑ 24240 24593; 🛜) Mellow verandah bar and gallery over the waterfront mixes music, mojitos and straight-up margaritas.

☆ Entertainment

Ouzerie Anatoli   TRADITIONAL MUSIC
(⊙ 8pm-2am summer) Wait till at least 11pm, then head to this breezy outdoor *ouzerie*, high above the *kastro*, to hear traditional *rembetika* music sung by Skopelos' own exponent of the Greek blues and bouzouki master, Georgos Xindaris.

🔒 Shopping

Two waterfront stand-bys are Ploumisti Shop and Archipelagos Shop for quality ceramics, small paintings, icons and handmade jewellery.

ℹ Information

There are four ATMs along the waterfront, which is also wired for free wi-fi access.
Health Centre (☑ 24240 22222; Ring Rd, opposite fire station)
Police (☑ 24240 22235; above National Bank)
Port Police (☑ 24240 22180; Quay)
Post Office (opposite Panagia Church; ⊙ 7.30am-2pm)

TRAVEL AGENCIES
Madro Travel (☑ 24240 22300; www.madro travel.com) At the end of the old port, Madro does accommodation and ticketing, arranges walking trips, island boat excursions, cooking lessons and even marriages (partners extra).
Thalpos Holidays (☑ 24240 29036; www. holidayislands.com) The helpful staff at this full-service waterfront agency also help with apartment and villa accommodation, boat hire, island excursions and weddings.

Glossa & Loutraki
Γλώσσα & Λουτράκι

Glossa, Skopelos' other settlement, is a whitewashed delight with a cluster of shops and eateries. A 2km road winds down from the small square to the laid-back port of Loutraki ('Glossa' in timetables). A shorter *kalderimi* (cobblestoned path) connects both villages as well. Fans of the 2008 movie *Mamma Mia!* can start their pilgrimage in Glossa to reach the film's little church, Agios Ioannis sto Kastri (St John of the Castle).

Loutraki means 'small bath' and you will find the remains of ancient Roman baths at the archaeological kiosk on the port.

🛌 Sleeping & Eating

To sleep nearer the Loutraki ferry dock, try Rania Studios (☑ 24240 33710; Loutraki; studio/apt from €35/50; P ✴ 🛜) or Hotel Selenunda (☑ 24240 34073; www.skopelosweb. gr/selenunda; Loutraki; d/tr/f from €45/60/75; P ✴ @ 🛜), both reliable and friendly.

Pansion Platana   PENSION $
(☑ 24240 33188; pansionplatana@hotmail.com; Glossa; r from €35; ✴) Between the bakery and Elefteria church, this cosy and welcoming domatia has overhead fans, kitchenettes and balcony views. Greek-Australian owner Eleni provides tea and tips.

★ Flisvos Taverna   TAVERNA $
(Loutraki; mains €3.50-7.50) Perched above the seawall 50m north of the car park, family-friendly Flisvos offers fresh fish, *mousakas* (baked layers of eggplant or zucchini, minced meat and potatoes topped with cheese sauce) and perfect appetisers such as tzatziki (sauce of grated cucumber, yoghurt and garlic) and *taramasalata*. Simple Greek fare at its best.

Agnanti Taverna & Bar   GREEK FUSION $$
(☑ 24240 33076; Glossa; mains €8-14) Enjoy the views of Evia from swank Agnanti's rooftop terrace, along with superb Greek fusion dishes like grilled sardines on pitta with sea fennel and sun-dried tomatoes.

Around Skopelos

Skopelos has several monasteries that can be visited on a beautiful scenic drive or daylong trek above Skopelos Town. Begin by following Monastery Rd, which skirts the bay and then climbs inland to the 18th-century Moni Evangelistrias, now a convent. The monastery's prize, aside from the superb views, is a gilded iconostasis containing an 11th-century icon of the Virgin Mary.

Further on, the 16th-century Moni Metamorfosis Sotiros is the oldest monastery on the island. From here a narrow road leads to

17th-century **Moni Varvaras**, with a view to the sea, and 18th-century **Moni Prodromou** (now a convent), 8km from Skopelos Town.

Most of Skopelos' best beaches are on the sheltered southwest and west coasts. The first one you come to is sand-and-pebble **Stafylos Beach**, 4km southeast of Skopelos Town. From its eastern end, a path leads over a small headland to the quieter **Velanio Beach**, the island's official nudist beach and a great snorkelling spot. Lovely **Agnontas**, 3km west of Stafylos, has a pebble-and-sand beach from where caïques sail to the superior and sandy **Limnonari Beach**, in a sheltered bay flanked by rocky outcrops.

From Agnontas the road cuts inland through pine forests before re-emerging at pretty **Panormos Beach**, with a few tavernas and domatia. One kilometre further, little **Andrines Beach** is sandy and less crowded. The next two bays, Milia and Kastani, are excellent for swimming. On the island's northeast coast, serene **Perivioliou Beach** is a 25-minute drive from Glossa.

☞ Tours

If you can't tell a twin-tailed pascha butterfly from a leopard orchid, join one of Heather Parsons' **guided walks** (☑ 6945249328; www.skopelos-walks.com; tours €15-20). Her four-hour Panormos walk follows a centuries-old path across the island, ending at a beach taverna, with wonderful views to Alonnisos and Evia along the way. Her book, *Skopelos Trails,* has graded trail descriptions. Heather also offers **Mamma Mia! jeep tours** to several of the movie's filming locations.

🛏 Sleeping & Eating

There are small hotels, domatia, tavernas and beach canteens at Stafylos, Agnontas, Limnonari, Panormos, Andrines and Milia.

Limnonari Rooms & Taverna   APARTMENT $
(☑ 24240 23046; www.skopelos.net/limnonari rooms; Limnonari Beach; d/tr/ste from €35/60/80; P ❄ ☎) This cluster of well-equipped apartments faces beautiful and sandy Limnonari Bay. The family's garden taverna serves vegetarian *mousakas,* fish and meat grills, along with owner Kostas' homemade olives and feta.

★ Mando Rooms   APARTMENT $$
(☑ 24240 23917; www.skopelos.cc/mando; Stafylos; d/tr/f incl breakfast from €60/80/100; P ❄ ☎) Having its own cove on Stafylos Bay is a good start at this well-managed family-oriented lodging, with private verandahs, communal kitchen, satellite TV and a solid platform over the rocks to enter the sea for swimming and snorkelling.

Alonnisos   Αλόννησος

POP 2700

Alonnisos rises from the sea in a mountain of greenery, with thick stands of aleppo pine and kermes oak, mastic and arbutus bushes, vineyards, olive and fruit trees, threaded with perfumy patches of wild oregano, sage and thyme. The west and north coasts are mostly steep and rocky, but the east coast is speckled with small bays and pebble-and-sand beaches.

As lovely as it is, Alonnisos has had its share of bad luck. In 1952 a thriving cottage wine industry came to a halt when vines imported from California were infested with phylloxera insects. Robbed of their livelihood, many islanders moved away. Then, in 1965, an earthquake destroyed the hilltop capital of Alonnisos Town (known as Old Alonnisos or Hora). The inhabitants were subsequently rehoused in temporary dwellings at Patitiri, which has since evolved into a quaint island port.

❶ Getting There & Away

Alonnisos' main port of Patitiri has links to Volos and Agios Konstantinos on the mainland and the other Sporades isles of Skiathos, Skopelos and Skyros, as well as the port of Paralia Kymis on Evia.

Tickets can be purchased from **Alkyon Travel** (☑ 24240 65220) or **Alonnisos Travel** (☑ 24240 65188) in Patitiri.

Boat Services from Alonnisos

DESTINATION	TIME	FARE	FREQUENCY
Agios Konstantinos**	4hr	€50	1 daily
Evia (Paralia Kymis)	6hr	€30	3 weekly
Skopelos (Glossa)*	45min	€14	3-4 daily
Skiathos	2hr	€11	4 weekly
Skiathos*	1½hr	€17	4-5 daily
Skopelos	40min	€6	1 daily
Skopelos*	20min	€9.50	2-3 daily
Volos	5hr	€28	1 daily
Volos*	3hr	€48	3 daily

*hydrofoil services
**fast-ferry services

Alonnisos

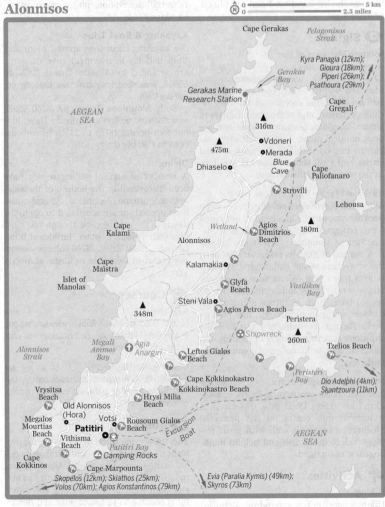

Getting Around

BUS

One bus plies the route between Patitiri and Old Alonnisos (€1.50), and then to Steni Vala (€1.90). Additionally, a summer beach bus (☑ 6973805610; €5) leaves Patitiri around 10.30am for points north and returns after 4pm.

CAR & MOTORCYCLE

Several motorcycle-hire outlets cluster near the waterfront, including reliable **I'm Bike** (☑ 24240 65010). For cars, try **Albedo Travel** (☑ 24240 65804) in Patitiri.

TAXI

The four taxis on the island (driven by Georgos, Periklis, Theodoros and Spyros) congregate opposite the quay. It's about €6 to Old Alonnisos (Hora), €10 to Leftos Gialos and €13 to Steni Vala.

Patitiri   Πατητήρι

Patitiri ('wine press') sits between two sandstone cliffs at the southern end of the east coast. The quay is in the centre of the waterfront, from where two roads lead inland. There are no road signs: people refer to them as the left-hand road and right-hand, or main, road.

◉ Sights

Folklore Museum of the Northern Sporades
MUSEUM

(☏ 24240 66250; www.alonissosmuseum.com; adult/child €4/free; ⊙11am-6pm May & Sep, to 9pm Jun-Aug) This exceptional museum includes extensive and well-signed displays of pirates' weapons, blacksmith tools and antique nautical maps. A small cafe overlooking the harbour exhibits the work of local artists, and a gift shop is open to the public. At the west end of the harbour.

National Marine Park of Alonnisos-Northern Sporades
PARK

(www.alonissos-park.gr) In a country not noted for its ecological foresight, the National Marine Park of Alonnisos is a welcome innovation. Started in 1992, its prime aim has been the protection of the endangered Mediterranean monk seal (*Monachus monachus*) and several rare seabirds. In summer, licensed boats from Alonnisos and Skopelos conduct excursions through the pristine park. Though it's unlikely you'll find the shy monk seal, your chances of spotting dolphins (striped, bottlenose and common) are fairly good.

MOM Information Centre
MUSEUM

(☏ 24240 66350; www.mom.gr; Patitiri; ⊙10am-10pm 1 Jun-30 Sep) Don't miss this excellent waterfront info centre on the protected Mediterranean monk seal, with great displays, videos in English and helpful multilingual staff on hand.

🏃 Activities

Hiking

Hiking opportunities abound on Alonnisos and over a dozen trails have been waymarked. At the bus stop in Old Alonnisos, a blue noticeboard details several walks. From Patitiri, a 2km *kalderimi donkey track* winds up through shrubbery and orchards before bringing you to Old Alonnisos. From Agios Dimitrios Beach to the wetland at Kastanorema, a **circular walk** with striking views takes about two hours. Popular trails are highlighted on both the excellent Anavasi and Terrain maps of Alonnisos.

Consider a **guided walk** (☏ 6979162443; www.alonnisoswalks.co.uk; walks €15-30) with island resident Chris Browne. His book *Alonnisos Through the Souls of Your Feet* con-

tains trail descriptions plus snorkelling and kayaking sites.

Kayaking & Boat Trips

Sea kayaking excursions around Alonnisos, from half-day to overnight cove camping, are arranged by **Albedo Travel** (☏ 24240 65804; www.albedotravel.com; sea kayaking per half-day €30).

Both **Alonnisos Travel** (☏ 24240 65188; www.alonnisostravel.gr) and Albedo Travel hire out four-person 18Hp to 25Hp motorboats (€48 to €60 per day).

Diving

A number of ancient sailing vessels have been discovered at the bottom of the shallow sea around Alonnisos. Several areas have opened (or are scheduled to open) for diving in the marine park, though you must dive with a guide. Contact Hariklea at **Ikion Diving** (☏ 6984181598, 24240 65158; www.ikiondiving.gr/en) in Steni Vala, or Kostas at Albedo Travel.

🎓 Courses

Kali Thea
YOGA

(☏ 6975930108, 24240 65513; www.kalithea.org; ⊙May-Oct) Hatha yoga and massage on outskirts of Old Alonnisos.

Christopher Hughes
ART

(☏ 6978645776; www.paintingalonissos.com; ⊙May-Oct) Runs five-day painting courses (watercolours and oils).

👉 Tours

Two full-service travel agencies on the waterfront provide maps and arrange popular marine park excursions. Albedo Travel (p620) and Alonnisos Travel (p620) run marine park trips, plus snorkelling and swimming excursions to Skantzoura and nearby islands.

Popular round-the-island excursions (€40) aboard the *Gorgona,* a classic Greek boat captained by charming island native **Pakis Athanasiou** (☏ 6978386588), visit the **Blue Cave** on the northeast coast and the islets of **Kyra Panagia** and **Peristera** in the marine park, with lunch and swimming breaks along the way.

🛌 Sleeping

★ Liadromia Hotel
HOTEL $

(☏ 24240 65521; www.liadromia.gr; d/tr/ste incl breakfast from €40/60/75; P ❄ @ 🛜) This welcoming and impeccably maintained hotel

THE MONK SEAL

Once populating hundreds of colonies in the Black Sea, the Mediterranean Sea and along Africa's Atlantic coast, the Mediterranean monk seal has been reduced to about 600 individuals. Half of these live in the seas around Greece.

One of the earth's rarest mammals, the seal is now one of the 20 most endangered species worldwide. Major threats include incidental capture in fishing gear, decreasing food supply as fisheries decline, habitat destruction and pollution. However, once common killings by fishermen – who saw the seal as a pest that tore holes in their nets and robbed their catch – have diminished with the recognition that protecting the seal also promotes recovery of fish stocks.

For more information, visit the website of **MOM** (Hellenic Society for the Study & Protection of the Monk Seal; www.mom.gr).

overlooking the harbour was Patitiri's first. All the rooms have character to spare, from hand-embroidered curtains to period furnishings. The gracious owner, Maria, takes obvious delight in making it all work.

Pension Pleiades PENSION **$**
(☑ 24240 65235; www.pleiadeshotel.gr; s/d/tr from €25/35/50; ❄️ @) Take the stairway behind the newsstand to find this bright budget option with views over Patitiri Bay and a sunset happy hour.

Camping Rocks CAMPGROUND **$**
(☑ 6973230977, 24240 65410; camp sites per adult/tent €7.50/3) Follow the signposts 1km south to this clean and shaded coastal spot with cafe.

Paradise Hotel HOTEL **$$**
(☑ 24240 65213; www.paradise-hotel.gr; s/d incl breakfast from €45/60; P ❄️ 🛜 🏊) Wood ceilings and stone-tiled floors give a rustic feel to these comfortable rooms, along with modern bathrooms and shuttered balconies which overlook both bay and harbour. Beyond the pool bar, a stairway leads to a small bay.

🍽 Eating & Drinking

⭐ **Ouzerie Archipelagos** GREEK **$**
(mains €4-8) To get the feel of this very Greek establishment, pick a table towards the back where locals gather to order round after round of excellent mezedhes, always-fresh grilled fish and local favourite *tsipouro* as the night rolls on.

Pi & Fi QUICK EATS **$**
(snacks €2-4) Pi & Fi roughly means quick and easy, such as their grab-and-go kebabs and pitta souvlakia. Located opposite the police station.

To Kamaki Ouzerie TAVERNA **$$**
(mains €5-15) This longtime local favourite, next to the National Bank, offers well-priced fresh fish and tasty vegetarian plates. Weekends often feature a family bouzouki player.

Cafe Bistro Helios BAR
(snacks €3-7) Snappy bistro hidden in plain view, up the steps from the National Bank. Well-priced small plates, with an international twist.

ℹ️ Information

National Bank of Greece ATM (main road)
Police (☑ 24240 65205; main road)
Port Police (☑ 24240 65595; Quay)
Post Office (main road; ⊙ 7.30am-2pm)

Old Alonnisos   Παλιά Αλόννησος

Old Alonnisos (aka Palia Alonnisos and Hora) is an enchanting place with panoramic views and winding stepped alleys. From the main road just outside the village, an old donkey path leads down to pebbled Megalos Mourtias Beach.

🛏 Sleeping

Elma's Houses APARTMENT **$**
(☑ 6945466776, 24240 66108; elmashouses@yahoo.gr; d/q from €55/70) Families will appreciate either of Elma's two roomy stone houses, each smartly decorated, with full kitchen, comfy beds and great views from the courtyard. Near the old school in the village.

⭐ **Konstantina Studios** APARTMENT **$$**
(☑ 6932271540, 24240 66165; www.konstantinastudios.gr; s/d incl breakfast from €50/85; P ❄️ 🛜) Among the nicest accommodation on Alonnisos, these handsome and quiet studios with fully equipped kitchens come

THE ORIGINAL CHEESE PIE

Tyropita (cheese pie), almost deified in its birthplace of the northern Sporades, is made with goat cheese rolled in delicate filo dough, coiled up, fried quickly and served hot – a method that evolved in the wood-fired ovens of Alonnisos. Eventually the pies found their way to the country kitchens of Skopelos.

In the 1990s a daytime TV host touted the pie, but credited Skopelos with its origin. Frozen 'Skopelos Cheese Pie' soon showed up in mainland supermarkets, even in the Athens' airport snack bars. Stunned Alonnisos folk still can't get over what's happened to their simple recipe. As Mahi, a Skopelos business woman, confided, 'Basically, we stole it!'

with balcony views of the southwest coast. The owner, Konstantina, fetches her guests from the dock, serves homemade breakfasts and offers loads of tips for navigating Alonnisos.

🍴 Eating & Drinking

⭐ **Hayati**　　　　　　　　　CONFECTIONERY **$**
(snacks €2-4; ⊙9am-2am) Hayati is a *glyko-poleio* (sweets shop) by day and a piano bar by night, with knock-out views of the island round the clock. Morning fare includes made-to-order *tyropita*. Later, you'll find homemade pastas, grills, custards and cakes, along with the gracious hospitality of owner-cooks Meni and Angela. It's a five-minute walk from the village square.

Astrofengia　　　　　　　　　GREEK **$$**
(mains €5-13) Patitiri residents think nothing of driving up to the Hora for well-prepared Greek standards, including a vegie *mousakas*. Some just go for the *galaktoboureko* dessert (custard slice).

Aerides Cafe-Bar　　　　　　　　　BAR
(⊙9am-5pm & 7pm-2am) Maria and Yiannis make the drinks, pick the music and scoop the ice cream in summer at this hip hole-in-the-wall on the square.

Sunset Cafe　　　　　　　　　CAFE
(⊙10am-2am) Between the Hora and Patitiri. Summer weekends feature live music in the courtyard.

Around Alonnisos

Alonnisos' main road reaches the northern tip of the island at Gerakas (19km), home to an EU-funded marine research station. North of Patitiri, several roads descend to small fishing bays and secluded beaches.

Along the east coast, the first bay from Patitiri is tiny **Rousoum Gialos**, tucked between Patitiri and Votsi. Next is **Votsi**, home to **Maria's Votsi Pension** (⊘24240 65510; www.pension-votsi.gr; Votsi; d/tr from €40/50; P❀@❂), with immaculate rooms and hospitality to spare. Two kilometres on, **Cape Kokkinokastro** is the site of the ancient and submerged city of Ikos. Continuing north, the road reaches **Leftos Gialos**, with a pebble beach and the superb **Taverna Eleonas** (mains €5-11), with exceptional *pites* (pies) and wine made by owner Nikos.

Steni Vala, a small fishing village and deep-water yacht port, has 50-odd rooms in domatia. Try **Ikaros Cafe & Market** (⊘24240 65390) for reliable lodging information. Four busy tavernas overlook the small marina, with **Taverna Fanari** (mains €4-9) claiming the best views. Small and sandy **Agios Petros Beach**, just south of the village, is home to flower-adorned and hidden luxe lodging, **Ilya Studios** (⊘210 803 0272, 6938327401; www.ilyasuites.gr; ste/villla from €80/160).

Kalamakia, 2km further north and the last village of note, has a few domatia and three fine dockside fish tavernas where the morning catch seems to jump from boat to plate.

Beyond Kalamakia, the sealed road continues 3km to a **wetland** marsh and **Agios Dimitrios Beach**, with a truck-canteen and domatia opposite a graceful stretch of white pebbles. Beyond this, the road narrows to a footpath heading inland.

Islets Around Alonnisos

Alonnisos is surrounded by eight uninhabited islets, all rich in flora and fauna. **Piperi**, the furthest island northeast of Alonnisos, is a refuge for the monk seal and is strictly off limits. Gioura, also off limits, is home to an unusual species of wild goat known for the crucifix-shaped marking on its spine. Excursion boats visit an old monastery and olive press on Kyra Panagia. The most remote of the group, Psathoura, boasts the submerged remains of an ancient city and the brightest lighthouse in the Aegean.

Peristera, just off Alonnisos' east coast, has sandy beaches and the remains of a castle. Nearby Lehousa is known for its stalactite-filled sea caves. Skantzoura, to the southeast of Alonnisos, is the habitat of the Eleonora's falcon and the rare Audouin's seagull. The eighth island in the group, situated between Peristera and Skantzoura, is known as Dio Adelphi (Two Brothers). Each 'brother' is actually a small island.

Skyros Σκύρος

POP 2888

Skyros, the largest of the Sporades group, can seem like two separate islands: the north has small bays, rolling farmland and pine forests while the south features arid hills and a rocky shoreline. In Greek mythology, Skyros was hiding place of the young Achilles.

Skyros was also the last port of call for the English poet Rupert Brooke (1887–1915), who died of septicaemia on a French hospital ship off the coast of Skyros en route to the Battle of Gallipoli.

ℹ Getting There & Away

AIR

In addition to domestic flights, Skyros airport has occasional charter flights from Oslo and Amsterdam.

For tickets, contact **Sky Express** (☑ 28102 23500; www.skyexpress.gr) or visit Skyros Travel Agency (p626).

Domestic Flights from Skyros

DESTINATION	TIME	FARE	FREQUENCY
Athens	25min	€28	3 weekly
Thessaloniki	35min	€91	2-3 weekly

BOAT

Skyros' main port is Linaria, with ferry links to Evia (Paralia Kymis), and Alonnisos and Skopelos in summer.

Purchase tickets from Skyros Travel (p626) in Skyros Town or the ticket kiosk at the dock in Linaria or in Paralia Kymis (Evia).

Boat Services from Skyros

DESTINATION	TIME	FARE	FREQUENCY
Evia (Paralia Kymis)	1¾hr	€9	1-2 daily
Alonnisos	6hr	€25	3 weekly
Skopelos	6½hr	€25	3 weekly

ℹ Getting Around

BUS & TAXI

A bus runs from Linaria to Skyros Town, Magazia and Molos (€2); and from Skyros Town to the airport (€2.50). A taxi from Skyros Town to Linaria is €18; to the airport, €25.

CAR & MOTORCYCLE

Cars, motorbikes and mountain bikes can all be hired in Skyros Town from **Martina's Rentals** (☑ 6974752380, 22220 92022), **Vayos Motorbikes** (☑ 22220 92957) (and bicycles) and **Angelis Cars** (☑ 22220 91888).

Skyros Town Σκύρος

Skyros' capital is draped over a high rocky bluff. It's topped by a 13th-century Venetian fortress, and is laced with labyrinthine, smooth cobblestone streets that invite wandering, but were designed to keep out the elements, including pirates.

The main thoroughfare (Agoras) is a lively jumble of people, tavernas, bars and shops flanked by winding alleyways. About 100m past the *plateia*, the main drag of Agoras forks left and zigzags to two small

THE GREEK BLUES

For one week in mid-July, the Manos Faltaïts Folk Museum is host to a rembetika music festival (www.rebetikoseminar.com/index.php) celebrating a music which started in Smyrna, and came to Greece with refugee musicians who found their way to the dens and dives of the Greek underground during the 1920s. This often melancholy and blues-tinged music is closely tied to the history and soul of Greece. There are daily instrument and voice workshops, films and seminars. Dinner at local tavernas and more music fill the evening hours, and the week concludes with a Saturday night concert, open to the public.

Skyros

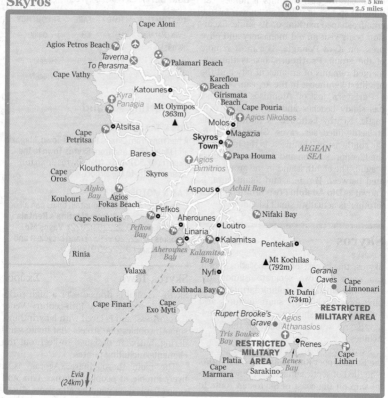

museums adjacent to Plateia Rupert Brooke, from where the steps descend 1km to Magazia Beach.

Sights & Activities

Manos Faltaïts Folk Museum MUSEUM
(22220 91232; www.faltaits.gr/english/museum.htm; Plateia Rupert Brooke; admission €2, incl tour €5; 10am-2pm & 6-9pm) This not-to-be-missed gem houses the collection of Skyrian ethnologist Manos Faltaïts, detailing the mythology and folklore of Skyros. The 19th-century mansion is a multi-level labyrinth of Skyrian costumes and embroidery, antique furniture and ceramics, daggers and cooking pots, vintage photographs and a small gift shop and cafe overlooking the sea.

Archaeological Museum MUSEUM
(Plateia Rupert Brooke; admission €2; 8.30am-3pm Tue-Sun) Along with Mycenaean pottery found near Magazia, there is a traditional Skyrian house interior, transported in its entirety from the benefactor's home.

Half-Marathon RACE
(22220 92707; nikonisi@hotmail.com) Each year on the last Saturday in September, Skyros hosts what could also be termed half-marathon, half-party. The race starts in Linaria and ends at the plateia in Skyros Town. A mini-marathon for the children sets the tone, all followed by music and dancing, which is the real point.

Courses

Reiki courses, lodging included, are offered year-round by longtime island resident and reiki master Janet Smith (6979292976, 22220 93510; www.reikisosimple.com).

Tours

Local owner Chrysanthi Zygogianni started Feel ingreece (22220 93100; www.feelin

greece.gr) in 2008, dedicated to helping sustain the best of Skyrian culture. The focus is on the local arts and the island's natural environment, in cooperation with the EU-supported Skyros Life Project. The office arranges hiking excursions to glimpse wild Skyrian horses and organises wetland bird-watching trips around the island. Pottery, woodcarving, Skyrian cooking, Greek dance lessons and boat trips are among the many offerings. Prices begin at €20.

Contact the well-informed and resourceful **Niko Sekkes** (☑ 6976983712, 22220 92707; nikonisi@hotmail.com) for details on his impromptu tours of the island, town and the remarkable Manos Faltaïts Folk Museum.

🛌 Sleeping

Pension Nikolas   PENSION $
(☑ 22220 91778; s/d/tr €35/50/60; P ❄ 🛜) Set back on a quiet road, this friendly pension is only a five-minute walk to busy Agoras. Upper rooms have air-conditioning and balconies; the lower rooms have fans and open onto a shady garden.

Elena Hotel   HOTEL $
(☑ 22220 91738; hotel.elena@yahoo.gr; s/d/tr from €25/35/45; P ❄ 🛜) The convenient Elena is just 100m from the main square, easy to find after a night on the town. Rooms are simple and clean, and a rooftop bar doubles as a breakfast spot on summer mornings.

★Hotel Nefeli & Skyrian Studios   BOUTIQUE HOTEL $$
(☑ 22220 91964; www.skyros-nefeli.gr; d/studio/ste incl breakfast from €70/90/240; P ❄ @ 🛜 ⚊) This smart and welcoming hotel on the edge of town has an easy minimalist-meets-Skyrian feel to it, with handsome furnishings

and swank bathrooms. The hotel and adjacent studios share a saltwater swimming pool and outdoor bar. Breakfast includes savoury and sweet Greek favourites, plus fresh-squeezed juice.

🍴 Eating

Skyros welcomes a steady number of visiting Athenians, with the pleasant result that island cooks do not cater to touristy tongues.

★Maryetis Restaurant   GREEK $
(Agoras; mains €6-9) The local favourite in town for grilled fish and octopus *stifadho* (stew), tasty pork dishes and great mezedhes such as black-eyed beans and fava dip. Wines and service both excellent.

Cafe Barba Yiannis   GREEK $
(Agoras; mains €4-8) Past the National Bank, this traditional *ouzerie* serves fresh mezedhes and juicy grills, along with excellent Skyrian bread, dips and drink.

Taverna Lambros   TAVERNA $
(mains €5-9) Hospitable family-run Lambros, 3km south towards Linaria, draws local favour for its generous grills, fresh fish and lobster, and Skyrian cheese bread.

🍷 Drinking & Nightlife

Nightlife in Skyros Town centres mostly around the bars on Agoras; the further north you go from the *plateia,* the more mellow the sounds.

Kalypso   BAR
(Agoras) Classy Kalypso plays lots of jazz and blues, and owner-bartender Hristos makes a fine margarita along with homemade sangria.

EVIA & THE SPORADES SKYROS

ARTISTS & PIRATES

Skyros has a lively community of working artists, from potters and painters to sculptors and weavers. The island artistry dates from Byzantine times when passing pirates collaborated with rogue residents, whose houses became virtual galleries for stolen booty looted from merchant ships: hand-carved furniture, ceramic plates and copper ornaments from Europe, the Middle East and Asia. Today, similar items adorn almost every Skyrian house.

To see the legacy of this very Skyrian tradition, check out these favourites: **George Lambrou** (sculptor and painter); **Stamatis Ftoulis** (ceramics); **Olga Zacharaiki** (embroidery, ceramic); **Lefteris & Emanueleou** (woodcarving); **Amersa Panagiotou** (embroider).

For details on finding these working artists, contact Chrysanthi at Feel ingreece (22220 93100), just off upper Agora.

SKYROS CARNIVAL

In this wild pre-Lenten festival, which takes place on the last four weekends before Lent and Orthodox Easter, young men portray their elders' vigour as they don goat masks, hairy jackets and dozens of copper goat bells. They then proceed to clank and dance through the town, each with a male partner dressed up as a Skyrian bride but also wearing a goat mask. The overtly pagan revelries include much singing and dancing, and even more drinking and feasting.

The transvestism evident in the carnival derives from the cult of Achilles associated in Greek mythology with Skyros, the childhood hiding place for the boy Achilles, whose mother, Thetis, feared a prophecy requiring her son's skills in the Trojan War. The boy was given to the care of King Lykomides, who raised him disguised as one of his own daughters. Young Achilles was outwitted, however, by Odysseus, who arrived with jewels and finery for the girls, along with a sword and shield. When Achilles alone showed interest in the weapons, Odysseus discovered his secret and persuaded him to go to Troy. The festival draws over 2000 visitors for the final weekend, so book early.

Artistiko BAR
(Agoras) This long and narrow hole-in-the-wall buzzes till dawn with Greek music and strong drink.

Agora Cafe-Bar BAR
(Plateia; 🛜) Next to the post office; cosy bar that escapes the thump of the main drag.

🛍 Shopping

Olga Zacharaiki CRAFT
(☑ 6974666113) Smart corner shop with handmade embroidery and high-quality copies of Skyrian pottery.

ℹ️ Information

National Bank of Greece ATM (Agoras)
Police (☑ 22220 91274; Agoras)
Post Office (Agoras; ⊙ 7.30am-2pm)
Skyros Travel Agency (☑ 69448 84588, 22220 91600; www.skyrostravel.com; Agoras; ⊙ 9.30am-1.30pm & 7-10pm) Helpful full-service agency arranges accommodation, transfers and onward travel, car and motorbike hire, and jeep and boat excursions around Skyros.

Magazia & Molos
Μαγαζιά & Μώλος

The resort of Magazia is a compact and colourful maze of winding alleys that skirts the southern end of a long, sandy beach just north of Skyros Town. Skinny-dippers can leave it all behind at **Papa Houma** near the southern end of Magazia.

Near the northern end of the beach, once-sleepy Molos now has its own share of decent tavernas and rooms. Its landmark windmill and adjacent rock-hewn church of **Agios Nikolaos** are easy to spot. The road ends at nearby **Girismata Beach**.

👁 Sights

There is a flourishing and diverse arts scene in Skyros, from traditional pottery, woodworking and embroidery, to modern painting and sculpture. Exceptional painter and sculptor **George Lambrou** (☑ 22220 93100) has pieces at the Benaki Museum in Athens, but you can visit his modest studio in Magazia throughout the summer. And facing the beach is the studio-workshop of ceramic artist **Stamatis Ftoulis** (☑ 22220 92220, 22220 91559), who also has a showroom in Skyros Town.

🛏 Sleeping

Two good options in Magazia are **Ariadne Apartments** (☑ 22220 91113; www.ariadnestudios.gr; Magazia; d/apt from €55/80; ❄ @ 🛜) with garden setting, and **Deidamia Hotel** (☑ 22220 92008; www.deidamia.com; d/tr/f from €45/50/70; P ❄ @ 🛜), just off the main road.

⭐ Perigiali Hotel & Studios HOTEL $
(☑ 22220 92075; www.perigiali.com; Magazia; d/tr/apt incl breakfast from €55/80/115; P ❄ 🛜 🏊) Perigiali feels secluded despite being only 60m from Magazia beach. The leafy compound features Skyrian-style rooms overlooking a garden with pear and apricot trees, while an upscale wing sports a pool with luxe apartments. Owner Amalia is full of ideas for travellers.

Georgia's Rooms

PENSION $

(☑ 6973819787, 22220 91357; www.georgiashouse.com; r from €30; ❄❓) You can't get much closer to the sea than at these well-managed and geranium-adorned domatia 20m from the beach, opposite a handy car park and cafe.

Ammos Hotel

HOTEL $$

(☑ 22220 91234; www.skyrosammoshotel.gr; Magazia; d/f incl breakfast from €60/80; ❄❓❆) This strikingly well-designed lodging is low-key and inviting, with modern bathrooms, overhead fans and a homemade Skyrian breakfast to start the day. Just 50m from lovely Yialos Beach. Prices vary according to sea or garden view, good value regardless.

🍴 Eating & Drinking

Stefanos Taverna

TAVERNA $

(mains €4.50-8) Sit on the terrace of this well-regarded eatery overlooking Magazia beach and choose from a range of point-and-eat dishes, wild greens and fresh fish. Breakfast omelettes start at €3.50.

Oi Istories Tou Barba

TAVERNA $

(My Uncle's Stories; Molos; mains €4-10) Look for the light-blue railing above the beach in Molos to find this excellent cafe-*tsipouradhiko* (*ouzerie*) with fine mezedhes.

Juicy Beach Bar

JUICE BAR

(Magazia; snacks €2-5) Escape the midday sun or chill under the stars at busy Juicy, with all-day breakfasts.

Thalassa Beach Bar

BAR

(Molos; snacks €3-7) Modern and sandy with mojitos and full-moon parties.

Linaria   Λιναριά

Linaria, the port of Skyros, is tucked into a small bay filled with bobbing fishing boats and a few low-key tavernas and *ouzeries*. Things perk up briefly whenever the *Achileas* ferry comes in, its surreal arrival announced with the sound of Richard Strauss' *Also Sprach Zarathustra* booming from hillside speakers above the port.

Just opposite the ferry dock, look for King Lykomides Rooms-to-Let (☑ 22220 93249, 6972694434; soula@skyrosnet.gr; r incl breakfast from €40-60; P ❄ @ ❓), an efficient domatio managed by the hospitable Soula Pappas, with spotless rooms and balconies.

Join the port regulars under the big plane tree at the friendly Taverna O Platanos (mains €5-7), for Greek taverna standards and generous salads. Next to the dock, try Taverna Ivilai (mains €4-9) for fine mezedhes and grills.

Kavos Bar (drinks & snacks €2-5), overlooking the port, pulls in Skyrians from across the island for sunset drinks.

Kalamitsa   Καλαμίτσα

This low wetland area, the largest on Skyros, takes its name from the Greek '*kalamia*' or reed. It's an important Aegean stopover for migrating egrets, herons and falcons. In ancient times, young Achilles set off for Troy from nearby Achili Bay, a legend at the heart of Skyrian folklore.

Taverna Mouries serves traditional Greek fare – generous and tasty. '*Mouries*' means mulberry, and several rambling old trees, planted by owner Manolis' grandfather,

---

ENDANGERED: A RARE BREED

The small-bodied Skyrian horse (*Equus Cabalus Skyriano*), often mistaken for a pony, is valued for its intelligence, beauty and gentleness. Though common across Greece in ancient times, today there are fewer than 300 of these horses, the majority living on the southern slopes of Mt Kochilas on Skyros.

Several Skyrians are working to save the endangered species. In 2006, Amanda Simpson and Stathis Katsarelias started with just three horses. Their modest facilities have expanded to accommodate around 40 horses as they seek to re-establish a herd of wild, pure-bred Skyrian horses. Visitors are welcome (☑ 6986051678; amasimpson@hotmail.com). Check out their Facebook page at 'Friends of the Skyrian Horse, Katsarelia-Simpson-Project'.

Eleni and Nikos Kritikos of the Skyrian Horse Society (☑ 6974694023, 22220 92345; www.skyrianhorsesociety.gr) oversee a popular 'Adopt a Skyrian Horse' program to help promote the breed. You can visit their office in Skyros Town, and horse farm at nearby Playa. Several of the horses can be glimpsed in Kalamitsa, opposite Taverna Mouries.

provide welcome shade in summer. Lamb and goat grills are specialities.

Nearby **Amersa's Traditional House** (Amersa Panagiotou; ☑ 6973397693) displays and sells the artist's fine handmade embroidery with traditonal motifs.

Atsitsa   Ατσίτσα

The picturesque port village of Atsitsa on the island's west coast occupies a woody shoreline setting. The snappy all-organic **Sunset Cafe** (Atsitsa; drinks & snacks €1.50-4) overlooking the bay offers Greek coffee and wine, fresh juices, ice cream, delicate cakes and salads, all compliments of Mariana and family.

Tris Boukes Bay
Τρεις Μπούκες Ορμος

The southernmost corner of the island is a windswept landscape partly restricted by a Greek naval station.

One of the main reasons to come here is to visit English poet **Rupert Brooke's grave**. The well-tended marble grave is in a quiet olive grove just inland from the bay; it's marked with a wooden sign in Greek on the roadside. The gravestone is inscribed with Brooke's most famous sonnet, 'The Soldier', beginning with the following epitaph:

If I should die think only this of me:
That there's some corner of a foreign field
That is forever England.

When Brooke's fellow naval officers buried him, they erected a simple wooden cross (now in England) with an inscription originally in Greek: 'Here lies the servant of God, sub-lieutenant in the English Navy, who died for the deliverance of Constantinople from the Turks'.

A nearby rough dirt road (4WD recommended) leads to **Renes Bay**, from where a 5km **hiking trail** skirts a coastal plateau, ending at the **lighthouse** at **Cape Lithari**. Small herds of wild Skyrian horses are often glimpsed here, along with rare Eleonora's falcons that nest in the steep cliffs nearby from April to October.

Beaches

On the northwest coast, near **Agios Petros Beach**, find the outstanding **Taverna Agios Petros** (☑ 6972842116; mains €5-8), set among a grove of pines and featuring its own produce, meat and cheese.

At azure-blue **Cape Petritsa**, 1.5km south of Atsitsa, the coastal road turns inland, finding the sea again at sandy **Agios Fokas Bay**, with a taverna and great swimming.

A beautiful horseshoe-shaped beach graces **Pefkos Bay**, 10km southeast of Atsitsa. Nearby, the beach at **Aherounes** has a gentle kid-friendly sandy bottom, along with two tavernas and domatia.

To the north near the airport, **Palamari** is a graceful uncrowded stretch of sandy beach. It's also the location of a well-signed **archaeological excavation** (http://geomor phologie.revues.org/668) of a fortified Early Bronze Age town dating from 2500 BC. The adjacent **wetland** is the remnant of an ancient alluvial lagoon which supported this fishing and hunting community. Today it remains a birdwatching mecca, especially for long-legged waders like herons and ibises. At the airport junction, roadside **Taverna To Perasma** (mains €5-10) serves excellent *mayirefta* dishes.

Ionian Islands

Best Places to Eat

➡ Vasilis (p645)

➡ Casa Grec (p654)

➡ Klimataria (p641)

➡ Tassia (p658)

➡ La Cucina (p638)

Best Places to Stay

➡ Emelisse Hotel (p658)

➡ Niforos (p656)

➡ Siorra Vittoria (p637)

➡ Boschetto Hotel (p648)

➡ Torri E Merli (p645)

Why Go?

The Ionian Islands (Τα Ιόνια Νησιά) stand apart from mainstream Greek life. With their cooler climate, abundant olive groves, cypress trees and beautifully forested mountains, the Ionians are a lighter, greener version of Greece. The Venetians, French and British have shaped the architecture, culture and (excellent) cuisine, and the unique feel of Ionian life has been evoked from Homer to the Durrells.

Though the islands appear linked in a chain down the west coast of mainlaind Greece (with the exception of Kythira, which sits at the southern tip of the Peloponnese), each has a distinct landscape and cultural history. Corfu Town has Parisian-style arcades, Venetian alleyways and Italian-inspired delicacies. Kefallonia, Paxi and Ithaki preserve wild terrain and a relaxed feel. Lefkada has some of the best beaches in Greece, if not the world. Kythira feels off-the-beaten-path, and full of surprises. The Ionians offer something for adventure seekers, food lovers, culture vultures and beach bums alike.

When to Go
Corfu Town

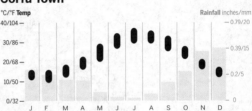

May Life is still quiet and the wildflowers are in full bloom everywhere.

Jul Escape the heat in the rest of Greece and head to its coolest islands.

Sep Leaves change colour, and the Robola grapes are being harvested in Kefallonia.

Ionian Islands Highlights

❶ Explore world-class museums, fortresses, restaurants and Venetian, French and British architecture in **Corfu Town** (p634)

❷ Hop from one gorgeous harbour to another in pastoral **Paxi** (p643)

❸ Treat yourself to top restaurants in Kefallonia's charming **Fiskardo** (p657) and striking **Assos** (p657)

❹ Learn to windsurf at **Vasiliki** (Lefkada; p649) or kayak and cave in **Kefallonia** (p651)

❺ Rank your favourite beaches, from the busiest on Corfu or Zakynthos to the quieter joys of Paxi or **Lefkada's west coast** (p649)

❻ Walk the paths of Homer in **Ithaki** (p658)

❼ Discover the tiny villages, waterfalls and remote coves of **Kythira** (p665)

History

The origin of the name 'Ionian' is obscure, but it's thought to derive from the goddess Io. One of Zeus' paramours, Io fled the wrath of a jealous Hera, passing through the waters now known as the Ionian Sea.

According to Homer, the islands were important during Mycenaean times, though only tombs (no villages or palaces) have been unearthed.

By the 8th century BC, the islands were in the hands of mighty city-state Corinth. A century later, Corfu staged a successful revolt. The Peloponnesian Wars (431–404 BC) left Corfu as little more than a staging post for whoever happened to be controlling Greece.

By the end of the 3rd century BC, the Romans ruled the Ionian region and, following the decline of the empire, the islands suffered waves of invaders: the Byzantine Empire (until the fall of Constantinople), Venice, Napoleon (in 1797), Russia (from 1799 to 1807), Napoleon again. In 1815, after Napoleon's downfall, the Ionians became a British protectorate.

The British constructed roads, bridges, schools and hospitals, established trade links, and developed agriculture and industry. But their rule was oppressive, nationalists wanted independence, and by 1864 Britain relinquished the islands to Greece.

WWII was rough on the Ionians and the islands saw mass emigration, and again following devastating earthquakes in 1948 and 1953. By the 1960s foreign holidaymakers were visiting in increasing numbers, and the tourist trade flourished.

❶ Information

USEFUL WEBSITES

Countless websites are devoted to the Ionians; here are some of the better ones:

Corfu www.corfu.gr, www.allcorfu.com, www.corfuland.gr (in Greek)

Ionian Islands www.greeka.com/ionian

Ithaki www.ithacagreece.com

Kefallonia www.kefalonia.net.gr

Lefkada www.lefkada.gr, www.lefkas.net

Paxi www.paxos-greece.com, www.paxos.tk

Zakynthos www.zakynthos-net.gr, www.zanteweb.gr

CORFU   ΚΕΡΚΥΡΑ

POP 101,080

Magnificent, verdant Corfu, or Kerkyra (*ker*-kih-rah) in Greek, was Homer's 'beautiful and rich land'. Mountains dominate the northern half where the coastlines can be steep and dramatic and where the island's interior is a rolling expanse of peaceful countryside. Stately cypresses, used for masts by the Venetians, rise from shimmering olive groves (also a Venetian inspiration). South of Corfu Town the island narrows and flattens.

Beaches with sometimes oppressively thick development punctuate the entire coastline. Development is most intensive north of Corfu Town and along the northernmost coast.

Corfu was a seat of European learning in the early days of modern Greece. While the rest of the nation struggled simply to get by, the Corfiots established cultural institutions such as libraries and centres of learning, and many major Greek figures like Ioannis Kapodistrias, the first head of independent Greece, hailed from Corfu. To this day, Corfiots remain proud of their intellectual and artistic roots. This legacy is visible from its fine museums and cultural life to its high-calibre, Italian-influenced cuisine.

❶ Getting There & Away

AIR

Corfu's **airport** (CFU; ☑ 26610 89600; www.corfu-airport.com) is about 2km southwest of the town centre.

Domestic

Aegean Airlines (☑ 26610 27100) Direct flights to Thessaloniki.

Astra Airlines (A2; www.astra-airlines.gr) Flies to Thessaloniki.

Olympic Air (☑ 801 801 0101) At the airport.

Sky Express (☑ 2810 223500; www.sky-express.gr) Operates a route to Preveza, Kefallonia and Zakynthos and (from June to September) to Iraklio, Crete.

Domestic Flights from Corfu

DESTINATION	TIME	FARE	FREQUENCY
Athens	1hr	€100	2-4 daily
Iraklio	1¾hr	€139	3 weekly, high season
Kefallonia	1hr 5min	€55	3 weekly
Kythira	3¾hr	€74	3 weekly
Preveza	30min	€55	3 weekly
Thessaloniki	55min	€88	3 weekly
Zakynthos	2hrs	€68	3 weekly

International

EasyJet (www.easyjet.com) has daily direct flights between the UK and Corfu (May to

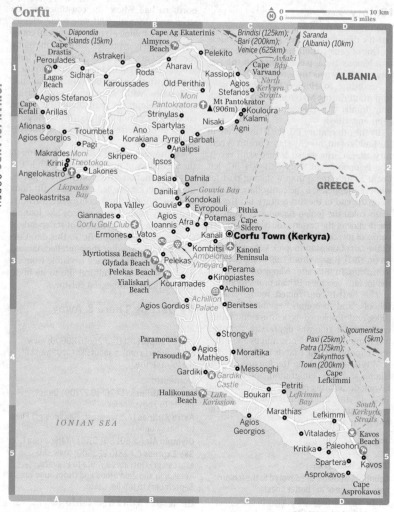

October) and high-season flights to Milan, Rome and Paris. **Air Berlin** (AB; ☑ 210 353 5264; www.airberlin.com) serves Germany. From May to September, many charter flights come from northern Europe and the UK.

BOAT

Neo Limani (New Port), with all ferry departures, lies west of hulking Neo Frourio (New Fortress).

Domestic

Ticket agencies in Corfu Town are near the new port, along Xenofondos Stratigou and Ethnikis Antistaseos. **Agoudimos Lines/GLD Travel**

(☑ 26610 80030; tickets@gld.gr; Ethnikis Antistaseos 1) has helpful staff.

Ilida (☑ Corfu 26610 49800, Paxi 26620 32401) hydrofoil goes between Corfu New Port and Paxi from mid-March until mid-October (see Petrakis Lines. **Despina** (☑ 26620 32114, 6980344759; http://bouastours.gr) serves Corfu New Port, Lefkimmi, Igoumenitsa and Paxi. Book ahead: places fill quickly.

Some international ferries from Corfu also call in at Igoumenitsa, Kefallonia, Patra and Zakynthos. For schedules see www.openseas.gr or the **ferry information office** (☑ 26650 26280) in Igoumenitsa.

BOAT SERVICES FROM CORFU

DESTINATION	PORT	TIME	FARE	FREQUENCY
Igoumenitsa	Corfu	1¼hr	€10	hourly
Igoumenitsa	Lefkimmi	1hr 10min	€8	6 daily
Patra	Corfu	6½hr	€35	2 weekly
Paxi*	Corfu	55min	€20	1-3 daily
Zakynthos	Corfu	8¾hr	€38	1 weekly

*high-speed services

International

Italy

Corfu has regular connections with Brindisi, Bari and Ancona, operated by a handful of companies sailing between Italy and Igoumenitsa and/or Patra. Some also go to Venice. Check with the domestic shipping agents or online. You can also sail between Italy and Igoumenitsa or Patra, then transfer to a local ferry.

Agoudimos Lines (☎210 414 1301; www.agoudimos-lines.com)

Endeavor Lines (☎210 940 5222, Corfu 26610 25000; www.endeavor-lines.com; Ethnikis Antistaseos 2, Sea Pilot Travel)

Superfast (☎26610 81222; www.superfast.com; Ethnikis Antistaseos 18)

Albania

Petrakis Lines (☎26610 31649; Ethnikis Antistaseos 4) operates daily hydrofoils to Saranda, Albania. In addition to the ticket, travellers also pay €10 for a temporary Albanian visa.

Boat Services from Corfu to Italy & Albania

DESTINATION	TIME	FARE	FREQUENCY
Ancona (Italy)	14½hr	€70	2 weekly
Bari (Italy)	8hr	€56	3 weekly
Brindisi (Italy)	5½-6¼hr	€61	2 weekly
Saranda (Albania)	25min	€19	1 daily

BUS

KTEL (☎26610 28927, 26610 28898; www.ktelkerkyras.gr) services go to Athens (€44.30, 8½ hours, three daily; on Monday, Thursday and Friday one goes via Lefkimmi) and Thessaloniki (€35.30, eight hours, daily). For both, budget another €10 for the ferry to the mainland. Purchase tickets from Corfu Town's long-distance bus station.

Getting Around

TO/FROM THE AIRPORT

Corfu local bus 19 goes between the airport and Plateia San Rocco in Corfu Town (buy tickets on board; €1.50, seven daily Monday to Friday, four or five Saturday and Sunday). The schedule is posted at the stop. If you miss bus 19, buses 6 and 10 stop on the main road 800m from the airport (en route to Benitses and Achillion). Taxis from the airport to Corfu Town cost €7 to €10.

BUS

Long-Distance Buses

Long-distance KTEL buses (known as green buses) travel from Corfu Town's **long-distance bus station** (☎26610 28927; www.ktelkerkyras.gr; Ioannou Theotoki), between Plateia San Rocco and the new port.

Fares cost €1.60 to €4.10. Timetables are at the ticket kiosk or online. Saturday services are reduced, Sunday and holidays are reduced considerably, or nonexistent.

Long-Distance Bus Services from Corfu

DESTINATION	TIME	FREQUENCY
Agios Gordios	45min	4 daily
Agios Stefanos	1½hr	4 daily
Aharavi (via Roda)	1¼hr	6 daily
Arillas (via Afionas)	1¼hr	2 daily
Barbati	45min	7 daily
Ermones	30min	6 daily
Glyfada	30min	4 daily
Kassiopi	45min	6 daily
Kavos	1½hr	8 daily
Messonghi	45min	8 daily
Paleokastritsa	45min	6 daily
Pyrgi	30min	5 daily
Sidhari	1¼hr	7 daily
Spartera	45min	2 daily

Local Buses

Local blue buses depart from the **local bus station** (☎26610 31595; Plateia San Rocco) in Corfu Old Town.

Tickets are €1.10 or €1.50 depending on journey length; purchase them at the booth on Plateia San Rocco (although tickets for Achillion, Benitses and Kouramades are bought on the bus). All trips are under 30 minutes. Service is reduced on weekends.

Local Bus Services from Corfu

DESTINATION	VIA	BUS NO	FREQUENCY
Agios Ioannis	Afra	8	13 daily
Achillion		10	6 daily
Benitses		6	14 daily
Evropouli	Potamas	4	11 daily
Kanoni		2a	half-hourly
Kombitsi	Kanalia	14	3 daily
Kondokali & Dasia	Gouvia	7	half-hourly
Kouramades	Kinopiastes	5	16 daily
Pelekas		11	11 daily

CAR & MOTORCYCLE

Car- and motorbike-hire outlets abound at the airport (Alamo, Hertz, Europcar etc.), in Corfu Town and resort towns. Prices start at around €40 per day (less for longer-term). Most local companies have offices along the northern waterfront.

Budget (☑ 26610 22062; www.budgetrentacar. gr; Eleftheriou Venizelou 50)

Sunrise (☑ 26610 44325, 26610 26511; www. corfusunrise.com; Ethnikis Antistaseos 6)

Top Cars (☑ 26610 35237; www.carrental-corfu.com; Donzelot 25)

Corfu Town   Κέρκυρα

POP 31,359

Charming, cosmopolitan Corfu Town (also known as Kerkyra) takes hold of you and never lets go. If you approach by sea, you will be met by the majesty of the famous Palaio Frourio (Old Fortress). Take a wander after the day-trippers leave to discover enchanting pastel-hued Venetian-era mansions, top museums and artistic life, and a buoyant year-round cosmopolitan spirit. Don't miss some of the region's finest restaurants.

ⓘ CORFU TOWN SIGHTS PASS

A joint sights pass (adult/concession €8/4) is good for the Palaio Frourio (Old Fortress), Antivouniotissa Museum, the Archaeological Museum and the Museum of Asian Art. Get it at any of the included sights.

◉ Sights & Activities

The grand seaside esplanade, known as the Spianada, is lined by an arcaded promenade, the Liston. Built by the French as a precursor to Paris' Rue de Rivoli, today the Liston, with its swathe of packed cafes, is the town's social hub. At the Spianada's northern end stands the grand neoclassical Palace of St Michael and St George. Inland, marble-paved streets lined with shops lead to the bustling modern town, centred around busy Plateia San Rocco (G Theotoki Sq).

At the time of writing, Corfu's Archaeological Museum was closed for extended renovations.

There is a striking memorial to Corfu's Jews in Plateia Solomou, near the Old Port in the area still known as Evraiki, the Jewish Quarter.

People swim off the point just north of the Palaio Frourio.

★ Palace of St Michael & St George   PALACE

Originally the residence of a succession of British high commissioners, this palace now houses the world-class Museum of Asian Art, founded in 1929.

Expertly curated with extensive, informative English-language placards, the collection's approximately 10,000 artefacts collected from all over Asia include priceless prehistoric bronzes, ceramics, jade figurines, coins and works of art in onyx, ivory and enamel. Additionally, the palace's throne room and rotunda are impressively adorned in period furnishings and art.

Behind the eastern side of the palace, the Municipal Art Gallery (admission €2; ⊙ 9am-5pm Tue-Sun) houses a fine collection featuring the work of leading Corfiot painters, a collection of splendid icons, rotating exhibitions, and a lovely seafront cafe.

★ Palaio Frourio   FORT

(☑ 26610 48310; adult/concession €4/2; ⊙ 8am-5pm Apr-Oct, 8.30am-3pm Nov-Mar) Constructed by the Venetians in the 15th century on the remains of a Byzantine castle and further altered by the British, this spectacular landmark offers respite from the crowds and superb views of the region. Climb to the summit of the inner outcrop which is crowned by a lighthouse for a 360-degree panorama. The gatehouse contains a Byzantine museum.

★ Antivouniotissa Museum   MUSEUM

(☑ 26610 38313; off Arseniou; adult/child €2/1; ⊙ 9am-4pm Tue-Sun) The exquisite timber-

MUSEUM TOUR: MUSEUM OF ASIAN ART

Length Two hours

As you enter the museum's grand foyer, on the left, stop into the Ionian Senate Conference Room, designed by palace architect Sir George Whitmore. On the upstairs landing, head left to begin the China Exhibit, crammed with priceless artefacts, like the ceremonial food vessel dating from the 12th to 11th century BC (case 6). The third room houses Ming vases, but don't miss the sculpted ivory, or, in the fifth room, the spectacular Miniature Art. Snuff bottles and carved semiprecious stones sit alongside coral-handled spoons and spectacular carved ivory spheres.

Back on the landing, head to the Throne Room with its elaborate trompe l'oleil murals and the Rotunda with its inlaid ceiling. This area often houses temporary exhibitions.

Next, the India Exhibit features fine examples of temple carvings, and the second room houses interesting Graeco-Buddhist Art from Afghanistan and Pakistan, such as the blue-grey schist Buddha showing Greek artistic influence. Visit the Tibetan thangkas (ritual banners) on your way to the Japanese Exhibit. Folding byobu screens lead to superb ukiyo-e woodblock prints and an excellent explanatory video of these 'Pictures of the Floating World'. At the time of research, the top floor of the museum was being renovated to contain the Japanese Exhibit. When it opens, be sure to find the beautiful Samurai armour.

roofed 15th-century Church of Our Lady of Antivouniotissa holds an outstanding collection of Byzantine and post-Byzantine icons and artefacts dating from the 13th to the 17th centuries.

★ **Church of Agios Spyridon** CHURCH
(Agios Spyridonos) The sacred relic of Corfu's beloved patron saint, St Spyridon, lies in an elaborate silver casket in the 16th-century basilica.

Neo Frourio FORT
(New Fortress; admission €3; ⊙ 9am-5pm May-Oct) A steep climb leads to this austere example of Venetian military architecture, added to extensively by the British. The interior is an eerie mass of tunnels, rooms and staircases, and the exterior has fine views.

★ **Mon Repos Estate** PARK
(Kanoni Peninsula; ⊙ 8am-7pm May-Oct, to 5pm Nov-Apr) FREE On the southern outskirts of town on the Kanoni Peninsula, an extensive wooded parkland estate surrounds an elegant neoclassical villa housing the Museum of Palaeopolis (☑ 26610 41369; www.corfu. gr; adult/concession €3/2; ⊙ 8am-7pm Tue-Sun May-Oct), with entertaining archaeological displays and exhibits on the history of Corfu Town. Paths lead through lush grounds to the ruins of two Doric temples; the first is truly a ruin, but the southerly Temple of Artemis is serenely impressive.

Take a picnic and plenty of water, as there are no nearby shops. Buses go to Kanoni from the Spianada (every 20 minutes).

Corfu Philharmonic Society MUSEUM
(☑ 26610 39289; www.fek.gr; N Theotoki 10; ⊙ 9.30am-1.30pm Mon-Sat) FREE Founded in 1840 by Nikolaos Mantzaros, the forward-thinking composer of the Greek national anthem, the society funds free music programs and hosts a museum dedicated to the vibrant musical history of the island.

Corfu Reading Society HISTORIC BUILDING
(☑ 26610 39528; www.anagnostikicorfu.com; Kapodistriou 120; ⊙ 9.30am-1.30pm Mon-Sat) FREE Founded in 1836, the oldest cultural institution in modern Greece houses 30,000 volumes. The art-filled mansion's upstairs map room houses the first map of Corfu, from the 15th century. Also hosts concerts and lectures.

Vidos Island ISLAND
Boats from the old port (€5) go to Vidos Island, off the coast, for beaches or a ramble through fortresses and a WWI Serbian cemetery.

☞ Tours

Day Trips COACH & BOAT TOURS
Petrakis Lines (☑ 26610 31649; www.ioniancruises.com; Ethnikis Antistaseos 4) and Sarris Cruises (☑ 26610 25317; Eleftheriou Venizelou 13)

Corfu Old Town

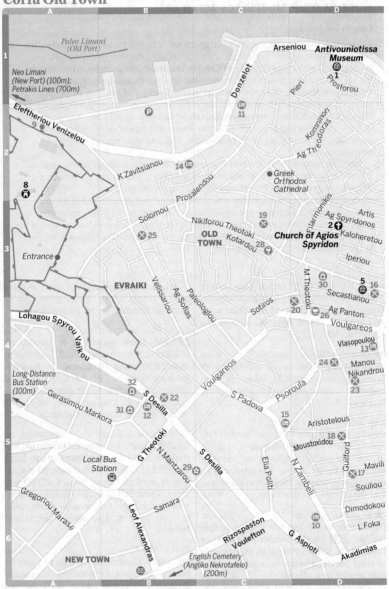

organise day trips from Corfu Town, including excursions to the Butrint Unesco World Heritage ancient ruins in Albania (€59; passports required); and **boat trips** to Paxi, the Blue Caves and Antipaxi (€40; go on a calm day). Transfers included.

🛏 Sleeping

Corfu Town tends towards the pricey. Book ahead in high season.

Hotel Konstantinoupolis   PENSION **$$**
(☎ 26610 48716; www.konstantinoupolis.gr; K Zavitsianou 11; s/d/tr incl breakfast €54/62/88; ❋ 🗢)

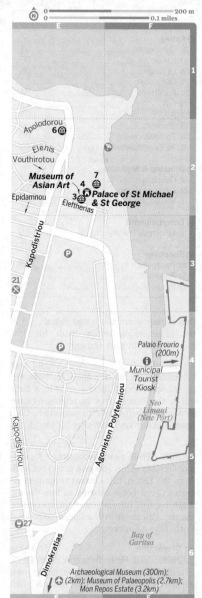

€165-190; P❄🛜) Expect luxury and style at this quiet 19th-century mansion where painstakingly restored traditional architecture and modern amenities meet. Marble bathrooms, crisp linens and genteel service make for a relaxed stay. Breakfast is in the peaceful garden beneath an ancient magnolia tree. The Vittoria suite encompasses the atelier and has views to the sea.

Bella Venezia　　　　　　BOUTIQUE HOTEL **$$**
(☏26610 46500; www.bellaveneziahotel.com; N Zambeli 4; s/d incl breakfast from €100/120; ⊖❄🛜) In a neoclassical former girls' school, the Venezia has comfy rooms and an elegant ambience. Conscientious staff welcome you, and the gazebo breakfast room in the garden is delightful.

City Marina Hotel　　　　　　HOTEL **$$**
(☏26610 39505; www.citymarina.gr; Donzelot 15; r incl breakfast €80; ❄🛜) Centrally located and with views of the New Fortress and the sea, these airy, comfortable rooms (some with balconies) are popular with large groups.

Hermes Hotel　　　　　　HOTEL **$$**
(☏26610 39268; www.hermes-hotel.gr; Markora 12; s/d/tr €50/70/90; ❄🛜) In a busy part of the new town, overlooking the market, the Hermes has had a complete makeover in recent years. Simple, tidy rooms with double glazing are especially atmospheric in the old wing.

Hotel Arcadion　　　　　　HOTEL **$$**
(☏26610 37670; www.arcadionhotel.com; Vlasopoulou 2; s/d/tr incl breakfast €80/85/115; ❄🛜) Straightforward clean rooms are not the enticement here; it's the location. Right on the Liston's busiest corner, balconies overlook the hubbub and the old fort.

🍴 Eating

Corfiot cuisine has been deliciously influenced by many cultures, particularly Italian. Dig in. A horde of good options cluster on Guilford (eg Del Sole and Giardino Citta). **Panetteria** (☏26610 22654; Vrahlioti 3) is an excellent bakery.

⭐**To Tavernaki tis Marinas**　　　　TAVERNA **$**
(☏6981656001; 4th Parados, Agias Sofias 1; mains €6-16; ⊙lunch & dinner) Restored stone walls, smooth hardwood floors and cheerful staff lift the ambience of this taverna a cut above the rest. Check daily specials or choose anything from *mousakas* (baked layers of eggplant or zucchini, minced meat and

Some of the rumpled rooms at this old Corfiot hotel overlook Plateia Palaio Limani and the sea.

⭐**Siorra Vittoria**　　　　BOUTIQUE HOTEL **$$**
(☏26610 36300; www.siorravittoria.com; Stefanou Padova 36; s/d incl breakfast from €95/135, ste

potatoes topped with cheese sauce) or grilled sardines to steak. Accompany it all with a dram of ouzo or *tsipouro* (distilled spirit similar to ouzo).

Chrisomalis TAVERNA $
(☑ 26610 30342; N Theotoki 6; mains €8-13; ⊙ lunch & dinner) Smack in the heart of the old town, this ma and pa operation dishes out the classics. Cruise inside to choose from what's fresh.

Rouvas TAVERNA $
(☑ 26610 31182; S Desilla 13; mains €5-8; ⊙ 9am-5pm) Excellent traditional cooking makes this a renowned lunch or takeaway stop for locals.

Starenio BAKERY $
(☑ 26610 47370; Guilford 59) Huge selection of gourmet pies, breads and the *best* cakes.

★**La Cucina** ITALIAN $$
(mains €13-25; ⊙ dinner) Guilford (☑ 26610 45029; Guilford 17); Moustoxidou (☑ 26610 45799; cnr Guilford & Moustoxidou) A long-established favourite, well-run La Cucina shines for its creative cuisine, with hand-rolled pasta dishes at the fore. Cajun shrimp with cherry tomatoes, spring onions and mascarpone is delicious, or try the range of innovative appetisers, salads and pizzas. Excellent wines accompany it all. The original Guilford loca-tion is cosy warm tones and murals, while the Moustoxidou annex (with identical menu) is chic in glass and grey.

La Famiglia ITALIAN $$
(☑ 26610 30270; Maniarizi-Arlioti 26; mains €9-18; ⊙ lunch & dinner) Tucked away in a back street, this homey spot highlights creative salads and pastas done to perfection. Cool tunes and low-key chatter set the mood.

Rex MEDITERRANEAN $$
(☑ 26610 39649; www.rexrestaurant.gr; Kapodis-triou 66; mains €12-18; ⊙ lunch & dinner) Set back from the Liston, this elegant restaurant el-evates Greek home cooking to fine dining. Attentive staff inform you of the specials of the day. Pair them with a fine wine or local Corfu Beer microbrews.

To Dimarchio ITALIAN $$
(☑ 26610 39031; Plateia Dimarchio; mains €9-25; ⊙ lunch & dinner) Relax in a luxuriant rose garden on a charming square. Attentive staff serve elegant, inventive dishes, both Ital-ian and Greek, prepared with the freshest ingredients.

🍷 Drinking & Nightlife

An enduring Corfu experience is preening and people-watching at Liston cafe-bars, al-though you'll pay €3.50 to €5 for a coffee or fresh juice.

Corfu Beer (www.corfubeer.com), the local microbrewery, does a delicious range of ales.

For dance venues, after 11pm head to Corfu's disco strip, 2km northwest of the new port, along Ethnikis Antistaseos (take a taxi; it's a busy unlit road without walkways). A €10 admission fee usually includes one drink.

★**Café Bristol** CAFE
(Voulgareos 40, cnr M Theotoki; ⊙9am-late) This Parisian-style cafe and bar, just off the beaten path, fills with a cool 20- to 30-something crowd.

★**Mikro Café** BAR
(☑26610 31009; N Theotoki 42, cnr Kotardou) Laid-back locals gather at this convivial cafe-bar with occasional live entertainment. Mikro's tables clamber up a narrow lane to a leafy raised terrace.

Cavalieri Hotel BAR
(Kapodistriou 4) Have mellow predinner drinks with excellent views from the rooftop garden bar.

Au Bar CLUB
(☑26610 80909; www.aubarcorfu.com; Ethnikis Antistaseos 34; ⊙Thu-Sat) Cool crowds come for house, R&B, Greek music and the occasional live show.

Edem Beach Nightclub CLUB
(☑26610 93013; www.edemclub.com; Dasia; ⊙nightly summer, closed winter) Dance the night away at Dasia Beach.

☆ **Entertainment**

Corfu Town has a lively cultural life of concerts, readings and so on. Check www.corfuland.gr (in Greek, use a web-based translator) for current listings.

Municipal Theatre PERFORMING ARTS
(☑26610 33598; Mantzarou) Corfu's cultural powerhouse stages classical music, opera, dance and drama here and at the theatre next to Mon Repos.

🔒 **Shopping**

Sweet shops and tourist haunts cram the streets of the tourist-oriented old town – there's something for every taste and budget. Fashion shops cluster along G Theotoki.

Papagiorgis FOOD, DRINK
(N Theotoki 32) Delectable local sweets and ice cream.

Public Market MARKET
(⊙morning Mon-Sat) North of Plateia San Rocco; sells fresh fruit, vegetables and fish.

Pogoniou FOOD & DRINK
(☑26610 31320; G Markora 17) Crammed with cheeses, cold cuts, spices, olive oil and other goodies.

ℹ️ **Information**

EMERGENCY
Tourist Police (☑26610 30265; Samartzi 4, 3rd fl) Off Plateia San Rocco.

INTERNET ACCESS
Bits & Bytes (☑26610 36812; cnr Mantzarou & Rizospaston Voulefton; per hr €3; ⊙24hr; 🛜)

MEDICAL SERVICES
Corfu General Hospital (☑26613 60400; Kondokali) About 7km north of Corfu Town.

TOURIST INFORMATION
Get *Corfiot* (€2), an English-language monthly newspaper with listings, at kiosks.
All Ways Travel (☑26610 33955; www.corfu allwaystravel.com; Plateia San Rocco 34) Helpful English-speaking staff.
Municipal Tourist Kiosk (Palaio Frourio; ⊙9am-4pm Mon-Sat Jun-Sep)

North & Northwest of Corfu Town

To explore fully all regions of the island outside Corfu Town your own transport is best. Much of the coast just north of Corfu Town is overwhelmed with beach resorts such as **Gouvia**, **Dasia** and the linked resorts of **Ipsos** and **Pyrgi**, all with close-quarters humanity and narrow beaches, but with everything for a family holiday.

Beyond Pyrgi the tawny slopes of **Mt Pantokrator** (906m), the island's highest peak, crowd down to the sea and reclaim the coast at some lovely scenic stretches along a winding road. Just beyond Pyrgi, the road corkscrews upwards and eventually passes through the picturesque villages **Spartylas** and **Strinylas**. It then climbs through stark terrain that is transformed by wildflowers in spring to the mountain's summit and the monastery, **Moni Pantokrator**, which is now dominated by a massive telecommunications tower. Superb all-round views stretch as far as the mountains of Albania and the Greek mainland.

ISLAND ACTIVITIES

Corfu brims with great outdoor action. Dinghy **sailing** and **windsurfing** buffs should find **Greek Sailing Holidays** (☑26630 81877; www.corfu-sailing-events.com) at Avlaki. For charters try **Corfu Sea School** (☑26610 97628; www.corfuseaschool.com) or **Sailing Holidays Ltd** (www.sailingholidays.com), both at Gouvia marina.

For **diving** in crystal-clear waters you'll find top operators at Kassiopi, Agios Gordios, Agios Georgios, Ipsos, Gouvia and Paleokastritsa.

Corfu has excellent **walking**. The **Corfu Trail** (www.thecorfutrail.com) traverses the island north to south and takes between eight and 12 days to complete. For help with accommodation along the trail, contact **Aperghi Travel** (☑26610 48713; www.travelling.gr/aperghi). The book *In the Footsteps of Lawrence Durrell and Gerald Durrell in Corfu* (Hilary Whitton Paipeti, 1999) is an excellent buy.

For **mountain biking**, especially off-road, the **Corfu Mountainbike Shop** (☑26610 93344; www.mountainbikecorfu.gr), in Dasia, rents bikes and organises day trips and cycling holidays.

Horse riding through olive groves and on quiet trails is offered through **Trailriders** (☑26630 23090; www.trailriderscorfu.gr), in Ano Korakiana.

Corfu Golf Club (☑26610 94220; www.corfugolfclub.com) is near Ermones, on Corfu's west coast.

Hugging the coast north from Pyrgi, the first decent spot is **Barbati** with its shingle beach and water-sports centre. The bay-side village of **Kalami** is famous for the former home of Lawrence and Nancy Durrell, called White House and now a rental villa (www.corfu-kalami.gr).

North again is **Agios Stefanos**, another attractive fishing village and resort nestled in a sheltered bay with a shingle beach.

Gorgeous little **Avlaki** lies beyond a wooded headland north of Agios Stefanos and has a substantial beach with very little development and only a couple of tavernas. It is popular for windsurfing.

Kassiopi is now crammed with shops, tavernas and bars but its strategic headland saw Roman and Venetian settlement. Nero is said to have holidayed outrageously here; nowadays British politicians visit the Rothschild estate nearby. Kassiopi is noted for its fine **embroidery**, sold in several shops. In the main street, opposite the church of the Blessed Virgin, steps climb to the ruins of the **Venetian castle**. Walks over the headland bring you to nearby **Battaria** and **Kanoni** beaches.

Beyond Kassiopi, the main road heads west along Corfu's north coast past the hugely popular resorts of **Aharavi**, **Roda** and **Sidhari**, all served by a succession of crowded beaches. **St George's Bay Country Club** (☑26630 63203; www.stgeorgesbay.com), in Aharavi, makes for a deluxe pool or spa outing, and has a seaside restaurant, and studios. Drive the winding road inland to magnificent **Old Perithia** to see a carefully restored Venetian village.

Corfu's other **Agios Stefanos**, on the island's northwest coast, has a large sandy beach. From the nearby fishing harbour regular excursion boats head for the **Diapondia Islands**, a cluster of little-known satellite islands. Contact **San Stefano Travel** (☑26630 51910; www.san-stefano.gr).

🛏 Sleeping

To rent a villa in a restored mountain hamlet with swimming pools and a spa, contact **Rou Estate** (www.rouestate.co.uk).

Dionysus Camping Village　CAMPGROUND $
(☑26610 91417; www.dionysuscamping.gr; Dafnilas Bay; camp sites per adult/car/tent €6.50/4/4.50, huts per person €12; 🐾🐕) The closest campground to Corfu Town, signposted between Tzavros and Dasia and well served by bus 7. It has good facilities in a mature olive grove.

★**Manessis Apartments**　APARTMENT $$
(☑26610 34990; http://manessiskassiopi.com; Kassiopi; 4-person apt €70-100; 🕸🐕) The friendly Greek-Irish owner maintains flower-filled gardens and bougainvillea-draped two-bedroom apartments (some with waterfront balconies). The location, at the end of Kassiopi's picturesque harbour, makes a lovely base.

Casa Lucia
APARTMENT, BUNGALOW **$$**

(☑ 26610 91419; www.casa-lucia-corfu.com; Sgombou; studios & cottages €70-120; ⊙ Apr-Oct; P 🏊)

🌿 A garden complex of lovely studios and cottages, Casa Lucia has a strong artistic and community ethos. There are yoga, t'ai chi and Pilates sessions and cultural events. It's on the road to Paleokastritsa.

✗ Eating

Corfu Town's northern suburbs hold a few good finds such as **Roula** (☑ 26610 91832; http://taverna-roula.gr; Kondokali) for fish and **Etrusco** (☑ 26610 93342; www.etrusco.gr; Kato Korakiana; mains €18-30) for fine dining. Agni's three competing tavernas, **Toula** (☑ 26630 91350), **Nikolas** (☑ 26630 91243) and **Agni** (☑ 26630 91142) all serve excellent food.

Taverna Galini
SEAFOOD **$**

(☑ 26630 81492; www.galinitaverna.gr; Agios Stefanos; mains €5-12; ⊙ lunch & dinner) Fresh local fish, fine seafood pasta, creative salads and hefty steaks on the northeast side of the island.

Cavo Barbaro
SEAFOOD **$$**

(☑ 26630 81905; Avlaki; mains €10-14; ⊙ lunch & dinner) Take a peaceful break on the water's edge at this relaxed little seafood joint.

Little Italy
ITALIAN **$$**

(☑ 26630 81749; Kassiopi; mains €6-18; ⊙ lunch & dinner) A long-standing Kassiopi favourite for fresh pasta and other pleasures like duck breast with caramelised oranges.

Piedra del Mar
MEDITERRANEAN **$$**

(☑ 26630 91566; www.piedradelmar.gr; Barbati; mains €7-22; ⊙ lunch & dinner Jul-Aug or Sep) Dust off your best togs for a dose of the good life... Beachfront chic melds perfectly with terrific Mediterranean cuisine.

South of Corfu Town

The coast road south from Corfu Town leads to well-signposted **Achillion Palace** (☑ 26610 56210; Gastouri; adult/child €7/2, audioguide €3; ⊙ 8am-8pm Apr-Oct, 8.45am-4pm Nov-Mar) near the village of Gastouri. It was built in the 1890s by Empress Elisabeth of Austria, known as Sisi, as a retreat and in tribute to her hero, Achilles. (Poor Sisi was later assassinated on the shores of Lake Geneva by a deranged anarchist.) Kaiser Wilhelm II bought the palace in 1907, and added a ferocious statue of Achilles Triumphant. Arrive early for fewer crowds and journey through neoclassicism, fabulous furnishings and bold statuary (style or kitsch?).

South of the Achillion, the resort of **Benitses** is enhanced by its pleasant old village, from where tracks and paths lead into the steep, wooded slopes above.

★ **Klimataria** (Bellos; ☑ 26610 71201; mains €8-14; ⊙ dinner), in Benitses, is worth a pilgrimage in its own right. Often simply called Bellos, after its unassuming owner, Kostas, every item in the tiny, humble taverna is absolutely delicious. From the olive oil and specially sourced feta to the tender octopus or array of mezedhes (appetisers), Bellos will not serve anything that he cannot find fresh. Book ahead in summer. If you can't get into Bellos, nearby **O Paxinos** (☑ 26610 72339; mains €9-16; ⊙ lunch & dinner) is noted for its mezedhes and fish dishes.

Further south again are the popular beach resorts of **Moraïtika** and **Messonghi**, from where the winding coastal road leads to tranquil **Boukari** with its little harbour. Walk back into the kitchen at the excellent *psarotaverna* (fish taverna) **Spiros Karidis** (☑ 26620 51205; fish per kg €35-50; ⊙ lunch & dinner) to select from the day's catch. The pleasant **Golden Sunset Hotel** (☑ 26620 51853; www.korfusunset.de; r incl breakfast €60) has upper-floor rooms with fantastic views.

Lefkimmi, in the southern part of the island, is one of Corfu's most down-to-earth towns, and still gets on with everyday life. Fascinating churches dot the older section, and it's divided by a rather quaint, but sometimes odorous, canal.

West Coast

Some of Corfu's prettiest countryside, villages and beaches are found along the west coast. The scenic and very popular resort

---

THE DURRELLS

The writers Lawrence and Gerald Durrell, prominently associated with Corfu, lived in Kalami for many years prior to WWII. Lawrence's nonfiction *Prospero's Cell* is a lyrical evocation of Corfu; his brother Gerald's equally excellent *My Family and Other Animals* was based on the Durrell family's eccentric and idyllic life on the island during the 1930s.

area, Paleokastritsa, 26km from Corfu Town, rambles for nearly 3km down a valley to a series of small, picturesque coves between tall cliffs. Craggy mountains swathed in cypresses and olive trees tower above. Venture to nearby grottoes or one of the dozen or so local beaches by small boat (per person €8.50, 30min); water taxis take you to your beach of choice; or partake in a range of water sports.

Perched on the rocky promontory at the end of Paleokastritsa is the icon-filled Moni Theotokou (⊙9am-1pm & 3-8pm), a monastery founded in the 13th century (although the present building dates from the 18th century). Just off the monastery's lovely garden, a small museum (⊙Apr-Oct) and olive mill exhibition have a shop selling oils and herbs.

From Paleokastritsa a path ascends 5km inland to the unspoilt village of Lakones which is fantastic for coastal views.

Quaint Doukades has a historic square and atmospheric tavernas. The 6km road north from Paleokastritsa to Krini and Makrades climbs steeply to spectacular views (many restaurants capitalise on the vistas). A left turn towards the coast leads through Krini's miniature town square and down to Angelokastro, the ruins of a Byzantine castle and the western-most bastion on Corfu.

Further north, via the village of Pagi, are the pleasant beach resorts of Agios Georgios and Arillas straddling the knuckly headland of Cape Arillas with the little village of Afionas straggling up its spine.

South of Paleokastritsa, the pebbly beach at Ermones is dominated by heavy development, but clings to its claim of being the beach on which Odysseus washed ashore and met Nausicaa, daughter of King Alcinous (who happened to be sunning herself).

Hilltop Pelekas, 4km south, is perched above wooded cliffs and one-time hippy beaches. At the summit, the Kaiser's Throne was the spot to which Kaiser Wilhelm rode his horse to get 360-degree island views. This area still attracts independent travellers.

The delightful old estate at Ambelonas (⊙6932158888; mezedhes €8-12, prix fixe incl wine €16-27; ⊙from 6.30pm Wed-Fri, otherwise by appointment), 6km from Corfu Town on the Pelekas road near Karoubatika, produces enticing local products, from vinegars to olives and sweets. Tour the olive-oil mill and winery, and sample the wares, including wines

from local grapes such as Kakotrygis, and Corfiot mezedhes.

Near Pelekas village are two sandy beaches, Glyfada and Kontogialos (also called Pelekas), a resort with water sports and sun beds galore. These quite-developed beaches are backed by large hotels and other accommodation. A free shuttle runs to them from Pelekas village.

Further north is the breathtaking, but dwindling (due to erosion) Myrtiotissa beach. It's a long slog down a steep, partly surfaced road (drivers use the parking area on the hilltop). The taverna and bar, Elia, partway down, makes a welcome break.

Agios Gordios is a popular resort south of Glyfada where a long sandy beach copes with the crowds.

Just along the turn-off from the main road to Halikounas Beach is the Byzantine Gardiki Castle, which has a picturesque entranceway, but is a ruin inside. Just south of the castle is the vast Lake Korission, separated from the sea by a narrow spit fronted by a long sandy beach where you can usually escape from the crowds.

🛏 Sleeping

Paleokastritsa and Pelekas are loaded with accommodation.

Yialiskari Beach Studios   APARTMENT $
(☑26610 54901; Yialiskari Beach; studios €60; ✳🛜) Studios with great views are perfect for those who want seclusion away from neighbouring Pelekas Beach.

Sunrock   HOSTEL $
(☑26610 94637; Pelekas Beach; dm/r per person incl breakfast €18/25; @🛜✳) Funky, laid-back and a bit worn. Crash out on the terrace at sunset or party on the beach.

Jimmy's Restaurant & Rooms   PENSION $
(☑26610 94284; www.jimmyspelekas.com; Pelekas village; s/d/tr €30/40/50; ⊙Apr-Oct; ✳) Decent rooms with rooftop views sit above a popular restaurant (mains €6 to €12).

Pink Palace   HOSTEL, HOTEL $
(☑26610 53103; www.thepinkpalace.com; Agios Gordios Beach; dm & r per person incl breakfast & dinner €21-45; ✳@) Consuming the whole town in pink, and a party place par excellence, Pink Palace offers a range of utilitarian rooms, quad bikes, activities galore...and loads of backpackers.

Paleokastritsa Camping
CAMPGROUND $

(📞26630 41204; www.paleokastritsa-bliss.com; Paleokastritsa; camp sites per adult/car/tent €5/3.10/3.50; ⊙late-May–mid-Oct; 🅿) On the right of the main road to town, this shady and well-organised campground in historic olive terraces also has pool access.

Rolling Stone
PENSION $

(📞26610 94942; www.pelekasbeach.com; Pelekas Beach; r/apt €35/88; @🛜) Simple, colourful apartments and double rooms surround a big sun terrace with funky trappings and a shared kitchen at this laid-back place.

Hotel Zefiros
HOTEL $$

(📞26630 41244; www.hotel-zefiros.gr; Paleokastritsa; d/tr/q incl breakfast €75/95/115; ❄🛜) Near the seafront and a delight, with immaculate, stylish rooms, some with a massive terrace, and a bright cafe.

Levant Hotel
HOTEL $$

(📞26610 94230; www.levantcorfu.com; Pelekas village; d incl breakfast €80; ⊙May–mid-Oct; 🅿❄🛜🌊) Simple rooms in this formerly grand old hotel sit up near the Kaiser's Throne; the sea-facing ones have glorious sunset views.

★ Kallisto Resort
APARTMENT $$$

(📞6977443555; www.corfuresorts.gr; Pelekas Beach; apt/villa from €160/220; 🅿❄🌊) A well-appointed array of apartments and villas sleep two to 12, and cascade down the hillside overlooking the north end of Pelekas Beach. Villas have private pools, gardens are manicured and life is good at this quietly luxurious getaway with all the mod cons.

✕ Eating & Drinking

★ Alonaki Bay Taverna
TAVERNA $

(📞26610 75872; Alonaki; mains €8-10; ⊙lunch & dinner) Follow the dirt roads to the point north of Lake Korission for this simple family-run taverna with a small menu of home-cooked meat and *mayirefta* (ready-cooked meals). Clean rooms and apartments overlook a garden and dramatic cliffs.

To Stavrodromi
TAVERNA $

(📞26610 94274; Pelekas; mains €7-11; ⊙dinner) At the crossroads of the Pelekas and Corfu Town roads, this homey joint offers delicious local specialities. It's known for the best *kontosouvli* (pork on a spit) on the island.

Nereids
TAVERNA $

(📞26630 41013; Paleokastritsa; mains €6-11; ⊙lunch & dinner) Halfway down the winding road to Paleokastritsa beach is this smart place with a huge leafy courtyard. Specialities include pork in mustard sauce with oregano and lemon.

Limani
TAVERNA $

(📞26630 42080; Paleokastritsa Harbour; mains €5-11; ⊙lunch & dinner) Local dishes with a sure hand on a rose-bedecked terrace.

★ Spyros & Vasilis
FRENCH $$

(📞26610 52552; www.spirosvasilis.com; Agios Ioannis; mains €15-21; ⊙lunch & dinner) It may seem odd to go to a French restaurant in Greece, but this understated, upscale restaurant may make the best steaks on the island. Indulge. The patios have gentle valley views and service is attentive. Signposted across from Aqualand on the road from Corfu Town to Paleokastritsa.

La Grotta
CAFE

(www.lagrottabar.com; Paleokastritsa) Cool sun-seekers hang out at this cafe-bar set in a beautiful rocky cove with sun beds and diving board. Located down steps opposite the Hotel Paleokastritsa driveway.

PAXI ΠΑΞΟΙ

POP 2200

Paxi lives up to its reputation as one of the Ionians' most idyllic islands. At only 10km by 4km it's the smallest of the main holiday islands and makes a fine escape from Corfu's quicker-paced pleasures. Three colourful harbour towns, Gaïos, Loggos and Lakka, have charming waterfronts with pink-and-cream buildings set against lush green hills. Gemlike coves can be reached by motorboat, if not by car or on foot. The dispersed inland villages sit within centuries-old olive groves, accented by winding stone walls, ancient windmills and olive presses. On the less accessible west coast, sheer limestone cliffs punctuated by caves and grottoes plunge hundreds of metres into the azure sea. Old mule trails are a walker's delight. Find *Bleasdale Walking Map of Paxos* (€12) at travel agencies.

ⓘ Getting There & Away

BOAT
Ferries dock at Gaïos' new port, 1km east of the central square. Excursion boats dock along the waterfront.

Paxi & Antipaxi

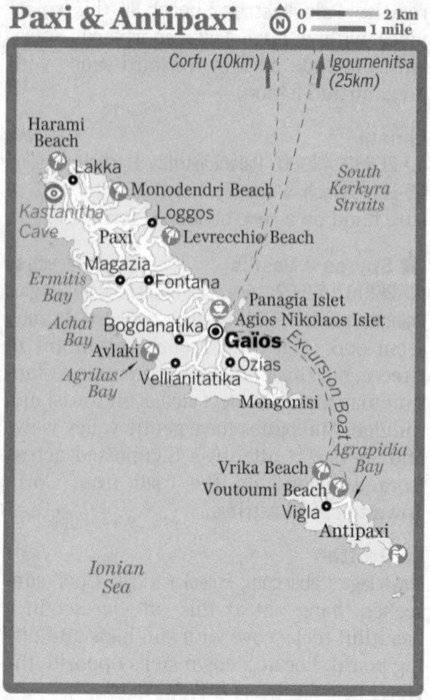

Two busy passenger-only hydrofoils link Corfu and Paxi (€20, 55 minutes, one to three daily May to mid-October), and occasionally Igoumenitsa. Arvanitakis Travel (p644) and Petrakis Lines (in Corfu) handle *Ilida;* and **Bouas Tours** (☎26620 32401; www.bouastours.gr; Gaïos) and **Zefi** (☎26620 32114; Gaïos) handle *Despina*.

Two daily car ferries link Paxi and Igoumenitsa (€10). For schedules try the ferry information office (p632) in Igoumenitsa.

Fast sea taxis are priced by boat. Corfu to Paxi costs €300; try **Nikos** (☎6932232072, 26620 32444; www.paxosseataxi.com; Gaïos).

BUS

Twice-weekly direct buses go between Athens and Paxi (€55, plus €7.50 for the ferry between Paxi and Igoumenitsa, seven hours) in high season. On Paxi, get tickets from Bouas Tours.

Getting Around

A bus links Gaïos and Lakka via Loggos up to four times daily (€2.50). Taxis between Gaïos and Lakka or Loggos cost around €12. The taxi rank in Gaïos is by the inland car park and bus stop. Many travel agencies rent small boats (€40 to €90 depending on engine capacity) – great for accessing coves.

Daily car hire starts at €38 in high season.

Alfa Hire (☎26620 32505; Gaïos)

Arvanitakis Travel (☎26620 32007; Gaïos)

Gaïos Γαϊος

POP 560

Gaïos, the island's main town, hardly needs to try for the 'picturesque' label. Pink, cream and whitewashed buildings line the edge of an emerald bay on either side of the Venetian square. The village is protected by the wooded **islet of Agios Nikolaos**, named after its monastery. Gaïos has the liveliest nightlife on the island, and cafes and tavernas line the waterfront.

Sleeping & Eating

★San Giorgio Apartments PENSION $

(☎26620 32223; s/d studios €40/50; ❄) Pink, blue and white are the colours of these peaceful, airy and clean studios with basic cooking facilities. Rooms 1 and 2 have fantastic balconies over the channel, others share a terrace.

Theklis Studios PENSION $$

(Clara Studios; ☎26620 32313; http://theklisstudios.com; studios €60-80; ❄) Thekli, a local fisher-diver, runs these immaculate, well-equipped studios. She'll meet you at the port if you call ahead.

Paxos Beach Hotel HOTEL $$$

(☎26620 32211; www.paxosbeachhotel.gr; d incl breakfast €130-190, ste €200-230; ❄≋) On a tiny cove with private beach, jetty, swimming pool, tennis court and restaurant, 1.5km south of Gaïos; bungalow-style rooms step down to the sea. Port transfers are available.

Karkaletzos TAVERNA $

(☎26620 32129; mains €7-10; ⏰7.45-11pm) Walk up an appetite to this grill house, a local favourite, 1km behind town. Meat dishes are balanced by creative fish cuisine.

Carnayo MEDITERRANEAN $$

(☎26620 32376; www.carnayopaxos.gr; mains €8-16; ⏰lunch & dinner) Striving for a higher level of service and a broader range of dishes than usual, Carnayo usually succeeds.

Information

The main street (Panagioti Kanga) runs inland from the square towards the back of town, where you'll find the bus stop, taxi rank and car park. Banks and ATMs are near the square. There's no tourist office, but travel agencies, such as **Paxos Magic Holidays** (☎26620 32269; www.paxosmagic.com), organise excursions, book tickets and arrange accommodation.

Loggos · Λόγγος

Exquisite Loggos sits 5km northwest of Gaïos and is a gem of a place with a dainty waterfront curled round a small bay. Bars and restaurants overlook the water and wooded slopes climb steeply above. Explore coves and pebble beaches nearby.

🛏 Sleeping & Eating

Hit waterside cafe-bars for cocktails and music.

Arthur House · APARTMENT **$$**
(☑ 26620 31330; http://paxos-arthur.blogspot.gr; studios €60; ℗) Modest, spotless studios sit above the owner's house, a 50m walk inland from the waterfront.

O Gios · TAVERNA **$**
(☑ 26620 31735; mains €8-12; ⊙ lunch & dinner) Home-cooked, good-value seafood and grill dishes.

★ Vasilis · MEDITERRANEAN **$$**
(☑ 26620 31587; mains €9-16; ⊙ lunch & dinner) You may have your best meal in the Ionians here. The waterside ambience is distinctly low-key, but the food is excellent. Lighter-than-air zucchini balls are to die for; salads are perfectly balanced; and everything is fresh, fresh, fresh. Specialities include octopus in red-wine sauce, lamb casserole, pasta and risotto. Reserve ahead in summer.

ℹ Information

The village and **Café Bar Four Seasons** (☑ 26620 31829; 🛜) has wi-fi. Hire boats (€50 to €70) and scooters (€20) from Julia's Boat & Bike at Arthur House.

Magazia · Μαγαζιά

Barely more than a crossroads several kilometres southwest of Loggos, on the western side of the island, Magazia makes a great pit stop for its two cafe-bars.

🍴 Eating & Drinking

★ Erimitis Bar · MEDITERRANEAN **$$**
(☑ 6977753499; www.erimitis.com; mains €13-16; ⊙ noon-10pm May-Oct) Rumble down dirt roads under olive trees to find this spectacular spot overlooking majestic cliffs plunging straight into the bluest of seas. Whether for sunset or an afternoon drink, it's well worth the journey if you have your own wheels.

Kafeneio Burnaos · CAFE
Don't blink or you'll miss this wonderful 60-year-old *kafeneio* (coffee house). There are no set hours, but locals gather here to play cards and backgammon (one set dates from 1957).

Lakka · Λάκκα

The picturesque, tranquil harbour of Lakka lies at the end of a shielding bay on the north coast. Yachts dot ice-blue waters, small beaches like **Harami Beach** lie round the bay's headland, and pleasant walks criss-cross the area.

🛏 Sleeping & Eating

Yorgos Studios · APARTMENT **$**
(☑ 26620 31807; www.routsis-holidays.com; d €50-70; ❉🛜) Immaculate and comfy, it's next door and run by Routsis Holidays, which represents many studios and apartments.

Torri E Merli · BOUTIQUE HOTEL **$$$**
(☑ 26212 34123; www.torriemerli.com; ste from €290; ⊙ May-Oct; ℗❉🛜🏊) The island's premier lodging – a tiny, perfect boutique hotel in a renovated stone mansion tucked into the hills 800m south of Lakka.

Diogenis · TAVERNA **$**
(☑ 26620 31442; mains €4-10; ⊙ lunch & dinner Jun-Sep) This popular eatery in the square in the centre of the village dishes out cuttlefish with spinach and lamb in lemon sauce, among other well-done classics.

ℹ Information

Helpful **Routsis Holidays** (☑ 26620 31807; www.routsis-holidays.com) books well-appointed apartments and villas for all budgets and arranges transport and excursions.

Paxos Blue Waves (☑ 26620 31162; www.paxos-studios.gr) rents boats (€35 to €65) and scooters (€20).

ANTIPAXI · ΑΝΤΙΠΑΞΟΙ

POP 25

The stunning and diminutive island of Antipaxi, 2km south of Paxi, is covered with vineyards and olive groves with the occasional hamlet here and there. Caïques and tourist boats run daily, in high season, from Gaïos and Lakka, and go to two beach coves – the small, sandy **Vrika Beach** and the pebbly **Voutoumi Beach**. Floating in the water here, with its dazzling clarity, is a sensational experience.

An inland path links the two beaches (a 30-minute walk) or, for the very energetic, walk up to the village of Vigla, or as far as the lighthouse at the southernmost tip. Take plenty of water and allow 1½ hours minimum each way.

Voutoumi and Vrika each have two restaurants (mains €7 to €15). Accommodation is available through tavernas.

ℹ️ Getting There & Away

Boats to Antipaxi (€7 return, high season only) leave Gaïos at 10am and return around 4.30pm (more services in July and August).

LEFKADA   ΛΕΥΚΑΔΑ

POP 22,710

Lefkada (or Lefkas) is the sleeper hit of the Ionians. Mountainous and remote in the centre, with gorgeous vistas and forests, the island is lined on its west coast with some of the best beaches in Greece. Holiday resorts tend to cling to the east coast where 10 satellite islets dot the sea.

Lefkada is less insular than most islands; it was once attached to the nearby mainland by a narrow isthmus until occupying Corinthians breached it with a canal in the 8th century BC. A causeway now spans the 25m strait, yet Lefkada remains steadfastly islandlike in the best of ways. In remote villages older women sport traditional dress and the main town, Lefkada Town, has a refreshing mid-20th-century appeal.

ℹ️ Getting There & Away

AIR

The closest airport is 20km north of Lefkada, near Preveza (Aktion; PVK) on the mainland. The only domestic airline serving Preveza is **Sky Express** (✆28102 23500; www.skyexpress.gr) with services to Corfu (€55, 25 minutes), Kefallonia (€49, 20 minutes), Zakynthos (€55, one hour), Kythira (€60, 2½ hours) and Sitia (Crete; €99, two hours, June to September only).

Air Berlin has occasional flights. May to September charter flights from northern Europe and the UK serve Preveza.

BOAT

West Ferry (www.westferry.gr) runs daily boats on an ever-changing schedule from Vasiliki to Kefallonia and Ithaki. Some months, the ferry

Ionian Pelagos (✆26450 31520) goes from Vasiliki via Piso Aetos in Ithaki to Sami in Kefallonia. For information and booking try **Samba Tours** (✆26450 31520; www.sambatours.gr; Vasiliki).

Boat Services from Vasiliki, Lefkada

DESTINATION	TIME	FARE	FREQUENCY
Fiskardo (Kefallonia)	1hr	€8	2 daily
Frikes (Ithaki)	2hr	€8	5 weekly
Piso Aetos (Ithaki)	1hr	€8	2 weekly
Sami (Kefallonia)	1¾hr	€8	1 daily

BUS

Lefkada Town's **KTEL bus station** (✆26450 22364; www.ktel-lefkadas.gr; Ant Tzeveleki), 1km from the centre, opposite the new marina serves Athens (€33.80, 5½ hours, four daily), Patra (€16.20, three hours, two weekly), Thessaloniki (€35.40, eight hours, three weekly), Preveza (€2.70, 30 minutes, six daily) and Igoumenitsa (€12.20, two hours, daily).

ℹ️ Getting Around

There's no bus between Lefkada and Preveza's Aktion airport. Taxis cost €37 to Lefkada Town, €55 to Nydri. From the airport, it's cheaper to take a taxi to Preveza and then a bus to Lefkada.

BUS

From Lefkada Town, frequent buses ply the east coast in high season. Sunday and low-season services are greatly reduced. Services go to Agios Nikitas (€1.60, 30 minutes, three daily), Karya (€1.60, 30 minutes, four daily), Nydri (€1.60, 30 minutes, 20 daily), Vasiliki (€3.40, one hour, four daily) and Vlicho (€1.60, 40 minutes, 11 daily).

CAR

Rentals start at €35 per day; there are countless car- and bike-hire companies in Nydri and several in Vasiliki.

It's possible to arrange for hire-car delivery at Preveza's Aktion Airport and then return it in Vasiliki if you are catching a ferry south (or vice versa).

Europcar (✆26450 23581; www.lefkaseuropcar.gr; Panagou 16, Lefkada Town)

Santas (✆26450 25250; www.ilovesantas.gr; Lefkada Town) For bikes or scooters, from €16 per day. Next to Ionian Star Hotel.

Lefkada & Its Satellites

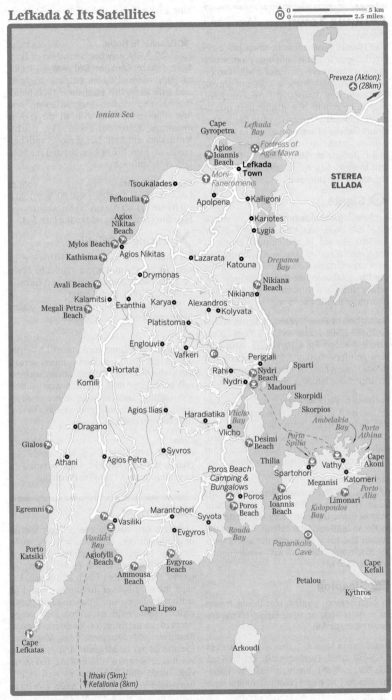

N
0 — 5 km
0 — 2.5 miles

Preveza (Aktion);
(28km)

Ionian Sea

Lefkada Bay

Cape Gyropetra

Agios Ioannis Beach

Fortress of Agia Mavra

Lefkada Town

Moni Faneromenis

Tsoukalades

Pefkoulia

Apolpena

Kalligoni

STEREA ELLADA

Kariotes

Lygia

Agios Nikitas Beach

Mylos Beach

Kathisma

Agios Nikitas

Lazarata

Katouna

Drepanos Bay

Drymonas

Nikiana Beach

Avali Beach

Nikiana

Kalamitsi

Exanthia

Karya

Alexandros

Megali Petra Beach

Platistoma

Kolyvata

Englouvi

Vafkeri

Perigiali

Sparti

Rahi

Nydri Beach

Hortata

Nydri

Madouri

Komili

Skorpidi

Skorpios

Agios Ilias

Haradiatika

Vlicho Bay

Ambelakia Bay

Porto Athina

Dragano

Vlicho

Desimi Beach

Porto Spilia

Gialos

Syvros

Thilia

Vathy

Cape Akoni

Athani

Agios Petra

Spartohori

Katomeri

Poros Beach Camping & Bungalows

Meganisi

Porto Alia

Egremni

Poros

Poros Beach

Agios Ioannis Beach

Limonari

Marantohori

Syvota

Kolopoulos Bay

Porto Katsiki

Vasiliki

Evgyros

Rouda Bay

Papanikolis Cave

Vasiliki Bay

Agiofylli Beach

Evgyros Beach

Petalou

Cape Kefali

Ammousa Beach

Cape Lipso

Kythros

Cape Lefkatas

Arkoudi

Ithaki (5km);
Kefallonia (8km)

Lefkada Town   Λευκάδα

POP 6938

The island's bustling main town has a relaxed, happy feel. It is built on a promontory at the southeastern corner of a salty lagoon where earthquakes are a constant threat. The town was devastated by one in 1948, only to be rebuilt in a distinctively quake-proof and attractive style with the upper-storey facades of some buildings in brightly painted corrugated tin. Stroll the vibrant main pedestrian thoroughfare, Dorpfeld, and lively Plateia Agiou Spyridonos or visit the handsome churches.

⊙ Sights

Archaeological Museum   MUSEUM
(☑26450 21635; adult/child €3/2; ⊙8am-3pm Tue-Sun) Housed in the cultural centre at the western end of Agelou Sikelianou, the museum contains island artefacts spanning the Palaeolithic to late-Roman periods. The prize exhibit is a 6th-century BC terracotta figurine of a flute player with nymphs.

Collection of Post-Byzantine Icons MUSEUM
(☑26450 22502; Rontogianni; ⊙8.30am-3.30pm Tue-Sat, 6-8.15pm Tue & Thu) FREE Works by icon painters from the Ionian school and Russia dating back to 1500 are displayed in an impressive building off Ioannou Mela.

Fortress of Agia Mavra   FORT
(⊙9am-1pm) FREE This 14th-century Venetian fortress squats immediately across the causeway. It was first established by the crusaders, but the remains mainly date from the Venetian and Turkish occupations.

Moni Faneromenis   MONASTERY
(☑26450 21305; ⊙museum 9am-1pm Mon-Sat) FREE Founded in 1634, on a hilltop 3km west of town, the monastery was destroyed by fire in 1886 and later rebuilt. Views of the lagoon and town are worth the ascent as is the monastery's museum with a collection of ecclesiastical art.

🛏 Sleeping

In high season, request rear-facing rooms for a quiet stay, or front-facing rooms for views of the action.

Hotel Santa Maura   HOTEL $$
(☑26450 21308; Dorpfeld; s/d/tr incl breakfast €50/60/70; ✱🕾) Enjoy a vaguely Bahamanian feel in pastel-coloured rooms with long balconies overlooking Dorpfeld's busy evening scene.

★Boschetto Hotel   BOUTIQUE HOTEL $$
(☑26450 20244; www.boschettohotel.com; Dorpfeld 1; d incl breakfast from €80; ✱@🕾) Painstakingly restored by an efficient husband and wife team, this exquisite c 1900 building has four custom-designed rooms and one suite tricked out with all the coolest amenities. Enjoy flat-screen TVs, marble bathrooms and front-facing rooms with balconies over the bright blue sea and the hub-bub of the cafe scene.

Pension Pirofani   HOTEL $$
(☑26450 25844; Dorpfeld; r €60-80; ✱🕾) Stylish rooms in lush colours fill this small hotel. Sparkling bathrooms add to the luxe feel.

🍴 Eating & Drinking

On Golemi find well-prepared Greek classics (mains €8 to €16) at **Frini Sto Molo** (☑26450 24879; ⊙lunch & dinner) and **Burano** (☑26450 26025; ⊙lunch & dinner).

Bars and cafes line the western waterfront and Plateia Agiou Spyridonos.

Ey Zhn   INTERNATIONAL $
(☑6974641160; Filarmonikis 8; mains €7-12; ⊙dinner Jan-Oct) Think roadhouse meets artist's loft at this ambience-rich restaurant with excellent, eclectic food. Exposed wood floors, soft lighting and jamming music complement dishes from mushroom risotto to tender tandoori chicken.

Ciao   ICE CREAM $
(Mitropoleos 8) Scoops up fresh-made ice cream, just off Dorpfeld: from *mastiha* (a sweet liquor from Chios) to chocolate.

East Coast

Lefkada's east coast has seen heavy tourist development over the years with the main focus at Nydri, once a gorgeously placed fishing village but now a crowded strip of tourist shops without much of a beach. Escape inland, however, to another world of scattered villages, small tavernas and pretty walks. From Nydri itself, you can escape seaward to the islets of **Madouri**, **Sparti**, **Skorpidi** and **Skorpios**, plus **Meganisi**. Excursions go to Meganisi and stop for a swim near Skorpios (€15 to €25), and some visit Ithaki and Kefallonia as well (€20). **Borsalino Travel** (☑26450 92528; www.borsa

linotravel.gr; internet per 20min €1) on Nydri's main street organises just about everything.

Amblers enjoy the lovely walk to **waterfalls** 3km out of Nydri.

Fishing boats bob alongside yachts in the relaxed harbour of **Syvota**, 15km south of Nydri (it is best reached with your own transport).

Sleeping & Eating

Galini Sivota Apartments   PENSION **$**
(☑ 26450 31347; Syvota; studios €45, 4-person apt €70; ✳) Super-tidy, homey apartments are set up from the waterfront, near the supermarket. Balconies have excellent harbour views.

Poros Beach Camping & Bungalows   CAMPGROUND **$**
(☑ 26450 95452; www.porosbeach.com.gr; Poros Beach; camp site per adult/car/tent €6/4/4, studios from €45; P✳@☂) Near Syvota and overlooking pretty Poros Beach, simple facilities include studios, shaded camping, restaurant and swimming pool.

★ Minas Taverna   TAVERNA **$$**
(☑ 26450 71480; www.minas-restaurant.gr; Nikiana; mains €6-14; ⊙ dinner nightly, lunch Sat & Sun, reduced hours in low season) Find this top-notch taverna 5km north of Nydri, just south of Nikiana. It's known island-wide for excellent everything – from pasta to grilled meat and seafood. Tables fill the restored stone building and terrace on the inland side of the road overlooking the sea.

Stavros   TAVERNA **$**
(☑ 26450 31181; Syvota; mains €7.50-13; ⊙ breakfast, lunch & dinner Easter-Oct) Come to Syvota's harbour-side taverna for the best fish soup on the island.

Vasiliki   Βασιλική

Vasiliki has a stony beach but is one of the best windsurfing venues in the Mediterranean. The enormous bay has soft breezes in the morning which are ideal for instructing beginners, and in the afternoon winds whip down flanking mountains for serious aficionados. The winding waterfront, with eucalyptus and canopy-covered eateries, is a pleasant place to relax.

Activities

Caïques take visitors to the island's better beaches and coves including **Agiofylli**

Beach, south of Vasiliki. Helpful Samba Tours (p646) organises car and bike hire, sells boat tickets and answers queries.

Along the beach, water-sports outfits stake their claims with flags, equipment and their own hotels for their clients.

Club Vass   WATER SPORTS
(☑ 26450 31588; www.clubvass.com) Sailboard hire (per hour/day €40/80), private lessons (€50) and one-week program (€190).

Nautilus Diving Club   DIVING, KAYAKING
(☑ 6936181775; www.underwater.gr) Options include snorkelling trips (€40 including lunch), single dive (€45), open-water course (€410) and sea-kayak hire (per hour single/double €15/20).

Sleeping & Eating

★ Pension Holidays   PENSION **$**
(☑ 26450 31426; www.pensionholidays.gr; r incl breakfast €40; ✳☎) Friendly Spiros and family offer Greek hospitality, breakfast on the balcony and excellent views of the bay and harbour. Find these simply furnished but kitchen-equipped rooms above the ferry dock.

Delfini   TAVERNA **$**
(☑ 26450 31430; mains €8-12; ⊙ breakfast, lunch & dinner) The best of the harbour haul with fresh-cooked traditional food.

Drinking

155   BAR
(www.155cocktailbar.com; ⊙ May-Oct) Excellent cocktails (€8), opposite ecofriendly Melina's Little Shop, in from the waterfront.

West Coast

Serious beach bums should head straight for Lefkada's west coast where the sea lives up to every cliché: it's an incredible turquoise and the beaches range from arcs of cliff and white stone to broad expanses of uninterrupted sand. The long stretches of **Pefkoulia** and **Kathisma** in the north are lovely (the latter is becoming more developed and has a few studios for rent), as are **Megali Petra** and **Avali**, south of Kalamitsi. Or find remote **Egremni** and breathtaking **Porto Katsiki** in the south. Explore! You'll pass local stalls selling olive oil, honey and wine.

Word is out about the picturesque town of **Agios Nikitas**, and people flock here to enjoy the pleasant atmosphere of this holiday village, plus attractive **Mylos Beach** just around the headland. To walk, take the path by Taverna Poseidon; it's about 15 minutes up and over the peninsula, or take a water taxi (€3) from tiny Agios Nikitas Beach.

🛌 Sleeping

Agios Nikitas is loaded with lodgings.

Aloni Studios APARTMENT $
(🖉26450 33604; www.alonistudios-lefkada.com; Athani; studio/5-person apt €45/60; [P]❄) One of the better of Athani's rooms for let and surrounded by potted flowers, Aloni's ship-shape studios have kitchens and terraces, overlooking the sea.

Olive Tree Hotel HOTEL $
(🖉26450 97453; www.olivetreehotel.gr; Agios Nikitas; s/d/studio from €50/60/75; ☺May-Sep; ❄🤶) Modest rooms run by friendly Greek-Canadians.

★Mira Resort APARTMENT $$
(🖉26450 24967, 6977075881; www.miraresort. com; Tsoukalades; maisonette incl breakfast from €80; ☺May-Oct; [P]❄🤶🏊) Well-run, super-clean secluded maisonettes terrace a hillside overlooking a large pool and the open sea. Friendly owners gear the resort towards longer stays, so guests can get comfortable and unwind. Find it 6km southwest of Lefkada Town.

Hotel Agios Nikitas HOTEL $$
(🖉26450 97460; www.agiosnikitas.gr; Agios Nikitas; d incl breakfast €70; ☺May-Sep; ❄🤶) Renovated in 2011 and perched in the back part of town; some rooms have sea views.

🍴 Eating & Drinking

T'Agnantio TAVERNA $
(🖉26450 97383; www.tagnantio.gr; Agios Nikitas; mains €6-10; ☺lunch & dinner Easter-Oct) Agios Nikitas' best taverna sits up on the south side of the beach. Expect fresh seafood and Greek standards in a mellow atmosphere with sea views and a grapevine-covered pergola.

Akrotiri TAVERNA $
(🖉26450 33149; Athani; mains €7-12; ☺lunch & dinner May-Sep) Fresh fish, grilled meat and *mayirefta* are worth the stop. Tables overlook the open sea.

Kambos Taverna TAVERNA $
(🖉26450 97278; Tsoukalades; mains €5-7; ☺lunch & dinner mid-May–Sep) Follow the small lane

from the main road just south of the Tsou-kalades church to find this tiny, family-run taverna tucked among vineyards and olive groves.

Rahi CAFE $
(🖉26450 99439; www.rachi.gr; Exanthia; dishes €6-8; ☺10am-1am May-Sep) Break the journey along the coast on the terrace open to the sky, mountains and vast, blue sea, and servng cafe food and mezedhes.

Central Lefkada

The spectacular central spine of Lefkada, with its traditional farming villages, lush green peaks, fragrant pine trees, olive groves and vineyards, plus fleeting views of the islets, is well worth exploring if you have time and transport.

The small village of **Karya** is the most touristy, but has a pretty square with plane trees and tavernas and is famous for its **embroidery**, introduced in the 19th century by a remarkable one-handed local woman, Maria Koutsochero, and commemorated by a **museum** in a traditional house. For rooms, ask British Brenda Sherry at **Café Pierros** (🖉6938605898).

The island's highest village, **Englouvi**, a few kilometres south of Karya, is renowned for its honey and lentil production.

Book ahead for a guided **Herbal Walk** (🖉6934287446; www.lefkas.cc) or workshop near quaint **Alexandros**.

★Kolyvata Taverna (Maria's Taverna; 🖉6984056686, 26450 41228; mains €5-8; ☺Apr-Oct) offers a rural, culinary dream for the truly intrepid. Gregarious Kiria Maria opens the front terrace of her home to guests (reserve ahead to be sure she's there), and serves up fresh, perfectly cooked treats – whatever's ready in her garden. The *koutsoupia* (Judas) tree blooms purple in springtime, and the views of the nearby hills are idyllic. Find the tiny stone hamlet of **Kolyvata**, signposted off the road between Alexandros and Nikiana.

MEGANISI ΜΕΓΑΝΗΣΙ

POP 1040

Meganisi, with its verdant landscape and deep turquoise bays fringed by pebbled beaches, is the easiest escape from too much Nydri. It can fit into a day visit or a longer, more relaxed stay. The narrow lanes and bougainvillea-bedecked houses of **Spartohori** perch on a plateau above Porto Spilia (where the ferry docks; follow the steep road or steps behind). Pretty **Vathy** is the island's second harbour, 800m behind which sits the village of **Katomeri**. With time to spare, visit remote beaches such as **Limonari**.

Asteria Holidays (☑ 26450 51107; www.asteria.gr), at Porto Spilia, can help with everything related to the island. **Hotel Meganisi** (☑ 26450 51240; www.hotelmeganisi.gr; Katomeri; d incl breakfast €60; ❋ 🛜 ☲) has simple rooms with some sea views. The undisputed favourite fish taverna **Porto Vathy** (☑ 26450 51125; Vathy; mains €6-14; ☉ lunch & dinner) is cast out on a small quay in Vathy.

❶ Getting There & Around

The ferry runs between Nydri and Meganisi (per person/car €2/14, 25 to 40 minutes, five daily) to Porto Spilia and Vathy.

A local bus runs five to seven times daily between Spartohori and Vathy (via Katomeri) but it's worth bringing your own transport on the ferry.

KEFALLONIA
ΚΕΦΑΛΛΟΝΙΑ

POP 35,590

Wild, beautiful Kefallonia, the largest of the Ionian Islands, feels like an independent land. Its intriguing bounty includes friendly people, bucolic villages, rugged mountains, rich vineyards, soaring coastal cliffs and golden beaches. The 1953 earthquake devastated many of the island's settlements and

much of the architecture is relatively modern. Surviving villages such as Assos and Fiskardo, and the ebullient quality of life as in rebuilt Argostoli, the capital, enliven everything. Under-explored areas like Paliki Peninsula, excellent unique cuisine, and great wines round out a spectacular island.

❶ Getting There & Away

AIR

The **airport** (EFL; ☑ 26710 41511) is 9km south of Argostoli.

Air Berlin has high season flights. From May to September, many charter flights come from northern Europe and the UK.

Olympic Air (☑ 26710 41511; www.olympicair.com) Serves Athens.

Sky Express (☑ 28102 23500; www.skyexpress.gr) Serves Corfu, Preveza and Zakynthos.

Domestic Flights from Kefallonia

DESTINATION	TIME	FARE	FREQUENCY
Athens	55min	€110	2 daily
Corfu	1hr	€55	3 weekly
Kythira	1¾hr	€57	3 weekly
Preveza	20min	€49	3 weekly
Zakynthos	25min	€55	3 weekly

BOAT
Port Authority (☑ 26710 22224)

Domestic

Frequent **Ionian Ferries** (www.ionianferries.gr) connect Poros and Argostoli to Kyllini in the Peloponnese. The ferry **Ionian Pelagos** (☑ in Sami, Kefallonia 26740 23405, in Vasiliki, Lefkada 26450 31520) links Sami with Astakos in the Peloponnese (sometimes via Piso Aetos in

BOAT SERVICES FROM KEFALLONIA

DESTINATION	PORT	TIME	FARE	FREQUENCY
Agios Nikolaos (Zakynthos)	Pesada	1½hr	€8	2 daily (May-Sep)
Astakos (mainland)	Sami	3hr	€10	1-2 daily
Igoumenitsa (mainland)	Sami	4¼hr	€15	1 weekly
Kyllini (Peloponnese)	Argostoli	3hr	€14	1 daily
Kyllini	Poros	1½hr	€10	5-6 daily
Patra (Peloponnese)	Sami	2¾hr	€18.20	1 daily
Piso Aetos (Ithaki)	Sami	30min	€3	2 weekly
Vasiliki (Lefkada)	Fiskardo	1hr	€8	2-3 daily
Vasiliki	Sami	1¾hr	€8	2 weekly (seasonal)
Vathy (Ithaki)	Sami	45min	€5.70	1 daily

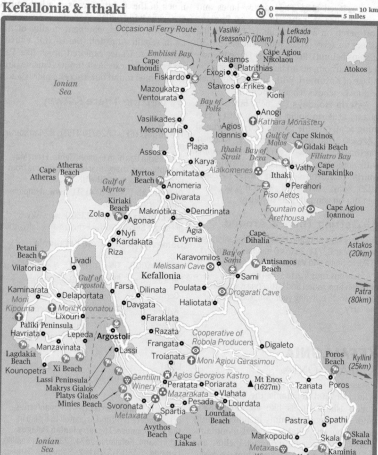

Ithaki). Some months, **ferries** (☑ 26450 31520) go directly from Sami to Vasiliki (Lefkada).

Strintzis Lines (www.strintzisferries.gr) has two ferries daily connecting Sami with Patra in the Peloponnese and Vathy or Piso Aetos in Ithaki.

West Ferry (www.westferry.gr) goes from Fiskardo, and sometimes Sami, to Vasiliki (Lefkada). It sometimes serves Frikes (Ithaki), usually from Vasiliki, but occasioanally from Fiskardo. Get information and tickets at **Nautilus Travel** (☑ 26740 41440; Fiskardo).

May to September, two daily **ferries** (☑ 26710 91280) connect the remote port of Pesada in the south to Agios Nikolaos on the northern tip

of Zakynthos. Buses to the ports are rare, so an alternative is to sail from Argostoli to Kyllini in the Peloponnese, and from there to Zakynthos Town.

Some Italy ferries stop in Sami on their way to/from Corfu or Igoumenitsa.

International

In high season, ferries like Ventouris (p737) connect Sami and Bari, Italy. **Endeavor Lines** (www.endeavor-lines.com) sometimes serves Brindisi via Corfu and Igoumenitsa. To get to other ports in Italy, take the ferry first from Sami to Patra.

Blue Sea Travel (☑ 26740 23007; www.sami star.com; Sami) On Sami's waterfront.

Vassilatos Shipping (☑ 26710 22618; Antoni Tritsi 54, Argostoli) Opposite Argostoli port authority.

BUS

Three daily buses connect Argostoli with Athens (€45, seven hours), via Patra (€27, four hours) using the ferry; buses also go to Athens from Sami (two daily), Poros (daily) and Lixouri (daily). **Argostoli KTEL bus station** (☑ 26710 22276; www.ktelkefallonias.gr; Antoni Tritsi 5) On Argostoli's southern waterfront. Excellent printed schedule.

ℹ Getting Around

TO/FROM THE AIRPORT
There's no airport bus; taxis cost around €18.

BOAT
Car ferries connect Argostoli and Lixouri, on the island's western Paliki Peninsula (per person/car €3.50/4.50, 30 minutes, hourly from 7.30am to 10.30pm, plus half-hourly to midnight July and August).

BUS
KTEL Buses (p653) serve Lassi Peninsula (€1.60, seven daily), Sami (€4.50, four daily), Poros (€5, two daily), Skala (€5, two daily) and Fiskardo (€6, daily). Once-daily east-coast service links Katelios with Skala, Poros, Sami, Agia Evfymia and Fiskardo. No buses run on Sunday.

CAR & MOTORCYCLE
Car- and bike-hire companies fill major resorts. **Europcar** (☑ 26710 42020) At the airport. **Hertz** (☑ 26710 42142) At the airport. **Karavomilos** (☑ 26740 22779; Sami) Does deliveries.

Argostoli Αργοστόλι
POP 8932

Animated and appealing Argostoli bubbles with activity in its pastel-bright streets. It was laid flat during the 1953 earthquake and is now a town of broad boulevards and pedestrianised shopping streets, like **Lithostroto**, centring on lively inland **Plateia Valianou**. In summer, *kantadoroi* amble the streets singing *kantades*, traditional songs accompanied by guitar and mandolin.

◉ Sights

Pick up the events booklet from the EOT to see what's on.

★**Korgialenio History & Folklore Museum** MUSEUM
(☑ 26710 28835; www.corgialenios.gr; Ilia Zervou 12; admission €3; ⊙ 9am-2pm Mon-Sat) Dedicated to preserving Kefallonian art and culture, this fine museum houses icons and pre-earthquake furniture, clothes and artwork from the homes of gentry and farmworkers.

★**Focas-Kosmetatos Foundation** MUSEUM
(☑ 26710 26595; Valianou; adult/child €3/free; ⊙ 10am-1pm Mon-Fri, low season by appointment) See displays on Kefallonia's cultural and political history in a pre-earthquake building. Its **Cephalonia Botanica** (⊙ 8.30am-2.30pm Mon-Fri) **FREE**, a lovely botanical garden, is about 2km from Argostoli centre.

Archaeological Museum MUSEUM
(☑ 26710 28300; Rokou Vergoti; admission €3; ⊙ 8am-3pm Tue-Sun) A collection of island relics, including Mycenaean finds.

Beaches BEACH
The town's closest, largest sandy beaches are crowded **Makrys Gialos** and **Platys Gialos**, 5km south on Lassi Peninsula. **Lourdata**, 16km from Argostoli on the Argostoli–Poros road, also has an attractive expansive beach set against a mountainous green backdrop.

🛏 Sleeping

★**Vivian Villa** PENSION $
(☑ 26710 23396; www.kefalonia-vivianvilla.gr; Deladetsima 11; d/studio €45/55; ✳ ☎) Friendly owners operate big, bright, tidy rooms, some with kitchens. The top-floor two-bedroom apartment is excellent; there's a lift. Located in a residential neighbourhood near the centre. Prices are discounted for longer stays.

Mirabel Hotel HOTEL $
(☑ 26710 25381; www.mirabelhotel.com; Plateia Valianou; d incl breakfast €60; ✳ @ ☎) Straightforward rooms sit on the main square in this busy business hotel.

Camping Argostoli CAMPGROUND $
(☑ 26710 23487; www.campingargostoli.gr; camp sites per adult/car/tent €6/3/5; ⊙ Jun-Oct; P ☎) Pleasant, quiet spot near the lighthouse on the northernmost point of the peninsula.

Hotel Ionian Plaza HOTEL $$
(☑ 26710 25581; www.ionianplaza.gr; Plateia Valianou; d/tr/q incl breakfast from €85/100/115; P ✳ @ ☎) Argostoli's smartest hotel, smack on the square, has a stylish marble-decorated lobby and small well-appointed rooms

Argostoli

Argostoli

◎ Top Sights
1 Focas-Kosmetatos Foundation B3
2 Korgialenio History & Folklore
   Museum B4

◎ Sights
3 Archaeological Museum B3

⊜ Sleeping
4 Hotel Ionian Plaza B2
5 Mirabel Hotel B3
6 Vivian Villa A1

⊗ Eating
7 Arhontiko B2
8 Casa Grec C3
9 Ladokolla B1
10 Produce & Meat Markets D4
11 Spathis C4

⊕ Entertainment
12 Bass Club C3

with balconies. Top-floor rooms have the best views.

✗ Eating

The waterfront produce and meat **markets** have nearby supermarkets and bakeries (such as the local powerhouse, Spathis).

Ladokolla   SOUVLAKI $
(☑26710 25522; Xarokopou 13; dishes €2-8; ☺12.30pm-2am) Piping-hot chicken, pork or lamb kebabs and pittas are delivered without plates onto table-top covers. Staff bring a plate for anything saucy, but this is down-to-earth nosh, popular locally and with lively service.

★ Casa Grec   MEDITERRANEAN $$
(☑26710 24091; S Metaxa 12; mains €12-22; ☺dinner, reduced hours in low season) Elegant, magical lighting, textiles and murals and a candlelit courtyard set the stage for refined dishes, each made from scratch by the chef-

owner, Costas. Pasta is dressed with nuanced sauces, steaks are succulent, desserts a dream. The chef's Greek-Canadian wife assists tableside with charm and humour, and the wine list is excellent.

Arhontiko KEFALLONIAN $$
(☑26710 27213; Risospaston 5; mains €7-17; ⊙breakfast, lunch & dinner) Tuck into top Kefallonian cuisine with starters such as a soufflé of spinach and excellent mains such as the whopping Kefallonian meat pie or *exohiko* (pork stuffed with tomatoes, onions, peppers and feta). Good house wines, relaxed, helpful service, and a cosy atmosphere round out the experience.

 Drinking & Nightlife

Cafes line Plateia Valianou and Lithostroto and bounce by late evening. **Bass Club** (www.bassclub.gr; cnr S Metaxa & Vergoti) draws the younger set. The popular club-restaurant **Katavothres** (☑26710 22221; waterfront) contains unusual geological formations, top-name DJs and a mixed crowd. **Stavento**, in Makrys Gialos, hops in summer.

 Information

The main ferry quay is at the northern end of the waterfront and the bus station is at its southern end. Banks with ATMs line the northern waterfront and Lithostroto.

EOT (☑26710 22248; ⊙7am-2.30pm Mon-Fri) On the northern waterfront by the port police.

Around Argostoli

You can make a gorgeous loop connecting Agios Georgios Kastro, Moni Agiou Gerasimou, Robola vineyards and the sea coast, or walks in **Mt Ainos**.

 Sights

★**Agios Georgios Kastro** RUIN
(Castle of St George; ⊙8.30am-3pm Tue-Sun) **FREE** This Venetian *kastro* (castle) from the 1500s sits atop a hill southeast of Argostoli and was the capital of Kefallonia for about 200 years. Well worth a visit for its stellar views, the castle is surrounded by a small village with Byzantine churches and restaurants (also with stunning vistas). **Palatino** (☑26710 68490; mains €7-10; ⊙lunch & dinner May-Oct) creates home-cooked Kefallonian specialities. **Astraios** (☑26710 69152; ⊙9pm-late) is a live Greek music bar owned by venerated musician Dionysos Frangopoulos.

Moni Agiou Gerasimou MONASTERY
(⊙9am-1pm & 3.30-8pm) Dedicated to Kefallonia's patron saint, the monastery, 16km east of Argostoli, is cared for by nuns. Inside the chapel lies the famous cave where Gerasimos escaped from the rigours of monastic life to even greater self-abnegation. Descend via a steep metal ladder into a small chamber 6m below.

Paliki Peninsula
Χερσόνησος Παλική

Anchored by the bustling gulf-side town of **Lixouri**, the Paliki Peninsula is an under-explored region of spectral white, cream and red clay cliffs, verdant farmland and vineyards, and hilltop villages. Beaches such as white-sanded **Petani** in the north and red-sanded **Xi** in the south add to the spice,

IONIAN ON THE VINE

The Ionian Islands would not be the same without wine, and Kefallonia especially has outstanding vintages, most notably from the unique Robola grape (VQRPD). Other varieties like Mavrodaphne (AOC) and Muscat (AOC) enhance the viniculture.

High in the mountains southeast of Argostoli, at the heart of verdant Omala Valley, lies the fascinating winery of the **Cooperative of Robola Producers of Kefallonia** (☑26710 86301; www.robola.gr; Omala; ⊙9am-8pm May-Sep, to 3pm Mon-Fri Oct-Apr) **FREE**. Here, grapes from about 300 independent growers are transformed into the yellow-green Robola, a dry white wine of subtle yet lively flavours. The grape is said to have been introduced by the Venetians and its wine was a favourite of the doge. It grows exuberantly on high ground, and the light soils, wet winters and arid summers of Kefallonia are ideal for its cultivation.

The smaller, very distinguished **Gentilini** (☑26710 41618; Minies) is 2km south of Argostoli on the airport road in a charming setting, with a range of superb wines including the scintillating Classico.

though Xi gets packed in summer. **Moni Kipouria**, a monastery built by a lone monk, overlooks stark cliffs, azure seas and robust vineyards, and is worth the trip to the far west of the peninsula.

Lixouri's central square sits waterside and throngs with life. The easiest way to access the peninsula from Argostoli is by the car ferry (per person/car €3.50/4.50, 30 minutes, hourly September to June, half-hourly July and August), and makes a fun half-day trip even if you don't have your own wheels. **Perdikis Travel** (26710 91097; tvrperdi@hol.gr), on Lixouri's southern seafront, helps with accommodation and arrangements.

Sleeping & Eating

Xi Village PENSION $
(26710 93830; www.xi-village.gr; Xi; d/tr/q €60/70/100; P❄️🛜🏊) Grab a tidy spot overlooking Xi Beach, with a pool.

★**Niforos** APARTMENT $$
(26710 97350; Petani; studios €75; ☺May-Oct; P❄️🛜🏊) Spacious, immaculate studios above Petani Beach have balconies overlooking the open sea. Friendly owners, large pool and on-site restaurant add to the charm.

Erasmia TAVERNA $
(26710 97372; Petani Beach; mains €6-8; ☺lunch & dinner May-Sep) Humble it may be at this beachside shack in Petani, but reserve ahead in August if you want a table and delish home-cooked treats. Great sunsets.

Apolafsi SEAFOOD $
(26710 91691; www.apolafsi.gr; Lepeda; mains €8-10; ☺lunch & dinner; P❄️🛜) Recommended as both a great restaurant with fresh seafood and grilled meats, and as a convenient hotel. Rooms (doubles including breakfast €50 to €60) have kitchens and splashed-out bathrooms; 2km south of Lixouri.

Mavroeidis BAKERY $
Perfect pit stop on the main square in Lixouri for the best *amygdalopita* (sweet almond cake) on the island.

Oi Nisoi Vardianoi TAVERNA $$
(6986948528; Xi; mains €8-15; ☺1.30pm-late) Excellent alfresco dining above Xi Beach. Reserve in summer.

Sami & Surrounds Σάμη
POP 1245

Sami, 25km northeast of Argostoli and the main port of Kefallonia, has a waterside strip loaded with tourist-oriented cafes, but beyond this it's an attractive town, nestled in a bright bay and flanked by steep hills. There are several monasteries, ancient castle ruins, walks and nearby beaches (such as **Antisamos Beach**) that are worth a trip. **Agia Evfymia** on the north side of the bay makes for a quieter alternative. Nearby **Melissani** and **Drogarati** caves are rather overrated.

Activities

The tourist office offers brochures outlining **walks** through the area; one covers Sami and Antisamos, another the trail from Agia Evfymia to Myrtos.

Sleeping & Eating

Karavomilos Beach Camping CAMPGROUND $
(26740 22480; www.camping-karavomilos.gr; Sami–Karavomilos Rd; camp sites per adult/car/tent €8.50/3.50/6; ☺May-Sep; @🛜🏊) This is a large, award-winning campground in a great beachfront location, with fantastic bathrooms and loads of facilities.

Gerasimos Dendrinos APARTMENT $
(26740 61455; Agia Evfymia; d €45; ❄️) This quiet option sits on the north side of Agia Evfymia. A gentle couple tends the rose

gardens and these tidy studios with unobstructed bay views.

Hotel Athina
HOTEL $$

(☑26740 22779; www.athinahotel.gr; Karavomilos; d incl breakfast from €60; ☺May-Oct; ❋@) Painted in cool greys, this simple resort hotel has studios overlooking the bay. Guests use the pool next door at swank **Ionian Emerald Resort** (☑26740 22708; www.ionian emerald.gr; d incl breakfast from €150) which has the same owner.

Melissani Hotel
HOTEL $$

(☑26740 22464; Dihalion 23, Sami; s/d/tr €50/65/75; ☺May-Oct; ❋) Unashamed retro style welcomes you at this slim building two blocks in from the waterfront. The smallish rooms have balconies with views of either mountains or sea.

★ Paradise Beach
KEFALLONIAN $

(Dendrinos; ☑26740 61392; Agia Evfymia; mains €6-13; ☺lunch & dinner mid-May–mid-Oct) Bear right past the Agia Evfymia harbourfront and continue until the road ends at famous Dendrinos, overlooking the Bay of Sami. The cheerful Dendrinos family offer outstanding local specialities, including dolmadhes (vine leaves stuffed with rice and sometimes meat), Kefallonian meat pie, or braised rabbit. Choose from what's fresh and save room for chocolate soufflé with rich citrus cream. Penelope Cruz and Nicholas Cage were regulars when filming *Captain Corelli's Mandolin* here.

ℹ Information

All facilities, including post office and banks, are in Sami. Buses for Argostoli usually meet ferries. Hire cars through Karavomilos (p653).

Port Authority (☑26740 22031; Sami)

Assos
Ασσος

Tiny, gorgeous Assos is an upmarket gem of whitewashed and pastel houses, many of them pre-earthquake. Baby Italian cypresses dot the steep mountain descending to the town which straddles the isthmus of a peninsula topped by a **Venetian fortress**. The fortress makes a great hike, with superlative views and old-world ambience, and the tiny green bay is eminently swimmable.

🛏 Sleeping & Eating

Apartment Linardos
APARTMENT $$

(☑26740 51563; www.linardosapartments.gr; d €70; ☺May-Sep; ❋) Spotless studios with

---

MYRTOS BEACH

One of Greece's most breathtaking picture-perfect beaches is **Myrtos**, 8km south of Assos along an exciting stretch of the west coast road. From a roadside viewing area, admire the white sand and shimmering blue water set between tall limestone cliffs far below. Reach the beach down a zigzagging road. The beach drops off sharply, but once you're in the water it's heavenly. Think clichéd turquoise and aqua water. And hordes in summer.

---

kitchens have beautiful views of town, the beach and the fortress.

Platanos
TAVERNA $

(mains €6-15; ☺breakfast, lunch & dinner Easter-Oct) Admired island-wide for its locally sourced, fresh ingredients and top-notch cooking, Platanos fills part of an attractive shady plaza near the waterfront. Strong on meat dishes, there are also fish and vegetarian options such as vegetable *mousakas*.

Fiskardo
Φισκάρδο

POP 230

Tiny, precious Fiskardo, 50km north of Argostoli, was the only Kefallonian village left largely intact after the 1953 earthquake. Its fine Venetian buildings, framed by cypress-mantled hills, have an authentic picturesque appeal and it's popular with well-heeled yachting fans. The outstanding restaurants and chilled-out feel might entice you to stay a while.

🛏 Sleeping

Rooms are deeply discounted in low season.

Villa Romantza
PENSION $

(☑26740 41322; www.villa-romantza.gr; r/studio/ apt €35/45/60; ❋) An excellent budget choice with simple, spacious clean rooms and studios.

Regina's Rooms
PENSION $

(☑26740 41125; www.regina-studios-boats.gr; d/tr €50/60; ❋☎) Friendly Regina runs a popular place with colourful rooms dotted with plastic flowers. Some have kitchenettes (add €5) and/or balconies with views to the port.

Archontiko
PENSION $$

(☑ 26740 41342; www.archontiko-fiskardo.gr; d without/with sea view €50/70; ☼) Overlooking the harbour, balconies of these luxurious rooms in a restored stone mansion are perfect for people-watching.

Stella Apartments
APARTMENT $$

(☑ 26740 41211; www.stella-apartments.gr; studio/apt from €65/130; ☼ @ ☎) On the quiet southern outskirts, these immaculate, spacious studios have full kitchens and balconies with outstanding sea views.

★ Emelisse Hotel
RESORT $$$

(☑ 26740 41200; www.arthotel.gr; Emblissi Bay; d/ste from €265/285, 4-person apt from €750, all incl breakfast; ⊙ mid-Apr–mid-Oct; P ☼ @ ☎ ☒) Situated in a superb position overlooking unspoiled Emblissi Bay, 1km west of Fiskardo, this stylish, luxurious hotel has every facility for the pampered holiday. Beautifully appointed rooms (think sleek comfort) tuck into immaculately cultivated terraces leading down to the crowning glory: a lavish swimming pool and restaurant (both open for day use) with fantastic sea views to Lefkada, Ithaki and beyond.

✖ Eating & Drinking

Fiskardo has some seriously top-level restaurants. Bars and cafes dot the doll-house waterfront for great people-watching.

★ Tassia
MEDITERRANEAN $$

(☑ 26740 41205; mains €7-25; ⊙ lunch & dinner May-Oct) Tassia Dendrinou, celebrated chef and writer on Greek cuisine, runs this portside Fiskardo institution. Everything is a refined delight, but specialities include baby marrow croquettes and a fisherman's pasta dish incorporating finely chopped squid, octopus, mussels and prawns in a magic combination that includes a dash of cognac.

Meat dishes are equally splendid and Tassia's desserts are rightfully famous.

Café Tselenti
ITALIAN $$

(☑ 26740 41344; mains €10-23; ⊙ lunch & dinner May-Oct) Housed in a lovely 19th-century building owned by the Tselenti family since 1893, this noted restaurant has a romantic outdoor terrace at the heart of the village. Outstanding cuisine includes aubergine rolls and terrific linguine with prawns, mussels and crayfish.

Vasso's
SEAFOOD $$

(☑ 26740 41276; mains €10-40; ⊙ lunch & dinner May-Oct) Whether it's fresh grilled fish or pasta with crayfish, Vasso's is *the* place to head for exceptional seafood.

ℹ Information

Nautilus Travel (p652) and **Pama Travel** (☑ 26740 41033; www.pamatravel.com; Fiskardo) arrange everything. Both have internet access (€2 per 30 minutes). Visit www.fiscardo.com for town info.

ITHAKI ΙΘΑΚΗ

POP 3180

Sheltered Ithaki dreams happily between Kefallonia and mainland Greece. The island is celebrated as the mythical home of Homer's Odysseus, where loyal wife Penelope waited patiently, besieged by unsavoury suitors, for Odysseus' much-delayed homecoming. This tranquil island is made up of two large bodies of land joined by a narrow isthmus. Sheer cliffs, precipitous, arid mountains and occasional olive groves gild this Ionian jewel. Diminutive villages (much rebuilt after the 1953 earthquake) and hidden coves with pebbly beaches add to the charm, while monasteries and churches offer Byzantine delights and splendid views.

BOAT SERVICES FROM ITHAKI

DESTINATION	PORT	TIME	FARE	FREQUENCY
Astakos (mainland)	Piso Aetos	2hr 20min	€10	1-2 daily
Patra (Peloponnese)	Piso Aetos	3¼hr	€21	1 daily
Sami (Kefallonia)	Piso Aetos	30min	€3	2 daily
Vasiliki (Lefkada)	Frikes	1hr	€8	5 weekly
Vasiliki	Piso Aetos	1¼hr	€8	2 weekly, seasonal

❶ Getting There & Away

BOAT

Strintzis Lines (www.strintzisferries.gr) has two ferries daily connecting Vathy or Piso Aetos with Patra in the Peloponnese via Sami on Kefallonia.

The ferry **Ionian Pelagos** (✆ 26740 32104) runs daily (sometimes twice a day) in high season between Piso Aetos, Sami and Astakos on the mainland.

West Ferry (www.westferry.gr) runs an ever-changing schedule from Frikes to Vasiliki, Lefkada. Sometimes ferries go from Frikes to Fiskardo, but usually you have to go via Vasiliki.

You can get information and tickets from Vathy's two travel agencies; they each serve different ferry companies.

Port Authority (✆ 26740 32909)

BUS

You can buy a bus ticket to Athens (€22, plus €18.60 for the ferry, daily), which requires boarding the ferry to Patra in Vathy; then, at Sami the bus loads on and you must find it.

❶ Getting Around

Piso Aetos, on Ithaki's west coast, has no settlement; taxis often meet boats, as does the municipal bus in high season only.

The island's one bus runs twice daily (weekdays only, more often in high season) between Kioni and Vathy via Stavros and Frikes (€3.90). Its limited schedule is not suited to day-trippers.

To travel around the island your best bet is to hire a moped or car (high season from €35), or motorboat. Companies will make deliveries for a fee (€10 to €15).

AGS (✆ 26740 32702; Vathy) On the western harbourfront.

Alpha Bike & Car Hire (✆ 26740 33243; www.alphacarsgreece.com; Vathy) Behind Alpha Bank.

Sea Taxi (✆ 6972142374, 26740 33581)

Taxis (✆ 6944790943, 6944686504, 6945700214) Taxis are relatively expensive (about €30 for the Vathy–Frikes trip).

Vathy   Βαθύ

POP 1820

Ithaki's laid-back main town sprawls along its elongated waterfront. The central square, Plateia Efstathiou Drakouli, buzzes with seafront traffic and cafes, and narrow lanes wriggle inland from the quay. Somewhat bedraggled, despite its gorgeous waters and surrounding mountains, Vathy is the only

place on the island with nightclubs, banks, travel agencies and the like.

Activities

★ Island Walks   WALKING

Ithaki's compact nature ensures dramatic scenery changes over short distances on walks that can reveal 360-degree views of the sea and surrounding islands. Several marked trails exist, and guided walks, including the popular Homer's Walk, explore little-seen parts of the island and are organised through **Island Walks** (www.islandwalks.com; €15-18). Routes range from 5km to 13km.

Day Trips   BOAT TOURS

Albatross (✆ 6976901643) and **Mana Korina** (✆ 6976654351) sail from Vathy in high season around Ithaki and in various combinations to Fiskardo, Lefkada and 'unknown islands' including Atokos and Kalamos (€45). They also make runs to **Gidaki Beach** (€10). To access Gidaki on foot, follow the walking track from **Skinari Beach**.

🛏 Sleeping

Grivas Gerasimos Rooms   PENSION $

(✆ 26740 33328; d/tr €40/45) A friendly proprietress maintains spacious studios with small balconies and sea views. Go right at the Century Club on the waterfront, then first left at the road parallel to the sea, then another 50m.

Odyssey Apartments   APARTMENT $$

(✆ 26740 33400; www.odysseyapartments.gr; studio €100, 1-/2-bedroom apt €130/160; P ❄ ☀) Perched on a hill 500m out of town, but worth it for its jovial owner, spotless studios and apartments (some for five people) and balconies with magical views of the yacht harbour and beyond. Signposted at the eastern end of the waterfront.

Hotel Familia   BOUTIQUE HOTEL $$

(✆ 26740 33366; www.hotel-familia.com; Odysseos 60; s/d incl breakfast from €90/105; ❄ ☎) This olive press has been turned into a swank boutique hotel. Chic slate is juxtaposed with soft tapestries and gentle lighting to create a wow effect. Family-run and friendly, but only one room has a courtyard, and there are no sea views.

Hotel Mentor   HOTEL $$

(✆ 26740 32433; www.hotelmentor.gr; s/d/tr/q incl breakfast €75/85/105/135; ❄ ☎) No-nonsense, tidy rooms on the harbourfront; some have views.

★**Hotel Perantzada** BOUTIQUE HOTEL $$$
(☑26740 33496; www.arthotel.gr/perantzada; Odyssea Androutsou; s/d incl breakfast from €135/170; ☉Easter–mid-Oct; ❋@☎☙) Three renovated buildings strung together create different moods: classic-quaint to sleek modern. Each is custom-fitted to highlight art, architecture and oh, yes, the views of the bay and mountains. Whether glorying in your modernist Ingo Maurer accoutrements or lazing by the decadent infinity pool, you will be casually pampered. Buffet breakfasts are every bit as decadent.

 Eating

Ithaki and Vathy's food situation is fairly ho-hum, so count on people-watching for satiation. For a sweet experience, try *rovani*, the local speciality made with rice, honey and cloves, at one of the patisseries on or near the main square.

Trehantiri TAVERNA $
(☑26740 33444; mains €5-8; ☉lunch & dinner) Old-school good eats flourish at this tiny backstreet taverna, across from the flower shop. Check behind the counter to see what's fresh and gab with the locals.

🛈 **Information**

Ithaki has no tourist office. **Delas Tours** (☑26740 32104) and **Polyctor Tours** (☑26740 33120; www.ithakiholidays.com), both on the main square, help with information. The square has the island's only banks (with ATMs) and the post office.

Around Ithaki

Ithaki reaches back into the mythical past to claim several sites associated with Homer's 'Odyssey'. Finding them can be an epic journey of its own: signage is scant. The **Fountain of Arethousa**, in the island's south, is where Odysseus' swineherd, Eumaeus, is believed to have brought his pigs to drink. The exposed and isolated hike, through unspoilt landscape with great sea views, takes 1½ to two hours (return) from the turn-off; this excludes the hilly 5km trudge up the road to the sign itself.

The location of Odysseus' palace has been much disputed and archaeologists have been unable to find conclusive evidence; some present-day archaeologists speculate that it was on **Pelikata Hill** near Stavros, while German archaeologist Heinrich Schliemann believed it to be at **Alalkomenes**, near Piso Aetos.

Take a break from Homeric myth and head north from Vathy along a fabulously scenic mountain road to sleepy **Anogi**, the old capital. Its restored church of **Agia Panagia** (claimed to be from the 12th century) has incredible Byzantine frescoes and a Venetian bell tower. Obtain keys from the neighbouring *kafeneio*. About 200m uphill, the small but evocative ruins of **Old Anogi** fill a rock-studded landscape.

Further north again, the inland village of **Stavros**, above the Bay of Polis, is also reachable via the west-coast road, and has the only ATM outside of Vathy. Visit its small, interesting **archaeological museum** (☑26740 31305; ☉8.30am-3pm Tue-Sun) FREE, with local artefacts dating from 3000 BC to the Roman period.

Driving north, make your way to the top of **Exogi** for panoramic views; on the way you'll pass the **House of Homer** archaeological dig, down a dirt road signposted on the right.

Heading northeast from Stavros takes you to the tiny, scrubby seafront village of **Frikes**, the ferry departure point for Lefkada. Clasped between windswept cliffs, it has a swathe of waterfront restaurants and busy bars.

From Frikes a twisting road hugs the beautiful coastline to end at lovely **Kioni**, perhaps the island's most picturesque seafront village. It spills down a verdant hillside to a miniature harbour where yachts overnight and sailors fill the few tavernas and cafes.

🛏 **Sleeping**

Ourania Apartments APARTMENT $
(☑26740 31027; www.ithacagreece.com/ourania/ourania.htm; Stavros; apt from €40; ℗❋) These homey studios are maintained by a friendly English-speaking proprietress. Views from the fantastic garden sweep over olive groves down to the sea.

Captain's Apartments APARTMENT $$
(☑26740 31481; www.captains-apartments.gr; Kioni; 2-/4-person apt €70/95; ❋☎) Well run and definitely shipshape are these well-maintained studios and apartments with forest views. They're signposted halfway down the twisting road to Kioni's harbour.

Kioni Apartments APARTMENT $$
(☑26740 31144; www.ithacagreece.eu; Kioni; apt €80; ☺May-Oct; ❋) Simple, centrally located studios sit right on the Kioni harbourfront. Four-night minimum occasionally enforced.

Eating & Drinking

In Kioni, comfy **Cafe Spavento** (☑26740 31427; Kioni; ☎) has wi-fi.

Stavros has a collection of basic eateries including **Ithaki Restaurant** (☑26740 31080; mains €8-14; ☺lunch & dinner) with home-cooked taverna food, garden restaurant **Polyphemus** (☑26740 31794; mains €10-16; ☺lunch & dinner), and cafes like **Sunset** for views and **To Kentro** for jawing locals.

★**Yefuri** TAVERNA $$
(☑26740 31131; Platrithias; mains €7-16; ☺dinner Tue-Sun, reduced hours low season) Perhaps the best restaurant outside of Vathy is Yefuri, with its fresh produce and rotating menu. It's on the road between Stavros and Platrithias.

Mythos TAVERNA $
(☑26740 31122; Kioni; mains €6-10; ☺lunch & dinner) In Kioni, Mythos has excellent *pastitsio* and other Greek staples.

Rementzo TAVERNA $
(☑26740 31719; Frikes; mains €6-12; ☺lunch & dinner) Located in Frikes, Rementzo does good-value Greek standards.

ZAKYNTHOS ΖΑΚΥΝΘΟΣ

POP 40,650

Zakynthos, also known by its Italian name Zante, battles against heavy package tourism along its eastern and southeast coasts. Underneath the brouhaha it is essentially a beautiful island with western and central regions of forested mountains dropping off to unreal turquoise waters. The northern and southern capes remain verdant and less exploited, and Zante Town adds a bit of sparkle to the overrun east, where the loggerhead turtle population struggles in the face of development.

ℹ Getting There & Away

AIR
Domestic
Astra Airlines (www.astra-airlines.gr) Flies to Thessaloniki.
Olympic Air (☑26950 42617, 801 801 0101; www.olympicair.com; Zakynthos Airport; ☺8am-10pm Mon-Fri) Flies to Athens.
Sky Express (☑28102 23500; www.skyexpress.gr) Flies to Corfu via Kefallonia and Preveza, and to Kythira.

International
May to September, charter flights come from northern Europe and the UK.
Air Berlin (www.airberlin.com) Flies to Germany.
EasyJet (www.easyjet.com) Flies to Gatwick and Milan in high season.

BOAT
Domestic
Ionian Ferries (☑26950 22083; www.ionianferries.gr; Lomvardou 40 & 72, Zakynthos Town) runs between four and eight ferries daily, depending on the season, between Zakynthos Town and Kyllini in the Peloponnese. Occasional international ferries call in on their way to/from Corfu, Igoumenitsa, Sami (Kefallonia), and Bari and Brindisi, Italy.

From the northern port of Agios Nikolaos a ferry serves Pesada in southern Kefallonia twice daily from May to October. **Chionis Tours** (☑26950 48996; Lomvardou 8, Zakynthos Town) sells tickets. There are barely any buses to the two ports, though, so unless you have wheels or a ride, it's better to cross to Kyllini and catch another ferry to Kefallonia.
Port Authority (☑26950 42556)

International
Ionian Ferries sells tickets for high-season services to Brindisi, Italy via Igoumenitsa and Corfu on Minoan Lines (p737), Superfast (p737) and Blue Star Ferries (p737). Ventouris (p737) goes to Bari.

BUS
Zakynthos KTEL bus station (☑26950 22255; www.ktel-zakynthos.gr) On the bypass to the west of Zakynthos Town. A bus runs from St Denis church at the harbour to the station. Services include Athens (€26, six hours, three

BOAT SERVICES FROM ZAKYNTHOS

DESTINATION	PORT	TIME	FARE	FREQUENCY
Kyllini (Peloponnese)	Zakynthos Town	1hr	€8	6 daily
Pesada (Kefallonia)	Agios Nikolaos	1½hr	€8	2 daily, seasonal

Zakynthos

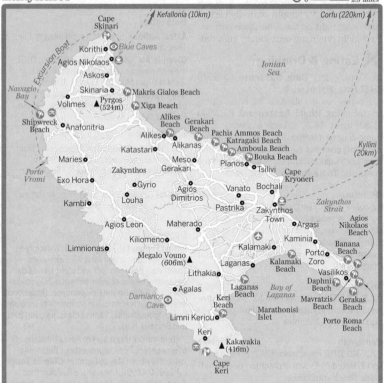

daily; can stop at Corinth KTEL), Patra (€8, 3½ hours, three daily) and Thessaloniki (€50, 10 hours, two weekly). Budget an additional €8 for the ferry to Kyllini.

ⓘ Getting Around

There's no bus between Zakynthos Town and the airport, 6km to the southwest. A taxi costs around €12.

Frequent buses go from Zakynthos Town's KTEL bus station to the developed resorts of Alikes (€1.70), Tsilivi, Argasi, Laganas and Kalamaki (all €1.60). Several useful local buses take the upper or lower main roads to Katastari and Volimes. Bus services to other villages are infrequent.

Rent cars (from €40 in high season) and motorcycles at the airport or in larger resorts.

Europcar (☑26950 41541; Ferry Quay, Zakynthos Town) Delivers to the airport.

Hertz Zakynthos Town (☑26950 45706); Airport (☑26950 24287)

Zakynthos Town Ζάκυνθος

POP 10,765

Zippy Zakynthos Town is the capital and port of the island and wraps round an enormous blue bay. The town was devastated by the 1953 earthquake, but was reconstructed with arcaded streets, imposing squares and gracious neoclassical public buildings. A Venetian fortress looks down from a hill on the hubbub of town life.

◉ Sights & Activities

The central square, Plateia Agiou Markou, is the place to people-watch.

★**Byzantine Museum**　　　　MUSEUM
(☑26950 42714; Plateia Solomou; admission €3; ◷8.30am-3pm Tue-Sun) Visit two levels of fabulous ecclesiastical art, rescued from churches razed by the earthquake. The beautiful building overlooks the main plaza.

Inside, the 16th-century St Andreas Monastery has been artfully 'replicated' to house its restored frescoes.

Museum of Solomos MUSEUM
(☑ 26950 48982; www.museumsolomos.gr; Plateia Agiou Markou 15; adult/child €4/free; ☺ 9am-2pm) The museum houses the memorabilia and archives of Dionysios Solomos (1798–1857), who was born on Zakynthos and is regarded as the father of modern Greek poetry. His *Hymn to Liberty* became the Greek national anthem.

Church of Dionysios CHURCH
(museum admission €2; ☺ museum 9am-1pm & 5-9pm) The church for the patron saint of the island, in Zakynthos Town's south, holds amazing giltwork and frescoes. Its ecclesiastical museum contains intriguing icons from the Monastery of Strofades (home to Dionysios for several years) plus scrolls from the 13th and 14th centuries.

Kastro RUIN
(☑ 26950 48099; admission €3; ☺ 8am-3pm Tue-Sun) This peaceful, shady and pine tree–filled ruined Venetian fortress sits high above Zakynthos Town. It's 2.5km from town; use the car park in Bochali and walk 300m.

🛌 Sleeping

Hotel Alba PENSION $
(☑ 26950 26641; www.albahotel.gr; L Ziva 38; d from €44; ❄ @) Polished, creamy marble and a cheery, well-lit feel brighten up simple rooms and even simpler bathrooms in this hotel in the centre.

Hotel Palatino HOTEL $$
(☑ 26950 27780; www.palatinohotel.gr; Kolokotroni 10; d/q from €75/130; ❄ @ 🛜) Spotless and in a quiet, residential neighbourhood near the centre. Smooth decor, with-it staff and some sea-view balconies.

Hotel Strada Marina HOTEL $$
(☑ 26950 42761; www.stradamarina.gr; Lombardou 14; d from €95; ❄ 🛜 🏊) Smack on the main harbourfront with a rooftop terrace and pool, plus well-equipped rooms. Upper balconies have great views of the bay and the action.

Hotel Diana HOTEL $$
(☑ 26950 28547; www.dianahotels.gr; Plateia Agiou Markou; r incl breakfast from €70; ❄ @ 🛜) This comfortable and well-appointed hotel in a central location has a two-bedroom family suite (€110).

🍴 Eating & Drinking

Restaurants abound but, as in most of the island, they tend to be overpriced and not overly inspiring.

★ Malanos TAVERNA $
(☑ 26950 45936; www.malanos.gr; Agiou Athanasiou, Kiri area; mains €5-10; ☺ noon-4pm & 8pm-late) Popular island-wide for Zakynthos specialities, this family-run taverna with simple plaid-covered tables and a covered porch serves up hits like rooster, rabbit and wild boar. Find it on the south edge of town, in the countryside (ask a local for directions).

Mesathes MEDITERRANEAN $$
(☑ 26950 49315; Ethnikis Antistaseos; mains €9-11; ☺ lunch & dinner) Elegant and tucked into the walking street behind the Byzantine Museum; a range of Greek and seafood dishes.

Base BAR
(http://basecafe.gr) Base commands the flow through Plateia Agiou Markou, dispensing coffees, drinks and music to a people-watching local crowd.

Around Zakynthos

Transport of your own is really necessary to unlock the charms of Zakynthos.

◉ Sights

Amid all of the southern sprawl, **Vasilikos Peninsula**, bordering the Bay of Laganas, remains the most forested and serene. Nevertheless it has started to become developed. For example, **Banana Beach**, a long, narrow strip of golden sand on the peninsula's northern side, sees crowds, water sports and umbrellas. **Kaminia** is a decent option. Zakynthos' best beach, long, sandy **Gerakas**, is on the other side of the peninsula, facing into Laganas Bay. Please note, however, that this is one of the main turtle-nesting beaches, and access is forbidden between dusk and dawn from May to October; follow conservation recommendations, available at the booth near the beach access path.

With transport, you can reach the raw terrain of the far southwest of the island. Beyond the traditional village of **Keri**, a tiny road leads (past a taverna claiming the

AT LOGGERHEADS

The Ionian Islands are home to the Mediterranean's loggerhead turtle *(Caretta caretta)*, one of Europe's most endangered marine species. The turtles bury their eggs on large tracts of clean, flat sand, unfortunately also the favoured habitat of basking tourists. Zakynthos hosts the largest density of nests, an estimated 1100 along the 5km Bay of Laganas area, part of the **National Marine Park of Zakynthos** (NMPZ; www.nmp-zak.org).

Strict regulations limit building, boating, fishing and water sports in designated zones. During hatching (July to October) conservation agencies place frames with warning notes over buried nests, yet many nests are still destroyed by visitors. Also, hatchlings often don't reach the water, becoming disoriented by sun beds, noise and lights. Similarly, boats kill or torment turtles.

Volunteers from **Archelon** (www.archelon.gr) and NMPZ run education/volunteer programs, and there is an information centre at Gerakas Beach (www.earthseasky.org).

➡ Designated nesting beaches are off limits between dusk and dawn during breeding season (May to October).

➡ Avoid using umbrellas on dry sand (use the wet part of the beach).

➡ Avoid boating trips in the Bay of Laganas.

---

biggest Greek flag in the country) to **Cape Keri** and its lighthouse above sheer cliffs.

Scenic and sometimes happily confusing roads lead north from here through beautiful wooded hill country where locals sell honey and other seasonal products. The route leads to the few land-accessible westcoast coves such as **Limnionas** or **Kambi** and to inland gems like **Kiliomeno**, whose church of **St Nikolaos** features an unusual roofless campanile. The bell tower of the church in **Agios Leon** was formerly a windmill. Lovely **Louha** tumbles down a valley surrounded by woodlands and pastures. **Exo Hora** has a collection of dry wells and what is reputed to be the oldest olive tree on the island. **Volimes** is the unabashed sales centre for traditional products.

The east coast north of Zakynthos Town is filled with resorts but the further north you go, the more remote and charming the island becomes. The road narrows at the ferry village, **Agios Nikolaos**, where development is slight. Carry on to reach pastoral, breezy **Cape Skinari**.

Boats leave from Agios Nikolaos and Cape Skinari for the **Blue Caves**, sea-level caverns that pierce the limestone coastal cliffs. Boats enter the caves, where the water turns a translucent blue from 9am to 2pm when sunlight shines in.

The boats also go to famous **Shipwreck Beach**, magnificent photos of which grace every tourist brochure about Zakynthos and even Greece. It is in **Navagio Bay**, about 3km west of Volimes at the northwest tip of the island. In low season it is, indeed, gorgeous, but in high season some say it feels like a D-Day beach landing at Normandy, so crowded are the waters. Go early in the day. From land, a precariously perched **lookout platform** (signposted between Anafonitria and Volimes) gives great views. **Potamitis Trips** (26950 31132; www.potamitisbros.gr; Cape Skinari) and **Karidis** (6974492193; Agios Nikolaos) run boats (Blue Caves €7.50, Shipwreck Beach and Blue Caves €15).

🛏 Sleeping

Book villas through **Aresti Club** (26950 26151; www.aresti.com.gr), and houses around the Vasilikos Peninsula through **Ionian Eco Villagers** (in UK 0871 711 5065; www.relaxing-holidays.com).

⭐ **Villa Christina**   APARTMENT **$**

(26950 49208; www.villachristina.gr; Limni Keriou; studio €45-50, apt €55-85, 5-person maisonette €110-160; ⊙May-Oct; P ❋ @ ☒) Super-friendly owners speak English and Italian and keep up a bodacious garden and immaculate studios in an ancient olive grove. Library/TV room, barbecue areas, and a sparkling pool augment the various accommodation options, all with kitchen facilities. Between Limni Keriou and the Laganas road.

Panorama Studios   APARTMENT **$**

(26950 31013; www.panorama-studios.gr; Agios Nikolaos; studios €40; P ❋ 🛜) English-speaking hosts offer excellent studios with sea views, on the main road 600m uphill from Agios Nikolaos, set back in a lovely garden.

Windmill PENSION $$
(26950 31132; www.potamitisbros.gr; d €70; ※)
This converted windmill and old stone house enjoy a fantastic cliff-top location in Cape Skinari. Quaint rooms all have stunning views. Steps lead to a lovely swimming area. There are cooking facilities and a cafe-bar.

Revera Villas HOTEL $$
(6974875171, 26950 27524; www.revera-zante.com; studio €70; P※🖥🌐🏊) Stone villas that have seen better days sit 500m southwest of Keri, just off the road to the lighthouse. Pristine location makes up for tatty textiles and spotty plumbing.

✖ Eating

Restaurants around Zakynthos are pretty bland. Keri, Limnionas and Kambi have good basic tavernas in high season only.

Alitzerinoi TAVERNA $
(26950 48552; www.alitzerinoi.gr; Kiliomeno; mains €7-12; 9am-late, only dinner Fri-Sun winter)
Locals make the trek to the tiny hamlet of Kiliomeno for great island cooking, using local produce and cheeses, in a quaint terraced courtyard spilling down the hillside.

Louha's Coffee Shop CAFE $
(26950 48426; Louha; mains €4-7; May-Oct)
Eat or drink under a vine-shaded terrace opposite the Church of St John the Theologian. Good local wine accompanies one daily special, salads and soothing views of cypress-dotted hills.

KYTHIRA ΚΥΘΗΡΑ

POP 4030
The island of Kythira (kee-thih-rah) dangles 12km off the tip of the Peloponnese's Lakonian peninsula between the Aegean and Ionian Seas. It is, despite its proximity to the Peloponnese, considered a part of the Ionian Island group, and the stands of cypress trees help remind you. Genuinely unspoilt, the rolling, central plateau that covers most of the island is farmed in places, and raw in others (with wild fennel and garlic). Towards the coast the land drops, forming cliffs to the sea and hidden beaches. The island's population is spread among more than 40 relatively rural villages, and benefits from potable water and lush valleys. The villages have a white-cube Cycladic feel, punctuated by neoclassical manors and old-style *kafeneia*, and are linked by narrow, winding lanes.

Tourism remains very low-key except in July and August, when the island goes mad. Descending visitors include the Kythiran diaspora returning from abroad (especially Australia). For the rest of the year, Kythira and its fine beaches are wonderfully peaceful.

ℹ Information

For more detail on Kythira visit www.kythira.gr, www.kithera.gr, www.kythira.info or www.visitkythera.gr. The informative English-language newspaper *Kythera* is available in some travel agencies, hotels and shops.

Walkers should find *Kythira on Foot: 32 Carefully Selected Walking Routes* (€10) by Frank van Weerde, and check www.kytherahiking.com which also guides walks.

ℹ Getting There & Away

AIR
The **airport** (KIT), 10km southeast of Potamos, has **Olympic Air** (801 801 0101; www.olympicair.com) flights to Athens (€81, 50 minutes, two daily). Sky Express (p120) operates a route to Zakynthos, Kefallonia, Preveza, Corfu (from June to September) and occasionally Iraklio, Crete.

BOAT SERVICES FROM KYTHIRA

DESTINATION	TIME	FARE	FREQUENCY
Gythio	2½hr	€11	1 weekly
Kalamata	5hr	€20	1 weekly
Kissamos-Kastelli	2½-4hr	€20	4 weekly (2 via Antikythira, €9)
Monemvasia	2hr	€10	1 weekly
Neapoli	1¼hr	€11	1 daily
Piraeus	6½hr	€24	2 weekly

Kythira & Antikythira

0 — 5 km
0 — 2.5 miles

Gythio (55km);
Kalamata (100km)

Neapoli
(25km)

Diakofti (50km)

Crete
(55km)

Potamos

Harhaliana

Galaniana

Antikythira

0 — 2 km

Antikythira

Cape Spathi

Platia Ammos

*Kythira
Strait*

Piraeus
(230km)

Fourni
Beach

Karavas

*Myrtoön
Sea*

Gerakari

Agia Pelagia

Petrouni

Agios Nikolaos

Lagada
Beach

*Antikythira
(50km) (see inset);
Crete (100km)*

Stavli

Trifyllianika

Potamos

Paliohora

Katsoulianika

Lykodimou
Beach

Logothetianika

Hristoforianika

458m

Makronisi
Island

Lianianika

*Ionian
Sea*

Pitsinades

Vamvakaradika

Aroniadika

Kastrisianika

Frilingianika

490m

Diakofti

Agia Moni

*Cave of
Agia Sofia*

Mitata

Kythira

389m

Kato
Hora

Mylopotamos

Viaradika

507m

Cape
Limnionas

*Temple of
Aphrodite*

Avlemonas

Fratsia

Paleopoli
Beach

Cape
Modoni

Pitsinianika

Karvounades

Kaladi
Beach

Kalokerines

Goudianika

Alexandrades

*Moni
Myrtidion*

Tsikalaria

Travasarianika

Skoulianika

Kombonada
Beach

*Sea of
Crete*

Fatsadika

410m

Katouni Bridge

Kato Livadi

Livadi

Kominianika

Katelouzianika

Fyri Ammos

Pourko

Strapodi

Agia Elesis

477m

Manitohori

Melidoni
Beach

Kalamos

Hora (Kythira)

Kapsali

Vroulea

Cape
Trahilos

Cape
Kapello

*Mediterranean
Sea*

BOAT

The main boat connection is between Diakofti and Neapoli in the Peloponnese. Get tickets at the port just before departure, or at Kithira Travel (p667).

LANE Lines calls at Diakofti on its weekly routes between Piraeus, Kythira, Antikythira, Kissamos–Kastelli (Crete) and Kalamata, Monemvasia and Gythio (Peloponnese). Get info and tickets from **Porfyra Travel** (☑ 27360 31888; www.kythira.info) in Livadi.

ℹ Getting Around

Occasional buses operate in August. There are pricey **taxis** (☑ 6944305433), but the island is large and the best way to see it is with your own transport. Car-hire companies can pick up from the port or airport.

Drakakis Tours (☑ 27360 31160; www.drakakistours.gr; Livadi) Cars, vans and 4WDs.

Panayotis Rent A Car (☑ 27360 31600; www.panayotis-rent-a-car.gr) Cars and mopeds. Has an airport branch.

Hora (Kythira)
Χώρα (Κύθηρα)

POP 267

Hora (or Kythira), the island's capital, is a vibrant village of whitewashed houses, perched on a long, slender ridge that stretches north from an impressive 13th-century Venetian *kastro* overlooking the sea.

◉ Sights

★ **Kastro** CASTLE
(⊙ 8am-3pm) FREE Hora's beautiful Venetian *kastro* was built in the 13th century and is one of Kythira's cultural highlights. If you walk to its southern extremity, passing the **Church of Panagia**, you will come to a sheer cliff with a stunning view of Kapsali and, on a clear day, Antikythira.

🛏 Sleeping & Eating

Castello Rooms PENSION $
(☑ 27360 31069; www.kythera-castelloapts.gr; Spyridonos Staï; studios from €40; ❄ 🛜) These seven comfortable rooms with kitchen facilities are set back from the main street and surrounded by a well-tended garden of flowers and fruit trees.

Hotel Margarita PENSION $$
(☑ 27360 31711; www.hotel-margarita.com; off Spyridonos Staï; s/d/tr €60/90/110; ⊙ Easter-

---

Oct; ❄ @) White-walled, blue-shuttered and generally charming, this hotel offers atmospheric rooms (all with TV and telephone) in a renovated 19th-century mansion, featuring B&W marble floors and a quirky old spiral staircase. The terrace affords fantastic *kastro* and sea views.

Corte O Suites APARTMENT $$
(☑ 27360 39139; www.corteo.gr; studio/2-bed apt incl breakfast €85/150; ⊙ Apr-Oct; ❄ @ 🛜) Modern, minimal decor keeps things simple at these beautiful kitchen-equipped apartments with private terraces and sea or valley views. Near the *kastro*.

Zorba's TAVERNA $
(☑ 27360 31655; mains €6-11; ⊙ dinner Tue-Sun) The pick of the town's eateries, and highly recommended by locals for grilled meat.

🍷 Drinking

Fos Fanari CAFE
(☑ 27360 31644; ⊙ 8am-late; 🛜) Avail yourself of wi-fi with spectacular valley views.

ℹ Information

Banks with ATMs and the post office are on the central square.

Kithira Travel (☑ Hora 27360 31390, Potamos 27360 31848; www.kithiratravel.gr)

Police Station (☑ 27360 31206) Near the *kastro*.

Kapsali Καψάλι

POP 34

The picturesque village of Kapsali, 2km south of Hora, is made spectacular by its twin sandy bays and sparkling waters. The protected harbour served as Hora's port in Venetian times, and the ochre beach has sheltered swimming. Kapsali's curving bays,

DON'T MISS

MYLOPOTAMOS
ΜΥΛΟΠΟΤΑΜΟΣ

Do not miss quaint Mylopotamos, nestled in a small valley, 13km north of Hora. Its central square is flanked by a charming church and bell tower, and by authentically traditional **Kafeneio O Platanos** (☑ 27360 33397), which in summer becomes an outdoor restaurant (mains €6 to €8). Staff can help with accommodation.

The Neraïda (water nymph) **waterfall**, with luxuriant greenery along the path, and an aquamarine pool, feels magical as it changes colour in shifting light. Take the right-hand fork in the road after the church and follow the signs.

A portal leads into Mylopotamos' cool, crumbling **kastro** (Kato Hora) `FREE`, a warren of well-preserved (locked) little churches along a spectaular promontory which has views down a gorge and to the sea. To reach it, take the left-hand fork in the road after the church and follow the signs to Kato Hora.

Other fabulous walks start in Mylopotamos; refer to *Kythira on Foot: 32 Carefully Selected Walking Routes*. The most picturesque and challenging walk heads along a gorge with ruins of former flour mills. You pass waterfalls and swimming holes along the way.

---

lined with restaurants and cafes, look dazzling when viewed from Hora's *kastro*.

The rocky island offshore is known as **Itra** (cooking pot) because when clouds gather above it locals say it looks like a steaming cooking pot.

Panayotis Rent a Car (p667) on the waterfront rents canoes, pedal boats, cars, mopeds and bicycles. **Kaptain Spiros** (☑ 6974022079) takes daily cruises on his glass-bottomed boat (from €12 per person), including to Itra, where you can swim.

🛌 Sleeping

Spitia Vassili   PENSION $
(☑ 27360 31125; www.kythirabungalowsvasili.gr; d/tr incl breakfast from €45/55; ❄ 🐾 🛜) This tree-lined complex has the perfect setting: away from the hordes and overlooking Kapsali Beach. The more expensive larger rooms feature bay views.

Aphrodite Apartments   APARTMENT $
(☑ 27360 31328; www.hotel-aphrodite.gr; d/tr/q from €55/70/75; ❄ 🐾 🛜) Overlooking the main road, but facing the sea, these pleasant apartments with kitchens are run by a friendly, English-speaking local. The top floor has super views.

★ El Sol Hotel   HOTEL $$
(☑ 27360 31766; www.elsolhotels.gr; d/5-person apt incl breakfast €120/160; 🅿 ❄ 🛜 ♿) This luxurious Cycladic-style resort has a view of Hora's *kastro* and the sea, a sparkling pool, decadent breakfasts and mod decor. Signposted off the Hora–Kapsali road.

🍴 Eating & Drinking

Hytra   TAVERNA $
(☑ 27360 37200; mains €4-8; ⊙ lunch & dinner; 🛜) Home-cooked platters of Greek staples at this simple waterfront taverna draw locals year-round.

Filio   TAVERNA $
(☑ 27360 31549; Kalamos; mains €6-9; ⊙ lunch & dinner Jun-Sep) Find tasty fresh taverna fare 5km outside of Kapsali, signposted near Kalamos. Popular with visitors and locals alike, it has a beautiful garden and friendly proprietors.

Fox Anglais   BAR
(Kapsali waterfront; 🛜) Feel-good music moves inside as it gets late.

Potamos
Ποταμός

POP 680

Potamos is the island's commercial hub. Its Sunday morning **flea market** attracts just about everyone on the island, and its central square is great for people-watching.

Super-popular **Taverna Panaretos** (☑ 27360 34290; mains €7-12; ⊙ lunch & dinner Mar-Oct, Thu-Sun Nov-Feb) is a natural: it uses home-grown everything, from oil to veggies and cheese. Try wild goat with olive oil and oregano.

Happenin' **Kafe Astikon** (☑ 27360 33141; ⊙ 7am-late; 🛜) anchors the town's cafe-bars and hosts occasional live music.

Agia Pelagia   Αγία Πελαγία

POP 280

Kythira's northern port of Agia Pelagia is a simple waterfront village set amid stunning cliffs and wooded inland valleys. Its sand-and-pebble beaches have vibrant azure waters, but better still are the magnificent volcanic beaches south of the headland, ending at Lagada Beach. The red, pink and tawny beaches are backed by cliffs, and also make for a good walk.

🛏 Sleeping & Eating

Hotel Pelagia Aphrodite   HOTEL $$
(☑27360 33926; www.pelagia-aphrodite.com; s/d/tr incl breakfast €48/60/78; ☉Easter-Oct; P❋❄) This Greek-Australian-run hotel is on a gorgeous bluff on the south end of town and has spotless large rooms, most with balconies overlooking the sea. At time of research, nearby construction created noise.

Maneas Beach Hotel   HOTEL $$
(☑27360 33503; www.kytherahotel.com; d incl breakfast €70; ❋❄) Harbourfront and sleek, it's a convenient vacation spot.

Kaleris   GREEK $$
(☑27360 33461; mains €6-14; ☉lunch & dinner Easter-Oct) Owner-chef Yiannis uses the best local products creatively: delectable parcels of feta drizzled with local thyme-infused honey, *vrechtoladea* (traditional rusks) and homemade beef tortellini.

Around Kythira

Get your own transport to explore beautiful back roads: hills, cliffs, hidden beaches, stands of cypress, and olive groves. The monasteries of Agia Moni and especially Agia Elesis are mountain refuges with superb views, and beautiful Moni Myrtidion stands on peaceful grounds on a plateau above the sea.

North of Hora, in Kato Livadi, find a small but excellent collection of artwork in the Museum of Byzantine and Post-Byzantine Art on Kythira (☑27360 31731; adult/child €2/free; ☉8.30am-2.30pm Tue-Sun). Just north of Kato Livadi make a detour to see iconic Katouni Bridge. The largest stone bridge in Greece, it was built by the British in the 19th century when Kythira was part of the British Protectorate.

Continue northeast through Paleopoli with its wide, pebbled beach, to the pretty fishing village, Avlemonas. Archaeologists spent years searching for evidence of a temple near Avlemonas, Aphrodite's birthplace. See if you can spot the kofinidia (two small rock protrusions): the sex organs of Uranus that Cronos tossed into the sea foam. Top beaches include nearby Kaladi Beach with its grey-brown stones. It takes a spectacular drive down twisty roads to reach Fyri Ammos with its mauve-grey stones. Kombonada Beach is another good bet.

The island's port, Diakofti, is picturesque to zip through, especially with its offshore shipwreck, but there's no need to linger.

In the island's northeast, the spectacularly situated ruins of the Byzantine capital of Paliohora are amazing to explore – they sit atop an isolated promontory surrounded by gorges.

Further north, the verdant, attractive village of Karavas is near the broad grey beach at Platia Ammos.

🛏 Sleeping & Eating

Maryianni   APARTMENT $$
(☑27360 33316; http://maryianni.gr; Avlemonas; 3-person studio/apt €90/120; P❋) Cycladic-style white and blue studios stack above the Avlemonas seaside. They have kitchens and terraces with spectacular sea views.

Skandia   TAVERNA $
(☑27360 33700; Paleopoli; mains €6-11; ☉lunch & dinner Apr-Oct, Fri-Sun Nov-Mar) Relax away from the madding crowds, under the spreading elm trees.

Psarotaverna O Manolis   SEAFOOD $
(☑27360 33748; Diakofti; mains €6-9; ☉lunch & dinner; ❄) Locals head here for the excellent fresh fish and to watch the boat pull in from Piraeus under moonlight.

Pierros   TAVERNA $
(☑27360 31014; http://pieros.gr; Livadi; mains €6-8; ☉lunch & dinner) Since 1933 this family-run favourite has served no-nonsense Greek staples.

Sotiris   SEAFOOD $
(☑27360 33722; Avlemonas; fish per kg €30-75; ☉lunch & dinner, reduced hours low season) A popular spot for lobster, seafood and fish soup. If you can't get in here, try Koralis.

Varkoula TAVERNA **$**

(☑ 27360 34224; Platia Ammos; mains €6-12; ☉ hours vary) Sup on freshly cooked fish accompanied by the tunes of the bouzouki-strumming owner. Ring ahead to confirm erratic hours.

ANTIKYTHIRA
ΑΝΤΙΚΥΘΗΡΑ

POP 45

Few people venture to the tiny island of Antikythira, the most remote island in the Ionians, 38km southeast of Kythira. It has only one settlement, **Potamos**, one doctor, one police officer, one telephone, one *kafeneio*-cum-taverna, and a monastery. It has no post office or bank. Rooms for rent open in summer only. Check www.antikythira.gr for details.

❶ Getting There & Away

LANE Lines calls at Antikythira on its route between Kythira (€9, 1¾ hours) and Kissamos-Kastelli in Crete (€10, two hours, one weekly). Some boats stop at Monemvasia and Gythio in the Peloponnese, or Piraeus (€24, 10½ hours). Contact Porfyra Travel (p667) in Livadi (Kythira).

Understand Greece

Greece Today

The Greeks are hurting and in a state of collective shock – their economic crisis has followed a period of unprecedented growth and prosperity, rampant consumerism and optimism. Greece's complex political and economic restructure is taking its toll on virtually every aspect of society. Few have been unaffected by savage wage and pension cuts, new taxes, record joblessness and thousands of shops and businesses closing.

Best in Print

The Odyssey (Homer; 8th century BC) Plagued by Poseidon, Odysseus struggles to return home to Ithaca.

Zorba the Greek (Nikos Kazantzakis; 1946) A spiritual bible to many; one man's unquenchable lust for life.

The Magus (John Fowles; 1966) Creepy mind games set on fictional island Phraxos.

Falling For Icarus: A Journey among the Cretans (Rory MacLean; 2004) A travel writer fulfills his ambition to build his own plane in the land of Icarus.

Best on Film

300 (2007) Testosterone-fuelled retelling of the Spartans' epic stand against the might of the Persian army in the Battle of Thermopylae, 480 BC.

Mamma Mia (2008) The island of Skopelos shines to the soundtrack of Abba.

Guns of Navarone (1961) Allied soldiers enter Nazi-occupied Greece in this compelling boy's-own thriller.

Shirley Valentine (1989) Classic Greek island romance on Mykonos.

Captain Corelli's Mandolin (2001) Lavish retelling of Louis de Bernières' novel, awash with romance in occupied Greece.

Austerity Measures

Between 2011 and 2013, Greeks took to the streets of Athens to protest the proposed cuts in wages, pensions and jobs outlined by the government in an attempt to satisfy its EU and IMF creditors and secure the country's 130bn euro rescue package.

In 2012–13 average Athenians, whether doctors or office workers, saw their wages severely cut, some say as much as 30%, while living costs were soaring at an unpalatable rate. At the same time, the rising unemployment rate has reached around 27% and there are plans to shell one in four public-sector jobs to help cut the deficit. No surprise then that the Greek psyche has shifted from relaxed to anxious. 'A state,' one Athenian told us, 'that we're just not used to.'

The austerity measures and declining living standards have also widened Greece's stark economic and social disparities – the hedonistic lifestyles of Athenians taking weekend jaunts to Mykonos bear no resemblance to struggling pensioners or workers in rural Greece. Homelessness, suicides and once-rare violent crime are on the rise. Growing anger and social unrest has sparked mass demonstrations and violent clashes with police. Disillusioned young Greeks are bearing the brunt of years of economic mismanagement – the country's most educated generation (30% of 20- and early 30-somethings are university graduates) face bleak employment prospects as youth unemployment tips 60%.

New Political Landscape

Many Greeks have suffered for so long in the grip of the economic crisis that they see nothing but gloom ahead, and have no belief in any of the current political entities.

Nothing highlights the surreal state of Greek politics in the wake of the economic crisis more than the unthinkable marriage of convenience between arch political rivals New Democracy and PASOK – who have alternately governed for nearly 40 years. Is the fragile coalition is a sign that Greek politicians can work together for the greater good? Many already cynical Greeks will tell you it's the troika of Greece's creditors really running the show. Lost faith in the major parties has changed Greece's political paradigm, shifting support to new parties, from radical left SYRIZA to far-right Golden Dawn.

Recent anti-government protests have escalated into violent clashes, often involving fringe anarchist groups; images of Athens in a haze of tear gas, and riot police clashing with hooded youths hurling rocks and petrol bombs have been beamed around the world. While most demonstrations are peaceful, visitors should steer clear of big rallies, which usually take place in the streets leading to the Greek Parliament.

Immigration & Asylum
A current hot potato of debate is immigration. As the main gateway to Europe, Greece is grappling with rampant illegal migration via the porous Turkish border and Greece's remote islands, and people from Afghanistan, Iraq and Africa are flooding into the country. Despite the number of arrivals, Greece has the lowest acceptance rate of any EU country for asylum requests, and draws international criticism for its immigrant and asylum policies and procedures.

Economic decline, concerns about immigrant crime and urban degradation have fuelled xenophobia and extremism, sparking anti-immigrant rallies, growing hostility and vigilante attacks on African and Asian immigrants, particularly in downtown Athens, where foreigners occupy abandoned buildings, town squares and parks.

Return to the Land
A trickle of ideologically driven city-dwellers had begun moving back to the land well before Greece's economic woes. Now, the country's once-shrinking villages are welcoming a new wave of nouveau-poor Greeks. Families of out-of-work professionals and tradesmen are returning to ancestral homes where they can live rent-free, grow their own vegetables or start farming ventures on family plots of land. An increase in agricultural employment is one of the by-products of the times, going back to Greece's traditional strength and way of life (though agriculture now accounts for only 3.8 percent of GDP). New arrivals, especially educated young women, may face a culture shock, as life has stayed more traditional in regional Greece.

POPULATION: **10.7 MILLION**

PERCENTAGE OF WOMEN: **50%**

LIFE EXPECTANCY: **80 YEARS**

INHABITANTS PER SQ KM: **82**

TOURISTS: **15.5 MILLION ANNUALLY**

if Greece were 100 people

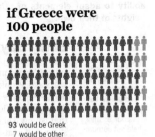

93 would be Greek
7 would be other

belief systems
(% of population)

98
Greek Orthodox

1.3
Muslim

0.7
Other

population per sq km

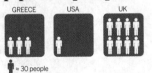

GREECE   USA   UK

≈ 30 people

History

A doorstep between Asia Minor and Europe, through ancient and modern times Greece has been tied to the rising and waning fortunes of its neighbours. In the 5th century BC Greece was almost devoured by the unstoppable spread of the Persian Empire, only reversed by Alexander. Later still, the Roman Empire overwhelmed old Hellas, but the nation revived once more under Byzantine rule. However, the Greeks' genius was their ability to adapt elements of other cultures' architecture and craft, taking it to new heights of their own.

Early Days

The epic Battle of Thermopylae, near today's Lamia, saw the Spartans redefine 'valour' as they held out outnumbered against King Xerxes' Persian force.

The discovery of a Neanderthal skull in a cave on the Halkidiki peninsula of Macedonia confirmed the presence of humans in Greece 700,000 years ago. People from the Palaeolithic times (around 6500 BC) left bones and tools in the Pindos Mountains, while pastoral communities emerged during neolithic times (7000–3000 BC), primarily in the fertile region that is now Thessaly. Agriculturally sophisticated, they grew crops, bred sheep and goats, and used clay to produce pots, vases and stylised representations of idols as figures of worship.

Artistic & Cultural Legacies

Ancient Civilisations

By 3000 BC settlements had developed into streets, squares and mud-brick houses. Adding to this momentum, Indo-European migrants introduced the processing of bronze into Greece and from there began three remarkable civilisations: Cycladic, Minoan and Mycenaean.

Cycladic Civilisation

The Cycladic civilisation was a cluster of fishing and farming island communities with a sophisticated artistic temperament. The most striking legacy of this civilisation is the carving of the statuettes from Parian marble – the famous Cycladic figurines. Cycladic sculptors are also renowned for their impressive, life-sized *kouroi* (marble statues), carved during the Archaic period.

TIMELINE	7000–3000 BC	3000–1100 BC	2000 BC
	For 4000 years the early inhabitants of the Greek peninsula live a simple agrarian life, growing crops and herding animals. Communities with housing and planned streets appear by around 3000 BC.	The discovery of blending copper and tin into a strong alloy heralds the Bronze Age. Trade gains traction; increased prosperity sees the birth of the Cycladic, Minoan and Mycenaean civilisations.	Minoan civilisation reaches its peak in Crete: architectural advances lead to the palaces in Knossos, Phaestos, Malia and Zakros, pottery-making improves and Crete's first script emerges.

Minoan Civilisation

Named after King Minos, the mythical ruler of Crete (and stepfather of the Minotaur), the Minoans were Europe's first advanced civilisation. Around 1900 BC the splendid complex of Knossos was first built (allegedly by Icarus' father, Daedalus), its frescoes, ventilation shafts, sewerage systems and ambitious designs marking an abrupt acceleration from neolithic life. Through their use of bronze the Minoans were able to build great sea vessels establishing a formidable profile as sailors and traders, whose reach extended across Asia Minor and North Africa.

The jury is out on what happened to trigger the demise of this great civilisation. Was it the tsunami and ash fallout caused by the volcanic eruption in Thira, Santorini in 1500 BC? Or perhaps the invading force of Mycenae?

Scholars divide the Cycladic civilisation into three periods: Early (3000–2000 BC), Middle (2000–1500 BC) and Late (1500–1100 BC).

Mycenaean Civilisation

The decline of the Minoan civilisation coincided with the rise of Mycenae (1600–1100 BC), which reached its peak between 1500 and 1200 BC with mainland city-states like Corinth, Tiryns (where Heracles was forced to report to collect his famous labours) and Mycenae. Warrior kings, who measured their wealth in weapons, now ruled from imposing palaces heavily fortified upon hills. The interiors featured impressive frescoes, and commercial transactions were documented on tablets in Linear B (a form of Greek language 500 years older than the Ionic Greek used by Homer). The Mycenaean's most impressive legacy is their magnificent gold masks, refined jewellery and metal ornaments, the best of which are in the National Archaeological Museum in Athens.

Geometric & Archaic Ages

The Dorians were an ancient Hellenic people who settled in the Peloponnese by the 8th century BC. In the 11th or 12th century BC these warrior-like people fanned out to occupy much of the mainland, seizing control of the Mycenaean kingdoms and enslaving the inhabitants. The following 400-year period is often referred to as Greece's 'dark age'; however, in their favour, the Dorians introduced iron and developed a new intricate style of pottery, decorated with striking geometric designs. Significantly they were to introduce the practice of *polytheism* (the worship of many gods), paving the foundations for Zeus and his pantheon of 12 principal deities.

During the following Archaic period, about 1000–800 BC, Greek culture developed rapidly; many of the advancements in literature, sculpture, theatre, architecture and intellectual endeavour began. This revival overlapped with the Classical age (the two eras are often classified as the

Homer's classic work, the 'Iliad', written in the 8th century BC, relates in poetic epithet a mythical episode of the Trojan War. Its sequel, the 'Odyssey', recounts the epic adventures of Odysseus and his companions in their journey home from the Trojan War.

1700–1550 BC	1500–1200 BC	1400 BC	1200–800 BC
Santorini erupts with a cataclysmic volcanic explosion, causing a Mediterranean-wide tsunami that scholars suggest contributed to the destruction of Minoan civilisation.	The authoritarian Mycenaean culture from the Peloponnese usurps much of the Cretan and Cycladic cultures. Goldsmithing is a predominant feature of Mycenaean life.	The Mycenaeans colonise Crete, building cities such as Kydonia (Hania) and Polyrrinia. Weapons manufacture flourishes; fine arts fall into decline. Greek gods replace worship of the Mother Goddess.	The Dorians herald 400 years of obscurity in terms of international trade, but excel in the use of iron weaponry and ironwork in architecture, and develop striking geometric designs on pottery.

Hellenic period). Advances included the Greek alphabet, the verses of Homer (the 'Odyssey' was possibly the world's first epic work of literature), the founding of the Olympic Games, and central sanctuaries such as Delphi. These common bonds gave Greeks a sense of national identity and intellectual vigour.

By about 800 BC, Greece had been divided into a series of independent city-states, the most powerful being Argos, Athens, Corinth, Elis, Sparta and Thiva (Thebes). Most abolished monarchic rule and aristocratic monopoly, establishing a set of laws that redistributed wealth and allowed the city's citizens to regain control over their lands.

Democracy

The seafaring city-state of Athens was still in the hands of aristocrats when Athens' greatest reformist, Solon, was appointed chief magistrate in 594 BC. His mandate was to defuse the mounting tensions between the haves and have-nots. In a high-risk strategy Solon cancelled all debts, liberating those who'd become enslaved because of them. Declaring all free Athenians equal by law, Solon abolished inherited privileges and restructured political power, establishing four classes based on wealth. Although only the first two classes were eligible for office, all four could elect magistrates and vote on legislation. Solon's reforms have become regarded as a blueprint of the ideological democratic system aspired to in most of today's Western societies.

Classical Age

An explosion in form and light, Greece's Golden Age, from the 6th to 4th centuries BC, saw a renaissance in cultural creativity. Literature and drama blossomed as many city-states enjoyed increased economic reform, political prosperity and a surge in mental agility, led by the noble works of Aeschylus, Euripides and Sophocles who contributed dramatic tragedies, and Aristophanes who inspired political satire with his comedies. Today the potency of this fertile era still resonates – many ideas discussed today were debated by these great minds. And that's not forgetting the journalistic blogs of historians Herodotus – widely regarded as the father of history – and Thucydides.

Athens reached its zenith after the monumental defeat of the Persians at the Battle of Marathon in 490 BC, founding the Delian League, a naval alliance formed to liberate city-states still occupied by Persia. Many Aegean and Ionian city-states swore an allegiance to Athens, making an annual contribution to the treasury of ships, bringing it fantastic wealth unrivalled by its poor neighbour, Sparta, and also turning it into something of an empire.

The Histories, written by Herodotus in the 5th century BC, chronicles the conflicts between the Ancient Greek city-states and Persia. The work is considered to be the first narrative of historical events ever written.

1100 BC	800–700 BC
The Dorians overrun the Mycenaean cities in Crete. They reorganise the political system, dividing society into classes. A rudimentary democracy replaces monarchical government.	Homer composes the 'Iliad' and the 'Odyssey' around this time. The two epic poems are Greece's earliest pieces of literary art, and are still praised for their poetic genius.

DANITA DELIMONT/GETTY IMAGES ©

➡ Scene from the 'Iliad' – the Trojan War

When Pericles became leader of Athens in 461 BC, he moved the treasury from Delos to the Acropolis, reappropriating funds to construct grander temples upon it, including the majestic Parthenon, and elsewhere, including the Temple of Zeus at Olympia. It was also during this Classical period that sculptors developed a more naturalistic, aesthetic style for marble pieces and bronze casts, and it was Pericles who commissioned the Athenian sculptor Pheidias to create the enduring marble friezes of the Parthenon and the sculpture of the city's patroness, Athena.

With the Aegean Sea safely under its wing, Athens began to look westwards for further expansion, bringing it into conflict with the Sparta-dominated Peloponnesian League. A series of skirmishes and provocations subsequently led to the Peloponnesian Wars.

Persian Fire, by Tom Holland, is a compelling account of the warring city-states of Athens and Sparta and how they had to finally pull together to face the Persian threat.

War & Conquest

The Persian Wars

Athens' rapid growth as a major city-state also meant heavy reliance on food imports from the Black Sea; and Persia's imperial expansion westward threatened strategic coastal trade routes across Asia Minor. Athens' support for a rebellion in the Persian colonies of Asia Minor sparked the Persian drive to destroy the city. Persian Emperor Darius spent five years suppressing the revolt and remained determined to succeed. A 25,000-strong Persian army reached Attica in 490 BC, but was defeated when an Athenian force of 10,000 outmanoeuvred it at the Battle of Marathon.

THE OLYMPIA OLYMPICS

The Olympic tradition emerged around the 11th century BC as a paean to Zeus, in the form of contests, attended initially by notable men – and women – who assembled before the sanctuary priests and swore to uphold solemn oaths. By the 8th century attendance had grown from a wide confederacy of city-states, and the festival morphed into a male-only major event lasting five days at the site of Olympia. First prize might have been a simple laurel wreath, but it was the esteem of the people that most mattered, for Greek olympiads were as venerated as Roman gladiators. A ceremonial truce was enforced for the duration of the games. Crowds of spectators lined the tracks, where competitors vied for an honourable (and at times dishonourable) victory in athletics, chariot races, wrestling and boxing (back then there were no gloves but simple leather straps). Three millennia later, while the scale and scope of the games may have expanded considerably, and bar the fact that the ancient games were always held in Olympia, the basic format is essentially unchanged. To visit the original site, with its still extant track and fallen columns, is amazingly evocative.

800–650 BC	700–500 BC	594 BC	490 BC
Independent city-states emerge in the Archaic Age as the Dorians develop. Aristocrats rule these ministates while tyrants occasionally take power by force. Greek alphabet emerges from Phoenician script.	Having originated around 1000 BC in the Peloponnese, the Spartans come to play a decisive role in Greek history. Politically and militarily, the Spartans dominate for around 200 years.	Solon, a ruling aristocrat in Athens, introduces rules of fair play to his citizenry. His radical rule-changing – in effect creating human and political rights – is credited as being the first step to real democracy.	Athens invokes the ire of the Persians by supporting insurgencies within Persian territorial domains. Seeking revenge, the Persian King Darius sends an army to teach Greece a lesson but is defeated at Marathon.

When Darius died in 485 BC, his son Xerxes resumed the quest to conquer Greece. In 480 BC Xerxes gathered men from every nation of his empire and launched a massive, coordinated invasion by land and sea. Some 30 city-states met in Corinth to devise a defence (others, including Delphi, sided with the Persians). This joint alliance, the Hellenic League, agreed on a combined army and navy under Spartan command, with the strategy provided by the brilliant Athenian leader, Themistocles. The Spartan king Leonidas led the army to the pass at Thermopylae, near present-day Lamia, the main passage into central Greece from the north. This bottleneck was easy to defend and, although the Greeks were greatly outnumbered, they held the pass – until a traitor showed the Persians another way over the mountains, from where they turned to attack the Greeks. The Greeks retreated, but Leonidas, along with 300 of his elite Spartan troops, fought to the death in a heroic last stand.

The Spartans and their Peloponnesian allies fell back on their second line of defence, an earthen wall across the Isthmus of Corinth, while the Persians advanced upon Athens. Themistocles ordered his people to flee the city, the women and children to seek refuge at Salamis (today's Salamina) and the men to sea with the Athenian naval fleet, while the Persians razed Athens to the ground. The Persian naval campaign, however, was not successful. By skilful manoeuvring, the Greek warships trapped the larger Persian ships in the narrow waters off Salamis, where the smaller, more agile Greek vessels carried the advantage. Xerxes returned to Persia in disgust, leaving his general Mardonius to subdue Greece. The result was quite the reverse: a year later, the Greeks, under the command of the Spartan general Pausanias, obliterated the Persian army at the Battle of Plataea.

The Peloponnesian Wars

The Peloponnesian League was essentially a military coalition governed by the iron hand of Sparta, who maintained political dominance over the Peloponnesian region. Athens' growing imperialism threatened Spartan hegemony; the ensuing power struggle was to last almost 30 years.

First Peloponnesian War

In The Peloponnesian War, Thucydides sets out a historical narrative of the quarrels and warfare between Athens and Sparta.

One of the major triggers of the first Peloponnesian War (431–421 BC) was the Corcyra incident, in which Athens supported Corcyra (present-day Corfu) in a row with Corinth, its mother city. Corinth called on Sparta to help and the Spartans, whose power depended to a large extent on Corinth's wealth and allegiance, duly rallied to the cause.

Athens knew it couldn't defeat the Spartans on land, so it abandoned Attica and withdrew behind its mighty walls, opting to rely on its navy to put pressure on Sparta by blockading the Peloponnese. Athens suffered

480 BC	479 BC	477 BC	461–32 BC
Darius' son and heir Xerxes seeks revenge for the Marathon defeat. The enormous forces sent to crush Greece defeat Leonidas at Thermopylae and then sack Athens, but are routed at sea off Salamis (Salamina).	The Greeks pay back their defeat at the hands of Xerxes by smashing the Persian army of Mardonius at the decisive Battle of Plataea under the Spartan leader Pausanias. The Persian Wars are finally over.	Seeking security while building a de facto empire, the Athenians establish a political and military alliance called the Delian League. Many city-states and islands join the new club.	New Athenian leader Pericles shifts power from Delos to Athens and uses the treasury wealth of the Delian League to fund massive works, including the construction of the magnificent Parthenon, an enduring legacy.

badly during the siege; plague broke out in the overcrowded city, killing a third of the population – including Pericles – but the defences held firm. The blockade of the Peloponnese eventually began to hurt and the two cities negotiated an uneasy truce.

Second Peloponnesian War

The truce lasted until 413 BC, when the Spartans went to the aid of the Sicilian city of Syracuse, which the Athenians had been besieging for three years. The Spartans ended the siege, and destroyed the Athenian fleet and army in the process.

Despite this, Athens fought on for a further nine years before it finally surrendered to Sparta in 404 BC. Corinth urged the total destruction of Athens, but the Spartans felt honour-bound to spare the city that had

THE SPARTANS

Maybe you saw the gory but brilliant film *300*, imaginatively based on the battle of Thermopylae in 480 BC; one of the most talked about battles in history. Three hundred elite Spartan soldiers held an entire Persian army (whose force numbered several thousand) at bay at the pass ('hot gates') of Thermopylae, near today's Lamia. For three days, wave upon wave of Persian soldiers fell upon their deadly spears and unbridgeable tortoise-shell formation. What kind of soldiers could display such bravery? Ones raised in the war-mongering/honour-based regime of Sparta.

The Spartans were held in mythic awe by their fellow Greeks for their ferocious, self-sacrificing martial supremacy, marching into battle in a disciplined, lock-stepped phalanx, living (and very often dying) by the motto 'return with your shield or on it'. The product of harsh ideology, every male Spartan was by definition a soldier (hoplite), who began his training almost from birth. Poor recruits were weeded out early – a citizens' committee decided which newborn babies did not pass muster (they would then be left on the Taÿgetos Mountains to die). The surviving children, from the age of seven, endured 13 years of training to foster supreme physical fitness, and suffered institutionalised beating 'competitions' to toughen them up. Sparta, fearing no one, was without city walls or fortification. Gold and silver coins, in an antimercenary measure to throttle any sign of material greed, were corrupted with lead to render them useless for trade with passing merchants. The same could be said about interactions with outsiders: inter-marriage with other tribes was equally forbidden, particularly with the Athenians, who the Spartans considered morally corrupt and too lavish. Spartan women, on the other hand, were accorded with more equality and respect than anywhere else in Greece at the time. But it was Sparta's inward, xenophobic character – along with the exhausting Peloponnesian Wars – that ultimately led to the decline and genetic weakening of this master race. The Battle of Leuctra in 371 BC was the first major defeat of the Spartans in open battle and marked the beginning of the collapse of their power.

431–21 BC	431–386 BC	413–404 BC	399 BC
The military might of Sparta runs afoul of the commercial and artistic clout of Athens over an alliance with Corcyra, becoming a full-blown war of attrition, with Athens barricaded and the Peloponnese embargoed.	Crete also sees internal strife: Knossos against Lyttos, Phaestos against Gortyna, Kydonia against Apollonia and Itanos against Ierapetra. An earthquake wreaks havoc in 386 BC.	A second war between Sparta and Athens breaks out over the distant colony of Sicily, ending an eight-year truce. The Spartans break the Athenian siege and Sparta assumes total dominance.	Socrates stands trial, accused of corrupting the young with pedagogical speeches. A jury condemns him to death. Rather than appealing for voluntary exile, Socrates defiantly accepts a cup of hemlock.

saved Greece from the Persians. Instead, they crippled it by confiscating its fleet, abolishing the Delian League and tearing down the walls between the city and Piraeus.

The Hellenistic Age

In the century following the Peloponnesian Wars (431–404 BC) between Athens and Sparta, the battle-weary city-states came under the rule of the Macedonian warrior king, Philip II. But it would be his extraordinary young son and successor, Alexander the Great, who would extend the Hellenistic idea across a vast empire. Alexander was obsessed with carrying the ideal of Hellenism to as far a horizon as his genius and his horse, Bucephalus, would take him. However, in Alexander's unstoppable blaze of glory, Athens and its counterparts began to feel they were again ruled by a king. The city-states felt disempowered by the loss of autonomy under the monarch. The Greeks now perceived themselves as part of a larger empire, and it is this concept that characterises the Hellenistic society. Contemporary arts, drama, sculpture and philosophy reflected growing awareness of a new definition of Greek identity.

The Trial of Socrates by IF Stone frames in a contemporary investigative light Plato's version of events surrounding the philosopher Socrates' life and death.

Hellenism would continue to prosper even under Roman rule. As the Roman province of Achaea, Greece experienced an unprecedented period of peace for almost 300 years, known as the Pax Romana. The Romans had always venerated Greek art, literature and philosophy, and aristocratic Romans sent their offspring to the many schools in Athens. Indeed, the Romans adopted most aspects of Hellenistic culture, from its dress to its gods, spreading its unifying traditions throughout their empire.

The Romans were also the first to refer to the Hellenes as Greeks, derived from the word *graikos* – the name of a prehistoric tribe.

The Rise of Macedon & Alexander the Great

By the late 4th century BC, the Greeks were engineering their own decline. Sparta began a doomed campaign to reclaim the cities of Asia Minor from Persian rule, bringing the Persians back into Greek affairs where they found willing allies in Athens and an increasingly powerful Thebes (Thiva). The rivalry between Sparta and Thebes culminated in the decisive Battle of Leuctra in 371 BC, where Thebes, led by Epaminondas, inflicted Sparta's first defeat in a pitched land battle. Spartan influence collapsed and Thebes filled the vacuum. In a surprise about-turn, Athens now allied itself with Sparta, and their combined forces met the Theban army at Mantinea in the Peloponnese in 362 BC. Thebes won the battle, but Epaminondas was killed; and without him, Theban power soon crumbled.

371–62 BC	359 BC	336 BC	334–23 BC
Thiva (Thebes), a small city-state, is in ascendancy and gains control after it wins against Sparta. But nine years of Theban dominance ends at the hands of a Spartan–Athenian alliance.	In the north, the Macedonians are on the rise as King Philip II seizes the initiative in the power vacuum. He seeks alliances with Sparta and Athens on a promise to wage war again on Persia.	Philip's son Alexander assumes leadership of Macedonia following the untimely murder of his father. Within a few years the new king takes up the challenge against Persia laid down by the slain Philip.	Alexander the Great sets out to conquer the known world. Thebes (Thiva) is the first victim, followed by the Persians, the Egyptians and finally the peoples of today's central Asia. He dies in 323 BC.

However, the political influence of the major city-states had by now been significantly eroded. Their strength waning, they were unable to combat the new power in the north, Macedon – geographically the modern *nomós* (prefecture) of Macedonia – which was gathering strength under its aggressive monarch, Philip II.

In 338 BC, Philip II marched into Greece and defeated a combined army of Athenians and Thebans at the Battle of Chaeronea. In a move that signalled the beginning of the end of the autonomous city-state structure, Philip called together all the city-states (except Sparta who resisted alliance) at Corinth and persuaded them to swear allegiance to Macedonia by promising to campaign against Persia. But before the monarch could realise those ambitions, a Macedonian noble assassinated Philip in 336 BC. His 20-year-old son, Alexander – brilliantly talented as a fighter and scholar – became king.

Philip II's death had been the signal for rebellions throughout the budding empire, but Alexander wasted no time in crushing them, making an example of Thebes by razing it to the ground. Upon his black stallion he was always the first into battle ahead of his men, and was renowned for his valour, cunning and recklessness. After restoring order in Thebes, he turned his attention to the Persian Empire and marched his seasoned army of 40,000 men into Asia Minor in 334 BC.

After a few bloody battles with the Persians, most notably at Issus (333 BC), Alexander succeeded in conquering Syria, Palestine and Egypt – where he was proclaimed pharaoh and founded the city of Alexandria. One of Alexander's tactics to minimise future resistance from his new subjects was to interbreed his soldiers with his new subjects, which forced a union between former foes. After Alexandria he maniacally pursued the Persian king, Darius III, defeating his army in 331 BC. Alexander continued his reign east into what is now Uzbekistan, Balkh in Afghanistan and northern India. His ambition was now to conquer the world, which he believed ended at the sea beyond India, but his now aged soldiers grew weary and in 324 BC forced him to return to Mesopotamia, where he settled in Babylon. The following year, at the age of 33, he fell ill suddenly and died. There had never been a leader like him, achieving such reach in such a short space of time. However, despite this powerful, expanded dynasty, his generals swooped like vultures on the empire and, when the dust settled, Alexander's empire was carved up into fractious, independent kingdoms.

Macedonia lost control of the Greek city-states to the south, which banded together into the Aetolian League, centred on Delphi, and the Achaean League, based in the Peloponnese. Athens and Sparta joined neither.

ALEXANDER THE GREAT

Alexander the Great is considered to be one of the best military leaders of all time: he was never beaten in battle, and by the age of 30 he reigned over one of the largest ancient empires stretching from Greece to the Himalayas.

86 BC–AD 224	67 BC
Roman expansion includes Greek territory. First defeating Macedonia at Pydna in 168 BC, the Romans ultimately overtake the mainland and establish the Pax Romana. It lasts 300 years.	The Romans finally conquer Crete after invading two years earlier at Kydonia. Gortyna becomes the capital and most powerful city. The 'Pax Romana' ends internal wars.

IMAGE SOURCE/GETTY IMAGES ©

➡ Statue of Alexander the Great, Thessaloniki (p239)

Foreign Rule

Roman Era

While Alexander the Great was forging his vast empire in the east, the Romans had been expanding theirs to the west, and now they were keen to start making inroads into Greece. After several inconclusive clashes, they defeated Macedon in 168 BC at the Battle of Pydna.

The Achaean League was defeated in 146 BC and the Roman consul Mummius made an example of the rebellious Corinthians by destroying their city. In 86 BC Athens joined an ill-fated rebellion against the Romans in Asia Minor staged by the king of the Black Sea region, Mithridates VI. In retribution, the Roman statesman Sulla invaded Athens and took off with its most valuable sculptures. Greece now became the Graeco-Roman province of Achaea. Although officially under the auspices of Rome, some major Greek cities were given the freedom to self-govern to some extent. As the Romans revered Greek culture, Athens retained its status as a centre of learning. During a succession of Roman emperors, namely Augustus, Nero and Hadrian, Greece experienced a period of relative peace, the Pax Romana, which was to last until the middle of the 3rd century AD.

> Philip II engaged the philosopher Aristotle to tutor the teenage Alexander, who was greatly inspired by Homer's 'Iliad'. Alexander retained a strong interest in the arts and culture throughout his life.

The Byzantine Empire & the Crusades

The Pax Romana began to crumble in AD 250 when the Goths invaded Greece, the first of a succession of invaders spurred on by the 'great migrations' of the Visigoths and then the Ostrogoths from the middle Balkans.

In an effort to resolve the conflict in the region, in AD 324 the Roman Emperor Constantine I, a Christian convert, transferred the capital of the empire from Rome to Byzantium, a city on the western shore of the Bosphorus, which was renamed Constantinople (present-day İstanbul). While Rome went into terminal decline, the eastern capital began to grow in wealth and strength as a Christian state. In the ensuing centuries, Byzantine Greece faced continued pressure from the Persians and Arabs, but it managed to retain its stronghold over the region.

It is ironic that the demise of the Byzantine Empire was accelerated by fellow Christians from the west – the Frankish Crusaders. The stated mission of the Crusades was to liberate the Holy Land from the Muslims, but in reality they were driven as much by greed as by religious zeal. The first three Crusades passed by without affecting the area, but the leaders of the Fourth Crusade (in the early part of the 13th century) decided that Constantinople presented richer pickings than Jerusalem and struck a deal with Venice, who had helped prop up the Crusades.

27 BC	AD 63	250	324
Crete is united with eastern Libya to form the Roman province of Creta et Cyrenaica, re-organising population centres and ushering in a new era of prosperity.	Christianity emerges after St Paul visits Crete and leaves his disciple, Titus, to convert the island. St Titus becomes Crete's first bishop.	The first Christian martyrs, the so-called Agii Deka (Ten Saints) are killed in the Cretan village of the same name, as Roman officials begin major Christian persecutions.	The AD 250 invasion of Greece by the Goths signals the decline of the Pax Romana and in 324 the capital of the Roman Empire is moved to Byzantium (later renamed Constantinople). Christianity gains traction.

Constantinople was sacked in 1204 and much of the Byzantine Empire was partitioned into fiefdoms ruled by self-styled 'Latin' (mostly Frankish or western-Germanic) princes. The Venetians, meanwhile, had also secured a foothold in Greece. Over the next few centuries they acquired all the key Greek ports, including Methoni, Koroni and Monemvasia in the Peloponnese (then known as the Morea), and the island of Crete, and became the wealthiest and most powerful traders in the Mediterranean.

Despite this sorry state of affairs, Byzantium was not yet dead. In 1259 the Byzantine Emperor Michael VIII Palaeologos recaptured the Peloponnese and made the city of Mystras his headquarters. Many eminent Byzantine artists, architects, intellectuals and philosophers converged on the city for a final burst of Byzantine creativity. Michael VIII managed to reclaim Constantinople in 1261, but by this time Byzantium was a shadow of its former self.

Ottoman Rule

Constantinople was soon facing a much greater threat from the east. The Seljuk Turks, a tribe from central Asia, had first appeared on the eastern fringes of the empire in the middle of the 11th century. The Ottomans (the followers of Osman, who ruled from 1289 to 1326) supplanted the Seljuks as the dominant Turkish tribe. The Muslim Ottomans began to rapidly expand the areas under their control and by the mid-15th century were harassing the Byzantine Empire on all sides.

On 29 May 1453, Constantinople fell under Turkish Ottoman rule (referred to by Greeks as *turkokratia*). Once more Greece became a battleground, this time fought over by the Turks and Venetians. Eventually, with the exception of the Ionian Islands (where the Venetians retained control), Greece became part of the Ottoman Empire.

Ottoman power reached its zenith under Sultan Süleyman the Magnificent, who ruled between 1520 and 1566. His successor, Selim the Sot, added Cyprus to their dominions in 1570, but his death in 1574 marked an end to serious territorial expansion. Although they captured Crete in 1669 after a 25-year campaign, the ineffectual sultans that followed in the late 16th and 17th centuries saw the empire go into steady decline.

Venice expelled the Turks from the Peloponnese in a three-year campaign (1685–87) that saw Venetian troops advance as far as Athens. During this campaign, Venetian artillery struck gunpowder stored inside the ruins of the Acropolis and badly damaged the Parthenon.

The Ottomans restored rule in 1715, but never regained their former authority. By the end of the 18th century, pockets of Turkish officials and aristocrats had emerged throughout Greece as self-governing cliques that made cursory gestures of obligation to the sultan in Constantinople.

The Green Line separating Greece and Turkey in modern-day Cyprus is a ghost town, a desert of silence where the clock stopped in 1974. Greeks still peer through the barbwire partition to the place they were born and banished from, but are unlikely to return to.

394	395	529	960
Christianity is declared the official religion. All pagan worship of Greek and Roman gods is outlawed. Christian theology supplants classical philosophy.	The Roman Empire splits and Crete is ruled by Byzantium. Crete becomes a self-governing province. Gortyna is its administrative centre. Piracy decreases, trade flourishes; many churches are built.	Athens' cultural influence is dealt a fatal blow when Emperor Justinian outlaws the teaching of classical philosophy in favour of Christian theology, by now regarded as the ultimate form of intellectual endeavour.	Byzantine General Nikiforos Fokas launches the 'Expedition to Crete', liberating the island. Coastal defences are fortified, and Chandax becomes the capital. A powerful land-holding class emerges.

Also, some Greeks had gained influence under the sultan's lax leadership or enjoyed privileged administrative status; they were influential church clerics, wealthy merchants, landowners or governors, ruling over the provincial Greek peasants. But there also existed an ever-increasing group of Greeks, including many intellectual expatriates, who aspired to emancipation.

Russia campaigned to liberate its fellow Christians in the south, and sent Russian agents to foment rebellion, first in the Peloponnese in 1770 and then in Epiros in 1786. Both insurrections were crushed ruthlessly – the latter by Ali Pasha (1741–1822), the Ottoman governor of Ioannina (who would proceed to set up his own power base in defiance of the sultan).

Independence

In 1814 businessmen Athanasios Tsakalof, Emmanuel Xanthos and Nikolaos Skoufas founded the first Greek independence party, the Filiki Eteria (Friendly Society). The underground organisation's message spread quickly. Supporters believed that armed force was the only effective means of liberation, and made generous financial contributions to the Greek fighters.

Ali Pasha's private rebellion against the sultan in 1820 gave the Greeks the impetus they needed. On 25 March 1821, the Greeks launched the War of Independence. Uprisings broke out almost simultaneously across most of Greece and the occupied islands. The fighting was savage and atrocities were committed on both sides; in the Peloponnese 12,000 Turkish inhabitants were killed after the capture of the city of Tripolitsa (present-day Tripoli), while the Turks retaliated with massacres in Asia Minor, most notoriously on the island of Chios.

The campaign escalated, and within a year the Greeks had captured the fortresses of Monemvasia, Navarino (modern Pylos) and Nafplio in the Peloponnese, and Messolongi, Athens and Thebes. The Greeks proclaimed independence on 13 January 1822 at Epidavros.

Regional differences over national governance twice escalated into civil war (in 1824 and 1825). The Ottomans took advantage and by 1827 the Turks (with Egyptian reinforcements) had recaptured most of the Peloponnese, as well as Messolongi and Athens. The Western powers intervened and a combined Russian, French and British naval fleet sunk the Turkish–Egyptian fleet in the Battle of Navarino in October 1827. Sultan Mahmud II defied the odds and proclaimed a holy war, prompting Russia to send troops into the Balkans to engage the Ottoman army. Fighting continued until 1829 when, with Russian troops at the gates of Constantinople, the sultan accepted Greek independence with the Treaty of Adrianople (independence was formally recognised in 1830).

Greece is home to the oldest mosque in Europe. The Bayezit's Mosque at Didymotiho was built by Ottoman Sultan Bayezit I in the late 14th century.

1204	1209	1453	1460
Marauding Frankish Crusaders sack Constantinople. Trading religious fervour for self-interest, the Crusaders strike a blow that sets Constantinople on the road to a slow demise.	Geoffrey de Villehardouin parcels out the Peloponnese into fiefs; he paves the way for his nephew, another Geoffrey, who appoints himself Prince of Morea (the name given to medieval Peloponnese).	Greece becomes a dominion of the Ottoman Turks after they seize control of Constantinople, sounding the death knell for the Byzantine Empire.	By 1460 the Morea falls to the Turks and centuries of power struggles between the Turks and Venetians follow.

The Modern Greek Nation

The Greeks, meanwhile, had been busy organising the independent state they had proclaimed several years earlier. In April 1827 the Greeks elected Ioannis Kapodistrias, a Corfiot and former diplomat of Russian Tsar Alexander I, as the first president of the republic; and chose Nafplio, in the Peloponnese, as the capital.

However, there was much dissension within Greek ranks. Kapodistrias was assassinated in 1831 after he had ordered the imprisonment of a Maniot chieftain, part of a response to undermine rising discontent and rebellion among the many parties (including leaders of the independence movement) whose authority had been weakened by the new state.

Amid the ensuing anarchy, Britain, France and Russia declared Greece a monarchy. They set on the throne a non-Greek, 17-year-old Bavarian Prince Otto, who arrived in Nafplio in January 1833. The new kingdom (established by the London Convention of 1832) consisted of the Peloponnese, Sterea Ellada, the Cyclades and the Sporades.

After moving the capital to Athens in 1834, King Otto proved to be an abrasive ruler who had alienated the independence veterans by giving the most prestigious official posts to his Bavarian court. However, by the end of the 1850s most of the stalwarts of the War of Independence had been replaced by a new breed of university graduates (Athens University was founded in 1817).

> The best-seller *Eleni*, written by Nicholas Gage, tells the gripping personal account of his family's life in the village of Lia, and the events leading to the execution of Gage's mother by communist guerillas during the Greek Civil War.

HISTORY THE MODERN GREEK NATION

A FEMALE FORCE

Greek women have played a strong role in Greek resistance movements throughout history and Laskarina Bouboulina (1771–1825), a celebrated seafarer, is one such woman. She became a member of Filiki Eteria (Friendly Society), a major organisation striving for independence against Ottoman rule. Originally from Hydra, she settled in Spetses, from where she commissioned the construction of and commanded – as a lady admiral – several warships that were used in significant naval blockades (the most famous vessel being the *Agamemnon*). She helped maintain the crews of her ships and a small army of soldiers, and supplied the revolutionaries with food, weapons and ammunition, using her ships for transportation. Her role in maritime operations significantly helped the independence movement. However, political factionism within the government led to her postwar arrest and subsequent exile to Spetses, where she died.

Distinguished as a national heroine, streets across Greece bear her name and her image appeared commemoratively on the (now-disused) one-drachma coin. Moreover, her great-granddaughter, Lela Karagiannis, also fought with the resistance in WWII. There are statues dedicated to both women in Spetses Town, and Bouboulina's home is now a private museum.

1541

Dominikos Theotokopoulos, later known as 'El Greco', is born in Candia; his subsequent creations in Italy and Spain are marked by both Cretan School influence and bold personal innovation.

1684–87

The Venetians expel the Turks from the Peloponnese in a campaign that sees Venetian troops advance as far as Athens.

WALTER BIBIKOW/GETTY IMAGES ©

→ El Greco Museum, Crete

The Great Idea

Greece's foreign policy (dubbed the 'Great Idea') was to assert sovereignty over its dispersed Greek populations. Set against the background of the Crimean conflict, British and French interests were nervous at the prospect of a Greek alliance with Russia against the Ottomans, especially as in 1862 Otto had been ousted in a bloodless coup.

The poet Lord Byron was one of a large group of philhellenic volunteers who played an active role in fanning the independence cause. Byron's war effort was cut short when he died in 1824.

British influence in the Ionian Islands had begun in 1815 (following a spell of political ping-pong between the Venetians, Russians and French). The British did improve the islands' infrastructure and many locals adopted British customs (such as afternoon tea and cricket). But, Greek independence put pressure on Britain to give sovereignty to the Greek nation, and in 1864 the British left. Meanwhile, Britain simultaneously eased onto the Greek throne the young Danish Prince William, crowned King George I in 1863. His 50-year reign eventually brought some stability to the country, beginning with a new constitution in 1864 that established the power of democratically elected representatives.

In 1881 Greece acquired Thessaly and part of Epiros as a result of a Russo–Turkish war. But Greece failed miserably when, in 1897, it tried to attack Turkey in the north in an effort to reach *enosis* (union) with Crete (who had persistently agitated for liberation from the Ottomans). The bid drained much of the country's resources, and timely diplomatic intervention by the great powers prevented the Turkish army from taking Athens.

Crete was placed under international administration, but the government of the island was gradually handed over to the Greeks, and in 1905 the president of the Cretan assembly, Eleftherios Venizelos, announced Crete's union with Greece (although this was not recognised by international law until 1913). Venizelos went on to become prime minister of Greece in 1910 and was the country's leading politician until his republican sympathies brought about his downfall in 1935.

Balkan Wars

Although the Ottoman Empire was in its death throes at the beginning of the 20th century, it had still retained Macedonia. This was a prize coveted by the newly formed Balkan countries of Serbia and Bulgaria, as well as by Greece, and led to the outbreak of the Balkan Wars (1912 and 1913). The outcome was the Treaty of Bucharest (August 1913), which greatly expanded Greek territory (and with it, its fertile agricultural resources). Its borders now took in the southern part of Macedonia (which included Thessaloniki, the vital cultural centre strategically positioned on the Balkan trade routes), part of Thrace, another chunk of Epiros, and the northeastern Aegean Islands, as well as recognising the union with Crete.

1770s & 1780s	1814	1821	1822–29
Catherine the Great of Russia dislodges the Turks from the Black Sea coast and assigns several towns with Ancient Greek names. She offers Greeks financial incentives and free land to settle the region.	The underground Hellenic Independence organisation known as the Filiki Eteria (Friendly Society) is established in the town of Odessa on the Black Sea coast. Its influence spreads throughout Greece.	On 25 March, Bishop Germanos of Patra (a member of the Filiki Eteria) signals the beginning of the War of Independence on the mainland. Greece celebrates this date as its national day of Independence.	Independence is declared at Epidavros on 13 January 1822, but fighting continues for another seven years. The Ottomans capitulate and accept the terms of the Treaty of Adrianople.

WWI & Smyrna

In March 1913 a man assassinated King George, and his son Constantine became the monarch. King Constantine, who was married to the sister of the German emperor, insisted that Greece remain neutral when WWI broke out in August 1914. As the war dragged on, the Allies (Britain, France and Russia) put increasing pressure on Greece to join forces with them against Germany and Turkey, promising concessions in Asia Minor in return. Prime Minister Venizelos favoured the Allied cause, placing him at loggerheads with the king. The king left Greece in June 1917, replaced by his second-born son, Alexander, who was more amenable to the Allies.

Greek troops served with distinction on the Allied side, but when the war ended in 1918 the promised land in Asia Minor was not forthcoming. Venizelos then led a diplomatic campaign to further the case and, with Allied acquiescence, landed troops in Smyrna (present-day İzmir in Turkey) in May 1919, under the guise of protecting the half a million Greeks living in the city. (However, the occupation of Smyrna stirred internal resentments and helped spark a series of sanguinary reprisals against its local Muslim population.) With a seemingly viable hold in Asia Minor, Venizelos ordered his troops to march ahead, and by September 1921 they'd advanced as far as Ankara. But by this stage foreign support for Venizelos had ebbed and Turkish forces, commanded by Mustafa Kemal (later to become Atatürk), halted the offensive. The Greek army retreated but Smyrna fell in 1922, and tens of thousands of its Greek inhabitants were killed.

The outcome of these hostilities was the Treaty of Lausanne in July 1923, whereby Turkey recovered eastern Thrace and the islands of Imvros and Tenedos, while Italy kept the Dodecanese (which it had temporarily acquired in 1912 and would hold until 1947).

The treaty also called for a population exchange between Greece and Turkey to prevent any future disputes. Almost 1.5 million Greeks left Turkey and almost 400,000 Turks left Greece. The exchange put a tremendous strain on the Greek economy and caused great bitterness and hardship for the individuals concerned. Many Greeks abandoned a privileged life in Asia Minor for one of extreme poverty in emerging urban shanty towns in Athens and Thessaloniki.

The Republic of 1924–35

The arrival of the Greek refugees from Turkey coincided with, and compounded, a period of political instability unprecedented even by Greek standards. In October 1920 King Alexander died from a monkey bite and his father Constantine was restored to the throne. But the ensuing political crisis deepened and Constantine abdicated (again) after the fall of

Eugène Delacroix' oil canvas *The Massacre at Chios* (1824) was inspired by the events in Asia Minor during Greece's War of Independence in 1821. The painting hangs in the Louvre Museum in Paris.

WAR OF INDEPENDENCE

1827	1827–31	1833	1862–63
British, French and Russian forces sink the combined Turkish-Egyptian naval fleet in the Battle of Navarino (at Pylos, in the Peloponnese), a decisive action in the War of Independence.	Ioannis Kapodistrias is appointed prime minister of a fledgling government with its capital in the Peloponnesian town of Nafplio. Discontent ensues and Kapodistrias is assassinated.	The powers of the Entente (Britain, France and Russia) decree that Greece should be a monarchy and dispatch Prince Otto of Bavaria to Greece to be the first appointed monarch in modern Greece.	The monarchy takes a nosedive and King Otto is deposed in a bloodless coup. The British return the Ionian Islands (a British protectorate since 1815) to Greece in an effort to quell Greece's expansionist urges.

Smyrna. He was replaced by his first son, George II, who was no match for the group of army officers who seized power after the war. A republic was proclaimed in March 1924 amid a series of coups and counter-coups.

A measure of stability was attained with Venizelos' return to power in 1928. He pursued a policy of economic and educational reform, but progress was inhibited by the Great Depression. His antiroyalist Liberal Party began to face a growing challenge from the monarchist Popular Party, culminating in defeat at the polls in March 1933. The new government was preparing for the restoration of the monarchy when Venizelos and his supporters staged an unsuccessful coup in March 1935. Venizelos was exiled to Paris, where he died a year later. In November 1935 King George II reassumed the throne (by a likely gerrymander of a plebiscite) and he installed the right-wing General Ioannis Metaxas as prime minister. Nine months later, Metaxas assumed dictatorial powers with the king's consent, under what many believed to be the pretext of preventing a communist-inspired republican coup.

WWII

Metaxas' grandiose vision was to create a utopian Third Greek Civilisation, based on its glorious ancient and Byzantine past, but what he actually created was more like a Greek version of the Third Reich. He exiled or imprisoned opponents, banned trade unions and the recently established Kommounistiko Komma Elladas (KKE, the Greek Communist Party), imposed press censorship, and created a secret police force and fascist-style youth movement. But Metaxas is best known for his reply of *ohi* (no) to Mussolini's ultimatum to allow Italians passage through Greece at the beginning of WWII, thus maintaining Greece's policy of strict neutrality. The Italians invaded Greece, but the Greeks drove them back into Albania.

A prerequisite of Hitler's plan to invade the Soviet Union was a secure southern flank in the Balkans. The British, realising this, asked Metaxas if they could land troops in Greece. He gave the same reply as he had given the Italians, but then died suddenly in January 1941. The king replaced him with the more timid Alexandros Koryzis, who agreed to British forces landing in Greece. Koryzis committed suicide when German troops invaded Greece on 6 April 1941. The Nazis vastly outnumbered the defending Greek, British, Australian and New Zealand troops, and the whole country was under Nazi occupation within a few weeks. The civilian population suffered appallingly during the occupation, many dying of starvation. The Nazis rounded up more than half the Jewish population and transported them to death camps.

Numerous resistance movements sprang up. The dominant three were Ellinikos Laïkos Apeleftherotikos Stratos (ELAS), Ethnikon Ape-

On 25 November 1942, a coalition of Greek resistance groups, aided by the British, blew up the Gorgopotamos railway bridge near Lamia in Sterea Ellada, sabotaging for weeks German supply routes through the country.

DEAN SUC/GETTY IMAGES ©

➧ Corinth Canal (p135)

leftherotikon Metopon (EAM) and the Ethnikos Dimokratikos Ellinikos Syndesmos (EDES). Although ELAS was founded by communists, not all of its members were left-wing, whereas EAM consisted of Stalinist KKE members who had lived in Moscow in the 1930s and harboured ambitions of establishing a postwar communist Greece. EDES consisted of right-wing and monarchist resistance fighters. These groups fought one another with as much venom as they fought the Germans, often with devastating results for the civilian Greek population.

The Germans began to retreat from Greece in October 1944, but the communist and monarchist resistance groups continued to fight one another.

Civil War

By late 1944 the royalists, republicans and communists were polarised by interparty division and locked in a serious battle for control. The British-backed provisional government was in an untenable position: the left was threatening revolt, and the British were pushing to prevent the communists from further legitimising their hold over the administration – influence the communists gained during the German occupation – in an effort to augment British hopes to reinstate the Greek monarchy.

On 3 December 1944 the police fired on a communist demonstration in Plateia Syntagmatos (Syntagma Sq) in Athens, killing several people. The ensuing six weeks of fighting between the left and the right, known as the Dekemvriana (events of December), marked the first round of the Greek Civil War. British troops intervened and prevented an ELAS–EAM coalition victory.

In February 1945 formal negotiations for reconciliation between the government and the communists fell flat, and the friction continued. Many civilians on all political sides were subjected to bitter reprisals at the hands of leftist groups, the army or rogue right-wing vigilantes, who threatened political enemies with widespread intimidation and violence. The royalists won the March 1946 election (which the communists had unsuccessfully boycotted), and a plebiscite (widely reported as rigged) in September put George II back on the throne.

In October the left-wing Democratic Army of Greece (DSE) was formed to resume the fight against the monarchy and its British supporters. Under the leadership of Markos Vafiadis, the DSE swiftly occupied a large swathe of land along Greece's northern border with Albania and Yugoslavia.

In 1947 the US intervened and the civil war developed into a setting for the new Cold War theatre. Communism was declared illegal and the government introduced its notorious Certificate of Political Reliability (which remained valid until 1962), which declared that the document

Inside Hitler's Greece: The Experience of Occupation, 1941-44, by Mark Mazower, is an intimate and comprehensive account of Greece under Nazi occupation and the rise of the resistance movement.

1883	1896	1900	1912–13
Greece's most famous writer, Nikos Kazantzakis, is born in Iraklio. He becomes famous for works like *Zorba the Greek* and *The Last Temptation of Christ* in the mid-20th century.	The staging of the first modern Olympic Games in Athens marks Greece's coming of age. Winners receive a silver medal and olive crown, and second and third places receive a bronze medal and a laurel branch, respectively.	Sir Arthur Evans begins excavations at Knossos, quickly unearthing the palace and stunning the archaeological world with the discovery of the advanced Minoan civilisation.	The Balkan Wars erupt when Greece and Serbia initially side with Bulgaria against Turkey over Macedonia. Then Greece and Serbia fight for the same territory against Bulgaria. Greece's territory expands.

bearer was not a left-wing sympathiser; without this certificate Greeks could not vote and found it almost impossible to get work. US aid did little to improve the situation on the ground. The DSE continued to be supplied from the north (by Yugoslavia, Bulgaria and indirectly by the Soviets through the Balkan states), and by the end of 1947 large chunks of the mainland were under its control, as well as parts of the islands of Crete, Chios and Lesvos.

In 1949 the tide began to turn when the forces of the central government drove the DSE out of the Peloponnese; but the fighting dragged on in the mountains of Epiros until October 1949, when Yugoslavia fell out with the Soviet Union and cut the DSE's supply lines.

The civil war left Greece politically frayed and economically shattered. More Greeks had been killed in three years of bitter civil war than in WWII, and a quarter of a million people were homeless.

The sense of despair became the trigger for a mass exodus. Almost a million Greeks headed off in search of a better life elsewhere, primarily to countries such as Australia, Canada and the US.

Reconstruction & the Cyprus Issue

After a series of unworkable coalitions, the electoral system was changed to majority voting in 1952 – which excluded the communists from future governments. The November 1952 election was a victory for the right-wing Ellinikos Synagermos (Greek Rally) party, led by General Alexander Papagos (a former civil-war field marshal). General Papagos remained in power until his death in 1955, when he was replaced by Konstandinos Karamanlis.

Greece joined NATO in 1952, and in 1953 the US was granted the right to operate sovereign bases. Intent on maintaining support for the anti-communist government, the US gave generous economic and military aid.

Cyprus resumed centre stage in Greece's foreign affairs. Since the 1930s Greek Cypriots (four-fifths of the island's population) had demanded union with Greece, while Turkey had maintained its claim to the island ever since it became a British protectorate in 1878 (it became a British crown colony in 1925). Greek public opinion was overwhelmingly in favour of union, a notion strongly opposed by Britain and the US on strategic grounds.

In 1956 the right-wing Greek Cypriot National Organisation of Cypriot Freedom Fighters (EOKA) took up arms against the British. In 1959, after extensive negotiations, Britain, Greece and Turkey finally agreed on a compromise solution whereby Cyprus would become an independent republic the following August, with Greek Cypriot Archbishop Makarios as president and a Turk, Faisal Kükük, as vice president. The changes did

1914	1919–23	1924–34	1935
The outbreak of WWI sees Greece initially neutral but eventually siding with the Western Allies against Germany and Turkey on the promise of land in Asia Minor.	Greece embarks on the 'Great Idea' to unite former Hellenic regions, including those in Asia Minor. It fails and leads to a population exchange between Greece and Turkey in 1923, referred to as the Asia Minor catastrophe.	Greece is proclaimed a republic and King George II leaves Greece. The Great Depression counters the nation's return to stability. Monarchists and parliamentarians under Venizelos tussle for control.	The monarchy is restored and King George II is reappointed to the throne. Right-wing General Ioannis Metaxas adopts the role of prime minister while introducing dictatorial measures of governance.

little to appease either side. EOKA resolved to keep fighting, while Turkish Cypriots clamoured for partition of the island.

Back in Greece, Georgios Papandreou, a former Venizelos supporter, founded the broadly based Centre Union (EK) in 1958, but elections in 1961 returned the National Radical Union (ERE), Karamanlis' new name for Greek Rally, to power for the third time in succession. Papandreou accused the ERE of ballot rigging, and the political turmoil that followed culminated in the murder, in May 1963, of Grigoris Lambrakis, the deputy of the communist Union of the Democratic Left (EDA). All this proved too much for Karamanlis, who resigned and went to live in Paris.

The EK finally came to power in February 1964 and Papandreou wasted no time in implementing a series of radical changes. He freed political prisoners and allowed exiles to come back to Greece, reduced income tax and the defence budget, and increased spending on social services and education.

Colonels, Monarchs & Democracy

The political right in Greece was rattled by Papandreou's tolerance of the left, and a group of army colonels, led by Georgios Papadopoulos and Stylianos Patakos, staged a coup on 21 April 1967. They established a military junta with Papadopoulos as prime minister. King Constantine tried an unsuccessful counter-coup in December, after which he fled to Rome, then London.

The colonels declared martial law, banned political parties and trade unions, imposed censorship and imprisoned, tortured and exiled thousands of dissidents. In June 1972 Papadopoulos declared Greece a republic and appointed himself president.

On 17 November 1973 tanks stormed a building at the Athens Polytechnio (Technical University) to quell a student occupation calling for an uprising against the US-backed junta. While the number of casualties is still in dispute (more than 20 students were reportedly killed and hundreds injured), the act spelt the death knell for the junta.

Shortly after, the head of the military security police, Dimitrios Ioannidis, deposed Papadopoulos. In July 1974 Ioannidis tried to impose unity with Cyprus by attempting to topple the Makarios government in Cyprus; Makarios got wind of an assassination attempt and escaped. The junta replaced him with the extremist Nikos Sampson (a former EOKA leader) as president. Consequently, mainland Turkey sent in troops until they occupied northern Cyprus, partitioning the country and displacing almost 200,000 Greek Cypriots who fled their homes for the safety of the south (reportedly more than 1500 Cypriots remain missing).

The junta dictatorship collapsed. Karamanlis was summoned from Paris to take office and his New Democracy (ND) party won a large

The 1963 political assassination of Grigoris Lambrakis is described in Vassilis Vassilikos' novel *Z*, which later became an award-winning film.

1940	1941–44	1944–49	1967–74
On 28 October Metaxas famously rebuffs the Italian request to traverse Greece at the beginning of WWII. The Italians engage Greek forces and are driven back into Albania.	Germany invades and occupies Greece. Monarchists, republicans and communists form resistance groups that, despite infighting, drive out the Germans after three years.	The end of WWII sees Greece descend into civil war, pitching monarchists against communists. The monarchists recover in 1946, but the civil war takes its toll and many Greeks emigrate in search of a better life.	Right- and left-wing factions continue to bicker, provoking in April 1967 a right-wing military coup d'état by army generals who establish a junta. They impose martial law and abolish many civil rights.

majority at the November elections in 1974 against the newly formed Panhellenic Socialist Union (PASOK), led by Andreas Papandreou (son of Georgios). A plebiscite voted 69% against the restoration of the monarchy and the ban on communist parties was lifted. (The exiled former royal family still lives in London, where it continues to use its royal titles. A dispute between the former king, Constantine, and the government over the family's assets was settled in 2002 and the royal family members now often return to Greece as private citizens.)

The 1980s & 1990s

Prince Philip, the Duke of Edinburgh, was part of the Greek royal family – born on Corfu as Prince Philip of Greece and Denmark in 1921. Former king of Greece, Constantine, is Prince William's godfather and Prince Charles' third cousin.

When Greece became the 10th member of the EU in 1981, it was the smallest and poorest member. In October 1981, Andreas Papandreou's PASOK party was elected as Greece's first socialist government. PASOK ruled for almost two decades (except for 1990–93). PASOK promised ambitious social reform, to close the US air bases and to withdraw from NATO. US military presence was reduced, but unemployment was high and reforms in education and welfare were limited. Women's issues fared better: the dowry system was abolished, abortion legalised, and civil marriage and divorce were implemented.

Economic scandal, a series of general strikes and fundamental policy wrangling over the country's education system damaged PASOK, and in 1990 Konstandinos Mitsotakis led the ND back to office. Intent on redressing the country's economic problems – high inflation and high government spending – the government imposed austerity measures, including a wage freeze for civil servants and steep increases in public-utility costs and basic services.

By late 1992 corruption allegations were being levelled against the government. By mid-1993 Mitsotakis supporters had abandoned the ND for the new Political Spring party; the ND lost its parliamentary majority and an early election in October returned Andreas Papandreou's PASOK party.

Papandreou stepped down in early 1996 due to ill health and he died on 26 June. His departure produced a dramatic change of direction for PASOK, with the party abandoning Papandreou's left-leaning politics and electing experienced economist and lawyer Costas Simitis as the new prime minister (who won a comfortable majority at the October 1996 polls).

The 21st Century

The new millenium saw Greece join the eurozone in 2001, amid rumblings from existing members that it was not ready economically to join – its public borrowing was too high, as was its inflation level. Membership had already been denied in 1999, and many Greeks were keen to

1973	1974	1981	1981–90
On 17 November tanks ram the gates of the Athens Polytechnio (Technical University) and troops storm the school buildings in a bid to quash a student uprising against the junta. More than 20 students die.	A botched plan to unite Cyprus with Greece prompts the invasion of Cyprus by Turkish troops and results in the fall of the military junta. This acts as a catalyst for the restoration of parliamentary democracy in Greece.	Greece joins the EU, effectively removing protective trade barriers and opening up the Greek economy to the wider world for the first time. The economy grows smartly.	Greece acquires its first elected socialist government (PASOK) under the leadership of Andreas Papandreou. The honeymoon lasts nine years. The conservatives ultimately reassume power.

ditch the drachma and nestle under the stable umbrella of the euro. In hindsight, many look back on that year and bemoan the mis-callibration of the drachma against the euro, claiming Greece's currency was under-valued, and that, overnight, living became disproportionately more expensive. That said, billions of euros poured into large-scale infrastructure projects across Greece, including the redevelopment of Athens – spurred on largely by its hosting of the 2004 Olympic Games, which was a tremendous boost for the city. However, rising unemployment, ballooning public debt, slowing inflation and the squeezing of consumer credit took their toll. Public opinion soured further in 2007 when Kostas Karamanlis' (the nephew of Konstandinos Karamanlis) conservative government (who had come to power in 2004) was widely criticised for its handling of the emergency response to severe summer fires, which were responsible for widespread destruction throughout Greece. Nevertheless, snap elections held in September 2007 returned the conservatives, albeit with a diminished majority.

> Greek is Europe's oldest written language, second only to Chinese in the world. It is traceable back to the Linear B script of the Minoans and Mycenaeans. For more on Linear B script, try www.ancientscripts.com/linearb.html.

Over recent years, a series of massive general strikes and blockades highlighted mounting electoral discontent. Hundreds of thousands of people protested against proposed radical labour and pension reforms and privatisation plans that analysts claim would help curb public debt. The backlash against the government reached boiling point in December 2008, when urban rioting broke out across the country, led by youths outraged by the police shooting of a 15-year-old boy in Athens following an alleged exchange between police and a group of teenagers. Youths hurled stones and firebombs at riot police who responded with tear gas. Concern continued over political tangles in investigations regarding alleged corruption among state executives (on both sides of the political fence) in connection with the Siemens Hellas group. This followed another controversy that involved land-swap deals between a monastery and the government, which some commentators believe to have gone heavily in the monastery's favour, at the expense of taxpayers. A general election held in October 2009, midway through Karamanlis' term, saw PASOK (under Georgios Papandreou) take back the reins in a landslide win against the conservatives.

Neighbourly Relations

Greece continues to face the challenge of resolving an abrasive relationship with its Balkan neighbour, Former Yugoslav Republic of Macedonia (FYROM), over the contentious issue of it adopting the nomenclature of Macedonia (a topic negotiated between the two nations via UN-mediated dialogue). Despite the fact Alexander's home of Pella still stands in the province of Macedonia in northern Greece, FYROM is still insisting Greece's favourite son is from their country.

1999	2004		2007
Turkey and Greece experience powerful earthquakes within weeks of each other that result in hundreds of deaths. By pledging mutual aid and support, the two nations initiate a warming of diplomatic relations.	Greece successfully hosts the 28th Summer Olympic Games amid much muffled rumour that infrastructure would not be complete in time. Greece also wins the European football championship.	ΑΘΗΝΑ 2004	Vast forest fires devastate much of the western Peloponnese as well as parts of Evia and Epiros, causing Greece's worst ecological disaster in decades. Thousands lose their homes and 66 people perish.

→ Athens Olympics poster

ANCIENT
GREECE

Relations with Turkey these days are more neighbourly. Greece supports Turkey's steps towards EU-ascension, and is urging joint action between the two nations to manage illegal immigration across Greece's borders. However, Turkey is expressing concerns over Greece's intentions of drilling for hydrocarbons in Cypriot waters, sparking a diplomatic headache. Given the desperate state of the Greek economy, utilising natural assets might be just what the beleaguered country's coffers need to set it back on track.

Sink or Swim

In 2009 a lethal cocktail of high public spending and widespread tax evasion, combined with the credit crunch of global recession, threatened to cripple Greece's economy. In 2010 Greece's fellow eurozone countries agreed to a US$145 billion package (half of Greece's GDP) to get the country back on its feet, though with strict conditions – the ruling government, PASOK, still lead by Georgios Papandreou, would have to impose austere measures of reform to receive these handouts and reduce Greece's bloated deficit. Huge cuts followed, including 10% off public workers' salaries, but it was too little too late and foreign creditors continued to demand ever higher interest rates for their loans.

The web portal www.ancient greece.com is great for all things ancient and Greek.

Greece was stuck between a real-life Scylla and Charybdis – to receive yet another bailout, which was absolutely essential to stop them toppling the euro as a credible currency, they had to effect reforms that penalised the average Greek even further (pushing formerly non-political citizens towards revolution). Some longed for a return to the drachma (the former currency); however, many believe that Greece would still be saddled with massive debt and a monetary system with absolutely no standing, if this was the case.

Georgios Papandreou asked the people for a referendum on the EU bailout, then failed to form a coalition government and stepped down from office. In November 2011, Lucas Papademos – a former vice president of the European Central Bank – took on the poisoned chalice of steering Greece's economy and prime ministerial duties. Antonis Samaras, leader of the New Democracy party, succeeded him the following year and in June 2012 assembled a coalition with third-placed PASOK and smaller groups to pursue the austerity program. By now the Greek public was reeling in despair with complete distrust of any political entity, as Athens again saw major strikes aimed at the massive cuts – 22% off the minimum wage, 15% off pensions and the axing of 15,000 public sector jobs. Suicide rates in the capital were up by 40%. Also up was support for the far-right fascist organisation, the Golden Dawn, bringing with them a rising tide of racism aimed squarely at Greece's immigrant population.

2007	2008	2009	2011
General elections are held in September and the conservative government of Kostas Karamanlis returns to power for a second consecutive term.	Police shoot and kill a 15-year-old boy in Athens following an alleged exchange between police and youths. This sparks a series of urban riots nationwide.	Eurozone countries approve a $US145 billion (€110 billion) rescue package for the country's economic crisis, in exchange for tougher austerity laws.	Tens of thousands of protesters march on parliament to oppose government efforts to pass new austerity laws. Prime Minister Papandreou resigns.

In June 2013, the Hellenic Broadcasting Corp or ERT was temporarily shut down after 70 years of operation, with the government saying it would shave off about 2500 workers (as part of a cost-cutting drive demanded by Greece's international creditors) before reopening it. The closure prompted journalist unions to stage a 24-hour strike in solidarity, creating a nationwide news blackout. These are indeed brutal times for the average Greek, with wage cuts of around 30% and up to 17 'new' taxes now crippling monthly income. The good news is that following the successful implementation of the austerity drive, the EU and the IMF predicts Greece will finally return to growth in 2014.

2011	2012	2012	2013
A coalition government is formed by Antonis Samaras of the New Democracy party.	Parliament passes a €13.5bn austerity plan aimed at securing the next round of EU and IMF bailout loans.	Proposed government cuts include 22% off the minimum wage, 15% off pensions and 15,000 public sector jobs.	Unemployment rises to 26.8% – the highest rate in the EU. Youth unemployment climbs to almost 60%. However, the EU and IMF predict Greece will return to growth in 2014.

Ancient Greek Culture

When the Roman Empire assimilated Greece it did so with considerable respect and idealism. The Romans in many ways based themselves on the Ancient Greeks, absorbing their deities (and renaming them), literature, myths, philosophy, fine arts and architecture. So what made the Ancient Greeks so special?

Mythology

Ancient Greece revolved around careful worship of 12 central gods and goddesses, all of which played a major role in the *mythos* (mythology). Each city-state had its own patron god or goddess to appease and flatter, while on a personal level a farmer might make sacrifice to the goddess Demeter to bless his crops, or a fisherman to Poseidon to bring him fish and safe passage on the waves.

The Ancient Pantheon

Here is a quick guide to the 12 central gods and goddesses of Greek mythology – their Roman names are in brackets.

➡ **Zeus (Jupiter)** Heavyweight champ of Mt Olympus, lord of the skies and master of disguise in pursuit of mortal maidens. Wardrobe includes shower of gold, bull, eagle and swan.

➡ **Poseidon (Neptune)** God of the seas, master of the mists and younger brother of Zeus. He dwelt in a glittering underwater palace.

➡ **Hera (Juno)** Protector of women and family, the queen of heaven is also the embattled wife of Zeus. She was the prototype of the jealous, domineering wife.

➡ **Hades (Pluto)** God of death, he ruled the underworld, bringing in newly dead with the help of his skeletal ferryman, Charon. Serious offenders were sent for torture in Tartarus, while heroes enjoyed eternal R&R in the Elysian Fields.

➡ **Athena (Minerva)** Goddess of wisdom, war, science and Guardian of Athens. The antithesis of Ares, Athena was deliberate and, where possible, diplomatic in

---

TOP FIVE MYTHICAL CREATURES

Medusa She of the bad hair day, punished by the gods for her inflated vanity. Even dead, her blood is lethal.

Cyclops A one-eyed giant. Odysseus and his crew were trapped in the cave of one such cyclops, Polyphemus.

Cerberus The three-headed dog of hell, he guards the entrance to the underworld – under his watch no one gets in or out.

Minotaur This half-man-half-bull mutant leads a life of existential angst in the abysmal labyrinth, tempered only by the occasional morsel of human flesh.

Hydra Cut one of its nine heads off and another two will grow in its place. Heracles solved the problem by cauterising each stump with his burning brand.

MUST-SEE THEATRES

Argos Dating from Classical times; could seat up to 20,000 people.

Ancient Delphi A well-preserved 4th-century-BC theatre,

Odeon of Herodes Atticus Built in AD 161 by Roman Herodes Atticus.

Theatre of Dionysos Once held seating for 17,000 spread over 64 tiers,

Theatre of Dodoni A colossal, 3rd-century-BC ancient site.

Theatre of Epidavros One of the best-preserved Classical Greek structures.

the art of war. Heracles, Jason (of Jason and the Argonauts fame) and Perseus all benefited from her patronage.

➡ **Aphrodite (Venus)** Goddess of love and beauty. The curvy lady of the shell was said to have been born whole on the waves. When she wasn't cuckolding her unfortunate husband, Hephaestus, she and her cherubic son Eros (Cupid) were enflaming hearts and causing trouble (cue the Trojan War).

➡ **Apollo** God of music, the arts and fortune-telling, Apollo was also the god of light and an expert shot with a bow and arrow. It was his steady hand which guided Paris' arrow towards Achilles' only weak spot – his heel – thus killing him.

➡ **Artemis (Diana)** The goddess of the hunt and twin sister of Apollo was, ironically, patron saint of wild animals. By turns spiteful and magnanimous, she was closely associated with the sinister Hecate, patroness of witchcraft.

➡ **Ares (Mars)** God of war. Zeus' least favourite of his progeny. Not surprisingly, Ares was worshipped by the bellicose Spartans and may today have felt at home among soccer hooligans.

➡ **Hermes (Mercury)** Messenger of the gods, patron saint of travellers, the handsome one with a winged hat and sandals. He was always on hand to smooth over the affairs of Zeus, his father.

➡ **Hephaestus (Vulcan)** God of craftsmanship, metallurgy and fire, this deformed and oft derided son of Zeus made the world's first woman of clay, Pandora, as a punishment for man. Inside that box of hers were the evils of mankind.

➡ **Hestia (Vesta)** Goddess of the hearth, she protected state fires in city halls from where citizens of Greece could light their brands. She remained unmarried, inviolate.

The Myths, the Myths!

Some of the greatest stories of all time – and some say the wellspring of story itself – are to be found in the Greek myths. For many of us, the fantastical stories of Heracles and Odysseus we heard as kids still linger in our imagination, and contemporary writers continue to reinterpret these stories and characters for books and films. Standing in the ancient ruins of an acropolis and peering across the watery horizon, it's not difficult to picture the Kraken (Poseidon's pet monster) rising from the Aegean, nor to imagine that fishing boat you see heading into the sunset as Jason's Argo en route to Colchis for the Golden Fleece.

The average Greek is fiercely proud of their myths and will love entertaining you with a list of the gods, but they'll love it even more if you know a few of them yourself. Here are a few of the most famous heroes and their stories to refresh your memory, but it is only the start of a rich, fantastical tapestry, that stretches all the way from the mists of Mt Olympus down to the farthest reaches of Hades.

Heracles (Hercules)

The most celebrated, endearing hero of ancient Greece, Heracles was set 12 labours for mistakenly killing his family. These included slaying the Nemean Lion and the Lernian Hydra; capturing the Ceryneian Hind and the Erymanthian Boar; cleaning the Augean Stables in one day; slaying the Stymphalian Birds; capturing the Cretan Bull; stealing the man-eating Mares of Diomedes; obtaining the Girdle of Hippolyta and the oxen of Geryon; stealing the Apples of the Hesperides; and capturing Cerberus.

Theseus

The Athenian hero volunteered himself as a one of seven men and maidens in the annual sacrifice to the Minotaur, the crazed half-bull-half-man offspring of King Minos of Crete. Once inside its forbidding labyrinth (from which none had returned), Theseus, aided by Princess Ariadne (who had a crush on him induced by Aphrodite's dart), loosened a spool of thread to find his way out once he'd killed the monster.

Poseidon

Icarus

Along with Daedalus (his father), Icarus flew off the cliffs of Crete pursued by King Minos and his troops. Using wings made of feathers and wax, his father instructed him to fly away from the midday sun. Boys will be boys, Icarus thinks he's Jonathan Livingston Seagull...glue melts, feathers separate, bird-boy drowns. And the moral is: listen to your father.

Perseus

Perseus' impossible task was to kill the gorgon, Medusa. With a head of snakes she could turn a man to stone with a single glance. Armed with an invisibility cap and a pair of flying sandals from Hermes, Perseus used his reflective shield to avoid Medusa's stare. Having cut off her head and secreted it in a bag, it was shortly unsheathed to save Andromeda, a princess bound to a rock and about to be sacrificed to a sea monster. Medusa's head turns the sea monster to stone, Perseus gets the girl.

Hera

Oedipus

You can run but you can't hide... Having been abandoned at birth, Oedipus learned from the Delphic oracle that he would one day slay his father and marry his mother. On the journey back to his birthplace, Thiva (Thebes), he killed a rude stranger and then discovered the city was plagued by a murderous Sphinx (a winged lion with a woman's head). The creature gave unsuspecting travellers and citizens a riddle; if they couldn't answer it they were dashed on the rocks. Oedipus succeeded in solving the riddle, felled the Sphinx and so gained the queen of Thiva's hand in marriage. On discovering the stranger he'd killed was his father and that his new wife was in fact his mother, Oedipus ripped out his eyes and exiled himself.

The Golden Age

In the 5th century BC, Athens had a cultural renaissance that has never been equalled – in fact, such was the diversity of its achievements that modern classical scholars refer to it as 'the miracle'. The era started with a vastly outnumbered Greek army defeating the Persian horde in the battles of Marathon and Salamis and ended with the beginning of the inevitable war between Athens and Sparta. It's often said that Athens' 'Golden Age' is the bedrock of Western civilization and had the Persians won,

Athena

Europe today would have been a vastly different place. Like Paris in the 1930s, Athens was a hotbed of talent. Any artist or writer worth their salt left their hometown and travelled to the great city of wisdom to share their thoughts and hear the great minds of the day express themselves.

Drama

The great dramatists such as Aeschylus, Aristophanes, Euripides and Sophocles redefined theatre from religious ritual to become a compelling form of entertainment. They were to be found at the Theatre of Dionysos at the foot of the Acropolis, and their comedies and tragedies reveal a great deal about the psyche of the ancient Greeks.

Across the country large open-air theatres were built on the sides of hills, designed to accommodate plays with increasingly sophisticated backdrops and props, choruses and themes, and to maximise sound so that even the people in the back row might hear the actors on stage. The dominant genres of theatre were tragedy and comedy. The first known actor was a man called Thespis, from whose name we derive the word 'thespian'.

Aphrodite

Philosophy

While the dramatists were cutting their thespian cloth, late-5th- and early-4th-century-BC philosophers Aristotle, Plato and Socrates were introducing new trains of thought rooted not in the mysticism of the myths, but rather in rationality, as the new Greek mind focused on logic and reason. Athens' greatest, most noble citizen, Socrates (469–399 BC), was forced to drink hemlock for his disbelief in the old gods, but before he died he left behind a school of hypothetical reductionism that is still used today.

Plato (427–347 BC), his star student, was responsible for documenting his teacher's thoughts, and without his work in books such as the *Symposium*, they would have been lost to us. Considered an idealist, Plato wrote *The Republic* as a warning to the city-state of Athens that unless its people respected law, leadership and educated its youth sufficiently, it would be doomed.

Plato's student Aristotle (384–322 BC), at the end of the Golden Age, focused his gifts on astronomy, physics, zoology, ethics and politics. Aristotle was also the personal physician to Philip II, King of Macedon, and the tutor of Alexander the Great. The greatest gift of the Athenian philosophers to modern-day thought is their spirit of rational inquiry.

Apollo

Sculpture

Classical sculpture began to gather pace in Greece in the 6th century BC with the renderings of nudes in marble. Most statues were created to revere a particular god or goddess and many were robed in grandiose garments. The statues of the preceding Archaic period, known as *kouroi*, had focused on symmetry and form, but in the early 5th century BC artists sought to create expression and animation. As temples demanded elaborate carvings, sculptors were called upon to create large reliefs upon them.

During the 5th century BC the craft became yet more sophisticated, as sculptors were taught to successfully map a face and create a likeness of their subject in marble busts. Perhaps the most famous Greek sculptor was Pheidias, whose reliefs upon the Parthenon depicting the Greek and Persian Wars – now known as the Parthenon Marbles – are celebrated as among the finest of the Golden Age.

Hermes

The Delphic Oracle

Near the modern-day village of Delphi is the site of the Delphic oracle, the most important oracle in ancient Greece. Its beginnings are shrouded in myth; some say Apollo, when looking for an earthly abode, found a home here but not before doing battle with the python who guarded the entrance to the centre of the earth. After he slew the python and threw it into the chasm it began to rot, producing noxious vapours. From this fissure came intoxicating fumes that the sibyl, or Pythia (a clairvoyant priestess, or seer), would sit above on a tripod. On inhaling the fumes, she would fall into a trance and allow herself to be possessed by Apollo. While in this state the sibyl raved and her mumblings were interpreted by attendant priests.

Citizens, politicians and kings paid a fee to consult the sibyl on personal affairs and matters of state – from whether to go to war or colonise a new country, to more prosaic matters. For more than six centuries, until it was destroyed by a Christian emperor, the Delphic oracle shaped the history of the world with its often eerily prescient prophecies.

Visiting today is a magical experience. Best seen early morning before the day-trippers arrive, or late afternoon, climb up past the temple of Apollo to the place the *Pythia* used to receive her Apollonian messages.

The World of the Ancient Greeks (2002), by archaeologists John Camp and Elizabeth Fisher, is a broad and in-depth look at how the Greeks have left their imprint on politics, philosophy, theatre, art, medicine and architecture.

Architecture

Cast your eyes around most major Western cities and you'll find a reinterpretation of classical Greek architecture. The Renaissance was inspired by the ancient style, as was the neoclassical movement and the British Greek Revival. For those of you with an eye to the past, part of the allure of Greece is the sheer volume of its well-preserved temples. Stand in the ruins of the Parthenon and with a little imagination it's easy to transport yourself back to classical 5th-century Greece.

Minoan Magnificence

Most of our knowledge of Greek architecture proper begins at around 2000 BC with the Minoans, who were based in Crete but whose influence spread throughout the Aegean to include the Cyclades. Minoan architects are famous for having constructed technologically advanced, labyrinthine palace complexes. The famous site at Knossos is one of the largest. Usually characterised as 'palaces', these sites were in fact multifunctional settlements that were the primary residences of royalty and priests, but housed some plebs, too. Large Minoan villages, such as those of Gournia and Palekastro in Crete, also included internal networks of paved roads that extended throughout the countryside to link the settlements with the palaces. More Minoan palace-era sophistication exists at Phaestos, Malia and Ancient Zakros also in Crete, and at the Minoan outpost of Ancient Akrotiri on the south of Santorini.

Several gigantic volcanic eruptions rocked the region in the mid-15th century BC, causing geological ripple-effects that at the very least caused big chunks of palace to fall to the ground. The Minoans resolutely rebuilt their crumbling palaces on an even grander scale, only to have more nat-

GRANDEUR OF KNOSSOS

According to myth, the man tasked with designing a maze to withhold the dreaded Minotaur was famous Athenian inventor Daedalus, father of Icarus. He also designed the Palace of Knossos (p425) for King Minos.

First discovered by a Cretan, Milos Kalokirinos, in 1878, it wasn't until 1900 that the ruins of Knossos were unearthed by an Englishman, Sir Arthur Evans. The elaborate palace complex at Knossos was originally formed largely as an administrative settlement surrounding the main palace, which comprised the main buildings arranged around a large central courtyard (1250 sq metres). Over time the entire settlement was rebuilt and extended. Long, raised causeways formed main corridors; narrow labyrinthine chambers flanked the palace walls (this meandering floor plan, together with the graphic ritual importance of bulls, inspired the myth of the labyrinth and the Minotaur). The compound featured strategically placed interior light wells, sophisticated ventilation systems, aqueducts, freshwater irrigation wells, and bathrooms with extensive plumbing and drainage systems. The ground levels consisted mostly of workshops, cylindrical grain silos and storage magazines.

Thanks to its restoration, today's Knossos is one of the easiest ruins for your imagination to take hold of.

ural disasters wipe them out again. The latter effected an architectural chasm that was filled by the emerging Mycenaean rivals on mainland Greece.

Mycenaean Engineering

The Mycenaeans had a fierce reputation as builders of massive masonry. These war-mongering people roamed southern mainland Greece, picking off the choice vantage points for their austere palaces, fenced within formidable citadels. The citadels' fortified Cyclopean-stone walls were on average an unbreachable 3m (10ft) to 7m (25ft) thick. The immense royal beehive tomb of the Treasury of Atreus (aka Tomb of Agamemnon) at Mycenae was constructed using tapered limestone blocks weighing up to 120 tonnes. The palace at Tiryns has stupendous corbel-vaulted galleries and is riddled with secret passageways; and the incredibly well-preserved Nestor's Palace, near modern Pylos, also illustrates the Mycenaeans' structural expertise.

Classic Compositions

The classical age (5th to 4th centuries BC) is when most Greek architectural clichés converge. This is when temples became characterised by the famous orders of columns, particularly the Doric, Ionic and Corinthian.

The mother of all Doric structures is the 5th-century-BC Parthenon, the ultimate in architectural bling: a gleaming, solid marble crown. To this day, it's probably *the* most obsessively photographed jewel in all of Greece.

In the meantime, the Greek colonies of the Asia Minor coast were creating their own Ionic order, designing a column base in several tiers and adding more flutes. This more graceful order's capital (the head) received an ornamented necking, and Iktinos fused elements of its design in the Parthenon. This order is used on the Acropolis' Temple of Athena Nike and the Erechtheion, where the famous Caryatids regally stand.

Towards the tail end of the classical period, the Corinthian column was in limited vogue. Featuring a single or double row of ornate leafy scrolls (usually the very sculptural acanthus), the order was subsequently adopted by the Romans and used only on Corinthian temples in Athens. The Temple of Olympian Zeus, completed during Emperor Hadrian's reign, is a grand, imposing structure. Another temple design, the graceful, circular temple *tholos* (dome) style, was used for the great Sanctuary of Athena Pronea at Delphi.

The Greek theatre design is a hallmark of the classical period (an example is the 4th-century-BC theatre at Epidavros) and had a round stage,

---

TOP FIVE PROVINCIAL ORIGINALS

Pyrgi See the medieval, labyrinthine, vaulted island village of Pyrgi in Chios, for its unique Genoese designs of intricate, geometric, grey-and-white facades.

Zagorohoria Gaze at the slate mansions of the Zagorohoria: schist-slab roofs, stone-slab walls and fortified courtyards.

Vathia Watch out for the lovely Vathia in Mani, for its startling meercat-esque stone tower houses with round turrets as sentry posts.

Oia Squint at the volcanic rock–hewn clifftop village of Oia in Santorini, with its dazzlingly whitewashed island streetscapes and homes.

Lefkada Town Discover the strangely attractive wooden-framed houses of Lefkada Town; the lower floors are panelled in wood; the upper floors are lined in painted sheet metal or corrugated iron.

KNOW YOUR DORIC FROM YOUR CORINTHIAN

Doric The most simple of the three styles. The shaft (the main part of the column) is plain and has 20 sides, while the capital (the head) is formed in a simple circle. Also there's no base. An obvious example of this is the Parthenon.

Ionic Look out for the ridged flutes carved into the column from top to bottom. The capital is also distinctive for its scrolls, while the base looks like a stack of rings.

Corinthian The most decorative and popular of all three orders. The column is ridged, however the distinctive feature is the capital's flowers and leaves, beneath a small scroll. The base is like that of the Ionic style.

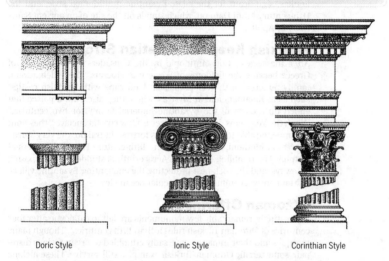

Doric Style   Ionic Style   Corinthian Style

radiating a semicircle of steeply banked stone benches that seated many thousands. Cleverly engineered acoustics meant every spectator could monitor every syllable uttered on the stage below. Most ancient Greek theatres are still used for summer festivals, music concerts and plays.

Hellenistic Citizens

In the twilight years of the classical age (from about the late 4th century BC), cosmopolitan folks started to weary of temples, casting their gaze towards a more decadent urban style. The Hellenistic architect was in hot demand for private homes and palace makeovers as wealthy citizens, dignitaries and political heavyweights lavishly remodelled their abodes in marble, and striking mosaics were displayed as status symbols (read *more* bling). The best Hellenistic ancient home displays are the grand houses at Delos.

Byzantine Zeal

Church-building was particularly expressive during Byzantium in Greece (from around AD 700). The original Greek Byzantine model features a distinctive cross-shape; essentially a central dome supported by four arches on piers and flanked by vaults, with smaller domes at the four corners and three apses to the east. Theologian architects opted for spectacular devotional mosaics and frescoes instead of carvings for the stylistic religious interiors. In Athens, the very appealing 12th-century Church of Agios Eleftherios incorporates fragments of a classical frieze in Pentelic marble. The charming 11th-century Church of Kapnikarea sits stranded, smack bang in the middle of downtown Athens – its interior flooring is of coloured marble and the external brickwork, which alternates with stone, is set in patterns. Thessaloniki's 8th-century Church of Agia Sofia, with her 30m-high dome, is a humble version of her sister namesake in İstanbul. There are numerous Byzantine chapels in Mystras, many of which were originally private chapels attached to enchanting 17th- and 18th-century *arhontika* (mansions once owned by *arhons,* wealthy bourgeoisie merchants).

Several Byzantine monastic sites have made it to the Unesco World Heritage register, including the *katholikon* (main churches) of Osios Loukas, significant for their late-Byzantine multidomed style, and the 11th-century Moni Dafniou, which stands on the site of an ancient Sanctuary of Apollo.

Frankish Keeps & Venetian Strongholds

After the sack of Constantinople by the Crusaders in 1204, much of Greece became the fiefdoms of Western aristocrats. The Villehardouin family punctuated the Peloponnesian landscape with Frankish castles, such as at Kalamata and at Mystras, where they also built a palace that ended up a court of the Byzantine imperial family for two centuries. When the Venetians dropped by to seize a few coastal enclaves, they built the impenetrable 16th-century Koules fortress in Iraklio, the very sturdy fortress at Methoni, and the imposing 18th-century Palamidi fortress at Nafplio. The rambling defence at Acrocorinth is studded with imposing gateways, and the rock-nest protecting the enchanting Byzantine village at Monemvasia commands spectacular ocean views.

Ottoman Offerings

Interestingly, remarkably few monuments are left to catalogue after four centuries of Ottoman Turkish rule (16th to 19th centuries). Though many mosques and their minarets have sadly crumbled or are in serious disrepair, some terrific Ottoman-Turkish examples still survive. These include the prominent pink-domed Mosque of Süleyman in Rhodes' Old Town. The Fethiye Mosque and Turkish Baths are two of Athens' few surviving Ottoman reminders, and the architect for the 16th-century Koursoun Tzami in Trikala also designed the Blue Mosque in İstanbul. The Turkish quarter of Varousi in Trikala, and the streets of Thessaloniki and of

BEST FUTURISTIC ATHENS

Acropolis Museum (p78) This new space houses Greece's antiquities. Designed by Bernard Tschumi, the museum features an internal glass cella (inner room) mirroring the Parthenon with the same number of columns (clad in steel) and a glass floor overlooking excavated ruins in situ.

Stavros Niarchos Foundation's Cultural Center The Pritzker Prize–winning architect Renzo Piano is designing the SNFCC. Plans include new venues for the National Library of Greece, the National Opera and the National Ballet School, to be set amid natural surroundings that will also feature an *agora* (market) and a canal that will link the park (at the old horse-racing tracks in Faliro) with the sea. Completion is due in 2015.

Planetarium (p94) This is the world's largest digital hemispherical dome, providing 360-degree 3D virtual rides through the galaxy.

Athens Olympic Complex (OAKA; ☎210 683 4777; www.oaka.com.gr; Marousi; mtero Irini) Notable for Spanish architect Santiago Calavrata's striking ultramodern glass-and-steel roof, which is suspended by cables from large arches.

Didymotiho, near the Turkish border, showcase superb Turkish-designed homes with stained-glass windows, wooden overhangs on buttresses, decorated plasterwork and painted woodwork.

Neoclassical Splendour

Regarded by experts as the most beautiful neoclassical building world-wide, the 1885 Athens Academy reflects Greece's post-Independence yearnings for grand and geometric forms, and Hellenistic detail. Renowned Danish architect Theophile Hansen drew inspiration from the Erechtheion to design the Academy's Ionic-style column entrance (guarded over by Apollo and Athena); the great interior oblong hall is lined with marble seating, and Austrian painter Christian Griepenkerl was commissioned to decorate its elaborate ceiling and wall paintings. In a similar vein, the Doric columns of the Temple of Hephaestus influenced Theophile's solid marble National Library, while Christian Hansen (Theophile's brother) was responsible for the handsome but more sedate Athens University, with its clean lines.

Meticulously restored neoclassical mansions house notable museums, such as the acclaimed Benaki Museum and the Ernst Ziller–built Numismatic Museum, which contains beautiful frescoes and mosaic floors.

Many provincial towns also display beautiful domestic adaptations of neoclassicism. In Symi, the harbour at Gialos is flanked by colourful neoclassical facades (still striking even if a little derelict) and Nafplio is also embellished with neoclassical buildings.

Modern Ideas

Athens today is embracing a sophisticated look-both-ways architectural aesthetic by showcasing its vast collection of antiquities and archaeological heritage in evolutionary buildings, and by beautifying landscapes for pedestrian zones to improve the urban environment. Examples include the well-designed facelift of the historic centre, including its spectacular floodlighting (designed by the renowned Pierre Bideau) of the ancient promenade, and the cutting-edge spaces emerging from once-drab and derelict industrial zones, such as the Technopolis gasworks arts complex in Gazi.

The distinctive blue-and-white Cycladic-style architecture most associated with the Greek islands was pragmatic and functional. The cuboid flat-roofed houses, huddled together along labyrinthine alleys, were designed to guard against the elements: strong winds and pirates.

ARCHITECTURE NEOCLASSICAL SPLENDOUR

The Arts

Greece is revered for its artistic and cultural legacy, and the arts remain a vibrant and evolving element of Greek culture, identity and self-expression. Despite, or because of, Greece's current economic woes, it has seen a palpable burst of artistic activity and creativity. While savage cuts in meagre state-arts funding have some sectors reeling, an alternative cultural scene is fighting back with low-budget films, artistic collectives, and small underground theatres and galleries popping up in the capital.

Modern Greek Art

Athens' metro stations feature an impressive showcase of Greek art from prominent artists including Yannis Gaitis (Larisa), Giorgos Zongolopoulos (Syntagma) and Alekos Fassianos (Metaxourgio), whose work fetches record prices for a living Greek artist.

Until the start of the 19th century, the primary art form in Greece was Byzantine religious painting. There was little artistic output under Ottoman rule, during which Greece essentially missed the Renaissance.

Byzantine church frescoes and icons depicted scenes from the life of Christ and figures of the saints. The 'Cretan school' of icon painting, influenced by the Italian Renaissance and artists fleeing to Crete after the fall of Constantinople, combined technical brilliance and dramatic richness. Cretan-born Renaissance painter El Greco ('The Greek' in Spanish), née Dominikos Theotokopoulos, got his grounding in the tradition of late-Byzantine fresco painting before moving to Spain in 1577.

Modern Greek art per se evolved after Independence, when painting became more secular, focusing on portraits, nautical themes and the War of Independence. Major 19th-century painters included Dionysios Tsokos, Theodoros Vryzakis, Nikiforos Lytras and Nicholas Gyzis, a leading artist of the Munich School (where many Greek artists of the day studied).

Early 20th-century artists such as Konstantinos Parthenis, Fotis Kontoglou, Konstantinos Kaleas and, later, the expressionist George Bouzianis, drew on their heritage and incorporated developments in modern art.

Leading 20th-century artists include cubist Nikos Hatzikyriakos-Ghikas, surrealist artist and poet Nikos Engonopoulos, Yiannis Tsarouhis, Panayiotis Tetsis, Yannis Moralis, Dimitris Mytaras and pioneer of the Arte Provera movement, Yiannis Kounellis.

The National Art Gallery has the most extensive collection of Greek 20th-century art, with significant collections at the New Art Gallery in Rhodes and the Museum of Contemporary Art in Andros.

Modern and contemporary sculpture is shown at the National Sculpture Gallery. Greece's marble sculpture tradition endures on Tinos, birthplace of foremost modern sculptors Dimitrios Filippotis and Yannoulis Halepas, as well as Costas Tsoclis, whose work fills the island's new museum.

Contemporary Greek Art Scene

Contemporary Greek art has been gaining exposure in Greece and abroad, with a growing number of Greek artists participating in international art events. The Greek arts scene has become more vibrant, less isolated and more experimental, and Athens street art is gaining recognition.

Greeks have had unprecedented exposure to global art through major international exhibitions held in impressive new art venues, small private galleries and artist-run initiatives such as the annual Hydra School Project. Since 2007, Biennials in Athens and Thessaloniki have put the cities on the international contemporary-arts circuit, while the National Museum of Contemporary Art was to move into its permanent home in 2014.

Many Greek artists have studied and made their homes and reputations abroad, but a new wave is returning or staying put, contributing to a fresh artistic energy. See the boxed text on p93 for more information.

Modern Greek Literature

Greek literature virtually ceased under Ottoman rule, and was then stifled by conflict over language – ancient Greek versus the vernacular Demotic or *katharevousa*, a compromise between the two (*dimotiki* won in 1976).

One of the most important works of early Greek literature is the 17th-century 10,000-line epic poem 'Erotokritos', by Crete's Vitsenzos Kornaros. Its 15-syllable rhyming verses are still recited in Crete's famous *mantinadhes* (rhyming couplets) and put to music.

Greece's most celebrated (and translated) 20th-century novelist is the controversial Nikos Kazantzakis, whose novels are full of drama and larger-than-life characters, such as the magnificent title character in *Alexis Zorbas* (Zorba the Greek). Another great novelist of the time, Stratis Myrivilis, wrote the classics *Vasilis Arvanitis* and *The Mermaid Madonna*.

Eminent 20th-century Greek poets include Egypt-born Constantine Cavafy and Nobel-prize laureates George Seferis and Odysseus Elytis, awarded in 1963 and 1979 respectively.

Greece's literary giants include Iakovos Kambanellis, Alexandros Papadiamantis, Kostis Palamas and poet-playwright Angelos Sikelianos. The plays of Yiorgos Skourtis and Pavlos Matessis have been translated and performed abroad.

The quirky, Rebus-like Inspector Haritos in Petros Markaris' popular crime series provides an enjoyable insight into crime and corruption in Athens. *Che Committed Suicide* (2010), *The Late Night News* (2005) and *Zone Defence* (2007) have been translated into English.

Contemporary Writers

Greece has a prolific publishing industry but scant fiction is translated into English.

GREECE ON SCREEN

Greece's new generation filmmakers have been gaining attention for what some critics have dubbed the 'weird wave' of Greek cinema. The award-winning films of Yorgos Lanthimos *(Alps, Dogtooth)* and Athina Rachel Tsangari *(Attenburg)*, at the weirder end of the scale, represent a new style of independent films emerging from Greece.

While Ektoras Kygizos' extraordinary *Boy Eating Bird Food* is an allegory for Greece's current plight, other notable recent films are a product of it – small, creative collaborations largely produced in the absence of state or industry funding.

The focus on Greek film comes in the wake of the loss of Greece's most critically acclaimed filmmaker, Theo Angelopoulos, who was hit by a motorcycle during a film shoot in 2012. Angelopoulos was renowned for his epic, dreamlike cinematic style and long takes and his melancholy symbolism and commentary on modern Greek history and society.

International festivals may be lauding arthouse Greek films, but domestic audiences prefer comedies such as box-office hits *Nisos* (2009) and *Sirens in the Aegean* (2005).

Few Greek films get commercial releases abroad. Recent exceptions were Tasos Boulmetis' *A Touch of Spice* (2003), Pantelis Voulgaris' *Brides* (2004), and Yannis Smaragdis' big-budget *El Greco* (2007). Greece's most internationally acclaimed film remains the classic 1964 Oscar winner *Zorba the Greek*.

Contemporary Greek writers have made small inroads into foreign markets, such as Apostolos Doxiadis with his international bestseller *Uncle Petros and Goldbach's Conjecture*, and award-winning children's writer Eugene Trivizas.

Greek publisher Kedros' modern literature translation series includes Dido Sotiriou's *Farewell Anatolia*, Maro Douka's *Fool's God* and Kostas Mourselas' bestselling *Red-Dyed Hair*, which was made into a popular TV series. Other prominent writers in translation include Ersi Sotiropoulou, Thanassis Valtinos, Rhea Galanaki, Ziranna Ziteli, Petros Markaris and Ioanna Karystiani.

Bypassing the translation issue, London-based Panos Karnezis (*The Maze*; *The Birthday Party*; *The Convent*) and Soti Triandafyllou (*Poor Margo*) write in English. Other notable contemporary authors available in translation include Alexis Stamatis (*Bar Flaubert*; *American Fugue*) and Vangelis Hatziyiannidis (*Four Walls*; *Stolen Time*).

Music

For most people, Greek music and dance evokes images of spirited, high-kicking laps around the dance floor to the tune of the bouzouki (a musical instrument in the lute family). Greece's strong and enduring music tradition, however, is a rich mosaic of musical influences and styles.

While many leading performers draw on traditional folk, *laïka* (popular urban folk) and *rembetika* (blues), Greece's vibrant music scene is also pumping out its share of pop, club dance music, jazz, rock and even hip-hop.

Traditional Folk Music

Traditional folk music was shunned by the Greek bourgeoisie after Independence, when they looked to Europe – and classical music and opera – rather than their Eastern or 'peasant' roots.

Greece's regional folk music is generally divided into *nisiotika*, the lighter, upbeat music of the islands, and the more grounded *dimotika* of the mainland – where the *klarino* (clarinet) is prominent and lyrics refer to hard times, war and rural life. The spirited music of Crete, dominated by the Cretan *lyra* (pear-shaped, three-string, bowed instrument) and lute, remains a dynamic musical tradition, with regular performances and recordings by new-generation exponents.

Laïka & Entehna

Laïka (popular or urban folk music) is Greece's most popular music. A mainstream offshoot of *rembetika, laïka* emerged in the late 1950s and 60s, when clubs in Athens became bigger and glitzier, and the music more commercial. The bouzouki went electric and the sentimental tunes about love, loss, pain and emigration came to embody the nation's spirit. The late Stelios Kazantzidis was the big voice of this era, along with Grigoris Bithikotsis.

Classically-trained composers Mikis Theodorakis and Manos Hatzidakis led a new style known as *entehni mousiki* ('artistic' music). They drew on *rembetika* and used instruments such as the bouzouki in more symphonic arrangements, and created popular hits from the poetry of Seferis, Elytis, Ritsos and Kavadias.

Composer Yiannis Markopoulos later introduced rural folk-music and traditional instruments such as the *lyra, santouri,* violin and *kanonaki* into the mainstream, and brought folk performers such as Crete's legendary Nikos Xylouris to the fore.

During the junta years the music of Theodorakis and Markopoulos became a form of political expression (Theodorakis' music was banned and the composer jailed).

MISIRLOU

The memorable opening-credits track from the 1994 film *Pulp Fiction* was based on surf guitar legend Dirk Dale's 1960s version of 'Misirlou', originally recorded by a Greek *rembetika* band around 1930.

Contemporary & Pop Music

While few Greek performers have made it big internationally – 1970s genre-defying icons Nana Mouskouri and Demis Roussos remain the best known – Greece has a strong local music scene, from traditional and pop music to Greek rock, heavy metal, rap and electronic dance.

Some of the most interesting music emerging from Greece fuses elements of folk, *laïka* and *entehna* with Western influences. One of the most whimsical examples was Greece's tongue-in-cheek 2013 Eurovision contender, in which *rembetika* veteran Agathonas Iakovidis teamed up with the ska-Balkan rhythms of Thessaloniki's kilt-wearing Koza Mostra.

Big names in contemporary Greek music include Dionysis Savopoulos, dubbed the Bob Dylan of Greece, and veteran George Dalaras and Haris Alexiou.

Stand-out contemporary performers include Cypriot-born Alkinoos Ioannides, Eleftheria Arvanitakiis, Savina Yannatou, and ethnic jazz fusion artists Kristi Stasinopoulou, Mode Plagal and the Cretan-inspired Haïnides.

Mihalis Hatziyiannis is the current darling of the pop scene, while headline *laïka* performers include Yiannis Ploutarhos, Antonis Remos and Thanos Petrelis.

The sound of the bouzouki, immortalised in Mikis Theodorakis' 1960s soundtrack to *Zorba the Greek*, has become synonymous with Greece. The long-necked lute-like instrument became central to *rembetika* and dominates *laïka*.

Classical Music & Opera

Despite classical music and opera appealing to an (albeit growing) minority of Greeks, this field is where Greece has made the most significant

---

REMBETIKA: THE GREEK BLUES

Known as the Greek 'blues', *rembetika* emerged in Greece's urban underground and has strongly influenced the sound of Greek popular music

Two styles make up what is broadly known as *rembetika*. *Smyrneika* or Café Aman music emerged in the mid- to late-19th century in the thriving port cities of Smyrna and Constantinople, which had large Greek populations, and in Thessaloniki, Volos, Syros and Athens. With a rich vocal style, haunting *amanedhes* (vocal improvisations) and occasional Turkish lyrics, its sound had more Eastern influence. Predominant instruments were the violin, *outi* (oud), guitar, mandolin, *kanonaki* and *santouri* (a flat multistringed instrument). The second style, dominated by the six-stringed bouzouki, evolved in Piraeus.

After the influx of refugees from Asia Minor in Piraeus following the 1922 population exchange (many also went to America, where *rembetika* was recorded in the 1920s), the two styles somewhat overlapped and *rembetika* became the music of the ghettos. Infused with defiance, nostalgia and lament, the songs reflected life's bleaker themes and the *manges* (street-wise outcasts) who sang and danced in the *tekedhes* (hash dens that inspired many songs).

In the mid-1930s, the Metaxas dictatorship tried to wipe out the subculture through censorship, police harassment and raids on *tekedhes*. People were arrested for carrying a bouzouki. Many artists stopped performing and recording, though the music continued clandestinely. After WWII a new wave of *rembetika* emerged that eliminated much of its seedy side.

Rembetika legends include Markos Vamvakaris, who became popular with the first bouzouki group in the early 1930s, composers Vasilis Tsitsanis, Apostolos Kaldaras, Yiannis Papaioannou, Giorgos Mitsakis and Apostolos Hatzihristou, and songtresses Sotiria Bellou and Marika Ninou, whose life inspired Costas Ferris' 1983 film *Rebetiko*.

Interest in genuine *rembetika* revived in the late 1970s to early 1980s – particularly among students and intellectuals – and it continues to be rediscovered by new generations.

Rembetika ensembles perform seated in a row and traditionally play acoustically. A characteristic feature is an improvised introduction called a *taxim*.

THE ARTS MUSIC

Byzantine music is mostly heard in Greek churches these days, though Byzantine choirs perform in concerts in Greece and abroad, and the music has influenced folk music.

international contribution, most notably composers Mikis Theodorakis and Manos Hatzidakis and opera diva Maria Callas.

Dimitris Mitropoulos led the New York Philharmonic in the 1950s, while distinguished composers include Stavros Xarhakos and the late Yannis Xenakis. Leading contemporary performers include pianist Dimitris Sgouros, tenor Mario Frangoulis and sopranos Elena Kelessidi and Irini Tsirakidou.

The country's concert halls and major cultural festivals such as the Hellenic Festival offer rich international programs, while opera buffs have the Greek National Opera and Syros' Apollo Theatre.

Greek Dance

Greeks have danced since the dawn of Hellenism. Some folk dances derive from the ritual dances performed in ancient temples – ancient vases depict a version of the well-known *syrtos* folk dance. Dancing was later part of military education; in times of occupation it became an act of defiance and a covert way to keep fit.

Regional dances, like musical styles, vary across Greece. In Epiros, the slow and dignified *tsamikos* reflects the often cold and insular nature of mountain life, while the brighter islands gave rise to light, springy dances such as the *ballos* and the *syrtos*. The Pontian Greeks' vigorous and warlike dances such as the *kotsari* reflect years of altercations with their Turkish neighbours. Crete has its graceful *syrtos,* the fast and triumphant *maleviziotiko* and the dynamic *pentozali,* with its agility-testing high kicks and leaps. The graceful *kalamatianos,* originally from Kalamata, reflects years of proud Peloponnese tradition.

Men dance the often spectacular solo *zeïmbekiko* (whirling, meditative improvisations with roots in *rembetika*). Women do the sensuous *tsifteteli*, a svelte, sinewy show of femininity evolved from the Middle Eastern belly dance.

The so-called 'Zorba dance', or *syrtaki,* is a stylised dance for two or three dancers with arms linked on each other's shoulders, though the modern variation is danced in a long circle with an ever-quickening beat.

Women and men traditionally danced separately, and had their own dances, except in courtship dances such as the *sousta.*

Folk dance groups throughout Greece preserve regional traditions. The best place to see folk dancing is at regional festivals and the Dora Stratou Dance Theatre in Athens.

Contemporary dance is gaining prominence in Greece, with leading local troupes taking their place among the international line-up at the prestigious Kalamata International Dance Festival and the Athens International Dance Festival.

Greek Cuisine

Simple, nutritious and flavoursome, the food is one of the pleasures of travel through Greece. Rustic Greek cooking reflects the history and bounty of its diverse regions and relies on fresh, seasonal, local produce. Traditional home-style cooking is enjoying a renaissance, with a greater focus on regional specialities and local produce. While the humble souvlaki remains ever-popular, the nation's new generation of chefs is also taking its culinary heritage up a notch, reinterpreting Greek classics with contemporary flair.

The Greek Kitchen

The essence of traditional Greek cuisine lies in fresh, seasonal home-grown produce and generally simple, unfussy cooking that brings out the rich flavours of the Mediterranean.

Greek dishes are simply seasoned. Lemon juice, garlic, pungent Greek oregano and extra virgin olive oil are the quintessential flavours, along with tomato, parsley and dill, and spices such as cinnamon, allspice and cloves.

Extra virgin olive oil, the elixir of Greece, is used liberally in cooking and salads and is also the secret to making tasty vegetables, pulses and legumes – key elements of the healthy Mediterranean diet.

Once reserved for special occasions, meat has become more prominent in the modern diet. Local free-range lamb and pork dominate, though kid goat is also popular (beef is largely imported).

Traditional tavernas normally offer a selection of mezedhes, food cooked *tis oras* (to order), such as grilled meat and seafood, and ready-cooked home-style dishes known as *mayirefta*.

A fresh loaf of (usually white) crusty bread is a mandatory feature of every meal.

Feta, the national cheese, has been produced for about 6000 years from sheep's and/or goat's milk. Only feta made in Greece can be called feta, an EU ruling giving it the same protected status as Parma ham and Champagne.

Mayirefta

Mayirefta is a catch-all term for a variety of home-style, one-pot, baked or casserole dishes. Some *mayirefta*, mostly braised vegetable dishes, are also referred to as *ladhera* (oven-baked or one-pot dishes), literally 'oily' dishes, because of the liberal use of olive oil. *Mayirefta* are prepared early and left to cool, which enhances the flavour (they are often better served lukewarm).

Most tavernas will offer a range of popular *mayirefta,* including Greece's signature dish, *mousakas* (baked layers of eggplant, minced meat and potatoes topped with cheese and béchamel sauce) and the summer favourite, *yemista* (tomatoes and seasonal vegetables stuffed with rice and herbs).

Common pasta dishes include *pastitsio* (a thick spaghetti and meat bake) and *youvetsi*, slow-cooked chicken, lamb or beef in a tomato sauce with *kritharaki* (risone or rice-shaped pasta).

Staple meat dishes include tasty tomato-based stews *(kokkinista)*, roast lamb or chicken *lemonato* (with lemon and oregano) with baked potatoes, rabbit or beef *stifadho* (sweet stew cooked with tomato and onions), *soutzoukakia* (spicy meatballs in tomato sauce) and pork or lamb *fricassee* (braised with celery, lettuce and *avgolemono*).

Hearty Greek soups such as *fasoladha* (bean soup), *fakes* (lentils) or chicken soup with rice and *avgolemono* (egg and lemon) are regrettably seldom found in restaurants.

Greek Grills

Greeks are masterful with grilled and spit-roasted meats, and the distinctive smoky aromas waft through every neighbourhood restaurant strip and celebration.

The souvlaki – arguably the national dish – comes in many forms, from cubes of grilled meat on a skewer to the pita-wrapped snack with pork or chicken *gyros* (kebab-style meat cooked on a vertical rotisserie).

At tavernas, tasty *païdakia* (lamb cutlets) and *brizoles* (pork chops) are usually ordered by the kilo.

Some places also make the delicacy *kokoretsi*, a spicy, spit-roasted or baked seasoned lamb or goat offal, wrapped in intestines.

Fish & Seafood

With such an expanse of islands and coastline, it's no surprise fish and seafood feature prominently in Greek cooking. Fish from the Mediterranean and Aegean Seas are incredibly tasty and best cooked with minimum fuss – grilled whole and drizzled with *ladholemono* (a lemon and oil dressing). Smaller fish such as *barbounia* (red mullet) and *maridha* (whitebait) are usually lightly fried.

Due to overfishing and high summer demand, fresh local fish isn't plentiful or cheap. Smaller fish such as sardines, whitebait and anchovies remain good value. On the islands, the best way to avoid imports is to seek out tavernas run by local fishing families.

Octopus hung out to dry like washing outside tavernas is one of the iconic images of Greece. Grilled or marinated, it makes a fine *mezes* (appetiser), and is also stewed in a wine sauce with macaroni.

Popular seafood dishes include grilled *soupies* (cuttlefish), calamari or squid stuffed with cheese and herbs or rice, and a winter favourite: fried salted cod served with *skordalia* (a lethal garlic and potato dip). Island tavernas will often have *psarosoupa* (fish soup) or a delectable *kakavia* (a bouillabaisse-style speciality laden with various fish and seafood; usually made to order). Greek *avgotaraho* (botargo), a distinctive fish roe (usually grey mullet) preserved in beeswax, is a delicacy exported from Messolongi, on the west coast.

MEZEDHES

Sharing a range of mezedhes (appetisers) is a great way to dine and try new dishes. Beyond the classic dips of tzatziki (yoghurt, cucumber and garlic), *melitzanosalata* (aubergine) and pink or white *taramasalata* (fish roe), you should also try *fava*, a creamy split-pea purée served with lemon juice and finely cut red onions. Named after the pan it is cooked in, *saganaki* is a wedge of fried hard cheese, but you will also come across *saganaki* mussels and prawns, cooked in tomato sauce with cheese.

Common meat mezedhes include *bekri mezes* (spicy meat morsels cooked in tomato and red wine), *keftedhes* (meatballs), *loukaniko* (pork sausage) and *spetsofai* (spicy sausage and pepper stew). Crispy fried or grilled calamari, whitebait (eaten whole like fries), marinated or grilled *gavros* (white anchovies), octopus and *lakerda* (cured fish) are popular seafood mezedhes. Vegetarians are well catered for with *dolmadhes* (vine-wrapped rice parcels), *yigantes* (giant lima beans in tomato and herb sauce), *kolokythokeftedhes* (zucchini fritters) and Cycladic specialties, *revythokeftedhes* (chickpea fritters) and *domatokeftedhes* (tomato fritters).

TASTES OF THE ISLANDS

Each Greek island group – and sometimes each island – has its own specialities.

Islanders in the arid Cyclades relied on beans and pulses as the foundation of their winter diet. Santorini is renowned for *fava* (split-pea purée served with lemon juice and finely cut red onions), fritters made from its unique waterless tomatoes and wild capers. Sifnos' trademark *revythadha* (chickpea stew) is slow-cooked overnight in a specially shaped clay pot. Spaghetti with lobster is another Cycladic speciality, while Mykonos makes a mean sausage, as well as *kopanisti* (spicy creamy cheese).

The Venetian influence in the Ionian Islands is reflected in dishes such as Corfu's spicy braised beef or rooster *pastitsada* (red sauce pasta), and *sofrito* (braised veal with garlic and wine sauce). Grilled pancetta (pork spare ribs) is popular in Zakynthos.

Crete's herb-rich dishes include *anthoi* (stuffed zucchini flowers), *soupies* (cuttlefish) with wild fennel, and the local delicacy, *hohlioi bourbouristoi* (snails with vinegar and rosemary). Lamb is cooked *tsigariasto* (sautéed) or *ofto* (grilled upright around hot coals), or stewed with *stamnagathi* (wild mountain greens), or broad beans and artichokes. *Kalitsounia* are the local *pita* (filled with *myzithra* or wild greens). Celebrations invariably involve spit-roasted and boiled lamb, the stock of which is used to make *pilafi*, or *gamopilafo* (wedding rice).

Greek Salad

Greece's sun-kissed fresh produce makes for delicious salads. The ubiquitous Greek salad (*horiatiki* or 'village salad') is *the* summer salad, made of tomatoes, cucumber, onions, feta and olives (sometimes garnished with purslane, peppers or capers). Lettuce and cabbage salads are served outside the summer, while beetroot salad is also popular, occasionally garnished with feta and walnuts. *Horta* (wild or cultivated greens) are delicious warm or cold, drizzled with olive oil and lemon, and go particularly well with fish.

Regional Cuisine

Provincial Greek cuisine is invariably influenced by local produce and microclimates, from the oil-rich foods of the Peloponnese and sweet red peppers of Florina, to the giant lima beans of northern Prespa and the foraged wild greens and herbs of the barren Cyclades.

While in some areas you will find only subtle variations of the Greek staples, others make dishes unheard of elsewhere, such as Serres' *kavourma* (smoked water buffalo) or northern Greece's stinging nettle pies.

The cuisine of northern Greece, influenced by the eastern flavours introduced by Asia Minor refugees, uses less olive oil and more peppers and spices. Thessaloniki's mezes culture has long had the gastronomic upper hand over Athens, while coastal towns like Volos are known for seafood mezedhes such as fried mussels or mussel pilaf. Ioannina's specialities include crayfish, frogs' legs and *kokoretsi* (grilled lamb offal wrapped in intestines).

Fertile Crete has the most distinctive regional cuisine, while the Peloponnese is known for simpler herb-rich, one-pot dishes and *ladhera*.

The preservation of food was integral to survival during the winter, especially on the isolated islands where sun-dried and cured fish is a speciality. Excellent cured meats include vinegar-cured pork *apaki* in Crete, olive-oil stored *pasto* (the Mani), spicy wine-marinated and smoked *louza* (pork) in Tinos and Mykonos and *siglino* (Crete and Peloponnese).

Barley, rye or wheat *paximadhia* (hard rusks), double-baked to keep for years, are moistened with water and topped with tomato and olive oil (and feta or *myzithra* cheese in the Cretan *dakos*).

Greece's exceptional tangy, thick-strained yoghurt, usually made from sheep's milk, is rich and flavourful and ideal for a healthy breakfast, topped with aromatic thyme honey, walnuts and fruit.

GREEK WINE

The Greek wine renaissance has been gaining international attention and awards, with first-class wines being produced from age-old indigenous varietals with unique character. The latest generation of internationally trained winemakers are producing great wines from Greece's premiere wine regions, from Nemea in the Peloponnese to Naoussa in the north.

Greek white varieties include *moschofilero*, *assyrtiko*, *athiri*, *roditis*, *robola* and *savatiano*; the popular reds include *xynomavro*, *agiorgitiko* and *kotsifali*.

House or barrel wine varies dramatically in quality (white is the safer bet), and is ordered by the kilo/carafe. Few places serve wine by the glass.

Greek dessert wines include excellent muscats from Samos, Limnos and Rhodes, Santorini's Vinsanto, Mavrodafne wine (often used in cooking) and Monemvasia's Malmsey sweet wine.

Retsina, the resin-flavoured wine that became popular in the 1960s, retains a largely folkloric significance with foreigners. It does go well with strongly flavoured food (especially seafood) and some winemakers make a modern version.

Greece's regions produce many different types of cheeses, most using goat's and sheep's milk, with infinite variations in taste. Apart from feta, local cheeses include *graviera*, a nutty, mild Gruyère-like sheep's-milk cheese (the best is made in Crete, Naxos and Tinos), *kaseri*, similar to provolone, the ricotta-like whey cheese *myzithra* (also dried and hardened for pastas), and creamy *manouri* from the north. *Saganaki* is made from firm, sharp cheeses such as *kefalotyri* or *kefalograviera*.

Every region also has variations of the *pita* (pie), from the pastry to the choice of fillings, though cheese, and cheese and spinach, are the most common.

> For an online feast of Greek recipes and food and travel snippets go to www.gourmed.com. You'll also find a large collection of Greek recipes at www.greek-recipe.com.

Sweet Treats

Greeks traditionally serve fruit rather than sweets after a meal, but there's no shortage of delectable Greek sweets and cakes.

Traditional sweets include baklava, *loukoumadhes* (ball-shaped doughnuts served with honey and cinnamon), *kataïfi* (chopped nuts inside shredded angel-hair pastry), *rizogalo* (rice pudding) and *galaktoboureko* (custard-filled pastry). Syrupy fruit preserves, *ghlika kutalyu* (spoon sweets), are served on tiny plates as a welcome offering, but are also delicious as a topping on yoghurt or ice cream.

Look out for regional specialities such as almond *amygdhalota* from Andros and Mykonos or Syros' renowned 'Grecian delight' (aka Turkish delight). Mastiha – mastic-flavoured *ypovryhio* (submarine) sugar confectionary from Chios – is served on a spoon dipped in a glass of water, or try the chilled mastic liqueur. Thessaloniki's famous *bougatsa* (baked creamy semolina custard–filled pastry sprinkled with icing sugar) can be found around Greece.

> Diane Kochilas' *The Country Cooking of Greece* is a beautifully presented and authoritative culinary guide to Greece's regional cuisine, produce and food traditions, with engaging stories and great recipes.

Festive Food

Greece's religious and cultural celebrations inevitably involve a feast and many have their own culinary traditions.

The 40-day Lenten fast spawned *nistisima*, foods without meat or dairy (or oil if you go strictly by the book). Lenten sweets include *halva*, both the Macedonian-style version (sold in delis) made from tahini and the semolina dessert often served after a meal.

Red-dyed boiled Easter eggs decorate the *tsoureki*, a brioche-style bread flavoured with *mahlepi* (mahaleb cherry kernels) and mastic. Saturday night's post-Resurrection Mass supper includes *mayiritsa* (offal soup), while Easter Sunday sees whole lambs cooking on spits all over the countryside.

A golden-glazed *vasilopita* cake is cut at midnight on New Year's Eve, giving good fortune to whoever gets the lucky coin inside.

Vegetarian-Friendly

While vegetarians are an oddity in Greece, they are well catered for, as vegetables feature prominently in Greek cooking – a legacy of lean times and the Orthodox faith's fasting traditions.

Look for popular vegetable dishes, such *fasolakia yiahni* (braised green beans), *bamies* (okra), *briam* (oven-baked vegetable casserole) and vine-leaf dolmadhes. Of the nutritious wild greens, *vlita* (amaranth) are the sweetest, but other common varieties include wild radish, dandelion, stinging nettle and sorrel.

Eating with Kids

Greeks love children and tavernas are very family-friendly, You may find children's menus in some tourist areas, but the Greek way of sharing dishes is a good way to feed the kids. Most tavernas will accommodate variations for children.

Greek coffee is traditionally brewed in a *briki* (narrow-top pot) on a hot-sand apparatus called a *hovoli* – and served in a small cup. Order a *metrio* (medium, with one sugar) and sip slowly until you reach the mudlike grounds (don't drink them).

Nature & Wildlife

While Greece is a perfect place to rub shoulders with ancient statues, it's equally ideal for getting up close to nature. Hike through the wildflowers, come eye-to-eye with a loggerhead turtle or simply stretch out on a beach. Greece has something for everyone who wants to get out and explore.

Nature Conservation

Pelicans and pygmy cormorants (www.spp.gr)

Birdlife (www.ornithologiki.gr)

Wildflowers (www.greekmountainflora.info)

Sea turtles (www.archelon.gr)

Going green (www.cleanupgreece.org.gr)

Experiencing the Outdoors

Greek Geography

No matter where you go in Greece, it's impossible to be much more than 100km from the sea. Rugged mountains, indigo water and seemingly innumerable islands dominate the Greek landscape, which was shaped by submerging seas, volcanic explosions and mineral-rich terrain. The mainland covers 131,944 sq km, with an indented coastline stretching for 15,020km. Mountains rise over 2000m and occasionally tumble down into plains, particularly in Thessaly and Thrace. Meanwhile, the Aegean and Ionian Seas flow between and link together the country's 1400 islands, with just 169 of them inhabited. These islands fill 400,000 sq km of territorial waters.

For those with a penchant for geography, Greece rocks. During the Triassic, Jurassic, Cretaceous and even later geological periods, Greece was a shallow oxygen-rich sea. The continuous submerging of land created large tracts of limestone through the whole submarine land mass. Later, as the land emerged from the sea to form the backbone of the current topography, a distinctly eroded landscape with crystalline rocks and other valuable minerals began to appear, marking the spine that links the north and south of the mainland today. Limestone caves are

---

GREEN ISSUES

Environmental awareness is beginning to seep into the fabric of Greece society, leading to slow but positive change. Environmental education has begun in schools, recycling is more common in cities, and even in the smallest villages you may find organic and environmentally sustainable restaurants and businesses. However, long-standing problems such as deforestation and soil erosion date back thousands of years. Live cultivation and goats have been the main culprits, while firewood gathering, shipbuilding, housing and industry have all taken their toll.

Illegal development of mainly coastal areas and building in forested or protected areas has gained momentum in Greece since the 1970s. Despite attempts at introducing laws and protests by locals and environmental groups, corruption and the lack of an infrastructure to enforce the laws means little is done to abate the land-grab. The issue is complicated by population growth and increased urban sprawl. The developments often put a severe strain on water supplies and endangered wildlife. A few developments have been torn down in recent years; however in more cases, the illegal buildings have been legalised, deemed necessary due to social need, whereby demolition would leave residents with no alternative affordable housing.

NATIONAL PARKS

National Parks were first established in Greece in 1938 with the creation of Mt Olympus National Park and followed quickly by the establishment of Parnassos National Park. There are now 10 national parks and two marine parks, which aim to protect the unique flora and fauna of Greece.

Facilities for visitors are often basic; abundant walking trails are not always maintained and the clutch of basic refuges is very simple. To most, the facilities matter little when compared to nature's magnificent backdrop. If you have the opportunity, it's well worth experiencing the wild side of Greece in one of these settings:

Mt Olympus National Park (p266) Home to Greece's tallest mountain, rich flora and considered the home of the gods.

Mt Parnitha National Park (p127) Very popular wooded parkland north of Athens; home to the red deer.

National Marine Park of Alonnisos (p620) Covers six islands and 22 islets in the Sporades and is home to monk seals, dolphins and rare birdlife.

Parnassos National Park (p197) Towering limestone and scenic views down to Delphi.

Prespa Lakes (p271) One of Europe's oldest lakes, steeped in wildlife and tranquillity.

Samaria Gorge (p449) Spectacular gorge in Crete and a refuge for the *kri-kri* (Cretan goat).

Cape Sounion (p127) A cape with panoramic views and home to the Temple of Poseidon.

Vikos-Aoös National Park (p291) Excellent hiking with caves, canyons and dense forest.

Bay of Laganas (p664) An Ionian refuge for loggerhead turtles.

Iti National Park (p205) Tranquil stretches of forest, meadows and pools. Home to eagles, deer and boar.

---

a major feature of this karst landscape, shaped by the dissolution of a soluble layer of bedrock.

Volcanic activity once regularly hit Greece with force – one of the world's largest volcanic explosions was on Santorini around 1650 BC. Today, earthquakes continue to shake the country on a smaller scale but with almost predictable frequency. In 1999, a 5.9-magnitude earthquake near Athens killed nearly 150 people and left thousands homeless. In 2008, three separate quakes of 6.5-magnitude shook the Peloponnese but caused little damage. To check out Greece's explosive past, visit the craters of Santorini, Nisyros and Polyvotis.

Greece is short on rivers, with none that are navigable, although they've become popular locations for white-water rafting. The largest rivers are the Aheloös, Aliakmonas, Aoös and Arahthos, all of which have their source in the Pindos Mountains of Epiros.

> Greece is the most seismically active country in Europe, with more than half of the continent's volcanic activity.

The long plains of the river valleys, and those between the mountains and the coast, form Greece's only lowlands. The mountainous terrain, dry climate and poor soil leave farmers at a loss and less than a quarter of the land is cultivated. Greece is, however, rich in minerals, with reserves of oil, manganese, bauxite and lignite.

Wildflowers

Greece is endowed with a variety of flora unrivaled elsewhere in Europe. The wildflowers are spectacular, with more than 6000 species, some of which occur nowhere else, and more than 100 varieties of orchid. They continue to thrive because most of the land is inadequate for intensive agriculture and has therefore escaped the ravages of chemical fertilisers.

The regions with the most wildflowers are the Lefka Ori Mountains in Crete and the Mani area of the Peloponnese. Trees begin to blossom as early as the end of February in warmer areas and the wildflowers start to appear in March. During spring the hillsides are carpeted with flowers, which seem to sprout even from the rocks. By summer the flowers have disappeared from everywhere but the northern mountainous regions. Autumn brings a new period of blossoming.

Herbs grow wild throughout much of Greece and you'll see locals out picking fresh herbs for their kitchen. Locally grown herbs are also increasingly sold as souvenirs and are generally organic.

Herbs in Cooking is an illustrative book by Maria and Nikos Psilakis that can be used as both an iden-tification guide and a cookbook for Greek dishes seasoned with local herbs.

Forests

It seems as if every village on the mainland has a plane tree shading its central square; however, the lush forests that once covered ancient Greece are increasingly rare. Having been decimated by thousands of years of clearing for grazing, boat building and housing, they've more recently suffered from severe forest fires. Northern Greece is the only region that has retained significant areas of native forest, and here you can experience mountainsides covered with dense thickets of hop hornbeam (*Ostrya carpinifolia*), noted for its lavish display of white-clustered flowers. Another common species is the Cyprus plane (*Platanus orientalis insularis*), which thrives wherever there is ample water.

Watching for Wildlife

On the Ground

In areas widely inhabited by humans, you are unlikely to spot any wild animals other than the odd fox, weasel, hare or rabbit scurrying out of your way. The more remote mountains of northern Greece continue to support a wide range of wildlife, including wild dogs and shepherds' dogs with bad attitudes, which often roam the higher pastures on grazing mountains and should be given a wide berth if encountered.

The brown bear, Europe's largest land mammal, still manages to survive in very small numbers in the Pindos Mountains, the Peristeri Range that rises above the Prespa Lakes, and in the mountains that lie along the Bulgarian border. It is estimated that only around 200 survive; if you want to see a bear in Greece nowadays, you're better off heading for the **Arcturos Bear Sanctuary** (www.arcturos.gr) in the village of Nymfeo in Macedonia.

A BURNING ISSUE

Each year, forest fires rage across Greece, destroying many thousands of hectares, often in some of the most picturesque areas of Greece. Mt Parnitha and the Peloponnese are still recovering from fires in 2007 that changed the face of the landscape. In the summer of 2012, more than 170 fast burning fires swept across the country, swallowing entire villages and leaving more than 50 dead. One of the worst hit islands was Chios, where more than 64 sq km of forest and farmland were destroyed, nine villages were evacuated and the island's mastic forests were threatened. As the fires reached the outskirts of Athens, the government declared a state of emergency and asked for water-bombing aircraft from Spain and Italy. By early in the summer of 2013, more than 20 fires had already ignited.

The increasing scale of recent fires is blamed on rising Mediterranean temperatures and high winds. Many locals argue that the government is ill-prepared and that its attempts to address the annual fires are slow. Fearing they won't receive help, many locals refuse to leave areas being evacuated, preferring to take the risk and attempt to fight the flames themselves.

DON'T BE A BOAR

Greece's relationship with its wildlife has not been a happy one. Hunting of wild animals is a popular activity with Greeks as a means of providing food. This is particularly true in mountainous regions where the partisanship of hunters is legendary. Despite signs forbidding hunting, Greek hunters often shoot freely at any potential game. While this can include rare and endangered species, the main game is often wild boars, which have been around since antiquity. Considered destructive and cunning animals, the number of wild boars has increased in recent decades, likely due to a lower number of predators. Many argue that hunting is an important means of culling them. There is also an increasing number of wild boar breeding farms and you will find boar on many menus.

The grey wolf, which is protected under the European Bern Convention, is officially classified as stable. However, at last count, there were only an estimated 200 to 300 surviving in the wild and it's believed that up to 100 are killed annually by farmers' indiscriminate (and illegal) use of poison baits in retaliation for the occasional marauding and mauling of their flocks. The Greek Government and insurance companies pay compensation for livestock lost to wolves but it doesn't appear to slow the killings. The surviving wolves live in small numbers in the forests of the Pindos Mountains in Epiros, as well as in the Dadia Forest Reserve area. Head to the Arcturos Wolf Sanctuary in Agrapidia, near Florina, which houses nine wolves rescued from illegal captivity.

The golden jackal is a strong candidate for Greece's most misunderstood mammal. Although its diet is 50% vegetarian (and the other 50% is made up of carrion, reptiles and small mammals), it has traditionally shouldered much of the blame for attacks on stock and has been hunted by farmers as a preventative measure. Near the brink of extinction, it was declared a protected species in 1990 and now survives only in the Fokida district of central Greece and on the island of Samos.

Once roaming across all of mainland Greece, the graceful Red Deer is now restricted to the Sithonia peninsula, the Rhodope Mountain bordering Bulgaria and Mt Parnitha north of Athens. As the largest herbivore in Greece, its population is under constant threat from illegal hunters, making attempts at population redistribution unsuccessful.

Greece has an active snake population and in spring and summer you will inevitably spot these wriggling reptiles on roads and pathways all over the country. Fortunately the majority are harmless, though the viper and the coral snake can cause fatalities. Lizards are in abundance and there is hardly a dry-stone wall without one of these curious creatures clambering around.

The **Hellenic Wildlife Hospital** (www.ekpazp.gr) is the oldest and largest wildlife rehabilitation centre in Greece and southern Europe.

In the Air

Birdwatchers have a field day in Greece as the country is on many north–south migratory paths. Lesvos (Mytilini) in particular draws a regular following of birders from all over Europe who come to spot some of more than 279 recorded species that stop off at the island annually. Storks are more visible visitors, arriving in early spring from Africa and returning to the same nests year after year. These are built on electricity poles, chimney tops and church towers, and can weigh up to 50kg; keep an eye out for them in northern Greece, especially in Thrace in Macedonia. Thrace has the richest colony of fish-eating birds in Europe, including species such as egrets, herons, cormorants and ibises, as well as the rare Dalmatian pelican – Turkey and Greece are now the only countries in

Europe where this large bird is found. The wetlands at the mouth of the Evros River, close to the border with Turkey, are home to two easily identifiable wading birds – the avocet, which has a long curving beak, and the black-winged stilt, which has extremely long pink legs.

Upstream on the Evros River in Thrace, the dense forests and rocky outcrops of the 72-sq-km Dadia Forest Reserve play host to the largest range of birds of prey in Europe. Thirty-six of the 38 European species can be seen here, and it is a breeding ground for 23 of them. Permanent residents include the giant black vulture, whose wingspan reaches 3m, the griffon vulture and the golden eagle. Europe's last 15 pairs of royal eagle nest on the river delta.

About 350 pairs of the rare Eleonora's falcon (60% of the world's population) nest on the island of Piperi in the Sporades and on Tilos, which is also home to the very rare Bonelli's eagle and the shy, cormorant-like Mediterranean shag.

The Greek Orthodox Church is the second-largest landowner in Greece.

Under the Sea

As Europe's most endangered marine mammal, the monk seal *(Monachus monachus)* ekes out an extremely precarious existence in Greece. Approximately 200 to 250 monk seals, about 50% of the world's population, are found in both the Ionian and Aegean Seas. Small colonies also live on the island of Alonnisos and there have been reported sightings on Tilos. Pervasive habitat encroachment is the main culprit for their diminished numbers, along with hunting by fishermen competing for declining fish stocks.

Loggerhead turtle hatchlings use the journey from the nest to the sea to build up their strength. Helping the baby turtles to the sea can actually lower their chances of survival.

The waters around Zakynthos are home to the last large sea turtle colony in Europe, that of the endangered loggerhead turtle *(Caretta caretta)*. The loggerhead also nests in smaller numbers in the Peloponnese and on Kefallonia and Crete. Greece's turtles have many hazards to dodge – entanglement in fishing nets and boat propellers, consumption of floating rubbish, and the destruction of their nesting beaches by sun-loungers and beach umbrellas that threaten their eggs. It doesn't help that the turtles' nesting time coincides with the European summer holiday season.

There is still the chance that you will spot dolphins from the ferry deck, however, a number of the species are now considered vulnerable. The number of common dolphins *(Delphinus delphis)* has dropped from 150 to 15 in the past decade. The main threats to dolphins are a diminished food supply and entanglement in fishing nets.

The Greek Way of Life

What crisis? Visitors may be forgiven for wondering about the state of the nation when they see Athens' bustling cafes and what appears to be business as usual on the Greek islands. The Greek way of life took a major hit as austerity measures further sunk the country into recession, but it's not in the Greeks' nature to retreat into the gloom.

National Psyche

Greeks have always shared good and bad times in the company of family and friends; they've danced when sad or defiant and sought solace in their country's rich culture and simple pleasures. Someone will always buy an unemployed youth a coffee, or their yiayia (grandmother) will give them hatziliki (pocket money) from her shrunken pension.

Greek values and the national character came under attack during the crisis – with Greeks universally characterised as lazy, leisure-loving, corrupt tax-evaders recklessly bringing Europe to the brink of economic collapse. The realities are far more complex – for every 'lazy' Greek there are hard-working people juggling two jobs to provide for their families.

Greeks pride themselves on their *filotimo*, a hard-to-translate Greek concept that underpins society's cultural norms. It encompasses personal and family honour, respect and loyalty to parents and grandparents, sacrifice and help for friends and strangers alike, pride in country and heritage, and gratitude and hospitality. Though some would argue it has been eroded, the concept remains an important part of Greek identity.

The Greeks also generously extend their *filoxenia* (hospitality). Despite the current fiscal problems, the average Greeks will still lavish you with free drinks, fresh cake from their kitchen, and the warmth they have always been famous for. Curious by nature, as well as passionate, loyal and fiery, Greeks engage in animated personal and political discussions rather than polite small-talk. Nothing is off limits for conversation, and you may find yourself quizzed as to why you haven't got children, why you're not married and how much you earn. They can be fervently patriotic, nationalistic and ethnocentric. Issues are debated with strong will. Greeks are unashamed about staring and blatantly observing (and commenting on) the comings and goings of people around them. They prefer spontaneity to making plans and are notoriously unpunctual (turning up on time is referred to as 'being English').

Social & Family Life

Greek life has always taken place in the public sphere, whether it's men talking politics at the local kafeneio or the elderly gathering in neighbourhood squares while their grandchildren play into the evening. While entertainment spending has been seriously curtailed, the gregarious Greeks nonetheless enjoy a vibrant social and cultural life and infamously lively nightlife.

Debunking the myth of the lazy Greek, OECD research suggests Greeks actually work longer hours than their European and US counterparts, though they have lower productivity and labour participation rates. Greek wages are amongst Europe's lowest and living costs amongst the highest.

It can be said that rather than living to work, Greeks work to live, with an emphasis on fun and shared company rather than slaving all hours in an office. People of all ages take their afternoon volta (outing) along seafront promenades or town centres, dressed up and refreshed from a siesta (albeit a dying institution). On weekends they flock to the beach and seaside tavernas, and summer holidays are the highlight of the year – traditionally, the capital virtually shuts down mid-August as people take off for the islands, beach towns or their ancestral villages. A peculiarly Greek social talking point is how many swims you've had that summer.

The word *xenos* means both stranger and guest, and Greeks see *filoxenia* (hospitality, welcome, shelter) almost as a duty and matter of personal pride and honour.

Greek society remains dominated by the family, and while many men may appear soaked with machismo, the matriarchal domestic model is still very much commonplace, with women subtly pulling the strings in the background. These strong family ties and kinship are helping Greeks survive testing times. Greece's weak welfare system means Greeks rely on families and social groups for support. Most Greek businesses are small, family-run operations. Parents strive to provide homes for their children when they get married.

Greeks rarely move out of home before they marry, unless they go to university or work in another city. While this was changing among professionals and people marrying later, low wages and rising unemployment have forced many young people to stay – or return – home.

Showing solidarity in the face of austerity, enterprising locals in Volos have developed an alternative currency unit to the EURO (the TEM), establishing a novel informal bartering system for goods and services, where participants exchange anything from olive oil to car repairs.

Greeks retain strong regional identities and ties to their ancestral villages. One of the first questions Greeks will ask a stranger is what part of Greece they come from. Even the country's most remote villages are bustling during holidays. Greece's large diaspora plays a significant role in the life of many islands and villages, returning each summer in droves.

The State

Personal freedom and the right to protest and protect their democratic rights are sacrosanct to Greeks. Trade-union activism, mass demonstrations and crippling general strikes are a routine part of life in Athens and other major cities, with police and property normally bearing the brunt of anti-establishment sentiment.

This rebellious spirit came to the fore during anti-austerity protests, as Greeks resisted economic reforms crucial to help curb Greece's soaring national debt.

The nation's capacity to overcome its economic woes has been stifled by systemic problems with Greece's political and civil life, aspects of society that Greeks have long criticised and perpetuated. A residual

PROUD HERITAGE

Today's Greeks cherish the achievements of their ancient forbears, and so they should. Without the Golden Age of Ancient Greece (about 500–300 BC), the world would arguably not have developed its classical sculpture, mathematics, geometry, philosophy, drama and politics. Not to mention the rich tapestry that Greek myths brought to the well of story and imagination. Show just a little appreciation of this to the average Greek and they'll love you for it.

Greeks are also proud of their long history of democratic rights (*demos* meaning people, and *cratos* meaning power). This concept of political freedom was hard-fought for by the likes of Solon of Athens and later built upon by Cleisthenes in the 5th and 4th centuries BC.

SPORTING PASSIONS

If the streets are quiet, you can't get a taxi or you hear a mighty roar coming from nearby cafes, chances are there's a football (soccer) game underway. Greece's most popular spectator sport inspires local passions and often unedifying fan hooliganism.

Football's first division is dominated by the big clubs: Olympiakos of Piraeus and arch rivals Panathinaikos of Athens, along with AEK Athens and Thessaloniki's PAOK.

While the top clubs have won European championships, Greece has remained in the shadow of Europe's soccer heavyweights since its 2004 European Cup win.

Greece is also one of the powerhouses of European basketball. Panathinaikos has won six Euroleague championships, while Olypiakos claimed its third title in 2013. Nigerian-born Greek basketballer Giannis Antetokounmpo became the poster boy for Greece's immigrants in 2013, when he was picked for the Milwaukee Bucks in the NBA draft (having had his Greek citizenship fast-tracked).

mistrust of the state and its institutions is a legacy of years of foreign occupation, while political instability fostered a weak civil society based on tax evasion, political patronage and nepotism, and a black market economy. Merit has long taken second place to political interests when allocating coveted public-sector jobs or EU funds. Making headway with Greece's bloated and inefficient bureaucracy required *meson* (the help of someone working in the system). The infamous *fakelaki* (envelope of cash) became a common way to cut red tape. At its worst, the system fed corruption and profiteering.

Aversion to the perceived over-regulated approach of Western nations is also part of the national psyche. An undercurrent of civil disobedience extends to lax attitudes to road rules or parking restrictions (you will see motorcyclists carrying their helmets as they chat on their mobile phones). As for the EU smoking ban for restaurants? It's as if it never happened.

The New Greeks

Since the 1990s, an influx of economic migrants has changed the face of a largely homogenous society. Greece's official immigrant population is now pushing one million, the majority coming from Albania, the Balkans and Eastern Europe.

It's not uncommon to find Bulgarian women looking after the elderly in remote villages, Polish workers propping up island tourism, Albanians dominating the manual labour force and in many villages, Eastern European brides filling the void left by Greek women who have moved to the cities. Undocumented migrants are also widely exploited as cheap labour in Greece's seasonal workforce, particularly in construction and agriculture.

While the early waves gained begrudging acceptance, more recent immigrants have largely struggled to integrate into mainstream society, existing on the fringe.

Faith & Identity

Families flock to church for lively Easter celebrations, weddings, baptisms and annual festivals, but it's largely women and the elderly who attend church services regularly. While most Greeks aren't devout, the Orthodox faith – the official religion of Greece – remains an important part of their identity and culture.

The Greek year revolves around saints' days and festivals of the Orthodox church calendar. Easter is bigger than Christmas and name days (celebrating your namesake saint) are more important than birthdays. Most people are named after a saint, as are boats, suburbs and train stations.

Religious rituals are part of daily life. You will notice taxi drivers, motorcyclists and people on public transport making the sign of the cross when they pass a church; compliments to babies and adults are followed by the *'ftou ftou'* (spitting) gesture to ward off the evil eye; people light church candles in memory of loved ones. Hundreds of privately-built small chapels dot the countryside, while the tiny roadside *iconostases* (chapels) are either shrines to road accidents victims or dedications to saints.

> *"Religious rituals are part of daily life"*

During consecutive foreign occupations the Church and was the principal upholder of Greek culture, language and traditions, and the church still exerts significant social, political and economic influence, though recent scandals have taken their toll.

Survival Guide

Directory A–Z

Accommodation

There is a range of accommodation available in Greece to suit every taste and pocket. All places to stay are subject to strict price controls set by the tourist police. By law, a notice must be displayed in every room, stating the category of the room and the price charged in each season. It's difficult to generalise accommodation prices in Greece as rates depend entirely on the season and location. Don't expect to pay the same price for a double on one of the islands as you would in central Greece or Athens.

Other points to note when considering hotel prices:

➡ Prices include community tax and VAT (value added tax).

➡ A 10% surcharge may be added for stays of fewer than three nights, but this is not mandatory.

➡ A mandatory charge of 20% is levied for an additional bed (although this is often waived if the bed is for a child).

➡ During July and August accommodation owners will charge the maximum price.

➡ In spring and autumn prices can drop by 20%.

➡ Prices can drop even further in winter.

➡ Rip-offs are rare; if you suspect that you have been exploited make a report to the tourist or the regular police, and they will act swiftly.

Camping

Camping is a good option, especially in summer. There are almost 350 campgrounds in Greece, found on the majority of islands (with the notable exception of the Saronic Gulf Islands). Standard facilities include hot showers, kitchens, restaurants and mini-markets – and often a swimming pool.

Most camping grounds are open only between April and October. The **Panhellenic Camping Association** (☑ 210 362 1560; www. panhellenic-camping-union.gr; Solonos 102, Exarhia, Athens) publishes an annual booklet listing all its campgrounds, their facilities and months of operation.

If you're camping in the height of summer, bring a silver fly sheet to reflect the heat off your tent (the dark tents that are all the rage in colder countries become sweat lodges). Between May and mid-September the weather is warm enough to sleep out under the stars. Many campgrounds have covered areas where tourists who don't have tents can sleep in summer; you can get by with a lightweight sleeping bag. It's a good idea to have a foam pad to lie on and a waterproof cover for your sleeping bag.

Some other points:

➡ Camping fees are highest from mid-June through to the end of August.

➡ Campgrounds charge €5 to €7 per adult and €3 to €4 for children aged four to 12. There's no charge for children under four.

➡ Tent sites cost from €4 per night for small tents, and from €5 per night for large tents.

➡ You can often rent tents for around €5.

➡ Caravan sites start at around €6; car costs are typically €4 to €5.

PRICE RANGES

We have divided accommodation into budgets based on the rate for a double room in high season (May to August). Unless otherwise stated, all rooms have private bathroom facilities.

€ Under €60 (under €80 in Athens)

€€ €60–150 (€80–150 in Athens)

€€€ Over €150

Domatia

Domatia (literally 'rooms') are the Greek equivalent of the British B&B, minus the breakfast. Once upon a time, domatia were little more than spare rooms in the family home; nowadays, many are purpose-built appendages with fully equipped kitchens. Standards of cleanliness are generally high.

Domatia remain a popular option for budget travellers. Expect to pay from €25 to €50 for a single, and €35 to €65 for a double, depending on whether bathrooms are shared or private, the season and how long you plan to stay. Domatia are found throughout the mainland (except in large cities) and on almost every island that has a permanent population. Many domatia are open only between April and October.

From June to September domatia owners are out in force, touting for customers. They meet buses and boats, shouting 'room, room!' and often carrying photographs of their rooms. In peak season it can prove a mistake not to take up an offer – but be wary of owners who are vague about the location of their accommodation.

Hostels

Most youth hostels in Greece are run by the **Greek Youth Hostel Organisation** (210 751 9530; www.athens-yhostel. com; Damareos 75, Pangrati, Athens). There are affiliated hostels in Athens, Olympia, Patra and Thessaloniki on the mainland, and on the islands of Crete and Santorini.

Hostel rates vary from around €10 to €20 for a bed in a dorm and you don't have to be a member to stay in them. Few have curfews.

Hotels

Hotels in Greece are divided into six categories: deluxe, A, B, C, D and E. Hotels are categorised according to the size of the rooms, whether or not they have a bar, and the

BOOK YOUR STAY ONLINE

For more accommodation reviews by Lonely Planet authors, check out http://lonelyplanet.com/hotels/. You'll find independent reviews, as well as recommendations on the best places to stay. Best of all, you can book online.

ratio of bathrooms to beds, rather than standards of cleanliness, comfort of beds and friendliness of staff – all elements that may be of greater relevance to guests.

➔ A- and B-class hotels have full amenities, private bathrooms and constant hot water; prices range from €50 to €85 for singles and from €90 and up for doubles.

➔ C-class hotels have a snack bar and rooms with private bathrooms, but not necessarily constant hot water; prices range from €35 to €60 for a single in high season and €45 to €80 for a double.

➔ D-class hotels generally have shared bathrooms and they may have solar-heated water, meaning hot water is not guaranteed; prices are comparable with domatia.

➔ E-class hotels have shared bathrooms and you may have to pay extra for hot water; prices are comparable with budget domatia.

Mountain Refuges

There are 55 mountain refuges dotted around the Greek mainland, Crete and Evia. They range from small huts with outdoor toilets and no cooking facilities to very comfortable modern lodges. They are run by the country's various mountaineering and skiing clubs. Prices start at around €10 per person, depending on the facilities. The EOT (Greek National Tourist Organisation) publication *Greece: Mountain Refuges & Ski Centres* has details about each refuge; copies are available at all EOT branches.

Pensions

Pensions are indistinguishable from hotels. They are categorised as A, B or C class. An A-class pension is equivalent in amenities and price to a B-class hotel, a B-class pension is equivalent to a C-class hotel, and a C-class pension is equivalent to a D- or E-class hotel.

Rental Accommodation

A really practical way to save money and maximise comfort is to rent a furnished apartment or villa. Many are purpose-built for tourists while others (villas in particular) may be owners' homes that they are not using. Some owners may insist on a minimum stay of a week. A good site to spot prospective villas is www.greekislands.com.

Business Hours

While opening hours can vary depending on the season, day or mood of the proprietor, some generalisations can be made (see p729). Note that while the government establishes opening hours for major sites, at the time of research these hours were inconsistent across many of the major sites due to issues with staffing and wages. Always try to double-check opening hours before visiting.

Customs Regulations

There are no longer duty-free restrictions within the EU. Upon entering the country from outside the EU, customs inspection is usually cursory for foreign tourists and a verbal declaration is generally all that is required. Random searches are still occasionally made for drugs. Import regulations for medicines are strict; if you are taking medication, make sure you get a statement from your doctor before you leave home. It is illegal, for instance, to take codeine into Greece without an accompanying doctor's certificate.

It is strictly forbidden to export antiquities (anything more than 100 years old) without an export permit. This crime is second only to drug smuggling in the penalties imposed. It is an offence to remove even the smallest article from an archaeological site. The place to apply for an export permit is the Antique Dealers and Private Collections section of the **Athens Archaeological Service** (Polygnotou 13, Plaka, Athens).

Vehicles

Cars can be brought into Greece for six months without a carnet; only a green card (international third-party insurance) is required. If arriving from Italy your only proof of entry into the country will be your ferry ticket stub, so don't lose it. From other countries, a passport stamp will be ample evidence.

Discount Cards

Camping Card International (CCI; www.campingcardinternational.com) Gives up to 25% savings in camping fees and third-party liability insurance while in the campground.

European Youth Card (www.eyca.org) Available for anyone up to the age of 30 (you don't have to be a resident of Europe); provides discounts of up to 20% at sights, shops and for some transport. Available from the kiosk website (kiosk.eyca.org) or travel agencies in Athens for €14.

International Student Identity Card (ISIC; www.isic.org) Entitles the holder to half-price admission to museums and ancient sites, and discounts at some budget hotels and hostels. Available online or from travel agencies in Athens. Applicants are required to provide documents proving student status, a passport photo and €10.

Seniors Cards Card-carrying EU pensioners can claim a range of benefits such as reduced admission to ancient sites and museums, and discounts on bus and train fares.

Electricity

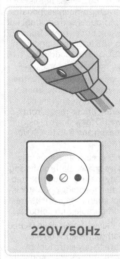

220V/50Hz

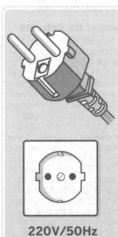

220V/50Hz

Embassies & Consulates

All foreign embassies in Greece are in Athens and its suburbs, with a few consulates in Thessaloniki.

Albanian Embassy (210 687 6200; embassy.athens@mfa.gov.al; Vekiareli 7, Athens)

Australian Embassy (210 870 4000; www.greece.embassy.gov.au; Ambelokipi, 6th fl, Thon Building, cnr Leoforos Alexandras & Leoforos Kifisias)

Bulgarian Embassy (210 674 8105; www.mfa.bg/embassies/greece; Stratigou Kalari 33a, Psyhiko, Athens)

Canadian Embassy (210 727 3400; www.greece.gc.ca; Ioannou Gennadiou 4)

Cypriot Embassy (210 723 7883; www.mfa.gov.cy/mfa/Embassies/Embassy_Athens.nsf; Irodotou 16, Athens)

French Embassy (210 361 1663; www.ambafrance-gr.org; Leoforos Vasilissis Sofias 7, Athens)

German Embassy (210 728 5111; www.athen.diplo.de; Dimitriou 3, cnr Karaoli, Kolonaki, Athens)

Irish Embassy (210 723 2771; www.embassyofireland.gr; Leoforos Vasileos Konstantinou 5-7, Athens)

Italian Embassy (210 361 7260; www.ambatene.esteri.it; Sekeri 2, Athens)

Netherlands Embassy (210 725 4900; www.dutchembassy.gr; Leoforos Vasileos Konstantinou 5-7, Athens)

New Zealand Embassy ((+39) 06 853 7501; www.nzembassy.com/italy; Via Clitunno 44 Rome) Travellers from New Zealand should contact the embassy in Rome.

Turkish Embassy (210 726 3000; embassy.athens@mfa.gov.tr; Vassileos Gheorgiou B'8, Athens) Has an additional branch in Athens (210 724 5915; turkbaskon@kom.forthnet.gr; Leoforos Vasileos Georgiou 8, Athens) and one in Thessaloniki (2310 248 452; turkbaskon@kom.forthnet.gr; Agiou Dimitriou 151).

UK Embassy (☎210 727 2600; www.ukingreece.fco. gov.uk/en; 1 Ploutarchou, Athens) Also has a branch at Thessaloniki (☎2310 278 006; www.ukingreece.fco.gov.uk/en; Tsimiski 43).

US Embassy (☎210 721 2951; http://athens.usembassy.gov; 91 Vasilisis Sophias, Athens) Also has a branch at Thessaloniki (☎2310 242 905; http://athens. us embassy.gov; Tsimiski 43).

Gay & Lesbian Travellers

In a country where the church still plays a prominent role in shaping society's views on issues such as sexuality, it comes as no surprise that homosexuality is generally frowned upon by many locals, especially outside the major cities. While there is no legislation against homosexual activity, it pays to be discreet.

Some areas of Greece are, however, extremely popular destinations for gay and lesbian travellers. Athens has a busy gay scene, but most gay and lesbian travellers head for the islands. Mykonos has long been famous for its bars, beaches and general hedonism, while Skiathos also has its share of gay hang-outs. The island of Lesvos (Mytilini), birthplace of the lesbian poet Sappho, has become something of a place of pilgrimage for lesbians.

The *Spartacus International Gay Guide*, published by Bruno Gmünder (Berlin) and on-line (www.spartacusworld.com/en), is widely regarded as the leading authority on the gay travel. The Greek section contains a wealth of information on gay venues everywhere from Alexandroupoli to Xanthi.

Health
Availability & Cost of Health Care

Although medical training is of a high standard in Greece,

STANDARD OPENING HOURS

Reviews do not contain business hours unless they differ from those listed here.

Banks 8am-2.30pm Mon-Thu, 8am-2pm Fri

Bars 8pm-late

Cafes 10am-midnight

Clubs 10pm-4am

Post offices Rural areas 7.30am-2pm Mon-Fri; urban offices 7.30am-8pm Mon-Fri, 7.30am-2pm Sat

Restaurants 11am-3pm & 7pm-1am

Shops 8am-3pm Mon, Wed & Sat; 8am-2.30pm & 5pm-8.30pm Tue, Thu & Fri (in Crete: 9am-2pm Mon-Sat. On Tue, Thu & Fri shops open again in the afternoon around 5.30pm & stay open until 8.30pm or 9pm; all day in summer in resorts)

---

the public health service is badly underfunded. Hospitals can be overcrowded, hygiene is not always what it should be and relatives are expected to bring in food for the patient, which can be a problem for a tourist. Conditions and treatment are much better in private hospitals, which are expensive. All this means that a good health-insurance policy is essential.

➡ If you need an ambulance in Greece call 166.

➡ There is at least one doctor on every island and larger islands have hospitals.

➡ Pharmacies can dispense medicines that are available only on prescription in most European countries.

➡ Consult a pharmacist for minor ailments.

Environmental Hazards

➡ Dangerous snakes include the adder and the less common viper and coral snakes. To minimise the possibilities of being bitten, always wear boots, socks and long trousers when walking through undergrowth where snakes may be present.

➡ Mosquitoes can be an annoying problem,

---

though there is no danger of contracting malaria. The electric mosquito-repellent devices are usually sufficient to keep the insects at bay at night. Choose accommodation that has fly screen on the windows wherever possible. Some mosquitoes in northern Greece can provoke a severe reaction. The Asian tiger mosquito *(Aedes albopictus)* may be encountered in mountainous areas, can be a voracious daytime biter, and is known to carry several viruses, including Eastern equine encephalitis, which can affect the central nervous system and cause severe complications and death. Use protective sprays or lotion if you suspect you are being bitten during the day.

Insurance

If you're an EU citizen, a European Health Insurance Card (EHIC; formerly the E111) covers you for most medical care but not emergency repatriation or non-emergencies. It is available from health centres, and post offices in the UK. Citizens from other countries should find out if there is a reciprocal arrangement for free medical care between their country and Greece. If you do need health insurance, make sure you get a policy that covers you for the worst possible scenario, such as an accident requiring an emergency flight home. Find out in advance if your insurance plan will make payments directly to providers or reimburse you later for overseas health expenditures.

Worldwide travel insurance is available at www.lonelyplanet.com/travel_services. You can buy, extend and claim online anytime – even if you're already on the road.

Water

Tap water is drinkable and safe in much of Greece but not always in small villages and on some of the islands. Always ask locally if the water is safe and, if in doubt, drink boiled or bought water. Even when water is safe, the substances and bacteria in it may be different from those you are used to and can cause vomiting or diarrhoea. Bottled water is widely available.

Internet Access

Greece has long embraced the convenience of the internet. There has been a huge increase in the number of hotels and businesses using the internet, and internet cafes are everywhere. Many hotels also offer wi-fi access, although hot spots are often located in the lobby rather than in your room. You'll also find many cafes offering wi-fi.

Legal Matters

Arrests

It is a good idea to have your passport with you at all times in case you are stopped by the police and questioned. Greek citizens are presumed always to have identification on them; foreign visitors are similarly presumed to by the police. If you are arrested by police insist on an interpreter

(the-lo dhi-ermi-nea) and/or a lawyer (the-lo dhi-ki-go-ro).

Drugs

Greek drug laws are the strictest in Europe. Greek courts make no distinction between possession and pushing. Possession of even a small amount of marijuana is likely to land you in jail.

Maps

Unless you are going to hike or drive, the free maps given out by the EOT will probably suffice, although they are not 100% accurate. Maps offering excellent coverage are published by an Athens-based company, Anavasi. Hikers should consider their *Topo* series, which have durable plasticised paper and detailed walking trails for many of the Aegean islands. Also look for Terrain maps, published in Athens and offering equally good coverage. All maps can be bought online or at major bookstores in Greece.

Money

ATMs

ATMs are found in every town large enough to support a bank and in almost all the tourist areas. If you've got MasterCard or Visa, there are plenty of places to withdraw money. Cirrus and Maestro users can make withdrawals in all major towns and tourist areas. Be aware that many ATMs on the islands can lose their connection for a day or two at a time, making it impossible for anyone (locals included) to withdraw money. It's useful to have a backup source of money.

Automated foreign-exchange machines are common in major tourist areas. They take all the major European currencies, Australian and US dollars and Japanese yen, and are useful in an emergency, although they charge a hefty commission.

Cash

Nothing beats cash for convenience – or for risk. If you lose cash, it's gone for good and very few travel insurers will come to your rescue. Those that will, normally limit the amount to approximately US$300. It's best to carry no more cash than you need for the next few days. It's also a good idea to set aside a small amount of cash, say US$100, as an emergency stash.

Note that Greek shopkeepers and small-business owners have a perennial problem with having any small change. If buying small items it is better to tender coins or small-denomination notes.

Credit Cards

Credit cards are now an accepted part of the commercial scene in Greece, although they're often not accepted on many of the smaller islands or in small villages. In larger places, credit cards can be used at top-end hotels, restaurants and shops. Some C-class hotels will accept credit cards, but D- and E-class hotels very seldom do.

The main credit cards are MasterCard and Visa, both of which are widely accepted in Greece. They can also be used as cash cards to draw cash from the ATMs of affiliated Greek banks in the same way as at home. Daily withdrawal limits are set by the issuing bank and are given in local currency only.

WITHDRAWALS

Be warned that many card companies can put an automatic block on your card after your first withdrawal abroad, as an antifraud mechanism. To avoid this happening, inform your bank of your travel plans.

Tipping

In restaurants a service charge is normally included in the bill, and while a tip is not expected (as it is in North America), it is always appreciated and should be left if the service has been good. Taxi drivers normally expect you to round up the fare, while bellhops who help you carry your luggage to your hotel room or stewards on ferries who take you to your cabin normally expect a small gratuity of between €1 and €3.

Travellers Cheques

The main reason to carry travellers cheques rather than cash is the protection they offer against theft. They are, however, losing popularity as more and more travellers opt to put their money in a bank at home and withdraw it at ATMs as they go. American Express, Visa and Thomas Cook cheques are available in euros and are all widely accepted and have efficient replacement policies.

Photography & Video

→ Digital memory cards are readily available from camera stores.

→ Never photograph a military installation or anything else that has a sign forbidding photography.

→ Flash photography is not allowed inside churches, and it's considered taboo to photograph the main altar.

→ Greeks usually love having their photos taken, but always ask permission first.

→ At archaeological sites you will be stopped from using a tripod as it marks you as a 'professional'.

Public Holidays

All banks and shops and most museums and ancient sites close on public holidays.

Many sites (including the ancient sites in Athens) offer free entry on the first Sunday of the month, with the exception of July and August. You may also gain free entry on other locally celebrated holidays, although this varies across the country.

National public holidays:

New Year's Day 1 January

Epiphany 6 January

First Sunday in Lent February

Greek Independence Day 25 March

Good Friday March/April

Orthodox Easter Sunday 20 April 2014, 12 April 2015, 1 May 2016, 16 April 2017, 8 April 2018, 28 April 2019

May Day (Protomagia) 1 May

Whit Monday (Agiou Pnevmatos) 50 days after Easter Sunday

Feast of the Assumption 15 August

Ohi Day 28 October

Christmas Day 25 December

St Stephen's Day 26 December

Safe Travel

Adulterated & Spiked Drinks

Adulterated drinks (known as *bombes*) are served in some bars and clubs in Athens and at resorts known for partying. These drinks are diluted with cheap illegal imports that leave you feeling worse for wear the next day.

At many of the party resorts catering to large budget-tour groups, spiked drinks are not uncommon; keep your hand over the top of your glass. More often than not, the perpetrators are foreign tourists rather than locals.

Tourist Police

The tourist police work in cooperation with the regular Greek police. Each tourist police office has at least one member of staff who speaks English. Hotels, restaurants, travel agencies, tourist shops, tourist guides, waiters, taxi drivers and bus drivers all come under the jurisdiction of the tourist police. If you have a complaint about any of these, report it to the tourist police and they will investigate. If you need to report a theft or loss of passport, go to the tourist police first, and they will act as interpreters between you and the regular police.

Smoking

In July 2009 Greece brought in antismoking laws similar to those found throughout most of Europe. Smoking is now banned inside public places, with the penalty being fines placed on the business owners. Greece is home to some of the heaviest smokers in Europe, so it is a challenge for these laws to be enforced and they are often imposed in only a nominal way in remote locations.

Telephone

The Greek telephone service is maintained by the public corporation known as OTE (pronounced o-*teh;* Organismos Tilepikoinonion Ellados). There are public telephones just about everywhere, including in some unbelievably isolated spots. The phones are easy to operate and can be used for local, long-distance and international calls. The 'i' at the top left of the push-button dialing panel brings up the operating instructions in English. Note that in Greece the area code must always be dialled when making a call (ie all Greek phone numbers are 10-digit).

Mobile Phones

There are several mobile service providers in Greece, among which Panafon, CosmOTE and Wind are the best known. Of these three, CosmOTE tends to have the best coverage in remote areas. All offer 2G connectivity and pay-as-you-talk services by which you can buy a rechargeable SIM card and have your own Greek mobile number. The use of a mobile phone while driving in Greece is prohibited, but the use of a Bluetooth headset is allowed.

Phonecards

All public phones use OTE phonecards, known as *telekarta,* not coins. These cards are widely available at *periptera* (street kiosks), corner shops and tourist shops. A local call costs around €0.30 for three minutes.

It's also possible to use payphones with the growing range of discount-card schemes. This involves dialling an access code and then punching in your card number. The OTE version of this card is known as 'Hronokarta'. The cards come with instructions in Greek and English and the talk time is enormous compared to the standard phonecard rates.

Time

Greece maintains one time zone throughout the country. It is two hours ahead of GMT/UTC and three hours ahead on daylight-saving time – which begins on the last Sunday in March, when clocks are put forward one hour.

Daylight saving ends on the last Sunday in October.

Toilets

➡ Most places in Greece have Western-style toilets, especially hotels and restaurants that cater for tourists. You'll occasionally come across Asian-style squat toilets in older houses, *kafeneia* (coffee houses) and public toilets.

➡ Public toilets are a rarity, except at airports and bus and train stations. Cafes are the best option if you get caught short, but you'll be expected to buy something for the privilege.

➡ The Greek plumbing system can't handle toilet paper; apparently the pipes are too narrow and anything larger than a postage stamp seems to cause a problem. Toilet paper etc should be placed in the small bin provided next to every toilet.

Tourist Information

Tourist information is handled by the Greek National Tourist Organisation, known by the initials GNTO abroad and EOT within Greece. The quality of service from office to office varies dramatically; in some you'll get information aplenty and in others you'll be hard pressed to find anyone behind the desk. EOT offices can be found in major tourist locations, though they are increasingly being supplemented or even replaced by local municipality tourist offices (such as in the Peloponnese).

The tourist police also fulfil the same functions as the EOT and municipal tourist offices, dispensing maps and brochures, and giving information on transport. If you're really stuck, the tourist police can help to find accommodation.

Travellers with Disabilities

Access for travellers with disabilities has improved somewhat in recent years, largely thanks to the Olympics. Improvements are mostly restricted to Athens, where there are more accessible sights, hotels and restaurants. Much of the rest of Greece remains inaccessible to wheelchairs, and the abundance of stones, marble, slippery cobbles and stepped alleys creates a further challenge. People who have visual or hearing impairments are also rarely catered to.

Careful planning before you go can make a world of difference. Check out www.greecetravel.com/handicapped for links to local articles, resorts and tour groups catering to tourists with physical disabilities.

Sailing Holidays (www.charterayachtingreece.com/DRYachting/index.html) Two-day to two-week sailing trips around the Greek islands in fully accessible yachts.

Sirens Resort (www.hotelsofgreece.com/central/loutraki/sirens-wheelchair-accessable-resort/index.html; Skaloma, Loutraki, Corinthia) Family-friendly resort with accessible apartments, tours and ramps into the sea.

Visas

The list of countries whose nationals can stay in Greece for up to three months without a visa includes Australia, Canada, all EU countries,

Iceland, Israel, Japan, New Zealand, Norway, Switzerland and the USA. Other countries included are the European principalities of Monaco and San Marino and most South American countries. The list changes – contact Greek embassies for the full list.

Visa Extensions

If you wish to stay in Greece for longer than three months, apply at a consulate abroad or at least 20 days in advance at the **Aliens Bureau** (☏210 770 5711; Leoforos Alexandras 173, Ambelokipi, Athens; ☺8am-1pm Mon-Fri) in the Athens Central Police Station. Take your passport and four passport photographs along. You may be asked for proof that you can support yourself financially, so keep all your bank exchange slips (or the equivalent from a post office). These slips are not always automatically given – you may have to ask for them. Elsewhere in Greece apply to the local police authority. You will likely be given a permit that will authorise you to stay in the country for a period of up to six months.

Many travellers get around the need for an extension by visiting Bulgaria or Turkey briefly and then re-entering Greece. If you overstay your visa, you will be slapped with a huge fine upon leaving the country.

Women Travellers

Many women travel alone in Greece. The crime rate remains relatively low and solo travel is probably safer than in most European countries. This does not mean that you should be lulled into complacency; bag snatching and rapes do occur, particu-

larly at party resorts on the islands.

The biggest nuisance to foreign women travelling alone is the guys the Greeks have nicknamed *kamaki*. The word means 'fishing trident' and refers to the *kamaki*'s favourite pastime: 'fishing' for foreign women. You'll find them everywhere there are lots of tourists: young (for the most part), smooth-talking guys who aren't in the least bashful about approaching women in the street. They can be very persistent, but they are usually a hassle rather than a threat. The majority of Greek men treat foreign women with respect.

Work

EU nationals don't need a work permit, but they need a residency permit and a Greek tax file number if they intend to stay longer than three months. Nationals of other countries are supposed to have a work permit.

Bar & Hostel Work

The bars of the Greek islands could not survive without foreign workers and there are thousands of summer jobs up for grabs every year. The pay is not fantastic, but you get to spend a summer in the islands. April and May are the times to go looking. Hostels and travellers' hotels are other places that regularly employ foreign workers.

English Tutoring

If you're looking for a permanent job, the most widely available option is to teach English. A TEFL (Teaching English as a Foreign Language) certificate or a university degree is an advantage but not essential. In the UK,

look through the *Times* educational supplement or Tuesday's edition of the *Guardian* newspaper for opportunities; in other countries, contact the Greek embassy.

Another possibility is to find a job teaching English once you are in Greece. You will see language schools everywhere. Strictly speaking, you need a licence to teach in these schools, but many will employ teachers without one. The best time to look around for such a job is late summer.

The noticeboard at the Compendium in Athens sometimes has advertisements looking for private English lessons.

Volunteer Work

Earth Sea & Sky (www. earthseasky.org) Conservation and research based in the Ionian Islands.

Hellenic Society for the Study & Protection of the Monk Seal (Map p68; ☏210 522 2888; www.mom.gr; Solomou 53, Exarhia, Athens) Volunteers are used for monitoring programs on the Ionian Islands.

Hellenic Wildlife Hospital (Elliniko Kentro Perithalpsis Agrion Zoön; ☏22970 28367; www.ekpazp.gr; ☺10am-7pm) Volunteers head (particularly during the winter months) to Aegina to this large wildlife rehabilitation centre.

Sea Turtle Protection Society of Greece (☏tel/fax 21052 31342; www.archelon.gr) Includes monitoring sea turtles in the Peloponnese.

WWOOF (World Wide Opportunities on Organic Farms; www.wwoofgreece.org) Offers opportunities for volunteers at one of around 57 farms in Greece.

Transport

GETTING THERE & AWAY

Entering the Country

Visitors to Greece with EU passports are rarely given more than a cursory glance, but customs and police may be interested in what you are carrying. EU citizens may also enter Greece on a national identity card.

Visitors from outside the EU may require a visa. This must be checked with consular authorities before you arrive.

Air

Airports & Airlines

Greece has four main international airports that take chartered and scheduled flights.

Many of Greece's other international airports, including Corfu, Crete and Mykonos, have begun taking scheduled international flights with easyJet. Kos and Araxos also take direct flights from Germany. Other international airports across the country include Santorini (Thira), Karpathos, Samos, Skiathos, Hrysoupoli, Aktion, Kefallonia and Zakynthos. These airports are most often used for charter flights from the UK, Germany and Scandinavia.

Eleftherios Venizelos International Airport (ATH; ☑210 353 0000; www.aia.gr) Athens' Eleftherios Venizelos International Airport lies near Spata, 27km east of Athens.

Nikos Kazantzakis International Airport (☑28103 97800; www.heraklion-airport. info) Crete's biggest airport is about 5km east of Iraklio's centre. It has a well-stocked duty-free shop.

Diagoras Airport (RHO; ☑22410 88700; Rhodes, Dodecanese)

Macedonia International Airport (SKG; ☑2310 473 212, 2310 473 700; www.thessalo-nikiairport.com; Thessaloniki, Northern Greece)

GREEK AIRLINES

Olympic Air (OA; ☑801 801 0101; www.olympicair.com) is the country's national airline with the majority of flights to and from Athens. Olympic flies direct between Athens and destinations throughout Europe, as well as to Cairo, İstanbul, Tel Aviv, New York and Toronto. **Aegean Airlines** (A3; ☑801 112 0000; www.aegeanair.com) has flights to/from destinations in Spain, Germany and Italy as well as to Paris, London, Cairo and İstanbul. The safety record of both airlines is exemplary. The contact details for local Olympic and Aegean offices are listed throughout the guide.

CLIMATE CHANGE & TRAVEL

Every form of transport that relies on carbon-based fuel generates CO_2, the main cause of human-induced climate change. Modern travel is dependent on aeroplanes, which might use less fuel per kilometre per person than most cars but travel much greater distances. The altitude at which aircraft emit gases (including CO_2) and particles also contributes to their climate change impact. Many websites offer 'carbon calculators' that allow people to estimate the carbon emissions generated by their journey and, for those who wish to do so, to offset the impact of the greenhouse gases emitted with contributions to portfolios of climate-friendly initiatives throughout the world. Lonely Planet offsets the carbon footprint of all staff and author travel.

OVERLAND FROM WESTERN EUROPE

If you're keen to reach Greece without taking to the air, and enjoy the independence of a road trip, you can reach Greece by heading overland to an Italian port and hopping on a ferry. A high-speed ferry trip from Venice to Patra can be completed in around 26 hours. From Patra to Athens is a further 3½ hours' driving.

If you fancy a bit more convenience and speed than that offered by buses and cars, it's easily done. Overland enthusiasts can reach Greece on a fascinating rail route through the Balkan peninsula, passing through Croatia, Serbia and the Former Yugoslav Republic of Macedonia. Or head to the western coast of Italy (there are connections throughout most of Europe) and then take a ferry to Greece. Not only will you be doing your bit for the Earth, but you'll see some gorgeous scenery from your window as well.

A sample itinerary from London would see you catching the Eurostar to Paris and then an overnight sleeper train to Bologna in Italy. From there, a coastal train takes you to Bari where there's an overnight boat to Patra on the Peloponnese. From Patra, it's a 4½-hour train journey to Athens. The journey will land you in Athens within two days of leaving London. See www.raileurope.com for more routes and tickets.

Greece is part of the Eurail network (www.eurail.com). Eurail passes can only be bought by residents of non-European countries and are supposed to be purchased before arriving in Europe but can be bought in Europe if your passport proves that you've been here for less than six months. Greece is also part of the Inter-Rail Pass system (www.interrailnet.com), available to those who have resided in Europe for six months or more. See the websites for full details of passes and prices.

TICKETS

EasyJet offers some of the cheapest tickets between Greece and the rest of Europe and covers a huge range of destinations. If you're coming from outside Europe, consider a cheap flight to a European hub like London and then an onward ticket with easyJet. Some airlines also offer cheap deals to students. If you're planning to travel between June and September, it's wise to book ahead.

Land

Travelling by land offers you the chance to really appreciate the landscape, as well as the many experiences that go along with train or bus travel. International train travel, in particular, has become much more feasible in recent years with speedier trains and better connections. You can now travel from London to Athens by train and ferry in less than two days. By choosing to travel on the ground instead of the air, you'll also be re-ducing your carbon footprint. It's a win-win situation.

Border Crossings

ALBANIA

The main crossing at Kakavia can have intensely slow queues.

Kakavia 60km northwest of Ioannina

Krystallopigi 14km west of Kotas on the Florina-Kastoria road

Mertziani 17km west of Konitsa

Sagiada 28km north of Igoumenitsa

BULGARIA

As Bulgaria is part of the EU, crossings are usually quick and hassle-free.

Exohi a new 448m tunnel border crossing 50km north of Drama

Ormenio 41km from Serres in northeastern Thrace

Promahonas 109km northeast of Thessaloniki

FORMER YUGOSLAV REPUBLIC OF MACEDONIA (FYROM)

Doïrani 31km north of Kilkis

Evzoni 68km north of Thessaloniki

Niki 16km north of Florina

TURKEY

Kipi is more convenient if you're heading for İstanbul, but the route through Kastanies goes via the fascinating towns of Soufli and Didymotiho in Greece, and Edirne (ancient Adrianoupolis) in Turkey.

Kastanies 139km northeast of Alexandroupoli

Kipi 43km east of Alexandroupoli

Bus

The Greek railways organisation **OSE** (Organismos Sidirodromon Ellados; www.ose.gr) once operated international buses from Greece. However, along with the cessation of international train services in 2011, the buses are no longer running. It's worth checking the website to see if the buses return to the road but don't hold your breath.

Train

The Greek railways organisation **OSE** (Organismos Sidirodromon Ellados; www.ose.gr)

has been seriously affected by the country's financial problems, with international trains eliminated and domestic routes severely curtailed. The situation is fluid, so check ahead.

Sea

Ferries can get very crowded in summer. If you want to take a vehicle across it's wise to make a reservation beforehand. The services indicated are for high season (July and August). Please note that tickets for all ferries to Turkey must be bought a day in advance and you will almost certainly be asked to turn in your passport the night before the trip. It will be returned the next day before you board the boat. Port tax for departures to Turkey is around €15.

Another way to visit Greece by sea is to join one of the many cruises that ply the Aegean.

GETTING AROUND

Greece is an easy place to travel around thanks to a comprehensive public transport system. Buses are the mainstay of land transport, with a network that reaches out to the smallest villages. Trains are a good alternative, where available. If you're in a hurry, Greece also has an extensive domestic air network. To most visitors, though, travelling in Greece means island hopping on the multitude of ferries that crisscross the Adriatic and the Aegean.

Air

The vast majority of domestic mainland flights are handled by the country's national carrier, **Olympic Air** (OA; ☑801 801 0101; www. olympicair.com), and its main competitor, **Aegean Airlines** (A3; ☑801 112 0000; www. aegeanair.com). Both offer

competitive rates. Olympic Air has offices wherever there are flights, as well as in other major towns.

The prices listed in this guide are for full-fare economy, and include domestic taxes and charges. There are discounts for return tickets for travel between Monday and Thursday, and bigger discounts for trips that include a Saturday night away. You'll find full details on the airline's website, as well as information on timetables.

The baggage allowance on domestic flights is 15kg, or 20kg if the domestic flight is part of an international journey. Olympic Air offers a 25% student discount on domestic flights, but only if the flight is part of an international journey.

Bicycle

Cycling is not popular among Greeks; however, it's gaining kudos with tourists. You'll need strong leg muscles to

INTERNATIONAL FERRY ROUTES

DESTINATION	DEPARTURE POINT	ARRIVAL POINT	TIME	FREQUENCY
Albania	Corfu	Saranda	25min	1 daily
Italy	Patra	Ancona	20hr	3 daily
Italy	Patra	Bari	14½hr	1 daily
Italy	Corfu	Bari	8hr	1 daily
Italy	Kefallonia	Bari	14hr	1 daily
Italy	Corfu	Bari	10hr	1 daily
Italy	Igoumenitsa	Bari	11½hr	1 daily
Italy	Patra	Brindisi	15hr	1 daily
Italy	Corfu	Brindisi	6hr	1 daily
Italy	Kefallonia	Brindisi	12hr	1 daily
Italy	Zakynthos	Brindisi	15hr	1 daily
Italy	Patra	Venice	30hr	12 weekly
Italy	Corfu	Venice	25hr	12 weekly
Turkey	Chios	Çeşme	1½hr	1 daily
Turkey	Kos	Bodrum	1hr	1 daily
Turkey	Lesvos	Dikeli	1hr	1 daily
Turkey	Rhodes	Marmaris	50min	2 daily
Turkey	Samos	Kuşadası	1½hr	2 daily

tackle the mountains or you can stick to some of the flatter coastal routes. Bike lanes are rare to nonexistent and helmets are not compulsory. The island of Kos is about the most bicycle-friendly place in Greece, as is anywhere flat, such as the plains of Thessaly or Thrace.

➡ You can hire bicycles in most tourist places, but they are not as widely available as cars and motorcycles. Prices range from €5 to €12 per day, depending on the type and age of the bike.

➡ Bicycles are carried free on ferries. You can buy decent mountain or touring bikes in Greece's major towns, though you may have a problem finding a ready buyer if you wish to sell it on. Bike prices are much the same as across the rest of Europe: anywhere from €300 to €2000.

Boat

Greece has an extensive network of ferries which are the only means of reaching many of the islands. Schedules are often subject to delays due to poor weather and industrial action and prices fluctuate regularly. In summer, ferries are regular between all but the most out-of-the-way destinations; however, services seriously slow down in winter and, in some cases, stop completely.

Domestic Ferry Operators

Ferry companies have local offices on many of the islands; see the relevant destination chapter for details of these as well as small, local ferries and caïques (little boats).

Aegean Flying Dolphins (☑210 422 1766; www.aegeanflyingdolphins.gr) Hydrofoils linking Samos with Kos and islands in between.

Aegean Speed Lines (☑210 969 0950; www.

aegeanspeedlines.gr) Superspeedy boats between Athens and the Cyclades.

Agoudimos Lines (☑210 414 1300; www.agoudimoslines.com) Ferries connecting the Cyclades and mainland. Also travels to Italy via Corfu.

Aigaion Pelagos (www.anek.gr) A subsidiary of ANEK Lines.

Alpha Ferries (☑210 428 4002, 210 428 4001; www.alphaferries.gr) Traditional ferries from Athens to the Cyclades.

ANE Kalymnou (☑22430 29384; www.anekalymnou.gr) Kalymnos-based hydrofoils and old-style ferries linking some of the Dodecanese and the Cyclades.

ANEK Lines (☑210 419 7420; www.anek.gr) Crete-based long-haul ferries.

ANES (☑210 422 5625; www.anes.gr) Symi-based old-style ferries servicing the Dodecanese.

Anna Express (☑22470 41215; www.lipsi-annaexpress.com) Small, fast ferry connecting the northern Dodecanese.

Blue Star Ferries (☑210 891 9800; www.bluestarferries.com) Long-haul, high-speed ferries and Seajet catamarans between the mainland and the Cyclades.

Cyclades Fast Ferries (☑210 418 2005; www.fastferries.com.gr) Comfortable ferries to the most popular Cyclades.

Dodekanisos Seaways (☑22410 70590; www.12ne.gr) Runs luxurious catamarans in the Dodecanese.

Euroseas (☑210 413 2188; www.ferries.gr/euroseas) Linking the Saronics with services to the mainland.

Evoikos Lines (☑210 413 4483; www.ferriesglyfa.gr) Comfortable short-haul ferry services between Glyfa on the mainland and Agiokambos in northern Evia.

GA Ferries (☑210 419 9100; www.gaferries.com) Old-style, long-haul ferries serving a huge number of islands.

Hellenic Seaways (☑210 419 9000; www.hellenicsea-

ways.gr) Conventional long-haul ferries and catamarans from the mainland to the Cyclades and between the Sporades and Saronic islands.

Ionian Ferries (☑210 324 9997; www.ionianferries.gr) Large ferries serving the Ionian Islands.

LANE Lines (☑210 427 4011; www.ferries.gr/lane) Long-haul ferries.

Minoan Lines (☑210 414 5700; www.minoan.gr) High-speed luxury ferries between Piraeus and Iraklio, and Patra, Igoumenitsa and Corfu.

NEL Lines (☑22510 26299; www.nel.gr) High-speed, long-haul ferries with services between northern Greece and Limnos, Lesvos, Chios, Samos and the Sporades.

SAOS Lines (☑210 625 0000; www.saos.gr) Big, slow boats calling in at many of the islands.

Sea Jets (☑210 412 1001; www.seajets.gr) Catamarans calling at Athens, Crete, Santorini (Thira), Paros and many islands in between.

Sea Star (☑22460 44000; www.net-club.gr/tilosseastar.htm) High-speed catamaran connecting Tilos with Rhodes, Halki and Nisyros.

Skyros Shipping Company (☑22220 921164; www.sne.gr) Slow boat between Skyros and Kymi on Evia.

Strintzis Ferries (☑26102 40000; www.strintzisferries.gr) Larger, older ferries in the Sporades.

Superfast Ferries (www.superfast.com) As the name implies, speedy ferries from the mainland to Crete, Corfu and Patra.

Ventouris Ferries (☑210 411 4911; www.ventourissealines.gr) Big boats from the mainland to the Cyclades.

Zante Ferries (☑26950 49500, in Athens 210 410 0211; www.zanteferries.gr) Older ferries connecting the mainland with the western Cyclades.

Bus

The bus network is comprehensive. All long-distance buses, on the mainland and the islands, are operated by regional collectives known as **KTEL** (Koino Tamio Eispraxeon Leoforion; www.ktel.org). Details of inter-urban buses throughout Greece are available by dialling ☎14505. Bus fares are fixed by the government and bus travel is very reasonably priced. A journey costs approximately €5 per 100km.

Services

Every prefecture on the mainland has a KTEL, which operates local services within the prefecture and to the main towns of other prefectures. With the exception of towns in Thrace, which are serviced by Thessaloniki, all the major towns on the mainland have frequent connections to Athens. The islands of Corfu, Kefallonia and Zakynthos can also be reached directly from Athens by bus – the fares include the price of the ferry ticket.

Most villages have a daily bus service of some sort, although remote areas may have only one or two buses a week. They operate for the benefit of people going to town to shop, rather than for tourists, and consequently leave the villages very early in the morning and return early in the afternoon.

Practicalities

➡ It is important to note that big cities like Athens, Iraklio, Patra and Thessaloniki may have more than one bus station, each serving different regions. Make sure you find the correct station for your destination. In small towns and villages the 'bus station' may be no more than a bus stop outside a *kafeneio* (coffee house) or taverna that doubles as a booking office.

➡ In remote areas, the timetable may be in Greek only, but most booking offices have timetables in both Greek and Roman script.

➡ It's best to turn up at least 20 minutes before departure to make sure you get a seat, and buses have been known to leave a few minutes before their scheduled departure.

➡ When you buy a ticket you may be allotted a seat number, which is noted on the ticket. The seat number is indicated on the *back* of each seat of the bus, not on the back of the seat in front; this causes confusion among Greeks and tourists alike.

➡ You can board a bus without a ticket and pay on board but, on a popular route or during high season, this may mean that you have to stand.

➡ The KTEL buses are safe and modern, and these days most are air conditioned – at least on the major routes. In more-remote rural areas they tend to be older and less comfortable. Buses on less-frequented routes do not usually have toilets on board and stop about every three hours on long journeys.

➡ Smoking is prohibited on all buses in Greece.

Car & Motorcycle

No one who has travelled on Greece's roads will be surprised to hear that the country's road fatality rate is one of the highest in Europe. More than 1000 people die on the roads every year, with ten times that number of people injured. Overtaking is listed as the greatest cause of accidents.

Heart-stopping moments aside, your own car is a great way to explore off the beaten track. The road network has improved enormously in recent years; many roads marked as dirt tracks on older maps have now been asphalted and many of the islands have very little traffic. There are regular (if costly) car-ferry services to almost all islands.

Practicalities

Automobile Association

Greece's domestic automobile association is **ELPA** (Elliniki Leschi Aftokinitou kai Periigiseon;☎210 606 8800; www.elpa.gr; Leoforos Mesogion 395, Agia Paraskevi, Athens).

Entry EU-registered vehicles enter free for up to six months without road taxes being due. A green card (international third-party insurance) is required along with proof of date of entry (ferry ticket or your passport stamp). Non-EU-registered vehicles may be logged in your passport.

Driving Licence EU driving licences are valid in Greece. Drivers from outside the EU may require International Driving Permits, which should be obtained before you leave home.

Fuel Available widely throughout the country, though service stations may be closed on weekends and public holidays. On the islands, there may be only one petrol station; check where it is

---

MOTORCYCLE WARNING

Greece is not the best place to initiate yourself into motorcycling. There are still a lot of gravel roads – particularly on the islands, and dozens of tourists have accidents every year. Scooters are particularly prone to sliding on gravelly bends. Try to hire a motorcycle with thinner profile tyres. If you are planning to use a motorcycle or moped, check that your travel insurance covers you. Many insurance companies don't offer cover for motorcycle accidents, so check the fine print!

ROAD DISTANCES (KM)

City	Alexandroupoli	Athens	Corinth	Edessa	Florina	Igoumenitsa	Ioannina	Kalamata	Kastoria	Kavala	Lamia	Larisa	Monemvasia	Nafplio	Patra	Pyrgos	Sparta	Thessaloniki	Trikala	Tripoli
Athens	854																			
Corinth	884	84																		
Edessa	427	569	596																	
Florina	497	592	251	353																
Igoumenitsa	816	473	393	380	353															
Ioannina	702	447	364	298	320	96														
Kalamata	1055	284	175	767	763	501	467													
Kastoria	535	489	519	108	67	286	204	690												
Kavala	177	682	655	250	320	615	525	878	358											
Lamia	643	214	244	355	360	353	263	415	274	466										
Larisa	493	361	389	218	231	309	209	561	239	323	151									
Monemvasia	1156	350	266	869	855	613	579	156	756	976	505	655								
Nafplio	947	165	63	659	664	482	427	163	582	770	307	455	215							
Patra	828	220	138	567	513	281	247	220	483	664	193	341	332	201						
Pyrgos	924	320	234	636	643	367	347	119	542	747	284	432	275	208	96					
Sparta	1025	225	145	737	759	517	483	60	660	848	385	533	96	119	236	180				
Thessaloniki	349	513	544	89	159	452	362	715	220	169	303	154	807	610	488	584	711			
Trikala	554	330	356	227	233	247	148	520	159	377	115	62	597	419	310	400	501	216		
Tripoli	964	194	110	713	681	457	430	90	639	820	324	472	157	81	176	155	61	624	466	
Volos	556	326	355	278	293	371	271	518	301	383	115	62	620	417	308	408	524	214	124	435

TRANSPORT CAR & MOTORCYCLE

before you head out. Self-service and credit-card pumps are not the norm in Greece. Petrol in Greece is cheaper than in many European countries, but expensive by American or Australian standards.

Petrol types:

➡ *Super* leaded

➡ *amolyvdi* unleaded

➡ *petreleo kinisis* diesel

Hire

CARS

➡ All the big multinational companies are represented in Athens, and most have branches in major towns and popular tourist destinations. The majority of islands have at least one outlet.

➡ By Greek law, rental cars have to be replaced every six years, so most vehicles you rent will be relatively new.

➡ The minimum driving age in Greece is 18 years, but most car-hire firms require you to be at least 21, or 23 for larger vehicles.

➡ High-season weekly rates with unlimited mileage start at about €280 for the smallest models, such as a Fiat Seicento, dropping to about €200 per week in winter. These prices don't include local tax (known as VAT). You can often find great deals at local companies. Their advertised rates can be up to 50% cheaper than the multinationals and they are normally open to negotiation, especially if business is slow.

➡ On the islands, you can rent a car for the day for

around €30 to €50, including all insurance and taxes.

➡ Always check what the insurance includes; there are often rough roads or dangerous routes that you can only tackle with a 4WD.

➡ If you want to take a hire car to another country or onto a ferry, you will need advance written authorisation from the hire company, as the insurance may not cover you. Unless you pay with a credit card, most hire companies will require a minimum deposit of €120 per day.

For current rates of some of the major car-hire players in Greece, see the following websites:

Avis (☏210 322 4951; www. avis.gr)

Budget (📞210 349 8800; www.budget.gr)

Europcar (📞210 960 2382; www.europcar.gr)

Hertz (📞210 626 4000; www.hertz.gr)

MOTORCYCLES

➡ Mopeds, motorcycles and scooters are available for hire wherever there are tourists to rent them. Most machines are newish and in good condition. Nonetheless, check brakes at the earliest opportunity.

➡ You must produce a licence that shows proficiency to ride the category of bike you wish to rent; this applies to everything from 50cc up. British citizens must obtain a Category A licence from the Driver and Vehicle Licensing Agency (www.dft.gov.uk/dvla) in the UK (in most other EU countries separate licences are automatically issued).

➡ Rates start from about €15 per day for a moped or 50cc motorcycle, to €30 per day for a 250cc motorcycle. Out of season these prices drop considerably, so use your bargaining skills.

➡ Most motorcycle hirers include third-party insurance in the price, but it's wise to check this. This insurance will not include medical expenses.

➡ Helmets are compulsory and rental agencies are obliged to offer one as part of the hire deal.

Road Conditions

➡ Main highways in Greece have been improving steadily over the years but many still don't offer smooth sailing.

➡ Some main roads retain the two-lane/hard shoulder format of the 1960s which can be confusing and even downright dangerous.

➡ Roadworks can take years and years in Greece, especially on the islands where funding often only trickles in. In other cases, excellent new tarmac roads may have appeared that are not on any local maps.

Road Hazards

➡ Slow drivers – many of them unsure and hesitant tourists – can cause serious traffic events on Greece's roads.

➡ Road surfaces can change rapidly when a section of road has succumbed to subsidence or weathering. Snow and ice can be a serious challenge in winter, and drivers are advised to carry snow chains. Animals in rural areas may wander onto roads, so extra vigilance is required.

➡ Roads passing through mountainous areas are often littered with fallen rocks that can cause extensive damage to a vehicle's underside or throw a bike rider.

Road Rules

➡ In Greece, as throughout Continental Europe, you drive on the right and overtake on the left.

➡ Outside built-up areas, traffic on a main road has right of way at intersections. In towns, vehicles coming from the right have right of way. This includes roundabouts – even if you're in the roundabout, you must give way to drivers coming onto the roundabout to your right.

➡ Seat belts must be worn in front seats, and in back seats if the car is fitted with them.

➡ Children under 12 years of age are not allowed in the front seat.

➡ It is compulsory to carry a first-aid kit, fire extinguisher and warning triangle, and it is forbidden to carry cans of petrol.

➡ Helmets are compulsory for motorcyclists if the motorcycle is 50cc or more. Police will book you if you're caught without a helmet.

➡ Outside residential areas the speed limit is 120km/h on highways, 90km/h on other roads and 50km/h in built-up areas. The speed limit for motorcycles up to 100cc is 70km/h and for larger motorcycles, 90km/h. Drivers exceeding the speed limit by 20% are liable to receive a fine of €60; exceeding it by 40% costs €150.

➡ A blood-alcohol content of 0.05% can incur a fine of €150, and over 0.08% is a criminal offence.

➡ If you are involved in an accident and no one is hurt, the police will not be required to write a report, but it is advisable to go to a nearby police station and explain what happened. You may need a police report for insurance purposes. If an accident involves injury, a driver who does not stop and does not inform the police may face a prison sentence.

Hitching

Hitching is never entirely safe in any country in the world, and we don't recommend it. Travellers who decide to hitch should understand that they are taking a small but potentially serious risk. People who do choose to hitch will be safer if they travel in pairs and they should let someone know where they are planning to go. In particular, it is unwise for females to hitch alone; women are better off hitching with a male companion.

Some parts of Greece are much better for hitching than others. Getting out of major cities tends to be hard work and Athens is notoriously difficult. Hitching is much easier in remote areas and on islands with poor public transport. On country roads it is not unknown for someone to stop and ask if you want a lift, even if you haven't stuck a thumb out.

Local Transport

Bus

Most Greek towns are small enough to get around on foot. All the major towns have local buses, but the only places you're likely to need them are Athens, Patra, Kalamata and Thessaloniki.

Metro

Athens is the only city in Greece large enough to warrant the building of an underground system. Note that only Greek student cards are valid for a student ticket on the metro.

Taxi

Taxis are widely available in Greece except on very small or remote islands. They are reasonably priced by European standards, especially if three or four people share costs. Many taxi drivers now have sat-nav systems in their cars, so finding a destination is a breeze as long as you have the exact address.

Yellow city cabs are metered, with rates doubling between midnight and 5am. Additional costs are charged for trips from an airport or a bus, port or train station, as well as for each piece of luggage over 10kg. Grey rural taxis do not have meters, so you should always settle on a price before you get in.

Some taxi drivers in Athens have been known to overcharge unwary travellers. If you have a complaint about a taxi driver, take the cab number and report your complaint to the tourist police. Taxi drivers in other towns in Greece are, on the whole, friendly, helpful and honest.

Tours

Tours are worth considering if your time is very limited or if you fancy somebody else doing the planning. In Athens, you'll find countless day tours, with some agencies offering two- or three-day trips to nearby sights. For something on a larger scale, try **Intrepid Travel** (www.intrepidtravel. com). With offices in Australia, the UK and the USA, Intrepid offers an eight-day tour from Athens to Santorini (€1100) and an eight/10-day sailing tour through the Cyclades (€800/1230), including everything except meals and flights. **Encounter Greece** (www.encountergreece.com) offers a plethora of tours; a 10-day tour across the country costs €1350 while three days on the mainland is €385. Flights to Greece are not included.

More adventurous tours include guided activities such as hiking, climbing, white-water rafting, kayaking, canoeing or canyoning.

The following options are also available:

Alpin Club (www.alpinclub. gr) In Athens; operates out of Karitena in the Peloponnese.

Robinson Expeditions (www.robinson.gr) Run tours from the centre and north of Greece.

Train

Trains are operated by the Greek railways organisation **OSE** (Organismos Sidirodromon Ellados; www.ose.gr). The Greek railway network is limited with essentially only two main lines: the standard-gauge service from Athens to Alexandroupoli via Thessaloniki, and the Peloponnese network. Due to financial in-

stability, services have been greatly reduced and prices and schedules are changeable. When you can, double-check on the OSE website. Information on departures from Athens or Thessaloniki can also be sought by calling ☎1440.

Classes

There are two types of service: regular (slow) trains that stop at all stations and faster, modern intercity (IC) trains that link most major cities. The slow trains represent the country's cheapest form of public transport: 2nd-class fares are absurdly cheap, and even 1st class is cheaper than bus travel.

The IC trains that link the major Greek cities are an excellent way to travel. The services are not necessarily fast – Greece is far too mountainous for that – but the trains are modern and comfortable. There are 1st- and 2nd-class tickets and a cafe-bar on board. On some services, meals can be ordered and delivered to your seat. The night service between Athens and Thessaloniki also offers a choice of couchettes, two-bed compartments and single compartments.

Train Passes

➡ Eurail and Inter-Rail cards are valid in Greece, but it's generally not worth buying one if Greece is the only place where you plan to use them. For IC and sleeper cars, you still require a costly supplement.

➡ On presentation of ID or passports, passengers more than 60 years old are entitled to a 25% discount on all lines except in July and August and over the Easter week.

➡ Whatever pass you have, you must have a reservation to board the train.

Language

The Greek language is believed to be one of the oldest European languages, with an oral tradition of 4000 years and a written tradition of approximately 3000 years. Due to its centuries of influence, Greek constitutes the origin of a large part of the vocabulary of many Indo-European languages (including English). It is the official language of Greece and co-official language of Cyprus (alongside Turkish), and is spoken by many migrant communities throughout the world.

The Greek alphabet is explained on the following page, but if you read the pronunciation guides given with each phrase in this chapter as if they were English, you'll be understood. Note that dh is pronounced as 'th' in 'there'; gh is a softer, slightly throaty version of 'g'; and kh is a throaty sound like the 'ch' in the Scottish 'loch'. All Greek words of two or more syllables have an acute accent ('), which indicates where the stress falls. In our pronunciation guides, stressed syllables are in italics.

In this chapter, masculine, feminine and neuter forms of words are included where necessary, separated with a slash and indicated with 'm', 'f' and 'n' respectively. Polite and informal options are indicated where relevant with 'pol' and 'inf'.

BASICS

Hello.	Γειά σας.	ya·sas (pol)
	Γειά σου.	ya·su (inf)
Goodbye.	Αντίο.	an·di·o
Yes./No.	Ναι./Όχι.	ne/o·hi

WANT MORE?

For in-depth language information and handy phrases, check out Lonely Planet's *Greek Phrasebook*. You'll find it at **shop.lonelyplanet.com**, or you can buy Lonely Planet's iPhone phrasebooks at the Apple App Store.

Please.	Παρακαλώ.	pa·ra·ka·lo
Thank you.	Ευχαριστώ.	ef·ha·ri·sto
You're welcome.	Παρακαλώ.	pa·ra·ka·lo
Excuse me.	Με συγχωρείτε.	me sing·kho·ri·te
Sorry.	Συγγνώμη.	sigh·no·mi

What's your name?

Πώς σας λένε;		pos sas le·ne
My name is ...		
Με λένε ...		me le·ne ...
Do you speak English?		
Μιλάτε αγγλικά;		mi·la·te an·gli·ka
I don't understand.		
Δεν καταλαβαίνω.		dhen ka·ta·la·ve·no

ACCOMMODATION

campsite	χώρος για κάμπινγκ	kho·ros yia kam·ping
hotel	ξενοδοχείο	kse·no·dho·khi·o
youth hostel	γιουθ χόστελ	yuth kho·stel

a ... room	ένα ... δωμάτιο	e·na ... dho·ma·ti·o
single	μονόκλινο	mo·no·kli·no
double	δίκλινο	dhi·kli·no

How much is it ...?	Πόσο κάνει ...;	po·so ka·ni ...
per night	τη βραδιά	ti·vra·dhya
per person	το άτομο	to a·to·mo

air-con	έρκοντίσιον	er·kon·di·si·on
bathroom	μπάνιο	ba·nio
fan	ανεμιστήρας	a·ne·mi·sti·ras
window	παράθυρο	pa·ra·thi·ro

DIRECTIONS

Where is ...?
Πού είναι …;   pu *i*·ne ...

What's the address?
Ποια είναι η διεύθυνση;   pia *i*·ne i dhi·*ef*·thin·si

Can you show me (on the map)?
Μπορείς να μου δείξεις   bo·*ris* na mu *dhik*·sis
(στο χάρτη);   (sto *khar*·ti)

Turn left.
Στρίψτε αριστερά.   *strips*·te a·ri·ste·*ra*

Turn right.
Στρίψτε δεξιά.   *strips*·te dhe·*ksia*

at the next corner
στην επόμενη γωνία   stin e·*po*·me·ni gho·*ni*·a

at the traffic lights
στα φώτα   sta *fo*·ta

behind	πίσω	*pi*·so
far	μακριά	ma·kri·a
in front of	μπροστά	bro·*sta*
near (to)	κοντά	kon·*da*
next to	δίπλα	*dhi*·pla
opposite	απέναντι	a·*pe*·nan·di
straight ahead	ολο ευθεία	o·lo ef·*thi*·a

EATING & DRINKING

a table for ...   Ενα τραπέζι   e·na tra·*pe*·zi
   για …   ya …

   (eight) o'clock   τις (οχτώ)   stis (okh·*to*)
   (two) people   (δύο) άτομα   (*dhi*·o) a·to·ma

I don't eat ...   Δεν τρώγω …   dhen tro·*gho* ...
   fish   ψάρι   *psa*·ri
   (red) meat   (κόκκινο)   (*ko*·ki·no)
   κρέας   *kre*·as
   peanuts   φυστίκια   fi·*sti*·kia
   poultry   πουλερικά   pu·le·ri·*ka*

What would you recommend?
Τι θα συνιστούσες;   ti tha si·ni·*stu*·ses

What's in that dish?
Τι περιέχει αυτό το   ti pe·ri·e·hi af·*to* to
φαγητό;   fa·ghi·*to*

Cheers!
Εις υγείαν!   is i·*yi*·an

That was delicious.
Ήταν νοστιμότατο!   *i*·tan no·sti·*mo*·ta·to

Please bring the bill.
Το λογαριασμό,   to lo·ghar·ya·*zmo*
παρακαλώ.   pa·ra·ka·*lo*

GREEK APLHABET

The Greek alphabet has 24 letters, shown below in their upper- and lower-case forms. Be aware that some letters look like English letters but are pronounced very differently, such as **B**, which is pronounced v; and **P**, pronounced r. As in English, how letters are pronounced is also influenced by the way they are combined, for example the **ου** combination is pronounced u as in 'put', and **οι** is pronounced ee as in 'feet'.

Α α	a	as in 'father'	**Ξ ξ**	x	as in 'ox'	
Β β	v	as in 'vine'	**Ο ο**	o	as in 'hot'	
Γ γ	gh	a softer, throaty 'g', or	**Π π**	p	as in 'pup'	
	y	as in 'yes'	**Ρ ρ**	r	as in 'road',	
Δ δ	dh	as in 'there'			slightly trilled	
Ε ε	e	as in 'egg'	**Σ σ, ς**	s	as in 'sand'	
Ζ ζ	z	as in 'zoo'	**Τ τ**	t	as in 'tap'	
Η η	i	as in 'feet'	**Υ υ**	i	as in 'feet'	
Θ θ	th	as in 'throw'	**Φ φ**	f	as in 'find'	
Ι ι	i	as in 'feet'	**Χ χ**	kh	as the 'ch' in the	
Κ κ	k	as in 'kite'			Scottish 'loch', or	
Λ λ	l	as in 'leg'		h	like a rough 'h'	
Μ μ	m	as in 'man'	**Ψ ψ**	ps	as in 'lapse'	
Ν ν	n	as in 'net'	**Ω ω**	o	as in 'hot'	

Note that the letter **Σ** has two forms for the lower case – **σ** and **ς**. The second one is used at the end of words. The Greek question mark is represented with the English equivalent of a semicolon (;).

Key Words

appetisers	ορεκτικά	o·rek·ti·*ka*
bar	μπαρ	bar
beef	βοδινό	vo·dhi·*no*
beer	μπύρα	*bi*·ra
bottle	μπουκάλι	bu·*ka*·li
bowl	μπωλ	bol
bread	ψωμί	pso·*mi*
breakfast	πρόγευμα	*pro*·yev·ma
cafe	καφετέρια	ka·fe·*te*·ri·a
cheese	τυρί	ti·*ri*
chicken	κοτόπουλο	ko·*to*·pu·lo
coffee	καφές	ka·*fes*
cold	κρυωμένος	kri·o·*me*·nos
cream	κρέμα	*kre*·ma
delicatessen	ντελικατέσεν	de·li·ka·*te*·sen
desserts	επιδόρπια	e·pi·*dhor*·pi·a
dinner	δείπνο	*dhip*·no
egg	αβγό	av·*gho*
fish	ψάρι	*psa*·ri
food	φαγητό	fa·yi·*to*
fork	πιρούνι	pi·*ru*·ni
fruit	φρούτα	*fru*·ta
glass	ποτήρι	po·*ti*·ri
grocery store	οπωροπωλείο	o·po·ro·po·*li*·o
herb	βότανο	*vo*·ta·no
high chair	καρέκλα	ka·*re*·kla
	για μωρά	yia mo·*ro*
hot	ζεστός	ze·*stos*
juice	χυμός	hi·*mos*
knife	μαχαίρι	ma·*he*·ri
lamb	αρνί	ar·*ni*
lunch	μεσημεριανό	me·si·me·ria·*no*
	φαγητό	fa·yi·*to*
main courses	κύρια φαγητά	*ki*·ri·a fa·yi·ta
market	αγορά	a·gho·*ra*
menu	μενού	me·*nu*
milk	γάλα	*gha*·la
nut	καρύδι	ka·*ri*·dhi
oil	λάδι	*la*·dhi
pepper	πιπέρι	pi·*pe*·ri
plate	πιάτο	*pia*·to
pork	χοιρινό	hi·ri·*no*
red wine	κόκκινο κρασί	*ko*·ki·no kra·*si*
restaurant	εστιατόριο	e·sti·a·*to*·ri·o
salt	αλάτι	a·*la*·ti
soft drink	αναψυκτικό	a·nap·sik·ti·*ko*

KEY PATTERNS

To get by in Greek, mix and match these simple patterns with words of your choice:

When's (the next bus)?

Πότε είναι	*po*·te *i*·ne
(το επόμενο	(to e·*po*·me·no
λεωφορείο);	le·o·fo·*ri*·o)

Where's (the station)?

| Πού είναι (ο σταθμός); | pu *i*·ne (o stath·*mos*) |

Do you have (a local map)?

| Έχετε οδικό | *e*·he·te o·dhi·*ko* |
| (τοπικό χάρτη); | (to·pi·*ko* *khar*·ti) |

Is there a (lift)?

| Υπάρχει (ασανσέρ); | i·*par*·hi (a·san·*ser*) |

Can I (try it on)?

| Μπορώ να | bo·*ro* na |
| (το προβάρω); | (to pro·*va*·ro) |

Could you (please help)?

Μπορείς να	bo·*ris* na
(βοηθήσεις,	(vo·i·*thi*·sis
παρακαλώ);	pa·ra·ka·*lo*)

Do I need (to book)?

| Χρειάζεται | khri·*a*·ze·te |
| (να κλείσω θέση); | (na *kli*·so *the*·si) |

I need (assistance).

| Χρειάζομαι | khri·*a*·zo·me |
| (βοήθεια). | (vo·*i*·thi·a) |

I'd like (to hire a car).

Θα ήθελα (να	tha *i*·the·la (na
ενοικιάσω ένα	e·ni·ki·a·so e·na
αυτοκίνητο).	af·to·*ki*·ni·to)

How much is it (per night)?

| Πόσο είναι (για | *po*·so *i*·ne (yia |
| κάθε νύχτα); | *ka*·the *nikh*·ta) |

spoon	κουτάλι	ku·*ta*·li
sugar	ζάχαρη	*za*·kha·ri
tea	τσάι	*tsa*·i
vegetable	λαχανικά	la·kha·ni·*ka*
vegetarian	χορτοφάγος	khor·to·*fa*·ghos
vinegar	ξύδι	*ksi*·dhi
water	νερό	ne·*ro*
white wine	άσπρο κρασί	a·spro kra·*si*
with/without	με/χωρίς	me/kho·*ris*

EMERGENCIES

Help!	Βοήθεια!	vo·*i*·thya
Go away!	Φύγε!	*fi*·ye
I'm lost.	Έχω χαθεί.	e·kho kha·*thi*
Where's the toilet?	Πού είναι η τουαλέτα;	pu *i*·ne i tu·a·*le*·ta

Signs

ΕΙΣΟΔΟΣ	**Entry**
ΕΞΟΔΟΣ	**Exit**
ΠΛΗΡΟΦΟΡΙΕΣ	**Information**
ΑΝΟΙΧΤΟ	**Open**
ΚΛΕΙΣΤΟ	**Closed**
ΑΠΑΓΟΡΕΥΕΤΑΙ	**Prohibited**
ΑΣΤΥΝΟΜΙΑ	**Police**
ΓΥΝΑΙΚΩΝ	**Toilets (Women)**
ΑΝΔΡΩΝ	**Toilets (Men)**

Call ...!	Φωνάξτε ...!	fo·*nak*·ste ...
a doctor	ένα γιατρό	e·na yi·a·*tro*
the police	την	tin
	αστυνομία	a·sti·no·*mi*·a

I'm ill.
Είμαι άρρωστος.　　　*i*·me a·ro·stos

I'm allergic to (antibiotics).
Είμαι αλλεργικός/　　*i*·me a·ler·yi·*kos*/
αλλεργική　　　　　　a·ler·yi·*ki*
(στα αντιβιωτικά)　　(sta an·di·vi·o·ti·*ka*) (m/f)

SHOPPING & SERVICES

I'd like to buy ...
Θέλω ν' αγοράσω ...　　*the*·lo na·gho·*ra*·so ...

I'm just looking.
Απλώς κοιτάζω.　　ap·*los* ki·*ta*·zo

Can I see it?
Μπορώ να το δω;　　bo·*ro* na to dho

I don't like it.
Δεν μου αρέσει.　　dhen mu a·*re*·si

How much is it?
Πόσο κάνει;　　*po*·so *ka*·ni

It's too expensive.
Είναι πολύ ακριβό.　　*i*·ne po·*li* a·kri·*vo*

Can you lower the price?
Μπορείς να κατεβάσεις　bo·*ris* na ka·te·va·sis
την τιμή;　　　　　　　tin ti·*mi*

ATM	αυτόματη	af·*to*·ma·ti
	μηχανή	mi·kha·*ni*
	χρημάτων	khri·*ma*·ton
bank	τράπεζα	*tra*·pe·za
credit card	πιστωτική	pi·sto·ti·*ki*
	κάρτα	*kar*·ta
internet cafe	καφενείο	ka·fe·*ni*·o
	διαδικτύου	dhi·a·dhik·*ti*·u
mobile phone	κινητό	ki·ni·*to*
post office	ταχυδρομείο	ta·hi·dhro·*mi*·o
tourist office	τουριστικό	tu·ri·sti·*ko*
	γραφείο	ghra·*fi*·o

TIME & DATES

What time is it?
Τι ώρα είναι;　　　ti o·ra *i*·ne

It's (two) o'clock.
Είναι (δύο) η ώρα.　　*i*·ne (*dhi*·o) i o·ra

It's half past (10).
(Δέκα) και μισή.　　(*dhe*·ka) ke mi·*si*

morning	πρωί	pro·*i*
(this)	(αυτό το)	(af·*to* to)
afternoon	απόγευμα	a·*po*·yev·ma
evening	βράδυ	*vra*·dhi

yesterday	χθες	hthes
today	σήμερα	*si*·me·ra
tomorrow	αύριο	*av*·ri·o

Monday	Δευτέρα	dhef·*te*·ra
Tuesday	Τρίτη	*tri*·ti
Wednesday	Τετάρτη	te·*tar*·ti
Thursday	Πέμπτη	*pemp*·ti
Friday	Παρασκευή	pa·ras·ke·*vi*
Saturday	Σάββατο	*sa*·va·to
Sunday	Κυριακή	ky·ri·a·*ki*

January	Ιανουάριος	ia·nu·*ar*·i·os
February	Φεβρουάριος	fev·ru·*ar*·i·os
March	Μάρτιος	*mar*·ti·os
April	Απρίλιοςα	a·*pri*·li·os
May	Μάιος	*mai*·os
June	Ιούνιος	i·*u*·ni·os
July	Ιούλιος	i·*u*·li·os
August	Αύγουστος	*av*·ghus·tos
September	Σεπτέμβριος	sep·*tem*·vri·os
October	Οκτώβριος	ok·*to*·vri·os
November	Νοέμβριος	no·*em*·vri·os
December	Δεκέμβριος	dhe·*kem*·vri·os

Question Words

How?	Πώς;	pos
What?	Τι;	ti
When?	Πότε;	*po*·te
Where?	Πού;	pu
Who?	Ποιος;	pi·*os* (m)
	Ποια;	pi·*a* (f)
	Ποιο;	pi·*o* (n)
Why?	Γιατί;	yi·a·*ti*

TRANSPORT

Public Transport

boat	πλοίο	pli·o
city bus	αστικό	a·sti·ko
intercity bus	λεωφορείο	le·o·fo·ri·o
plane	αεροπλάνο	ae·ro·pla·no
train	τραίνο	tre·no

Where do I buy a ticket?
Πού αγοράζω εισιτήριο; pu a·gho·ra·zo i·si·ti·ri·o

I want to go to ...
Θέλω να πάω στο/στη ... the·lo na pao sto/sti...

What time does it leave?
Τι ώρα φεύγει; ti o·ra fev·yi

Does it stop at (Iraklio)?
Σταματάει στο sta·ma·ta·i sto
(Ηράκλειο); (i·ra·kli·o)

I'd like to get off at (Iraklio).
Θα ήθελα να κατεβώ tha i·the·la na ka·te·vo
στο (Ηράκλειο). sto (i·ra·kli·o)

I'd like	Θα ήθελα	tha i·the·la
(a) ...	(ένα) ...	(e·na) ...
1st class	πρώτη θέση	pro·ti the·si
2nd class	δεύτερη θέση	def·te·ri the·si
one-way ticket	απλό εισιτήριο	a·plo i·si·ti·ri·o
return ticket	εισιτήριο με	i·si·ti·ri·o me
	επιστροφή	e·pi·stro·fi

cancelled	ακυρώθηκε	a·ki·ro·thi·ke
delayed	καθυστέρησε	ka·thi·ste·ri·se
platform	πλατφόρμα	plat·for·ma
ticket office	εκδοτήριο	ek·dho·ti·ri·o
	εισιτηρίων	i·si·ti·ri·on
timetable	δρομολόγιο	dhro·mo·lo·gio
train station	σταθμός	stath·mos
	τρένου	tre·nu

Driving & Cycling

I'd like to hire	Θα ήθελα να	tha i·the·la na
a ...	νοικιάσω ...	ni·ki·a·so ...
4WD	ένα τέσσερα	e·na tes·se·ra
	επί τέσσερα	e·pi tes·se·ra
bicycle	ένα	e·na
	ποδήλατο	po·dhi·la·to
car	ένα	e·na
	αυτοκίνητο	af·ti·ki·ni·to
jeep	ένα τζιπ	e·na tzip
motorbike	μια	mya
	μοτοσυκλέττα	mo·to·si·klet·ta

Numbers

1	ένας	e·nas (m)
	μία	mi·a (f)
	ένα	e·na (n)
2	δύο	dhi·o
3	τρεις	tris (m&f)
	τρία	tri·a (n)
4	τέσσερεις	te·se·ris (m&f)
	τέσσερα	te·se·ra (n)
5	πέντε	pen·de
6	έξη	e·xi
7	επτά	ep·ta
8	οχτώ	oh·to
9	εννέα	e·ne·a
10	δέκα	dhe·ka
20	είκοσι	ik·o·si
30	τριάντα	tri·an·da
40	σαράντα	sa·ran·da
50	πενήντα	pe·nin·da
60	εξήντα	ek·sin·da
70	εβδομήντα	ev·dho·min·da
80	ογδόντα	ogh·dhon·da
90	ενενήντα	e·ne·nin·da
100	εκατό	e·ka·to
1000	χίλιοι	hi·li·i (m)
	χίλιες	hi·li·ez (f)
	χίλια	hi·li·a (n)

Do I need a helmet?
Χρειάζομαι κράνος; khri·a·zo·me kra·nos

Is this the road to ...?
Αυτός είναι ο af·tos i·ne o
δρόμος για ... ; dhro·mos ya ...

Where's a petrol station?
Πού είναι ένα πρατήριο pu i·ne e·na pra·ti·ri·o
βενζίνας; ven·zi·nas

(How long) Can I park here?
(Πόση ώρα) Μπορώ να (po·si o·ra) bo·ro na
παρκάρω εδώ; par·ka·ro e·dho

The car/motorbike has broken down (at ...).
Το αυτοκίνητο/ to af·to·ki·ni·to/
η μοτοσυκλέττα i mo·to·si·klet·ta
χάλασε (στο ...). kha·la·se (sto ...)

I need a mechanic.
Χρειάζομαι μηχανικό. khri·a·zo·me mi·kha·ni·ko

I have a flat tyre.
Έπαθα λάστιχο. e·pa·tha la·sti·cho

I've run out of petrol.
Έμεινα από βενζίνη. e·mi·na a·po ven·zi·ni

GLOSSARY

For culinary terms, see Eat Like a Local (p46) and Greek Cuisine (p711).

Achaean civilisation – see *Mycenaean civilisation*

acropolis – citadel, highest point of an ancient city

agia (f), agios (m), agii (pl) – saint(s)

agora – commercial area of an ancient city; shopping precinct in modern Greece

amphora – large two-handled vase in which wine or oil was kept

Archaic period – also known as the *Middle Age* (800–480 BC); period in which the city-states emerged from the *dark age* and traded their way to wealth and power; the city-states were unified by a Greek alphabet and common cultural pursuits, engendering a sense of national identity

arhon – leading citizen of a town, often a wealthy bourgeois merchant; chief magistrate

arhontika – 17th- and 18th-century-AD mansions, which belonged to *arhons*

askitiria – mini-chapels or hermitages; places of solitary worship

asklepion – ancient medical complex

baglamas – small stringed instrument like a mini bouzouki

basilica – early Christian church

bouzouki – long-necked, stringed lute-like instrument associated with *rembetika* music

bouzoukia – any nightclub where the *bouzouki* is played and low-grade blues songs are sung

Byzantine Empire – characterised by the merging of Hellenistic culture and Christianity and named after Byzantium, the city on the Bosphorus that became the capital of the Roman Empire in AD 324; when the Roman Empire was formally divided in AD 395, Rome went into decline and the eastern capital, renamed Constantinople after Emperor Constantine I, flourished; the Byzantine Empire (324 BC–AD 1453) dissolved after the fall of Constantinople to the Turks in 1453

caïque – small, sturdy fishing boat often used to carry passengers

capital – top of a column

Classical period – era in which the Greek city-states reached the height of their wealth and power after the defeat of the Persians in the 5th century BC; the Classical period (480–323 BC) ended with the decline of the city-states as a result of the Peloponnesian Wars, and the expansionist aspirations of Philip II, King of Macedon (r 359–336 BC) and his son, Alexander the Great (r 336–323 BC)

Corinthian – order of Greek architecture recognisable by columns with bell-shaped capitals with sculpted elaborate ornaments based on acanthus leaves; see also *Doric* and *Ionic*

Cycladic civilisation – the civilisation (3000–1100 BC) that emerged following the settlement of Phoenician colonists on the Cycladic islands

cyclops (s), cyclopes (pl) – mythical one-eyed giants

dark age (1200–800 BC) – period in which Greece was under *Dorian* rule

domatio (s), domatia (pl) – room, often in a private home; a cheap form of accommodation

Dorians – Hellenic warriors who invaded Greece around 1200 BC, demolishing the city-states and destroying the *Mycenaean civilisation*; heralded Greece's *dark age*, when the artistic and cultural advancements of the *Mycenaean* and *Minoan civilisations* were abandoned; the Dorians later developed into land-holding aristocrats, encouraging the resurgence of independent city-states led by wealthy aristocrats

Doric – order of Greek architecture characterised by a column that has no base, a fluted shaft and a relatively plain capital, when compared with the flourishes evident on *Ionic* and *Corinthian* capitals

Ellada or Ellas – see *Hellas*

ELPA – Elliniki Leschi Aftokinitou kai Periigiseon; Greek motoring and touring club

ELTA – Ellinika Tahydromia; Greek post office organisation

EOS – Ellinikos Orivatikos Syllogos; the association of Greek Mountaineering Clubs

EOT – Ellinikos Organismos Tourismou; main tourist office (has offices in most major towns), known abroad as *GNTO* (Greek National Tourist Organisation)

estiatorio – restaurant serving ready-made food as well as à la carte

Filiki Eteria – Friendly Society; a group of Greeks in exile; formed during Ottoman rule to organise an uprising against the Turks

filoxenia – hospitality

frourio – fortress; sometimes also referred to as a *kastro*

Geometric period – the period (1200–800 BC) characterised by pottery decorated with geometric designs; sometimes referred to as Greece's *dark age*

GNTO – Greek National Tourist Organisation; see also *EOT*

Hellas – the Greek name for Greece; also known as Ellada or Ellas

Hellenistic period – prosperous, influential period (323–146 BC) of Greek civilisation ushered in by Alexander the Great's empire-building and lasting until the Roman sacking of Corinth

hora – main town, usually on an island

horio – village

Ionic – order of Greek architecture characterised by a column with truncated flutes and capitals with ornaments resembling scrolls; see also *Doric* and *Corinthian*

kastro – walled-in town; also describes a fortress or castle

katholikon – principal church of a monastic complex

kore – female statue of the *Archaic period*; see also *kouros*

kouros (s), kouroi (pl) – male statue of the *Archaic period*, characterised by a stiff body posture and enigmatic smile; see also *kore*

kri-kri – endemic Cretan animal with large horns similar to a wild goat; also known as the *agrimi*

KTEL – Koino Tamio Eispraxeon Leoforion; national bus cooperative, which runs all long-distance bus services

laïka – literally 'popular (songs)'; mainstream songs that have either been around for years or are of recent origin; also referred to as urban folk music

leoforos – avenue; commonly shortened to 'leof'

libation – in ancient Greece, wine or food that was offered to the gods

limenarhio – port police

Linear A – Minoan script; so far undeciphered

Linear B – Mycenaean script; has been deciphered

lyra – small violin-like instrument or lyre, played on the knee; common in Cretan and Pontian music

megaron – central room or quarters of a Mycenaean palace

meltemi – dry northerly wind that blows throughout much of Greece in the summer

mezedhopoleio – restaurant specialising in mezedhes

Middle Age – see *Archaic period*

Minoan civilisation – Bronze Age (3000–1200 BC) culture of Crete named after the mythical King Minos, and characterised by pottery and metalwork of great beauty and artisanship; it has three periods: Protopalatial (3400–2100 BC), Neopalatial (2100–1580 BC) and Postpalatial (1580–1200 BC)

moni – monastery or convent

Mycenaean civilisation – first great civilisation (1600–1100 BC) of the Greek mainland, characterised by powerful independent city-states ruled by kings; also known as the *Achaean civilisation*

New Democracy – Nea Dimodratia; conservative political party

necropolis – literally 'city of the dead'; ancient cemetery

nisi – island

nymphaeum – in ancient Greece, building containing a fountain and often dedicated to nymphs

odeion – ancient Greek indoor theatre

odos – street

OSE – Organismos Sidirodromon Ellados; the name of Greek Railways Organisation

ouzerie – place that serves ouzo and light snacks

OTE – Organismos Tilepikoinonion Ellados; Greece's major telecommunications carrier

Panagia – Mother of God or Virgin Mary; name frequently used for churches

paralia – waterfront

panigyri (s), panigyria (p) – festival; the most common ones celebrate annual saints' days

pediment – triangular section, often filled with sculpture above the columns, found at the front and back of a classical Greek temple

periptero (s), periptera (pl) – street kiosk

peristyle – columns surrounding a building, usually a temple or courtyard

plateia – square

pithos (s), pithoi (pl) – large Minoan storage jar or urn

propylon (s), propylaia (pl) – elaborately built main entrance to an ancient city or sanctuary; a propylon had one gateway and a propylaia more than one

prytaneion – the administrative centre of the city-state

rembetika – blues songs, commonly associated with the underworld of the 1920s

rhyton – another name for a *libation* vessel

rizitika – traditional, patriotic songs of western Crete

Sarakatsani – Greek-speaking nomadic shepherd community from northern Greece

stele (s), stelae (pl) – upright stone (or pillar) decorated with inscriptions or figures

stoa – long colonnaded building, usually in an *agora;* used as a meeting place and shelter in ancient Greece

taverna – the most common type of traditional restaurant that serves food and wine

tholos – Mycenaean tomb shaped like a beehive

Vlach – traditional, seminomadic shepherds from Northern Greece who speak a Latin-based dialect

Behind the Scenes

SEND US YOUR FEEDBACK

We love to hear from travellers – your comments keep us on our toes and help make our books better. Our well-travelled team reads every word on what you loved or loathed about this book. Although we cannot reply individually to postal submissions, we always guarantee that your feedback goes straight to the appropriate authors, in time for the next edition. Each person who sends us information is thanked in the next edition – the most useful submissions are rewarded with a selection of digital PDF chapters.

Visit **lonelyplanet.com/contact** to submit your updates and suggestions or to ask for help. Our award-winning website also features inspirational travel stories, news and discussions.

Note: We may edit, reproduce and incorporate your comments in Lonely Planet products such as guidebooks, websites and digital products, so let us know if you don't want your comments reproduced or your name acknowledged. For a copy of our privacy policy visit lonelyplanet.com/privacy.

OUR READERS

Many thanks to the travellers who used the last edition and wrote to us with helpful hints, useful advice and interesting anecdotes:

Alan Graham, Andy White, Anette Uddqvist, Anita Vriend, Apostolos Spyros, Christopher Hansen, David Mason, Dimitris Efstratiadis, Eberhard Zantke, Efrat Ben Shalom, Ester van Zuylen, George & Linda Moss, George Moss, Jeroen Meeboer, Jesse Naiman, Jim Maas, JJ Wytrwal, Joske de Roode, Judith Bowman, Katarzyna Podgorska, Katy Tydeman, Kit Arthur, Lia Spartali, Linda Swinn, Lorna Hitchin, Marina Metalios, Marjatta Reinius, Martijn Huijnen, Martin Kummel, Megan van Rooyen, Melike Sayman, Nicola Long, Philip Howard, Ralf Kaefer, Roland Keller, Roy Sayegh, Sofia Lizzio, Stephen Lioy, Stephen Strand, Susan Howard, Walter Lars

AUTHOR THANKS

Korina Miller

An enormous thank you to Mum and Dad for minding the fort while I was away and making it possible for me to take this project on. Thank you to my fabulous daughters, Simone and Monique, for letting me work and also encouraging me to take breaks. Thank you to Katie, Anna, Angela and Anthony at Lonely Planet for their support and to my co-authors for their insights and camaraderie. A warm *efharisto* to all of the people I met on the road – both locals and travellers – who shared their stories, knowledge and enthusiasm for Greece. And to Kirk, my own personal Bukowski.

Kate Armstrong

In the Pelops, my warmest thanks yet again to Petros and the Zotos family for their support, and to Vaso, Nena and Koula, dear friends; in Central Greece, Alexandra Groth, Yiannis and Soyla at Alsos House. In Delphi – Penny Kolomvotsos, Sotiris and Apostolos – this couldn't have been done without you; Chris and Kathy in Pelion, Chrisoula in Galaxidi. *Efharisto* Anna Tyler, Angela Tinson, Korina Miller and fellow scribes. Finally, to 'SB' (aka Kian) for his driving skills, intellect and humour, and bringing out my inner Greco- and omega-philes.

Alexis Averbuck

Honour to Alexandra Stamopoulou for always-inspiring tips and overall inspiration. Marina Flenga is, yet again, a fairy godmother, connecting me to islanders everywhere. Marilee Anargyrou Kyriazakou and Cali Doxiadis (Kerkyra), Olga Karayiannis and Eleni Masselou (Andros), Elina Dallas, Dimitris Foussekis and Maria Liarikos (Tinos), Michail Karampatsos and Michalis Pateras (Syros), Christiana Sofianopoulou and Dimitris Liaroutsos (Serifos), Vula Bolou and Sotiris Iliadis (Sifnos), Manita

Scocimara-Ponghis (Kefallonia), and Petros Haritatos and Mike Tsanas (Spetses) shared their love and knowledge of their islands. In Athens, Ilias Nikolaidis and Elina Lychoudi were the King and Queen of Nightlife. Margarita, Kostas and Zisis, and Anthy and Costas made it home.

Michael Stamatios Clark

Ευχαριστω, thank you, to those who helped make the road a welcoming destination – in particular, Heather Parsons, George and Mahi (Skopelos); Gisela (Skiathos), Chrysanthi Zygogianni, Niko Sekkes (Skyros); Kostas and Bessie (Alonnisos) and Kyrillos on Evia; the Fouskas family, Vasillis and Demetra, Kostas and Nana Vatsis (Ikaria). Special thanks to fellow authors Kate and Chris, and to Korina Miller for coordinating grace. And to my family – Janet, Melina and Alexander – Greek kisses on both cheeks for all.

Chris Deliso

Many Greek friends provided invaluable advice – many of whom share popular Greek names. Special credit goes to Lefteris 1 and 2, Georgios 1, 2 and 3, Maria 1 and 2, Anna and Panos, Periklis, Christina, Fotis, Miltos, Daniel, and the bar DJs who tolerated my Sonic Youth requests. I also must thank my fellow Lonely Planet scribes, especially coordinating author Korina Miller, commissioning editor Anna Tyler, managing editor Angela Tinson and everyone on the map-making, production and tech-support teams for their good cheer.

Victoria Kyriakopoulos

Thanks to the great Greek author team for sharing their food views and experiences, and to the Lonely Planet editors for another opportunity to write about Greek food and culture. Thanks to my ever-supportive husband Chris, and my Greek family and friends and the special and generous people who have made travelling in Greece such a joy. *Kali antamosi* – next time my son Kostas will get his first taste of the Greece I love.

Andrea Schulte-Peevers

Fond thanks to all the wonderful friends and strangers who've provided valuable local insights about Crete before and during my research ramblings around the island. These include (in no particular order): Miriam Bers, Utha Herzbruch-Ruess, Yiannis Zervakis, the Papadospiridaki family, Stravroula (Kissamos), Lynn (Elounda), Madalina (Elounda) and Vaggelis Alegakis.

Richard Waters

My special thanks to everyone who made my trip more colourful with their *filoxenia* and generosity. In no particular order, Efi and Spyros, Marianna Angelou, Mikalis Melenos, Antonios, George, Rena Kioulafi, the Greek Tourist Board in London, Lily Alicabiotis, Ioannis at Kilindra, Enetikon Travel, Alexis at Afendoulis, Fokas, Ilidi Rock. My thanks, too, to the mapping and editorial team, and commissioning editors Katie O'Connell and Anna Tyler.

ACKNOWLEDGMENTS

Climate map data adapted from Peel MC, Finlayson BL & McMahon TA (2007) 'Updated World Map of the Köppen-Geiger Climate Classification', *Hydrology and Earth System Sciences*, 11, 163344.

Illustrations pp72–3, pp426–7 by Javier Martinez Zarracina. Illustration pp194–5 by Michael Weldon.

Cover photograph: Moni Agias Varvaras Rousanou, Meteora; Michele Falzone/Getty Images.

THIS BOOK

This guidebook was commissioned in Lonely Planet's London office, and produced by the following:

Commissioning Editors Katie O'Connell, Anna Tyler

Coordinating Editors Kate Mathews, Branislava Vladisavljevic

Senior Cartographer Valentina Kremenchutskaya

Coordinating Layout Designer Nicholas Colicchia

Managing Editors Bruce Evans, Angela Tinson

Managing Layout Designer Chris Girdler

Assisting Editors Andrew Bain, Penny Cordner, Laura Gibb, Carly Hall, Kellie Langdon, Anne Mulvaney, Rosie Nicholson, Erin Richards, Sam Trafford

Assisting Cartographers Jeff Cameron, Julie Dodkins, Mick Garrett, Rachel Imeson, Jackson James

Assisting Layout Designers Clara Monitto, Carlos Solarte

Cover Research Naomi Parker

Internal Image Research Rebecca Skinner

Thanks to Anita Banh, Barbara Di Castro, Brigitte Ellemor, Ryan Evans, Larissa Frost, Genesys India, Jouve India, Andi Jones, Wayne Murphy, Catherine Naghten, Trent Paton, Martine Power, Gina Tsarouhas, Gerard Walker

Index

Map Pages **000**
Photo Pages **000**

Map Legend

Sights

- Beach
- Bird Sanctuary
- Buddhist
- Castle/Palace
- Christian
- Confucian
- Hindu
- Islamic
- Jain
- Jewish
- Monument
- Museum/Gallery/Historic Building
- Ruin
- Sento Hot Baths/Onsen
- Shinto
- Sikh
- Taoist
- Winery/Vineyard
- Zoo/Wildlife Sanctuary
- Other Sight

Activities, Courses & Tours

- Bodysurfing
- Diving
- Canoeing/Kayaking
- Course/Tour
- Skiing
- Snorkelling
- Surfing
- Swimming/Pool
- Walking
- Windsurfing
- Other Activity

Sleeping

- Sleeping
- Camping

Eating

- Eating

Drinking & Nightlife

- Drinking & Nightlife
- Cafe

Entertainment

- Entertainment

Shopping

- Shopping

Information

- Bank
- Embassy/Consulate
- Hospital/Medical
- Internet
- Police
- Post Office
- Telephone
- Toilet
- Tourist Information
- Other Information

Geographic

- Beach
- Hut/Shelter
- Lighthouse
- Lookout
- Mountain/Volcano
- Oasis
- Park
- Pass
- Picnic Area
- Waterfall

Population

- Capital (National)
- Capital (State/Province)
- City/Large Town
- Town/Village

Transport

- Airport
- Border crossing
- Bus
- Cable car/Funicular
- Cycling
- Ferry
- Metro station
- Monorail
- Parking
- Petrol station
- S-Bahn/S-train/Subway station
- Taxi
- T-bane/Tunnelbana station
- Train station/Railway
- Tram
- Tube station
- U-Bahn/Underground station
- Other Transport

Note: Not all symbols displayed above appear on the maps in this book

Routes

- Tollway
- Freeway
- Primary
- Secondary
- Tertiary
- Lane
- Unsealed road
- Road under construction
- Plaza/Mall
- Steps
- Tunnel
- Pedestrian overpass
- Walking Tour
- Walking Tour detour
- Path/Walking Trail

Boundaries

- International
- State/Province
- Disputed
- Regional/Suburb
- Marine Park
- Cliff
- Wall

Hydrography

- River, Creek
- Intermittent River
- Canal
- Water
- Dry/Salt/Intermittent Lake
- Reef

Areas

- Airport/Runway
- Beach/Desert
- Cemetery (Christian)
- Cemetery (Other)
- Glacier
- Mudflat
- Park/Forest
- Sight (Building)
- Sportsground
- Swamp/Mangrove

Chris Deliso

Northern Greece Chris was drawing maps of the Aegean by age five. Twenty years later he ended up in Greece, during an Oxford MPhil in Byzantine Studies. Ever since studying Greek in Thessaloniki (1998) and spending a year in Crete, he's visited Greece frequently. For this edition, he matched wits with the tortoise guarding Platamonas' Byzantine castle, absorbed the beauty of Ioannina's lake island, and almost got beaten by Kastoria bar thugs who pegged him as an under-cover Greek tax policeman. Visit his website: www.chrisdeliso.com.

Read more about Chris at:
lonelyplanet.com/members/chrisdeliso

Victoria Kyriakopoulos

Victoria is a Melbourne-based writer, journalist and foodie who has lived, worked and travelled extensively in her ancestral home, feeding her passion and sharing her insight on Greece. She's written for newspapers and magazines around the globe and worked on Lonely Planet guides to Greece since 2001. Victoria wrote the Eat Like a Local, Arts, Greek Cuisine and Greek Way of Life chapters.

Andrea Schulte-Peevers

Crete Andrea has travelled the distance to the moon and back in her visits to around 70 countries, but she'll forever cherish the memory of first setting foot on Crete some 17 years ago and being instantly charmed by its people, the rich tapestry of their traditions and their long and proud history. She has written or contributed to some 60 Lonely Planet books, including the Crete regional guide. Her current home is Berlin.

Richard Waters

Dodecanese Richard is an award-winning journalist and works for *The Independent, Sunday Times, Wanderlust* and *National Geographic Traveller.* He lives with his fiancée and two kids in the Cotswolds. His spiritual home is Greece thanks to more than 20 visits, the first of which was as a kid in the '70s on the isles of Corfu, Rhodes and Zakynthos. He loves their myths, cuisine and, most of all, the Greeks themselves. Even in the midst of the crisis, he found them to possess their usual humour, warmth and stoicism. Richard also wrote the Greece Today, History, Ancient Greek Culture and Architecture chapters.

OUR STORY

A beat-up old car, a few dollars in the pocket and a sense of adventure. In 1972 that's all Tony and Maureen Wheeler needed for the trip of a lifetime – across Europe and Asia overland to Australia. It took several months, and at the end – broke but inspired – they sat at their kitchen table writing and stapling together their first travel guide, *Across Asia on the Cheap*. Within a week they'd sold 1500 copies. Lonely Planet was born.

Today, Lonely Planet has offices in Melbourne, London and Oakland, with more than 600 staff and writers. We share Tony's belief that 'a great guidebook should do three things: inform, educate and amuse'.

OUR WRITERS

Korina Miller

Coordinating Author, Cyclades Korina first ventured to Greece as a backpacking teenager, sleeping on ferry decks and hiking in the mountains. Since then she's found herself drawn back to soak up the timelessness of the old towns and drink coffee with locals in seaside *kafeneio*. Korina grew up on Vancouver Island and has been exploring the globe independently since she was 16, visiting or living in 36 countries and picking up a degree in Communications and Canadian Studies and a MA in Migration Studies en route. Korina has written nearly 30 titles for Lonely Planet and also works as a Commissioning Editor and a children's writing coach. Korina also wrote the Plan Your Trip section, Nature & Wildlife chapter and the Survival Guide.

Kate Armstrong

Peloponnese, Central Greece Having studied history and fine arts, Kate headed to Greece aeons ago to view a *kouros*, and fell in love with the country. The *pythia* at Delphi told her she'd return; she has, frequently. For this edition she climbed rock pinnacles at Meteora and tackled donkey paths in the Pelion. She met mythical beings in the Peloponnese, devoured kilos of seafood, covered 6000km and received Aphrodite-style hospitality. See www.katearmstrong.com.au.

Read more about Kate at:
lonelyplanet.com/members/kate_armstrong

Alexis Averbuck

Athens & Around, Saronic Gulf Islands, Cyclades, Ionian Islands Alexis lives in Hydra, Greece, takes regular reverse R&R in Athens, and makes any excuse she can to travel the isolated back roads of her adopted land. She is committed to dispelling the stereotype that Greece is simply a string of sandy beaches. A travel writer for two decades, Alexis has lived in Antarctica for a year, crossed the Pacific by sailboat and written books on her journeys through Asia and the Americas. She's also a painter – visit www.alexisaverbuck.com.

Read more about Alexis at:
lonelyplanet.com/members/alexisaverbuck

Michael Stamatios Clark

Northeastern Aegean Islands, Evia & the Sporades Michael's Greek roots go back to the village of Karavostamo on the island of Ikaria, home of his maternal grandparents, and one of his destinations for this guide. His first trip to the islands was as a deckhand aboard a Greek freighter, trading Greek lessons for English over backgammon. For this edition, Michael chewed mastic on Chios, listened to *rembetika* music on Skyros and tested the thermal sea waters of Ikaria, sampling Greek coffee and *retsina* along the way.

OVER PAGE — MORE WRITERS

Published by Lonely Planet Publications Pty Ltd
ABN 36 005 607 983
11th edition – March 2014
ISBN 978 1 74220 726 1
© Lonely Planet 2014   Photographs © as indicated 2014
10 9 8 7 6 5 4 3 2 1
Printed in China